CONSTITUTIONAL CRIMINAL PROCEDURE: FROM INVESTIGATION TO TRIAL

Fourth Edition

By

Phillip E. Johnson
Jefferson E. Peyser Professor Emeritus
University of California, Berkeley

Morgan Cloud
Charles Howard Candler Professor of Law
Emory University

AMERICAN CASEBOOK SERIES®

THOMSON
WEST

Mat #18196476

American Casebook Series and West Group are trademarks
registered in the U.S. Patent and Trademark Office.

COPYRIGHT © 1994 WEST PUBLISHING CO.
© West, a Thomson business, 2000
© 2005 Thomson/West
        610 Opperman Drive
        P.O. Box 64526
        St. Paul, MN 55164–0526
        1–800–328–9352

Printed in the United States of America

ISBN 0–314–25660–1

 *TEXT IS PRINTED ON 10% POST
CONSUMER RECYCLED PAPER*

To my mother, Marjorie Cloud

M.C.

*

Preface

Although the Fourth Edition of this book is in many ways an entirely new volume, it embodies many of the aspirations of the previous editions. This book is designed to provide teachers and students with a sophisticated presentation of fundamental issues in constitutional criminal procedure in a succinct and efficient text. It is structured to permit the reader to learn the rules currently governing each topic of constitutional law, but also to supply the historical and jurisprudential contexts which produced current doctrine. Students should finish their criminal procedure course with a deep understanding of constitutional law as it works in the context of the criminal justice system.

The Fourth Edition has been designed intentionally to provide comprehensive coverage of fundamental topics of constitutional criminal procedure—including judicial review, federalism, the exclusionary rule, due process of law, search and seizure, interrogation and confession, the right to counsel, identification procedures, pretrial detention, grand jury proceedings, and the impact of the contemporary "war on terror" upon these topics—in approximately 750 pages. To accomplish these goals, the book emphasizes the judicial decisions which have produced the fundamental theories in each of these areas of law. Excerpts from scholarly writings and the authors' commentaries and notes are used sparingly to provide students necessary guidance. As a result, the book avoids a problem that plagues many law school casebooks—the accretion of textual materials that become so voluminous that they obstruct the professors' efforts to teach and the students' efforts to learn.

To permit comprehensive but concise coverage, cases have been edited rigorously to provide students with the materials they need, but no more. Most citations and footnotes have been eliminated. These condensed opinions are edited for effective teaching and learning, not for use as sources to be cited in other legal materials. On the other hand, the factual background of individual cases are often presented in detail, because the facts are frequently critical for our understanding of judicial opinions. Where the original opinion's recitation of the facts is unnecessarily lengthy, a more succinct summary of the facts is provided in brackets.

Constitutional criminal procedure should be one of the most engaging and interesting of law school courses. Nowhere in the law are the fundamental conflicts between the need for social order and the desire for individual liberty presented with such clarity and power. Our hope is that those using the Fourth Edition will find, as we have, that this is one of the most challenging, provocative, and exciting courses in the law school curriculum.

Morgan Cloud

Emory University
Atlanta, Georgia

*

v

Summary of Contents

*

Table of Contents

PART IV.   THE CONSTITUTION IN A TIME OF CRISIS: THE WAR ON TERROR

*

Selected Constitutional Amendments

Amendment I

Congress shall make no law respecting an establishment of religion, or prohibiting the free exercise thereof; or abridging the freedom of speech, or of the press; or the right of the people peaceably to assemble, and to petition the Government for a redress of grievances.

Amendment II

A well regulated Militia, being necessary to the security of a free State, the right of the people to keep and bear Arms, shall not be infringed.

Amendment III

No Soldier shall, in time of peace be quartered in any house, without the consent of the Owner, nor in time of war, but in a manner to be prescribed by law.

Amendment IV

The right of the people to be secure in their persons, houses, papers, and effects, against unreasonable searches and seizures, shall not be violated, and no Warrants shall issue, but upon probable cause, supported by Oath or affirmation, and particularly describing the place to be searched, and the persons or things to be seized.

Amendment V

No person shall be held to answer for a capital, or otherwise infamous crime, unless on a presentment or indictment of a Grand Jury, except in cases arising in the land or naval forces, or in the Militia, when in actual service in time of War or public danger; nor shall any person be subject for the same offence to be twice put in jeopardy of life or limb; nor shall be compelled in any criminal case to be a witness against himself, nor be deprived of life, liberty, or property, without due process of law; nor shall private property be taken for public use, without just compensation.

Amendment VI

In all criminal prosecutions, the accused shall enjoy the right to a speedy and public trial, by an impartial jury of the State and district wherein the crime shall have been committed, which district shall have been previously ascertained by law, and to be informed of the nature and cause of the accusation; to be confronted with the witnesses against him; to have compulsory process for obtaining witnesses in his favor, and to have the Assistance of Counsel for his defence.

Amendment VII

In Suits at common law, where the value in controversy shall exceed twenty dollars, the right of trial by jury shall be preserved, and no fact tried by jury, shall be otherwise re-examined in any Court of the United States, than according to the rules of the common law.

Amendment VIII

Excessive bail shall not be required, nor excessive fines imposed, nor cruel and unusual punishments inflicted.

Amendment IX

The enumeration in the Constitution, of certain rights, shall not be construed to deny or disparage others retained by the people.

*　*　*

Amendment XIV

Section 1.　All persons born or naturalized in the United States, and subject to the jurisdiction thereof, are citizens of the United States and of the State wherein they reside.　No State shall make or enforce any law which shall abridge the privileges or immunities of citizens of the United States; nor shall any State deprive any person of life, liberty, or property, without due process of law; nor deny to any person within its jurisdiction the equal protection of the laws.

*　*　*

Section 5.　The Congress shall have power to enforce, by appropriate legislation, the provisions of this article.

Table of Cases

The principal cases are in bold type. Cases cited or discussed in the text are in roman type. References are to pages. Cases cited in principal cases and within other quoted materials are not included.

*

CONSTITUTIONAL CRIMINAL PROCEDURE: FROM INVESTIGATION TO TRIAL

Fourth Edition

*

Part I

SEARCH AND SEIZURE

Chapter 1

CONSTITUTIONAL JUDICIAL REVIEW

A. THE EXCLUSIONARY RULE AND CONSTITUTIONAL JUDICIAL REVIEW

Commentary

It is impossible to understand contemporary constitutional criminal procedure without addressing the debate about appropriate remedies for violations of constitutional rights by those investigating crimes and prosecuting criminals. A number of possible remedies exist. These include civil suits seeking damages from individual government agents and from the governmental entities that employ them, criminal prosecutions of individual law enforcers who violate constitutional rules, and administrative sanctions against those officers. The most commonly used remedy, however, is also the most controversial. It is the exclusionary rule. This remedy was first explicitly employed by the Supreme Court in 1914, yet the debate over its efficacy continues almost a century later. We begin our study of the rules governing the investigation of crimes by exploring the nature, scope and functions of the exclusionary rule.

In recent years, the Supreme Court has declared that the sole justification for the exclusionary rule is to deter police misconduct. These recent opinions generally rest on an interrelated set of propositions: (1) the exclusionary remedy is merely a judge-made rule of evidence and not an essential element of the rights protected by the Fourth Amendment; (2) the exclusionary remedy is directed at police officers, not judges, and can only be justified to the extent that it deters police officers from violating the Constitution; (3) the rule's success as a deterrent is essentially an empirical question that can be answered by "balancing" the rule's costs against its deterrent benefits in a particular setting; (4) similarly, the rights protected by the Fourth Amendment can be treated as mere interests to be balanced against competing government claims of authority; and (5) although unlawful searches and seizures violate the Fourth Amendment, using items obtained from those illegal searches as evidence does not.

2

Like the remedy of suppression itself, the deterrence theory has its critics. Some critics argue that the Supreme Court did not rely exclusively on the deterrence theory until the 1970s; that the theory has been misapplied to limit the application of the exclusionary rule; and regardless of the merits or weaknesses of the deterrence theory, the language of the Supreme Court's earlier opinions suggest that the Supreme Court initially adopted the exclusionary rule for reasons other than deterrence.

According to this theory, the Supreme Court originally adopted the exclusionary rule as a method of constitutional judicial review of the acts of the other branches of government, particularly law enforcers in the executive branch. From this perspective, the exclusionary rule was adopted as a means of exercising constitutional judicial review in the criminal procedure context. The suppression remedy permitted judges to enforce the rights of individual claimants by crafting a remedy relevant to the lawsuits before them—criminal prosecutions brought by the state against individual defendants. Other possible remedies required separate proceedings, and typically were directed at police officers who were not even parties in the criminal prosecutions in which suppression was sought. A classic example was the common law trespass suit seeking civil damages. This remedy was available only if the civil claimant, typically the defendant in the criminal case, maintained separate judicial proceedings in which the named defendants usually would be government searchers. The third reason was perhaps the most important. Suppressing illegally obtained evidence was a remedy that judges controlled. They could apply the remedy within the context of cases being litigated before them without being forced to rely upon other branches of government to enforce individual constitutional rights. In contrast, other actors in the justice system (prosecutors, police departments, and juries) controlled the application of other possible remedies.

As you read each of the following cases, consider which of these theories the Court relied upon to justify its holding and which approach is preferable.

WEEKS v. UNITED STATES

Supreme Court of the United States, 1914.
232 U.S. 383, 34 S.Ct. 341, 58 L.Ed. 652.

Mr. Justice Day delivered the opinion of the court.

An indictment was returned against the plaintiff in error, defendant below, and herein so designated, in the District Court of the United States for the Western District of Missouri, containing nine counts. The seventh count, upon which a conviction was had, charged the use of the mails for the purpose of transporting certain coupons or tickets representing chances or shares in a lottery or gift enterprise, in violation of § 213 of the Criminal Code. Sentence of fine and imprisonment was imposed. This writ of error is to review that judgment.

The defendant was arrested by a police officer, so far as the record shows, without warrant, at the Union Station in Kansas City, Missouri, where he was employed by an express company. Other police officers had gone to the house of the defendant and being told by a neighbor where the key was kept, found it and entered the house. They searched the defendant's room and took possession of various papers and articles found there, which were afterwards turned over to the United States Marshal. Later in the same day police officers returned with the Marshal, who thought he might find additional evidence, and, being admitted by someone in the house, probably a boarder, in response to a rap, the Marshal searched the defendant's room and carried away certain letters and envelopes found in the drawer of a chiffonier. Neither the Marshal nor the police officers had a search warrant. * * *

After the jury had been sworn and before any evidence had been given, the defendant again urged his petition for the return of his property, which was denied by the court. Upon the introduction of such papers during the trial, the defendant objected on the ground that the papers had been obtained without a search warrant and by breaking open his home, in violation of the Fourth and Fifth Amendments to the Constitution of the United States, which objection was overruled by the court. Among the papers retained and put in evidence were a number of lottery tickets and statements with reference to the lottery, taken at the first visit of the police to the defendant's room, and a number of letters written to the defendant in respect to the lottery, taken by the Marshal upon his search of defendant's room.

The defendant assigns error, among other things, in the court's refusal to grant his petition for the return of his property and in permitting the papers to be used at the trial.

* * *

The effect of the Fourth Amendment is to put the courts of the United States and Federal officials, in the exercise of their power and authority, under limitations and restraints as to the exercise of such power and authority, and to forever secure the people, their persons, houses, papers and effects against all unreasonable searches and seizures under the guise of law. This protection reaches all alike, whether accused of crime or not, and the duty of giving to it force and effect is obligatory upon all entrusted under our Federal system with the enforcement of the laws. The tendency of those who execute the criminal laws of the country to obtain conviction by means of unlawful seizures and enforced confessions, the latter often obtained after subjecting accused persons to unwarranted practices destructive of rights secured by the Federal Constitution, should find no sanction in the judgments of the courts which are charged at all times with the support of the Constitution and to which people of all conditions have a right to appeal for the maintenance of such fundamental rights. * * * The United States Marshal could only have invaded the house of the accused when armed with a warrant issued as required by the Constitution, upon sworn information and describing with reasonable particularity the thing for which the search was to be made. Instead, he acted without sanction of law, doubtless prompted by the desire to bring further proof to the aid of the Government, and under color of his office undertook to make a seizure of private papers in direct violation of the constitutional prohibition against such action. Under such circumstances, without sworn information and particular description, not even an order of court would have justified such procedure, much less was it within the authority of the United States Marshal to thus invade the house and privacy of the accused. * * *

We therefore reach the conclusion that the letters in question were taken from the house of the accused by an official of the United States acting under color of his office in direct violation of the constitutional rights of the defendant; that having made a seasonable application for their return, which was heard and passed upon by the court, there was involved in the order refusing the application a denial of the constitutional rights of the accused, and that the court should have restored these letters to the accused. In holding them and permitting their use upon the trial, we think prejudicial error was committed. As to the papers and property seized by the policemen, it does not appear that they acted under any claim of Federal authority such as would make the Amendment applicable to such unauthorized seizures. The record shows that what they did by way of arrest and search and seizure was done before the finding of the indictment in the Federal court, under what supposed right or authority does not appear. What remedies the defendant may have against them we need not inquire, as the Fourth Amendment is not directed to individual misconduct of such officials. Its limitations reach the Federal Government and its agencies.

It results that the judgment of the court below must be reversed, and the case remanded for further proceedings in accordance with this opinion. *Reversed*.

B. INCORPORATION OF THE BILL OF RIGHTS

Commentary

Until the 1860s, it was accepted that the Bill of Rights limited the power of the national government, but not of the States. Barron v. Mayor of Baltimore, 32 U.S. (7 Pet.) 243 (1833). Adoption of the Fourteenth Amendment upended this consensus, and litigants began to claim that provisions contained in the first eight Amendments now were imposed on the states. After the Supreme Court rejected claims based upon the Fourteenth Amendment's Privileges or Immunities Clause in the Slaughterhouse Cases, litigants shifted their focus to the Amendment's Due Process Clause, typically arguing that it imposed rights found in the original Amendments on the States. By the end of the 1930s, the Supreme Court had refused to "incorporate" the Bill of Rights into the Due Process Clause but its decisions had established that some rights were so fundamental to the concept of ordered liberty that the States could not infringe upon them without violating the requirements of due process. In *Wolf v. Colorado*, the Supreme Court addressed two related questions: were the right to be free from unreasonable searches and seizures and the exclusionary remedy such fundamental rights? Twelve years later the Court revisited these questions in *Mapp v. Ohio*.

WOLF v. COLORADO

Supreme Court of the United States, 1949.
338 U.S. 25, 69 S.Ct. 1359, 93 L.Ed. 1782.

MR. JUSTICE FRANKFURTER delivered the opinion of the Court.

The precise question for consideration is this: Does a conviction by a State court for a State offense deny the "due process of law" required by the Fourteenth Amendment, solely because evidence that was admitted at the trial was obtained under circumstances which would have rendered it inadmissible in a prosecution for violation of a federal law in a court of the United States because there deemed to be an infraction of the Fourth Amendment as applied in *Weeks v. United States*, 232 U.S. 383, 34 S.Ct. 341, 58 L.Ed. 652 (1914). The Supreme Court of Colorado has sustained convictions in which such evidence was admitted, and we brought the cases here.

Unlike the specific requirements and restrictions placed by the Bill of Rights (Amendments I to VIII) upon the administration of criminal justice by federal authority, the Fourteenth Amendment did not subject criminal justice in the States to specific limitations. The notion that the "due process of law" guaranteed by the Fourteenth Amendment is shorthand for the first eight amendments of the Constitution and thereby incorporates them has been rejected by this Court again and again, after impressive consideration. * * *

For purposes of ascertaining the restrictions which the Due Process Clause imposed upon the States in the enforcement of their criminal law, we adhere to the views expressed in *Palko v. Connecticut*, 302 U.S. 319, 58 S.Ct. 149, 82 L.Ed. 288 (1937). That decision speaks to us with the great weight of the authority, particularly in matters of civil liberty, of a court that included Mr. Chief Justice Hughes, Mr. Justice Brandeis, Mr. Justice Stone and Mr. Justice Cardozo, to name only the dead. In rejecting the suggestion that the Due Process Clause incorporated the original Bill of Rights, Mr. Justice Cardozo reaffirmed on behalf of that Court a different but deeper and more pervasive conception of the Due Process Clause. This Clause exacts from the States for the lowliest and the most outcast all that is "implicit in the concept of ordered liberty." 302 U.S. at 325.

Due process of law thus conveys neither formal nor fixed nor narrow requirements. It is the compendious expression for all those rights which the courts must enforce because they are basic to our free society. But basic rights do not become petrified as of any one time, even though, as a matter of human experience, some may not too rhetorically be called eternal verities. It is of the very nature of a free society to advance in its standards of what is deemed reasonable and right. Representing as it does a living principle, due process is not confined within a permanent catalogue of what may at a given time be deemed the limits or the essentials of fundamental rights.

* * *

The security of one's privacy against arbitrary intrusion by the police—which is at the core of the Fourth Amendment—is basic to a free society. It is therefore implicit in "the concept of ordered liberty" and as such enforceable against the States through the Due Process Clause. The knock at the door, whether by day or by night, as a prelude to a search, without authority of law but solely on the authority of the police, did not need the commentary of recent history to be condemned as inconsistent with the conception of human rights enshrined in the history and the basic constitutional documents of English-speaking peoples.

Accordingly, we have no hesitation in saying that were a State affirmatively to sanction such police incursion into privacy it would run counter to the guaranty of the Fourteenth Amendment. But the ways of enforcing such a basic right raise questions of a different order. How such arbitrary conduct should be checked, what remedies against it should be afforded, the means by which the right should be made effective, are all questions that are not to be so dogmatically answered as to preclude the varying solutions which spring from an allowable range of judgment on issues not susceptible of quantitative solution.

In *Weeks* this Court held that in a federal prosecution the Fourth Amendment barred the use of evidence secured through an illegal search and seizure. This ruling was made for the first time in 1914. It was not derived from the explicit requirements of the Fourth Amendment; it was not based on legislation expressing Congressional policy in the enforcement of the Constitution. The decision was a matter of judicial implication. Since then it has been frequently applied and we stoutly adhere to it. But the immediate question is whether the basic right to protection against arbitrary intrusion by the police demands the exclusion of logically relevant evidence obtained by an unreasonable search and seizure because, in a federal prosecution for a federal crime, it would be excluded. As a matter of inherent reason, one would suppose this to be an issue as to which men with complete devotion to the protection of the right of privacy might give different answers. When we find that in fact most of the English-speaking world does not regard as vital to such protection the exclusion of evidence thus obtained, we must hesitate to treat this remedy as an essential ingredient of the right. The contrariety of views of the States is particularly impressive in view of the careful reconsideration which they have given the problem in the light of the *Weeks* decision. * * * As of today 31 States reject the *Weeks* doctrine, 16 States are in agreement with it. Of 10 jurisdictions within the United Kingdom and the British Commonwealth of Nations which have passed on the question, none has held evidence obtained by illegal search and seizure inadmissible.

The jurisdictions which have rejected the *Weeks* doctrine have not left the right to privacy without other means of protection. Indeed, the exclusion of evidence is a remedy which directly serves only to protect those upon whose person or premises something incriminating has been found. We cannot, therefore, regard it as a departure from basic standards to remand such persons, together with those who emerge scatheless from a search, to the remedies of private action and such protection as the internal discipline of the police, under the eyes of an alert public opinion, may afford. Granting that in practice the exclusion of evidence may be an effective way of deterring unreasonable searches, it is not for this Court to condemn as falling below the minimal standards assured by the Due Process Clause a State's reliance upon other methods which, if consistently enforced, would be equally effective. * * * We cannot brush aside the experience of States which deem the incidence of such conduct by the police too slight to call for a deterrent remedy not by way of disciplinary measures but by overriding the relevant rules of evidence. There are, moreover, reasons for excluding evidence unreasonably obtained by the federal police which are less compelling in the case of police under State or local authority. The public opinion of a community can far more effectively be exerted against oppressive conduct on the part of police directly responsible to the community itself than can local opinion, sporadically aroused, be brought to bear upon remote authority pervasively exerted throughout the country.

We hold, therefore, that in a prosecution in a State court for a State crime the Fourteenth Amendment does not forbid the admission of evidence obtained by an unreasonable search and seizure. * * * Affirmed.

[The concurring opinion of JUSTICE BLACK, and the dissenting opinion of JUSTICE DOUGLAS, are omitted.]

MR. JUSTICE MURPHY, with whom MR. JUSTICE RUTLEDGE joins, dissenting.

It is disheartening to find so much that is right in an opinion which seems to me so fundamentally wrong. Of course I agree with the Court that the Fourteenth Amendment prohibits activities which are proscribed by the search and seizure clause of the Fourth Amendment. See my dissenting views, and those of MR. JUSTICE BLACK, in *Adamson v. California*, 332 U.S. 46, 68, 123, 67 S.Ct. 1672, 91 L.Ed. 1903 (1947). Quite apart from the blanket application of the Bill of Rights to the States, a devotee of democracy would ill suit his name were he to suggest that his home's protection against unlicensed governmental invasion was not "of the very essence of a scheme of ordered liberty." It is difficult for me to understand how the Court can go this far and yet be unwilling to make the step which can give some meaning to the pronouncements it utters.

Imagination and zeal may invent a dozen methods to give content to the commands of the Fourth Amendment. But this Court is limited to the remedies currently available. It cannot legislate the ideal system. If we would attempt the enforcement of the search and seizure clause in the ordinary case today, we are limited to three devices: judicial exclusion of the illegally obtained evidence; criminal prosecution of violators; and civil action against violators in the action of trespass.

Alternatives are deceptive. Their very statement conveys the impression that one possibility is as effective as the next. In this case their statement is blinding. For there is but one alternative to the rule of exclusion. That is no sanction at all.

* * *

* * * Little need be said concerning the possibilities of criminal prosecution. Self-scrutiny is a lofty ideal, but its exaltation reaches new heights if we expect a District Attorney to prosecute himself or his associates for well-meaning violations of the search and seizure clause during a raid the District Attorney or his associates have ordered. But there is an appealing ring in another alternative. A trespass action for damages is a venerable means of securing reparation for unauthorized invasion of the home. Why not put the old writ to a new use? When the Court cites cases permitting the action, the remedy seems complete.

But what an illusory remedy this is, if by "remedy" we mean a positive deterrent to police and prosecutors tempted to violate the Fourth Amendment. The appealing ring softens when we recall that in a trespass action the measure of damages is simply the extent of the injury to physical property. If the officer searches with care, he can avoid all but nominal damages—a penny, or a dollar. Are punitive damages possible? Perhaps. But a few states permit none, whatever the circumstances. In those that do, the plaintiff must show the real ill will or malice of the defendant, and surely it is not unreasonable to assume that one in honest pursuit of crime bears no malice toward the search victim. If that burden is carried, recovery may yet be defeated by the rule that there must be physical damages before punitive damages may be awarded. In addition, some states limit punitive damages to the actual expenses of litigation. Others demand some arbitrary ratio between actual and punitive damages before a verdict may stand. Even assuming the ill will of the officer, his reasonable grounds for belief that the home he searched harbored evidence of crime is admissible in mitigation of punitive damages. The bad reputation of the plaintiff is likewise admissible. If the evidence seized was actually used at a trial, that fact has been held a complete justification of the search, and a defense against the trespass action. And even if the plaintiff hurdles all these obstacles, and gains a substantial verdict, the individual officer's finances may well make the judgment useless—for the municipality, of course, is not liable without its consent. Is it surprising that there is so little in the books concerning trespass actions for violation of the search and seizure clause?

The conclusion is inescapable that but one remedy exists to deter violations of the search and seizure clause. That is the rule which excludes illegally obtained evidence. Only by exclusion can we impress upon the zealous prosecutor that violation of the Constitution will do him no good. And only when that point is driven home can the prosecutor be expected to emphasize the importance of observing constitutional demands in his instructions to the police. * * *

I cannot believe that we should decide due process questions by simply taking a poll of the rules in various jurisdictions, even if we follow the *Palko* "test." Today's decision will do inestimable harm to the cause of fair police methods in our cities and states. Even more important, perhaps, it must have tragic effect upon public respect for our judiciary. For the Court now allows what is indeed shabby business: lawlessness by officers of the law.

Since the evidence admitted was secured in violation of the Fourth Amendment, the judgment should be reversed.

MAPP v. OHIO

Supreme Court of the United States, 1961.
367 U.S. 643, 81 S.Ct. 1684, 6 L.Ed.2d 1081.

MR. JUSTICE CLARK delivered the opinion of the Court.

Appellant stands convicted of knowingly [possessing obscene books and photographs].

On May 23, 1957, three Cleveland police officers arrived at appellant's residence in that city pursuant to information that "a person [was] hiding out in the home, who was wanted for questioning in connection with a recent bombing, and that there was a large amount of policy paraphernalia being hidden in the home." Miss Mapp and her daughter by a former marriage lived on the top floor of the two-family dwelling. Upon their arrival at that house, the officers knocked on the door and demanded entrance but appellant, after telephoning her attorney, refused to admit them without a search warrant. They advised their headquarters of the situation and undertook a surveillance of the house.

The officers again sought entrance some three hours later when four or more additional officers arrived on the scene. When Miss Mapp did not come to the door immediately, at least one of the several doors to the house was forcibly opened and the policemen gained admittance. Meanwhile Miss Mapp's attorney arrived, but the officers, having secured their own entry, and continuing in their defiance of the law, would permit him neither to see Miss Mapp nor to enter the house. It appears that Miss Mapp was halfway down the stairs from the upper floor to the front door when the officers, in this highhanded manner, broke into the hall. She demanded to see the search warrant. A paper, claimed to be a warrant, was held up by one of the officers. She grabbed the "warrant" and placed it in her bosom. A struggle ensued in which the officers recovered the piece of paper and as a result of which they handcuffed appellant because she had been "belligerent" in resisting their official rescue of the "warrant" from her person. Running roughshod over appellant, a policeman "grabbed" her, "twisted [her] hand," and she "yelled [and] pleaded with him" because "it was hurting." Appellant, in handcuffs, was then forcibly taken upstairs to her bedroom where the officers searched a dresser, a chest of drawers, a closet and some suitcases. They also looked into a photo album and through personal papers belonging to the appellant. The search spread to the rest of the second floor including the child's bedroom, the living room, the kitchen and a dinette. The basement of the building and a trunk found therein were also searched. The obscene materials for possession of which she was ultimately convicted were discovered in the course of that widespread search.

At the trial no search warrant was produced by the prosecution, nor was the failure to produce one explained or accounted for. * * *

The State says that even if the search were made without authority, or otherwise unreasonably, it is not prevented from using the unconstitutionally seized evidence at trial, citing *Wolf v. Colorado*, 338 U.S. 25, 69 S.Ct. 1359, 93 L.Ed.1782 (1949), in which this Court did indeed hold "that in a prosecution in a State court for a State crime the Fourteenth Amendment does not forbid the admission of evidence obtained by an unreasonable search and seizure." On this appeal, * * * it is urged once again that we review that holding. * * * While in 1949, prior to the *Wolf* case, almost two-thirds of the States were opposed to the use of the exclusionary rule, now, despite the *Wolf* case, more than half of those since passing upon it, by their own legislative or judicial decision, have wholly or partly adopted or adhered to the *Weeks* rule. Significantly, among those now following the rule is California, which, according to its highest court, was "compelled to reach that conclusion because other remedies have completely failed to secure compliance with the constitutional provisions." In connection with this California case, we note that the second basis elaborated in *Wolf* in support of its failure to enforce the exclusionary doctrine against the States was that "other means of protection" have been afforded "the right to privacy." The experience of California that such other remedies have been worthless and futile is buttressed by the experience of other States. The obvious futility of relegating the Fourth Amendment to the protection of other remedies has, moreover, been recognized by this Court since *Wolf*. See *Irvine v. California*, 347 U.S. 128, 137, 74 S.Ct. 381, 98 L.Ed. 561 (1954).

* * *

[T]he factual considerations supporting the failure of the *Wolf* Court to include the *Weeks* exclusionary rule when it recognized the enforceability of the right to privacy against the States in 1949, while not basically relevant to the constitutional consideration, could not, in any analysis, now be deemed controlling. * * *

IV

Since the Fourth Amendment's right of privacy has been declared enforceable against the States through the Due Process Clause of the Fourteenth, it is enforceable against them by the same sanction of exclusion as is used against the Federal Government. Were it otherwise, then just as without the *Weeks* rule the assurance against unreasonable federal searches and seizures would be "a form of words," valueless and undeserving of mention in a perpetual charter of inestimable human liberties, so too, without that rule the freedom from state invasions of privacy would be so ephemeral and so neatly severed from its conceptual nexus with the freedom from all brutish means of coercing evidence as not to merit this Court's high regard as a freedom "implicit in the concept of ordered liberty." At the time that the Court held in *Wolf* that the Amendment was applicable to the States through the Due Process Clause, the cases of this Court, as we have seen, had steadfastly held that as to federal officers the Fourth Amendment included the exclusion of the evidence seized in violation of its provisions. Even *Wolf* "stoutly adhered" to that proposition. The right to privacy, when conceded operatively enforceable against the States, was not susceptible of destruction by avulsion of the sanction upon which its protection and enjoyment had always been deemed dependent under the *Boyd, Weeks* and *Silverthorne* cases. Therefore, in extending the substantive protections of due process to all constitutionally unreasonable searches—state or federal—it was logically and constitutionally necessary that the exclusion doctrine—an essential part of the right to privacy—be also insisted upon as an essential ingredient of the right newly recognized by the *Wolf* case. In short, the admission of the new constitutional right by *Wolf* could not consistently tolerate denial of its most important constitutional privilege, namely, the exclusion of the evidence which an accused had been forced to give by reason of the unlawful seizure. To hold otherwise is to grant the right but in reality to withhold its privilege and enjoyment. Only last year the Court itself recognized that the purpose of the exclusionary rule "is to deter—to compel respect for the constitutional guaranty in the only effectively available way—by removing the incentive to disregard it." *Elkins v. United States*.

Indeed, we are aware of no restraint, similar to that rejected today, conditioning the enforcement of any other basic constitutional right. The right to privacy, no less important than any other right carefully and particularly reserved to the people, would stand in marked contrast to all other rights declared as "basic to a free society." This Court has not hesitated to enforce as strictly against the States as it does against the Federal Government the rights of free speech and of a free press, the rights to notice and to a fair, public trial, including, as it does, the right not to be convicted by use of a coerced confession, however logically relevant it be, and without regard to its reliability. And nothing could be more certain than that when a coerced confession is involved, "the relevant rules of evidence" are overridden without regard to "the incidence of such conduct by the police," slight or frequent. Why should not the same rule apply to what is tantamount to coerced testimony by way of unconstitutional seizure of goods, papers, effects, documents, etc.? We find that, as to the Federal Government, the Fourth and Fifth Amendments and, as to the States, the freedom from unconscionable invasions of privacy and the freedom from convictions based upon coerced confessions do enjoy an "intimate relation" in their perpetuation of "principles of humanity and civil liberty [secured] * * * only after years of struggle," *Bram v. United States*, 168 U.S. 532, 543–544, 18 S.Ct. 183, 42 L.Ed. 568 (1897). They express "supplementing phases of the same constitutional purpose—to maintain inviolate large areas of personal privacy." *Feldman v. United States*, 322 U.S. 487, 489–490, 64 S.Ct. 1082, 88 L.Ed.1408 (1944). The philosophy of each Amendment and of each freedom is complementary to, although not dependent upon, that of the other in its sphere of influence—the very least that together they assure in either sphere is that no man is to be convicted on unconstitutional evidence.

V.

Moreover, our holding that the exclusionary rule is an essential part of both the Fourth and Fourteenth Amendments is not only the logical dictate of prior cases, but it also makes very good sense. There is no war between the Constitution and common sense. Presently, a federal prosecutor may make no use of evidence illegally seized, but a State's attorney across the street may, although he supposedly is operating under the enforceable prohibitions of the same Amendment. Thus the State, by admitting evidence unlawfully seized, serves to encourage disobedience to the Federal Constitution which it is bound to uphold. * * *

There are those who say, as did Justice (then Judge) Cardozo, that under our constitutional exclusionary doctrine "[t]he criminal is to go free because the constable has blundered." *People v. Defore*, 242 N.Y., at 21, 150 N.E., at 587. In some cases this will undoubtedly be the result. But, as was said in *Elkins* [v. United States, 364 U.S. 206 (1960)], "there is another consideration—the imperative of judicial integrity." The criminal goes free, if he must, but it is the law that sets him free. Nothing can destroy a government more quickly than its failure to observe its own laws, or worse, its disregard of the charter of its own existence. As Mr. Justice Brandeis, dissenting, said in *Olmstead v. United States*, 277 U.S. 438, 485, 48 S.Ct. 564, 72 L.Ed. 944 (1928): "Our Government is the potent, the omnipresent teacher. For good or for ill, it teaches the whole people by its example. * * * If the Government becomes a lawbreaker, it breeds contempt for law; it invites every man to become a law unto himself; it invites anarchy." Nor can it lightly be assumed that, as a practical matter, adoption of the exclusionary rule fetters law enforcement. Only last year this Court expressly considered that contention and found that "pragmatic evidence of a sort" to the contrary was not wanting. *Elkins v. United States.* The Court noted that

"The federal courts themselves have operated under the exclusionary rule of *Weeks* for almost half a century; yet it has not been suggested either that the Federal Bureau of Investigation has thereby been rendered ineffective, or that the administration of criminal justice in the federal courts has thereby been disrupted. Moreover, the experience of the states is impressive. * * * The movement towards the rule of exclusion has been halting but seemingly inexorable."

The ignoble shortcut to conviction left open to the State tends to destroy the entire system of constitutional restraints on which the liberties of the people rest. Having once recognized that the right to privacy embodied in the Fourth Amendment is enforceable against the States, and that the right to be secure against rule invasions of privacy by state officers is, therefore, constitutional in origin, we can no longer permit that right to remain an empty promise. Because it is enforceable in the same manner and to like effect as other basic rights secured by the Due Process Clause, we can no longer permit it to be revocable at the whim of any police officer who, in the name of law enforcement itself, chooses to suspend its enjoyment. Our decision, founded on reason and truth, gives to the individual no more than that which the Constitution guarantees him, to the police officer no less than that to which honest law enforcement is entitled, and, to the courts, that judicial integrity so necessary in the true administration of justice. * * *

Reversed and Remanded.

[The concurring opinions of Justices Douglas and Black, and the dissenting opinion of Justice Harlan, with whom Justices Frankfurter and Whittaker joined, are omitted.]

C.   LIMITING THE IMPACT OF THE EXCLUSIONARY RULE

1.   Balancing Costs and Benefits: The Deterrence Theory

UNITED STATES v. CALANDRA

Supreme Court of the United States, 1974.
414 U.S. 338, 94 S.Ct. 613, 38 L.Ed.2d 561.

MR. JUSTICE POWELL delivered the opinion of the Court.

* * *

I

[Federal agents obtained a warrant authorizing a search of Calandra's place of business, where they seized various items. A federal grand jury subpoenaed Calandra, who appeared but refused to testify, invoking his Fifth Amendment privilege against self-incrimination. The Government sought an immunity order to compel Calandra to testify. Calandra moved to suppress the evidence seized in the search, arguing that the affidavit supporting the warrant was insufficient and that the search exceeded the scope of the warrant. The Court of Appeals affirmed the District Court's order suppressing the evidence and ordering that Calandra need not answer grand jury's questions based upon the suppressed evidence. The Supreme Court reversed the Court of Appeals.]

II

The institution of the grand jury is deeply rooted in Anglo–American history. In England, the grand jury served for centuries both as a body of accusers sworn to discover and present for trial persons suspected of criminal wrongdoing and as a protector of citizens against arbitrary and oppressive governmental action. In this country the Founders thought the grand jury so essential to basic liberties that they provided in the Fifth Amendment that federal prosecution for serious crimes can only be instituted by "a presentment or indictment of a Grand Jury." The grand jury's historic functions survive to this day. Its responsibilities continue to include both the determination whether there is probable cause to believe a crime has been committed and the protection of citizens against unfounded criminal prosecutions.

Traditionally the grand jury has been accorded wide latitude to inquire into violations of criminal law. No judge presides to monitor its proceedings. It deliberates in secret and may determine alone the course of its inquiry. The grand jury may compel the production of evidence or the testimony of witnesses as it considers appropriate, and its operation generally is unrestrained by the technical procedural and evidentiary rules governing the conduct of criminal trials. * * *

* * *

"The role of the grand jury as an important instrument of effective law enforcement necessarily includes an investigatory function with respect to determining whether a crime has been committed and who committed it. . . . 'When the grand jury is performing its investigatory function into a general problem area . . . society's interest is best served by a thorough and extensive investigation.' A grand jury investigation 'is not fully carried out until every available clue has been run down and all witnesses examined in every proper way to find if a crime has been committed.' Such an investigation may be triggered by tips, rumors, evidence proffered by the prosecutor, or the personal knowledge of the grand jurors. It is only after the grand jury has examined the evidence that a determination of whether the proceeding will result in an indictment can be made. . . . "

The grand jury's sources of information are widely drawn, and the validity of an indictment is not affected by the character of the evidence considered. Thus, an indictment valid on its face is not subject to challenge on the ground that the grand jury acted on the basis of inadequate or incompetent evidence, or even on the basis of information obtained in violation of a defendant's Fifth Amendment privilege against self-incrimination.

The power of a federal court to compel persons to appear and testify before a grand jury is also firmly established. *Kastigar* v. *United States*, 406 U.S. 441 (1972). [T]he duty to testify has been regarded as "so necessary to the administration of justice" that the witness' personal interest in privacy must yield to the public's overriding interest in full disclosure. * * *

Of course, the grand jury's subpoena power is not unlimited. It may consider incompetent evidence, but it may not itself violate a valid privilege, whether established by the Constitution, statutes, or the common law. Although, for example, an indictment based on evidence obtained in violation of a defendant's Fifth Amendment privilege is nevertheless valid, the grand jury may not force a witness to answer questions in violation of that constitutional guarantee. Rather, the grand jury may override a Fifth Amendment claim only if the witness is granted immunity co-extensive with the privilege against self-incrimination. Similarly, a grand jury may not compel a person to produce books and papers that would incriminate him. *Boyd* v. *United States*, 116 U.S. 616, 633–635 (1886). The grand jury is also without power to invade a legitimate privacy interest protected by the Fourth Amendment. A grand jury's subpoena *duces tecum* will be disallowed if it is "far too sweeping in its terms to be regarded as reasonable" under the Fourth Amendment. *Hale* v. *Henkel*, 201 U.S. 43, 76 (1906). Judicial supervision is properly exercised in such cases to prevent the wrong before it occurs.

* * *

The purpose of the exclusionary rule is not to redress the injury to the privacy of the search victim:

> "The ruptured privacy of the victims' homes and effects cannot be restored. Reparation comes too late." *Linkletter* v. *Walker*, 381 U.S. 618, 637 (1965).

Instead, the rule's prime purpose is to deter future unlawful police conduct and thereby effectuate the guarantee of the Fourth Amendment against unreasonable searches and seizures:

> "The rule is calculated to prevent, not to repair. Its purpose is to deter—to compel respect for the constitutional guaranty in the only effectively available way—by removing the incentive to disregard it."

In sum, the rule is a judicially created remedy designed to safeguard Fourth Amendment rights generally through its deterrent effect, rather than a personal constitutional right of the party aggrieved.

Despite its broad deterrent purpose, the exclusionary rule has never been interpreted to proscribe the use of illegally seized evidence in all proceedings or against all persons. As with any remedial device, the application of the rule has been restricted to those areas where its remedial objectives are thought most efficaciously served. The balancing process implicit in this approach is expressed in the contours of the standing requirement. Thus, standing to invoke the exclusionary rule has been confined to situations where the Government seeks to use such evidence to incriminate the victim of the unlawful search. This standing rule is premised on a recognition that the need for deterrence and hence the rationale for excluding the evidence are strongest where the Government's unlawful conduct would result in imposition of a criminal sanction on the victim of the search.

IV

In deciding whether to extend the exclusionary rule to grand jury proceedings, we must weigh the potential injury to the historic role and functions of the grand jury against the potential benefits of the rule as applied in this context. It is evident that this extension of the exclusionary rule would seriously impede the grand jury. Because the grand jury does not finally adjudicate guilt or innocence, it has traditionally been allowed to pursue its investigative and accusatorial functions unimpeded by the evidentiary and procedural restrictions applicable to a criminal trial. Permitting witnesses to invoke the exclusionary rule before a grand jury would precipitate adjudication of issues hitherto reserved for the trial on the merits and would delay and disrupt grand jury proceedings. Suppression hearings would halt the orderly progress of an investigation and might necessitate extended litigation of issues only tangentially related to the grand jury's primary objective. The probable result would be "protracted interruption of grand jury proceedings," effectively transforming them into preliminary trials on the merits. In some cases the delay might be fatal to the enforcement of the criminal law. * * *

* * *

Any incremental deterrent effect which might be achieved by extending the rule to grand jury proceedings is uncertain at best. Whatever deterrence of police misconduct may result from the exclusion of illegally seized evidence from criminal trials, it is unrealistic to assume that application of the rule to grand jury proceedings would significantly further that goal. Such an extension would deter only police investigation consciously directed toward the discovery of evidence solely for use in a grand jury investigation. The incentive to disregard the requirement of the Fourth Amendment solely to obtain an indictment from a grand jury is substantially negated by the inadmissibility of the illegally seized evidence in a subsequent criminal prosecution of the search victim. For the most part, a prosecutor would be unlikely to request an indictment where a conviction could not be obtained. We therefore decline to embrace a view that would achieve a speculative and undoubtedly minimal advance in the deterrence of police misconduct at the expense of substantially impeding the role of the grand jury.

* * *

Mr. Justice Brennan, with whom Mr. Justice Douglas and Mr. Justice Marshall join, dissenting.

The Court holds that the exclusionary rule in search-and-seizure cases does not apply to grand jury proceedings because the principal objective of the rule is "to deter future unlawful police conduct," and "it is unrealistic to assume that application of the rule to grand jury proceedings would significantly further that goal." This downgrading of the exclusionary rule to a determination whether its application in a particular type of proceeding furthers deterrence of future police misconduct reflects a startling misconception, unless it is a purposeful rejection, of the historical objective and purpose of the rule.

The commands of the Fourth Amendment are, of course, directed solely to public officials. Necessarily, therefore, only official violations of those commands could have created the evil that threatened to make the Amendment a dead letter. But curtailment of the evil, if a consideration at all, was at best only a hoped-for effect of the exclusionary rule, not its ultimate objective. Indeed, there is no evidence that the possible deterrent effect of the rule was given any attention by the judges chiefly responsible for its formulation. Their concern as guardians of the Bill of Rights was to fashion an enforcement tool to give content and meaning to the Fourth Amendment's guarantees. They thus bore out James Madison's prediction in his address to the First Congress on June 8, 1789:

> "If they [the rights] are incorporated into the Constitution, independent tribunals of justice will consider themselves in a peculiar manner the guardians of those rights; they will be an impenetrable bulwark against every assumption of power in the Legislative or Executive; they will be naturally led to resist every encroachment upon rights expressly stipulated for in the Constitution by the declaration of rights." 1 Annals of Cong. 439 (1789).

Since, however, those judges were without power to direct or control the conduct of law enforcement officers, the enforcement tool had necessarily to be one capable of administration by judges. The exclusionary rule, if not perfect, accomplished the twin goals of enabling the judiciary to avoid the taint of partnership in official lawlessness and of assuring the people—all potential victims of unlawful government conduct—that the government would not profit from its lawless behavior, thus minimizing the risk of seriously undermining popular trust in government.

That these considerations, not the rule's possible deterrent effect, were uppermost in the minds of the framers of the rule clearly emerges from the decision which fashioned it:

> The effect of the Fourth Amendment is to put the courts of the United States and Federal officials, in the exercise of their power and authority, under limitations and restraints as to the exercise of such power and authority, and to forever secure the people, their persons, houses, papers and effects against all unreasonable searches and seizures under the guise of law. . . . The tendency of those who execute the criminal laws of the country to obtain conviction by means of unlawful seizures . . . *should find no sanction in the judgments of the courts which are charged at all times with the support of the Constitution and to which people of all conditions have a right to appeal for the maintenance of such fundamental rights* . . . .
>
> This protection is equally extended to the action of the Government and officers of the law acting under it. . . . *To sanction such proceedings would be to affirm by judicial decision a manifest neglect if not an open defiance of the prohibitions of the Constitution, intended for the protection of the people against such unauthorized action. Weeks* v. *United States*, 232 U.S. 383, 391–392, 394 (1914) (emphasis added).

* * *

Thus, the Court seriously errs in describing the exclusionary rule as merely "a judicially created remedy designed to safeguard Fourth Amendment rights generally through its deterrent effect...." Rather, the exclusionary rule is "part and parcel of the Fourth Amendment's limitation upon [governmental] encroachment of individual privacy,", and "an essential part of both the Fourth and Fourteenth Amendments," that "gives to the individual no more than that which the Constitution guarantees him, to the police officer no less than that to which honest law enforcement is entitled, and, to the courts, that judicial integrity so necessary in the true administration of justice."]

* * *

The exclusionary rule gave life to Madison's prediction that "independent tribunals of justice ... will be naturally led to resist every encroachment upon rights expressly stipulated for in the Constitution by the declaration of rights." 1 Annals of Cong. 439 (1789). We betray the trust upon which that prediction rested by today's long step toward abandonment of the exclusionary rule. * * *

I dissent and would affirm the judgment of the Court of Appeals.

2. Balancing Costs and Benefits of Exclusion: The "Good Faith" Exception

UNITED STATES v. LEON

Supreme Court of the United States, 1984.
468 U.S. 897, 104 S.Ct. 3405, 82 L.Ed.2d 677.

JUSTICE WHITE delivered the opinion of the Court.

This case presents the question whether the Fourth Amendment exclusionary rule should be modified so as not to bar the use in the prosecution's case-in-chief of evidence obtained by officers acting in reasonable reliance on a search warrant issued by a detached and neutral magistrate but ultimately found to be unsupported by probable cause. * * *

I

[An officer of the Burbank, California Police Department received a tip that two people were selling large quantities of cocaine and methaqualone from their residence in that city. Although the informant had not been proven to be reliable, he claimed to have witnessed criminal activity, and also said that small quantities of drugs were kept at the residence. Officers attempted to corroborate the tip by conducting extensive surveillance of that home, two other residences, people associated with the three homes, and the airline travels of one of the suspects. As a result of the investigation, they prepared an extensive application for search warrants for the residences, which was reviewed by several Deputy District Attorneys. A state superior court judge issued a facially valid search warrant. The ensuing searches uncovered drugs and other evidence at the three residences. Several people were indicted by a grand jury in the District Court for the Central District of California and charged with conspiracy to possess and distribute cocaine and a variety of substantive counts.

The defendants filed motions to suppress the evidence seized pursuant to the warrant. The District Court concluded that the case was a close one, but granted the motions to suppress in part, on the ground that the affidavit was insufficient to establish probable cause. "In response to a request from the Government, the court made clear that Officer Rombach had acted in good faith, but it rejected the Government's suggestion that the Fourth Amendment exclusionary rule should not apply where evidence is seized in reasonable, good-faith reliance on a search warrant." The Court of Appeals affirmed the suppression order. "The government, wishing to obtain a decision on the "good faith exception" issue, declined to seek review of the holding that the affidavit did not establish probable cause." The Supreme Court for the first time adopted a "good faith" exception to the exclusionary rule.]

II

A

The Fourth Amendment contains no provision expressly precluding the use of evidence obtained in violation of its commands, and an examination of its origin and purposes makes clear that the use of fruits of a past unlawful search or seizure "work[s] no new Fourth Amendment wrong." *United States v. Calandra*, 414 U.S. 338, 354, 94 S.Ct. 613, 38 L.Ed.2d 561 (1974). The wrong condemned by the Amendment is "fully accomplished" by the unlawful search or seizure itself, and the exclusionary rule is neither intended nor able to cure the invasion of the defendant's rights which he has already suffered. The rule thus operates as a judicially created remedy designed to safeguard Fourth Amendment rights generally through its deterrent effect, rather than a personal constitutional right of the person aggrieved. * * *

The substantial social costs exacted by the exclusionary rule for the vindication of Fourth Amendment rights have long been a source of concern. * * * An objectionable collateral consequence of this interference with the criminal justice system's truth-finding function is that some guilty defendants may go free or receive reduced sentences as a result of favorable plea bargains.[6] Particularly when law enforcement

---

6. Researchers have only recently begun to study extensively the effects of the exclusionary rule on the disposition of felony arrests. One study suggests that the rule results in the nonprosecution or nonconviction of between 0.6% and 2.35% of individuals arrested for felonies. Davies, A Hard Look at What We Know (and Still Need to Learn) About the "Costs" of the Exclusionary Rule: The NIJ Study and Other Studies of "Lost" Arrests, 1983 A.B.F.Res.J. 611, 621. The estimates are higher for particular crimes the prosecution of which depends heavily on physical evidence. Thus, the cumulative loss due to nonprosecution or nonconviction of individuals arrested on felony drug charges is probably in the range of 2.8% to 7.1%. *Id.*, at 680. Davies' analysis of California data suggests that screening by police and prosecutors results in the release because of illegal searches or seizures of as many as 1.4% of all felony arrestees, *id.*, at

officers have acted in objective good faith or their transgressions have been minor, the magnitude of the benefit conferred on such guilty defendants offends basic concepts of the criminal justice system. Indiscriminate application of the exclusionary rule, therefore, may well generate disrespect for the law and the administration of justice. * * *

B

Close attention to those remedial objectives has characterized our recent decisions concerning the scope of the Fourth Amendment exclusionary rule. The Court has, to be sure, not seriously questioned, "in the absence of a more efficacious sanction, the continued application of the rule to suppress evidence from the [prosecution's] case where a Fourth Amendment violation has been substantial and deliberate...." Nevertheless, the balancing approach that has evolved in various contexts—including criminal trials—forcefully suggests that the exclusionary rule be more generally modified to permit the introduction of evidence obtained in the reasonable good-faith belief that a search or seizure was in accord with the Fourth Amendment.

In *Stone v. Powell,* 428 U.S. 465, 96 S.Ct. 3037, 49 L.Ed.2d 1067 (1976), the Court emphasized the costs of the exclusionary rule, expressed its view that limiting the circumstances under which Fourth Amendment claims could be raised in federal habeas corpus proceedings would not reduce the rule's deterrent effect, and held that a state prisoner who has been afforded a full and fair opportunity to litigate a Fourth Amendment claim may not obtain federal habeas relief on the ground that unlawfully obtained evidence had been introduced at his trial. * * * Proposed extensions of the exclusionary rule to proceedings other than the criminal trial itself have been evaluated and rejected under the same analytic approach. * * *

* * *

III

A

Because a search warrant "provides the detached scrutiny of a neutral magistrate, which is a more reliable safeguard against improper

650, that 0.9% of felony arrestees are released because of illegal searches or seizures at the preliminary hearing or after trial, *id.,* at 653, and that roughly 0.05% of all felony arrestees benefit from reversals on appeal because of illegal searches. *Id.,* at 654. See also K. Brosi, A Cross–City Comparison of Felony Case Processing 16, 18–19 (1979); Report of the Comptroller General of the United States, Impact of the Exclusionary Rule on Federal Criminal Prosecutions 10–11, 14 (1979); F. Feeney, F. Dill & A. Weir, Arrests Without Convictions: How Often They Occur and Why 203–206 (1983); National Institute of Justice, The Effects of the Exclusionary Rule: A Study in California 1–2 (1982); Nardulli, The Societal Cost of the Exclusionary Rule: An Empirical Assessment, 1983 A.B.F.Res.J. 585, 600. The exclusionary rule also has been found to affect the plea-bargaining process. S. Schlesinger, Exclusionary Injustice: The Problem of Illegally Obtained Evidence 63 (1977). But see Davies, *supra,* at 668–669; Nardulli, *supra,* at 604–606.

Many of these researchers have concluded that the impact of the exclusionary rule is insubstantial, but the small percentages with which they deal mask a large absolute number of felons who are released because the cases against them were based in part on illegal searches or seizures. * * *

searches than the hurried judgment of a law enforcement officer 'engaged in the often competitive enterprise of ferreting out crime,' '' we have expressed a strong preference for warrants and declared that ''in a doubtful or marginal case a search under a warrant may be sustainable where without one it would fail.'' * * *

Deference to the magistrate, however, is not boundless. It is clear, first, that the deference accorded to a magistrate's finding of probable cause does not preclude inquiry into the knowing or reckless falsity of the affidavit on which that determination was based. *Franks v. Delaware*, 438 U.S. 154 (1978). Second, the courts must also insist that the magistrate purport to perform his ''neutral and detached'' function and not serve merely as a rubber stamp for the police. A magistrate failing to ''manifest that neutrality and detachment demanded of a judicial officer when presented with a warrant application'' and who acts instead as ''an adjunct law enforcement officer'' cannot provide valid authorization for an otherwise unconstitutional search.

Third, reviewing courts will not defer to a warrant based on an affidavit that does not ''provide the magistrate with a substantial basis for determining the existence of probable cause.'' * * *

Only in the first of these three situations, however, has the Court set forth a rationale for suppressing evidence obtained pursuant to a search warrant; in the other areas, it has simply excluded such evidence without considering whether Fourth Amendment interests will be advanced. To the extent that proponents of exclusion rely on its behavioral effects on judges and magistrates in these areas, their reliance is misplaced. First, the exclusionary rule is designed to deter police misconduct rather than to punish the errors of judges and magistrates. Second, there exists no evidence suggesting that judges and magistrates are inclined to ignore or subvert the Fourth Amendment or that lawlessness among these actors requires application of the extreme sanction of exclusion.

Third, and most important, we discern no basis, and are offered none, for believing that exclusion of evidence seized pursuant to a warrant will have a significant deterrent effect on the issuing judge or magistrate. Many of the factors that indicate that the exclusionary rule cannot provide an effective ''special'' or ''general'' deterrent for individual offending law enforcement officers apply as well to judges or magistrates. And, to the extent that the rule is thought to operate as a ''systemic'' deterrent on a wider audience, it clearly can have no such effect on individuals empowered to issue search warrants. Judges and magistrates are not adjuncts to the law enforcement team; as neutral judicial officers, they have no stake in the outcome of particular criminal prosecutions. The threat of exclusion thus cannot be expected significantly to deter them. Imposition of the exclusionary sanction is not necessary meaningfully to inform judicial officers of their errors, and we cannot conclude that admitting evidence obtained pursuant to a warrant while at the same time declaring that the warrant was somehow defective will in any way reduce judicial officers' professional incentives to comply with the Fourth Amendment, encourage them to repeat their mistakes, or lead to the granting of all colorable warrant requests.

B

* * *

We have frequently questioned whether the exclusionary rule can have any deterrent effect when the offending officers acted in the objectively reasonable belief that their conduct did not violate the Fourth Amendment. * * * But even assuming that the rule effectively deters some police misconduct and provides incentives for the law enforcement profession as a whole to conduct itself in accord with the Fourth Amendment, it cannot be expected, and should not be applied, to deter objectively reasonable law enforcement activity. * * * [20]

* * *

This is particularly true, we believe, when an officer acting with objective good faith has obtained a search warrant from a judge or magistrate and acted within its scope. In most such cases, there is no police illegality and thus nothing to deter. It is the magistrate's responsibility to determine whether the officer's allegations establish probable cause and, if so, to issue a warrant comporting in form with the requirements of the Fourth Amendment. In the ordinary case, an officer cannot be expected to question the magistrate's probable-cause determination or his judgment that the form of the warrant is technically sufficient. * * *

C

We conclude that the marginal or nonexistent benefits produced by suppressing evidence obtained in objectively reasonable reliance on a subsequently invalidated search warrant cannot justify the substantial costs of exclusion. We do not suggest, however, that exclusion is always inappropriate in cases where an officer has obtained a warrant and abided by its terms. * * * Suppression therefore remains an appropriate remedy if the magistrate or judge in issuing a warrant was misled by information in an affidavit that the affiant knew was false or would have known was false except for his reckless disregard of the truth. The exception we recognize today will also not apply in cases where the issuing magistrate wholly abandoned his judicial role in the manner condemned in *Lo-Ji Sales, Inc. v. New York*, 442 U.S. 319, 99 S.Ct. 2319, 60 L.Ed.2d 920 (1979); in such circumstances, no reasonably well-trained officer should rely on the warrant. Nor would an officer manifest objective good faith in relying on a warrant based on an affidavit so lacking in indicia of probable cause as to render official belief in its

---

20. We emphasize that the standard of reasonableness we adopt is an objective one. Many objections to a good-faith exception assume that the exception will turn on the subjective good faith of individual officers.

* * * The objective standard we adopt, moreover, requires officers to have a reasonable knowledge of what the law prohibits.

existence entirely unreasonable. Finally, depending on the circumstances of the particular case, a warrant may be so facially deficient—*i.e.*, in failing to particularize the place to be searched or the things to be seized—that the executing officers cannot reasonably presume it to be valid.

* * *

[The concurring opinion of JUSTICE BLACKMUN and the dissenting opinion of JUSTICE BRENNAN, with whom JUSTICE MARSHALL joined, and JUSTICE STEVENS' opinion, concurring in the judgment and dissenting in part, are omitted]

Note

The Supreme Court addressed a related question in *Leon's* companion case, Massachusetts v. Sheppard, 468 U.S. 981 (1984), in which it applied the rules articulated in that opinion "to a situation in which police officers seize items pursuant to a warrant subsequently invalidated because of a technical error on the part of the issuing judge." Officers investigating a homicide developed probable cause to believe that Sheppard was guilty of the crime. On the basis of the evidence, they prepared an application for an arrest warrant and a search warrant authorizing a search of Sheppard's residence. The affidavit included a description of the evidence the officers wanted to search for in the home, which included liquor, marijuana, items of clothing, wire, rope and a blunt instrument. The district attorney, the district attorney's first assistant, and a sergeant each reviewed the application, and all concluded that it set forth probable cause for the search and the arrest. The Supreme Court described the events that led to the production of a deficient warrant:

"Because it was Sunday, the local court was closed, and the police had a difficult time finding a warrant application form. Detective O'Malley finally found a warrant form previously in use in the Dorchester District. The form was entitled "Search Warrant—Controlled Substance." Realizing that some changes had to be made before the form could be used to authorize the search requested in the affidavit, Detective O'Malley deleted the subtitle "controlled substance" with a typewriter. He also substituted "Roxbury" for the printed "Dorchester" and typed Sheppard's name and address into blank spaces provided for that information. However, the reference to "controlled substance" was not deleted in the portion of the form that constituted the warrant application and that, when signed, would constitute the warrant itself.

"Detective O'Malley then took the affidavit and the warrant form to the residence of a judge who had consented to consider the warrant application. The judge examined the affidavit and stated that he would authorize the search as requested. Detective O'Malley offered the warrant form and stated that he knew the form as presented dealt with controlled substances. He showed the judge where he had crossed out the subtitles. After unsuccessfully searching for a more suitable form, the judge informed O'Malley that he would make the necessary changes so as to provide a proper search warrant. The judge then took the form, made some changes on it, and dated and signed the warrant. However, he did not change the substantive portion of the warrant, which continued to authorize a search for controlled substances.[2] The warrant directed the officers to "search for any controlled substance, article, implement or other paraphernalia used in, for, or in connection with the unlawful possession or use of any controlled substance, and to seize and securely keep the same until final action.... " nor did he alter the form so as to incorporate the affidavit. The judge returned the affidavit and the warrant to O'Malley, informing him that the warrant was sufficient authority in form and content to carry out the search as requested. O'Malley took the two documents and, accompanied by other officers, proceeded to Sheppard's residence. The scope of the ensuing search was limited to the items listed in the affidavit, and several incriminating pieces of evidence were discovered. Sheppard was then charged with first-degree murder."

The Supreme Court concluded that the officers had taken all the steps "that could reasonably be expected of them, and as a result" a reasonable police officer would have concluded, as O'Malley did, that the warrant authorized a search for the materials outlined in the affidavit. Applying the principles articulated in *Leon*, the majority decided that in this case probable cause did exist, and that "[s]uppressing evidence because the judge failed to make all the necessary clerical corrections despite his assurances that such changes would be made will not serve the deterrent function that the exclusionary rule was designed to achieve. Accordingly, federal law does not require the exclusion of the disputed evidence in this case." Justices Brennan and Marshall again dissented vigorously to the admission of evidence obtained under the authority of a search warrant that failed to comply with the requirement of particularity required by the text of the Fourth Amendment. Among their arguments, the dissenters objected to the majority's characterization of the exclusionary rule as a judicially created remedy justified only by its deterrent effect. They argued that from its adoption in *Weeks*, the exclusionary rule was part of the personal rights protected by the Fourth Amendment, and that adherence to the particularity requirements of the Amendment was necessary to protect those rights.

As you read the following case, consider whether it merely is an application of *Leon* and *Sheppard*, or instead is a restriction on the scope of the "good faith" exception to the exclusionary rule.

GROH v. RAMIREZ

Supreme Court of the United States, 2004.
540 U.S. 551, 124 S.Ct. 1284, 157 L.Ed.2d 1068.

JUSTICE STEVENS delivered the opinion of the Court.

Petitioner conducted a search of respondents' home pursuant to a warrant that failed to describe the "persons or things to be seized." The questions presented are (1) whether the search violated the Fourth

---

2. The warrant directed the officers to "search for any controlled substance, article, implement or other paraphernalia used in, for, or in connection with the unlawful possession or use of any controlled substance, and to seize and securely keep the same until final action.... "

Amendment, and (2) if so, whether petitioner nevertheless is entitled to qualified immunity, given that a Magistrate Judge (Magistrate), relying on an affidavit that particularly described the items in question, found probable cause to conduct the search.

I

Respondents, Joseph Ramirez and members of his family, live on a large ranch in Butte–Silver Bow County, Montana. Petitioner, Jeff Groh, has been a Special Agent for the Bureau of Alcohol, Tobacco and Firearms (ATF) since 1989. In February 1997, a concerned citizen informed petitioner that on a number of visits to respondents' ranch the visitor had seen a large stock of weaponry, including an automatic rifle, grenades, a grenade launcher, and a rocket launcher. Based on that information, petitioner prepared and signed an application for a warrant to search the ranch. The application stated that the search was for "any automatic firearms or parts to automatic weapons, destructive devices to include but not limited to grenades, grenade launchers, rocket launchers, and any and all receipts pertaining to the purchase or manufacture of automatic weapons or explosive devices or launchers." Petitioner supported the application with a detailed affidavit, which he also prepared and executed, that set forth the basis for his belief that the listed items were concealed on the ranch. Petitioner then presented these documents to a Magistrate, along with a warrant form that petitioner also had completed. The Magistrate signed the warrant form.

Although the application particularly described the place to be searched and the contraband petitioner expected to find, the warrant itself was less specific; it failed to identify any of the items that petitioner intended to seize. In the portion of the form that called for a description of the "person or property" to be seized, petitioner typed a description of respondents' two-story blue house rather than the alleged stockpile of firearms. The warrant did not incorporate by reference the itemized list contained in the application. It did, however, recite that the Magistrate was satisfied the affidavit established probable cause to believe that contraband was concealed on the premises, and that sufficient grounds existed for the warrant's issuance.

The day after the Magistrate issued the warrant, petitioner led a team of law enforcement officers, including both federal agents and members of the local sheriff's department, in the search of respondents' premises. Although respondent Joseph Ramirez was not home, his wife and children were. Petitioner states that he orally described the objects of the search to Mrs. Ramirez in person and to Mr. Ramirez by telephone. According to Mrs. Ramirez, however, petitioner explained only that he was searching for " 'an explosive device in a box.' " At any rate, the officers' search uncovered no illegal weapons or explosives. When the officers left, petitioner gave Mrs. Ramirez a copy of the search warrant, but not a copy of the application, which had been sealed. The following day, in response to a request from respondents' attorney, petitioner faxed the attorney a copy of the page of the application that listed the items to be seized. No charges were filed against the Ramirezes.

Respondents sued petitioner and the other officers under *Bivens* v. *Six Unknown Fed. Narcotics Agents,* 403 U.S. 388, 29 L.Ed.2d 619, 91 S.Ct. 1999 (1971), and 42 USC § 1983, raising eight claims, including violation of the Fourth Amendment. * * *

* * *

II

The warrant was plainly invalid. The Fourth Amendment states unambiguously that "no Warrants shall issue, but upon probable cause, supported by Oath or affirmation, and *particularly describing* the place to be searched, and *the persons or things to be seized.*" (Emphasis added.) The warrant in this case complied with the first three of these requirements: It was based on probable cause and supported by a sworn affidavit, and it described particularly the place of the search. On the fourth requirement, however, the warrant failed altogether. Indeed, petitioner concedes that "the warrant ... was deficient in particularity because it provided no description of the type of evidence sought."

The fact that the *application* adequately described the "things to be seized" does not save the *warrant* from its facial invalidity. The Fourth Amendment by its terms requires particularity in the warrant, not in the supporting documents. And for good reason: "The presence of a search warrant serves a high function," and that high function is not necessarily vindicated when some other document, somewhere, says something about the objects of the search, but the contents of that document are neither known to the person whose home is being searched nor available for her inspection. We do not say that the Fourth Amendment forbids a warrant from cross-referencing other documents. Indeed, most Courts of Appeals have held that a court may construe a warrant with reference to a supporting application or affidavit if the warrant uses appropriate words of incorporation, and if the supporting document accompanies the warrant. But in this case the warrant did not incorporate other documents by reference, nor did either the affidavit or the application (which had been placed under seal) accompany the warrant. Hence, we need not further explore the matter of incorporation.

Petitioner argues that even though the warrant was invalid, the search nevertheless was "reasonable" within the meaning of the Fourth Amendment. He notes that a Magistrate authorized the search on the basis of adequate evidence of probable cause, that petitioner orally described to respondents the items to be seized, and that the search did not exceed the limits intended by the Magistrate and described by petitioner. Thus, petitioner maintains, his search of respondents' ranch was functionally equivalent to a search authorized by a valid warrant.

We disagree. This warrant did not simply omit a few items from a list of many to be seized, or misdescribe a few of several items. Nor did it make what fairly could be characterized as a mere technical mistake or typographical error. Rather, in the space set aside for a description of the items to be seized, the warrant stated that the items consisted of a "single dwelling residence ... blue in color." In other words, the warrant did not describe the items to be seized *at all*. In this respect the warrant was so obviously deficient that we must regard the search as "warrantless" within the meaning of our case law. "We are not dealing with formalities." Because " 'the right of a man to retreat into his own home and there be free from unreasonable governmental intrusion' " stands " '[a]t the very core' of the Fourth Amendment," our cases have firmly established the " 'basic principle of Fourth Amendment law' that searches and seizures inside a home without a warrant are presumptively unreasonable." Thus, "absent exigent circumstances, a warrantless entry to search for weapons or contraband is unconstitutional even when a felony has been committed and there is probable cause to believe that incriminating evidence will be found within." We have clearly stated that the presumptive rule against warrantless searches applies with equal force to searches whose only defect is a lack of particularity in the warrant. * * *

Petitioner asks us to hold that a search conducted pursuant to a warrant lacking particularity should be exempt from the presumption of unreasonableness if the goals served by the particularity requirement are otherwise satisfied. He maintains that the search in this case satisfied those goals—which he says are "to prevent general searches, to prevent the seizure of one thing under a warrant describing another, and to prevent warrants from being issued on vague or dubious information," because the scope of the search did not exceed the limits set forth in the application. But unless the particular items described in the affidavit are also set forth in the warrant itself (or at least incorporated by reference, and the affidavit present at the search), there can be no written assurance that the Magistrate actually found probable cause to search for, and to seize, every item mentioned in the affidavit. In this case, for example, it is at least theoretically possible that the Magistrate was satisfied that the search for weapons and explosives was justified by the showing in the affidavit, but not convinced that any evidentiary basis existed for rummaging through respondents' files and papers for receipts pertaining to the purchase or manufacture of such items. Or, conceivably, the Magistrate might have believed that some of the weapons mentioned in the affidavit could have been lawfully possessed and therefore should not be seized. The mere fact that the Magistrate issued a warrant does not necessarily establish that he agreed that the scope of the search should be as broad as the affiant's request. Even though petitioner acted with restraint in conducting the search, "the inescapable fact is that this restraint was imposed by the agents themselves, not by a judicial officer."

We have long held, moreover, that the purpose of the particularity requirement is not limited to the prevention of general searches. A particular warrant also "assures the individual whose property is searched or seized of the lawful authority of the executing officer, his need to search, and the limits of his power to search."

* * *

It is incumbent on the officer executing a search warrant to ensure the search is lawfully authorized and lawfully conducted. Because petitioner did not have in his possession a warrant particularly describing the things he intended to seize, proceeding with the search was clearly "unreasonable" under the Fourth Amendment. The Court of Appeals correctly held that the search was unconstitutional.

* * *

Accordingly, the judgment of the Court of Appeals is affirmed. It is so ordered.

[The dissenting opinion of Justice Kennedy, with whom The Chief Justice joined, is omitted.]

Justice Thomas, with whom Justice Scalia joins, and with whom The Chief Justice joins as to Part III, dissenting.

The Fourth Amendment provides: "The right of the people to be secure in their persons, houses, papers, and effects, against unreasonable searches and seizures, shall not be violated, and no Warrants shall issue, but upon probable cause, supported by Oath or affirmation, and particularly describing the place to be searched, and the persons or things to be seized." The precise relationship between the Amendment's Warrant Clause and Unreasonableness Clause is unclear. But neither Clause explicitly requires a warrant. While "it is of course textually possible to consider [a warrant requirement] implicit within the requirement of reasonableness," the text of the Fourth Amendment certainly does not mandate this result. Nor does the Amendment's history, which is clear as to the Amendment's principal target (general warrants), but not as clear with respect to when warrants were required, if ever. Indeed, because of the very different nature and scope of federal authority and ability to conduct searches and arrests at the founding, it is possible that neither the history of the Fourth Amendment nor the common law provides much guidance.

As a result, the Court has vacillated between imposing a categorical warrant requirement and applying a general reasonableness standard. The Court has most frequently held that warrantless searches are presumptively unreasonable, but has also found a plethora of exceptions to presumptive unreasonableness. That is, our cases stand for the illuminating proposition that warrantless searches are *per se* unreasonable, except, of course, when they are not.

Today the Court holds that the warrant in this case was "so obviously deficient" that the ensuing search must be regarded as a warrantless search and thus presumptively unreasonable. However, the text of the Fourth Amendment, its history, and the sheer number of exceptions to the Court's categorical warrant requirement seriously undermine the bases upon which the Court today rests its holding. Instead of adding to this confusing jurisprudence, as the Court has done, I would turn to first principles in order to determine the relationship between the Warrant Clause and the Unreasonableness Clause. But even within the Court's current framework, a search conducted pursuant to a defective warrant is constitutionally different from a "warrantless search." Consequently, despite the defective warrant, I would still ask whether this search was unreasonable and would conclude that it was not. * * *

* * *

3. Balancing Costs and Benefits of Exclusion: The Independent Source and Inevitable Discovery Exceptions

NIX v. WILLIAMS

Supreme Court of the United States, 1984.
467 U.S. 431, 104 S.Ct. 2501, 81 L.Ed.2d 377.

CHIEF JUSTICE BURGER DELIVERED THE OPINION OF THE COURT.

[Williams was convicted of murdering a 10–year-old girl. The United States Supreme Court reversed his conviction because police had elicited incriminating statements leading to the discovery of the child's body by violating Williams' Sixth Amendment right to counsel. That case, *Brewer v. Williams*, is discussed in Chapter 6, *infra*. Williams was retried by the State of Iowa, and convicted a second time for the murder.]

I.

* * *

C

Second Trial

At Williams' second trial in 1977 in the Iowa court, the prosecution did not offer Williams' statements into evidence, nor did it seek to show that Williams had directed the police to the child's body. However, evidence of the condition of her body as it was found, articles and photographs of her clothing, and the results of post mortem medical and chemical tests on the body were admitted. The trial court concluded that the State had proved by a preponderance of the evidence that, if the search had not been suspended and Williams had not led the police to the victim, her body would have been discovered *"within a short time"* in essentially the same condition as it was actually found. The trial court also ruled that if the police had not located the body, "the search would clearly have been taken up again where it left off, given the extreme circumstances of this case and the body would [have] been found *in short order*."

In finding that the body would have been discovered in essentially the same condition as it was actually found, the court noted that freezing temperatures had prevailed and tissue deterioration would have been suspended. The challenged evidence was admitted and the jury again found Williams guilty of first-degree murder; he was sentenced to life in prison.

* * *

II

A

The Iowa Supreme Court correctly stated that the "vast majority" of all courts, both state and federal, recognize an inevitable discovery exception to the exclusionary rule. We are now urged to adopt and apply the so-called ultimate or inevitable discovery exception to the exclusionary rule.

* * *

B

The doctrine requiring courts to suppress evidence as the tainted "fruit" of unlawful governmental conduct had its genesis in *Silverthorne Lumber Co.* v. *United States*, 251 U.S. 385, 40 S.Ct. 182, 64 L.Ed.319 (1920); there, the Court held that the exclusionary rule applies not only to the illegally obtained evidence itself, but also to other incriminating evidence derived from the primary evidence. The holding of *Silverthorne* was carefully limited, however, for the Court emphasized that such information does not automatically become "sacred and inaccessible."

"If knowledge of [such facts] is gained from an *independent source*, they may be proved like any others...." (emphasis added).

* * *

The core rationale consistently advanced by this Court for extending the exclusionary rule to evidence that is the fruit of unlawful police conduct has been that this admittedly drastic and socially costly course is needed to deter police from violations of constitutional and statutory protections. This Court has accepted the argument that the way to ensure such protections is to exclude evidence seized as a result of such violations notwithstanding the high social cost of letting persons obviously guilty go unpunished for their crimes. On this rationale, the prosecution is not to be put in a better position than it would have been in if no illegality had transpired.

By contrast, the derivative evidence analysis ensures that the prosecution is not put in a *worse* position simply because of some earlier police error or misconduct. The independent source doctrine allows admission of evidence that has been discovered by means wholly independent of any constitutional violation. That doctrine, although closely related to the inevitable discovery doctrine, does not apply here; Williams' statements to Leaming indeed led police to the child's body, but that is not the whole story. The independent source doctrine teaches us that the interest of society in deterring unlawful police conduct and the public interest in having juries receive all probative evidence of a crime are properly balanced by putting the police in the same, not a *worse*, position that they would have been in if no police error or misconduct had occurred. When the challenged evidence has an independent source, exclusion of such evidence would put the police in a worse position than they would have been in absent any error or violation. There is a functional similarity between these two doctrines in that exclusion of evidence that would inevitably have been discovered would also put the government in a worse position, because the police would have obtained that evidence if no misconduct had taken place. Thus, while the independent source exception would not justify admission of evidence in this case, its rationale is wholly consistent with and justifies our adoption of the ultimate or inevitable discovery exception to the exclusionary rule.

It is clear that the cases implementing the exclusionary rule "begin with the premise that the challenged evidence is *in some sense* the product of illegal governmental activity." Of course, this does not end the inquiry. If the prosecution can establish by a preponderance of the evidence that the information ultimately or inevitably would have been discovered by lawful means—here the volunteers' search—then the deterrence rationale has so little basis that the evidence should be received. Anything less would reject logic, experience, and common sense.

* * *

[W]hen an officer is aware that the evidence will inevitably be discovered, he will try to avoid engaging in any questionable practice. In that situation, there will be little to gain from taking any dubious "shortcuts" to obtain the evidence. Significant disincentives to obtaining evidence illegally—including the possibility of departmental discipline and civil liability—also lessen the likelihood that the ultimate or inevitable discovery exception will promote police misconduct. In these circumstances, the societal costs of the exclusionary rule far outweigh any possible benefits to deterrence that a good-faith requirement might produce.

Williams contends that because he did not waive his right to the assistance of counsel, the Court may not balance competing values in deciding whether the challenged evidence was properly admitted. He argues that, unlike the exclusionary rule in the Fourth Amendment context, the essential purpose of which is to deter police misconduct, the Sixth Amendment exclusionary rule is designed to protect the right to a fair trial and the integrity of the factfinding process. Williams contends that, when those interests are at stake, the societal costs of excluding evidence obtained from responses presumed involuntary are irrelevant in determining whether such evidence should be excluded. We disagree.

Exclusion of physical evidence that would inevitably have been discovered adds nothing to either the integrity or fairness of a criminal trial. The Sixth Amendment right to counsel protects against unfairness by preserving the adversary process in which the reliability of proffered evidence may be tested in cross-examination. Here, however, Detective Leaming's conduct did nothing to impugn the reliability of the evidence in question—the body of the child and its condition as it was found, articles of clothing found on the body, and the autopsy. No one would seriously contend that the presence of counsel in the police car when Leaming appealed to Williams' decent human instincts would have had any bearing on the reliability of the body as evidence. Suppression, in these circumstances, would do nothing whatever to promote the integrity of the trial process, but would inflict a wholly unacceptable burden on the administration of criminal justice.

Nor would suppression ensure fairness on the theory that it tends to safeguard the adversary system of justice. To assure the fairness of trial proceedings, this Court has held that assistance of counsel must be available at pretrial confrontations where "the subsequent trial [cannot] cure [an otherwise] one-sided confrontation between prosecuting authorities and the uncounseled defendant." Fairness can be assured by placing the State and the accused in the same positions they would have been in had the impermissible conduct not taken place. However, if the government can prove that the evidence would have been obtained inevitably and, therefore, would have been admitted regardless of any overreaching by the police, there is no rational basis to keep that evidence from the jury in order to ensure the fairness of the trial proceedings. In that situation, the State has gained no advantage at trial and the defendant has suffered no prejudice. Indeed, suppression of the evidence would operate to undermine the adversary system by putting the State in a *worse* position than it would have occupied without any police misconduct. Williams' argument that inevitable discovery constitutes impermissible balancing of values is without merit.

* * *

C

[T]hree courts independently reviewing the evidence have found that the body of the child inevitably would have been found by the searchers. Williams challenges these findings, asserting that the record contains only the "*post hoc* rationalization" that the search efforts would have proceeded two and one-half miles into Polk County where Williams had led police to the body.

When that challenge was made at the suppression hearing preceding Williams' second trial, the prosecution offered the testimony of Agent Ruxlow of the Iowa Bureau of Criminal Investigation. Ruxlow had organized and directed some 200 volunteers who were searching for the child's body. The searchers were instructed "to check all the roads, the ditches, any culverts.... If they came upon any abandoned farm buildings, they were instructed to go onto the property and search those abandoned farm buildings or any other places where a small child could be secreted." Ruxlow testified that he marked off highway maps of

Poweshiek and Jasper Counties in grid fashion, divided the volunteers into teams of four to six persons, and assigned each team to search specific grid areas. Ruxlow also testified that, if the search had not been suspended because of Williams' promised cooperation, it would have continued into Polk County, using the same grid system. Although he had previously marked off into grids only the highway maps of Poweshiek and Jasper Counties, Ruxlow had obtained a map of Polk County, which he said he would have marked off in the same manner had it been necessary for the search to continue.

The search had commenced at approximately 10 a. m. and moved westward through Poweshiek County into Jasper County. At approximately 3 p. m., after Williams had volunteered to cooperate with the police, Detective Leaming, who was in the police car with Williams, sent word to Ruxlow and the other Special Agent directing the search to meet him at the Grinnell truck stop and the search was suspended at that time. Ruxlow also stated that he was "under the impression that there was a possibility" that Williams would lead them to the child's body at that time. The search was not resumed once it was learned that Williams had led the police to the body, which was found two and one-half miles from where the search had stopped in what would have been the easternmost grid to be searched in Polk County. There was testimony that it would have taken an additional three to five hours to discover the body if the search had continued; the body was found near a culvert, one of the kinds of places the teams had been specifically directed to search.

On this record it is clear that the search parties were approaching the actual location of the body, and we are satisfied, along with three courts earlier, that the volunteer search teams would have resumed the search had Williams not earlier led the police to the body and the body inevitably would have been found. * * *

* * *

[Concurring opinions of JUSTICE WHITE AND Justice Stevens are omitted.]

JUSTICE BRENNAN, WITH WHOM Justice Marshall joins, dissenting.

* * *

To the extent that today's decision adopts this "inevitable discovery" exception to the exclusionary rule, it simply acknowledges a doctrine that is akin to the "independent source" exception first recognized by the Court in *Silverthorne Lumber Co.* v. *United States.* In particular, the Court concludes that unconstitutionally obtained evidence may be admitted at trial if it inevitably would have been discovered in the same condition by an independent line of investigation that was already being pursued when the constitutional violation occurred. As has every Federal Court of Appeals previously addressing this issue, I agree that in these circumstances the "inevitable discovery" exception to the exclusionary rule is consistent with the requirements of the Constitution.

In its zealous efforts to emasculate the exclusionary rule, however, the Court loses sight of the crucial difference between the "inevitable discovery" doctrine and the "independent source" exception from which it is derived. When properly applied, the "independent source" exception allows the prosecution to use evidence only if it was, in fact, obtained by fully lawful means. It therefore does no violence to the constitutional protections that the exclusionary rule is meant to enforce. The "inevitable discovery" exception is likewise compatible with the Constitution, though it differs in one key respect from its next of kin: specifically, the evidence sought to be introduced at trial has not actually been obtained from an independent source, but rather would have been discovered as a matter of course if independent investigations were allowed to proceed.

In my view, this distinction should require that the government satisfy a heightened burden of proof before it is allowed to use such evidence. The inevitable discovery exception necessarily implicates a hypothetical finding that differs in kind from the factual finding that precedes application of the independent source rule. To ensure that this hypothetical finding is narrowly confined to circumstances that are functionally equivalent to an independent source, and to protect fully the fundamental rights served by the exclusionary rule, I would require clear and convincing evidence before concluding that the government had met its burden of proof on this issue. Increasing the burden of proof serves to impress the factfinder with the importance of the decision and thereby reduces the risk that illegally obtained evidence will be admitted. Because the lower courts did not impose such a requirement, I would remand this case for application of this heightened burden of proof by the lower courts in the first instance. I am therefore unable to join either the Court's opinion or its judgment.

Chapter 2

PROTECTED INTERESTS: PROPERTY AND PRIVACY

A. ORIGINAL THEORIES: PROPERTY RIGHTS, LIBERTY, AND PRIVACY

Commentary

Today no one disputes that the Fourth Amendment protects some aspects of liberty and privacy, although neither word is mentioned in the Amendment's text. As the cases in this Chapter will demonstrate, since 1967 the Supreme Court has generally rejected the notion that Fourth Amendment rights are rooted in property rights, although the constitutional text itself appears to define the rights protected by the Amendment largely in terms of property, and a person's relationship to it:

> The right of the people to be secure in their *persons, houses, papers, and effects*, against unreasonable searches and seizures, shall not be violated, and no Warrants shall issue, but upon probable cause, supported by Oath or affirmation, and *particularly describing the place to be searched, and the persons or things to be seized.* (Emphasis supplied)

Obviously he Fourth Amendment text associates protected rights— liberty and privacy—with identifiable types of real and personal property. Until the 1960s, the Supreme Court placed the relationship between property, privacy, and liberty near the center of its Fourth Amendment jurisprudence. The relationship had two faces, one procedural and one substantive. Searches and seizures were unconstitutional if they failed to satisfy procedural requirements, typically those set out in the Warrant Clause. But even proper procedures could not justify intrusions upon some substantive rights and some kinds of property. And from the nineteenth century until the 1920s, one kind of property mentioned explicitly in the Fourth Amendment—papers—received special treatment in the Supreme Court's opinions.

In these opinions, the Supreme Court limited searches and seizures of private papers by declaring that the Fourth Amendment and the Fifth Amendment privilege against self-incrimination ran together to create a zone of privacy into which the government could not lawfully intrude. Even a valid warrant could not authorize the seizure of some private papers. The Court justified these opinions in part by relying upon common law notions about papers as a species of property, but the extra protection the Court awarded papers derived from concerns about compelled revelations of the papers' contents. This early view of the significance of property expressing ideas has been abandoned in recent decades, when the Supreme Court has been more deferential to government efforts to obtain private papers, both in the exercise of regulatory powers and for use as evidence in criminal cases. The first case in this Chapter not only was the Supreme Court's first attempt to articulate a broad theory of the Fourth Amendment, but also established doctrines that influenced the Court's jurisprudence for more than eighty years.

BOYD v. UNITED STATES

Supreme Court of the United States, 1886.
116 U.S. 616, 6 S.Ct. 524, 29 L.Ed. 746.

JUSTICE BRADLEY delivered the opinion of the court.

[The United States brought a civil forfeiture action alleging that E.A. Boyd & Sons (the Boyds) had violated customs laws by importing thirty-five cases of plate glass without paying the required duties, and sought civil forfeiture of the glass. The Boyds had supplied plate glass for a new federal building erected in Philadelphia. They had paid import duties for the glass actually used in the project, which was taken from their existing inventory. Their agreement with the federal government permitted the Boyds to import replacement glass without paying duties. The government asserted that the Boyds had attempted to defraud it by importing more replacement glass than the agreement permitted. At the government's request and pursuant to a federal statute, the District Court issued a subpoena commanding the Boyds to produce an invoice for an earlier shipment of imported glass. The Boyds complied, but objected to the compelled production of the invoice and its introduction into evidence, claiming that the statute authorizing the subpoena violated both the Fourth Amendment prohibition against unreasonable searches and seizures and the Fifth Amendment privilege against self-incrimination. The relevant statute provided that "if the defendant or claimant shall fail or refuse to produce such book, invoice, or paper * * * the allegations stated in the said motion shall be taken as confessed, [and the government attorney was permitted to examine the papers] and may offer the same in evidence on behalf of the United States. But the owner of said books and papers, his agent or attorney [retained custody of the papers] except pending their examination in court.... " The invoice was introduced into evidence over the Boyds' objections. The jury decided in the government's favor, and the 35 cases of plate glass were forfeited to the government. The Circuit Court affirmed the judgment of forfeiture.]

The clauses of the Constitution, to which it is contended that these laws are repugnant, are the Fourth and Fifth Amendments. The Fourth declares, "The right of the people to be secure in their persons, houses, papers, and effects, against unreasonable searches and seizures, shall not be violated, and no warrants shall issue, but upon probable cause, supported by oath or affirmation, and particularly describing the place to be searched, and the persons or things to be seized." The Fifth Article, amongst other things, declares that no person "shall be compelled in any criminal case to be a witness against himself."

But, in regard to the Fourth Amendment, it is contended that, whatever might have been alleged against the constitutionality of the [statutes] under which the order in the present case was made, is free from constitutional objection, because it does not authorize the search and seizure of books and papers, but only requires the defendant or claimant to produce them. That is so; but it declares that if he does not produce them, the allegations which it is affirmed they will prove shall be taken as confessed. This is tantamount to compelling their production; for the prosecuting attorney will always be sure to state the evidence expected to be derived from them as strongly as the case will admit of. It is true that certain aggravating incidents of actual search and seizure, such as forcible entry into a man's house and searching amongst his papers, are wanting, and to this extent the proceeding under the act of 1874 is a mitigation of that which was authorized by the former acts; but it accomplishes the substantial object of those acts in forcing from a party evidence against himself. It is our opinion, therefore, that a compulsory production of a man's private papers to establish a criminal charge against him, or to forfeit his property, is within the scope of the Fourth Amendment to the Constitution, in all cases in which a search and seizure would be; because it is a material ingredient, and effects the sole object and purpose of search and seizure.

* * * As before stated, the act of 1863 was the first act in this country, and, we might say, either in this country or in England, so far as we have been able to ascertain, which authorized the search and seizure of a man's private papers, or the compulsory production of them, for the purpose of using them in evidence against him in a criminal case, or in a proceeding to enforce the forfeiture of his property. Even the act under which the obnoxious writs of assistance were issued did not go as far as this, but only authorized the examination of ships and vessels, and persons found therein, for the purpose of finding goods prohibited to be imported or exported, or on which the duties were not paid, and to enter into and search any suspected vaults, cellars, or warehouses for such goods. The search for and seizure of stolen or forfeited goods, or goods liable to duties and concealed to avoid the payment thereof, are totally different things from a search for and seizure of a man's private books and papers for the purpose of obtaining information therein contained, or of using them as evidence against him. The two things differ toto coelo. In the one case, the government is entitled to the possession of the property; in the other it is not. The seizure of stolen goods is authorized by the common law; and the seizure of goods forfeited for a breach of the revenue laws, or concealed to avoid the duties payable on them, has been

authorized by English statutes for at least two centuries past; and the like seizures have been authorized by our own revenue acts from the commencement of the government. * * *

But, when examined with care, it is manifest that there is a total unlikeness of these official acts and proceedings to that which is now under consideration. In the case of stolen goods, the owner from whom they were stolen is entitled to their possession; and in the case of excisable or dutiable articles, the government has an interest in them for the payment of the duties thereon, and until such duties are paid has a right to keep them under observation, or to pursue and drag them from concealment; and in the case of goods seized on attachment or execution, the creditor is entitled to their seizure in satisfaction of his debt; and the examination of a defendant under oath to obtain a discovery of concealed property or credits is a proceeding merely civil to effect the ends of justice, and is no more than what the court of chancery would direct on a bill for discovery. Whereas, by the proceeding now under consideration, the court attempts to extort from the party his private books and papers to make him liable for a penalty or to forfeit his property.

In order to ascertain the nature of the proceedings intended by the Fourth Amendment to the Constitution under the terms "unreasonable searches and seizures," it is only necessary to recall the contemporary or then recent history of the controversies on the subject, both in this country and in England. The practice had obtained in the colonies of issuing writs of assistance to the revenue officers, empowering them, in their discretion, to search suspected places for smuggled goods, which James Otis pronounced "the worst instrument of arbitrary power, the most destructive of English liberty, and the fundamental principles of law, that ever was found in an English law book;" since they placed "the liberty of every man in the hands of every petty officer." This was in February, 1761, in Boston, and the famous debate in which it occurred was perhaps the most prominent event which inaugurated the resistance of the colonies to the oppressions of the mother country. "Then and there," said John Adams, "then and there was the first scene of the first act of opposition to the arbitrary claims of Great Britain. Then and there the child Independence was born."

These things, and the events which took place in England immediately following the argument about writs of assistance in Boston, were fresh in the memories of those who achieved our independence and established our form of government. * * * The case, however, which will always be celebrated as being the occasion of Lord Camden's memorable discussion of the subject, was that of Entick v. Carrington and Three Other King's Messengers, 19 Howell's State Trials, 1029. The action was trespass for entering the plaintiff's dwelling-house in November, 1762, and breaking open his desks, boxes, & c., and searching and examining his papers. The jury rendered a special verdict, and the case was twice solemnly argued at the bar. Lord Camden pronounced the judgment of the court in * * * 1765, and the law as expounded by him has been regarded as settled from that time to this, and his great judgment on that occasion is considered as one of the landmarks of English liberty. It was welcomed and applauded by the lovers of liberty in the colonies as well as in the mother country. It is regarded as one of the permanent monuments of the British Constitution, and is quoted as such by the English authorities on that subject down to the present time.

* * *

After describing the power claimed by the Secretary of State for issuing general search warrants, and the manner in which they were executed, Lord Camden says: * * *

"The great end for which men entered into society was to secure their property. That right is preserved sacred and incommunicable in all instances where it has not been taken away or abridged by some public law for the good of the whole. * * * According to this reasoning, it is now incumbent upon the defendants to show the law by which this seizure is warranted. If that cannot be done, it is a trespass.

"Papers are the owner's goods and chattels; they are his dearest property; and are so far from enduring a seizure, that they will hardly bear an inspection; and though the eye cannot by the laws of England be guilty of a trespass, yet where private papers are removed and carried away the secret nature of those goods will be an aggravation of the trespass, and demand more considerable damages in that respect. Where is the written law that gives any magistrate such a power? I can safely answer, there is none; and, therefore, it is too much for us, without such authority, to pronounce a practice legal which would be subversive of all the comforts of society.

* * *

"Lastly, it is urged as an argument of utility, that such a search is a means of detecting offenders by discovering evidence. I wish some cases had been shown, where the law forceth evidence out of the owner's custody by process. There is no process against papers in civil causes. It has been often tried, but never prevailed. Nay, where the adversary has by force or fraud got possession of your own proper evidence, there is no way to get it back but by action. In the criminal law such a proceeding was never heard of; and yet there are some crimes, such, for instance, as murder, rape, robbery, and house-breaking, to say nothing of forgery and perjury, that are more atrocious than libelling. But our law has provided no paper-search in these cases to help forward the conviction. Whether this proceeds from the gentleness of the law towards criminals, or from a consideration that such a power would be more pernicious to the innocent than useful to the public, I will not say. It is very certain that the law obliges no man to accuse himself; because the necessary means of compelling self-accusation, falling upon the innocent as well as the guilty, would be both cruel and unjust; and it would seem, that search for evidence is disallowed upon the same principle. Then, too, the innocent would be confounded with the guilty."

* * *

The principles laid down in this opinion affect the very essence of constitutional liberty and security. They reach farther than the concrete form of the case then before the court, with its adventitious circumstances; they apply to all invasions on the part of the government and its employes of the sanctity of a man's home and the privacies of life. It is not the breaking of his doors, and the rummaging of his drawers, that constitutes the essence of the offence; but it is the invasion of his indefeasible right of personal security, personal liberty and private property, where that right has never been forfeited by his conviction of some public offence,—it is the invasion of this sacred right which underlies and constitutes the essence of Lord Camden's judgment. Breaking into a house and opening boxes and drawers are circumstances of aggravation; but any forcible and compulsory extortion of a man's own testimony or of his private papers to be used as evidence to convict him of crime or to forfeit his goods, is within the condemnation of that judgment. In this regard the Fourth and Fifth Amendments run almost into each other.

Can we doubt that when the Fourth and Fifth Amendments to the Constitution of the United States were penned and adopted, the language of Lord Camden was relied on as expressing the true doctrine on the subject of searches and seizures, and as furnishing the true criteria of the reasonable and "unreasonable" character of such seizures? Could the men who proposed those amendments, in the light of Lord Camden's opinion, have [approved the statute in dispute in *Boyd*]? It seems to us that the question cannot admit of a doubt. They never would have approved of them. The struggles against arbitrary power in which they had been engaged for more than twenty years, would have been too deeply engraved in their memories to have allowed them to approve of such insidious disguises of the old grievance which they had so deeply abhorred.

* * *

[A]ny compulsory discovery by extorting the party's oath, or compelling the production of his private books and papers, to convict him of crime, or to forfeit his property, is contrary to the principles of a free government. It is abhorrent to the instincts of an Englishman; it is abhorrent to the instincts of an American. It may suit the purposes of despotic power; but it cannot abide the pure atmosphere of political liberty and personal freedom.

* * *

Reverting then to the peculiar phraseology of this act, and to the information in the present case, which is founded on it, we have to deal with an act which expressly excludes criminal proceedings from its operation (though embracing civil suits for penalties and forfeitures), and with an information not technically a criminal proceeding, and neither, therefore, within the literal terms of the Fifth Amendment to the Constitution any more than it is within the literal terms of the Fourth. Does this relieve the proceedings or the law from being obnoxious to the prohibitions of either? We think not; we think they are within the spirit of both.

We have already noticed the intimate relation between the two amendments. They throw great light on each other. For the "unreasonable searches and seizures" condemned in the Fourth Amendment are almost always made for the purpose of compelling a man to give evidence against himself, which in criminal cases is condemned in the Fifth Amendment; and compelling a man "in a criminal case to be a witness against himself," which is condemned in the Fifth Amendment, throws light on the question as to what is an "unreasonable search and seizure" within the meaning of the Fourth Amendment. And we have been unable to perceive that the seizure of a man's private books and papers to be used in evidence against him is substantially different from compelling him to be a witness against himself. We think it is within the clear intent and meaning of those terms. We are also clearly of opinion that proceedings instituted for the purpose of declaring the forfeiture of a man's property by reason of offences committed by him, though they may be civil in form, are in their nature criminal. * * * The information, though technically a civil proceeding, is in substance and effect a criminal one. * * * As, therefore, suits for penalties and forfeitures incurred by the commission of offences against the law, are of this quasi-criminal nature, we think that they are within the reason of criminal proceedings for all the purposes of the Fourth Amendment of the Constitution, and of that portion of the Fifth Amendment which declares that no person shall be compelled in any criminal case to be a witness against himself; and we are further of opinion that a compulsory production of the private books and papers of the owner of goods sought to be forfeited in such a suit is compelling him to be a witness against himself, within the meaning of the Fifth Amendment to the Constitution, and is the equivalent of a search and seizure—and an unreasonable search and seizure—within the meaning of the Fourth Amendment. Though the proceeding in question is divested of many of the aggravating incidents of actual search and seizure, yet, as before said, it contains their substance and essence, and effects their substantial purpose. It may be that it is the obnoxious thing in its mildest and least repulsive form; but illegitimate and unconstitutional practices get their first footing in that way, namely, by silent approaches and slight deviations from legal modes of procedure. This can only be obviated by adhering to the rule that constitutional provisions for the security of person and property should be liberally construed. A close and literal construction deprives them of half their efficacy, and leads to gradual depreciation of the right, as if it consisted more in sound than in substance. It is the duty of courts to be watchful for the constitutional rights of the citizen, and against any stealthy encroachments thereon. Their motto should be obsta principiis. We have no doubt that the legislative body is actuated by the same motives; but the vast accumulation of public business brought before it sometimes prevents it, on a first presentation, from noticing objections which become developed by time and the practical application of the objectionable law.

* * *

[The concurring opinion of JUSTICE MILLER, with whom the CHIEF JUSTICE joined, is omitted.]

OLMSTEAD ET AL. v. UNITED STATES

Supreme Court of the United States, 1928.
277 U.S. 438, 48 S.Ct. 564, 72 L.Ed. 944.

CHIEF JUSTICE TAFT delivered the opinion of the Court.

[Olmstead and his co-defendants were convicted of conspiring to violate the federal prohibition laws. The government's evidence revealed that Olmstead was the general manager of a criminal enterprise with annual revenues exceeding two million dollars, a substantial figure in the 1920s. The enterprise employed more than fifty persons, owned two seagoing vessels for the transportation of liquor to British Columbia, several smaller vessels for coastwise transportation to the State of Washington, and a ranch with a large underground cache for storage. The enterprise also maintained a number of smaller caches in that city, as well as a central office manned with operators to handle the telephones. It employed executives, salesmen, deliverymen, dispatchers, scouts, bookkeepers, collectors and an attorney. "One of the chief men was always on duty at the main office to receive orders by telephones and to direct their filling by a corps of men stationed in another room— the 'bull pen.' The call numbers of the telephones were given to those known to be likely customers. At times the sales amounted to 200 cases of liquor per day." Wiretaps of the conspirators' telephone conversations were a critical source of the evidence establishing the conspiracy. "Small wires were inserted along the ordinary telephone wires from the residences of four of the petitioners and those leading from the chief office. The insertions were made without trespass upon any property of the defendants. They were made in the basement of the large office building. The taps from house lines were made in the streets near the houses." The sole issue before the Court was whether the use "of evidence of private telephone conversations between the defendants and others, intercepted by means of wire tapping, amounted to a violation of the Fourth and Fifth Amendments. "]

* * *

The well known historical purpose of the Fourth Amendment, directed against general warrants and writs of assistance, was to prevent the use of governmental force to search a man's house, his person, his papers and his effects; and to prevent their seizure against his will. This phase of the misuse of governmental power of compulsion is the emphasis of the opinion of the Court in * * * *Boyd v. United States*, 116 U.S. 616, 6 S.Ct. 524, 29 L.Ed. 746 (1886). * * *

* * *

The Amendment itself shows that the search is to be of material things—the person, the house, his papers or his effects. The description of the warrant necessary to make the proceeding lawful, is that it must specify the place to be searched and the person or *things* to be seized.

* * *

By the invention of the telephone, fifty years ago, and its application for the purpose of extending communications, one can talk with another at a far distant place. The language of the Amendment can not be extended and expanded to include telephone wires reaching to the whole world from the defendant's house of office. The intervening wires are not part of his house of office any more than are the highways along which they are stretched.

* * *

"The Fourth Amendment is to be construed in the light of what was deemed an unreasonable search and seizure when it was adopted and in a manner which will conserve public interests as well as the interests and rights of individual citizens."

Justice Bradley in the *Boyd* case and Justice Clarke in the *Gouled* case, said that the Fifth Amendment and the Fourth Amendment were to be liberally construed to effect the purpose of the framers of the Constitution in the interest of liberty. But that can not justify enlargement of the language employed beyond the possible practical meaning of houses, persons, papers, and effects, or so to apply the words search and seizure as to forbid hearing or sight.

* * *

Neither the cases we have cited nor any of the many federal decisions brought to our attention hold the Fourth Amendment to have been violated as against a defendant unless there has been an official search and seizure of his person, or such a seizure of his papers or his tangible material effects, or an actual physical invasion of his house "or curtilage" for the purpose of making a seizure.

We think, therefore, that the wire tapping here disclosed did not amount to a search or seizure within the meaning of the Fourth Amendment.

* * *

A standard which would forbid the reception of evidence if obtained by other than nice ethical conduct by government officials would make society suffer and give criminals greater immunity than has been known heretofore. In the absence of controlling legislation by Congress, those who realize the difficulties in bringing offenders to justice may well deem it wise that the exclusion of evidence should be confined to cases where rights under the Constitution would be violated by admitting it.

* * *

[The dissenting opinions of JUSTICE HOLMES, JUSTICE BUTLER, and JUSTICE STONE are omitted.]

JUSTICE BRANDEIS, dissenting.

* * *

The Government makes no attempt to defend the methods employed by its officers. Indeed, it concedes that if wire-tapping can be deemed a search and seizure within the Fourth Amendment, such wire-tapping as was practiced in the case at bar was an unreasonable search and seizure, and that the evidence thus obtained was inadmissible. But it relies on the language of the Amendment; and it claims that the protection given thereby cannot properly be held to include a telephone conversation.

"We must never forget," said MR. CHIEF JUSTICE MARSHALL in *McCulloch* v. *Maryland*, 17 U.S. 316, 4 L.Ed. 579 (1819), "that it is a constitution we are expounding." * * * "Time works changes, brings into existence new conditions and purposes. Therefore a principle to be vital must be capable of wider application than the mischief which gave it birth. This is peculiarly true of constitutions. They are not ephemeral enactments, designed to meet passing occasions. They are, to use the words of Chief Justice Marshall 'designed to approach immortality as nearly as human institutions can approach it.' The future is their care and provision for events of good and bad tendencies of which no prophecy can be made. In the application of a constitution, therefore, our contemplation cannot be only of what has been but of what may be. Under any other rule a constitution would indeed be as easy of application as it would be deficient in efficacy and power. Its general principles would have little value and be converted by precedent into impotent and lifeless formulas. Rights declared in words might be lost in reality."

When the Fourth and Fifth Amendments were adopted, "the form that evil had theretofore taken," had been necessarily simple. Force and violence were then the only means known to man by which a Government could directly effect self-incrimination. It could compel the individual to testify—a compulsion effected, if need be, by torture. It could secure possession of his papers and other articles incident to his private life—a seizure effected, if need be, by breaking and entry. Protection against such invasion of "the sanctities of a man's home and the privacies of life" was provided in the Fourth and Fifth Amendments by specific language. But "time works changes, brings into existence new conditions and purposes." Subtler and more far-reaching means of invading privacy have become available to the Government. Discovery and invention have made it possible for the Government, by means far more effective than stretching upon the rack, to obtain disclosure in court of what is whispered in the closet.

Moreover, "in the application of a constitution, our contemplation cannot be only of what has been but of what may be." The progress of science in furnishing the Government with means of espionage is not likely to stop with wire-tapping. Ways may some day be developed by which the Government, without removing papers from secret drawers, can reproduce them in court, and by which it will be enabled to expose to a jury the most intimate occurrences of the home. Advances in the psychic and related sciences may bring means of exploring unexpressed beliefs, thoughts and emotions. "That places the liberty of every man in the hands of every petty officer" was said by James Otis of much lesser intrusions than these. To Lord Camden, a far slighter intrusion seemed "subversive of all the comforts of society." Can it be that the Constitution affords no protection against such invasions of individual security?

A sufficient answer is found in *Boyd*, a case that will be remembered as long as civil liberty lives in the United States. * * *

* * * The evil incident to invasion of the privacy of the telephone is far greater than that involved in tampering with the mails. Whenever a telephone line is tapped, the privacy of the persons at both ends of the line is invaded and all conversations between them upon any subject, and although proper, confidential and privileged, may be overheard. Moreover, the tapping of one man's telephone line involves the tapping of the telephone of every other person whom he may call or who may call him. As a means of espionage, writs of assistance and general warrants are but puny instruments of tyranny and oppression when compared with wire-tapping.

Time and again, this Court in giving effect to the principle underlying the Fourth Amendment, has refused to place an unduly literal construction upon it. This was notably illustrated in the *Boyd* case itself. Taking language in its ordinary meaning, there is no "search" or "seizure" when a defendant is required to produce a document in the orderly process of a court's procedure. "The right of the people to be secure in their persons, houses, papers, and effects, against unreasonable searches and seizures," would not be violated, under any ordinary construction of language, by compelling obedience to a subpoena. But this Court holds the evidence inadmissible simply because the information leading to the issue of the subpoena has been unlawfully secured. * * * The provision against self-incrimination in the Fifth Amendment has been given an equally broad construction. The language is: "No person ... shall be compelled in any criminal case to be a witness against himself." Yet we have held, not only that the protection of the Amendment extends to a witness before a grand jury, although he has not been charged with crime, but that: "It applies alike to civil and criminal proceedings, wherever the answer might tend to subject to criminal responsibility him who gives it. The privilege protects a mere witness as fully as it does one who is also a party defendant." The narrow language of the Amendment has been consistently construed in the light of its object, "to insure that a person should not be compelled, when acting as a witness in any investigation, to give testimony which might tend to show that he himself had committed a crime. The privilege is limited to criminal matters, but it is as broad as the mischief against which it seeks to guard."

* * *

* * * The makers of our Constitution undertook to secure conditions favorable to the pursuit of happiness. They recognized the significance of man's spiritual nature, of his feelings and of his intellect. They knew that only a part of the pain, pleasure and satisfactions of life are to be found in material things. They sought to protect Americans in their beliefs, their thoughts, their emotions and their sensations. They conferred, as against the Government, the right to be let alone—the most comprehensive of rights and the right most valued by civilized men. To protect that right, every unjustifiable intrusion by the Government upon the privacy of the individual, whatever the means employed, must be deemed a violation of the Fourth Amendment. And the use, as evidence in a criminal proceeding, of facts ascertained by such intrusion must be deemed a violation of the Fifth.

Applying to the Fourth and Fifth Amendments the established rule of construction, the defendants' objections to the evidence obtained by wire-tapping must, in my opinion, be sustained. It is, of course, immaterial where the physical connection with the telephone wires leading into the defendants' premises was made. And it is also immaterial that the intrusion was in aid of law enforcement. Experience should teach us to be most on our guard to protect liberty when the Government's purposes are beneficent. Men born to freedom are naturally alert to repel invasion of their liberty by evil-minded rulers. The greatest dangers to liberty lurk in insidious encroachment by men of zeal, well-meaning but without understanding.

* * *

The door of a court is not barred because the plaintiff has committed a crime. The confirmed criminal is as much entitled to redress as his most virtuous fellow citizen; no record of crime, however long, makes one an outlaw. * * *

B. PRIVACY SUPPLANTS PROPERTY IN FOURTH AMENDMENT THEORY

Commentary

By abandoning the liberal interpretive approach of earlier cases like *Boyd* and *Weeks* while preserving the link between property and privacy rights, the Supreme Court's decision in *Olmstead* guaranteed that the Fourth Amendment would be irrelevant as a device for regulating the use of new technologies that allowed the government to invade formerly private places without committing a common law trespass. As new technologies permitted investigators to intrude directly into the lives of people, and as their use became more common, it was almost inevitable that the Court would eventually abandon this restrictive property-based theory of the Fourth Amendment to permit constitutional judicial review of technological searches. The Court took that step in 1967 in its decision in *Katz v. United States*, *infra*, where it overruled the trespass theory announced in *Olmstead*. Earlier the same year, the Supreme Court laid the groundwork for its famous *Katz* opinion by overruling another "relic" of its 1920s jurisprudence, the "mere evidence rule."

1. Procedural versus Substantive Fourth Amendment Rights

WARDEN, MARYLAND PENITENTIARY v. HAYDEN

Supreme Court of the United States, 1967.
387 U.S. 294, 87 S.Ct. 1642, 18 L.Ed.2d 782.

MR. JUSTICE BRENNAN delivered the opinion of the Court.

[Police officers in hot pursuit of a fleeing felon entered and searched the defendants multi-story home. One officer searched the basement, and "found in a washing machine a jacket and trousers of the type the fleeing man was said to have worn." Other officers found a gun hidden in a toilet and also discovered a "clip of ammunition for the pistol and a cap * * * under the mattress of Hayden's bed, and ammunition for the shotgun was found in a bureau drawer in Hayden's room. All these items of evidence were introduced against respondent at his trial."]

III.

We come, then, to the question whether, even though the search was lawful, the Court of Appeals was correct in holding that the seizure and introduction of the items of clothing violated the Fourth Amendment because they are "mere evidence." The distinction made by some of our cases between seizure of items of evidential value only and seizure of instrumentalities, fruits, or contraband has been criticized by courts and commentators. The Court of Appeals, however, felt "obligated to adhere to it." We today reject the distinction as based on premises no longer accepted as rules governing the application of the Fourth Amendment.

* * *

In *Gouled* v. *United States*, 255 U.S. 298, 309, 41 S.Ct. 261, 65 L.Ed. 647 (1921), the Court said that search warrants "may not be used as a means of gaining access to a man's house or office and papers solely for the purpose of making search to secure evidence to be used against him in a criminal or penal proceeding. . . . " The Court derived from *Boyd* the proposition that warrants "may be resorted to only when a primary right to such search and seizure may be found in the interest which the public or the complainant may have in the property to be seized, or in the right to the possession of it, or when a valid exercise of the police power renders possession of the property by the accused unlawful and provides that it may be taken," that is, when the property is an instrumentality or fruit of crime, or contraband. Since it was "impossible to say, on the record . . . that the Government had any interest" in the papers involved "other than as evidence against the accused . . . ," "to permit them to be used in evidence would be, in effect, as ruled in * * * *Boyd,* to compel the defendant to become a witness against himself."

The items of clothing involved in this case are not "testimonial" or "communicative" in nature, and their introduction therefore did not compel respondent to become a witness against himself in violation of the Fifth Amendment. This case thus does not require that we consider whether there are items of evidential value whose very nature precludes them from being the object of a reasonable search and seizure.

The Fourth Amendment ruling in *Gouled* was based upon the dual, related premises that historically the right to search for and seize property depended upon the assertion by the Government of a valid claim of superior interest, and that it was not enough that the purpose of the search and seizure was to obtain evidence to use in apprehending and convicting criminals. The common law of search and seizure after *Entick* v. *Carrington,* 19 How. St. Tr. 1029, reflected Lord Camden's view, derived no doubt from the political thought of his time, that the "great end, for which men entered into society, was to secure their property." Warrants were "allowed only where the primary right to such a search and seizure is in the interest which the public or complainant may have in the property seized." Thus stolen property—the fruits of crime—was always subject to seizure. And the power to search for stolen property was gradually extended to cover "any property which the private citizen was not permitted to possess," which included instrumentalities of crime (because of the early notion that items used in crime were forfeited to the State) and contraband. No separate governmental interest in seizing evidence to apprehend and convict criminals was recognized; it was required that some property interest be asserted. The remedial structure also reflected these dual premises. Trespass, replevin, and the other means of redress for persons aggrieved by searches and seizures, depended upon proof of a superior property interest. And since a lawful seizure presupposed a superior claim, it was inconceivable that a person could recover property lawfully seized. As Lord Camden pointed out in *Entick,* a general warrant enabled "the party's own property [to be] seized before and without conviction, and he has no power to reclaim his goods, even after his innocence is cleared by acquittal."

The premise that property interests control the right of the Government to search and seize has been discredited. Searches and seizures may be "unreasonable" within the Fourth Amendment even though the Government asserts a superior property interest at common law. We have recognized that the principal object of the Fourth Amendment is the protection of privacy rather than property, and have increasingly discarded fictional and procedural barriers rested on property concepts. See *Jones* v. *United States,* 362 U.S. 257, 266, 80 S.Ct. 725, 4 L.Ed.2d

697 (1960); *Silverman* v. *United States*, 365 U.S. 505, 511, 81 S.Ct. 679, 5 L.Ed.2d 734 (1961). This shift in emphasis from property to privacy has come about through a subtle interplay of substantive and procedural reform. The remedial structure at the time even of *Weeks* v. *United States*, 232 U.S. 383, 34 S.Ct. 341, 58 L.Ed. 652 (1914), was arguably explainable in property terms. * * *

The development of search and seizure law since *Silverthorne Lumber Co. v. United States*, 251 U.S. 385, 40 S.Ct. 182, 64 L.Ed. 319 (1920) and *Gouled* is replete with examples of the transformation in substantive law brought about through the interaction of the felt need to protect privacy from unreasonable invasions and the flexibility in rulemaking made possible by the remedy of exclusion. We have held, for example, that intangible as well as tangible evidence may be suppressed, and that an actual trespass under local property law is unnecessary to support a remediable violation of the Fourth Amendment. * * * And with particular relevance here, we have given recognition to the interest in privacy despite the complete absence of a property claim by suppressing the very items which at common law could be seized with impunity: stolen goods, instrumentalities, and contraband.

The premise in *Gouled* that government may not seize evidence simply for the purpose of proving crime has likewise been discredited. The requirement that the Government assert in addition some property interest in material it seizes has long been a fiction, obscuring the reality that government has an interest in solving crime. * * * The requirements of the Fourth Amendment can secure the same protection of privacy whether the search is for "mere evidence" or for fruits, instrumentalities or contraband. There must, of course, be a nexus—automatically provided in the case of fruits, instrumentalities or contraband—between the item to be seized and criminal behavior. Thus in the case of "mere evidence," probable cause must be examined in terms of cause to believe that the evidence sought will aid in a particular apprehension or conviction. * * *

The remedy of suppression, moreover, which made possible protection of privacy from unreasonable searches without regard to proof of a superior property interest, likewise provides the procedural device necessary for allowing otherwise permissible searches and seizures conducted solely to obtain evidence of crime. * * *

* * *

[But if rejection of the mere evidence rule] does enlarge the area of permissible searches, the intrusions are nevertheless made after fulfilling the probable cause and particularity requirements of the Fourth Amendment and after the intervention of "a neutral and detached magistrate. . . . " The Fourth Amendment allows intrusions upon privacy under these circumstances, and there is no viable reason to distinguish intrusions to secure "mere evidence" from intrusions to secure fruits, instrumentalities, or contraband.

* * *

[The concurring opinion by JUSTICE FORTAS, with whom THE CHIEF JUSTICE joined, and JUSTICE BLACK's concurrence in the result, are omitted.]

MR. JUSTICE DOUGLAS, dissenting.

* * *

[The Fourth Amendment] has been thought, until today, to have two faces of privacy:

(1) One creates a zone of privacy that may not be invaded by the police through raids, by the legislators through laws, or by magistrates through the issuance of warrants.

(2) A second creates a zone of privacy that may be invaded either by the police in hot pursuit or by a search incident to arrest or by a warrant issued by a magistrate on a showing of probable cause.

The *first* has been recognized from early days in Anglo–American law. Search warrants, for seizure of stolen property, though having an ancient lineage, were criticized even by Coke.

As stated by Lord Camden in *Entick*, even warrants authorizing seizure of stolen goods were looked upon with disfavor but "crept into the law by imperceptible practice." By the time of Charles II they had burst their original bounds and were used by the Star Chamber to find evidence among the files and papers of political suspects. * * * From this use of papers as evidence there grew up the practice of the Star Chamber empowering a person "to search in all places, where books were printing, in order to see if the printer had a licence; and if upon such search he found any books which he suspected to be libellous against the church or state, he was to seize them, and carry them before the proper magistrate." Thus the general warrant became a powerful instrument in proceedings for seditious libel against printers and authors. John Wilkes led the campaign against the general warrant. Wilkes won [*Entick*]; and Lord Camden's opinion not only outlawed the general warrant but went on to condemn searches "for evidence" with or without a general warrant[.]

* * *

Lord Camden's twofold classification of zones of privacy was said by Cooley to be reflected in the Fourth Amendment:

"The warrant is not allowed for the purpose of obtaining evidence of an intended crime; but only after lawful evidence of an offence actually committed. Nor even then is it allowable to invade one's privacy for the sole purpose of obtaining evidence against him, except in a few special cases where that which is the subject of the crime is supposed to be concealed, and the public or the complainant has an interest in it or in its destruction."

And that was the holding of the Court in *Boyd*. * * *

* * *

* * * Our question is whether the Government, though armed with a proper search warrant or though making a search incident to an arrest, may seize, and use at the trial, testimonial evidence, whether it would otherwise be barred by the Fifth Amendment or would be free from such strictures. The teaching of *Boyd* is that such evidence, though seized pursuant to a lawful search, is inadmissible.

* * *

2.   The Emergence of "Expectation of Privacy" Analysis

KATZ v. UNITED STATES

Supreme Court of the United States, 1967.
389 U.S. 347, 88 S.Ct. 507, 19 L.Ed.2d 576.

MR. JUSTICE STEWART delivered the opinion of the Court.

The petitioner was convicted in the District Court for the Southern District of California under an eight-count indictment charging him with transmitting wagering information by telephone from Los Angeles to Miami and Boston, in violation of a federal statute. At trial the Government was permitted, over the petitioner's objection, to introduce evidence of the petitioner's end of telephone conversations, overheard by FBI agents who had attached an electronic listening and recording device to the outside of the public telephone booth from which he had placed his calls. In affirming his conviction, the Court of Appeals rejected the contention that the recordings had been obtained in violation of the Fourth Amendment, because "there was no physical entrance into the area occupied by [the petitioner]." We granted certiorari in order to consider the constitutional questions thus presented.

The petitioner has phrased those questions as follows:

"A. Whether a public telephone booth is a constitutionally protected area so that evidence obtained by attaching an electronic listening recording device to the top of such a booth is obtained in violation of the right to privacy of the user of the booth.

"B. Whether physical penetration of a constitutionally protected area is necessary before a search and seizure can be said to be violative of the Fourth Amendment to the United States Constitution."

We decline to adopt this formulation of the issues. In the first place, the correct solution of Fourth Amendment problems is not necessarily promoted by incantation of the phrase "constitutionally protected area." Secondly, the Fourth Amendment cannot be translated into a general constitutional "right to privacy." That Amendment protects individual privacy against certain kinds of governmental intrusion, but its protections go further, and often have nothing to do with privacy at all. Other provisions of the Constitution protect personal privacy from other forms of governmental invasion. But the protection of a person's *general* right to privacy—his right to be let alone by other people—is, like the protection of his property and of his very life, left largely to the law of the individual States.

Because of the misleading way the issues have been formulated, the parties have attached great significance to the characterization of the telephone booth from which the petitioner placed his calls. The petitioner has strenuously argued that the booth was a "constitutionally protected area." The Government has maintained with equal vigor that it was not. But this effort to decide whether or not a given "area," viewed in the abstract, is "constitutionally protected" deflects attention from the problem presented by this case.[9] For the Fourth Amendment protects people, not places. What a person knowingly exposes to the public, even in his own home or office, is not a subject of Fourth Amendment protection. But what he seeks to preserve as private, even in an area accessible to the public, may be constitutionally protected.

The Government stresses the fact that the telephone booth from which the petitioner made his calls was constructed partly of glass, so that he was as visible after he entered it as he would have been if he had remained outside. But what he sought to exclude when he entered the booth was not the intruding eye—it was the uninvited ear. He did not shed his right to do so simply because he made his calls from a place where he might be seen. No less than an individual in a business office, in a friend's apartment, or in a taxicab, a person in a telephone booth may rely upon the protection of the Fourth Amendment. One who occupies it, shuts the door behind him, and pays the toll that permits him to place a call is surely entitled to assume that the words he utters into the mouthpiece will not be broadcast to the world. To read the Constitution more narrowly is to ignore the vital role that the public telephone has come to play in private communication.

The Government contends, however, that the activities of its agents in this case should not be tested by Fourth Amendment requirements, for the surveillance technique they employed involved no physical penetration of the telephone booth from which the petitioner placed his calls. It is true that the absence of such penetration was at one time thought to foreclose further Fourth Amendment inquiry, *Olmstead* v. *United States*, 277 U.S. 438, 457, 464, 466, 48 S.Ct. 564, 72 L.Ed. 944 (1928); *Goldman* v. *United States*, 316 U.S. 129, 134–136, 62 S.Ct. 993,

---

9. It is true that this Court has occasionally described its conclusions in terms of "constitutionally protected areas," see, e. g., *Silverman* v. *United States*, 365 U.S. 505, 510, 512, 81 S.Ct. 679, 5 L.Ed.2d 734 (1961); *Lopez* v. *United States*, 373 U.S. 427, 438–439, 83 S.Ct. 1381, 10 L.Ed.2d 462 (1963); *Berger* v. *New York*, 388 U.S. 41, 57, 59, 87 S.Ct. 1873, 18 L.Ed.2d 1040 (1967), but we have never suggested that this concept can serve as a talismanic solution to every Fourth Amendment problem.

86 L.Ed. 1322 (1942), for that Amendment was thought to limit only searches and seizures of tangible property. But "the premise that property interests control the right of the Government to search and seize has been discredited." *Warden* v. *Hayden*, 387 U.S. 294, 304, 87 S.Ct. 1642, 18 L.Ed.2d 782 (1967). Thus, although a closely divided Court supposed in *Olmstead* that surveillance without any trespass and without the seizure of any material object fell outside the ambit of the Constitution, we have since departed from the narrow view on which that decision rested. Indeed, we have expressly held that the Fourth Amendment governs not only the seizure of tangible items, but extends as well to the recording of oral statements, overheard without any "technical trespass under ... local property law." *Silverman* v. *United States*, 365 U.S. 505, 511, 81 S.Ct. 679, 5 L.Ed.2d 734 (1961). Once this much is acknowledged, and once it is recognized that the Fourth Amendment protects people—and not simply "areas"—against unreasonable searches and seizures, it becomes clear that the reach of that Amendment cannot turn upon the presence or absence of a physical intrusion into any given enclosure.

We conclude that the underpinnings of *Olmstead* and *Goldman* have been so eroded by our subsequent decisions that the "trespass" doctrine there enunciated can no longer be regarded as controlling. The Government's activities in electronically listening to and recording the petitioner's words violated the privacy upon which he justifiably relied while using the telephone booth and thus constituted a "search and seizure" within the meaning of the Fourth Amendment. The fact that the electronic device employed to achieve that end did not happen to penetrate the wall of the booth can have no constitutional significance.

The question remaining for decision, then, is whether the search and seizure conducted in this case complied with constitutional standards. In that regard, the Government's position is that its agents acted in an entirely defensible manner: They did not begin their electronic surveillance until investigation of the petitioner's activities had established a strong probability that he was using the telephone in question to transmit gambling information to persons in other States, in violation of federal law. Moreover, the surveillance was limited, both in scope and in duration, to the specific purpose of establishing the contents of the petitioner's unlawful telephonic communications. The agents confined their surveillance to the brief periods during which he used the telephone booth, and they took great care to overhear only the conversations of the petitioner himself.

Accepting this account of the Government's actions as accurate, it is clear that this surveillance was so narrowly circumscribed that a duly authorized magistrate, properly notified of the need for such investigation, specifically informed of the basis on which it was to proceed, and clearly apprised of the precise intrusion it would entail, could constitutionally have authorized, with appropriate safeguards, the very limited search and seizure that the Government asserts in fact took place. Only last Term we sustained the validity of such an authorization, holding that, under sufficiently "precise and discriminate circumstances," a federal court may empower government agents to employ a concealed electronic device "for the narrow and particularized purpose of ascertaining the truth of the . . . allegations" of a "detailed factual affidavit alleging the commission of a specific criminal offense." *Osborn* v. *United States*, 385 U.S. 323, 329–330, 87 S.Ct. 429, 17 L.Ed.2d 394 (1966). Discussing that holding, the Court in *Berger* v. *New York*, 388 U.S. 41, 87 S.Ct. 1873, 18 L.Ed.2d 1040 (1967), said that "the order authorizing the use of the electronic device" in *Osborn* "afforded similar protections to those . . . of conventional warrants authorizing the seizure of tangible evidence." Through those protections, "no greater invasion of privacy was permitted than was necessary under the circumstances." *Id.*, at 57. Here, too, a similar judicial order could have accommodated "the legitimate needs of law enforcement" by authorizing the carefully limited use of electronic surveillance.

The Government urges that, because its agents relied upon the decisions in *Olmstead* and *Goldman*, and because they did no more here than they might properly have done with prior judicial sanction, we should retroactively validate their conduct. That we cannot do. It is apparent that the agents in this case acted with restraint. Yet the inescapable fact is that this restraint was imposed by the agents themselves, not by a judicial officer. They were not required, before commencing the search, to present their estimate of probable cause for detached scrutiny by a neutral magistrate. They were not compelled, during the conduct of the search itself, to observe precise limits established in advance by a specific court order. Nor were they directed, after the search had been completed, to notify the authorizing magistrate in detail of all that had been seized. In the absence of such safeguards, this Court has never sustained a search upon the sole ground that officers reasonably expected to find evidence of a particular crime and voluntarily confined their activities to the least intrusive means consistent with that end. Searches conducted without warrants have been held unlawful "notwithstanding facts unquestionably showing probable cause," for the Constitution requires "that the deliberate, impartial judgment of a judicial officer . . . be interposed between the citizen and the police. . . . " "Over and again this Court has emphasized that the mandate of the [Fourth] Amendment requires adherence to judicial processes," and that searches conducted outside the judicial process, without prior approval by judge or magistrate, are *per se* unreasonable under the Fourth Amendment—subject only to a few specifically established and well-delineated exceptions.

It is difficult to imagine how any of those exceptions could ever apply to the sort of search and seizure involved in this case. Even electronic surveillance substantially contemporaneous with an individual's arrest could hardly be deemed an "incident" of that arrest. Nor could the use of electronic surveillance without prior authorization be justified on grounds of "hot pursuit." And, of course, the very nature of electronic surveillance precludes its use pursuant to the suspect's consent.

* * *

These considerations do not vanish when the search in question is transferred from the setting of a home, an office, or a hotel room to that of a telephone booth. Wherever a man may be, he is entitled to know that he will remain free from unreasonable searches and seizures. The government agents here ignored "the procedure of antecedent justification . . . that is central to the Fourth Amendment," a procedure that we hold to be a constitutional precondition of the kind of electronic surveillance involved in this case. Because the surveillance here failed to meet that condition, and because it led to the petitioner's conviction, the judgment must be reversed.

It is so ordered.

MR. JUSTICE MARSHALL took no part in the consideration or decision of this case.

[The concurring opinions of JUSTICE DOUGLAS and JUSTICE WHITE are omitted.]

MR. JUSTICE HARLAN, concurring.

I join the opinion of the Court, which I read to hold only (a) that an enclosed telephone booth is an area where, like a home, and unlike a field, a person has a constitutionally protected reasonable expectation of privacy; (b) that electronic as well as physical intrusion into a place that is in this sense private may constitute a violation of the Fourth Amendment; and (c) that the invasion of a constitutionally protected area by federal authorities is, as the Court has long held, presumptively unreasonable in the absence of a search warrant.

As the Court's opinion states, "the Fourth Amendment protects people, not places." The question, however, is what protection it affords to those people. Generally, as here, the answer to that question requires reference to a "place." My understanding of the rule that has emerged from prior decisions is that there is a twofold requirement, first that a person have exhibited an actual (subjective) expectation of privacy and, second, that the expectation be one that society is prepared to recognize as "reasonable." Thus a man's home is, for most purposes, a place where he expects privacy, but objects, activities, or statements that he exposes to the "plain view" of outsiders are not "protected" because no intention to keep them to himself has been exhibited. On the other hand, conversations in the open would not be protected against being overheard, for the expectation of privacy under the circumstances would be unreasonable.

The critical fact in this case is that "one who occupies it, [a telephone booth] shuts the door behind him, and pays the toll that permits him to place a call is surely entitled to assume" that his conversation is not being intercepted. The point is not that the booth is "accessible to the public" at other times, but that it is a temporarily private place whose momentary occupants' expectations of freedom from intrusion are recognized as reasonable.

* * *

[Mr. Justice Black's dissenting opinion is omitted.]

C. TECHNOLOGY AND THE *KATZ* "EXPECTATION OF PRIVACY TEST"

CALIFORNIA v. CIRAOLO

Supreme Court of the United States, 1986.
476 U.S. 207, 106 S.Ct. 1809, 90 L.Ed.2d 210.

Chief Justice Burger delivered the opinion of the Court.

We granted certiorari to determine whether the Fourth Amendment is violated by aerial observation without a warrant from an altitude of 1,000 feet of a fenced-in backyard within the curtilage of a home.

I

On September 2, 1982, Santa Clara Police received an anonymous telephone tip that marijuana was growing in respondent's backyard. Police were unable to observe the contents of respondent's yard from ground level because of a 6–foot outer fence and a 10–foot inner fence completely enclosing the yard. Later that day, Officer Shutz, who was assigned to investigate, secured a private plane and flew over respondent's house at an altitude of 1,000 feet, within navigable airspace; he was accompanied by Officer Rodriguez. Both officers were trained in marijuana identification. From the overflight, the officers readily identified marijuana plants 8 feet to 10 feet in height growing in a 15–by 25–foot plot in respondent's yard; they photographed the area with a standard 35mm camera.

On September 8, 1982, Officer Shutz obtained a search warrant on the basis of an affidavit describing the anonymous tip and their observations; a photograph depicting respondent's house, the backyard, and neighboring homes was attached to the affidavit as an exhibit. The warrant was executed the next day and 73 plants were seized; it is not disputed that these were marijuana.

After the trial court denied respondent's motion to suppress the evidence of the search, respondent pleaded guilty to a charge of cultivation of marijuana. The California Court of Appeal reversed, however, on the ground that the warrantless aerial *observation* of respondent's yard which led to the issuance of the warrant violated the Fourth Amendment. * * * The court emphasized that the height and existence of the two fences constituted "objective criteria from which we may conclude he manifested a reasonable expectation of privacy by any standard."

Examining the particular method of surveillance undertaken, the court then found it "significant" that the flyover "was not the result of a routine patrol conducted for any other legitimate law enforcement or public safety objective, but was undertaken for the specific purpose of observing this particular enclosure within [respondent's] curtilage." It held this focused observation was "a direct and unauthorized intrusion into the sanctity of the home" which violated respondent's reasonable expectation of privacy. * * *

* * *

II

The touchstone of Fourth Amendment analysis is whether a person has a "constitutionally protected reasonable expectation of privacy." *Katz* v. *United States*, 389 U.S. 347, 360, 88 S.Ct. 507, 19 L.Ed.2d 576 (1967) (HARLAN, J., concurring). *Katz* posits a two-part inquiry: first, has the individual manifested a subjective expectation of privacy in the object of the challenged search? Second, is society willing to recognize that expectation as reasonable?

Clearly—and understandably—respondent has met the test of manifesting his own subjective intent and desire to maintain privacy as to his unlawful agricultural pursuits. However, we need not address that issue, for the State has not challenged the finding of the California Court of Appeal that respondent had such an expectation. It can reasonably be assumed that the 10–foot fence was placed to conceal the marijuana crop from at least street-level views. So far as the normal sidewalk traffic was concerned, this fence served that purpose, because respondent "took normal precautions to maintain his privacy."

Yet a 10–foot fence might not shield these plants from the eyes of a citizen or a policeman perched on the top of a truck or a two-level bus. Whether respondent therefore manifested a subjective expectation of privacy from *all* observations of his backyard, or whether instead he manifested merely a hope that no one would observe his unlawful gardening pursuits, is not entirely clear in these circumstances. Respondent appears to challenge the authority of government to observe his activity from any vantage point or place if the viewing is motivated by a law enforcement purpose, and not the result of a casual, accidental observation.

We turn, therefore, to the second inquiry under *Katz, i. e.*, whether that expectation is reasonable. In pursuing this inquiry, we must keep in mind that "[the] test of legitimacy is not whether the individual chooses to conceal assertedly 'private' activity," but instead "whether the government's intrusion infringes upon the personal and societal values protected by the Fourth Amendment."

Respondent argues that because his yard was in the curtilage of his home, no governmental aerial observation is permissible under the Fourth Amendment without a warrant. The history and genesis of the curtilage doctrine are instructive. "At common law, the curtilage is the area to which extends the intimate activity associated with the 'sanctity of a man's home and the privacies of life.' " (*Boyd* v. *United States*, 116 U.S. 616, 630, 6 S.Ct. 524, 29 L.Ed. 746 (1886)). The protection afforded the curtilage is essentially a protection of families and personal privacy in an area intimately linked to the home, both physically and psychologically, where privacy expectations are most heightened. The claimed area here was immediately adjacent to a suburban home, surrounded by high double fences. This close nexus to the home would appear to encompass this small area within the curtilage. Accepting, as the State does, that this yard and its crop fall within the curtilage, the question remains whether naked-eye observation of the curtilage by police from an aircraft lawfully operating at an altitude of 1,000 feet violates an expectation of privacy that is reasonable.

That the area is within the curtilage does not itself bar all police observation. The Fourth Amendment protection of the home has never been extended to require law enforcement officers to shield their eyes when passing by a home on public thoroughfares. Nor does the mere fact that an individual has taken measures to restrict some views of his activities preclude an officer's observations from a public vantage point where he has a right to be and which renders the activities clearly visible. "What a person knowingly exposes to the public, even in his own home or office, is not a subject of Fourth Amendment protection."

The observations by Officers Shutz and Rodriguez in this case took place within public navigable airspace, in a physically nonintrusive manner; from this point they were able to observe plants readily discernible to the naked eye as marijuana. That the observation from aircraft was directed at identifying the plants and the officers were trained to recognize marijuana is irrelevant. Such observation is precisely what a judicial officer needs to provide a basis for a warrant. Any member of the public flying in this airspace who glanced down could have seen everything that these officers observed. On this record, we readily conclude that respondent's expectation that his garden was protected from such observation is unreasonable and is not an expectation that society is prepared to honor.

* * *

JUSTICE POWELL, with whom JUSTICE BRENNAN, JUSTICE MARSHALL, and JUSTICE BLACKMUN join, dissenting.

Concurring in *Katz*, JUSTICE HARLAN warned that any decision to construe the Fourth Amendment as proscribing only physical intrusions by police onto private property "is, in the present day, bad physics as well as bad law, for reasonable expectations of privacy may be defeated by electronic as well as physical invasion." Because the Court today ignores that warning in an opinion that departs significantly from the standard developed in *Katz* for deciding when a Fourth Amendment violation has occurred, I dissent.

* * *

II

A

The Fourth Amendment protects "[the] right of the people to be secure in their persons, houses, papers, and effects, against unreasonable searches and seizures." While the familiar history of the Amendment need not be recounted here, we should remember that it reflects a choice that our society should be one in which citizens "dwell in reasonable security and freedom from surveillance." Since that choice was made by the Framers of the Constitution, our cases construing the Fourth Amendment have relied in part on the common law for instruction on "what sorts of searches the Framers ... regarded as reasonable." But we have repeatedly refused to freeze " 'into constitutional law those enforcement practices that existed at the time of the Fourth Amendment's passage.' " Rather, we have construed the Amendment " 'in light of contemporary norms and conditions,' " in order to prevent "any stealthy encroachments" on our citizens' right to be free of arbitrary official intrusion. *Boyd*. Since the landmark decision in *Katz*, the Court has fulfilled its duty to protect Fourth Amendment rights by asking if police surveillance has intruded on an individual's reasonable expectation of privacy.

* * * Technological advances have enabled police to see people's activities and associations, and to hear their conversations, without being in physical proximity. Moreover, the capability now exists for police to conduct intrusive surveillance without any physical penetration of the walls of homes or other structures that citizens may believe shelters their privacy. Looking to the Fourth Amendment for protection against such "broad and unsuspected governmental incursions" into the "cherished privacy of law-abiding citizens," the Court in *Katz* abandoned its inquiry into whether police had committed a physical trespass. *Katz* announced a standard under which the occurrence of a search turned not on the physical position of the police conducting the surveillance, but on whether the surveillance in question had invaded a constitutionally protected reasonable expectation of privacy.

* * *

The second question under *Katz* has been described as asking whether an expectation of privacy is "legitimate in the sense required by the Fourth Amendment." The answer turns on "whether the government's intrusion infringes upon the personal and societal values protected by the Fourth Amendment." While no single consideration has been regarded as dispositive, "the Court has given weight to such factors as the intention of the Framers of the Fourth Amendment, ... the uses to which the individual has put a location, ... and our societal understanding that certain areas deserve the most scrupulous protection from government invasion."[5] Our decisions have made clear that this inquiry

---

5. "Legitimation of expectations of privacy by law must have a source outside of the Fourth Amendment, either by reference to concepts of real or personal property law

often must be decided by "reference to a 'place,' " and that a home is a place in which a subjective expectation of privacy virtually always will be legitimate. "At the very core [of the Fourth Amendment] stands the right of a [person] to retreat into his own home and there be free from unreasonable governmental intrusion."

B

This case involves surveillance of a home, for * * * the curtilage "has been considered part of the home itself for Fourth Amendment purposes." In *Dow Chemical Co.* v. *United States*, 476 U.S. 227, 106 S.Ct. 1819, 90 L.Ed.2d 226 (1986), decided today, the Court reaffirms that the "curtilage doctrine evolved to protect much the same kind of privacy as that covering the interior of a structure." The Court in *Dow* emphasizes, moreover, that society accepts as reasonable citizens' expectations of privacy in the area immediately surrounding their homes.

In deciding whether an area is within the curtilage, courts "have defined the curtilage, as did the common law, by reference to the factors that determine whether an individual reasonably may expect that an area immediately adjacent to the home will remain private. The lower federal courts have agreed that the curtilage is "an area of domestic use immediately surrounding a dwelling and usually but not always fenced in with the dwelling." Those courts also have held that whether an area is within the curtilage must be decided by looking at all of the facts. Relevant facts include the proximity between the area claimed to be curtilage and the home, the nature of the uses to which the area is put, and the steps taken by the resident to protect the area from observation by people passing by.

III

A

* * *

The Court's holding, therefore, must rest solely on the fact that members of the public fly in planes and may look down at homes as they fly over them. The Court does not explain why it finds this fact to be significant. One may assume that the Court believes that citizens bear the risk that air travelers will observe activities occurring within backyards that are open to the sun and air. This risk, the Court appears to hold, nullifies expectations of privacy in those yards even as to purposeful police surveillance from the air. * * *

This line of reasoning is flawed. First, the actual risk to privacy from commercial or pleasure aircraft is virtually nonexistent. Travelers on commercial flights, as well as private planes used for business or personal reasons, normally obtain at most a fleeting, anonymous, and nondiscriminating glimpse of the landscape and buildings over which they pass.

or to understandings that are recognized and permitted by society." This inquiry necessarily focuses on personal interests in privacy and liberty recognized by a free society.

The risk that a passenger on such a plane might observe private activities, and might connect those activities with particular people, is simply too trivial to protect against. It is no accident that, as a matter of common experience, many people build fences around their residential areas, but few build roofs over their backyards. Therefore, contrary to the Court's suggestion, people do not " 'knowingly [expose]' " their residential yards " 'to the public' " merely by failing to build barriers that prevent aerial surveillance.

[T]he Court fails to acknowledge the qualitative difference between police surveillance and other uses made of the airspace. Members of the public use the airspace for travel, business, or pleasure, not for the purpose of observing activities taking place within residential yards. Here, police conducted an overflight at low altitude solely for the purpose of discovering evidence of crime within a private enclave into which they were constitutionally forbidden to intrude at ground level without a warrant. It is not easy to believe that our society is prepared to force individuals to bear the risk of this type of warrantless police intrusion into their residential areas.

B

Since respondent had a reasonable expectation of privacy in his yard, aerial surveillance undertaken by the police for the purpose of discovering evidence of crime constituted a "search" within the meaning of the Fourth Amendment. "Warrantless searches are presumptively unreasonable, though the Court has recognized a few limited exceptions to this general rule." This case presents no such exception. The indiscriminate nature of aerial surveillance, illustrated by Officer Shutz' photograph of respondent's home and enclosed yard as well as those of his neighbors, poses "far too serious a threat to privacy interests in the home to escape entirely some sort of Fourth Amendment oversight." Therefore, I would affirm the judgment of the California Court of Appeal ordering suppression of the marijuana plants.

* * *

FLORIDA v. RILEY

Supreme Court of the United States, 1989.
488 U.S. 445, 109 S.Ct. 693, 102 L.Ed.2d 835.

JUSTICE WHITE announced the judgment of the Court and delivered an opinion, in which THE CHIEF JUSTICE, JUSTICE SCALIA, and JUSTICE KENNEDY join.

* * *

Respondent Riley lived in a mobile home located on five acres of rural property. A greenhouse was located 10 to 20 feet behind the mobile home. Two sides of the greenhouse were enclosed. The other two sides were not enclosed but the contents of the greenhouse were obscured from view from surrounding property by trees, shrubs, and the mobile home. The greenhouse was covered by corrugated roofing panels, some translucent and some opaque. At the time relevant to this case, two of the panels, amounting to approximately 10% of the roof area, were missing. A wire fence surrounded the mobile home and the greenhouse, and the property was posted with a "DO NOT ENTER" sign.

This case originated with an anonymous tip to the Pasco County Sheriff's office that marijuana was being grown on respondent's property. When an investigating officer discovered that he could not see the contents of the greenhouse from the road, he circled twice over respondent's property in a helicopter at the height of 400 feet. With his naked eye, he was able to see through the openings in the roof and one or more of the open sides of the greenhouse and to identify what he thought was marijuana growing in the structure. A warrant was obtained based on these observations, and the ensuing search revealed marijuana growing in the greenhouse. Respondent was charged with possession of marijuana under Florida law. The trial court granted his motion to suppress; the Florida Court of Appeals reversed but certified the case to the Florida Supreme Court, which quashed the decision of the Court of Appeals and reinstated the trial court's suppression order.

We agree with the State's submission that our decision in *California v. Ciraolo* controls this case. * * * As a general proposition, the police may see what may be seen "from a public vantage point where [they have] a right to be." Thus the police, like the public, would have been free to inspect the backyard garden from the street if their view had been unobstructed. They were likewise free to inspect the yard from the vantage point of an aircraft flying in the navigable airspace as this plane was. * * *

* * * In this case, as in *Ciraolo*, the property surveyed was within the curtilage of respondent's home. Riley no doubt intended and expected that his greenhouse would not be open to public inspection, and the precautions he took protected against ground-level observation. Because the sides and roof of his greenhouse were left partially open, however, what was growing in the greenhouse was subject to viewing from the air. Under the holding in *Ciraolo*, Riley could not reasonably have expected the contents of his greenhouse to be immune from examination by an officer seated in a fixed-wing aircraft flying in navigable airspace at an altitude of 1,000 feet or * * * at an altitude of 500 feet, the lower limit of the navigable airspace for such an aircraft. Here, the inspection was made from a helicopter, but as is the case with fixed-wing planes, "private and commercial flight [by helicopter] in the public airways is routine" in this country, and there is no indication that such flights are unheard of in Pasco County, Florida. Riley could not reasonably have expected that his greenhouse was protected from public or official observation from a helicopter had it been flying within the navigable airspace for fixed-wing aircraft.

Nor on the facts before us, does it make a difference for Fourth Amendment purposes that the helicopter was flying at 400 feet when the officer saw what was growing in the greenhouse through the partially open roof and sides of the structure. We would have a different case if flying at that altitude had been contrary to law or regulation. But helicopters are not bound by the lower limits of the navigable airspace allowed to other aircraft.[3] Any member of the public could legally have been flying over Riley's property in a helicopter at the altitude of 400 feet and could have observed Riley's greenhouse. The police officer did no more. This is not to say that an inspection of the curtilage of a house from an aircraft will always pass muster under the Fourth Amendment simply because the plane is within the navigable airspace specified by law. But it is of obvious importance that the helicopter in this case was *not* violating the law, and there is nothing in the record or before us to suggest that helicopters flying at 400 feet are sufficiently rare in this country to lend substance to respondent's claim that he reasonably anticipated that his greenhouse would not be subject to observation from that altitude. Neither is there any intimation here that the helicopter interfered with respondent's normal use of the greenhouse or of other parts of the curtilage. As far as this record reveals, no intimate details connected with the use of the home or curtilage were observed, and there was no undue noise, and no wind, dust, or threat of injury. In these circumstances, there was no violation of the Fourth Amendment.

The judgment of the Florida Supreme Court is accordingly reversed.

JUSTICE O'CONNOR, concurring in the judgment.

I concur in the judgment reversing the Supreme Court of Florida because I agree that police observation of the greenhouse in Riley's curtilage from a helicopter passing at an altitude of 400 feet did not violate an expectation of privacy "that society is prepared to recognize as 'reasonable.'" I write separately, however, to clarify the standard I believe follows from *Ciraolo*. In my view, the plurality's approach rests the scope of Fourth Amendment protection too heavily on compliance with FAA regulations whose purpose is to promote air safety, not to protect "[t]he right of the people to be secure in their persons, houses, papers, and effects, against unreasonable searches and seizures." U.S. Const., Amdt. 4.

* * *

Observations of curtilage from helicopters at very low altitudes are not perfectly analogous to ground-level observations from public roads or sidewalks. While in both cases the police may have a legal right to occupy the physical space from which their observations are made, the two

---

3. While Federal Aviation Administration regulations permit fixed-wing aircraft to be operated at an altitude of 1,000 feet while flying over congested areas and at an altitude of 500 feet above the surface in other than congested areas, helicopters may be operated at less than the minimums for fixed-wing aircraft "if the operation is conducted without hazard to persons or property on the surface. In addition, each person operating a helicopter shall comply with routes or altitudes specifically prescribed for helicopters by the [FAA] Administrator." 14 CFR § 91.79 (1988).

situations are not necessarily comparable in terms of whether expectations of privacy from such vantage points should be considered reasonable. Public roads, even those less traveled by, are clearly demarked public thoroughfares. Individuals who seek privacy can take precautions, tailored to the location of the road, to avoid disclosing private activities to those who pass by. They can build a tall fence, for example, and thus ensure private enjoyment of the curtilage without risking public observation from the road or sidewalk. If they do not take such precautions, they cannot reasonably expect privacy from public observation. In contrast, even individuals who have taken effective precautions to ensure against ground-level observations cannot block off all conceivable aerial views of their outdoor patios and yards without entirely giving up their enjoyment of those areas. To require individuals to completely cover and enclose their curtilage is to demand more than the "precautions customarily taken by those seeking privacy." The fact that a helicopter could conceivably observe the curtilage at virtually any altitude or angle, without violating FAA regulations, does not in itself mean that an individual has no reasonable expectation of privacy from such observation.

In determining whether Riley had a reasonable expectation of privacy from aerial observation, the relevant inquiry after *Ciraolo* is not whether the helicopter was where it had a right to be under FAA regulations. Rather, consistent with *Katz v. United States,* we must ask whether the helicopter was in the public airways at an altitude at which members of the public travel with sufficient regularity that Riley's expectation of privacy from aerial observation was not "one that society is prepared to recognize as 'reasonable.'" Thus, in determining " 'whether the government's intrusion infringes upon the personal and societal values protected by the Fourth Amendment,'" it is not conclusive to observe, as the plurality does, that "[a]ny member of the public could legally have been flying over Riley's property in a helicopter at the altitude of 400 feet and could have observed Riley's greenhouse." Nor is it conclusive that police helicopters may often fly at 400 feet. If the public rarely, if ever, travels overhead at such altitudes, the observation cannot be said to be from a vantage point generally used by the public and Riley cannot be said to have "knowingly exposed[d]" his greenhouse to public view. However, if the public can generally be expected to travel over residential backyards at an altitude of 400 feet, Riley cannot reasonably expect his curtilage to be free from such aerial observation.

In my view, the defendant must bear the burden of proving that his expectation of privacy was a reasonable one, and thus that a "search" within the meaning of the Fourth Amendment even took place.

* * *

Justice Brennan, with whom Justice Marshall and Justice Stevens join, dissenting.

* * *

I

The opinion for a plurality of the Court reads almost as if *Katz* had never been decided. * * * [T]he relevant inquiry is whether the police surveillance "violated the privacy upon which [the defendant] justifiably relied" * * *. The result of that inquiry in any given case depends ultimately on the judgment "whether, if the particular form of surveillance practiced by the police is permitted to go unregulated by constitutional restraints, the amount of privacy and freedom remaining to citizens would be diminished to a compass inconsistent with the aims of a free and open society."

* * *

* * * Under the plurality's exceedingly grudging Fourth Amendment theory, the expectation of privacy is defeated if a single member of the public could conceivably position herself to see into the area in question without doing anything illegal. It is defeated whatever the difficulty a person would have in so positioning herself, and however infrequently anyone would in fact do so. In taking this view the plurality ignores the very essence of *Katz*. The reason why there is no reasonable expectation of privacy in an area that is exposed to the public is that little diminution in "the amount of privacy and freedom remaining to citizens" will result from police surveillance of something that any passerby readily sees. To pretend, as the plurality opinion does, that the same is true when the police use a helicopter to peer over high fences is, at best, disingenuous. [C]an it seriously be questioned that Riley enjoyed virtually complete privacy in his backyard greenhouse, and that that privacy was invaded solely by police helicopter surveillance? Is the theoretical possibility that any member of the public (with sufficient means) could also have hired a helicopter and looked over Riley's fence of any relevance at all in determining whether Riley suffered a serious loss of privacy and personal security through the police action?

* * *

III

Perhaps the most remarkable passage in the plurality opinion is its suggestion that the case might be a different one had any "intimate details connected with the use of the home or curtilage [been] observed." What, one wonders, is meant by "intimate details"? If the police had observed Riley embracing his wife in the backyard greenhouse, would we then say that his reasonable expectation of privacy had been infringed? Where in the Fourth Amendment or in our cases is there any warrant for imposing a requirement that the activity observed must be "intimate" in order to be protected by the Constitution?

* * *

IV

* * *

What separates me from JUSTICE O'CONNOR is essentially an empirical matter concerning the extent of public use of the airspace at that altitude, together with the question of how to resolve that issue. I do not think the constitutional claim should fail simply because "there is reason to believe" that there is "considerable" public flying this close to earth or because Riley "introduced no evidence to the contrary before the Florida courts." * * * If so, I think we could take judicial notice that, while there may be an occasional privately owned helicopter that flies over populated areas at an altitude of 400 feet, such flights are a rarity and are almost entirely limited to approaching or leaving airports or to reporting traffic congestion near major roadways. * * *

If, however, we are to resolve the issue by considering whether the appropriate party carried its burden of proof, I again think that Riley must prevail. Because the State has greater access to information concerning customary flight patterns and because the coercive power of the State ought not be brought to bear in cases in which it is unclear whether the prosecution is a product of an unconstitutional, warrantless search. * * *

* * *

[JUSTICE BLACKMUN'S dissenting opinion is omitted.]

DOW CHEMICAL CO. v. UNITED STATES

Supreme Court of the United States, 1986.
476 U.S. 227, 106 S.Ct. 1819, 90 L.Ed.2d 226.

CHIEF JUSTICE BURGER delivered the opinion of the Court.

* * *

I

Petitioner Dow Chemical Co. operates a 2,000–acre facility manufacturing chemicals at Midland, Michigan. The facility consists of numerous covered buildings, with manufacturing equipment and piping conduits located between the various buildings exposed to visual observation from the air. At all times, Dow has maintained elaborate security around the perimeter of the complex barring ground-level public views of these areas. It also investigates any low-level flights by aircraft over the facility. Dow has not undertaken, however, to conceal all manufacturing equipment within the complex from aerial views. Dow maintains that the cost of covering its exposed equipment would be prohibitive.

In early 1978, enforcement officials of EPA, with Dow's consent, made an on-site inspection of two powerplants in this complex. A subsequent EPA request for a second inspection, however, was denied, and EPA did not thereafter seek an administrative search warrant.

Instead, EPA employed a commercial aerial photographer, using a standard floor-mounted, precision aerial mapping camera, to take photographs of the facility from altitudes of 12,000, 3,000, and 1,200 feet. At all times the aircraft was lawfully within navigable airspace.

* * *

II

The photographs at issue in this case are essentially like those commonly used in mapmaking. Any person with an airplane and an aerial camera could readily duplicate them. In common with much else, the technology of photography has changed in this century. These developments have enhanced industrial processes, and indeed all areas of life; they have also enhanced law enforcement techniques. Whether they may be employed by competitors to penetrate trade secrets is not a question presented in this case. Governments do not generally seek to appropriate trade secrets of the private sector, and the right to be free of appropriation of trade secrets is protected by law.

* * *

IV

We turn now to Dow's contention that taking aerial photographs constituted a search without a warrant, thereby violating Dow's rights under the Fourth Amendment. In making this contention, however, Dow concedes that a simple flyover with naked-eye observation, or the taking of a photograph from a nearby hillside overlooking such a facility, would give rise to no Fourth Amendment problem.

* * *

Two lines of cases are relevant to the inquiry: the curtilage doctrine and the "open fields" doctrine. The curtilage area immediately surrounding a private house has long been given protection as a place where the occupants have a reasonable and legitimate expectation of privacy that society is prepared to accept.

As the curtilage doctrine evolved to protect much the same kind of privacy as that covering the interior of a structure, the contrasting "open fields" doctrine evolved as well. From *Hester* v. *United States*, 265 U.S. 57, 44 S.Ct. 445, 68 L.Ed. 898 (1924), to *Oliver* [v. *United States*, 466 U.S. 170, (1984)], the Court has drawn a line as to what expectations are reasonable in the open areas beyond the curtilage of a dwelling: "open fields do not provide the setting for those intimate activities that the [Fourth] Amendment is intended to shelter from governmental interference or surveillance." In *Oliver*, we held that "an individual may not legitimately demand privacy for activities out of doors in fields, except in the area immediately surrounding the home." To fall within the "open fields" doctrine the area "need be neither 'open' nor a 'field' as those terms are used in common speech."

Dow plainly has a reasonable, legitimate, and objective expectation of privacy within the interior of its covered buildings, and it is equally clear that expectation is one society is prepared to observe. Moreover, it could hardly be expected that Dow would erect a huge cover over a 2,000–acre tract. In contending that its entire enclosed plant complex is an "industrial curtilage," Dow argues that its exposed manufacturing facilities are analogous to the curtilage surrounding a home because it has taken every possible step to bar access from ground level.

* * * In *Oliver*, the Court described the curtilage of a dwelling as "the area to which extends the intimate activity associated with the 'sanctity of a man's home and the privacies of life.' " The intimate activities associated with family privacy and the home and its curtilage simply do not reach the outdoor areas or spaces between structures and buildings of a manufacturing plant.

Admittedly, Dow's enclosed plant complex, like the area in *Oliver*, does not fall precisely within the "open fields" doctrine. The area at issue here can perhaps be seen as falling somewhere between "open fields" and curtilage, but lacking some of the critical characteristics of both.[3] Dow's inner manufacturing areas are elaborately secured to ensure they are not open or exposed to the public from the ground. Any actual physical entry by EPA into any enclosed area would raise significantly different questions, because "[the] businessman, like the occupant of a residence, has a constitutional right to go about his business free from unreasonable official entries upon his private commercial property." The narrow issue raised by Dow's claim of search and seizure, however, concerns aerial observation of a 2,000–acre outdoor manufacturing facility *without* physical entry.

* * *

We pointed out in *Donovan* v. *Dewey*, 452 U.S. 594, 598–599, 101 S.Ct. 2534, 69 L.Ed.2d 262 (1981), that the Government has "greater latitude to conduct warrantless inspections of commercial property" because "the expectation of privacy that the owner of commercial property enjoys in such property differs significantly from the sanctity accorded an individual's home." We emphasized that unlike a homeowner's interest in his dwelling, "[the] interest of the owner of commercial property is not one in being free from any inspections." And with regard to regulatory inspections, we have held that "[what] is observable by the public is observable without a warrant, by the Government inspector as well."

3. In *Oliver*, we observed that "for most homes, the boundaries of the curtilage will be clearly marked; and the conception defining the curtilage—as the area around the home to which the activity of home life extends—is a familiar one easily understood from our daily experience." While we did not attempt to definitively mark the boundaries of what constitutes an open field, we noted that "[it] is clear ... that the term 'open fields' may include any unoccupied or undeveloped area outside of the curtilage." As *Oliver* recognized, the curtilage surrounding a home is generally a well-defined, limited area. In stark contrast, the areas for which Dow claims enhanced protection cover the equivalent of a half dozen family farms.

Oliver recognized that in the open field context, "the public and police lawfully may survey lands from the air." Here, EPA was not employing some unique sensory device that, for example, could penetrate the walls of buildings and record conversations in Dow's plants, offices, or laboratories, but rather a conventional, albeit precise, commercial camera commonly used in mapmaking. The Government asserts it has not yet enlarged the photographs to any significant degree, but Dow points out that simple magnification permits identification of objects such as wires as small as 1/2–inch in diameter.

It may well be, as the Government concedes, that surveillance of private property by using highly sophisticated surveillance equipment not generally available to the public, such as satellite technology, might be constitutionally proscribed absent a warrant. But the photographs here are not so revealing of intimate details as to raise constitutional concerns. Although they undoubtedly give EPA more detailed information than naked-eye views, they remain limited to an outline of the facility's buildings and equipment. The mere fact that human vision is enhanced somewhat, at least to the degree here, does not give rise to constitutional problems.[5] An electronic device to penetrate walls or windows so as to hear and record confidential discussions of chemical formulae or other trade secrets would raise very different and far more serious questions; other protections such as trade secret laws are available to protect commercial activities from private surveillance by competitors.

* * *

We hold that the taking of aerial photographs of an industrial plant complex from navigable airspace is not a search prohibited by the Fourth Amendment. *Affirmed.*

JUSTICE POWELL, with whom JUSTICE BRENNAN, JUSTICE MARSHALL, and JUSTICE BLACKMUN join, concurring in part, and dissenting in part.

* * *

I

* * *

Short of erecting a roof over the Midland complex, Dow has, as the Court states, undertaken "elaborate" precautions to secure the facility

---

5. The partial dissent emphasizes Dow's claim that under magnification power lines as small as 1/2–inch in diameter can be observed. But a glance at the photographs in issue shows that those power lines are observable only because of their stark contrast with the snow-white background. No objects as small as 1/2–inch in diameter such as a class ring, for example, are recognizable, nor are there any identifiable human faces or secret documents captured in such a fashion as to implicate more serious privacy concerns. Fourth Amendment cases must be decided on the facts of each case, not by extravagant generalizations. "[We] have never held that potential, as opposed to actual, invasions of privacy constitute searches for purposes of the Fourth Amendment." *United States v. Karo,* 468 U.S. 705, 712, 104 S.Ct. 3296, 82 L.Ed.2d 530 (1984). On these facts, nothing in these photographs suggests that any reasonable expectations of privacy have been infringed.

from unwelcome intrusions. In fact, Dow appears to have done everything commercially feasible to protect the confidential business information and property located within the borders of the facility. Security measures include an 8-foot-high chain link fence completely surrounding the facility that is guarded by security personnel and monitored by closed-circuit television, alarm systems that are triggered by unauthorized entry into the facility, motion detectors that indicate movement of persons within restricted areas, a prohibition on use of camera equipment by anyone other than authorized Dow personnel, and a strict policy under which no photographs of the facility may be taken or released without prior management review and approval. In addition to these precautions, the open-air plants were placed within the internal portion of the 2,000-acre complex to conceal them from the view of members of the public outside the perimeter fence.

Dow's security program also includes procedures designed to protect the facility from aerial photography. Dow has instructed its employees that it is "concerned when other than commercial passenger flights pass over the plant property." When "suspicious" overflights occur, such as where a plane makes several passes over the facility, employees try to obtain the plane's identification number and description. Working with personnel from the State Police and local airports, Dow employees then locate the pilot to determine if he has photographed the facility. If Dow learns that he has done so, Dow takes steps to prevent dissemination of photographs that show details of its proprietary technology.

* * *

Using a sophisticated aerial mapping camera,[4] this firm [hired by the EPA] took approximately 75 color photographs of various parts of the plant. The District Court found that "some of the photographs taken from directly above the plant at 1,200 feet are capable of enlargement to a scale of 1 inch equals 20 feet *or greater*, without significant loss of detail or resolution. When enlarged in this manner, and viewed under magnification, it is possible to discern equipment, pipes, and power lines as small as 1/2 inch in diameter." Observation of these minute details is, as the District Court found, "a near physical impossibility" from anywhere "but *directly above*" the complex. (emphasis in original). Because of the complicated details captured in the photographs, the District Court concluded, "the camera saw a great deal more than the human eye could ever see," even if the observer was located directly above the facility.

* * *

4. The District Court believed it was "important to an understanding of this case to provide a description of the highly effective equipment used" in photographing Dow's facility. "The aircraft used was a twin engine Beechcraft," which is "able to 'provide photographic stability, fast mobility and flight endurance required for precision photography.' " The camera used "cost in excess of $22,000.00 and is described by the company as the 'finest precision aerial camera available.' … The camera was mounted to the floor inside the aircraft and was capable of taking several photographs in precise and rapid succession." This technique facilitates stereoscopic examination, a type of examination that permits depth perception.

KYLLO v. UNITED STATES

Supreme Court of the United States, 2001.
533 U.S. 27, 121 S.Ct. 2038, 150 L.Ed.2d 94.

JUSTICE SCALIA delivered the opinion of the Court.

This case presents the question whether the use of a thermal-imaging device aimed at a private home from a public street to detect relative amounts of heat within the home constitutes a "search" within the meaning of the Fourth Amendment.

I

In 1991 Agent William Elliott of the United States Department of the Interior came to suspect that marijuana was being grown in the home belonging to petitioner Danny Kyllo * * *. Indoor marijuana growth typically requires high-intensity lamps. In order to determine whether an amount of heat was emanating from petitioner's home consistent with the use of such lamps, at 3:20 a.m. on January 16, 1992, Agent Elliott and Dan Haas used an Agema Thermovision 210 thermal imager to scan the triplex. Thermal imagers detect infrared radiation, which virtually all objects emit but which is not visible to the naked eye. The imager converts radiation into images based on relative warmth— black is cool, white is hot, shades of gray connote relative differences; in that respect, it operates somewhat like a video camera showing heat images. The scan of Kyllo's home took only a few minutes and was performed from the passenger seat of Agent Elliott's vehicle across the street from the front of the house and also from the street in back of the house. The scan showed that the roof over the garage and a side wall of petitioner's home were relatively hot compared to the rest of the home and substantially warmer than neighboring homes in the triplex. Agent Elliott concluded that petitioner was using halide lights to grow marijuana in his house, which indeed he was. Based on tips from informants, utility bills, and the thermal imaging, a Federal Magistrate Judge issued a warrant authorizing a search of petitioner's home, and the agents found an indoor growing operation involving more than 100 plants. Petitioner was indicted on one count of manufacturing marijuana * * *. He unsuccessfully moved to suppress the evidence seized from his home and then entered a conditional guilty plea.

* * *

II

The Fourth Amendment provides that "the right of the people to be secure in their persons, houses, papers, and effects, against unreasonable searches and seizures, shall not be violated." "At the very core" of the Fourth Amendment "stands the right of a man to retreat into his own home and there be free from unreasonable governmental intrusion." * * *

On the other hand, the antecedent question of whether or not a Fourth Amendment "search" has occurred is not so simple under our precedent. The permissibility of ordinary visual surveillance of a home used to be clear because, well into the 20th century, our Fourth Amendment jurisprudence was tied to common-law trespass. Visual surveillance was unquestionably lawful because " 'the eye cannot by the laws of England be guilty of a trespass.' " We have since decoupled violation of a person's Fourth Amendment rights from trespassory violation of his property, but the lawfulness of warrantless visual surveillance of a home has still been preserved. As we observed in *California v. Ciraolo*, 476 U.S. 207, 213, 106 S.Ct. 1809, 90 L.Ed.2d 210 (1986), "the Fourth Amendment protection of the home has never been extended to require law enforcement officers to shield their eyes when passing by a home on public thoroughfares."

One might think that the new validating rationale would be that examining the portion of a house that is in plain public view, while it is a "search" despite the absence of trespass, is not an "unreasonable" one under the Fourth Amendment. But in fact we have held that visual observation is no "search" at all—perhaps in order to preserve somewhat more intact our doctrine that warrantless searches are presumptively unconstitutional. * * *

* * *

III

It would be foolish to contend that the degree of privacy secured to citizens by the Fourth Amendment has been entirely unaffected by the advance of technology. For example, as the cases discussed above make clear, the technology enabling human flight has exposed to public view (and hence, we have said, to official observation) uncovered portions of the house and its curtilage that once were private. The question we confront today is what limits there are upon this power of technology to shrink the realm of guaranteed privacy.

The *Katz* test—whether the individual has an expectation of privacy that society is prepared to recognize as reasonable—has often been criticized as circular, and hence subjective and unpredictable. While it may be difficult to refine *Katz* when the search of areas such as telephone booths, automobiles, or even the curtilage and uncovered portions of residences are at issue, in the case of the search of the interior of homes—the prototypical and hence most commonly litigated area of protected privacy—there is a ready criterion, with roots deep in the common law, of the minimal expectation of privacy that *exists*, and that is acknowledged to be *reasonable*. To withdraw protection of this minimum expectation would be to permit police technology to erode the privacy guaranteed by the Fourth Amendment. We think that obtaining by sense-enhancing technology any information regarding the interior of the home that could not otherwise have been obtained without physical "intrusion into a constitutionally protected area," constitutes a search—

at least where (as here) the technology in question is not in general public use. This assures preservation of that degree of privacy against government that existed when the Fourth Amendment was adopted. On the basis of this criterion, the information obtained by the thermal imager in this case was the product of a search.

The Government maintains, however, that the thermal imaging must be upheld because it detected "only heat radiating from the external surface of the house." The dissent makes this its leading point, contending that there is a fundamental difference between what it calls "off-the-wall" observations and "through-the-wall surveillance." But just as a thermal imager captures only heat emanating from a house, so also a powerful directional microphone picks up only sound emanating from a house-and a satellite capable of scanning from many miles away would pick up only visible light emanating from a house. We rejected such a mechanical interpretation of the Fourth Amendment in *Katz*, where the eavesdropping device picked up only sound waves that reached the exterior of the phone booth. Reversing that approach would leave the homeowner at the mercy of advancing technology—including imaging technology that could discern all human activity in the home. While the technology used in the present case was relatively crude, the rule we adopt must take account of more sophisticated systems that are already in use or in development.[3] * * *

The Government also contends that the thermal imaging was constitutional because it did not "detect private activities occurring in private areas." It points out that in *Dow Chemical* we observed that the enhanced aerial photography did not reveal any "intimate details." *Dow Chemical*, however, involved enhanced aerial photography of an industrial complex, which does not share the Fourth Amendment sanctity of the home. The Fourth Amendment's protection of the home has never been tied to measurement of the quality or quantity of information obtained. * * * In the home, our cases show, *all* details are intimate details, because the entire area is held safe from prying government eyes. * * * These were intimate details because they were details of the home, just as was the detail of how warm—or even how relatively warm—Kyllo was heating his residence.

Limiting the prohibition of thermal imaging to "intimate details" would not only be wrong in principle; it would be impractical in application, failing to provide "a workable accommodation between the needs of law enforcement and the interests protected by the Fourth Amend-

---

3. The ability to "see" through walls and other opaque barriers is a clear, and scientifically feasible, goal of law enforcement research and development. The National Law Enforcement and Corrections Technology Center, a program within the United States Department of Justice, features on its Internet Website projects that include a "Radar–Based Through-the-Wall Surveillance System," "Handheld Ultra-sound Through the Wall Surveillance," and a "Radar Flashlight" that "will enable law officers to detect individuals through interior building walls." www.nlectc.org/techproj/ (visited May 3, 2001). Some devices may emit low levels of radiation that travel "through-the-wall," but others, such as more sophisticated thermal imaging devices, are entirely passive, or "off-the-wall" as the dissent puts it.

ment." To begin with, there is no necessary connection between the sophistication of the surveillance equipment and the "intimacy" of the details that it observes—which means that one cannot say (and the police cannot be assured) that use of the relatively crude equipment at issue here will always be lawful. The Agema Thermovision 210 might disclose, for example, at what hour each night the lady of the house takes her daily sauna and bath—a detail that many would consider "intimate"; and a much more sophisticated system might detect nothing more intimate than the fact that someone left a closet light on. * * *[6]

* * *

We have said that the Fourth Amendment draws "a firm line at the entrance to the house." That line, we think, must be not only firm but also bright—which requires clear specification of those methods of surveillance that require a warrant. While it is certainly possible to conclude from the videotape of the thermal imaging that occurred in this case that no "significant" compromise of the homeowner's privacy has occurred, we must take the long view, from the original meaning of the Fourth Amendment forward.

> "The Fourth Amendment is to be construed in the light of what was deemed an unreasonable search and seizure when it was adopted, and in a manner which will conserve public interests as well as the interests and rights of individual citizens."

Where, as here, the Government uses a device that is not in general public use, to explore details of the home that would previously have been unknowable without physical intrusion, the surveillance is a "search" and is presumptively unreasonable without a warrant.

Since we hold the Thermovision imaging to have been an unlawful search, it will remain for the District Court to determine whether, without the evidence it provided, the search warrant issued in this case was supported by probable cause—and if not, whether there is any other basis for supporting admission of the evidence that the search pursuant to the warrant produced.

The judgment of the Court of Appeals is reversed; the case is remanded for further proceedings consistent with this opinion.

Justice Stevens, with whom The Chief Justice, Justice O'Connor, and Justice Kennedy join, dissenting.

There is, in my judgment, a distinction of constitutional magnitude between "through-the-wall surveillance" that gives the observer or listener direct access to information in a private area, on the one hand, and

---

6. The dissent argues that we have injected potential uncertainty into the constitutional analysis by noting that whether or not the technology is in general public use may be a factor. That quarrel, however, is not with us but with this Court's precedent. See *Ciraolo, supra,* at 215 ("In an age where private and commercial flight in the public airways is routine, it is unreasonable for respondent to expect that his marijuana plants were constitutionally protected from being observed with the naked eye from an altitude of 1,000 feet"). Given that we can quite confidently say that thermal imaging is not "routine," we decline in this case to reexamine that factor.

the thought processes used to draw inferences from information in the public domain, on the other hand. The Court has crafted a rule that purports to deal with direct observations of the inside of the home, but the case before us merely involves indirect deductions from "off-the-wall" surveillance, that is, observations of the exterior of the home. Those observations were made with a fairly primitive thermal imager that gathered data exposed on the outside of petitioner's home but did not invade any constitutionally protected interest in privacy. Moreover, I believe that the supposedly "bright-line" rule the Court has created in response to its concerns about future technological developments is unnecessary, unwise, and inconsistent with the Fourth Amendment.

I

There is no need for the Court to craft a new rule to decide this case, as it is controlled by established principles from our Fourth Amendment jurisprudence. One of those core principles, of course, is that "searches and seizures *inside a home* without a warrant are presumptively unreasonable." But it is equally well settled that searches and seizures of property in plain view are presumptively reasonable. Whether that property is residential or commercial, the basic principle is the same: " 'What a person knowingly exposes to the public, even in his own home or office, is not a subject of Fourth Amendment protection.' " That is the principle implicated here.

* * * All that the infrared camera did in this case was passively measure heat emitted from the exterior surfaces of petitioner's home; all that those measurements showed were relative differences in emission levels, vaguely indicating that some areas of the roof and outside walls were warmer than others. As still images from the infrared scans show, no details regarding the interior of petitioner's home were revealed. Unlike an x-ray scan, or other possible "through-the-wall" techniques, the detection of infrared radiation emanating from the home did not accomplish "an unauthorized physical penetration into the premises," nor did it "obtain information that it could not have obtained by observation from outside the curtilage of the house."

Indeed, the ordinary use of the senses might enable a neighbor or passerby to notice the heat emanating from a building, particularly if it is vented, as was the case here. Additionally, any member of the public might notice that one part of a house is warmer than another part or a nearby building if, for example, rainwater evaporates or snow melts at different rates across its surfaces. * * *

* * *

To be sure, the homeowner has a reasonable expectation of privacy concerning what takes place within the home, and the Fourth Amendment's protection against physical invasions of the home should apply to their functional equivalent. But the equipment in this case did not penetrate the walls of petitioner's home, and while it did pick up "details of the home" that were exposed to the public, it did not obtain "any information regarding the *interior* of the home." * * *

* * *

II

* * * As I have suggested, I would not erect a constitutional impediment to the use of sense-enhancing technology unless it provides its user with the functional equivalent of actual presence in the area being searched.

Despite the Court's attempt to draw a line that is "not only firm but also bright," the contours of its new rule are uncertain because its protection apparently dissipates as soon as the relevant technology is "in general public use." Yet how much use is general public use is not even hinted at by the Court's opinion, which makes the somewhat doubtful assumption that the thermal imager used in this case does not satisfy that criterion.[5] In any event, putting aside its lack of clarity, this criterion is somewhat perverse because it seems likely that the threat to privacy will grow, rather than recede, as the use of intrusive equipment becomes more readily available.

* * *

D. PRIVACY EXPECTATIONS AND ASSUMPTION OF THE RISK OF DISCLOSURE

1. Assumption of the Risk and Technological Surveillance

UNITED STATES v. WHITE

Supreme Court of the United States, 1971.
401 U.S. 745, 91 S.Ct. 1122, 28 L.Ed.2d 453.

MR. JUSTICE WHITE announced the judgment of the Court and an opinion in which THE CHIEF JUSTICE, MR. JUSTICE STEWART, and MR. JUSTICE BLACKMUN join.

* * * The issue before us is whether the Fourth Amendment bars from evidence the testimony of governmental agents who related certain conversations which had occurred between defendant White and a government informant, Harvey Jackson, and which the agents overheard by monitoring the frequency of a radio transmitter carried by Jackson and concealed on his person. On four occasions the conversations took place in Jackson's home; each of these conversations was overheard by an

---

5. The record describes a device that numbers close to a thousand manufactured units; that has a predecessor numbering in the neighborhood of 4,000 to 5,000 units; that competes with a similar product numbering from 5,000 to 6,000 units; and that is "readily available to the public" for commercial, personal, or law enforcement pur-poses, and is just an 800–number away from being rented from "half a dozen national companies" by anyone who wants one. Since, by virtue of the Court's new rule, the issue is one of first impression, perhaps it should order an evidentiary hearing to determine whether these facts suffice to establish "general public use."

agent concealed in a kitchen closet with Jackson's consent and by a second agent outside the house using a radio receiver. Four other conversations—one in respondent's home, one in a restaurant, and two in Jackson's car—were overheard by the use of radio equipment. The prosecution was unable to locate and produce Jackson at the trial and the trial court overruled objections to the testimony of the agents who conducted the electronic surveillance. The jury returned a guilty verdict and defendant appealed.

* * *

I

* * *

[Katz v. United States, 389 U.S. 347, 88 S.Ct. 507, 19 L.Ed.2d 576 (1967)], however, finally swept away doctrines that electronic eavesdropping is permissible under the Fourth Amendment unless physical invasion of a constitutionally protected area produced the challenged evidence. In that case government agents, without petitioner's consent or knowledge, attached a listening device to the outside of a public telephone booth and recorded the defendant's end of his telephone conversations. In declaring the recordings inadmissible in evidence in the absence of a warrant authorizing the surveillance, the Court overruled *Olmstead* and *Goldman* and held that the absence of physical intrusion into the telephone booth did not justify using electronic devices in listening to and recording Katz' words, thereby violating the privacy on which he justifiably relied while using the telephone in those circumstances.

* * *

Hoffa v. United States, 385 U.S. 293, 87 S.Ct. 408, 17 L.Ed.2d 374 (1966), which was left undisturbed by *Katz*, held that however strongly a defendant may trust an apparent colleague, his expectations in this respect are not protected by the Fourth Amendment when it turns out that the colleague is a government agent regularly communicating with the authorities. In these circumstances, "no interest legitimately protected by the Fourth Amendment is involved," for that amendment affords no protection to "a wrongdoer's misplaced belief that a person to whom he voluntarily confides his wrongdoing will not reveal it." No warrant to "search and seize" is required in such circumstances, nor is it when the Government sends to defendant's home a secret agent who conceals his identity and makes a purchase of narcotics from the accused, *Lewis v. United States*, 385 U.S. 206, 87 S.Ct. 424, 17 L.Ed.2d 312 (1966), or when the same agent, unbeknown to the defendant, carries electronic equipment to record the defendant's words and the evidence so gathered is later offered in evidence. *Lopez v. United States*, 373 U.S. 427, 83 S.Ct. 1381, 10 L.Ed.2d 462 (1963).

Conceding that *Hoffa, Lewis*, and *Lopez* remained unaffected by *Katz*, the Court of Appeals nevertheless read both *Katz* and the Fourth

Amendment to require a different result if the agent not only records his conversations with the defendant but instantaneously transmits them electronically to other agents equipped with radio receivers. Where this occurs, the Court of Appeals held, the Fourth Amendment is violated and the testimony of the listening agents must be excluded from evidence.

* * *

Our problem is not what the privacy expectations of particular defendants in particular situations may be or the extent to which they may in fact have relied on the discretion of their companions. Very probably, individual defendants neither know nor suspect that their colleagues have gone or will go to the police or are carrying recorders or transmitters. Otherwise, conversation would cease and our problem with these encounters would be nonexistent or far different from those now before us. Our problem, in terms of the principles announced in *Katz*, is what expectations of privacy are constitutionally "justifiable"—what expectations the Fourth Amendment will protect in the absence of a warrant. So far, the law permits the frustration of actual expectations of privacy by permitting authorities to use the testimony of those associates who for one reason or another have determined to turn to the police, as well as by authorizing the use of informants in the manner exemplified by *Hoffa* and *Lewis*. If the law gives no protection to the wrongdoer whose trusted accomplice is or becomes a police agent, neither should it protect him when that same agent has recorded or transmitted the conversations which are later offered in evidence to prove the State's case.

* * *

* * * An electronic recording will many times produce a more reliable rendition of what a defendant has said than will the unaided memory of a police agent. It may also be that with the recording in existence it is less likely that the informant will change his mind, less chance that threat or injury will suppress unfavorable evidence and less chance that cross-examination will confound the testimony. Considerations like these obviously do not favor the defendant, but we are not prepared to hold that a defendant who has no constitutional right to exclude the informer's unaided testimony nevertheless has a Fourth Amendment privilege against a more accurate version of the events in question.

It is thus untenable to consider the activities and reports of the police agent himself, though acting without a warrant, to be a "reasonable" investigative effort and lawful under the Fourth Amendment but to view the same agent with a recorder or transmitter as conducting an "unreasonable" and unconstitutional search and seizure. * * *

* * *

The judgment of the Court of Appeals is reversed.

[Concurring opinions of Justice Black and Justice Brennan, and a dissenting opinion of Justice Douglas, are omitted.]

Mr. Justice Harlan, dissenting.

* * *

* * * The analysis must, in my view, transcend the search for subjective expectations or legal attribution of assumptions of risk. Our expectations, and the risks we assume, are in large part reflections of laws that translate into rules the customs and values of the past and present.

Since it is the task of the law to form and project, as well as mirror and reflect, we should not, as judges, merely recite the expectations and risks without examining the desirability of saddling them upon society. The critical question, therefore, is whether under our system of government, as reflected in the Constitution, we should impose on our citizens the risks of the electronic listener or observer without at least the protection of a warrant requirement.

* * *

B

The impact of the practice of third-party bugging, must, I think, be considered such as to undermine that confidence and sense of security in dealing with one another that is characteristic of individual relationships between citizens in a free society. It goes beyond the impact on privacy occasioned by the ordinary type of "informer" investigation upheld in *Lewis* and *Hoffa*. The argument of the plurality opinion, to the effect that it is irrelevant whether secrets are revealed by the mere tattletale or the transistor, ignores the differences occasioned by third-party monitoring and recording which insures full and accurate disclosure of all that is said, free of the possibility of error and oversight that inheres in human reporting.

Authority is hardly required to support the proposition that words would be measured a good deal more carefully and communication inhibited if one suspected his conversations were being transmitted and transcribed. Were third-party bugging a prevalent practice, it might well smother that spontaneity—reflected in frivolous, impetuous, sacrilegious, and defiant discourse—that liberates daily life. Much off-hand exchange is easily forgotten and one may count on the obscurity of his remarks, protected by the very fact of a limited audience, and the likelihood that the listener will either overlook or forget what is said, as well as the listener's inability to reformulate a conversation without having to contend with a documented record. All these values are sacrificed by a rule of law that permits official monitoring of private discourse limited only by the need to locate a willing assistant.

* * *

Finally, it is too easy to forget—and, hence, too often forgotten—that the issue here is whether to interpose a search warrant procedure between law enforcement agencies engaging in electronic eavesdropping and the public generally. By casting its "risk analysis" solely in terms of the expectations and risks that "wrongdoers" or "one contemplating illegal activities" ought to bear, the plurality opinion, I think, misses the mark entirely. * * * The interest [left unprotected] is the expectation of the ordinary citizen, who has never engaged in illegal conduct in his life, that he may carry on his private discourse freely, openly, and spontaneously without measuring his every word against the connotations it might carry when instantaneously heard by others unknown to him and unfamiliar with his situation or analyzed in a cold, formal record played days, months, or years after the conversation. Interposition of a warrant requirement is designed not to shield "wrongdoers," but to secure a measure of privacy and a sense of personal security throughout our society.

The Fourth Amendment does, of course, leave room for the employment of modern technology in criminal law enforcement, but in the stream of current developments in Fourth Amendment law I think it must be held that third-party electronic monitoring, subject only to the self-restraint of law enforcement officials, has no place in our society.

* * *

Commentary

The Supreme Court has also decided cases involving the use of electronic tracking devices (beepers) to assist agents in following movements of vehicles or containers. The Fourth Amendment issue might be raised either with respect to the installation of the beeper, or with respect to the subsequent activities of the police in following the container with the aid of the beeper.

In United States v. Knotts, 460 U.S. 276 (1983), the police obtained the consent of a chemical company to install a beeper into a container of chloroform (used to make illegal drugs) which was subsequently sold to a suspect. With the assistance of the beeper, the police were then able to follow the suspect to the location of an illicit drug laboratory in a remote area. Given that merely following the suspect's automobile raises no Fourth Amendment issue, the Supreme Court majority held that nothing in the Fourth Amendment prohibits the police from making use of this kind of scientific assistance to augment their senses.

In a second "beeper" case, the Court decided two questions left unresolved in *Knotts*: (1) Whether installation of a beeper in a container of chemicals with the consent of its original owner constitutes a search or seizure when the container is subsequently delivered to a buyer having no knowledge of its presence; and (2) whether monitoring of a beeper constitutes a Fourth Amendment search when it reveals information that could not have been obtained through unaided visual surveillance (the movements of the container inside a building, which police could not see but could follow electronically). The majority opinion held that the installation violated no

Fourth Amendment right of the ultimate recipient, but that the subsequent monitoring required prior judicial authorization to the extent that the police continue to monitor the beeper when the container has been taken inside private premises. The Court observed that it would be obviously desirable for police to obtain warrants for the installation and monitoring of beepers in all cases, because it would often be important to continue monitoring to determine precisely where the container is located in a place not open to visual surveillance. The majority left open the possibility that warrants might be obtainable on a showing of reasonable suspicion rather than probable cause, given that the invasion of privacy in such cases is not as great as it is with a traditional search. United States v. Karo, 468 U.S. 705 (1984). However, the Supreme Court's recent decision in *Kyllo v. United States, supra*, appears to preclude this limitation on the holding in Karo.

Of course, holding that an activity is not a search or seizure means not only that it is not regulated by the warrant requirement, but also that it is not regulated by the Fourth Amendment at all. It would be possible to say that, for example, surreptitious recording of conversations as occurred in *United States v. White* is a search, but may be conducted with probable cause under an exception to the warrant requirement. The significance or utility of such a requirement would depend upon whether arbitrary recording of conversations by law enforcement agencies occurs with any frequency, and whether it is enough of a danger to privacy that after-the-fact judicial review is desirable. Conceivably, bringing consensual electronic surveillance within the scope of the Fourth Amendment would curtail excessive employment of the practice. On the other hand, it might merely add another issue to be litigated in criminal trials without substantially affecting law enforcement practice.

2. Privacy Expectations, Public Transportation, and Luggage

BOND v. UNITED STATES

Supreme Court of the United States, 2000.
529 U.S. 334, 120 S.Ct. 1462, 146 L.Ed.2d 365.

CHIEF JUSTICE REHNQUIST delivered the opinion of the Court.

This case presents the question whether a law enforcement officer's physical manipulation of a bus passenger's carry-on luggage violated the Fourth Amendment's proscription against unreasonable searches. We hold that it did.

Petitioner Steven Dewayne Bond was a passenger on a Greyhound bus that left California bound for Little Rock, Arkansas. The bus stopped, as it was required to do, at the permanent Border Patrol checkpoint in Sierra Blanca, Texas. Border Patrol Agent Cesar Cantu boarded the bus to check the immigration status of its passengers. After reaching the back of the bus, having satisfied himself that the passengers were lawfully in the United States, Agent Cantu began walking toward the front. Along the way, he squeezed the soft luggage which passengers had placed in the overhead storage space above the seats.

Petitioner was seated four or five rows from the back of the bus. As Agent Cantu inspected the luggage in the compartment above petitioner's seat, he squeezed a green canvas bag and noticed that it contained a "brick-like" object. Petitioner admitted that the bag was his and agreed to allow Agent Cantu to open it. Upon opening the bag, Agent Cantu discovered a "brick" of methamphetamine. The brick had been wrapped in duct tape until it was oval-shaped and then rolled in a pair of pants.

[Bond's motion to suppress was denied, and he was convicted of conspiracy to possess, and possession with intent to distribute, methamphetamine.]

The Fourth Amendment provides that "[t]he right of the people to be secure in their persons, houses, papers, and effects, against unreasonable searches and seizures, shall not be violated.... " A traveler's personal luggage is clearly an "effect" protected by the Amendment. Indeed, it is undisputed here that petitioner possessed a privacy interest in his bag.

But the Government asserts that by exposing his bag to the public, petitioner lost a reasonable expectation that his bag would not be physically manipulated. The Government relies on our decisions in *California* v. *Ciraolo*, 476 U.S. 207, 106 S.Ct. 1809, 90 L.Ed.2d 210 (1986), and *Florida* v. *Riley*, 488 U.S. 445, 109 S.Ct. 693, 102 L.Ed.2d 835 (1989), for the proposition that matters open to public observation are not protected by the Fourth Amendment. In *Ciraolo*, we held that police observation of a backyard from a plane flying at an altitude of 1,000 feet did not violate a reasonable expectation of privacy. Similarly, in *Riley*, we relied on *Ciraolo* to hold that police observation of a greenhouse in a home's curtilage from a helicopter passing at an altitude of 400 feet did not violate the Fourth Amendment. We reasoned that the property was "not necessarily protected from inspection that involves no physical invasion," and determined that because any member of the public could have lawfully observed the defendants' property by flying overhead, the defendants' expectation of privacy was "not reasonable and not one 'that society is prepared to honor.' "

But *Ciraolo* and *Riley* are different from this case because they involved only visual, as opposed to tactile, observation. Physically invasive inspection is simply more intrusive than purely visual inspection. For example, in *Terry* v. *Ohio*, 392 U.S. 1, 88 S.Ct. 1868, 20 L.Ed.2d 889 (1968), we stated that a "careful [tactile] exploration of the outer surfaces of a person's clothing all over his or her body" is a "serious intrusion upon the sanctity of the person, which may inflict great indignity and arouse strong resentment, and is not to be undertaken lightly." Although Agent Cantu did not "frisk" petitioner's person, he did conduct a probing tactile examination of petitioner's carry-on luggage. Obviously, petitioner's bag was not part of his person. But travelers are particularly concerned about their carry-on luggage; they generally use it to transport personal items that, for whatever reason, they prefer to keep close at hand.

Here, petitioner concedes that, by placing his bag in the overhead compartment, he could expect that it would be exposed to certain kinds of touching and handling. But petitioner argues that Agent Cantu's physical manipulation of his luggage "far exceeded the casual contact [petitioner] could have expected from other passengers." * * *

Our Fourth Amendment analysis embraces two questions. First, we ask whether the individual, by his conduct, has exhibited an actual expectation of privacy; that is, whether he has shown that "he [sought] to preserve [something] as private." Here, petitioner sought to preserve privacy by using an opaque bag and placing that bag directly above his seat. Second, we inquire whether the individual's expectation of privacy is "one that society is prepared to recognize as reasonable." When a bus passenger places a bag in an overhead bin, he expects that other passengers or bus employees may move it for one reason or another. Thus, a bus passenger clearly expects that his bag may be handled. He does not expect that other passengers or bus employees will, as a matter of course, feel the bag in an exploratory manner. But this is exactly what the agent did here. We therefore hold that the agent's physical manipulation of petitioner's bag violated the Fourth Amendment.

The judgment of the Court of Appeals is Reversed.

JUSTICE BREYER, with whom JUSTICE SCALIA joins, dissenting.

Does a traveler who places a soft-sided bag in the shared overhead storage compartment of a bus have a "reasonable expectation" that strangers will not push, pull, prod, squeeze, or otherwise manipulate his luggage? Unlike the majority, I believe that he does not.

Petitioner argues—and the majority points out—that, even if bags in overhead bins are subject to general "touching" and "handling," this case is special because "Agent Cantu's physical manipulation of [petitioner's] luggage 'far exceeded the casual contact [he] could have expected from other passengers.' "But the record shows the contrary. Agent Cantu testified that border patrol officers (who routinely enter buses at designated checkpoints to run immigration checks) "conduct an inspection of the overhead luggage by squeezing the bags as we're going out." * * * Agent Cantu * * * explained that he felt "the edges of the brick in the bag," and that it was a "[b]rick-like object . . . that, when squeezed, you could feel an outline of something of a different mass inside of it." Although the agent acknowledged that his practice was to "squeeze [bags] very hard," he testified that his touch ordinarily was not "[h]ard enough to break something inside that might be fragile." Petitioner also testified that Agent Cantu "reached for my bag, and he shook it a little, and squeezed it."

How does the "squeezing" just described differ from the treatment that overhead luggage is likely to receive from strangers in a world of travel that is somewhat less gentle than it used to be? I think not at all. * * *

* * * The law is clear that the Fourth Amendment protects against government intrusion that upsets an "actual (subjective) expectation of privacy" that is objectively " 'reasonable.' " * * * [A]n individual cannot reasonably expect privacy in respect to objects or activities that he "knowingly exposes to the public."

* * *

Of course, the agent's *purpose* here–searching for drugs–differs dramatically from the intention of a driver or fellow passenger who squeezes a bag in the process of making more room for another parcel. But in determining whether an expectation of privacy is reasonable, it is the *effect*, not the purpose, that matters. ("[T]he issue is not [the agent's] state of mind, but the objective effect of his actions"). Few individuals with something to hide wish to expose that something to the police, however careless or indifferent they may be in respect to discovery by other members of the public. Hence, a Fourth Amendment rule that turns on purpose could prevent police alone from intruding where other strangers freely tread. * * *

Nor can I accept the majority's effort to distinguish "tactile" from "visual" interventions, even assuming that distinction matters here. Whether tactile manipulation (say, of the exterior of luggage) is more intrusive or less intrusive than visual observation (say, through a lighted window) necessarily depends on the particular circumstances.

Chapter 3

INTERPRETING THE FOURTH AMENDMENT: THE WARRANT PREFERENCE MODEL

A. THE WARRANT PREFERENCE MODEL

Introduction

The text of the Fourth Amendment regulates only two types of government conduct: searches and seizures (affecting persons, houses, papers, and effects), and only prohibits searches and seizures that are unreasonable. Those interpreting the Fourth Amendment must determine not only what government conduct constitutes searches and seizures, but also must define which are unreasonable. One important interpretive approach has been to define the "reasonableness" required in the Amendment's first clause in terms of the requirements prescribed in its second clause—the Warrant Clause. As you read the following materials, consider whether this interpretive approach is a legitimate textual interpretation, that is both consistent with the Amendment's history and appropriate as policy—or is, instead, defective from each of these perspectives.

1. Anthony Amsterdam, *Perspectives on the Fourth Amendment*, 58 MINN L REV. 349, 410–411 (1974).

"The Court's construction of the amendment as embodying an overriding preference for search warrants is supportable, in my view, because the Court is obliged to give an internally coherent reading to the unreasonableness clause and the warrant clause as expressions of repudiation of the general warrant. In this view, the fourth amendment condemns searches conducted under general warrants and writs of assistance as 'unreasonable.' It also forbids unreasonable warrantless searches. That is all the amendment says about warrantless searches, and the word 'unreasonable' is hardly self-illuminating. Surely then the Court has done right to seek some part of the meaning of an 'unreasonable' warrantless search by asking what the condemnation of general warrants and writs implies about the nature of 'unreasonable' searches and seizures. [W]arrantless searches exhibiting the same characteristics

86

as general warrants and writs must be deemed unreasonable if there is no principled basis for distinguishing them from general warrants and writs.

"The framers of the fourth amendment accepted specific warrants as reasonable: the second clause of the amendment tells us so. Therefore, the objectionable feature of general warrants and writs must be their indiscriminate character. Warrants are not to issue indiscriminately: that is the office of the probable cause requirement. Nor may indiscriminate searches be made under them: that is why particularity of description of the persons or things to be seized is demanded. * * *

"Indiscriminate searches or seizures might be thought to be bad for either or both of two reasons. The first is that they expose people and their possessions to interferences by government when there is no good reason to do so. The concern here is against *unjustified* searches and seizures: it rests upon the principle that every citizen is entitled to security of his person and property unless and until an adequate justification for disturbing the security is shown. The second is that indiscriminate searches and seizures are conducted at the discretion of executive officials, who may act despotically and capriciously in the exercise of the power to search and seize. This latter concern runs against *arbitrary* searches and seizures: it condemns the petty tyranny of unregulated rummagers." (emphasis in original).

2. Adapted from Morgan Cloud, *Searching through History; Searching for History*, 63 U. CHI. L. REV. 1707 (1996).

The Fourth Amendment is a compound sentence consisting of two related clauses. Its text commands:

> The right of the people to be secure in their persons, houses, papers, and effects, against unreasonable searches and seizures, shall not be violated, and no Warrants shall issue, but upon probable cause, supported by Oath or affirmation, and particularly describing the place to be searched, and the persons or things to be seized.

Identifying the relationship between these two clauses has been a fundamental task in Fourth Amendment theory. For most of the twentieth century the Supreme Court employed a "warrant model" that employed a "conjunctive" theory in which the more specific language of the Warrant Clause defines the procedural attributes of reasonable searches and seizures. According to this theory, a search or seizure is procedurally reasonable if authorized by a valid, properly executed warrant. But warrants are not required in all circumstances. Warrantless intrusions that satisfy some fundamental requirements embodied in the Warrant Clause also can be constitutional. Probable cause is perhaps the most important of these requirements. It exists when " 'the facts and circumstances within their [the officers'] knowledge and of which they had reasonably trustworthy information [are] sufficient in themselves to warrant a man of reasonable caution in the belief that' an offense has been or is being committed.''[a] By requiring fact-based suspicion, the probable cause standard precludes many kinds of general searches.

This conjunctive theory recognizes that many searches and seizures are justified by the combination of probable cause and an exception to the warrant requirement. Most of these exceptions rest upon some kind of exigency. For instance, warrantless searches and seizures are reasonable when securing a warrant would permit a suspect to escape or dispose of contraband, or would create a threat to public safety. A classic example is the automobile exception permitting searches of automobiles when officers have probable cause to believe they contain contraband. Conversely, when the place searched is a home, the Supreme Court has been less willing to permit warrantless intrusions.

PAYTON v. NEW YORK

Supreme Court of the United States, 1980.
445 U.S. 573, 100 S.Ct. 1371, 63 L.Ed.2d 639.

Mr. Justice Stevens delivered the opinion of the Court.

These appeals challenge the constitutionality of New York statutes that authorize police officers to enter a private residence without a warrant and with force, if necessary, to make a routine felony arrest. [The Supreme Court held that the Fourth Amendment prohibits the police from making a warrantless and nonconsensual entry into a suspect's home in order to make a routine felony arrest.]

I

On January 14, 1970, after two days of intensive investigation, New York detectives had assembled evidence sufficient to establish probable cause to believe that Theodore Payton had murdered the manager of a gas station two days earlier. At about 7:30 a. m. on January 15, six officers went to Payton's apartment in the Bronx, intending to arrest him. They had not obtained a warrant. Although light and music emanated from the apartment, there was no response to their knock on the metal door. They summoned emergency assistance and, about 30 minutes later, used crowbars to break open the door and enter the apartment. No one was there. In plain view, however, was a .30–caliber shell casing that was seized and later admitted into evidence at Payton's murder trial.

* * *

II

It is familiar history that indiscriminate searches and seizures conducted under the authority of ''general warrants'' were the immediate evils that motivated the framing and adoption of the Fourth Amend-

---

a. Brinegar v. United States, 338 U.S. 160, 175–76 (1949), quoting Carroll v. Unit-   ed States, 267 U.S. 132, 162 (1925).

ment. Indeed, as originally proposed in the House of Representatives, the draft contained only one clause, which directly imposed limitations on the issuance of warrants, but imposed no express restrictions on warrantless searches or seizures. As it was ultimately adopted, however, the Amendment contained two separate clauses, the first protecting the basic right to be free from unreasonable searches and seizures and the second requiring that warrants be particular and supported by probable cause. * * *

It is thus perfectly clear that the evil the Amendment was designed to prevent was broader than the abuse of a general warrant. Unreasonable searches or seizures conducted without any warrant at all are condemned by the plain language of the first clause of the Amendment. Almost a century ago the Court stated in resounding terms that the principles reflected in the Amendment "reached farther than the concrete form" of the specific cases that gave it birth, and "apply to all invasions on the part of the government and its employees of the sanctity of a man's home and the privacies of life." *Boyd v. United States,* 116 U.S. 616, 630, 6 S.Ct. 524, 29 L.Ed. 746 (1886). Without pausing to consider whether that broad language may require some qualification, it is sufficient to note that the warrantless arrest of a person is a species of seizure required by the Amendment to be reasonable. * * *

The simple language of the Amendment applies equally to seizures of persons and to seizures of property. Our analysis in this case may therefore properly commence with rules that have been well established in Fourth Amendment litigation involving tangible items. As the Court reiterated just a few years ago, the "physical entry of the home is the chief evil against which the wording of the Fourth Amendment is directed." And we have long adhered to the view that the warrant procedure minimizes the danger of needless intrusions of that sort.

It is a "basic principle of Fourth Amendment law" that searches and seizures inside a home without a warrant are presumptively unreasonable. Yet it is also well settled that objects such as weapons or contraband found in a public place may be seized by the police without a warrant. The seizure of property in plain view involves no invasion of privacy and is presumptively reasonable, assuming that there is probable cause to associate the property with criminal activity. * * *

* * *

[T]he critical point is that any differences in the intrusiveness of entries to search and entries to arrest are merely ones of degree rather than kind. The two intrusions share this fundamental characteristic: the breach of the entrance to an individual's home. The Fourth Amendment protects the individual's privacy in a variety of settings. In none is the zone of privacy more clearly defined than when bounded by the unambiguous physical dimensions of an individual's home—a zone that finds its roots in clear and specific constitutional terms: "The right of the people to be secure in their ... houses ... shall not be violated." That language unequivocally establishes the proposition that "[at] the very core of the Fourth Amendment stands the right of a man to retreat into his own home and there be free from unreasonable governmental intrusion." In terms that apply equally to seizures of property and to seizures of persons, the Fourth Amendment has drawn a firm line at the entrance to the house. Absent exigent circumstances, that threshold may not reasonably be crossed without a warrant.

* * *

IV

The parties have argued at some length about the practical consequences of a warrant requirement as a precondition to a felony arrest in the home. In the absence of any evidence that effective law enforcement has suffered in those States that already have such a requirement, we are inclined to view such arguments with skepticism. More fundamentally, however, such arguments of policy must give way to a constitutional command that we consider to be unequivocal.

Finally, we note the State's suggestion that only a search warrant based on probable cause to believe the suspect is at home at a given time can adequately protect the privacy interests at stake, and since such a warrant requirement is manifestly impractical, there need be no warrant of any kind. We find this ingenious argument unpersuasive. It is true that an arrest warrant requirement may afford less protection than a search warrant requirement, but it will suffice to interpose the magistrate's determination of probable cause between the zealous officer and the citizen. If there is sufficient evidence of a citizen's participation in a felony to persuade a judicial officer that his arrest is justified, it is constitutionally reasonable to require him to open his doors to the officers of the law. Thus, for Fourth Amendment purposes, an arrest warrant founded on probable cause implicitly carries with it the limited authority to enter a dwelling in which the suspect lives when there is reason to believe the suspect is within.

Because no arrest warrant was obtained in either of these cases, the judgments must be reversed and the cases remanded to the New York Court of Appeals for further proceedings not inconsistent with this opinion.

* * *

[The concurring opinion of JUSTICE BLACKMUN, and the dissenting opinion of JUSTICE REHNQUIST are omitted.]

MR. JUSTICE WHITE, with whom THE CHIEF JUSTICE and MR. JUSTICE REHNQUIST join, dissenting.

The Court today holds that absent exigent circumstances officers may never enter a home during the daytime to arrest for a dangerous felony unless they have first obtained a warrant. This hard-and-fast rule, founded on erroneous assumptions concerning the intrusiveness of home arrest entries, finds little or no support in the common law or in the text and history of the Fourth Amendment. I respectfully dissent.

I

As the Court notes, he common law of searches and seizures, as evolved in England, as transported to the Colonies, and as developed among the States, is highly relevant to the present scope of the Fourth Amendment. Today's decision virtually ignores these centuries of common-law development, and distorts the historical meaning of the Fourth Amendment, by proclaiming for the first time a rigid warrant requirement for all nonexigent home arrest entries.

A

As early as the 15th century the common law had limited the Crown's power to invade a private dwelling in order to arrest. A Year Book case of 1455 held that in civil cases the sheriff could not break doors to arrest for debt or trespass, for the arrest was then only in the private interests of a party. * * * The holdings of these cases were condensed in the maxim that "every man's house is his castle."

However, this limitation on the Crown's power applied only to private civil actions. In cases directly involving the Crown, the rule was that "[the] king's keys unlock all doors." * * * Likewise, *Semayne's Case* stated in dictum:

> "In all cases when the King is party, the Sheriff (if the doors be not open) may break the party's house, either to arrest him, or to do other execution of the King's process, if otherwise he cannot enter."
> 5 Co. Rep., at 91b, 77 Eng. Rep., at 195.

Although these cases established the Crown's power to enter a dwelling in criminal cases, they did not directly address the question of whether a constable could break doors to arrest without authorization by a warrant. * * * The warrant authorized the constable to take actions beyond his inherent powers. It also ensured that he actually carried out his instructions, by giving him clear notice of his duty, for the breach of which he could be punished, and by relieving him from civil liability even if probable cause to arrest were lacking. For this reason, warrants were sometimes issued even when the act commanded was within the constable's inherent authority.

* * *

A second school of thought, on which the Court relies, held that the constable could not break doors on mere "bare suspicion." * * * These authorities can be read as imposing a somewhat more stringent requirement of probable cause for arrests in the home than for arrests elsewhere. But they would not bar nonexigent, warrantless home arrests in all circumstances, as the Court does today. * * *

* * *

B

The history of the Fourth Amendment does not support the rule announced today. At the time that Amendment was adopted the constable possessed broad inherent powers to arrest. The limitations on those powers derived, not from a warrant "requirement," but from the generally ministerial nature of the constable's office at common law. Far from restricting the constable's arrest power, the institution of the warrant was used to expand that authority by giving the constable delegated powers of a superior officer such as a justice of the peace. Hence at the time of the Bill of Rights, the warrant functioned as a powerful tool of law enforcement rather than as a protection for the rights of criminal suspects.

In fact, it was the abusive use of the warrant power, rather than any excessive zeal in the discharge of peace officers' inherent authority, that precipitated the Fourth Amendment. That Amendment grew out of colonial opposition to the infamous general warrants known as writs of assistance, which empowered customs officers to search at will, and to break open receptacles or packages, wherever they suspected uncustomed goods to be. The writs did not specify where searches could occur and they remained effective throughout the sovereign's lifetime. In effect, the writs placed complete discretion in the hands of executing officials. Customs searches of this type were beyond the inherent power of common-law officials and were the subject of court suits when performed by colonial customs agents not acting pursuant to a writ.

* * *

That the Framers were concerned about warrants, and not about the constable's inherent power to arrest, is also evident from the text and legislative history of the Fourth Amendment. That provision first reaffirms the basic principle of common law, that "[the] right of the people to be secure in their persons, houses, papers, and effects, against unreasonable searches and seizures, shall not be violated.... " The Amendment does not here purport to limit or restrict the peace officer's inherent power to arrest or search, but rather assumes an existing right against actions in excess of that inherent power and ensures that it remain inviolable. As I have noted, it was not generally considered "unreasonable" at common law for officers to break doors in making warrantless felony arrests. The Amendment's second clause is directed at the actions of officers taken in their ministerial capacity pursuant to writs of assistance and other warrants. In contrast to the first Clause, the second Clause does purport to alter colonial practice: "and no Warrants shall issue, but upon probable cause, supported by Oath or affirmation, and particularly describing the place to be searched, and the persons or things to be seized."

* * *

II

* * *

[F]our restrictions on home arrests—felony, knock and announce, daytime, and stringent probable cause—constitute powerful and complementary protections for the privacy interests associated with the home. The felony requirement guards against abusive or arbitrary enforcement and ensures that invasions of the home occur only in case of the most serious crimes. The knock-and-announce and daytime requirements protect individuals against the fear, humiliation, and embarrassment of being roused from their beds in states of partial or complete undress. And these requirements allow the arrestee to surrender at his front door, thereby maintaining his dignity and preventing the officers from entering other rooms of the dwelling. The stringent probable-cause requirement would help ensure against the possibility that the police would enter when the suspect was not home, and, in searching for him, frighten members of the family or ransack parts of the house, seizing items in plain view. In short, these requirements, taken together, permit an individual suspected of a serious crime to surrender at the front door of his dwelling and thereby avoid most of the humiliation and indignity that the Court seems to believe necessarily accompany a house arrest entry. * * *

* * *

Notes

1. One year after deciding *Payton*, the Supreme Court reviewed a case in which the police had obtained an arrest warrant—but not for the person whose home was searched. In Steagald v. United States, 451 U.S. 204 (1981), Drug Enforcement Administration agents executing an arrest warrant for one Lyons entered Steagald's home to search for Lyons without first obtaining a search warrant for the house. While searching Steagald's home, the agents found cocaine and other incriminating evidence but did not find Lyons. Steagald was indicted, tried and convicted on federal drug charges. The trial judge denied his motion to suppress the evidence uncovered during the search of his home and the Court of Appeals affirmed. The Supreme Court reversed, holding that absent exigent circumstances or consent, a home may not be searched without a warrant. The Court emphasized that two distinct interests were implicated by this search. Lyons' liberty interest in being free from an unreasonable seizure was distinct from Steagald's privacy interest in being free from an unreasonable search of his home. The arrest warrant adequately protected Lyon's liberty interest, but did nothing to protect Steagald's constitutionally protected privacy interest. In an opinion by Justice Marshall, the Court concluded that "the search of his home was no more reasonable from petitioner's perspective than it would have been if conducted in the absence of any warrant." The search therefore violated the Fourth Amendment.

2. The Fourth Amendment specifies the constitutional requirements for a valid warrant. Not only must the issuance of the warrant satisfy

constitutional standards, so must the execution of the warrant. In recent years the Supreme Court has issued a series of opinions construing these standards, particularly the "knock and announce" rule. The most recent of these opinion, *United States v. Banks*, also discusses the earlier opinions.

UNITED STATES v. BANKS

Supreme Court of the United States, 2003.
540 U.S. 31, 124 S.Ct. 521, 157 L.Ed.2d 343.

JUSTICE SOUTER delivered the opinion of the Court.

Officers executing a warrant to search for cocaine in respondent Banks's apartment knocked and announced their authority. The question is whether their 15–to–20–second wait before a forcible entry satisfied the Fourth Amendment * * *. We hold that it did.

I

With information that Banks was selling cocaine at home, North Las Vegas Police Department officers and Federal Bureau of Investigation agents got a warrant to search his two-bedroom apartment. As soon as they arrived there, about 2 o'clock on a Wednesday afternoon, officers posted in front called out "police search warrant" and rapped hard enough on the door to be heard by officers at the back door. There was no indication whether anyone was home, and after waiting for 15 to 20 seconds with no answer, the officers broke open the front door with a battering ram. Banks was in the shower and testified that he heard nothing until the crash of the door, which brought him out dripping to confront the police. The search produced weapons, crack cocaine, and other evidence of drug dealing.

[The District Court denied Banks' suppression motion, which claimed that the officers executing the search warrant waited an unreasonably short time before forcing entry, which violated the Fourth Amendment. Banks pleaded guilty, reserving his right to challenge the search on appeal. The Ninth Circuit reversed, and set forth a nonexhaustive list of factors that officers reasonably should consider when deciding when they could enter premises identified in a warrant, after knocking and announcing their presence but receiving no response. The factors listed included the size and location of the residence, the location of the officers in relation to the main living or sleeping areas of the residence; the time of day and the nature of the suspected offense, the evidence demonstrating the suspect's guilt, the suspect's prior convictions and the type of offense for which he was convicted, and "any other observations triggering the senses of the officers that reasonably would lead one to believe that immediate entry was necessary." The Supreme Court granted certiorari to consider how to apply the standard of reasonableness to the length of time police with a warrant must wait before entering without permission after knocking and announcing their intent in a felony case, and it reversed the Ninth Circuit.]

II

* * *

In *Wilson* v. *Arkansas*, 514 U.S. 927, 131 L.Ed.2d 976, 115 S.Ct. 1914 (1995), we held that the common law knock-and-announce principle is one focus of the reasonableness enquiry; and we subsequently decided that although the standard generally requires the police to announce their intent to search before entering closed premises, the obligation gives way when officers "have a reasonable suspicion that knocking and announcing their presence, under the particular circumstances, would be dangerous or futile, or . . . would inhibit the effective investigation of the crime by, for example, allowing the destruction of evidence," *Richards* v. *Wisconsin*, 520 U.S. 385, 394, 137 L.Ed.2d 615, 117 S.Ct. 1416 (1997). When a warrant applicant gives reasonable grounds to expect futility or to suspect that one or another such exigency already exists or will arise instantly upon knocking, a magistrate judge is acting within the Constitution to authorize a "no-knock" entry. And even when executing a warrant silent about that, if circumstances support a reasonable suspicion of exigency when the officers arrive at the door, they may go straight in.

Since most people keep their doors locked, entering without knocking will normally do some damage, a circumstance too common to require a heightened justification when a reasonable suspicion of exigency already justifies an unwarned entry. We have accordingly held that police in exigent circumstances may damage premises so far as necessary for a no-knock entrance without demonstrating the suspected risk in any more detail than the law demands for an unannounced intrusion simply by lifting the latch. Either way, it is enough that the officers had a reasonable suspicion of exigent circumstances.

III

[H]ere the Government claims that a risk of losing evidence arose shortly after knocking and announcing. Although the police concededly arrived at Banks's door without reasonable suspicion of facts justifying a no-knock entry, they argue that announcing their presence started the clock running toward the moment of apprehension that Banks would flush away the easily disposable cocaine, prompted by knowing the police would soon be coming in. * * *

Banks does not, of course, deny that exigency may develop in the period beginning when officers with a warrant knock to be admitted, and the issue comes down to whether it was reasonable to suspect imminent loss of evidence after the 15 to 20 seconds the officers waited prior to forcing their way. Though we agree with Judge Fisher's dissenting opinion that this call is a close one, we think that after 15 or 20 seconds without a response, police could fairly suspect that cocaine would be gone if they were reticent any longer. Courts of Appeals have, indeed, routinely held similar wait times to be reasonable in drug cases with similar facts including easily disposable evidence (and some courts have found even shorter ones to be reasonable enough).

A look at Banks's counterarguments shows why these courts reached sensible results, for each of his reasons for saying that 15 to 20 seconds was too brief rests on a mistake about the relevant enquiry: the fact that he was actually in the shower and did not hear the officers is not to the point, and the same is true of the claim that it might have taken him longer than 20 seconds if he had heard the knock and headed straight for the door. As for the shower, it is enough to say that the facts known to the police are what count in judging reasonable waiting time, and there is no indication that the police knew that Banks was in the shower and thus unaware of an impending search that he would otherwise have tried to frustrate.

And the argument that 15 to 20 seconds was too short for Banks to have come to the door ignores the very risk that justified prompt entry. True, if the officers were to justify their timing here by claiming that Banks's failure to admit them fairly suggested a refusal to let them in, Banks could at least argue that no such suspicion can arise until an occupant has had time to get to the door, a time that will vary with the size of the establishment, perhaps five seconds to open a motel room door, or several minutes to move through a townhouse. In this case, however, the police claim exigent need to enter, and the crucial fact in examining their actions is not time to reach the door but the particular exigency claimed. On the record here, what matters is the opportunity to get rid of cocaine, which a prudent dealer will keep near a commode or kitchen sink. The significant circumstances include the arrival of the police during the day, when anyone inside would probably have been up and around, and the sufficiency of 15 to 20 seconds for getting to the bathroom or the kitchen to start flushing cocaine down the drain. That is, when circumstances are exigent because a pusher may be near the point of putting his drugs beyond reach, it is imminent disposal, not travel time to the entrance, that governs when the police may reasonably enter; since the bathroom and kitchen are usually in the interior of a dwelling, not the front hall, there is no reason generally to peg the travel time to the location of the door, and no reliable basis for giving the proprietor of a mansion a longer wait than the resident of a bungalow, or an apartment like Banks's. And 15 to 20 seconds does not seem an unrealistic guess about the time someone would need to get in a position to rid his quarters of cocaine.

Once the exigency had matured, of course, the officers were not bound to learn anything more or wait any longer before going in, even though their entry entailed some harm to the building. [T]he exigent need of law enforcement trumps a resident's interest in avoiding all property damage, and there is no reason to treat a post-knock exigency differently from the no-knock counterpart * * *.

IV

* * * At common law, the knock-and-announce rule was traditionally "justified in part by the belief that announcement generally would avoid 'the destruction or breaking of any house ... by which great damage and inconvenience might ensue.'" One point in making an officer knock and announce, then, is to give a person inside the chance to save his door. That is why, in the case with no reason to suspect an immediate risk of frustration or futility in waiting at all, the reasonable wait time may well be longer when police make a forced entry, since they ought to be more certain the occupant has had time to answer the door. It is hard to be more definite than that, without turning the notion of a reasonable time under all the circumstances into a set of sub-rules as the Ninth Circuit has been inclined to do. Suffice it to say that the need to damage property in the course of getting in is a good reason to require more patience than it would be reasonable to expect if the door were open. Police seeking a stolen piano may be able to spend more time to make sure they really need the battering ram.

* * *

ILLINOIS v. McARTHUR

Supreme Court of the United States, 2001.
531 U.S. 326, 121 S.Ct. 946, 148 L.Ed.2d 838.

JUSTICE BREYER delivered the opinion of the Court.

* * *

I

A

On April 2, 1997, Tera McArthur asked two police officers to accompany her to the trailer where she lived with her husband, Charles, so that they could keep the peace while she removed her belongings. The two officers, Assistant Chief John Love and Officer Richard Skidis, arrived with Tera at the trailer at about 3:15 p.m. Tera went inside, where Charles was present. The officers remained outside.

When Tera emerged after collecting her possessions, she spoke to Chief Love, who was then on the porch. She suggested he check the trailer because "Chuck had dope in there." She added (in Love's words) that she had seen Chuck "slid[e] some dope underneath the couch."

Love knocked on the trailer door, told Charles what Tera had said, and asked for permission to search the trailer, which Charles denied. Love then sent Officer Skidis with Tera to get a search warrant.

Love told Charles, who by this time was also on the porch, that he could not reenter the trailer unless a police officer accompanied him. Charles subsequently reentered the trailer two or three times (to get cigarettes and to make phone calls), and each time Love stood just inside the door to observe what Charles did.

Officer Skidis obtained the warrant by about 5 p.m. He returned to the trailer and, along with other officers, searched it. The officers found under the sofa a marijuana pipe, a box for marijuana (called a "one-hitter" box), and a small amount of marijuana. They then arrested Charles.

[McArthur was charged with two misdemeanors: possessing drug paraphernalia and marijuana (less than 2.5 grams). The trial court granted McArthur's motion to suppress the pipe, box, and marijuana on the ground that they were the "fruit" of an unlawful police seizure—the officers' refusal to let him reenter his trailer unaccompanied, "which would have permitted him, he said, to 'have destroyed the marijuana.'" The state Appellate Court of Illinois affirmed, and the Illinois Supreme Court denied the State's petition for leave to appeal. The Supreme Court granted certiorari to determine whether the Fourth Amendment prohibits this type of temporary seizure.]

II

A

The Fourth Amendment says that the "right of the people to be secure in their persons, houses, papers, and effects, against unreasonable searches and seizures, shall not be violated." Its "central requirement" is one of reasonableness. In order to enforce that requirement, this Court has interpreted the Amendment as establishing rules and presumptions designed to control conduct of law enforcement officers that may significantly intrude upon privacy interests. Sometimes those rules require warrants. We have said, for example, that in "the ordinary case," seizures of personal property are "unreasonable within the meaning of the Fourth Amendment," without more, "unless ... accomplished pursuant to a judicial warrant," issued by a neutral magistrate after finding probable cause.

We nonetheless have made it clear that there are exceptions to the warrant requirement. When faced with special law enforcement needs, diminished expectations of privacy, minimal intrusions, or the like, the Court has found that certain general, or individual, circumstances may render a warrantless search or seizure reasonable.

In the circumstances of the case before us, we cannot say that the warrantless seizure was *per se* unreasonable. It involves a plausible claim of specially pressing or urgent law enforcement need, *i.e.*, "exigent circumstances." Moreover, the restraint at issue was tailored to that need, being limited in time and scope, and avoiding significant intrusion into the home itself. Consequently, rather than employing a *per se* rule of unreasonableness, we balance the privacy-related and law enforcement-related concerns to determine if the intrusion was reasonable.

We conclude that the restriction at issue was reasonable, and hence lawful, in light of the following circumstances, which we consider in combination. First, the police had probable cause to believe that McArthur's trailer home contained evidence of a crime and contraband, namely, unlawful drugs. The police had had an opportunity to speak with Tera McArthur and make at least a very rough assessment of her reliability. They knew she had had a firsthand opportunity to observe her husband's behavior, in particular with respect to the drugs at issue. And they thought, with good reason, that her report to them reflected that opportunity.

Second, the police had good reason to fear that, unless restrained, McArthur would destroy the drugs before they could return with a warrant. They reasonably might have thought that McArthur realized that his wife knew about his marijuana stash; observed that she was angry or frightened enough to ask the police to accompany her; saw that after leaving the trailer she had spoken with the police; and noticed that she had walked off with one policeman while leaving the other outside to observe the trailer. They reasonably could have concluded that McArthur, consequently suspecting an imminent search, would, if given the chance, get rid of the drugs fast.

Third, the police made reasonable efforts to reconcile their law enforcement needs with the demands of personal privacy. They neither searched the trailer nor arrested McArthur before obtaining a warrant. Rather, they imposed a significantly less restrictive restraint, preventing McArthur only from entering the trailer unaccompanied. They left his home and his belongings intact—until a neutral Magistrate, finding probable cause, issued a warrant.

Fourth, the police imposed the restraint for a limited period of time, namely, two hours. As far as the record reveals, this time period was no longer than reasonably necessary for the police, acting with diligence, to obtain the warrant * * * Given the nature of the intrusion and the law enforcement interest at stake, this brief seizure of the premises was permissible.

* * *

[JUSTICE SOUTER's concurring opinion is omitted.]

JUSTICE STEVENS, dissenting.

The Illinois General Assembly has decided that the possession of less than 2.5 grams of marijuana is a class C misdemeanor. In so classifying the offense, the legislature made a concerted policy judgment that the possession of small amounts of marijuana for personal use does not constitute a particularly significant public policy concern. While it is true that this offense—like feeding livestock on a public highway or offering a movie for rent without clearly displaying its rating—may warrant a jail sentence of up to 30 days, the detection and prosecution of possessors of small quantities of this substance is by no means a law enforcement priority in the State of Illinois.

Because the governmental interest implicated by the particular criminal prohibition at issue in this case is so slight, this is a poor vehicle for probing the boundaries of the government's power to limit an individual's possessory interest in his or her home pending the arrival of a search warrant. Given my preference, I would, therefore, dismiss the writ of certiorari as improvidently granted. * * * I would affirm.

B. THE MEANING AND FUNCTIONS OF THE PROBABLE CAUSE STANDARD

Countless judicial opinions recite this classic definition of probable cause: "If the facts and circumstances before the officer are such as to warrant a man of prudence and caution in believing that the offense has been committed, it is sufficient." Carroll v. United States, 267 U.S. 132, 162 (1925). Determining whether probable cause exists in a particular case inevitably requires a fact sensitive analysis. In the following pair of cases, the Supreme Court attempted to define what information must be provided by police and prosecutors to judges conducting this fact sensitive analysis, and what "test" the judges should apply in deciding whether probable cause exists—particularly in cases where probable cause depends (at least in part) upon information provided by informers.

SPINELLI v. UNITED STATES

Supreme Court of the United States, 1969.
393 U.S. 410, 89 S.Ct. 584, 21 L.Ed.2d 637.

MR. JUSTICE HARLAN delivered the opinion of the Court.

William Spinelli was convicted * * * of traveling to St. Louis, Missouri, from a nearby Illinois suburb with the intention of conducting gambling activities proscribed by Missouri law. At every appropriate stage in the proceedings in the lower courts, the petitioner challenged the constitutionality of the warrant which authorized the FBI search that uncovered the evidence necessary for his conviction. * * *

In *Aguilar v. Texas,* 378 U.S. 108, 84 S.Ct. 1509, 12 L.Ed.2d 723 (1964), a search warrant had issued upon an affidavit of police officers who swore only that they had "received reliable information from a credible person and do believe" that narcotics were being illegally stored on the described premises. While recognizing that the constitutional requirement of probable cause can be satisfied by hearsay information, this Court held the affidavit inadequate for two reasons. First, the application failed to set forth any of the "underlying circumstances" necessary to enable the magistrate independently to judge of the validity of the informant's conclusion that the narcotics were where he said they were. Second, the affiant-officers did not attempt to support their claim that their informant was " 'credible' or his information 'reliable.' " The Government is, however, quite right in saying that the FBI affidavit in the present case is more ample than that in *Aguilar.* Not only does it contain a report from an anonymous informant, but it also contains a report of an independent FBI investigation which is said to corroborate the informant's tip. We are, then, required to delineate the manner in which *Aguilar*'s two-pronged test should be applied in these circumstances.

In essence, the affidavit, reproduced in full in the Appendix to this opinion, contained the following allegations:

1. The FBI had kept track of Spinelli's movements on five days during the month of August 1965. On four of these occasions, Spinelli was seen crossing one of two bridges leading from Illinois into St. Louis, Missouri, between 11 a. m. and 12:15 p. m. On four of the five days, Spinelli was also seen parking his car in a lot used by residents of an apartment house at 1108 Indian Circle Drive in St. Louis, between 3:30 p.m. and 4:45 p.m. On one day, Spinelli was followed further and seen to enter a particular apartment in the building.

2. An FBI check with the telephone company revealed that this apartment contained two telephones listed under the name of Grace P. Hagen, and carrying the numbers WYdown 4–0029 and WYdown 4–0136.

3. The application stated that "William Spinelli is known to this affiant and to federal law enforcement agents and local law enforcement agents as a bookmaker, an associate of bookmakers, a gambler, and an associate of gamblers."

4. Finally, it was stated that the FBI "has been informed by a confidential reliable informant that William Spinelli is operating a hand-book and accepting wagers and disseminating wagering information by means of the telephones which have been assigned the numbers WY-down 4–0029 and WYdown 4–0136."

There can be no question that the last item mentioned, detailing the informant's tip, has a fundamental place in this warrant application. Without it, probable cause could not be established. The first two items reflect only innocent-seeming activity and data. Spinelli's travels to and from the apartment building and his entry into a particular apartment on one occasion could hardly be taken as bespeaking gambling activity; and there is surely nothing unusual about an apartment containing two separate telephones. Many a householder indulges himself in this petty luxury. Finally, the allegation that Spinelli was "known" to the affiant and to other federal and local law enforcement officers as a gambler and an associate of gamblers is but a bald and unilluminating assertion of suspicion that is entitled to no weight in appraising the magistrate's decision.

So much indeed the Government does not deny. Rather, following the reasoning of the Court of Appeals, the Government claims that the informant's tip gives a suspicious color to the FBI's reports detailing Spinelli's innocent-seeming conduct and that, conversely, the FBI's surveillance corroborates the informant's tip, thereby entitling it to more weight. It is true, of course, that the magistrate is obligated to render a judgment based upon a common-sense reading of the entire affidavit. We believe, however, that the "totality of circumstances" approach taken by the Court of Appeals paints with too broad a brush. Where, as here, the informer's tip is a necessary element in a finding of probable cause, its proper weight must be determined by a more precise analysis.

* * * *Aguilar* is relevant at this stage of the inquiry as well because the tests it establishes were designed to implement the long-standing principle that probable cause must be determined by a "neutral and detached magistrate," and not by "the officer engaged in the often competitive enterprise of ferreting out crime." *Johnson v. United States,* 333 U.S. 10, 14, 68 S.Ct. 367, 92 L.Ed. 436 (1948). A magistrate cannot be said to have properly discharged his constitutional duty if he relies on an informer's tip which—even when partially corroborated—is not as reliable as one which passes *Aguilar's* requirements when standing alone.

Applying these principles to the present case, we first consider the weight to be given the informer's tip when it is considered apart from the rest of the affidavit. It is clear that a Commissioner could not credit it without abdicating his constitutional function. Though the affiant swore that his confidant was "reliable," he offered the magistrate no reason in support of this conclusion. Perhaps even more important is the fact that *Aguilar's* other test has not been satisfied. The tip does not contain a sufficient statement of the underlying circumstances from which the informer concluded that Spinelli was running a bookmaking operation. We are not told how the FBI's source received his information—it is not alleged that the informant personally observed Spinelli at work or that he had ever placed a bet with him. Moreover, if the informant came by the information indirectly, he did not explain why his sources were reliable. In the absence of a statement detailing the manner in which the information was gathered, it is especially important that the tip describe the accused's criminal activity in sufficient detail that the magistrate may know that he is relying on something more substantial than a casual rumor circulating in the underworld or an accusation based merely on an individual's general reputation.

The detail provided by the informant in *Draper v. United States,* 358 U.S. 307, 79 S.Ct. 329, 3 L.Ed.2d 327 (1959), provides a suitable benchmark. While Hereford, the Government's informer in that case, did not state the way in which he had obtained his information, he reported that Draper had gone to Chicago the day before by train and that he would return to Denver by train with three ounces of heroin on one of two specified mornings. Moreover, Hereford went on to describe, with minute particularity, the clothes that Draper would be wearing upon his arrival at the Denver station. A magistrate, when confronted with such detail, could reasonably infer that the informant had gained his information in a reliable way. Such an inference cannot be made in the present case. Here, the only facts supplied were that Spinelli was using two specified telephones and that these phones were being used in gambling operations. This meager report could easily have been obtained from an offhand remark heard at a neighborhood bar.

Nor do we believe that the patent doubts *Aguilar* raises as to the report's reliability are adequately resolved by a consideration of the allegations detailing the FBI's independent investigative efforts. At most, these allegations indicated that Spinelli could have used the telephones specified by the informant for some purpose. This cannot by itself be said to support both the inference that the informer was generally trustworthy and that he had made his charge against Spinelli on the basis of information obtained in a reliable way. Once again, *Draper* provides a relevant comparison. Independent police work in that case corroborated much more than one small detail that had been provided by the informant. There, the police, upon meeting the inbound Denver train on the second morning specified by informer Hereford, saw a man whose dress corresponded precisely to Hereford's detailed description. It was then apparent that the informant had not been fabricating his report out of whole cloth; since the report was of the sort which in common experience may be recognized as having been obtained in a reliable way, it was perfectly clear that probable cause had been established.

We conclude, then, that in the present case the informant's tip—even when corroborated to the extent indicated—was not sufficient to provide the basis for a finding of probable cause. This is not to say that the tip was so insubstantial that it could not properly have counted in the magistrate's determination. Rather, it needed some further support. When we look to the other parts of the application, however, we find nothing alleged which would permit the suspicions engendered by the informant's report to ripen into a judgment that a crime was probably being committed. As we have already seen, the allegations detailing the FBI's surveillance of Spinelli and its investigation of the telephone company records contain no suggestion of criminal conduct when taken by themselves—and they are not endowed with an aura of suspicion by virtue of the informer's tip. Nor do we find that the FBI's reports take on a sinister color when read in light of common knowledge that bookmaking is often carried on over the telephone and from premises ostensibly used by others for perfectly normal purposes. Such an argument would carry weight in a situation in which the premises contain an unusual number of telephones or abnormal activity is observed, but it does not fit this case where neither of these factors is present. All that remains to be considered is the flat statement that Spinelli was "known" to the FBI and others as a gambler. But just as a simple assertion of police suspicion is not itself a sufficient basis for a magistrate's finding of probable cause, we do not believe it may be used to give additional weight to allegations that would otherwise be insufficient.

The affidavit, then, falls short of the standards set forth in *Aguilar, Draper,* and our other decisions that give content to the notion of probable cause. In holding as we have done, we do not retreat from the established propositions that only the probability, and not a prima facie showing, of criminal activity is the standard of probable cause; that affidavits of probable cause are tested by much less rigorous standards than those governing the admissibility of evidence at trial; that in judging probable cause issuing magistrates are not to be confined by niggardly limitations or by restrictions on the use of their common sense; and that their determination of probable cause should be paid great deference by reviewing courts. But we cannot sustain this warrant without diluting important safeguards that assure that the judgment of a disinterested judicial officer will interpose itself between the police and the citizenry.

* * *

MR. JUSTICE MARSHALL took no part in the consideration or decision of this case.

MR. JUSTICE WHITE, concurring.

An investigator's affidavit that he has seen gambling equipment being moved into a house at a specified address will support the issuance of a search warrant. The oath affirms the honesty of the statement and negatives the lie or imagination. Personal observation attests to the facts asserted—that there is gambling equipment on the premises at the named address.

But if the officer simply avers, without more, that there is gambling paraphernalia on certain premises, the warrant should not issue, even though the belief of the officer is an honest one, as evidenced by his oath, and even though the magistrate knows him to be an experienced, intelligent officer who has been reliable in the past. * * * Because an affidavit asserting, without more, the location of gambling equipment at a particular address does not claim personal observation of any of the facts by the officer, and because of the likelihood that the information came from an unidentified third party, affidavits of this type are unacceptable.

Neither should the warrant issue if the officer states that there is gambling equipment in a particular apartment and that his information comes from an informant, named or unnamed, since the honesty of the informant and the basis for his report are unknown. Nor would the missing elements be completely supplied by the officer's oath that the informant has often furnished reliable information in the past. This attests to the honesty of the informant, but *Aguilar* requires something more—did the information come from observation, or did the informant in turn receive it from another? Absent additional facts for believing the informant's report, his assertion stands no better than the oath of the officer to the same effect. Indeed, if the affidavit of an officer, known by the magistrate to be honest and experienced, stating that gambling equipment is located in a certain building is unacceptable, it would be quixotic if a similar statement from an honest informant were found to furnish probable cause. A strong argument can be made that both should be acceptable under the Fourth Amendment, but under our cases neither is. The past reliability of the informant can no more furnish probable cause for believing his current report than can previous experience with the officer himself.

* * *

I am inclined to agree with the majority that there are limited special circumstances in which an "honest" informant's report, if sufficiently detailed, will in effect verify itself—that is, the magistrate when confronted with such detail could reasonably infer that the informant had gained his information in a reliable way. Detailed information may sometimes imply that the informant himself has observed the facts. Suppose an informant with whom an officer has had satisfactory experience states that there is gambling equipment in the living room of a specified apartment and describes in detail not only the equipment itself but also the appointments and furnishings in the apartment. Detail like this, if true at all, must rest on personal observation either of the informant or of someone else. If the latter, we know nothing of the third person's honesty or sources; he may be making a wholly false report. But it is arguable that on these facts it was the informant himself who has perceived the facts, for the information reported is not usually the subject of casual, day-to-day conversation. Because the informant is honest and it is probable that he has viewed the facts, there is probable cause for the issuance of a warrant.

* * *

* * * The thrust of *Draper* is not that the verified facts have independent significance with respect to proof of the tenth. The argument instead relates to the reliability of the source: because an informant is right about some things, he is more probably right about other facts, usually the critical, unverified facts.

* * *

[The dissenting opinions of JUSTICES BLACK, FORTAS and STEWART are omitted.]

ILLINOIS v. GATES

Supreme Court of the United States, 1983.
462 U.S. 213, 103 S.Ct. 2317, 76 L.Ed.2d 527.

JUSTICE REHNQUIST delivered the opinion of the Court.

Respondents Lance and Susan Gates were indicted for violation of state drug laws after police officers, executing a search warrant, discovered marihuana and other contraband in their automobile and home. Prior to trial the Gateses moved to suppress evidence seized during this search. The Illinois Supreme Court affirmed the decisions of lower state courts granting the motion. It held that the affidavit submitted in support of the State's application for a warrant to search the Gateses' property was inadequate under this Court's decisions in *Aguilar v. Texas,* 378 U.S. 108, 84 S.Ct. 1509, 12 L.Ed.2d 723 (1964) and *Spinelli v. United States,* 393 U.S. 410, 89 S.Ct. 584, 21 L.Ed.2d 637 (1969). * * *

* * *

II

* * * Bloomingdale, Ill., is a suburb of Chicago located in Du Page County. On May 3, 1978, the Bloomingdale Police Department received by mail an anonymous handwritten letter which read as follows:

"This letter is to inform you that you have a couple in your town who strictly make their living on selling drugs. They are Sue and Lance Gates, they live on Greenway, off Bloomingdale Rd. in the condominiums. Most of their buys are done in Florida. Sue his wife drives their car to Florida, where she leaves it to be loaded up with drugs, then Lance flys down and drives it back. Sue flys back after she drops the car off in Florida. May 3 she is driving down there again and Lance will be flying down in a few days to drive it back. At the time Lance drives the car back he has the trunk loaded with over $100,000.00 in drugs. Presently they have over $100,000.00 worth of drugs in their basement.

"They brag about the fact they never have to work, and make their entire living on pushers.

"I guarantee if you watch them carefully you will make a big catch. They are friends with some big drugs dealers, who visit their house often.

"Lance & Susan Gates" Greenway "in Condominiums"

The letter was referred by the Chief of Police of the Bloomingdale Police Department to Detective Mader, who decided to pursue the tip. Mader learned, from the office of the Illinois Secretary of State, that an Illinois driver's license had been issued to one Lance Gates, residing at a stated address in Bloomingdale. He contacted a confidential informant, whose examination of certain financial records revealed a more recent address for the Gateses, and he also learned from a police officer assigned to O'Hare Airport that "L. Gates" had made a reservation on Eastern Airlines Flight 245 to West Palm Beach, Fla., scheduled to depart from Chicago on May 5 at 4:15 p.m.

Mader then made arrangements with an agent of the Drug Enforcement Administration for surveillance of the May 5 Eastern Airlines flight. The agent later reported to Mader that Gates had boarded the flight, and that federal agents in Florida had observed him arrive in West Palm Beach and take a taxi to the nearby Holiday Inn. They also reported that Gates went to a room registered to one Susan Gates and that, at 7 o'clock the next morning, Gates and an unidentified woman left the motel in a Mercury bearing Illinois license plates and drove northbound on an interstate highway frequently used by travelers to the Chicago area. In addition, the DEA agent informed Mader that the license plate number on the Mercury was registered to a Hornet station wagon owned by Gates. The agent also advised Mader that the driving time between West Palm Beach and Bloomingdale was approximately 22 to 24 hours.

Mader signed an affidavit setting forth the foregoing facts, and submitted it to a judge of the Circuit Court of Du Page County, together with a copy of the anonymous letter. The judge of that court thereupon issued a search warrant for the Gateses' residence and for their automobile. The judge, in deciding to issue the warrant, could have determined that the *modus operandi* of the Gateses had been substantially corroborated. As the anonymous letter predicted, Lance Gates had flown from Chicago to West Palm Beach late in the afternoon of May 5th, had checked into a hotel room registered in the name of his wife, and, at 7 o'clock the following morning, had headed north, accompanied by an unidentified woman, out of West Palm Beach on an interstate highway used by travelers from South Florida to Chicago in an automobile bearing a license plate issued to him.

At 5:15 a.m. on March 7, only 36 hours after he had flown out of Chicago, Lance Gates, and his wife, returned to their home in Bloomingdale, driving the car in which they had left West Palm Beach some 22 hours earlier. The Bloomingdale police were awaiting them, searched the trunk of the Mercury, and uncovered approximately 350 pounds of marihuana. A search of the Gateses' home revealed marihuana, weapons, and other contraband. * * *

* * *

The Illinois Supreme Court concluded—and we are inclined to agree—that, standing alone, the anonymous letter sent to the Bloomingdale Police Department would not provide the basis for a magistrate's determination that there was probable cause to believe contraband would be found in the Gateses' car and home. The letter provides virtually nothing from which one might conclude that its author is either honest or his information reliable; likewise, the letter gives absolutely no indication of the basis for the writer's predictions regarding the Gateses' criminal activities. Something more was required, then, before a magistrate could conclude that there was probable cause to believe that contraband would be found in the Gateses' home and car.

The Illinois Supreme Court also properly recognized that Detective Mader's affidavit might be capable of supplementing the anonymous letter with information sufficient to permit a determination of probable cause. In holding that the affidavit in fact did not contain sufficient additional information to sustain a determination of probable cause, the Illinois court applied a "two-pronged test," derived from our decision in *Spinelli*. The Illinois Supreme Court, like some others, apparently understood *Spinelli* as requiring that the anonymous letter satisfy each of two independent requirements before it could be relied on. According to this view, the letter, as supplemented by Mader's affidavit, first had to adequately reveal the "basis of knowledge" of the letterwriter—the particular means by which he came by the information given in his report. Second, it had to provide facts sufficiently establishing either the "veracity" of the affiant's informant, or, alternatively, the "reliability" of the informant's report in this particular case.

The Illinois court * * * found that the test had not been satisfied. First, the "veracity" prong was not satisfied because, "[t]here was simply no basis [for] [concluding] that the anonymous person [who wrote the letter to the Bloomingdale Police Department] was credible." The court indicated that corroboration by police of details contained in the letter might never satisfy the "veracity" prong, and in any event, could not do so if, as in the present case, only "innocent" details are corroborated. In addition, the letter gave no indication of the basis of its writer's knowledge of the Gateses' activities. * * * Thus, it concluded that no showing of probable cause had been made.

We agree with the Illinois Supreme Court that an informant's "veracity," "reliability," and "basis of knowledge" are all highly relevant in determining the value of his report. We do not agree, however, that these elements should be understood as entirely separate and independent requirements to be rigidly exacted in every case, which the opinion of the Supreme Court of Illinois would imply. Rather, as detailed below, they should be understood simply as closely intertwined issues that may usefully illuminate the common-sense, practical question whether there is "probable cause" to believe that contraband or evidence is located in a particular place. * * *

* * *

III

* * *

[A]ffidavits "are normally drafted by nonlawyers in the midst and haste of a criminal investigation. Technical requirements of elaborate specificity once exacted under common law pleadings have no proper place in this area." Likewise, search and arrest warrants long have been issued by persons who are neither lawyers nor judges, and who certainly do not remain abreast of each judicial refinement of the nature of "probable cause." The rigorous inquiry into the *Spinelli* prongs and the complex superstructure of evidentiary and analytical rules that some have seen implicit in our *Spinelli* decision, cannot be reconciled with the fact that many warrants are—quite properly—issued on the basis of nontechnical, common-sense judgments of laymen applying a standard less demanding than those used in more formal legal proceedings. * * *

* * *

If the affidavits submitted by police officers are subjected to the type of scrutiny some courts have deemed appropriate, police might well resort to warrantless searches, with the hope of relying on consent or some other exception to the Warrant Clause that might develop at the time of the search. In addition, the possession of a warrant by officers conducting an arrest or search greatly reduces the perception of unlawful or intrusive police conduct, by assuring the individual whose property is searched or seized of the lawful authority of the executing officer, his need to search, and the limits of his power to search. Reflecting this preference for the warrant process, the traditional standard for review of an issuing magistrate's probable-cause determination has been that so long as the magistrate had a "substantial basis for ... [concluding]" that a search would uncover evidence of wrongdoing, the Fourth Amendment requires no more. We think reaffirmation of this standard better serves the purpose of encouraging recourse to the warrant procedure and is more consistent with our traditional deference to the probable-cause determinations of magistrates than is the "two-pronged test."

Finally, the direction taken by decisions following *Spinelli* poorly serves "[t]he most basic function of any government": "to provide for the security of the individual and of his property." The strictures that inevitably accompany the "two-pronged test" cannot avoid seriously impeding the task of law enforcement. If, as the Illinois Supreme Court apparently thought, that test must be rigorously applied in every case, anonymous tips would be of greatly diminished value in police work. Ordinary citizens, like ordinary witnesses, generally do not provide extensive recitations of the basis of their everyday observations. Like-wise, as the Illinois Supreme Court observed in this case, the veracity of persons supplying anonymous tips is by hypothesis largely unknown, and unknowable. As a result, anonymous tips seldom could survive a rigorous application of either of the *Spinelli* prongs. Yet, such tips, particularly when supplemented by independent police investigation, frequently con-tribute to the solution of otherwise "perfect crimes." While a conscien-tious assessment of the basis for crediting such tips is required by the Fourth Amendment, a standard that leaves virtually no place for anony-mous citizen informants is not.

For all these reasons, we conclude that it is wiser to abandon the "two-pronged test" established by our decisions in *Aguilar* and *Spinelli*. In its place we reaffirm the totality-of-the-circumstances analysis that traditionally has informed probable-cause determinations. The task of the issuing magistrate is simply to make a practical, common-sense decision whether, given all the circumstances set forth in the affidavit before him, including the "veracity" and "basis of knowledge" of per-sons supplying hearsay information, there is a fair probability that contraband or evidence of a crime will be found in a particular place. And the duty of a reviewing court is simply to ensure that the magistrate had a "substantial basis for conclud[ing]" that probable cause existed. We are convinced that this flexible, easily applied standard will better achieve the accommodation of public and private interests that the Fourth Amendment requires than does the approach that has developed from *Aguilar* and *Spinelli*.

Our earlier cases illustrate the limits beyond which a magistrate may not venture in issuing a warrant. A sworn statement of an affiant that "he has cause to suspect and does believe" that liquor illegally brought into the United States is located on certain premises will not do. An affidavit must provide the magistrate with a substantial basis for determining the existence of probable cause * * *. An officer's statement that "[a]ffiants have received reliable information from a credible person and do believe" that heroin is stored in a home, is likewise inadequate. [T]his is a mere conclusory statement that gives the magistrate virtually no basis at all for making a judgment regarding probable cause. Suffi-cient information must be presented to the magistrate to allow that official to determine probable cause; his action cannot be a mere ratifica-tion of the bare conclusions of others. In order to ensure that such an abdication of the magistrate's duty does not occur, courts must continue to conscientiously review the sufficiency of affidavits on which warrants are issued. * * *

* * *

IV

* * *

The showing of probable cause in the present case was fully as compelling as that in [Draper v. United States, 358 U.S. 307, 79 S.Ct. 329, 3 L.Ed.2d 327 (1959)]. Even standing alone, the facts obtained through the independent investigation of Mader and the DEA at least suggested that the Gateses were involved in drug trafficking. In addition to being a popular vacation site, Florida is well known as a source of narcotics and other illegal drugs. Lance Gates' flight to Palm Beach, his brief, overnight stay in a motel, and apparent immediate return north to Chicago in the family car, conveniently awaiting him in West Palm Beach, is as suggestive of a prearranged drug run, as it is of an ordinary vacation trip.

In addition, the judge could rely on the anonymous letter, which had been corroborated in major part by Mader's efforts * * *. The corroboration of the letter's predictions that the Gates's car would be in Florida, that Lance Gates would fly to Florida in the next day or so, and that he would drive the car north toward Bloomingdale all indicated, albeit not with certainty, that the informant's other assertions also were true. * * *

Finally, the anonymous letter contained a range of details relating not just to easily obtained facts and conditions existing at the time of the tip, but to future actions of third parties ordinarily not easily predicted. The letterwriter's accurate information as to the travel plans of each of the Gateses was of a character likely obtained only from the Gateses themselves, or from someone familiar with their not entirely ordinary travel plans. If the informant had access to accurate information of this type a magistrate could properly conclude that it was not unlikely that he also had access to reliable information of the Gateses' alleged illegal activities. Of course, the Gateses' travel plans might have been learned from a talkative neighbor or travel agent; under the "two-pronged test" developed from *Spinelli*, the character of the details in the anonymous letter might well not permit a sufficiently clear inference regarding the letterwriter's "basis of knowledge." But, as discussed previously, probable cause does not demand the certainty we associate with formal trials. It is enough that there was a fair probability that the writer of the anonymous letter had obtained his entire story either from the Gateses or someone they trusted. And corroboration of major portions of the letter's predictions provides just this probability. It is apparent, therefore, that the judge issuing the warrant had a "substantial basis for . . . [concluding]" that probable cause to search the Gateses' home and car existed. The judgment of the Supreme Court of Illinois therefore must be reversed.

[JUSTICE WHITE's opinion concurring in the judgment, and JUSTICE BRENNAN's dissenting opinion, with whom JUSTICE MARSHALL joined, are omitted.]

JUSTICE STEVENS, with whom JUSTICE BRENNAN joins, dissenting.

The fact that Lance and Sue Gates made a 22–hour nonstop drive from West Palm Beach, Florida, to Bloomingdale, Illinois, only a few hours after Lance had flown to Florida provided persuasive evidence that they were engaged in illicit activity. That fact, however, was not known to the judge when he issued the warrant to search their home.

What the judge did know at that time was that the anonymous informant had not been completely accurate in his or her predictions. The informant had indicated that "Sue ... drives their car to Florida *where she leaves it to be loaded up with drugs .... Sue [flies] back after she drops the car off in Florida.*" Yet Detective Mader's affidavit reported that she "left the West Palm Beach area driving the Mercury northbound."

The discrepancy between the informant's predictions and the facts known to Detective Mader is significant for three reasons. First, it cast doubt on the informant's hypothesis that the Gates already had "over [$100,000] worth of drugs in their basement." The informant had predicted an itinerary that always kept one spouse in Bloomingdale, suggesting that the Gates did not want to leave their home unguarded because something valuable was hidden within. That inference obviously could not be drawn when it was known that the pair was actually together over a thousand miles from home.

Second, the discrepancy made the Gates' conduct seem substantially less unusual than the informant had predicted it would be. It would have been odd if, as predicted, Sue had driven down to Florida on Wednesday, left the car, and flown right back to Illinois. But the mere facts that Sue was in West Palm Beach with the car, that she was joined by her husband at the Holiday Inn on Friday, and that the couple drove north together the next morning are neither unusual nor probative of criminal activity.

Third, the fact that the anonymous letter contained a material mistake undermines the reasonableness of relying on it as a basis for making a forcible entry into a private home.

Of course, the activities in this case did not stop when the judge issued the warrant. The Gates drove all night to Bloomingdale, the officers searched the car and found 400 pounds of marihuana, and then they searched the house. However, none of these subsequent events may be considered in evaluating the warrant, and the search of the house was legal only if the warrant was valid. I cannot accept the Court's casual conclusion that, *before the Gates arrived in Bloomingdale,* there was probable cause to justify a valid entry and search of a private home. No one knows who the informant in this case was, or what motivated him or her to write the note. Given that the note's predictions were faulty in one significant respect, and were corroborated by nothing except ordinary innocent activity, I must surmise that the Court's evaluation of the warrant's validity has been colored by subsequent events.

* * *

Commentary

1. The issue presented in *Gates* is substantially different from the issues presented in *Aguilar* and *Spinelli*. In those cases the police may well have been in possession of information amounting to probable cause, but the conclusory affidavits did not communicate enough of the background information for a magistrate to make an informed judgment. The Supreme Court's holdings were intended to require the police to supply sufficiently detailed information to permit the magistrate to make an independent determination of probable cause.

In *Gates*, on the other hand, the police *did* provide the magistrate in the affidavit with the relevant background information which they had obtained. The problem is not that the police held back information and communicated only conclusions; the problem is that the essential corroborating detail was inconclusive. But what degree of certainty is required to establish probable cause? The essential point in the majority opinion in *Gates* is not the abandonment of the two-prong analysis but the insistence that only a "fair probability" is required. If we require only that the information be sufficient to indicate that there is a fairly good chance that the search will uncover contraband, then we accept a risk that innocent people suspected of criminal activity may be searched. If we require virtual certainty, then we protect possibly innocent persons from searches but pay a price in law enforcement effectiveness.

In his concurring opinion in *Gates*, Justice White concluded that the affidavit satisfied the *Aguilar–Spinelli* test because of the way in which he evaluated the success of police efforts to corroborate the tip. The dissenters, on the other hand, concluded that the affidavit failed even the flexible "totality of the circumstances" test because of the importance they attached to the acknowledged discrepancies between the tip and the corroborating circumstances.

Another way to approach the case is to ask what (if anything) the officers should have done differently. Should they have ignored the anonymous letter on the theory that it was insufficiently reliable to justify the expenditure of substantial police resources in obtaining corroboration? Should Detective Mader have anticipated the importance which reviewing courts would attach to the discrepancy in the travel arrangements, and obtained a warrant authorizing a search only if the suspects returned home within 24 hours? Should Mader have ignored the warrant procedure, waited until the *Gates* couple arrived at home, and then searched their car with probable cause under the automobile exception to the warrant requirement? (After being caught in possession of 350 pounds of marijuana, one or both of the suspects might well have consented to a search of the house, considering that little would be gained by a refusal.) How do you think the dissenters would prefer the police to have acted?

Commentators were mostly critical of *Gates*. See e.g. Kamisar, "Gates, 'Probable Cause,' 'Good Faith,' and Beyond," 69 Iowa L.Rev. 557 (1984); Wasserstrom, "The Incredible Shrinking Fourth Amendment," 21 Am.Crim. L.Rev. 257 (1984); 1 LaFave & Israel Criminal Procedure 192–203 (1984). But see, Joseph Grano, "Probable Cause and Common Sense: A Reply to the Critics of Illinois v. Gates," 17 U.Mich.J.L.Ref. 465 (1984) (defending the decision.)

2. *Some state courts went in a different direction.* The Supreme Court applied the *Gates* standard in Massachusetts v. Upton, 466 U.S. 727 (1984). A Lt. Beland had participated in a search of a motel room reserved by one Richard Kelleher, in the course of which the police recovered some items stolen from two recently burglarized homes. Later than day, he received a telephone call from an unidentified woman who told him that there was "a motor home full of stolen stuff" parked behind the home of one George Upton. She said that the stolen items included jewelry, silver and gold (similar items had been taken in the two burglaries previously mentioned). She further told Lt. Beland that Upton was going to move the motor home soon because he had learned of the raid on Kelleher's motel room and he had purchased the stolen items from Kelleher. She said she had seen the stolen items but refused to identify herself because Upton would kill her. Lt. Beland responded that he knew that the caller was Upton's girlfriend Lynn Alberico, whom he had previously met. The caller admitted that she was that person, and said that she had "broken up" with Upton and wanted to "burn him."

Following the telephone call, Beland went to the Upton house to verify that a motor home was parked on the property. Then, while other officers watched the premises, he prepared an affidavit setting out the information related above. He also attached the police reports on the two prior burglaries, along with lists of the stolen property. A magistrate issued the search warrant, and a subsequent search of the motor home produced the items described by the caller and other stolen property.

The Massachusetts Supreme Court held the warrant invalid, explaining that probable cause was lacking for the following reasons: (1) The basis of the informant's knowledge was not "forcefully apparent.... Although she said that she had seen the stolen property, she did not say that she had seen it in the motor home or when she had seen it." (2) The informer's reliability was not sufficiently demonstrated. She was essentially anonymous, despite her unverified assent to the proposition that she was Lynn Alberico. Beland did not state that he really did know who she was, and she may have been covering up her true identity. (3) The corroboration was insufficient to cure the preceding deficiencies. Commonwealth v. Upton, 390 Mass. 562, 458 N.E.2d 717 (1983).

The Supreme Court reversed per curiam, emphasizing that *Gates* had abandoned the two-pronged test, and that the information in the affidavit taken as a whole satisfied the new standard announced in *Gates*. After the remand, the Massachusetts Supreme Court held the warrant invalid under the search and seizure provision of the *state* constitution. Commonwealth v.

Upton, 394 Mass. 363, 476 N.E.2d 548 (1985). The Massachusetts court observed that the *Gates* standard was "unacceptably shapeless and permissive," and announced that it would continue to apply the two-pronged test of the *Aguilar* and *Spinelli* cases in interpreting the state constitution. Several other states courts have also declined to follow *Gates* when interpreting their state constitutions.

The New York Court of Appeals also declined to follow *Gates* in interpreting its state constitutional search and seizure provision in People v. Griminger, 71 N.Y.2d 635, 529 N.Y.S.2d 55, 524 N.E.2d 409 (1988). In that case a counterfeiting suspect gave U.S. Secret Service agents a detailed statement describing drugs which he had observed in Griminger's bedroom. One of the agents then obtained a warrant to search Griminger's home. According to the affidavit this agent prepared, a confidential informant known as "Source A" had observed the drugs in the bedroom and attic and had observed the defendant selling drugs as recently as seven days ago. The affidavit also stated that, pursuant to a consent search, about four pounds of marijuana were found in a garbage can at the same residence. Although the agent did not personally know the counterfeiting suspect, his affidavit identified the informer as "a person known to your deponent." The agent did not say that the informer was under arrest when he provided the information, and gave no other information pertaining to reliability. The New York court affirmed findings by lower courts that this information failed to establish the reliability prong, and defended the *Aguilar–Spinelli* test against charges that it is excessively technical. The New York court also held that the state constitutional standard would apply even though the warrant was issued by a federal judge at the request of a federal officer.

3. *Anticipatory warrants*. Should Detective Mader have obtained an "anticipatory search warrant," allowing a search of the Gates residence only if the automobile arrived from Florida on schedule? At the time such warrants were highly unusual, but after *Gates* they became common. The United States Court of Appeals for the Seventh Circuit discussed anticipatory warrants in United States v. Leidner, 99 F.3d 1423 (7th Cir.1996). In that case, Missouri police found 200 pounds of marijuana in a car driven by Sapp. Sapp said that he was transporting the marijuana to Leidner's home in Illinois, and agreed to make a controlled delivery to Leidner. On the basis of those facts Illinois police obtained a warrant to search Leidner's residence. The issuing magistrate orally told them that they should not execute the warrant until the delivery occurred, but the warrant itself did not contain this limitation. Sapp made the delivery and the police then made the search.

A federal district judge held the ASW invalid because it did not state that the search was to be made only if the delivery occurred. The Court of Appeals reversed this holding, reasoning that it was implicit in all the circumstances that the controlled delivery would precede the search. A more difficult issue was that there was no independent evidence, other than the word of the informer, that the marijuana really had been intended for Leidner. Leidner's counsel argued that Sapp could have named anyone he knew in an effort to transfer the blame from himself after being caught with the contraband, in hope of getting a better deal from the authorities. The Court of Appeals held that Sapp's information was sufficiently detailed and credible to meet the probable cause standard of *Gates*.

The Ninth Circuit took a different view of the anticipatory warrant in United States v. Hotal, 143 F.3d 1223 (9th Cir.1998). The defendant had ordered videotapes containing child pornography from a mailed offer which was part of a government sting operation. A postal inspector obtained a warrant authorizing a search of the defendant's home "forthwith." The warrant also incorporated by reference the inspector's affidavit, which said that the search would be conducted only after the defendant received the tapes and took them into his home. Case law in the Ninth Circuit does not permit the government to cure a defective warrant by using information contained in the affidavit unless there is proof that the affidavit accompanied the warrant at the time of the search. There was no such proof in this case, and so the Ninth Circuit held that the warrant was invalid even though the search was actually conducted only after the triggering event.

See also, United States v. Gendron, 18 F.3d 955, 965 (1st Cir.1994), where Chief Judge Breyer, now Justice Breyer, wrote that "the simple fact that a warrant is 'anticipatory'—i.e., that it takes effect, not upon issuance, but at a specified future time—does not invalidate a warrant or make it somehow suspect or legally disfavored."

C. EXCEPTIONS TO THE WARRANT RULE

The Supreme Court has frequently stated the rule that a search conducted without a warrant issued upon probable cause is *"per se unreasonable . . .* subject only to a few specifically established and well-delineated exceptions." After reading the materials in this Chapter and in Chapter 4, you may conclude that the exceptions have swallowed the rule. In reality, most searches and seizures are conducted without the prior authority of a warrant issued by a judge. In many encounters, police officers simply do not have time to obtain a warrant. In those circumstances, it is necessary to avoid a rigid per se rule commanding that warrants are always required. The automobile and exigent circumstances exceptions to the warrant requirement, which are covered later in this Chapter, exemplify this kind of "escape route" from the general rule requiring warrants.

The Court also has affirmed the validity of many warrantless arrests, as the following cases demonstrate. What is the justification for these seizures? Do they present a type of exigency? Or does the Court simply follow blindly the common law rules announced in medieval England? Or is there some other justification?

1. Warrantless Arrests

MARYLAND v. PRINGLE

Supreme Court of the United States, 2003.
540 U.S. 366, 124 S.Ct. 795, 157 L.Ed.2d 769.

CHIEF JUSTICE REHNQUIST delivered the opinion of the Court.

In the early morning hours a passenger car occupied by three men was stopped for speeding by a police officer. The officer, upon searching the car, seized $763 of rolled-up cash from the glove compartment and five glassine baggies of cocaine from between the back-seat armrest and the back seat. After all three men denied ownership of the cocaine and money, the officer arrested each of them. We hold that the officer had probable cause to arrest Pringle—one of the three men.

At 3:16 a.m. on August 7, 1999, a Baltimore County Police officer stopped a Nissan Maxima for speeding. There were three occupants in the car: Donte Partlow, the driver and owner, respondent Pringle, the front-seat passenger, and Otis Smith, the back-seat passenger. The officer asked Partlow for his license and registration. When Partlow opened the glove compartment to retrieve the vehicle registration, the officer observed a large amount of rolled-up money in the glove compartment. The officer returned to his patrol car with Partlow's license and registration to check the computer system for outstanding violations. The computer check did not reveal any violations. The officer returned to the stopped car, had Partlow get out, and issued him an oral warning.

After a second patrol car arrived, the officer asked Partlow if he had any weapons or narcotics in the vehicle. Partlow indicated that he did not. Partlow then consented to a search of the vehicle. The search yielded $763 from the glove compartment and five plastic glassine baggies containing cocaine from behind the back-seat armrest. When the officer began the search the armrest was in the upright position flat against the rear seat. The officer pulled down the armrest and found the drugs, which had been placed between the armrest and the back seat of the car.

The officer questioned all three men about the ownership of the drugs and money, and told them that if no one admitted to ownership of the drugs he was going to arrest them all. The men offered no information regarding the ownership of the drugs or money. All three were placed under arrest and transported to the police station.

Later that morning, Pringle waived his rights under *Miranda* v. *Arizona*, 384 U.S. 436, 16 L.Ed.2d 694, 86 S.Ct. 1602 (1966), and gave an oral and written confession in which he acknowledged that the cocaine belonged to him, that he and his friends were going to a party, and that he intended to sell the cocaine or "[u]se it for sex." Pringle maintained that the other occupants of the car did not know about the drugs, and they were released.

The trial court denied Pringle's motion to suppress his confession as the fruit of an illegal arrest, holding that the officer had probable cause to arrest Pringle. A jury convicted Pringle of possession with intent to distribute cocaine and possession of cocaine. He was sentenced to 10 years' incarceration without the possibility of parole. * * *

* * *

It is uncontested in the present case that the officer, upon recovering the five plastic glassine baggies containing suspected cocaine, had probable cause to believe a felony had been committed. The sole question is whether the officer had probable cause to believe that Pringle committed that crime.

The long-prevailing standard of probable cause protects "citizens from rash and unreasonable interferences with privacy and from unfounded charges of crime," while giving "fair leeway for enforcing the law in the community's protection." On many occasions, we have reiterated that the probable-cause standard is a " 'practical, nontechnical conception' " that deals with " 'the factual and practical considerations of everyday life on which reasonable and prudent men, not legal technicians, act.' " "[P]robable cause is a fluid concept—turning on the assessment of probabilities in particular factual contexts—not readily, or even usefully, reduced to a neat set of legal rules."

The probable-cause standard is incapable of precise definition or quantification into percentages because it deals with probabilities and depends on the totality of the circumstances. We have stated, however, that "[t]he substance of all the definitions of probable cause is a reasonable ground for belief of guilt," and that the belief of guilt must be particularized with respect to the person to be searched or seized * * *.

To determine whether an officer had probable cause to arrest an individual, we examine the events leading up to the arrest, and then decide "whether these historical facts, viewed from the standpoint of an objectively reasonable police officer, amount to" probable cause.

In this case, Pringle was one of three men riding in a Nissan Maxima at 3:16 a.m. There was $763 of rolled-up cash in the glove compartment directly in front of Pringle. Five plastic glassine baggies of cocaine were behind the back-seat armrest and accessible to all three men. Upon questioning, the three men failed to offer any information with respect to the ownership of the cocaine or the money.

We think it an entirely reasonable inference from these facts that any or all three of the occupants had knowledge of, and exercised dominion and control over, the cocaine. Thus a reasonable officer could conclude that there was probable cause to believe Pringle committed the crime of possession of cocaine, either solely or jointly.

Pringle's attempt to characterize this case as a guilt-by-association case is unavailing. His reliance on *Ybarra* v. *Illinois,* [444 U.S. 85 (1979)] * * * is misplaced. In *Ybarra*, police officers obtained a warrant to search a tavern and its bartender for evidence of possession of a controlled substance. Upon entering the tavern, the officers conducted patdown searches of the customers present in the tavern, including Ybarra. Inside a cigarette pack retrieved from Ybarra's pocket, an officer found six tinfoil packets containing heroin. We stated:

> "[A] person's mere propinquity to others independently suspected of criminal activity does not, without more, give rise to probable cause to search that person. Where the standard is probable cause, a search or seizure of a person must be supported by probable cause particularized with respect to that person. This requirement cannot

be undercut or avoided by simply pointing to the fact that coinciden-tally there exists probable cause to search or seize another or to search the premises where the person may happen to be."

We held that the search warrant did not permit body searches of all of the tavern's patrons and that the police could not pat down the patrons for weapons, absent individualized suspicion.

This case is quite different from *Ybarra.* Pringle and his two companions were in a relatively small automobile, not a public tavern. In *Wyoming* v. *Houghton,* 526 U.S. 295, 143 L.Ed.2d 408, 119 S.Ct. 1297 (1999), we noted that "a car passenger—unlike the unwitting tavern patron in *Ybarra*—will often be engaged in a common enterprise with the driver, and have the same interest in concealing the fruits or the evidence of their wrongdoing." Here we think it was reasonable for the officer to infer a common enterprise among the three men. The quantity of drugs and cash in the car indicated the likelihood of drug dealing, an enterprise to which a dealer would be unlikely to admit an innocent person with the potential to furnish evidence against him.

* * *

UNITED STATES v. WATSON

Supreme Court of the United States, 1976.
423 U.S. 411, 96 S.Ct. 820, 46 L.Ed.2d 598.

Mr. Justice White delivered the opinion of the Court.

[Watson was convicted of illegally possessing two stolen credit cards seized from his car. His suppression motion rested on several theories, including the argument that the arrest itself was invalid because the federal officers had not obtained an arrest warrant.]

II

* * *

Under the Fourth Amendment, the people are to be "secure in their persons, houses, papers, and effects, against unreasonable searches and seizures, . . . and no Warrants shall issue, but upon probable cause. . . . " Section 3061 represents a judgment by Congress that it is not unreason-able under the Fourth Amendment for postal inspectors to arrest with-out a warrant provided they have probable cause to do so. This was not an isolated or quixotic judgment of the legislative branch. Other federal law enforcement officers have been expressly authorized by statute for many years to make felony arrests on probable cause but without a warrant. This is true of United States marshals, and of agents of the Federal Bureau of Investigation; the Drug Enforcement Administration; the Secret Service; and the Customs Service.

Because there is a "strong presumption of constitutionality due to an Act of Congress, especially when it turns on what is 'reasonable,'" "[o]bviously the Court should be reluctant to decide that a search thus authorized by Congress was unreasonable and that the Act was therefore unconstitutional." Moreover, there is nothing in the Court's prior cases indicating that under the Fourth Amendment a warrant is required to make a valid arrest for a felony. Indeed, the relevant prior decisions are uniformly to the contrary.

"The usual rule is that a police officer may arrest without warrant one believed by the officer upon reasonable cause to have been guilty of a felony.... " * * * Just last Term, while recognizing that maximum protection of individual rights could be assured by requiring a magistrate's review of the factual justification prior to any arrest, we stated that "such a requirement would constitute an intolerable handicap for legitimate law enforcement" and noted that the Court "has never invalidated an arrest supported by probable cause solely because the officers failed to secure a warrant."

The cases construing the Fourth Amendment thus reflect the ancient common-law rule that a peace officer was permitted to arrest without a warrant for a misdemeanor or felony committed in his presence as well as for a felony not committed in his presence if there was reasonable ground for making the arrest. This has also been the prevailing rule under state constitutions and statutes. "The rule of the common law, that a peace officer or a private citizen may arrest a felon without a warrant, has been generally held by the courts of the several States to be in force in cases of felony punishable by the civil tribunals."

* * *

Because the common-law rule authorizing arrests without a warrant generally prevailed in the States, it is important for present purposes to note that in 1792 Congress invested United States marshals and their deputies with "the same powers in executing the laws of the United States, as sheriffs and their deputies in the several states have by law, in executing the laws of their respective states." Act of May 2, 1792, c. 28, § 9, 1 Stat. 265. The Second Congress thus saw no inconsistency between the Fourth Amendment and legislation giving United States marshals the same power as local peace officers to arrest for a felony without a warrant. * * *

The balance struck by the common law in generally authorizing felony arrests on probable cause, but without a warrant, has survived substantially intact. * * *

* * *

Watson's arrest did not violate the Fourth Amendment, and the Court of Appeals erred in holding to the contrary.

* * *

[Concurring opinions of JUSTICE POWELL and JUSTICE STEWART are omitted.]

MR. JUSTICE MARSHALL, with whom MR. JUSTICE BRENNAN joins, dissenting.

* * *

II

* * *

The Court * * * relies on the English common-law rule of arrest and the many state and federal statutes following it. There are two serious flaws in this approach. First, as a matter of factual analysis, the substance of the ancient common-law rule provides no support for the far-reaching modern rule that the Court fashions on its model. Second, as a matter of doctrine, the longstanding existence of a Government practice does not immunize the practice from scrutiny under the mandate of our Constitution.

The common-law rule was indeed as the Court states it:

"[A] peace officer was permitted to arrest without a warrant for a misdemeanor or felony committed in his presence as well as for a felony not committed in his presence if there was reasonable ground for making the arrest."

To apply the rule blindly today, however, makes as much sense as attempting to interpret Hamlet's admonition to Ophelia, "Get thee to a nunnery, go," without understanding the meaning of Hamlet's words in the context of their age.[3] For the fact is that a felony at common law and a felony today bear only slight resemblance, with the result that the relevance of the common-law rule of arrest to the modern interpretation of our Constitution is minimal.

* * *

This difference reflects more than changing notions of penology. It reflects a substantive change in the kinds of crimes called felonies. Only the most serious crimes were felonies at common law, and many crimes now classified as felonies under federal or state law were treated as misdemeanors. * * *

To make an arrest for any of these crimes at common law, the police officer was required to obtain a warrant, unless the crime was committed in his presence. Since many of these same crimes are commonly classified as felonies today, however, under the Court's holding a warrant is no longer needed to make such arrests, a result in contravention of the common law.

Thus the lesson of the common law, and those courts in this country that have accepted its rule, is an ambiguous one. Applied in its original context, the common-law rule would allow the warrantless arrest of

3. Nunnery was Elizabethan slang for house of prostitution. 7 Oxford English Dictionary 264 (1933).

some, but not all, of those we call felons today. Accordingly, the Court is simply historically wrong when it tells us that "[t]he balance struck by the common law in generally authorizing felony arrests on probable cause, but without a warrant, has survived substantially intact." As a matter of substance, the balance struck by the common law in accommodating the public need for the most certain and immediate arrest of criminal suspects with the requirement of magisterial oversight to protect against mistaken insults to privacy decreed that only in the most serious of cases could the warrant be dispensed with. This balance is not recognized when the common-law rule is unthinkingly transposed to our present classifications of criminal offenses. Indeed, the only clear lesson of history is contrary to the one the Court draws: the common law considered the arrest warrant far more important than today's decision leaves it.

* * *

III

* * *

A warrant requirement for arrests would, of course, minimize the possibility that such an intrusion into the individual's sacred sphere of personal privacy would occur on less than probable cause. Primarily for this reason, a warrant is required for searches. Surely there is no reason to place greater trust in the partisan assessment of a police officer that there is probable cause for an arrest than in his determination that probable cause exists for a search. * * *

We come then to the second part of the warrant test: whether a warrant requirement would unduly burden legitimate law enforcement interests. * * * I believe, however, that the suggested concerns are wholly illusory. Indeed, the argument that a warrant requirement for arrests would be an onerous chore for the police seems somewhat anomalous in light of the Government's concession that "it is the standard practice of the Federal Bureau of Investigation [FBI] to present its evidence to the United States Attorney, and to obtain a warrant, before making an arrest." * * *

* * *

2. Consent

SCHNECKLOTH v. BUSTAMONTE

Supreme Court of the United States, 1973.
412 U.S. 218, 93 S.Ct. 2041, 36 L.Ed.2d 854.

Mr. Justice Stewart delivered the opinion of the Court.

It is well settled under the Fourth and Fourteenth Amendments that a search conducted without a warrant issued upon probable cause is "*per se* unreasonable ... subject only to a few specifically established and well-delineated exceptions." It is equally well settled that one of the specifically established exceptions to the requirements of both a warrant and probable cause is a search that is conducted pursuant to consent. The constitutional question in the present case concerns the definition of "consent" in this Fourth and Fourteenth Amendment context.

I

* * *

While on routine patrol in Sunnyvale, California, at approximately 2:40 in the morning, Police Officer James Rand stopped an automobile when he observed that one headlight and its license plate light were burned out. Six men were in the vehicle. Joe Alcala and the respondent, Robert Bustamonte, were in the front seat with Joe Gonzales, the driver. Three older men were seated in the rear. When, in response to the policeman's question, Gonzales could not produce a driver's license, Officer Rand asked if any of the other five had any evidence of identification. Only Alcala produced a license, and he explained that the car was his brother's. After the six occupants had stepped out of the car at the officer's request and after two additional policemen had arrived, Officer Rand asked Alcala if he could search the car. Alcala replied, "Sure, go ahead." Prior to the search no one was threatened with arrest and, according to Officer Rand's uncontradicted testimony, it "was all very congenial at this time." Gonzales testified that Alcala actually helped in the search of the car, by opening the trunk and glove compartment. In Gonzales' words: "The police officer asked Joe Alcala, he goes, 'Does the trunk open?' And Joe said, 'Yes.' He went to the car and got the keys and opened up the trunk." Wadded up under the left rear seat, the police officers found three checks that had previously been stolen from a car wash.

The trial judge denied the motion to suppress, and the checks in question were admitted in evidence at Bustamonte's trial. On the basis of this and other evidence he was convicted. * * * "Not only officer Rand, but Gonzales, the driver of the automobile, testified that Alcala's assent to the search of his brother's automobile was freely, even casually given. At the time of the request to search the automobile the atmosphere, according to Rand, was 'congenial' and there had been no discussion of any crime. As noted, Gonzales said Alcala even attempted to aid in the search." * * *

* * *

II

[T]he State concedes that "when a prosecutor seeks to rely upon consent to justify the lawfulness of a search, he has the burden of proving that the consent was, in fact, freely and voluntarily given."

The precise question in this case, then, is what must the prosecution prove to demonstrate that a consent was "voluntarily" given. * * *

A

The most extensive judicial exposition of the meaning of "voluntariness" has been developed in those cases in which the Court has had to determine the "voluntariness" of a defendant's confession for purposes of the Fourteenth Amendment. * * *

* * *

"[V]oluntariness" has reflected an accommodation of the complex of values implicated in police questioning of a suspect. At one end of the spectrum is the acknowledged need for police questioning as a tool for the effective enforcement of criminal laws. Without such investigation, those who were innocent might be falsely accused, those who were guilty might wholly escape prosecution, and many crimes would go unsolved. In short, the security of all would be diminished. At the other end of the spectrum is the set of values reflecting society's deeply felt belief that the criminal law cannot be used as an instrument of unfairness, and that the possibility of unfair and even brutal police tactics poses a real and serious threat to civilized notions of justice. "In cases involving involuntary confessions, this Court enforces the strongly felt attitude of our society that important human values are sacrificed where an agency of the government, in the course of securing a conviction, wrings a confession out of an accused against his will."

This Court's decisions reflect a frank recognition that the Constitution requires the sacrifice of neither security nor liberty. The Due Process Clause does not mandate that the police forgo all questioning, or that they be given carte blanche to extract what they can from a suspect. "The ultimate test remains that which has been the only clearly established test in Anglo–American courts for two hundred years: the test of voluntariness. Is the confession the product of an essentially free and unconstrained choice by its maker? If it is, if he has willed to confess, it may be used against him. If it is not, if his will has been overborne and his capacity for self-determination critically impaired, the use of his confession offends due process."

In determining whether a defendant's will was over-borne in a particular case, the Court has assessed the totality of all the surrounding circumstances—both the characteristics of the accused and the details of the interrogation. Some of the factors taken into account have included the youth of the accused, his lack of education, or his low intelligence, the lack of any advice to the accused of his constitutional rights, the length of detention, the repeated and prolonged nature of the questioning, and the use of physical punishment such as the deprivation of food or sleep. In all of these cases, the Court determined the factual circumstances surrounding the confession, assessed the psychological impact on the accused, and evaluated the legal significance of how the accused reacted.

The significant fact about all of these decisions is that none of them turned on the presence or absence of a single controlling criterion; each reflected a careful scrutiny of all the surrounding circumstances. In none of them did the Court rule that the Due Process Clause required the prosecution to prove as part of its initial burden that the defendant knew he had a right to refuse to answer the questions that were put. While the state of the accused's mind, and the failure of the police to advise the accused of his rights, were certainly factors to be evaluated in assessing the "voluntariness" of an accused's responses, they were not in and of themselves determinative.

B

[T]he question whether a consent to a search was in fact "voluntary" or was the product of duress or coercion, express or implied, is a question of fact to be determined from the totality of all the circumstances. While knowledge of the right to refuse consent is one factor to be taken into account, the government need not establish such knowledge as the *sine qua non* of an effective consent. As with police questioning, two competing concerns must be accommodated in determining the meaning of a "voluntary" consent—the legitimate need for such searches and the equally important requirement of assuring the absence of coercion.

In situations where the police have some evidence of illicit activity, but lack probable cause to arrest or search, a search authorized by a valid consent may be the only means of obtaining important and reliable evidence. In the present case for example, while the police had reason to stop the car for traffic violations, the State does not contend that there was probable cause to search the vehicle or that the search was incident to a valid arrest of any of the occupants. Yet, the search yielded tangible evidence that served as a basis for a prosecution, and provided some assurance that others, wholly innocent of the crime, were not mistakenly brought to trial. And in those cases where there is probable cause to arrest or search, but where the police lack a warrant, a consent search may still be valuable. If the search is conducted and proves fruitless, that in itself may convince the police that an arrest with its possible stigma and embarrassment is unnecessary, or that a far more extensive search pursuant to a warrant is not justified. In short, a search pursuant to consent may result in considerably less inconvenience for the subject of the search, and, properly conducted, is a constitutionally permissible and wholly legitimate aspect of effective police activity.

But the Fourth and Fourteenth Amendments require that a consent not be coerced, by explicit or implicit means, by implied threat or covert force. For, no matter how subtly the coercion was applied, the resulting "consent" would be no more than a pretext for the unjustified police intrusion against which the Fourth Amendment is directed. * * *

* * *

One alternative that would go far toward proving that the subject of a search did know he had a right to refuse consent would be to advise him of that right before eliciting his consent. That, however, is a suggestion that has been almost universally repudiated by both federal and state courts, and, we think, rightly so. For it would be thoroughly impractical to impose on the normal consent search the detailed requirements of an effective warning. Consent searches are part of the standard investigatory techniques of law enforcement agencies. They normally occur on the highway, or in a person's home or office, and under informal and unstructured conditions. The circumstances that prompt the initial request to search may develop quickly or be a logical extension of investigative police questioning. The police may seek to investigate further suspicious circumstances or to follow up leads developed in questioning persons at the scene of a crime. These situations are a far cry from the structured atmosphere of a trial where, assisted by counsel if he chooses, a defendant is informed of his trial rights. And, while surely a closer question, these situations are still immeasurably far removed from "custodial interrogation" where, in *Miranda v. Arizona,* 384 U.S. 436, 86 S.Ct. 1602, 16 L.Ed.2d 694 (1966), we found that the Constitution required certain now familiar warnings as a prerequisite to police interrogation. * * *

Consequently, we cannot accept * * * that proof of knowledge of the right to refuse consent is a necessary prerequisite to demonstrating a "voluntary" consent. Rather, it is only by analyzing all the circumstances of an individual consent that it can be ascertained whether in fact it was voluntary or coerced. It is this careful sifting of the unique facts and circumstances of each case that is evidenced in our prior decisions involving consent searches.

* * *

C

It is said, however, that a "consent" is a "waiver" of a person's rights under the Fourth and Fourteenth Amendments. The argument is that by allowing the police to conduct a search, a person "waives" whatever right he had to prevent the police from searching. It is argued that under the doctrine of *Johnson v. Zerbst,* 304 U.S. 458, 464, 58 S.Ct. 1019, 82 L.Ed. 1461 (1938), to establish such a "waiver" the State must demonstrate "an intentional relinquishment or abandonment of a known right or privilege."

* * *

The requirement of a "knowing" and "intelligent" waiver was articulated in a case involving the validity of a defendant's decision to forgo a right constitutionally guaranteed to protect a fair trial and the reliability of the truth-determining process. *Johnson* dealt with the denial of counsel in a federal criminal trial. There the Court held that under the Sixth Amendment a criminal defendant is entitled to the assistance of counsel, and that if he lacks sufficient funds to retain counsel, it is the Government's obligation to furnish him with a lawyer. As Mr. Justice Black wrote for the Court: "The Sixth Amendment stands as a constant admonition that if the constitutional safeguards it provides be lost, justice will not 'still be done.' It embodies a realistic recognition of the obvious truth that the average defendant does not have the professional legal skill to protect himself when brought before a tribunal with power to take his life or liberty, wherein the prosecution is presented by experienced and learned counsel. That which is simple, orderly and necessary to the lawyer, to the untrained layman may appear intricate, complex and mysterious.'' To preserve the fairness of the trial process the Court established an appropriately heavy burden on the Government before waiver could be found—''an intentional relinquishment or abandonment of a known right or privilege.''

Almost without exception, the requirement of a knowing and intelligent waiver has been applied only to those rights which the Constitution guarantees to a criminal defendant in order to preserve a fair trial. Hence, and hardly surprisingly in view of the facts of *Johnson* itself, the standard of a knowing and intelligent waiver has most often been applied to test the validity of a waiver of counsel, either at trial, or upon a guilty plea. And the Court has also applied the *Johnson* criteria to assess the effectiveness of a waiver of other trial rights such as the right to confrontation, to a jury trial, and to a speedy trial, and the right to be free from twice being placed in jeopardy. Guilty pleas have been carefully scrutinized to determine whether the accused knew and understood all the rights to which he would be entitled at trial, and that he had intentionally chosen to forgo them. And the Court has evaluated the knowing and intelligent nature of the waiver of trial rights in trial-type situations, such as the waiver of the privilege against compulsory self-incrimination before an administrative agency or a congressional committee, or the waiver of counsel in a juvenile proceeding.

* * *

There is a vast difference between those rights that protect a fair criminal trial and the rights guaranteed under the Fourth Amendment. Nothing, either in the purposes behind requiring a ''knowing'' and ''intelligent'' waiver of trial rights, or in the practical application of such a requirement suggests that it ought to be extended to the constitutional guarantee against unreasonable searches and seizures.

* * *

The protections of the Fourth Amendment are of a wholly different order, and have nothing whatever to do with promoting the fair ascertainment of truth at a criminal trial. Rather, the Fourth Amendment protects the ''security of one's privacy against arbitrary intrusion by the police. . . . '' * * * The Fourth Amendment ''is not an adjunct to the ascertainment of truth.'' The guarantees of the Fourth Amendment stand ''as a protection of quite different constitutional values—values reflecting the concern of our society for the right of each individual to be let alone. To recognize this is no more than to accord those values undiluted respect.''

[T]he community has a real interest in encouraging consent, for the resulting search may yield necessary evidence for the solution and prosecution of crime, evidence that may insure that a wholly innocent person is not wrongly charged with a criminal offense.

* * *

[The concurring opinions of JUSTICE BLACKMUN and JUSTICE POWELL and the dissenting opinions of JUSTICE DOUGLAS and JUSTICE BRENNAN are omitted.]

JUSTICE MARSHALL, dissenting.

"[T]he Constitution guarantees . . . a society of free choice. Such a society presupposes the capacity of its members to choose." I would have thought that the capacity to choose necessarily depends upon knowledge that there is a choice to be made. But today the Court reaches the curious result that one can choose to relinquish a constitutional right— the right to be free of unreasonable searches—without knowing that he has the alternative of refusing to accede to a police request to search. I cannot agree, and therefore dissent.

* * *

II

My approach to the case is straightforward and, to me, obviously required by the notion of consent as a relinquishment of Fourth Amendment rights. I am at a loss to understand why consent "cannot be taken literally to mean a 'knowing' choice." In fact, I have difficulty in comprehending how a decision made without knowledge of available alternatives can be treated as a choice at all.

If consent to search means that a person has chosen to forgo his right to exclude the police from the place they seek to search, it follows that his consent cannot be considered a meaningful choice unless he knew that he could in fact exclude the police. The Court appears, however, to reject even the modest proposition that, if the subject of a search convinces the trier of fact that he did not know of his right to refuse assent to a police request for permission to search, the search must be held unconstitutional. For it says only that "knowledge of the right to refuse consent is one factor to be taken into account." I find this incomprehensible. I can think of no other situation in which we would say that a person agreed to some course of action if he convinced us that he did not know that there was some other course he might have pursued. I would therefore hold, at a minimum, that the prosecution may not rely on a purported consent to search if the subject of the search did not know that he could refuse to give consent. * * * Where the police claim authority to search yet in fact lack such authority, the subject does not know that he may permissibly refuse them entry, and it is this lack of knowledge that invalidates the consent.

If one accepts this view, the question then is a simple one: must the Government show that the subject knew of his rights, or must the subject show that he lacked such knowledge?

I think that any fair allocation of the burden would require that it be placed on the prosecution. On this question, the Court indulges in what might be called the "straw man" method of adjudication. * * *

* * *

The burden on the prosecutor would disappear, of course, if the police, at the time they requested consent to search, also told the subject that he had a right to refuse consent and that his decision to refuse would be respected. The Court's assertions to the contrary notwithstanding, there is nothing impractical about this method of satisfying the prosecution's burden of proof. It must be emphasized that the decision about informing the subject of his rights would lie with the officers seeking consent. If they believed that providing such information would impede their investigation, they might simply ask for consent, taking the risk that at some later date the prosecutor would be unable to prove that the subject knew of his rights or that some other basis for the search existed.

The Court contends that if an officer paused to inform the subject of his rights, the informality of the exchange would be destroyed. I doubt that a simple statement by an officer of an individual's right to refuse consent would do much to alter the informality of the exchange, except to alert the subject to a fact that he surely is entitled to know. It is not without significance that for many years the agents of the Federal Bureau of Investigation have routinely informed subjects of their right to refuse consent, when they request consent to search. The reported cases in which the police have informed subjects of their right to refuse consent show, also, that the information can be given without disrupting the casual flow of events. What evidence there is, then, rather strongly suggests that nothing disastrous would happen if the police, before requesting consent, informed the subject that he had a right to refuse consent and that his refusal would be respected.

I must conclude, with some reluctance, that when the Court speaks of practicality, what it really is talking of is the continued ability of the police to capitalize on the ignorance of citizens so as to accomplish by subterfuge what they could not achieve by relying only on the knowing relinquishment of constitutional rights. Of course it would be "practical" for the police to ignore the commands of the Fourth Amendment, if by practicality we mean that more criminals will be apprehended, even though the constitutional rights of innocent people also go by the board. But such a practical advantage is achieved only at the cost of permitting the police to disregard the limitations that the Constitution places on their behavior, a cost that a constitutional democracy cannot long absorb.

* * *

ILLINOIS v. RODRIGUEZ

Supreme Court of the United States, 1990.
497 U.S. 177, 110 S.Ct. 2793, 111 L.Ed.2d 148.

JUSTICE SCALIA delivered the opinion of the Court.

* * * The present case presents [the issue]: Whether a warrantless entry is valid when based upon the consent of a third party whom the police, at the time of the entry, reasonably believe to possess common authority over the premises, but who in fact does not do so.

I

Respondent Edward Rodriguez was arrested in his apartment by law enforcement officers and charged with possession of illegal drugs. The police gained entry to the apartment with the consent and assistance of Gail Fischer, who had lived there with respondent for several months. The relevant facts leading to the arrest are as follows.

On July 26, 1985, police were summoned to the residence of Dorothy Jackson on South Wolcott in Chicago. They were met by Ms. Jackson's daughter, Gail Fischer, who showed signs of a severe beating. She told the officers that she had been assaulted by respondent Edward Rodriguez earlier that day in an apartment on South California Avenue. Fischer stated that Rodriguez was then asleep in the apartment, and she consented to travel there with the police in order to unlock the door with her key so that the officers could enter and arrest him. During this conversation, Fischer several times referred to the apartment on South California as "our" apartment, and said that she had clothes and furniture there. It is unclear whether she indicated that she currently lived at the apartment, or only that she used to live there.

The police officers drove to the apartment on South California, accompanied by Fischer. They did not obtain an arrest warrant for Rodriguez, nor did they seek a search warrant for the apartment. At the apartment, Fischer unlocked the door with her key and gave the officers permission to enter. They moved through the door into the living room, where they observed in plain view drug paraphernalia and containers filled with white powder that they believed (correctly, as later analysis showed) to be cocaine. They proceeded to the bedroom, where they found Rodriguez asleep and discovered additional containers of white powder in two open attache cases. The officers arrested Rodriguez and seized the drugs and related paraphernalia.

* * *

II

The Fourth Amendment generally prohibits the warrantless entry of a person's home, whether to make an arrest or to search for specific objects. The prohibition does not apply, however, to situations in which voluntary consent has been obtained, either from the individual whose property is searched, or from a third party who possesses common authority over the premises. The State of Illinois contends that that exception applies in the present case.

"[C]ommon authority" rests "on mutual use of the property by persons generally having joint access or control for most purposes.... " The burden of establishing that common authority rests upon the State. On the basis of this record, it is clear that burden was not sustained. The evidence showed that although Fischer, with her two small children, had lived with Rodriguez beginning in December 1984, she had moved out on July 1, 1985, almost a month before the search at issue here, and had gone to live with her mother. She took her and her children's clothing with her, though leaving behind some furniture and household effects. During the period after July 1 she sometimes spent the night at Rodriguez's apartment, but never invited her friends there, and never went there herself when he was not home. Her name was not on the lease nor did she contribute to the rent. She had a key to the apartment, which she said at trial she had taken without Rodriguez's knowledge (though she testified at the preliminary hearing that Rodriguez had given her the key). On these facts the State has not established that, with respect to the South California apartment, Fischer had "joint access or control for most purposes." To the contrary, the Appellate Court's determination of no common authority over the apartment was obviously correct.

III

* * *

What Rodriguez is assured by the trial right of the exclusionary rule, where it applies, is that no evidence seized in violation of the Fourth Amendment will be introduced at his trial unless he consents. What he is assured by the Fourth Amendment itself, however, is not that no government search of his house will occur unless he consents; but that no such search will occur that is "unreasonable." There are various elements, of course, that can make a search of a person's house "reasonable"—one of which is the consent of the person or his cotenant. The essence of respondent's argument is that we should impose upon this element a requirement that we have not imposed upon other elements that regularly compel government officers to exercise judgment regarding the facts: namely, the requirement that their judgment be not only responsible but correct.

The fundamental objective that alone validates all unconsented government searches is, of course, the seizure of persons who have committed or are about to commit crimes, or of evidence related to crimes. But "reasonableness," with respect to this necessary element, does not demand that the government be factually correct in its assessment that that is what a search will produce. Warrants need only be supported by "probable cause," which demands no more than a proper "assessment of probabilities in particular factual contexts.... " If a magistrate, based upon seemingly reliable but factually inaccurate information, issues a warrant for the search of a house in which the sought-after felon is not present, has never been present, and was never likely to have been present, the owner of that house suffers one of the inconveniences we all expose ourselves to as the cost of living in a safe society; he does not suffer a violation of the Fourth Amendment.

Another element often, though not invariably, required in order to render an unconsented search "reasonable" is, of course, that the officer be authorized by a valid warrant. Here also we have not held that "reasonableness" precludes error with respect to those factual judgments that law enforcement officials are expected to make. In *Maryland v. Garrison,* 480 U.S. 79, 107 S.Ct. 1013, 94 L.Ed.2d 72 (1987), a warrant supported by probable cause with respect to one apartment was erroneously issued for an entire floor that was divided (though not clearly) into two apartments. We upheld the search of the apartment not properly covered by the warrant. We said:

> "The validity of the search of respondent's apartment pursuant to a warrant authorizing the search of the entire third floor depends on whether the officers' failure to realize the overbreadth of the warrant was objectively understandable and reasonable. Here it unquestionably was. The objective facts available to the officers at the time suggested no distinction between [the suspect's] apartment and the third-floor premises."

* * *

It would be superfluous to multiply these examples. It is apparent that in order to satisfy the "reasonableness" requirement of the Fourth Amendment, what is generally demanded of the many factual determinations that must regularly be made by agents of the government— whether the magistrate issuing a warrant, the police officer executing a warrant, or the police officer conducting a search or seizure under one of the exceptions to the warrant requirement—is not that they always be correct, but that they always be reasonable. As we put it in *Brinegar v. United States,* 338 U.S. 160, 176, 69 S.Ct. 1302, 93 L.Ed.1879 (1949):

> "Because many situations which confront officers in the course of executing their duties are more or less ambiguous, room must be allowed for some mistakes on their part. But the mistakes must be those of reasonable men, acting on facts leading sensibly to their conclusions of probability."

We see no reason to depart from this general rule with respect to facts bearing upon the authority to consent to a search. Whether the basis for such authority exists is the sort of recurring factual question to which law enforcement officials must be expected to apply their judgment; and all the Fourth Amendment requires is that they answer it reasonably. The Constitution is no more violated when officers enter without a warrant because they reasonably (though erroneously) believe that the person who has consented to their entry is a resident of the premises, than it is violated when they enter without a warrant because they reasonably (though erroneously) believe they are in pursuit of a violent felon who is about to escape.

* * *

[W]hat we hold today does not suggest that law enforcement officers may always accept a person's invitation to enter premises. Even when the invitation is accompanied by an explicit assertion that the person lives there, the surrounding circumstances could conceivably be such that a reasonable person would doubt its truth and not act upon it without further inquiry. As with other factual determinations bearing upon search and seizure, determination of consent to enter must "be judged against an objective standard: would the facts available to the officer at the moment ... 'warrant a man of reasonable caution in the belief' " that the consenting party had authority over the premises? If not, then warrantless entry without further inquiry is unlawful unless authority actually exists. But if so, the search is valid.

* * *

JUSTICE MARSHALL, with whom JUSTICE BRENNAN and JUSTICE STEVENS join, dissenting.

Dorothy Jackson summoned police officers to her house to report that her daughter Gail Fischer had been beaten. Fischer told police that Ed Rodriguez, her boyfriend, was her assaulter. During an interview with Fischer, one of the officers asked if Rodriguez dealt in narcotics. Fischer did not respond. Fischer did agree, however, to the officers' request to let them into Rodriguez's apartment so that they could arrest him for battery. The police, without a warrant and despite the absence of an exigency, entered Rodriguez's home to arrest him. As a result of their entry, the police discovered narcotics that the State subsequently sought to introduce in a drug prosecution against Rodriguez.

* * * The majority's [decision] rests on a misconception of the basis for third-party consent searches. That such searches do not give rise to claims of constitutional violations rests not on the premise that they are "reasonable" under the Fourth Amendment, but on the premise that a person may voluntarily limit his expectation of privacy by allowing others to exercise authority over his possessions. Thus, an individual's decision to permit another "joint access [to] or control [over the property] for most purposes," limits that individual's reasonable expectation of privacy and to that extent limits his Fourth Amendment protections. If an individual has not so limited his expectation of privacy, the police may not dispense with the safeguards established by the Fourth Amendment.

The baseline for the reasonableness of a search or seizure in the home is the presence of a warrant. Indeed, "searches and seizures inside a home without a warrant are presumptively unreasonable." Exceptions to the warrant requirement must therefore serve "compelling" law enforcement goals. Because the sole law enforcement purpose underlying third-party consent searches is avoiding the inconvenience of securing a warrant, a departure from the warrant requirement is not justified simply because an officer reasonably believes a third party has consented to a search of the defendant's home. In holding otherwise, the majority ignores our long-standing view that "the informed and deliberate determinations of magistrates ... as to what searches and seizures are permissible under the Constitution are to be preferred over the hurried action of officers and others who may happen to make arrests."

I

* * * We have recognized that the "physical entry of the home is the chief evil against which the wording of the Fourth Amendment is directed." We have further held that "a search or seizure carried out on a suspect's premises without a warrant is *per se* unreasonable, unless the police can show that it falls within one of a carefully defined set of exceptions." Those exceptions must be crafted in light of the warrant requirement's purposes. * * *

* * *

In the absence of an exigency, then, warrantless home searches and seizures are unreasonable under the Fourth Amendment. The weighty constitutional interest in preventing unauthorized intrusions into the home overrides any law enforcement interest in relying on the reasonable but potentially mistaken belief that a third party has authority to consent to such a search or seizure. Indeed, as the present case illustrates, only the minimal interest in avoiding the inconvenience of obtaining a warrant weighs in on the law enforcement side.

* * * The concerns of expediting police work and avoiding paperwork "are never very convincing reasons and, in these circumstances, certainly are not enough to by-pass the constitutional requirement." In this case, * * * "no suspect was fleeing or likely to take flight. The search was of permanent premises, not of a movable vehicle. No evidence or contraband was threatened with removal or destruction.... If the officers in this case were excused from the constitutional duty of presenting their evidence to a magistrate, it is difficult to think of a case in which it should be required."

Unlike searches conducted pursuant to the recognized exceptions to the warrant requirement, third-party consent searches are not based on an exigency and therefore serve no compelling social goal. Police officers, when faced with the choice of relying on consent by a third party or securing a warrant, should secure a warrant and must therefore accept the risk of error should they instead choose to rely on consent.

* * *

FLORIDA v. JIMENO

Supreme Court of the United States, 1991.
500 U.S. 248, 111 S.Ct. 1801, 114 L.Ed.2d 297.

CHIEF JUSTICE REHNQUIST delivered the opinion of the Court.

In this case we decide whether a criminal suspect's Fourth Amendment right to be free from unreasonable searches is violated when, after he gives a police officer permission to search his automobile, the officer opens a closed container found within the car that might reasonably hold the object of the search. We find that it is not. The Fourth Amendment is satisfied when, under the circumstances, it is objectively reasonable for the officer to believe that the scope of the suspect's consent permitted him to open a particular container within the automobile.

This case began when a Dade County police officer, Frank Trujillo, overheard respondent, Enio Jimeno, arranging what appeared to be a drug transaction over a public telephone. Believing that Jimeno might be involved in illegal drug trafficking, Officer Trujillo followed his car. The officer observed respondents make a right turn at a red light without stopping. He then pulled Jimeno over to the side of the road in order to issue him a traffic citation. Officer Trujillo told Jimeno that he had been stopped for committing a traffic infraction. The officer went on to say that he had reason to believe that Jimeno was carrying narcotics in his car, and asked permission to search the car. He explained that Jimeno did not have to consent to a search of the car. Jimeno stated that he had nothing to hide and gave Trujillo permission to search the automobile. After Jimeno's spouse, respondent Luz Jimeno, stepped out of the car, Officer Trujillo went to the passenger side, opened the door, and saw a folded, brown paper bag on the floorboard. The officer picked up the bag, opened it, and found a kilogram of cocaine inside.

The Jimenos were charged with possession with intent to distribute cocaine in violation of Florida law. Before trial, they moved to suppress the cocaine found in the bag on the ground that Jimeno's consent to search the car did not extend to the closed paper bag inside of the car. The trial court granted the motion. It found that although Jimeno "could have assumed that the officer would have searched the bag" at the time he gave his consent, his mere consent to search the car did not carry with it specific consent to open the bag and examine its contents.

The Florida District Court of Appeal affirmed the trial court's decision to suppress the evidence of the cocaine. In doing so, the court established a *per se* rule that "consent to a general search for narcotics does not extend to 'sealed containers within the general area agreed to by the defendant.'" The Florida Supreme Court affirmed * * *. We granted certiorari to determine whether consent to search a vehicle may extend to closed containers found inside the vehicle, and we now reverse the judgment of the Supreme Court of Florida.

The touchstone of the Fourth Amendment is reasonableness. The Fourth Amendment does not proscribe all state-initiated searches and seizures; it merely proscribes those which are unreasonable. Thus, we have long approved consensual searches because it is no doubt reasonable for the police to conduct a search once they have been permitted to do so. The standard for measuring the scope of a suspect's consent under the Fourth Amendment is that of "objective" reasonableness—what would the typical reasonable person have understood by the exchange between the officer and the suspect? The question before us, then, is whether it is reasonable for an officer to consider a suspect's general consent to a search of his car to include consent to examine a paper bag lying on the floor of the car. We think that it is.

The scope of a search is generally defined by its expressed object. In this case, the terms of the search's authorization were simple. Respondent granted Officer Trujillo permission to search his car, and did not place any explicit limitation on the scope of the search. Trujillo had informed Jimeno that he believed Jimeno was carrying narcotics, and that he would be looking for narcotics in the car. We think that it was objectively reasonable for the police to conclude that the general consent to search respondents' car included consent to search containers within that car which might bear drugs. A reasonable person may be expected to know that narcotics are generally carried in some form of a container. "Contraband goods rarely are strewn across the trunk or floor of a car." The authorization to search in this case, therefore, extended beyond the surfaces of the car's interior to the paper bag lying on the car's floor.

The facts of this case are therefore different from those in *State* v. *Wells,* 495 U.S. 1, 110 S.Ct. 1632, 109 L.Ed.2d 1 (1990), * * * [w]here the Supreme Court of Florida held that consent to search the trunk of a car did not include authorization to pry open a locked briefcase found inside the trunk. It is very likely unreasonable to think that a suspect, by consenting to the search of his trunk, has agreed to the breaking open of a locked briefcase within the trunk, but it is otherwise with respect to a closed paper bag.

Respondents argue, and the Florida trial court agreed, that if the police wish to search closed containers within a car they must separately request permission to search each container. But we see no basis for adding this sort of superstructure to the Fourth Amendment's basic test of objective reasonableness. A suspect may of course delimit as he chooses the scope of the search to which he consents. But if his consent would reasonably be understood to extend to a particular container, the Fourth Amendment provides no grounds for requiring a more explicit authorization. "The community has a real interest in encouraging consent, for the resulting search may yield necessary evidence for the solution and prosecution of crime, evidence that may insure that a wholly innocent person is not wrongly charged with a criminal offense."

* * *

Justice Marshall, with whom Justice Stevens joins, dissenting.

The question in this case is whether an individual's general consent to a search of the interior of his car for narcotics should reasonably be understood as consent to a search of closed containers inside the car. Nothing in today's opinion dispels my belief that the two are not one and the same from the consenting individual's standpoint. Consequently, an individual's consent to a search of the interior of his car should not be understood to authorize a search of closed containers inside the car. I dissent.

In my view, analysis of this question must start by identifying the differing expectations of privacy that attach to cars and closed containers. It is well established that an individual has but a limited expectation of privacy in the interior of his car. A car ordinarily is not used as a residence or repository for one's personal effects, and its passengers and contents are generally exposed to public view. Moreover, cars "are subjected to pervasive and continuing governmental regulation and controls," and may be seized by the police when necessary to protect public safety or to facilitate the flow of traffic.

In contrast, it is equally well established that an individual has a heightened expectation of privacy in the contents of a closed container. Luggage, handbags, paper bags, and other containers are common repositories for one's papers and effects, and the protection of these items from state intrusion lies at the heart of the Fourth Amendment. By placing his possessions inside a container, an individual manifests an intent that his possessions be "preserved as private," and thus kept "free from public examination."

The distinct privacy expectations that a person has in a car as opposed to a closed container do not merge when the individual uses his car to transport the container. In this situation, the individual still retains a heightened expectation of privacy in the container. Nor does an individual's heightened expectation of privacy turn on the type of container in which he stores his possessions. Notwithstanding the majority's suggestion to the contrary, this Court has soundly rejected any distinction between "worthy" containers, like locked briefcases, and "unworthy" containers, like paper bags.

Because an individual's expectation of privacy in a container is distinct from, and far greater than, his expectation of privacy in the interior of his car, it follows that an individual's consent to a search of the interior of his car cannot necessarily be understood as extending to containers in the car. At the very least, general consent to search the car is ambiguous with respect to containers found inside the car. In my view, the independent and divisible nature of the privacy interests in cars and containers mandates that a police officer who wishes to search a suspicious container found during a consensual automobile search obtain additional consent to search the container. If the driver intended to authorize search of the container, he will say so; if not, then he will say no. The only objection that the police could have to such a rule is that it would prevent them from exploiting the ignorance of a citizen who simply did not anticipate that his consent to search the car would be understood to authorize the police to rummage through his packages.

According to the majority, it nonetheless is reasonable for a police officer to construe generalized consent to search an automobile for narcotics as extending to closed containers, because "[a] reasonable person may be expected to know that narcotics are generally carried in some form of a container." This is an interesting contention. By the same logic a person who consents to a search of the car from the driver's seat could also be deemed to consent to a search of his person or indeed of his body cavities, since a reasonable person may be expected to know that drug couriers frequently store their contraband on their persons or in their body cavities. * * *

The majority also argues that the police should not be required to secure specific consent to search a closed container, because " 'the community has a real interest in encouraging consent.' " * * * Apparently, the majority's real concern is that if the police were required to ask for additional consent to search a closed container found during the consensual search of an automobile, an individual who did not mean to authorize such additional searching would have an opportunity to say no. In essence, then, the majority is claiming that "the community has a real interest" not in encouraging citizens to *consent* to investigatory efforts of their law enforcement agents, but rather in encouraging individuals to be *duped* by them. This is not the community that the Fourth Amendment contemplates.

* * *

3. "Plain View" Searches and Seizures

ARIZONA v. HICKS

Supreme Court of the United States, 1987.
480 U.S. 321, 107 S.Ct. 1149, 94 L.Ed.2d 347.

JUSTICE SCALIA delivered the opinion of the Court.

In *Coolidge v. New Hampshire,* 403 U.S. 443, 91 S.Ct. 2022, 29 L.Ed.2d 564 (1971), we said that in certain circumstances a warrantless seizure by police of an item that comes within plain view during their lawful search of a private area may be reasonable under the Fourth Amendment. We granted certiorari in the present case to decide whether this "plain view" doctrine may be invoked when the police have less than probable cause to believe that the item in question is evidence of a crime or is contraband.

I

On April 18, 1984, a bullet was fired through the floor of respondent's apartment, striking and injuring a man in the apartment below. Police officers arrived and entered respondent's apartment to search for the shooter, for other victims, and for weapons. They found and seized three weapons, including a sawed-off rifle, and in the course of their search also discovered a stocking-cap mask.

One of the policemen, Officer Nelson, noticed two sets of expensive stereo components, which seemed out of place in the squalid and otherwise ill-appointed four-room apartment. Suspecting that they were stolen, he read and recorded their serial numbers—moving some of the components, including a Bang and Olufsen turntable, in order to do so— which he then reported by phone to his headquarters. On being advised that the turntable had been taken in an armed robbery, he seized it immediately. It was later determined that some of the other serial numbers matched those on other stereo equipment taken in the same armed robbery, and a warrant was obtained and executed to seize that equipment as well. Respondent was subsequently indicted for the robbery. [The trial court granted his suppression motion, and the state appellate courts affirmed this ruling.]

II

As an initial matter, the State argues that Officer Nelson's actions constituted neither a "search" nor a "seizure" within the meaning of the Fourth Amendment. We agree that the mere recording of the serial numbers did not constitute a seizure. To be sure, that was the first step in a process by which respondent was eventually deprived of the stereo equipment. In and of itself, however, it did not "meaningfully interfere" with respondent's possessory interest in either the serial numbers or the equipment, and therefore did not amount to a seizure.

Officer Nelson's moving of the equipment, however, did constitute a "search" separate and apart from the search for the shooter, victims, and weapons that was the lawful objective of his entry into the apartment. Merely inspecting those parts of the turntable that came into view during the latter search would not have constituted an independent search, because it would have produced no additional invasion of respondent's privacy interest. But taking action, unrelated to the objectives of the authorized intrusion, which exposed to view concealed portions of the apartment or its contents, did produce a new invasion of respondent's privacy unjustified by the exigent circumstance that validated the entry. This is why * * * the "distinction between 'looking' at a suspicious object in plain view and 'moving' it even a few inches" is much more than trivial for purposes of the Fourth Amendment. It matters not that the search uncovered nothing of any great personal value to respondent—serial numbers rather than (what might conceivably have been hidden behind or under the equipment) letters or photographs. A search is a search, even if it happens to disclose nothing but the bottom of a turntable.

III

The remaining question is whether the search was "reasonable" under the Fourth Amendment. On this aspect of the case we reject, at the outset, the apparent position of the Arizona Court of Appeals that because the officers' action directed to the stereo equipment was unrelated to the justification for their entry into respondent's apartment, it was *ipso facto* unreasonable. That lack of relationship *always* exists with regard to action validated under the "plain view" doctrine; where action is taken for the purpose justifying the entry, invocation of the doctrine is superfluous. * * *

We turn, then, to application of the doctrine to the facts of this case. "It is well established that under certain circumstances the police may *seize* evidence in plain view without a warrant." Those circumstances include situations "[where] the initial intrusion that brings the police within plain view of such [evidence] is supported ... by one of the recognized exceptions to the warrant requirement," such as the exigent-circumstances intrusion here. It would be absurd to say that an object could lawfully be seized and taken from the premises, but could not be moved for closer examination. It is clear, therefore, that the search here was valid if the "plain view" doctrine would have sustained a seizure of the equipment.

There is no doubt it would have done so if Officer Nelson had probable cause to believe that the equipment was stolen. The State has conceded, however, that he had only a "reasonable suspicion," by which it means something less than probable cause. We have not ruled on the question whether probable cause is required in order to invoke the "plain view" doctrine. * * *

We now hold that probable cause is required. To say otherwise would be to cut the "plain view" doctrine loose from its theoretical and practical moorings. The theory of that doctrine consists of extending to nonpublic places such as the home, where searches and seizures without a warrant are presumptively unreasonable, the police's longstanding authority to make warrantless seizures in public places of such objects as weapons and contraband. And the practical justification for that extension is the desirability of sparing police, whose viewing of the object in the course of a lawful search is as legitimate as it would have been in a public place, the inconvenience and the risk—to themselves or to preservation of the evidence—of going to obtain a warrant. Dispensing with the need for a warrant is worlds apart from permitting a lesser standard of *cause* for the seizure than a warrant would require, *i.e.*, the standard of probable cause. No reason is apparent why an object should routinely be seizable on lesser grounds, during an unrelated search and seizure, than would have been needed to obtain a warrant for that same object if it had been known to be on the premises.

We do not say, of course, that a seizure can never be justified on less than probable cause. We have held that it can—where, for example, the seizure is minimally intrusive and operational necessities render it the only practicable means of detecting certain types of crime. No special operational necessities are relied on here, however—but rather the mere fact that the items in question came lawfully within the officer's plain view. That alone cannot supplant the requirement of probable cause.

The same considerations preclude us from holding that, even though probable cause would have been necessary for a *seizure*, the *search* of objects in plain view that occurred here could be sustained on lesser grounds. A dwelling-place search, no less than a dwelling-place seizure, requires probable cause, and there is no reason in theory or practicality why application of the "plain view" doctrine would supplant that requirement. Although the interest protected by the Fourth Amendment injunction against unreasonable searches is quite different from that protected by its injunction against unreasonable seizures, neither the one nor the other is of inferior worth or necessarily requires only lesser protection. We have not elsewhere drawn a categorical distinction between the two insofar as concerns the degree of justification needed to establish the reasonableness of police action, and we see no reason for a distinction in the particular circumstances before us here. Indeed, to treat searches more liberally would especially erode the plurality's warning in *Coolidge* that "the 'plain view' doctrine may not be used to extend a general exploratory search from one object to another until something incriminating at last emerges." In short, whether legal authority to move the equipment could be found only as an inevitable concomitant of the authority to seize it, or also as a consequence of some independent power to search certain objects in plain view, probable cause to believe the equipment was stolen was required.

Justice O'Connor's dissent suggests that we uphold the action here on the ground that it was a "cursory inspection" rather than a "full-blown search," and could therefore be justified by reasonable suspicion instead of probable cause. As already noted, a truly cursory inspection— one that involves merely looking at what is already exposed to view, without disturbing it—is not a "search" for Fourth Amendment purposes, and therefore does not even require reasonable suspicion. We are unwilling to send police and judges into a new thicket of Fourth Amendment law, to seek a creature of uncertain description that is neither a "plain view" inspection nor yet a "full-blown search." * * *

Justice Powell's dissent reasonably asks what it is we would have had Officer Nelson do in these circumstances. The answer depends, of course, upon whether he had probable cause to conduct a search, a question that was not preserved in this case. If he had, then he should have done precisely what he did. If not, then he should have followed up his suspicions, if possible, by means other than a search—just as he would have had to do if, while walking along the street, he had noticed the same suspicious stereo equipment sitting inside a house a few feet away from him, beneath an open window. It may well be that, in such circumstances, no effective means short of a search exist. But there is nothing new in the realization that the Constitution sometimes insulates the criminality of a few in order to protect the privacy of us all. Our disagreement with the dissenters pertains to where the proper balance should be struck; we choose to adhere to the textual and traditional standard of probable cause.

* * *

[JUSTICE WHITE's concurring opinion is omitted.]

JUSTICE POWELL, with whom THE CHIEF JUSTICE and JUSTICE O'CONNOR join, dissenting.

I join JUSTICE O'CONNOR's dissenting opinion, and write briefly to highlight what seem to me the unfortunate consequences of the Court's decision.

Today the Court holds for the first time that the requirement of probable cause operates as a separate limitation on the application of the plain-view doctrine. The plurality opinion in *Coolidge v. New Hampshire* required only that it be "immediately apparent to the police that they have evidence before them; the 'plain view' doctrine may not be used to extend a general exploratory search from one object to another until something incriminating at last emerges." There was no general exploratory search in this case, and I would not approve such a search. All the pertinent objects were in plain view and could be identified as objects frequently stolen. There was no looking into closets, opening of drawers or trunks, or other "rummaging around." * * *

The officers' suspicion that the stereo components at issue were stolen was both reasonable and based on specific, articulable facts. Indeed, the State was unwise to concede the absence of probable cause. The police lawfully entered respondent's apartment under exigent circumstances that arose when a bullet fired through the floor of the apartment struck a man in the apartment below. What they saw in the apartment hardly suggested that it was occupied by law-abiding citizens. A .25–caliber automatic pistol lay in plain view on the living room floor. During a concededly lawful search, the officers found a .45–caliber automatic, a .22–caliber, sawed-off rifle, and a stocking-cap mask. The apartment was littered with drug paraphernalia. The officers also observed two sets of expensive stereo components of a type that frequently was stolen.

It is fair to ask what Officer Nelson should have done in these circumstances. Accepting the State's concession that he lacked probable cause, he could not have obtained a warrant to seize the stereo components. Neither could he have remained on the premises and forcibly prevented their removal. * * * To read the serial number on a Bang and Olufsen turntable [Officer Nelson] had to "turn it around or turn it upside down." Officer Nelson noted the serial numbers on the stereo components and telephoned the National Crime Information Center to check them against the Center's computerized listing of stolen property. The computer confirmed his suspicion that at least the Bang and Olufsen turntable had been stolen. On the basis of this information, the officers obtained a warrant to seize the turntable and other stereo components that also proved to be stolen.

The Court holds that there was an unlawful search of the turntable. It agrees that the "mere recording of the serial numbers did not constitute a seizure." Thus, if the computer had identified as stolen property a component with a visible serial number, the evidence would have been admissible. But the Court further holds that "Officer Nelson's moving of the equipment ... did constitute a 'search'.... " It perceives a constitutional distinction between reading a serial number on an object and moving or picking up an identical object to see its serial number. To make its position unmistakably clear, the Court concludes that a "search is a search, even if it happens to disclose nothing but the bottom of a turntable." With all respect, this distinction between "looking" at a suspicious object in plain view and "moving" it even a few inches trivializes the Fourth Amendment. The Court's new rule will cause uncertainty, and could deter conscientious police officers from lawfully obtaining evidence necessary to convict guilty persons. Apart from the importance of rationality in the interpretation of the Fourth Amendment, today's decision may handicap law enforcement without enhancing privacy interests. Accordingly, I dissent.

JUSTICE O'CONNOR, with whom THE CHIEF JUSTICE and JUSTICE POWELL join, dissenting.

The Court today gives the right answer to the wrong question. The Court asks whether the police must have probable cause before either seizing an object in plain view or conducting a full-blown search of that object, and concludes that they must. I agree. In my view, however, this case presents a different question: whether police must have probable cause before conducting a cursory inspection of an item in plain view. Because I conclude that such an inspection is reasonable if the police are aware of facts or circumstances that justify a reasonable suspicion that the item is evidence of a crime, I would reverse the judgment of the Arizona Court of Appeals, and therefore dissent.

In *Coolidge v. New Hampshire,* Justice Stewart summarized three requirements that the plurality thought must be satisfied for a plain-view search or seizure. First, the police must lawfully make an initial intrusion or otherwise be in a position from which they can view a particular area. Second, the officer must discover incriminating evidence "inadvertently." Third, it must be "immediately apparent" to the police that the items they observe may be evidence of a crime, contraband, or otherwise subject to seizure. * * * There is no dispute in this case that the first two requirements have been satisfied. The officers were lawfully in the apartment pursuant to exigent circumstances, and the discovery of the stereo was inadvertent—the officers did not " 'know in advance the location of [certain] evidence and intend to seize it,' relying on the plain-view doctrine only as a pretext." Instead, the dispute in this case focuses on the application of the "immediately apparent" requirement; at issue is whether a police officer's reasonable suspicion is adequate to justify a cursory examination of an item in plain view.

The purpose of the "immediately apparent" requirement is to prevent "general, exploratory rummaging in a person's belongings." If an officer could indiscriminately search every item in plain view, a search justified by a limited purpose—such as exigent circumstances—could be used to eviscerate the protections of the Fourth Amendment. In order to prevent such a general search, therefore, we require that the relevance of the item be "immediately apparent." * * *

Thus, I agree with the Court that even under the plain-view doctrine, probable cause is required before the police seize an item, or conduct a full-blown search of evidence in plain view. Such a requirement of probable cause will prevent the plain-view doctrine from authorizing general searches. This is not to say, however, that even a mere inspection of a suspicious item must be supported by probable cause. When a police officer makes a cursory inspection of a suspicious item in plain view in order to determine whether it is indeed evidence of a crime, there is no "exploratory rummaging." Only those items that the police officer "reasonably suspects" as evidence of a crime may be inspected, and perhaps more importantly, the scope of such an inspection is quite limited. In short, if police officers have a reasonable, articulable suspicion that an object they come across during the course of a lawful search is evidence of crime, in my view they may make a cursory examination of the object to verify their suspicion. If the officers wish to go beyond such a cursory examination of the object, however, they must have probable cause.

* * *

HORTON v. CALIFORNIA

Supreme Court of the United States, 1990.
496 U.S. 128, 110 S.Ct. 2301, 110 L.Ed.2d 112.

Stevens, J., delivered the opinion of the Court.

In this case we revisit an issue that was considered, but not conclusively resolved, in *Coolidge v. New Hampshire,* 403 U.S. 443, 91 S.Ct. 2022, 29 L.Ed.2d 564 (1971): Whether the warrantless seizure of evidence of crime in plain view is prohibited by the Fourth Amendment if the discovery of the evidence was not inadvertent. We conclude that even though inadvertence is a characteristic of most legitimate "plain view" seizures, it is not a necessary condition.

I

Petitioner was convicted of the armed robbery of Erwin Wallaker, the treasurer of the San Jose Coin Club. When Wallaker returned to his home after the Club's annual show, he entered his garage and was accosted by two masked men, one armed with a machine gun and the other with an electrical shocking device, sometimes referred to as a "stun gun." The two men shocked Wallaker, bound and handcuffed him, and robbed him of jewelry and cash. During the encounter sufficient conversation took place to enable Wallaker subsequently to identify petitioner's distinctive voice. His identification was partially corroborated by a witness who saw the robbers leaving the scene, and by evidence that petitioner had attended the coin shows.

Sergeant LaRault, an experienced police officer, investigated the crime and determined that there was probable cause to search petitioner's home for the proceeds of the robbery and for the weapons used by the robbers. His affidavit for a search warrant referred to police reports that described the weapons as well as the proceeds, but the warrant issued by the Magistrate only authorized a search for the proceeds, including three specifically described rings.

Pursuant to the warrant, LaRault searched petitioner's residence, but he did not find the stolen property. During the course of the search, however, he discovered the weapons in plain view and seized them. Specifically, he seized an Uzi machine gun, a .38 caliber revolver, two stun guns, a handcuff key, a San Jose Coin Club advertising brochure, and a few items of clothing identified by the victim.[1] LaRault testified that while he was searching for the rings, he also was interested in finding other evidence connecting petitioner to the robbery. Thus, the seized evidence was not discovered "inadvertently."

The trial court refused to suppress the evidence found in petitioner's home and, after a jury trial, petitioner was found guilty and sentenced to prison.* * *

II

* * *

The right to security in person and property protected by the Fourth Amendment may be invaded in quite different ways by searches and seizures. A search compromises the individual interest in privacy; a seizure deprives the individual of dominion over his or her person or property. The "plain view" doctrine is often considered an exception to the general rule that warrantless searches are presumptively unreasonable, but this characterization overlooks the important difference between searches and seizures. If an article is already in plain view, neither its observation nor its seizure would involve any invasion of privacy. A seizure of the article, however, would obviously invade the owner's possessory interest. If "plain view" justifies an exception from an otherwise applicable warrant requirement, therefore, it must be an exception that is addressed to the concerns that are implicated by seizures rather than by searches.

* * *

III

Justice Stewart concluded that the inadvertence requirement was necessary to avoid a violation of the express constitutional requirement that a valid warrant must particularly describe the things to be seized. He explained:

---

1. Although the officer viewed other handguns and rifles, he did not seize them because there was no probable cause to believe they were associated with criminal activity. *Arizona v. Hicks*, 480 U.S. 321, 327, 107 S.Ct. 1149, 94 L.Ed.2d 347 (1987).

"The rationale of the exception to the warrant requirement, as just stated, is that a plain-view seizure will not turn an initially valid (and therefore limited) search into a 'general' one, while the inconvenience of procuring a warrant to cover an inadvertent discovery is great. But where the discovery is anticipated, where the police know in advance the location of the evidence and intend to seize it, the situation is altogether different. The requirement of a warrant to seize imposes no inconvenience whatever, or at least none which is constitutionally cognizable in a legal system that regards warrantless searches as 'per se unreasonable' in the absence of 'exigent circumstances.'

"If the initial intrusion is bottomed upon a warrant that fails to mention a particular object, though the police know its location and intend to seize it, then there is a violation of the express constitutional requirement of 'Warrants ... particularly describing .. [the] things to be seized.' "

We find two flaws in this reasoning. First, evenhanded law enforcement is best achieved by the application of objective standards of conduct, rather than standards that depend upon the subjective state of mind of the officer. The fact that an officer is interested in an item of evidence and fully expects to find it in the course of a search should not invalidate its seizure if the search is confined in area and duration by the terms of a warrant or a valid exception to the warrant requirement. If the officer has knowledge approaching certainty that the item will be found, we see no reason why he or she would deliberately omit a particular description of the item to be seized from the application for a search warrant. Specification of the additional item could only permit the officer to expand the scope of the search. On the other hand, if he or she has a valid warrant to search for one item and merely a suspicion concerning the second, whether or not it amounts to probable cause, we fail to see why that suspicion should immunize the second item from seizure if it is found during a lawful search for the first. * * *

Second, the suggestion that the inadvertence requirement is necessary to prevent the police from conducting general searches, or from converting specific warrants into general warrants, is not persuasive because that interest is already served by the requirements that no warrant issue unless it "particularly describes the place to be searched and the persons or things to be seized," and that a warrantless search be circumscribed by the exigencies which justify its initiation. Scrupulous adherence to these requirements serves the interests in limiting the area and duration of the search that the inadvertence requirement inadequately protects. Once those commands have been satisfied and the officer has a lawful right of access, however, no additional Fourth Amendment interest is furthered by requiring that the discovery of evidence be inadvertent. If the scope of the search exceeds that permitted by the terms of a validly issued warrant or the character of the relevant exception from the warrant requirement, the subsequent seizure is unconstitutional without more. Thus, in the case of a search incident to a lawful arrest, "if the police stray outside the scope of an authorized *Chimel* search they are already in violation of the Fourth Amendment, and evidence so seized will be excluded; adding a second reason for excluding evidence hardly seems worth the candle." * * *

In this case, the scope of the search was not enlarged in the slightest by the omission of any reference to the weapons in the warrant. Indeed, if the three rings and other items named in the warrant had been found at the outset—or petitioner had them in his possession and had responded to the warrant by producing them immediately—no search for weapons could have taken place. * * *

* * *

In this case the items seized from petitioner's home were discovered during a lawful search authorized by a valid warrant. When they were discovered, it was immediately apparent to the officer that they constituted incriminating evidence. He had probable cause, not only to obtain a warrant to search for the stolen property, but also to believe that the weapons and handguns had been used in the crime he was investigating. The search was authorized by the warrant, the seizure was authorized by the "plain view" doctrine. The judgment is affirmed.

JUSTICE BRENNAN, with whom JUSTICE MARSHALL joins, dissenting.

I remain convinced that Justice Stewart correctly articulated the plain view doctrine in *Coolidge v. New Hampshire*. The Fourth Amendment permits law enforcement officers to seize items for which they do not have a warrant when those items are found in plain view and (1) the officers are lawfully in a position to observe the items, (2) the discovery of the items is "inadvertent," and (3) it is immediately apparent to the officers that the items are evidence of a crime, contraband, or otherwise subject to seizure. In eschewing the inadvertent discovery requirement, the majority ignores the Fourth Amendment's express command that warrants particularly describe not only the places to be searched, but also the things to be seized. I respectfully dissent from this rewriting of the Fourth Amendment.

I

* * * The [Fourth] Amendment protects two distinct interests. The prohibition against unreasonable searches and the requirement that a warrant "particularly describe the place to be searched" protect an interest in privacy. The prohibition against unreasonable seizures and the requirement that a warrant "particularly describe ... the ... things to be seized" protect a possessory interest in property.[1] The Fourth Amendment, by its terms, declares the privacy and possessory interests to be equally important. As this Court recently stated, "Although the

---

1. As the majority recognizes, the requirement that warrants particularly describe the things to be seized also protects privacy interests by preventing general searches.* * *

interest protected by the Fourth Amendment injunction against unreasonable searches is quite different from that protected by its injunction against unreasonable seizures, neither the one nor the other is of inferior worth or necessarily requires only lesser protection.''

The Amendment protects these equally important interests in precisely the same manner: by requiring a neutral and detached magistrate to evaluate, before the search or seizure, the government's showing of probable cause and its particular description of the place to be searched and the items to be seized. Accordingly, just as a warrantless search is *per se* unreasonable absent exigent circumstances, so too a seizure of personal property is *''per se* unreasonable within the meaning of the Fourth Amendment unless it is accomplished pursuant to a judicial warrant issued upon probable cause and particularly describing the items to be seized.'' * * *

The plain view doctrine is an exception to the general rule that a seizure of personal property must be authorized by a warrant. As Justice Stewart explained in Coolidge, we accept a warrantless seizure when an officer is lawfully in a location and inadvertently sees evidence of a crime because of ''the inconvenience of procuring a warrant'' to seize this newly discovered piece of evidence. But ''where the discovery is anticipated, where the police know in advance the location of the evidence and intend to seize it,'' the argument that procuring a warrant would be ''inconvenient'' loses much, if not all, of its force. Barring an exigency, there is no reason why the police officers could not have obtained a warrant to seize this evidence before entering the premises. The rationale behind the inadvertent discovery requirement is simply that we will not excuse officers from the general requirement of a warrant to seize if the officers know the location of evidence, have probable cause to seize it, intend to seize it, and yet do not bother to obtain a warrant particularly describing that evidence. To do so would violate ''the express constitutional requirement of 'Warrants ... particularly describing ... [the] things to be seized,' '' and would ''fly in the face of the basic rule that no amount of probable cause can justify a warrantless seizure.''

* * *

4. Exigent Circumstances

WARDEN, MARYLAND PENITENTIARY v. HAYDEN

Supreme Court of the United States, 1967.
387 U.S. 294, 87 S.Ct. 1642, 18 L.Ed.2d 782.

MR. JUSTICE BRENNAN delivered the opinion of the Court.

* * *

I

About 8 a. m. on March 17, 1962, an armed robber entered the business premises of the Diamond Cab Company in Baltimore, Maryland. He took some $363 and ran. Two cab drivers in the vicinity, attracted by shouts of "Holdup," followed the man to 2111 Cocoa Lane. One driver notified the company dispatcher by radio that the man was a Negro about 5'8' tall, wearing a light cap and dark jacket, and that he had entered the house on Cocoa Lane. The dispatcher relayed the information to police who were proceeding to the scene of the robbery. Within minutes, police arrived at the house in a number of patrol cars. An officer knocked and announced their presence. Mrs. Hayden answered, and the officers told her they believed that a robber had entered the house, and asked to search the house. She offered no objection.

The officers spread out through the first and second floors and the cellar in search of the robber. Hayden was found in an upstairs bedroom feigning sleep. He was arrested when the officers on the first floor and in the cellar reported that no other man was in the house. Meanwhile an officer was attracted to an adjoining bathroom by the noise of running water, and discovered a shotgun and a pistol in a flush tank; another officer who, according to the District Court, "was searching the cellar for a man or the money" found in a washing machine a jacket and trousers of the type the fleeing man was said to have worn. A clip of ammunition for the pistol and a cap were found under the mattress of Hayden's bed, and ammunition for the shotgun was found in a bureau drawer in Hayden's room. All these items of evidence were introduced against respondent at his trial.

II

We agree with the Court of Appeals that neither the entry without warrant to search for the robber, nor the search for him without warrant was invalid. Under the circumstances of this case, "the exigencies of the situation made that course imperative." The police were informed that an armed robbery had taken place, and that the suspect had entered 2111 Cocoa Lane less than five minutes before they reached it. They acted reasonably when they entered the house and began to search for a man of the description they had been given and for weapons which he had used in the robbery or might use against them. The Fourth Amendment does not require police officers to delay in the course of an investigation if to do so would gravely endanger their lives or the lives of others. Speed here was essential, and only a thorough search of the house for persons and weapons could have insured that Hayden was the only man present and that the police had control of all weapons which could be used against them or to effect an escape.

[T]he seizures occurred prior to or immediately contemporaneous with Hayden's arrest, as part of an effort to find a suspected felon, armed, within the house onto which he had run only minutes before the police arrived. The permissible scope of search must, therefore, at the least, be as broad as may reasonably be necessary to prevent the dangers that the suspect at large in the house may resist or escape.

It is argued that, while the weapons, ammunition, and cap may have been seized in the course of a search for weapons, the officer who seized the clothing was searching neither for the suspect nor for weapons when he looked into the washing machine in which he found the clothing. But even if we assume, although we do not decide, that the exigent circumstances in this case made lawful a search without warrant only for the suspect or his weapons, it cannot be said on this record that the officer who found the clothes in the washing machine was not searching for weapons. He testified that he was searching for the man or the money, but his failure to state explicitly that he was searching for weapons, in the absence of a specific question to that effect, can hardly be accorded controlling weight. He knew that the robber was armed and he did not know that some weapons had been found at the time he opened the machine.[5] In these circumstances the inference that he was in fact also looking for weapons is fully justified.

* * *

VALE v. LOUISIANA

Supreme Court of the United States, 1970.
399 U.S. 30, 90 S.Ct. 1969, 26 L.Ed.2d 409.

MR. JUSTICE STEWART delivered the opinion of the Court.

[Police officers possessing two warrants for Vale's arrest conducted a surveillance of his home. They observed what they believed was a drug sale by Vale to the driver of an automobile parked outside Vale's house. The officers believed the drugs had been stored in Vale's home. As Vale returned to his house, the officers arrested him on the front steps of the house. The officers told him they were going to search the house. According to the Louisiana Supreme Court, "[a]fter they all entered the front room, Officer Laumann made a cursory inspection of the house to ascertain if anyone else was present and within about three minutes Mrs. Vale and James Vale, mother and brother of Donald Vale, returned home carrying groceries and were informed of the arrest and impending search. The search of a rear bedroom revealed a quantity of narcotics." The Supreme Court first held that the search incident to arrest doctrine could not justify a search inside a home when the arrest occurred outside the building.]

The Louisiana Supreme Court thought the search independently supportable because it involved narcotics, which are easily removed, hidden, or destroyed. It would be unreasonable, the Louisiana court concluded, "to require the officers under the facts of the case to first secure a search warrant before searching the premises, as time is of the essence inasmuch as the officers never know whether there is anyone on

---

5. The officer was asked in the District Court whether he found the money. He answered that he did not, and stated: "By the time I had gotten down into the basement I heard someone say upstairs, 'There's a man up here.'" He was asked: "What did you do then?" and answered:

"By this time I had already discovered some clothing which fit the description of the clothing worn by the subject that we were looking for...." It is clear from the record and from the findings that the weapons were found after or at the same time the police found Hayden.

the premises to be searched who could very easily destroy the evidence." Such a rationale could not apply to the present case, since by their own account the arresting officers satisfied themselves that no one else was in the house when they first entered the premises. But entirely apart from that point, our past decisions make clear that only in "a few specifically established and well-delineated" situations, may a warrantless search of a dwelling withstand constitutional scrutiny, even though the authorities have probable cause to conduct it. The burden rests on the State to show the existence of such an exceptional situation. And the record before us discloses none.

There is no suggestion that anyone consented to the search. The officers were not responding to an emergency. They were not in hot pursuit of a fleeing felon. The goods ultimately seized were not in the process of destruction.

The officers were able to procure two warrants for Vale's arrest. They also had information that he was residing at the address where they found him. There is thus no reason, so far as anything before us appears, to suppose that it was impracticable for them to obtain a search warrant as well. We decline to hold that an arrest on the street can provide its own "exigent circumstance" so as to justify a warrantless search of the arrestee's house.

The Louisiana courts committed constitutional error in admitting into evidence the fruits of the illegal search. * * *

[The dissenting opinion by MR. JUSTICE BLACK, with whom THE CHIEF JUSTICE joined, is omitted.]

5. Searches of Automobiles and Containers

a. Searches of Automobiles

CARROLL v. UNITED STATES

Supreme Court of the United States, 1925.
267 U.S. 132, 45 S.Ct. 280, 69 L.Ed. 543.

CHIEF JUSTICE TAFT delivered the opinion of the Court.

[The National Prohibition Act, enacted to enforce the Eighteenth Amendment, criminalized possession of "any liquor intended for use in violating the Act," and provided "that no property rights shall exist in such liquor." The act authorized issuance of search warrantless seizures of "intoxicating liquors in any wagon, buggy, automobile, water or air craft, or other vehicle," and authorized law enforcers to "take possession of the vehicle and team or automobile, boat, air or water craft, or any other conveyance, and shall arrest any person in charge thereof." CHIEF JUSTICE TAFT quoted from the report of a legislative committee.]

In its report the Committee spoke in part as follows:

* * *

* * * "It is impossible to get a warrant to stop an automobile. Before a warrant could be secured the automobile would be beyond the reach of the officer with its load of illegal liquor disposed of."

[T]he guaranty of freedom from unreasonable searches and seizures by the Fourth Amendment has been construed, practically since the beginning of the Government, as recognizing a necessary difference between a search of a store, dwelling house or other structure in respect of which a proper official warrant readily may be obtained, and a search of a ship, motor boat, wagon or automobile, for contraband goods, where it is not practicable to secure a warrant because the vehicle can be quickly moved out of the locality or jurisdiction in which the warrant must be sought.

Having thus established that contraband goods concealed and illegally transported in an automobile or other vehicle may be searched for without a warrant, we come now to consider under what circumstances such search may be made. It would be intolerable and unreasonable if a prohibition agent were authorized to stop every automobile on the chance of finding liquor and thus subject all persons lawfully using the highways to the inconvenience and indignity of such a search. Travellers may be so stopped in crossing an international boundary because of national self protection reasonably requiring one entering the country to identify himself as entitled to come in, and his belongings as effects which may be lawfully brought in. But those lawfully within the country, entitled to use the public highways, have a right to free passage without interruption or search unless there is known to a competent official authorized to search, probable cause for believing that their vehicles are carrying contraband or illegal merchandise. * * *

* * *

Such a rule fulfills the guaranty of the Fourth Amendment. In cases where the securing of a warrant is reasonably practicable, it must be used, and when properly supported by affidavit and issued after judicial approval protects the seizing officer against a suit for damages. In cases where seizure is impossible except without warrant, the seizing officer acts unlawfully and at his peril unless he can show the court probable cause.

* * *

Finally, was there probable cause? * * *

We know in this way that Grand Rapids is about 152 miles from Detroit and that Detroit and its neighborhood along the Detroit River, which is the International Boundary, is one of the most active centers for introducing illegally into this country spirituous liquors for distribution into the interior. It is obvious from the evidence that the prohibition agents were engaged in a regular patrol along the important highways from Detroit to Grand Rapids to stop and seize liquor carried in automobiles. They knew or had convincing evidence to make them believe that the Carroll boys, as they called them, were so-called "bootleggers" in Grand Rapids, i.e., that they were engaged in plying the unlawful trade of selling such liquor in that city. The officers had soon after noted their going from Grand Rapids half way to Detroit and attempted to follow them to that city to see where they went, but they escaped observation. Two months later these officers suddenly met the same men on their way westward presumably from Detroit. The partners in the original combination to sell liquor in Grand Rapids were together in the same automobile they had been in the night when they tried to furnish the whisky to the officers which was thus identified as part of the firm equipment. They were coming from the direction of the great source of supply for their stock to Grand Rapids where they plied their trade. That the officers when they saw the defendants believed that they were carrying liquor we can have no doubt, and we think it is equally clear that they had reasonable cause for thinking so. Emphasis is put by defendants' counsel on the statement made by one of the officers that they were not looking for defendants at the particular time when they appeared. We do not perceive that it has any weight. As soon as they did appear, the officers were entitled to use their reasoning faculties upon all the facts of which they had previous knowledge in respect to the defendants.

The necessity for probable cause in justifying seizures on land or sea, in making arrests without warrant for past felonies, and in malicious prosecution and false imprisonment cases has led to frequent definition of the phrase. [T]his Court defined probable cause as follows:

> "If the facts and circumstances before the officer are such as to warrant a man of prudence and caution in believing that the offense has been committed, it is sufficient." * * *

* * *

In the light of these authorities, and what is shown by this record, it is clear the officers here had justification for the search and seizure. This is to say that the facts and circumstances within their knowledge and of which they had reasonably trustworthy information were sufficient in themselves to warrant a man of reasonable caution in the belief that intoxicating liquor was being transported in the automobile which they stopped and searched.

* * *

[The dissenting opinion of JUSTICE MCREYNOLDS, in which JUSTICE SUTHERLAND joined, is omitted.]

CHAMBERS v. MARONEY
Supreme Court of the United States, 1970.
399 U.S. 42, 90 S.Ct. 1975, 26 L.Ed.2d 419.

JUSTICE WHITE delivered the opinion of the Court.

* * *

I

During the night of May 20, 1963, a Gulf service station in North Braddock, Pennsylvania, was robbed by two men, each of whom carried and displayed a gun. The robbers took the currency from the cash register; the service station attendant, one Stephen Kovacich, was directed to place the coins in his right-hand glove, which was then taken by the robbers. Two teen-agers, who had earlier noticed a blue compact station wagon circling the block in the vicinity of the Gulf station, then saw the station wagon speed away from a parking lot close to the Gulf station. About the same time, they learned that the Gulf station had been robbed. They reported to police, who arrived immediately, that four men were in the station wagon and one was wearing a green sweater. Kovacich told the police that one of the men who robbed him was wearing a green sweater and the other was wearing a trench coat. A description of the car and the two robbers was broadcast over the police radio. Within an hour, a light blue compact station wagon answering the description and carrying four men was stopped by the police about two miles from the Gulf station. Petitioner was one of the men in the station wagon. He was wearing a green sweater and there was a trench coat in the car. The occupants were arrested and the car was driven to the police station. In the course of a thorough search of the car at the station, the police found concealed in a compartment under the dashboard two .38–caliber revolvers (one loaded with dumdum bullets), a right-hand glove containing small change, and certain cards bearing the name of Raymond Havicon, the attendant at a Boron service station in McKeesport, Pennsylvania, who had been robbed at gunpoint on May 13, 1963. In the course of a warrant-authorized search of petitioner's home the day after petitioner's arrest, police found and seized certain .38–caliber ammunition, including some dumdum bullets similar to those found in one of the guns taken from the station wagon.

* * *

II

[T]he search that produced the incriminating evidence was made at the police station some time after the arrest and cannot be justified as a search incident to an arrest: "Once an accused is under arrest and in custody, then a search made at another place, without a warrant, is simply not incident to the arrest." [T]he reasons that have been thought sufficient to justify warrantless searches carried out in connection with an arrest no longer obtain when the accused is safely in custody at the station house.

[T]he police had probable cause to believe that the robbers, carrying guns and the fruits of the crime, had fled the scene in a light blue compact station wagon which would be carrying four men, one wearing a green sweater and another wearing a trench coat. As the state courts correctly held, there was probable cause to arrest the occupants of the station wagon that the officers stopped; just as obviously was there probable cause to search the car for guns and stolen money.

In terms of the circumstances justifying a warrantless search, the Court has long distinguished between an automobile and a home or office. In *Carroll v. United States,* 267 U.S. 132, 45 S.Ct. 280, 69 L.Ed.543 (1925), the issue was the admissibility in evidence of contraband liquor seized in a warrantless search of a car on the highway. [T]he Court held that automobiles and other conveyances may be searched without a warrant in circumstances that would not justify the search without a warrant of a house or an office, provided that there is probable cause to believe that the car contains articles that the officers are entitled to seize. * * *

* * *

[T]he circumstances that furnish probable cause to search a particular auto for particular articles are most often unforeseeable; moreover, the opportunity to search is fleeting since a car is readily movable. Where this is true, as in *Carroll* and the case before us now, if an effective search is to be made at any time, either the search must be made immediately without a warrant or the car itself must be seized and held without a warrant for whatever period is necessary to obtain a warrant for the search.

In enforcing the Fourth Amendment's prohibition against unreasonable searches and seizures, the Court has insisted upon probable cause as a minimum requirement for a reasonable search permitted by the Constitution. As a general rule, it has also required the judgment of a magistrate on the probable-cause issue and the issuance of a warrant before a search is made. Only in exigent circumstances will the judgment of the police as to probable cause serve as a sufficient authorization for a search. *Carroll,* holds a search warrant unnecessary where there is probable cause to search an automobile stopped on the highway; the car is movable, the occupants are alerted, and the car's contents may never be found again if a warrant must be obtained. Hence an immediate search is constitutionally permissible.

Arguably, because of the preference for a magistrate's judgment, only the immobilization of the car should be permitted until a search warrant is obtained; arguably, only the "lesser" intrusion is permissible until the magistrate authorizes the "greater." But which is the "greater" and which the "lesser" intrusion is itself a debatable question and the answer may depend on a variety of circumstances. For constitutional purposes, we see no difference between on the one hand seizing and holding a car before presenting the probable cause issue to a magistrate and on the other hand carrying out an immediate search without a warrant. Given probable cause to search, either course is reasonable under the Fourth Amendment.

On the facts before us, the blue station wagon could have been searched on the spot when it was stopped since there was probable cause to search and it was a fleeting target for a search. The probable-cause factor still obtained at the station house and so did the mobility of the car unless the Fourth Amendment permits a warrantless seizure of the car and the denial of its use to anyone until a warrant is secured. In that event there is little to choose in terms of practical consequences between an immediate search without a warrant and the car's immobilization until a warrant is obtained.[10] The same consequences may not follow where there is unforeseeable cause to search a house. Compare *Vale* v. *Louisiana, ante,* p. 30. But as *Carroll, supra,* held, for the purposes of the Fourth Amendment there is a constitutional difference between houses and cars.

* * *

[JUSTICE STEWART's concurring opinion is omitted.]

MR. JUSTICE HARLAN, concurring in part and dissenting in part.

* * *

II

In sustaining the search of the automobile I believe the Court ignores the framework of our past decisions circumscribing the scope of permissible search without a warrant. The Court has long read the Fourth Amendment's proscription of "unreasonable" searches as imposing a general principle that a search without a warrant is not justified by the mere knowledge by the searching officers of facts showing probable cause. The "general requirement that a search warrant be obtained" is basic to the Amendment's protection of privacy, and " 'the burden is on those seeking [an] exemption . . . to show the need for it.' "

Fidelity to this established principle requires that, where exceptions are made to accommodate the exigencies of particular situations, those exceptions be no broader than necessitated by the circumstances presented. For example, the Court has recognized that an arrest creates an emergency situation justifying a warrantless search of the arrestee's person and of "the area from within which he might gain possession of a weapon or destructible evidence"; however, because the exigency giving rise to this exception extends only that far, the search may go no further. * * *

Where officers have probable cause to search a vehicle on a public way, a further limited exception to the warrant requirement is reasonable because "the vehicle can be quickly moved out of the locality or jurisdiction in which the warrant must be sought." *Carroll v. United States.* Because the officers might be deprived of valuable evidence if required to obtain a warrant before effecting any search or seizure, I

---

10. It was not unreasonable in this case to take the car to the station house. All occupants in the car were arrested in a dark parking lot in the middle of the night. A careful search at that point was impractical and perhaps not safe for the officers, and it would serve the owner's convenience and the safety of his car to have the vehicle and the keys together at the station house.

agree with the Court that they should be permitted to take the steps necessary to preserve evidence and to make a search possible. The Court holds that those steps include making a warrantless search of the entire vehicle on the highway—a conclusion reached by the Court in *Carroll* without discussion—and indeed appears to go further and to condone the removal of the car to the police station for a warrantless search there at the convenience of the police. I cannot agree that this result is consistent with our insistence in other areas that departures from the warrant requirement strictly conform to the exigency presented.

The Court concedes that the police could prevent removal of the evidence by temporarily seizing the car for the time necessary to obtain a warrant. It does not dispute that such a course would fully protect the interests of effective law enforcement; rather it states that whether temporary seizure is a "lesser" intrusion than warrantless search "is itself a debatable question and the answer may depend on a variety of circumstances." I believe it clear that a warrantless search involves the greater sacrifice of Fourth Amendment values.

The Fourth Amendment proscribes, to be sure, unreasonable "seizures" as well as "searches." However, in the circumstances in which this problem is likely to occur, the lesser intrusion will almost always be the simple seizure of the car for the period—perhaps a day—necessary to enable the officers to obtain a search warrant. In the first place, as this case shows, the very facts establishing probable cause to search will often also justify arrest of the occupants of the vehicle. Since the occupants themselves are to be taken into custody, they will suffer minimal further inconvenience from the temporary immobilization of their vehicle. Even where no arrests are made, persons who wish to avoid a search—either to protect their privacy or to conceal incriminating evidence—will almost certainly prefer a brief loss of the use of the vehicle in exchange for the opportunity to have a magistrate pass upon the justification for the search. To be sure, one can conceive of instances in which the occupant, having nothing to hide and lacking concern for the privacy of the automobile, would be more deeply offended by a temporary immobilization of his vehicle than by a prompt search of it. However, such a person always remains free to consent to an immediate search, thus avoiding any delay. Where consent is not forthcoming, the occupants of the car have an interest in privacy that is protected by the Fourth Amendment even where the circumstances justify a temporary seizure. The Court's endorsement of a warrantless invasion of that privacy where another course would suffice is simply inconsistent with our repeated stress on the Fourth Amendment's mandate of " 'adherence to judicial processes.' "

* * *

CALIFORNIA v. CARNEY

Supreme Court of the United States, 1985.
471 U.S. 386, 105 S.Ct. 2066, 85 L.Ed.2d 406.

CHIEF JUSTICE BURGER delivered the opinion of the Court.

We granted certiorari to decide whether law enforcement agents violated the Fourth Amendment when they conducted a warrantless search, based on probable cause, of a fully mobile "motor home" located in a public place.

I

On May 31, 1979, Drug Enforcement Agency Agent Robert Williams watched respondent, Charles Carney, approach a youth in downtown San Diego. The youth accompanied Carney to a Dodge Mini Motor Home parked in a nearby lot. Carney and the youth closed the window shades in the motor home, including one across the front window. Agent Williams had previously received uncorroborated information that the same motor home was used by another person who was exchanging marihuana for sex. Williams, with assistance from other agents, kept the motor home under surveillance for the entire one and one-quarter hours that Carney and the youth remained inside. When the youth left the motor home, the agents followed and stopped him. The youth told the agents that he had received marihuana in return for allowing Carney sexual contacts.

At the agents' request, the youth returned to the motor home and knocked on its door; Carney stepped out. The agents identified themselves as law enforcement officers. Without a warrant or consent, one agent entered the motor home and observed marihuana, plastic bags, and a scale of the kind used in weighing drugs on a table. Agent Williams took Carney into custody and took possession of the motor home. A subsequent search of the motor home at the police station revealed additional marihuana in the cupboards and refrigerator.

* * *

II

The Fourth Amendment protects the "right of the people to be secure in their persons, houses, papers, and effects, against unreasonable searches and seizures." This fundamental right is preserved by a requirement that searches be conducted pursuant to a warrant issued by an independent judicial officer. There are, of course, exceptions to the general rule that a warrant must be secured before a search is undertaken; one is the so-called "automobile exception" at issue in this case. This exception to the warrant requirement was first set forth by the Court 60 years ago in *Carroll v. United States,* 267 U.S. 132, 45 S.Ct. 280, 69 L.Ed. 543 (1925). * * *

* * *

The capacity to be "quickly moved" was clearly the basis of the holding in *Carroll*, and our cases have consistently recognized ready mobility as one of the principal bases of the automobile exception. * * *

However, although ready mobility alone was perhaps the original justification for the vehicle exception, our later cases have made clear that ready mobility is not the only basis for the exception. The reasons for the vehicle exception, we have said, are twofold. "Besides the element of mobility, less rigorous warrant requirements govern because the expectation of privacy with respect to one's automobile is significantly less than that relating to one's home or office."

Even in cases where an automobile was not immediately mobile, the lesser expectation of privacy resulting from its use as a readily mobile vehicle justified application of the vehicular exception. In some cases, the configuration of the vehicle contributed to the lower expectations of privacy; for example, * * * because the passenger compartment of a standard automobile is relatively open to plain view, there are lesser expectations of privacy. But even when enclosed "repository" areas have been involved, we have concluded that the lesser expectations of privacy warrant application of the exception. We have applied the exception in the context of a locked car trunk, a sealed package in a car trunk, a closed compartment under the dashboard, the interior of a vehicle's upholstery, or sealed packages inside a covered pickup truck.

These reduced expectations of privacy derive not from the fact that the area to be searched is in plain view, but from the pervasive regulation of vehicles capable of traveling on the public highways. As we explained in *South Dakota* v. *Opperman*, 428 U.S. 364, 96 S.Ct. 3092, 49 L.Ed.2d 1000 (1976), an inventory search case:

> "Automobiles, unlike homes, are subjected to pervasive and continuing governmental regulation and controls, including periodic inspection and licensing requirements. As an everyday occurrence, police stop and examine vehicles when license plates or inspection stickers have expired, or if other violations, such as exhaust fumes or excessive noise, are noted, or if headlights or other safety equipment are not in proper working order."

The public is fully aware that it is accorded less privacy in its automobiles because of this compelling governmental need for regulation. Historically, "individuals always [have] been on notice that movable vessels may be stopped and searched on facts giving rise to probable cause that the vehicle contains contraband, without the protection afforded by a magistrate's prior evaluation of those facts." In short, the pervasive schemes of regulation, which necessarily lead to reduced expectations of privacy, and the exigencies attendant to ready mobility justify searches without prior recourse to the authority of a magistrate so long as the overriding standard of probable cause is met.

When a vehicle is being used on the highways, or if it is readily capable of such use and is found stationary in a place not regularly used for residential purposes—temporary or otherwise—the two justifications for the vehicle exception come into play. First, the vehicle is obviously readily mobile by the turn of an ignition key, if not actually moving. Second, there is a reduced expectation of privacy stemming from its use as a licensed motor vehicle subject to a range of police regulation inapplicable to a fixed dwelling. At least in these circumstances, the overriding societal interests in effective law enforcement justify an immediate search before the vehicle and its occupants become unavailable.

While it is true that respondent's vehicle possessed some, if not many of the attributes of a home, it is equally clear that the vehicle falls clearly within the scope of the exception laid down in *Carroll* and applied in succeeding cases. Like the automobile in *Carroll*, respondent's motor home was readily mobile. Absent the prompt search and seizure, it could readily have been moved beyond the reach of the police. Furthermore, the vehicle was licensed to "operate on public streets; [was] serviced in public places; ... and [was] subject to extensive regulation and inspection." And the vehicle was so situated that an objective observer would conclude that it was being used not as a residence, but as a vehicle.

Respondent urges us to distinguish his vehicle from other vehicles within the exception because it was *capable of functioning as a home.* In our increasingly mobile society, many vehicles used for transportation can be and are being used not only for transportation but for shelter, *i. e.*, as a "home" or "residence." To distinguish between respondent's motor home and an ordinary sedan for purposes of the vehicle exception would require that we apply the exception depending upon the size of the vehicle and the quality of its appointments. Moreover, to fail to apply the exception to vehicles such as a motor home ignores the fact that a motor home lends itself easily to use as an instrument of illicit drug traffic and other illegal activity. * * *

Our application of the vehicle exception has never turned on the other uses to which a vehicle might be put. The exception has historically turned on the ready mobility of the vehicle, and on the presence of the vehicle in a setting that objectively indicates that the vehicle is being used for transportation.[3] These two requirements for application of the exception ensure that law enforcement officials are not unnecessarily hamstrung in their efforts to detect and prosecute criminal activity, and that the legitimate privacy interests of the public are protected. Applying the vehicle exception in these circumstances allows the essential purposes served by the exception to be fulfilled, while assuring that the exception will acknowledge legitimate privacy interests.

3. We need not pass on the application of the vehicle exception to a motor home that is situated in a way or place that objectively indicates that it is being used as a residence. Among the factors that might be relevant in determining whether a warrant would be required in such a circumstance is its location, whether the vehicle is readily mobile or instead, for instance, elevated on blocks, whether the vehicle is licensed, whether it is connected to utilities, and whether it has convenient access to a public road.

III

* * *

This search was not unreasonable; it was plainly one that the magistrate could authorize if presented with these facts. The DEA agents had fresh, direct, uncontradicted evidence that the respondent was distributing a controlled substance from the vehicle, apart from evidence of other possible offenses. The agents thus had abundant probable cause to enter and search the vehicle for evidence of a crime notwithstanding its possible use as a dwelling place.

* * *

JUSTICE STEVENS, with whom JUSTICE BRENNAN and JUSTICE MARSHALL join, dissenting.

The character of "the place to be searched" plays an important role in Fourth Amendment analysis. In this case, police officers searched a Dodge/Midas Mini Motor Home. The California Supreme Court correctly characterized this vehicle as a "hybrid" which combines "the mobility attribute of an automobile ... with most of the privacy characteristics of a house."

The hybrid character of the motor home places it at the crossroads between the privacy interests that generally forbid warrantless invasions of the home, and the law enforcement interests that support the exception for warrantless searches of automobiles based on probable cause. By choosing to follow the latter route, the Court errs * * *.

* * *

II

* * *

If the motor home were parked in the exact middle of the intersection between the general rule and the exception for automobiles, priority should be given to the rule rather than the exception.

III

The motor home, however, was not parked in the middle of that intersection. Our prior cases teach us that inherent mobility is not a sufficient justification for the fashioning of an exception to the warrant requirement, especially in the face of heightened expectations of privacy in the location searched. Motor homes, by their common use and construction, afford their owners a substantial and legitimate expectation of privacy when they dwell within. When a motor home is parked in a location that is removed from the public highway, I believe that society is prepared to recognize that the expectations of privacy within it are not unlike the expectations one has in a fixed dwelling. As a general rule, such places may only be searched with a warrant based upon probable cause. Warrantless searches of motor homes are only reasonable when the motor home is traveling on the public streets or highways, or when exigent circumstances otherwise require an immediate search without the expenditure of time necessary to obtain a warrant.

* * *

In this case, the motor home was parked in an off-the-street lot only a few blocks from the courthouse in downtown San Diego where dozens of magistrates were available to entertain a warrant application. The officers clearly had the element of surprise with them, and with curtains covering the windshield, the motor home offered no indication of any imminent departure. The officers plainly had probable cause to arrest the respondent and search the motor home, and on this record, it is inexplicable why they eschewed the safe harbor of a warrant.

* * *

Unlike a brick bungalow or a frame Victorian, a motor home seldom serves as a permanent lifetime abode. The motor home in this case, however, was designed to accommodate a breadth of ordinary everyday living. Photographs in the record indicate that its height, length, and beam provided substantial living space inside: stuffed chairs surround a table; cupboards provide room for storage of personal effects; bunk beds provide sleeping space; and a refrigerator provides ample space for food and beverages. Moreover, curtains and large opaque walls inhibit viewing the activities inside from the exterior of the vehicle. The interior configuration of the motor home establishes that the vehicle's size, shape, and mode of construction should have indicated to the officers that it was a vehicle containing mobile living quarters.

* * *

b.   Searches of Containers in Automobiles

UNITED STATES v. ROSS

Supreme Court of the United States, 1982.
456 U.S. 798, 102 S.Ct. 2157, 72 L.Ed.2d 572.

JUSTICE STEVENS delivered the opinion of the Court.

* * * In this case, we consider the extent to which police officers—who have legitimately stopped an automobile and who have probable cause to believe that contraband is concealed somewhere within it—may conduct a probing search of compartments and containers within the vehicle whose contents are not in plain view. We hold that they may conduct a search of the vehicle that is as thorough as a magistrate could authorize in a warrant "particularly describing the place to be searched."

I

In the evening of November 27, 1978, an informant who had previously proved to be reliable telephoned Detective Marcum of the

District of Columbia Police Department and told him that an individual known as "Bandit" was selling narcotics kept in the trunk of a car parked at 439 Ridge Street. The informant stated that he had just observed "Bandit" complete a sale and that "Bandit" had told him that additional narcotics were in the trunk. The informant gave Marcum a detailed description of "Bandit" and stated that the car was a "purplish maroon" Chevrolet Malibu with District of Columbia license plates.

Accompanied by Detective Cassidy and Sergeant Gonzales, Marcum immediately drove to the area and found a maroon Malibu parked in front of 439 Ridge Street. A license check disclosed that the car was registered to Albert Ross; a computer check on Ross revealed that he fit the informant's description and used the alias "Bandit." In two passes through the neighborhood the officers did not observe anyone matching the informant's description. To avoid alerting persons on the street, they left the area.

[When the officers returned, they saw the maroon Malibu departing and that the driver matched the description of Ross. They stopped the car and searched the interior of the vehicle, where they found a handgun and a bullet. The officers arrested Ross and searched the vehicle's trunk. They searched a brown paper bag located in the trunk, and found several glassine bags containing a white powder that the police laboratory later identified as heroin. At the station they searched the automobile thoroughly, and in the trunk found a zippered leather pouch containing $3,200 in cash. The officers did not obtain a warrant.]

II

* * *

[T]he probable-cause determination must be based on objective facts that could justify the issuance of a warrant by a magistrate and not merely on the subjective good faith of the police officers. " '[As] we have seen, good faith is not enough to constitute probable cause. That faith must be grounded on facts within knowledge of the [officer], which in the judgment of the court would make his faith reasonable.' "

[T]he exception to the warrant requirement established in *Carroll*— the scope of which we consider in this case—applies only to searches of vehicles that are supported by probable cause. In this class of cases, a search is not unreasonable if based on facts that would justify the issuance of a warrant, even though a warrant has not actually been obtained.

III

The rationale justifying a warrantless search of an automobile that is believed to be transporting contraband arguably applies with equal force to any movable container that is believed to be carrying an illicit substance. That argument, however, was squarely rejected in *United States* v. *Chadwick*, 433 U.S. 1, 97 S.Ct. 2476, 53 L.Ed.2d 538 (1977).

Chadwick involved the warrantless search of a 200–pound footlocker secured with two padlocks. Federal railroad officials in San Diego became suspicious when they noticed that a brown footlocker loaded onto a train bound for Boston was unusually heavy and leaking talcum powder, a substance often used to mask the odor of marihuana. Narcotics agents met the train in Boston and a trained police dog signaled the presence of a controlled substance inside the footlocker. The agents did not seize the footlocker, however, at this time; they waited until respondent Chadwick arrived and the footlocker was placed in the trunk of Chadwick's automobile. Before the engine was started, the officers arrested Chadwick and his two companions. The agents then removed the footlocker to a secured place, opened it without a warrant, and discovered a large quantity of marihuana.

In a subsequent criminal proceeding, Chadwick claimed that the warrantless search of the footlocker violated the Fourth Amendment. [T]he Government argued that as soon as the footlocker was placed in the automobile a warrantless search was permissible under *Carroll* [and also contended] that the warrant requirement of the Fourth Amendment applied only to searches of homes and other "core" areas of privacy. The Court unanimously rejected that contention. Writing for the Court, THE CHIEF JUSTICE stated:

> "[If] there is little evidence that the Framers intended the Warrant Clause to operate outside the home, there is no evidence at all that they intended to exclude from protection of the Clause all searches occurring outside the home. The absence of a contemporary outcry against warrantless searches in public places was because, aside from searches incident to arrest, such warrantless searches were not a large issue in colonial America. Thus, silence in the historical record tells us little about the Framers' attitude toward application of the Warrant Clause to the search of respondents' footlocker. What we do know is that the Framers were men who focused on the wrongs of that day but who intended the Fourth Amendment to safeguard fundamental values which would far outlast the specific abuses which gave it birth."

* * *

The facts in *Arkansas* v. *Sanders*, 442 U.S. 753, 99 S.Ct. 2586, 61 L.Ed.2d 235 (1979), were similar to those in *Chadwick*. In *Sanders*, a Little Rock police officer received information from a reliable informant that Sanders would arrive at the local airport on a specified flight that afternoon carrying a green suitcase containing marihuana. The officer went to the airport. Sanders arrived on schedule and retrieved a green suitcase from the airline baggage service. Sanders gave the suitcase to a waiting companion, who placed it in the trunk of a taxi. Sanders and his companion drove off in the cab; police officers followed and stopped the taxi several blocks from the airport. The officers opened the trunk, seized the suitcase, and searched it on the scene without a warrant. As predicted, the suitcase contained marihuana.

* * * As in *Chadwick*, the mere fact that the suitcase had been placed in the trunk of the vehicle did not render the automobile exception of *Carroll* applicable; the police had probable cause to seize the suitcase before it was placed in the trunk of the cab and did not have probable cause to search the taxi itself. Since the suitcase had been placed in the trunk, no danger existed that its contents could have been secreted elsewhere in the vehicle. As THE CHIEF JUSTICE noted in his opinion concurring in the judgment:

> "Because the police officers had probable cause to believe that respondent's green suitcase contained marihuana before it was placed in the trunk of the taxicab, their duty to obtain a search warrant before opening it is clear under *United States* v. *Chadwick*....

> "... Here, as in *Chadwick*, it was the *luggage* being transported by respondent at the time of the arrest, not the automobile in which it was being carried, that was the suspected locus of the contraband. The relationship between the automobile and the contraband was purely coincidental, as in *Chadwick*. The fact that the suitcase was resting in the trunk of the automobile at the time of respondent's arrest does not turn this into an 'automobile' exception case. The Court need say no more."

* * *

Robbins v. California, 453 U.S. 420, 101 S.Ct. 2841, 69 L.Ed.2d 744 (1981), however, was a case in which suspicion was not directed at a specific container. In that case the Court for the first time was forced to consider whether police officers who are entitled to conduct a warrantless search of an automobile stopped on a public roadway may open a container found within the vehicle. In the early morning of January 5, 1975, police officers stopped Robbins' station wagon because he was driving erratically. Robbins got out of the car, but later returned to obtain the vehicle's registration papers. When he opened the car door, the officers smelled marihuana smoke. One of the officers searched Robbins and discovered a vial of liquid; in a search of the interior of the car the officer found marihuana. The police officers then opened the tailgate of the station wagon and raised the cover of a recessed luggage compartment. In the compartment they found two packages wrapped in green opaque plastic. The police unwrapped the packages and discovered a large amount of marihuana in each.

* * *

This Court * * * rejected the argument that the outward appearance of the packages precluded Robbins from having a reasonable expectation of privacy in their contents [and] the argument that there is a constitutional distinction between searches of luggage and searches of "less worthy" containers. JUSTICE STEWART reasoned that all containers are equally protected by the Fourth Amendment unless their contents are in plain view. The plurality concluded that the warrantless search was impermissible because *Chadwick* and *Sanders* had established that "a closed piece of luggage found in a lawfully searched car is constitutionally protected to the same extent as are closed pieces of luggage found anywhere else."

* * *

* * * Unlike *Chadwick* and *Sanders*, in this case police officers had probable cause to search respondent's entire vehicle. Unlike *Robbins*, in this case the parties have squarely addressed the question whether, in the course of a legitimate warrantless search of an automobile, police are entitled to open containers found within the vehicle. We now address that question. Its answer is determined by the scope of the search that is authorized by the exception to the warrant requirement set forth in *Carroll*.

IV

* * *

A lawful search of fixed premises generally extends to the entire area in which the object of the search may be found and is not limited by the possibility that separate acts of entry or opening may be required to complete the search. Thus, a warrant that authorizes an officer to search a home for illegal weapons also provides authority to open closets, chests, drawers, and containers in which the weapon might be found. A warrant to open a footlocker to search for marihuana would also authorize the opening of packages found inside. A warrant to search a vehicle would support a search of every part of the vehicle that might contain the object of the search. When a legitimate search is under way, and when its purpose and its limits have been precisely defined, nice distinctions between closets, drawers, and containers, in the case of a home, or between glove compartments, upholstered seats, trunks, and wrapped packages, in the case of a vehicle, must give way to the interest in the prompt and efficient completion of the task at hand.

This rule applies equally to all containers, as indeed we believe it must. One point on which the Court was in virtually unanimous agreement in *Robbins* was that a constitutional distinction between "worthy" and "unworthy" containers would be improper. Even though such a distinction perhaps could evolve in a series of cases in which paper bags, locked trunks, lunch buckets, and orange crates were placed on one side of the line or the other, the central purpose of the Fourth Amendment forecloses such a distinction. For just as the most frail cottage in the kingdom is absolutely entitled to the same guarantees of privacy as the most majestic mansion, so also may a traveler who carries a toothbrush and a few articles of clothing in a paper bag or knotted scarf claim an equal right to conceal his possessions from official inspection as the sophisticated executive with the locked attache case.

[T]he Fourth Amendment provides protection to the owner of every container that conceals its contents from plain view. But the protection afforded by the Amendment varies in different settings. The luggage carried by a traveler entering the country may be searched at random by a customs officer; the luggage may be searched no matter how great the traveler's desire to conceal the contents may be. A container carried at the time of arrest often may be searched without a warrant and even without any specific suspicion concerning its contents. A container that may conceal the object of a search authorized by a warrant may be opened immediately; the individual's interest in privacy must give way to the magistrate's official determination of probable cause.

In the same manner, an individual's expectation of privacy in a vehicle and its contents may not survive if probable cause is given to believe that the vehicle is transporting contraband. Certainly the privacy interests in a car's trunk or glove compartment may be no less than those in a movable container. An individual undoubtedly has a significant interest that the upholstery of his automobile will not be ripped or a hidden compartment within it opened. These interests must yield to the authority of a search, however, which—in light of *Carroll*—does not itself require the prior approval of a magistrate. The scope of a warrantless search based on probable cause is no narrower—and no broader— than the scope of a search authorized by a warrant supported by probable cause. Only the prior approval of the magistrate is waived; the search otherwise is as the magistrate could authorize.

The scope of a warrantless search of an automobile thus is not defined by the nature of the container in which the contraband is secreted. Rather, it is defined by the object of the search and the places in which there is probable cause to believe that it may be found. Just as probable cause to believe that a stolen lawnmower may be found in a garage will not support a warrant to search an upstairs bedroom, probable cause to believe that undocumented aliens are being transported in a van will not justify a warrantless search of a suitcase. Probable cause to believe that a container placed in the trunk of a taxi contains contraband or evidence does not justify a search of the entire cab.

V

* * *

* * * We hold that the scope of the warrantless search authorized by [the automobile] exception is no broader and no narrower than a magistrate could legitimately authorize by warrant. If probable cause justifies the search of a lawfully stopped vehicle, it justifies the search of every part of the vehicle and its contents that may conceal the object of the search.

* * *

[The concurring opinions of JUSTICE BLACKMAN and JUSTICE POWELL and the dissenting opinion of Justice White are omitted.]

JUSTICE MARSHALL, with whom JUSTICE BRENNAN joins, dissenting.

The majority today not only repeals all realistic limits on warrant-less automobile searches, it repeals the Fourth Amendment warrant requirement itself. By equating a police officer's estimation of probable cause with a magistrate's, the Court utterly disregards the value of a neutral and detached magistrate. For as we recently, and unanimously, reaffirmed:

> "The warrant traditionally has represented an independent assurance that a search and arrest will not proceed without probable cause to believe that a crime has been committed and that the person or place named in the warrant is involved in the crime. Thus, an issuing magistrate must meet two tests. He must be neutral and detached, and he must be capable of determining whether probable cause exists for the requested arrest or search. This Court long has insisted that inferences of probable cause be drawn by 'a neutral and detached magistrate instead of being judged by the officer engaged in the often competitive enterprise of ferreting out crime.' "

A police officer on the beat hardly satisfies these standards. In adopting today's new rule, the majority opinion shows contempt for these Fourth Amendment values, ignores this Court's precedents, is internally inconsistent, and produces anomalous and unjust consequences. I therefore dissent.

I

According to the majority, whenever police have probable cause to believe that contraband may be found within an automobile that they have stopped on the highway, they may search not only the automobile but also any container found inside it, without obtaining a warrant. The scope of the search, we are told, is as broad as a magistrate could authorize in a warrant to search the automobile. The majority makes little attempt to justify this rule in terms of recognized Fourth Amendment values. The Court simply ignores the critical function that a magistrate serves. And although the Court purports to rely on the mobility of an automobile and the impracticability of obtaining a warrant, it never explains why these concerns permit the warrantless search of a *container*, which can easily be seized and immobilized while police are obtaining a warrant.

* * *

A

* * *

The requirement of prior review by a detached and neutral magistrate limits the concentration of power held by executive officers over the individual, and prevents some overbroad or unjustified searches from occurring at all. Prior review may also "prevent hindsight from coloring the evaluation of the reasonableness of a search or seizure." Furthermore, even if a magistrate would have authorized the search that the

police conducted, the interposition of a magistrate's neutral judgment reassures the public that the orderly process of law has been respected
* * *

* * *

B

* * *

The majority's sleight-of-hand ignores the obvious differences between the function served by a magistrate in making a determination of probable cause and the function of the automobile exception. It is irrelevant to a magistrate's function whether the items subject to search are mobile, may be in danger of destruction, or are impractical to store, or whether an immediate search would be less intrusive than a seizure without a warrant. A magistrate's only concern is whether there is probable cause to search them. Where suspicion has focused not on a particular item but only on a vehicle, home, or office, the magistrate might reasonably authorize a search of closed containers at the location as well. But an officer on the beat who searches an automobile without a warrant is not entitled to conduct a broader search than the exigency obviating the warrant justifies. After all, what justifies the warrantless search is not probable cause alone, but *probable cause coupled with the mobility of the automobile*. Because the scope of a *warrantless* search should depend on the scope of the justification for dispensing with a warrant, the entire premise of the majority's opinion fails to support its conclusion.

The majority's rule masks the startling assumption that a policeman's determination of probable cause is the functional equivalent of the determination of a neutral and detached magistrate. This assumption ignores a major premise of the warrant requirement—the importance of having a neutral and detached magistrate determine whether probable cause exists. The majority's explanation that the scope of the warrantless automobile search will be "limited" to what a magistrate could authorize is thus inconsistent with our cases, which firmly establish that an on-the-spot determination of probable cause is *never* the same as a decision by a neutral and detached magistrate.

* * *

III

* * *

The only convincing explanation I discern for the majority's broad rule is expediency: it assists police in conducting automobile searches, ensuring that the private containers into which criminal suspects often place goods will no longer be a Fourth Amendment shield. "When a legitimate search is under way," the Court instructs us, "nice distinctions between ... glove compartments, upholstered seats, trunks, and wrapped packages ... must give way to the interest in the prompt and efficient completion of the task at hand." No "nice distinctions" are necessary, however, to comprehend the well-recognized differences between movable containers (which, even after today's decision, would be subject to the warrant requirement if located outside an automobile), and the automobile itself, together with its integral parts. Nor can I pass by the majority's glib assertion that the "prompt and efficient completion of the task at hand" is paramount to the Fourth Amendment interests of our citizens. I had thought it well established that "the mere fact that law enforcement may be made more efficient can never by itself justify disregard of the Fourth Amendment."

This case will have profound implications for the privacy of citizens traveling in automobiles, as the Court well understands. "For countless vehicles are stopped on highways and public streets every day and our cases demonstrate that it is not uncommon for police officers to have probable cause to believe that contraband may be found in a stopped vehicle." A closed paper bag, a toolbox, a knapsack, a suitcase, and an attache case can alike be searched without the protection of the judgment of a neutral magistrate, based only on the rarely disturbed decision of a police officer that he has probable cause to search for contraband in the vehicle. The Court derives satisfaction from the fact that its rule does not exalt the rights of the wealthy over the rights of the poor. A rule so broad that all citizens lose vital Fourth Amendment protection is no cause for celebration.

CALIFORNIA v. ACEVEDO

Supreme Court of the United States, 1991.
500 U.S. 565, 111 S.Ct. 1982, 114 L.Ed.2d 619.

JUSTICE BLACKMUN delivered the opinion of the Court.

This case requires us once again to consider the so-called "automobile exception" to the warrant requirement of the Fourth Amendment and its application to the search of a closed container in the trunk of a car.

I

On October 28, 1987, Officer Coleman of the Santa Ana, Cal., Police Department received a telephone call from a federal drug enforcement agent in Hawaii. The agent informed Coleman that he had seized a package containing marijuana which was to have been delivered to the Federal Express Office in Santa Ana and which was addressed to J. R. Daza at 805 West Stevens Avenue in that city. The agent arranged to send the package to Coleman instead. Coleman then was to take the package to the Federal Express office and arrest the person who arrived to claim it.

Coleman received the package on October 29, verified its contents, and took it to the Senior Operations Manager at the Federal Express office. At about 10:30 a.m. on October 30, a man, who identified himself as Jamie Daza, arrived to claim the package. He accepted it and drove to his apartment on West Stevens. He carried the package into the apartment.

At 11:45 a.m., officers observed Daza leave the apartment and drop the box and paper that had contained the marijuana into a trash bin. Coleman at that point left the scene to get a search warrant. About 12:05 p.m., the officers saw Richard St. George leave the apartment carrying a blue knapsack which appeared to be half full. The officers stopped him as he was driving off, searched the knapsack, and found 1 1/2 pounds of marijuana.

At 12:30 p.m., respondent Charles Steven Acevedo arrived. He entered Daza's apartment, stayed for about 10 minutes, and reappeared carrying a brown paper bag that looked full. The officers noticed that the bag was the size of one of the wrapped marijuana packages sent from Hawaii. Acevedo walked to a silver Honda in the parking lot. He placed the bag in the trunk of the car and started to drive away. Fearing the loss of evidence, officers in a marked police car stopped him. They opened the trunk and the bag, and found marijuana.

* * *

II

* * *

In *United States v. Ross,* 456 U.S. 798, 102 S.Ct. 2157, 72 L.Ed.2d 572, [the Court determined that] "if probable cause justifies the search of a lawfully stopped vehicle, it justifies the search of every part of the vehicle and its contents that may conceal the object of the search." In *Ross,* therefore, we clarified the scope of the *Carroll* doctrine as properly including a "probing search" of compartments and containers within the automobile so long as the search is supported by probable cause.

In addition to this clarification, *Ross* distinguished the *Carroll* doctrine from the separate rule that governed the search of closed containers. The Court had announced this separate rule, unique to luggage and other closed packages, bags, and containers, in *United States v. Chadwick,* 433 U.S. 1, 97 S.Ct. 2476, 53 L.Ed.2d 538 (1977). [The Court reviewed the facts and holdings of *Chadwick* and *Arkansas v. Sanders,* 442 U.S. 753, 99 S.Ct. 2586, 61 L.Ed.2d 235 (1979), which are discussed in *Ross, supra.*]

In *Ross,* the Court endeavored to distinguish between *Carroll,* which governed the *Ross* automobile search, and *Chadwick,* which governed the *Sanders* automobile search. It held that the *Carroll* doctrine covered searches of automobiles when the police had probable cause to search an entire vehicle, but that the *Chadwick* doctrine governed searches of luggage when the officers had probable cause to search only a container within the vehicle. Thus, in a *Ross* situation, the police could conduct a reasonable search under the Fourth Amendment without obtaining a warrant, whereas in a *Sanders* situation, the police had to obtain a warrant before they searched.

* * *

III

* * *

This Court in *Ross* rejected *Chadwick*'s distinction between containers and cars. It concluded that the expectation of privacy in one's vehicle is equal to one's expectation of privacy in the container, and noted that "the privacy interests in a car's trunk or glove compartment may be no less than those in a movable container." It also recognized that it was arguable that the same exigent circumstances that permit a warrantless search of an automobile would justify the warrantless search of a movable container. In deference to the rule of *Chadwick* and *Sanders*, however, the Court put that question to one side. It concluded that the time and expense of the warrant process would be misdirected if the police could search every cubic inch of an automobile until they discovered a paper sack, at which point the Fourth Amendment required them to take the sack to a magistrate for permission to look inside. We now must decide the question deferred in *Ross:* whether the Fourth Amendment requires the police to obtain a warrant to open the sack in a movable vehicle simply because they lack probable cause to search the entire car. We conclude that it does not.

IV

Dissenters in *Ross* asked why the suitcase in *Sanders* was "more private, less difficult for police to seize and store, or in any other relevant respect more properly subject to the warrant requirement, than a container that police discover in a probable-cause search of an entire automobile?" We now agree that a container found after a general search of the automobile and a container found in a car after a limited search for the container are equally easy for the police to store and for the suspect to hide or destroy. In fact, we see no principled distinction in terms of either the privacy expectation or the exigent circumstances between the paper bag found by the police in *Ross* and the paper bag found by the police here. Furthermore, by attempting to distinguish between a container for which the police are specifically searching and a container which they come across in a car, we have provided only minimal protection for privacy and have impeded effective law enforcement.

The line between probable cause to search a vehicle and probable cause to search a package in that vehicle is not always clear, and separate rules that govern the two objects to be searched may enable the police to broaden their power to make warrantless searches and disserve privacy interests. We noted this in *Ross* in the context of a search of an entire vehicle. Recognizing that under *Carroll*, the "entire vehicle itself . . . could be searched without a warrant," we concluded that "prohibiting police from opening immediately a container in which the object of the search is most likely to be found and instead forcing them first to comb the entire vehicle would actually exacerbate the intrusion on privacy interests." At the moment when officers stop an automobile, it may be less than clear whether they suspect with a high degree of certainty that the vehicle contains drugs in a bag or simply contains drugs. If the police know that they may open a bag only if they are actually searching the entire car, they may search more extensively than they otherwise would in order to establish the general probable cause required by *Ross*.

* * *

To the extent that the *Chadwick-Sanders* rule protects privacy, its protection is minimal. Law enforcement officers may seize a container and hold it until they obtain a search warrant. "Since the police, by hypothesis, have probable cause to seize the property, we can assume that a warrant will be routinely forthcoming in the overwhelming majority of cases." And the police often will be able to search containers without a warrant, despite the *Chadwick-Sanders* rule, as a search incident to a lawful arrest. * * *

Finally, the search of a paper bag intrudes far less on individual privacy than does the incursion sanctioned long ago in *Carroll*. In that case, prohibition agents slashed the upholstery of the automobile. This Court nonetheless found their search to be reasonable under the Fourth Amendment. If destroying the interior of an automobile is not unreasonable, we cannot conclude that looking inside a closed container is. In light of the minimal protection to privacy afforded by the *Chadwick-Sanders* rule, and our serious doubt whether that rule substantially serves privacy interests, we now hold that the Fourth Amendment does not compel separate treatment for an automobile search that extends only to a container within the vehicle.

V

* * *

The discrepancy between the two rules has led to confusion for law enforcement officers. For example, when an officer, who has developed probable cause to believe that a vehicle contains drugs, begins to search the vehicle and immediately discovers a closed container, which rule applies? The defendant will argue that the fact that the officer first chose to search the container indicates that his probable cause extended only to the container and that *Chadwick* and *Sanders* therefore require a warrant. On the other hand, the fact that the officer first chose to search in the most obvious location should not restrict the propriety of the search. * * * We have noted the virtue of providing " '"clear and unequivocal" guidelines to the law enforcement profession.' " The *Chad-*

wick-Sanders rule is the antithesis of a " 'clear and unequivocal' guideline."

* * *

VI

* * *

Our holding today neither extends the *Carroll* doctrine nor broadens the scope of the permissible automobile search delineated in *Carroll, Chambers,* and *Ross.* It remains a "cardinal principle that 'searches conducted outside the judicial process, without prior approval by judge or magistrate, are *per se* unreasonable under the Fourth Amendment— subject only to a few specifically established and well-delineated exceptions.' " * * *.

Until today, this Court has drawn a curious line between the search of an automobile that coincidentally turns up a container and the search of a container that coincidentally turns up in an automobile. The protections of the Fourth Amendment must not turn on such coincidences. We therefore interpret *Carroll* as providing one rule to govern all automobile searches. The police may search an automobile and the containers within it where they have probable cause to believe contraband or evidence is contained.

[Justice Scalia's concurring opinion and Justice White's dissenting opinion are omitted.]

Justice Stevens, with whom Justice Marshall joins, dissenting.

* * *

I

The Fourth Amendment is a restraint on Executive power. The Amendment constitutes the Framers' direct constitutional response to the unreasonable law enforcement practices employed by agents of the British Crown. Over the years—particularly in the period immediately after World War II and particularly in opinions authored by Justice Jackson after his service as a special prosecutor at the Nuremburg trials—the Court has recognized the importance of this restraint as a bulwark against police practices that prevail in totalitarian regimes. This history is, however, only part of the explanation for the warrant requirement. The requirement also reflects the sound policy judgment that, absent exceptional circumstances, the decision to invade the privacy of an individual's personal effects should be made by a neutral magistrate rather than an agent of the Executive. In his opinion for the Court in *Johnson* v. *United States,* 333 U.S. 10, 68 S.Ct. 367, 92 L.Ed.436 (1948) Justice Jackson explained:

"The point of the Fourth Amendment, which often is not grasped by zealous officers, is not that it denies law enforcement the support of the usual inferences which reasonable men draw from evidence. Its protection consists in requiring that those inferences be drawn by a neutral and detached magistrate instead of being judged by the officer engaged in the often competitive enterprise of ferreting out crime.''

Our decisions have always acknowledged that the warrant requirement imposes a burden on law enforcement. And our cases have not questioned that trained professionals normally make reliable assessments of the existence of probable cause to conduct a search. We have repeatedly held, however, that these factors are outweighed by the individual interest in privacy that is protected by advance judicial approval. The Fourth Amendment dictates that the privacy interest is paramount, no matter how marginal the risk of error might be if the legality of warrantless searches were judged only after the fact.

* * *

II

In its opinion today, the Court recognizes that the police did not have probable cause to search respondent's vehicle and that a search of anything but the paper bag that respondent had carried from Daza's apartment and placed in the trunk of his car would have been unconstitutional. Moreover, as I read the opinion, the Court assumes that the police could not have made a warrantless inspection of the bag before it was placed in the car. Finally, the Court also does not question the fact that, under our prior cases, it would have been lawful for the police to seize the container and detain it (and respondent) until they obtained a search warrant. Thus, all of the relevant facts that governed our decisions in *Chadwick* and *Sanders* are present here whereas the relevant fact that justified the vehicle search in *Ross* is not present.

The Court does not attempt to identify any exigent circumstances that would justify its refusal to apply the general rule against warrantless searches. Instead, it advances these three arguments: First, the rules identified in the foregoing cases are confusing and anomalous. Second, the rules do not protect any significant interest in privacy. And, third, the rules impede effective law enforcement. None of these arguments withstands scrutiny.

* * *

To the extent there was any ''anomaly'' in our prior jurisprudence, the Court has ''cured'' it at the expense of creating a more serious paradox. For surely it is anomalous to prohibit a search of a briefcase while the owner is carrying it exposed on a public street yet to permit a search once the owner has placed the briefcase in the locked trunk of his car. One's privacy interest in one's luggage can certainly not be diminished by one's removing it from a public thoroughfare and placing it— out of sight—in a privately owned vehicle. Nor is the danger that evidence will escape increased if the luggage is in a car rather than on the street. In either location, if the police have probable cause, they are authorized to seize the luggage and to detain it until they obtain judicial approval for a search. Any line demarking an exception to the warrant requirement will appear blurred at the edges, but the Court has certainly erred if it believes that, by erasing one line and drawing another, it has drawn a clearer boundary.

* * *

Under the Court's holding today, the privacy interest that protects the contents of a suitcase or a briefcase from a warrantless search when it is in public view simply vanishes when its owner climbs into a taxicab. Unquestionably the rejection of the *Sanders* line of cases by today's decision will result in a significant loss of individual privacy.

* * *

6. Seizures of Automobiles and Their Occupants

WHREN v. UNITED STATES

Supreme Court of the United States, 1996.
517 U.S. 806, 116 S.Ct. 1769, 135 L.Ed.2d 89.

JUSTICE SCALIA delivered the opinion of the Court.

In this case we decide whether the temporary detention of a motorist who the police have probable cause to believe has committed a civil traffic violation is inconsistent with the Fourth Amendment's prohibition against unreasonable seizures unless a reasonable officer would have been motivated to stop the car by desire to enforce the traffic laws.

I

On the evening of June 10, 1993, plainclothes vice-squad officers of the District of Columbia Metropolitan Police Department were patrolling a "high drug area" of the city in an unmarked car. Their suspicions were aroused when they passed a dark Pathfinder truck with temporary license plates and youthful occupants waiting at a stop sign, the driver looking down into the lap of the passenger at his right. The truck remained stopped at the intersection for what seemed an unusually long time—more than 20 seconds. When the police car executed a U-turn in order to head back toward the truck, the Pathfinder turned suddenly to its right, without signalling, and sped off at an "unreasonable" speed. The policemen followed, and in a short while overtook the Pathfinder when it stopped behind other traffic at a red light. They pulled up alongside, and Officer Ephraim Soto stepped out and approached the driver's door, identifying himself as a police officer and directing the driver, petitioner Brown, to put the vehicle in park. When Soto drew up to the driver's window, he immediately observed two large plastic bags of what appeared to be crack cocaine in petitioner Whren's hands. Petitioners were arrested, and quantities of several types of illegal drugs were retrieved from the vehicle.

* * *

II

* * * Petitioners accept that Officer Soto had probable cause to believe that various provisions of the District of Columbia traffic code had been violated. They argue, however, that "in the unique context of civil traffic regulations" probable cause is not enough. Since, they contend, the use of automobiles is so heavily and minutely regulated that total compliance with traffic and safety rules is nearly impossible, a police officer will almost invariably be able to catch any given motorist in a technical violation. This creates the temptation to use traffic stops as a means of investigating other law violations, as to which no probable cause or even articulable suspicion exists. Petitioners, who are both black, further contend that police officers might decide which motorists to stop based on decidedly impermissible factors, such as the race of the car's occupants. To avoid this danger, they say, the Fourth Amendment test for traffic stops should be, not the normal one (applied by the Court of Appeals) of whether probable cause existed to justify the stop; but rather, whether a police officer, acting reasonably, would have made the stop for the reason given.

A

[The Court discussed earlier cases which it interpreted as rejecting the argument that a search or seizure could be invalidated because it was pretextual, that is motivated by some purpose other than the asserted law enforcement rationale.]

We think these cases foreclose any argument that the constitutional reasonableness of traffic stops depends on the actual motivations of the individual officers involved. We of course agree with petitioners that the Constitution prohibits selective enforcement of the law based on considerations such as race. But the constitutional basis for objecting to intentionally discriminatory application of laws is the Equal Protection Clause, not the Fourth Amendment. Subjective intentions play no role in ordinary, probable-cause Fourth Amendment analysis.

B

Recognizing that we have been unwilling to entertain Fourth Amendment challenges based on the actual motivations of individual officers, petitioners disavow any intention to make the individual officer's subjective good faith the touchstone of "reasonableness." They insist that the standard they have put forward—whether the officer's conduct deviated materially from usual police practices, so that a reasonable officer in the same circumstances would not have made the stop for the reasons given-is an "objective" one.

But although framed in empirical terms, this approach is plainly and indisputably driven by subjective considerations. Its whole purpose is to prevent the police from doing under the guise of enforcing the traffic code what they would like to do for different reasons. Petitioners' proposed standard may not use the word "pretext," but it is designed to combat nothing other than the perceived "danger" of the pretextual stop, albeit only indirectly and over the run of cases. Instead of asking whether the individual officer had the proper state of mind, the petitioners would have us ask, in effect, whether (based on general police practices) it is plausible to believe that the officer had the proper state of mind.

[T]he Fourth Amendment's concern with "reasonableness" allows certain actions to be taken in certain circumstances, whatever the subjective intent. [I]t seems to us somewhat easier to figure out the intent of an individual officer than to plumb the collective consciousness of law enforcement in order to determine whether a "reasonable officer" would have been moved to act upon the traffic violation. While police manuals and standard procedures may sometimes provide objective assistance, ordinarily one would be reduced to speculating about the hypothetical reaction of a hypothetical constable—an exercise that might be called virtual subjectivity.

Moreover, police enforcement practices, even if they could be practicably assessed by a judge, vary from place to place and from time to time. We cannot accept that the search and seizure protections of the Fourth Amendment are so variable, and can be made to turn upon such trivialities. The difficulty is illustrated by petitioners' arguments in this case. Their claim that a reasonable officer would not have made this stop is based largely on District of Columbia police regulations which permit plainclothes officers in unmarked vehicles to enforce traffic laws "only in the case of a violation that is so grave as to pose an immediate threat to the safety of others." This basis of invalidation would not apply in jurisdictions that had a different practice. And it would not have applied even in the District of Columbia, if Officer Soto had been wearing a uniform or patrolling in a marked police cruiser.

* * *

III

* * *

Where probable cause has existed, the only cases in which we have found it necessary actually to perform the "balancing" analysis involved searches or seizures conducted in an extraordinary manner, unusually harmful to an individual's privacy or even physical interests—such as, for example, seizure by means of deadly force, unannounced entry into a home, entry into a home without a warrant, or physical penetration of the body. The making of a traffic stop out-of-uniform does not remotely qualify as such an extreme practice, and so is governed by the usual rule that probable cause to believe the law has been broken "outbalances" private interest in avoiding police contact.

Petitioners urge as an extraordinary factor in this case that the "multitude of applicable traffic and equipment regulations" is so large and so difficult to obey perfectly that virtually everyone is guilty of violation, permitting the police to single out almost whomever they wish for a stop. But we are aware of no principle that would allow us to decide at what point a code of law becomes so expansive and so commonly violated that infraction itself can no longer be the ordinary measure of the lawfulness of enforcement. And even if we could identify such exorbitant codes, we do not know by what standard (or what right) we would decide, as petitioners would have us do, which particular provisions are sufficiently important to merit enforcement.

For the run-of-the-mine case, which this surely is, we think there is no realistic alternative to the traditional common-law rule that probable cause justifies a search and seizure.

* * *

Commentary

Police officers in some departments routinely ask drivers stopped for traffic offenses for consent to search their vehicles for drugs or weapons. The Supreme Court has held that the officer is not required to advise the motorist that he or she is free to leave before requesting consent to search the automobile. *Ohio v. Robinette*, 519 U.S. 33 (1996). When an officer makes a lawful traffic stop, he or she may routinely order both the driver and any passengers to exit the vehicle—and presumably, to frisk them for weapons. See *Pennsylvania v. Mimms*, 434 U.S. 106 (1977); *Maryland v. Wilson*, 519 U.S. 408 (1997). In *Wilson* the Supreme Court observed in a footnote: "Respondent argues that, because we have generally eschewed bright-line rules in the Fourth Amendment context, see, e.g., *Ohio v. Robinette*, 519 U.S. 33, we should not here conclude that passengers may constitutionally be ordered out of lawfully stopped vehicles. But, that we typically avoid per se rules concerning searches and seizures does not mean that we have always done so; *Mimms* itself drew a bright line, and we believe the principles that underlay that decision apply to passengers as well." The Supreme Court has adopted other bright line rules permitting officers to seize motor vehicles. In *Whren*, the Court approved traffic stops as long as the officer observed a violation of the traffic laws. In the following case, the Court extended this notion to authorize warrantless custodial arrests for even minor violations of the traffic laws.

ATWATER v. CITY OF LAGO VISTA

Supreme Court of the United States, 2001.
532 U.S. 318, 121 S.Ct. 1536, 149 L.Ed.2d 549.

JUSTICE SOUTER delivered the opinion of the Court.

The question is whether the Fourth Amendment forbids a warrantless arrest for a minor criminal offense, such as a misdemeanor seatbelt violation punishable only by a fine. We hold that it does not.

I

A

In Texas, if a car is equipped with safety belts, a front-seat passenger must wear one, and the driver must secure any small child riding in front. Violation of either provision is "a misdemeanor punishable by a fine not less than $25 or more than $50." Texas law expressly authorizes "[a]ny peace officer [to] arrest without warrant a person found committing a violation" of these seatbelt laws, although it permits police to issue citations in lieu of arrest.

In March 1997, Petitioner Gail Atwater was driving her pickup truck in Lago Vista, Texas, with her 3–year-old son and 5–year-old daughter in the front seat. None of them was wearing a seatbelt. Respondent Bart Turek, a Lago Vista police officer at the time, observed the seatbelt violations and pulled Atwater over. According to Atwater's complaint (the allegations of which we assume to be true for present purposes), Turek approached the truck and "yell[ed]" something to the effect of "[w]e've met before" and "[y]ou're going to jail."[1] He then called for backup and asked to see Atwater's driver's license and insurance documentation, which state law required her to carry. When Atwater told Turek that she did not have the papers because her purse had been stolen the day before, Turek said that he had "heard that story two-hundred times."

Atwater asked to take her "frightened, upset, and crying" children to a friend's house nearby, but Turek told her, "[y]ou're not going anywhere." As it turned out, Atwater's friend learned what was going on and soon arrived to take charge of the children. Turek then handcuffed Atwater, placed her in his squad car, and drove her to the local police station, where booking officers had her remove her shoes, jewelry, and eyeglasses, and empty her pockets. Officers took Atwater's "mug shot" and placed her, alone, in a jail cell for about one hour, after which she was taken before a magistrate and released on $310 bond.

Atwater was charged with driving without her seatbelt fastened, failing to secure her children in seatbelts, driving without a license, and failing to provide proof of insurance. She ultimately pleaded no contest to the misdemeanor seatbelt offenses and paid a $50 fine; the other charges were dismissed.

B

Atwater and her husband, petitioner Michael Haas, filed suit * * * under 42 U.S.C. § 1983 against Turek and respondents City of Lago Vista and Chief of Police Frank Miller * * * [alleging] that respondents

---

1. Turek had previously stopped Atwater for what he had thought was a seatbelt violation, but had realized that Atwater's son, although seated on the vehicle's armrest, was in fact belted in. Atwater acknowledged that her son's seating position was unsafe, and Turek issued a verbal warning.

had violated Atwater's Fourth Amendment "right to be free from unreasonable seizure," and sought compensatory and punitive damages.

* * *

We granted certiorari to consider whether the Fourth Amendment, either by incorporating common-law restrictions on misdemeanor arrests or otherwise, limits police officers' authority to arrest without warrant for minor criminal offenses. * * *

* * *

III

While it is true here that history, if not unequivocal, has expressed a decided, majority view that the police need not obtain an arrest warrant merely because a misdemeanor stopped short of violence or a threat of it, Atwater does not wager all on history. Instead, she asks us to mint a new rule of constitutional law on the understanding that when historical practice fails to speak conclusively to a claim grounded on the Fourth Amendment, courts are left to strike a current balance between individual and societal interests by subjecting particular contemporary circumstances to traditional standards of reasonableness. Atwater accordingly argues for a modern arrest rule, one not necessarily requiring violent breach of the peace, but nonetheless forbidding custodial arrest, even upon probable cause, when conviction could not ultimately carry any jail time and when the government shows no compelling need for immediate detention.

If we were to derive a rule exclusively to address the uncontested facts of this case, Atwater might well prevail. She was a known and established resident of Lago Vista with no place to hide and no incentive to flee, and common sense says she would almost certainly have buckled up as a condition of driving off with a citation. In her case, the physical incidents of arrest were merely gratuitous humiliations imposed by a police officer who was (at best) exercising extremely poor judgment. Atwater's claim to live free of pointless indignity and confinement clearly outweighs anything the City can raise against it specific to her case.

But we have traditionally recognized that a responsible Fourth Amendment balance is not well served by standards requiring sensitive, case-by-case determinations of government need, lest every discretionary judgment in the field be converted into an occasion for constitutional review. Often enough, the Fourth Amendment has to be applied on the spur (and in the heat) of the moment, and the object in implementing its command of reasonableness is to draw standards sufficiently clear and simple to be applied with a fair prospect of surviving judicial second-guessing months and years after an arrest or search is made. Courts attempting to strike a reasonable Fourth Amendment balance thus credit the government's side with an essential interest in readily administrable rules.

At first glance, Atwater's argument may seem to respect the values of clarity and simplicity, so far as she claims that the Fourth Amendment generally forbids warrantless arrests for minor crimes not accompanied by violence or some demonstrable threat of it (whether "minor crime" be defined as a fine-only traffic offense, a fine-only offense more generally, or a misdemeanor). But the claim is not ultimately so simple, nor could it be, for complications arise the moment we begin to think about the possible applications of the several criteria Atwater proposes for drawing a line between minor crimes with limited arrest authority and others not so restricted.

One line, she suggests, might be between "jailable" and "fine-only" offenses, between those for which conviction could result in commitment and those for which it could not. The trouble with this distinction, of course, is that an officer on the street might not be able to tell. It is not merely that we cannot expect every police officer to know the details of frequently complex penalty schemes, but that penalties for ostensibly identical conduct can vary on account of facts difficult (if not impossible) to know at the scene of an arrest. Is this the first offense or is the suspect a repeat offender? Is the weight of the marijuana a gram above or a gram below the fine-only line? Where conduct could implicate more than one criminal prohibition, which one will the district attorney ultimately decide to charge? And so on.

* * *

One may ask, of course, why these difficulties may not be answered by a simple tie breaker for the police to follow in the field: if in doubt, do not arrest. The first answer is that in practice the tie breaker would boil down to something akin to a least-restrictive-alternative limitation, which is itself one of those "ifs, ands, and buts" rules, generally thought inappropriate in working out Fourth Amendment protection. Beyond that, whatever help the tie breaker might give would come at the price of a systematic disincentive to arrest in situations where even Atwater concedes that arresting would serve an important societal interest. An officer not quite sure that the drugs weighed enough to warrant jail time or not quite certain about a suspect's risk of flight would not arrest, even though it could perfectly well turn out that, in fact, the offense called for incarceration and the defendant was long gone on the day of trial. Multiplied many times over, the costs to society of such underenforcement could easily outweigh the costs to defendants of being needlessly arrested and booked, as Atwater herself acknowledges.

* * *

The upshot of all these influences, combined with the good sense (and, failing that, the political accountability) of most local lawmakers and law-enforcement officials, is a dearth of horribles demanding redress. Indeed, when Atwater's counsel was asked at oral argument for any indications of comparably foolish, warrantless misdemeanor arrests, he could offer only one. We are sure that there are others, but just as surely the country is not confronting anything like an epidemic of unnecessary minor-offense arrests. That fact caps the reasons for rejecting Atwater's request for the development of a new and distinct body of constitutional law.

Accordingly, we confirm today what our prior cases have intimated: the standard of probable cause "applies to all arrests, without the need to 'balance' the interests and circumstances involved in particular situations." If an officer has probable cause to believe that an individual has committed even a very minor criminal offense in his presence, he may, without violating the Fourth Amendment, arrest the offender.

IV

Atwater's arrest satisfied constitutional requirements. There is no dispute that Officer Turek had probable cause to believe that Atwater had committed a crime in his presence. * * * Turek was accordingly authorized (not required, but authorized) to make a custodial arrest without balancing costs and benefits or determining whether or not Atwater's arrest was in some sense necessary.

Nor was the arrest made in an "extraordinary manner, unusually harmful to [her] privacy or ... physical interests." * * * [T]he question whether a search or seizure is "extraordinary" turns, above all else, on the manner in which the search or seizure is executed. Atwater's arrest was surely "humiliating," as she says in her brief, but it was no more "harmful to ... privacy or ... physical interests" than the normal custodial arrest. She was handcuffed, placed in a squad car, and taken to the local police station, where officers asked her to remove her shoes, jewelry, and glasses, and to empty her pockets. They then took her photograph and placed her in a cell, alone, for about an hour, after which she was taken before a magistrate, and released on $310 bond. The arrest and booking were inconvenient and embarrassing to Atwater, but not so extraordinary as to violate the Fourth Amendment.

The Court of Appeals's en banc judgment is affirmed. It is so ordered.

JUSTICE O'CONNOR, with whom JUSTICE STEVENS, JUSTICE GINSBURG, and JUSTICE BREYER join, dissenting.

* * *

I

A full custodial arrest, such as the one to which Ms. Atwater was subjected, is the quintessential seizure. When a full custodial arrest is effected without a warrant, the plain language of the Fourth Amendment requires that the arrest be reasonable. It is beyond cavil that "the touchstone of our analysis under the Fourth Amendment is always 'the reasonableness in all the circumstances of the particular governmental invasion of a citizen's personal security.' "

* * *

Our decision in *Whren* v. *United States*, 517 U.S. 806, 116 S.Ct. 1769, 135 L.Ed.2d 89 (1996), is not to the contrary. The specific question presented there was whether, in evaluating the Fourth Amendment reasonableness of a traffic stop, the subjective intent of the police officer is a relevant consideration. We held that it is not, and stated that "[t]he making of a traffic stop . . . is governed by the usual rule that probable cause to believe the law has been broken 'outbalances' private interest in avoiding police contact."

We of course did not have occasion in *Whren* to consider the constitutional preconditions for warrantless arrests for fine-only offenses. Nor should our words be taken beyond their context. There are significant qualitative differences between a traffic stop and a full custodial arrest. While both are seizures that fall within the ambit of the Fourth Amendment, the latter entails a much greater intrusion on an individual's liberty and privacy interests. * * * Thus, when there is probable cause to believe that a person has violated a minor traffic law, there can be little question that the state interest in law enforcement will justify the relatively limited intrusion of a traffic stop. It is by no means certain, however, that where the offense is punishable only by fine, "probable cause to believe the law has been broken [will] 'outbalanc[e]' private interest in avoiding" a full custodial arrest. Justifying a full arrest by the same quantum of evidence that justifies a traffic stop— even though the offender cannot ultimately be imprisoned for her conduct—defies any sense of proportionality and is in serious tension with the Fourth Amendment's proscription of unreasonable seizures.

A custodial arrest exacts an obvious toll on an individual's liberty and privacy, even when the period of custody is relatively brief. The arrestee is subject to a full search of her person and confiscation of her possessions. If the arrestee is the occupant of a car, the entire passenger compartment of the car, including packages therein, is subject to search as well. The arrestee may be detained for up to 48 hours without having a magistrate determine whether there in fact was probable cause for the arrest. Because people arrested for all types of violent and nonviolent offenses may be housed together awaiting such review, this detention period is potentially dangerous. And once the period of custody is over, the fact of the arrest is a permanent part of the public record.

We have said that "the penalty that may attach to any particular offense seems to provide the clearest and most consistent indication of the State's interest in arresting individuals suspected of committing that offense." If the State has decided that a fine, and not imprisonment, is the appropriate punishment for an offense, the State's interest in taking a person suspected of committing that offense into custody is surely limited, at best. * * *

* * * I would require that when there is probable cause to believe that a fine-only offense has been committed, the police officer should issue a citation unless the officer is "able to point to specific and articulable facts which, taken together with rational inferences from

those facts, reasonably warrant [the additional] intrusion" of a full custodial arrest.

* * *

II

The record in this case makes it abundantly clear that Ms. Atwater's arrest was constitutionally unreasonable. * * * While Turek was justified in stopping Atwater, neither law nor reason supports his decision to arrest her instead of simply giving her a citation. The officer's actions cannot sensibly be viewed as a permissible means of balancing Atwater's Fourth Amendment interests with the State's own legitimate interests.

There is no question that Officer Turek's actions severely infringed Atwater's liberty and privacy. Turek was loud and accusatory from the moment he approached Atwater's car. Atwater's young children were terrified and hysterical. Yet when Atwater asked Turek to lower his voice because he was scaring the children, he responded by jabbing his finger in Atwater's face and saying, "You're going to jail." Having made the decision to arrest, Turek did not inform Atwater of her right to remain silent. He instead asked for her license and insurance information.

Atwater asked if she could at least take her children to a friend's house down the street before going to the police station. But Turek—who had just castigated Atwater for not caring for her children—refused and said he would take the children into custody as well. Only the intervention of neighborhood children who had witnessed the scene and summoned one of Atwater's friends saved the children from being hauled to jail with their mother.

With the children gone, Officer Turek handcuffed Ms. Atwater with her hands behind her back, placed her in the police car, and drove her to the police station. Ironically, Turek did not secure Atwater in a seat belt for the drive. At the station, Atwater was forced to remove her shoes, relinquish her possessions, and wait in a holding cell for about an hour. A judge finally informed Atwater of her rights and the charges against her, and released her when she posted bond. Atwater returned to the scene of the arrest, only to find that her car had been towed.

Ms. Atwater ultimately pleaded no contest to violating the seatbelt law and was fined $50. Even though that fine was the maximum penalty for her crime, and even though Officer Turek has never articulated any justification for his actions, the city contends that arresting Atwater was constitutionally reasonable because it advanced two legitimate interests: "the enforcement of child safety laws and encouraging [Atwater] to appear for trial."

It is difficult to see how arresting Atwater served either of these goals any more effectively than the issuance of a citation. * * *

With respect to the related goal of child welfare, the decision to arrest Atwater was nothing short of counterproductive. Atwater's children witnessed Officer Turek yell at their mother and threaten to take them all into custody. Ultimately, they were forced to leave her behind with Turek, knowing that she was being taken to jail. Understandably, the 3–year-old boy was "very, very, very traumatized." After the incident, he had to see a child psychologist regularly, who reported that the boy "felt very guilty that he couldn't stop this horrible thing ... he was powerless to help his mother or sister." Both of Atwater's children are now terrified at the sight of any police car. According to Atwater, the arrest "just never leaves us. It's a conversation we have every other day, once a week, and it's—it raises its head constantly in our lives."

* * *

III

* * *

[U]nbounded discretion carries with it grave potential for abuse. [A]s the recent debate over racial profiling demonstrates all too clearly, a relatively minor traffic infraction may often serve as an excuse for stopping and harassing an individual. After today, the arsenal available to any officer extends to a full arrest and the searches permissible concomitant to that arrest. An officer's subjective motivations for making a traffic stop are not relevant considerations in determining the reasonableness of the stop. But it is precisely because these motivations are beyond our purview that we must vigilantly ensure that officers' poststop actions—which are properly within our reach—comport with the Fourth Amendment's guarantee of reasonableness.

* * *

7. Searches Incident to Arrest

UNITED STATES v. ROBINSON

Supreme Court of the United States, 1973.
414 U.S. 218, 94 S.Ct. 467, 38 L.Ed.2d 427.

Mr. Justice Rehnquist delivered the opinion of the Court.* * *

On April 23, 1968, at approximately 11 p. m., Officer Richard Jenks, a 15–year veteran of the District of Columbia Metropolitan Police Department, observed the respondent driving a 1965 Cadillac near the intersection of 8th and C Streets, N. E., in the District of Columbia. Jenks, as a result of previous investigation following a check of respondent's operator's permit four days earlier, determined there was reason to believe that respondent was operating a motor vehicle after the revocation of his operator's permit. This is an offense defined by statute in the District of Columbia which carries a mandatory minimum jail term, a mandatory minimum fine, or both.

Jenks signaled respondent to stop the automobile, which respondent did, and all three of the occupants emerged from the car. At that point

Jenks informed respondent that he was under arrest for "operating after revocation and obtaining a permit by misrepresentation." It was assumed by the Court of Appeals, and is conceded by the respondent here, that Jenks had probable cause to arrest respondent, and that he effected a full-custody arrest.

In accordance with procedures prescribed in police department instructions, Jenks then began to search respondent. * * * During this patdown, Jenks felt an object in the left breast pocket of the heavy coat respondent was wearing, but testified that he "couldn't tell what it was" and also that he "couldn't actually tell the size of it." Jenks then reached into the pocket and pulled out the object, which turned out to be a "crumpled up cigarette package." * * *

The officer then opened the cigarette pack and found 14 gelatin capsules of white powder which he thought to be, and which later analysis proved to be, heroin. * * *

* * *

I

It is well settled that a search incident to a lawful arrest is a traditional exception to the warrant requirement of the Fourth Amendment. This general exception has historically been formulated into two distinct propositions. The first is that a search may be made of the *person* of the arrestee by virtue of the lawful arrest. The second is that a search may be made of the area within the control of the arrestee.

Examination of this Court's decisions shows that these two propositions have been treated quite differently. The validity of the search of a person incident to a lawful arrest has been regarded as settled from its first enunciation, and has remained virtually unchallenged until the present case. The validity of the second proposition, while likewise conceded in principle, has been subject to differing interpretations as to the extent of the area which may be searched.

* * *

Throughout the series of cases in which the Court has addressed the second proposition relating to a search incident to a lawful arrest—the permissible area beyond the person of the arrestee which such a search may cover—no doubt has been expressed as to the unqualified authority of the arresting authority to search the person of the arrestee. In *Chimel v. California* 395 U.S. 752, 89 S.Ct. 2034, 23 L.Ed.2d 685 (1969) * * * full recognition was again given to the authority to search the person of the arrestee:

> "When an arrest is made, it is reasonable for the arresting officer to search the person arrested in order to remove any weapons that the latter might seek to use in order to resist arrest or effect his escape. Otherwise, the officer's safety might well be endangered, and the arrest itself frustrated. In addition, it is entirely reasonable for the

arresting officer to search for and seize any evidence on the arrestee's person in order to prevent its concealment or destruction."

* * *

III

* * *

The Court of Appeals in effect determined that the *only* reason supporting the authority for a *full* search incident to lawful arrest was the possibility of discovery of evidence or fruits. Concluding that there could be no evidence or fruits in the case of an offense such as that with which respondent was charged, it held that any protective search would have to be limited by the conditions laid down in *Terry* [*v. Ohio*, 392 U.S. 1, 88 S.Ct. 1868, 20 L.Ed.2d 889 (1968)] for a search upon less than probable cause to arrest. * * *

The justification or reason for the authority to search incident to a lawful arrest rests quite as much on the need to disarm the suspect in order to take him into custody as it does on the need to preserve evidence on his person for later use at trial. * * *

Nor are we inclined, on the basis of what seems to us to be a rather speculative judgment, to qualify the breadth of the general authority to search incident to a lawful custodial arrest on an assumption that persons arrested for the offense of driving while their licenses have been revoked are less likely to possess dangerous weapons than are those arrested for other crimes.[5] It is scarcely open to doubt that the danger to an officer is far greater in the case of the extended exposure which follows the taking of a suspect into custody and transporting him to the police station than in the case of the relatively fleeting contact resulting from the typical *Terry*-type stop. This is an adequate basis for treating all custodial arrests alike for purposes of search justification.

* * *[A]uthority to search the person incident to a lawful custodial arrest, while based upon the need to disarm and to discover evidence, does not depend on what a court may later decide was the probability in a particular arrest situation that weapons or evidence would in fact be found upon the person of the suspect. A custodial arrest of a suspect based on probable cause is a reasonable intrusion under the Fourth Amendment; that intrusion being lawful, a search incident to the arrest requires no additional justification. It is the fact of the lawful arrest which establishes the authority to search, and we hold that in the case of

---

5. Such an assumption appears at least questionable in light of the available statistical data concerning assaults on police officers who are in the course of making arrests. The danger to the police officer flows from the fact of the arrest, and its attendant proximity, stress, and uncertainty, and not from the grounds for arrest. One study concludes that approximately 30% of the shootings of police officers occur when an officer stops a person in an automobile. [T]he Uniform Crime Reports, prepared by the Federal Bureau of Investigation, indicate that a significant percentage of murders of police officers occurs when the officers are making traffic stops. Those reports indicate that during January–March 1973, 35 police officers were murdered; 11 of those officers were killed while engaged in making traffic stops.

a lawful custodial arrest a full search of the person is not only an exception to the warrant requirement of the Fourth Amendment, but is also a "reasonable" search under that Amendment.

* * *

[The concurring opinion of Justice Powell is omitted.]

Mr. Justice Marshall, with whom Mr. Justice Douglas and Mr. Justice Brennan join, dissenting.

Certain fundamental principles have characterized this Court's Fourth Amendment jurisprudence over the years. Perhaps the most basic of these [is]: "There is no formula for the determination of reasonableness. Each case is to be decided on its own facts and circumstances." * * * "The constitutional validity of a warrantless search is preeminently the sort of question which can only be decided in the concrete factual context of the individual case." And the intensive, at times painstaking, case-by-case analysis characteristic of our Fourth Amendment decisions bespeaks our "jealous regard for maintaining the integrity of individual rights."

In the present case, however, the majority turns its back on these principles, holding that "the fact of the lawful arrest" always establishes the authority to conduct a full search of the arrestee's person, regardless of whether in a particular case "there was present one of the reasons supporting the authority for a search of the person incident to a lawful arrest." The majority's approach represents a clear and marked departure from our long tradition of case-by-case adjudication of the reasonableness of searches and seizures under the Fourth Amendment. I continue to believe that "the scheme of the Fourth Amendment becomes meaningful only when it is assured that at some point the conduct of those charged with enforcing the laws can be subjected to the more detached, neutral scrutiny of a judge who must evaluate the reasonableness of a particular search or seizure in light of the particular circumstances." * * *

I

* * * Officer Richard Jenks stopped a 1965 Cadillac driven by respondent * * * for what was called a "routine spot check." At that time, Officer Jenks examined respondent's temporary operator's permit, automobile registration card, and Selective Service classification card. Although he permitted respondent to go on his way, Officer Jenks pursued a discrepancy he had noted between the "1938" date of birth given on the operator's permit and the "1927" date of birth given on the Selective Service card. A check of police traffic records showed that an operator's permit issued to one Willie Robinson, Jr., born in 1927, had been revoked, and that a temporary operator's permit had subsequently been issued to one Willie Robinson, born in 1938. The pictures on the revoked permit and on the application for the temporary permit were of the same man—the person stopped by Jenks for the routine check on April 19. Having investigated the matter himself in this fashion, it is clear that Officer Jenks had probable cause to believe that respondent had violated a provision of the District of Columbia Motor Vehicle Code making it unlawful for any person to operate a motor vehicle in the District during the period for which his operator's permit is revoked.

Four days later, on April 23, 1968, while on duty in their patrol car, Officer Jenks and his partner saw respondent driving the same vehicle. They pulled up behind respondent's car and signaled it to stop. * * *

* * *

The first step in the search was for Jenks to place both his hands on respondent's chest and begin to pat him down. During this patdown, Jenks felt something in the left breast pocket of respondent's heavy overcoat. Jenks later testified that he could not immediately tell what was in the pocket. The record does indicate, however, that the object did not feel like a gun and that Jenks had no particular indication it was a weapon of any kind. Nonetheless, he reached into the pocket and took the object out. It turned out to be a crumpled-up cigarette package.

With the package now in his hands, Jenks could feel objects inside but could not tell what they were. It does not appear that Jenks had any reason to believe, or did in fact believe, that the objects were weapons of any sort. He nevertheless opened up the package and looked inside, thereby finding the gelatin capsules of heroin which were introduced against respondent at his trial for the possession and facilitation of concealment of heroin.

II

* * *

* * * There is always the possibility that a police officer, lacking probable cause to obtain a search warrant, will use a traffic arrest as a pretext to conduct a search. I suggest this possibility not to impugn the integrity of our police, but merely to point out that case-by-case adjudication will always be necessary to determine whether a full arrest was effected for purely legitimate reasons or, rather, as a pretext for searching the arrestee. "An arrest may not be used as a pretext to search for evidence."

* * *

CHIMEL v. CALIFORNIA

Supreme Court of the United States, 1969.
395 U.S. 752, 89 S.Ct. 2034, 23 L.Ed.2d 685.

MR. JUSTICE STEWART delivered the opinion of the Court.

This case raises basic questions concerning the permissible scope under the Fourth Amendment of a search incident to a lawful arrest.

The relevant facts are essentially undisputed. Late in the afternoon of September 13, 1965, three police officers arrived at the Santa Ana,

California, home of the petitioner with a warrant authorizing his arrest for the burglary of a coin shop. The officers knocked on the door, identified themselves to the petitioner's wife, and asked if they might come inside. She ushered them into the house, where they waited 10 or 15 minutes until the petitioner returned home from work. When the petitioner entered the house, one of the officers handed him the arrest warrant and asked for permission to "look around." The petitioner objected, but was advised that "on the basis of the lawful arrest," the officers would nonetheless conduct a search. No search warrant had been issued.

Accompanied by the petitioner's wife, the officers then looked through the entire three-bedroom house, including the attic, the garage, and a small workshop. In some rooms the search was relatively cursory. In the master bedroom and sewing room, however, the officers directed the petitioner's wife to open drawers and "to physically move contents of the drawers from side to side so that [they] might view any items that would have come from [the] burglary." After completing the search, they seized numerous items—primarily coins, but also several medals, tokens, and a few other objects. The entire search took between 45 minutes and an hour.

At the petitioner's subsequent state trial on two charges of burglary, the items taken from his house were admitted into evidence against him, over his objection that they had been unconstitutionally seized. He was convicted, and the judgments of conviction were affirmed by both the California Court of Appeal and the California Supreme Court. * * *

[Justice Stewart reviewed a number of authorities construing the permissible scope of searches incident to arrest, including a number of contradictory Supreme Court decisions decided over the previous half century. After reviewing the Court's decision the previous year in *Terry v. Ohio*, that permitted warrantless "frisks" on less than probable cause, the *Chimel* opinion announced a rule defining the area that might be searched under the search incident to arrest doctrine.]

* * * When an arrest is made, it is reasonable for the arresting officer to search the person arrested in order to remove any weapons that the latter might seek to use in order to resist arrest or effect his escape. Otherwise, the officer's safety might well be endangered, and the arrest itself frustrated. In addition, it is entirely reasonable for the arresting officer to search for and seize any evidence on the arrestee's person in order to prevent its concealment or destruction. And the area into which an arrestee might reach in order to grab a weapon or evidentiary items must, of course, be governed by a like rule. A gun on a table or in a drawer in front of one who is arrested can be as dangerous to the arresting officer as one concealed in the clothing of the person arrested. There is ample justification, therefore, for a search of the arrestee's person and the area "within his immediate control"—construing that phrase to mean the area from within which he might gain possession of a weapon or destructible evidence.

There is no comparable justification, however, for routinely searching any room other than that in which an arrest occurs—or, for that matter, for searching through all the desk drawers or other closed or concealed areas in that room itself. Such searches, in the absence of well-recognized exceptions, may be made only under the authority of a search warrant. The "adherence to judicial processes" mandated by the Fourth Amendment requires no less.

* * *

"The rule allowing contemporaneous searches is justified, for example, by the need to seize weapons and other things which might be used to assault an officer or effect an escape, as well as by the need to prevent the destruction of evidence of the crime—things which might easily happen where the weapon or evidence is on the accused's person or under his immediate control. But these justifications are absent where a search is remote in time or place from the arrest."

* * *

It is argued in the present case that it is "reasonable" to search a man's house when he is arrested in it. But that argument is founded on little more than a subjective view regarding the acceptability of certain sorts of police conduct, and not on considerations relevant to Fourth Amendment interests. Under such an unconfined analysis, Fourth Amendment protection in this area would approach the evaporation point. It is not easy to explain why, for instance, it is less subjectively "reasonable" to search a man's house when he is arrested on his front lawn—or just down the street—than it is when he happens to be in the house at the time of arrest. * * *

Thus, although "the recurring questions of the reasonableness of searches" depend upon "the facts and circumstances—the total atmosphere of the case," those facts and circumstances must be viewed in the light of established Fourth Amendment principles.

* * *

The petitioner correctly points out that one result of decisions such as *Rabinowitz* and *Harris* is to give law enforcement officials the opportunity to engage in searches not justified by probable cause, by the simple expedient of arranging to arrest suspects at home rather than elsewhere. We do not suggest that the petitioner is necessarily correct in his assertion that such a strategy was utilized here, but the fact remains that had he been arrested earlier in the day, at his place of employment rather than at home, no search of his house could have been made without a search warrant. In any event, even apart from the possibility of such police tactics, the general point so forcefully made by Judge Learned Hand remains:

"After arresting a man in his house, to rummage at will among his papers in search of whatever will convict him, appears to us to be indistinguishable from what might be done under a general warrant;

indeed, the warrant would give more protection, for presumably it must be issued by a magistrate. True, by hypothesis the power would not exist, if the supposed offender were not found on the premises; but it is small consolation to know that one's papers are safe only so long as one is not at home."

* * *

Application of sound Fourth Amendment principles to the facts of this case produces a clear result. The search here went far beyond the petitioner's person and the area from within which he might have obtained either a weapon or something that could have been used as evidence against him. There was no constitutional justification, in the absence of a search warrant, for extending the search beyond that area. The scope of the search was, therefore, "unreasonable" under the Fourth and Fourteenth Amendments, and the petitioner's conviction cannot stand.

[JUSTICE HARLAN'S concurring opinion is omitted]

MR. JUSTICE WHITE with whom MR. JUSTICE BLACK joins, dissenting.

Few areas of the law have been as subject to shifting constitutional standards over the last 50 years as that of the search "incident to an arrest." There has been a remarkable instability in this whole area, which has seen at least four major shifts in emphasis. Today's opinion makes an untimely fifth. In my view, the Court should not now abandon the old rule.

* * *

II

The rule which has prevailed, but for very brief or doubtful periods of aberration, is that a search incident to an arrest may extend to those areas under the control of the defendant and where items subject to constitutional seizure may be found. The justification for this rule must, under the language of the Fourth Amendment, lie in the reasonableness of the rule. * * *

* * *

In terms, then, the Court must decide whether a given search is reasonable. The Amendment does not proscribe "warrantless searches" but instead it proscribes "unreasonable searches" and this Court has never held nor does the majority today assert that warrantless searches are necessarily unreasonable.

Applying this reasonableness test to the area of searches incident to arrests, one thing is clear at the outset. Search of an arrested man and of the items within his immediate reach must in almost every case be reasonable. There is always a danger that the suspect will try to escape, seizing concealed weapons with which to overpower and injure the arresting officers, and there is a danger that he may destroy evidence vital to the prosecution. Circumstances in which these justifications would not apply are sufficiently rare that inquiry is not made into searches of this scope, which have been considered reasonable throughout.

The justifications which make such a search reasonable obviously do not apply to the search of areas to which the accused does not have ready physical access. This is not enough, however, to prove such searches unconstitutional. The Court has always held, and does not today deny, that when there is probable cause to search and it is "impracticable" for one reason or another to get a search warrant, then a warrantless search may be reasonable.

This is not to say that a search can be reasonable without regard to the probable cause to believe that seizable items are on the premises. But when there are exigent circumstances, and probable cause, then the search may be made without a warrant, reasonably. An arrest itself may often create an emergency situation making it impracticable to obtain a warrant before embarking on a related search. Again assuming that there is probable cause to search premises at the spot where a suspect is arrested, it seems to me unreasonable to require the police to leave the scene in order to obtain a search warrant when they are already legally there to make a valid arrest, and when there must almost always be a strong possibility that confederates of the arrested man will in the meanwhile remove the items for which the police have probable cause to search. This must so often be the case that it seems to me as unreasonable to require a warrant for a search of the premises as to require a warrant for search of the person and his very immediate surroundings.

This case provides a good illustration of my point that it is unreasonable to require police to leave the scene of an arrest in order to obtain a search warrant when they already have probable cause to search and there is a clear danger that the items for which they may reasonably search will be removed before they return with a warrant. * * * There was doubtless probable cause not only to arrest petitioner, but also to search his house. He had obliquely admitted, both to a neighbor and to the owner of the burglarized store, that he had committed the burglary. In light of this, and the fact that the neighbor had seen other admittedly stolen property in petitioner's house, there was surely probable cause on which a warrant could have issued to search the house for the stolen coins. Moreover, had the police simply arrested petitioner, taken him off to the station house, and later returned with a warrant, it seems very likely that petitioner's wife, who in view of petitioner's generally garrulous nature must have known of the robbery, would have removed the coins. For the police to search the house while the evidence they had probable cause to search out and seize was still there cannot be considered unreasonable.

* * *

IV

If circumstances so often require the warrantless arrest that the law generally permits it, the typical situation will find the arresting officers lawfully on the premises without arrest or search warrant. Like the majority, I would permit the police to search the person of a suspect and the area under his immediate control either to assure the safety of the officers or to prevent the destruction of evidence. And like the majority, I see nothing in the arrest alone furnishing probable cause for a search of any broader scope. However, where as here the existence of probable cause is independently established and would justify a warrant for a broader search for evidence, I would follow past cases and permit such a search to be carried out without a warrant, since the fact of arrest supplies an exigent circumstance justifying police action before the evidence can be removed, and also alerts the suspect to the fact of the search so that he can immediately seek judicial determination of probable cause in an adversary proceeding, and appropriate redress.

* * *

NEW YORK v. BELTON

Supreme Court of the United States, 1981.
453 U.S. 454, 101 S.Ct. 2860, 69 L.Ed.2d 768.

JUSTICE STEWART delivered the opinion of the Court.

* * *

I

On April 9, 1978, Trooper Douglas Nicot, a New York State policeman driving an unmarked car on the New York Thruway, was passed by another automobile traveling at an excessive rate of speed. Nicot gave chase, overtook the speeding vehicle, and ordered its driver to pull it over to the side of the road and stop. There were four men in the car, one of whom was Roger Belton, the respondent in this case. The policeman asked to see the driver's license and automobile registration, and discovered that none of the men owned the vehicle or was related to its owner. Meanwhile, the policeman had smelled burnt marihuana and had seen on the floor of the car an envelope marked "Supergold" that he associated with marihuana. He therefore directed the men to get out of the car, and placed them under arrest for the unlawful possession of marihuana. He patted down each of the men and "split them up into four separate areas of the Thruway at this time so they would not be in physical touching area of each other." He then picked up the envelope marked "Supergold" and found that it contained marihuana. * * * He then searched the passenger compartment of the car. On the back seat he found a black leather jacket belonging to Belton. He unzipped one of the pockets of the jacket and discovered cocaine. Placing the jacket in his automobile, he drove the four arrestees to a nearby police station.

* * *

II

It is a first principle of Fourth Amendment jurisprudence that the police may not conduct a search unless they first convince a neutral magistrate that there is probable cause to do so. This Court has recognized, however, that "the exigencies of the situation" may sometimes make exemption from the warrant requirement "imperative." Specifically, the Court held in *Chimel v. California* 395 U.S. 752, 89 S.Ct. 2034, 23 L.Ed.2d 685 (1969) that a lawful custodial arrest creates a situation which justifies the contemporaneous search without a warrant of the person arrested and of the immediately surrounding area. Such searches have long been considered valid because of the need "to remove any weapons that [the arrestee] might seek to use in order to resist arrest or effect his escape" and the need to prevent the concealment or destruction of evidence.

The Court's opinion in *Chimel* emphasized the principle that * * * "[the] scope of [a] search must be 'strictly tied to and justified by' the circumstances which rendered its initiation permissible." Thus while the Court in *Chimel* found "ample justification" for a search of "the area from within which [an arrestee] might gain possession of a weapon or destructible evidence," the Court found "no comparable justification . . . for routinely searching any room other than that in which an arrest occurs—or, for that matter, for searching through all the desk drawers or other closed or concealed areas in that room itself."

* * *

* * * "[A] single familiar standard is essential to guide police officers, who have only limited time and expertise to reflect on and balance the social and individual interests involved in the specific circumstances they confront."

So it was that, in *United States v. Robinson,* 414 U.S. 218, 94 S.Ct. 467, 38 L.Ed.2d 427 (1973) the Court hewed to a straightforward rule, easily applied, and predictably enforced: "[In] the case of a lawful custodial arrest a full search of the person is not only an exception to the warrant requirement of the Fourth Amendment, but is also a 'reasonable' search under that Amendment."

But no straightforward rule has emerged from the litigated cases respecting the question involved here—the question of the proper scope of a search of the interior of an automobile incident to a lawful custodial arrest of its occupants. * * *

* * * In order to establish the workable rule this category of cases requires, * * * we hold that when a policeman has made a lawful custodial arrest of the occupant of an automobile, he may, as a contemporaneous incident of that arrest, search the passenger compartment of that automobile.

It follows from this conclusion that the police may also examine the contents of any containers found within the passenger compartment, for if the passenger compartment is within reach of the arrestee, so also will containers in it be within his reach.[4] Such a container may, of course, be

---

4. "Container" here denotes any object capable of holding another object. It thus includes closed or open glove compartments, consoles, or other receptacles located

searched whether it is open or closed, since the justification for the search is not that the arrestee has no privacy interest in the container, but that the lawful custodial arrest justifies the infringement of any privacy interest the arrestee may have. Thus, while the Court in *Chimel* held that the police could not search all the drawers in an arrestee's house simply because the police had arrested him at home, the Court noted that drawers within an arrestee's reach could be searched because of the danger their contents might pose to the police.

It is true, of course, that these containers will sometimes be such that they could hold neither a weapon nor evidence of the criminal conduct for which the suspect was arrested. However, in *United States* v. *Robinson*, the Court rejected the argument that such a container—there a "crumpled up cigarette package"—located during a search of Robinson incident to his arrest could not be searched: "The authority to search the person incident to a lawful custodial arrest, while based upon the need to disarm and to discover evidence, does not depend on what a court may later decide was the probability in a particular arrest situation that weapons or evidence would in fact be found upon the person of the suspect. A custodial arrest of a suspect based on probable cause is a reasonable intrusion under the Fourth Amendment; that intrusion being lawful, a search incident to the arrest requires no additional justification."

* * *

III

It is not questioned that the respondent was the subject of a lawful custodial arrest on a charge of possessing marihuana. The search of the respondent's jacket followed immediately upon that arrest. The jacket was located inside the passenger compartment of the car in which the respondent had been a passenger just before he was arrested. The jacket was thus within the area which we have concluded was "within the arrestee's immediate control" within the meaning of the *Chimel* case. The search of the jacket, therefore, was a search incident to a lawful custodial arrest, and it did not violate the Fourth and Fourteenth Amendments. * * *

[JUSTICE REHNQUIST'S concurring opinion is omitted.]

JUSTICE BRENNAN with whom JUSTICE MARSHALL joins, dissenting.

In *Chimel v. California,* this Court carefully analyzed more than 50 years of conflicting precedent governing the permissible scope of warrantless searches incident to custodial arrest. The Court today turns its back on the product of that analysis, formulating an arbitrary "bright-line" rule applicable to "recent" occupants of automobiles that fails to reflect *Chimel*'s underlying policy justifications. While the Court claims

anywhere within the passenger compartment, as well as luggage, boxes, bags, clothing, and the like. Our holding encompasses only the interior of the passenger compartment of an automobile and does not encompass the trunk.

to leave *Chimel* intact, I fear that its unwarranted abandonment of the principles underlying that decision may signal a wholesale retreat from our carefully developed search-incident-to-arrest analysis. I dissent.

I

It has long been a fundamental principle of Fourth Amendment analysis that exceptions to the warrant requirement are to be narrowly construed. Predicated on the Fourth Amendment's essential purpose of "[shielding] the citizen from unwarranted intrusions into his privacy," this principle carries with it two corollaries. First, for a search to be valid under the Fourth Amendment, it must be " 'strictly tied to and justified by' the circumstances which rendered its initiation permissible." Second, in determining whether to grant an exception to the warrant requirement, courts should carefully consider the facts and circumstances of each search and seizure, focusing on the reasons supporting the exception rather than on any bright-line rule of general application.

The *Chimel* exception to the warrant requirement was designed with two principal concerns in mind: the safety of the arresting officer and the preservation of easily concealed or destructible evidence. Recognizing that a suspect might have access to weapons or contraband at the time of arrest, the Court declared:

> "When an arrest is made, it is reasonable for the arresting officer to search the person arrested in order to remove any weapons that the latter might seek to use in order to resist arrest or effect his escape. Otherwise, the officer's safety might well be endangered, and the arrest itself frustrated. In addition, it is entirely reasonable for the arresting officer to search for and seize any evidence on the arrestee's person in order to prevent its concealment or destruction. And the area into which an arrestee might reach in order to grab a weapon or evidentiary items must, of course, be governed by a like rule."

* * * When the arrest has been consummated and the arrestee safely taken into custody, the justifications underlying *Chimel*'s limited exception to the warrant requirement cease to apply: at that point there is no possibility that the arrestee could reach weapons or contraband.

In its attempt to formulate a " 'single, familiar standard . . . to guide police officers, who have only limited time and expertise to reflect on and balance the social and individual interests involved in the specific circumstances they confront,' " the Court today disregards these principles, and instead adopts a fiction—that the interior of a car is *always* within the immediate control of an arrestee who has recently been in the car. * * *

* * *

II

As the facts of this case make clear, the Court today substantially expands the permissible scope of searches incident to arrest by permitting police officers to search areas and containers the arrestee could not possibly reach at the time of arrest. These facts demonstrate that at the time Belton and his three companions were placed under custodial arrest—which was *after* they had been removed from the car, patted down, and separated—none of them could have reached the jackets that had been left on the back seat of the car. * * *

* * *

By approving the constitutionality of the warrantless search in this case, the Court carves out a dangerous precedent that is not justified by the concerns underlying *Chimel*. Disregarding the principle "that the scope of a warrantless search must be commensurate with the rationale that excepts the search from the warrant requirement," the Court for the first time grants police officers authority to conduct a warrantless "area" search under circumstances where there is no chance that the arrestee "might gain possession of a weapon or destructible evidence." Under the approach taken today, the result would presumably be the same even if Officer Nicot had handcuffed Belton and his companions in the patrol car before placing them under arrest, and even if his search had extended to locked luggage or other inaccessible containers located in the back seat of the car.

This expansion of the *Chimel* exception is both analytically unsound and inconsistent with every significant search-incident-to-arrest case we have decided in which the issue was whether the police could lawfully conduct a warrantless search of the area surrounding the arrestee. [T]he crucial question under *Chimel* is not whether the arrestee could *ever* have reached the area that was searched, but whether he could have reached it at the time of arrest and search. If not, the officer's failure to obtain a warrant may not be excused. * * *

III

The Court seeks to justify its departure from the principles underlying *Chimel* by proclaiming the need for a new "bright-line" rule to guide the officer in the field. As we pointed out in *Mincey v. Arizona,* 437 U.S. 385, 98 S.Ct. 2408, 57 L.Ed.2d 290 (1978) however, "the mere fact that law enforcement may be made more efficient can never by itself justify disregard of the Fourth Amendment." Moreover, the Court's attempt to forge a "bright-line" rule fails on its own terms. While the "interior/trunk" distinction may provide a workable guide in certain routine cases—for example, where the officer arrests the driver of a car and then immediately searches the seats and floor—in the long run, I suspect it will create far more problems than it solves. The Court's new approach leaves open too many questions and, more important, it provides the police and the courts with too few tools with which to find the answers.

Thus, although the Court concludes that a warrantless search of a car may take place even though the suspect was arrested outside the car, it does not indicate how long after the suspect's arrest that search may validly be conducted.* * * Are special rules necessary for station wagons and hatchbacks, where the luggage compartment may be reached through the interior, or taxicabs, where a glass panel might separate the driver's compartment from the rest of the car? Are the only containers that may be searched those that are large enough to be "capable of holding another object"? Or does the new rule apply to any container, even if it "could hold neither a weapon nor evidence of the criminal conduct for which the suspect was arrested"?

The Court does not give the police any "bright-line" answers to these questions. More important, because the Court's new rule abandons the justifications underlying *Chimel, it offers no guidance to the police officer seeking to work out these answers for himself.* As we warned in *Chimel*: "No consideration relevant to the Fourth Amendment suggests any point of rational limitation, once the search is allowed to go beyond the area from which the person arrested might obtain weapons or evidentiary items." By failing to heed this warning, the Court has undermined rather than furthered the goal of consistent law enforcement: it has failed to offer any principles to guide the police and the courts in their application of the new rule to nonroutine situations.

[JUSTICE WHITE's dissenting opinion is omitted.]

THORNTON v. UNITED STATES

Supreme Court of the United States, 2004.
541 U.S. 615, 124 S.Ct. 2127, 158 L.Ed.2d 905.

CHIEF JUSTICE REHNQUIST delivered the opinion of the Court [except as to footnote 4, which is omitted here].

[The Court held that its opinion in *New York* v. *Belton,* 453 U.S. 454, 69 L.Ed.2d 768, 101 S.Ct. 2860 (1981), controls even when an officer does not make contact until the person arrested has left the vehicle.]

Officer Deion Nichols of the Norfolk, Virginia, Police Department, who was in uniform but driving an unmarked police car, first noticed petitioner Marcus Thornton when petitioner slowed down so as to avoid driving next to him. Nichols suspected that petitioner knew he was a police officer and for some reason did not want to pull next to him. His suspicions aroused, Nichols pulled off onto a side street and petitioner passed him. After petitioner passed him, Nichols ran a check on petitioner's license tags, which revealed that the tags had been issued to a 1982 Chevy two-door and not to a Lincoln Town Car, the model of car petitioner was driving. Before Nichols had an opportunity to pull him over, petitioner drove into a parking lot, parked, and got out of the vehicle. Nichols saw petitioner leave his vehicle as he pulled in behind him. He parked the patrol car, accosted petitioner, and asked him for his driver's license. He also told him that his license tags did not match the vehicle that he was driving.

Petitioner appeared nervous. He began rambling and licking his lips; he was sweating. Concerned for his safety, Nichols asked petitioner if he had any narcotics or weapons on him or in his vehicle. Petitioner said no. Nichols then asked petitioner if he could pat him down, to which petitioner agreed. Nichols felt a bulge in petitioner's left front pocket and again asked him if he had any illegal narcotics on him. This time petitioner stated that he did, and he reached into his pocket and pulled out two individual bags, one containing three bags of marijuana and the other containing a large amount of crack cocaine. Nichols handcuffed petitioner, informed him that he was under arrest, and placed him in the back seat of the patrol car. He then searched petitioner's vehicle and found a BryCo .9–millimeter handgun under the driver's seat. [Thornton moved to suppress the firearm as the fruit of an unconstitutional search.]

[The Court discussed the search incident to arrest doctrine developed in *Belton*, *Chimel* v. *California*, 395 U.S. 752, 23 L.Ed.2d 685, 89 S.Ct. 2034 (1969), and *United States* v. *Robinson*, 414 U.S. 218, 38 L.Ed.2d 427, 94 S.Ct. 467 (1973). Both are discussed *supra*.]

In all relevant aspects, the arrest of a suspect who is next to a vehicle presents identical concerns regarding officer safety and the destruction of evidence as the arrest of one who is inside the vehicle. An officer may search a suspect's vehicle under *Belton* only if the suspect is arrested. A custodial arrest is fluid and "the danger to the police officer flows from *the fact of the arrest*, and its attendant proximity, stress, and uncertainty," The stress is no less merely because the arrestee exited his car before the officer initiated contact, nor is an arrestee less likely to attempt to lunge for a weapon or to destroy evidence if he is outside of, but still in control of, the vehicle. In either case, the officer faces a highly volatile situation. It would make little sense to apply two different rules to what is, at bottom, the same situation.

* * *

Petitioner argues, however, that *Belton* will fail to provide a "bright-line" rule if it applies to more than vehicle "occupants." But *Belton* allows police to search the passenger compartment of a vehicle incident to a lawful custodial arrest of both "occupants" and "recent occupants." Indeed, the respondent in *Belton* was not inside the car at the time of the arrest and search; he was standing on the highway. In any event, while an arrestee's status as a "recent occupant" may turn on his temporal or spatial relationship to the car at the time of the arrest and search, it certainly does not turn on whether he was inside or outside the car at the moment that the officer first initiated contact with him.

To be sure, not all contraband in the passenger compartment is likely to be readily accessible to a "recent occupant." It is unlikely in this case that petitioner could have reached under the driver's seat for his gun once he was outside of his automobile. But the firearm and the passenger compartment in general were no more inaccessible than were the contraband and the passenger compartment in *Belton*. The need for a clear rule, readily understood by police officers and not depending on differing estimates of what items were or were not within reach of an arrestee at any particular moment, justifies the sort of generalization which *Belton* enunciated. Once an officer determines that there is probable cause to make an arrest, it is reasonable to allow officers to ensure their safety and to preserve evidence by searching the entire passenger compartment.

Rather than clarifying the constitutional limits of a *Belton* search, petitioner's "contact initiation" rule would obfuscate them. Under petitioner's proposed rule, an officer approaching a suspect who has just alighted from his vehicle would have to determine whether he actually confronted or signaled confrontation with the suspect while he remained in the car, or whether the suspect exited his vehicle unaware of, and for reasons unrelated to, the officer's presence. This determination would be inherently subjective and highly fact specific, and would require precisely the sort of ad hoc determinations on the part of officers in the field and reviewing courts that *Belton* sought to avoid. Experience has shown that such a rule is impracticable, and we refuse to adopt it. So long as an arrestee is the sort of "recent occupant" of a vehicle such as petitioner was here, officers may search that vehicle incident to the arrest.

The judgment of the Court of Appeals is affirmed.

[JUSTICE O'CONNOR'S opinion, concurring in part, is omitted.]

JUSTICE SCALIA, with whom JUSTICE GINSBURG joins, concurring in the judgment.

* * *

When petitioner's car was searched in this case, he was neither in, nor anywhere near, the passenger compartment of his vehicle. Rather, he was handcuffed and secured in the back of the officer's squad car. The risk that he would nevertheless "grab a weapon or evidentiary item" from his car was remote in the extreme. The Court's effort to apply our current doctrine to this search stretches it beyond its breaking point, and for that reason I cannot join the Court's opinion.

I

I see three reasons why the search in this case might have been justified to protect officer safety or prevent concealment or destruction of evidence. None ultimately persuades me.

The first is that, despite being handcuffed and secured in the back of a squad car, petitioner might have escaped and retrieved a weapon or evidence from his vehicle—a theory that calls to mind Judge Goldberg's reference to the mythical arrestee "possessed of the skill of Houdini and the strength of Hercules." The United States, endeavoring to ground this seemingly speculative fear in reality, points to a total of seven instances over the past 13 years in which state or federal officers were attacked with weapons by handcuffed or formerly handcuffed arrestees. These instances do not, however, justify the search authority claimed. Three involved arrestees who retrieved weapons concealed *on their own person*. Three more involved arrestees who seized a weapon *from the arresting officer*. Authority to search the arrestee's own person is beyond question; and of course no search could prevent seizure of the officer's gun. Only one of the seven instances involved a handcuffed arrestee who escaped from a squad car to retrieve a weapon from somewhere else * * *.

[T]he Government's inability to come up with even a single example of a handcuffed arrestee's retrieval of arms or evidence from his vehicle undermines its claims. The risk that a suspect handcuffed in the back of a squad car might escape and recover a weapon from his vehicle is surely no greater than the risk that a suspect handcuffed in his residence might escape and recover a weapon from the next room—a danger we held insufficient to justify a search in *Chimel*.

The second defense of the search in this case is that, since the officer could have conducted the search at the time of arrest (when the suspect was still near the car), he should not be penalized for having taken the sensible precaution of securing the suspect in the squad car first. As one Court of Appeals put it: " 'It does not make sense to prescribe a constitutional test that is entirely at odds with safe and sensible police procedures.' " The weakness of this argument is that it assumes that, one way or another, the search must take place. But conducting a *Chimel* search is not the Government's right; it is an exception—justified by necessity—to a rule that would otherwise render the search unlawful. If "sensible police procedures" require that suspects be handcuffed and put in squad cars, then police should handcuff suspects, put them in squad cars, and not conduct the search. Indeed, if an officer leaves a suspect unrestrained nearby just to manufacture authority to search, one could argue that the search is unreasonable *precisely because* the dangerous conditions justifying it existed only by virtue of the officer's failure to follow sensible procedures.

The third defense of the search is that, even though the arrestee posed no risk here, *Belton* searches in general are reasonable, and the benefits of a bright-line rule justify upholding that small minority of searches that, on their particular facts, are not reasonable. The validity of this argument rests on the accuracy of *Belton*'s claim that the passenger compartment is "in fact generally, even if not inevitably," within the suspect's immediate control. By the United States' own admission, however, "the practice of restraining an arrestee on the scene before searching a car that he just occupied is so prevalent that holding that *Belton* does not apply in that setting would ... 'largely render *Belton* a dead letter.' " Reported cases involving this precise factual scenario—a motorist handcuffed and secured in the back of a squad car when the search takes place—are legion. Some courts uphold such searches even when the squad car carrying the handcuffed arrestee has already left the scene.

* * *

II

* * *

* * * When officer safety or imminent evidence concealment or destruction is at issue, officers should not have to make fine judgments in the heat of the moment. But in the context of a general evidence-gathering search, the state interests that might justify any overbreadth are far less compelling. A motorist may be arrested for a wide variety of offenses; in many cases, there is no reasonable basis to believe relevant evidence might be found in the car. I would therefore limit *Belton* searches to cases where it is reasonable to believe evidence relevant to the crime of arrest might be found in the vehicle.

In this case, as in *Belton*, petitioner was lawfully arrested for a drug offense. It was reasonable for Officer Nichols to believe that further contraband or similar evidence relevant to the crime for which he had been arrested might be found in the vehicle from which he had just alighted and which was still within his vicinity at the time of arrest. I would affirm the decision below on that ground.

[JUSTICE STEVENS dissenting opinion, in which JUSTICE SOUTER joined, is omitted.]

* * *

8.   Inventory Searches

ILLINOIS v. LAFAYETTE

Supreme Court of the United States, 1983.
462 U.S. 640, 103 S.Ct. 2605, 77 L.Ed.2d 65.

Chief Justice Burger delivered the opinion of the Court.

I

On September 1, 1980, at about 10 p.m., Officer Maurice Mietzner of the Kankakee City Police arrived at the Town Cinema in Kankakee, Ill., in response to a call about a disturbance. There he found respondent involved in an altercation with the theater manager. He arrested respondent for disturbing the peace, handcuffed him, and took him to the police station. Respondent carried a purse-type shoulder bag on the trip to the station.

At the police station respondent was taken to the booking room; there, Officer Mietzner removed the handcuffs from respondent and ordered him to empty his pockets and place the contents on the counter. After doing so, respondent took a package of cigarettes from his shoulder bag and placed the bag on the counter. Mietzner then removed the contents of the bag, and found 10 amphetamine pills inside the plastic wrap of a cigarette package.

[T]he trial court ordered the suppression of the amphetamine pills.

* * *

II

The question here is whether, consistent with the Fourth Amendment, it is reasonable for police to search the personal effects of a person under lawful arrest as part of the routine administrative procedure at a police station house incident to booking and jailing the suspect. The justification for such searches does not rest on probable cause, and hence the absence of a warrant is immaterial to the reasonableness of the search. Indeed, we have previously established that the inventory search constitutes a well-defined exception to the warrant requirement.

A so-called inventory search is not an independent legal concept but rather an incidental administrative step following arrest and preceding incarceration. To determine whether the search of respondent's shoulder bag was unreasonable we must "[balance] its intrusion on the individual's Fourth Amendment interests against its promotion of legitimate governmental interests."

* * *

The governmental interests underlying a station-house search of the arrestee's person and possessions may in some circumstances be even greater than those supporting a search immediately following arrest. Consequently, the scope of a station-house search will often vary from that made at the time of arrest. Police conduct that would be impractical or unreasonable—or embarrassingly intrusive—on the street can more readily—and privately—be performed at the station. For example, the interests supporting a search incident to arrest would hardly justify disrobing an arrestee on the street, but the practical necessities of routine jail administration may even justify taking a prisoner's clothes before confining him, although that step would be rare. "With or without probable cause, the authorities were entitled [at the station house] not only to search [the arrestee's] clothing but also to take it from him and keep it in official custody."

At the station house, it is entirely proper for police to remove and list or inventory property found on the person or in the possession of an arrested person who is to be jailed. A range of governmental interests supports an inventory process. It is not unheard of for persons employed in police activities to steal property taken from arrested persons; similarly, arrested persons have been known to make false claims regarding what was taken from their possession at the station house. A standardized procedure for making a list or inventory as soon as reasonable after reaching the station house not only deters false claims but also inhibits theft or careless handling of articles taken from the arrested person. Arrested persons have also been known to injure themselves—or others—with belts, knives, drugs, or other items on their person while being detained. Dangerous instrumentalities—such as razor blades, bombs, or weapons—can be concealed in innocent-looking articles taken from the arrestee's possession. The bare recital of these mundane realities justifies reasonable measures by police to limit these risks—either while the items are in police possession or at the time they are returned to the arrestee upon his release. Examining all the items removed from the arrestee's person or possession and listing or inventorying them is an entirely reasonable administrative procedure. It is immaterial whether the police actually fear any particular package or container; the need to protect against such risks arises independently of a particular officer's subjective concerns. Finally, inspection of an arrestee's personal property may assist the police in ascertaining or verifying his identity. In short, every consideration of orderly police administration benefiting both police and the public points toward the appropriateness of the examination of respondent's shoulder bag prior to his incarceration.

Our prior cases amply support this conclusion. In *South Dakota* v. *Opperman*, 428 U.S. 364, 96 S.Ct. 3092, 49 L.Ed.2d 1000 (1976), we upheld a search of the contents of the glove compartment of an abandoned automobile lawfully impounded by the police. We held that the search was reasonable because it served legitimate governmental interests that outweighed the individual's privacy interests in the contents of his car. Those measures protected the owner's property while it was in the custody of the police and protected police against possible false claims of theft. We found no need to consider the existence of less intrusive means of protecting the police and the property in their custody—such as locking the car and impounding it in safe storage under guard. Similarly, standardized inventory procedures are appropriate to serve legitimate governmental interests at stake here.

The Illinois court held that the search of respondent's shoulder bag was unreasonable because "preservation of the defendant's property and protection of police from claims of lost or stolen property, 'could have been achieved in a less intrusive manner.' For example, ... the defendant's shoulder bag could easily have been secured by sealing it within a plastic bag or box and placing it in a secured locker." Perhaps so, but the real question is not what "could have been achieved," but whether the Fourth Amendment *requires* such steps; it is not our function to write a manual on administering routine, neutral procedures of the station house. Our role is to assure against violations of the Constitution.

The reasonableness of any particular governmental activity does not necessarily or invariably turn on the existence of alternative "less intrusive" means. In *Cady* v. *Dombrowski*, 413 U.S. 433, 93 S.Ct. 2523, 37 L.Ed.2d 706 (1973), for example, we upheld the search of the trunk of a car to find a revolver suspected of being there. We rejected the contention that the public could equally well have been protected by the posting of a guard over the automobile. In language equally applicable to this case, we held, "[the] fact that the protection of the public might, in the abstract, have been accomplished by 'less intrusive' means does not, by itself, render the search unreasonable." We are hardly in a position to second-guess police departments as to what practical administrative method will best deter theft by and false claims against its employees and preserve the security of the station house. It is evident that a station-house search of every item carried on or by a person who has lawfully been taken into custody by the police will amply serve the important and legitimate governmental interests involved.

Even if less intrusive means existed of protecting some particular types of property, it would be unreasonable to expect police officers in the everyday course of business to make fine and subtle distinctions in deciding which containers or items may be searched and which must be sealed as a unit. Only recently in we stated that " '[a] single familiar standard is essential to guide police officers, who have only limited time and expertise to reflect on and balance the social and individual interests involved in the specific circumstances they confront.' "

Applying these principles, we hold that it is not "unreasonable" for police, as part of the routine procedure incident to incarcerating an arrested person, to search any container or article in his possession, in accordance with established inventory procedures.

COLORADO v. BERTINE

Supreme Court of the United States, 1987.
479 U.S. 367, 107 S.Ct. 738, 93 L.Ed.2d 739.

Chief Justice Rehnquist delivered the opinion of the Court.

On February 10, 1984, a police officer in Boulder, Colorado, arrested respondent Steven Lee Bertine for driving while under the influence of alcohol. After Bertine was taken into custody and before the arrival of a tow truck to take Bertine's van to an impoundment lot, a backup officer inventoried the contents of the van. The officer opened a closed backpack in which he found controlled substances, cocaine paraphernalia, and a large amount of cash. Bertine was subsequently charged with driving while under the influence of alcohol, unlawful possession of cocaine with intent to dispense, sell, and distribute, and unlawful possession of methaqualone. We are asked to decide whether the Fourth Amendment prohibits the State from proving these charges with the evidence discovered during the inventory of Bertine's van. We hold that it does not.

The backup officer inventoried the van in accordance with local police procedures, which require a detailed inspection and inventory of impounded vehicles. He found the backpack directly behind the frontseat of the van. Inside the pack, the officer observed a nylon bag containing metal canisters. Opening the canisters, the officer discovered that they contained cocaine, methaqualone tablets, cocaine paraphernalia, and $700 in cash. In an outside zippered pouch of the backpack, he also found $210 in cash in a sealed envelope. After completing the inventory of the van, the officer had the van towed to an impound lot and brought the backpack, money, and contraband to the police station.

* * *

* * *[A]n inventory search may be "reasonable" under the Fourth Amendment even though it is not conducted pursuant to a warrant based upon probable cause. In *South Dakota* v. *Opperman*, 428 U.S. 364, 96 S.Ct. 3092, 49 L.Ed.2d 1000 (1976), this Court assessed the reasonableness of an inventory search of the glove compartment in an abandoned automobile impounded by the police. We found that inventory procedures serve to protect an owner's property while it is in the custody of the police, to insure against claims of lost, stolen, or vandalized property, and to guard the police from danger. * * *

In our more recent decision, *Illinois v. LaFayette* 462 U.S. 640, 103 S.Ct. 2605, 77 L.Ed.2d 65 (1983), a police officer conducted an inventory search of the contents of a shoulder bag in the possession of an individual being taken into custody. In deciding whether this search was reasonable, we recognized that the search served legitimate governmental interests similar to those identified in *Opperman*. We determined that those interests outweighed the individual's Fourth Amendment interests and upheld the search.

In the present case, as in *Opperman* and *Lafayette*, there was no showing that the police, who were following standardized procedures, acted in bad faith or for the sole purpose of investigation. In addition, the governmental interests justifying the inventory searches in *Opperman* and *Lafayette* are nearly the same as those which obtain here. In each case, the police were potentially responsible for the property taken into their custody. By securing the property, the police protected the property from unauthorized interference. Knowledge of the precise nature of the property helped guard against claims of theft, vandalism, or negligence. Such knowledge also helped to avert any danger to police or others that may have been posed by the property.

* * *

The Supreme Court of Colorado also expressed the view that the search in this case was unreasonable because Bertine's van was towed to a secure, lighted facility and because Bertine himself could have been offered the opportunity to make other arrangements for the safekeeping of his property. But the security of the storage facility does not completely eliminate the need for inventorying; the police may still wish to protect themselves or the owners of the lot against false claims of theft or dangerous instrumentalities. And while giving Bertine an opportunity to make alternative arrangements would undoubtedly have been possible, we said in *Lafayette*:

> "[The] real question is not what 'could have been achieved,' but whether the Fourth Amendment *requires* such steps. . . .

We conclude that here, as in *Lafayette*, reasonable police regulations relating to inventory procedures administered in good faith satisfy the Fourth Amendment, even though courts might as a matter of hindsight be able to devise equally reasonable rules requiring a different procedure.

The Supreme Court of Colorado also thought it necessary to require that police, before inventorying a container, weigh the strength of the individual's privacy interest in the container against the possibility that the container might serve as a repository for dangerous or valuable items. We think that such a requirement is contrary to our decisions in

Opperman and *Lafayette*, and by analogy to our decision in *United States v. Ross*, 456 U.S. 798, 102 S.Ct. 2157, 72 L.Ed.2d 572 (1982):

> "Even if less intrusive means existed of protecting some particular types of property, it would be unreasonable to expect police officers in the everyday course of business to make fine and subtle distinctions in deciding which containers or items may be searched and which must be sealed as a unit."

> "When a legitimate search is under way, and when its purpose and its limits have been precisely defined, nice distinctions between closets, drawers, and containers, in the case of a home, or between glove compartments, upholstered seats, trunks, and wrapped packages, in the case of a vehicle, must give way to the interest in the prompt and efficient completion of the task at hand."

We reaffirm these principles here: " '[a] single familiar standard is essential to guide police officers, who have only limited time and expertise to reflect on and balance the social and individual interests involved in the specific circumstances they confront.' "

Bertine finally argues that the inventory search of his van was unconstitutional because departmental regulations gave the police officers discretion to choose between impounding his van and parking and locking it in a public parking place. Nothing in *Opperman* or *Lafayette* prohibits the exercise of police discretion so long as that discretion is exercised according to standard criteria and on the basis of something other than suspicion of evidence of criminal activity. Here, the discretion afforded the Boulder police was exercised in light of standardized criteria, related to the feasibility and appropriateness of parking and locking a vehicle rather than impounding it.[7] There was no showing that the police chose to impound Bertine's van in order to investigate suspected criminal activity.

[The concurring opinions of JUSTICE BLACKMUN, JUSTICE POWELL, and JUSTICE O'CONNOR are omitted]

JUSTICE MARSHALL, with whom JUSTICE BRENNAN joins, dissenting.

I

As the Court acknowledges, inventory searches are reasonable only if conducted according to standardized procedures. In both *Opperman* and *Lafayette*, the Court relied on the absence of police discretion in determining that the inventory searches in question were reasonable.

---

7. In arguing that the Boulder Police Department procedures set forth no standardized criteria guiding an officer's decision to impound a vehicle, the dissent selectively quotes from the police directive concerning the care and security of vehicles taken into police custody. The dissent fails to mention that the directive establishes several conditions that must be met before an officer may pursue the park-and-lock alternative. For example, police may not park and lock the vehicle where there is reasonable risk of damage or vandalism to the vehicle or where the approval of the arrestee cannot be obtained. Not only do such conditions circumscribe the discretion of individual officers, but they also protect the vehicle and its contents and minimize claims of property loss.

* * * In assessing the reasonableness of searches conducted in limited situations such as these, where we do not require probable cause or a warrant, we have consistently emphasized the need for such set procedures: "standardless and unconstrained discretion is the evil the Court has discerned when in previous cases it has insisted that the discretion of the official in the field be circumscribed, at least to some extent."

The Court today attempts to evade these clear prohibitions on unfettered police discretion by declaring that "the discretion afforded the Boulder police was exercised in light of standardized criteria, related to the feasibility and appropriateness of parking and locking a vehicle rather than impounding it." This vital assertion is flatly contradicted by the record in this case. The officer who conducted the inventory, Officer Reichenbach, testified at the suppression hearing that the decision not to "park and lock" respondent's vehicle was his "own individual discretionary decision." Indeed, application of these supposedly standardized "criteria" upon which the Court so heavily relies would have yielded a different result in this case. Since there was ample public parking adjacent to the intersection where respondent was stopped, consideration of "feasibility" would certainly have militated in favor of the "park and lock" option, not against it. I do not comprehend how consideration of "appropriateness" serves to channel a field officer's discretion; nonetheless, the "park and lock" option would seem particularly appropriate in this case, where respondent was stopped for a traffic offense and was not likely to be in custody for a significant length of time.

Indeed, the record indicates that *no* standardized criteria limit a Boulder police officer's discretion. According to a departmental directive, after placing a driver under arrest, an officer has three options for disposing of the vehicle. First, he can allow a third party to take custody. Second, the officer or the driver (depending on the nature of the arrest) may take the car to the nearest public parking facility, lock it, and take the keys. Finally, the officer can do what was done in this case: impound the vehicle, and search and inventory its contents, including closed containers.

Under the first option, the police have no occasion to search the automobile. Under the "park and lock" option, "[closed] containers that give no indication of containing either valuables or a weapon *may not be opened and the contents searched* (i.e., inventoried)." Only if the police choose the third option are they entitled to search closed containers in the vehicle. Where the vehicle is not itself evidence of a crime, as in this case, the police apparently have totally unbridled discretion as to which procedure to use. Consistent with this conclusion, Officer Reichenbach testified that such decisions were left to the discretion of the officer on the scene.

Once a Boulder police officer has made this initial completely discretionary decision to impound a vehicle, he is given little guidance as to which areas to search and what sort of items to inventory. The arresting officer, Officer Toporek, testified at the suppression hearing as to what items would be inventoried: "That would I think be very individualistic as far as what an officer may or may not go into. I think whatever arouses his suspicious *[sic]* as far as what may be contained in any type of article in the car." In application, these so-called procedures left the breadth of the "inventory" to the whim of the individual officer. Clearly, "[the] practical effect of this system is to leave the [owner] subject to the discretion of the official in the field."

Inventory searches are not subject to the warrant requirement because they are conducted by the government as part of a "community caretaking" function, "totally divorced from the detection, investigation, or acquisition of evidence relating to the violation of a criminal statute." Standardized procedures are necessary to ensure that this narrow exception is not improperly used to justify, after the fact, a warrantless investigative foray. Accordingly, to invalidate a search that is conducted without established procedures, it is not necessary to establish that the police actually acted in bad faith, or that the inventory was in fact a "pretext." By allowing the police unfettered discretion, Boulder's discretionary scheme, like the random spot checks in *Delaware* v. *Prouse*, is unreasonable because of the " 'grave danger' of abuse of discretion."

* * *

Chapter 4

THE "REASONABLENESS" MODEL AND FOURTH AMENDMENT BALANCING

Introduction

The warrant preference model discussed in Chapter 3 creates problems for anyone interpreting the Fourth Amendment. On a practical level, the many exceptions engrafted onto the warrant rule demonstrate that circumstances frequently do not permit law enforcers to obtain a warrant before they act. The warrant model also creates problems on more theoretical levels. For example, it is relatively inflexible. According to this theory, any government conduct regulated by the Amendment must satisfy the requirements of probable cause and a warrant or exception. In recent decades, the Supreme Court has employed a more flexible, but also less rule-bound, approach that emphasizes the reasonableness standard found in the Fourth Amendment's first clause. Consider the following commentaries discussing this development and the justifications for this new interpretive theory.

1. Akhil Reed Amar, Fourth Amendment First Principles, 107 Harv. L. Rev. 757, 761, 782–783, 801 (1994).

"The words of the Fourth Amendment really do mean what they say. They do not require warrants, even presumptively, for searches and seizures. They do not require probable cause for all searches and seizures without warrants. They do not require—or even invite—exclusions of evidence, contraband, or stolen goods. All this is relatively obvious if only we read the Amendment's words carefully and take them seriously * * *

* * *

"In recognizing various exceptions to its so-called warrant requirement, the modern Court has routinely said that even warrantless searches and seizures ordinarily must be backed by 'probable cause' But like its kindred warrant requirement, the probable cause requirement stands the Fourth Amendment on its head.

"Begin with the text. The 'probable cause' standard applies only to 'warrants' not to all 'searches' and 'seizures' None of the other warrant rules—oath or affirmation, particular description, and so forth—sensibly applies to all searches and seizures; and the Court, bowing to the text and common sense, has never so applied them.

"Why, then, has the Court tried to wrench the words 'probable cause' from one Clause and force them into another? Because of the 'fundamental and obvious' notion that 'less stringent standards for reviewing the officer's discretion in effecting a warrantless arrest and search would discourage resort to the procedures for obtaining a warrant.' In the words of a leading commentator,' the concept of probable cause lies at the heart of the fourth amendment' and it would be 'incongruous' if police officers have "greater power to make seizures than magistrates have to authorize them."

* * *

Of course, certain intrusive subcategories of warrantless action—arrests, for example—might generally require "probable cause" at common law, but this is a far cry from the idea that *all* searches and seizures must meet this standard to be reasonable. Supporters of a global probable cause requirement have yet to identify even a single early case, treatise, or state constitution that explicitly proclaims "probable cause" as the prerequisite for all "searches and seizures." And let us recall once again the apparent common law rule that a warrantless intrusion could be justified after the fact, even in the absence of objective probable cause ex ante, if it succeeded in turning up an actual felon.

Rights first. The core of the Fourth Amendment, as we have seen, is neither a warrant nor probable cause, but reasonableness. Because of the Court's preoccupation with warrants and probable cause—ordaining these with one hand while chiseling out exception after exception with the other—the Justices have spent surprisingly little time self-consciously reflecting on what, exactly, makes for a substantively unreasonable search or seizure.

2. Adapted from Morgan Cloud, Searching through History; Searching for History, 63 U. Chi. L. Rev. 1707 (1996).

In recent years, the "warrant model" employing the conjunctive theory linking the two clauses has lost its central role in the Supreme Court's Fourth Amendment jurisprudence. In a number of different settings, the Supreme Court has adopted a "disjunctive" theory that cleaves the Amendment's two clauses. Rather than focus upon the characteristics of reasonable searches and seizures outlined in the Warrant Clause, the Supreme Court has concluded that whether a particular search is unreasonable "is judged by balancing its intrusion on the individual's Fourth Amendment interests against its promotion of legitimate governmental interests." The warrant model now is treated merely as an example of balancing, imposed on some, but not all, criminal investigations.

The following passage from Skinner v. Railway Labor Executives' Ass'n, 489 U.S. 602, 618–619 (1989), exemplifies this increasingly common method of constitutional interpretation:

> [T]he Fourth Amendment does not proscribe all searches and seizures, but only those that are unreasonable. What is reasonable, of course, "depends on all of the circumstances surrounding the search or seizure and the nature of the search or seizure itself." Thus, the permissibility of a particular practice "is judged by balancing its intrusion on the individual's Fourth Amendment interests against its promotion of legitimate governmental interests."
>
> In most criminal cases, we strike this balance in favor of the procedures described by the Warrant Clause of the Fourth Amendment. Except in certain well-defined circumstances, a search or seizure in such a case is not reasonable unless it is accomplished pursuant to a judicial warrant issued upon probable cause. We have recognized exceptions to this rule, however, "when 'special needs, beyond the normal need for law enforcement, make the warrant and probable-cause requirement impracticable.' " When faced with such special needs, we have not hesitated to balance the governmental and privacy interests to assess the practicality of the warrant and probable-cause requirements in the particular context.

With increasing frequency, the Court has decided that the rules found in the Warrant Clause, including the fundamental requirement of probable cause, are irrelevant for judging the reasonableness of many government searches and seizures. "[A] warrant is not required to establish the reasonableness of *all* government searches; and when a warrant is not required (and the Warrant Clause therefore not applicable), probable cause is not invariably required either."

This argument rests upon tautological reasoning and the assumption that the Amendment's two clauses apply to discrete categories of searches and seizures. The argument posits that the requirements imposed by the Warrant Clause are relevant only to searches and seizures conducted pursuant to warrants. Searches conducted without a warrant or probable cause are reasonable whenever a decision maker determines that "special needs" make that conduct reasonable. Freed from the constraints of the Warrant Clause, judges applying the increasingly malleable standard of reasonableness can adopt whatever policies they prefer.

3. The Supreme Court's initial steps in this doctrinal revolution were taken in a case involving enforcement of public health and safety rules and not enforcement of traditional criminal laws. In Camara v. Municipal Court, 387 U.S. 523, 87 S.Ct. 1727, 18 L.Ed.2d 930 (1967), the Court reconsidered its recent decision in Frank v. Maryland, 359 U.S. 360, 79 S.Ct. 804, 3 L.Ed.2d 877 (1959), which had upheld a state court conviction of a property owner who refused to permit a municipal health inspector to enter and inspect his premises without a search warrant. In reversing its earlier decision, the *Camara* Court concluded that the

Fourth Amendment, imposed upon the States through the Fourteenth Amendment, regulated administrative building inspection programs, and announced a new "balancing" method to justify this expansion of the scope of the Fourth Amendment. One year later, in Terry v. Ohio, 392 U.S. 1, 88 S.Ct. 1868, 20 L.Ed.2d 889 (1968), the Court relied upon *Camara* to extend the balancing process to the enforcement of criminal laws. Once again, the decision extended the courts' power of constitutional judicial review over previously unregulated government practices.

As you read the materials in this Chapter, consider the following questions: Were the Court's decisions extending its power of constitutional judicial review into areas previously unregulated by Fourth Amendment consistent with the constitutional text? Were they necessary? Do the problems created by this exercise of judicial authority justify weakening or abandoning the warrant model?

A. BALANCING EMERGES IN FOURTH AMENDMENT THEORY: ADMINISTRATIVE SEARCHES

CAMARA v. MUNICIPAL COURT

Supreme Court of the United States, 1967.
387 U.S. 523, 87 S.Ct. 1727, 18 L.Ed.2d 930.

Mr. Justice White delivered the opinion of the Court.

[A housing inspector from the San Francisco Department of Public Health entered an apartment building to make a routine annual inspection for possible violations of the city's Housing Code. The building's manager informed the inspector that appellant, lessee of the ground floor, was using the rear of his leasehold as a personal residence. Claiming that the building's occupancy permit did not allow residential use of the ground floor, the inspector demanded that Camara permit an inspection of the premises. Camara refused to allow the inspection because the inspector lacked a search warrant. Camara was charged with refusing to permit a lawful inspection in violation of the city housing code.]

I.

* * * The basic purpose of [the Fourth] Amendment, as recognized in countless decisions of this Court, is to safeguard the privacy and security of individuals against arbitrary invasions by governmental officials. The Fourth Amendment thus gives concrete expression to a right of the people which "is basic to a free society." * * *

Though there has been general agreement as to the fundamental purpose of the Fourth Amendment, translation of the abstract prohibition against "unreasonable searches and seizures" into workable guidelines for the decision of particular cases is a difficult task which has for many years divided the members of this Court. Nevertheless, one governing principle, justified by history and by current experience, has consistently been followed: except in certain carefully defined classes of cases, a search of private property without proper consent is "unreasonable" unless it has been authorized by a valid search warrant. * * *

* * *

* * * It is surely anomalous to say that the individual and his private property are fully protected by the Fourth Amendment only when the individual is suspected of criminal behavior. For instance, even the most law-abiding citizen has a very tangible interest in limiting the circumstances under which the sanctity of his home may be broken by official authority, for the possibility of criminal entry under the guise of official sanction is a serious threat to personal and family security. * * * Like most regulatory laws, fire, health, and housing codes are enforced by criminal processes. In some cities, discovery of a violation by the inspector leads to a criminal complaint. Even in cities where discovery of a violation produces only an administrative compliance order, refusal to comply is a criminal offense, and the fact of compliance is verified by a second inspection, again without a warrant. Finally, as this case demonstrates, refusal to permit an inspection is itself a crime, punishable by fine or even by jail sentence.

* * *

In our opinion, these arguments unduly discount the purposes behind the warrant machinery contemplated by the Fourth Amendment. Under the present system, when the inspector demands entry, the occupant has no way of knowing whether enforcement of the municipal code involved requires inspection of his premises, no way of knowing the lawful limits of the inspector's power to search, and no way of knowing whether the inspector himself is acting under proper authorization. These are questions which may be reviewed by a neutral magistrate without any reassessment of the basic agency decision to canvass an area. Yet, only by refusing entry and risking a criminal conviction can the occupant at present challenge the inspector's decision to search. And even if the occupant possesses sufficient fortitude to take this risk, as appellant did here, he may never learn any more about the reason for the inspection than that the law generally allows housing inspectors to gain entry. The practical effect of this system is to leave the occupant subject to the discretion of the official in the field. This is precisely the discretion to invade private property which we have consistently circumscribed by a requirement that a disinterested party warrant the need to search. We simply cannot say that the protections provided by the warrant procedure are not needed in this context; broad statutory safeguards are no substitute for individualized review, particularly when those safeguards may only be invoked at the risk of a criminal penalty.

The final justification suggested for warrantless administrative searches is that the public interest demands such a rule: it is vigorously argued that the health and safety of entire urban populations is dependent upon enforcement of minimum fire, housing, and sanitation standards, and that the only effective means of enforcing such codes is by routine systematized inspection of all physical structures. Of course, in applying any reasonableness standard, including one of constitutional dimension, an argument that the public interest demands a particular rule must receive careful consideration. But we think this argument misses the mark. The question is not, at this stage at least, whether these inspections may be made, but whether they may be made without a warrant. * * * It has nowhere been urged that fire, health, and housing code inspection programs could not achieve their goals within the confines of a reasonable search warrant requirement. Thus, we do not find the public need argument dispositive.

In summary, we hold that administrative searches of the kind at issue here are significant intrusions upon the interests protected by the Fourth Amendment, that such searches when authorized and conducted without a warrant procedure lack the traditional safeguards which the Fourth Amendment guarantees to the individual, and that the reasons put forth in *Frank* v. *Maryland* and in other cases for upholding these warrantless searches are insufficient to justify so substantial a weakening of the Fourth Amendment's protections. Because of the nature of the municipal programs under consideration, however, these conclusions must be the beginning, not the end, of our inquiry. The *Frank* majority gave recognition to the unique character of these inspection programs by refusing to require search warrants; to reject that disposition does not justify ignoring the question whether some other accommodation between public need and individual rights is essential.

II.

The Fourth Amendment provides that, "no Warrants shall issue, but upon probable cause." Borrowing from more typical Fourth Amendment cases, appellant argues not only that code enforcement inspection programs must be circumscribed by a warrant procedure, but also that warrants should issue only when the inspector possesses probable cause to believe that a particular dwelling contains violations of the minimum standards prescribed by the code being enforced. We disagree.

In cases in which the Fourth Amendment requires that a warrant to search be obtained, "probable cause" is the standard by which a particular decision to search is tested against the constitutional mandate of reasonableness. To apply this standard, it is obviously necessary first to focus upon the governmental interest which allegedly justifies official intrusion upon the constitutionally protected interests of the private citizen. For example, in a criminal investigation, the police may undertake to recover specific stolen or contraband goods. But that public interest would hardly justify a sweeping search of an entire city conducted in the hope that these goods might be found. Consequently, a search for these goods, even with a warrant, is "reasonable" only when there is "probable cause" to believe that they will be uncovered in a particular dwelling.

Unlike the search pursuant to a criminal investigation, the inspection programs at issue here are aimed at securing city-wide compliance with minimum physical standards for private property. The primary governmental interest at stake is to prevent even the unintentional development of conditions which are hazardous to public health and safety. Because fires and epidemics may ravage large urban areas, because unsightly conditions adversely affect the economic values of neighboring structures, numerous courts have upheld the police power of municipalities to impose and enforce such minimum standards even upon existing structures. In determining whether a particular inspection is reasonable—and thus in determining whether there is probable cause to issue a warrant for that inspection—the need for the inspection must be weighed in terms of these reasonable goals of code enforcement.

* * *

* * * Unfortunately, there can be no ready test for determining reasonableness other than by balancing the need to search against the invasion which the search entails. But we think that a number of persuasive factors combine to support the reasonableness of area code-enforcement inspections. First, such programs have a long history of judicial and public acceptance. Second, the public interest demands that all dangerous conditions be prevented or abated, yet it is doubtful that any other canvassing technique would achieve acceptable results. Many such conditions—faulty wiring is an obvious example—are not observable from outside the building and indeed may not be apparent to the inexpert occupant himself. Finally, because the inspections are neither personal in nature nor aimed at the discovery of evidence of crime, they involve a relatively limited invasion of the urban citizen's privacy. * * *

" ... This is not to suggest that a health official need show the same kind of proof to a magistrate to obtain a warrant as one must who would search for the fruits or instrumentalities of crime. Where considerations of health and safety are involved, the facts that would justify an inference of 'probable cause' to make an inspection are clearly different from those that would justify such an inference where a criminal investigation has been undertaken. Experience may show the need for periodic inspections of certain facilities without a further showing of cause to believe that substandard conditions dangerous to the public are being maintained. The passage of a certain period without inspection might of itself be sufficient in a given situation to justify the issuance of a warrant. The test of 'probable cause' required by the Fourth Amendment can take into account the nature of the search that is being sought."

Having concluded that the area inspection is a "reasonable" search of private property within the meaning of the Fourth Amendment, it is obvious that "probable cause" to issue a warrant to inspect must exist if reasonable legislative or administrative standards for conducting an area inspection are satisfied with respect to a particular dwelling. Such standards, which will vary with the municipal program being enforced, may be based upon the passage of time, the nature of the building (e. g., a multi-family apartment house), or the condition of the entire area, but they will not necessarily depend upon specific knowledge of the condition of the particular dwelling. It has been suggested that so to vary the probable cause test from the standard applied in criminal cases would be to authorize a "synthetic search warrant" and thereby to lessen the overall protections of the Fourth Amendment. But we do not agree. The warrant procedure is designed to guarantee that a decision to search private property is justified by a reasonable governmental interest. But reasonableness is still the ultimate standard. If a valid public interest justifies the intrusion contemplated, then there is probable cause to issue a suitably restricted search warrant. Such an approach neither endangers time-honored doctrines applicable to criminal investigations nor makes a nullity of the probable cause requirement in this area. It merely gives full recognition to the competing public and private interests here at stake and, in so doing, best fulfills the historic purpose behind the constitutional right to be free from unreasonable government invasions of privacy.

III.

Since our holding emphasizes the controlling standard of reasonableness, nothing we say today is intended to foreclose prompt inspections, even without a warrant, that the law has traditionally upheld in emergency situations. On the other hand, in the case of most routine area inspections, there is no compelling urgency to inspect at a particular time or on a particular day. Moreover, most citizens allow inspections of their property without a warrant. Thus, as a practical matter and in light of the Fourth Amendment's requirement that a warrant specify the property to be searched, it seems likely that warrants should normally be sought only after entry is refused unless there has been a citizen complaint or there is other satisfactory reason for securing immediate entry. Similarly, the requirement of a warrant procedure does not suggest any change in what seems to be the prevailing local policy, in most situations, of authorizing entry, but not entry by force, to inspect.

IV.

In this case, appellant has been charged with a crime for his refusal to permit housing inspectors to enter his leasehold without a warrant. There was no emergency demanding immediate access; in fact, the inspectors made three trips to the building in an attempt to obtain appellant's consent to search. Yet no warrant was obtained and thus appellant was unable to verify either the need for or the appropriate limits of the inspection. No doubt, the inspectors entered the public portion of the building with the consent of the landlord, through the building's manager, but appellee does not contend that such consent was sufficient to authorize inspection of appellant's premises. [W]e therefore conclude that appellant had a constitutional right to insist that the inspectors obtain a warrant to search and that appellant may not constitutionally be convicted for refusing to consent to the inspection.
* * *

[MR. JUSTICE CLARK's dissenting opinion is omitted.]

B.　THE *TERRY* REVOLUTION

Introduction

"The tendency of a principle to expand itself to the limit of its logic may be counteracted by the tendency to confine itself within the limits of its history." Benjamin Cardozo, THE NATURE OF THE JUDICIAL PROCESS 51 (1921).

The year after it extended the reach of the Fourth Amendment to include the administrative searches at issue in *Camara*, the Supreme Court explicitly employed a balancing methodology in a criminal case to uphold a warrantless search and seizure not justified by probable cause. As you read *Terry v. Ohio* and the cases following it in this Chapter, consider whether each principle adopted in *Terry* has expanded over the years "to the limit of its logic," or instead has been constrained by the facts and issues which the Court cited in *Terry* to justify this break with traditional Fourth Amendment theory.

TERRY v. OHIO

Supreme Court of the United States, 1968.
392 U.S. 1, 88 S.Ct. 1868, 20 L.Ed.2d 889.

MR. CHIEF JUSTICE WARREN delivered the opinion of the Court.

This case presents serious questions concerning the role of the Fourth Amendment in the confrontation on the street between the citizen and the policeman investigating suspicious circumstances.

Petitioner Terry was convicted of carrying a concealed weapon and sentenced to the statutorily prescribed term of one to three years in the penitentiary. Following the denial of a pretrial motion to suppress, the prosecution introduced in evidence two revolvers and a number of bullets seized from Terry and a codefendant, Richard Chilton, by Cleveland Police Detective Martin McFadden. At the hearing on the motion to suppress this evidence, Officer McFadden testified that while he was patrolling in plain clothes in downtown Cleveland at approximately 2:30 in the afternoon of October 31, 1963, his attention was attracted by two men, Chilton and Terry, standing on the corner of Huron Road and Euclid Avenue. He had never seen the two men before, and he was unable to say precisely what first drew his eye to them. However, he testified that he had been a policeman for 39 years and a detective for 35 and that he had been assigned to patrol this vicinity of downtown Cleveland for shoplifters and pickpockets for 30 years. He explained that he had developed routine habits of observation over the years and that he would "stand and watch people or walk and watch people at many intervals of the day." He added: "Now, in this case when I looked over they didn't look right to me at the time."

His interest aroused, Officer McFadden took up a post of observation in the entrance to a store 300 to 400 feet away from the two men. "I get more purpose to watch them when I seen their movements," he testified. He saw one of the men leave the other one and walk southwest on Huron Road, past some stores. The man paused for a moment and looked in a store window, then walked on a short distance, turned around and walked back toward the corner, pausing once again to look in the same store window. He rejoined his companion at the corner, and the two conferred briefly. Then the second man went through the same series of motions, strolling down Huron Road, looking in the same window, walking on a short distance, turning back, peering in the store window again, and returning to confer with the first man at the corner. The two men repeated this ritual alternately between five and six times apiece—in all, roughly a dozen trips. At one point, while the two were standing together on the corner, a third man approached them and engaged them briefly in conversation. This man then left the two others and walked west on Euclid Avenue. Chilton and Terry resumed their measured pacing, peering, and conferring. After this had gone on for 10 to 12 minutes, the two men walked off together, heading west on Euclid Avenue, following the path taken earlier by the third man.

By this time Officer McFadden had become thoroughly suspicious. He testified that after observing their elaborately casual and oft-repeated reconnaissance of the store window on Huron Road, he suspected the two men of "casing a job, a stick-up," and that he considered it his duty as a police officer to investigate further. He added that he feared "they may have a gun." Thus, Officer McFadden followed Chilton and Terry and saw them stop in front of Zucker's store to talk to the same man who had conferred with them earlier on the street corner. Deciding that the situation was ripe for direct action, Officer McFadden approached the three men, identified himself as a police officer and asked for their names. At this point his knowledge was confined to what he had observed. He was not acquainted with any of the three men by name or by sight, and he had received no information concerning them from any other source. When the men "mumbled something" in response to his inquiries, Officer McFadden grabbed petitioner Terry, spun him around so that they were facing the other two, with Terry between McFadden and the others, and patted down the outside of his clothing. In the left breast pocket of Terry's overcoat Officer McFadden felt a pistol. He reached inside the overcoat pocket, but was unable to remove the gun. At this point, keeping Terry between himself and the others, the officer ordered all three men to enter Zucker's store. As they went in, he removed Terry's overcoat completely, removed a .38–caliber revolver from the pocket and ordered all three men to face the wall with their hands raised. Officer McFadden proceeded to pat down the outer clothing of Chilton and the third man, Katz. He discovered another revolver in the outer pocket of Chilton's overcoat, but no weapons were found on Katz. The officer testified that he only patted the men down to see whether they had weapons, and that he did not put his hands beneath the outer garments of either Terry or Chilton until he felt their guns. So far as appears from the record, he never placed his hands beneath Katz' outer garments. Officer McFadden seized Chilton's gun, asked the proprietor of the store to call a police wagon, and took all three men to the station, where Chilton and Terry were formally charged with carrying concealed weapons.

* * *

I.

* * *

We have recently held that "the Fourth Amendment protects people, not places," and wherever an individual may harbor a reasonable "expectation of privacy," he is entitled to be free from unreasonable governmental intrusion. Of course, the specific content and incidents of this right must be shaped by the context in which it is asserted. For "what the Constitution forbids is not all searches and seizures, but unreasonable searches and seizures." Unquestionably petitioner was entitled to the protection of the Fourth Amendment as he walked down the street in Cleveland. The question is whether in all the circumstances of this on-the-street encounter, his right to personal security was violated by an unreasonable search and seizure.

We would be less than candid if we did not acknowledge that this question thrusts to the fore difficult and troublesome issues regarding a sensitive area of police activity—issues which have never before been squarely presented to this Court. Reflective of the tensions involved are the practical and constitutional arguments pressed with great vigor on both sides of the public debate over the power of the police to "stop and frisk"—as it is sometimes euphemistically termed—suspicious persons.

On the one hand, it is frequently argued that in dealing with the rapidly unfolding and often dangerous situations on city streets the police are in need of an escalating set of flexible responses, graduated in relation to the amount of information they possess. For this purpose it is urged that distinctions should be made between a "stop" and an "arrest" (or a "seizure" of a person), and between a "frisk" and a "search." Thus, it is argued, the police should be allowed to "stop" a person and detain him briefly for questioning upon suspicion that he may be connected with criminal activity. Upon suspicion that the person may be armed, the police should have the power to "frisk" him for weapons. If the "stop" and the "frisk" give rise to probable cause to believe that the suspect has committed a crime, then the police should be empowered to make a formal "arrest," and a full incident "search" of the person. This scheme is justified in part upon the notion that a "stop" and a "frisk" amount to a mere "minor inconvenience and petty indignity," which can properly be imposed upon the citizen in the interest of effective law enforcement on the basis of a police officer's suspicion.

* * *

On the other side the argument is made that the authority of the police must be strictly circumscribed by the law of arrest and search as it has developed to date in the traditional jurisprudence of the Fourth Amendment. It is contended with some force that there is not—and cannot be—a variety of police activity which does not depend solely upon the voluntary cooperation of the citizen and yet which stops short of an arrest based upon probable cause to make such an arrest. The heart of the Fourth Amendment, the argument runs, is a severe requirement of specific justification for any intrusion upon protected personal security, coupled with a highly developed system of judicial controls to enforce upon the agents of the State the commands of the Constitution. Acquiescence by the courts in the compulsion inherent in the field interrogation practices at issue here, it is urged, would constitute an abdication of judicial control over, and indeed an encouragement of, substantial interference with liberty and personal security by police officers whose judgment is necessarily colored by their primary involvement in "the often competitive enterprise of ferreting out crime." This, it is argued, can only serve to exacerbate police-community tensions in the crowded centers of our Nation's cities.

In this context we approach the issues in this case mindful of the limitations of the judicial function in controlling the myriad daily situations in which policemen and citizens confront each other on the street. The State has characterized the issue here as "the right of a police officer ... to make an on-the-street stop, interrogate and pat down for weapons (known in street vernacular as 'stop and frisk')." But this is only partly accurate. For the issue is not the abstract propriety of the police conduct, but the admissibility against petitioner of the evidence uncovered by the search and seizure. Ever since its inception, the rule excluding evidence seized in violation of the Fourth Amendment has been recognized as a principal mode of discouraging lawless police conduct. Thus its major thrust is a deterrent one, and experience has taught that it is the only effective deterrent to police misconduct in the criminal context, and that without it the constitutional guarantee against unreasonable searches and seizures would be a mere "form of words." The rule also serves another vital function—"the imperative of judicial integrity." Courts which sit under our Constitution cannot and will not be made party to lawless invasions of the constitutional rights of citizens by permitting unhindered governmental use of the fruits of such invasions. Thus in our system evidentiary rulings provide the context in which the judicial process of inclusion and exclusion approves some conduct as comporting with constitutional guarantees and disapproves other actions by state agents. A ruling admitting evidence in a criminal trial, we recognize, has the necessary effect of legitimizing the conduct which produced the evidence, while an application of the exclusionary rule withholds the constitutional imprimatur.

The exclusionary rule has its limitations, however, as a tool of judicial control. It cannot properly be invoked to exclude the products of legitimate police investigative techniques on the ground that much conduct which is closely similar involves unwarranted intrusions upon constitutional protections. Moreover, in some contexts the rule is ineffective as a deterrent. Street encounters between citizens and police officers are incredibly rich in diversity. They range from wholly friendly exchanges of pleasantries or mutually useful information to hostile confrontations of armed men involving arrests, or injuries, or loss of life. Moreover, hostile confrontations are not all of a piece. Some of them begin in a friendly enough manner, only to take a different turn upon the injection of some unexpected element into the conversation. Encounters are initiated by the police for a wide variety of purposes, some of which are wholly unrelated to a desire to prosecute for crime.[9] Doubtless some police "field interrogation" conduct violates the Fourth Amendment. But a stern refusal by this Court to condone such activity does not necessarily render it responsive to the exclusionary rule. Regardless of how effective the rule may be where obtaining convictions is an important objective of the police, it is powerless to deter invasions of constitutionally guaranteed rights where the police either have no interest in prosecuting or are willing to forgo successful prosecution in the interest of serving some other goal.

Proper adjudication of cases in which the exclusionary rule is invoked demands a constant awareness of these limitations. The wholesale harassment by certain elements of the police community, of which minority groups, particularly Negroes, frequently complain,[11] will not be stopped by the exclusion of any evidence from any criminal trial. Yet a rigid and unthinking application of the exclusionary rule, in futile protest against practices which it can never be used effectively to control, may exact a high toll in human injury and frustration of efforts to prevent crime. No judicial opinion can comprehend the protean variety of the street encounter, and we can only judge the facts of the case before us. Nothing we say today is to be taken as indicating approval of

9. See L. Tiffany, D. McIntyre & D. Rotenberg, Detection of Crime: Stopping and Questioning, Search and Seizure, Encouragement and Entrapment 18–56 (1967). This sort of police conduct may, for example, be designed simply to help an intoxicated person find his way home, with no intention of arresting him unless he becomes obstreperous. Or the police may be seeking to mediate a domestic quarrel which threatens to erupt into violence. They may accost a woman in an area known for prostitution as part of a harassment campaign designed to drive prostitutes away without the considerable difficulty involved in prosecuting them. Or they may be conducting a dragnet search of all teenagers in a particular section of the city for weapons because they have heard rumors of an impending gang fight.

11. The President's Commission on Law Enforcement and Administration of Justice found that "in many communities, field interrogations are a major source of friction between the police and minority groups." President's Commission on Law Enforcement and Administration of Justice, Task Force Report: The Police 183 (1967). It was reported that the friction caused by "misuse of field interrogations" increases "as more police departments adopt 'aggressive patrol' in which officers are encouraged routinely to stop and question persons on the street who are unknown to them, who are suspicious, or whose purpose for being abroad is not readily evident." Id., at 184. While the frequency with which "frisking" forms a part of field interrogation practice varies tremendously with the locale, the objective of the interrogation, and the particular officer, see Tiffany, McIntyre & Rotenberg, supra, n. 9, at 47–48, it cannot help but be a severely exacerbating factor in police-community tensions. This is particularly true in situations where the "stop and frisk" of youths or minority group members is "motivated by the officers' perceived need to maintain the power image of the beat officer, an aim sometimes accomplished by humiliating anyone who attempts to undermine police control of the streets."

police conduct outside the legitimate investigative sphere. Under our decision, courts still retain their traditional responsibility to guard against police conduct which is overbearing or harassing, or which trenches upon personal security without the objective evidentiary justification which the Constitution requires. * * *

II.

Our first task is to * * * decide whether and when Officer McFadden "seized" Terry and whether and when he conducted a "search." There is some suggestion in the use of such terms as "stop" and "frisk" that such police conduct is outside the purview of the Fourth Amendment because neither action rises to the level of a "search" or "seizure" within the meaning of the Constitution. We emphatically reject this notion. It is quite plain that the Fourth Amendment governs "seizures" of the person which do not eventuate in a trip to the station house and prosecution for crime—"arrests" in traditional terminology. It must be recognized that whenever a police officer accosts an individual and restrains his freedom to walk away, he has "seized" that person. And it is nothing less than sheer torture of the English language to suggest that a careful exploration of the outer surfaces of a person's clothing all over his or her body in an attempt to find weapons is not a "search." Moreover, it is simply fantastic to urge that such a procedure performed in public by a policeman while the citizen stands helpless, perhaps facing a wall with his hands raised, is a "petty indignity."[13] It is a serious intrusion upon the sanctity of the person, which may inflict great indignity and arouse strong resentment, and it is not to be undertaken lightly.

* * *

The danger in the logic which proceeds upon distinctions between a "stop" and an "arrest," or "seizure" of the person, and between a "frisk" and a "search" is twofold. It seeks to isolate from constitutional scrutiny the initial stages of the contact between the policeman and the citizen. And by suggesting a rigid all-or-nothing model of justification and regulation under the Amendment, it obscures the utility of limitations upon the scope, as well as the initiation, of police action as a means of constitutional regulation. This Court has held in the past that a search which is reasonable at its inception may violate the Fourth Amendment by virtue of its intolerable intensity and scope. The scope of the search must be "strictly tied to and justified by" the circumstances which rendered its initiation permissible.

In our view the sounder course is to recognize that the Fourth Amendment governs all intrusions by agents of the public upon personal

13. Consider the following apt description:

"[T]he officer must feel with sensitive fingers every portion of the prisoner's body. A thorough search must be made of the prisoner's arms and armpits, waistline and back, the groin and area about the testicles, and entire surface of the legs down to the feet." Priar & Martin, Searching and Disarming Criminals, 45 J. Crim. L. C. & P. S. 481 (1954).

security, and to make the scope of the particular intrusion, in light of all the exigencies of the case, a central element in the analysis of reasonableness. * * *

The distinctions of classical "stop-and-frisk" theory thus serve to divert attention from the central inquiry under the Fourth Amendment—the reasonableness in all the circumstances of the particular governmental invasion of a citizen's personal security. "Search" and "seizure" are not talismans. We therefore reject the notions that the Fourth Amendment does not come into play at all as a limitation upon police conduct if the officers stop short of something called a "technical arrest" or a "full-blown search."

In this case there can be no question, then, that Officer McFadden "seized" petitioner and subjected him to a "search" when he took hold of him and patted down the outer surfaces of his clothing. We must decide whether at that point it was reasonable for Officer McFadden to have interfered with petitioner's personal security as he did. And in determining whether the seizure and search were "unreasonable" our inquiry is a dual one—whether the officer's action was justified at its inception, and whether it was reasonably related in scope to the circumstances which justified the interference in the first place.

III.

If this case involved police conduct subject to the Warrant Clause of the Fourth Amendment, we would have to ascertain whether "probable cause" existed to justify the search and seizure which took place. However, that is not the case. We do not retreat from our holdings that the police must, whenever practicable, obtain advance judicial approval of searches and seizures through the warrant procedure, or that in most instances failure to comply with the warrant requirement can only be excused by exigent circumstances. But we deal here with an entire rubric of police conduct—necessarily swift action predicated upon the on-the-spot observations of the officer on the beat—which historically has not been, and as a practical matter could not be, subjected to the warrant procedure. Instead, the conduct involved in this case must be tested by the Fourth Amendment's general proscription against unreasonable searches and seizures.

Nonetheless, the notions which underlie both the warrant procedure and the requirement of probable cause remain fully relevant in this context. In order to assess the reasonableness of Officer McFadden's conduct as a general proposition, it is necessary "first to focus upon the governmental interest which allegedly justifies official intrusion upon the constitutionally protected interests of the private citizen," for there is "no ready test for determining reasonableness other than by balancing the need to search [or seize] against the invasion which the search [or seizure] entails." *Camara* v. *Municipal Court*, 387 U.S. 523, 534–535, 536–537, 87 S.Ct. 1727, 18 L.Ed.2d 930 (1967). And in justifying the particular intrusion the police officer must be able to point to specific and articulable facts which, taken together with rational inferences from those facts, reasonably warrant that intrusion. The scheme of the Fourth Amendment becomes meaningful only when it is assured that at some point the conduct of those charged with enforcing the laws can be subjected to the more detached, neutral scrutiny of a judge who must evaluate the reasonableness of a particular search or seizure in light of the particular circumstances. And in making that assessment it is imperative that the facts be judged against an objective standard: would the facts available to the officer at the moment of the seizure or the search "warrant a man of reasonable caution in the belief" that the action taken was appropriate? Anything less would invite intrusions upon constitutionally guaranteed rights based on nothing more substantial than inarticulate hunches, a result this Court has consistently refused to sanction. And simple " 'good faith on the part of the arresting officer is not enough.' . . . If subjective good faith alone were the test, the protections of the Fourth Amendment would evaporate, and the people would be 'secure in their persons, houses, papers, and effects,' only in the discretion of the police."

Applying these principles to this case, we consider first the nature and extent of the governmental interests involved. One general interest is of course that of effective crime prevention and detection; it is this interest which underlies the recognition that a police officer may in appropriate circumstances and in an appropriate manner approach a person for purposes of investigating possibly criminal behavior even though there is no probable cause to make an arrest. It was this legitimate investigative function Officer McFadden was discharging when he decided to approach petitioner and his companions. He had observed Terry, Chilton, and Katz go through a series of acts, each of them perhaps innocent in itself, but which taken together warranted further investigation. There is nothing unusual in two men standing together on a street corner, perhaps waiting for someone. Nor is there anything suspicious about people in such circumstances strolling up and down the street, singly or in pairs. Store windows, moreover, are made to be looked in. But the story is quite different where, as here, two men hover about a street corner for an extended period of time, at the end of which it becomes apparent that they are not waiting for anyone or anything; where these men pace alternately along an identical route, pausing to stare in the same store window roughly 24 times; where each completion of this route is followed immediately by a conference between the two men on the corner; where they are joined in one of these conferences by a third man who leaves swiftly; and where the two men finally follow the third and rejoin him a couple of blocks away. It would have been poor police work indeed for an officer of 30 years' experience in the detection of thievery from stores in this same neighborhood to have failed to investigate this behavior further.

The crux of this case, however, is not the propriety of Officer McFadden's taking steps to investigate petitioner's suspicious behavior, but rather, whether there was justification for McFadden's invasion of Terry's personal security by searching him for weapons in the course of that investigation. We are now concerned with more than the governmental interest in investigating crime; in addition, there is the more immediate interest of the police officer in taking steps to assure himself that the person with whom he is dealing is not armed with a weapon that could unexpectedly and fatally be used against him. Certainly it would be unreasonable to require that police officers take unnecessary risks in the performance of their duties. American criminals have a long tradition of armed violence, and every year in this country many law enforcement officers are killed in the line of duty, and thousands more are wounded. Virtually all of these deaths and a substantial portion of the injuries are inflicted with guns and knives.

In view of these facts, we cannot blind ourselves to the need for law enforcement officers to protect themselves and other prospective victims of violence in situations where they may lack probable cause for an arrest. When an officer is justified in believing that the individual whose suspicious behavior he is investigating at close range is armed and presently dangerous to the officer or to others, it would appear to be clearly unreasonable to deny the officer the power to take necessary measures to determine whether the person is in fact carrying a weapon and to neutralize the threat of physical harm.

We must still consider, however, the nature and quality of the intrusion on individual rights which must be accepted if police officers are to be conceded the right to search for weapons in situations where probable cause to arrest for crime is lacking. Even a limited search of the outer clothing for weapons constitutes a severe, though brief, intrusion upon cherished personal security, and it must surely be an annoying, frightening, and perhaps humiliating experience. * * *

* * * A search for weapons in the absence of probable cause to arrest, however, must, like any other search, be strictly circumscribed by the exigencies which justify its initiation. Thus it must be limited to that which is necessary for the discovery of weapons which might be used to harm the officer or others nearby, and may realistically be characterized as something less than a "full" search, even though it remains a serious intrusion.

A second, and related, objection to petitioner's argument is that it assumes that the law of arrest has already worked out the balance between the particular interests involved here—the neutralization of danger to the policeman in the investigative circumstance and the sanctity of the individual. But this is not so. An arrest is a wholly different kind of intrusion upon individual freedom from a limited search for weapons, and the interests each is designed to serve are likewise quite different. An arrest is the initial stage of a criminal prosecution. It is intended to vindicate society's interest in having its laws obeyed, and it is inevitably accompanied by future interference with the individual's freedom of movement, whether or not trial or conviction ultimately follows. The protective search for weapons, on the other hand, constitutes a brief, though far from inconsiderable, intrusion upon the sanctity of the person. It does not follow that because an officer may lawfully arrest a person only when he is apprised of facts sufficient to warrant a belief that the person has committed or is committing a crime, the officer is equally unjustified, absent that kind of evidence, in making any intrusions short of an arrest. Moreover, a perfectly reasonable apprehension of danger may arise long before the officer is possessed of adequate information to justify taking a person into custody for the purpose of prosecuting him for a crime. * * *

Our evaluation of the proper balance that has to be struck in this type of case leads us to conclude that there must be a narrowly drawn authority to permit a reasonable search for weapons for the protection of the police officer, where he has reason to believe that he is dealing with an armed and dangerous individual, regardless of whether he has probable cause to arrest the individual for a crime. The officer need not be absolutely certain that the individual is armed; the issue is whether a reasonably prudent man in the circumstances would be warranted in the belief that his safety or that of others was in danger. And in determining whether the officer acted reasonably in such circumstances, due weight must be given, not to his inchoate and unparticularized suspicion or "hunch," but to the specific reasonable inferences which he is entitled to draw from the facts in light of his experience.

IV.

We must now examine the conduct of Officer McFadden in this case to determine whether his search and seizure of petitioner were reasonable, both at their inception and as conducted. He had observed Terry, together with Chilton and another man, acting in a manner he took to be preface to a "stick-up." We think on the facts and circumstances Officer McFadden detailed before the trial judge a reasonably prudent man would have been warranted in believing petitioner was armed and thus presented a threat to the officer's safety while he was investigating his suspicious behavior. The actions of Terry and Chilton were consistent with McFadden's hypothesis that these men were contemplating a daylight robbery—which, it is reasonable to assume, would be likely to involve the use of weapons—and nothing in their conduct from the time he first noticed them until the time he confronted them and identified himself as a police officer gave him sufficient reason to negate that hypothesis. Although the trio had departed the original scene, there was nothing to indicate abandonment of an intent to commit a robbery at some point. Thus, when Officer McFadden approached the three men gathered before the display window at Zucker's store he had observed enough to make it quite reasonable to fear that they were armed; and nothing in their response to his hailing them, identifying himself as a police officer, and asking their names served to dispel that reasonable belief. * * *

The manner in which the seizure and search were conducted is, of course, as vital a part of the inquiry as whether they were warranted at all. The Fourth Amendment proceeds as much by limitations upon the scope of governmental action as by imposing preconditions upon its initiation. The entire deterrent purpose of the rule excluding evidence seized in violation of the Fourth Amendment rests on the assumption that "limitations upon the fruit to be gathered tend to limit the quest itself." Thus, evidence may not be introduced if it was discovered by means of a seizure and search which were not reasonably related in scope to the justification for their initiation.

* * *[A] search, unlike a search without a warrant incident to a lawful arrest, is not justified by any need to prevent the disappearance or destruction of evidence of crime. The sole justification of the search in the present situation is the protection of the police officer and others nearby, and it must therefore be confined in scope to an intrusion reasonably designed to discover guns, knives, clubs, or other hidden instruments for the assault of the police officer.

The scope of the search in this case presents no serious problem in light of these standards. Officer McFadden patted down the outer clothing of petitioner and his two companions. He did not place his hands in their pockets or under the outer surface of their garments until he had felt weapons, and then he merely reached for and removed the guns. He never did invade Katz' person beyond the outer surfaces of his clothes, since he discovered nothing in his pat-down which might have been a weapon. Officer McFadden confined his search strictly to what was minimally necessary to learn whether the men were armed and to disarm them once he discovered the weapons. He did not conduct a general exploratory search for whatever evidence of criminal activity he might find.

* * *

[Concurring opinions of JUSTICE BLACK and JUSTICE HARLAN are omitted.]

MR. JUSTICE WHITE, concurring.

* * * There is nothing in the Constitution which prevents a policeman from addressing questions to anyone on the streets. Absent special circumstances, the person approached may not be detained or frisked but may refuse to cooperate and go on his way. However, given the proper circumstances, such as those in this case, it seems to me the person may be briefly detained against his will while pertinent questions are directed to him. Of course, the person stopped is not obliged to answer, answers may not be compelled, and refusal to answer furnishes no basis for an arrest, although it may alert the officer to the need for continued observation. * * *

MR. JUSTICE DOUGLAS, dissenting.

I agree that petitioner was "seized" within the meaning of the Fourth Amendment. I also agree that frisking petitioner and his companions for guns was a "search." But it is a mystery how that "search" and that "seizure" can be constitutional by Fourth Amendment standards, unless there was "probable cause" to believe that (1) a crime had been committed or (2) a crime was in the process of being committed or (3) a crime was about to be committed.

The opinion of the Court disclaims the existence of "probable cause." If loitering were in issue and that was the offense charged, there would be "probable cause" shown. But the crime here is carrying concealed weapons; and there is no basis for concluding that the officer had "probable cause" for believing that that crime was being committed. Had a warrant been sought, a magistrate would, therefore, have been unauthorized to issue one, for he can act only if there is a showing of "probable cause." We hold today that the police have greater authority to make a "seizure" and conduct a "search" than a judge has to authorize such action. We have said precisely the opposite over and over again.

* * *

The infringement on personal liberty of any "seizure" of a person can only be "reasonable" under the Fourth Amendment if we require the police to possess "probable cause" before they seize him. Only that line draws a meaningful distinction between an officer's mere inkling and the presence of facts within the officer's personal knowledge which would convince a reasonable man that the person seized has committed, is committing, or is about to commit a particular crime. "In dealing with probable cause, ... as the very name implies, we deal with probabilities. These are not technical; they are the factual and practical considerations of everyday life on which reasonable and prudent men, not legal technicians, act."

* * *

C. THE MEANING OF REASONABLE SUSPICION

UNITED STATES v. SOKOLOW

Supreme Court of the United States, 1989.
490 U.S. 1, 109 S.Ct. 1581, 104 L.Ed.2d 1.

CHIEF JUSTICE REHNQUIST delivered the opinion of the Court.

* * *

This case involves a typical attempt to smuggle drugs through one of the Nation's airports. On a Sunday in July 1984, respondent went to the United Airlines ticket counter at Honolulu Airport, where he purchased two round-trip tickets for a flight to Miami leaving later that day. The tickets were purchased in the names of "Andrew Kray" and "Janet Norian," and had open return dates. Respondent paid $2,100 for the tickets from a large roll of $20 bills, which appeared to contain a total of $4,000. He also gave the ticket agent his home telephone number. The ticket agent noticed that respondent seemed nervous; he was about 25 years old; he was dressed in a black jumpsuit and wore gold jewelry; and he was accompanied by a woman, who turned out to be Janet Norian.

Neither respondent nor his companion checked any of their four pieces of luggage.

After the couple left for their flight, the ticket agent informed Officer John McCarthy of the Honolulu Police Department of respondent's cash purchase of tickets to Miami. Officer McCarthy determined that the telephone number respondent gave to the ticket agent was subscribed to a "Karl Herman," who resided at 348–A Royal Hawaiian Avenue in Honolulu. Unbeknownst to McCarthy (and later to the DEA agents), respondent was Herman's roommate. The ticket agent identified respondent's voice on the answering machine at Herman's number. Officer McCarthy was unable to find any listing under the name "Andrew Kray" in Hawaii. McCarthy subsequently learned that return reservations from Miami to Honolulu had been made in the names of Kray and Norian, with their arrival scheduled for July 25, three days after respondent and his companion had left. He also learned that Kray and Norian were scheduled to make stopovers in Denver and Los Angeles.

On July 25, during the stopover in Los Angeles, DEA agents identified respondent. He "appeared to be very nervous and was looking all around the waiting area." Later that day, at 6:30 p.m., respondent and Norian arrived in Honolulu. As before, they had not checked their luggage. Respondent was still wearing a black jumpsuit and gold jewelry. The couple proceeded directly to the street and tried to hail a cab, where Agent Richard Kempshall and three other DEA agents approached them. Kempshall displayed his credentials, grabbed respondent by the arm and moved him back onto the sidewalk. Kempshall asked respondent for his airline ticket and identification; respondent said that he had neither. He told the agents that his name was "Sokolow," but that he was traveling under his mother's maiden name, "Kray."

Respondent and Norian were escorted to the DEA office at the airport. There, the couple's luggage was examined by "Donker," a narcotics detector dog, which alerted to respondent's brown shoulder bag. The agents arrested respondent. He was advised of his constitutional rights and declined to make any statements. The agents obtained a warrant to search the shoulder bag. They found no illicit drugs, but the bag did contain several suspicious documents indicating respondent's involvement in drug trafficking. The agents had Donker reexamine the remaining luggage, and this time the dog alerted to a medium sized Louis Vuitton bag. By now, it was 9:30 p.m., too late for the agents to obtain a second warrant. They allowed respondent to leave for the night, but kept his luggage. The next morning, after a second dog confirmed Donker's alert, the agents obtained a warrant and found 1,063 grams of cocaine inside the bag.

* * *

The United States Court of Appeals for the Ninth Circuit reversed respondent's conviction by a divided vote, holding that the DEA agents did not have a reasonable suspicion to justify the stop. The majority divided the facts bearing on reasonable suspicion into two categories. In the first category, the majority placed facts describing "ongoing criminal activity," such as the use of an alias or evasive movement through an airport; the majority believed that at least one such factor was always needed to support a finding of reasonable suspicion. In the second category, it placed facts describing "personal characteristics" of drug couriers, such as the cash payment for tickets, a short trip to a major source city for drugs, nervousness, type of attire, and unchecked luggage. The majority believed that such facts, "shared by drug couriers and the public at large," were only relevant if there was evidence of ongoing criminal behavior and the Government offered "[e]mpirical documentation" that the combination of facts at issue did not describe the behavior of "significant numbers of innocent persons." Applying this two-part test to the facts of this case, the majority found that there was no evidence of ongoing criminal behavior, and thus that the agents' stop was impermissible. * * *

The rule enunciated by the Court of Appeals, in which evidence available to an officer is divided into evidence of "ongoing criminal behavior," on the one hand, and "probabilistic" evidence, on the other, * * * seems to us to draw a sharp line between types of evidence, the probative value of which varies only in degree. The Court of Appeals classified evidence of traveling under an alias, or evidence that the suspect took an evasive or erratic path through an airport, as meeting the test for showing "ongoing criminal activity." But certainly instances are conceivable in which traveling under an alias would not reflect ongoing criminal activity: for example, a person who wished to travel to a hospital or clinic for an operation and wished to conceal that fact. One taking an evasive path through an airport might be seeking to avoid a confrontation with an angry acquaintance or with a creditor. * * *

On the other hand, the factors in this case that the Court of Appeals treated as merely "probabilistic" also have probative significance. Paying $2,100 in cash for two airplane tickets is out of the ordinary, and it is even more out of the ordinary to pay that sum from a roll of $20 bills containing nearly twice that amount of cash. Most business travelers, we feel confident, purchase airline tickets by credit card or check so as to have a record for tax or business purposes, and few vacationers carry with them thousands of dollars in $20 bills. We also think the agents had a reasonable ground to believe that respondent was traveling under an alias; the evidence was by no means conclusive, but it was sufficient to warrant consideration. While a trip from Honolulu to Miami, standing alone, is not a cause for any sort of suspicion, here there was more: surely few residents of Honolulu travel from that city for 20 hours to spend 48 hours in Miami during the month of July.

Any one of these factors is not by itself proof of any illegal conduct and is quite consistent with innocent travel. But we think taken together they amount to reasonable suspicion. * * *

We do not agree with respondent that our analysis is somehow changed by the agents' belief that his behavior was consistent with one of the DEA's "drug courier profiles." A court sitting to determine the existence of reasonable suspicion must require the agent to articulate the factors leading to that conclusion, but the fact that these factors may be set forth in a "profile" does not somehow detract from their evidentiary significance as seen by a trained agent. * * * The judgment of the Court of Appeals is therefore reversed and the case remanded for further proceedings consistent with our decision.

JUSTICE MARSHALL, with whom JUSTICE BRENNAN joins, dissenting.

* * *

* * *It is highly significant that the DEA agents stopped Sokolow because he matched one of the DEA's "profiles" of a paradigmatic drug courier. In my view, a law enforcement officer's mechanistic application of a formula of personal and behavioral traits in deciding whom to detain can only dull the officer's ability and determination to make sensitive and fact-specific inferences in light of his experience, particularly in ambiguous or borderline cases. Reflexive reliance on a profile of drug courier characteristics runs a far greater risk than does ordinary, case-by-case police work, of subjecting innocent individuals to unwarranted police harassment and detention. * * * In asserting that it is not "somehow" relevant that the agents who stopped Sokolow did so in reliance on a prefabricated profile of criminal characteristics, the majority thus ducks serious issues relating to a questionable law enforcement practice * * *.

The remaining circumstantial facts known about Sokolow, considered either singly or together, are scarcely indicative of criminal activity. * * * The fact that Sokolow took a brief trip to a resort city for which he brought only carry-on luggage also describes a very large category of presumably innocent travelers. That Sokolow embarked from Miami, "a source city for illicit drugs," is no more suggestive of illegality; thousands of innocent persons travel from "source cities" every day and, judging from the DEA's testimony in past cases, nearly every major city in the country may be characterized as a source or distribution city. That Sokolow had his phone listed in another person's name also does not support the majority's assertion that the DEA agents reasonably believed Sokolow was using an alias; it is commonplace to have one's phone registered in the name of a roommate, which, it later turned out, was precisely what Sokolow had done. That Sokolow was dressed in a black jumpsuit and wore gold jewelry also provides no grounds for suspecting wrongdoing, the majority's repeated and unexplained allusions to Sokolow's style of dress notwithstanding. For law enforcement officers to base a search, even in part, on a pop guess that persons dressed in a particular fashion are likely to commit crimes not only stretches the concept of reasonable suspicion beyond recognition, but also is inimical to the self-expression which the choice of wardrobe may provide.

Finally, that Sokolow paid for his tickets in cash indicates no imminent or ongoing criminal activity. The majority "feel[s] confident" that "[m]ost business travelers ... purchase airline tickets by credit card or check." Why the majority confines its focus only to "business travelers" I do not know, but I would not so lightly infer ongoing crime from the use of legal tender. Making major cash purchases, while surely less common today, may simply reflect the traveler's aversion to, or inability to obtain, plastic money. Conceivably, a person who spends large amounts of cash may be trying to launder his proceeds from *past* criminal enterprises by converting them into goods and services. But, as I have noted, investigating completed episodes of crime goes beyond the appropriately limited purview of the brief, *Terry*-style seizure. Moreover, it is unreasonable to suggest that, had Sokolow left the airport, he would have been gone forever and thus immune from subsequent investigation. Sokolow, after all, had given the airline his phone number, and the DEA, having ascertained that it was indeed Sokolow's voice on the answering machine at that number, could have learned from that information where Sokolow resided.

UNITED STATES v. ARVIZU

United States Supreme Court, 2002.
534 U.S. 266, 122 S.Ct. 744, 151 L.Ed.2d 740.

CHIEF JUSTICE REHNQUIST delivered the opinion of the Court.

Respondent Ralph Arvizu was stopped by a border patrol agent while driving on an unpaved road in a remote area of southeastern Arizona. A search of his vehicle turned up more than 100 pounds of marijuana. The District Court for the District of Arizona denied respondent's motion to suppress, but the Court of Appeals for the Ninth Circuit reversed. In the course of its opinion, it categorized certain factors relied upon by the District Court as simply out of bounds in deciding whether there was "reasonable suspicion" for the stop. We hold that the Court of Appeals' methodology was contrary to our prior decisions and that it reached the wrong result in this case.

On an afternoon in January 1998, Agent Clinton Stoddard was working at a border patrol checkpoint along U.S. Highway 191 approximately 30 miles north of Douglas, Arizona. Douglas has a population of about 13,000 and is situated on the United States–Mexico border in the southeastern part of the State. Only two highways lead north from Douglas. Highway 191 leads north to Interstate 10, which passes through Tucson and Phoenix. State Highway 80 heads northeast through less populated areas toward New Mexico, skirting south and east of the portion of the Coronado National Forest that lies approximately 20 miles northeast of Douglas.

The checkpoint is located at the intersection of 191 and Rucker Canyon Road, an unpaved east-west road that connects 191 and the Coronado National Forest. When the checkpoint is operational, border patrol agents stop the traffic on 191 as part of a coordinated effort to stem the flow of illegal immigration and smuggling across the international border. Agents use roving patrols to apprehend smugglers trying to circumvent the checkpoint by taking the backroads, including those roads through the sparsely populated area between Douglas and the national forest. Magnetic sensors, or "intrusion devices," facilitate agents' efforts in patrolling these areas. Directionally sensitive, the sensors signal the passage of traffic that would be consistent with smuggling activities.

* * *

Around 2:15 p.m., Stoddard received a report via Douglas radio that a Leslie Canyon Road sensor had triggered. This was significant to Stoddard for two reasons. First, it suggested to him that a vehicle might be trying to circumvent the checkpoint. Second, the timing coincided with the point when agents begin heading back to the checkpoint for a shift change, which leaves the area unpatrolled. Stoddard knew that alien smugglers did extensive scouting and seemed to be most active when agents were en route back to the checkpoint. Another border patrol agent told Stoddard that the same sensor had gone off several weeks before and that he had apprehended a minivan using the same route and witnessed the occupants throwing bundles of marijuana out the door.

Stoddard drove eastbound on Rucker Canyon Road to investigate. * * * He pulled off to the side of the road at a slight slant so he could get a good look at the oncoming vehicle as it passed by.

It was a minivan, a type of automobile that Stoddard knew smugglers used. As it approached, it slowed dramatically, from about 50–55 to 25–30 miles per hour. He saw five occupants inside. An adult man was driving, an adult woman sat in the front passenger seat, and three children were in the back. The driver appeared stiff and his posture very rigid. He did not look at Stoddard and seemed to be trying to pretend that Stoddard was not there. Stoddard thought this suspicious because in his experience on patrol most persons look over and see what is going on, and in that area most drivers give border patrol agents a friendly wave. Stoddard noticed that the knees of the two children sitting in the very back seat were unusually high, as if their feet were propped up on some cargo on the floor.

At that point, Stoddard decided to get a closer look, so he began to follow the vehicle * * *. Shortly thereafter, all of the children, though still facing forward, put their hands up at the same time and began to wave at Stoddard in an abnormal pattern. It looked to Stoddard as if the children were being instructed. Their odd waving continued on and off for about four to five minutes.

Several hundred feet before the Kuykendall Cutoff Road intersection, the driver signaled that he would turn. * * * The turn was significant to Stoddard because it was made at the last place that would have allowed the minivan to avoid the checkpoint. Also, Kuykendall, though passable by a sedan or van, is rougher than either Rucker Canyon or Leslie Canyon roads, and the normal traffic is four-wheel-drive vehicles. * * *

Stoddard radioed for a registration check and learned that the minivan was registered to an address in Douglas that was four blocks north of the border in an area notorious for alien and narcotics smuggling. After receiving the information, Stoddard decided to make a vehicle stop. He approached the driver and learned that his name was Ralph Arvizu. Stoddard asked if respondent would mind if he looked inside and searched the vehicle. Respondent agreed, and Stoddard discovered marijuana in a black duffel bag under the feet of the two children in the back seat. Another bag containing marijuana was behind the rear seat. In all, the van contained 128.85 pounds of marijuana, worth an estimated $99,080.

[Aruizu was charged with possession with intent to distribute marijuana in violation of 21 U.S.C. § 841(a)(1) (1994 ed.). The District Court denied his motion to suppress the marijuana, which argued, among other things, that Stoddard did not have reasonable suspicion to stop the vehicle as required by the Fourth Amendment.]

The Court of Appeals for the Ninth Circuit reversed. In its view, fact-specific weighing of circumstances or other multifactor tests introduced "a troubling degree of uncertainty and unpredictability" into the Fourth Amendment analysis. It therefore "attempted . . . to describe and clearly delimit the extent to which certain factors may be considered by law enforcement officers in making stops such as the stop involving" respondent. After characterizing the District Court's analysis as relying on a list of 10 factors, the Court of Appeals proceeded to examine each in turn. It held that 7 of the factors, including respondent's slowing down, his failure to acknowledge Stoddard, the raised position of the children's knees, and their odd waving carried little or no weight in the reasonable-suspicion calculus. The remaining factors—the road's use by smugglers, the temporal proximity between respondent's trip and the agents' shift change, and the use of minivans by smugglers—were not enough to render the stop permissible. We granted certiorari to review the decision of the Court of Appeals because of its importance to the enforcement of federal drug and immigration laws.

The Fourth Amendment prohibits "unreasonable searches and seizures" by the Government, and its protections extend to brief investigatory stops of persons or vehicles that fall short of traditional arrest. Because the "balance between the public interest and the individual's right to personal security," tilts in favor of a standard less than probable cause in such cases, the Fourth Amendment is satisfied if the officer's action is supported by reasonable suspicion to believe that criminal activity " 'may be afoot.' " When discussing how reviewing courts should make reasonable-suspicion determinations, we have said repeatedly that they must look at the "totality of the circumstances" of each case to see whether the detaining officer has a "particularized and objective basis" for suspecting legal wrongdoing. This process allows officers to draw on their own experience and specialized training to make inferences from and deductions about the cumulative information available to them that "might well elude an untrained person."

* * *

We think that the approach taken by the Court of Appeals here departs sharply from the teachings of these cases. The court's evaluation and rejection of seven of the listed factors in isolation from each other does not take into account the "totality of the circumstances," as our cases have understood that phrase. The court appeared to believe that each observation by Stoddard that was by itself readily susceptible to an innocent explanation was entitled to "no weight." *Terry*, however, precludes this sort of divide-and-conquer analysis. * * * Although each of the series of acts was "perhaps innocent in itself," we held that, taken together, they "warranted further investigation."

* * *

But the Court of Appeals' approach would * * * seriously undercut the "totality of the circumstances" principle which governs the existence *vel non* of "reasonable suspicion." Take, for example, the court's positions that respondent's deceleration could not be considered because "slowing down after spotting a law enforcement vehicle is an entirely normal response that is in no way indicative of criminal activity" and that his failure to acknowledge Stoddard's presence provided no support because there were "no 'special circumstances' rendering 'innocent avoidance . . . improbable.'" We think it quite reasonable that a driver's slowing down, stiffening of posture, and failure to acknowledge a sighted law enforcement officer might well be unremarkable in one instance (such as a busy San Francisco highway) while quite unusual in another (such as a remote portion of rural southeastern Arizona). Stoddard was entitled to make an assessment of the situation in light of his specialized training and familiarity with the customs of the area's inhabitants. * * *

* * *

Respondent argues that we must rule in his favor because the facts suggested a family in a minivan on a holiday outing. A determination that reasonable suspicion exists, however, need not rule out the possibility of innocent conduct. Undoubtedly, each of these factors alone is susceptible to innocent explanation, and some factors are more probative than others. Taken together, we believe they sufficed to form a particularized and objective basis for Stoddard's stopping the vehicle, making the stop reasonable within the meaning of the Fourth Amendment.

The judgment of the Court of Appeals is therefore reversed, and the case is remanded for further proceedings consistent with this opinion. It is so ordered.

[Justice Scalia's concurring opinion has been omitted.]

ILLINOIS v. WARDLOW

Supreme Court of the United States, 2000.
528 U.S. 119, 120 S.Ct. 673, 145 L.Ed.2d 570.

CHIEF JUSTICE REHNQUIST delivered the opinion of the Court. * * *

Respondent Wardlow fled upon seeing police officers patrolling an area known for heavy narcotics trafficking. Two of the officers caught up with him, stopped him and conducted a protective pat-down search for weapons. Discovering a .38–caliber handgun, the officers arrested Wardlow. We hold that the officers' stop did not violate the Fourth Amendment to the United States Constitution.

On September 9, 1995, Officers Nolan and Harvey were working as uniformed officers in the special operations section of the Chicago Police Department. The officers were driving the last car of a four car caravan converging on an area known for heavy narcotics trafficking in order to investigate drug transactions. The officers were traveling together because they expected to find a crowd of people in the area, including lookouts and customers.

As the caravan passed 4035 West Van Buren, Officer Nolan observed respondent Wardlow standing next to the building holding an opaque bag. Respondent looked in the direction of the officers and fled. Nolan and Harvey turned their car southbound, watched him as he ran through the gangway and an alley, and eventually cornered him on the street. Nolan then exited his car and stopped respondent. He immediately conducted a protective pat-down search for weapons because in his experience it was common for there to be weapons in the near vicinity of narcotics transactions. During the frisk, Officer Nolan squeezed the bag respondent was carrying and felt a heavy, hard object similar to the shape of a gun. The officer then opened the bag and discovered a .38–caliber handgun with five live rounds of ammunition. The officers arrested Wardlow.

The Illinois trial court denied respondent's motion to suppress, finding the gun was recovered during a lawful stop and frisk. Following a stipulated bench trial, Wardlow was convicted of unlawful use of a weapon by a felon. The Illinois Appellate Court reversed Wardlow's conviction, concluding that the gun should have been suppressed because Officer Nolan did not have reasonable suspicion sufficient to justify an investigative stop pursuant to *Terry v. Ohio*, 392 U.S. 1, 88 S.Ct. 1868, 20 L.Ed.2d 889 (1968).

The Illinois Supreme Court agreed. * * * We granted certiorari, and now reverse.[1]

---

1. The state courts have differed on whether unprovoked flight is sufficient grounds to constitute reasonable suspicion. See, *e.g.*, *State* v. *Anderson*, 155 Wis. 2d 77, 454 N.W.2d 763 (Wis. 1990) (flight alone is sufficient); *Platt* v. *State*, 589 N.E.2d 222 (Ind. 1992) (same); *Harris* v. *State*, 205 Ga. App. 813, 423 S.E.2d 723 (1992) (flight in high crime area sufficient); *State* v. *Hicks*, 241 Neb. 357, 488 N.W.2d 359 (1992) (flight

This case, involving a brief encounter between a citizen and a police officer on a public street, is governed by the analysis we first applied in *Terry*. In *Terry*, we held that an officer may, consistent with the Fourth Amendment, conduct a brief, investigatory stop when the officer has a reasonable, articulable suspicion that criminal activity is afoot. While "reasonable suspicion" is a less demanding standard than probable cause and requires a showing considerably less than preponderance of the evidence, the Fourth Amendment requires at least a minimal level of objective justification for making the stop. The officer must be able to articulate more than an "inchoate and unparticularized suspicion or 'hunch' " of criminal activity.

Nolan and Harvey were among eight officers in a four car caravan that was converging on an area known for heavy narcotics trafficking, and the officers anticipated encountering a large number of people in the area, including drug customers and individuals serving as lookouts. It was in this context that Officer Nolan decided to investigate Wardlow after observing him flee. An individual's presence in an area of expected criminal activity, standing alone, is not enough to support a reasonable, particularized suspicion that the person is committing a crime. But officers are not required to ignore the relevant characteristics of a location in determining whether the circumstances are sufficiently suspicious to warrant further investigation. Accordingly, we have previously noted the fact that the stop occurred in a "high crime area" among the relevant contextual considerations in a *Terry* analysis.

In this case, moreover, it was not merely respondent's presence in an area of heavy narcotics trafficking that aroused the officers' suspicion but his unprovoked flight upon noticing the police. Our cases have also recognized that nervous, evasive behavior is a pertinent factor in determining reasonable suspicion. Headlong flight—wherever it occurs—is the consummate act of evasion: it is not necessarily indicative of wrongdoing, but it is certainly suggestive of such. In reviewing the propriety of an officer's conduct, courts do not have available empirical studies dealing with inferences drawn from suspicious behavior, and we cannot reasonably demand scientific certainty from judges or law enforcement officers where none exists. Thus, the determination of reasonable suspicion must be based on commonsense judgments and inferences about human behavior. We conclude Officer Nolan was justified in suspecting that Wardlow was involved in criminal activity, and, therefore, in investigating further.

Such a holding is entirely consistent with our decision in *Florida* v. *Royer*, 460 U.S. 491, 103 S.Ct. 1319, 75 L.Ed.2d 229 (1983), where we held that when an officer, without reasonable suspicion or probable cause, approaches an individual, the individual has a right to ignore the police and go about his business. And any "refusal to cooperate, without more, does not furnish the minimal level of objective justification needed

is not enough); *State* v. *Tucker*, 136 N.J. 158, 642 A.2d 401 (1994) (same); *People* v. *Shabaz*, 424 Mich. 42, 378 N.W.2d 451 (1985) (same); *People* v. *Wilson*, 784 P.2d 325 (Colo. 1989) (same).

for a detention or seizure." *Florida* v. *Bostick*, 501 U.S. 429, 111 S.Ct. 2382, 115 L.Ed.2d 389 (1991). But unprovoked flight is simply not a mere refusal to cooperate. Flight, by its very nature, is not "going about one's business"; in fact, it is just the opposite. Allowing officers confronted with such flight to stop the fugitive and investigate further is quite consistent with the individual's right to go about his business or to stay put and remain silent in the face of police questioning.

Respondent and *amici* also argue that there are innocent reasons for flight from police and that, therefore, flight is not necessarily indicative of ongoing criminal activity. This fact is undoubtedly true, but does not establish a violation of the Fourth Amendment. Even in *Terry*, the conduct justifying the stop was ambiguous and susceptible of an innocent explanation. The officer observed two individuals pacing back and forth in front of a store, peering into the window and periodically conferring. All of this conduct was by itself lawful, but it also suggested that the individuals were casing the store for a planned robbery. *Terry* recognized that the officers could detain the individuals to resolve the ambiguity.

In allowing such detentions, *Terry* accepts the risk that officers may stop innocent people. Indeed, the Fourth Amendment accepts that risk in connection with more drastic police action; persons arrested and detained on probable cause to believe they have committed a crime may turn out to be innocent. The *Terry* stop is a far more minimal intrusion, simply allowing the officer to briefly investigate further. If the officer does not learn facts rising to the level of probable cause, the individual must be allowed to go on his way. But in this case the officers found respondent in possession of a handgun, and arrested him for violation of an Illinois firearms statute. No question of the propriety of the arrest itself is before us.

The judgment of the Supreme Court of Illinois is reversed, and the cause is remanded for further proceedings not inconsistent with this opinion.

Justice Stevens, with whom Justice Souter, Justice Ginsburg, and Justice Breyer join, concurring in part and dissenting in part.

The State of Illinois asks this Court to announce a "bright-line rule" authorizing the temporary detention of anyone who flees at the mere sight of a police officer. Respondent counters by asking us to adopt the opposite *per se* rule—that the fact that a person flees upon seeing the police can never, by itself, be sufficient to justify a temporary investigative stop of the kind authorized by *Terry* v. *Ohio*.

The Court today wisely endorses neither *per se* rule. Instead, it rejects the proposition that "flight is ... necessarily indicative of ongoing criminal activity," adhering to the view that "the concept of reasonable suspicion ... is not readily, or even usefully, reduced to a neat set of legal rules," but must be determined by looking to "the totality of the circumstances—the whole picture." Abiding by this framework, the

Court concludes that "Officer Nolan was justified in suspecting that Wardlow was involved in criminal activity."

Although I agree with the Court's rejection of the *per se* rules proffered by the parties, unlike the Court, I am persuaded that in this case the brief testimony of the officer who seized respondent does not justify the conclusion that he had reasonable suspicion to make the stop. Before discussing the specific facts of this case, I shall comment on the parties' requests for a *per se* rule.

I

In *Terry* v. *Ohio*, we first recognized "that a police officer may in appropriate circumstances and in an appropriate manner approach a person for purposes of investigating possibly criminal behavior even though there is no probable cause to make an arrest," an authority permitting the officer to "stop and briefly detain a person for investigative purposes." We approved as well "a reasonable search for weapons for the protection of the police officer, where he has reason to believe that he is dealing with an armed and dangerous individual, regardless of whether he has probable cause to arrest the individual for a crime." * * *

Accordingly, we recognized only a "narrowly drawn authority" that is "limited to that which is necessary for the discovery of weapons." An officer conducting an investigatory stop, we further explained, must articulate "a particularized and objective basis for suspecting the particular person stopped of criminal activity." * * * "The relevant inquiry" concerning the inferences and conclusions a court draws "is not whether particular conduct is 'innocent' or 'guilty,' but the degree of suspicion that attaches to particular types of noncriminal acts."

The question in this case concerns "the degree of suspicion that attaches to" a person's flight—or, more precisely, what "commonsense conclusions" can be drawn respecting the motives behind that flight. A pedestrian may break into a run for a variety of reasons—to catch up with a friend a block or two away, to seek shelter from an impending storm, to arrive at a bus stop before the bus leaves, to get home in time for dinner, to resume jogging after a pause for rest, to avoid contact with a bore or a bully, or simply to answer the call of nature—any of which might coincide with the arrival of an officer in the vicinity. A pedestrian might also run because he or she has just sighted one or more police officers. * * *

Given the diversity and frequency of possible motivations for flight, it would be profoundly unwise to endorse either *per se* rule. The inference we can reasonably draw about the motivation for a person's flight, rather, will depend on a number of different circumstances. Factors such as the time of day, the number of people in the area, the character of the neighborhood, whether the officer was in uniform, the way the runner was dressed, the direction and speed of the flight, and whether the person's behavior was otherwise unusual might be relevant in specific cases. This number of variables is surely sufficient to preclude either a bright-line rule that always justifies, or that never justifies, an investigative stop based on the sole fact that flight began after a police officer appeared nearby

* * *

Even assuming we know that a person runs because he sees the police, the inference to be drawn may still vary from case to case. Flight to escape police detection, we have said, may have an entirely innocent motivation:

> "[I]t is a matter of common knowledge that men who are entirely innocent do sometimes fly from the scene of a crime through fear of being apprehended as the guilty parties, or from an unwillingness to appear as witnesses. * * * "

In addition to these concerns, a reasonable person may conclude that an officer's sudden appearance indicates nearby criminal activity. And where there is criminal activity there is also a substantial element of danger—either from the criminal or from a confrontation between the criminal and the police. These considerations can lead to an innocent and understandable desire to quit the vicinity with all speed.

Among some citizens, particularly minorities and those residing in high crime areas, there is also the possibility that the fleeing person is entirely innocent, but, with or without justification, believes that contact with the police can itself be dangerous, apart from any criminal activity associated with the officer's sudden presence. For such a person, unprovoked flight is neither "aberrant" nor "abnormal." Moreover, these concerns and fears are known to the police officers themselves, and are validated by law enforcement investigations into their own practices.[10]

10. New Jersey's Attorney General, in a recent investigation into allegations of racial profiling on the New Jersey Turnpike, concluded that "minority motorists have been treated differently [by New Jersey State Troopers] than non-minority motorists during the course of traffic stops on the New Jersey Turnpike." "The problem of disparate treatment is real—not imagined," declared the Attorney General. Not surprisingly, the report concluded that this disparate treatment "engenders feelings of fear, resentment, hostility, and mistrust by minority citizens." See Interim Report 4, 7. Recently, the United States Department of Justice, citing this very evidence, announced that it would appoint an outside monitor to oversee the actions of the New Jersey State Police and ensure that it enacts policy changes advocated by the Interim Report, and keeps records on racial statistics and traffic stops. See Kocieniewski, U.S. Will Monitor New Jersey Police on Race Profiling, N. Y. Times, Dec. 23, 1999, p. A1, col. 6.

Likewise, the Massachusetts Attorney General investigated similar allegations of egregious police conduct toward minorities. The report stated:

"We conclude that Boston police officers engaged in improper, and unconstitutional, conduct in the 1989–90 period with respect to stops and searches of minority individuals. . . . Although we cannot say with precision how widespread this illegal conduct was, we believe that it was sufficiently common to justify changes in certain Department practices.

"Perhaps the most disturbing evidence was that the scope of a number of *Terry* searches went far beyond anything authorized by that case and indeed, beyond anything that we believe would be acceptable under the federal and state constitutions even where probable cause existed to conduct a full search incident to an arrest. Forcing young men to lower their trousers, or otherwise searching inside their underwear, on public streets or in public hall-

Accordingly, the evidence supporting the reasonableness of these beliefs is too pervasive to be dismissed as random or rare, and too persuasive to be disparaged as inconclusive or insufficient. In any event, just as we do not require "scientific certainty" for our commonsense conclusion that unprovoked flight can sometimes indicate suspicious motives, neither do we require scientific certainty to conclude that unprovoked flight can occur for other, innocent reasons.

* * *

"Unprovoked flight," in short, describes a category of activity too broad and varied to permit a *per se* reasonable inference regarding the motivation for the activity. While the innocent explanations surely do not establish that the Fourth Amendment is always violated whenever someone is stopped solely on the basis of an unprovoked flight, neither do the suspicious motivations establish that the Fourth Amendment is never violated when a *Terry* stop is predicated on that fact alone. For these reasons, the Court is surely correct in refusing to embrace either *per se* rule advocated by the parties. The totality of the circumstances, as always, must dictate the result.

II

Guided by that totality-of-the-circumstances test, the Court concludes that Officer Nolan had reasonable suspicion to stop respondent. In this respect, my view differs from the Court's. * * *

Respondent Wardlow was arrested a few minutes after noon on September 9, 1995. Nolan was part of an eight-officer, four-car caravan patrol team. The officers were headed for "one of the areas in the 11th District [of Chicago] that's high [in] narcotics traffic." The reason why four cars were in the caravan was that "normally in these different areas there's an enormous amount of people, sometimes lookouts, customers." Officer Nolan testified that he was in uniform on that day, but he did not recall whether he was driving a marked or an unmarked car.

* * * Nolan first observed respondent "in front of 4035 West Van Buren." Wardlow "looked in our direction and began fleeing." Nolan then "began driving southbound down the street observing [respondent] running through the gangway and the alley southbound," and observed that Wardlow was carrying a white, opaque bag under his arm. After the car turned south and intercepted respondent as he "ran right towards us," Officer Nolan stopped him and conducted a "protective search," which revealed that the bag under respondent's arm contained a loaded handgun.

* * *

ways, is so demeaning and invasive of fundamental precepts of privacy that it can only be condemned in the strongest terms. The fact that not only the young men themselves, but independent witnesses complained of strip searches, should be deeply alarming to all members of this community." J. Shannon, Attorney General of Massachusetts, Report of the Attorney General's Civil Rights Division on Boston Police Department Practices 60–61 (Dec. 18, 1990).

No other factors sufficiently support a finding of reasonable suspicion. Though respondent was carrying a white, opaque bag under his arm, there is nothing at all suspicious about that. Certainly the time of day—shortly after noon—does not support Illinois' argument. Nor were the officers "responding to any call or report of suspicious activity in the area." * * *

* * *

D. *TERRY* SEIZURES OF PEOPLE

FLORIDA v. BOSTICK

Supreme Court of the United States, 1991.
501 U.S. 429, 111 S.Ct. 2382, 115 L.Ed.2d 389.

JUSTICE O'CONNOR delivered the opinion of the Court.

* * *

I

Drug interdiction efforts have led to the use of police surveillance at airports, train stations, and bus depots. Law enforcement officers stationed at such locations routinely approach individuals, either randomly or because they suspect in some vague way that the individuals may be engaged in criminal activity, and ask them potentially incriminating questions. Broward County has adopted such a program. County Sheriff's Department officers routinely board buses at scheduled stops and ask passengers for permission to search their luggage.

In this case, two officers discovered cocaine when they searched a suitcase belonging to Bostick. The underlying facts of the search are in dispute, but the Florida Supreme Court, whose decision we review here, stated explicitly the factual premise for its decision:

"Two officers, complete with badges, insignia and one of them holding a recognizable zipper pouch containing a pistol, boarded a bus bound from Miami to Atlanta during a stopover in Fort Lauderdale. Eyeing the passengers, the officers admittedly without articulable suspicion, picked out the defendant passenger and asked to inspect his ticket and identification. The ticket, from Miami to Atlanta, matched the defendant's identification and both were immediately returned to him as unremarkable. However, the two police officers persisted and explained their presence as narcotics agents on the lookout for illegal drugs. In pursuit of that aim, they then requested the defendant's consent to search his luggage. Needless to say, there is a conflict in the evidence about whether the defendant consented to the search of the second bag in which the contraband was found and as to whether he was informed of his right to refuse consent. However, any conflict must be resolved in favor of the state, it being a question of fact decided by the trial judge."

Two facts are particularly worth noting. First, the police specifically advised Bostick that he had the right to refuse consent. Bostick appears to have disputed the point, but, as the Florida Supreme Court noted explicitly, the trial court resolved this evidentiary conflict in the State's favor. Second, at no time did the officers threaten Bostick with a gun. The Florida Supreme Court indicated that one officer carried a zipper pouch containing a pistol—the equivalent of carrying a gun in a holster—but the court did not suggest that the gun was ever removed from its pouch, pointed at Bostick, or otherwise used in a threatening manner. The dissent's characterization of the officers as "gun-wielding inquisitors," is colorful, but lacks any basis in fact.

Bostick was arrested and charged with trafficking in cocaine. [The Florida Supreme Court held that "an impermissible seizure results when police mount a drug search on buses during scheduled stops and question boarded passengers without articulable reasons for doing so, thereby obtaining consent to search the passengers' luggage."] * * *

II

* * *

* * * Our cases make it clear that a seizure does not occur simply because a police officer approaches an individual and asks a few questions. So long as a reasonable person would feel free "to disregard the police and go about his business," the encounter is consensual and no reasonable suspicion is required. * * * There is no doubt that if this same encounter had taken place before Bostick boarded the bus or in the lobby of the bus terminal, it would not rise to the level of a seizure. The Court has dealt with similar encounters in airports and has found them to be the sort of consensual encounters that implicate no Fourth Amendment interest. We have stated that even when officers have no basis for suspecting a particular individual, they may generally ask questions of that individual, ask to examine the individual's identification, and request consent to search his or her luggage—as long as the police do not convey a message that compliance with their requests is required. [Citations omitted]

Bostick insists that this case is different because it took place in the cramped confines of a bus. A police encounter is much more intimidating in this setting, he argues, because police tower over a seated passenger and there is little room to move around. Bostick claims to find support in language from *Michigan v. Chesternut*, 486 U.S. 567, 108 S.Ct. 1975, 100 L.Ed.2d 565 (1988), and other cases, indicating that a seizure occurs when a reasonable person would believe that he or she is not "free to leave." Bostick maintains that a reasonable bus passenger would not have felt free to leave under the circumstances of this case because there is nowhere to go on a bus. Also, the bus was about to depart. Had Bostick disembarked, he would have risked being stranded and losing whatever baggage he had locked away in the luggage compartment.

The Florida Supreme Court found this argument persuasive, so much so that it adopted a per se rule prohibiting the police from randomly boarding buses as a means of drug interdiction. The state court erred, however, in focusing on whether Bostick was "free to leave" rather than on the principle that those words were intended to capture. When police attempt to question a person who is walking down the street or through an airport lobby, it makes sense to inquire whether a reasonable person would feel free to continue walking. But when the person is seated on a bus and has no desire to leave, the degree to which a reasonable person would feel that he or she could leave is not an accurate measure of the coercive effect of the encounter.

Here, for example, the mere fact that Bostick did not feel free to leave the bus does not mean that the police seized him. Bostick was a passenger on a bus that was scheduled to depart. He would not have felt free to leave the bus even if the police had not been present. Bostick's movements were "confined" in a sense, but this was the natural result of his decision to take the bus; it says nothing about whether or not the police conduct at issue was coercive. * * * In such a situation, the appropriate inquiry is whether a reasonable person would feel free to decline the officers' requests or otherwise terminate the encounter. * * * Where the encounter takes place is one factor, but it is not the only one. And, as the Solicitor General correctly observes, an individual may decline an officer's request without fearing prosecution. We have consistently held that a refusal to cooperate, without more, does not furnish the minimal level of objective justification needed for a detention or seizure. [Citations]

The facts of this case, as described by the Florida Supreme Court, leave some doubt whether a seizure occurred. Two officers walked up to Bostick on the bus, asked him a few questions, and asked if they could search his bags. As we have explained, no seizure occurs when police ask questions of an individual, ask to examine the individual's identification, and request consent to search his or her luggage—so long as the officers do not convey a message that compliance with their requests is required. Here, the facts recited by the Florida Supreme Court indicate that the officers did not point guns at Bostick or otherwise threaten him and that they specifically advised Bostick that he could refuse consent.

Nevertheless, we refrain from deciding whether or not a seizure occurred in this case. The trial court made no express findings of fact, and the Florida Supreme Court rested its decision on a single fact—that the encounter took place on a bus—rather than on the totality of the circumstances. We remand so that the Florida courts may evaluate the seizure question under the correct legal standard. We do reject, however, Bostick's argument that he must have been seized because no reasonable person would freely consent to a search of luggage that he or she knows contains drugs. This argument cannot prevail because the "reasonable person" test presupposes an *innocent* person. * * *

The dissent characterizes our decision as holding that police may board buses and by an *"intimidating* show of authority," demand of passengers their "voluntary" cooperation. That characterization is incorrect. Clearly, a bus passenger's decision to cooperate with law enforcement officers authorizes the police to conduct a search without first obtaining a warrant *only* if the cooperation is voluntary. "Consent" that is the product of official intimidation or harassment is not consent at all. Citizens do not forfeit their constitutional rights when they are coerced to comply with a request that they would prefer to refuse. The question to be decided by the Florida courts on remand is whether Bostick chose to permit the search of his luggage.

The dissent also attempts to characterize our decision as applying a lesser degree of constitutional protection to those individuals who travel by bus, rather than by other forms of transportation. This, too, is an erroneous characterization. Our Fourth Amendment inquiry in this case—whether a reasonable person would have felt free to decline the officers' requests or otherwise terminate the encounter—applies equally to police encounters that take place on trains, planes, and city streets. It is the dissent that would single out this particular mode of travel for differential treatment by adopting a per se rule that random bus searches are unconstitutional.

The dissent reserves its strongest criticism for the proposition that police officers can approach individuals as to whom they have no reasonable suspicion and ask them potentially incriminating questions. But this proposition is by no means novel; it has been endorsed by the Court any number of times. * * * Unless the dissent advocates overruling a long, unbroken line of decisions dating back more than 20 years, its criticism is not well taken.

We adhere to the rule that, in order to determine whether a particular encounter constitutes a seizure, a court must consider all the circumstances surrounding the encounter to determine whether the police conduct would have communicated to a reasonable person that the person was not free to decline the officers' requests or otherwise terminate the encounter. That rule applies to encounters that take place on a city street or in an airport lobby, and it applies equally to encounters on a bus. The Florida Supreme Court erred in adopting a per se rule.

The judgment of the Florida Supreme Court is reversed, and the case remanded for further proceedings not inconsistent with this opinion.

JUSTICE MARSHALL, with whom JUSTICE BLACKMUN and JUSTICE STEVENS join, dissenting.

I.

At issue in this case is a new and increasingly common tactic in the war on drugs: the suspicionless police sweep of buses in interstate or intrastate travel. Typically under this technique, a group of state or federal officers will board a bus while it is stopped at an intermediate point on its route. Often displaying badges, weapons or other indicia of authority, the officers identify themselves and announce their purpose to intercept drug traffickers. They proceed to approach individual passengers, requesting them to show identification, produce their tickets, and explain the purpose of their travels. Never do the officers advise the passengers that they are free not to speak with the officers. An "interview" of this type ordinarily culminates in a request for consent to search the passenger's luggage.

These sweeps are conducted in "dragnet" style. The police admittedly act without an "articulable suspicion" in deciding which buses to board and which passengers to approach for interviewing. By proceeding systematically in this fashion, the police are able to engage in a tremendously high volume of searches. The percentage of successful drug interdictions is low.

To put it mildly, these sweeps are inconvenient, intrusive, and intimidating. They occur within cramped confines, with officers typically placing themselves in between the passenger selected for an interview and the exit of the bus. Because the bus is only temporarily stationed at a point short of its destination, the passengers are in no position to leave as a means of evading the officers' questioning. Undoubtedly, such a sweep holds up the progress of the bus. Thus, this new and increasingly common tactic, burdens the experience of traveling by bus with a degree of governmental interference to which, until now, our society has been proudly unaccustomed.* * *

* * *

II.

I have no objection to the manner in which the majority frames the test for determining whether a suspicionless bus sweep amounts to a Fourth Amendment "seizure." I agree that the appropriate question is whether a passenger who is approached during such a sweep "would feel free to decline the officers' requests or otherwise terminate the encounter." What I cannot understand is how the majority can possibly suggest an affirmative answer to this question.

* * * Inexplicably, the majority repeatedly stresses the trial court's implicit finding that the police officers advised respondent that he was free to refuse permission to search his travel bag. This aspect of the exchange between respondent and the police is completely irrelevant to the issue before us. For as the State concedes, and as the majority purports to "accept," if respondent was unlawfully seized when the officers approached him and initiated questioning, the resulting search was likewise unlawful no matter how well advised respondent was of his right to refuse it. Consequently, the issue is not whether a passenger in respondent's position would have felt free to deny consent to the search of his bag, but whether such a passenger—without being apprised of his rights—would have felt free to terminate the antecedent encounter with the police.

Unlike the majority, I have no doubt that the answer to this question is no. Apart from trying to accommodate the officers, respondent had only two options. First, he could have remained seated while obstinately refusing to respond to the officers' questioning. But in light of the intimidating show of authority that the officers made upon boarding the bus, respondent reasonably could have believed that such behavior would only arouse the officers' suspicions and intensify their interrogation. Indeed, officers who carry out bus sweeps like the one at issue here frequently admit that this is the effect of a passenger's refusal to cooperate. The majority's observation that a mere refusal to answer questions, "without more," does not give rise to a reasonable basis for seizing a passenger, is utterly beside the point, because a passenger unadvised of his rights and otherwise unversed in constitutional law has no reason to know that the police cannot hold his refusal to cooperate against him.

Second, respondent could have tried to escape the officers' presence by leaving the bus altogether. But because doing so would have required respondent to squeeze past the gunwielding inquisitor who was blocking the aisle of the bus, this hardly seems like a course that respondent reasonably would have viewed as available to him. The majority lamely protests that nothing in the stipulated facts shows that the questioning officer *pointed* his gun at respondent or otherwise *threatened* him with the weapon. Our decisions recognize the obvious point, however, that the choice of the police to "display" their weapons during an encounter exerts significant coercive pressure on the confronted citizen. We have never suggested that the police must go so far as to put a citizen in immediate apprehension of being shot before a court can take account of the intimidating effect of being questioned by an officer with weapon in hand.

Even if respondent had perceived that the officers would *let* him leave the bus, moreover, he could not reasonably have been expected to resort to this means of evading their intrusive questioning. For so far as respondent knew, the bus' departure from the terminal was imminent. Unlike a person approached by the police on the street, or at a bus or airport terminal after reaching his destination, a passenger approached by the police at an intermediate point in a long bus journey cannot simply leave the scene and repair to a safe haven to avoid unwanted probing by law enforcement officials. The vulnerability that an intrastate or interstate traveler experiences when confronted by the police outside of his "own familiar territory" surely aggravates the coercive quality of such an encounter.

* * *

* * * Withdrawing this particular weapon from the government's drug-war arsenal would hardly leave the police without any means of combating the use of buses as instrumentalities of the drug trade. The police would remain free, for example, to approach passengers whom they have a reasonable, articulable basis to suspect of criminal wrongdo-

ing. Alternatively, they could continue to confront passengers without suspicion so long as they took simple steps, like advising the passengers confronted of their right to decline to be questioned, to dispel the aura of coercion and intimidation that pervades such encounters. There is no reason to expect that such requirements would render the Nation's buses law enforcement-free zones.

* * *

Commentary

The preceding case illustrates one way that the long running "war on drugs" has affected search and seizure theory. The general pattern is that the officers approach a person and engage in questioning, hoping either to obtain consent to a search or to uncover facts sufficient to constitute probable cause. The cases recognize three levels or tiers of police-citizen contact in these situations:

1. *No Fourth Amendment intrusion.* Mere conversation between the officer and the citizen that involves no element of coercion or detention does not implicate the Fourth Amendment at all. Officers do not need to have reasonable suspicion to observe citizens closely, or follow them about an airport, or even to engage them in conversation. According to *Florida v. Royer*, 460 U.S. 491 (1983), "there is no Constitutional infringement when an officer merely approaches and speaks to an individual in a public place."

2. *Temporary detention.* According to the oft-cited standard of *United States v. Mendenhall*, 446 U.S. 544 (1980), a seizure of this type has occurred if "in view of all the circumstances surrounding the incident, a reasonable person would have believed he was not free to leave." The moment at which a mere conversation becomes a detention may turn on a subjective assessment, because the officer rarely says in so many words that the citizen may not leave. A detention will ordinarily be found where the officer retains the citizen's travel ticket or identification, or asks the citizen to accompany him to another location, or otherwise signals he is exercising authority.

3. *Full-scale arrest.* In *Florida v. Royer,* 460 U.S. 491, 497 (1983), the suspect gave consent to search his luggage after being removed to an interrogation room at the airport. The Supreme Court opinion by Justice White held that at this point the encounter had escalated beyond a temporary investigative detention into an arrest, and that the fact that the suspect was traveling under an assumed name and had paid cash for a one-way ticket did not amount to probable cause. The consent was thus invalid as the product of an unlawful arrest.

4. Other Seizure Tests. As *Bostick* demonstrates, the almost infinite variety of contacts between law enforcers and the public has led the Supreme Court to enunciate a variety of tests for determining whether a Fourth Amendment seizure occurred in an individual case.

In California v. Hodari D., 499 U.S. 621 (1991), the defendant discarded cocaine while being pursued by a police officer. The defendant argued that the officer's pursuit was a seizure under the *Mendenhall* test because it constituted a show of authority that called upon Hodari to halt. The

Supreme Court held that in the absence of physical contact, a display of authority was a seizure only if the person submitted to it. Because Hodari D. had not submitted to the officer's show of authority, but instead had attempted to escape, the Court held that "he was not seized until he was tackled. The cocaine abandoned while he was running was in this case not the fruit of a seizure, and his motion to exclude evidence of it was properly denied."

In Tennessee v. Garner, 471 U.S. 1 (1985), a police officer shot and killed a fleeing suspect. The Court concluded that this conduct constituted a Fourth Amendment seizure: "Whenever an officer restrains the freedom of a person to walk away, he has seized that person. While it is not always clear just when minimal police interference becomes a seizure, see United States v. Mendenhall, 446 U.S. 544 (1980), there can be no question that apprehension by the use of deadly force is a seizure subject to the reasonableness requirement of the Fourth Amendment."

In Brower v. County of Inyo, 489 U.S. 593 (1989), a fleeing motorist was killed when the stolen car that he had driven at high speeds for approximately 20 miles in an attempt to escape from pursuing police officers crashed into a police roadblock. The Supreme Court noted that although "a Fourth Amendment seizure does not occur whenever there is a governmentally caused termination of an individual's freedom of movement (the innocent passerby), nor even whenever there is a governmentally caused and governmentally *desired* termination of an individual's freedom of movement (the fleeing felon), but only when there is a governmental termination of freedom of movement *through means intentionally applied*." In applying this standard to the case before it, the Court held that it was "enough for a seizure that a person be stopped by the very instrumentality set in motion or put in place in order to achieve that result. It was enough here, therefore, that, according to the allegations of the complaint, Brower was meant to be stopped by the physical obstacle of the roadblock—and that he was so stopped."

* * *

HIIBEL v. SIXTH JUDICIAL DISTRICT COURT OF NEVADA

Supreme Court of the United States, 2004.
542 U.S. 177, 124 S.Ct. 2451, 159 L.Ed.2d 292.

JUSTICE KENNEDY delivered the opinion of the Court.

The petitioner was arrested and convicted for refusing to identify himself during a stop allowed by *Terry v. Ohio*, 392 U.S. 1, 20 L.Ed.2d 889, 88 S.Ct. 1868 (1968). He challenges his conviction under the Fourth and Fifth Amendments to the United States Constitution, applicable to the States through the Fourteenth Amendment.

I

The sheriff's department in Humboldt County, Nevada, received an afternoon telephone call reporting an assault. The caller reported seeing a man assault a woman in a red and silver GMC truck on Grass Valley Road. Deputy Sheriff Lee Dove was dispatched to investigate. When the officer arrived at the scene, he found the truck parked on the side of the road. A man was standing by the truck, and a young woman was sitting inside it. The officer observed skid marks in the gravel behind the vehicle, leading him to believe it had come to a sudden stop.

The officer approached the man and explained that he was investigating a report of a fight. The man appeared to be intoxicated. The officer asked him if he had "any identification on [him]," which we understand as a request to produce a driver's license or some other form of written identification. The man refused and asked why the officer wanted to see identification. The officer responded that he was conducting an investigation and needed to see some identification. The unidentified man became agitated and insisted he had done nothing wrong. The officer explained that he wanted to find out who the man was and what he was doing there. After continued refusals to comply with the officer's request for identification, the man began to taunt the officer by placing his hands behind his back and telling the officer to arrest him and take him to jail. This routine kept up for several minutes: the officer asked for identification 11 times and was refused each time. After warning the man that he would be arrested if he continued to refuse to comply, the officer placed him under arrest.

We now know that the man arrested on Grass Valley Road is Larry Dudley Hiibel. Hiibel was charged with "willfully resisting, delaying, or obstructing a public officer in discharging or attempting to discharge any legal duty of his office" in violation of Nev. Rev. Stat. (NRS) § 199.280 (2003). The government reasoned that Hiibel had obstructed the officer in carrying out his duties under § 171.123, a Nevada statute that defines the legal rights and duties of a police officer in the context of an investigative stop. Section 171.123 provides in relevant part:

> "1. Any peace officer may detain any person whom the officer encounters under circumstances which reasonably indicate that the person has committed, is committing or is about to commit a crime.

* * *

> "3. The officer may detain the person pursuant to this section only to ascertain his identity and the suspicious circumstances surrounding his presence abroad. Any person so detained shall identify himself, but may not be compelled to answer any other inquiry of any peace officer."

[A state court concluded that Hiibel's refusal to identify himself "obstructed and delayed a public officer attempting to discharge his duty." Hiibel was convicted and fined $250.]

II

NRS § 171.123(3) is an enactment sometimes referred to as a "stop and identify" statute. [Citations to statutes in another 20 states are omitted.] Stop and identify statutes often combine elements of traditional vagrancy laws with provisions intended to regulate police behavior in the course of investigatory stops. The statutes vary from State to State, but all permit an officer to ask or require a suspect to disclose his identity. * * * In some States, a suspect's refusal to identify himself is a misdemeanor offense or civil violation; in others, it is a factor to be considered in whether the suspect has violated loitering laws. In other States, a suspect may decline to identify himself without penalty.

Stop and identify statutes have their roots in early English vagrancy laws that required suspected vagrants to face arrest unless they gave "a good Account of themselves," a power that itself reflected common-law rights of private persons to "arrest any suspicious night-walker, and detain him till he give a good account of himself. . . . " In recent decades, the Court has found constitutional infirmity in traditional vagrancy laws. In *Papachristou* v. *Jacksonville,* 405 U.S. 156, 31 L.Ed.2d 110, 92 S.Ct. 839 (1972), the Court held that a traditional vagrancy law was void for vagueness. Its broad scope and imprecise terms denied proper notice to potential offenders and permitted police officers to exercise unfettered discretion in the enforcement of the law.

The Court has recognized similar constitutional limitations on the scope and operation of stop and identify statutes. In *Brown* v. *Texas,* 443 U.S. 47, 52, 61 L.Ed.2d 357, 99 S.Ct. 2637 (1979), the Court invalidated a conviction for violating a Texas stop and identify statute on Fourth Amendment grounds. The Court ruled that the initial stop was not based on specific, objective facts establishing reasonable suspicion to believe the suspect was involved in criminal activity. Absent that factual basis for detaining the defendant, the Court held, the risk of "arbitrary and abusive police practices" was too great and the stop was impermissible. Four Terms later, the Court invalidated a modified stop and identify statute on vagueness grounds. See *Kolender* v. *Lawson,* 461 U.S. 352, 75 L.Ed.2d 903, 103 S.Ct. 1855 (1983). The California law in *Kolender* required a suspect to give an officer " 'credible and reliable' " identification when asked to identify himself. The Court held that the statute was void because it provided no standard for determining what a suspect must do to comply with it, resulting in " 'virtually unrestrained power to arrest and charge persons with a violation.' "

The present case begins where our prior cases left off. Here there is no question that the initial stop was based on reasonable suspicion, satisfying the Fourth Amendment requirements noted in *Brown.* Further, the petitioner has not alleged that the statute is unconstitutionally vague, as in *Kolender.* Here the Nevada statute is narrower and more precise. The statute in *Kolender* had been interpreted to require a suspect to give the officer "credible and reliable" identification. In contrast, the Nevada Supreme Court has interpreted NRS § 171.123(3) to require only that a suspect disclose his name. As we understand it, the statute does not require a suspect to give the officer a driver's license or any other document. Provided that the suspect either states his name or communicates it to the officer by other means—a choice, we assume, that the suspect may make—the statute is satisfied and no violation occurs.

III

Hiibel argues that his conviction cannot stand because the officer's conduct violated his Fourth Amendment rights. We disagree.

Asking questions is an essential part of police investigations. In the ordinary course a police officer is free to ask a person for identification without implicating the Fourth Amendment. "Interrogation relating to one's identity or a request for identification by the police does not, by itself, constitute a Fourth Amendment seizure." Beginning with *Terry* v. *Ohio*, the Court has recognized that a law enforcement officer's reasonable suspicion that a person may be involved in criminal activity permits the officer to stop the person for a brief time and take additional steps to investigate further. To ensure that the resulting seizure is constitutionally reasonable, a *Terry* stop must be limited. The officer's action must be " 'justified at its inception, and . . . reasonably related in scope to the circumstances which justified the interference in the first place.' " For example, the seizure cannot continue for an excessive period of time, or resemble a traditional arrest.

Our decisions make clear that questions concerning a suspect's identity are a routine and accepted part of many *Terry* stops.

Obtaining a suspect's name in the course of a *Terry* stop serves important government interests. Knowledge of identity may inform an officer that a suspect is wanted for another offense, or has a record of violence or mental disorder. On the other hand, knowing identity may help clear a suspect and allow the police to concentrate their efforts elsewhere. Identity may prove particularly important in cases such as this, where the police are investigating what appears to be a domestic assault. Officers called to investigate domestic disputes need to know whom they are dealing with in order to assess the situation, the threat to their own safety, and possible danger to the potential victim.

Although it is well established that an officer may ask a suspect to identify himself in the course of a *Terry* stop, it has been an open question whether the suspect can be arrested and prosecuted for refusal to answer. * * *

* * *

The principles of *Terry* permit a State to require a suspect to disclose his name in the course of a *Terry* stop. The reasonableness of a seizure under the Fourth Amendment is determined "by balancing its intrusion on the individual's Fourth Amendment interests against its promotion of legitimate government interests." The Nevada statute satisfies that standard. The request for identity has an immediate relation to the purpose, rationale, and practical demands of a *Terry* stop. The threat of criminal sanction helps ensure that the request for identity does not become a legal nullity. On the other hand, the Nevada statute does not alter the nature of the stop itself: it does not change its duration, or its location. A state law requiring a suspect to disclose his name in the course of a valid *Terry* stop is consistent with Fourth Amendment prohibitions against unreasonable searches and seizures.

Petitioner argues that the Nevada statute circumvents the probable cause requirement, in effect allowing an officer to arrest a person for being suspicious. According to petitioner, this creates a risk of arbitrary police conduct that the Fourth Amendment does not permit. These are familiar concerns; they were central to the opinion in *Papachristou,* and also to the decisions limiting the operation of stop and identify statutes in *Kolender* and *Brown.* Petitioner's concerns are met by the requirement that a *Terry* stop must be justified at its inception and "reasonably related in scope to the circumstances which justified" the initial stop. Under these principles, an officer may not arrest a suspect for failure to identify himself if the request for identification is not reasonably related to the circumstances justifying the stop. * * * It is clear in this case that the request for identification was "reasonably related in scope to the circumstances which justified" the stop. The officer's request was a commonsense inquiry, not an effort to obtain an arrest for failure to identify after a *Terry* stop yielded insufficient evidence. The stop, the request, and the State's requirement of a response did not contravene the guarantees of the Fourth Amendment.

IV

Petitioner further contends that his conviction violates the Fifth Amendment's prohibition on compelled self-incrimination. * * * To qualify for the Fifth Amendment privilege, a communication must be testimonial, incriminating, and compelled.

Respondents urge us to hold that the statements NRS § 171.123(3) requires are nontestimonial, and so outside the Clause's scope. We decline to resolve the case on that basis. "To be testimonial, an accused's communication must itself, explicitly or implicitly, relate a factual assertion or disclose information." Stating one's name may qualify as an assertion of fact relating to identity. Production of identity documents might meet the definition as well. [A]cts of production may yield testimony establishing "the existence, authenticity, and custody of items [the police seek]." Even if these required actions are testimonial, however, petitioner's challenge must fail because in this case disclosure of his name presented no reasonable danger of incrimination.

* * *

As we stated in *Kastigar* v. *United States,* 406 U.S. 441, 445, 32 L.Ed.2d 212, 92 S.Ct. 1653 (1972), the Fifth Amendment privilege against compulsory self-incrimination "protects against any disclosures that the witness reasonably believes could be used in a criminal prosecution or could lead to other evidence that might be so used." Suspects who have been granted immunity from prosecution may, therefore, be compelled to answer; with the threat of prosecution removed, there can be no reasonable belief that the evidence will be used against them.

In this case petitioner's refusal to disclose his name was not based on any articulated real and appreciable fear that his name would be used to incriminate him, or that it "would furnish a link in the chain of evidence needed to prosecute" him. As best we can tell, petitioner refused to identify himself only because he thought his name was none of the officer's business. Even today, petitioner does not explain how the disclosure of his name could have been used against him in a criminal case. While we recognize petitioner's strong belief that he should not have to disclose his identity, the Fifth Amendment does not override the Nevada Legislature's judgment to the contrary absent a reasonable belief that the disclosure would tend to incriminate him.

The narrow scope of the disclosure requirement is also important. One's identity is, by definition, unique; yet it is, in another sense, a universal characteristic. Answering a request to disclose a name is likely to be so insignificant in the scheme of things as to be incriminating only in unusual circumstances. In every criminal case, it is known and must be known who has been arrested and who is being tried. Even witnesses who plan to invoke the Fifth Amendment privilege answer when their names are called to take the stand. Still, a case may arise where there is a substantial allegation that furnishing identity at the time of a stop would have given the police a link in the chain of evidence needed to convict the individual of a separate offense. In that case, the court can then consider whether the privilege applies, and, if the Fifth Amendment has been violated, what remedy must follow. We need not resolve those questions here.

The judgment of the Nevada Supreme Court is Affirmed.

[The dissenting opinions by Justice Stevens and by Justice Breyer, with whom Justice Souter and Justice Ginsburg joined, are omitted.]

E. *TERRY* SEARCHES OF PEOPLE

FLORIDA v. J.L.

Supreme Court of the United States, 2000.
529 U.S. 266, 120 S.Ct. 1375, 146 L.Ed.2d 254.

Justice Ginsburg, delivered the opinion of the Court.

The question presented in this case is whether an anonymous tip that a person is carrying a gun is, without more, sufficient to justify a police officer's stop and frisk of that person. We hold that it is not.

I

On October 13, 1995, an anonymous caller reported to the Miami–Dade Police that a young black male standing at a particular bus stop and wearing a plaid shirt was carrying a gun. So far as the record reveals, there is no audio recording of the tip, and nothing is known about the informant. Sometime after the police received the tip—the record does not say how long—two officers were instructed to respond. They arrived at the bus stop about six minutes later and saw three black males "just hanging out [there]." One of the three, respondent J.L., was wearing a plaid shirt. Apart from the tip, the officers had no reason to suspect any of the three of illegal conduct. The officers did not see a firearm, and J.L. made no threatening or otherwise unusual movements. One of the officers approached J.L., told him to put his hands up on the bus stop, frisked him, and seized a gun from J.L.'s pocket. The second officer frisked the other two individuals, against whom no allegations had been made, and found nothing.

J.L., who was at the time of the frisk "10 days shy of his 16th birthday," was charged under state law with carrying a concealed firearm without a license and possessing a firearm while under the age of 18. [The Florida Supreme Court "held the search invalid under the Fourth Amendment."]

Anonymous tips, the Florida Supreme Court stated, are generally less reliable than tips from known informants and can form the basis for reasonable suspicion only if accompanied by specific indicia of reliability, for example, the correct forecast of a subject's "not easily predicted" movements. The tip leading to the frisk of J.L., the court observed, provided no such predictions, nor did it contain any other qualifying indicia of reliability. Two justices dissented. The safety of the police and the public, they maintained, justifies a "firearm exception" to the general rule barring investigatory stops and frisks on the basis of bareboned anonymous tips.

* * * We granted certiorari, and now affirm the judgment of the Florida Supreme Court.

II

Our "stop and frisk" decisions begin with *Terry v. Ohio*, 392 U.S. 1, 88 S.Ct. 1868, 20 L.Ed.2d 889 (1968). This Court held in *Terry*

> "Where a police officer observes unusual conduct which leads him reasonably to conclude in light of his experience that criminal activity may be afoot and that the persons with whom he is dealing may be armed and presently dangerous, where in the course of investigating this behavior he identifies himself as a policeman and makes reasonable inquiries, and where nothing in the initial stages of the encounter serves to dispel his reasonable fear for his own safety, he is entitled for the protection of himself and others in the area to conduct a carefully limited search of the outer clothing of such persons in an attempt to discover weapons which might be used to assault him."

In the instant case, the officers' suspicion that J.L. was carrying a weapon arose not from any observations of their own but solely from a call made from an unknown location by an unknown caller. Unlike a tip from a known informant whose reputation can be assessed and who can be held responsible if her allegations turn out to be fabricated, "an anonymous tip alone seldom demonstrates the informant's basis of knowledge or veracity". As we have recognized, however, there are situations in which an anonymous tip, suitably corroborated, exhibits "sufficient indicia of reliability to provide reasonable suspicion to make the investigatory stop." The question we here confront is whether the tip pointing to J.L. had those indicia of reliability.

In *Alabama v. White,* 496 U.S. 325, 110 S.Ct. 2412, 110 L.Ed.2d 301 (1990) the police received an anonymous tip asserting that a woman was carrying cocaine and predicting that she would leave an apartment building at a specified time, get into a car matching a particular description, and drive to a named motel. Standing alone, the tip would not have justified a *Terry* stop. Only after police observation showed that the informant had accurately predicted the woman's movements, we explained, did it become reasonable to think the tipster had inside knowledge about the suspect and therefore to credit his assertion about the cocaine. Although the court held that the suspicion in *White* became reasonable after police surveillance, we regarded the case as borderline. Knowledge about a person's future movements indicates some familiarity with that person's affairs, but having such knowledge does not necessarily imply that the informant knows, in particular, whether that person is carrying hidden contraband. * * *

The tip in the instant case lacked the moderate indicia of reliability present in *White* and essential to the Court's decision in that case. The anonymous call concerning J.L. provided no predictive information and therefore left the police without means to test the informant's knowledge or credibility. That the allegation about the gun turned out to be correct does not suggest that the officers, prior to the frisks, had a reasonable basis for suspecting J.L. of engaging in unlawful conduct: The reasonableness of official suspicion must be measured by what the officers knew before they conducted their search. All the police had to go on in this case was the bare report of an unknown, unaccountable informant who neither explained how he knew of the gun nor supplied any basis for believing he had inside information about J.L. If *White* was a close case on the reliability of anonymous tips, this one surely falls on the other side of the line.

Florida contends that the tip was reliable because its description of the suspect's visible attributes proved accurate: There really was a young black male wearing a plaid shirt at the bus stop. The United States as amicus curiae makes a similar argument, proposing that a stop and frisk should be permitted "when (1) an anonymous tip provides a description of a particular person at a particular location illegally carrying a concealed firearm, (2) police promptly verify the pertinent details of the tip except the existence of the firearm, and (3) there are no factors that cast doubt on the reliability of the tip. . . . " These contentions misapprehend the reliability needed for a tip to justify *Terry* stop.

An accurate description of a subject's readily observable location and appearance is of course reliable in this limited sense: It will help the police correctly identify the person whom the tipster means to accuse. Such a tip, however, does not show that the tipster has knowledge of concealed criminal activity. The reasonable suspicion here at issue requires that a tip be reliable in its assertion of illegality, not just in its tendency to identify a determinate person.

A second major argument advanced by Florida and the United States as amicus is, in essence, that the standard *Terry* analysis should be modified to license a "firearm exception." Under such an exception, a tip alleging an illegal gun would justify a stop and frisk even if the accusation would fail standard pre-search reliability testing. We decline to adopt this position.

Firearms are dangerous, and extraordinary dangers sometimes justify unusual precautions. Our decisions recognize the serious threat that armed criminals pose to public safety; *Terry*'s rule, which permits protective police searches on the basis of reasonable suspicion rather than demanding that officers meet the higher standard of probable cause, responds to this very concern. But an automatic firearm exception to our established reliability analysis would rove too far. Such an exception would enable any person seeking to harass another to set in motion an intrusive, embarrassing police search of the targeted person simply by placing an anonymous call falsely reporting the target's unlawful carriage of a gun. Nor could one securely confine such an exception to allegations involving firearms. Several Courts of Appeals have held it per se foreseeable for people carrying significant amounts of illegal drugs to be carrying guns as well. If police officers may properly conduct *Terry* frisks on the basis of bare-boned tips about guns, it would be reasonable to maintain under the above-cited decisions that the police should similarly have discretion to frisk based on bare-boned tips about narcotics. [T]he Fourth Amendment is not so easily satisfied.

Finally, the requirement that an anonymous tip bear standard indicia of reliability in order to justify a stop in no way diminishes a police officer's prerogative, in accord with *Terry*, to conduct a protective search of a person who has already been legitimately stopped. We speak in today's decision only of cases in which the officer's authority to make the initial stop is at issue. In that context, we hold that an anonymous tip lacking indicia of reliability of the kind contemplated in *Adams* and *White* does not justify a stop and frisk whenever and however it alleges the illegal possession of a firearm.

The judgment of the Florida Supreme Court is affirmed.

JUSTICE KENNEDY, with whom THE CHIEF JUSTICE joins, concurring.

On the record created at the suppression hearing, the Court's decision is correct. The Court says all that is necessary to resolve this case, and I join the opinion in all respects. It might be noted, however, that there are many indicia of reliability respecting anonymous tips that we have yet to explore in our cases.

When a police officer testifies that a suspect aroused the officer's suspicion, and so justifies a stop and frisk, the courts can weigh the officer's credibility and admit evidence seized pursuant to the frisk even if no one, aside from the officer and defendant themselves, was present or observed the seizure. An anonymous telephone tip without more is different, however; for even if the officer's testimony about receipt of the tip is found credible, there is a second layer of inquiry respecting the reliability of the informant that cannot be pursued. If the telephone call is truly anonymous, the informant has not placed his credibility at risk and can lie with impunity. The reviewing court cannot judge the credibility of the informant and the risk of fabrication becomes unacceptable.

On this record, then, the Court is correct in holding that the telephone tip did not justify the arresting officer's immediate stop and frisk of respondent. There was testimony that an anonymous tip came in by a telephone call and nothing more. The record does not show whether some notation or other documentation of the call was either by a voice recording or tracing the call to a telephone number. * * *

[A] tip might be anonymous in some sense yet have certain other features, either supporting reliability or narrowing the likely class of informants, so that the tip does provide the lawful basis for some police action. One such feature, as the Court recognizes, is that the tip predicts future conduct of the alleged criminal. There may be others. For example, if an unnamed caller with a voice which sounds the same each time tells police on two successive nights about criminal activity which in fact occurs each night, a similar call on the third night ought not be treated automatically like the tip in the case now before us. In the instance supposed, there would be a plausible argument that experience cures some of the uncertainty surrounding the anonymity, justifying a proportionate police response. * * *

If an informant places his anonymity at risk, a court can consider this factor in weighing the reliability of the tip. An instance where a tip might be considered anonymous but nevertheless sufficiently reliable to justify a proportionate police response may be when an unnamed person driving a car the police officer later describes stops for a moment and, face to face, informs the police that criminal activity is occurring. This too seems different from the tip in the present case.

Instant caller identification is widely available to police, and, if anonymous tips are proving unreliable and distracting to police, squad cars can be sent within seconds to the location of the telephone used by the informant. Voice recording of telephone tips might, in appropriate cases, be used by police to locate the caller. It is unlawful to make false reports to the police, and the ability of the police to trace the identity of anonymous telephone informants may be a factor which lends reliability to what, years earlier, might have been considered unreliable anonymous tips.

* * *

MINNESOTA v. DICKERSON

Supreme Court of the United States, 1993.
508 U.S. 366, 113 S.Ct. 2130, 124 L.Ed.2d 334.

JUSTICE WHITE delivered the opinion of the Court.

In this case, we consider whether the Fourth Amendment permits the seizure of contraband detected through a police officer's sense of touch during a protective patdown search.

I

On the evening of November 9, 1989, two Minneapolis police officers were patrolling an area on the city's north side in a marked squad car. At about 8:15 p.m., one of the officers observed respondent leaving a 12–unit apartment building on Morgan Avenue North. The officer, having previously responded to complaints of drug sales in the building's hallways and having executed several search warrants on the premises, considered the building to be a notorious "crack house." According to testimony credited by the trial court, respondent began walking toward the police but, upon spotting the squad car and making eye contact with one of the officers, abruptly halted and began walking in the opposite direction. His suspicion aroused, this officer watched as respondent turned and entered an alley on the other side of the apartment building. Based upon respondent's seemingly evasive actions and the fact that he had just left a building known for cocaine traffic, the officers decided to stop respondent and investigate further.

The officers pulled their squad car into the alley and ordered respondent to stop and submit to a patdown search. The search revealed no weapons, but the officer conducting the search did take an interest in a small lump in respondent's nylon jacket. The officer later testified:

> "[A]s I pat-searched the front of his body, I felt a lump, a small lump, in the front pocket. I examined it with my fingers and it slid and it felt to be a lump of crack cocaine in cellophane."

The officer then reached into respondent's pocket and retrieved a small plastic bag containing one fifth of one gram of crack cocaine. Respondent was arrested and charged in Hennepin County District Court with possession of a controlled substance.

Before trial, respondent moved to suppress the cocaine. * * * His suppression motion having failed, respondent proceeded to trial and was found guilty.

* * *

II

A

The Fourth Amendment guarantees "the right of the people to be secure in their persons, houses, papers, and effects, against unreasonable searches and seizures." Time and again, this Court has observed that searches and seizures " 'conducted outside the judicial process, without prior approval by judge or magistrate, are *per se* unreasonable under the Fourth Amendment—subject only to a few specifically established and well delineated exceptions.' " One such exception was recognized in *Terry* v. *Ohio* 392 U.S. 1, 88 S Ct. 1868, 20 L.Ed.2d 889 (1968) which held that "where a police officer observes unusual conduct which leads him reasonably to conclude in light of his experience that criminal activity may be afoot ... ," the officer may briefly stop the suspicious person and make "reasonable inquiries" aimed at confirming or dispelling his suspicions.

Terry further held that "when an officer is justified in believing that the individual whose suspicious behavior he is investigating at close range is armed and presently dangerous to the officer or to others," the officer may conduct a patdown search "to determine whether the person is in fact carrying a weapon." "The purpose of this limited search is not to discover evidence of crime, but to allow the officer to pursue his investigation without fear of violence.... " Rather, a protective search— permitted without a warrant and on the basis of reasonable suspicion less than probable cause—must be strictly "limited to that which is necessary for the discovery of weapons which might be used to harm the officer or others nearby." If the protective search goes beyond what is necessary to determine if the suspect is armed, it is no longer valid under *Terry* and its fruits will be suppressed.

* * * The question presented today is whether police officers may seize nonthreatening contraband detected during a protective patdown search of the sort permitted by *Terry*. We think the answer is clearly that they may, so long as the officers' search stays within the bounds marked by *Terry*.

B

We have already held that police officers, at least under certain circumstances, may seize contraband detected during the lawful execution of a *Terry* search. In *Michigan* v. *Long,* 463 U.S. 1032, 103 S.Ct. 3469, 77 L.Ed.2d 1201 (1983) [t]he Court held first that, in the context of a roadside encounter, where police have reasonable suspicion based on specific and articulable facts to believe that a driver may be armed and dangerous, they may conduct a protective search for weapons not only of the driver's person but also of the passenger compartment of the automobile. Of course, the protective search of the vehicle, being justified solely by the danger that weapons stored there could be used against the officers or bystanders, must be "limited to those areas in which a weapon may be placed or hidden." The Court then held: "If, while conducting a legitimate *Terry* search of the interior of the automobile, the officer should, as here, discover contraband other than weapons, he clearly cannot be required to ignore the contraband, and the Fourth Amendment does not require its suppression in such circumstances."

The Court in *Long* justified this latter holding by reference to our cases under the "plain-view" doctrine. Under that doctrine, if police are lawfully in a position from which they view an object, if its incriminating character is immediately apparent, and if the officers have a lawful right of access to the object, they may seize it without a warrant. If, however, the police lack probable cause to believe that an object in plain view is contraband without conducting some further search of the object—*i.e.*, if "its incriminating character [is not] 'immediately apparent,' " the plain-view doctrine cannot justify its seizure.

We think that this doctrine has an obvious application by analogy to cases in which an officer discovers contraband through the sense of touch during an otherwise lawful search. The rationale of the plain-view doctrine is that if contraband is left in open view and is observed by a police officer from a lawful vantage point, there has been no invasion of a legitimate expectation of privacy and thus no "search" within the meaning of the Fourth Amendment—or at least no search independent of the initial intrusion that gave the officers their vantage point. The warrantless seizure of contraband that presents itself in this manner is deemed justified by the realization that resort to a neutral magistrate under such circumstances would often be impracticable and would do little to promote the objectives of the Fourth Amendment. The same can be said of tactile discoveries of contraband. If a police officer lawfully pats down a suspect's outer clothing and feels an object whose contour or mass makes its identity immediately apparent, there has been no invasion of the suspect's privacy beyond that already authorized by the officer's search for weapons; if the object is contraband, its warrantless seizure would be justified by the same practical considerations that inhere in the plain-view context.

The Minnesota Supreme Court rejected an analogy to the plain-view doctrine on two grounds: first, its belief that "the sense of touch is inherently less immediate and less reliable than the sense of sight," and second, that "the sense of touch is far more intrusive into the personal privacy that is at the core of the Fourth Amendment." 481 N.W.2d at 845. We have a somewhat different view. First, *Terry* itself demonstrates that the sense of touch is capable of revealing the nature of an object with sufficient reliability to support a seizure. The very premise of *Terry*, after all, is that officers will be able to detect the presence of weapons through the sense of touch and *Terry* upheld precisely such a seizure. Even if it were true that the sense of touch is generally less reliable than the sense of sight, that only suggests that officers will less often be able to justify seizures of unseen contraband. Regardless of whether the officer detects the contraband by sight or by touch, however, the Fourth Amendment's requirement that the officer have probable cause to believe that the item is contraband before seizing it ensures against excessively speculative seizures. The court's second concern—that touch is more intrusive into privacy than is sight—is inapposite in light of the fact that the intrusion the court fears has already been authorized by the lawful search for weapons. The seizure of an item whose identity is already known occasions no further invasion of privacy. Accordingly, the suspect's privacy interests are not advanced by a categorical rule barring the seizure of contraband plainly detected through the sense of touch.

III

It remains to apply these principles to the facts of this case. Respondent has not challenged the finding made by the trial court and affirmed by both the Court of Appeals and the State Supreme Court that the police were justified under *Terry* in stopping him and frisking him for weapons. Thus, the dispositive question before this Court is whether the officer who conducted the search was acting within the lawful bounds marked by *Terry* at the time he gained probable cause to believe that the lump in respondent's jacket was contraband. The State District Court did not make precise findings on this point, instead finding simply that the officer, after feeling "a small, hard object wrapped in plastic" in respondent's pocket, "formed the opinion that the object . . . was crack . . . cocaine." The District Court also noted that the officer made "no claim that he suspected this object to be a weapon," a finding affirmed on appeal, (the officer "never thought the lump was a weapon"). The Minnesota Supreme Court, after "a close examination of the record," held that the officer's own testimony "belies any notion that he 'immediately' " recognized the lump as crack cocaine. Rather, the court concluded, the officer determined that the lump was contraband only after "squeezing, sliding and otherwise manipulating the contents of the defendant's pocket"—a pocket which the officer already knew contained no weapon. *Ibid.*

Under the State Supreme Court's interpretation of the record before it, it is clear that the court was correct in holding that the police officer in this case overstepped the bounds of the "strictly circumscribed" search for weapons allowed under *Terry*. Where, as here, "an officer who is executing a valid search for one item seizes a different item," this Court rightly "has been sensitive to the danger . . . that officers will enlarge a specific authorization, furnished by a warrant or an exigency, into the equivalent of a general warrant to rummage and seize at will." Here, the officer's continued exploration of respondent's pocket after having concluded that it contained no weapon was unrelated to "the sole justification of the search [under *Terry*:] . . . the protection of the police officer and others nearby." It therefore amounted to the sort of evidentiary search that *Terry* expressly refused to authorize * * *.

Once again, the analogy to the plain-view doctrine is apt. * * * Although the officer was lawfully in a position to feel the lump in respondent's pocket, because *Terry* entitled him to place his hands upon respondent's jacket, the court below determined that the incriminating character of the object was not immediately apparent to him. Rather, the officer determined that the item was contraband only after conducting a further search, one not authorized by *Terry* or by any other exception to the warrant requirement. Because this further search of respondent's pocket was constitutionally invalid, the seizure of the cocaine that followed is likewise unconstitutional.

* * *

JUSTICE SCALIA, concurring.

I take it to be a fundamental principle of constitutional adjudication that the terms in the Constitution must be given the meaning ascribed to them at the time of their ratification. Thus, when the Fourth Amendment provides that "the right of the people to be secure in their persons, houses, papers, and effects, against *unreasonable searches and seizures*, shall not be violated" (emphasis added), it "is to be construed in the light of what was deemed an unreasonable search and seizure when it was adopted," The purpose of the provision, in other words, is to preserve that degree of respect for the privacy of persons and the inviolability of their property that existed when the provision was adopted—even if a later, less virtuous age should become accustomed to considering all sorts of intrusion "reasonable."

My problem with the present case is that I am not entirely sure that the physical search—the "frisk"—that produced the evidence at issue here complied with that constitutional standard. The decision of ours that gave approval to such searches, *Terry*, made no serious attempt to determine compliance with traditional standards, but rather, according to the style of this Court at the time, simply adjudged that such a search was "reasonable" by current estimations.

There is good evidence, I think, that the "stop" portion of the *Terry* "stop-and-frisk" holding accords with the common law—that it had long been considered reasonable to detain suspicious persons for the purpose of demanding that they give an account of themselves. This is suggested, in particular, by the so-called night-walker statutes, and their common-law antecedents.

I am unaware, however, of any precedent for a physical search of a person thus temporarily detained for questioning. Sometimes, of course, the temporary detention of a suspicious character would be elevated to a full custodial arrest on probable cause—as, for instance, when a suspect was unable to provide a sufficient accounting of himself. At *that* point, it is clear that the common law would permit not just a protective "frisk," but a full physical search incident to the arrest. When, however, the detention did not rise to the level of a full-blown arrest (and was not supported by the degree of cause needful for that purpose), there appears to be no clear support at common law for physically searching the suspect.

I frankly doubt, moreover, whether the fiercely proud men who adopted our Fourth Amendment would have allowed themselves to be subjected, on mere *suspicion* of being armed and dangerous, to such indignity—which is described as follows in a police manual:

"Check the subject's neck and collar. A check should be made under the subject's arm. Next a check should be made of the upper back. The lower back should also be checked.

"A check should be made of the upper part of the man's chest and the lower region around the stomach. The belt, a favorite concealment spot, should be checked. The inside thigh and crotch area also should be searched. The legs should be checked for possible weapons. The last items to be checked are the shoes and cuffs of the subject." J. Moynahan, Police Searching Procedures 7 (1963) (citations omitted).

* * *

I adhere to original meaning, however. And though I do not favor the mode of analysis in *Terry*, I cannot say that its result was wrong. Constitutionality of the "frisk" in the present case was neither challenged nor argued. Assuming, therefore, that the search was lawful, I agree with the Court's premise that any evidence incidentally discovered in the course of it would be admissible, and join the Court's opinion in its entirety.

[CHIEF JUSTICE REHNQUIST'S opinion concurring in part and dissenting in part is omitted].

F. *TERRY* SEARCHES AND SEIZURES OF PROPERTY

MICHIGAN v. LONG

Supreme Court of the United States, 1983.
463 U.S. 1032, 103 S.Ct. 3469, 77 L.Ed.2d 1201.

JUSTICE O'CONNOR delivered the opinion of the Court.

* * *

I

Deputies Howell and Lewis were on patrol in a rural area one evening when, shortly after midnight, they observed a car traveling erratically and at excessive speed.[1] The officers observed the car turning down a side road, where it swerved off into a shallow ditch. The officers stopped to investigate. Long, the only occupant of the automobile, met the deputies at the rear of the car, which was protruding from the ditch onto the road. The door on the driver's side of the vehicle was left open.

---

1. It is clear, and the respondent concedes, that if the officers had arrested Long for speeding or for driving while intoxicated, they could have searched the passenger compartment under *New York v. Belton, 453 U.S. 454 (1981),* and the trunk under *United States v. Ross, 456 U.S. 798 (1982),* if they had probable cause to believe that the trunk contained contraband. However, at oral argument, the State informed us that while Long could have been arrested for a speeding violation under Michigan law, he was *not* arrested because "[as] a matter of practice," police in Michigan do not arrest for speeding violations unless "more" is involved. The officers did issue Long an appearance ticket.* * *

Deputy Howell requested Long to produce his operator's license, but he did not respond. After the request was repeated, Long produced his license. Long again failed to respond when Howell requested him to produce the vehicle registration. After another repeated request, Long, who Howell thought "appeared to be under the influence of something," turned from the officers and began walking toward the open door of the vehicle. The officers followed Long and both observed a large hunting knife on the floorboard of the driver's side of the car. The officers then stopped Long's progress and subjected him to a *Terry* protective pat-down, which revealed no weapons.

Long and Deputy Lewis then stood by the rear of the vehicle while Deputy Howell shined his flashlight into the interior of the vehicle, but did not actually enter it. The purpose of Howell's action was "to search for other weapons." The officer noticed that something was protruding from under the armrest on the front seat. He knelt in the vehicle and lifted the armrest. He saw an open pouch on the front seat, and upon flashing his light on the pouch, determined that it contained what appeared to be marihuana. After Deputy Howell showed the pouch and its contents to Deputy Lewis, Long was arrested for possession of marihuana. A further search of the interior of the vehicle, including the glovebox, revealed neither more contraband nor the vehicle registration. The officers decided to impound the vehicle. Deputy Howell opened the trunk, which did not have a lock, and discovered inside it approximately 75 pounds of marihuana.

[The state trial court denied Long's motion to suppress the marihuana taken from both the interior of the car and its trunk and he was convicted of possession of marihuana. The Michigan Supreme Court reversed, concluding that "the sole justification of the *Terry* search, protection of the police officers and others nearby, cannot justify the search in this case."]

We granted certiorari in this case to consider the important question of the authority of a police officer to protect himself by conducting a *Terry*-type search of the passenger compartment of a motor vehicle during the lawful investigatory stop of the occupant of the vehicle.

II

Before reaching the merits, we must consider Long's argument that we are without jurisdiction to decide this case because the decision below rests on an adequate and independent state ground. The court below referred twice to the State Constitution in its opinion, but otherwise relied exclusively on federal law. Long argues that the Michigan courts have provided greater protection from searches and seizures under the State Constitution than is afforded under the Fourth Amendment, and the references to the State Constitution therefore establish an adequate and independent ground for the decision below.

* * *

Respect for the independence of state courts, as well as avoidance of rendering advisory opinions, have been the cornerstones of this Court's refusal to decide cases where there is an adequate and independent state ground. It is precisely because of this respect for state courts, and this desire to avoid advisory opinions, that we do not wish to continue to decide issues of state law that go beyond the opinion that we review, or to require state courts to reconsider cases to clarify the grounds of their decisions. Accordingly, when, as in this case, a state court decision fairly appears to rest primarily on federal law, or to be interwoven with the federal law, and when the adequacy and independence of any possible state law ground is not clear from the face of the opinion, we will accept as the most reasonable explanation that the state court decided the case the way it did because it believed that federal law required it to do so. If a state court chooses merely to rely on federal precedents as it would on the precedents of all other jurisdictions, then it need only make clear by a plain statement in its judgment or opinion that the federal cases are being used only for the purpose of guidance, and do not themselves compel the result that the court has reached. In this way, both justice and judicial administration will be greatly improved. If the state court decision indicates clearly and expressly that it is alternatively based on bona fide separate, adequate, and independent grounds, we, of course, will not undertake to review the decision.

[The Court then concluded that "in this case that the Michigan Supreme Court rested its decision primarily on federal law."]

* * *

III

* * *

[T]he search of the passenger compartment of an automobile, limited to those areas in which a weapon may be placed or hidden, is permissible if the police officer possesses a reasonable belief based on "specific and articulable facts which, taken together with the rational inferences from those facts, reasonably warrant" the officer in believing that the suspect is dangerous and the suspect may gain immediate control of weapons.[14] * * *

14. We stress that our decision does not mean that the police may conduct automobile searches *whenever* they conduct an investigative stop, although the "bright line" that we drew in *Belton* clearly authorizes such a search whenever officers effect a custodial arrest. An additional interest exists in the arrest context, *i. e.*, preservation of evidence, and this justifies an "automatic" search. However, that additional interest does not exist in the *Terry* context. A *Terry* search, "unlike a search without a warrant incident to a lawful arrest, is not justified by any need to prevent the disappearance or destruction of evidence of crime.... The sole justification of the search ... is the protection of the police officer and others nearby...." 392 U.S., at 29. What we borrow now from *Chimel v. California, 395 U.S. 752 (1969),* and *Belton* is merely the recognition that part of the reason to allow area searches incident to an arrest is that the arrestee, who may not himself be armed, may be able to gain access to weapons to injure officers or others nearby, or otherwise to hinder legitimate police activity. This recognition applies as well in the *Terry* context. However, because the interest in collecting and preserving

The circumstances of this case clearly justified Deputies Howell and Lewis in their reasonable belief that Long posed a danger if he were permitted to reenter his vehicle. The hour was late and the area rural. Long was driving his automobile at excessive speed, and his car swerved into a ditch. The officers had to repeat their questions to Long, who appeared to be "under the influence" of some intoxicant. Long was not frisked until the officers observed that there was a large knife in the interior of the car into which Long was about to reenter. The subsequent search of the car was restricted to those areas to which Long would generally have immediate control, and that could contain a weapon. The trial court determined that the leather pouch containing marihuana could have contained a weapon. It is clear that the intrusion was "strictly circumscribed by the exigencies which [justified] its initiation."

[T]he balancing required by *Terry* clearly weighs in favor of allowing the police to conduct an area search of the passenger compartment to uncover weapons, as long as they possess an articulable and objectively reasonable belief that the suspect is potentially dangerous.

* * *

The judgment of the Michigan Supreme Court is reversed, and the case is remanded for further proceedings not inconsistent with this opinion. *It is so ordered.*

[JUSTICE BLACKMUN'S opinion concurring in part and concurring in the judgment is omitted.]

JUSTICE BRENNAN, with whom JUSTICE MARSHALL JOINS, dissenting.

The Court today holds that "the protective search of the passenger compartment" of the automobile involved in this case "was reasonable under the principles articulated in *Terry* and other decisions of this Court." I disagree. *Terry v. Ohio* does not support the Court's conclusion and the reliance on "other decisions" is patently misplaced. Plainly, the Court is simply continuing the process of distorting *Terry* beyond recognition and forcing it into service as an unlikely weapon against the Fourth Amendment's fundamental requirement that searches and seizures be based on probable cause. I, therefore, dissent.

* * *

In *Terry*, the Court confronted the "quite narrow question" of "whether it is always unreasonable for a policeman to seize a person and subject him to a *limited* search for weapons unless there is probable cause for an arrest." Because the Court was dealing "with an entire rubric of police conduct ... which historically [had] not been, and as a practical matter could not be, subjected to the warrant procedure," the Court tested the conduct at issue "by the Fourth Amendment's general proscription against unreasonable searches and seizures." * * *

evidence is not present in the *Terry* context, we require that officers who conduct area searches during investigative detentions must do so only when they have the level of suspicion identified in *Terry*.

It is clear that *Terry* authorized only limited searches of the person for weapons. In light of what *Terry* said, relevant portions of which the Court neglects to quote, the Court's suggestion that *"Terry* need not be read as restricting the preventive search to the person of the detained suspect" can only be described as disingenuous. Nothing in *Terry* authorized police officers to search a suspect's car based on reasonable suspicion. * * *

The Court's reliance on *Chimel v. California* and *New York v. Belton* as support for its new "area search" rule within the context of a *Terry* stop is misplaced. * * *

* * *

The critical distinction between this case and *Terry* on the one hand, and *Chimel* and *Belton* on the other, is that the latter two cases arose within the context of lawful custodial arrests supported by probable cause. The Court in *Terry* expressly recognized the difference between a search incident to arrest and the "limited search for weapons," involved in that case. * * *

* * *

As these cases recognize, there is a vital difference between searches incident to lawful custodial arrests and *Terry* protective searches. The Court deliberately ignores that difference in relying on principles developed within the context of intrusions supported by probable cause to arrest to construct an "area search" rule within the context of a *Terry* stop.

* * *

The Court suggests no limit on the "area search" it now authorizes. The Court states that a "search of the passenger compartment of an automobile, limited to those areas in which a weapon may be placed or hidden, is permissible if the police officer possesses a reasonable belief based on 'specific and articulable facts which, taken together with the rational inferences from those facts, reasonably warrant' the officers in believing that the suspect is dangerous and the suspect may gain immediate control of weapons." Presumably a weapon "may be placed or hidden" anywhere in a car. A weapon also might be hidden in a container in the car. * * * An individual can lawfully possess many things that can be used as weapons. A hammer, or a baseball bat, can be used as a very effective weapon. [T]he implications of the Court's decision are frightening.

* * *

JUSTICE STEVENS, dissenting.

The jurisprudential questions presented in this case are far more important than the question whether the Michigan police officer's search of respondent's car violated the Fourth Amendment. The case raises profoundly significant questions concerning the relationship between two sovereigns—the State of Michigan and the United States of America.

The Supreme Court of the State of Michigan expressly held "that the deputies' search of the vehicle was proscribed by the Fourth Amendment to the United States Constitution and *art 1, § 11 of the Michigan Constitution*." The state law ground is clearly adequate to support the judgment, but the question whether it is independent of the Michigan Supreme Court's understanding of federal law is more difficult. * * *

[W]e are left with a choice between two presumptions: one in favor of our taking jurisdiction, and one against it. Historically, the latter presumption has always prevailed. The rule * * * was as follows:

> "Where the judgment of the state court rests on two grounds, one involving a federal question and the other not, or if it does not appear upon which of two grounds the judgment was based, and the ground independent of a federal question is sufficient in itself to sustain it, this Court will not take jurisdiction.

* * *

The nature of the case before us hardly compels a departure from tradition. These are not cases in which an American citizen has been deprived of a right secured by the United States Constitution or a federal statute. Rather, they are cases in which a state court has upheld a citizen's assertion of a right, finding the citizen to be protected under both federal and state law. * * *

UNITED STATES v. PLACE

Supreme Court of the United States, 1983.
462 U.S. 696, 103 S.Ct. 2637, 77 L.Ed.2d 110.

JUSTICE O'CONNOR delivered the opinion of the Court.

* * *

I

Respondent Raymond J. Place's behavior aroused the suspicions of law enforcement officers as he waited in line at the Miami International Airport to purchase a ticket to New York's La Guardia Airport. As Place proceeded to the gate for his flight, the agents approached him and requested his airline ticket and some identification. Place complied with the request and consented to a search of the two suitcases he had checked. Because his flight was about to depart, however, the agents decided not to search the luggage.

Prompted by Place's parting remark that he had recognized that they were police, the agents inspected the address tags on the checked luggage and noted discrepancies in the two street addresses. Further investigation revealed that neither address existed and that the telephone number Place had given the airline belonged to a third address on the same street. On the basis of their encounter with Place and this information, the Miami agents called Drug Enforcement Administration (DEA) authorities in New York to relay their information about Place.

Two DEA agents waited for Place at the arrival gate at La Guardia Airport in New York. There again, his behavior aroused the suspicion of the agents. After he had claimed his two bags and called a limousine, the agents decided to approach him. They identified themselves as federal narcotics agents, to which Place responded that he knew they were "cops" and had spotted them as soon as he had deplaned. One of the agents informed Place that, based on their own observations and information obtained from the Miami authorities, they believed that he might be carrying narcotics. After identifying the bags as belonging to him, Place stated that a number of police at the Miami Airport had surrounded him and searched his baggage. The agents responded that their information was to the contrary. The agents requested and received identification from Place—a New Jersey driver's license, on which the agents later ran a computer check that disclosed no offenses, and his airline ticket receipt. When Place refused to consent to a search of his luggage, one of the agents told him that they were going to take the luggage to a federal judge to try to obtain a search warrant and that Place was free to accompany them. Place declined, but obtained from one of the agents telephone numbers at which the agents could be reached.

The agents then took the bags to Kennedy Airport, where they subjected the bags to a "sniff test" by a trained narcotics detection dog. The dog reacted positively to the smaller of the two bags but ambiguously to the larger bag. Approximately 90 minutes had elapsed since the seizure of respondent's luggage. Because it was late on a Friday afternoon, the agents retained the luggage until Monday morning, when they secured a search warrant from a Magistrate for the smaller bag. Upon opening that bag, the agents discovered 1,125 grams of cocaine.

[The trial court denied the defendant's motion to suppress the cocaine, and Place was convicted of possession of cocaine with intent to distribute. The Court of Appeals reversed.]

II

* * * In the ordinary case, the Court has viewed a seizure of personal property as *per se* unreasonable within the meaning of the Fourth Amendment unless it is accomplished pursuant to a judicial warrant issued upon probable cause and particularly describing the items to be seized. Where law enforcement authorities have probable cause to believe that a container holds contraband or evidence of a crime, but have not secured a warrant, the Court has interpreted the Amendment to permit seizure of the property, pending issuance of a warrant to examine its contents, if the exigencies of the circumstances demand it or some other recognized exception to the warrant requirement is present. * * *

In this case, the Government asks us to recognize the reasonableness under the Fourth Amendment of warrantless seizures of personal luggage from the custody of the owner on the basis of less than probable cause, for the purpose of pursuing a limited course of investigation, short of opening the luggage, that would quickly confirm or dispel the authorities' suspicion. Specifically, we are asked to apply the principles of *Terry* v. *Ohio,* to permit such seizures on the basis of reasonable, articulable suspicion, premised on objective facts, that the luggage contains contraband or evidence of a crime. In our view, such application is appropriate.

* * *

The exception to the probable-cause requirement for limited seizures of the person recognized in *Terry* and its progeny rests on a balancing of the competing interests to determine the reasonableness of the type of seizure involved within the meaning of "the Fourth Amendment's general proscription against unreasonable searches and seizures." We must balance the nature and quality of the intrusion on the individual's Fourth Amendment interests against the importance of the governmental interests alleged to justify the intrusion. When the nature and extent of the detention are minimally intrusive of the individual's Fourth Amendment interests, the opposing law enforcement interests can support a seizure based on less than probable cause.

* * * The Government contends that, where the authorities possess specific and articulable facts warranting a reasonable belief that a traveler's luggage contains narcotics, the governmental interest in seizing the luggage briefly to pursue further investigation is substantial. We agree. "[The] public has a compelling interest in detecting those who would traffic in deadly drugs for personal profit."

Respondent suggests that, absent some special law enforcement interest such as officer safety, a generalized interest in law enforcement cannot justify an intrusion on an individual's Fourth Amendment interests in the absence of probable cause. Our prior cases, however, do not support this proposition. In *Terry,* we described the governmental interests supporting the initial seizure of the person as "effective crime prevention and detection; it is this interest which underlies the recognition that a police officer may in appropriate circumstances and in an appropriate manner approach a person for purposes of investigating possibly criminal behavior even though there is no probable cause to make an arrest." * * * The test is whether those interests are sufficiently "substantial," not whether they are independent of the interest in investigating crimes effectively and apprehending suspects. * * * Because of the inherently transient nature of drug courier activity at airports, allowing police to make brief investigative stops of persons at airports on reasonable suspicion of drug-trafficking substantially enhances the likelihood that police will be able to prevent the flow of narcotics into distribution channels.

Against this strong governmental interest, we must weigh the nature and extent of the intrusion upon the individual's Fourth Amendment rights when the police briefly detain luggage for limited investigative purposes. On this point, respondent Place urges that the rationale for a *Terry* stop of the person is wholly inapplicable to investigative detentions of personality. Specifically, the *Terry* exception to the probable-cause requirement is premised on the notion that a *Terry*-type stop of the person is substantially less intrusive of a person's liberty interests than a formal arrest. In the property context, however, Place urges, there are no degrees of intrusion. Once the owner's property is seized, the dispossession is absolute.

We disagree. The intrusion on possessory interests occasioned by a seizure of one's personal effects can vary both in its nature and extent. The seizure may be made after the owner has relinquished control of the property to a third party or, as here, from the immediate custody and control of the owner. Moreover, the police may confine their investigation to an on-the-spot inquiry—for example, immediate exposure of the luggage to a trained narcotics detection dog—or transport the property to another location. Given the fact that seizures of property can vary in intrusiveness, some brief detentions of personal effects may be so minimally intrusive of Fourth Amendment interests that strong countervailing governmental interests will justify a seizure based only on specific articulable facts that the property contains contraband or evidence of a crime.

* * *

The purpose for which respondent's luggage was seized, of course, was to arrange its exposure to a narcotics detection dog. Obviously, if this investigative procedure is itself a search requiring probable cause, the initial seizure of respondent's luggage for the purpose of subjecting it to the sniff test—no matter how brief—could not be justified on less than probable cause.

The Fourth Amendment "protects people from unreasonable government intrusions into their legitimate expectations of privacy." We have affirmed that a person possesses a privacy interest in the contents of personal luggage that is protected by the Fourth Amendment. A "canine sniff" by a well-trained narcotics detection dog, however, does not require opening the luggage. It does not expose noncontraband items that otherwise would remain hidden from public view, as does, for example, an officer's rummaging through the contents of the luggage. Thus, the manner in which information is obtained through this investigative technique is much less intrusive than a typical search. Moreover, the sniff discloses only the presence or absence of narcotics, a contraband item. Thus, despite the fact that the sniff tells the authorities something about the contents of the luggage, the information obtained is limited. This limited disclosure also ensures that the owner of the property is not subjected to the embarrassment and inconvenience entailed in less discriminate and more intrusive investigative methods.

In these respects, the canine sniff is *sui generis*. We are aware of no other investigative procedure that is so limited both in the manner in which the information is obtained and in the content of the information revealed by the procedure. Therefore, we conclude that the particular course of investigation that the agents intended to pursue here—exposure of respondent's luggage, which was located in a public place, to a trained canine—did not constitute a "search" within the meaning of the Fourth Amendment.

III

There is no doubt that the agents made a "seizure" of Place's luggage for purposes of the Fourth Amendment when, following his refusal to consent to a search, the agent told Place that he was going to take the luggage to a federal judge to secure issuance of a warrant. As we observed in *Terry*, "[the] manner in which the seizure . . . [was] conducted is, of course, as vital a part of the inquiry as whether [it was] warranted at all." We therefore examine whether the agents' conduct in this case was such as to place the seizure within the general rule requiring probable cause for a seizure or within *Terry*'s exception to that rule.

* * * The precise type of detention we confront here is seizure of personal luggage from the immediate possession of the suspect for the purpose of arranging exposure to a narcotics detection dog. Particularly in the case of detention of luggage within the traveler's immediate possession, the police conduct intrudes on both the suspect's possessory interest in his luggage as well as his liberty interest in proceeding with his itinerary. The person whose luggage is detained is technically still free to continue his travels or carry out other personal activities pending release of the luggage. Moreover, he is not subjected to the coercive atmosphere of a custodial confinement or to the public indignity of being personally detained. Nevertheless, such a seizure can effectively restrain the person since he is subjected to the possible disruption of his travel plans in order to remain with his luggage or to arrange for its return. Therefore, when the police seize luggage from the suspect's custody, we think the limitations applicable to investigative detentions of the person should define the permissible scope of an investigative detention of the person's luggage on less than probable cause. Under this standard, it is clear that the police conduct here exceeded the permissible limits of a *Terry*-type investigative stop.

The length of the detention of respondent's luggage alone precludes the conclusion that the seizure was reasonable in the absence of probable cause. Although we have recognized the reasonableness of seizures longer than [] momentary ones * * *, the brevity of the invasion of the individual's Fourth Amendment interests is an important factor in determining whether the seizure is so minimally intrusive as to be justifiable on reasonable suspicion. Moreover, in assessing the effect of the length of the detention, we take into account whether the police diligently pursue their investigation. We note that here the New York agents knew the time of Place's scheduled arrival at La Guardia, had ample time to arrange for their additional investigation at that location, and thereby could have minimized the intrusion on respondent's Fourth Amendment interests. Thus, although we decline to adopt any outside time limitation for a permissible *Terry* stop, we have never approved a seizure of the person for the prolonged 90–minute period involved here and cannot do so on the facts presented by this case.

Although the 90–minute detention of respondent's luggage is sufficient to render the seizure unreasonable, the violation was exacerbated by the failure of the agents to accurately inform respondent of the place to which they were transporting his luggage, of the length of time he might be dispossessed, and of what arrangements would be made for return of the luggage if the investigation dispelled the suspicion. In short, we hold that the detention of respondent's luggage in this case went beyond the narrow authority possessed by police to detain briefly luggage reasonably suspected to contain narcotics.

IV

We conclude that, under all of the circumstances of this case, the seizure of respondent's luggage was unreasonable under the Fourth Amendment. Consequently, the evidence obtained from the subsequent search of his luggage was inadmissible, and Place's conviction must be reversed. * * * *It is so ordered.*

[The concurring opinions of JUSTICE BRENNAN, with whom JUSTICE MARSHALL joined, and of JUSTICE BLACKMUN, with whom JUSTICE MARSHALL joined, are omitted.]

* * *

G. BALANCING REPLACES THE WARRANT MODEL: "SPECIAL NEEDS" AND SUSPICIONLESS SEARCHES AND SEIZURES

1. Suspicionless Searches: Mandatory Drug–Testing

SKINNER v. RAILWAY LABOR EXECUTIVES' ASSOCIATION

Supreme Court of the United States, 1989.
489 U.S. 602, 109 S.Ct. 1402, 103 L.Ed.2d 639.

JUSTICE KENNEDY delivered the opinion of the Court.

The Federal Railroad Safety Act of 1970 authorizes the Secretary of Transportation to "prescribe, as necessary, appropriate rules, regulations, orders, and standards for all areas of railroad safety." Finding that alcohol and drug abuse by railroad employees poses a serious threat to safety, the Federal Railroad Administration (FRA) has promulgated regulations that mandate blood and urine tests of employees who are involved in certain train accidents. The FRA also has adopted regulations that do not require, but do authorize, railroads to administer breath and urine tests to employees who violate certain safety rules. The question presented by this case is whether these regulations violate the Fourth Amendment.

I

A

The problem of alcohol use on American railroads is as old as the industry itself, and efforts to deter it by carrier rules began at least a century ago. For many years, railroads have prohibited operating employees from possessing alcohol or being intoxicated while on duty and from consuming alcoholic beverages while subject to being called for duty. More recently, these proscriptions have been expanded to forbid possession or use of certain drugs. These restrictions are embodied in "Rule G," an industry-wide operating rule promulgated by the Association of American Railroads, and are enforced, in various formulations, by virtually every railroad in the country. The customary sanction for Rule G violations is dismissal.

In July 1983, the FRA expressed concern that these industry efforts were not adequate to curb alcohol and drug abuse by railroad employees. The FRA pointed to evidence indicating that on-the-job intoxication was a significant problem in the railroad industry. The FRA also found, after a review of accident investigation reports, that from 1972 to 1983 "the nation's railroads experienced at least 21 significant train accidents involving alcohol or drug use as a probable cause or contributing factor," and that these accidents "resulted in 25 fatalities, 61 non-fatal injuries, and property damage estimated at $19 million (approximately $27 million in 1982 dollars)." 48 Fed. Reg. 30726 (1983). The FRA further identified "an additional 17 fatalities to operating employees working on or around rail rolling stock that involved alcohol or drugs as a contributing factor." *Ibid.* * * *.

* * * "Even without the benefit of regular post-accident testing," the FRA "identified 34 fatalities, 66 injuries and over $28 million in property damage (in 1983 dollars) that resulted from the errors of alcohol and drug-impaired employees in 45 train accidents and train incidents during the period 1975 through 1983." Some of these accidents resulted in the release of hazardous materials and, in one case, the ensuing pollution required the evacuation of an entire Louisiana community. In view of the obvious safety hazards of drug and alcohol use by railroad employees, the FRA announced in June 1984 its intention to promulgate federal regulations on the subject.

B

* * *

[T]wo subparts of the regulations relate to testing. Subpart C, which is entitled "Post–Accident Toxicological Testing," is mandatory. It provides that railroads "shall take all practicable steps to assure that all covered employees of the railroad directly involved ... provide blood and urine samples for toxicological testing by FRA," upon the occurrence of certain specified events. Toxicological testing is required following a "major train accident," which is defined as any train accident that involves (i) a fatality, (ii) the release of hazardous material accompanied by an evacuation or a reportable injury, or (iii) damage to railroad property of $500,000 or more. The railroad has the further duty of collecting blood and urine samples for testing after an "impact accident," which is defined as a collision that results in a reportable injury, or in damage to railroad property of $50,000 or more. Finally, the railroad is also obligated to test after "[a]ny train incident that involves a fatality to any onduty railroad employee."

After occurrence of an event which activates its duty to test, the railroad must transport all crew members and other covered employees directly involved in the accident or incident to an independent medical facility, where both blood and urine samples must be obtained from each employee. The samples have been collected, the railroad is required to ship them by prepaid air freight to the FRA laboratory for analysis. There, the samples are analyzed using "state-of-the-art equipment and techniques" to detect and measure alcohol and drugs. The FRA proposes to place primary reliance on analysis of blood samples, as blood is "the only available body fluid . . . that can provide a clear indication not only of the presence of alcohol and drugs but also their current impairment effects." Urine samples are also necessary, however, because drug traces remain in the urine longer than in blood, and in some cases it will not be possible to transport employees to a medical facility before the time it takes for certain drugs to be eliminated from the bloodstream. In those instances, a "positive urine test, taken with specific information on the pattern of elimination for the particular drug and other information on the behavior of the employee and the circumstances of the accident, may be crucial to the determination of" the cause of an accident.

* * *

Subpart D of the regulations * * * authorizes railroads to require covered employees to submit to breath or urine tests in certain circumstances not addressed by Subpart C. Breath or urine tests, or both, may be ordered (1) after a reportable accident or incident, where a supervisor has a "reasonable suspicion" that an employee's acts or omissions contributed to the occurrence or severity of the accident or incident; or (2) in the event of certain specific rule violations, including noncompliance with a signal and excessive speeding. A railroad also may require breath tests where a supervisor has a "reasonable suspicion" that an employee is under the influence of alcohol, based upon specific, personal observations concerning the appearance, behavior, speech, or body odors of the employee. Where impairment is suspected, a railroad, in addition, may require urine tests * * *.

* * *

II

* * *

A

Although the Fourth Amendment does not apply to a search or seizure, even an arbitrary one, effected by a private party on his own initiative, the Amendment protects against such intrusions if the private party acted as an instrument or agent of the Government. A railroad that complies with the provisions of Subpart C of the regulations does so by compulsion of sovereign authority, and the lawfulness of its acts is controlled by the Fourth Amendment. * * *

* * * Whether a private party should be deemed an agent or instrument of the Government for Fourth Amendment purposes necessarily turns on the degree of the Government's participation in the private party's activities, a question that can only be resolved "in light of all the circumstances." * * * Here, specific features of the regulations combine to convince us that the Government did more than adopt a passive position toward the underlying private conduct.

* * *

B

* * *

We have long recognized that a "compelled intrusio[n] into the body for blood to be analyzed for alcohol content" must be deemed a Fourth Amendment search. *See Schmerber* v. *California*, 384 U.S. 757, 767–768, 86 S.Ct. 1826, 16 L.Ed.2d 908 (1966). In light of our society's concern for the security of one's person, it is obvious that this physical intrusion, penetrating beneath the skin, infringes an expectation of privacy that society is prepared to recognize as reasonable. The ensuing chemical analysis of the sample to obtain physiological data is a further invasion of the tested employee's privacy interests. Much the same is true of the breath-testing procedures required under Subpart D of the regulations. Subjecting a person to a breathalyzer test, which generally requires the production of alveolar or "deep lung" breath for chemical analysis, implicates similar concerns about bodily integrity and, like the blood-alcohol test we considered in *Schmerber*, should also be deemed a search.

Unlike the blood-testing procedure at issue in *Schmerber*, the procedures prescribed by the FRA regulations for collecting and testing urine samples do not entail a surgical intrusion into the body. It is not disputed, however, that chemical analysis of urine, like that of blood, can reveal a host of private medical facts about an employee, including whether he or she is epileptic, pregnant, or diabetic. Nor can it be disputed that the process of collecting the sample to be tested, which may in some cases involve visual or aural monitoring of the act of urination, itself implicates privacy interests. As the Court of Appeals for the Fifth Circuit has stated:

> "There are few activities in our society more personal or private than the passing of urine. Most people describe it by euphemisms if they talk about it at all. It is a function traditionally performed

without public observation; indeed, its performance in public is generally prohibited by law as well as social custom." (this is a block quote that is indented in the lexis version)

Because it is clear that the collection and testing of urine intrudes upon expectations of privacy that society has long recognized as reasonable, * * * these intrusions must be deemed searches under the Fourth Amendment.

* * *

III

A

To hold that the Fourth Amendment is applicable to the drug and alcohol testing prescribed by the FRA regulations is only to begin the inquiry into the standards governing such intrusions. For the Fourth Amendment does not proscribe all searches and seizures, but only those that are unreasonable. What is reasonable, of course, "depends on all of the circumstances surrounding the search or seizure and the nature of the search or seizure itself." Thus, the permissibility of a particular practice "is judged by balancing its intrusion on the individual's Fourth Amendment interests against its promotion of legitimate governmental interests."

In most criminal cases, we strike this balance in favor of the procedures described by the Warrant Clause of the Fourth Amendment. Except in certain well-defined circumstances, a search or seizure in such a case is not reasonable unless it is accomplished pursuant to a judicial warrant issued upon probable cause. We have recognized exceptions to this rule, however, "when 'special needs, beyond the normal need for law enforcement, make the warrant and probable-cause requirement impracticable.' " When faced with such special needs, we have not hesitated to balance the governmental and privacy interests to assess the practicality of the warrant and probable-cause requirements in the particular context.

The Government's interest in regulating the conduct of railroad employees to ensure safety, like its supervision of probationers or regulated industries, or its operation of a government office, school, or prison, "likewise presents 'special needs' beyond normal law enforcement that may justify departures from the usual warrant and probable-cause requirements." The hours of service employees covered by the FRA regulations include persons engaged in handling orders concerning train movements, operating crews, and those engaged in the maintenance and repair of signal systems. It is undisputed that these and other covered employees are engaged in safety-sensitive tasks. * * *

* * * This governmental interest in ensuring the safety of the traveling public and of the employees themselves plainly justifies prohibiting covered employees from using alcohol or drugs on duty, or while subject to being called for duty. This interest also "require[s] and

justif[ies] the exercise of supervision to assure that the restrictions are in fact observed." The question that remains, then, is whether the Government's need to monitor compliance with these restrictions justifies the privacy intrusions at issue absent a warrant or individualized suspicion.

B

An essential purpose of a warrant requirement is to protect privacy interests by assuring citizens subject to a search or seizure that such intrusions are not the random or arbitrary acts of government agents. A warrant assures the citizen that the intrusion is authorized by law, and that it is narrowly limited in its objectives and scope. A warrant also provides the detached scrutiny of a neutral magistrate, and thus ensures an objective determination whether an intrusion is justified in any given case. In the present context, however, a warrant would do little to further these aims. Both the circumstances justifying toxicological testing and the permissible limits of such intrusions are defined narrowly and specifically in the regulations that authorize them, and doubtless are well known to covered employees. Indeed, in light of the standardized nature of the tests and the minimal discretion vested in those charged with administering the program, there are virtually no facts for a neutral magistrate to evaluate.

We have recognized, moreover, that the government's interest in dispensing with the warrant requirement is at its strongest when, as here, "the burden of obtaining a warrant is likely to frustrate the governmental purpose behind the search." As the FRA recognized, alcohol and other drugs are eliminated from the bloodstream at a constant rate, and blood and breath samples taken to measure whether these substances were in the bloodstream when a triggering event occurred must be obtained as soon as possible. Although the metabolites of some drugs remain in the urine for longer periods of time and may enable the FRA to estimate whether the employee was impaired by those drugs at the time of a covered accident, incident, or rule violation, the delay necessary to procure a warrant nevertheless may result in the destruction of valuable evidence.

The Government's need to rely on private railroads to set the testing process in motion also indicates that insistence on a warrant requirement would impede the achievement of the Government's objective. Railroad supervisors * * * are not in the business of investigating violations of the criminal laws or enforcing administrative codes, and otherwise have little occasion to become familiar with the intricacies of this Court's Fourth Amendment jurisprudence. "Imposing unwieldy warrant procedures ... upon supervisors, who would otherwise have no reason to be familiar with such procedures, is simply unreasonable."

[I]mposing a warrant requirement in the present context would add little to the assurances of certainty and regularity already afforded by the regulations, while significantly hindering, and in many cases frustrating, the objectives of the Government's testing program. * * *

C

Our cases indicate that even a search that may be performed without a warrant must be based, as a general matter, on probable cause to believe that the person to be searched has violated the law. When the balance of interests precludes insistence on a showing of probable cause, we have usually required "some quantum of individualized suspicion" before concluding that a search is reasonable. We made it clear, however, that a showing of individualized suspicion is not a constitutional floor, below which a search must be presumed unreasonable. In limited circumstances, where the privacy interests implicated by the search are minimal, and where an important governmental interest furthered by the intrusion would be placed in jeopardy by a requirement of individualized suspicion, a search may be reasonable despite the absence of such suspicion. We believe this is true of the intrusions in question here.

* * *

* * * [I]n *Schmerber*, * * * we held that a State could direct that a blood sample be withdrawn from a motorist suspected of driving while intoxicated, despite his refusal to consent to the intrusion. We noted that the test was performed in a reasonable manner, as the motorist's "blood was taken by a physician in a hospital environment according to accepted medical practices." We said also that the intrusion occasioned by a blood test is not significant, since such "tests are a commonplace in these days of periodic physical examinations and experience with them teaches that the quantity of blood extracted is minimal, and that for most people the procedure involves virtually no risk, trauma, or pain." *Schmerber* thus confirmed "society's judgment that blood tests do not constitute an unduly extensive imposition on an individual's privacy and bodily integrity."

The breath tests authorized by Subpart D of the regulations are even less intrusive than the blood tests prescribed by Subpart C. Unlike blood tests, breath tests do not require piercing the skin and may be conducted safely outside a hospital environment and with a minimum of inconvenience or embarrassment. * * * In all the circumstances, we cannot conclude that the administration of a breath test implicates significant privacy concerns.

A more difficult question is presented by urine tests. Like breath tests, urine tests are not invasive of the body and, under the regulations, may not be used as an occasion for inquiring into private facts unrelated to alcohol or drug use. We recognize, however, that the procedures for collecting the necessary samples, which require employees to perform an excretory function traditionally shielded by great privacy, raise concerns not implicated by blood or breath tests. While we would not characterize these additional privacy concerns as minimal in most contexts, we note that the regulations endeavor to reduce the intrusiveness of the collection process. The regulations do not require that samples be furnished under the direct observation of a monitor, despite the desirability of such a procedure to ensure the integrity of the sample. The sample is also collected in a medical environment, by personnel unrelated to the railroad employer, and is thus not unlike similar procedures encountered often in the context of a regular physical examination.

More importantly, the expectations of privacy of covered employees are diminished by reason of their participation in an industry that is regulated pervasively to ensure safety, a goal dependent, in substantial part, on the health and fitness of covered employees. * * *

* * * We conclude, therefore, that the testing procedures contemplated by Subparts C and D pose only limited threats to the justifiable expectations of privacy of covered employees.

By contrast, the Government interest in testing without a showing of individualized suspicion is compelling. Employees subject to the tests discharge duties fraught with such risks of injury to others that even a momentary lapse of attention can have disastrous consequences. Much like persons who have routine access to dangerous nuclear power facilities, employees who are subject to testing under the FRA regulations can cause great human loss before any signs of impairment become noticeable to supervisors or others. * * *

* * *

A requirement of particularized suspicion of drug or alcohol use would seriously impede an employer's ability to obtain this information, despite its obvious importance. Experience confirms the FRA's judgment that the scene of a serious rail accident is chaotic. Investigators who arrive at the scene shortly after a major accident has occurred may find it difficult to determine which members of a train crew contributed to its occurrence. Obtaining evidence that might give rise to the suspicion that a particular employee is impaired, a difficult endeavor in the best of circumstances, is most impracticable in the aftermath of a serious accident. While events following the rule violations that activate the testing authority of Subpart D may be less chaotic, objective indicia of impairment are absent in these instances as well. Indeed, any attempt to gather evidence relating to the possible impairment of particular employees likely would result in the loss or deterioration of the evidence furnished by the tests. It would be unrealistic, and inimical to the Government's goal of ensuring safety in rail transportation, to require a showing of individualized suspicion in these circumstances.

* * *

We conclude that the compelling Government interests served by the FRA's regulations would be significantly hindered if railroads were required to point to specific facts giving rise to a reasonable suspicion of impairment before testing a given employee. In view of our conclusion that, on the present record, the toxicological testing contemplated by the regulations is not an undue infringement on the justifiable expectations of privacy of covered employees, the Government's compelling interests outweigh privacy concerns.

* * *

[JUSTICE STEVENS' concurring opinion is omitted.]

JUSTICE MARSHALL, with whom JUSTICE BRENNAN joins, dissenting.

The issue in this case is not whether declaring a war on illegal drugs is good public policy. The importance of ridding our society of such drugs is, by now, apparent to all. Rather, the issue here is whether the Government's deployment in that war of a particularly Draconian weapon—the compulsory collection and chemical testing of railroad workers' blood and urine—comports with the Fourth Amendment. Precisely because the need for action against the drug scourge is manifest, the need for vigilance against unconstitutional excess is great. History teaches that grave threats to liberty often come in times of urgency, when constitutional rights seem too extravagant to endure. The World War II relocation-camp cases, and the Red scare and McCarthy-era internal subversion cases, are only the most extreme reminders that when we allow fundamental freedoms to be sacrificed in the name of real or perceived exigency, we invariably come to regret it.

In permitting the Government to force entire railroad crews to submit to invasive blood and urine tests, even when it lacks any evidence of drug or alcohol use or other wrongdoing, the majority today joins those shortsighted courts which have allowed basic constitutional rights to fall prey to momentary emergencies. The majority holds that the need of the Federal Railroad Administration (FRA) to deter and diagnose train accidents outweighs any "minimal" intrusions on personal dignity and privacy posed by mass toxicological testing of persons who have given no indication whatsoever of impairment. In reaching this result, the majority ignores the text and doctrinal history of the Fourth Amendment, which require that highly intrusive searches of this type be based on probable cause, not on the evanescent cost-benefit calculations of agencies or judges. But the majority errs even under its own utilitarian standards, trivializing the raw intrusiveness of, and overlooking serious conceptual and operational flaws in, the FRA's testing program. These flaws cast grave doubts on whether that program, though born of good intentions, will do more than ineffectually symbolize the Government's opposition to drug use.

* * *

I

The Court today takes its longest step yet toward reading the probable-cause requirement out of the Fourth Amendment. For the fourth time in as many years, a majority holds that a " 'special nee[d], beyond the normal need for law enforcement,' " makes the " 'require-ment' " of probable cause " 'impracticable.' " With the recognition of "[t]he Government's interest in regulating the conduct of railroad employees to ensure safety" as such a need, the Court has now permitted "special needs" to displace constitutional text in each of the four categories of searches enumerated in the Fourth Amendment * * *.

* * * As this Court has long recognized, the Framers intended the provisions of [the Warrant] Clause—a warrant and probable cause—to "provide the yardstick against which official searches and seizures are to be measured." Without the content which those provisions give to the Fourth Amendment's overarching command that searches and seizures be "reasonable," the Amendment lies virtually devoid of meaning, subject to whatever content shifting judicial majorities, concerned about the problems of the day, choose to give to that supple term. Constitutional requirements like probable cause are not fair-weather friends, present when advantageous, conveniently absent when "special needs" make them seem not.

Until recently, an unbroken line of cases had recognized probable cause as an indispensable prerequisite for a full-scale search, regardless of whether such a search was conducted pursuant to a warrant or under one of the recognized exceptions to the warrant requirement. Only where the government action in question had a "substantially less intrusive" impact on privacy, and thus clearly fell short of a full-scale search, did we relax the probable-cause standard. Even in this class of cases, we almost always required the government to show some individualized suspicion to justify the search. The few searches which we upheld in the absence of individualized justification were routinized, fleeting, and nonintrusive encounters conducted pursuant to regulatory programs which entailed no contact with the person.

* * *

In widening the "special needs" exception to probable cause to authorize searches of the human body unsupported by *any* evidence of wrongdoing, the majority today completes the process * * * of eliminating altogether the probable-cause requirement for civil searches—those undertaken for reasons "beyond the normal need for law enforcement." In its place, the majority substitutes a manipulable balancing inquiry under which, upon the mere assertion of a "special need," even the deepest dignitary and privacy interests become vulnerable to governmental incursion. By its terms, however, the Fourth Amendment—unlike the Fifth and Sixth—does not confine its protections to either criminal or civil actions. Instead, it protects generally "[t]he right of the people to be secure."

* * *

II

The proper way to evaluate the FRA's testing regime is to use the same analytic framework which we have traditionally used to appraise Fourth Amendment claims involving full-scale searches, at least until the recent "special needs" cases. Under that framework, we inquire, serially, whether search has taken place; whether the search was based on a valid warrant or undertaken pursuant to a recognized exception to the warrant requirement; whether the search was based on probable cause or validly based on lesser suspicion because it was minimally intrusive; and, finally, whether the search was conducted in a reasonable manner.

* * *

VERNONIA SCHOOL DISTRICT 47J v. ACTON

Supreme Court of the United States, 1995.
515 U.S. 646, 115 S.Ct. 2386, 132 L.Ed.2d 564.

JUSTICE SCALIA delivered the opinion of the Court.

The Student Athlete Drug Policy adopted by School District 47J in the town of Vernonia, Oregon, authorizes random urinalysis drug testing of students who participate in the District's school athletics programs. We granted certiorari to decide whether this violates the Fourth and Fourteenth Amendments to the United States Constitution.

I

A

Petitioner Vernonia School District 47J (District) operates one high school and three grade schools in the logging community of Vernonia, Oregon. As elsewhere in small-town America, school sports play a prominent role in the town's life, and student athletes are admired in their schools and in the community.

Drugs had not been a major problem in Vernonia schools. In the mid-to-late 1980's, however, teachers and administrators observed a sharp increase in drug use. Students began to speak out about their attraction to the drug culture, and to boast that there was nothing the school could do about it. Along with more drugs came more disciplinary problems. Between 1988 and 1989 the number of disciplinary referrals in Vernonia schools rose to more than twice the number reported in the early 1980's, and several students were suspended. Students became increasingly rude during class; outbursts of profane language became common.

Not only were student athletes included among the drug users but, as the District Court found, athletes were the leaders of the drug culture. This caused the District's administrators particular concern, since drug use increases the risk of sports-related injury. Expert testimony at the trial confirmed the deleterious effects of drugs on motivation, memory, judgment, reaction, coordination, and performance. The high school football and wrestling coach witnessed a severe sternum injury suffered by a wrestler, and various omissions of safety procedures and misexecutions by football players, all attributable in his belief to the effects of drug use.

Initially, the District responded to the drug problem by offering special classes, speakers, and presentations designed to deter drug use. It even brought in a specially trained dog to detect drugs, but the drug problem persisted. * * *

[In the fall of 1989, the District implemented a drug-testing program. Its express purpose was to prevent student athletes from using drugs, to protect their health and safety, and to provide drug users with assistance programs.]

B

The Policy applies to all students participating in interscholastic athletics. Students wishing to play sports must sign a form consenting to the testing and must obtain the written consent of their parents. Athletes are tested at the beginning of the season for their sport. In addition, once each week of the season the names of the athletes are placed in a "pool" from which a student, with the supervision of two adults, blindly draws the names of 10% of the athletes for random testing. Those selected are notified and tested that same day, if possible.

The student to be tested completes a specimen control form which bears an assigned number. Prescription medications that the student is taking must be identified by providing a copy of the prescription or a doctor's authorization. The student then enters an empty locker room accompanied by an adult monitor of the same sex. Each boy selected produces a sample at a urinal, remaining fully clothed with his back to the monitor, who stands approximately 12 to 15 feet behind the student. Monitors may (though do not always) watch the student while he produces the sample, and they listen for normal sounds of urination. Girls produce samples in an enclosed bathroom stall, so that they can be heard but not observed. After the sample is produced, it is given to the monitor, who checks it for temperature and tampering and then transfers it to a vial.

The samples are sent to an independent laboratory, which routinely tests them for amphetamines, cocaine, and marijuana. Other drugs, such as LSD, may be screened at the request of the District, but the identity of a particular student does not determine which drugs will be tested. The laboratory's procedures are 99.94% accurate. The District follows strict procedures regarding the chain of custody and access to test results. The laboratory does not know the identity of the students whose samples it tests. It is authorized to mail written test reports only to the superintendent and to provide test results to District personnel by telephone only after the requesting official recites a code confirming his authority. Only the superintendent, principals, vice-principals, and athletic directors have access to test results, and the results are not kept for more than one year.

If a sample tests positive, a second test is administered as soon as possible to confirm the result. If the second test is negative, no further action is taken. If the second test is positive, the athlete's parents are notified, and the school principal convenes a meeting with the student and his parents, at which the student is given the option of (1) participating for six weeks in an assistance program that includes weekly urinalysis, or (2) suffering suspension from athletics for the remainder of the current season and the next athletic season. The student is then retested prior to the start of the next athletic season for which he or she is eligible. The Policy states that a second offense results in automatic imposition of option (2); a third offense in suspension for the remainder of the current season and the next two athletic seasons.

C

In the fall of 1991, respondent James Acton, then a seventh-grader, signed up to play football at one of the District's grade schools. He was denied participation, however, because he and his parents refused to sign the testing consent forms. The Actons filed suit, seeking declaratory and injunctive relief from enforcement of the Policy on the grounds that it violated the Fourth and Fourteenth Amendments to the United States Constitution and Article I, § 9, of the Oregon Constitution. [The Supreme Court reversed a decision by the United States Court of Appeals for the Ninth Circuit, which had held that the Policy violated both the Fourth and Fourteenth Amendments and Article I, § 9, of the Oregon Constitution.]

II

* * * In *Skinner v. Railway Labor Executives' Assn.*, 489 U.S. 602, 617, 109 S.Ct. 1402, 103 L.Ed.2d 639 (1989), we held that state-compelled collection and testing of urine, such as that required by the Student Athlete Drug Policy, constitutes a "search" subject to the demands of the Fourth Amendment.

As the text of the Fourth Amendment indicates, the ultimate measure of the constitutionality of a governmental search is "reasonableness." At least in a case such as this, where there was no clear practice, either approving or disapproving the type of search at issue, at the time the constitutional provision was enacted, whether a particular search meets the reasonableness standard is judged by balancing its intrusion on the individual's Fourth Amendment interests against its promotion of legitimate governmental interests. Where a search is undertaken by law enforcement officials to discover evidence of criminal wrongdoing, this Court has said that reasonableness generally requires the obtaining of a judicial warrant. Warrants cannot be issued, of course, without the showing of probable cause required by the Warrant Clause. But a warrant is not required to establish the reasonableness of all government searches; and when a warrant is not required (and the Warrant Clause therefore not applicable), probable cause is not invariably required either. A search unsupported by probable cause can be constitutional, we have said, "when special needs, beyond the normal need for law enforcement, make the warrant and probable-cause requirement impracticable."

We have found such "special needs" to exist in the public-school context. There, the warrant requirement "would unduly interfere with the maintenance of the swift and informal disciplinary procedures [that are] needed," and "strict adherence to the requirement that searches be based upon probable cause" would undercut "the substantial need of teachers and administrators for freedom to maintain order in the schools." * * * As we explicitly acknowledged, however, the Fourth Amendment imposes no irreducible requirement of such [individualized] suspicion. We have upheld suspicionless searches and seizures to conduct drug testing of railroad personnel involved in train accidents, to conduct random drug testing of federal customs officers who carry arms or are involved in drug interdiction, and to maintain automobile checkpoints looking for illegal immigrants and contraband, and drunk drivers.

III

The first factor to be considered is the nature of the privacy interest upon which the search here at issue intrudes. The Fourth Amendment does not protect all subjective expectations of privacy, but only those that society recognizes as "legitimate." What expectations are legitimate varies, of course, with context, depending, for example, upon whether the individual asserting the privacy interest is at home, at work, in a car, or in a public park. In addition, the legitimacy of certain privacy expectations vis-a-vis the State may depend upon the individual's legal relationship with the State. * * * Central, in our view, to the present case is the fact that the subjects of the Policy are (1) children, who (2) have been committed to the temporary custody of the State as schoolmaster.

Traditionally at common law, and still today, unemancipated minors lack some of the most fundamental rights of self-determination—including even the right of liberty in its narrow sense, i.e., the right to come and go at will. They are subject, even as to their physical freedom, to the control of their parents or guardians. When parents place minor children in private schools for their education, the teachers and administrators of those schools stand in loco parentis over the children entrusted to them. In fact, the tutor or schoolmaster is the very prototype of that status. As Blackstone describes it, a parent "may * * * delegate part of his parental authority, during his life, to the tutor or schoolmaster of his child; who is then in loco parentis, and has such a portion of the power of the parent committed to his charge, viz. that of restraint and correction, as may be necessary to answer the purposes for which he is employed."

* * *

Fourth Amendment rights, no less than First and Fourteenth Amendment rights, are different in public schools than elsewhere; the "reasonableness" inquiry cannot disregard the schools' custodial and tutelary responsibility for children. For their own good and that of their classmates, public school children are routinely required to submit to various physical examinations, and to be vaccinated against various diseases. * * *

Legitimate privacy expectations are even less with regard to student athletes. School sports are not for the bashful. They require "suiting up" before each practice or event, and showering and changing afterwards. Public school locker rooms, the usual sites for these activities, are not notable for the privacy they afford. The locker rooms in Vernonia are typical: no individual dressing rooms are provided; shower heads are lined up along a wall, unseparated by any sort of partition or curtain; not even all the toilet stalls have doors. * * *

There is an additional respect in which school athletes have a reduced expectation of privacy. By choosing to "go out for the team," they voluntarily subject themselves to a degree of regulation even higher than that imposed on students generally. In Vernonia's public schools, they must submit to a preseason physical exam (James testified that his included the giving of a urine sample), they must acquire adequate insurance coverage or sign an insurance waiver, maintain a minimum grade point average, and comply with any "rules of conduct, dress, training hours and related matters as may be established for each sport by the head coach and athletic director with the principal's approval." Somewhat like adults who choose to participate in a "closely regulated industry," students who voluntarily participate in school athletics have reason to expect intrusions upon normal rights and privileges, including privacy.

IV

Having considered the scope of the legitimate expectation of privacy at issue here, we turn next to the character of the intrusion that is complained of. We recognized in *Skinner* that collecting the samples for urinalysis intrudes upon "an excretory function traditionally shielded by great privacy." We noted, however, that the degree of intrusion depends upon the manner in which production of the urine sample is monitored. Under the District's Policy, male students produce samples at a urinal along a wall. They remain fully clothed and are only observed from behind, if at all. Female students produce samples in an enclosed stall, with a female monitor standing outside listening only for sounds of tampering. These conditions are nearly identical to those typically encountered in public restrooms, which men, women, and especially school children use daily. Under such conditions, the privacy interests compromised by the process of obtaining the urine sample are in our view negligible.

The other privacy-invasive aspect of urinalysis is, of course, the information it discloses concerning the state of the subject's body, and the materials he has ingested. In this regard it is significant that the tests at issue here look only for drugs, and not for whether the student is, for example, epileptic, pregnant, or diabetic. Moreover, the drugs for which the samples are screened are standard, and do not vary according to the identity of the student. And finally, the results of the tests are disclosed only to a limited class of school personnel who have a need to know; and they are not turned over to law enforcement authorities or used for any internal disciplinary function.

* * *

V

* * *

* * * School years are the time when the physical, psychological, and addictive effects of drugs are most severe. And of course the effects of a drug-infested school are visited not just upon the users, but upon the entire student body and faculty, as the educational process is disrupted. In the present case, moreover, the necessity for the State to act is magnified by the fact that this evil is being visited not just upon individuals at large, but upon children for whom it has undertaken a special responsibility of care and direction. Finally, it must not be lost sight of that this program is directed more narrowly to drug use by school athletes, where the risk of immediate physical harm to the drug user or those with whom he is playing his sport is particularly high. Apart from psychological effects, which include impairment of judgment, slow reaction time, and a lessening of the perception of pain, the particular drugs screened by the District's Policy have been demonstrated to pose substantial physical risks to athletes. * * *

* * *

VI

Taking into account all the factors we have considered above—the decreased expectation of privacy, the relative unobtrusiveness of the search, and the severity of the need met by the search—we conclude Vernonia's Policy is reasonable and hence constitutional.

We caution against the assumption that suspicionless drug testing will readily pass constitutional muster in other contexts. The most significant element in this case is the first we discussed: that the Policy was undertaken in furtherance of the government's responsibilities, under a public school system, as guardian and tutor of children entrusted to its care. [W]hen the government acts as guardian and tutor the relevant question is whether the search is one that a reasonable guardian and tutor might undertake. Given the findings of need made by the District Court, we conclude that in the present case it is.

* * *

JUSTICE GINSBURG, concurring.

The Court constantly observes that the School District's drug-testing policy applies only to students who voluntarily participate in interscholastic athletics. Correspondingly, the most severe sanction allowed under the District's policy is suspension from extracurricular athletic programs. I comprehend the Court's opinion as reserving the question whether the District, on no more than the showing made here, constitutionally could impose routine drug testing not only on those seeking to engage with others in team sports, but on all students required to attend school.

[JUSTICE O'CONNOR's dissenting opinion, in which JUSTICE STEVENS and JUSTICE SOUTER joined, is omitted.]

Commentary

1.   Two years later, the Supreme Court refused to extend the reach of its holding in *Vernonia* outside the school setting. In *Chandler v. Miller*, 520 U.S. 305 (1997), the Court examined a Georgia law requiring that candidates for election to certain state offices must certify that they tested negative (by urinalysis) for drugs within 30 days prior to qualifying for nomination. Justice Ginsburg's opinion for the majority applied the reasoning of *Vernonia* and its predecessors to hold that a suspicionless search is unconstitutional unless it is based on "special needs" beyond the general need for effective law enforcement. The majority opinion rejected the State's argument that unlawful drug use calls into question a public official's judgment and integrity, and thus jeopardizes the discharge of public functions. The majority reasoned that "nothing in the record hints that the hazards respondents broadly describe are real and not simply hypothetical for Georgia's polity." Only Chief Justice Rehnquist dissented, arguing that the Georgia statutory policy was as compelling as the interest asserted by the federal government in *National Treasury Employees Union v. Von Raab*, 489 U.S. 656 (1989). In *Von Raab*, the Supreme Court upheld (5–4) a U.S. Treasury Department regulation requiring mandatory urine testing for drugs for certain government employees involved in drug law enforcement, carrying of firearms, or handling of classified material.

2.   Only five years after Chandler v. Miller, the Supreme Court upheld another school district's mandatory, suspicionless drug testing program. In Board of Education v. Earls, 536 U.S. 822 (2002), the Court reviewed a program not limited to students participating in interscholastic athletics. The Board of Education of Tecumseh, Oklahoma had implemented a Student Activities Drug Testing Policy that required all middle and high school students who participate in any extracurricular activities to submit to drug testing. While the policy had "been applied only to competitive extracurricular activities sanctioned by the Oklahoma Secondary Schools Activities Association," this was an expansive list, including "the Academic Team, Future Farmers of America, Future Homemakers of America, band, choir, pom pon, cheerleading, and athletics." The policy required students to submit to urinalysis tests designed to detect the use of illegal drugs, including amphetamines, marijuana, cocaine, opiates, and barbituates, but not medical conditions or the presence of authorized prescription medications. Students were required to take a drug test before participating in an extracurricular activity, submit to random drug testing while participating in that activity, and agree to be tested at any time upon reasonable suspicion. Lindsay Earls was a member of the show choir, the marching band, the Academic Team, and the National Honor Society. In an opinion by Justice Thomas, the majority invoked the "special needs" analysis used in *Vernonia*,

and reversed a decision by the United States Court of Appeals for the Tenth Circuit. The Supreme Court held that the Policy was constitutional because it "reasonably serves the School District's important interest in detecting and preventing drug use among its students...."

The Court emphasized that "Fourth Amendment rights ... are different in public schools than elsewhere; the 'reasonableness' inquiry cannot disregard the schools' custodial and tutelary responsibility for children." In particular, a finding of individualized suspicion may not be necessary when a school conducts drug testing.

The dissenters pointed out that in *Vernonia*, the Court had emphasized that drug use "increased the risk of sports-related injury" and that Vernonia's athletes were the "leaders" of an aggressive local "drug culture" that had reached "'epidemic proportions.'" In contrast, the Tecumseh school superintendent repeatedly described the problem as "not ... major," yet the drug testing policy was applied to academic team members solely because they participated in a nonathletic, competitive extracurricular activity— participation associated with neither special dangers from, nor particular predilections for, drug use. In dissent, Justice Ginsburg argued that the "policy targets for testing a student population least likely to be at risk from illicit drugs and their damaging effects.

2. Suspicionless Seizures: Highway Roadblocks

MICHIGAN DEPARTMENT OF STATE POLICE v. SITZ

Supreme Court of the United States, 1990.
496 U.S. 444, 110 S.Ct. 2481, 110 L.Ed.2d 412.

* * *

Petitioners, the Michigan Department of State Police and its Director, established a sobriety checkpoint pilot program in early 1986. The Director appointed a Sobriety Checkpoint Advisory Committee comprising representatives of the State Police force, local police forces, state prosecutors, and the University of Michigan Transportation Research Institute. Pursuant to its charge, the Advisory Committee created guidelines setting forth procedures governing checkpoint operations, site selection, and publicity.

Under the guidelines, checkpoints would be set up at selected sites along state roads. All vehicles passing through a checkpoint would be stopped and their drivers briefly examined for signs of intoxication. In cases where a checkpoint officer detected signs of intoxication, the motorist would be directed to a location out of the traffic flow where an officer would check the motorist's driver's license and car registration and, if warranted, conduct further sobriety tests. Should the field tests and the officer's observations suggest that the driver was intoxicated, an arrest would be made. All other drivers would be permitted to resume their journey immediately.

The first—and to date the only—sobriety checkpoint operated under the program was conducted in Saginaw County with the assistance of the Saginaw County Sheriff's Department. During the hour-and-fifteen-minute duration of the checkpoint's operation, 126 vehicles passed through the checkpoint. The average delay for each vehicle was approximately 25 seconds. Two drivers were detained for field sobriety testing, and one of the two was arrested for driving under the influence of alcohol. A third driver who drive through without stopping was pulled over by an officer in an observation vehicle and arrested for driving under the influence.

On the day before the operation of the Saginaw County checkpoint, respondents filed a compliant in the Circuit Court of Wayne County seeking declaratory and injunctive relief from potential subjection to the checkpoints. Each of the respondents "is a licensed driver in the State of Michigan ... who regularly travels throughout the State in his automobile." During pretrial proceedings, petitioners agreed to delay further implementation of the checkpoint program pending the outcome of this litigation.

After the trial, at which the court heard extensive testimony concerning, inter alia, the "effectiveness" of highway sobriety checkpoint programs, the court ruled that the Michigan program violated the Fourth Amendment and Art. 1, § 11, of the Michigan Constitution. On appeal, the Michigan Court of Appeals affirmed the holding that the program violated the Fourth Amendment and, for that reason, did not consider whether the program violated the Michigan Constitution. After the Michigan Supreme Court denied petitioners' application for leave to appeal, we granted certiorari.

* * *

Petitioners concede, correctly in our view, that a Fourth Amendment "seizure" occurs when a vehicle is stopped at a checkpoint. The question thus becomes whether such seizures are "reasonable" under the Fourth Amendment.

* * * We address only the initial stop of each motorist passing through a checkpoint and the associated preliminary questioning and observation by checkpoint officers. Detention of particular motorists for more extensive field sobriety testing may require satisfaction of an individualized suspicion standard.

No one can seriously dispute the magnitude of the drunken driving problem or the States' interest in eradicating it. Media reports of alcohol-related death and mutilation on the Nation's roads are legion. The anecdotal is confirmed by the statistical. "Drunk drivers cause an annual death toll of over 25,000 and in the same time span cause nearly one million personal injuries and more than five billion dollars in property damage." For decades, this Court has "repeatedly lamented the tragedy."

Conversely, the weight bearing on the other scale—the measure of the intrusion on motorists stopped briefly at sobriety checkpoints—is slight. We reached a similar conclusion as to the intrusion on motorists subjected to a brief stop at a highway checkpoint for detecting illegal aliens. We see virtually no difference between the levels of intrusion on law-abiding motorists from the brief stops necessary to the effectuation of these two types of checkpoints, which to the average motorist would seem identical save for the nature of the questions the checkpoint officers might ask. The trial court and the Court of Appeals, thus, accurately gauged the "objective" intrusion, measured by the duration of the seizure and the intensity of the investigation, as minimal.

With respect to what it perceived to be the "subjective" intrusion on motorists, however, the Court of Appeals found such intrusion substantial. [The Michigan courts concluded] that the checkpoints have the potential to generate fear and surprise in motorists. This was so because the record failed to demonstrate that approaching motorists would be aware of their option to make U-turns or turnoffs to avoid the checkpoints. On that basis, the court deemed the subjective intrusion from the checkpoints unreasonable.

* * * The "fear and surprise" to be considered are not the natural fear of one who has been drinking over the prospect of being stopped at a sobriety checkpoint but, rather, the fear and surprise engendered in law abiding motorists by the nature of the stop. * * *

[The Supreme Court concluded that because the "checkpoints are selected pursuant to the guidelines, and uniformed police officers stop every approaching vehicle [t]he intrusion resulting from the brief stop at the sobriety checkpoint" is minimal.]

The Court of Appeals went on to consider as part of the balancing analysis the "effectiveness" of the proposed checkpoint program. Based on extensive testimony in the trial record, the court concluded that the checkpoint program failed the "effectiveness" part of the test, and that this failure materially discounted petitioners' strong interest in implementing the program. We think the Court of Appeals was wrong on this point as well.

* * * Experts in police science might disagree over which of several methods of apprehending drunken drivers is preferrable as an ideal. But for purposes of Fourth Amendment analysis, the choice among such reasonable alternatives remains with the governmental officials who have a unique understanding of, and a responsibility for, limited public resources, including a finite number of police officers. * * *

* * *

In sum, the balance of the State's interest in preventing drunken driving, the extent to which this system can reasonably be said to advance that interest, and the degree of intrusion upon individual motorists who are briefly stopped, weighs in favor of the state program. We therefore hold that it is consistent with the Fourth Amendment. The judgment of the Michigan Court of Appeals is accordingly reversed, and the cause is remanded for further proceedings not inconsistent with this opinion. Reversed.

[JUSTICE BLACKMUN'S opinion, concurring in the judgment, and JUSTICE BRENNAN's dissenting opinion, with whom JUSTICE MARSHALL joined, are omitted.]

JUSTICE STEVENS, with whom JUSTICE BRENNAN and JUSTICE MARSHALL join as to Parts I and II, dissenting.

* * *

[T]he record in this case makes clear that a decision holding these suspicionless seizures unconstitutional would not impede the law enforcement community's remarkable progress in reducing the death toll on our highways. Because the Michigan program was patterned after an older program in Maryland, the trial judge gave special attention to that State's experience. Over a period of several years, Maryland operated 125 checkpoints; of the 41,000 motorists passing through those checkpoints, only 143 persons (0.3%) were arrested. The number of man-hours devoted to these operations is not in the record, but it seems inconceivable that a higher arrest rate could not have been achieved by more conventional means. Yet, even if the 143 checkpoint arrests were assumed to involve a net increase in the number of drunk driving arrests per year, the figure would still be insignificant by comparison to the 71,000 such arrests made by Michigan State Police without checkpoints in 1984 alone.

Any relationship between sobriety checkpoints and an actual reduction in highway fatalities is even less substantial than the minimal impact on arrest rates. As the Michigan Court of Appeals pointed out, "Maryland had conducted a study comparing traffic statistics between a county using checkpoints and a control county. The results of the study showed that alcohol-related accidents in the checkpoint county decreased by ten percent, whereas the control county saw an eleven percent decrease; and while fatal accidents in the control county fell from sixteen to three, fatal accidents in the checkpoint county actually doubled from the prior year."

In light of these considerations, it seems evident that the Court today misapplies the balancing test * * *. The Court overvalues the law enforcement interest in using sobriety checkpoints, undervalues the citizen's interest in freedom from random, unannounced investigatory seizures, and mistakenly assumes that there is "virtually no difference" between a routine stop at a permanent, fixed checkpoint and a surprise stop at a sobriety checkpoint. I believe this case is controlled by our several precedents condemning suspicionless random stops of motorists for investigatory purposes.

* * *

III

The most disturbing aspect of the Court's decision today is that it appears to give no weight to the citizen's interest in freedom from suspicionless unannounced investigatory seizures. Although the author of the opinion does not reiterate his description of that interest as "diaphanous," the Court's opinion implicitly adopts that characterization. On the other hand, the Court places a heavy thumb on the law enforcement interest by looking only at gross receipts instead of net benefits. Perhaps this tampering with the scales of justice can be explained by the Court's obvious concern about the slaughter on our highways, and a resultant tolerance for policies designed to alleviate the problem by "setting an example" of a few motorists. This possibility prompts two observations.

First, my objections to random seizures or temporary checkpoints do not apply to a host of other investigatory procedures that do not depend upon surprise and are unquestionably permissible. These procedures have been used to address other threats to human life no less pressing than the threat posed by drunken drivers. It is, for example, common practice to require every prospective airline passenger, or every visitor to a public building, to pass through a metal detector that will reveal the presence of a firearm or an explosive. Permanent, nondiscretionary checkpoints could be used to control serious dangers at other publicly operated facilities. Because concealed weapons obviously represent one such substantial threat to public safety, I would suppose that all subway passengers could be required to pass through metal detectors, so long as the detectors were permanent and every passenger was subjected to the same search. Likewise, I would suppose that a State could condition access to its toll roads upon not only paying the toll but also taking a uniformly administered breathalizer test. That requirement might well keep all drunken drivers off the highways that serve the fastest and most dangerous traffic. This procedure would not be subject to the constitutional objections that control this case: the checkpoints would be permanently fixed, the stopping procedure would apply to all users of the toll road in precisely the same way, and police officers would not be free to make arbitrary choices about which neighborhoods should be targeted or about which individuals should be more thoroughly searched. Random, suspicionless seizures designed to search for evidence of firearms, drugs, or intoxication belong, however, in a fundamentally different category. These seizures play upon the detained individual's reasonable expectations of privacy, injecting a suspicionless search into a context where none would normally occur. The imposition that seems diaphanous today may be intolerable tomorrow. See Boyd v. United States, 116 U.S. 616, 635 (1886).

* * *

INDIANAPOLIS v. EDMOND

Supreme Court of the United States, 2000.
531 U.S. 32, 121 S.Ct. 447, 148 L.Ed.2d 333.

JUSTICE O'CONNOR delivered the opinion of the Court.

In *Michigan Dept. of State Police* v. *Sitz* 496 U.S. 444, 110 S.Ct. 2481, 110 L.Ed.2d 412 (1990) and *United States* v. *Martinez-Fuerte,* 428 U.S. 543, 96 S.Ct. 3074, 49 L.Ed.2d 1116 (1976) we held that brief, suspicionless seizures at highway checkpoints for the purposes of combating drunk driving and intercepting illegal immigrants were constitutional. We now consider the constitutionality of a highway checkpoint program whose primary purpose is the discovery and interdiction of illegal narcotics.

I

In August 1998, the city of Indianapolis began to operate vehicle checkpoints on Indianapolis roads in an effort to interdict unlawful drugs. The city conducted six such roadblocks between August and November that year, stopping 1,161 vehicles and arresting 104 motorists. Fifty-five arrests were for drug-related crimes, while 49 were for offenses unrelated to drugs. The overall "hit rate" of the program was thus approximately nine percent.

* * * At each checkpoint location, the police stop a predetermined number of vehicles. Approximately 30 officers are stationed at the checkpoint. Pursuant to written directives issued by the chief of police, at least one officer approaches the vehicle, advises the driver that he or she is being stopped briefly at a drug checkpoint, and asks the driver to produce a license and registration. The officer also looks for signs of impairment and conducts an open-view examination of the vehicle from the outside. A narcotics-detection dog walks around the outside of each stopped vehicle.

The directives instruct the officers that they may conduct a search only by consent or based on the appropriate quantum of particularized suspicion. The officers must conduct each stop in the same manner until particularized suspicion develops, and the officers have no discretion to stop any vehicle out of sequence. The city agreed * * * to operate the checkpoints in such a way as to ensure that the total duration of each stop, absent reasonable suspicion or probable cause, would be five minutes or less.

* * * According to [Indianapolis Police] Sergeant DePew, checkpoint locations are selected weeks in advance based on such considerations as area crime statistics and traffic flow. The checkpoints are generally operated during daylight hours and are identified with lighted signs reading, "NARCOTICS CHECKPOINT ___ MILE AHEAD, NARCOTICS K—9 IN USE, BE PREPARED TO STOP." Once a group of cars has been stopped, other traffic proceeds without interruption until

all the stopped cars have been processed or diverted for further processing. Sergeant DePew also stated that the average stop for a vehicle not subject to further processing lasts two to three minutes or less.

Respondents James Edmond and Joell Palmer were each stopped at a narcotics checkpoint in late September 1998. Respondents then filed a lawsuit on behalf of themselves and the class of all motorists who had been stopped or were subject to being stopped in the future at the Indianapolis drug checkpoints. Respondents claimed that the roadblocks violated the Fourth Amendment of the United States Constitution and the search and seizure provision of the Indiana Constitution. Respondents requested declaratory and injunctive relief for the class, as well as damages and attorney's fees for themselves.

[The United States Court of Appeals for the Seventh Circuit held that the checkpoints contravened the Fourth Amendment and the Supreme Court affirmed.]

II

The Fourth Amendment requires that searches and seizures be reasonable. A search or seizure is ordinarily unreasonable in the absence of individualized suspicion of wrongdoing. While such suspicion is not an "irreducible" component of reasonableness, we have recognized only limited circumstances in which the usual rule does not apply. For example, we have upheld certain regimes of suspicionless searches where the program was designed to serve "special needs, beyond the normal need for law enforcement." * * * We have also allowed searches for certain administrative purposes without particularized suspicion of misconduct, provided that those searches are appropriately limited.

* * *

In *Martinez-Fuerte,* we entertained Fourth Amendment challenges to stops at two permanent immigration checkpoints located on major United States highways less than 100 miles from the Mexican border. We noted * * * the "formidable law enforcement problems" posed by the northbound tide of illegal entrants into the United States. * * * We also stressed the impracticality of the particularized study of a given car to discern whether it was transporting illegal aliens, as well as the relatively modest degree of intrusion entailed by the stops.

Our subsequent cases have confirmed that considerations specifically related to the need to police the border were a significant factor in our *Martinez-Fuerte* decision. * * * Although the stops in *Martinez-Fuerte* did not occur at the border itself, the checkpoints were located near the border and served a border control function made necessary by the difficulty of guarding the border's entire length.

[The Court emphasized that the Michigan sobriety checkpoint in *Sitz* was constitutional because it was "aimed at reducing the immediate hazard posed by the presence of drunk drivers on the highways" and the State had a significant "interest in getting drunk drivers off the road."]

In [Delaware v. Prouse, 440 U.S. 648, 99 S.Ct. 1391, 59 L.Ed.2d 660 (197)] we invalidated a discretionary, suspicionless stop for a spot check of a motorist's driver's license and vehicle registration. The officer's conduct in that case was unconstitutional primarily on account of his exercise of "standardless and unconstrained discretion." We nonetheless acknowledged the States' "vital interest in ensuring that only those qualified to do so are permitted to operate motor vehicles, that these vehicles are fit for safe operation, and hence that licensing, registration, and vehicle inspection requirements are being observed." Accordingly, we suggested that "[q]uestioning of all oncoming traffic at roadblock-type stops" would be a lawful means of serving this interest in highway safety.

* * * Not only does the common thread of highway safety thus run through *Sitz* and *Prouse,* but *Prouse* itself reveals a difference in the Fourth Amendment significance of highway safety interests and the general interest in crime control.

III

It is well established that a vehicle stop at a highway checkpoint effectuates a seizure within the meaning of the Fourth Amendment. The fact that officers walk a narcotics-detection dog around the exterior of each car at the Indianapolis checkpoints does not transform the seizure into a search. Just as in *United States* v. *Place,* 462 U.S. 696, 103 S.Ct. 2637, 77 L.Ed.2d 110 (1983) an exterior sniff of an automobile does not require entry into the car and is not designed to disclose any information other than the presence or absence of narcotics. Like the dog sniff in *Place,* a sniff by a dog that simply walks around a car is "much less intrusive than a typical search." Rather, what principally distinguishes these checkpoints from those we have previously approved is their primary purpose.

As petitioners concede, the Indianapolis checkpoint program unquestionably has the primary purpose of interdicting illegal narcotics * * * In addition, the first document attached to the parties' stipulation is entitled "DRUG CHECKPOINT CONTACT OFFICER DIRECTIVES BY ORDER OF THE CHIEF OF POLICE." These directives instruct officers to "[a]dvise the citizen that they are being stopped briefly at a drug checkpoint." * * * Further, according to Sergeant DePew, the checkpoints are identified with lighted signs reading, "NARCOTICS CHECKPOINT ___ MILE AHEAD, NARCOTICS K–9 IN USE, BE PREPARED TO STOP." Finally, both the District Court and the Court of Appeals recognized that the primary purpose of the roadblocks is the interdiction of narcotics.

We have never approved a checkpoint program whose primary purpose was to detect evidence of ordinary criminal wrongdoing. Rather, our checkpoint cases have recognized only limited exceptions to the general rule that a seizure must be accompanied by some measure of individualized suspicion. We suggested in *Prouse* that we would not credit the "general interest in crime control" as justification for a regime of suspicionless stops. Consistent with this suggestion, each of the checkpoint programs that we have approved was designed primarily to serve purposes closely related to the problems of policing the border or the necessity of ensuring roadway safety. Because the primary purpose of the Indianapolis narcotics checkpoint program is to uncover evidence of ordinary criminal wrongdoing, the program contravenes the Fourth Amendment.

* * * Without drawing the line at roadblocks designed primarily to serve the general interest in crime control, the Fourth Amendment would do little to prevent such intrusions from becoming a routine part of American life.

Petitioners also emphasize the severe and intractable nature of the drug problem as justification for the checkpoint program * * * But the gravity of the threat alone cannot be dispositive of questions concerning what means law enforcement officers may employ to pursue a given purpose. Rather, in determining whether individualized suspicion is required, we must consider the nature of the interests threatened and their connection to the particular law enforcement practices at issue. We are particularly reluctant to recognize exceptions to the general rule of individualized suspicion where governmental authorities primarily pursue their general crime control ends.

* * *

* * * We decline to suspend the usual requirement of individualized suspicion where the police seek to employ a checkpoint primarily for the ordinary enterprise of investigating crimes. We cannot sanction stops justified only by the generalized and ever-present possibility that interrogation and inspection may reveal that any given motorist has committed some crime.

Of course, there are circumstances that may justify a law enforcement checkpoint where the primary purpose would otherwise, but for some emergency, relate to ordinary crime control. For example, * * * the Fourth Amendment would almost certainly permit an appropriately tailored roadblock set up to thwart an imminent terrorist attack or to catch a dangerous criminal who is likely to flee by way of a particular route. The exigencies created by these scenarios are far removed from the circumstances under which authorities might simply stop cars as a matter of course to see if there just happens to be a felon leaving the jurisdiction. While we do not limit the purposes that may justify a checkpoint program to any rigid set of categories, we decline to approve a program whose primary purpose is ultimately indistinguishable from the general interest in crime control.

* * *

* * * While reasonableness under the Fourth Amendment is predominantly an objective inquiry, our special needs and administrative

search cases demonstrate that purpose is often relevant when suspicion-less intrusions pursuant to a general scheme are at issue.[2]

It goes without saying that our holding today does nothing to alter the constitutional status of the sobriety and border checkpoints that we approved in *Sitz* and *Martinez-Fuerte*, or of the type of traffic checkpoint that we suggested would be lawful in *Prouse*. The constitutionality of such checkpoint programs still depends on a balancing of the competing interests at stake and the effectiveness of the program. When law enforcement authorities pursue primarily general crime control purposes at checkpoints such as here, however, stops can only be justified by some quantum of individualized suspicion.

Our holding also does not affect the validity of border searches or searches at places like airports and government buildings, where the need for such measures to ensure public safety can be particularly acute. Nor does our opinion speak to other intrusions aimed primarily at purposes beyond the general interest in crime control. Our holding also does not impair the ability of police officers to act appropriately upon information that they properly learn during a checkpoint stop justified by a lawful primary purpose, even where such action may result in the arrest of a motorist for an offense unrelated to that purpose. Finally, we caution that the purpose inquiry in this context is to be conducted only at the programmatic level and is not an invitation to probe the minds of individual officers acting at the scene.

Because the primary purpose of the Indianapolis checkpoint program is ultimately indistinguishable from the general interest in crime control, the checkpoints violate the Fourth Amendment. The judgment of the Court of Appeals is accordingly affirmed. It is so ordered.

[CHIEF JUSTICE REHNQUIST's dissenting opinion, in which JUSTICE THOMAS joined, and which JUSTICE SCALIA joined in part, is omitted.]

JUSTICE THOMAS, dissenting.

Taken together, our decisions in *Michigan Dept. of State Police v. Sitz* and *United States v. Martinez–Fuerte* stand for the proposition that suspicionless roadblock seizures are constitutionally permissible if conducted according to a plan that limits the discretion of the officers conducting the stops. I am not convinced that *Sitz* and *Martinez-Fuerte* were correctly decided. Indeed, I rather doubt that the Framers of the Fourth Amendment would have considered "reasonable" a program of indiscriminate stops of individuals not suspected of wrongdoing.

Respondents did not, however, advocate the overruling of *Sitz* and *Martinez-Fuerte*, and I am reluctant to consider such a step without the benefit of briefing and argument. For the reasons given by THE CHIEF

---

2. Because petitioners concede that the primary purpose of the Indianapolis checkpoints is narcotics detection, we need not decide whether the State may establish a checkpoint program with the primary purpose of checking licenses or driver sobriety and a secondary purpose of interdicting narcotics. Specifically, we express no view on the question whether police may expand the scope of a license or sobriety checkpoint seizure in order to detect the presence of drugs in a stopped car.

JUSTICE, I believe that those cases compel upholding the program at issue here. I, therefore, join his opinion.

ILLINOIS v. CABALLES

Supreme Court of the United States, 2005.
___ U.S. ___, 125 S.Ct. 834, 160 L.Ed.2d 842.

JUSTICE STEVENS delivered the opinion of the Court.

Illinois State Trooper Daniel Gillette stopped respondent for speeding on an interstate highway. When Gillette radioed the police dispatcher to report the stop, a second trooper, Craig Graham, a member of the Illinois State Police Drug Interdiction Team, overheard the transmission and immediately headed for the scene with his narcotics-detection dog. When they arrived, respondent's car was on the shoulder of the road and respondent was in Gillette's vehicle. While Gillette was in the process of writing a warning ticket, Graham walked his dog around respondent's car. The dog alerted at the trunk. Based on that alert, the officers searched the trunk, found marijuana, and arrested respondent. The entire incident lasted less than 10 minutes.

Respondent was convicted of a narcotics offense and sentenced to 12 years' imprisonment and a $256,136 fine. [The trial judge denied Caballes' motion to suppress the seized evidence, and the Illinois Supreme Court reversed, concluding that because the canine sniff was performed without any " 'specific and articulable facts' " to suggest drug activity, the use of the dog "unjustifiably enlarged the scope of a routine traffic stop into a drug investigation." The Supreme Court granted certiorari on a single issue: "Whether the Fourth Amendment requires reasonable, articulable suspicion to justify using a drug-detection dog to sniff a vehicle during a legitimate traffic stop."]

Here, the initial seizure of respondent when he was stopped on the highway was based on probable cause, and was concededly lawful. It is nevertheless clear that a seizure that is lawful at its inception can violate the Fourth Amendment if its manner of execution unreasonably infringes interests protected by the Constitution. A seizure that is justified solely by the interest in issuing a warning ticket to the driver can become unlawful if it is prolonged beyond the time reasonably required to complete that mission. [The Court agreed with an earlier decision by the state court holding that contraband discovered by a dog sniff conducted during an unreasonably prolonged traffic stop was the product of an unconstitutional seizure. In *Caballes*, however, the Supreme Court accepted the finding by the Illinois courts that the "duration of the stop in this case was entirely justified by the traffic offense and the ordinary inquiries incident to such a stop."]

Despite this conclusion, the Illinois Supreme Court held that the initially lawful traffic stop became an unlawful seizure solely as a result of the canine sniff that occurred outside respondent's stopped car. That is, the court characterized the dog sniff as the cause rather than the consequence of a constitutional violation. In its view, the use of the dog converted the citizen-police encounter from a lawful traffic stop into a drug investigation, and because the shift in purpose was not supported by any reasonable suspicion that respondent possessed narcotics, it was unlawful. In our view, conducting a dog sniff would not change the character of a traffic stop that is lawful at its inception and otherwise executed in a reasonable manner, unless the dog sniff itself infringed respondent's constitutionally protected interest in privacy. Our cases hold that it did not.

Official conduct that does not "compromise any legitimate interest in privacy" is not a search subject to the Fourth Amendment. We have held that any interest in possessing contraband cannot be deemed "legitimate," and thus, governmental conduct that *only* reveals the possession of contraband "compromises no legitimate privacy interest." [Citing *United States* v. *Jacobsen*, 466 U.S. 109, 123 (1984)]. This is because the expectation "that certain facts will not come to the attention of the authorities" is not the same as an interest in "privacy that society is prepared to consider reasonable." In *United States* v. *Place*, 462 U.S. 696 (1983), we treated a canine sniff by a well-trained narcotics-detection dog as "*sui generis*" because it "discloses only the presence or absence of narcotics, a contraband item." Respondent likewise concedes that "drug sniffs are designed, and if properly conducted are generally likely, to reveal only the presence of contraband." Although respondent argues that the error rates, particularly the existence of false positives, call into question the premise that drug-detection dogs alert only to contraband, the record contains no evidence or findings that support his argument. Moreover, respondent does not suggest that an erroneous alert, in and of itself, reveals any legitimate private information, and, in this case, the trial judge found that the dog sniff was sufficiently reliable to establish probable cause to conduct a full-blown search of the trunk.

Accordingly, the use of a well-trained narcotics-detection dog—one that "does not expose noncontraband items that otherwise would remain hidden from public view" during a lawful traffic stop, generally does not implicate legitimate privacy interests. In this case, the dog sniff was performed on the exterior of respondent's car while he was lawfully seized for a traffic violation. Any intrusion on respondent's privacy expectations does not rise to the level of a constitutionally cognizable infringement.

This conclusion is entirely consistent with our recent decision that the use of a thermal-imaging device to detect the growth of marijuana in a home constituted an unlawful search. *Kyllo* v. *United States*, 533 U.S. 27 (2001). Critical to that decision was the fact that the device was capable of detecting lawful activity—in that case, intimate details in a home, such as "at what hour each night the lady of the house takes her daily sauna and bath." The legitimate expectation that information about perfectly lawful activity will remain private is categorically distinguishable from respondent's hopes or expectations concerning the non-detection of contraband in the trunk of his car. A dog sniff conducted during a concededly lawful traffic stop that reveals no information other than the location of a substance that no individual has any right to possess does not violate the Fourth Amendment.

The judgment of the Illinois Supreme Court is vacated, and the case is remanded for further proceedings not inconsistent with this opinion. It is so ordered.

THE CHIEF JUSTICE took no part in the decision of this case.

JUSTICE SOUTER, dissenting.

In *United States* v. *Place,* 462 U.S. 696 (1983), we categorized the sniff of the narcotics-seeking dog as *"sui generis"* under the Fourth Amendment and held it was not a search. The classification rests not only upon the limited nature of the intrusion, but on a further premise that experience has shown to be untenable, the assumption that trained sniffing dogs do not err. What we have learned about the fallibility of dogs in the years since *Place* was decided would itself be reason to call for reconsidering *Place's* decision against treating the intentional use of a trained dog as a search. The portent of this very case, however, adds insistence to the call, for an uncritical adherence to *Place* would render the Fourth Amendment indifferent to suspicionless and indiscriminate sweeps of cars in parking garages and pedestrians on sidewalks; if a sniff is not preceded by a seizure subject to Fourth Amendment notice, it escapes Fourth Amendment review entirely unless it is treated as a search. We should not wait for these developments to occur before rethinking *Place's* analysis, which invites such untoward consequences.

At the heart both of *Place* and the Court's opinion today is the proposition that sniffs by a trained dog are *sui generis* because a reaction by the dog in going alert is a response to nothing but the presence of contraband. Hence, the argument goes, because the sniff can only reveal the presence of items devoid of any legal use, the sniff "does not implicate legitimate privacy interests" and is not to be treated as a search.

The infallible dog, however, is a creature of legal fiction. Although the Supreme Court of Illinois did not get into the sniffing averages of drug dogs, their supposed infallibility is belied by judicial opinions describing well-trained animals sniffing and alerting with less than perfect accuracy, whether owing to errors by their handlers, the limitations of the dogs themselves, or even the pervasive contamination of currency by cocaine. See, *e.g., United States* v. *Kennedy*, 131 F.3d 1371, 1378 (CA10 1997) (describing a dog that had a 71% accuracy rate); *United States* v. *Scarborough*, 128 F.3d 1373, 1378, n. 3 (CA10 1997) (describing a dog that erroneously alerted 4 times out of 19 while working for the postal service and 8% of the time over its entire career); *United States* v. *Limares*, 269 F.3d 794, 797 (CA7 2001) (accepting as reliable a dog that gave false positives between 7 and 38% of the time); *Laime* v. *State*, 347 Ark. 142, 159, 60 S. W. 3d 464, 476 (2001) (speaking of a dog that made between 10 and 50 errors); *United States* v. *$242,-484.00*, 351 F.3d 499, 511 (CA11 2003) (noting that because as much as

80% of all currency in circulation contains drug residue, a dog alert "is of little value"), vacated on other grounds by rehearing en banc, 357 F.3d 1225 (CA11 2004); *United States* v. *Carr*, 25 F.3d 1194, 1214–1217 (CA3 1994) (Becker, J., concurring in part and dissenting in part) ("[A] substantial portion of United States currency ... is tainted with sufficient traces of controlled substances to cause a trained canine to alert to their presence"). Indeed, a study cited by Illinois in this case for the proposition that dog sniffs are "generally reliable" shows that dogs in artificial testing situations return false positives anywhere from 12.5 to 60% of the time, depending on the length of the search. * * *

Once the dog's fallibility is recognized, however, that ends the justification claimed in *Place* for treating the sniff as *sui generis* under the Fourth Amendment: the sniff alert does not necessarily signal hidden contraband, and opening the container or enclosed space whose emanations the dog has sensed will not necessarily reveal contraband or any other evidence of crime. This is not, of course, to deny that a dog's reaction may provide reasonable suspicion, or probable cause, to search the container or enclosure; the Fourth Amendment does not demand certainty of success to justify a search for evidence or contraband. The point is simply that the sniff and alert cannot claim the certainty that *Place* assumed, both in treating the deliberate use of sniffing dogs as *sui generis* and then taking that characterization as a reason to say they are not searches subject to Fourth Amendment scrutiny. And when that aura of uniqueness disappears, there is no basis in *Place*'s reasoning, and no good reason otherwise, to ignore the actual function that dog sniffs perform. They are conducted to obtain information about the contents of private spaces beyond anything that human senses could perceive, even when conventionally enhanced. The information is not provided by independent third parties beyond the reach of constitutional limitations, but gathered by the government's own officers in order to justify searches of the traditional sort, which may or may not reveal evidence of crime but will disclose anything meant to be kept private in the area searched. Thus in practice the government's use of a trained narcotics dog functions as a limited search to reveal undisclosed facts about private enclosures, to be used to justify a further and complete search of the enclosed area. And given the fallibility of the dog, the sniff is the first step in a process that may disclose "intimate details" without revealing contraband, just as a thermal-imaging device might do, as described in *Kyllo* v. *United States*, 533 U.S. 27 (2001).[3]

3. *Kyllo* was concerned with whether a search occurred when the police used a thermal-imaging device on a house to detect heat emanations associated with high-powered marijuana-growing lamps. In concluding that using the device was a search, the Court stressed that the "Government [may not] use a device ... to explore details of the home that would previously have been unknowable without physical intrusion." 533 U.S., at 40. Any difference between the dwelling in *Kyllo* and the trunk of the car here may go to the issue of the reasonableness of the respective searches, but it has no bearing on the question of search or no search. Nor is it significant that *Kyllo*'s imaging device would disclose personal details immediately, whereas they would be revealed only in the further step of opening the enclosed space following the dog's alert reaction; in practical terms the same values protected by the Fourth Amendment are at

It makes sense, then, to treat a sniff as the search that it amounts to in practice, and to rely on the body of our Fourth Amendment cases, including *Kyllo*, in deciding whether such a search is reasonable. As a general proposition, using a dog to sniff for drugs is subject to the rule that the object of enforcing criminal laws does not, without more, justify suspicionless Fourth Amendment intrusions. See *Indianapolis* v. *Edmond*, 531 U.S. 32, 41–42 (2000). Since the police claim to have had no particular suspicion that Caballes was violating any drug law, this sniff search must stand or fall on its being ancillary to the traffic stop that led up to it. * * *

* * * While *Terry* authorized a restricted incidental search for weapons when reasonable suspicion warrants such a safety measure, the Court took care to keep a *Terry* stop from automatically becoming a foot in the door for all investigatory purposes; the permissible intrusion was bounded by the justification for the detention.[5] * * * That has to be the rule unless *Terry* is going to become an open-sesame for general searches, and that rule requires holding that the police do not have reasonable grounds to conduct sniff searches for drugs simply because they have stopped someone to receive a ticket for a highway offense. Since the police had no indication of illegal activity beyond the speed of the car in this case, the sniff search should be held unreasonable under the Fourth Amendment and its fruits should be suppressed.

* * *

The Court today does not go so far as to say explicitly that sniff searches by dogs trained to sense contraband always get a free pass under the Fourth Amendment, since it reserves judgment on the constitutional significance of sniffs assumed to be more intrusive than a dog's walk around a stopped car. For this reason, I do not take the Court's reliance on *Jacobsen* as actually signaling recognition of a broad authority to conduct suspicionless sniffs for drugs in any parked car, about which JUSTICE GINSBURG is rightly concerned, or on the person of any pedestrian minding his own business on a sidewalk. But the Court's stated reasoning provides no apparent stopping point short of such excesses. For the sake of providing a workable framework to analyze cases on facts like these, which are certain to come along, I would treat the dog sniff as the familiar search it is in fact, subject to scrutiny under the Fourth Amendment.

JUSTICE GINSBURG, with whom JUSTICE SOUTER joins, dissenting.

Illinois State Police Trooper Daniel Gillette stopped Roy Caballes for driving 71 miles per hour in a zone with a posted speed limit of 65 miles

---

stake in each case. The justifications required by the Fourth Amendment may or may not differ as between the two practices, but if constitutional scrutiny is in order for the imager, it is in order for the dog.

5. Thus, in *Place* itself, the Government officials had independent grounds to sus-

pect that the luggage in question contained contraband before they employed the dog sniff. 462 U.S., at 698 (describing how Place had acted suspiciously in line at the airport and had labeled his luggage with inconsistent and fictional addresses).

per hour. Trooper Craig Graham of the Drug Interdiction Team heard on the radio that Trooper Gillette was making a traffic stop. Although Gillette requested no aid, Graham decided to come to the scene to conduct a dog sniff. Gillette informed Caballes that he was speeding and asked for the usual documents—driver's license, car registration, and proof of insurance. Caballes promptly provided the requested documents but refused to consent to a search of his vehicle. After calling his dispatcher to check on the validity of Caballes' license and for outstanding warrants, Gillette returned to his vehicle to write Caballes a warning ticket. Interrupted by a radio call on an unrelated matter, Gillette was still writing the ticket when Trooper Graham arrived with his drug-detection dog. Graham walked the dog around the car, the dog alerted at Caballes' trunk, and, after opening the trunk, the troopers found marijuana.

[Justice Ginsburg concluded that the Illinois Supreme Court was correct in ruling that the police violated the Fourth Amendment because they "impermissibly broadened the scope of the traffic stop in this case into a drug investigation."]

* * *

"A routine traffic stop," the Court has observed, "is a relatively brief encounter and 'is more analogous to a so-called *Terry* stop . . . than to a formal arrest.' " *Knowles* v. *Iowa,* 525 U.S. 113, 117 (1998) (quoting *Berkemer* v. *McCarty,* 468 U.S. 420, 439 (1984). I would apply *Terry*'s reasonable-relation test, as the Illinois Supreme Court did, to determine whether the canine sniff impermissibly expanded the scope of the initially valid seizure of Caballes.

It is hardly dispositive that the dog sniff in this case may not have lengthened the duration of the stop. *Terry*, it merits repetition, instructs that any investigation must be "reasonably related in *scope* to the circumstances which justified the interference in the first place." The unwarranted and nonconsensual expansion of the seizure here from a routine traffic stop to a drug investigation broadened the scope of the investigation in a manner that, in my judgment, runs afoul of the Fourth Amendment.

The Court rejects the Illinois Supreme Court's judgment and, implicitly, the application of *Terry* to a traffic stop converted, by calling in a dog, to a drug search. The Court so rules, holding that a dog sniff does not render a seizure that is reasonable in time unreasonable in scope. Dog sniffs that detect only the possession of contraband may be employed without offense to the Fourth Amendment, the Court reasons, because they reveal no lawful activity and hence disturb no legitimate expectation of privacy.

In my view, the Court diminishes the Fourth Amendment's force by abandoning the second *Terry* inquiry (was the police action "reasonably related in scope to the circumstances [justifying] the [initial] interference"). A drug-detection dog is an intimidating animal. Injecting such an animal into a routine traffic stop changes the character of the encounter between the police and the motorist. The stop becomes broader, more adversarial, and (in at least some cases) longer. Caballes—who, as far as Troopers Gillette and Graham knew, was guilty solely of driving six miles per hour over the speed limit—was exposed to the embarrassment and intimidation of being investigated, on a public thoroughfare, for drugs. Even if the drug sniff is not characterized as a Fourth Amendment "search," the sniff surely broadened the scope of the traffic-violation-related seizure.

The Court has never removed police action from Fourth Amendment control on the ground that the action is well calculated to apprehend the guilty. Under today's decision, every traffic stop could become an occasion to call in the dogs, to the distress and embarrassment of the law-abiding population.

* * *

The dog sniff in this case, it bears emphasis, was for drug detection only. A dog sniff for explosives, involving security interests not presented here, would be an entirely different matter. Detector dogs are ordinarily trained not as all-purpose sniffers, but for discrete purposes. For example, they may be trained for narcotics detection or for explosives detection or for agricultural products detection. There is no indication in this case that the dog accompanying Trooper Graham was trained for anything other than drug detection.

This Court has distinguished between the general interest in crime control and more immediate threats to public safety. In *Michigan Dept. of State Police* v. *Sitz,* 496 U.S. 444 (1990), this Court upheld the use of a sobriety traffic checkpoint. Balancing the State's interest in preventing drunk driving, the extent to which that could be accomplished through the checkpoint program, and the degree of intrusion the stops involved, the Court determined that the State's checkpoint program was consistent with the Fourth Amendment. Ten years after *Sitz,* in *Indianapolis* v. *Edmond,* 531 U.S. 32, this Court held that a drug interdiction checkpoint violated the Fourth Amendment. Despite the illegal narcotics traffic that the Nation is struggling to stem, the Court explained, a "general interest in crime control" did not justify the stops. The Court distinguished the sobriety checkpoints in *Sitz* on the ground that those checkpoints were designed to eliminate an "immediate, vehicle-bound threat to life and limb."

* * *

Commentary

In *Edmond,* the Supreme Court emphasized that the roadblock was unconstitutional because it allowed the police to conduct suspicionless seizures "primarily for the ordinary enterprise of investigating crimes." Only two years later, the Court upheld the use of a roadblock employed solely for the purpose of investigating a specific crime. In Illinois v. Lidster, 540 U.S.

419 (2004), the Court approved a highway checkpoint at which police stopped motorists to ask them for information about a recent hit-and-run accident in which a motorist had killed a bicyclist. About a week after the accident, at about the same time of night, and at about the same place, local police set up a highway checkpoint designed to obtain more information about the accident from the public. "Police cars with flashing lights partially blocked the eastbound lanes of the highway. The blockage forced traffic to slow down, leading to lines of up to 15 cars in each lane. As each vehicle drew up to the checkpoint, an officer would stop it for 10 to 15 seconds, ask the occupants whether they had seen anything happen there the previous weekend, and hand each driver a flyer. The flyer said 'ALERT ... FATAL HIT & RUN ACCIDENT' and requested 'assistance in identifying the vehicle and driver in this accident which killed a 70 year old bicyclist.' "

As Robert Lidster approached the roadblock in a minivan, his van swerved, nearly hitting one of the officers. The officer smelled alcohol on Lidster's breath. He directed Lidster to a side street where another officer administered a sobriety test and then arrested Lidster. Lidster was tried and convicted in Illinois state court of driving under the influence of alcohol. Lidster challenged the lawfulness of his arrest and conviction on the ground that the government had obtained much of the relevant evidence through use of a checkpoint stop that violated the Fourth Amendment. The Supreme Court distinguished the Illinois roadblock from the drug checkpoint in Edmond, which the police had set up "to detect evidence of ordinary criminal wrongdoing," particularly possession of illegal drugs. The Supreme Court concluded that the Illinois checkpoint's "primary law enforcement purpose was *not* to determine whether a vehicle's occupants were committing a crime, but to ask vehicle occupants, as members of the public, for their help in providing information about a crime in all likelihood committed by others. The police expected the information elicited to help them apprehend, not the vehicle's occupants, but other individuals." The Court then noted that "unlike *Edmond*, the context here (seeking information from the public) is one in which, by definition, the concept of individualized suspicion has little role to play. Like certain other forms of police activity, say, crowd control or public safety, an information-seeking stop is not the kind of event that involves suspicion, or lack of suspicion, of the relevant individual." The Court also concluded that the roadblock "interfered only minimally with liberty of the sort the Fourth Amendment seeks to protect" and advanced the public interest.

H. THE BORDER

1. People at the Border

UNITED STATES v. MONTOYA DE HERNANDEZ

Supreme Court of the United States, 1985.
473 U.S. 531, 105 S.Ct. 3304, 87 L.Ed.2d 381.

JUSTICE REHNQUIST delivered the opinion of the Court.

Respondent Rosa Elvira Montoya de Hernandez was detained by customs officials upon her arrival at the Los Angeles airport on a flight from Bogota, Colombia. She was found to be smuggling 88 cocaine-filled balloons in her alimentary canal, and was convicted after a bench trial of various federal narcotics offenses. * * *

Respondent arrived at Los Angeles International Airport shortly after midnight, March 5, 1983, on Avianca Flight 080, a direct 10-hour flight from Bogota, Colombia. Her visa was in order so she was passed through Immigration and proceeded to the customs desk. At the customs desk she encountered Customs Inspector Talamantes, who reviewed her documents and noticed from her passport that she had made at least eight recent trips to either Miami or Los Angeles. Talamantes referred respondent to a secondary customs' desk for further questioning. At this desk Talamantes and another inspector asked respondent general questions concerning herself and the purpose of her trip. Respondent revealed that she spoke no English and had no family or friends in the United States. She explained in Spanish that she had come to the United States to purchase goods for her husband's store in Bogota. The customs inspectors recognized Bogota as a "source city" for narcotics. Respondent possessed $5,000 in cash, mostly $50 bills, but had no billfold. She indicated to the inspectors that she had no appointments with merchandise vendors, but planned to ride around Los Angeles in taxicabs visiting retail stores such as J. C. Penney and K-Mart in order to buy goods for her husband's store with the $5,000.

Respondent admitted that she had no hotel reservations, but stated that she planned to stay at a Holiday Inn. Respondent could not recall how her airline ticket was purchased. When the inspectors opened respondent's one small valise they found about four changes of "cold weather" clothing. Respondent had no shoes other than the high-heeled pair she was wearing. Although respondent possessed no checks, waybills, credit cards, or letters of credit, she did produce a Colombian business card and a number of old receipts, waybills, and fabric swatches displayed in a photo album.

At this point Talamantes and the other inspector suspected that respondent was a "balloon swallower," one who attempts to smuggle narcotics into this country hidden in her alimentary canal. Over the years Inspector Talamantes had apprehended dozens of alimentary canal smugglers arriving on Avianca Flight 080.

The inspectors requested a female customs inspector to take respondent to a private area and conduct a patdown and strip search. During the search the female inspector felt respondent's abdomen area and noticed a firm fullness, as if respondent were wearing a girdle. The search revealed no contraband but the inspector noticed that respondent was wearing two pair of elastic underpants with a paper towel lining the crotch area.

When respondent returned to the customs area and the female inspector reported her discoveries, the inspector in charge told respondent that he suspected she was smuggling drugs in her alimentary canal. Respondent agreed to the inspector's request that she be x rayed at a hospital but in answer to the inspector's query stated that she was pregnant. She agreed to a pregnancy test before the x ray. Respondent withdrew the consent for an x ray when she learned that she would have to be handcuffed en route to the hospital. The inspector then gave respondent the option of returning to Colombia on the next available flight, agreeing to an x ray, or remaining in detention until she produced a monitored bowel movement that would confirm or rebut the inspectors' suspicions. Respondent chose the first option and was placed in a customs' office under observation. She was told that if she went to the toilet she would have to use a wastebasket in the women's restroom, in order that female customs inspectors could inspect her stool for balloons or capsules carrying narcotics. The inspectors refused respondent's request to place a telephone call.

Respondent sat in the customs office, under observation, for the remainder of the night. During the night customs officials attempted to place respondent on a Mexican airline that was flying to Bogota via Mexico City in the morning. The airline refused to transport respondent because she lacked a Mexican visa necessary to land in Mexico City. Respondent was not permitted to leave, and was informed that she would be detained until she agreed to an x ray or her bowels moved. She remained detained in the customs office under observation, for most of the time curled up in a chair leaning to one side. She refused all offers of food and drink, and refused to use the toilet facilities. The Court of Appeals noted that she exhibited symptoms of discomfort consistent with "heroic efforts to resist the usual calls of nature."

At the shift change at 4:00 p.m. the next afternoon, almost 16 hours after her flight had landed, respondent still had not defecated or urinated or partaken of food or drink. At that time customs officials sought a court order authorizing a pregnancy test, an x ray, and a rectal examination. The Federal Magistrate issued an order just before midnight that evening, which authorized a rectal examination and involuntary x ray, provided that the physician in charge considered respondent's claim of pregnancy. Respondent was taken to a hospital and given a pregnancy test, which later turned out to be negative. Before the results of the pregnancy test were known, a physician conducted a rectal examination and removed from respondent's rectum a balloon containing a foreign substance. Respondent was then placed formally under arrest. By 4:10 a.m. respondent had passed 6 similar balloons; over the next 4 days she passed 88 balloons containing a total of 528 grams of 80% pure cocaine hydrochloride. * * *

Here the seizure of respondent took place at the international border. Since the founding of our Republic, Congress has granted the Executive plenary authority to conduct routine searches and seizures at the border, without probable cause or a warrant, in order to regulate the collection of duties and to prevent the introduction of contraband into this country. * * *

Consistently, therefore, with Congress' power to protect the Nation by stopping and examining persons entering this country, the Fourth Amendment's balance of reasonableness is qualitatively different at the international border than in the interior. Routine searches of the persons and effects of entrants are not subject to any requirement of reasonable suspicion, probable cause, or warrant, and first-class mail may be opened without a warrant on less than probable cause. Automotive travelers may be stopped at fixed check points near the border without individualized suspicion even if the stop is based largely on ethnicity, *United States v. Martinez–Fuerte,* 428 U.S. 543, 562–563, 96 S.Ct. 3074, 49 L.Ed.2d 1116 (1976), and boats on inland waters with ready access to the sea may be hailed and boarded with no suspicion whatever. *United States v. Villamonte–Marquez,* 462 U.S. 579, 103 S.Ct. 2573, 77 L.Ed.2d 22 (1983).

These cases reflect longstanding concern for the protection of the integrity of the border. This concern is, if anything, heightened by the veritable national crisis in law enforcement caused by smuggling of illicit narcotics, and in particular by the increasing utilization of alimentary canal smuggling. This desperate practice appears to be a relatively recent addition to the smugglers' repertoire of deceptive practices, and it also appears to be exceedingly difficult to detect. * * *

We have not previously decided what level of suspicion would justify a seizure of an incoming traveler for purposes other than a routine border search. * * *

We hold that the detention of a traveler at the border, beyond the scope of a routine customs search and inspection, is justified at its inception if customs agents, considering all the facts surrounding the traveler and her trip, reasonably suspect that the traveler is smuggling contraband in her alimentary canal.[4]

* * *

The facts, and their rational inferences, known to customs inspectors in this case clearly supported a reasonable suspicion that respondent was an alimentary canal smuggler. * * *

The final issue in this case is whether the detention of respondent was reasonably related in scope to the circumstances which justified it initially. In this regard we have cautioned that courts should not indulge in unrealistic second-guessing, and we have noted that creative judges, engaged in *post hoc* evaluations of police conduct can almost always imagine some alternative means by which the objectives of the police might have been accomplished. * * *

4. It is also important to note what we do *not* hold. Because the issues are not presented today we suggest no view on what level of suspicion, if any is required for nonroutine border searches such as strip, body cavity, or involuntary x-ray searches. Both parties would have us decide the issue of whether aliens possess lesser Fourth Amendment rights at the border; that question was not raised in either court below and we do not consider it today.

The rudimentary knowledge of the human body which judges possess in common with the rest of humankind tells us that alimentary canal smuggling cannot be detected in the amount of time in which other illegal activity may be investigated through brief *Terry*-type stops. It presents few, if any external signs; a quick frisk will not do, nor will even a strip search. In the case of respondent the inspectors had available, as an alternative to simply awaiting her bowel movement, an x ray. They offered her the alternative of submitting herself to that procedure. But when she refused that alternative, the customs inspectors were left with only two practical alternatives: detain her for such time as necessary to confirm their suspicions, a detention which would last much longer than the typical *"Terry"* stop, or turn her loose into the interior carrying the reasonably suspected contraband drugs.

The inspectors in this case followed this former procedure. They no doubt expected that respondent, having recently disembarked from a 10–hour direct flight with a full and stiff abdomen, would produce a bowel movement without extended delay. But her visible efforts to resist the call of nature, which the court below labeled "heroic," disappointed this expectation and in turn caused her humiliation and discomfort. Our prior cases have refused to charge police with delays in investigatory detention attributable to the suspect's evasive actions, and that principle applies here as well. Respondent alone was responsible for much of the duration and discomfort of the seizure.

Under these circumstances, we conclude that the detention in this case was not unreasonably long. * * *

[Justice Stevens' opinion concurring in the judgment is omitted.]

Justice Brennan, with whom Justice Marshall joins, dissenting. * * *

Travelers at the national border are routinely subjected to questioning, pat-downs, and thorough searches of their belongings. These measures, which involve relatively limited invasions of privacy and which typically are conducted on all incoming travelers, do not violate the Fourth Amendment given the interests of "national self-protection reasonably requiring one entering the country to identify himself as entitled to come in, and his belongings as effects which may lawfully be brought in." Individual travelers also may be singled out on "reasonable suspicion" and briefly held for further investigation. At some point, however, further investigation involves such severe intrusions on the values the Fourth Amendment protects that more stringent safeguards are required. For example, the length and nature of a detention may, at least when conducted for criminal-investigative purposes, ripen into something approximating a full-scale custodial arrest—indeed, the arrestee, unlike the detainee in cases such as this, is at least given such basic rights as a telephone call, *Miranda* warnings, a bed, a prompt hearing before the nearest federal magistrate, an appointed attorney, and consideration of bail. In addition, border detentions may involve the use of such highly intrusive investigative techniques as body-cavity searches, x-ray searches, and stomach-pumping.

I believe that detentions and searches falling into these more intrusive categories are presumptively "reasonable" within the meaning of the Fourth Amendment only if authorized by a judicial officer. * * *

[T]he available evidence suggests that the number of highly intrusive border searches of suspicious-looking but ultimately innocent travelers may be very high. One physician who at the request of customs officials conducted many "internal searches"—rectal and vaginal examinations and stomach-pumping—estimated that he had found contraband in only 15 to 20 percent of the persons he had examined. It has similarly been estimated that only 16 percent of women subjected to body-cavity searches at the border were in fact found to be carrying contraband. It is precisely to minimize the risk of harassing so many innocent people that the Fourth Amendment requires the intervention of a judicial officer. * * *

* * *

II

I believe that de Hernandez' detention violated the Fourth Amendment for an additional reason: it was not supported by probable cause. In the domestic context, a detention of the sort that occurred here would be permissible only if there were probable cause at the outset. * * *

To be sure, it is commonly asserted that as a result of the Fourth Amendment's "border exception" there is no requirement of probable cause for such investigations. But the justifications for the border exception necessarily limit its breadth. * * * As a condition of entry, the traveler may be subjected to exhaustive processing and examinations, and his belongings may be scrutinized with exacting care. I have no doubt as well that, *as a condition of entry*, travelers in appropriate circumstances may be required to excrete their bodily wastes for further scrutiny and to submit to diagnostic x-rays.

Contrary to the Court's reasoning, however, the Government in carrying out such immigration and customs functions does not simply have the two stark alternatives of either forcing a traveler to submit to such procedures or allowing him to pass into the interior. There is a third alternative: to instruct the traveler who refuses to submit to burdensome but reasonable conditions of entry that he is free to turn around and leave the country. In fact, I believe that the "reasonableness" of any burdensome requirement for entry is necessarily conditioned on the potential entrant's freedom to leave the country if he objects to that requirement. Surely the Government's manifest interest in preventing potentially excludable individuals carrying potential contraband from crossing our borders is fully vindicated if those individuals voluntarily decided not to cross the borders.

This does not, of course, mean that such individuals are not fully subject to the criminal laws while on American soil. If there is probable cause to believe they have violated the law, they may be arrested just like any other person within our borders. And if there is "reasonable suspicion" to believe they may be engaged in such violations, they may briefly be detained pursuant to *Terry* for further investigation, subject to the same limitations and conditions governing *Terry* stops anywhere else in the country. But if such *Terry* suspicion does not promptly ripen into probable cause, such travelers must be given a meaningful choice: either agree to further detention as a condition of eventual entry, or leave the country.

2. Property at the Border

UNITED STATES v. FLORES–MONTANO

Supreme Court of the United States, 2004.
541 U.S. 149, 124 S.Ct. 1582, 158 L.Ed.2d 311.

CHIEF JUSTICE REHNQUIST delivered the opinion of the Court.

Customs officials seized 37 kilograms—a little more than 81 pounds—of marijuana from respondent Manuel Flores–Montano's gas tank at the international border. The Court of Appeals for the Ninth Circuit * * * held that the Fourth Amendment forbade the fuel tank search absent reasonable suspicion. We hold that the search in question did not require reasonable suspicion.

Respondent, driving a 1987 Ford Taurus station wagon, attempted to enter the United States at the Otay Mesa Port of Entry in southern California. A customs inspector conducted an inspection of the station wagon, and requested respondent to leave the vehicle. The vehicle was then taken to a secondary inspection station.

At the secondary station, a second customs inspector inspected the gas tank by tapping it, and noted that the tank sounded solid. Subsequently, the inspector requested a mechanic under contract with Customs to come to the border station to remove the tank. Within 20 to 30 minutes, the mechanic arrived. He raised the car on a hydraulic lift, loosened the straps and unscrewed the bolts holding the gas tank to the undercarriage of the vehicle, and then disconnected some hoses and electrical connections. After the gas tank was removed, the inspector hammered off bondo (a putty-like hardening substance that is used to seal openings) from the top of the gas tank. The inspector opened an access plate underneath the bondo and found 37 kilograms of marijuana bricks. The process took 15 to 25 minutes.

[The defendant moved to suppress the marijuana recovered from the gas tank. Relying on Ninth Circuit precedent, the District Court held that reasonable suspicion was required to justify the search and granted the motion to suppress. The Ninth Circuit Court of Appeals affirmed.]

In *Molina-Tarazon*, the Court of Appeals decided a case presenting similar facts to the one at bar. It asked "whether [the removal and dismantling of the defendant's fuel tank] is a 'routine' border search for which no suspicion whatsoever is required." The Court of Appeals stated that "[i]n order to conduct a search that goes beyond the routine, an inspector must have reasonable suspicion," and the "critical factor" in determining whether a search is "routine" is the "degree of intrusiveness."

The Court of Appeals seized on language from our opinion in *United States* v. *Montoya de Hernandez*, 473 U.S. 531, 87 L.Ed.2d 381, 105 S.Ct. 3304 (1985), in which we used the word "routine" as a descriptive term in discussing border searches. ("Routine searches of the persons and effects of entrants are not subject to any requirement of reasonable suspicion, probable cause, or warrant"). The Court of Appeals took the term "routine," fashioned a new balancing test, and extended it to searches of vehicles. But the reasons that might support a requirement of some level of suspicion in the case of highly intrusive searches of the person—dignity and privacy interests of the person being searched—simply do not carry over to vehicles. Complex balancing tests to determine what is a "routine" search of a vehicle, as opposed to a more "intrusive" search of a person, have no place in border searches of vehicles.

The Government's interest in preventing the entry of unwanted persons and effects is at its zenith at the international border. Time and again, we have stated that "searches made at the border, pursuant to the longstanding right of the sovereign to protect itself by stopping and examining persons and property crossing into this country, are reasonable simply by virtue of the fact that they occur at the border." Congress, since the beginning of our Government, "has granted the Executive plenary authority to conduct routine searches and seizures at the border, without probable cause or a warrant, in order to regulate the collection of duties and to prevent the introduction of contraband into this country." The modern statute that authorized the search in this case derived from a statute passed by the First Congress, and reflects the "impressive historical pedigree" of the Government's power and interest. It is axiomatic that the United States, as sovereign, has the inherent authority to protect, and a paramount interest in protecting, its territorial integrity.

That interest in protecting the borders is illustrated in this case by the evidence that smugglers frequently attempt to penetrate our borders with contraband secreted in their automobiles' fuel tank. Over the past 5 1/2 fiscal years, there have been 18,788 vehicle drug seizures at the southern California ports of entry. Of those 18,788, gas tank drug seizures have accounted for 4,619 of the vehicle drug seizures, or approximately 25%. In addition, instances of persons smuggled in and around gas tank compartments are discovered at the ports of entry of San Ysidro and Otay Mesa at a rate averaging 1 approximately every 10 days.

Respondent asserts two main arguments with respect to his Fourth Amendment interests. First, he urges that he has a privacy interest in his fuel tank, and that the suspicionless disassembly of his tank is an invasion of his privacy. But on many occasions, we have noted that the expectation of privacy is less at the border than it is in the interior. We have long recognized that automobiles seeking entry into this country may be searched. See *Carroll* v. *United States,* 267 U.S. 132, 154, 69 L.Ed. 543, 45 S.Ct. 280 (1925). It is difficult to imagine how the search of a gas tank, which should be solely a repository for fuel, could be more of an invasion of privacy than the search of the automobile's passenger compartment.

Second, respondent argues that the Fourth Amendment "protects property as well as privacy," *Soldal* v. *Cook County,* 506 U.S. 56, 62, 121 L.Ed.2d 450, 113 S.Ct. 538 (1992), and that the disassembly and reassembly of his gas tank is a significant deprivation of his property interest because it may damage the vehicle. He does not, and on the record cannot, truly contend that the procedure of removal, disassembly, and reassembly of the fuel tank in this case or any other has resulted in serious damage to, or destruction of, the property. According to the Government, for example, in fiscal year 2003, 348 gas tank searches conducted along the southern border were negative (*i.e.,* no contraband was found), the gas tanks were reassembled, and the vehicles continued their entry into the United States without incident.

Respondent cites not a single accident involving the vehicle or motorist in the many thousands of gas tank disassemblies that have occurred at the border. A gas tank search involves a brief procedure that can be reversed without damaging the safety or operation of the vehicle. If damage to a vehicle were to occur, the motorist might be entitled to recovery. While the interference with a motorist's possessory interest is not insignificant when the Government removes, disassembles, and reassembles his gas tank, it nevertheless is justified by the Government's paramount interest in protecting the border.

For the reasons stated, we conclude that the Government's authority to conduct suspicionless inspections at the border includes the authority to remove, disassemble, and reassemble a vehicle's fuel tank. While it may be true that some searches of property are so destructive as to require a different result, this was not one of them. The judgment of the United States Court of Appeals for the Ninth Circuit is therefore reversed, and the case is remanded for further proceedings consistent with this opinion. It is so ordered.

[JUSTICE BREYER'S concurring opinion is omitted.]

Part II

INTERROGATION, CONFES-
SIONS, AND THE RIGHT
TO COUNSEL

Chapter 5

VOLUNTARINESS AND THE FIFTH AMENDMENT

Introduction.

For nearly a century, the Supreme Court's jurisprudence interpreting the rules governing interrogations and confessions employed a totalities of the circumstances analysis to determine the voluntariness of a suspect's statement. In a series of nineteenth-century opinions, the Court relied upon common law rules and the Fifth Amendment to prohibit the use of involuntary confessions. In federal cases, the Fifth Amendment provided an explicit textual basis for excluding self-incriminatory statements that were extracted from the suspect by coercive pressure.

The Court did not reverse a state court conviction on the grounds that it was based upon a coerced confession until its landmark decision in *Brown v. Mississippi*, 297 U.S. 278 (1936). In the three decades following *Brown*, the Court decided about one confession case a year, and typically used a "voluntariness" analysis to decide whether the confession had been obtained by unconstitutional coercion. This approach was supplanted for most interrogations and confessions by the famous decision in *Miranda v. Arizona*. The materials in this chapter trace the evolution of the constitutional rules governing interrogations and confessions from the nineteenth century to *Miranda*, and to the cases interpreting these rules in the decades following that seminal decision.

A. PRE-*MIRANDA* THEORIES:

1. The Fifth Amendment in Federal Cases

BRAM v. UNITED STATES
Supreme Court of the United States, 1897.
168 U.S. 532, 18 S.Ct. 183, 42 L.Ed. 568.

Justice White delivered the opinion of the court.

[Three people, including the captain, were killed on board the American ship Herbert Fuller, which was carrying a cargo of lumber from Boston to a port in South America. The murders occurred after midnight, while Bram, the first mate, was in charge of the vessel. The surviving crew members originally accused a seaman, Brown, of the crime. They put Brown in irons and sailed to one of the closest ports, Halifax, Nova Scotia. The trip to Halifax took about a week, and during this time Brown claimed that he was innocent and that he had seen Bram kill the captain while Brown was standing outside the ship's cabin and looking through a window. As a result, crew members overpowered Bram and also placed him in irons. Bram and Brown were both carried into Halifax in irons. When the ship arrived at Nova Scotia, Bram and Brown were held in custody by the chief of police and interrogated by a police detective. They were then sent to Boston, where Bram was tried and convicted of the murders. During the trial, a detective who questioned Bram in Halifax testified about Bram's statements during the interrogation for the prosecution and over the objections of Bram's attorney. The details of the interrogation are described later in the Court's opinion.]

In criminal trials, in the courts of the United States, where-ever a question arises whether a confession is incompetent because not voluntary, the issue is controlled by that portion of the Fifth Amendment to the Constitution of the United States, commanding that no person "shall be compelled in any criminal case to be a witness against himself." The legal principle by which the admissibility of the confession of an accused person is to be determined is expressed in the textbooks.

In 3 Russell on Crimes, (6th ed.) 478, it is stated as follows:

"But a confession, in order to be admissible, must be free and voluntary: that is, must not be extracted by any sort of threats or violence, nor obtained by any direct or implied promises, however slight, nor by the exertion of any improper influence.... A confession can never be received in evidence where the prisoner has been influenced by any threat or promise; for the law cannot measure the force of the influence used, or decide upon its effect upon the mind of the prisoner, and therefore excludes the declaration if any degree of influence has been exerted." * * *

A brief consideration of the reasons which gave rise to the adoption of the Fifth Amendment, of the wrongs which it was intended to prevent and of the safeguards which it was its purpose unalterably to secure, will make it clear that the generic language of the Amendment was but a crystallization of the doctrine as to confessions, well settled when the Amendment was adopted, and since expressed in the text writers and expounded by the adjudications, and hence that the statements on the subject by the text writers and adjudications but formulate the conceptions and commands of the Amendment itself. In Boyd v. United States, 116 U.S. 616, 6 S.Ct. 524, 29 L.Ed. 746 (1886), attention was called to the intimate relation existing between the provision of the Fifth Amendment securing one accused against being compelled to testify against himself, and those of the Fourth Amendment protecting against unreasonable searches and seizures; and it was in that case demonstrated that both of these Amendments contemplated perpetuating, in their full efficacy, by means of a constitutional provision, principles of humanity and civil liberty, which had been secured in the mother country only after years of struggle, so as to implant them in our institutions in the fullness of their integrity, free from the possibilities of future legislative change. In commenting on the same subject, in Brown v. Walker, 161 U.S. 591, 596, 16 S.Ct. 644, 40 L.Ed. 819 (1896), the court, speaking through Mr. Justice Brown, said:

"The maxim nemo tenetur seipsum accusare had its origin in a protest against the inquisitorial and manifestly unjust methods of interrogating accused persons, which has long obtained in the continental system, and until the expulsion of the Stuarts from the British throne in 1688, and the erection of additional barriers for the protection of the people against the exercise of arbitrary power, was not uncommon even in England. While the admissions or confessions of the prisoner, when voluntarily and freely made, have always ranked high in the scale of incriminating evidence, if an accused person be asked to explain his apparent connection with a crime under investigation, the ease with which the questions put to him may assume an inquisitorial character, the temptation to press the witness unduly, to browbeat him if he be timid or reluctant, to push him into a corner, and to entrap him into fatal contradictions * * * made the system so odious as to give rise to a demand for its total abolition. * * * So deeply did the iniquities of the ancient system impress themselves upon the minds of the American colonists that the States, with one accord, made a denial of the right to question an accused person a part of their fundamental law, so that a maxim, which in England was a mere rule of evidence, became clothed in this country with the impregnability of a constitutional enactment."

There can be no doubt that long prior to our independence the doctrine that one accused of crime could not be compelled to testify against himself had reached its full development in the common law, was there considered as resting on the law of nature, and was embedded in that system as one of its great and distinguishing attributes.

* * *

In approaching the adjudicated cases for the purpose of endeavoring to deduce from them what quantum of proof, in a case presented, is adequate to create, by the operation of hope or fear, an involuntary condition of the mind, the difficulty encountered is, that all the decided cases necessarily rest upon the state of facts which existed in the particular case, and, therefore, furnish no certain criterion, since the conclusion that a given state of fact was adequate to have produced an involuntary confession does not establish that the same result has been created by a different although somewhat similar condition of fact. Indeed, the embarrassment which comes from the varying state of fact, considered in the decided cases, has given rise to the statement that there was no general rule of law by which the admissibility of a confession could be determined, but that the courts had left the rule to be evolved from the facts of each particular case. * * *

* * * The rule is not that in order to render a statement admissible the proof must be adequate to establish that the particular communications contained in a statement were voluntarily made, but it must be sufficient to establish that the making of the statement was voluntary; that is to say, that from the causes, which the law treats as legally sufficient to engender in the mind of the accused hope or fear in respect to the crime charged, the accused was not involuntarily impelled to make a statement, when but for the improper influences he would have remained silent. * * *

* * *

We come, then, to a consideration of the circumstances surrounding, and the facts established to exist, in reference to the confession, in order to determine whether it was shown to have been voluntarily made. * * * On reaching port, these two suspected persons were delivered to the custody of the police authorities of Halifax and were there held in confinement awaiting the action of the United States consul * * *. [While in custody] the police detective caused Bram to be brought from jail to his private office, and when there alone with the detective he was stripped of his clothing, and either whilst the detective was in the act of so stripping him, or after he was denuded, the conversation offered as a confession took place. The detective repeats what he said to the prisoner, whom he had thus stripped, as follows:

"When Mr. Bram came into my office I said to him: 'Bram, we are trying to unravel this horrible mystery.' I said: 'Your position is rather an awkward one. I have had Brown in this office, and he made a statement that he saw you do the murder.' He said: 'He could not have seen me. Where was he?' I said: 'He states he was at the wheel.' 'Well,' He said, 'he could not see me from there.' "

The fact, then, is, that the language of the accused, which was offered in evidence as a confession, was made use of by him as a reply to the statement of the detective that Bram's co-suspect had charged him with the crime, and, although the answer was in the form of a denial, it was doubtless offered as a confession because of an implication of guilt which it was conceived the words of the denial might be considered to mean. But the situation of the accused, and the nature of the communication made to him by the detective, necessarily overthrows any possible implication that his reply to the detective could have been the result of a purely voluntary mental action; that is to say, when all the surrounding circumstances are considered in their true relations, not only is the claim that the statement was voluntary overthrown, but the impression is irresistibly produced that it must necessarily have been the result of either hope or fear, or both, operating on the mind.

It cannot be doubted that, placed in the position in which the accused was when the statement was made to him that the other suspected person had charged him with crime, the result was to produce upon his mind the fear that if he remained silent it would be considered an admission of guilt, and therefore render certain his being committed for trial as the guilty person, and it cannot be conceived that the converse impression would not also have naturally arisen, that by denying there was hope of removing the suspicion from himself. If this must have been the state of mind of one situated as was the prisoner when the confession was made, how in reason can it be said that the answer which he gave and which was required by the situation was wholly voluntary and in no manner influenced by the force of hope or fear? To so conclude would be to deny the necessary relation of cause and effect. Indeed, the implication of guilt resulting from silence has been considered by some state courts of last resort, in decided cases, to which we have already made reference, as so cogent that they have held that where a person is accused of guilt, under circumstances which call upon him to make denial, the fact of his silence is competent evidence as tending to establish guilt. [T]hat is to say, he would be impelled to speak either for fear that his failure to make answer would be considered against him, or of hope that if he did reply he would be benefited thereby. And these self-evident deductions are greatly strengthened by considering the place where the statements were made and the conduct of the detective towards the accused. Bram had been brought from confinement to the office of the detective, and there, when alone with him, in a foreign land, while he was in the act of being stripped or had been stripped of his clothing, was interrogated by the officer, who was thus, while putting the questions and receiving answers thereto, exercising complete authority and control over the person he was interrogating. Although these facts may not, when isolated each from the other, be sufficient to warrant the inference that an influence compelling a statement had been exerted, yet when taken as a whole, in conjunction with the nature of the communication made, they give room to the strongest inference that the statements of Bram were not made by one who in law could be considered a free agent. * * *. A plainer violation as well of the letter as of the spirit and purpose of the constitutional immunity could scarcely be conceived of.

Moreover, aside from the natural result arising from the situation of the accused and the communication made to him by the detective, the conversation conveyed an express intimation rendering the confession involuntary within the rule laid down by the authorities. What further was said by the detective? "Now, look here, Bram, I am satisfied that you killed the captain from all I have heard from Mr. Brown. But," I said, "some of us here think you could not have done all that crime alone. If you had an accomplice, you should say so, and not have the blame of this horrible crime on your own shoulders." But how could the weight of the whole crime be removed from the shoulders of the prisoner as a consequence of his speaking, unless benefit as to the crime and its punishment was to arise from his speaking? [In] light of the impression that it was calculated to produce on the mind of the accused, [the detective's comment suggested] some benefit as to the crime and its punishment as arising from making a statement.

* * * It, in substance, therefore, called upon the prisoner to disclose his accomplice, and might well have been understood as holding out an encouragement that by so doing he might at least obtain a mitigation of the punishment for the crime which otherwise would assuredly follow. As said in the passage from Russell on Crimes already quoted, "the law cannot measure the force of the influence used or decide upon its effect upon the mind of the prisoner, and, therefore, excludes the declaration if any degree of influence has been exerted." In the case before us we find that an influence was exerted, and as any doubt as to whether the confession was voluntary must be determined in favor of the accused, we cannot escape the conclusion that error was committed by the trial court in admitting the confession under the circumstances disclosed by the record.

* * *

The judgment is reversed and the cause remanded with directions to set aside the verdict and to order a new trial.

[JUSTICE BREWER's dissenting opinion, in which CHIEF JUSTICE FULLER and JUSTICE BROWN joined, is omitted.]

Note

The *Bram* opinion cited a long list of state court opinions that had found that confessions were involuntary because of improper inducements offered by interrogators. As the cases in this chapter illustrate, many of the tactics considered improper in the nineteenth century are permitted under contemporary interpretation of the Fifth Amendment privilege. The improper inducements in the state court opinions cited in *Bram* included: saying to the prisoner, "You have got your foot in it, and somebody else was with you; now, if you did break open the door, the best thing you can do is to tell all about it, and to tell who was with you, and to tell the truth, the whole truth, and nothing but the truth;" saying to the accused, "it will be better for you to make a full disclosure;" saying to the accused, "I don't think the truth will hurt anybody. It will be better for you to come out and tell all you know about it, if you feel that way;" advising the prisoner to make full restitution, and saying, "if you do so it will go easy with you; it will be better for you to confess; the door of mercy is open and that of justice closed;" threatening to arrest the accused and expose his family if he did not confess; saying to one suspected of crime, "the suspicion is general against you, and you had as well tell all about it, the prosecution will be no greater, I don't expect to do anything with you; I am going to send you home to your mother;" saying to the accused, "Edmund, if you know anything, it may be best for you to tell it;" or, "Edmund, if you know anything, go and tell it, and it may be best for you;" saying to the prisoner, "The best you can do is to own up; it will be better for you;" saying to the accused, "I believe you are guilty; if you are you had better say so; if you are not you had better say that;" saying to the prisoner, "if you are guilty, I would advise you to make an honest confession;

it might be easier for you. It is plain against you;" saying to the accused, "you had as well tell all about it." By the late twentieth century, such statements were typically accepted as proper methods of interrogation, and not treated as improper inducements or threats.

2. Fourteenth Amendment Due Process in State Cases

BROWN v. MISSISSIPPI

Supreme Court of the United States, 1936.
297 U.S. 278, 56 S.Ct. 461, 80 L.Ed. 682.

MR. CHIEF JUSTICE HUGHES delivered the opinion of the Court.

The question in this case is whether convictions, which rest solely upon confessions shown to have been extorted by officers of the State by brutality and violence, are consistent with the due process of law required by the Fourteenth Amendment of the Constitution of the United States.

Petitioners were indicted for the murder of one Raymond Stewart, whose death occurred on March 30, 1934. They were indicted on April 4, 1934, and were then arraigned and pleaded not guilty. Counsel were appointed by the court to defend them. Trial was begun the next morning and was concluded on the following day, when they were found guilty and sentenced to death.

Aside from the confessions, there was no evidence sufficient to warrant the submission of the case to the jury. [T]estimony as to the confessions was received over the objection of defendants' counsel. Defendants then testified that the confessions were false and had been procured by physical torture. The case went to the jury * * * . [The State Supreme Court rejected the defendants' arguments "that all the evidence against them was obtained by coercion and brutality known to the court and to the district attorney," and that the defendants had been denied due process guaranteed by the Fourteenth Amendment of the Constitution of the United States. The State Supreme Court affirmed the convictions and death sentences. It ruled "(1) that immunity from self-incrimination is not essential to due process of law, and (2) that the failure of the trial court to exclude the confessions after the introduction of evidence showing their incompetency, in the absence of a request for such exclusion, did not deprive the defendants of life or liberty without due process of law; and that even if the trial court had erroneously overruled a motion to exclude the confessions, the ruling would have been mere error reversible on appeal, but not a violation of constitutional right." Chief Justice Hughes described the coercion used to obtain the defendants' confessions by quoting from the dissenting opinion in the state supreme court case.]

* * * There is no dispute as to the facts upon this point and as they are clearly and adequately stated in the dissenting opinion of Judge Griffith (with whom Judge Anderson concurred)—showing both the extreme brutality of the measures to extort the confessions and the

participation of the state authorities—we quote this part of his opinion in full, as follows:

"The crime with which these defendants, all ignorant negroes, are charged, was discovered about one o'clock p.m. on Friday, March 30, 1934. On that night one Dial, a deputy sheriff, accompanied by others, came to the home of Ellington, one of the defendants, and requested him to accompany them to the house of the deceased, and there a number of white men were gathered, who began to accuse the defendant of the crime. Upon his denial they seized him, and with the participation of the deputy they hanged him by a rope to the limb of a tree, and having let him down, they hung him again, and when he was let down the second time, and he still protested his innocence, he was tied to a tree and whipped, and still declining to accede to the demands that he confess, he was finally released and he returned with some difficulty to his home, suffering intense pain and agony. The record of the testimony shows that the signs of the rope on his neck were plainly visible during the so-called trial. A day or two thereafter the said deputy, accompanied by another, returned to the home of the said defendant and arrested him, and departed with the prisoner towards the jail in an adjoining county, but went by a route which led into the State of Alabama; and while on the way, in that State, the deputy stopped and again severely whipped the defendant, declaring that he would continue the whipping until he confessed, and the defendant then agreed to confess to such a statement as the deputy would dictate, and he did so, after which he was delivered to jail.

"The other two defendants, Ed Brown and Henry Shields, were also arrested and taken to the same jail. On Sunday night, April 1, 1934, the same deputy, accompanied by a number of white men, one of whom was also an officer, and by the jailer, came to the jail, and the two last named defendants were made to strip and they were laid over chairs and their backs were cut to pieces with a leather strap with buckles on it, and they were likewise made by the said deputy definitely to understand that the whipping would be continued unless and until they confessed, and not only confessed, but confessed in every matter of detail as demanded by those present; and in this manner the defendants confessed the crime, and as the whippings progressed and were repeated, they changed or adjusted their confession in all particulars of detail so as to conform to the demands of their torturers. When the confessions had been obtained in the exact form and contents as desired by the mob, they left with the parting admonition and warning that, if the defendants changed their story at any time in any respect from that last stated, the perpetrators of the outrage would administer the same or equally effective treatment.

"Further details of the brutal treatment to which these helpless prisoners were subjected need not be pursued. It is sufficient to say that in pertinent respects the transcript reads more like pages torn from some medieval account, than a record made within the confines of a modern civilization which aspires to an enlightened constitutional government.

"All this having been accomplished, on the next day, that is, on Monday, April 2, when the defendants had been given time to recuperate somewhat from the tortures to which they had been subjected, the two sheriffs, one of the county where the crime was committed, and the other of the county of the jail in which the prisoners were confined, came to the jail, accompanied by eight other persons, some of them deputies, there to hear the free and voluntary confession of these miserable and abject defendants. The sheriff of the county of the crime admitted that he had heard of the whipping, but averred that he had no personal knowledge of it. He admitted that one of the defendants, when brought before him to confess, was limping and did not sit down, and that this particular defendant then and there stated that he had been strapped so severely that he could not sit down, and as already stated, the signs of the rope on the neck of another of the defendants were plainly visible to all. Nevertheless the solemn farce of hearing the free and voluntary confessions was gone through with, and these two sheriffs and one other person then present were the three witnesses used in court to establish the so-called confessions, which were received by the court and admitted in evidence over the objections of the defendants duly entered of record as each of the said three witnesses delivered their alleged testimony. There was thus enough before the court when these confessions were first offered to make known to the court that they were not, beyond all reasonable doubt, free and voluntary; and the failure of the court then to exclude the confessions is sufficient to reverse the judgment, under every rule of procedure that has heretofore been prescribed, and hence it was not necessary subsequently to renew the objections by motion or otherwise.

"The spurious confessions having been obtained—and the farce last mentioned having been gone through with on Monday, April 2d—the court, then in session, on the following day, Tuesday, April 3, 1934, ordered the grand jury to reassemble on the succeeding day, April 4, 1934, at nine o'clock, and on the morning of the day last mentioned the grand jury returned an indictment against the defendants for murder. Late that afternoon the defendants were brought from the jail in the adjoining county and arraigned, when one or more of them offered to plead guilty, which the court declined to accept, and, upon inquiry whether they had or desired counsel, they stated that they had none, and did not suppose that counsel could be of any assistance to them. The court thereupon appointed counsel, and set the case for trial for the following morning at nine o'clock, and the defendants were returned to the jail in the adjoining county about thirty miles away.

"The defendants were brought to the courthouse of the county on the following morning, April 5th, and the so-called trial was opened, and was concluded on the next day, April 6, 1934, and resulted in a pretended conviction with death sentences. The evidence upon which the conviction was obtained was the so-called confessions. Without this evidence a peremptory instruction to find for the defendants would have been inescapable. The defendants were put on the stand, and by their testimony the facts and the details thereof as to the manner by which the confessions were extorted from them were fully developed, and it is further disclosed by the record that the same deputy, Dial, under whose guiding hand and active participation the tortures to coerce the confessions were administered, was actively in the performance of the supposed duties of a court deputy in the courthouse and in the presence of the prisoners during what is denominated, in complimentary terms, the trial of these defendants. This deputy was put on the stand by the state in rebuttal, and admitted the whippings. It is interesting to note that in his testimony with reference to the whipping of the defendant Ellington, and in response to the inquiry as to how severely he was whipped, the deputy stated, 'Not too much for a negro; not as much as I would have done if it were left to me.' Two others who had participated in these whippings were introduced and admitted it—not a single witness was introduced who denied it. The facts are not only undisputed, they are admitted, and admitted to have been done by officers of the state, in conjunction with other participants, and all this was definitely well known to everybody connected with the trial, and during the trial, including the state's prosecuting attorney and the trial judge presiding.''

1. The State stresses the statement in *Twining* v. *New Jersey*, 211 U.S. 78, 114, 29 S.Ct. 14, 53 L.Ed. 97 (1908), that "exemption from compulsory self-incrimination in the courts of the States is not secured by any part of the Federal Constitution," and the statement in *Snyder* v. *Massachusetts*, 291 U.S. 97, 105, 54 S.Ct. 330, 78 L.Ed. 674 (1934), that "the privilege against self-incrimination may be withdrawn and the accused put upon the stand as a witness for the State." But the question of the right of the State to withdraw the privilege against self-incrimination is not here involved. The compulsion to which the quoted statements refer is that of the processes of justice by which the accused may be called as a witness and required to testify. Compulsion by torture to extort a confession is a different matter.

The State is free to regulate the procedure of its courts in accordance with its own conceptions of policy, unless in so doing it "offends some principle of justice so rooted in the traditions and conscience of our people as to be ranked as fundamental. The State may abolish trial by jury. It may dispense with indictment by a grand jury and substitute complaint or information. But the freedom of the State in establishing its policy is the freedom of constitutional government and is limited by the requirement of due process of law. Because a State may dispense with a jury trial, it does not follow that it may substitute trial by ordeal. The rack and torture chamber may not be substituted for the witness stand. The State may not permit an accused to be hurried to conviction under mob domination—where the whole proceeding is but a mask—without supplying corrective process. The State may not deny to the accused the aid of counsel. Nor may a State, through the action of its officers, contrive a conviction through the pretense of a trial which in truth is "but used as a means of depriving a defendant of liberty through a deliberate deception of court and jury by the presentation of testimony known to be perjured." And the trial equally is a mere pretense where the state authorities have contrived a conviction resting solely upon confessions obtained by violence. The due process clause requires "that state action, whether through one agency or another, shall be consistent with the fundamental principles of liberty and justice which lie at the base of all our civil and political institutions." It would be difficult to conceive of methods more revolting to the sense of justice than those taken to procure the confessions of these petitioners, and the use of the confessions thus obtained as the basis for conviction and sentence was a clear denial of due process.

2. It is in this view that the further contention of the State must be considered. That contention rests upon the failure of counsel for the accused, who had objected to the admissibility of the confessions, to move for their exclusion after they had been introduced and the fact of coercion had been proved. It is a contention which proceeds upon a misconception of the nature of petitioners' complaint. That complaint is not of the commission of mere error, but of a wrong so fundamental that it made the whole proceeding a mere pretense of a trial and rendered the conviction and sentence wholly void. We are not concerned with a mere question of state practice, or whether counsel assigned to petitioners were competent or mistakenly assumed that their first objections were sufficient. In an earlier case the Supreme Court of the State had recognized the duty of the court to supply corrective process where due process of law had been denied. In *Fisher* v. *State*, 145 Miss. 116, 134; 110 So. 361, 365, the court said: "Coercing the supposed state's criminals into confessions and using such confessions so coerced from them against them in trials has been the curse of all countries. It was the chief inequity, the crowning infamy of the Star Chamber, and the Inquisition, and other similar institutions. The constitution recognized the evils that lay behind these practices and prohibited them in this country.... The duty of maintaining constitutional rights of a person on trial for his life rises above mere rules of procedure and wherever the court is clearly satisfied that such violations exist, it will refuse to sanction such violations and will apply the corrective."

In the instant case, the trial court was fully advised by the undisputed evidence of the way in which the confessions had been procured. The trial court knew that there was no other evidence upon which conviction and sentence could be based. Yet it proceeded to permit conviction and to pronounce sentence. The conviction and sentence were void for want of the essential elements of due process, and the proceeding thus vitiated could be challenged in any appropriate manner. It was challenged before the Supreme Court of the State by the express invocation of the Fourteenth Amendment. That court entertained the challenge, considered the federal question thus presented, but declined to enforce petitioners' constitutional right. The court thus denied a federal right fully established and specially set up and claimed and the judgment must be *Reversed.*

*Commentary**

In the three decades that followed *Brown*, the Supreme Court decided about three dozen confession cases, but most were governed by the Fourteenth Amendment, not the Fifth. Chief Justice Rehnquist's opinion in Dickerson v. United States, 530 U.S. 428, 432–33 (2000) presented *infra* summarized this case law:

> Prior to *Miranda*, we evaluated the admissibility of a suspect's confession under a voluntariness test. . . . Over time, our cases recognized two constitutional bases for the requirement that a confession be voluntary to be admitted into evidence: the Fifth Amendment right against self-incrimination and the Due Process Clause of the Fourteenth Amendment.

He then noted that "for the middle third of the 20th century our cases based the rule against admitting coerced confessions primarily, if not exclusively, on notions of due process. We applied the due process voluntariness test in 'some 30 different cases decided during the era.'"

The due process test developed in those cases considered "the totality of all the surrounding circumstances—both the characteristics of the accused and the details of the interrogation." Applying the totality-of-the-circumstances test, courts examined "[a]ll the circumstances attendant upon the confession," and excluded the confession if "all the attendant circumstances indicate that the confession was coerced or compelled."

Inevitably this was a fact-sensitive, case-by-case method of adjudication. It was "retail" constitutional decisionmaking that produced few global rules. Nonetheless, over time the cumulative effect of this process appeared to influence police practices. In *Brown*, investigators tortured the suspects until they confessed. Twenty years later, the claims of coercion raised in the Supreme Court's confession cases typically alleged less egregious police misconduct. Suspects were not whipped or hanged as they had been in *Brown*, but abusive practices continued. Suspects were held incommunicado for days; subjected to lengthy interrogations without respite; denied sleep, food, and medical care; and forced to confess to avoid being turned over to an apparent lynch mob.

The incremental process of change embedded in the due process methodology was too gradual for some justices,[1] and as early as the late

---

* Adopted from Morgan Cloud, George B. Shepherd, Alison Nodvin Burkoff, and Justin Shur, Words Without Meaning: The Constitution, Confessions, and Mentally Retarded Suspects, 69 U.Chi.L.Rev. 495, 517–522 (2002).

1. See George E. Dix, *Federal Constitutional Confession Law: The 1986 and 1987 Supreme Court Terms*, 67 Tex L Rev 231, 235–36 (1988). Two other reasons motivated the Supreme Court to abandon the voluntariness standard. First, the Supreme Court "had been unable to stimulate sufficient lower-court awareness of the voluntariness doctrine's underlying concerns," especially the Court's increasing sensitivity to the risks that police practices posed to values protected by the federal constitution. Id at 235. Second, "the confession problem had outgrown the voluntariness rule. As the Court encountered fewer cases of physical coercion, its concern progressed to the more subtle risks that interrogation practices posed to constitutional values." Id at 235–36. Voluntariness analysis, "perhaps an efficient weapon against overt coercion, was

1940s the Court began to grope for more global rules that would eliminate abusive interrogation tactics.[2] The Court's efforts to find more comprehensive rules to regulate police practices intensified in the 1960s. Only two years before *Miranda*, the Court decided three cases that moved haltingly in that direction. Although the Supreme Court relied upon the Sixth Amendment—not the Fifth—in two of the these decisions,[3] they nonetheless foreshadowed the *Miranda* decision's emphasis upon the importance of defense counsel's presence during custodial interrogation. The third of these 1964 decisions played a more direct role in laying the doctrinal foundations for *Miranda*. In Malloy v. Hogan, 378 U.S. 1 (1964), the Court held that the Fifth Amendment's Self–Incrimination Clause was incorporated in the Due Process Clause of the Fourteenth Amendment and therefore was binding upon the states. This allowed the *Miranda* Court to define Fifth Amendment rules governing both federal and state interrogations.

far less effective when applied to psychological ploys." Id at 236.

2. The first attempt at devising a broad prophylactic rule was the "prompt appearance" rule, which was justified by evidence that most abusive interrogations occur in the period between arrest and the suspect's first appearance before a judicial officer. The prompt appearance rule ultimately should be viewed as a nonconstitutional rule that rested upon the Court's supervisory powers within the federal judicial system. As a result, it did not apply within the state systems. This principle is embodied in Rule 5(a) of the Federal Rules of Criminal Procedure. See also *McNabb v. United States*, 318 U.S. 332, 339–40 (1943) (holding that judicial supervision in the federal courts implies a duty to set aside convictions based on abusive interrogations); *Mallory v. United States*, 354 U.S. 449, 451–54 (1957) (applying Rule 5(a) and discussing its justifications). The Court's opinion in *Miranda v. Arizona*, 384 U.S. at 463, praised the prompt appearance rule's effect upon coercive interrogations:

> Because of the adoption by Congress of Rule 5(a) of the Federal Rules of Criminal Procedure, and this Court's effectuation of that Rule in *McNabb v. United States* ... and *Mallory v. United States*, we have had little occasion in the past quarter century to reach the constitutional issues in dealing with federal interrogations. These supervisory rules, requiring production of an arrested person before a commissioner "without unnecessary delay" and excluding evidence obtained in

default of that statutory obligation, were nonetheless responsive to the same considerations of Fifth Amendment policy that unavoidably face us now as to the States. In *McNabb* ... and in *Mallory* ... we recognized both the dangers of interrogation and the appropriateness of prophylaxis stemming from the very fact of interrogation itself.

3. The first opinion decreed that defendants have the right to have an attorney present during any "critical period" of the proceedings, including confrontations between defendants and undercover agents for the state, once formal adversarial proceedings had commenced. Relying on the Sixth Amendment right to counsel, the Court suppressed statements made to an undercover informer about crimes for which the defendant already had been indicted. *Massiah v. United States* 377 U.S. 201, 204, 207 (1964). In the second case, the defendant made incriminating statements during custodial interrogation, but before the commencement of formal adversarial proceedings. Once again the Sixth Amendment provided the constitutional basis for the decision. In an opinion that, in retrospect, looks like a bridge between the fact-based totality-of-the-circumstances approach and the creation of global rules in *Miranda*; the Court suppressed the defendant's confession because police had taken him into custody, had made him the focus of the investigation, and had refused to allow him to meet with his attorney. *Escobedo v. Illinois*, 378 U.S. 478, 490–91 (1964).

B. THE MIRANDA "REVOLUTION"

1. The Road to Miranda

MASSIAH v. UNITED STATES

Supreme Court of the United States, 1964.
377 U.S. 201, 84 S.Ct. 1199, 12 L.E.2d 246.

MR. JUSTICE STEWART delivered the opinion of the Court. * * *

[Federal authorities indicted Massiah and Colson for conspiring with others to import cocaine seized on a ship in New York harbor. Massiah retained a lawyer, pleaded not guilty, and was released on bail to await trial. Subsequently, Colson secretly agreed to cooperate with the continuing government investigation of the smuggling operation. He arranged to meet with Massiah to discuss their situation, and the two held a lengthy conversation while sitting in Colson's automobile parked on a city street. Colson was wearing a radio transmitter, and the entire conversation was overhead by a federal agent. This agent testified at Massiah's trial on a variety of narcotics charges, relating various incriminating statements that Massiah made in the conversation with Colson.]

* * *

In Spano v. New York, 360 U.S. 315, 79 S.Ct. 1202, 3 L.Ed.2d 1265 (1959), this Court reversed a state criminal conviction because a confession had been wrongly admitted into evidence against the defendant at his trial. * * * While the Court's opinion relied upon the totality of the circumstances under which the confession had been obtained, four concurring Justices pointed out that the Constitution required reversal of the conviction upon the sole and specific ground that the confession had been deliberately elicited by the police after the defendant had been indicted, and therefore at a time when he was clearly entitled to a lawyer's help. * * *

* * *

Here we deal not with a state court conviction, but with a federal case, where the specific guarantee of the Sixth Amendment directly applies. We hold that the petitioner was denied the basic protections of that guarantee when there was used against him at his trial evidence of his own incriminating words, which federal agents had deliberately elicited from him after he had been indicted and in the absence of his counsel. It is true that in the Spano case the defendant was interrogated in a police station, while here the damaging testimony was elicited from the defendant without his knowledge while he was free on bail. But, as Judge Hays pointed out in his dissent in the Court of Appeals, "if such a rule is to have any efficacy it must apply to indirect and surreptitious interrogations as well as those conducted in the jailhouse. In this case, Massiah was more seriously imposed upon . . . , because he did not even know that he was under interrogation by a government agent."

The Solicitor General, in his brief and oral argument, has strenuously contended that the federal law enforcement agents had the right, if not indeed the duty, to continue their investigation of the petitioner and his alleged criminal associates even though the petitioner had been indicted. He points out that the Government was continuing its investigation in order to uncover not only the source of narcotics found on the S.S. *Santa Maria*, but also their intended buyer. He says that the quantity of narcotics involved was such as to suggest that the petitioner was part of a large and well-organized ring, and indeed that the continuing investigation confirmed this suspicion, since it resulted in criminal charges against many defendants. Under these circumstances the Solicitor General concludes that the government agents were completely "justified in making use of Colson's cooperation by having Colson continue his normal associations and by surveilling them."

We may accept and, at least for present purposes, completely approve all that this argument implies * * *. We do not question that in this case, as in many cases, it was entirely proper to continue an investigation of the suspected criminal activities of the defendant and his alleged confederates, even though the defendant had already been indicted. All that we hold is that the defendant's own incriminating statements, obtained by federal agents under the circumstances here disclosed, could not constitutionally be used by the prosecution as evidence against *him* at his trial. *Reversed.*

[The dissenting opinion by JUSTICE WHITE, with whom JUSTICE CLARK and JUSTICE HARLAN join, is omitted.]

ESCOBEDO v. ILLINOIS

Supreme Court of the United States, 1964.
378 U.S. 478, 84 S.Ct. 1758, 12 L.Ed.2d 977.

MR. JUSTICE GOLDBERG delivered the opinion of the Court.

The critical question in this case is whether, under the circumstances, the refusal by the police to honor petitioner's request to consult with his lawyer during the course of an interrogation constitutes a denial of "the Assistance of Counsel" in violation of the Sixth Amendment to the Constitution as "made obligatory upon the States by the Fourteenth Amendment," *Gideon v. Wainwright*, 372 U.S. 335, 342, 83 S.Ct. 792; 9 L.Ed.2d 799 (1963), and thereby renders inadmissible in a state criminal trial any incriminating statement elicited by the police during the interrogation.

On the night of January 19, 1960, petitioner's brother-in-law was fatally shot. In the early hours of the next morning, at 2:30 a.m., petitioner was arrested without a warrant and interrogated. Petitioner made no statement to the police and was released at 5 that afternoon pursuant to a state court writ of habeas corpus obtained by Mr. Warren Wolfson, a lawyer who had been retained by petitioner.

On January 30, Benedict DiGerlando, who was then in police custody and who was later indicted for the murder along with petitioner, told the police that petitioner had fired the fatal shots. Between 8 and 9 that evening, petitioner and his sister, the widow of the deceased, were arrested and taken to police headquarters. En route to the police station, the police "had handcuffed the defendant behind his back," and "one of the arresting officers told defendant that DiGerlando had named him as the one who shot" the deceased. Petitioner testified, without contradiction, that the "detectives said they had us pretty well, up pretty tight, and we might as well admit to this crime," and that he replied, "I am sorry but I would like to have advice from my lawyer." A police officer testified that although petitioner was not formally charged "he was in custody" and "couldn't walk out the door."

Shortly after petitioner reached police headquarters, his retained lawyer arrived. [The lawyer testified that the police refused to allow him to talk to his client. He did catch a glimpse of Escobedo through an open door and they exchanged waves.]

Petitioner testified that during the course of the interrogation he repeatedly asked to speak to his lawyer and that the police said that his lawyer "didn't want to see" him. The testimony of the police officers confirmed these accounts in substantial detail.

Notwithstanding repeated requests by each, petitioner and his retained lawyer were afforded no opportunity to consult during the course of the entire interrogation. At one point, as previously noted, petitioner and his attorney came into each other's view for a few moments but the attorney was quickly ushered away. Petitioner testified "that he heard a detective telling the attorney the latter would not be allowed to talk to [him] 'until they were done' " and that he heard the attorney being refused permission to remain in the adjoining room. A police officer testified that he had told the lawyer that he could not see petitioner until "we were through interrogating" him.

There is testimony by the police that during the interrogation, petitioner, a 22–year-old of Mexican extraction with no record of previous experience with the police, "was handcuffed" in a standing position and that he "was nervous, he had circles under his eyes and he was upset" and was "agitated" because "he had not slept well in over a week."

It is undisputed that during the course of the interrogation Officer Montejano, who "grew up" in petitioner's neighborhood, who knew his family, and who uses "Spanish language in [his] police work," conferred alone with petitioner "for about a quarter of an hour ... " Petitioner testified that the officer said to him "in Spanish that my sister and I could go home if I pinned it on Benedict DiGerlando," that "he would see to it that we would go home and be held only as witnesses, if anything, if we had made a statement against DiGerlando..., that we would be able to go home that night." Petitioner testified that he made the statement in issue because of this assurance. Officer Montejano denied offering any such assurance.

A police officer testified that during the interrogation the following occurred:

> "I informed him of what DiGerlando told me and when I did, he told me that DiGerlando was [lying] and I said, 'Would you care to tell DiGerlando that?' and he said, 'Yes, I will.' So, I brought...Escobedo in and he confronted DiGerlando and he told him that he was lying and said, 'I didn't shoot Manuel, you did it.' "

In this way, petitioner, for the first time admitted to some knowledge of the crime. After that he made additional statements further implicating himself in the murder plot. At this point an Assistant State's Attorney, Theodore J. Cooper, was summoned "to take" a statement. Mr. Cooper, an experienced lawyer who was assigned to the Homicide Division to take "statements from some defendants and some prisoners that they had in custody," "took" petitioner's statement by asking carefully framed questions apparently designed to assure the admissibility into evidence of the resulting answers. Mr. Cooper testified that he did not advise petitioner of his constitutional rights, and it is undisputed that no one during the course of the interrogation so advised him.

Petitioner moved both before and during trial to suppress the incriminating statement, but the motions were denied. Petitioner was convicted of murder and he appealed the conviction.

* * *

The interrogation here was conducted before petitioner was formally indicted. But in the context of this case, that fact should make no difference. When petitioner requested, and was denied, an opportunity to consult with his lawyer, the investigation had ceased to be a general investigation of an unsolved crime. Petitioner had become the accused, and the purpose of the interrogation was to "get him" to confess his guilt despite his constitutional right not to do so. At the time of his arrest and throughout the course of the interrogation, the police told petitioner that they had convincing evidence that he had fired the fatal shots. Without informing him of his absolute right to remain silent in the face of this accusation, the police urged him to make a statement.
* * *

* * *

In Gideon v. Wainwright, we held that every person accused of a crime, whether state or federal, is entitled to a lawyer at trial. The rule sought by the State here, however, would make the trial no more than an appeal from the interrogation; and the "right to use counsel at the formal trial [would be] a very hollow thing [if], for all practical purposes, the conviction is already assured by pretrial examination." * * *

It is argued that if the right to counsel is afforded prior to indictment, the number of confessions obtained by the police will diminish significantly, because most confessions are obtained during the period between arrest and indictment, and "any lawyer worth his salt will tell the suspect in no uncertain terms to make no statement to police under any circumstances." *Watts v. Indiana,* 338 U.S. 49, 59, 69 S.Ct. 1347, 93 L.Ed. 1801 (1949) (Jackson, J., concurring in part and dissenting in part). This argument, of course, cuts two ways. The fact that many confessions are obtained during this period points up its critical nature as a stage when legal aid and advice are surely needed. The right to counsel would indeed be hollow if it began at a period when few confessions were obtained. There is necessarily a direct relationship between the importance of a stage to the police in their quest for a confession and the criticalness of that stage to the accused in his need for legal advice. Our Constitution, unlike some others, strikes the balance in favor of the right of the accused to be advised by his lawyer of his privilege against self-incrimination.

We have learned the lesson of history, ancient and modern, that a system of criminal law enforcement which comes to depend on the "confession" will, in the long run, be less reliable and more subject to abuses than a system which depends on extrinsic evidence independently secured through skillful investigation. * * * We have also learned the companion lesson of history that no system of criminal justice can, or should, survive if it comes to depend for its continued effectiveness on the citizens' abdication through unawareness of their constitutional rights. No system worth preserving should have to *fear* that if an accused is permitted to consult with a lawyer, he will become aware of, and exercise, these rights. If the exercise of constitutional rights will thwart the effectiveness of a system of law enforcement, then there is something very wrong with that system.

We hold, therefore, that where, as here, the investigation is no longer a general inquiry into an unsolved crime but has begun to focus on a particular suspect, the suspect has been taken into police custody, the police carry out a process of interrogations that lends itself to eliciting incriminating statements, the suspect has requested and been denied an opportunity to consult with his lawyer, and the police have not effectively warned him of his absolute constitutional right to remain silent, the accused has been denied "the Assistance of Counsel" in violation of the Sixth Amendment to the Constitution as made obligatory upon the States by the Fourteenth Amendment, and that no statement elicited by the police during the interrogation may be used against him at a criminal trial. * * * *Reversed and remanded.*

[The dissenting opinions of Justice Harlan, Justice Stewart, and Justice White, are omitted.]

2. *Miranda*

MIRANDA v. ARIZONA

Supreme Court of the United States, 1966.
384 U.S. 436, 86 S.Ct. 1602, 16 L.Ed.2d 694.

Mr. Chief Justice Warren delivered the opinion of the Court.

The cases before us raise questions which go to the roots of our concepts of American criminal jurisprudence: the restraints society must observe consistent with the Federal Constitution in prosecuting individuals for crime. More specifically, we deal with the admissibility of statements obtained from an individual who is subjected to custodial police interrogation and the necessity for procedures which assure that the individual is accorded his privilege under the Fifth Amendment to the Constitution not to be compelled to incriminate himself.

* * *

Our holding will be spelled out with some specificity in the pages which follow but briefly stated it is this: the prosecution may not use statements, whether exculpatory or inculpatory, stemming from custodial interrogation of the defendant unless it demonstrates the use of procedural safeguards effective to secure the privilege against self-incrimination. By custodial interrogation, we mean questioning initiated by law enforcement officers after a person has been taken into custody or otherwise deprived of his freedom of action in any significant way.[4] As for the procedural safeguards to be employed, unless other fully effective means are devised to inform accused persons of their right of silence and to assure a continuous opportunity to exercise it, the following measures are required. Prior to any questioning, the person must be warned that he has a right to remain silent, that any statement he does make may be used as evidence against him, and that he has a right to the presence of an attorney, either retained or appointed. The defendant may waive effectuation of these rights, provided the waiver is made voluntarily, knowingly and intelligently. If, however, he indicates in any manner and at any stage of the process that he wishes to consult with an attorney before speaking there can be no questioning. Likewise, if the individual is alone and indicates in any manner that he does not wish to be interrogated, the police may not question him. The mere fact that he may have answered some questions or volunteered some statements on his own does not deprive him of the right to refrain from answering any further inquiries until he has consulted with an attorney and thereafter consents to be questioned.

I

The constitutional issue we decide in each of these cases is the admissibility of statements obtained from a defendant questioned while

---

4. This is what we meant in *Escobedo* when we spoke of an investigation which had focused on an accused.

in custody or otherwise deprived of his freedom of action in any significant way. In each, the defendant was questioned by police officers, detectives, or a prosecuting attorney in a room in which he was cut off from the outside world. In none of these cases was the defendant given a full and effective warning of his rights at the outset of the interrogation process. In all the cases, the questioning elicited oral admissions, and in three of them, signed statements as well which were admitted at their trials. They all thus share salient features—incommunicado interrogation of individuals in a police-dominated atmosphere, resulting in self-incriminating statements without full warnings of constitutional rights.

An understanding of the nature and setting of this in-custody interrogation is essential to our decisions today. The difficulty in depicting what transpires at such interrogations stems from the fact that in this country they have largely taken place incommunicado. From extensive factual studies undertaken in the early 1930's, including the famous Wickersham Report to Congress by a Presidential Commission, it is clear that police violence and the "third degree" flourished at that time. In a series of cases decided by this Court long after these studies, the police resorted to physical brutality—beating, hanging, whipping—and to sustained and protracted questioning incommunicado in order to extort confessions. The Commission on Civil Rights in 1961 found much evidence to indicate that "some policemen still resort to physical force to obtain confessions." The use of physical brutality and violence is not, unfortunately, relegated to the past or to any part of the country. Only recently in Kings County, New York, the police brutally beat, kicked and placed lighted cigarette butts on the back of a potential witness under interrogation for the purpose of securing a statement incriminating a third party.

* * *

[T]he modern practice of in-custody interrogation is psychologically rather than physically oriented. [T]his Court has recognized that coercion can be mental as well as physical, and that the blood of the accused is not the only hallmark of an unconstitutional inquisition." Interrogation still takes place in privacy. Privacy results in secrecy and this in turn results in a gap in our knowledge as to what in fact goes on in the interrogation rooms. A valuable source of information about present police practices, however, may be found in various police manuals and texts which document procedures employed with success in the past, and which recommend various other effective tactics. These texts are used by law enforcement agencies themselves as guides. It should be noted that these texts professedly present the most enlightened and effective means presently used to obtain statements through custodial interrogation. By considering these texts and other data, it is possible to describe procedures observed and noted around the country.

The officers are told by the manuals that the "principal psychological factor contributing to a successful interrogation is *privacy*—being alone with the person under interrogation." The efficacy of this tactic has been explained as follows:

> "If at all practicable, the interrogation should take place in the investigator's office or at least in a room of his own choice. The subject should be deprived of every psychological advantage. In his own home he may be confident, indignant, or recalcitrant. He is more keenly aware of his rights and more reluctant to tell of his indiscretions or criminal behavior within the walls of his home. Moreover his family and other friends are nearby, their presence lending moral support. In his own office, the investigator possesses all the advantages. The atmosphere suggests the invincibility of the forces of the law."

To highlight the isolation and unfamiliar surroundings, the manuals instruct the police to display an air of confidence in the suspect's guilt and from outward appearance to maintain only an interest in confirming certain details. The guilt of the subject is to be posited as a fact. The interrogator should direct his comments toward the reasons why the subject committed the act, rather than court failure by asking the subject whether he did it. Like other men, perhaps the subject has had a bad family life, had an unhappy childhood, had too much to drink, had an unrequited desire for women. The officers are instructed to minimize the moral seriousness of the offense, to cast blame on the victim or on society. These tactics are designed to put the subject in a psychological state where his story is but an elaboration of what the police purport to know already—that he is guilty. Explanations to the contrary are dismissed and discouraged.

The texts thus stress that the major qualities an interrogator should possess are patience and perseverance. One writer describes the efficacy of these characteristics in this manner:

> "In the preceding paragraphs emphasis has been placed on kindness and stratagems. The investigator will, however, encounter many situations where the sheer weight of his personality will be the deciding factor. Where emotional appeals and tricks are employed to no avail, he must rely on an oppressive atmosphere of dogged persistence. He must interrogate steadily and without relent, leaving the subject no prospect of surcease. He must dominate his subject and overwhelm him with his inexorable will to obtain the truth. He should interrogate for a spell of several hours pausing only for the subject's necessities in acknowledgment of the need to avoid a charge of duress that can be technically substantiated. In a serious case, the interrogation may continue for days, with the required intervals for food and sleep, but with no respite from the atmosphere of domination. It is possible in this way to induce the subject to talk without resorting to duress or coercion. The method should be used only when the guilt of the subject appears highly probable."

* * *

The interrogators sometimes are instructed to induce a confession out of trickery. The technique here is quite effective in crimes which require identification or which run in series. In the identification situation, the interrogator may take a break in his questioning to place the subject among a group of men in a line-up. "The witness or complainant (previously coached, if necessary) studies the line-up and confidently points out the subject as the guilty party." Then the questioning resumes "as though there were now no doubt about the guilt of the subject." * * *

* * *

The manuals also contain instructions for police on how to handle the individual who refuses to discuss the matter entirely, or who asks for an attorney or relatives. The examiner is to concede him the right to remain silent. "This usually has a very undermining effect. [H]owever, the officer is told to point out the incriminating significance of the suspect's refusal to talk:

> "Joe, you have a right to remain silent. That's your privilege and I'm the last person in the world who'll try to take it away from you. If that's the way you want to leave this, O. K. But let me ask you this. Suppose you were in my shoes and I were in yours and you called me in to ask me about this and I told you, 'I don't want to answer any of your questions.' You'd think I had something to hide, and you'd probably be right in thinking that. That's exactly what I'll have to think about you, and so will everybody else. So let's sit here and talk this whole thing over."

* * *

Even without employing brutality, the "third degree" or the specific stratagems described above, the very fact of custodial interrogation exacts a heavy toll on individual liberty and trades on the weakness of individuals.[24] * * * In other settings, these individuals might have exercised their constitutional rights. In the incommunicado police-dominated atmosphere, they succumbed.

In these cases, we might not find the defendants' statements to have been involuntary in traditional terms. Our concern for adequate safeguards to protect precious Fifth Amendment rights is, of course, not lessened in the slightest. In each of the cases, the defendant was thrust into an unfamiliar atmosphere and run through menacing police interrogation procedures. The potentiality for compulsion is forcefully apparent, for example, in *Miranda*, where the indigent Mexican defendant was a seriously disturbed individual with pronounced sexual fantasies, and in

---

24. Interrogation procedures may even give rise to a false confession. The most recent conspicuous example occurred in New York, in 1964, when a Negro of limited intelligence confessed to two brutal murders and a rape which he had not committed. When this was discovered, the prosecutor was reported as saying: "Call it what you want—brain-washing, hypnosis, fright. They made him give an untrue confession. The only thing I don't believe is that Whitmore was beaten." N. Y. Times, Jan. 28, 1965, p. 1, col. 5. * * *

Stewart, in which the defendant was an indigent Los Angeles Negro who had dropped out of school in the sixth grade. To be sure, the records do not evince overt physical coercion or patent psychological ploys. The fact remains that in none of these cases did the officers undertake to afford appropriate safeguards at the outset of the interrogation to insure that the statements were truly the product of free choice.

It is obvious that such an interrogation environment is created for no purpose other than to subjugate the individual to the will of his examiner. This atmosphere carries its own badge of intimidation. To be sure, this is not physical intimidation, but it is equally destructive of human dignity. The current practice of incommunicado interrogation is at odds with one of our Nation's most cherished principles—that the individual may not be compelled to incriminate himself. Unless adequate protective devices are employed to dispel the compulsion inherent in custodial surroundings, no statement obtained from the defendant can truly be the product of his free choice.

From the foregoing, we can readily perceive an intimate connection between the privilege against self-incrimination and police custodial questioning. It is fitting to turn to history and precedent underlying the Self–Incrimination Clause to determine its applicability in this situation.

II

* * *

[T]he privilege against self-incrimination—the essential mainstay of our adversary system—is founded on a complex of values. All these policies point to one overriding thought: the constitutional foundation underlying the privilege is the respect a government—state or federal— must accord to the dignity and integrity of its citizens. To maintain a "fair state-individual balance," to require the government "to shoulder the entire load," to respect the inviolability of the human personality, our accusatory system of criminal justice demands that the government seeking to punish an individual produce the evidence against him by its own independent labors, rather than by the cruel, simple expedient of compelling it from his own mouth. In sum, the privilege is fulfilled only when the person is guaranteed the right "to remain silent unless he chooses to speak in the unfettered exercise of his own will."

* * *

III

Today, then, there can be no doubt that the Fifth Amendment privilege is available outside of criminal court proceedings and serves to protect persons in all settings in which their freedom of action is curtailed in any significant way from being compelled to incriminate themselves. We have concluded that without proper safeguards the process of in-custody interrogation of persons suspected or accused of crime contains inherently compelling pressures which work to undermine the individual's will to resist and to compel him to speak where he would not otherwise do so freely. In order to combat these pressures and to permit a full opportunity to exercise the privilege against self-incrimination, the accused must be adequately and effectively apprised of his rights and the exercise of those rights must be fully honored.

It is impossible for us to foresee the potential alternatives for protecting the privilege which might be devised by Congress or the States in the exercise of their creative rule-making capacities. Therefore we cannot say that the Constitution necessarily requires adherence to any particular solution for the inherent compulsions of the interrogation process as it is presently conducted. Our decision in no way creates a constitutional straitjacket which will handicap sound efforts at reform, nor is it intended to have this effect. We encourage Congress and the States to continue their laudable search for increasingly effective ways of protecting the rights of the individual while promoting efficient enforcement of our criminal laws. However, unless we are shown other procedures which are at least as effective in apprising accused persons of their right of silence and in assuring a continuous opportunity to exercise it, the following safeguards must be observed.

At the outset, if a person in custody is to be subjected to interrogation, he must first be informed in clear and unequivocal terms that he has the right to remain silent. For those unaware of the privilege, the warning is needed simply to make them aware of it—the threshold requirement for an intelligent decision as to its exercise. More important, such a warning is an absolute prerequisite in overcoming the inherent pressures of the interrogation atmosphere. It is not just the subnormal or woefully ignorant who succumb to an interrogator's imprecations, whether implied or expressly stated, that the interrogation will continue until a confession is obtained or that silence in the face of accusation is itself damning and will bode ill when presented to a jury. Further, the warning will show the individual that his interrogators are prepared to recognize his privilege should he choose to exercise it.

The Fifth Amendment privilege is so fundamental to our system of constitutional rule and the expedient of giving an adequate warning as to the availability of the privilege so simple, we will not pause to inquire in individual cases whether the defendant was aware of his rights without a warning being given. Assessments of the knowledge the defendant possessed, based on information as to his age, education, intelligence, or prior contact with authorities, can never be more than speculation; a warning is a clearcut fact. More important, whatever the background of the person interrogated, a warning at the time of the interrogation is indispensable to overcome its pressures and to insure that the individual knows he is free to exercise the privilege at that point in time.

The warning of the right to remain silent must be accompanied by the explanation that anything said can and will be used against the individual in court. This warning is needed in order to make him aware not only of the privilege, but also of the consequences of forgoing it. It is only through an awareness of these consequences that there can be any assurance of real understanding and intelligent exercise of the privilege. Moreover, this warning may serve to make the individual more acutely aware that he is faced with a phase of the adversary system—that he is not in the presence of persons acting solely in his interest.

The circumstances surrounding in-custody interrogation can operate very quickly to overbear the will of one merely made aware of his privilege by his interrogators. Therefore, the right to have counsel present at the interrogation is indispensable to the protection of the Fifth Amendment privilege under the system we delineate today. Our aim is to assure that the individual's right to choose between silence and speech remains unfettered throughout the interrogation process. A once-stated warning, delivered by those who will conduct the interrogation, cannot itself suffice to that end among those who most require knowledge of their rights. A mere warning given by the interrogators is not alone sufficient to accomplish that end. Prosecutors themselves claim that the admonishment of the right to remain silent without more "will benefit only the recidivist and the professional." Even preliminary advice given to the accused by his own attorney can be swiftly overcome by the secret interrogation process. Thus, the need for counsel to protect the Fifth Amendment privilege comprehends not merely a right to consult with counsel prior to questioning, but also to have counsel present during any questioning if the defendant so desires.

The presence of counsel at the interrogation may serve several significant subsidiary functions as well. If the accused decides to talk to his interrogators, the assistance of counsel can mitigate the dangers of untrustworthiness. With a lawyer present the likelihood that the police will practice coercion is reduced, and if coercion is nevertheless exercised the lawyer can testify to it in court. The presence of a lawyer can also help to guarantee that the accused gives a fully accurate statement to the police and that the statement is rightly reported by the prosecution at trial.

An individual need not make a pre-interrogation request for a lawyer. While such request affirmatively secures his right to have one, his failure to ask for a lawyer does not constitute a waiver. No effective waiver of the right to counsel during interrogation can be recognized unless specifically made after the warnings we here delineate have been given. The accused who does not know his rights and therefore does not make a request may be the person who most needs counsel. * * *

* * *

Accordingly we hold that an individual held for interrogation must be clearly informed that he has the right to consult with a lawyer and to have the lawyer with him during interrogation under the system for protecting the privilege we delineate today. As with the warnings of the right to remain silent and that anything stated can be used in evidence against him, this warning is an absolute prerequisite to interrogation. No amount of circumstantial evidence that the person may have been aware of this right will suffice to stand in its stead. Only through such a warning is there ascertainable assurance that the accused was aware of this right.

If an individual indicates that he wishes the assistance of counsel before any interrogation occurs, the authorities cannot rationally ignore or deny his request on the basis that the individual does not have or cannot afford a retained attorney. The financial ability of the individual has no relationship to the scope of the rights involved here. The privilege against self-incrimination secured by the Constitution applies to all individuals. The need for counsel in order to protect the privilege exists for the indigent as well as the affluent. In fact, were we to limit these constitutional rights to those who can retain an attorney, our decisions today would be of little significance. The cases before us as well as the vast majority of confession cases with which we have dealt in the past involve those unable to retain counsel. While authorities are not required to relieve the accused of his poverty, they have the obligation not to take advantage of indigence in the administration of justice. * * *

In order fully to apprise a person interrogated of the extent of his rights under this system then, it is necessary to warn him not only that he has the right to consult with an attorney, but also that if he is indigent a lawyer will be appointed to represent him. Without this additional warning, the admonition of the right to consult with counsel would often be understood as meaning only that he can consult with a lawyer if he has one or has the funds to obtain one. The warning of a right to counsel would be hollow if not couched in terms that would convey to the indigent—the person most often subjected to interrogation—the knowledge that he too has a right to have counsel present. As with the warnings of the right to remain silent and of the general right to counsel, only by effective and express explanation to the indigent of this right can there be assurance that he was truly in a position to exercise it.

Once warnings have been given, the subsequent procedure is clear. If the individual indicates in any manner, at any time prior to or during questioning, that he wishes to remain silent, the interrogation must cease.[44] At this point he has shown that he intends to exercise his Fifth Amendment privilege; any statement taken after the person invokes his privilege cannot be other than the product of compulsion, subtle or otherwise. Without the right to cut off questioning, the setting of in-custody interrogation operates on the individual to overcome free choice in producing a statement after the privilege has been once invoked. If the individual states that he wants an attorney, the interrogation must cease until an attorney is present. At that time, the individual must have

---

44. If an individual indicates his desire to remain silent, but has an attorney present, there may be some circumstances in which further questioning would be permissible. In the absence of evidence of overbearing, statements then made in the presence of counsel might be free of the compelling influence of the interrogation process and might fairly be construed as a waiver of the privilege for purposes of these statements.

an opportunity to confer with the attorney and to have him present during any subsequent questioning. If the individual cannot obtain an attorney and he indicates that he wants one before speaking to police, they must respect his decision to remain silent.

This does not mean, as some have suggested, that each police station must have a "station house lawyer" present at all times to advise prisoners. * * * If authorities conclude that they will not provide counsel during a reasonable period of time in which investigation in the field is carried out, they may refrain from doing so without violating the person's Fifth Amendment privilege so long as they do not question him during that time.

If the interrogation continues without the presence of an attorney and a statement is taken, a heavy burden rests on the government to demonstrate that the defendant knowingly and intelligently waived his privilege against self-incrimination and his right to retained or appointed counsel. This Court has always set high standards of proof for the waiver of constitutional rights, *Johnson* v. *Zerbst*, 304 U.S. 458, 58 S.Ct. 1019, 82 L.Ed. 1461 (1938), and we re-assert these standards as applied to in-custody interrogation. Since the State is responsible for establishing the isolated circumstances under which the interrogation takes place and has the only means of making available corroborated evidence of warnings given during incommunicado interrogation, the burden is rightly on its shoulders.

An express statement that the individual is willing to make a statement and does not want an attorney followed closely by a statement could constitute a waiver. But a valid waiver will not be presumed simply from the silence of the accused after warnings are given or simply from the fact that a confession was in fact eventually obtained. * * *

* * *

Whatever the testimony of the authorities as to waiver of rights by an accused, the fact of lengthy interrogation or incommunicado incarceration before a statement is made is strong evidence that the accused did not validly waive his rights. In these circumstances the fact that the individual eventually made a statement is consistent with the conclusion that the compelling influence of the interrogation finally forced him to do so. It is inconsistent with any notion of a voluntary relinquishment of the privilege. Moreover, any evidence that the accused was threatened, tricked, or cajoled into a waiver will, of course, show that the defendant did not voluntarily waive his privilege. The requirement of warnings and waiver of rights is a fundamental with respect to the Fifth Amendment privilege and not simply a preliminary ritual to existing methods of interrogation.

The warnings required and the waiver necessary in accordance with our opinion today are, in the absence of a fully effective equivalent, prerequisites to the admissibility of any statement made by a defendant. No distinction can be drawn between statements which are direct confessions and statements which amount to "admissions" of part or all of an offense. The privilege against self-incrimination protects the individual from being compelled to incriminate himself in any manner; it does not distinguish degrees of incrimination. Similarly, for precisely the same reason, no distinction may be drawn between inculpatory statements and statements alleged to be merely "exculpatory." If a statement made were in fact truly exculpatory it would, of course, never be used by the prosecution. In fact, statements merely intended to be exculpatory by the defendant are often used to impeach his testimony at trial or to demonstrate untruths in the statement given under interrogation and thus to prove guilt by implication. * * *

* * *

Our decision is not intended to hamper the traditional function of police officers in investigating crime. When an individual is in custody on probable cause, the police may, of course, seek out evidence in the field to be used at trial against him. Such investigation may include inquiry of persons not under restraint. General on-the-scene questioning as to facts surrounding a crime or other general questioning of citizens in the fact-finding process is not affected by our holding. It is an act of responsible citizenship for individuals to give whatever information they may have to aid in law enforcement. In such situations the compelling atmosphere inherent in the process of in-custody interrogation is not necessarily present.

In dealing with statements obtained through interrogation, we do not purport to find all confessions inadmissible. Confessions remain a proper element in law enforcement. Any statement given freely and voluntarily without any compelling influences is, of course, admissible in evidence. The fundamental import of the privilege while an individual is in custody is not whether he is allowed to talk to the police without the benefit of warnings and counsel, but whether he can be interrogated. There is no requirement that police stop a person who enters a police station and states that he wishes to confess to a crime, or a person who calls the police to offer a confession or any other statement he desires to make. Volunteered statements of any kind are not barred by the Fifth Amendment and their admissibility is not affected by our holding today.

* * *

IV

* * *

Over the years the Federal Bureau of Investigation has compiled an exemplary record of effective law enforcement while advising any suspect or arrested person, at the outset of an interview, that he is not required to make a statement, that any statement may be used against him in court, that the individual may obtain the services of an attorney of his own choice and, more recently, that he has a right to free counsel if he is unable to pay. * * *

* * *

The experience in some other countries also suggests that the danger to law enforcement in curbs on interrogation is overplayed. The English procedure since 1912 under the Judges' Rules is significant. As recently strengthened, the Rules require that a cautionary warning be given an accused by a police officer as soon as he has evidence that affords reasonable grounds for suspicion; they also require that any statement made be given by the accused without questioning by police. The right of the individual to consult with an attorney during this period is expressly recognized.

The safeguards present under Scottish law may be even greater than in England. Scottish judicial decisions bar use in evidence of most confessions obtained through police interrogation. In India, confessions made to police not in the presence of a magistrate have been excluded by rule of evidence since 1872, at a time when it operated under British law. Identical provisions appear in the Evidence Ordinance of Ceylon, enacted in 1895. Similarly, in our country the Uniform Code of Military Justice has long provided that no suspect may be interrogated without first being warned of his right not to make a statement and that any statement he makes may be used against him. Denial of the right to consult counsel during interrogation has also been proscribed by military tribunals. There appears to have been no marked detrimental effect on criminal law enforcement in these jurisdictions as a result of these rules. Conditions of law enforcement in our country are sufficiently similar to permit reference to this experience as assurance that lawlessness will not result from warning an individual of his rights or allowing him to exercise them. Moreover, it is consistent with our legal system that we give at least as much protection to these rights as is given in the jurisdictions described. We deal in our country with rights grounded in a specific requirement of the Fifth Amendment of the Constitution, whereas other jurisdictions arrived at their conclusions on the basis of principles of justice not so specifically defined.

* * *

Mr. Justice Clark, dissenting in [part] and concurring in [part].

* * *

III

* * * Under the "totality of circumstances" rule * * * I would consider in each case whether the police officer prior to custodial interrogation added the warning that the suspect might have counsel present at the interrogation and, further, that a court would appoint one at his request if he was too poor to employ counsel. In the absence of warnings, the burden would be on the State to prove that counsel was knowingly and intelligently waived or that in the totality of the circum-

stances, including the failure to give the necessary warnings, the confession was clearly voluntary.

Rather than employing the arbitrary Fifth Amendment rule which the Court lays down I would follow the more pliable dictates of the Due Process Clauses of the Fifth and Fourteenth Amendments which we are accustomed to administering and which we know from our cases are effective instruments in protecting persons in police custody. In this way we would not be acting in the dark nor in one full sweep changing the traditional rules of custodial interrogation which this Court has for so long recognized as a justifiable and proper tool in balancing individual rights against the rights of society. It will be soon enough to go further when we are able to appraise with somewhat better accuracy the effect of such a holding.

* * *

[The dissenting opinion of JUSTICE HARLAN, whom JUSTICE STEWART and JUSTICE WHITE joined, is omitted.]

MR. JUSTICE WHITE, with whom MR. JUSTICE HARLAN and MR. JUSTICE STEWART join, dissenting.

* * *

IV

* * *

The obvious underpinning of the Court's decision is a deep-seated distrust of all confessions. As the Court declares that the accused may not be interrogated without counsel present, absent a waiver of the right to counsel, and as the Court all but admonishes the lawyer to advise the accused to remain silent, the result adds up to a judicial judgment that evidence from the accused should not be used against him in any way, whether compelled or not. This is the not so subtle overtone of the opinion—that it is inherently wrong for the police to gather evidence from the accused himself. And this is precisely the nub of this dissent. I see nothing wrong or immoral, and certainly nothing unconstitutional, in the police's asking a suspect whom they have reasonable cause to arrest whether or not he killed his wife or in confronting him with the evidence on which the arrest was based, at least where he has been plainly advised that he may remain completely silent. Until today, "the admissions or confessions of the prisoner, when voluntarily and freely made, have always ranked high in the scale of incriminating evidence." Particularly when corroborated, as where the police have confirmed the accused's disclosure of the hiding place of implements or fruits of the crime, such confessions have the highest reliability and significantly contribute to the certitude with which we may believe the accused is guilty. Moreover, it is by no means certain that the process of confessing is injurious to the accused. To the contrary it may provide psychological relief and enhance the prospects for rehabilitation.

This is not to say that the value of respect for the inviolability of the accused's individual personality should be accorded no weight or that all confessions should be indiscriminately admitted. This Court has long read the Constitution to proscribe compelled confessions, a salutary rule from which there should be no retreat. But I see no sound basis, factual or otherwise, and the Court gives none, for concluding that the present rule against the receipt of coerced confessions is inadequate for the task of sorting out inadmissible evidence and must be replaced by the *per se* rule which is now imposed. Even if the new concept can be said to have advantages of some sort over the present law, they are far outweighed by its likely undesirable impact on other very relevant and important interests.

The most basic function of any government is to provide for the security of the individual and of his property. These ends of society are served by the criminal laws which for the most part are aimed at the prevention of crime. Without the reasonably effective performance of the task of preventing private violence and retaliation, it is idle to talk about human dignity and civilized values.

* * *

In some unknown number of cases the Court's rule will return a killer, a rapist or other criminal to the streets and to the environment which produced him, to repeat his crime whenever it pleases him. As a consequence, there will not be a gain, but a loss, in human dignity. The real concern is not the unfortunate consequences of this new decision on the criminal law as an abstract, disembodied series of authoritative proscriptions, but the impact on those who rely on the public authority for protection and who without it can only engage in violent self-help with guns, knives and the help of their neighbors similarly inclined. There is, of course, a saving factor: the next victims are uncertain, unnamed and unrepresented in this case.

* * *

3. *Miranda* Applied: Custodial Interrogation

a. Custody

BERKEMER v. McCARTY

Supreme Court of the United States, 1984.
468 U.S. 420, 104 S.Ct. 3138, 82 L.Ed.2d 317.

Justice Marshall delivered the opinion of the Court.

This case presents two related questions: First, does our decision in *Miranda v. Arizona*, 384 U.S. 436, 86 S.Ct. 1602, 16 L.Ed.2d 694 (1966), govern the admissibility of statements made during custodial interrogation by a suspect accused of a misdemeanor traffic offense? Second, does the roadside questioning of a motorist detained pursuant to a traffic stop constitute custodial interrogation for the purposes of the doctrine enunciated in *Miranda*?

I

A

The parties have stipulated to the essential facts. On the evening of March 31, 1980, Trooper Williams of the Ohio State Highway Patrol observed respondent's car weaving in and out of a lane on Interstate Highway 270. After following the car for two miles, Williams forced respondent to stop and asked him to get out of the vehicle. When respondent complied, Williams noticed that he was having difficulty standing. At that point, "Williams concluded that [respondent] would be charged with a traffic offense and, therefore, his freedom to leave the scene was terminated." However, respondent was not told that he would be taken into custody. Williams then asked respondent to perform a field sobriety test, commonly known as a "balancing test." Respondent could not do so without falling.

While still at the scene of the traffic stop, Williams asked respondent whether he had been using intoxicants. Respondent replied that "he had consumed two beers and had smoked several joints of marijuana a short time before." Respondent's speech was slurred, and Williams had difficulty understanding him. Williams thereupon formally placed respondent under arrest and transported him in the patrol car to the Franklin County Jail.

At the jail, respondent was given an intoxilyzer test to determine the concentration of alcohol in his blood. The test did not detect any alcohol whatsoever in respondent's system. Williams then resumed questioning respondent in order to obtain information for inclusion in the State Highway Patrol Alcohol Influence Report. Respondent answered affirmatively a question whether he had been drinking. When then asked if he was under the influence of alcohol, he said, "I guess, barely." Williams next asked respondent to indicate on the form whether the marihuana he had smoked had been treated with any chemicals. In the section of the report headed "Remarks," respondent wrote, "No [angel] dust or PCP in the pot. Rick McCarty."

At no point in this sequence of events did Williams or anyone else tell respondent that he had a right to remain silent, to consult with an attorney, and to have an attorney appointed for him if he could not afford one.

B

[McCarty was charged with the misdemeanor offense of operating a motor vehicle while under the influence of alcohol and/or drugs. His motion to exclude the various incriminating statements was denied, he pleaded "no contest" and was found guilty. The Supreme Court granted certiorari to resolve confusion in the federal and state courts regarding the applicability of our ruling in *Miranda* to interrogations involving minor offenses and traffic stops.]

II

* * *

Absent a compelling justification we surely would be unwilling so seriously to impair the simplicity and clarity of the holding of *Miranda*. Neither of the two arguments proffered by petitioner constitutes such a justification. Petitioner first contends that *Miranda* warnings are unnecessary when a suspect is questioned about a misdemeanor traffic offense, because the police have no reason to subject such a suspect to the sort of interrogation that most troubled the Court in *Miranda*. We cannot agree that the dangers of police abuse are so slight in this context. For example, the offense of driving while intoxicated is increasingly regarded in many jurisdictions as a very serious matter. Especially when the intoxicant at issue is a narcotic drug rather than alcohol, the police sometimes have difficulty obtaining evidence of this crime. Under such circumstances, the incentive for the police to try to induce the defendant to incriminate himself may well be substantial. Similar incentives are likely to be present when a person is arrested for a minor offense but the police suspect that a more serious crime may have been committed.

We do not suggest that there is any reason to think improper efforts were made in this case to induce respondent to make damaging admissions. More generally, we have no doubt that, in conducting most custodial interrogations of persons arrested for misdemeanor traffic offenses, the police behave responsibly and do not deliberately exert pressures upon the suspect to confess against his will. But the same might be said of custodial interrogations of persons arrested for felonies. The purposes of the safeguards prescribed by *Miranda* are to *ensure* that the police do not coerce or trick captive suspects into confessing, to relieve the " 'inherently compelling pressures' " generated by the custodial setting itself, " 'which work to undermine the individual's will to resist,' " and as much as possible to free courts from the task of scrutinizing individual cases to try to determine, after the fact, whether particular confessions were voluntary. Those purposes are implicated as much by in-custody questioning of persons suspected of misdemeanors as they are by questioning of persons suspected of felonies.

. Petitioner's second argument is that law enforcement would be more expeditious and effective in the absence of a requirement that persons arrested for traffic offenses be informed of their rights. Again, we are unpersuaded. The occasions on which the police arrest and then interrogate someone suspected only of a misdemeanor traffic offense are rare. The police are already well accustomed to giving *Miranda* warnings to persons taken into custody. Adherence to the principle that *all* suspects must be given such warnings will not significantly hamper the efforts of the police to investigate crimes.

We hold therefore that a person subjected to custodial interrogation is entitled to the benefit of the procedural safeguards enunciated in *Miranda*, regardless of the nature or severity of the offense of which he is suspected or for which he was arrested.

The implication of this holding is that the Court of Appeals was correct in ruling that the statements made by respondent at the County Jail were inadmissible. There can be no question that respondent was "in custody" at least as of the moment he was formally placed under arrest and instructed to get into the police car. Because he was not informed of his constitutional rights at that juncture, respondent's subsequent admissions should not have been used against him.

III

To assess the admissibility of the self-incriminating statements made by respondent prior to his formal arrest, we are obliged to address a second issue concerning the scope of our decision in *Miranda*: whether the roadside questioning of a motorist detained pursuant to a routine traffic stop should be considered "custodial interrogation." Respondent urges that it should, on the ground that *Miranda* by its terms applies whenever "a person has been taken into custody *or otherwise deprived of his freedom of action in any significant way*," (emphasis added). Petitioner contends that a holding that every detained motorist must be advised of his rights before being questioned would constitute an unwarranted extension of the *Miranda* doctrine.

It must be acknowledged at the outset that a traffic stop significantly curtails the "freedom of action" of the driver and the passengers, if any, of the detained vehicle. Under the law of most States, it is a crime either to ignore a policeman's signal to stop one's car or, once having stopped, to drive away without permission. Certainly few motorists would feel free either to disobey a directive to pull over or to leave the scene of a traffic stop without being told they might do so. Partly for these reasons, we have long acknowledged that "stopping an automobile and detaining its occupants constitute a 'seizure' within the meaning of [the Fourth] [Amendment], even though the purpose of the stop is limited and the resulting detention quite brief."

However, we decline to accord talismanic power to the phrase in the *Miranda* opinion emphasized by respondent. Fidelity to the doctrine announced in *Miranda* requires that it be enforced strictly, but only in those types of situations in which the concerns that powered the decision are implicated. Thus, we must decide whether a traffic stop exerts upon a detained person pressures that sufficiently impair his free exercise of his privilege against self-incrimination to require that he be warned of his constitutional rights.

Two features of an ordinary traffic stop mitigate the danger that a person questioned will be induced "to speak where he would not otherwise do so freely." First, detention of a motorist pursuant to a traffic stop is presumptively temporary and brief. The vast majority of roadside detentions last only a few minutes. A motorist's expectations, when he sees a policeman's light flashing behind him, are that he will be obliged to spend a short period of time answering questions and waiting while the officer checks his license and registration, that he may then be given a citation, but that in the end he most likely will be allowed to continue on his way. In this respect, questioning incident to an ordinary traffic stop is quite different from stationhouse interrogation, which frequently is prolonged, and in which the detainee often is aware that questioning will continue until he provides his interrogators the answers they seek.

Second, circumstances associated with the typical traffic stop are not such that the motorist feels completely at the mercy of the police. To be sure, the aura of authority surrounding an armed, uniformed officer and the knowledge that the officer has some discretion in deciding whether to issue a citation, in combination, exert some pressure on the detainee to respond to questions. But other aspects of the situation substantially offset these forces. Perhaps most importantly, the typical traffic stop is public, at least to some degree. Passersby, on foot or in other cars, witness the interaction of officer and motorist. This exposure to public view both reduces the ability of an unscrupulous policeman to use illegitimate means to elicit self-incriminating statements and diminishes the motorist's fear that, if he does not cooperate, he will be subjected to abuse. The fact that the detained motorist typically is confronted by only one or at most two policemen further mutes his sense of vulnerability. In short, the atmosphere surrounding an ordinary traffic stop is substantially less "police dominated" than that surrounding the kinds of interrogation at issue in *Miranda* itself, and in the subsequent cases in which we have applied *Miranda*.

In both of these respects, the usual traffic stop is more analogous to a so-called "*Terry* stop," see *Terry v. Ohio*, 392 U.S. 1, 88 S.Ct. 1868, 20 L.Ed.2d 889 (1968), than to a formal arrest. Under the Fourth Amendment, we have held, a policeman who lacks probable cause but whose "observations lead him reasonably to suspect" that a particular person has committed, is committing, or is about to commit a crime, may detain that person briefly in order to "investigate the circumstances that provoke suspicion." "[The] stop and inquiry must be 'reasonably related in scope to the justification for their initiation.' " Typically, this means that the officer may ask the detainee a moderate number of questions to determine his identity and to try to obtain information confirming or dispelling the officer's suspicions. But the detainee is not obliged to respond. And, unless the detainee's answers provide the officer with probable cause to arrest him, he must then be released. The comparatively nonthreatening character of detentions of this sort explains the absence of any suggestion in our opinions that *Terry* stops are subject to the dictates of *Miranda*. The similarly noncoercive aspect of ordinary traffic stops prompts us to hold that persons temporarily detained pursuant to such stops are not "in custody" for the purposes of *Miranda*.

Respondent contends that to "exempt" traffic stops from the coverage of *Miranda* will open the way to widespread abuse. Policemen will simply delay formally arresting detained motorists, and will subject them to sustained and intimidating interrogation at the scene of their initial detention. The net result, respondent contends, will be a serious threat to the rights that the *Miranda* doctrine is designed to protect.

We are confident that the state of affairs projected by respondent will not come to pass. It is settled that the safeguards prescribed by *Miranda* become applicable as soon as a suspect's freedom of action is curtailed to a "degree associated with formal arrest." If a motorist who has been detained pursuant to a traffic stop thereafter is subjected to treatment that renders him "in custody" for practical purposes, he will be entitled to the full panoply of protections prescribed by *Miranda*.

Admittedly, our adherence to the doctrine just recounted will mean that the police and lower courts will continue occasionally to have difficulty deciding exactly when a suspect has been taken into custody. Either a rule that *Miranda* applies to all traffic stops or a rule that a suspect need not be advised of his rights until he is formally placed under arrest would provide a clearer, more easily administered line. However, each of these two alternatives has drawbacks that make it unacceptable. The first would substantially impede the enforcement of the Nation's traffic laws—by compelling the police either to take the time to warn all detained motorists of their constitutional rights or to forgo use of self-incriminating statements made by those motorists— while doing little to protect citizens' Fifth Amendment rights. The second would enable the police to circumvent the constraints on custodial interrogations established by *Miranda*.

Turning to the case before us, we find nothing in the record that indicates that respondent should have been given *Miranda* warnings at any point prior to the time Trooper Williams placed him under arrest. For the reasons indicated above, we reject the contention that the initial stop of respondent's car, by itself, rendered him "in custody." And respondent has failed to demonstrate that, at any time between the initial stop and the arrest, he was subjected to restraints comparable to those associated with a formal arrest. Only a short period of time elapsed between the stop and the arrest. At no point during that interval was respondent informed that his detention would not be temporary. Although Trooper Williams apparently decided as soon as respondent stepped out of his car that respondent would be taken into custody and charged with a traffic offense, Williams never communicated his intention to respondent. A policeman's unarticulated plan has no bearing on the question whether a suspect was "in custody" at a particular time; the only relevant inquiry is how a reasonable man in the suspect's position would have understood his situation. Nor do other aspects of the interaction of Williams and respondent support the contention that respondent was exposed to "custodial interrogation" at the scene of the stop. From aught that appears in the stipulation of facts, a single police officer asked respondent a modest number of questions and requested him to perform a simple balancing test at a location visible to passing motorists. Treatment of this sort cannot fairly be characterized as the functional equivalent of formal arrest.

We conclude, in short, that respondent was not taken into custody for the purposes of *Miranda* until Williams arrested him. Consequently, the statements respondent made prior to that point were admissible against him.

* * *

[JUSTICE STEVENS's concurring opinion is omitted.]

YARBOROUGH, WARDEN v. ALVARADO

Supreme Court of the United States, 2004.
541 U.S. 652, 124 S.Ct. 2140, 158 L.Ed.2d 938.

JUSTICE KENNEDY delivered the opinion of the Court.

[The United States Court of Appeals for the Ninth Circuit ruled that a California state court unreasonably applied clearly established law when it held that the respondent was not in custody for *Miranda* purposes, and granted Alvarado a writ of habeas corpus. The Supreme Court reversed in a 4–1–4 decision that includes the Court's most recent analysis of the meaning of custody under *Miranda*.]

I

[Alvarado, who was 17 years old, was a suspect in a crime involving a carjacking and murder. Los Angeles County Sheriff's detective Comstock contacted Alvarado's mother at work with the message that she wished to speak with Alvarado, and Alvarado's parents brought him to a sheriff's station to be interviewed. Comstock took Alvarado to a small interview room and interviewed him while his parents waited in the lobby. Alvarado contended that his parents asked to be present during the interview but were rebuffed. The interview lasted about two hours, and was recorded by Comstock with Alvarado's knowledge. Alvarado was *not* given the warnings required under *Miranda* v. *Arizona*, 384 U.S. 436, 16 L.Ed.2d 694, 86 S.Ct. 1602 (1966) for custodial interrogations. At first Alvarado denied that he was present at the crime scene, but as the interrogation continued Alvarado slowly began to change his story. Eventually, Alvarado admitted he had helped Paul Soto try to steal the victim's truck by standing near the passenger side door, that he knew Soto was armed, and that he had helped hide the gun after the murder. Alvarado explained that he had expected Soto to scare the driver with the gun, but that he did not expect Soto to kill anyone.]

* * * California charged Soto and Alvarado with first-degree murder and attempted robbery. Citing *Miranda*, Alvarado moved to suppress his statements from the Comstock interview. The trial court denied the motion on the ground that the interview was non-custodial. [A]t the trial, Alvarado testified in his own defense. He offered an innocent explanation for his conduct, testifying that he happened to be standing in the parking lot of the mall when a gun went off nearby. The government's cross-examination relied on Alvarado's statement to Comstock. * * * When Alvarado denied particular statements, the prosecution countered by playing excerpts from the audio recording of the interview.

During cross-examination, Alvarado agreed that the interview with Comstock "was a pretty friendly conversation," that there was "sort of a free flow between [Alvarado] and Detective Comstock," and that Alvarado did not "feel coerced or threatened in any way" during the interview,

[Alvarado was convicted of first-degree murder and attempted robbery; the trial judge reduced his conviction to second-degree murder due to his comparatively minor role in the offense and sentenced Alvarado to a term of imprisonment of 15–years-to-life. The Court of Appeals reversed, and the Supreme Court in turn reversed the Ninth Circuit.]

II

* * *

Miranda itself held that preinterrogation warnings are required in the context of custodial interrogations given "the compulsion inherent in custodial surroundings." The Court explained that "custodial interrogation" meant "questioning initiated by law enforcement officers after a person has been taken into custody or otherwise deprived of his freedom of action in any significant way." The *Miranda* decision did not provide the Court with an opportunity to apply that test to a set of facts.

After *Miranda*, the Court first applied the custody test in *Oregon* v. *Mathiason*, 429 U.S. 492, 50 L.Ed.2d 714, 97 S.Ct. 711 (1977) *(per curiam)*. In *Mathiason,* a police officer contacted the suspect after a burglary victim identified him. The officer arranged to meet the suspect at a nearby police station. At the outset of the questioning, the officer stated his belief that the suspect was involved in the burglary but that he was not under arrest. During the 30–minute interview, the suspect admitted his guilt. He was then allowed to leave. The Court held that the questioning was not custodial because there was "no indication that the questioning took place in a context where [the suspect's] freedom to depart was restricted in any way." The Court noted that the suspect had come voluntarily to the police station, that he was informed that he was not under arrest, and that he was allowed to leave at the end of the interview.

* * *

Our more recent cases instruct that custody must be determined based on a how a reasonable person in the suspect's situation would perceive his circumstances. In *Berkemer* v. *McCarty,* 468 U.S. 420, 82 L.Ed.2d 317, 104 S.Ct. 3138 (1984), [t]he Court held the traffic stop noncustodial despite the officer's intent to arrest because he had not communicated that intent to the driver. "A policeman's unarticulated plan has no bearing on the question whether a suspect was 'in custody' at a particular time," the Court explained. "The only relevant inquiry is how a reasonable man in the suspect's position would have understood his situation." In a footnote, the Court cited a New York state case for the view that an objective test was preferable to a subjective test in part because it does not " 'place upon the police the burden of anticipating the frailties or idiosyncrasies of every person whom they question.' "

* * *

Finally, in *Thompson* v. *Keohane,* 516 U.S. 99 (1995), the Court offered the following description of the *Miranda* custody test:

"Two discrete inquiries are essential to the determination: first, what were the circumstances surrounding the interrogation; and second, given those circumstances, would a reasonable person have felt he or she was not at liberty to terminate the interrogation and leave. Once the scene is set and the players' lines and actions are reconstructed, the court must apply an objective test to resolve the ultimate inquiry: was there a formal arrest or restraint on freedom of movement of the degree associated with a formal arrest."

* * *

[W]e conclude that the state court's application of our clearly established law was reasonable. [F]air-minded jurists could disagree over whether Alvarado was in custody. On one hand, certain facts weigh against a finding that Alvarado was in custody. The police did not transport Alvarado to the station or require him to appear at a particular time. They did not threaten him or suggest he would be placed under arrest. Alvarado's parents remained in the lobby during the interview, suggesting that the interview would be brief. In fact, according to trial counsel for Alvarado, he and his parents were told that the interview was " 'not going to be long.' " During the interview, Comstock focused on Soto's crimes rather than Alvarado's. Instead of pressuring Alvarado with the threat of arrest and prosecution, she appealed to his interest in telling the truth and being helpful to a police officer. In addition, Comstock twice asked Alvarado if he wanted to take a break. At the end of the interview, Alvarado went home. All of these objective facts are consistent with an interrogation environment in which a reasonable person would have felt free to terminate the interview and leave. Indeed, a number of the facts echo those of *Mathiason*, a *per curiam* summary reversal in which we found it "clear from these facts" that the suspect was not in custody.

Other facts point in the opposite direction. Comstock interviewed Alvarado at the police station. The interview lasted two hours, four times longer than the 30–minute interview in *Mathiason*. Unlike the officer in *Mathiason*, Comstock did not tell Alvarado that he was free to leave. Alvarado was brought to the police station by his legal guardians rather than arriving on his own accord, making the extent of his control over his presence unclear. Counsel for Alvarado alleges that Alvarado's parents asked to be present at the interview but were rebuffed, a fact that— if known to Alvarado—might reasonably have led someone in Alvarado's position to feel more restricted than otherwise. These facts weigh in favor of the view that Alvarado was in custody.

These differing indications lead us to hold that the state court's application of our custody standard was reasonable. The Court of Appeals was nowhere close to the mark when it concluded otherwise. Although the question of what an "unreasonable application" of law might be difficult in some cases, it is not difficult here. The custody test is general, and the state court's application of our law fits within the matrix of our prior decisions. We cannot grant relief under [the Antiterrorism and Effective Death Penalty Act] by conducting our own independent inquiry into whether the state court was correct as a *de novo* matter. "[A] federal habeas court may not issue the writ simply because that court concludes in its independent judgment that the state-court decision applied [the law] incorrectly." Under that standard, relief cannot be granted.

III

* * *

* * * Our opinions applying the *Miranda* custody test have not mentioned the suspect's age, much less mandated its consideration. The only indications in the Court's opinions relevant to a suspect's experience with law enforcement have rejected reliance on such factors.

There is an important conceptual difference between the *Miranda* custody test and the line of cases from other contexts considering age and experience. The *Miranda* custody inquiry is an objective test [that] furthers "the clarity of [Miranda's] rule," ensuring that the police do not need "to make guesses as to [the circumstances] at issue before deciding how they may interrogate the suspect." * * *

[T]he argument that the custody inquiry states an objective rule designed to give clear guidance to the police, while consideration of a suspect's individual characteristics—including his age—could be viewed as creating a subjective inquiry. For these reasons, the state court's failure to consider Alvarado's age does not provide a proper basis for finding that the state court's decision was an unreasonable application of clearly established law.

* * *

The state court considered the proper factors and reached a reasonable conclusion. The judgment of the Court of Appeals is Reversed.

[JUSTICE O'CONNOR's concurring opinion is omitted.]

JUSTICE BREYER, with whom JUSTICE STEVENS, JUSTICE SOUTER, and JUSTICE GINSBURG join, dissenting.

In my view, Michael Alvarado clearly was "in custody" when the police questioned him (without *Miranda* warnings) about the murder of Francisco Castaneda. * * *

I

A

The law in this case asks judges to apply, not arcane or complex legal directives, but ordinary common sense. Would a reasonable person in Alvarado's position have felt free simply to get up and walk out of the small room in the station house at will during his 2–hour police interrogation? I ask the reader to put himself, or herself, in Alvarado's circumstances and then answer that question: Alvarado hears from his parents that he is needed for police questioning. His parents take him to the station. On arrival, a police officer separates him from his parents. His parents ask to come along, but the officer says they may not. Another officer says, " 'What do we have here; we are going to question a suspect.' "

The police take Alvarado to a small interrogation room, away from the station's public area. A single officer begins to question him, making clear in the process that the police have evidence that he participated in an attempted carjacking connected with a murder. When he says that he never saw any shooting, the officer suggests that he is lying, while adding that she is "giving [him] the opportunity to tell the truth" and "take care of himself." Toward the end of the questioning, the officer gives him permission to take a bathroom or water break. After two hours, by which time he has admitted he was involved in the attempted theft, knew about the gun, and helped to hide it, the questioning ends.

What reasonable person in the circumstances—brought to a police station by his parents at police request, put in a small interrogation room, questioned for a solid two hours, and confronted with claims that there is strong evidence that he participated in a serious crime, could have thought to himself, "Well, anytime I want to leave I can just get up and walk out"? If the person harbored any doubts, would he still think he might be free to leave once he recalls that the police officer has just refused to let his parents remain with him during questioning? Would he still think that he, rather than the officer, controls the situation?

There is only one possible answer to these questions. A reasonable person would *not* have thought he was free simply to pick up and leave in the middle of the interrogation. I believe the California courts were clearly wrong to hold the contrary, and the Ninth Circuit was right in concluding that those state courts unreasonably applied clearly established federal law.

* * *

C

What about Alvarado's youth? The fact that Alvarado was 17 helps to show that he was unlikely to have felt free to ignore his parents' request to come to the station. And a 17–year-old is more likely than, say, a 35–year-old, to take a police officer's assertion of authority to keep parents outside the room as an assertion of authority to keep their child inside as well.

The majority suggests that the law might *prevent* a judge from taking account of the fact that Alvarado was 17. I can find nothing in the law that supports that conclusion. Our cases do instruct lower courts to apply a "reasonable person" standard. But the "reasonable person" standard does not require a court to pretend that Alvarado was a 35–year-old * * *.

Rather, the precise legal definition of "reasonable person" may, depending on legal context, appropriately account for certain personal characteristics. In negligence suits, for example, the question is what would a "reasonable person" do " 'under the same or similar circumstances.' " In answering that question, courts enjoy "latitude" and may make "allowance not only for external facts, but sometimes for certain characteristics of the actor himself," including physical disability, youth, or advanced age. This allowance makes sense in light of the tort standard's recognized purpose: deterrence. Given that purpose, why pretend that a child is an adult or that a blind man can see?

In the present context, that of *Miranda*'s "in custody" inquiry, the law has introduced the concept of a "reasonable person" to avoid judicial inquiry into subjective states of mind, and to focus the inquiry instead upon objective circumstances that are known to both the officer and the suspect and that are likely relevant to the way a person would understand his situation.

In this case, Alvarado's youth is an objective circumstance that was known to the police. It is not a special quality, but rather a widely shared characteristic that generates commonsense conclusions about behavior and perception. To focus on the circumstance of age in a case like this does not complicate the "in custody" inquiry. And to say that courts should ignore widely shared, objective characteristics, like age, on the ground that only a (large) *minority* of the population possesses them would produce absurd results, the present instance being a case in point. I am not surprised that the majority points to no case suggesting any such limitation.

* * *

b. Interrogation

RHODE ISLAND v. INNIS

Supreme Court of the United States, 1980.
446 U.S. 291, 100 S.Ct. 1682, 64 L.Ed.2d 297.

Mr. Justice Stewart delivered the opinion of the Court.

In *Miranda v. Arizona*, 384 U.S. 436, 86 S.Ct. 1602, 16 L.Ed.2d 694 (1966), the Court held that, once a defendant in custody asks to speak with a lawyer, all interrogation must cease until a lawyer is present. The issue in this case is whether the respondent was "interrogated" in violation of the standards promulgated in the *Miranda* opinion.

I

On the night of January 12, 1975, John Mulvaney, a Providence, R. I., taxicab driver, disappeared after being dispatched to pick up a customer. His body was discovered four days later buried in a shallow grave in Coventry, R. I. He had died from a shotgun blast aimed at the back of his head.

On January 17, 1975, shortly after midnight, the Providence police received a telephone call from Gerald Aubin, also a taxicab driver, who reported that he had just been robbed by a man wielding a sawed-off shotgun. Aubin further reported that he had dropped off his assailant near Rhode Island College in a section of Providence known as Mount Pleasant. While at the Providence police station waiting to give a statement, Aubin noticed a picture of his assailant on a bulletin board. Aubin so informed one of the police officers present. The officer prepared a photo array, and again Aubin identified a picture of the same person. That person was the respondent. Shortly thereafter, the Providence police began a search of the Mount Pleasant area.

At approximately 4:30 a. m. on the same date, Patrolman Lovell, while cruising the streets of Mount Pleasant in a patrol car, spotted the respondent standing in the street facing him. When Patrolman Lovell stopped his car, the respondent walked towards it. Patrolman Lovell then arrested the respondent, who was unarmed, and advised him of his so-called *Miranda* rights. While the two men waited in the patrol car for other police officers to arrive, Patrolman Lovell did not converse with the respondent other than to respond to the latter's request for a cigarette.

Within minutes, Sergeant Sears arrived at the scene of the arrest, and he also gave the respondent the *Miranda* warnings. Immediately thereafter, Captain Leyden and other police officers arrived. Captain Leyden advised the respondent of his *Miranda* rights. The respondent stated that he understood those rights and wanted to speak with a lawyer. Captain Leyden then directed that the respondent be placed in a "caged wagon," a four-door police car with a wire screen mesh between the front and rear seats, and be driven to the central police station. Three officers, Patrolmen Gleckman, Williams, and McKenna, were assigned to accompany the respondent to the central station. They placed the respondent in the vehicle and shut the doors. Captain Leyden then instructed the officers not to question the respondent or intimidate or coerce him in any way. The three officers then entered the vehicle, and it departed.

While en route to the central station, Patrolman Gleckman initiated a conversation with Patrolman McKenna concerning the missing shotgun. As Patrolman Gleckman later testified:

"A. At this point, I was talking back and forth with Patrolman McKenna stating that I frequent this area while on patrol and [that because a school for handicapped children is located nearby,] there's a lot of handicapped children running around in this area, and God forbid one of them might find a weapon with shells and they might hurt themselves."

Patrolman McKenna apparently shared his fellow officer's concern:

"A. I more or less concurred with him [Gleckman] that it was a safety factor and that we should, you know, continue to search for the weapon and try to find it."

While Patrolman Williams said nothing, he overheard the conversation between the two officers:

"A. He [Gleckman] said it would be too bad if the little—I believe he said a girl—would pick up the gun, maybe kill herself."

The respondent then interrupted the conversation, stating that the officers should turn the car around so he could show them where the gun was located. At this point, Patrolman McKenna radioed back to Captain Leyden that they were returning to the scene of the arrest, and that the respondent would inform them of the location of the gun. At the time the respondent indicated that the officers should turn back, they had traveled no more than a mile, a trip encompassing only a few minutes.

The police vehicle then returned to the scene of the arrest where a search for the shotgun was in progress. There, Captain Leyden again advised the respondent of his *Miranda* rights. The respondent replied that he understood those rights but that he "wanted to get the gun out of the way because of the kids in the area in the school." The respondent then led the police to a nearby field, where he pointed out the shotgun under some rocks by the side of the road.

[The trial judge admitted the shotgun and testimony related to its discovery in evidence at Innis's trial and he was convicted.]

II

* * *

In the present case, the parties are in agreement that the respondent was fully informed of his *Miranda* rights and that he invoked his *Miranda* right to counsel when he told Captain Leyden that he wished to consult with a lawyer. It is also uncontested that the respondent was "in custody" while being transported to the police station.

The issue, therefore, is whether the respondent was "interrogated" by the police officers in violation of the respondent's undisputed right under *Miranda* to remain silent until he had consulted with a lawyer. In resolving this issue, we first define the term "interrogation" under *Miranda* before turning to a consideration of the facts of this case.

A

The starting point for defining "interrogation" in this context is, of course, the Court's *Miranda* opinion. There the Court observed that "[by] custodial interrogation, we mean *questioning* initiated by law enforcement officers after a person has been taken into custody or otherwise deprived of his freedom of action in any significant way." (emphasis added). This passage and other references throughout the opinion to "questioning" might suggest that the *Miranda* rules were to apply only to those police interrogation practices that involve express questioning of a defendant while in custody.

We do not, however, construe the *Miranda* opinion so narrowly. The concern of the Court in *Miranda* was that the "interrogation environment" created by the interplay of interrogation and custody would "subjugate the individual to the will of his examiner" and thereby undermine the privilege against compulsory self-incrimination. The police practices that evoked this concern included several that did not involve express questioning. For example, one of the practices discussed in *Miranda* was the use of lineups in which a coached witness would pick the defendant as the perpetrator. This was designed to establish that the defendant was in fact guilty as a predicate for further interrogation. * * *

This is not to say, however, that all statements obtained by the police after a person has been taken into custody are to be considered the product of interrogation. As the Court in *Miranda* noted:

"Confessions remain a proper element in law enforcement. Any statement given freely and voluntarily without any compelling influences is, of course, admissible in evidence. *The fundamental import of the privilege while an individual is in custody is not whether he is allowed to talk to the police without the benefit of warnings and counsel, but whether he can be interrogated.* . . . Volunteered statements of any kind are not barred by the Fifth Amendment and their admissibility is not affected by our holding today." (emphasis added).

It is clear therefore that the special procedural safeguards outlined in *Miranda* are required not where a suspect is simply taken into custody, but rather where a suspect in custody is subjected to interrogation. "Interrogation," as conceptualized in the *Miranda* opinion, must reflect a measure of compulsion above and beyond that inherent in custody itself.

We conclude that the *Miranda* safeguards come into play whenever a person in custody is subjected to either express questioning or its functional equivalent. That is to say, the term "interrogation" under *Miranda* refers not only to express questioning, but also to any words or actions on the part of the police (other than those normally attendant to arrest and custody) that the police should know are reasonably likely to elicit an incriminating response from the suspect. The latter portion of this definition focuses primarily upon the perceptions of the suspect, rather than the intent of the police. This focus reflects the fact that the *Miranda* safeguards were designed to vest a suspect in custody with an added measure of protection against coercive police practices, without regard to objective proof of the underlying intent of the police. A practice that the police should know is reasonably likely to evoke an incriminating response from a suspect thus amounts to interrogation.[7] But, since the police surely cannot be held accountable for the unforeseeable results of their words or actions, the definition of interrogation can extend only to words or actions on the part of police officers that they *should have known* were reasonably likely to elicit an incriminating response.[8]

B

Turning to the facts of the present case, we conclude that the respondent was not "interrogated" within the meaning of *Miranda*. It is undisputed that the first prong of the definition of "interrogation" was not satisfied, for the conversation between Patrolmen Gleckman and McKenna included no express questioning of the respondent. Rather, that conversation was, at least in form, nothing more than a dialogue between the two officers to which no response from the respondent was invited.

Moreover, it cannot be fairly concluded that the respondent was subjected to the "functional equivalent" of questioning. It cannot be said, in short, that Patrolmen Gleckman and McKenna should have known that their conversation was reasonably likely to elicit an incriminating response from the respondent. There is nothing in the record to suggest that the officers were aware that the respondent was peculiarly susceptible to an appeal to his conscience concerning the safety of handicapped children. Nor is there anything in the record to suggest that the police knew that the respondent was unusually disoriented or upset at the time of his arrest.

The case thus boils down to whether, in the context of a brief conversation, the officers should have known that the respondent would suddenly be moved to make a self-incriminating response. Given the fact that the entire conversation appears to have consisted of no more than a few offhand remarks, we cannot say that the officers should have known that it was reasonably likely that Innis would so respond. This is not a case where the police carried on a lengthy harangue in the presence of the suspect. * * *

* * *

7. This is not to say that the intent of the police is irrelevant, for it may well have a bearing on whether the police should have known that their words or actions were reasonably likely to evoke an incriminating response. In particular, where a police practice is designed to elicit an incriminating response from the accused, it is unlikely that the practice will not also be one which the police should have known was reasonably likely to have that effect.

8. Any knowledge the police may have had concerning the unusual susceptibility of a defendant to a particular form of persuasion might be an important factor in determining whether the police should have known that their words or actions were reasonably likely to elicit an incriminating response from the suspect.

[The concurring opinions of JUSTICE WHITE and CHIEF JUSTICE BURGER and a dissenting opinion of JUSTICE STEVENS are omitted.]

MR. JUSTICE MARSHALL, with whom MR. JUSTICE BRENNAN joins, dissenting.

I am substantially in agreement with the Court's definition of "interrogation" within the meaning of *Miranda v. Arizona*. In my view, the *Miranda* safeguards apply whenever police conduct is intended or likely to produce a response from a suspect in custody. As I read the Court's opinion, its definition of "interrogation" for *Miranda* purposes is equivalent, for practical purposes, to my formulation, since it contemplates that "where a police practice is designed to elicit an incriminating response from the accused, it is unlikely that the practice will not also be one which the police should have known was reasonably likely to have that effect." Thus, the Court requires an objective inquiry into the likely effect of police conduct on a typical individual, taking into account any special susceptibility of the suspect to certain kinds of pressure of which the police know or have reason to know.

I am utterly at a loss, however, to understand how this objective standard as applied to the facts before us can rationally lead to the conclusion that there was no interrogation. Innis was arrested at 4:30 a. m., handcuffed, searched, advised of his rights, and placed in the back seat of a patrol car. Within a short time he had been twice more advised of his rights and driven away in a four-door sedan with three police officers. Two officers sat in the front seat and one sat beside Innis in the back seat. Since the car traveled no more than a mile before Innis agreed to point out the location of the murder weapon, Officer Gleckman must have begun almost immediately to talk about the search for the shotgun.

The Court attempts to characterize Gleckman's statements as "no more than a few offhand remarks" which could not reasonably have been expected to elicit a response. If the statements had been addressed to respondent, it would be impossible to draw such a conclusion. The simple message of the "talking back and forth" between Gleckman and McKenna was that they had to find the shotgun to avert a child's death.

One can scarcely imagine a stronger appeal to the conscience of a suspect—*any* suspect—than the assertion that if the weapon is not found an innocent person will be hurt or killed. And not just any innocent person, but an innocent child—a little girl—a helpless, handicapped little girl on her way to school. The notion that such an appeal could not be expected to have any effect unless the suspect were known to have some special interest in handicapped children verges on the ludicrous. As a matter of fact, the appeal to a suspect to confess for the sake of others, to "display some evidence of decency and honor," is a classic interrogation technique.

Gleckman's remarks would obviously have constituted interrogation if they had been explicitly directed to respondent, and the result should not be different because they were nominally addressed to McKenna. This is not a case where police officers speaking among themselves are accidentally overheard by a suspect. These officers were "talking back and forth" in close quarters with the handcuffed suspect, traveling past the very place where they believed the weapon was located. They knew respondent would hear and attend to their conversation, and they are chargeable with knowledge of and responsibility for the pressures to speak which they created.

I firmly believe that this case is simply and aberration, and that in future cases the Court will apply the standard adopted today in accordance with its plain meaning.

4. Invoking and Waiving *Miranda* Rights

MICHIGAN v. MOSLEY

Supreme Court of the United States, 1975.
423 U.S. 96, 96 S.Ct. 321, 46 L.Ed.2d 313.

Mr. Justice Stewart delivered the opinion of the Court.

[The defendant, Richard Bert Mosley, was arrested in Detroit, Mich., by Detective James Cowie for armed robberies.] After effecting the arrest, Detective Cowie brought Mosley to the Robbery, Breaking and Entering Bureau of the Police Department, located on the fourth floor of the departmental headquarters building. The officer advised Mosley of his rights under this Court's decision in *Miranda* v. *Arizona,* and had him read and sign the department's constitutional rights notification certificate. After filling out the necessary arrest papers, Cowie began questioning Mosley about the robbery of the White Tower Restaurant. When Mosley said he did not want to answer any questions about the robberies, Cowie promptly ceased the interrogation. The completion of the arrest papers and the questioning of Mosley together took approximately 20 minutes. At no time during the questioning did Mosley indicate a desire to consult with a lawyer, and there is no claim that the procedures followed to this point did not fully comply with the strictures of the *Miranda* opinion. Mosley was then taken to a ninth-floor cell block.

Shortly after 6 p.m., Detective Hill of the Detroit Police Department Homicide Bureau brought Mosley from the cell block to the fifth-floor office of the Homicide Bureau for questioning about the fatal shooting of a man named Leroy Williams. * * * Mosley had not been arrested on this charge or interrogated about it by Detective Cowie. Before questioning Mosley about this homicide, Detective Hill carefully advised him of his *"Miranda* rights." Mosley read the notification form both silently and aloud, and Detective Hill then read and explained the warnings to him and had him sign the form. Mosley at first denied any involvement in the Williams murder, but after the officer told him that Anthony Smith had confessed to participating in the slaying and had named him as the "shooter," Mosley made a statement implicating himself in the homicide. The interrogation by Detective Hill lasted approximately 15 minutes, and at no time during its course did Mosley ask to consult with a lawyer or indicate that he did not want to discuss the homicide. In short, there is no claim that the procedures followed during Detective Hill's interrogation of Mosley, standing alone, did not fully comply with the strictures of the *Miranda* opinion.

[Mosley's motion to suppress his statement to Detective Hill was denied and a jury convicted him of first-degree murder.]

* * *

In the *Miranda* case this Court [held] that unless law enforcement officers give certain specified warnings before questioning a person in custody, and follow certain specified procedures during the course of an subsequent interrogation, any statement made by the person in custody cannot over his objection be admitted in evidence against him as a defendant at trial, even though the statement may in fact be wholly voluntary.

Neither party in the present case challenges the continuing validity of the *Miranda* decision, or of any of the so-called guidelines it established to protect what the Court there said was a person's constitutional privilege against compulsory self-incrimination. The issue in this case, rather, is whether the conduct of the Detroit police that led to Mosley's incriminating statement did in fact violate the *Miranda* "guidelines," so as to render the statement inadmissible in evidence against Mosley at his trial. Resolution of the question turns almost entirely on the interpretation of a single passage in the *Miranda* opinion, upon which the Michigan appellate court relied in finding a *per se* violation of *Miranda*:

> "Once warnings have been given, the subsequent procedure is clear. If the individual indicates in any manner, at any time prior to or during questioning, that he wishes to remain silent, the interrogation must cease. At this point he has shown that he intends to exercise his Fifth Amendment privilege; any statement taken after the person invokes his privilege cannot be other than the product of compulsion, subtle or otherwise. Without the right to cut off questioning, the setting of in-custody interrogation operates on the individual to overcome free choice in producing a statement after the privilege has been once invoked."

This passage states that "the interrogation must cease" when the person in custody indicates that "he wishes to remain silent." It does not state under what circumstances, if any, a resumption of questioning is permissible. The passage could be literally read to mean that a person who has invoked his "right to silence" can never again be subjected to custodial interrogation by any police officer at any time or place on any subject. Another possible construction of the passage would characterize "any statement taken after the person invokes his privilege" as "the product of compulsion" and would therefore mandate its exclusion from evidence, even if it were volunteered by the person in custody without any further interrogation whatever. Or the passage could be interpreted to require only the immediate cessation of questioning, and to permit a resumption of interrogation after a momentary respite.

It is evident that any of these possible literal interpretations would lead to absurd and unintended results. To permit the continuation of custodial interrogation after a momentary cessation would clearly frustrate the purposes of *Miranda* by allowing repeated rounds of questioning to undermine the will of the person being questioned. At the other extreme, a blanket prohibition against the taking of voluntary statements or a permanent immunity from further interrogation, regardless of the circumstances, would transform the *Miranda* safeguards into wholly irrational obstacles to legitimate police investigative activity, and deprive suspects of an opportunity to make informed and intelligent assessments of their interests. Clearly, therefore, neither this passage nor any other passage in the *Miranda* opinion can sensibly be read to create a *per se* proscription of indefinite duration upon any further questioning by any police officer on any subject, once the person in custody has indicated a desire to remain silent.

A reasonable and faithful interpretation of the *Miranda* opinion must rest on the intention of the Court in that case to adopt "fully effective means . . . to notify the person of his right of silence and to assure that the exercise of the right will be scrupulously honored. . . . " The critical safeguard identified in the passage at issue is a person's "right to cut off questioning." Through the exercise of his option to terminate questioning he can control the time at which questioning occurs, the subjects discussed, and the duration of the interrogation. The requirement that law enforcement authorities must respect a person's exercise of that option counteracts the coercive pressures of the custodial setting. We therefore conclude that the admissibility of statements obtained after the person in custody has decided to remain silent depends under *Miranda* on whether his "right to cut of questioning" was "scrupulously honored."

A review of the circumstances leading to Mosley's confession reveals that his "right to cut of questioning" was fully respected in this case. Before his initial interrogation, Mosley was carefully advised that he was under no obligation to answer any questions and could remain silent if he wished. He orally acknowledged that he understood the *Miranda* warnings and then signed a printed notification-of-rights form. When Mosley stated that he did not want to discuss the robberies, Detective Cowie immediately ceased the interrogation and did not try either to resume the questioning or in any way to persuade Mosley to reconsider his position. After an interval of more than two hours, Mosley was questioned by another police officer at another location about an unrelated holdup murder. He was given full and complete *Miranda* warnings at the outset of the second interrogation. He was thus reminded again that he could remain silent and could consult with a lawyer, and was carefully given a full and fair opportunity to exercise these options. The subsequent questioning did not undercut Mosley's previous decision not to answer Detective Cowie's inquiries. Detective Hill did not resume the interrogation about the [robberies], but instead focused exclusively on the Leroy Williams homicide, a crime different in nature and in time and place of occurrence from the robberies for which Mosley had been arrested and interrogated by Detective Cowie. Although it is not clear from the record how much Detective Hill knew about the earlier interrogation, his questioning of Mosley about an unrelated homicide was quite consistent with a reasonable interpretation of Mosley's earlier refusal to answer any questions about the robberies.

This is not a case, therefore, where the police failed to honor a decision of a person in custody to cut off questioning, either by refusing to discontinue the interrogation upon request or by persisting in repeated efforts to wear down his resistance and make him change his mind. In contrast to such practices, the police here immediately ceased the interrogation, resumed questioning only after the passage of a significant period of time and the provision of a fresh set of warnings, and restricted the second interrogation to a crime that had not been a subject of the earlier interrogation.

* * *

For these reasons, we conclude that the admission in evidence of Mosley's incriminating statement did not violate the principles of *Miranda* v. *Arizona.* * * *

[JUSTICE WHITE's concurring opinion is omitted.]

MR. JUSTICE BRENNAN, with whom MR. JUSTICE MARSHALL joins, dissenting.

The Court focuses on the correct passage from *Miranda* v. *Arizona*:

"Once warnings have been given, the subsequent procedure is clear. If the individual indicates in any manner, at any time prior to or during questioning, that he wishes to remain silent, the interrogation must cease. At this point he has shown that he intends to exercise his Fifth Amendment privilege; any statement taken after the person invokes his privilege cannot be other than the product of compulsion, subtle or otherwise. Without the right to cut off questioning, the setting of in-custody interrogation operates on the individual to overcome free choice in producing a statement after the privilege has been once invoked."

* * *

The *Miranda* guidelines were necessitated by the inherently coercive nature of in-custody questioning. * * * We "concluded that without proper safeguards the process of in-custody interrogation of persons suspected or accused of crime contains inherently compelling pressures which work to undermine the individual's will to resist and to compel him to speak where he would not otherwise do so freely." * * *

[T]he task confronting the Court is not whether voluntary statements will be excluded, but whether the procedures approved will be sufficient to assure with reasonable certainty that a confession is not obtained under the influence of the compulsion inherent in interrogation and detention. The procedures approved by the Court today fail to provide that assurance.

* * *

I agree that *Miranda* is not to be read, on the one hand, to impose an absolute ban on resumption of questioning "at any time or place on any subject," or on the other hand, "to permit a resumption of interrogation after a momentary respite." But this surely cannot justify adoption of a vague and ineffective procedural standard that falls somewhere between those absurd extremes, for *Miranda* in flat and unambiguous terms requires that questioning "cease" when a suspect exercises the right to remain silent. *Miranda's* terms, however, are not so uncompromising as to preclude the fashioning of guidelines to govern this case. Those guidelines must, of course, necessarily be sensitive to the reality that "[a]s a practical matter, the compulsion to speak in the isolated setting of the police station may well be greater than in courts or other official investigations, where there are often impartial observers to guard against intimidation or trickery."

The fashioning of guidelines for this case is an easy task. Adequate procedures are readily available. Michigan law requires that the suspect be arraigned before a judicial officer "without unnecessary delay," certainly not a burdensome requirement. Alternatively, a requirement that resumption of questioning should await appointment and arrival of counsel for the suspect would be an acceptable and readily satisfied precondition to resumption. *Miranda* expressly held that "[t]he presence of counsel . . . would be the adequate protective device necessary to make the process of police interrogation conform to the dictates of the privilege [against self-incrimination]." The Court expediently bypasses this alternative in its search for circumstances where renewed questioning would be permissible.

Indeed, language in *Miranda* suggests that the presence of counsel is the only appropriate alternative. In categorical language we held in *Miranda:* "If the individual indicates in any manner, at any time prior to or during questioning, that he wishes to remain silent, the interrogation must cease." We then immediately observed:

> "If an individual indicates his desire to remain silent but has an attorney present, there *may* be some circumstances in which further questioning would be permissible. In the absence of evidence of overbearing, statements then made in the presence of counsel *might* be free of the compelling influence of the interrogation process and *might* fairly be construed as a waiver of the privilege for purposes of these statements."

* * *

EDWARDS v. ARIZONA

Supreme Court of the United States, 1981.
451 U.S. 477, 101 S.Ct. 1880, 68 L.Ed.2d 378.

JUSTICE WHITE delivered the opinion of the Court. * * *

I

On January 19, 1976, a sworn complaint was filed against Edwards in Arizona state court charging him with robbery, burglary, and first-degree murder. An arrest warrant was issued pursuant to the complaint, and Edwards was arrested at his home later that same day. At the police station, he was informed of his rights as required by *Miranda v. Arizona*, 384 U.S. 436, 86 S.Ct. 1602, 16 L.Ed.2d 694 (1966). Petitioner stated that he understood his rights, and was willing to submit to questioning. After being told that another suspect already in custody had implicated him in the crime, Edwards denied involvement and gave a taped statement presenting an alibi defense. He then sought to "make a deal." The interrogating officer told him that he wanted a statement, but that he did not have the authority to negotiate a deal. The officer provided Edwards with the telephone number of a county attorney. Petitioner made the call, but hung up after a few moments. Edwards then said: "I want an attorney before making a deal." At that point, questioning ceased and Edwards was taken to county jail.

At 9:15 the next morning, two detectives, colleagues of the officer who had interrogated Edwards the previous night, came to the jail and asked to see Edwards. When the detention officer informed Edwards that the detectives wished to speak with him, he replied that he did not want to talk to anyone. The guard told him that "he had" to talk and then took him to meet with the detectives. The officers identified themselves, stated they wanted to talk to him, and informed him of his *Miranda* rights. Edwards was willing to talk, but he first wanted to hear the taped statement of the alleged accomplice who had implicated him. After listening to the tape for several minutes, petitioner said that he would make a statement so long as it was not tape-recorded. The detectives informed him that the recording was irrelevant since they could testify in court concerning whatever he said. Edwards replied: "I'll tell you anything you want to know, but I don't want it on tape." He thereupon implicated himself in the crime.

Prior to trial, Edwards moved to suppress his confession on the ground that his *Miranda* rights had been violated when the officers returned to question him after he had invoked his right to counsel. The trial court initially granted the motion to suppress, but reversed its ruling when presented with a supposedly controlling decision of a higher Arizona court. The court stated without explanation that it found Edwards' statement to be voluntary. [The Arizona Supreme Court affirmed Edwards' conviction.] Contrary to the holdings of the state courts, Edwards insists that having exercised his right on the 19th to have counsel present during interrogation, he did not validly waive that right on the 20th. For the following reasons, we agree.

First, the Arizona Supreme Court applied an erroneous standard for determining waiver where the accused has specifically invoked his right to counsel. It is reasonably clear under our cases that waivers of counsel must not only be voluntary, but must also constitute a knowing and intelligent relinquishment or abandonment of a known right or privilege * * *.

* * *

In referring to the necessity to find Edwards' confession knowing and intelligent, the State Supreme Court cited *Schneckloth v. Busta-monte*, 412 U.S. 218, 93 S.Ct. 2041, 36 L.Ed.2d 854 (1973). Yet, it is clear that *Schneckloth* does not control the issue presented in this case. The issue in *Schneckloth* was under what conditions an individual could be found to have consented to a search and thereby waived his Fourth Amendment rights. The Court declined to impose the "intentional relinquishment or abandonment of a known right or privilege" standard and required only that the consent be voluntary under the totality of the circumstances. The Court specifically noted that the right to counsel was a prime example of those rights requiring the special protection of the knowing and intelligent waiver standard, but held that "[t]he considerations that informed the Court's holding in *Miranda* are simply inapplicable in the present case." *Schneckloth* itself thus emphasized that the voluntariness of a consent or an admission on the one hand, and a knowing and intelligent waiver on the other, are discrete inquiries. Here, however sound the conclusion of the state courts as to the voluntariness of Edwards' admission may be, neither the trial court nor the Arizona Supreme Court undertook to focus on whether Edwards understood his right to counsel and intelligently and knowingly relinquished it. It is thus apparent that the decision below misunderstood the requirement for finding a valid waiver of the right to counsel, once invoked.

Second, although we have held that after initially being advised of his *Miranda* rights, the accused may himself validly waive his rights and respond to interrogation, the Court has strongly indicated that additional safeguards are necessary when the accused asks for counsel; and we now hold that when an accused has invoked his right to have counsel present during custodial interrogation, a valid waiver of that right cannot be established by showing only that he responded to further police-initiated custodial interrogation even if he has been advised of his rights. We further hold that an accused, such as Edwards, having expressed his desire to deal with the police only through counsel, is not subject to further interrogation by the authorities until counsel has been made available to him, unless the accused himself initiates further communication, exchanges, or conversations with the police.

* * *

Accordingly, the holding of the Arizona Supreme Court that Edwards had waived his right to counsel was infirm, and the judgment of that court is reversed. *So ordered*.

[The concurring opinion of CHIEF JUSTICE BURGER and the concurring opinion of JUSTICE POWELL, in which JUSTICE REHNQUIST joined, are omitted.]

OREGON v. BRADSHAW

Supreme Court of the United States, 1983.
462 U.S. 1039, 103 S.Ct. 2830, 77 L.Ed.2d 405.

JUSTICE REHNQUIST announced the judgment of the Court and delivered an opinion, in which THE CHIEF JUSTICE, JUSTICE WHITE, and JUSTICE O'CONNOR joined.

[Bradshaw was a suspect in the death of a minor, whose body had been found in the minor's wrecked pickup truck. Police took Bradwhaw to a police station, where he was advised of his *Miranda* rights. Bradshaw gave a statement in which he admitted that he had provided the minor and others with liquor for a party, but denied involvement in the traffic accident. The police arrested Bradshaw for furnishing liquor to a minor, again advised him of his *Miranda* rights, and told him that the police believed he had been driving the pickup truck at the time of the fatal accident. Bradshaw denied this, and said "I do want an attorney before it goes very much further." The officer immediately terminated the conversation. Police subsequently transferred Bradshaw to a different police station.]

[Either just before or during this trip to another police station] respondent inquired of a police officer, "Well, what is going to happen to me now?" The officer answered by saying: "You do not have to talk to me. You have requested an attorney and I don't want you talking to me unless you so desire because anything you say—because—since you have requested an attorney, you know, it has to be at your own free will." Respondent said he understood. There followed a discussion between respondent and the officer concerning where respondent was being taken and the offense with which he would be charged. The officer suggested that respondent might help himself by taking a polygraph examination. Respondent agreed to take such an examination, saying that he was willing to do whatever he could to clear up the matter.

The next day, following another reading to respondent of his *Miranda* rights, and respondent's signing a written waiver of those rights, the polygraph was administered. At its conclusion, the examiner told respondent that he did not believe respondent was telling the truth. Respondent then recanted his earlier story, admitting that he had been at the wheel of the vehicle in which Reynolds was killed, that he had consumed a considerable amount of alcohol, and that he had passed out at the wheel before the vehicle left the roadway and came to rest in the creek.

[Bradshaw was convicted of several crimes, including first-degree manslaughter. The Oregon Court of Appeals reversed, concluding that the statements had been obtained in violation of respondent's rights under *Edwards* v. *Arizona*, 451 U.S. 477 (1981). The state appellate court determined that Bradshaw's question, "Well, what is going to happen to me now?", was not a waiver of the right to counsel he had invoked.]

We think the Oregon Court of Appeals misapprehended the test laid down in *Edwards*. We did not there hold that the "initiation" of a conversation by a defendant such as respondent would amount to a waiver of a previously invoked right to counsel; we held that after the right to counsel had been asserted by an accused, further interrogation of the accused should not take place "unless the accused himself initiates further communication, exchanges, or conversations with the police." This was in effect a prophylactic rule, designed to protect an accused in police custody from being badgered by police officers in the manner in which the defendant in *Edwards* was. * * * But even if a conversation taking place after the accused has "expressed his desire to deal with the police only through counsel," is initiated by the accused, where reinterrogation follows, the burden remains upon the prosecution to show that subsequent events indicated a waiver of the Fifth Amendment right to have counsel present during the interrogation. * * *

* * *

There can be no doubt in this case that in asking, "Well, what is going to happen to me now?", respondent "initiated" further conversation in the ordinary dictionary sense of that word. [T]here are undoubtedly situations where a bare inquiry by either a defendant or by a police officer should not be held to "initiate" any conversation or dialogue. There are some inquiries, such as a request for a drink of water or a request to use a telephone, that are so routine that they cannot be fairly said to represent a desire on the part of an accused to open up a more generalized discussion relating directly or indirectly to the investigation. Such inquiries or statements, by either an accused or a police officer, relating to routine incidents of the custodial relationship, will not generally "initiate" a conversation in the sense in which that word was used in *Edwards*.

Although ambiguous, the respondent's question in this case as to what was going to happen to him evinced a willingness and a desire for a generalized discussion about the investigation; it was not merely a necessary inquiry arising out of the incidents of the custodial relationship. It could reasonably have been interpreted by the officer as relating generally to the investigation. That the police officer so understood it is apparent from the fact that he immediately reminded the accused that "[you] do not have to talk to me," and only after the accused told him that he "understood" did they have a generalized conversation. On these facts we believe that there was not a violation of the *Edwards* rule.

Since there was no violation of the *Edwards* rule in this case, the next inquiry was "whether a valid waiver of the right to counsel and the right to silence had occurred, that is, whether the purported waiver was knowing and intelligent and found to be so under the totality of the circumstances, including the necessary fact that the accused, not the police, reopened the dialogue with the authorities." As we have said many times before, this determination depends upon " 'the particular facts and circumstances surrounding [the] case, including the background, experience, and conduct of the accused.' "

[The Supreme Court affirmed the state trial court's conclusion that the statements Bradshaw made to the polygraph examiner were voluntary and the result of a knowing waiver of his right to remain silent.]

[The opinion of JUSTICE POWELL concurring in the judgment is omitted.]

JUSTICE MARSHALL, with whom JUSTICE BRENNAN, JUSTICE BLACKMUN, and JUSTICE STEVENS join, dissenting.

* * *

II

I agree with the plurality that, in order to constitute "initiation" under *Edwards*, an accused's inquiry must demonstrate a desire to discuss the subject matter of the criminal investigation. I am baffled, however, at the plurality's application of that standard to the facts of this case. The plurality asserts that respondent's question, "[What] is going to happen to me now?", evinced both "a willingness and a desire for a generalized discussion about the investigation." [U]nder the circumstances of this case, it is plain that respondent's only "desire" was to find out where the police were going to take him. As the Oregon Court of Appeals stated, respondent's query came only minutes after his invocation of the right to counsel and was simply "a normal reaction to being taken from the police station and placed in a police car, obviously for transport to some destination." On these facts, I fail to see how respondent's question can be considered "initiation" of a conversation about the subject matter of the criminal investigation.

* * *

DAVIS v. UNITED STATES

Supreme Court of the United States, 1994.
512 U.S. 452, 114 S.Ct. 2350, 129 L.Ed.2d 362.

JUSTICE O'CONNOR delivered the opinion of the Court.

[Investigators of the Naval Investigative Service (NIS) suspected that Davis, a member of the United States Navy, had committed a homicide. They interviewed Davis at an NIS office. As required by military law, the agents advised Davis that he was a suspect in the killing, that he was not required to make a statement, that any statement could be used against him at a trial by court-martial, and that he was entitled to speak with an attorney and have an attorney present during questioning. Petitioner waived his rights to remain silent and to counsel, both orally and in writing.]

I

* * *

About an hour and a half into the interview, petitioner said, "Maybe I should talk to a lawyer." According to the uncontradicted testimony of one of the interviewing agents, the interview then proceeded as follows:

"[We m]ade it very clear that we're not here to violate his rights, that if he wants a lawyer, then we will stop any kind of questioning with him, that we weren't going to pursue the matter unless we have it clarified is he asking for a lawyer or is he just making a comment about a lawyer, and he said, [']No, I'm not asking for a lawyer,' and then he continued on, and said, 'No, I don't want a lawyer.' "

After a short break, the agents reminded petitioner of his rights to remain silent and to counsel. The interview then continued for another hour, until petitioner said, "I think I want a lawyer before I say anything else." At that point, questioning ceased.

[Defendant's motion to suppress his statements was denied. He was convicted of homicide and was sentenced to confinement for life, a dishonorable discharge, forfeiture of all pay and allowances, and a reduction to the lowest pay grade.]

II

* * *

The right to counsel recognized in *Miranda*, 384 U.S. 436, 86 S.Ct. 1602, 16 L.Ed.2d. 694 (1966), is sufficiently important to suspects in criminal investigations, we have held, that it "requir[es] the special protection of the knowing and intelligent waiver standard." If the suspect effectively waives his right to counsel after receiving the *Miranda* warnings, law enforcement officers are free to question him. But if a suspect requests counsel at any time during the interview, he is not subject to further questioning until a lawyer has been made available or the suspect himself reinitiates conversation. This "second layer of prophylaxis for the *Miranda* right to counsel" is "designed to prevent police from badgering a defendant into waiving his previously asserted *Miranda* rights." To that end, we have held that a suspect who has invoked the right to counsel cannot be questioned regarding any offense unless an attorney is actually present. "It remains clear, however, that this prohibition on further questioning—like other aspects of *Miranda*—is not itself required by the Fifth Amendment's prohibition on coerced confessions, but is instead justified only by reference to its prophylactic purpose."

The applicability of the " 'rigid' prophylactic rule" of [*Edwards v. Arizona*, 451 U.S. 477, 101 S.Ct. 1880, 68 L.Ed.2d 378 (1981)] requires courts to "determine whether the accused *actually invoked* his right to counsel." To avoid difficulties of proof and to provide guidance to officers conducting interrogations, this is an objective inquiry. Invocation of the *Miranda* right to counsel "requires, at a minimum, some statement that can reasonably be construed to be an expression of a desire for the assistance of an attorney." But if a suspect makes a reference to an attorney that is ambiguous or equivocal in that a reasonable officer in light of the circumstances would have understood only that the suspect *might* be invoking the right to counsel, our precedents do not require the cessation of questioning.

Rather, the suspect must unambiguously request counsel. As we have observed, "a statement either is such an assertion of the right to counsel or it is not." Although a suspect need not "speak with the discrimination of an Oxford don," he must articulate his desire to have counsel present sufficiently clearly that a reasonable police officer in the circumstances would understand the statement to be a request for an attorney. If the statement fails to meet the requisite level of clarity, *Edwards* does not require that the officers stop questioning the suspect.

We decline petitioner's invitation to extend *Edwards* and require law enforcement officers to cease questioning immediately upon the making of an ambiguous or equivocal reference to an attorney. The rationale underlying *Edwards* is that the police must respect a suspect's wishes regarding his right to have an attorney present during custodial interrogation. But when the officers conducting the questioning reasonably do not know whether or not the suspect wants a lawyer, a rule requiring the immediate cessation of questioning "would transform the *Miranda* safeguards into wholly irrational obstacles to legitimate police investigative activity," because it would needlessly prevent the police from questioning a suspect in the absence of counsel even if the suspect did not wish to have a lawyer present. * * *

We recognize that requiring a clear assertion of the right to counsel might disadvantage some suspects who—because of fear, intimidation, lack of linguistic skills, or a variety of other reasons—will not clearly articulate their right to counsel although they actually want to have a lawyer present. But the primary protection afforded suspects subject to custodial interrogation is the *Miranda* warnings themselves. * * *

* * * The *Edwards* rule—questioning must cease if the suspect asks for a lawyer—provides a bright line that can be applied by officers in the real world of investigation and interrogation without unduly hampering the gathering of information. But if we were to require questioning to cease if a suspect makes a statement that *might* be a request for an attorney, this clarity and ease of application would be lost. Police officers would be forced to make difficult judgment calls about whether the suspect in fact wants a lawyer even though he has not said so, with the threat of suppression if they guess wrong. We therefore hold that, after a

knowing and voluntary waiver of the *Miranda* rights, law enforcement officers may continue questioning until and unless the suspect clearly requests an attorney.

Of course, when a suspect makes an ambiguous or equivocal statement it will often be good police practice for the interviewing officers to clarify whether or not he actually wants an attorney. That was the procedure followed by the NIS agents in this case. Clarifying questions help protect the rights of the suspect by ensuring that he gets an attorney if he wants one, and will minimize the chance of a confession being suppressed due to subsequent judicial second-guessing as to the meaning of the suspect's statement regarding counsel. But we decline to adopt a rule requiring officers to ask clarifying questions. If the suspect's statement is not an unambiguous or unequivocal request for counsel, the officers have no obligation to stop questioning him.

* * *

The courts below found that petitioner's remark to the NIS agents—"Maybe I should talk to a lawyer"—was not a request for counsel, and we see no reason to disturb that conclusion. The NIS agents therefore were not required to stop questioning petitioner, though it was entirely proper for them to clarify whether petitioner in fact wanted a lawyer. Because there is no ground for suppression of petitioner's statements, the judgment of the Court of Military Appeals is *Affirmed*.

[The concurring opinion of JUSTICE SCALIA is presented *infra*, in § C. The concurring opinion of JUSTICE SOUTER, with whom JUSTICE BLACKMUN, JUSTICE STEVENS, and JUSTICE GINSBURG joined, is omitted.]

5. Coercion and Waiver

ILLINOIS v. PERKINS

Supreme Court of the United States, 1990.
496 U.S. 292, 110 S.Ct. 2394, 110 L.Ed.2d 243.

JUSTICE KENNEDY delivered the opinion of the Court.

An undercover government agent was placed in the cell of respondent Perkins, who was incarcerated on charges unrelated to the subject of the agent's investigation. Respondent made statements that implicated him in the crime that the agent sought to solve. Respondent claims that the statements should be inadmissible because he had not been given Miranda warnings by the agent. We hold that the statements are admissible. Miranda warnings are not required when the suspect is unaware that he is speaking to a law enforcement officer and gives a voluntary statement.

I

In November 1984, Richard Stephenson was murdered in a suburb of East St. Louis, Illinois. The murder remained unsolved until March 1986, when one Donald Charlton told police that he had learned about a homicide from a fellow inmate at the Graham Correctional Facility, where Charlton had been serving a sentence for burglary. The fellow inmate was Lloyd Perkins, who is the respondent here. Charlton told police that, while at Graham, he had befriended respondent, who told him in detail about a murder that respondent had committed in East St. Louis. On hearing Charlton's account, the police recognized details of the Stephenson murder that were not well known, and so they treated Charlton's story as a credible one.

By the time the police heard Charlton's account, respondent had been released from Graham, but police traced him to a jail in Montgomery County, Illinois, where he was being held pending trial on a charge of aggravated battery, unrelated to the Stephenson murder. The police wanted to investigate further respondent's connection to the Stephenson murder, but feared that the use of an eavesdropping device would prove impracticable and unsafe. They decided instead to place an undercover agent in the cellblock with respondent and Charlton. The plan was for Charlton and undercover agent John Parisi to pose as escapees from a work release program who had been arrested in the course of a burglary. Parisi and Charlton were instructed to engage respondent in casual conversation and report anything he said about the Stephenson murder.

Parisi, using the alias "Vito Bianco," and Charlton, both clothed in jail garb, were placed in the cellblock with respondent at the Montgomery County jail. The cellblock consisted of 12 separate cells that opened onto a common room. Respondent greeted Charlton who, after a brief conversation with respondent, introduced Parisi by his alias. Parisi told respondent that he "wasn't going to do any more time," and suggested that the three of them escape. Respondent replied that the Montgomery County jail was "rinky-dink" and that they could "break out." The trio met in respondent's cell later that evening, after the other inmates were asleep, to refine their plan. Respondent said that his girlfriend could smuggle in a pistol. Charlton said "Hey, I'm not a murderer, I'm a burglar. That's your guys' profession." After telling Charlton that he would be responsible for any murder that occurred, Parisi asked respondent if he had ever "done" anybody. Respondent said that he had, and proceeded to describe at length the events of the Stephenson murder. Parisi and respondent then engaged in some casual conversation before respondent went to sleep. Parisi did not give respondent *Miranda* warnings before the conversations.

[Perkins was charged with the Stephenson murder. The trial court granted his motion to suppress his statements to Parisi in jail, and the State appealed and the Appellate Court of Illinois affirmed. The Supreme Court granted certiorari to decide whether an undercover law enforcement officer must give Miranda warnings to an incarcerated suspect before asking him questions that may elicit an incriminating response, and reversed the state courts.]

II

In *Miranda v. Arizona* [384 U.S. 436, 86 S.Ct. 1602, 16 L.Ed.2d 694 (1966)], the Court held that the Fifth Amendment privilege against self-incrimination prohibits admitting statements given by a suspect during "custodial interrogation" without a prior warning. Custodial interrogation means "questioning initiated by law enforcement officers after a person was been taken into custody.... ". The warning mandated by *Miranda* was meant to preserve the privilege during "incommunicado interrogation of individuals in a police-dominated atmosphere." That atmosphere is said to generate "inherently compelling pressures which work to undermine the individual's will to resist and to compel him to speak where he would not otherwise do so freely." "Fidelity to the doctrine announced in *Miranda* requires that it be enforced strictly, but only in those types of situations in which the concerns that powered the decision are implicated."

Conversations between suspects and undercover agents do not implicate the concerns underlying *Miranda*. The essential ingredients of a "police-dominated atmosphere" and compulsion are not present when an incarcerated person speaks freely to someone that he believes to be a fellow inmate. Coercion is determined from the perspective of the suspect. When a suspect considers himself in the company of cellmates and not officers, the coercive atmosphere is lacking. There is no empirical basis for the assumption that a suspect speaking to those whom he assumes are not officers will feel compelled to speak by the fear of reprisal for remaining silent or in the hope of more lenient treatment should be confess.

It is the premise of *Miranda* that the danger of coercion results from the interaction of custody and official interrogation. We reject the argument that *Miranda* warnings are required whenever a suspect is in custody in a technical sense and converses with someone who happens to be a government agent. Questioning by captors, who appear to control the suspect's fate, may create mutually reinforcing pressures that the Court has assumed will weaken the suspect's will, but where a suspect does not know that he is conversing with a government agent, these pressures do not exist. The State Court here mistakenly assumed that because the suspect was in custody, no undercover questioning could take place. When the suspect has no reason to think that the listeners have official power over him, it should not be assumed that his words are motivated by the reaction he expects from his listeners. "When the agent carries neither badge nor gun and wears not 'police blue,' but the same prison gray" as the suspect, there is no "interplay between police interrogation and police custody."

Miranda forbids coercion, but mere strategic deception by taking advantage of a suspect's misplaced trust in one he supposes to be a fellow prisoner. As we recognized in *Miranda*, "confessions remain a proper element in law enforcement. Any statement given freely and voluntarily without any compelling influences is, of course, admissible in evidence." Ploys to mislead a suspect or lull him into a false sense of security that do not rise to the level of compulsion or coercion to speak are not within *Miranda's* concerns.

Miranda was not meant to protect suspects from boasting about their criminal activities in front of persons whom they believe to be their cellmates. This case is illustrative. Respondent had no reason to feel that undercover agent Parisi had any legal authority to force him to answer questions or that Parisi could affect respondent's future treatment. Respondent viewed the cellmate-agent as an equal and showed no hint of being intimidated by the atmosphere of the jail. In recounting the details of the Stephenson murder, respondent was motivated solely by the desire to impress his fellow inmates. He spoke at his own peril.

* * *

This Court's Sixth Amendment decisions in *Massiah v. United States,* 377 U.S. 201, 84 S.Ct. 1199, 12 L.Ed.2d 246 (1964), *United States v. Henry,* 447 U.S. 264, 100 S.Ct. 2183, 65 L.Ed.2d 115 (1980), and *Maine v. Moulton,* 474 U.S. 159, 106 S.Ct. 477, 88 L.Ed.2d 481 (1985), also do not avail respondent. We held in those cases that the government may not use an undercover agent to circumvent the Sixth Amendment right to counsel once a suspect has been charged with the crime. After charges have been filed, the Sixth Amendment prevents the government from interfering with the accused's right to counsel. In the instant case no charges had been filed on the subject of the interrogation, and our Sixth Amendment precedents are not applicable.

* * *

We hold that an undercover law enforcement officer posing as a fellow inmate need not give *Miranda* warnings to an incarcerated suspect before asking questions that may elicit an incriminating response. The statements at issue in this case were voluntary, and there is no federal obstacle to their admissibility at trial. We now reverse and remand for proceedings not inconsistent with our opinion. It is so ordered.

[The concurring opinion of JUSTICE BRENNAN is omitted.]

JUSTICE MARSHALL, dissenting.

This Court clearly and simply stated its holding in *Miranda v. Arizona:* "The prosecution may not use statements, whether exculpatory or inculpatory, stemming from custodial interrogation of the defendant unless it demonstrates the use of procedural safeguards effective to secure the privilege against self-incrimination." The conditions that require the police to apprise a defendant of his constitutional rights— custodial interrogation conducted by an agent of the police—were present in this case. Because Lloyd Perkins received no *Miranda* warnings before he was subjected to custodial interrogation, his confession was not admissible.

* * *

While Perkins was confined, an undercover police officer, with the help of a police informant, questioned him about a serious crime. Although the Court does not dispute that Perkins was interrogated, it downplays the nature of the 35–minute questioning by disingenuously referring to it as a "conversation." The officer's narration of the "conversation" at Perkins' trial, however, reveals that it clearly was an interrogation.

"[Agent:] You ever do anyone?

"[Perkins:] Yeah, once in East St. Louis, in a rich white neighborhood.

"Informant: I didn't know they had any rich white neighborhoods in East St. Louis.

"Perkins: It wasn't in East St. Louis, it was by a race track in Fairview Heights. . . .

"[Agent]: You did a guy in Fairview Heights?

"Perkins: Yeah in a rich white section where most of the houses look the same.

"[Informant]: If all the houses look the same, how did you know you had the right house?

"Perkins: Me and two guys cased the house for about a week. I knew exactly which house, the second house on the left from the corner.

"[Agent]: How long ago did this happen?

"Perkins: Approximately about two years ago. I got paid $5,000 for that job.

"[Agent]: How did it go down?

"Perkins: I walked up to . . . this guy['s] house with a sawed-off under my trench coat.

"[Agent]: What type gun[?]

"Perkins: A .12 gauge Remmington [sic] Automatic Model 1100 sawed-off."

The police officer continued the inquiry, asking a series of questions designed to elicit specific information about the victim, the crime scene, the weapon, Perkins' motive, and his actions during and after the shooting. This interaction was not a "conversation"; Perkins, the officer, and the informant were not equal participants in a free-ranging discussion, with each man offering his views on different topics. Rather, it was an interrogation: Perkins was subjected to express questioning likely to evoke an incriminating response.

Because Perkins was interrogated by police while he was in custody, *Miranda* required that the officer inform him of his rights. In rejecting that conclusion, the Court finds that "conversations" between undercover agents and suspects are devoid of the coercion inherent in stationhouse interrogations conducted by law enforcement officials who openly represent the State. *Miranda* was not, however, concerned solely with police *coercion*. It dealt with *any* police tactics that may operate to compel a suspect in custody to make incriminating statements without full awareness of his constitutional rights. Thus, when a law enforcement agent structures a custodial interrogation so that a suspect feels compelled to reveal incriminating information, he must inform the suspect of his constitutional rights and give him an opportunity to decide whether or not to talk.

The compulsion proscribed by *Miranda* includes deception by the police. See *Miranda, supra, at* 453 (indicting police tactics "to induce a confession out of trickery," such as using fictitious witnesses or false accusations); *Berkemer v. McCarty,* 468 U.S. 420, 433, 104 S.Ct. 3138, 82 L.Ed.2d 317 (1984) ("The purposes of the safeguards prescribed by *Miranda* are to ensure that the police do not coerce *or* trick captive suspects into confessing") (emphasis deleted, emphasis added). Cf. *Moran v. Burbine,* 475 U.S. 412, 421, 106 S.Ct. 1135, 89 L.Ed.2d 410 (1986) ("The relinquishment of the right [protected by the *Miranda* warnings] must have been voluntary in the sense that it was the product of a free and deliberate choice rather than intimidation, coercion, *or* deception") (emphasis added). * * *

Custody works to the State's advantage in obtaining incriminating information. The psychological pressures inherent in confinement increase the suspect's anxiety, making him likely to seek relief by talking with others. The inmate is thus more susceptible to efforts by undercover agents to elicit information from him. Similarly, where the suspect is incarcerated, the constant threat of physical danger peculiar to the prison environment may make him demonstrate his toughness to other inmates by recounting or inventing past violent acts. "Because the suspect's ability to select people with whom he can confide is completely within their control, the police have a unique opportunity to exploit the suspect's vulnerability. In short, the police can insure that if the pressures of confinement lead the suspect to confide in anyone, it will be a police agent." * * *

Thus, the pressures unique to custody allow the police to use deceptive interrogation tactics to compel a suspect to make an incriminating statement. The compulsion is not eliminated by the suspect's ignorance of his interrogator's true identify. The Court therefore need not inquire past the bare facts of custody and interrogation to determine whether *Miranda* warnings are required.

* * *

ARIZONA v. FULMINANTE
Supreme Court of the United States, 1991.
499 U.S. 279, 111 S.Ct. 1246, 113 L.Ed.2d 302.

WHITE, J., delivered an opinion, Parts I, II, and IV of which are for the Court, and filed a dissenting opinion in Part III. MARSHALL, BLACKMUN, and STEVENS, JJ., joined Parts I, II, III, and IV of that opinion; SCALIA, J., joined Parts I and II; and KENNEDY, J., joined Parts I and IV. REHNQUIST, C.J., delivered an opinion, Part II of which is for the Court, and filed a dissenting opinion in Parts I and III. O'CONNOR, J., joined Parts I, II, and III of that opinion; KENNEDY and SOUTER, JJ., joined Parts I and II; and SCALIA, J., joined Parts II and III. KENNEDY, J., filed an opinion concurring in the judgment.

JUSTICE WHITE delivered the opinion of the Court.

The Arizona Supreme Court ruled in this case that respondent Oreste Fulminante's confession, received in evidence at his trial for murder, had been coerced and that its use against him was barred by the Fifth and Fourteenth Amendments to the United States Constitution. The court also held that the harmless-error rule could not be used to save the conviction. We affirm the judgment of the Arizona court, although for different reasons than those upon which that court relied.

I

[Local police in Mesa, Arizona suspected Fulminante of murdering his 11–year–old stepdaughter, Jeneane Michelle Hunt. When no charges were filed against him, Fulminante left Arizona for New Jersey. He was later convicted in New Jersey on federal charges of possession of a firearm by a felon. Fulminante was incarcerated in a federal prison in New York. He became friends with another inmate, Anthony Sarivola, a former police officer. Sarivola had been involved in loansharking for organized crime but then became a paid informant for the FBI. Sarivola heard a rumor that Fulminante was suspected of killing a child in Arizona and raised the subject with Fulminante in several conversations, but Fulminante repeatedly denied any involvement in Jeneane's death. An FBI agent instructed Sarivola to find out more. Sarivola subsequently offered to protect Fulminante from his fellow inmates, who had begun to threaten him because of the rumors of the Arizona child murder. Sarivola placed a condition on his help. He told Fulminane that "You have to tell me about it, you know. I mean, in other words, for me to give you any help." Fulminante then admitted to Sarivola that he had driven Jeneane to the desert on his motorcycle, where he choked her, sexually assaulted her, and made her beg for her life, before shooting her twice in the head. Sarivola was released from prison about a month later. A few months later, Fulminante was indicted in Arizona for the first-degree murder of Jeneane. The trial court denied Fulminante's motion to suppress the statement he had given to Sarivola in prison, as well as a second confession he had given to Donna Sarivola, then Anthony Sarivola's fiancee and later his wife, following Fulminante's release from prison in New York. He was convicted of murder and sentenced to death. The Arizona Supreme Court reversed his conviction, holding that the admission of a coerced confession required reversal regardless of the strength of the other evidence.]

* * * Because of differing views in the state and federal courts over whether the admission at trial of a coerced confession is subject to a

harmless-error analysis, we granted the State's petition for certiorari. Although a majority of this Court finds that such a confession is subject to a harmless error analysis, for the reasons set forth below, we affirm the judgment of the Arizona court.

II

* * *

Although the question is a close one, we agree with the Arizona Supreme Court's conclusion that Fulminante's confession was coerced. The Arizona Supreme Court found a credible threat of physical violence unless Fulminante confessed. Our cases have made clear that a finding of coercion need not depend upon actual violence by a government agent; a credible threat is sufficient. * * * As in *Payne v. Arkansas*, 356 U.S. 560, 78 S.Ct. 844, 2 L.Ed.2d 975 (1958), where the Court found that a confession was coerced because the interrogating police officer had promised that if the accused confessed, the officer would protect the accused from an angry mob outside the jailhouse door, so too here, the Arizona Supreme Court found that it was fear of physical violence, absent protection from his friend (and Government agent) Sarivola which motivated Fulminante to confess. Accepting the Arizona court's finding, permissible on this record, that there was a credible threat of physical violence, we agree with its conclusion that Fulminante's will was overborne in such a way as to render his confession the product of coercion.

III

Four of us, Justices Marshall, Blackmun, Stevens, and myself, would affirm the judgment of the Arizona Supreme Court on the ground that the harmless-error rule is inapplicable to erroneously admitted coerced confessions. We thus disagree with the Justices who have a contrary view. The majority today abandons what until now the Court has regarded as the axiomatic proposition that a defendant in a criminal case is deprived of due process of law if his conviction is founded, in whole or in part, upon an involuntary confession, without regard for the truth or falsity of the confession, and even though there is ample evidence aside from the confession to support the conviction. Today, a majority of the Court, without any justification, overrules this vast body of precedent without a word and in so doing dislodges one of the fundamental tenets of our criminal justice system. In extending to coerced confessions the harmless error rule of *Chapman v. California*, 386 U.S. 18, 87 S.Ct. 824, 17 L.Ed.2d 705 (1967), the majority declares that because the Court has applied that analysis to numerous other "trial errors," there is no reason that it should not apply to an error of this nature as well. The four of us remain convinced, however, that we should abide by our cases that have refused to apply the harmless error rule to coerced confessions, for a coerced confession is fundamentally different from other types of errone-ously admitted evidence to which the rule has been applied. * * *

Chapman specifically noted three constitutional errors that could not be categorized as harmless error: using a coerced confession against a defendant in a criminal trial, depriving a defendant of counsel, and trying a defendant before a biased judge. The majority attempts to distinguish the use of a coerced confession from the other two errors listed in *Chapman* first by distorting the decision in *Payne,* and then by drawing a meaningless dichotomy between "trial errors" and "structural defects" in the trial process. Viewing *Payne* as merely rejecting a test whereby the admission of a coerced confession could stand if there were "sufficient evidence," other than the confession to support the conviction, the majority suggests that the Court in *Payne* might have reached a different result had it been considering a harmless error test. It is clear, though, that in *Payne* the Court recognized that regardless of the amount of other evidence, "the admission in evidence, over objection, of the coerced confession vitiates the judgment," because "where, as here, a coerced confession constitutes a part of the evidence before the jury and a general verdict is returned, no one can say what credit and weight the jury gave to the confession." The inability to assess its effect on a conviction causes the admission at trial of a coerced confession to defy analysis by harmless-error standards, just as certainly as do deprivation of counsel and trial before a biased judge.

* * *

* * * A defendant's confession is "probably the most probative and damaging evidence that can be admitted against him," so damaging that a jury should not be expected to ignore it even if told to do so, and because in any event it is impossible to know what credit and weight the jury gave to the confession. * * *

* * *

* * *

[T]he four of us would adhere to the consistent line of authority that has recognized as a basic tenet of our criminal justice system, before and after both *Miranda* and *Chapman,* the prohibition against using a defendant's coerced confession against him at his criminal trial. Stare decisis is of fundamental importance to the rule of law; the majority offers no convincing reason for overturning our long line of decisions requiring the exclusion of coerced confessions.

IV

Since five Justices have determined that harmless error analysis applies to coerced confessions, it becomes necessary to evaluate under that ruling the admissibility of Fulminante's confession to Sarivola. * * * While some statements by a defendant may concern isolated aspects of the crime or may be incriminating only when linked to other evidence, a full confession in which the defendant discloses the motive for and means of the crime may tempt the jury to rely upon that evidence alone in reaching its decision. In the case of a coerced confession such as that given by Fulminante to Sarivola, the risk that the confession is unreliable, coupled with the profound impact that the confession has upon the jury, requires a reviewing court to exercise extreme caution before determining that the admission of the confession at trial was harmless.

* * * Our review of the record leads us to conclude that the State has failed to meet its burden of establishing, beyond a reasonable doubt, that the admission of Fulminante's confession to Anthony Sarivola was harmless error. Three considerations compel this result.

First, the transcript discloses that both the trial court and the State recognized that a successful prosecution depended on the jury believing the two confessions. Absent the confessions, it is unlikely that Fulminante would have been prosecuted at all, because the physical evidence from the scene and other circumstantial evidence would have been insufficient to convict. Indeed, no indictment was filed until nearly two years after the murder. Although the police had suspected Fulminante from the beginning, as the prosecutor acknowledged in his opening statement to the jury, "What brings us to Court, what makes this case fileable, and prosecutable and triable is that later, Mr. Fulminante confesses this crime to Anthony Sarivola and later, to Donna Sarivola, his wife." [I]n his closing argument, the prosecutor prefaced his discussion of the two confessions by conceding, "We have a lot of circumstantial evidence that indicates that this is our suspect, this is the fellow that did it, but it's a little short as far as saying that it's proof that he actually put the gun to the girl's head and killed her. So it's a little short of that. We recognize that."

Second, the jury's assessment of the confession to Donna Sarivola could easily have depended in large part on the presence of the confession to Anthony Sarivola. Absent the admission at trial of the first confession, the jurors might have found Donna Sarivola's story unbelievable. [She] testified that Fulminante, whom she had never before met, confessed in detail about Jeneane's brutal murder in response to her casual question concerning why he was going to visit friends in Pennsylvania instead of returning to his family in Arizona.

[I]t is clear that the jury might have believed that the two confessions reinforced and corroborated each other. For this reason, one confession was not merely cumulative of the other. While in some cases two confessions, delivered on different occasions to different listeners, might be viewed as being independent of each other, it strains credulity to think that the jury so viewed the two confessions in this case, especially given the close relationship between Donna and Anthony Sarivola.

The jurors could also have believed that Donna Sarivola had a motive to lie about the confession in order to assist her husband. Anthony Sarivola received significant benefits from federal authorities, including payment for information, immunity from prosecution, and eventual placement in the federal Witness Protection Program. In addition, the jury might have found Donna motivated by her own desire for favorable treatment, for she, too, was ultimately placed in the Witness Protection Program.

Third, the admission of the first confession led to the admission of other evidence prejudicial to Fulminante. For example, the State introduced evidence that Fulminante knew of Sarivola's connections with organized crime in an attempt to explain why Fulminante would have been motivated to confess to Sarivola in seeking protection. * * *

Finally, although our concern here is with the effect of the erroneous admission of the confession on Fulminante's conviction, it is clear that the presence of the confession also influenced the sentencing phase of the trial. Under Arizona law, the trial judge is the sentencer. * * * In this case, "based upon admissible evidence produced at the trial," the judge found that only one aggravating circumstance existed beyond a reasonable doubt, i.e., that the murder was committed in "an especially heinous, cruel, and depraved manner." In reaching this conclusion, the judge relied heavily on evidence concerning the manner of the killing and Fulminante's motives and state of mind which could only be found in the two confessions. * * *

* * *

Because a majority of the Court has determined that Fulminante's confession to Anthony Sarivola was coerced and because a majority has determined that admitting this confession was not harmless beyond a reasonable doubt, we agree with the Arizona Supreme Court's conclusion that Fulminante is entitled to a new trial at which the confession is not admitted. Accordingly the judgment of the Arizona Supreme Court is *Affirmed*.

CHIEF JUSTICE REHNQUIST, with whom JUSTICE O'CONNOR joins, JUSTICE KENNEDY and JUSTICE SOUTER join as to Parts I and II, and JUSTICE SCALIA joins as to Parts II and III, delivering the opinion of the Court as to Part II, and dissenting as to Parts I and III.

The Court today properly concludes that the admission of an "involuntary" confession at trial is subject to harmless error analysis. Nonetheless, the independent review of the record which we are required to make shows that respondent Fulminante's confession was not in fact involuntary. And even if the confession were deemed to be involuntary, the evidence offered at trial, including a second, untainted confession by Fulminante, supports the conclusion that any error here was certainly harmless.

* * *

II

Since this Court's landmark decision in *Chapman v. California*, in which we adopted the general rule that a constitutional error does not automatically require reversal of a conviction, the Court has applied harmless error analysis to a wide range of errors and has recognized that most constitutional errors can be harmless. The common thread connecting these cases is that each involved "trial error"—error which occurred during the presentation of the case to the jury, and which may therefore be quantitatively assessed in the context of other evidence presented in order to determine whether its admission was harmless beyond a reasonable doubt. In applying harmless error analysis to these many different constitutional violations, the Court has been faithful to the belief that the harmless-error doctrine is essential to preserve the principle that the central purpose of a criminal trial is to decide the factual question of the defendant's guilt or innocence, and promotes public respect for the criminal process by focusing on the underlying fairness of the trial rather than on the virtually inevitable presence of immaterial error.

In *Chapman* the Court stated [that] "Although our prior cases have indicated that there are some constitutional rights so basic to a fair trial that their infraction can never be treated as harmless error, this statement in itself belies any belief that all trial errors which violate the Constitution automatically call for reversal." See, e.g., *Payne v. Arkansas* (coerced confession); *Gideon v. Wainwright*, 372 U.S. 335, 83 S.Ct. 792, 9 L.Ed.2d 799 (1963) (right to counsel); *Tumey v. Ohio*, 273 U.S. 510, 47 S.Ct. 437, 71 L.Ed. 749 (1927) (impartial judge).

* * *

The admission of an involuntary confession—a classic "trial error"—is markedly different from the other two constitutional violations referred to in the *Chapman* footnote as not being subject to harmless-error analysis. One of those cases, *Gideon v. Wainwright*, involved the total deprivation of the right to counsel at trial. The other, *Tumey v. Ohio*, involved a judge who was not impartial. These are structural defects in the constitution of the trial mechanism, which defy analysis by "harmless-error" standards. The entire conduct of the trial from beginning to end is obviously affected by the absence of counsel for a criminal defendant, just as it is by the presence on the bench of a judge who is not impartial. Since our decision in *Chapman*, other cases have added to the category of constitutional errors which are not subject to harmless error the following: unlawful exclusion of members of the defendant's race from a grand jury, Vasquez v. Hillery; the right to self-representation at trial, *McKaskle v. Wiggins*, 465 U.S. 168, 104 S.Ct. 944. 79 L.Ed.2d 122 (1984); and the right to public trial, *Waller v. Georgia*. Each of these constitutional deprivations is a similar structural defect affecting the framework within which the trial proceeds, rather than simply an error in the trial process itself. * * *

* * *The admission of an involuntary confession is a "trial error," similar in both degree and kind to the erroneous admission of other types of evidence. The evidentiary impact of an involuntary confession, and its effect upon the composition of the record, is indistinguishable from that of a confession obtained in violation of the Sixth Amendment, of evidence seized in violation of the Fourth Amendment, or of a prosecutor's improper comment on a defendant's silence at trial in violation of the Fifth Amendment. When reviewing the erroneous admission of an involuntary confession, the appellate court, as it does with the admission of other forms of improperly admitted evidence, simply reviews the remainder of the evidence against the defendant to determine whether the admission of the confession was harmless beyond a reasonable doubt.

* * *

Of course an involuntary confession may have a more dramatic effect on the course of a trial than do other trial errors—in particular cases it may be devastating to a defendant—but this simply means that a reviewing court will conclude in such a case that its admission was not harmless error; it is not a reason for eschewing the harmless error test entirely. * * *

III

* * * [T]his seems to me to be a classic case of harmless error: a second confession giving more details of the crime than the first was admitted in evidence and found to be free of any constitutional objection. Accordingly, I would affirm the holding of the Supreme Court of Arizona in its initial opinion, and reverse the judgment which it ultimately rendered in this case.

[JUSTICE KENNEDY's opinion concurring in the judgment is omitted.]

6. Mental Capacity and Waiver

COLORADO v. CONNELLY

Supreme Court of the United States, 1986.
479 U.S. 157, 107 S.Ct. 515, 93 L.Ed.2d 473.

CHIEF JUSTICE REHNQUIST delivered the opinion of the Court.

In this case, the Supreme Court of Colorado held that the United States Constitution requires a court to suppress a confession when the mental state of the defendant, at the time he made the confession, interfered with his "rational intellect" and his "free will." Because this decision seemed to conflict with prior holdings of this Court, we granted certiorari. We conclude that the admissibility of this kind of statement is governed by state rules of evidence, rather than by our previous decisions regarding coerced confessions and *Miranda* waivers. We therefore reverse.

I

On August 18, 1983, Officer Patrick Anderson of the Denver Police Department was in uniform, working in an off-duty capacity in downtown Denver. Respondent Francis Connelly approached Officer Anderson and, without any prompting, stated that he had murdered someone and wanted to talk about it. Anderson immediately advised respondent that he had the right to remain silent, that anything he said could be used against him in court, and that he had the right to an attorney prior to any police questioning. Respondent stated that he understood these rights but he still wanted to talk about the murder. Understandably bewildered by this confession, Officer Anderson asked respondent several questions. Connelly denied that he had been drinking, denied that he had been taking any drugs, and stated that, in the past, he had been a patient in several mental hospitals. Officer Anderson again told Connelly that he was under no obligation to say anything. Connelly replied that it was "all right," and that he would talk to Officer Anderson because his conscience had been bothering him. To Officer Anderson, respondent appeared to understand fully the nature of his acts.

Shortly thereafter, Homicide Detective Stephen Antuna arrived. Respondent was again advised of his rights, and Detective Antuna asked him "what he had on his mind." Respondent answered that he had come all the way from Boston to confess to the murder of Mary Ann Junta, a young girl whom he had killed in Denver sometime during November 1982. Respondent was taken to police headquarters, and a search of police records revealed that the body of an unidentified female had been found in April 1983. Respondent openly detailed his story to Detective Antuna and Sergeant Thomas Haney, and readily agreed to take the officers to the scene of the killing. Under Connelly's sole direction, the two officers and respondent proceeded in a police vehicle to the location of the crime. Respondent pointed out the exact location of the murder. Throughout this episode, Detective Antuna perceived no indication whatsoever that respondent was suffering from any kind of mental illness.

Respondent was held overnight. During an interview with the public defender's office the following morning, he became visibly disoriented. He began giving confused answers to questions, and for the first time, stated that "voices" had told him to come to Denver and that he had followed the directions of these voices in confessing. Respondent was sent to a state hospital for evaluation. He was initially found incompetent to assist in his own defense. By March 1984, however, the doctors evaluating respondent determined that he was competent to proceed to trial.

At a preliminary hearing, respondent moved to suppress all of his statements. Doctor Jeffrey Metzner, a psychiatrist employed by the state hospital, testified that respondent was suffering from chronic schizophrenia and was in a psychotic state at least as of August 17, 1983, the day before he confessed. Metzner's interviews with respondent revealed that respondent was following the "voice of God." This voice instructed respondent to withdraw money from the bank, to buy an airplane ticket, and to fly from Boston to Denver. When respondent arrived from Boston, God's voice became stronger and told respondent either to confess to the killing or to commit suicide. Reluctantly following the command of the voices, respondent approached Officer Anderson and confessed.

Dr. Metzner testified that, in his expert opinion, respondent was experiencing "command hallucinations." This condition interfered with respondent's "volitional abilities; that is, his ability to make free and rational choices." Dr. Metzner further testified that Connelly's illness did not significantly impair his cognitive abilities. Thus, respondent understood the rights he had when Officer Anderson and Detective Antuna advised him that he need not speak. Dr. Metzner admitted that the "voices" could in reality be Connelly's interpretation of his own guilt, but explained that in his opinion, Connelly's psychosis motivated his confession.

On the basis of this evidence the Colorado trial court decided that respondent's statements must be suppressed because they were "involuntary." [The Colorado Supreme Court affirmed the suppression order, holding that the statements were involuntary and the *Miranda* waiver invalid.]

II

* * *

The difficulty with the approach of the Supreme Court of Colorado is that it fails to recognize the essential link between coercive activity of the State, on the one hand, and a resulting confession by a defendant, on the other. The flaw in respondent's constitutional argument is that it would expand our previous line of "voluntariness" cases into a far-ranging requirement that courts must divine a defendant's motivation for speaking or acting as he did even though there be no claim that governmental conduct coerced his decision.

The most outrageous behavior by a private party seeking to secure evidence against a defendant does not make that evidence inadmissible under the Due Process Clause. * * * Moreover, suppressing respondent's statements would serve absolutely no purpose in enforcing constitutional guarantees. The purpose of excluding evidence seized in violation of the Constitution is to substantially deter future violations of the Constitution. Only if we were to establish a brand new constitutional right—the right of a criminal defendant to confess to his crime only when totally rational and properly motivated—could respondent's present claim be sustained.

* * * A statement rendered by one in the condition of respondent might be proved to be quite unreliable, but this is a matter to be governed by the evidentiary laws of the forum, see, *e.g.*, Fed.Rule Evid. 601, and not by the Due Process Clause of the Fourteenth Amendment. * * *

* * *

III

A

[The Supreme Court of Colorado held that the State must bear its burden of proving waiver of these *Miranda* rights by "clear and convincing evidence." The United States Supreme Court held that the State only had the burden of proving waiver by the lesser standard of a preponderance of the evidence.]

B

We also think that the Supreme Court of Colorado was mistaken in its analysis of the question of whether respondent had waived his *Miranda* rights in this case. Of course, a waiver must at a minimum be "voluntary" to be effective against an accused. The Supreme Court of Colorado in addressing this question relied on the testimony of the court-appointed psychiatrist to the effect that respondent was not capable of making a "free decision with respect to his constitutional right of silence . . . and his constitutional right to confer with a lawyer before talking to the police."

We think that the Supreme Court of Colorado erred in importing into this area of constitutional law notions of "free will" that have no place there. There is obviously no reason to require more in the way of a "voluntariness" inquiry in the *Miranda* waiver context than in the Fourteenth Amendment confession context. The sole concern of the Fifth Amendment, on which *Miranda* was based, is governmental coercion. * * * Respondent's perception of coercion flowing from the "voice of God," however important or significant such a perception may be in other disciplines, is a matter to which the United States Constitution does not speak.

IV

The judgment of the Supreme Court of Colorado is accordingly reversed, and the cause remanded for further proceedings not inconsistent with this opinion. *It is so ordered.*

[The concurring opinions of JUSTICE BLACKMUN and JUSTICE STEVENS are omitted.]

JUSTICE BRENNAN, with whom JUSTICE MARSHALL joins, dissenting. * * *

Today's decision restricts the application of the term "involuntary" to those confessions obtained by police coercion. Confessions by mentally ill individuals or by persons coerced by parties other than police officers are now considered "voluntary." The Court's failure to recognize all forms of involuntariness or coercion as antithetical to due process reflects a refusal to acknowledge free will as a value of constitutional consequence. But due process derives much of its meaning from a conception of fundamental fairness that emphasizes the right to make vital choices voluntarily: "The Fourteenth Amendment secures against state invasion . . . the right of a person to remain silent unless he chooses to speak in the unfettered exercise of his own will. . ." *Malloy v. Hogan,* 378 U.S. 1, 8, 84 S.Ct. 1489, 12 L.Ed.2d 653 (1964). This right requires vigilant protection if we are to safeguard the values of private conscience and human dignity.

This Court's assertion that we would be required "to establish a brand new constitutional right" to recognize the respondent's claim ignores 200 years of constitutional jurisprudence. While it is true that police overreaching has been an element of every confession case to date, it is also true that in every case the Court has made clear that ensuring that a confession is a product of free will is an independent concern. * * *

* * *

Since the Court redefines voluntary confessions to include confessions by mentally ill individuals, the reliability of these confessions becomes a central concern. A concern for reliability is inherent in our criminal justice system, which relies upon accusatorial rather than inquisitorial practices. While an inquisitorial system prefers obtaining confessions from criminal defendants, an accusatorial system must place its faith in determinations of guilt by evidence independently and freely secured. * * *

* * *

The instant case starkly highlights the danger of admitting a confession by a person with a severe mental illness. The trial court made no findings concerning the reliability of Mr. Connelly's involuntary confession, since it believed that the confession was excludable on the basis of involuntariness. However, the overwhelming evidence in the record points to the unreliability of Mr. Connelly's delusional mind. Mr. Connelly was found incompetent to stand trial because he was unable to relate accurate information, and the court-appointed psychiatrist indicated that Mr. Connelly was actively hallucinating and exhibited delusional thinking at the time of his confession. * * *

Moreover, the record is barren of any corroboration of the mentally ill defendant's confession. No physical evidence links the defendant to the alleged crime. Police did not identify the alleged victim's body as the woman named by the defendant. Mr. Connelly identified the alleged scene of the crime, but it has not been verified that the unidentified body was found there or that a crime actually occurred there. There is not a shred of competent evidence in this record linking the defendant to the charged homicide. There is only Mr. Connelly's confession.

Minimum standards of due process should require that the trial court find substantial indicia of reliability, on the basis of evidence extrinsic to the confession itself, before admitting the confession of a mentally ill person into evidence. I would require the trial court to make such a finding on remand. To hold otherwise allows the State to imprison and possibly to execute a mentally ill defendant based solely upon an inherently unreliable confession.

* * *

C. MIRANDA CONSTRAINED

1. The Assault on *Miranda's* Constitutional Status

Introduction

The Supreme Court's decision in *Miranda* provoked immediate and continuing criticism. During the 1968 presidential campaign, Republican nominee Richard Nixon repeatedly attacked the Court's decisions in *Miranda* and *Escobedo v. Illinois*. In campaign speeches, Nixon complained that the effect of these decisions was to increase the amount of crime in the country by giving direct comfort to criminals: "The tragic lesson of guilty men walking free from hundreds of courtrooms across this country has not been lost on the criminal community." He argued that the "balance must be shifted back toward the peace forces in our society and a requisite step is to redress the imbalance created by these specific court decisions." Nixon proposed two solutions. The first—which is reviewed later in this Chapter in the Supreme Court's opinion in *Dickerson v. United States*—was passage of a provision of the Omnibus Crime Control and Safe Streets Act of 1968, which ostensibly overruled both *Miranda* and *Escobedo*. Congress enacted that provision as 18 U.S.C. § 3501.

Nixon's second solution was to appoint judges who would vote to reverse these decisions. President Nixon appointed four Justices to the Supreme Court. One of those was a prominent critic of the *Miranda* decision. While serving as Assistant Attorney General in the Justice Department, William Rehnquist publicly criticized *Miranda* and other criminal justice decisions by the Warren Court. Appearing before the Senate's Constitutional Rights Subcommittee, for example, Rehnquist testified that he supported "an effort by statute to modify all or part of the exclusionary rule which now prevents the use against a criminal defendant of evidence which is found to have [been] obtained in violation of his constitutional rights." After being appointed to the Supreme Court, Justice Rehnquist authored several influential opinions that laid a theoretical foundation for holding that 18 U.S.C. § 3501 had in fact overruled *Miranda*. The most influential of these opinions was *Michigan v. Tucker*.

MICHIGAN v. TUCKER

Supreme Court of the United States, 1974.
417 U.S. 433, 94 S.Ct. 2357, 41 L.Ed.2d 182.

MR. JUSTICE REHNQUIST delivered the opinion of the Court.

* * *

I

[Tucker was suspected of raping and severely beating a woman in her home. Police initially linked Tucker to the crime by following his dog from the crime scene to his home. The police arrested Tucker and brought him to the police station for questioning. Prior to the interrogation, officers advised him that any statements he might make could be used against him at a later date in court, but did not advise him that he would be furnished counsel free of charge if he could not pay for such services himself. When police officers questioned Tucker about his activities on the night of the rape and assault, he claimed that he had first been with one Robert Henderson and then later at home, alone, asleep. Officers then contacted Henderson, but his story served to discredit rather than to support Tucker's alibi. Although Henderson acknowledged he had been with Tucker on the night of the crime, he also said that Tucker had left early in the evening. In addition, Henderson reported that on the following day he asked Tucker how he had gotten scratches on his face, specifically asking Tucker whether "he got hold of a wild one or something?" and Tucker had answered: "Something like that." When Henderson asked "who it was?" Tucker replied: "Some woman lived the next block over," adding "[s]he is a widow woman." Police interrogated Tucker prior to the decision in *Miranda*, but his trial occurred after the decision. The Supreme Court had previously held that *Miranda* applied to such cases. Tucker's statements during interrogation were excluded, but the trial judge denied the motion to exclude Henderson's testimony. Henderson testified at trial, Tucker was convicted of rape, and he was sentenced to 20 to 40 years' imprisonment. Tucker's conviction was affirmed by the Michigan appellate courts, but the Federal District Court reversed on the grounds that exclusion of Henderson's testimony was required to protect Tucker's Fifth Amendment right against compulsory self-incrimination. The Court of Appeals for the Sixth Circuit affirmed the District Court, and the Supreme Court in turn reversed the Sixth Circuit.]

III

* * *

Where there has been genuine compulsion of testimony, the [privilege against compulsory self-incrimination] has been given broad scope. Although the constitutional language in which the privilege is cast might be construed to apply only to situations in which the prosecution seeks to call a defendant to testify against himself at his criminal trial, its application has not been so limited. The right has been held applicable to proceedings before a grand jury; to congressional investigations; to juvenile proceedings; and to other statutory inquiries. The privilege has also been applied against the States by virtue of the Fourteenth Amendment . .

* * *

[T]he Court in *Miranda*, for the first time, expressly declared that the Self–Incrimination Clause was applicable to state interrogations at a police station, and that a defendant's statements might be excluded at trial despite their voluntary character under traditional principles.

To supplement this new doctrine, and to help police officers conduct interrogations without facing a continued risk that valuable evidence would be lost, the Court in *Miranda* established a set of specific protective guidelines, now commonly known as the *Miranda* rules. The Court declared that "the prosecution may not use statements, whether exculpatory or inculpatory, stemming from custodial interrogation of the defendant unless it demonstrates the use of procedural safeguards effective to secure the privilege against self-incrimination." A series of recommended "procedural safeguards" then followed. The Court in particular stated:

> "Prior to any questioning, the person must be warned that he has a right to remain silent, that any statement he does make may be used as evidence against him, and that he has a right to the presence of an attorney, either retained or appointed."

The Court said that the defendant, of course, could waive these rights, but that any waiver must have been made "voluntarily, knowingly and intelligently."

The Court recognized that these procedural safeguards were not themselves rights protected by the Constitution but were instead measures to insure that the right against compulsory self-incrimination was protected. As the Court remarked: "We cannot say that the Constitution necessarily requires adherence to any particular solution for the inherent compulsions of the interrogation process as it is presently conducted."

The suggested safeguards were not intended to "create a constitutional straitjacket," but rather to provide practical reinforcement for the right against compulsory self-incrimination.

A comparison of the facts in this case with the historical circumstances underlying the privilege against compulsory self-incrimination strongly indicates that the police conduct here did not deprive respondent of his privilege against compulsory self-incrimination as such, but rather failed to make available to him the full measure of procedural safeguards associated with that right since *Miranda*. Certainly no one could contend that the interrogation faced by respondent bore any resemblance to the historical practices at which the right against compulsory self-incrimination was aimed. [H]is statements could hardly be termed involuntary as that term has been defined in the decisions of this Court. * * *

Our determination that the interrogation in this case involved no compulsion sufficient to breach the right against compulsory self-incrimination does not mean there was not a disregard, albeit an inadvertent disregard, of the procedural rules later established in *Miranda*. The question for decision is how sweeping the judicially imposed consequences of this disregard shall be. This Court said in *Miranda* that statements taken in violation of the *Miranda* principles must not be used to prove the prosecution's case at trial. That requirement was fully complied with by the state court here: respondent's statements, claiming that he was with Henderson and then asleep during the time period of the crime were not admitted against him at trial. This Court has also said, in *Wong Sun* v. *United States*, 371 U.S. 471 (1963), that the "fruits" of police conduct which actually infringed a defendant's Fourth Amendment rights must be suppressed. But we have already concluded that the police conduct at issue here did not abridge respondent's constitutional privilege against compulsory self-incrimination, but departed only from the prophylactic standards later laid down by this Court in *Miranda* to safeguard that privilege. Thus, in deciding whether Henderson's testimony must be excluded, there is no controlling precedent of this Court to guide us. We must therefore examine the matter as a question of principle.

IV

* * *

This Court has already recognized that a failure to give interrogated suspects full *Miranda* warnings does not entitle the suspect to insist that statements made by him be excluded in every conceivable context. In *Harris* v. *New York*, 401 U.S. 222 (1971), the Court was faced with the question of whether the statements of the defendant himself, taken without informing him of his right of access to appointed counsel, could be used to impeach defendant's direct testimony at trial. The Court concluded that they could, saying:

> "Some comments in the *Miranda* opinion can indeed be read as indicating a bar to use of an uncounseled statement for any purpose, but discussion of that issue was not at all necessary to the Court's holding and cannot be regarded as controlling. *Miranda* barred the prosecution from making its case with statements of an accused made while in custody prior to having or effectively waiving counsel. It does not follow from *Miranda* that evidence inadmissible against an accused in the prosecution's case in chief is barred for all purposes, provided of course that the trustworthiness of the evidence satisfies legal standards."

We believe that this reasoning is equally applicable here. * * * *Reversed.*

[The concurring opinions of Justice Stewart, of Justice White, and of Justice Brennan, with whom Justice Marshall joined, are omitted.].

MR. JUSTICE DOUGLAS, dissenting.

* * *

I

* * *

I cannot agree when the Court says that the interrogation here "did not abridge respondent's constitutional privilege against compulsory self-incrimination, but departed only from the prophylactic standards later laid down by this Court in *Miranda* to safeguard that privilege." The Court is not free to prescribe preferred modes of interrogation absent a constitutional basis. We held the "requirement of warnings and waiver of rights [to be] fundamental with respect to the Fifth Amendment privilege," and without so holding we would have been powerless to reverse Miranda's conviction. While *Miranda* recognized that police need not mouth the precise words contained in the Court's opinion, such warnings were held necessary "unless other fully effective means are adopted to notify the person" of his rights. There is no contention here that other means were adopted. The respondent's statements were thus obtained "under circumstances that did not meet *constitutional* standards for protection of the privilege [against self-incrimination]." (emphasis added).

II

With the premise that respondent was subjected to an unconstitutional interrogation, there remains the question whether not only the testimony elicited in the interrogation but also the fruits thereof must be suppressed. Mr. Justice Holmes first articulated the "fruits" doctrine in *Silverthorne Lumber Co.* v. *United States*, 251 U.S. 385 (1920). In that case the Government had illegally seized the petitioner's corporate books and documents. The Government photographed the items before returning them and used the photographs as a basis to subpoena the petitioner to produce the originals before the grand jury. The petitioner refused to comply and was cited for contempt. In reversing, the Court noted that "the essence of a provision forbidding the acquisition of evidence in a certain way is that not merely evidence so acquired shall not be used before the Court but that it shall not be used at all."

The principle received more recent recognition in *Wong Sun* v. *United States*, 371 U.S. 471 (1963). There one Toy had made statements to federal agents and the statements were held inadmissible against him. The statements led the agents to one Yee and at Yee's home the agents found narcotics which were introduced at trial against Toy. In reversing Toy's conviction the Court held that the narcotics discovered at Yee's home must be excluded just as Toy's statements which led to that discovery.

The testimony of the witness in this case was no less a fruit of unconstitutional police action than the photographs in *Silverthorne* or the narcotics in *Wong Sun*. The petitioner has stipulated that the identity and the whereabouts of the witness and his connection with the case were learned about only through the unconstitutional interrogation of the respondent. His testimony must be excluded to comply with *Miranda*'s mandate that "*no* evidence obtained as a result of interrogation [not preceded by adequate warnings] can be used against" an accused. (emphasis added).

* * *

DAVIS v. UNITED STATES

Supreme Court of the United States, 1994.
512 U.S. 452, 114 S.Ct. 2350, 129 L.Ed.2d 362.

[The opinion of the Supreme Court is presented earlier in this chapter. Justice Scalia's concurring opinion calling for enforcement of the federal statute that attempted to overrule *Miranda* introduces the Court's landmark decision in *Dickerson v. United States*.]

JUSTICE SCALIA, concurring.

Section 3501 of Title 18 of the United States Code is "the statute governing the admissibility of confessions in federal prosecutions." That provision declares that "a confession ... *shall be admissible in evidence if it is voluntarily given*," and that the issue of voluntariness shall be determined on the basis of "*all* the circumstances surrounding the giving of the confession, *including* whether or not [the] defendant was advised or knew that he was not required to make any statement ... [;] ... whether or not [the] defendant had been advised prior to questioning of his right to the assistance of counsel; and ... whether or not [the] defendant was without the assistance of counsel when questioned.... " § § 3501(a), (b) (emphases added). It continues (lest the import be doubtful): "The presence or absence of any of the above-mentioned factors ... need not be conclusive on the issue of voluntariness of the confession." § 3501(b). Legal analysis of the admissibility of a confession without reference to these provisions is equivalent to legal analysis of the admissibility of hearsay without consulting the Rules of Evidence; it is an unreal exercise. Yet as the Court observes, that is precisely what the United States has undertaken in this case. It did not raise § 3501(a) below and asserted that it is "not at issue" here.

This is not the first case in which the United States has declined to invoke § 3501 before us—nor even the first case in which that failure has been called to its attention. In fact, with limited exceptions the provision has been studiously avoided by every Administration, not only in this Court but in the lower courts, since its enactment more than 25 years ago.

I agree with the Court that it is *proper*, given the Government's failure to raise the point, to render judgment without taking account of § 3501. But the refusal to consider arguments not raised is a sound prudential practice, rather than a statutory or constitutional mandate, and there are times when prudence dictates the contrary. As far as I am concerned, such a time will have arrived when a case that comes within the terms of this statute is next presented to us.

For most of this century, voluntariness *vel non* was the touchstone of admissibility of confessions. Section 3501 of Title 18 *seems* to provide for that standard in federal criminal prosecutions today. I say "seems" because I do not wish to prejudge any issue of law. I am entirely open to the argument that § 3501 does not mean what it appears to say; that it is inapplicable for some other reason; or even that it is unconstitutional. But I will no longer be open to the argument that this Court should continue to ignore the commands of § 3501 simply because the Executive declines to insist that we observe them.

The Executive has the power (whether or not it has the right) effectively to nullify some provisions of law by the mere failure to prosecute—the exercise of so-called prosecutorial discretion. And it has the power (whether or not it has the right) to avoid application of § 3501 by simply declining to introduce into evidence confessions admissible under its terms. But once a prosecution has been commenced and a confession introduced, the Executive assuredly has neither the power nor the right to determine what objections to admissibility of the confession are valid in law. Section § 3501 of Title 18 is a provision of law directed *to the courts*, reflecting the people's assessment of the proper balance to be struck between concern for persons interrogated in custody and the needs of effective law enforcement. We shirk our duty if we systematically disregard that statutory command simply because the Justice Department systematically declines to remind us of it.

The United States' repeated refusal to invoke § 3501, combined with the courts' traditional (albeit merely prudential) refusal to consider arguments not raised, has caused the federal judiciary to confront a host of *"Miranda"* issues that might be entirely irrelevant under federal law. Worse still, it may have produced—during an era of intense national concern about the problem of runaway crime—the acquittal and the nonprosecution of many dangerous felons, enabling them to continue their depredations upon our citizens. There is no excuse for this. Perhaps (though I do not immediately see why) the Justice Department has good basis for believing that allowing prosecutions to be defeated on grounds that could be avoided by invocation of § 3501 is consistent with the Executive's obligation to "take Care that the Laws be faithfully executed," U.S. Const., Art. II, § 3. That is not the point. The point is whether *our* continuing refusal to *consider* § 3501 is consistent with the Third Branch's obligation to decide according to the law. I think it is not.

DICKERSON v. UNITED STATES

Supreme Court of the United States, 2000.
530 U.S. 428, 120 S.Ct. 2326, 147 L.Ed.2d 405.

CHIEF JUSTICE REHNQUIST delivered the opinion of the Court.

In *Miranda* v. *Arizona*, 384 U.S. 436, 86 S.Ct. 1602, 16 L.Ed.2d 694 (1966), we held that certain warnings must be given before a suspect's statement made during custodial interrogation could be admitted in evidence. In the wake of that decision, Congress enacted 18 U.S.C. § 3501, which in essence laid down a rule that the admissibility of such statements should turn only on whether or not they were voluntarily made. We hold that *Miranda*, being a constitutional decision of this Court, may not be in effect overruled by an Act of Congress, and we decline to overrule *Miranda* ourselves. We therefore hold that *Miranda* and its progeny in this Court govern the admissibility of statements made during custodial interrogation in both state and federal courts.

Petitioner Dickerson was indicted for bank robbery, conspiracy to commit bank robbery, and using a firearm in the course of committing a crime of violence, all in violation of the applicable provisions of Title 18 of the United States Code. Before trial, Dickerson moved to suppress a statement he had made at a Federal Bureau of Investigation field office, on the grounds that he had not received "*Miranda* warnings" before being interrogated. The District Court granted his motion to suppress, and the Government took an interlocutory appeal to the United States Court of Appeals for the Fourth Circuit. That court, by a divided vote, reversed the District Court's suppression order. It agreed with the District Court's conclusion that petitioner had not received *Miranda* warnings before making his statement. But it went on to hold that § 3501, which in effect makes the admissibility of statements such as Dickerson's turn solely on whether they were made voluntarily, was satisfied in this case. It then concluded that our decision in *Miranda* was not a constitutional holding, and that therefore Congress could by statute have the final say on the question of admissibility.

Because of the importance of the questions raised by the Court of Appeals' decision, we granted certiorari, and now reverse.

We begin with a brief historical account of the law governing the admission of confessions. Prior to *Miranda*, we evaluated the admissibility of a suspect's confession under a voluntariness test. The roots of this test developed in the common law, as the courts of England and then the United States recognized that coerced confessions are inherently untrustworthy * * * Over time, our cases recognized two constitutional bases for the requirement that a confession be voluntary to be admitted into evidence: the Fifth Amendment right against self-incrimination and the Due Process Clause of the Fourteenth Amendment. * * *

[F]or the middle third of the 20th century our cases based the rule against admitting coerced confessions primarily, if not exclusively, on notions of due process. We applied the due process voluntariness test in "some 30 different cases decided during the era that intervened between *Brown* [*v. Mississippi*], 297 U.S. 278, 80 L.Ed.682, 56 S.Ct. 461 (1936), and *Escobedo* v. *Illinois,* 378 U.S. 478, 84 S.Ct. 1758, 12 L.Ed.2d 977 (1964)." Those cases refined the test into an inquiry that examines "whether a defendant's will was overborne" by the circumstances surrounding the giving of a confession. The due process test takes into consideration "the totality of all the surrounding circumstances—both the characteristics of the accused and the details of the interrogation." The determination "depend[s] upon a weighing of the circumstances of pressure against the power of resistance of the person confessing."

We have never abandoned this due process jurisprudence, and thus continue to exclude confessions that were obtained involuntarily. But our decisions in *Malloy* v. *Hogan,* 378 U.S. 1, 84 S.Ct. 1489, 12 L.Ed.2d

653 (1964), and *Miranda* changed the focus of much of the inquiry in determining the admissibility of suspects' incriminating statements. In *Malloy*, we held that the Fifth Amendment's Self–Incrimination Clause is incorporated in the Due Process Clause of the Fourteenth Amendment and thus applies to the States. We decided *Miranda* on the heels of *Malloy*.

In *Miranda*, we noted that the advent of modern custodial police interrogation brought with it an increased concern about confessions obtained by coercion. Because custodial police interrogation, by its very nature, isolates and pressures the individual, we stated that "[e]ven without employing brutality, the 'third degree' or [other] specific stratagems, ... custodial interrogation exacts a heavy toll on individual liberty and trades on the weakness of individuals." We concluded that the coercion inherent in custodial interrogation blurs the line between voluntary and involuntary statements, and thus heightens the risk that an individual will not be "accorded his privilege under the Fifth Amendment ... not to be compelled to incriminate himself." Accordingly, we laid down "concrete constitutional guidelines for law enforcement agencies and courts to follow." Those guidelines established that the admissibility in evidence of any statement given during custodial interrogation of a suspect would depend on whether the police provided the suspect with four warnings. These warnings (which have come to be known colloquially as "*Miranda* rights") are: a suspect "has the right to remain silent, that anything he says can be used against him in a court of law, that he has the right to the presence of an attorney, and that if he cannot afford an attorney one will be appointed for him prior to any questioning if he so desires."

Two years after *Miranda* was decided, Congress enacted § 3501. That section provides, in relevant part:

"(a) In any criminal prosecution brought by the United States or by the District of Columbia, a confession ... shall be admissible in evidence if it is voluntarily given. Before such confession is received in evidence, the trial judge shall, out of the presence of the jury, determine any issue as to voluntariness. If the trial judge determines that the confession was voluntarily made it shall be admitted in evidence and the trial judge shall permit the jury to hear relevant evidence on the issue of voluntariness and shall instruct the jury to give such weight to the confession as the jury feels it deserves under all the circumstances.

"(b) The trial judge in determining the issue of voluntariness shall take into consideration all the circumstances surrounding the giving of the confession, including (1) the time elapsing between arrest and arraignment of the defendant making the confession, if it was made after arrest and before arraignment, (2) whether such defendant knew the nature of the offense with which he was charged or of which he was suspected at the time of making the confession, (3) whether or not such defendant was advised or knew that he was not required to make any statement and that any such statement could be used against him, (4) whether or not such defendant had been advised prior to questioning of his right to the assistance of counsel; and (5) whether or not such defendant was without the assistance of counsel when questioned and when giving such confession.

"The presence or absence of any of the above-mentioned factors to be taken into consideration by the judge need not be conclusive on the issue of voluntariness of the confession."

Given § 3501's express designation of voluntariness as the touchstone of admissibility, its omission of any warning requirement, and the instruction for trial courts to consider a nonexclusive list of factors relevant to the circumstances of a confession, we agree with the Court of Appeals that Congress intended by its enactment to overrule *Miranda*. Because of the obvious conflict between our decision in *Miranda* and § 3501, we must address whether Congress has constitutional authority to thus supersede *Miranda*. If Congress has such authority, § 3501's totality-of-the-circumstances approach must prevail over *Miranda*'s requirement of warnings; if not, that section must yield to *Miranda*'s more specific requirements.

The law in this area is clear. This Court has supervisory authority over the federal courts, and we may use that authority to prescribe rules of evidence and procedure that are binding in those tribunals. However, the power to judicially create and enforce nonconstitutional "rules of procedure and evidence for the federal courts exists only in the absence of a relevant Act of Congress." Congress retains the ultimate authority to modify or set aside any judicially created rules of evidence and procedure that are not required by the Constitution.

But Congress may not legislatively supersede our decisions interpreting and applying the Constitution. See, *e.g., City of Boerne* v. *Flores*, 521 U.S. 507, 517–521, 117 S.Ct. 2157, 138 L.Ed.2d 624 (1997). This case therefore turns on whether the *Miranda* Court announced a constitutional rule or merely exercised its supervisory authority to regulate evidence in the absence of congressional direction. Recognizing this point, the Court of Appeals surveyed *Miranda* and its progeny to determine the constitutional status of the *Miranda* decision. Relying on the fact that we have created several exceptions to *Miranda*'s warnings requirement and that we have repeatedly referred to the *Miranda* warnings as "prophylactic," and "not themselves rights protected by the Constitution," *Michigan* v. *Tucker*, 417 U.S. 433, 444, 94 S.Ct. 2357, 41 L.Ed.2d 182 (1974), the Court of Appeals concluded that the protections announced in *Miranda* are not constitutionally required.

We disagree with the Court of Appeals' conclusion, although we concede that there is language in some of our opinions that supports the view taken by that court. But first and foremost of the factors on the other side—that *Miranda* is a constitutional decision—is that both *Miranda* and two of its companion cases applied the rule to proceedings in state courts—to wit, Arizona, California, and New York. Since that time, we have consistently applied *Miranda*'s rule to prosecutions arising in state courts. It is beyond dispute that we do not hold a supervisory power over the courts of the several States. * * *

The *Miranda* opinion itself begins by stating that the Court granted certiorari "to explore some facets of the problems ... of applying the privilege against self-incrimination to in-custody interrogation, *and to give concrete constitutional guidelines for law enforcement agencies and courts to follow.*" In fact, the majority opinion is replete with statements indicating that the majority thought it was announcing a constitutional rule. Indeed, the Court's ultimate conclusion was that the unwarned confessions obtained in the four cases before the Court in *Miranda* "were obtained from the defendant under circumstances that did not meet constitutional standards for protection of the privilege."

Additional support for our conclusion that *Miranda* is constitutionally based is found in the *Miranda* Court's invitation for legislative action to protect the constitutional right against coerced self-incrimination. After discussing the "compelling pressures" inherent in custodial police interrogation, the *Miranda* Court concluded that, "[i]n order to combat these pressures and to permit a full opportunity to exercise the privilege against self-incrimination, the accused must be adequately and effectively appraised of his rights and the exercise of those rights must be fully honored." However, the Court emphasized that it could not foresee "the potential alternatives for protecting the privilege which might be devised by Congress or the States," and it accordingly opined that the Constitution would not preclude legislative solutions that differed from the prescribed *Miranda* warnings but which were "at least as effective in apprising accused persons of their right of silence and in assuring a continuous opportunity to exercise it."

The Court of Appeals also relied on the fact that we have, after our *Miranda* decision, made exceptions from its rule in cases * * *. But we have also broadened the application of the *Miranda* doctrine in cases * * *. These decisions illustrate the principle—not that *Miranda* is not a constitutional rule—but that no constitutional rule is immutable. No court laying down a general rule can possibly foresee the various circumstances in which counsel will seek to apply it, and the sort of modifications represented by these cases are as much a normal part of constitutional law as the original decision.

The Court of Appeals also noted that in *Oregon* v. *Elstad*, 470 U. S. 298, 105 S.Ct. 1285, 84 L.Ed.2d 222 (1985), we stated that " '[t]he *Miranda* exclusionary rule ... serves the Fifth Amendment and sweeps more broadly than the Fifth Amendment itself.' " Our decision in that case—refusing to apply the traditional "fruits" doctrine developed in Fourth Amendment cases—does not prove that *Miranda* is a nonconstitutional decision, but simply recognizes the fact that unreasonable searches under the Fourth Amendment are different from unwarned interrogation under the Fifth Amendment.

* * * *Miranda* requires procedures that will warn a suspect in custody of his right to remain silent and which will assure the suspect that the exercise of that right will be honored. As discussed above, § 3501 explicitly eschews a requirement of pre-interrogation warnings in favor of an approach that looks to the administration of such warnings as only one factor in determining the voluntariness of a suspect's confession. The additional remedies cited by *amicus* do not, in our view, render them, together with § 3501 an adequate substitute for the warnings required by *Miranda*.

The dissent argues that it is judicial overreaching for this Court to hold § 3501 unconstitutional unless we hold that the *Miranda* warnings are required by the Constitution, in the sense that nothing else will suffice to satisfy constitutional requirements. But we need not go farther than *Miranda* to decide this case. In *Miranda*, the Court noted that reliance on the traditional totality-of-the-circumstances test raised a risk of overlooking an involuntary custodial confession, a risk that the Court found unacceptably great when the confession is offered in the case in chief to prove guilt. The Court therefore concluded that something more than the totality test was necessary. As discussed above, § 3501 reinstates the totality test as sufficient. Section 3501 therefore cannot be sustained if *Miranda* is to remain the law.

Whether or not we would agree with *Miranda*'s reasoning and its resulting rule, were we addressing the issue in the first instance, the principles of *stare decisis* weigh heavily against overruling it now. While " '*stare decisis* is not an inexorable command,' " particularly when we are interpreting the Constitution, "even in constitutional cases, the doctrine carries such persuasive force that we have always required a departure from precedent to be supported by some 'special justification.' "

We do not think there is such justification for overruling *Miranda*. *Miranda* has become embedded in routine police practice to the point where the warnings have become part of our national culture. While we have overruled our precedents when subsequent cases have undermined their doctrinal underpinnings, we do not believe that this has happened to the *Miranda* decision. If anything, our subsequent cases have reduced the impact of the *Miranda* rule on legitimate law enforcement while reaffirming the decision's core ruling that unwarned statements may not be used as evidence in the prosecution's case in chief.

The disadvantage of the *Miranda* rule is that statements which may be by no means involuntary, made by a defendant who is aware of his "rights," may nonetheless be excluded and a guilty defendant go free as a result. But experience suggests that the totality-of-the-circumstances test which § 3501 seeks to revive is more difficult than *Miranda* for law enforcement officers to conform to, and for courts to apply in a consistent manner. The requirement that *Miranda* warnings be given does not, of course, dispense with the voluntariness inquiry. But * * * "[c]ases in which a defendant can make a colorable argument that a self-incriminating statement was 'compelled' despite the fact that the law enforcement authorities adhered to the dictates of *Miranda* are rare."

In sum, we conclude that *Miranda* announced a constitutional rule that Congress may not supersede legislatively. Following the rule of *stare decisis*, we decline to overrule *Miranda* ourselves. The judgment of the Court of Appeals is therefore *Reversed*.

JUSTICE SCALIA, with whom JUSTICE THOMAS joins, dissenting.

* * * Those who understand the judicial process will appreciate that today's decision is not a reaffirmation of *Miranda*, but a radical revision of the most significant element of *Miranda* (as of all cases): the rationale that gives it a permanent place in our jurisprudence.

Marbury v. *Madison*, 5 U.S. 137, 2 L.Ed. 60, 1 Cranch 137 (1803), held that an Act of Congress will not be enforced by the courts if what it prescribes violates the Constitution of the United States. That was the basis on which *Miranda* was decided. One will search today's opinion in vain, however, for a statement (surely simple enough to make) that what 18 U.S.C. § 3501 prescribes—the use at trial of a voluntary confession, even when a *Miranda* warning or its equivalent has failed to be given— violates the Constitution. The reason the statement does not appear is not only (and perhaps not so much) that it would be absurd, inasmuch as § 3501 excludes from trial precisely what the Constitution excludes from trial, viz., compelled confessions; but also that Justices whose votes are needed to compose today's majority are on record as believing that a violation of *Miranda* is *not* a violation of the Constitution. And so, to justify today's agreed-upon result, the Court must adopt a significant *new*, if not entirely comprehensible, principle of constitutional law. As the Court chooses to describe that principle, statutes of Congress can be disregarded, not only when what they prescribe violates the Constitution, but when what they prescribe contradicts a decision of this Court that "announced a constitutional rule." As I shall discuss in some detail, the only thing that can possibly mean in the context of this case is that this Court has the power, not merely to apply the Constitution but to expand it, imposing what it regards as useful "prophylactic" restrictions upon Congress and the States. That is an immense and frightening antidemocratic power, and it does not exist.

* * *

I

Early in this Nation's history, this Court established the sound proposition that constitutional government in a system of separated powers requires judges to regard as inoperative any legislative act, even of Congress itself, that is "repugnant to the Constitution."

* * *

The power we recognized in *Marbury* will thus permit us, indeed require us, to "disregar[d]" § 3501, a duly enacted statute governing the admissibility of evidence in the federal courts, only if it "be in opposition to the constitution"—here, assertedly, the dictates of the Fifth Amendment.

It was once possible to characterize the so-called *Miranda* rule as resting (however implausibly) upon the proposition that what the statute here before us permits—the admission at trial of un-*Mirandized* confessions—violates the Constitution. That is the fairest reading of the *Miranda* case itself * * *

* * *

II

As the Court today acknowledges, since *Miranda* we have explicitly, and repeatedly, interpreted that decision as having announced, not the circumstances in which custodial interrogation runs afoul of the Fifth or Fourteenth Amendment, but rather only "prophylactic" rules that go beyond the right against compelled self-incrimination. Of course the seeds of this "prophylactic" interpretation of *Miranda* were present in the decision itself. In subsequent cases, the seeds have sprouted and borne fruit: The Court has squarely concluded that it is possible—indeed not uncommon—for the police to violate Miranda without also violating the Constitution.

Michigan v. Tucker, 417 U.S. 433 (1974), an opinion for the Court written by then-Justice Rehnquist, rejected the true-to-*Marbury*, failure-to-warn-as-constitutional-violation interpretation of *Miranda*. It held that exclusion of the "fruits" of a *Miranda* violation—the statement of a witness whose identity the defendant had revealed while in custody—was not required. The opinion explained that the question whether the "police conduct complained of directly infringed upon respondent's right against compulsory self-incrimination" was a "separate question" from "whether it instead violated only the prophylactic rules developed to protect that right." The "procedural safeguards" adopted in *Miranda*, the Court said, "were not themselves rights protected by the Constitution but were instead measures to insure that the right against compulsory self-incrimination was protected," and to "provide practical reinforcement for the right." * * *

* * *

In light of these cases, and our statements to the same effect in others, it is simply no longer possible for the Court to conclude, even if it wanted to, that a violation of *Miranda*'s rules is a violation of the Constitution. But as I explained at the outset, that is what is required before the Court may disregard a law of Congress governing the admissibility of evidence in federal court. * * * By disregarding congressional action that concededly does not violate the Constitution, the Court flagrantly offends fundamental principles of separation of powers, and arrogates to itself prerogatives reserved to the representatives of the people.

* * *

IV

Thus, while I agree with the Court that § 3501 cannot be upheld without also concluding that *Miranda* represents an illegitimate exercise of our authority to review state-court judgments, I do not share the Court's hesitation in reaching that conclusion. For while the Court is also correct that the doctrine of *stare decisis* demands some "special justification" for a departure from longstanding precedent—even precedent of the constitutional variety—that criterion is more than met here. To repeat Justice Stevens' cogent observation, it is "[o]bviou[s]" that "the Court's power to reverse Miranda's conviction rested *entirely* on the determination that a violation of the Federal Constitution had occurred." * * *

* * *

Moreover, it is not clear why the Court thinks that the "totality-of-the-circumstances test ... is more difficult than *Miranda* for law enforcement officers to conform to, and for courts to apply in a consistent manner." * * *

But even were I to agree that the old totality-of-the-circumstances test was more cumbersome, it is simply not true that *Miranda* has banished it from the law and replaced it with a new test. Under the current regime, which the Court today retains in its entirety, courts are frequently called upon to undertake *both* inquiries. That is because, as explained earlier, voluntariness remains the *constitutional* standard, and as such continues to govern the admissibility for impeachment purposes of statements taken in violation of *Miranda*, the admissibility of the "fruits" of such statements, and the admissibility of statements challenged as unconstitutionally obtained *despite* the interrogator's compliance with *Miranda*.

* * *

I dissent from today's decision, and, until § 3501 is repealed, will continue to apply it in all cases where there has been a sustainable finding that the defendant's confession was voluntary.

Commentary

1. In the years preceding the Court's decision in *Dickerson*, prominent legal scholars debated vigorously the *Miranda* decision's empirical effects upon law enforcement and the securing of admissible confessions—often reaching very different conclusions. Some authors concluded that Miranda had led to the exclusion of a large percentage of confessions. See, e.g., Paul G. Cassell & Bret S. Hayman, *Police Interrogation in the 1990s: An Empirical Study of the Effects of Miranda*, 43 UCLA L. Rev. 839 (1996); Paul G. Cassell, *Miranda's Social Costs: An Empirical Reassessment*, 90 Nw. L. Rev. 387 (1996). Others concluded that the data indicated that Miranda had not produced a large percentage of excluded confessions. See, e.g., Stephen J. Schulhofer, *Miranda's Practical Effect: Substantial Benefits and Vanishingly*

Small Social Costs, 90 Nw. L. Rev. 501 (1996); George C. Thomas III, *Is Miranda a Real–World Failure? A Plea for More and Better Evidence*, 43 UCLA L. Rev. 821 (1996).

Chief Justice Rehnquist's opinion in *Dickerson* may have been the last word on the subject. Recall that he concluded that "[c]ases in which a defendant can make a colorable argument that a self-incriminating statement was 'compelled' despite the fact that the law enforcement authorities adhered to the dictates of *Miranda* are rare." Once the warnings are given and a suspect executes a valid waiver, absent some egregious misconduct by the police courts invariably conclude that the confession was voluntary, and therefore admissible. As a practical matter, the *Miranda* warnings serve as a license to admit, rather than a reason to exclude, confessions. Perhaps this is one reason that Chief Justice Rehnquist authored the opinion that preserved *Miranda* from being overruled by the statute he had championed more than a quarter century earlier.

2. In *Dickerson*, the Court appeared to resolve several longstanding debates about the constitutional status of the *Miranda* warnings and the nature of the rights protected by the Fifth Amendment. Subsequent cases demonstrate that conflicts about these issues persist among the Justices. For example, the apparent consensus reached in *Dickerson* was fractured in Chavez v. Martinez, 538 U.S. 760 (2003). Six Justices wrote opinions. Justice Thomas announced the Court's judgment, but failed to obtain a majority for any part of his opinion. Only Chief Justice Rehnquist joined Justice Thomas' opinion in its entirety. That fact is noteworthy, because portions of Justice Thomas' opinion appear to reject key elements of the reasoning contained in the Chief Justice's majority opinion in *Dickerson*. Part II of Justice Souter's concurring opinion attracted five votes, and thus constitutes a majority opinion for the Court, but the remainder of his opinion attracted only two votes. Concurring and dissenting opinions also were published by Justices Scalia, Kennedy, Stevens, and Ginsburg.

Martinez filed a *§ 1983* suit alleging that his constitutional rights were violated by a coercive interrogation by police officer Chavez. Martinez was shot during a fight with police officers and suffered severe injuries that left Martinez permanently blind and paralyzed from the waist down. The officers then placed Martinez under arrest. Chavez, a patrol supervisor, arrived on the scene minutes later with paramedics. Chavez accompanied Martinez to the hospital and then questioned Martinez there while he was receiving treatment from medical personnel. The interview lasted a total of about 10 minutes, over a 45–minute period, with Chavez leaving the emergency room for periods of time to permit medical personnel to attend to Martinez. At no point during the interview was Martinez given the *Miranda* warnings.

The plurality noted that at first, Martinez's answers generally were "I don't know," "I am dying," and "I am choking." Later in the interview, Martinez admitted that he had taken a gun from an officer's holster and pointed it at the police, and that he used heroin regularly. At one point, Martinez said "I am not telling you anything until they treat me," yet Chavez continued the interview.

In his opinion concurring in part and dissenting in part, JUSTICE STEVENS quoted at length from he transcript of the tape recorded interrogation that occurred in the emergency room of the hospital. The transcript included the following passages:

"Chavez: Can you hear? look listen, I am Benjamin Chavez with the police here in Oxnard, look.

"O. M.: I am dying, please.

* * *

"Chavez: OK, listen, listen I want to know what happened, OK??

"O. M.: I want them to treat me.

"Chavez: OK, they are do it (sic), look when you took out the gun from the tape (sic) of the police . . .

"O. M.: I am dying . . .

"Chavez: OK, look, what I want to know if you took out (sic) the gun of the police?

"O. M.: I am not telling you anything until they treat me.

"Chavez: Look, tell me what happened, I want to know, look well don't you want the police know (sic) what happened with you?

"O. M.: Uuuggghhh! My belly hurts . . .

* * *

"Chavez: Nothing, why did you run (sic) from the police?

"O. M.: I don't want to say anything anymore.

"Chavez: No?

"O. M.: I want them to treat me, it hurts a lot, please.

"Chavez: You don't want to tell (sic) what happened with you over there?

"O. M.: I don't want to die, I don't want to die."

Martinez was never charged with a crime, and his answers were never used against him in any criminal prosecution. Martinez filed suit under 42 U.S.C. § 1983, maintaining that Chavez's actions violated his Fifth Amendment right not to be "compelled in any criminal case to be a witness against himself," as well as his Fourteenth Amendment substantive due process right to be free from coercive questioning. Officer Chavez raised a qualified immunity defense. The District Court granted summary judgment in favor of Martinez, and the Ninth Circuit affirmed the District Court's denial of qualified immunity, concluding that Chavez's actions deprived Martinez of his rights under the Fifth and Fourteenth Amendments and that a reasonable officer "would have known that persistent interrogation of the suspect despite repeated requests to stop violated the suspect's Fifth and Fourteenth Amendment right to be free from coercive interrogation."

In the plurality opinion, Justice Thomas never mentioned Chief Justice Rehnquist's recent opinion in *Dickerson*, in which the Court had held that *Miranda* announced a constitutional rule. Instead, Justice Thomas focused upon the use of compelled statements, and concluded that Martinez's allegations failed to state a violation of his constitutional rights because "Martinez was never prosecuted for a crime, let alone compelled to be a witness against himself in a criminal case." In reaching this conclusion, the plurality rejected the argument that a "criminal case" within the meaning of the Fifth Amendment should encompass the entire criminal investigatory process, including police interrogations, and found that a "criminal case" requires at least the initiation of legal proceedings. "Statements compelled by police interrogations of course may not be used against a defendant at trial, but it is not until their use in a criminal case that a violation of the Self–Incrimination Clause occurs." Justice Thomas concluded that "mere coercion does not violate the text of the Self–Incrimination Clause absent use of the compelled statements in a criminal case against the witness."

The plurality found that the Fourteenth Amendment's Due Process Clause, rather than the Fifth Amendment's Self–Incrimination Clause, was the source of any legal remedy available to Martinez, and emphasized that this did "not mean that police torture or other abuse that results in a confession is constitutionally permissible so long as the statements are not used at trial; it simply means that" the Self–Incrimination Clause is not the source of that remedy. The plurality also concluded that "Chavez's questioning did not violate Martinez's due process rights."

As noted above, a majority of Justices joined in Part II of Justice Souter's opinion, which held that whether Martinez could pursue a claim of liability for a substantive due process violation was an issue to be addressed by the lower courts on remand. The majority did not, therefore, agree with the lower courts that Martinez already had established that his constitutional rights had been violated. Two Justices argued forcefully against this conclusion.

Justice Stevens, concurring in part and dissenting in part, argued that the interrogation of Martinez "was the functional equivalent of an attempt to obtain an involuntary confession from a prisoner by torturous methods. As a matter of law, that type of brutal police conduct constitutes an immediate deprivation of the prisoner's constitutionally protected interest in liberty. Because these propositions are so clear, the District Court and the Court of Appeals correctly held that petitioner is not entitled to qualified immunity."

Justice Kennedy, also concurring in part and dissenting in part, asserted that "[a] constitutional right is traduced the moment torture or its close equivalents are brought to bear. Constitutional protection for a tortured suspect is not held in abeyance until some later criminal proceeding takes place." Unlike the plurality, he emphasized that *Dickerson* had confirmed that the *Miranda* warnings are constitutional requirements. Justice Kennedy also emphasized that the Self–Incrimination Clause assures both

> that a person will not be compelled to testify against himself in a criminal proceeding and a continuing right against government conduct intended to bring about self-incrimination. The principle extends to forbid policies which exert official compulsion that might induce a person into forfeiting his rights under the Clause.

> The conclusion that the Self–Incrimination Clause is not violated until the government seeks to use a statement in some later criminal proceeding strips the Clause of an essential part of its force and

meaning. * * * To tell our whole legal system that when conducting a criminal investigation police officials can use severe compulsion or even torture with no present violation of the right against compelled self-incrimination can only diminish a celebrated provision in the Bill of Rights. A Constitution survives over time because the people share a common, historic commitment to certain simple but fundamental principles which preserve their freedom. Today's decision undermines one of those respected precepts.

In my view the Self–Incrimination Clause is applicable at the time and place police use compulsion to extract a statement from a suspect. The Clause forbids that conduct. A majority of the Court has now concluded otherwise, but that should not end this case.
* * *

2. Fifth Amendment Balancing: The Public Safety Exception

NEW YORK v. QUARLES

Supreme Court of the United States, 1984.
467 U.S. 649, 104 S.Ct. 2626, 81 L.Ed.2d 550.

JUSTICE REHNQUIST delivered the opinion of the Court.

Respondent Benjamin Quarles was charged in the New York trial court with criminal possession of a weapon. The trial court suppressed the gun in question, and a statement made by respondent, because the statement was obtained by police before they read respondent his "*Miranda* rights." That ruling was affirmed on appeal through the New York Court of Appeals. [W]e now reverse. We conclude that under the circumstances involved in this case, overriding considerations of public safety justify the officer's failure to provide *Miranda* warnings before he asked questions devoted to locating the abandoned weapon.

On September 11, 1980, at approximately 12:30 a. m., Officer Frank Kraft and Officer Sal Scarring were on road patrol in Queens, N. Y., when a young woman approached their car. She told them that she had just been raped by a black male, approximately six feet tall, who was wearing a black jacket with the name "Big Ben" printed in yellow letters on the back. She told the officers that the man had just entered an A & P supermarket located nearby and that the man was carrying a gun.

The officers drove the woman to the supermarket, and Officer Kraft entered the store while Officer Scarring radioed for assistance. Officer Kraft quickly spotted respondent, who matched the description given by the woman, approaching a checkout counter. Apparently upon seeing the officer, respondent turned and ran toward the rear of the store, and Officer Kraft pursued him with a drawn gun. When respondent turned the corner at the end of an aisle, Officer Kraft lost sight of him for several seconds, and upon regaining sight of respondent, ordered him to stop and put his hands over his head.

Although more than three other officers had arrived on the scene by that time, Officer Kraft was the first to reach respondent. He frisked him and discovered that he was wearing a shoulder holster which was then empty. After handcuffing him, Officer Kraft asked him where the gun was. Respondent nodded in the direction of some empty cartons and responded, "the gun is over there." Officer Kraft thereafter retrieved a loaded .38–caliber revolver from one of the cartons, formally placed respondent under arrest, and read him his *Miranda* rights from a printed card. Respondent indicated that he would be willing to answer questions without an attorney present. Officer Kraft then asked respondent if he owned the gun and where he had purchased it. Respondent answered that he did own it and that he had purchased it in Miami, Fla.

In the subsequent prosecution of respondent for criminal possession of a weapon, the judge excluded the statement, "the gun is over there," and the gun because the officer had not given respondent the warnings required by our decision in *Miranda v. Arizona*, 384 U.S. 436, 86 S.Ct. 1602, 16 L.Ed.2d 694 (1966), before asking him where the gun was located. The judge excluded the other statements about respondent's ownership of the gun and the place of purchase, as evidence tainted by the prior *Miranda* violation. * * *

[W]e believe that this case presents a situation where concern for public safety must be paramount to adherence to the literal language of the prophylactic rules enunciated in *Miranda*.

* * * In *Miranda* this Court for the first time extended the Fifth Amendment privilege against compulsory self-incrimination to individuals subjected to custodial interrogation by the police. The Fifth Amendment itself does not prohibit all incriminating admissions; "[absent] some officially *coerced* self-accusation, the Fifth Amendment privilege is not violated by even the most damning admissions." (emphasis added). The *Miranda* Court, however, presumed that interrogation in certain custodial circumstances is inherently coercive and held that statements made under those circumstances are inadmissible unless the suspect is specifically informed of his *Miranda* rights and freely decides to forgo those rights. The prophylactic *Miranda* warnings therefore are "not themselves rights protected by the Constitution but [are] instead measures to insure that the right against compulsory self-incrimination [is] protected." Requiring *Miranda* warnings before custodial interrogation provides "practical reinforcement" for the Fifth Amendment right.

In this case we have before us no claim that respondent's statements were actually compelled by police conduct which overcame his will to resist. Thus the only issue before us is whether Officer Kraft was justified in failing to make available to respondent the procedural safeguards associated with the privilege against compulsory self-incrimination since *Miranda*.

The New York Court of Appeals was undoubtedly correct in deciding that the facts of this case come within the ambit of the *Miranda* decision as we have subsequently interpreted it. We agree that respondent was in police custody because we have noted that "the ultimate inquiry is simply whether there is a 'formal arrest or restraint on freedom of movement' of the degree associated with a formal arrest," Here Quarles was surrounded by at least four police officers and was handcuffed when the questioning at issue took place. As the New York Court of Appeals observed, there was nothing to suggest that any of the officers were any longer concerned for their own physical safety. * * *

We hold that on these facts there is a "public safety" exception to the requirement that *Miranda* warnings be given before a suspect's answers may be admitted into evidence, and that the availability of that exception does not depend upon the motivation of the individual officers involved. In a kaleidoscopic situation such as the one confronting these officers, where spontaneity rather than adherence to a police manual is necessarily the order of the day, the application of the exception which we recognize today should not be made to depend on *post hoc* findings at a suppression hearing concerning the subjective motivation of the arresting officer. Undoubtedly most police officers, if placed in Officer Kraft's position, would act out of a host of different, instinctive, and largely unverifiable motives—their own safety, the safety of others, and perhaps as well the desire to obtain incriminating evidence from the suspect.

Whatever the motivation of individual officers in such a situation, we do not believe that the doctrinal underpinnings of *Miranda* require that it be applied in all its rigor to a situation in which police officers ask questions reasonably prompted by a concern for the public safety. The *Miranda* decision was based in large part on this Court's view that the warnings which it required police to give to suspects in custody would reduce the likelihood that the suspects would fall victim to constitutionally impermissible practices of police interrogation in the presumptively coercive environment of the station house. The dissenters warned that the requirement of *Miranda* warnings would have the effect of decreasing the number of suspects who respond to police questioning. The *Miranda* majority, however, apparently felt that whatever the cost to society in terms of fewer convictions of guilty suspects, that cost would simply have to be borne in the interest of enlarged protection for the Fifth Amendment privilege.

The police in this case, in the very act of apprehending a suspect, were confronted with the immediate necessity of ascertaining the whereabouts of a gun which they had every reason to believe the suspect had just removed from his empty holster and discarded in the supermarket. So long as the gun was concealed somewhere in the supermarket, with its actual whereabouts unknown, it obviously posed more than one danger to the public safety: an accomplice might make use of it, a customer or employee might later come upon it.

In such a situation, if the police are required to recite the familiar *Miranda* warnings before asking the whereabouts of the gun, suspects in Quarles' position might well be deterred from responding. Procedural safeguards which deter a suspect from responding were deemed acceptable in *Miranda* in order to protect the Fifth Amendment privilege; when the primary social cost of those added protections is the possibility of fewer convictions, the *Miranda* majority was willing to bear that cost. Here, had *Miranda* warnings deterred Quarles from responding to Officer Kraft's question about the whereabouts of the gun, the cost would have been something more than merely the failure to obtain evidence useful in convicting Quarles. Officer Kraft needed an answer to his question not simply to make his case against Quarles but to insure that further danger to the public did not result from the concealment of the gun in a public area.

We conclude that the need for answers to questions in a situation posing a threat to the public safety outweighs the need for the prophylactic rule protecting the Fifth Amendment's privilege against self-incrimination. We decline to place officers such as Officer Kraft in the untenable position of having to consider, often in a matter of seconds, whether it best serves society for them to ask the necessary questions without the *Miranda* warnings and render whatever probative evidence they uncover inadmissible, or for them to give the warnings in order to preserve the admissibility of evidence they might uncover but possibly damage or destroy their ability to obtain that evidence and neutralize the volatile situation confronting them.

In recognizing a narrow exception to the *Miranda* rule in this case, we acknowledge that to some degree we lessen the desirable clarity of that rule. * * * As we have in other contexts, we recognize here the importance of a workable rule "to guide police officers, who have only limited time and expertise to reflect on and balance the social and individual interests involved in the specific circumstances they confront." But as we have pointed out, we believe that the exception which we recognize today lessens the necessity of that on-the-scene balancing process. The exception will not be difficult for police officers to apply because in each case it will be circumscribed by the exigency which justifies it. We think police officers can and will distinguish almost instinctively between questions necessary to secure their own safety or the safety of the public and questions designed solely to elicit testimonial evidence from a suspect.

* * *

We hold that the Court of Appeals in this case erred in excluding the statement, "the gun is over there," and the gun because of the officer's failure to read respondent his *Miranda* rights before attempting to locate the weapon. Accordingly we hold that it also erred in excluding the subsequent statements as illegal fruits of a *Miranda* violation. We therefore reverse and remand for further proceedings not inconsistent with this opinion. *It is so ordered.*

JUSTICE O'CONNOR, concurring in the judgment in part and dissenting in part.

In *Miranda v. Arizona* the Court held unconstitutional, because inherently compelled, the admission of statements derived from in-custody questioning not preceded by an explanation of the privilege against self-incrimination and the consequences of forgoing it. Today, the Court concludes that overriding considerations of public safety justify the admission of evidence—oral statements and a gun—secured without the benefit of such warnings. In so holding, the Court acknowl-edges that it is departing from prior precedent, and that it is "[lessening] the desirable clarity of [the *Miranda*] rule." Were the Court writing from a clean slate, I could agree with its holding. But *Miranda* is now the law and, in my view, the Court has not provided sufficient justification for departing from it or for blurring its now clear strictures. Accordingly, I would require suppression of the initial statement taken from respon-dent in this case. On the other hand, nothing in *Miranda* or the privilege itself requires exclusion of nontestimonial evidence derived from infor-mal custodial interrogation, and I therefore agree with the Court that admission of the gun in evidence is proper.

I

* * *

Since the time *Miranda* was decided, the Court has repeatedly refused to bend the literal terms of that decision. To be sure, the Court has been sensitive to the substantial burden the *Miranda* rules place on local law enforcement efforts, and consequently has refused to extend the decision or to increase its strictures on law enforcement agencies in almost any way. Similarly, where "statements taken in violation of the *Miranda* principles [have] not [been] used to prove the prosecution's case at trial," the Court has allowed evidence derived from those statements to be admitted. But wherever an accused has been taken into "custody" and subjected to "interrogation" without warnings, the Court has consistently prohibited the use of his responses for prosecutorial purposes at trial. As a consequence, the "meaning of *Miranda* has become reasonably clear and law enforcement practices have adjusted to its strictures."

In my view, a "public safety" exception unnecessarily blurs the edges of the clear line heretofore established and makes *Miranda*'s requirements more difficult to understand. In some cases, police will benefit because a reviewing court will find that an exigency excused their failure to administer the required warnings. * * * "While the rigidity of the prophylactic rules was a principal weakness in the view of dissenters and critics outside the Court, ... that rigidity [has also been called a] strength of the decision. It [has] afforded police and courts clear guid-ance on the manner in which to conduct a custodial investigation: if it was rigid, it was also precise. . . . [This] core virtue of *Miranda* would be eviscerated if the prophylactic rules were freely [ignored] by ... courts under the guise of [reinterpreting] *Miranda* . . . . "

The justification the Court provides for upsetting the equilibrium that has finally been achieved—that police cannot and should not balance considerations of public safety against the individual's interest in avoiding compulsory testimonial self-incrimination—really misses the critical question to be decided. *Miranda* has never been read to prohibit the police from asking questions to secure the public safety. Rather, the critical question *Miranda* addresses is who shall bear the cost of securing the public safety when such questions are asked and answered: the defendant or the State. *Miranda*, for better or worse, found the resolution of that question implicit in the prohibition against compulsory self-incrimination and placed the burden on the State. When police ask custodial questions without administering the required warnings, *Miranda* quite clearly requires that the answers received be presumed compelled and that they be excluded from evidence at trial.

* * *

II

The court below assumed, without discussion, that the privilege against self-incrimination required that the gun derived from respondent's statement also be suppressed, whether or not the State could independently link it to him. That conclusion was, in my view, incorrect.

A

[Justice O'Connor discussed prior cases holding that the privilege against self-incrimination applies only to "testimonial" communications, and not to non-testimonial evidence.]

B

The gun respondent was compelled to supply is clearly evidence of the "real or physical" sort. What makes the question of its admissibility difficult is the fact that, in asking respondent to produce the gun, the police also "compelled" him, in the *Miranda* sense, to create an incriminating testimonial response. In other words, the case is problematic because police compelled respondent not only to provide the gun but also to admit that he knew where it was and that it was his.

* * *

To be sure, admission of nontestimonial evidence secured through informal custodial interrogation will reduce the incentives to enforce the *Miranda* code. But that fact simply begs the question of *how much* enforcement is appropriate. There are some situations, as the Court's struggle to accommodate a "public safety" exception demonstrates, in which the societal cost of administering the *Miranda* warnings is very high indeed. The *Miranda* decision quite practically does not express any societal interest in having those warnings administered for their own sake. Rather, the warnings and waiver are only required to ensure that "testimony" used against the accused at trial is voluntarily given. Therefore, if the testimonial aspects of the accused's custodial communications are suppressed, the failure to administer the *Miranda* warnings should cease to be of concern. The harm caused by failure to administer *Miranda* warnings relates only to admission of testimonial self-incriminations, and the suppression of such incriminations should by itself produce the optimal enforcement of the *Miranda* rule.

C

* * *

[I]f a suspect is subject to abusive police practices and actually or overtly compelled to speak, it is reasonable to infer both an unwillingness to speak and a perceptible assertion of the privilege. Thus, when the *Miranda* violation consists of a deliberate and flagrant abuse of the accused's constitutional rights, amounting to a denial of due process, application of a broader exclusionary rule is warranted. Of course, "a defendant raising [such] a coerced-confession claim ... must first prevail in a voluntariness hearing before his confession and evidence derived from it [will] become inadmissible." By contrast, where the accused proves only that the police failed to administer the *Miranda* warnings, exclusion of the statement itself is all that will and should be required. Limitation of the *Miranda* prohibition to testimonial use of the statements themselves adequately serves the purposes of the privilege against self-incrimination.

* * *

Justice Marshall, with whom Justice Brennan and Justice Stevens join, dissenting.

* * *

I

* * *

The majority's entire analysis rests on the factual assumption that the public was at risk during Quarles' interrogation. This assumption is completely in conflict with the facts as found by New York's highest court. Before the interrogation began, Quarles had been "reduced to a condition of physical powerlessness." Contrary to the majority's speculations, Quarles was not believed to have, nor did he in fact have, an accomplice to come to his rescue. When the questioning began, the arresting officers were sufficiently confident of their safety to put away their guns. As Officer Kraft acknowledged at the suppression hearing, "the situation was under control." * * *

* * *

[N]o customers or employees were wandering about the store in danger of coming across Quarles' discarded weapon. Although the supermarket was open to the public, Quarles' arrest took place during the middle of the night when the store was apparently deserted except for the clerks at the check-out counter. The police could easily have cordoned off the store and searched for the missing gun. Had they done so, they would have found the gun forthwith. The police were well aware that Quarles had discarded his weapon somewhere near the scene of the arrest. As the State acknowledged before the New York Court of Appeals: "After Officer Kraft had handcuffed and frisked the defendant in the supermarket, *he knew with a high degree of certainty that the defendant's gun was within the immediate vicinity of the encounter.* He undoubtedly would have searched for it in the carton a few feet away without the defendant having looked in that direction and saying that it was there."

* * *

IV

Having determined that the Fifth Amendment renders inadmissible Quarles' response to Officer Kraft's questioning, I have no doubt that our precedents require that the gun discovered as a direct result of Quarles' statement must be presumed inadmissible as well. The gun was the direct product of a coercive custodial interrogation. [T]his Court has held that the Government may not introduce incriminating evidence derived from an illegally obtained source. [The dissent cited cases applying the "fruit of the poisonous tree" doctrine, which is discussed in Chapter 7.]

D. COMPELLED TESTIMONY AND IMMUNITY

COUNSELMAN v. HITCHCOCK

Supreme Court of the United States, 1892.
142 U.S. 547, 12 S.Ct. 195, 35 L.Ed. 1110.

MR. JUSTICE BLATCHFORD, after stating the case, delivered the opinion of the court.

* * *

By § 10 or the Interstate Commerce Act, unlawful discrimination in rates, fares or charges, for the transportation of passengers or property, is made subject not only to a fine of not to exceed $5000 for each offence, but to imprisonment in the penitentiary for not over two years, or to both, in the discretion of the court. By § 12 of the act * * *, the Interstate Commerce Commission is authorized and required to execute and enforce the provisions of the act, and on the request of the commission, it is made the duty of any district attorney of the United States to whom the commission may apply, to institute in the proper court, and to prosecute under the direction of the Attorney General of the United States, all necessary proceedings for the enforcement of the provisions of the act and for the punishment of all violations thereof.

* * *

It is broadly contended on the part of the appellee that a witness is not entitled to plead the privilege of silence, except in a criminal case against himself; but such is not the language of the Constitution. Its provision is that no person shall be compelled in any criminal case to be a witness against himself. This provision must have a broad construction in favor of the right which it was intended to secure. The matter under investigation by the grand jury in this case was a criminal matter, to inquire whether there had been a criminal violation of the Interstate Commerce Act. If Counselman had been guilty of the matters inquired of in the questions which he refused to answer, he himself was liable to criminal prosecution under the act. The case before the grand jury was, therefore, a criminal case. The reason given by Counselman for his refusal to answer the questions was that his answers might tend to criminate him, and showed that his apprehension was that, if he answered the questions truly and fully (as he was bound to do if he should answer them at all), the answers might show that he had committed a crime against the Interstate Commerce Act, for which he might be prosecuted. His answers, therefore, would be testimony against himself, and he would be compelled to give them in a criminal case.

It is impossible that the meaning of the constitutional provision can only be, that a person shall not be compelled to be a witness against himself in a criminal prosecution against himself. It would doubtless cover such cases; but it is not limited to them. The object was to insure that a person should not be compelled, when acting as a witness in any investigation, to give testimony which might tend to show that he himself had committed a crime. The privilege is limited to criminal matters, but it is as broad as the mischief against which it seeks to guard.

* * *

But this provision distinctly means a criminal prosecution against a person who is accused and who is to be tried by a petit jury. A criminal prosecution under article 6 of the amendments, is much narrower than a "criminal case," under article 5 of the amendments. It is entirely consistent with the language of article 5, that the privilege of not being a witness against himself is to be exercised in a proceeding before a grand jury.

* * *

It is an ancient principle of the law of evidence, that a witness shall not be compelled, in any proceeding, to make disclosures or to give testimony which will tend to criminate him or subject him to fines, penalties or forfeitures.

The relations of Counselman to the subject of inquiry before the grand jury, as shown by the questions put to him, in connection with the provisions of the Interstate Commerce Act, entitled him to invoke the protection of the Constitution.

It remains to consider whether § 860 of the Revised Statutes removes the protection of the constitutional privilege of Counselman. That section must be construed as declaring that no evidence obtained from a witness by means of a judicial proceeding shall be given in evidence, or in any manner used against him or his property or estate, in any court of the United States, in any criminal proceeding, or for the enforcement of any penalty or forfeiture. It follows, that any evidence which might have been obtained from Counselman by means of his examination before the grand jury could not be given in evidence or used against him or his property in any court of the United States, in any criminal proceeding, or for the enforcement of any penalty or forfeiture. This, of course, protected him against the use of his testimony against him or his property in any prosecution against him or his property, in any criminal proceeding, in a court of the United States. But it had only that effect. It could not, and would not, prevent the use of his testimony to search out other testimony to be used in evidence against him or his property, in a criminal proceeding in such court. It could not prevent the obtaining and the use of witnesses and evidence which should be attributable directly to the testimony he might give under compulsion, and on which he might be convicted, when otherwise, and if he had refused to answer, he could not possibly have been convicted.

The constitutional provision distinctly declares that a person shall not "be compelled in any criminal case to be a witness against himself;" and the protection of § 860 is not coextensive with the constitutional provision. Legislation cannot detract from the privilege afforded by the Constitution. It would be quite another thing if the Constitution had provided that no person shall be compelled in any criminal case to be a witness against himself, unless it should be provided by statute that criminating evidence extracted from a witness against his will should not be used against him. But a mere act of Congress cannot amend the Constitution, even if it should engraft thereon such a proviso.

In some States, where there is a like constitutional provision, it has been attempted by legislation to remove the constitutional provision, by declaring that there shall be no future criminal prosecution against the witness, thus making it impossible for the criminal charge against him ever to come under the cognizance of any court, or at least enabling him to plead the statute in absolute bar of such prosecution.

* * *

* * * It is a reasonable construction, we think, of the constitutional provision, that the witness is protected "from being compelled to disclose the circumstances of his offence, the sources from which, or the means by which, evidence of its commission, or of his connection with it, may be obtained, or made effectual for his connection, without using his answers as direct admissions against him."

It is quite clear that legislation cannot abridge a constitutional privilege, and that it cannot replace or supply one, at least unless it is so broad as to have the same extent in scope and effect. It is to be noted of

§ 860 of the Revised Statutes that it does not undertake to compel self-criminating evidence from a party or a witness. In several of the state statutes above referred to, the testimony of the party or witness is made compulsory, and in some either all possibility of a future prosecution of the party or witness is distinctly taken away, or he can plead in bar or abatement the fact that he was compelled to testify.

We are clearly of opinion that no statute which leaves the party or witness subject to prosecution after he answers the criminating question put to him, can have the effect of supplanting the privilege conferred by the Constitution of the United States. Section 860 of the Revised Statutes does not supply a complete protection from all the perils against which the constitutional prohibition was designed to guard, and is not a full substitute for that prohibition. In view of the constitutional provision, a statutory enactment, to be valid, must afford absolute immunity against future prosecution for the offence to which the question relates. * * * Section 860, moreover, affords no protection against that use of compelled testimony which consists in gaining therefrom a knowledge of the details of a crime, and of sources of information which may supply other means of convicting the witness or party.

* * *

From a consideration of the language of the constitutional provision, and of all the authorities referred to, we are clearly of opinion that the appellant was entitled to refuse, as he did, to answer. The judgment of the Circuit Court must, therefore, be [r]eversed, and the case remanded to that court, with a direction to discharge the appellant from custody, on the writ of habeas corpus.

KASTIGAR v. UNITED STATES

Supreme Court of the United States, 1972.
406 U.S. 441, 92 S.Ct. 1653, 32 L.Ed.2d 212.

MR. JUSTICE POWELL delivered the opinion of the court.

* * *

[The petitioners were subpoenaed to appear before a United States grand jury, and prior to their appearances, the Government applied to the District Court for an order directing petitioners to answer questions and produce evidence before the grand jury under a grant of immunity conferred pursuant to 18 U. S. C. § § 6002–6003. Petitioners argued that the scope of the immunity provided by the statute was not coextensive with the scope of the privilege against self-incrimination, and therefore was not sufficient to supplant the privilege and compel their testimony. The District Court rejected this argument, and ordered the petitioners to appear before the grand jury and answer its questions under the grant of immunity. Despite the court's order, they asserted the privilege against compulsory self-incrimination and refused to answer questions before the grand jury, and the District Court found both in contempt, ordered them into custody until either they answered the grand jury's questions or the term of the grand jury expired, and the Court of Appeals for the Ninth Circuit affirmed. The Supreme Court granted certiorari to resolve the question of whether testimony may be compelled by granting "use and derivative use" immunity, or whether it is necessary to grant immunity from prosecution for offenses to which compelled testimony relates "transactional" immunity.]

The power of government to compel persons to testify in court or before grand juries and other governmental agencies is firmly established in Anglo–American jurisprudence. * * *

But the power to compel testimony is not absolute. There are a number of exemptions from the testimonial duty, the most important of which is the Fifth Amendment privilege against compulsory self-incrimination. The privilege reflects a complex of our fundamental values and aspirations, and marks an important advance in the development of our liberty. It can be asserted in any proceeding, civil or criminal, administrative or judicial, investigatory or adjudicatory; and it protects against any disclosures that the witness reasonably believes could be used in a criminal prosecution or could lead to other evidence that might be so used. This Court has been zealous to safeguard the values that underlie the privilege.[12]

Immunity statutes, which have historical roots deep in Anglo–American jurisprudence, are not incompatible with these values. Rather, they seek a rational accommodation between the imperatives of the privilege and the legitimate demands of government to compel citizens to testify. The existence of these statutes reflects the importance of testimony, and the fact that many offenses are of such a character that the only persons capable of giving useful testimony are those implicated in the crime. * * *

* * *

III

Petitioners' [contend] that the scope of immunity provided by the federal witness immunity statute, 18 U. S. C. § 6002, is not coextensive with the scope of the Fifth Amendment privilege against compulsory self-incrimination, and therefore is not sufficient to supplant the privilege and compel testimony over a claim of the privilege. The statute provides that when a witness is compelled by district court order to testify over a claim of the privilege:

> "the witness may not refuse to comply with the order on the basis of his privilege against self-incrimination; but no testimony or other information compelled under the order (or any information directly or indirectly derived from such testimony or other information) may

---

12. See, *e. g., Miranda* v. *Arizona,* 384 U.S. 436, 443–444 (1966); *Boyd* v. *United* *States,* 116 U.S. 616, 635 (1886).

be used against the witness in any criminal case, except a prosecution for perjury, giving a false statement, or otherwise failing to comply with the order." 18 U. S. C. § 6002.

The constitutional inquiry, rooted in logic and history, as well as in the decisions of this Court, is whether the immunity granted under this statute is coextensive with the scope of the privilege. * * *

Petitioners draw a distinction between statutes that provide transactional immunity and those that provide, as does the statute before us, immunity from use and derivative use. They contend that a statute must at a minimum grant full transactional immunity in order to be coextensive with the scope of the privilege. In support of this contention, they rely on *Counselman* v. *Hitchcock*, 142 U.S. 547 (1892), the first case in which this Court considered a constitutional challenge to an immunity statute. The statute * * * provided that no "evidence obtained from a party or witness by means of a judicial proceeding ... shall be given in evidence, or in any manner used against him ... in any court of the United States.... " [T]his Court construed the statute as affording a witness protection only against the use of the specific testimony compelled from him under the grant of immunity. This construction meant that the statute "could not, and would not, prevent the use of his testimony to search out other testimony to be used in evidence against him." Since the [statute] would permit the use against the immunized witness of evidence derived from his compelled testimony, it did not protect the witness to the same extent that a claim of the privilege would protect him. Accordingly, * * * the witness' refusal to testify was held proper. * * *

* * *

[In response to the *Counselman* decision, Congress enacted the Compulsory Testimony Act of 1893, which provided that "no person shall be prosecuted or subjected to any penalty or forfeiture for or on account of any transaction, matter or thing, concerning which he may testify, or produce evidence, documentary or otherwise.... "]

This transactional immunity statute became the basic form for the numerous federal immunity statutes until 1970, when, after re-examining applicable constitutional principles and the adequacy of existing law, Congress enacted the statute here under consideration. The new statute, which does not "afford [the] absolute immunity against future prosecution" referred to in *Counselman*, was drafted to meet what Congress judged to be the conceptual basis of *Counselman*, as elaborated in subsequent decisions of the Court, namely, that immunity from the use of compelled testimony and evidence derived therefrom is coextensive with the scope of the privilege.

The statute's explicit proscription of the use in any criminal case of "testimony or other information compelled under the order (or any information directly or indirectly derived from such testimony or other information)" is consonant with Fifth Amendment standards. We hold that such immunity from use and derivative use is coextensive with the scope of the privilege against self-incrimination, and therefore is sufficient to compel testimony over a claim of the privilege. While a grant of immunity must afford protection commensurate with that afforded by the privilege, it need not be broader. Transactional immunity, which accords full immunity from prosecution for the offense to which the compelled testimony relates, affords the witness considerably broader protection than does the Fifth Amendment privilege. The privilege has never been construed to mean that one who invokes it cannot subsequently be prosecuted. Its sole concern is to afford protection against being "forced to give testimony leading to the infliction of 'penalties affixed to ... criminal acts.'" Immunity from the use of compelled testimony, as well as evidence derived directly and indirectly therefrom, affords this protection. It prohibits the prosecutorial authorities from using the compelled testimony in *any* respect, and it therefore insures that the testimony cannot lead to the infliction of criminal penalties on the witness.

* * *

[In *Murphy* v. *Waterfront Comm'n*, 378 U.S. 52 (1964), the issue before the Court] was whether New Jersey and New York could compel the witnesses, whom these States had immunized from prosecution under their laws, to give testimony that might then be used to convict them of a federal crime. Since New Jersey and New York had not purported to confer immunity from federal prosecution, the Court was faced with the question what limitations the Fifth Amendment privilege imposed on the prosecutorial powers of the Federal Government, a nonimmunizing sovereign. After undertaking an examination of the policies and purposes of the privilege, the Court overturned the rule that one jurisdiction within our federal structure may compel a witness to give testimony which could be used to convict him of a crime in another jurisdiction. The Court held that the privilege protects state witnesses against incrimination under federal as well as state law, and federal witnesses against incrimination under state as well as federal law. Applying this principle to the state immunity legislation before it, the Court held the constitutional rule to be that:

> "[A] state witness may not be compelled to give testimony which may be incriminating under federal law unless the compelled testimony and its fruits cannot be used in any manner by federal officials in connection with a criminal prosecution against him. We conclude, moreover, that in order to implement this constitutional rule and accommodate the interests of the State and Federal Governments in investigating and prosecuting crime, the Federal Government must be prohibited from making any such use of compelled testimony and its fruits."

* * *

[B]oth the reasoning of the Court in *Murphy* and the result reached compel the conclusion that use and derivative-use immunity is constitutionally sufficient to compel testimony over a claim of the privilege. Since the privilege is fully applicable and its scope is the same whether invoked in a state or in a federal jurisdiction, the *Murphy* conclusion that a prohibition on use and derivative use secures a witness' Fifth Amendment privilege against infringement by the Federal Government demonstrates that immunity from use and derivative use is coextensive with the scope of the privilege. As the *Murphy* Court noted, immunity from use and derivative use "leaves the witness and the Federal Government in substantially the same position as if the witness had claimed his privilege" in the absence of a grant of immunity. * * * This protection coextensive with the privilege is the degree of protection that the Constitution requires, and is all that the Constitution requires even against the jurisdiction compelling testimony by granting immunity.

IV

* * *

Petitioners argue that use and derivative-use immunity will not adequately protect a witness from various possible incriminating uses of the compelled testimony: for example, the prosecutor or other law enforcement officials may obtain leads, names of witnesses, or other information not otherwise available that might result in a prosecution. It will be difficult and perhaps impossible, the argument goes, to identify, by testimony or cross-examination, the subtle ways in which the compelled testimony may disadvantage a witness, especially in the jurisdiction granting the immunity.

This argument presupposes that the statute's prohibition will prove impossible to enforce. The statute provides a sweeping proscription of any use, direct or indirect, of the compelled testimony and any information derived therefrom * * *.

This total prohibition on use provides a comprehensive safeguard, barring the use of compelled testimony as an "investigatory lead," and also barring the use of any evidence obtained by focusing investigation on a witness as a result of his compelled disclosures.

A person accorded this immunity under 18 U. S. C. § 6002, and subsequently prosecuted, is not dependent for the preservation of his rights upon the integrity and good faith of the prosecuting authorities. As stated in *Murphy*:

> "Once a defendant demonstrates that he has testified, under a state grant of immunity, to matters related to the federal prosecution, the federal authorities have the burden of showing that their evidence is not tainted by establishing that they had an independent, legitimate source for the disputed evidence."

This burden of proof, which we reaffirm as appropriate, is not limited to a negation of taint; rather, it imposes on the prosecution the affirmative duty to prove that the evidence it proposes to use is derived from a legitimate source wholly independent of the compelled testimony.

* * *

We conclude that the immunity provided by 18 U. S. C. § 6002 leaves the witness and the prosecutorial authorities in substantially the same position as if the witness had claimed the Fifth Amendment privilege. The immunity therefore is coextensive with the privilege and suffices to supplant it. The judgment of the Court of Appeals for the Ninth Circuit accordingly is *Affirmed*.

[JUSTICE BRENNAN and JUSTICE REHNQUIST took no part in the consideration or decision of this case. The dissenting opinion of JUSTICE DOUGLAS is omitted.]

MR. JUSTICE MARSHALL, dissenting.

Today the Court holds that the United States may compel a witness to give incriminating testimony, and subsequently prosecute him for crimes to which that testimony relates. I cannot believe the Fifth Amendment permits that result.

The Fifth Amendment gives a witness an absolute right to resist interrogation, if the testimony sought would tend to incriminate him. A grant of immunity may strip the witness of the right to refuse to testify, but only if it is broad enough to eliminate all possibility that the testimony will in fact operate to incriminate him. It must put him in precisely the same position, *vis-a-vis* the government that has compelled his testimony, as he would have been in had he remained silent in reliance on the privilege.

* * * The Court asserts that the witness is adequately protected by a rule imposing on the government a heavy burden of proof if it would establish the independent character of evidence to be used against the witness. But in light of the inevitable uncertainties of the factfinding process, a greater margin of protection is required in order to provide a reliable guarantee that the witness is in exactly the same position as if he had not testified. That margin can be provided only by immunity from prosecution for the offenses to which the testimony relates, *i.e.*, transactional immunity.

I do not see how it can suffice merely to put the burden of proof on the government. First, contrary to the Court's assertion, the Court's rule does leave the witness "dependent for the preservation of his rights upon the integrity and good faith of the prosecuting authorities." For the information relevant to the question of taint is uniquely within the knowledge of the prosecuting authorities. They alone are in a position to trace the chains of information and investigation that lead to the evidence to be used in a criminal prosecution. A witness who suspects that his compelled testimony was used to develop a lead will be hard pressed indeed to ferret out the evidence necessary to prove it. * * * The good faith of the prosecuting authorities is thus the sole safeguard of the witness' rights. Second, even their good faith is not a sufficient safeguard. For the paths of information through the investigative bureaucracy may well be long and winding, and even a prosecutor acting in the best of faith cannot be certain that somewhere in the depths of his investigative apparatus, often including hundreds of employees, there was not some prohibited use of the compelled testimony. * * *

* * *

UNITED STATES v. DOE

Supreme Court of the United States, 1984.
465 U.S. 605, 104 S.Ct. 1237, 79 L.Ed.2d 552.

JUSTICE POWELL delivered the opinion of the Court.

This case presents the issue whether, and to what extent, the Fifth Amendment privilege against compelled self-incrimination applies to the business records of a sole proprietorship.

I

Respondent is the owner of several sole proprietorships. In late 1980, a grand jury, during the course of an investigation of corruption in the awarding of county and municipal contracts, served five subpoenas on respondent. The first two demanded the production of the telephone records of several of respondent's companies and all records pertaining to four bank accounts of respondent and his companies. The subpoenas were limited to the period between January 1, 1977, and the dates of the subpoenas. The third subpoena demanded the production of a list of virtually all the business records of one of respondent's companies for the period between January 1, 1976, and the date of the subpoena.[1] The fourth subpoena sought production of a similar list of business records belonging to another company. The final subpoena demanded production of all bank statements and cancelled checks of two of respondent's companies that had accounts at a bank in the Grand Cayman Islands.

[Doe moved to quash the subpoenas. The District Court for the District of New Jersey granted his motion except with respect to those documents and records required by law to be kept or disclosed to a public agency. The Court of Appeals for the Third Circuit affirmed. The

---

1. The categories of records sought by the third subpoena were: (1) general ledgers; (2) general journals; (3) cash disbursement journals; (4) petty cash books and vouchers; (5) purchase journals; (6) vouchers; (7) paid bills; (8) invoices; (9) cash receipts journal; (10) billings; (11) bank statements; (12) canceled checks and check stubs; (13) payroll records; (14) contracts and copies of contracts, including all retainer agreements; (15) financial statements; (16) bank deposit tickets; (17) retained copies of partnership income tax returns; (18) retained copies of payroll tax returns; (19) accounts payable ledger; (20) accounts receivable ledger; (21) telephone company statement of calls and telegrams, and all telephone toll slips; (22) records of all escrow, trust, or fiduciary accounts maintained on behalf of clients; (23) safe deposit box records; (24) records of all purchases and sales of all stocks and bonds; (25) names and home addresses of all partners, associates, and employees; (26) W-2 forms of each partner, associate, and employee; (27) workpapers; and (28) copies of tax returns.

Supreme Court affirmed in part, reversed in part, and remanded for further proceedings.]

III

A

The Court [in Fisher v. United States, 425 U.S. 391 (1976)] expressly declined to reach the question whether the Fifth Amendment privilege protects the contents of an individual's tax records in his possession. The rationale underlying our holding in that case is, however, persuasive here. As we noted in *Fisher*, the Fifth Amendment protects the person asserting the privilege only from *compelled* self-incrimination. Where the preparation of business records is voluntary, no compulsion is present. A subpoena that demands production of documents "does not compel oral testimony; nor would it ordinarily compel the taxpayer to restate, repeat, or affirm the truth of the contents of the documents sought." * * *

* * * Respondent does not contend that he prepared the documents involuntarily or that the subpoena would force him to restate, repeat, or affirm the truth of their contents. The fact that the records are in respondent's possession is irrelevant to the determination of whether the creation of the records was compelled. We therefore hold that the contents of those records are not privileged.

B

Although the contents of a document may not be privileged, the act of producing the document may be. A government subpoena compels the holder of the document to perform an act that may have testimonial aspects and an incriminating effect. As we noted in *Fisher*:

"Compliance with the subpoena tacitly concedes the existence of the papers demanded and their possession or control by the taxpayer. It also would indicate the taxpayer's belief that the papers are those described in the subpoena. The elements of compulsion are clearly present, but the more difficult issues are whether the tacit averments of the taxpayer are both 'testimonial' and 'incriminating' for purposes of applying the Fifth Amendment. These questions perhaps do not lend themselves to categorical answers; their resolution may instead depend on the facts and circumstances of particular cases or classes thereof."

In *Fisher*, the Court explored the effect that the act of production would have on the taxpayer and determined that the act of production would have only minimal testimonial value and would not operate to incriminate the taxpayer. Unlike the Court in *Fisher*, we have the explicit finding of the District Court that the act of producing the documents would involve testimonial self-incrimination. The Court of Appeals agreed. The District Court's finding essentially rests on its determination of factual issues. Therefore, we will not overturn that finding unless it has no support in the record. Traditionally, we also have been reluctant to disturb findings of fact in which two courts below have concurred. We therefore decline to overturn the finding of the District Court in this regard, where, as here, it has been affirmed by the Court of Appeals.

IV

The Government, as it concedes, could have compelled respondent to produce the documents listed in the subpoena. Title 18 U. S. C. § § 6002 and 6003 provide for the granting of use immunity with respect to the potentially incriminating evidence. The Court upheld the constitutionality of the use immunity statute in *Kastigar* v. *United States*, 406 U.S. 441 (1972).

The Government did state several times before the District Court that it would not use respondent's act of production against him in any way. But counsel for the Government never made a statutory request to the District Court to grant respondent use immunity. We are urged to adopt a doctrine of constructive use immunity. Under this doctrine, the courts would impose a requirement on the Government not to use the incriminatory aspects of the act of production against the person claiming the privilege even though the statutory procedures have not been followed.

We decline to extend the jurisdiction of courts to include prospective grants of use immunity in the absence of the formal request that the statute requires. [I]n passing the use immunity statute, "Congress gave certain officials in the Department of Justice exclusive authority to grant immunities." "Congress foresaw the courts as playing only a minor role in the immunizing process. The decision to seek use immunity necessarily involves a balancing of the Government's interest in obtaining information against the risk that immunity will frustrate the Government's attempts to prosecute the subject of the investigation. Congress expressly left this decision exclusively to the Justice Department. If, on remand, the appropriate official concludes that it is desirable to compel respondent to produce his business records, the statutory procedure for requesting use immunity will be available.

V

We conclude that the Court of Appeals erred in holding that the contents of the subpoenaed documents were privileged under the Fifth Amendment. The act of producing the documents at issue in this case is privileged and cannot be compelled without a statutory grant of use immunity pursuant to 18 U. S. C. § § 6002 and 6003. The judgment of the Court of Appeals is, therefore, affirmed in part and reversed in part, and the case is remanded to the District Court for further proceedings consistent with this opinion. *It is so ordered* .

JUSTICE O'CONNOR, concurring.

I concur in both the result and reasoning of JUSTICE POWELL'S opinion for the Court. I write separately, however, just to make explicit what is implicit in the analysis of that opinion: that the Fifth Amendment provides absolutely no protection for the contents of private papers of any kind. The notion that the Fifth Amendment protects the privacy of papers originated in *Boyd* v. *United States*, 116 U.S. 616, 630 (1886), but our decision in *Fisher* v. *United States*, 425 U.S. 391 (1976), sounded the death knell for *Boyd*. "Several of *Boyd*'s express or implicit declarations [had] not stood the test of time," and its privacy of papers concept "[had] long been a rule searching for a rationale.... Today's decision puts a long overdue end to that fruitless search.

JUSTICE MARSHALL, with whom JUSTICE BRENNAN joins, concurring in part and dissenting in part.

* * *

Contrary to what JUSTICE O'CONNOR contends, I do not view the Court's opinion in this case as having reconsidered whether the Fifth Amendment provides protection for the contents of "private papers of any kind." This case presented nothing remotely close to the question that JUSTICE O'CONNOR eagerly poses and answers. First, as noted above, the issue whether the Fifth Amendment protects the contents of the documents was obviated by the Court of Appeals' rulings relating to the act of production and statutory use immunity. Second, the documents at stake here are business records which implicate a lesser degree of concern for privacy interests than, for example, personal diaries.

Were it true that the Court's opinion stands for the proposition that "the Fifth Amendment provides absolutely no protection for the contents of private papers of any kind," I would assuredly dissent. I continue to believe that under the Fifth Amendment "there are certain documents no person ought to be compelled to produce at the Government's request."

[JUSTICE STEVENS's opinion, concurring in part and dissenting in part, is omitted.]

Note

Although the Supreme Court has limited the scope of the communications protected by the Privilege Against Self–Incrimination in opinions like *Quarles* and *Doe*, the Court has applied the privilege expansively on other issues. For example, in Ohio v. Reiner, 532 U.S. 17 (2001), the Court reversed a decision by the Supreme Court of Ohio, which had held that a witness who denies all culpability does not have a valid Fifth Amendment privilege against self-incrimination. The Court concluded that "our precedents dictate that the privilege protects the innocent as well as the guilty." Reiner was charged with involuntary manslaughter in connection with the death of his 2–month-old son Alex. The defense theory was that the family's babysitter, Susan Batt, was the culpable party. Batt asserted her Fifth Amendment privilege and refused to testify until, at the State's request, the trial court granted her transactional immunity from prosecution. Batt denied any involvement in Alex's death. She testified that she had never shaken the victim at any time. The jury found respondent guilty of involuntary manslaughter, and he appealed. In a per curiam opinion, the Supreme Court found that the state court had determined that Batt did not have a valid Fifth Amendment privilege.

The Supreme Court acknowledged that under its precedents the privilege's protection extends only to witnesses who have " 'reasonable cause to apprehend danger from a direct answer'. That inquiry is for the court; the witness' assertion does not by itself establish the risk of incrimination. A danger of 'imaginary and unsubstantial character' will not suffice. But we have never held, as the Supreme Court of Ohio did, that the privilege is unavailable to those who claim innocence. To the contrary, we have emphasized that one of the Fifth Amendment's 'basic functions ... is to protect *innocent* men ... "who otherwise might be ensnared by ambiguous circumstances." ' * * * [T]ruthful responses of an innocent witness, as well as those of a wrongdoer, may provide the government with incriminating evidence from the speaker's own mouth."

Chapter 6

INTERROGATION AND CONFESSIONS: THE REVIVAL OF SIXTH AMENDMENT THEORIES

A. MASSIAH REVIVED

BREWER v. WILLIAMS

Supreme Court of the United States, 1977.
430 U.S. 387, 97 S.Ct. 1232, 51 L.Ed.2d 424.

MR. JUSTICE STEWART delivered the opinion of the Court. * * *

I

On the afternoon of December 24, 1968, a 10–year-old girl named Pamela Powers went with her family to the YMCA in Des Moines, Iowa, to watch a wrestling tournament in which her brother was participating. When she failed to return from a trip to the washroom, a search for her began. The search was unsuccessful.

Robert Williams, who had recently escaped from a mental hospital, was a resident of the YMCA. Soon after the girl's disappearance Williams was seen in the YMCA lobby carrying some clothing and a large bundle wrapped in a blanket. He obtained help from a 14–year-old boy in opening the street door of the YMCA and the door to his automobile parked outside. When Williams placed the bundle in the front seat of his car the boy "saw two legs in it and they were skinny and white." Before anyone could see what was in the bundle Williams drove away. His abandoned car was found the following day in Davenport, Iowa, roughly 160 miles east of Des Moines. A warrant was then issued in Des Moines for his arrest on a charge of abduction.

On the morning of December 26, a Des Moines lawyer named Henry McKnight went to the Des Moines police station and informed the officers present that he had just received a long-distance call from Williams, and that he had advised Williams to turn himself in to the Davenport police. Williams did surrender that morning to the police in

435

Davenport, and they booked him on the charge specified in the arrest warrant and gave him the warnings required by *Miranda* v. *Arizona,* 384 U.S. 436, 86 S.Ct. 1602, 16 L.Ed.2d 694 (1966). The Davenport police then telephoned their counterparts in Des Moines to inform them that Williams had surrendered. McKnight, the lawyer, was still at the Des Moines police headquarters, and Williams conversed with McKnight on the telephone. In the presence of the Des Moines chief of police and a police detective named Leaming, McKnight advised Williams that Des Moines police officers would be driving to Davenport to pick him up, that the officers would not interrogate him or mistreat him, and that Williams was not to talk to the officers about Pamela Powers until after consulting with McKnight upon his return to Des Moines. As a result of these conversations, it was agreed between McKnight and the Des Moines police officials that Detective Leaming and a fellow officer would drive to Davenport to pick up Williams, that they would bring him directly back to Des Moines, and that they would not question him during the trip.

In the meantime Williams was arraigned before a judge in Davenport on the outstanding arrest warrant. The judge advised him of his *Miranda* rights and committed him to jail. Before leaving the courtroom, Williams conferred with a lawyer named Kelly, who advised him not to make any statements until consulting with McKnight back in Des Moines.

Detective Leaming and his fellow officer arrived in Davenport about noon to pick up Williams and return him to Des Moines. Soon after their arrival they met with Williams and Kelly, who, they understood, was acting as Williams' lawyer. Detective Leaming repeated the *Miranda* warnings, and told Williams:

> "[W]e both know that you're being represented here by Mr. Kelly and you're being represented by Mr. McKnight in Des Moines, and ... I want you to remember this because we'll be visiting between here and Des Moines."

Williams then conferred again with Kelly alone, and after this conference Kelly reiterated to Detective Leaming that Williams was not to be questioned about the disappearance of Pamela Powers until after he had consulted with McKnight back in Des Moines. When Leaming expressed some reservations, Kelly firmly stated that the agreement with McKnight was to be carried out—that there was to be no interrogation of Williams during the automobile journey to Des Moines. Kelly was denied permission to ride in the police car back to Des Moines with Williams and the two officers.

The two detectives, with Williams in their charge, then set out on the 160–mile drive. At no time during the trip did Williams express a willingness to be interrogated in the absence of an attorney. Instead, he stated several times that "[w]hen I get to Des Moines and see Mr. McKnight, I am going to tell you the whole story." Detective Leaming knew that Williams was a former mental patient, and knew also that he was deeply religious.

The detective and his prisoner soon embarked on a wideranging conversation covering a variety of topics, including the subject of religion. Then, not long after leaving Davenport and reaching the interstate highway, Detective Leaming delivered what has been referred to in the briefs and oral arguments as the "Christian burial speech." Addressing Williams as "Reverend," the detective said:

> "I want to give you something to think about while we're traveling down the road ... Number one, I want you to observe the weather conditions, it's raining, it's sleeting, it's freezing, driving is very treacherous, visibility is poor, it's going to be dark early this evening. They are predicting several inches of snow for tonight, and I feel that you yourself are the only person that knows where this little girl's body is, that you yourself have only been there once, and if you get a snow on top of it you yourself may be unable to find it. And, since we will be going right past the area on the way into Des Moines, I feel that we could stop and locate the body, that the parents of this little girl should be entitled to a Christian burial for the little girl who was snatched away from them on Christmas [E]ve and murdered. And I feel we should stop and locate it on the way in rather than waiting until morning and trying to come back out after a snow storm and possibly not being able to find it at all. "

Williams asked Detective Leaming why he thought their route to Des Moines would be taking them past the girl's body, and Leaming responded that he knew the body was in the area of Mitchellville—a town they would be passing on the way to Des Moines. Leaming then stated: "I do not want you to answer me. I don't want to discuss it any further. Just think about it as we're riding down the road."

As the car approached Grinnell, a town approximately 100 miles west of Davenport, Williams asked whether the police had found the victim's shoes. When Detective Leaming replied that he was unsure, Williams directed the officers to a service station where he said he had left the shoes; a search for them proved unsuccessful. As they continued towards Des Moines, Williams asked whether the police had found the blanket, and directed the officers to a rest area where he said he had disposed of the blanket. Nothing was found. The car continued towards Des Moines, and as it approached Mitchellville, Williams said that he would show the officers where the body was. He then directed the police to the body of Pamela Powers.

[Williams was indicted for first-degree murder. The trial court denied the defense motion to suppress all evidence relating to or resulting from any statements Williams had made during the automobile ride from Davenport to Des Moines, Williams was found guilty of murder, and the conviction was affirmed by the Iowa Supreme Court, which found that Williams had waived his right to counsel on the automobile ride from Davenport to Des Moines.]

II

B

* * *

[The right to counsel] guaranteed by the Sixth and Fourteenth Amendments, is indispensable to the fair administration of our adversary system of criminal justice. Its vital need at the pretrial stage has perhaps nowhere been more succinctly explained than in Mr. Justice Sutherland's memorable words for the Court 44 years ago in *Powell* v. *Alabama,* 287 U.S. 45, 57, 53 S.Ct. 55, 77 L.Ed. 158 (1932):

> "[D]uring perhaps the most critical period of the proceedings against these defendants, that is to say, from the time of their arraignment until the beginning of their trial, when consultation, thoroughgoing investigation and preparation were vitally important, the defendants did not have the aid of counsel in any real sense, although they were as much entitled to such aid during that period as at the trial itself."

[T]he right to counsel granted by the Sixth and Fourteenth Amendments means at least that a person is entitled to the help of a lawyer at or after the time that judicial proceedings have been initiated against him—"whether by way of formal charge, preliminary hearing, indictment, information, or arraignment."

There can be no doubt in the present case that judicial proceedings had been initiated against Williams before the start of the automobile ride from Davenport to Des Moines. A warrant had been issued for his arrest, he had been arraigned on that warrant before a judge in a Davenport courtroom, and he had been committed by the court to confinement in jail. The State does not contend otherwise.

There can be no serious doubt, either, that Detective Leaming deliberately and designedly set out to elicit information from Williams just as surely as—and perhaps more effectively than—if he had formally interrogated him. Detective Leaming was fully aware before departing for Des Moines that Williams was being represented in Davenport by Kelly and in Des Moines by McKnight. Yet he purposely sought during Williams' isolation from his lawyers to obtain as much incriminating information as possible. Indeed, Detective Leaming conceded as much when he testified at Williams' trial * * *.

The state courts clearly proceeded upon the hypothesis that Detective Leaming's "Christian burial speech" had been tantamount to interrogation. Both courts recognized that Williams had been entitled to the assistance of counsel at the time he made the incriminating statements. Yet no such constitutional protection would have come into play if there had been no interrogation.

The circumstances of this case are thus constitutionally indistinguishable from those presented in *Massiah* v. *United States,* 377 U.S. 201, 84 S.Ct. 1199, 12 L.Ed.2d 246 (1964). The petitioner in that case was indicted for violating the federal narcotics law. He retained a lawyer, pleaded not guilty, and was released on bail. While he was free on bail a federal agent succeeded by surreptitious means in listening to incriminating statements made by him. Evidence of these statements was introduced against the petitioner at his trial, and he was convicted. This Court reversed the conviction, holding "that the petitioner was denied the basic protections of that guarantee [the right to counsel] when there was used against him at his trial evidence of his own incriminating words, which federal agents had deliberately elicited from him after he had been indicted and in the absence of his counsel."

That the incriminating statements were elicited surreptitiously in the *Massiah* case, and otherwise here, is constitutionally irrelevant. Rather, the clear rule of *Massiah* is that once adversary proceedings have commenced against an individual, he has a right to legal representation when the government interrogates him. It thus requires no wooden or technical application of the *Massiah* doctrine to conclude that Williams was entitled to the assistance of counsel guaranteed to him by the Sixth and Fourteenth Amendments.

III

* * *

[T]he proper standard to be applied in determining the question of waiver as a matter of federal constitutional law [makes it] incumbent upon the State to prove "an intentional relinquishment or abandonment of a known right or privilege." That standard has been reiterated in many cases. We have said that the right to counsel does not depend upon a request by the defendant, and that courts indulge in every reasonable presumption against waiver. This strict standard applies equally to an alleged waiver of the right to counsel whether at trial or at a critical stage of pretrial proceedings.

We conclude, finally, that the Court of Appeals was correct in holding that, judged by these standards, the record in this case falls far short of sustaining petitioner's burden. It is true that Williams had been informed of and appeared to understand his right to counsel. But waiver requires not merely comprehension but relinquishment, and Williams' consistent reliance upon the advice of counsel in dealing with the authorities refutes any suggestion that he waived that right. He consulted McKnight by long-distance telephone before turning himself in. He spoke with McKnight by telephone again shortly after being booked. After he was arraigned, Williams sought out and obtained legal advice from Kelly. Williams again consulted with Kelly after Detective Leaming and his fellow officer arrived in Davenport. Throughout, Williams was advised not to make any statements before seeing McKnight in Des Moines, and was assured that the police had agreed not to question him. His statements while in the car that he would tell the whole story *after* seeing McKnight in Des Moines were the clearest expressions by Williams himself that he desired the presence of an attorney before any interrogation took place. But even before making these statements, Williams had effectively asserted his right to counsel by having secured attorneys at both ends of the automobile trip, both of whom, acting as his agents, had made clear to the police that no interrogation was to occur during the journey. Williams knew of that agreement and, particularly in view of his consistent reliance on counsel, there is no basis for concluding that he disavowed it.

Despite Williams' express and implicit assertions of his right to counsel, Detective Leaming proceeded to elicit incriminating statements from Williams. Leaming did not preface this effort by telling Williams that he had a right to the presence of a lawyer, and made no effort at all to ascertain whether Williams wished to relinquish that right. The circumstances of record in this case thus provide no reasonable basis for finding that Williams waived his right to the assistance of counsel.

The Court of Appeals did not hold, nor do we, that under the circumstances of this case Williams *could not,* without notice to counsel, have waived his rights under the Sixth and Fourteenth Amendments. It only held, as do we, that he did not.

IV

The crime of which Williams was convicted was senseless and brutal, calling for swift and energetic action by the police to apprehend the perpetrator and gather evidence with which he could be convicted. No mission of law enforcement officials is more important. Yet "[d]isinterested zeal for the public good does not assure either wisdom or right in the methods it pursues." Although we do not lightly affirm the issuance of a writ of habeas corpus in this case, so clear a violation of the Sixth and Fourteenth Amendments as here occurred cannot be condoned. The pressures on state executive and judicial officers charged with the administration of the criminal law are great, especially when the crime is murder and the victim a small child. But it is precisely the predictability of those pressures that makes imperative a resolute loyalty to the guarantees that the Constitution extends to us all.

* * *

[The concurring opinions of JUSTICE MARSHALL, JUSTICE POWELL, and JUSTICE STEVENS are omitted.]

MR. CHIEF JUSTICE BURGER, dissenting.

The result in this case ought to be intolerable in any society which purports to call itself an organized society. It continues the Court—by the narrowest margin—on the much-criticized course of punishing the public for the mistakes and misdeeds of law enforcement officers, instead of punishing the officer directly, if in fact he is guilty of wrongdoing. It mechanically and blindly keeps reliable evidence from juries whether the claimed constitutional violation involves gross police misconduct or honest human error.

Williams is guilty of the savage murder of a small child; no member of the Court contends he is not. While in custody, and after no fewer than *five* warnings of his rights to silence and to counsel, he led police to the concealed body of his victim. The Court concedes Williams was not threatened or coerced and that he spoke and acted voluntarily and with full awareness of his constitutional rights. In the face of all this, the Court now holds that because Williams was prompted by the detective's statement—not interrogation but a statement—the jury must not be told how the police found the body.

* * *

MR. JUSTICE WHITE, with whom MR. JUSTICE BLACKMUN and MR. JUSTICE REHNQUIST join, dissenting.

* * *

II

The strictest test of waiver which might be applied to this case is that set forth in *Johnson* v. *Zerbst,* 304 U.S. 458, 464 (1938), and quoted by the majority. In order to show that a right has been waived under this test, the State must prove "an intentional relinquishment or abandonment of a known right or privilege." The majority creates no new rule preventing an accused who has retained a lawyer from waiving his right to the lawyer's presence during questioning. The majority simply finds that no waiver was proved in this case. I disagree. That respondent knew of his right not to say anything to the officers without advice and presence of counsel is established on this record to a moral certainty. He was advised of the right by three officials of the State—telling at least one that he understood the right—and by two lawyers. Finally, he further demonstrated his knowledge of the right by informing the police that he would tell them the story in the presence of McKnight when they arrived in Des Moines. The issue in this case, then, is whether respondent relinquished that right intentionally.

Respondent relinquished his right not to talk to the police about his crime when the car approached the place where he had hidden the victim's clothes. Men usually intend to do what they do, and there is nothing in the record to support the proposition that respondent's decision to talk was anything but an exercise of his own free will. Apparently, without any prodding from the officers, respondent—who had earlier said that he would tell the whole story when he arrived in Des Moines—spontaneously changed his mind about the timing of his disclosures when the car approached the places where he had hidden the evidence. [R]espondent's decision to talk in the absence of counsel can hardly be viewed as the product of an overborne will. The statement by Leaming was not coercive; it was accompanied by a request that respondent not respond to it; and it was delivered hours before respondent decided to make any statement. Respondent's waiver was thus knowing and intentional.

* * *

[The dissenting opinion of JUSTICE BLACKMUN, with whom JUSTICE WHILE and JUSTICE REHNQUIST joined, is omitted.]

MAINE v. MOULTON

Supreme Court of the United States, 1985.
474 U.S. 159, 106 S.Ct. 477, 88 L.Ed.2d 481.

JUSTICE BRENNAN delivered the opinion of the Court.

The question presented in this case is whether respondent's Sixth Amendment right to the assistance of counsel was violated by the admission at trial of incriminating statements made by him to his codefendant, a secret government informant, after indictment and at a meeting of the two to plan defense strategy for the upcoming trial.

I

[In April 1981, a grand jury indicted Moulton and Colson on four counts of theft by receiving stolen vehicles. Both defendants, who were represented by retained counsel, appeared before the Maine Superior Court and entered pleas of not guilty. Both were released on bail pending trial. In November 1982, while the trial was still pending, Colson reported to the police that he had received anonymous threatening telephone calls about these pending charges and said that he wanted to talk to the police—who told Colson to speak with his lawyer and to call back. Two days later, Colson and Moulton met at a restaurant to plan for their upcoming trial. According to Colson, Moulton proposed killing Gary Elwell, a government witness. A few days later, Colson and his lawyer met with police officers. Colson confessed that Moulton and he had committed the crimes for which they had been indicted. Colson also confessed to other crimes, including theft and arson. Colson agreed to cooperate with the prosecution in exchange for a deal that no further charges would be brought against him. Colson also discussed the anonymous threats he had received and Moulton's inchoate plan to kill Elwell. Police then placed a recording device on Colson's telephone, which allowed them to tape three of Colson's conversations with Moulton. The conversations were not directly incriminating, but during the last conversation, Moulton and Colson agreed to meet on December 26, 1982. The police equipped Colson with a body wire transmitter, which made it possible to record what was said at that meeting.]

[The December 26 meeting, consisted of a lengthy discussion of the pending charges and what Moulton and Colson could do to obtain an acquittal. Moulton and Colson decided to create false alibis as their defense at trial. In an effort to conform these alibis as closely as possible to what really happened, much of their discussion involved reviewing the details of their crimes. Although Colson had described these events in detail when he confessed to the police a month earlier, he now frequently professed to be unable to recall the events. Apologizing for his poor memory, he repeatedly asked Moulton to remind him about the details of what had happened, and this technique caused Moulton to make numerous incriminating statements. Each of these statements was later admitted into evidence against Moulton at trial.]

[The trial court denied Moulton's motion to suppress the recorded statements he made to Colson in the three telephone conversations and at the December 26 meeting. Prior to trial, the State had the pending indictments dismissed and obtained new indictments against Moulton that realleged the pending charges and charged Moulton in addition with burglary, arson, and three more thefts. Moulton pleaded guilty to some charges and the trial court dismissed others for improper venue. At Moulton's trial, the State offered portions of the tapes of the December 26 meeting, principally those involving direct discussion of the thefts for which Moulton was originally indicted. Moulton was found guilty of burglary and theft and he appealed on the ground that the admission into evidence of his statements to Colson violated his Sixth Amendment right to the assistance of counsel.]

II

A

The right to the assistance of counsel guaranteed by the Sixth and Fourteenth Amendments is indispensable to the fair administration of our adversarial system of criminal justice. Embodying "a realistic recognition of the obvious truth that the average defendant does not have the professional legal skill to protect himself," *Johnson* v. *Zerbst*, 304 U.S. 458, 462–463, 58 S.Ct. 1019, 82 L.Ed. 1461 (1938), the right to counsel safeguards the other rights deemed essential for the fair prosecution of a criminal proceeding. Justice Sutherland's oft-quoted explanation in *Powell* v. *Alabama*, 287 U.S. 45 (1932), bears repetition here:

> "The right to be heard would be, in many cases, of little avail if it did not comprehend the right to be heard by counsel. Even the intelligent and educated layman has small and sometimes no skill in the science of law. If charged with crime, he is incapable, generally, of determining for himself whether the indictment is good or bad. He is unfamiliar with the rules of evidence. Left without the aid of counsel he may be put on trial without a proper charge, and convicted upon incompetent evidence, or evidence irrelevant to the issue or otherwise inadmissible. He lacks both the skill and knowledge adequately to prepare his defense, even though he have a perfect one. He requires the guiding hand of counsel at every stage of the proceedings against him."

[T]he Court has also recognized that the assistance of counsel cannot be limited to participation in a trial; to deprive a person of counsel during the period prior to trial may be more damaging than denial of counsel during the trial itself. Recognizing that the right to the assistance of counsel is shaped by the need for the assistance of counsel, we have found that the right attaches at earlier, "critical" stages in the criminal justice process "where the results might well settle the accused's fate and reduce the trial itself to a mere formality." And, "[whatever] else it may mean, the right to counsel granted by the Sixth and Fourteenth Amendments means at least that a person is entitled to the help of a lawyer at or after the time that judicial proceedings have been initiated against him..." *Brewer* v. *Williams*, 430 U.S. 387, 398, 97 S.Ct. 1232, 51 L.Ed.2d 424 (1977). This is because, after the initiation of adversary criminal proceedings, " 'the government has committed itself to prosecute, and ... the adverse positions of government and defendant have solidified. It is then that a defendant finds himself faced with the prosecutorial forces of organized society, and immersed in the intricacies of substantive and procedural criminal law.' "

B

Once the right to counsel has attached and been asserted, the State must of course honor it. This means more than simply that the State cannot prevent the accused from obtaining the assistance of counsel. The Sixth Amendment also imposes on the State an affirmative obligation to respect and preserve the accused's choice to seek this assistance. We have on several occasions been called upon to clarify the scope of the State's obligation in this regard, and have made clear that, at the very least, the prosecutor and police have an affirmative obligation not to act in a manner that circumvents and thereby dilutes the protection afforded by the right to counsel.

* * *

C

* * *

* * * The Sixth Amendment guarantees the accused, at least after the initiation of formal charges, the right to rely on counsel as a "medium" between him and the State. As noted above, this guarantee includes the State's affirmative obligation not to act in a manner that circumvents the protections accorded the accused by invoking this right. The determination whether particular action by state agents violates the accused's right to the assistance of counsel must be made in light of this obligation. Thus, the Sixth Amendment is not violated whenever—by luck or happenstance—the State obtains incriminating statements from the accused after the right to counsel has attached. However, knowing exploitation by the State of an opportunity to confront the accused without counsel being present is as much a breach of the State's obligation not to circumvent the right to the assistance of counsel as is the intentional creation of such an opportunity. Accordingly, the Sixth Amendment is violated when the State obtains incriminating statements by knowingly circumventing the accused's right to have counsel present in a confrontation between the accused and a state agent.

III

Applying this principle to the case at hand, it is clear that the State violated Moulton's Sixth Amendment right when it arranged to record conversations between Moulton and its undercover informant, Colson. It was the police who suggested to Colson that he record his telephone conversations with Moulton. Having learned from these recordings that Moulton and Colson were going to meet, the police asked Colson to let them put a body wire transmitter on him to record what was said. Police Chief Keating admitted that, when they made this request, the police knew—as they must have known from the recorded telephone conversations—that Moulton and Colson were meeting for the express purpose of discussing the pending charges and planning a defense for the trial. The police thus knew that Moulton would make statements that he had a constitutional right not to make to their agent prior to consulting with counsel. [T]he fact that the police were "fortunate enough to have an undercover informant already in close proximity to the accused" does not excuse their conduct under these circumstances. By concealing the fact that Colson was an agent of the State, the police denied Moulton the opportunity to consult with counsel and thus denied him the assistance of counsel guaranteed by the Sixth Amendment.

IV

The Solicitor General argues that the incriminating statements obtained by the Maine police nevertheless should not be suppressed because the police had other, legitimate reasons for listening to Moulton's conversations with Colson, namely, to investigate Moulton's alleged plan to kill Gary Elwell and to insure Colson's safety. In *Massiah*, the Government also contended that incriminating statements obtained as a result of its deliberate efforts should not be excluded because law enforcement agents had "the right, if not indeed the duty, to continue their investigation of [Massiah] and his alleged criminal associates.... " There, as here, the Government argued that this circumstance justified its surveillance and cured any improper acts or purposes. We rejected this argument, and held:

> "We do not question that in this case, as in many cases, it was entirely proper to continue an investigation of the suspected criminal activities of the defendant and his alleged confederates, even though the defendant had already been indicted. All that we hold is that the defendant's own incriminating statements, obtained by federal agents under the circumstances here disclosed, could not constitutionally be used by the prosecution as evidence against him at his trial."

We reaffirm this holding, which states a sensible solution to a difficult problem. The police have an interest in the thorough investigation of crimes for which formal charges have already been filed. They also have an interest in investigating new or additional crimes. Investigations of either type of crime may require surveillance of individuals already under indictment. Moreover, law enforcement officials investigating an individual suspected of committing one crime and formally charged with having committed another crime obviously seek to discover evidence useful at a trial of either crime. In seeking evidence pertaining to pending charges, however, the Government's investigative powers are limited by the Sixth Amendment rights of the accused. To allow the admission of evidence obtained from the accused in violation of his Sixth Amendment rights whenever the police assert an alternative, legitimate reason for their surveillance invites abuse by law enforcement personnel in the form of fabricated investigations and risks the evisceration of the Sixth Amendment right recognized in *Massiah*. On the other hand, to exclude evidence pertaining to charges as to which the Sixth Amendment right to counsel had not attached at the time the evidence was obtained, simply because other charges were pending at that time, would unnecessarily frustrate the public's interest in the investigation of criminal activities. Consequently, incriminating statements pertaining to pending charges are inadmissible at the trial of those charges, notwithstanding the fact that the police were also investigating other crimes, if, in obtaining this evidence, the State violated the Sixth Amendment by knowingly circumventing the accused's right to the assistance of counsel.

* * *

[The dissenting opinion of CHIEF JUSTICE BURGER, with whom JUSTICE WHITE and JUSTICE REHNQUIST joined, and with whom JUSTICE O'CONNOR joined as to Parts I and III, is omitted.]

B. THE RIGHT TO COUNSEL UNDER THE FIFTH AND SIXTH AMENDMENTS

1. Drawing a Line Between the Two Amendments

MORAN v. BURBINE

Supreme Court of the United States, 1986.
475 U.S. 412, 106 S.Ct. 1135, 89 L.Ed.2d 410.

JUSTICE O'CONNOR delivered the opinion of the Court.

After being informed of his rights pursuant to *Miranda v. Arizona,* 384 U.S. 436, 86 S.Ct. 1602, 16 L.Ed.2d 694 (1966), and after executing a series of written waivers, respondent confessed to the murder of a young woman. At no point during the course of the interrogation, which occurred prior to arraignment, did he request an attorney. While he was in police custody, his sister attempted to retain a lawyer to represent him. The attorney telephoned the police station and received assurances that respondent would not be questioned further until the next day. In fact, the interrogation session that yielded the inculpatory statements began later that evening. The question presented is whether either the conduct of the police or respondent's ignorance of the attorney's efforts to reach him taints the validity of the waivers and therefore requires exclusion of the confessions.

I

[Shortly before Cranston, Rhode Island, police arrested Burbine and two others for a local burglary, they had received information linking Burbine to a homicide committed several months earlier in Providence Rhode Island. The arresting officer informed Burbine of his *Miranda* rights, and he refused to execute a written waiver. At approximately 6 p.m., on that same day, the same detective telephoned the Providence police to convey the information he had uncovered, and about an hour later, three officers from the Providence police department arrived at the Cranston headquarters for the purpose of questioning Burabine about the murder.]

That same evening, at about 7:45 p.m., respondent's sister telephoned the Public Defender's Office to obtain legal assistance for her brother. Her sole concern was the breaking and entering charge, as she was unaware that respondent was then under suspicion for murder. She asked for Richard Casparian who had been scheduled to meet with respondent earlier that afternoon to discuss another charge unrelated to either the break-in or the murder. As soon as the conversation ended, the attorney who took the call attempted to reach Mr. Casparian. When those efforts were unsuccessful, she telephoned Allegra Munson, another Assistant Public Defender, and told her about respondent's arrest and his sister's subsequent request that the office represent him.

At 8:15 p.m., Ms. Munson telephoned the Cranston police station and asked that her call be transferred to the detective division. * * *

[T]he conversation proceeded as follows:

"A male voice responded with the word 'Detectives.' Ms. Munson identified herself and asked if Brian Burbine was being held; the person responded affirmatively. Ms. Munson explained to the person that Burbine was represented by attorney Casparian who was not available; she further stated that she would act as Burbine's legal counsel in the event that the police intended to place him in a lineup or question him. The unidentified person told Ms. Munson that the police would not be questioning Burbine or putting him in a lineup and that they were through with him for the night. Ms. Munson was not informed that the Providence Police were at the Cranston police station or that Burbine was a suspect in Mary's murder."

At all relevant times, respondent was unaware of his sister's efforts to retain counsel and of the fact and contents of Ms. Munson's telephone conversation.

Less than an hour later, the police brought respondent to an interrogation room and conducted the first of a series of interviews concerning the murder. Prior to each session, respondent was informed of his *Miranda rights*, and on three separate occasions he signed a written form acknowledging that he understood his right to the presence of an attorney and explicitly indicating that he "[did] not want an attorney called or appointed for [him]" before he gave a statement.

Uncontradicted evidence at the suppression hearing indicated that at least twice during the course of the evening, respondent was left in a room where he had access to a telephone, which he apparently declined to use. Eventually, respondent signed three written statements fully admitting to the murder.

[Burbine's motion to suppress the statements was denied, and he was convicted of murder in the first degree. The appellate court reversed.] We granted certiorari to decide whether a prearraignment confession preceded by an otherwise valid waiver must be suppressed either because the police misinformed an inquiring attorney about their plans concerning the suspect or because they failed to inform the suspect of the attorney's efforts to reach him. We now reverse.

II

In *Miranda* v. *Arizona*, the Court recognized that custodial interrogations, by their very nature, generate "compelling pressures which work to undermine the individual's will to resist and to compel him to speak where he would not otherwise do so freely." To combat this inherent compulsion, and thereby protect the Fifth Amendment privilege against self-incrimination, *Miranda* imposed on the police an obligation to follow certain procedures in their dealings with the accused. In particular, prior to the initiation of questioning, they must fully apprise the suspect of the State's intention to use his statements to secure a conviction, and must inform him of his rights to remain silent and to "have counsel present . . . if [he] so desires." Beyond this duty to inform, *Miranda* requires that the police respect the accused's decision to exercise the rights outlined in the warnings. "If the individual indicates in any manner, at any time prior to or during questioning, that he wishes to remain silent, [or if he] states that he wants an attorney, the interrogation must cease."

* * *

A

Echoing the standard first articulated in *Johnson v. Zerbst,* 304 U.S. 458, 464, 58 S.Ct. 1019, 82 L.Ed. 1461 (1938), *Miranda* holds that "[the] defendant may waive effectuation" of the rights conveyed in the warnings "provided the waiver is made voluntarily, knowingly and intelligently." First, the relinquishment of the right must have been voluntary in the sense that it was the product of a free and deliberate choice rather than intimidation, coercion, or deception. Second, the waiver must have been made with a full awareness of both the nature of the right being abandoned and the consequences of the decision to abandon it. Only if the "totality of the circumstances surrounding the interrogation" reveals both an uncoerced choice and the requisite level of comprehension may a court properly conclude that the *Miranda* rights have been waived.

Under this standard, we have no doubt that respondent validly waived his right to remain silent and to the presence of counsel. The voluntariness of the waiver is not at issue. [T]he record is devoid of any suggestion that police resorted to physical or psychological pressure to elicit the statements. Indeed it appears that it was respondent, and not the police, who spontaneously initiated the conversation that led to the first and most damaging confession. Cf. *Edwards v. Arizona*, 451 U.S. 477, 101 S.Ct. 1880, 68 L.Ed.2d 378 (1981). Nor is there any question about respondent's comprehension of the full panoply of rights set out in the *Miranda* warnings and of the potential consequences of a decision to relinquish them. Nonetheless, the Court of Appeals believed that the "[deliberate] or reckless" conduct of the police, in particular their failure to inform respondent of the telephone call, fatally undermined the validity of the otherwise proper waiver. We find this conclusion untenable as a matter of both logic and precedent.

Events occurring outside of the presence of the suspect and entirely unknown to him surely can have no bearing on the capacity to comprehend and knowingly relinquish a constitutional right. Under the analysis of the Court of Appeals, the same defendant, armed with the same information and confronted with precisely the same police conduct, would have knowingly waived his *Miranda* rights had a lawyer not telephoned the police station to inquire about his status. Nothing in any of our waiver decisions or in our understanding of the essential components of a valid waiver requires so incongruous a result. No doubt the additional information would have been useful to respondent; perhaps even it might have affected his decision to confess. But we have never read the Constitution to require that the police supply a suspect with a flow of information to help him calibrate his self-interest in deciding whether to speak or stand by his rights. Once it is determined that a suspect's decision not to rely on his rights was uncoerced, that he at all times knew he could stand mute and request a lawyer, and that he was aware of the State's intention to use his statements to secure a conviction, the analysis is complete and the waiver is valid as a matter of law. The Court of Appeals' conclusion to the contrary was in error.

Nor do we believe that the level of the police's culpability in failing to inform respondent of the telephone call has any bearing on the validity of the waivers. In light of the state-court findings that there was no "conspiracy or collusion" on the part of the police, we have serious doubts about whether the Court of Appeals was free to conclude that their conduct constituted "deliberate or reckless irresponsibility." But whether intentional or inadvertent, the state of mind of the police is irrelevant to the question of the intelligence and voluntariness of respondent's election to abandon his rights. Although highly inappropriate, even deliberate deception of an attorney could not possibly affect a suspect's decision to waive his *Miranda* rights unless he were at least aware of the incident. Compare *Escobedo v. Illinois*, 378 U.S. 478, 481, 84 S.Ct. 1758, 12 L.Ed.2d 977 (1964) (excluding confession where police incorrectly told the *suspect* that his lawyer " 'didn't want to see' him"). Nor was the failure to inform respondent of the telephone call the kind of "[trickery]" that can vitiate the validity of a waiver. *Miranda*, 384

U.S., at 476. Granting that the "deliberate or reckless" withholding of information is objectionable as a matter of ethics, such conduct is only relevant to the constitutional validity of a waiver if it deprives a defendant of knowledge essential to his ability to understand the nature of his rights and the consequences of abandoning them. Because respondent's voluntary decision to speak was made with full awareness and comprehension of all the information *Miranda* requires the police to convey, the waivers were valid.

B

* * *

At the outset, while we share respondent's distaste for the deliberate misleading of an officer of the court, reading *Miranda* to forbid police deception of an *attorney* "would cut [the decision] completely loose from its own explicitly stated rationale." As is now well established, "[the] . . . *Miranda* warnings are 'not themselves rights protected by the Constitution but [are] instead measures to insure that the [suspect's] right against compulsory self-incrimination [is] protected.' " *New York v. Quarles*, 467 U.S. 649, 654, 104 S.Ct. 2626, 81 L.Ed.2d 550 (1984), quoting *Michigan v. Tucker*, 417 U.S. 433, 444, 94 S.Ct. 2357, 41 L.Ed.2d 182 (1974). Their objective is not to mold police conduct for its own sake. Nothing in the Constitution vests in us the authority to mandate a code of behavior for state officials wholly unconnected to any federal right or privilege. The purpose of the *Miranda* warnings instead is to dissipate the compulsion inherent in custodial interrogation and, in so doing, guard against abridgment of the suspect's Fifth Amendment rights. Clearly, a rule that focuses on how the police treat an attorney—conduct that has no relevance at all to the degree of compulsion experienced by the defendant during interrogation—would ignore both *Miranda*'s mission and its only source of legitimacy.

Nor are we prepared to adopt a rule requiring that the police inform a suspect of an attorney's efforts to reach him. While such a rule might add marginally to *Miranda*'s goal of dispelling the compulsion inherent in custodial interrogation, overriding practical considerations counsel against its adoption. As we have stressed on numerous occasions, "[one] of the principal advantages" of *Miranda* is the ease and clarity of its application. We have little doubt that the approach urged by respondent and endorsed by the Court of Appeals would have the inevitable consequence of muddying *Miranda*'s otherwise relatively clear waters. The legal questions it would spawn are legion: To what extent should the police be held accountable for knowing that the accused has counsel? Is it enough that someone in the station house knows, or must the interrogating officer himself know of counsel's efforts to contact the suspect? Do counsel's efforts to talk to the suspect concerning one criminal investigation trigger the obligation to inform the defendant before interrogation may proceed on a wholly separate matter? We are unwilling to modify *Miranda* in a manner that would so clearly undermine the decision's central "virtue of informing police and prosecutors with specificity ... what they may do in conducting [a] custodial interrogation, and of informing courts under what circumstances statements obtained during such interrogation are not admissible."

* * *

* * * Because, as *Miranda* holds, full comprehension of the rights to remain silent and request an attorney are sufficient to dispel whatever coercion is inherent in the interrogation process, a rule requiring the police to inform the suspect of an attorney's efforts to contact him would contribute to the protection of the Fifth Amendment privilege only incidentally, if at all. This minimal benefit, however, would come at a substantial cost to society's legitimate and substantial interest in securing admissions of guilt. * * *

We acknowledge that a number of state courts have reached a contrary conclusion. * * * Nothing we say today disables the States from adopting different requirements for the conduct of its employees and officials as a matter of state law. We hold only that the Court of Appeals erred in construing the Fifth Amendment to the Federal Constitution to require the exclusion of respondent's three confessions.

III

Respondent also contends that the Sixth Amendment requires exclusion of his three confessions. It is clear, of course, that, absent a valid waiver, the defendant has the right to the presence of an attorney during any interrogation occurring after the first formal charging proceeding, the point at which the Sixth Amendment right to counsel initially attaches. And we readily agree that once the right *has* attached, it follows that the police may not interfere with the efforts of a defendant's attorney to act as a " 'medium' between [the suspect] and the State" during the interrogation. *Maine v. Moulton,* 474 U.S. 159, 176, 106 S.Ct. 477, 88 L.Ed.2d 481 (1985). The difficulty for respondent is that the interrogation sessions that yielded the inculpatory statements took place *before* the initiation of "adversary judicial proceedings." He contends, however, that this circumstance is not fatal to his Sixth Amendment claim. At least in some situations, he argues, the Sixth Amendment protects the integrity of the attorney-client relationship regardless of whether the prosecution has in fact commenced "by way of formal charge, preliminary hearing, indictment, information or arraignment." * * * The right to noninterference with an attorney's dealings with a criminal suspect, he asserts, arises the moment that the relationship is formed, or, at the very least, once the defendant is placed in custodial interrogation.

* * *

[W]e find respondent's understanding of the Sixth Amendment both practically and theoretically unsound. As a practical matter, it makes little sense to say that the Sixth Amendment right to counsel attaches at different times depending on the fortuity of whether the suspect or his family happens to have retained counsel prior to interrogation. * * * The Sixth Amendment's intended function is not to wrap a protective cloak around the attorney-client relationship for its own sake any more than it is to protect a suspect from the consequences of his own candor. Its purpose, rather, is to assure that in any "criminal [prosecution]," the accused shall not be left to his own devices in facing the " 'prosecutorial forces of organized society.' " *Maine v. Moulton.* By its very terms, it becomes applicable only when the government's role shifts from investigation to accusation. For it is only then that the assistance of one versed in the "intricacies ... of law" is needed to assure that the prosecution's case encounters "the crucible of meaningful adversarial testing."

Indeed, in *Maine* v. *Moulton,* decided this Term, the Court again confirmed that looking to the initiation of adversary judicial proceedings, far from being mere formalism, is fundamental to the proper application of the Sixth Amendment right to counsel. There, we considered the constitutional implications of a surreptitious investigation that yielded evidence pertaining to two crimes. For one, the defendant had been indicted; for the other, he had not. Concerning the former, the Court reaffirmed that after the first charging proceeding the government may not deliberately elicit incriminating statements from an accused out of the presence of counsel. The Court made clear, however, that the evidence concerning the crime for which the defendant had not been indicted—evidence obtained in precisely the same manner from the identical suspect—would be admissible at a trial limited to those charges. [T]he Sixth Amendment right to counsel does not attach until after the initiation of formal charges. Moreover, because Moulton already had legal representation, the decision all but forecloses respondent's argument that the attorney-client relationship itself triggers the Sixth Amendment right.

Respondent contends, however, that custodial interrogations require a different rule. Because confessions elicited during the course of police questioning often seal a suspect's fate, he argues, the need for an advocate—and the concomitant right to noninterference with the attorney-client relationship—is at its zenith, regardless of whether the State has initiated the first adversary judicial proceeding. We do not doubt that a lawyer's presence could be of value to the suspect; and we readily agree that if a suspect confesses, his attorney's case at trial will be that much more difficult. [U]ntil such time as the " 'government has committed itself to prosecute, and ... the adverse positions of government and defendant have solidified' " the Sixth Amendment right to counsel does not attach.

Because, as respondent acknowledges, the events that led to the inculpatory statements preceded the formal initiation of adversary judicial proceedings, we reject the contention that the conduct of the police violated his rights under the Sixth Amendment.

* * *

JUSTICE STEVENS, with whom JUSTICE BRENNAN and JUSTICE MARSHALL join, dissenting.

This case poses fundamental questions about our system of justice. As this Court has long recognized, and reaffirmed only weeks ago, "ours is an accusatorial and not an inquisitorial system." The Court's opinion today represents a startling departure from that basic insight.

The Court concludes that the police may deceive an attorney by giving her false information about whether her client will be questioned, and that the police may deceive a suspect by failing to inform him of his attorney's communications and efforts to represent him. For the majority, this conclusion, though "[distasteful]," is not even debatable. The deception of the attorney is irrelevant because the attorney has no right to information, accuracy, honesty, or fairness in the police response to her questions about her client. The deception of the client is acceptable, because, although the information would affect the client's assertion of his rights, the client's actions in ignorance of the availability of his attorney are voluntary, knowing, and intelligent; additionally, society's interest in apprehending, prosecuting, and punishing criminals outweighs the suspect's interest in information regarding his attorney's efforts to communicate with him. Finally, even mendacious police interference in the communications between a suspect and his lawyer does not violate any notion of fundamental fairness because it does not shock the conscience of the majority.

* * *

The Court's holding focuses on the period after a suspect has been taken into custody and before he has been charged with an offense. The core of the Court's holding is that police interference with an attorney's access to her client during that period is not unconstitutional. The Court reasons that a State has a compelling interest, not simply in custodial interrogation, but in lawyer-free, incommunicado custodial interrogation. Such incommunicado interrogation is so important that a lawyer may be given false information that prevents her presence and representation; it is so important that police may refuse to inform a suspect of his attorney's communications and immediate availability. This conclusion flies in the face of this Court's repeated expressions of deep concern about incommunicado questioning. Until today, incommunicado questioning has been viewed with the strictest scrutiny by this Court; today, incommunicado questioning is embraced as a societal goal of the highest order that justifies police deception of the shabbiest kind.

* * *

Police interference with communications between an attorney and his client is a recurrent problem. The factual variations in the many state-court opinions condemning this interference as a violation of the Federal Constitution suggest the variety of contexts in which the problem emerges. In Oklahoma, police led a lawyer to several different locations while they interrogated the suspect; in Oregon, police moved a suspect to a new location when they learned that his lawyer was on his way; in Illinois, authorities failed to tell a suspect that his lawyer had arrived at the jail and asked to see him; in Massachusetts, police did not tell suspects that their lawyers were at or near the police station. In all these cases, the police not only failed to inform the suspect, but also misled the attorneys. The scenarios vary, but the core problem of police interference remains. "Its recurrence suggests that it has roots in some condition fundamental and general to our criminal system."

The near-consensus of state courts and the legal profession's Standards about this recurrent problem lends powerful support to the conclusion that police may not interfere with communications between an attorney and the client whom they are questioning. Indeed, at least two opinions from this Court seemed to express precisely that view. * * *

* * *

II

[T]he burden of proving the validity of a waiver of constitutional rights is always on the *government*. When such a waiver occurs in a custodial setting, that burden is an especially heavy one because custodial interrogation is inherently coercive, because disinterested witnesses are seldom available to describe what actually happened, and because history has taught us that the danger of overreaching during incommunicado interrogation is so real.

* * *

In short, settled principles about construing waivers of constitutional rights and about the need for strict presumptions in custodial interrogations, as well as a plain reading of the *Miranda* opinion itself, overwhelmingly support the conclusion reached by almost every state court that has considered the matter—a suspect's waiver of his right to counsel is invalid if police refuse to inform the suspect of his counsel's communications.

* * *

VII

This case turns on a proper appraisal of the role of the lawyer in our society. If a lawyer is seen as a nettlesome obstacle to the pursuit of wrongdoers—as in an inquisitorial society—then the Court's decision today makes a good deal of sense. If a lawyer is seen as an aid to the understanding and protection of constitutional rights—as in an accusatorial society—then today's decision makes no sense at all. * * * I respectfully dissent.

2. Blurring the Line Between the Two Amendments

MICHIGAN v. JACKSON

Supreme Court of the United States, 1986.
475 U.S. 625, 106 S.Ct. 1404, 89 L.Ed.2d 631.

JUSTICE STEVENS delivered the opinion of the Court.

In *Edwards* v. *Arizona*, 451 U.S. 477, 101 S.Ct. 1880, 68 L.Ed.2d 378 (1981), we held that an accused person in custody who has "expressed his desire to deal with the police only through counsel, is not subject to further interrogation by the authorities until counsel has been made available to him, unless the accused himself initiates further communication, exchanges, or conversations with the police." * * *

The question presented by these two cases is whether the same rule applies to a defendant who has been formally charged with a crime and who has requested appointment of counsel at his arraignment. In both cases, the Michigan Supreme Court held that postarraignment confessions were improperly obtained—and the Sixth Amendment violated—because the defendants had "requested counsel during their arraignments, but were not afforded an opportunity to consult with counsel before the police initiated further interrogations." We agree with that holding.

I

The relevant facts may be briefly stated. [Only the facts relating to the prosecution of Jackson are presented.]

Respondent Jackson was convicted of second-degree murder and conspiracy to commit second-degree murder. He was one of four participants in a wife's plan to have her husband killed on July 12, 1979. Arrested on an unrelated charge on July 30, 1979, he made a series of six statements in response to police questioning prior to his arraignment at 4:30 p.m. on August 1. During the arraignment, Jackson requested that counsel be appointed for him. The police involved in his investigation were present at the arraignment. On the following morning, before he had an opportunity to consult with counsel, two police officers obtained another statement from Jackson to "confirm" that he was the person who had shot the victim. As was true of the six prearraignment statements, the questioning was preceded by advice of his *Miranda* rights and Jackson's agreement to proceed without counsel being present.

* * *

II

The question is not whether respondents had a right to counsel at their postarraignment, custodial interrogations. The existence of that right is clear. It has two sources. The Fifth Amendment protection against compelled self-incrimination provides the right to counsel at

custodial interrogations. *Edwards*. The Sixth Amendment guarantee of
the assistance of counsel also provides the right to counsel at postarraignment interrogations. The arraignment signals "the initiation of
adversary judicial proceedings" and thus the attachment of the Sixth
Amendment, thereafter, government efforts to elicit information from
the accused, including interrogation, represent "critical stages" at which
the Sixth Amendment applies. *Maine* v. *Moulton*, 474 U.S. 159, 106 S.Ct.
477, 88 L.Ed.2d 481 (1985). The question in these cases is whether
respondents validly waived their right to counsel at the postarraignment
custodial interrogations.

In *Edwards*, the request for counsel was made to the police during
custodial interrogation, and the basis for the Court's holding was the
Fifth Amendment privilege against compelled self-incrimination. The
Court noted the relevance of various Sixth Amendment precedents, but
found it unnecessary to rely on the possible applicability of the Sixth
Amendment. In these cases, the request for counsel was made to a judge
during arraignment, and the basis for the Michigan Supreme Court
opinion was the Sixth Amendment's guarantee of the assistance of
counsel. The State argues that the *Edwards* rule should not apply to
these circumstances because there are legal differences in the basis for
the claims; because there are factual differences in the contexts of the
claims; and because respondents signed valid waivers of their right to
counsel at the postarraignment custodial interrogations. We consider
these contentions in turn.

The State contends that differences in the legal principles underlying the Fifth and Sixth Amendments compel the conclusion that the
Edwards rule should not apply to a Sixth Amendment claim. *Edwards*
flows from the Fifth Amendment's right to counsel at custodial interrogations, the State argues; its relevance to the Sixth Amendment's
provision of the assistance of counsel is far less clear, and thus the
Edwards principle for assessing waivers is unnecessary and inappropriate.

In our opinion, however, the reasons for prohibiting the interrogation of an uncounseled prisoner who has asked for the help of a lawyer
are even stronger after he has been formally charged with an offense
than before. The State's argument misapprehends the nature of the
pretrial protections afforded by the Sixth Amendment. In *United States*
v. *Gouveia*, 467 U.S. 180, 104 S.Ct. 2292, 81 L.Ed.2d 146 (1984). we
explained the significance of the formal accusation, and the corresponding attachment of the Sixth Amendment right to counsel:

> "[G]iven the plain language of the Amendment and its purpose
> of protecting the unaided layman at critical confrontations with his
> adversary, our conclusion that the right to counsel attaches at the
> initiation of adversary judicial criminal proceedings 'is far from a
> mere formalism.' It is only at that time 'that the government has
> committed itself to prosecute, and only then that the adverse posi-
> tions of government and defendant have solidified. It is then that a

defendant finds himself faced with the prosecutorial forces of organized society, and immersed in the intricacies of substantive and procedural criminal law.' "

As a result, the "Sixth Amendment guarantees the accused, at least after the initiation of formal charges, the right to rely on counsel as a 'medium' between him and the State." *Maine* v. *Moulton*. Thus, the Sixth Amendment right to counsel at a postarraignment interrogation requires at least as much protection as the Fifth Amendment right to counsel at any custodial interrogation.

Indeed, after a formal accusation has been made—and a person who had previously been just a "suspect" has become an "accused" within the meaning of the Sixth Amendment—the constitutional right to the assistance of counsel is of such importance that the police may no longer employ techniques for eliciting information from an uncounseled defendant that might have been entirely proper at an earlier stage of their investigation. * * * Far from undermining the *Edwards* rule, the difference between the legal basis for the rule applied in *Edwards* and the Sixth Amendment claim asserted in these cases actually provides additional support for the application of the rule in these circumstances.

The State also relies on the factual differences between a request for counsel during custodial interrogation and a request for counsel at an arraignment. The State maintains that respondents may not have actually intended their request for counsel to encompass representation during any further questioning by the police. This argument, however, must be considered against the backdrop of our standard for assessing waivers of constitutional rights. Almost a half century ago, in *Johnson* v. *Zerbst*, 304 U.S. 458, 58 S.Ct. 1019, 82 L.Ed. 1461 (1938), a case involving an alleged waiver of a defendant's Sixth Amendment right to counsel, the Court explained that we should "indulge every reasonable presumption against waiver of fundamental constitutional rights." For that reason, it is the State that has the burden of establishing a valid waiver. Doubts must be resolved in favor of protecting the constitutional claim. This settled approach to questions of waiver requires us to give a broad, rather than a narrow, interpretation to a defendant's request for counsel—we presume that the defendant requests the lawyer's services at every critical stage of the prosecution. We thus reject the State's suggestion that respondents' requests for the appointment of counsel should be construed to apply only to representation in formal legal proceedings.

* * *

III

Edwards is grounded in the understanding that "the assertion of the right to counsel [is] a significant event," and that "additional safeguards are necessary when the accused asks for counsel." We conclude that the assertion is no less significant, and the need for additional safeguards no less clear, when the request for counsel is made at an arraignment and when the basis for the claim is the Sixth Amendment. We thus hold that, if police initiate interrogation after a defendant's assertion, at an arraignment or similar proceeding, of his right to counsel, any waiver of the defendant's right to counsel for that police-initiated interrogation is invalid.

Although the *Edwards* decision itself rested on the Fifth Amendment and concerned a request for counsel made during custodial interrogation, the Michigan Supreme Court correctly perceived that the reasoning of that case applies with even greater force to these cases. The judgments are accordingly affirmed. *It is so ordered.*

[CHIEF JUSTICE BURGER'S concurring opinion is omitted.]

JUSTICE REHNQUIST, with whom JUSTICE POWELL and JUSTICE O'CONNOR join, dissenting.

The Court's decision today rests on the following deceptively simple line of reasoning: *Edwards* v. *Arizona* created a bright-line rule to protect a defendant's Fifth Amendment rights; Sixth Amendment rights are even more important than Fifth Amendment rights; therefore, we must also apply the *Edwards* rule to the Sixth Amendment. The Court prefers this neat syllogism to an effort to discuss or answer the only relevant question: Does the *Edwards* rule make sense in the context of the Sixth Amendment? I think it does not, and I therefore dissent from the Court's unjustified extension of the *Edwards* rule to the Sixth Amendment.

My disagreement with the Court stems from our differing understandings of *Edwards*. In *Edwards*, this Court held that once a defendant has invoked his right under *Miranda* v. *Arizona*, 384 U.S. 436, 86 S.Ct. 1602, 16 L.Ed.2d 694 (1966), to have counsel present during custodial interrogation, "a valid waiver of that right cannot be established by showing only that he responded to further police-initiated custodial interrogation even if he has been advised of his rights." This "prophylactic rule," was deemed necessary to prevent the police from effectively "overriding" a defendant's assertion of his *Miranda* rights by "badgering" him into waiving those rights. * * *

What the Court today either forgets or chooses to ignore is that the "constitutional guarantee" * * * is the Fifth Amendment's prohibition on compelled self-incrimination. This prohibition, of course, is also the constitutional underpinning for the set of prophylactic rules announced in *Miranda* itself. *Edwards*, like *Miranda*, imposes on the police a bright-line standard of conduct intended to help ensure that confessions obtained through custodial interrogation will not be "coerced" or "involuntary." Seen in this proper light, *Edwards* provides nothing more than a second layer of protection, in addition to those rights conferred by *Miranda*, for a defendant who might otherwise be compelled by the police to incriminate himself in violation of the Fifth Amendment.

The dispositive question in the instant cases, and the question the Court should address in its opinion, is whether the same kind of prophylactic rule is needed to protect a defendant's right to counsel under the Sixth Amendment. The answer to this question, it seems to me, is clearly "no." * * *

Not only does the Court today cut the *Edwards* rule loose from its analytical moorings, it does so in a manner that graphically reveals the illogic of the Court's position. The Court phrases the question presented in these cases as whether the *Edwards* rule applies "to a defendant who has been formally charged with a crime *and who has requested appointment of counsel at his arraignment."* And the Court ultimately limits its holding to those situations where the police "initiate interrogation *after a defendant's assertion, at an arraignment or similar proceeding, of his right to counsel."*

In other words, the Court most assuredly does *not* hold that the *Edwards per se* rule prohibiting all police-initiated interrogations applies from the moment the defendant's Sixth Amendment right to counsel attaches, with or without a request for counsel by the defendant. Such a holding would represent, after all, a shockingly dramatic restructuring of the balance this Court has traditionally struck between the rights of the defendant and those of the larger society. Applying the *Edwards* rule to situations in which a defendant has not made an explicit request for counsel would also render completely nugatory the extensive discussion of "waiver" in such prior Sixth Amendment cases as *Brewer* v. *Williams,* 430 U.S. 387, 401–406, 97 S.Ct. 1232, 51 L.Ed.2d 424 (1977).

This leaves the Court, however, in an analytical strait-jacket. The problem with the limitation the Court places on the Sixth Amendment version of the *Edwards* rule is that, unlike a defendant's "right to counsel" under *Miranda,* which does not arise until affirmatively invoked by the defendant during custodial interrogation, a defendant's Sixth Amendment right to counsel does not depend at all on whether the defendant has requested counsel. * * *

The Court provides no satisfactory explanation for its decision to extend the *Edwards* rule to the Sixth Amendment, yet limit that rule to those defendants foresighted enough, or just plain lucky enough, to have made an explicit request for counsel which we have always understood to be completely unnecessary for Sixth Amendment purposes. The Court attempts to justify its emphasis on the otherwise legally insignificant request for counsel by stating that "we construe the defendant's request for counsel as an extremely important fact in considering the validity of a subsequent waiver in response to police-initiated interrogation." This statement sounds reasonable, but it is flatly inconsistent with the remainder of the Court's opinion, in which the Court holds that there can be no waiver of the Sixth Amendment right to counsel after a request for counsel has been made. It is obvious that, for the Court, the defendant's request for counsel is not merely an "extremely important fact"; rather, it is the *only* fact that counts.

The truth is that there is no satisfactory explanation for the position the Court adopts in these cases. The glaring inconsistencies in the

Court's opinion arise precisely because the Court lacks a coherent, analytically sound basis for its decision. The prophylactic rule of *Edwards*, designed from its inception to protect a defendant's right under the Fifth Amendment not to be compelled to incriminate himself, simply does not meaningfully apply to the Sixth Amendment. I would hold that *Edwards* has no application outside the context of the Fifth Amendment, and would therefore reverse the judgment of the court below.

PATTERSON v. ILLINOIS

Supreme Court of the United States, 1988.
487 U.S. 285, 108 S.Ct. 2389, 101 L.Ed.2d 261.

JUSTICE WHITE delivered the opinion of the Court.

In this case, we are called on to determine whether the interrogation of petitioner after his indictment violated his Sixth Amendment right to counsel.

I

Before dawn on August 21, 1983, petitioner and other members of the "Vice Lords" street gang became involved in a fight with members of a rival gang, the "Black Mobsters." Some time after the fight, a former member of the Black Mobsters, James Jackson, went to the home where the Vice Lords had fled. A second fight broke out there, with petitioner and three other Vice Lords beating Jackson severely. The Vice Lords then put Jackson into a car, drove to the end of a nearby street, and left him face down in a puddle of water. Later that morning, police discovered Jackson, dead, where he had been left.

That afternoon, local police officers obtained warrants for the arrest of the Vice Lords, on charges of battery and mob action, in connection with the first fight. One of the gang members who was arrested gave the police a statement concerning the first fight; the statement also implicated several of the Vice Lords (including petitioner) in Jackson's murder. A few hours later, petitioner was apprehended. Petitioner was informed of his rights under *Miranda v. Arizona*, 384 U.S. 436, 86 S.Ct. 1602, 16 L.Ed.2d 694 (1966), and volunteered to answer questions put to him by the police. Petitioner gave a statement concerning the initial fight between the rival gangs, but denied knowing anything about Jackson's death. Petitioner was held in custody the following day, August 22, as law enforcement authorities completed their investigation of the Jackson murder.

On August 23, a Cook County grand jury indicted petitioner and two other gang members for the murder of James Jackson. Police Officer Michael Gresham, who had questioned petitioner earlier, removed him from the lockup where he was being held, and told petitioner that because he had been indicted he was being transferred to the Cook County jail. Petitioner asked Gresham which of the gang members had been charged with Jackson's murder, and upon learning that one particular Vice Lord had been omitted from the indictments, asked: "[W]hy wasn't he indicted, he did everything.'' Petitioner also began to explain that there was a witness who would support his account of the crime.

At this point, Gresham interrupted petitioner, and handed him a Miranda waiver form. The form contained five specific warnings, as suggested by this Court's Miranda decision, to make petitioner aware of his right to counsel and of the consequences of any statement he might make to police. Gresham read the warnings aloud, as petitioner read along with him. Petitioner initialed each of the five warnings, and signed the waiver form. Petitioner then gave a lengthy statement to police officers concerning the Jackson murder; petitioner's statement described in detail the role of each of the Vice Lords—including himself—in the murder of James Jackson.

Later that day, petitioner confessed involvement in the murder for a second time. This confession came in an interview with Assistant State's Attorney (ASA) George Smith. At the outset of the interview, Smith reviewed with petitioner the Miranda waiver he had previously signed, and petitioner confirmed that he had signed the waiver and understood his rights. Smith went through the waiver procedure once again: reading petitioner his rights, having petitioner initial each one, and sign a waiver form. In addition, Smith informed petitioner that he was a lawyer working with the police investigating the Jackson case. Petitioner then gave another inculpatory statement concerning the crime.

[The trial judge denied Patterson's motions to suppress his statements, the statements were used against him at trial where a jury convicted him of murder. Patterson was sentenced to a 24–year prison term.]

* * *

II

There can be no doubt that petitioner had the right to have the assistance of counsel at his postindictment interviews with law enforcement authorities. Our cases make it plain that the Sixth Amendment guarantees this right to criminal defendants.[3] Petitioner asserts that the questioning that produced his incriminating statements violated his Sixth Amendment right to counsel in two ways.

A

Petitioner's first claim is that because his Sixth Amendment right to counsel arose with his indictment, the police were thereafter barred from initiating a meeting with him. He equates himself with a preindictment suspect who, while being interrogated, asserts his Fifth Amendment

---

3. We note as a matter of some significance that petitioner had not retained, or accepted by appointment, a lawyer to represent him at the time he was questioned by authorities. Once an accused has a lawyer, a distinct set of constitutional safeguards aimed at preserving the sanctity of the attorney-client relationship takes effect. See *Maine v. Moulton, 474 U.S. 159, 176 (1985).* The State conceded as much at argument. Indeed, the analysis changes markedly once an accused even *requests* the assistance of counsel. See *Michigan v. Jackson.*

right to counsel; under *Edwards v. Arizona,* 451 U.S. 477. 101 S.Ct. 1880, 68 L.Ed.2d 378 (1981), such a suspect may not be questioned again unless he initiates the meeting.

Petitioner, however, at no time sought to exercise his right to have counsel present. The fact that petitioner's Sixth Amendment right came into existence with his indictment, *i. e.,* that he had such a right at the time of his questioning, does not distinguish him from the preindictment interrogatee whose right to counsel is in existence and available for his exercise while he is questioned. Had petitioner indicated he wanted the assistance of counsel, the authorities' interview with him would have stopped, and further questioning would have been forbidden (unless petitioner called for such a meeting). This was our holding in *Michigan v. Jackson,* 475 U.S. 625, 106 S.Ct. 1404, 89 L.Ed.2d 631 (1986), which applied *Edwards* to the Sixth Amendment context. We observe that the analysis in Jackson is rendered wholly unnecessary if petitioner's position is correct: under petitioner's theory, the officers in Jackson would have been completely barred from approaching the accused in that case unless he called for them. Our decision in Jackson, however, turned on the fact that the accused "ha[d] asked for the help of a lawyer" in dealing with the police.

At bottom, petitioner's theory cannot be squared with our rationale in *Edwards,* the case he relies on for support. *Edwards* rested on the view that once "an accused ... ha[s] expressed his desire to deal with the police only through counsel" he should "not [be] subject to further interrogation by the authorities until counsel has been made available to him, unless the accused himself initiates further communication." Preserving the integrity of an accused's choice to communicate with police only through counsel is the essence of *Edwards* and its progeny—not barring an accused from making an initial election as to whether he will face the State's officers during questioning with the aid of counsel, or go it alone. If an accused "knowingly and intelligently" pursues the latter course, we see no reason why the uncounseled statements he then makes must be excluded at his trial.

B

Petitioner's principal and more substantial claim is that questioning him without counsel present violated the Sixth Amendment because he did not validly waive his right to have counsel present during the interviews. Since it is clear that after the *Miranda* warnings were given to petitioner, he not only voluntarily answered questions without claiming his right to silence or his right to have a lawyer present to advise him but also executed a written waiver of his right to counsel during questioning, the specific issue posed here is whether this waiver was a "knowing and intelligent" waiver of his Sixth Amendment right.

In the past, this Court has held that a waiver of the Sixth Amendment right to counsel is valid only when it reflects "an intentional relinquishment or abandonment of a known right or privilege." In other words, the accused must "kno[w] what he is doing" so that "his choice is made with eyes open." In a case arising under the Fifth Amendment, we described this requirement as "a full awareness of both the nature of the right being abandoned and the consequences of the decision to abandon it." Whichever of these formulations is used, the key inquiry in a case such as this one must be: Was the accused, who waived his Sixth Amendment rights during postindictment questioning, made sufficiently aware of his right to have counsel present during the questioning, and of the possible consequences of a decision to forgo the aid of counsel? In this case, we are convinced that by admonishing petitioner with the *Miranda* warnings, respondent has met this burden and that petitioner's waiver of his right to counsel at the questioning was valid.

First, the *Miranda* warnings given petitioner made him aware of his right to have counsel present during the questioning. By telling petitioner that he had a right to consult with an attorney, to have a lawyer present while he was questioned, and even to have a lawyer appointed for him if he could not afford to retain one on his own, Officer Gresham and ASA Smith conveyed to petitioner the sum and substance of the rights that the Sixth Amendment provided him. "Indeed, it seems self-evident that one who is told he" has such rights to counsel "is in a curious posture to later complain" that his waiver of these rights was unknowing. There is little more petitioner could have possibly been told in an effort to satisfy this portion of the waiver inquiry.

Second, the *Miranda* warnings also served to make petitioner aware of the consequences of a decision by him to waive his Sixth Amendment rights during postindictment questioning. Petitioner knew that any statement that he made could be used against him in subsequent criminal proceedings. This is the ultimate adverse consequence petitioner could have suffered by virtue of his choice to make uncounseled admissions to the authorities. This warning also sufficed—contrary to petitioner's claim here—to let petitioner know what a lawyer could "do for him" during the postindictment questioning: namely, advise petitioner to refrain from making any such statements. By knowing what could be done with any statements he might make, and therefore, what benefit could be obtained by having the aid of counsel while making such statements, petitioner was essentially informed of the possible consequences of going without counsel during questioning. If petitioner nonetheless lacked "a full and complete appreciation of all of the consequences flowing" from his waiver, it does not defeat the State's showing that the information it provided to him satisfied the constitutional minimum.

* * *

As a general matter, then, an accused who is admonished with the warnings prescribed by this Court in *Miranda* has been sufficiently apprised of the nature of his Sixth Amendment rights, and of the consequences of abandoning those rights, so that his waiver on this basis will be considered a knowing and intelligent one. We feel that our conclusion in a recent Fifth Amendment case is equally apposite here:

"Once it is determined that a suspect's decision not to rely on his rights was uncoerced, that he at all times knew he could stand mute and request a lawyer, and that he was aware of the State's intention to use his statements to secure a conviction, the analysis is complete and the waiver is valid as a matter of law." *See Moran v. Burbine*, 475 U.S. 412, 106 S.Ct. 1135, 89 L.Ed.2d 410 (1986).

C

We consequently reject petitioner's argument, which has some acceptance from courts and commentators, that since "the sixth amendment right [to counsel] is far superior to that of the fifth amendment right" and since "[t]he greater the right the greater the loss from a waiver of that right," waiver of an accused's Sixth Amendment right to counsel should be "more difficult" to effectuate than waiver of a suspect's Fifth Amendment rights. While our cases have recognized a "difference" between the Fifth Amendment and Sixth Amendment rights to counsel, and the "policies" behind these constitutional guarantees, we have never suggested that one right is "superior" or "greater" than the other, nor is there any support in our cases for the notion that because a Sixth Amendment right may be involved, it is more difficult to waive than the Fifth Amendment counterpart.

* * *

Thus, we require a more searching or formal inquiry before permitting an accused to waive his right to counsel at trial than we require for a Sixth Amendment waiver during postindictment questioning—not because postindictment questioning is "less important" than a trial (the analysis that petitioner's "hierarchical" approach would suggest)—but because the full "dangers and disadvantages of self-representation" during questioning are less substantial and more obvious to an accused than they are at trial. Because the role of counsel at questioning is relatively simple and limited, we see no problem in having a waiver procedure at that stage which is likewise simple and limited. So long as the accused is made aware of the "dangers and disadvantages of self-representation" during postindictment questioning, by use of the Miranda warnings, his waiver of his Sixth Amendment right to counsel at such questioning is "knowing and intelligent."

* * *

[JUSTICE BLACKMUN's dissenting opinion is omitted]

JUSTICE STEVENS, with whom JUSTICE BRENNAN and JUSTICE MARSHALL join, dissenting.

The Court should not condone unethical forms of trial preparation by prosecutors or their investigators. In civil litigation it is improper for a lawyer to communicate with his or her adversary's client without either notice to opposing counsel or the permission of the court. An attempt to obtain evidence for use at trial by going behind the back of one's adversary would be not only a serious breach of professional ethics but also a manifestly unfair form of trial practice. In the criminal context, the same ethical rules apply and, in my opinion, notions of fairness that are at least as demanding should also be enforced.

After a jury has been empaneled and a criminal trial is in progress, it would obviously be improper for the prosecutor to conduct a private interview with the defendant for the purpose of obtaining evidence to be used against him at trial. By "private interview" I mean, of course, an interview initiated by the prosecutor, or his or her agents, without notice to the defendant's lawyer and without the permission of the court. Even if such an interview were to be commenced by giving the defendant the five items of legal advice that are mandated by Miranda, I have no doubt that this Court would promptly and unanimously condemn such a shabby practice. As our holding in *Michigan v. Jackson* suggests, such a practice would not simply constitute a serious ethical violation, but would rise to the level of an impairment of the Sixth Amendment right to counsel.

The question that this case raises, therefore, is at what point in the adversary process does it become impermissible for the prosecutor, or his or her agents, to conduct such private interviews with the opposing party? Several alternatives are conceivable: when the trial commences, when the defendant has actually met and accepted representation by his or her appointed counsel, when counsel is appointed, or when the adversary process commences. In my opinion, the Sixth Amendment right to counsel demands that a firm and unequivocal line be drawn at the point at which adversary proceedings commence.

In prior cases this Court has used strong language to emphasize the significance of the formal commencement of adversary proceedings. Such language has been employed to explain decisions denying the defendant the benefit of the protection of the Sixth Amendment in preindictment settings, but an evenhanded interpretation of the Amendment would support the view that additional protection should automatically attach the moment the formal proceedings begin. * * *

* * *

Most recently, in *Moran v. Burbine* the Court upheld a waiver of the right to counsel in a pretrial context even though the waiver "would not be valid" if the same situation had arisen after indictment. In the *Moran* opinion, the Court explained:

"It is clear, of course, that, absent a valid waiver, the defendant has the right to the presence of an attorney during any interrogation occurring after the first formal charging proceeding, the point at which the Sixth Amendment right to counsel initially attaches. And we readily agree that once the right has attached, it follows that the police may not interfere with the efforts of a defendant's attorney to act as a '"medium" between [the suspect] and the State' during the interrogation. The difficulty for respondent is that the interrogation sessions that yielded the inculpatory statements took place before the initiation of 'adversary judicial proceedings.' "

Today, however, in reaching a decision similarly favorable to the interest in law enforcement unfettered by process concerns, the Court backs away from the significance previously attributed to the initiation of formal proceedings. In the majority's view, the purported waiver of counsel in this case is properly equated with that of an unindicted suspect. Yet, as recognized in * * * *Moran*, important differences separate the two. The return of an indictment, or like instrument, substantially alters the relationship between the state and the accused. Only after a formal accusation has "the government . . . committed itself to prosecute, and only then [have] the adverse positions of government and defendant . . . solidified." Moreover, the return of an indictment also presumably signals the government's conclusion that it has sufficient evidence to establish a prima facie case. As a result, any further interrogation can only be designed to buttress the government's case; authorities are no longer simply attempting " 'to solve a crime.' " Given the significance of the initiation of formal proceedings and the concomitant shift in the relationship between the state and the accused, I think it quite wrong to suggest that *Miranda* warnings—or for that matter, any warnings offered by an adverse party—provide a sufficient basis for permitting the undoubtedly prejudicial—and, in my view, unfair—practice of permitting trained law enforcement personnel and prosecuting attorneys to communicate with as-of-yet unrepresented criminal defendants.

* * *

Yet, once it is conceded that certain advice is required and that after indictment the adversary relationship between the state and the accused has solidified, it inescapably follows that a prosecutor may not conduct private interviews with a charged defendant. As at least one Court of Appeals has recognized, there are ethical constraints that prevent a prosecutor from giving legal advice to an uncounseled adversary. Thus, neither the prosecutor nor his or her agents can ethically provide the unrepresented defendant with the kind of advice that should precede an evidence-gathering interview after formal proceedings have been commenced. Indeed, in my opinion even the Miranda warnings themselves are a species of legal advice that is improper when given by the prosecutor after indictment.

* * *

* * * It is true, of course, that the interest in effective law enforcement would benefit from an opportunity to engage in incommunicado questioning of defendants who, for reasons beyond their control, have not been able to receive the legal advice from counsel to which they are constitutionally entitled. But the Court's singleminded concentration on that interest might also lead to the toleration of similar practices at any stage of the trial. I think it clear that such private communications are intolerable not simply during trial, but at any point after adversary proceedings have commenced. I therefore respectfully dissent.

3.　Redrawing the Line Between the Two Amendments?

McNEIL v. WISCONSIN

Supreme Court of the United States, 1991.
501 U.S. 171, 111 S.Ct. 2204, 115 L.Ed.2d 158.

JUSTICE SCALIA delivered the opinion of the Court.

This case presents the question whether an accused's invocation of his Sixth Amendment right to counsel during a judicial proceeding constitutes an invocation of his *Miranda* right to counsel.

I

Petitioner Paul McNeil was arrested in Omaha, Nebraska, in May 1987, pursuant to a warrant charging him with an armed robbery in West Allis, Wisconsin, a suburb of Milwaukee. Shortly after his arrest, two Milwaukee County deputy sheriffs arrived in Omaha to retrieve him. After advising him of his *Miranda* rights, the deputies sought to question him. He refused to answer any questions, but did not request an attorney. The deputies promptly ended the interview.

Once back in Wisconsin, petitioner was brought before a Milwaukee County Court Commissioner on the armed robbery charge. The Commissioner set bail and scheduled a preliminary examination. An attorney from the Wisconsin Public Defender's Office represented petitioner at this initial appearance.

Later that evening, Detective Joseph Butts of the Milwaukee County Sheriff's Department visited petitioner in jail. Butts had been assisting the Racine County, Wisconsin, police in their investigation of a murder, attempted murder, and armed burglary in the town of Caledonia; petitioner was a suspect. Butts advised petitioner of his *Miranda* rights, and petitioner signed a form waiving them. In this first interview, petitioner did not deny knowledge of the Caledonia crimes, but said that he had not been involved.

Butts returned two days later with detectives from Caledonia. He again began the encounter by advising petitioner of his *Miranda* rights and providing a waiver form. Petitioner placed his initials next to each of the warnings and signed the form. This time, petitioner admitted that he had been involved in the Caledonia crimes, which he described in detail. He also implicated two other men, Willie Pope and Lloyd Crowley. The statement was typed up by a detective and given to petitioner to review. Petitioner placed his initials next to every reference to himself and signed every page.

Butts and the Caledonia Police returned two days later, having in the meantime found and questioned Pope, who convinced them that he had not been involved in the Caledonia crimes. They again began the interview by administering the *Miranda* warnings and obtaining petitioner's signature and initials on the waiver form. Petitioner acknowledged that he had lied about Pope's involvement to minimize his own role in the Caledonia crimes and provided another statement recounting the events, which was transcribed, signed, and initialed as before.

The following day, petitioner was formally charged with the Caledonia crimes and transferred to that jurisdiction. His pretrial motion to suppress the three incriminating statements was denied. He was convicted of second-degree murder, attempted first-degree murder, and armed robbery, and sentenced to 60 years in prison.

* * *

II

The Sixth Amendment provides that "in all criminal prosecutions, the accused shall enjoy the right ... to have the Assistance of Counsel for his defence." In *Michigan v. Jackson*, 475 U.S. 625, 106 S.Ct. 1404, 89 L.Ed.2d 631 (1986), we held that once this right to counsel has attached and has been invoked, any subsequent waiver during a police-initiated custodial interview is ineffective. It is undisputed, and we accept for purposes of the present case, that at the time petitioner provided the incriminating statements at issue, his Sixth Amendment right had attached and had been invoked with respect to the *West Allis armed robbery*, for which he had been formally charged.

The Sixth Amendment right, however, is offense specific. It cannot be invoked once for all future prosecutions, for it does not attach until a prosecution is commenced, that is, " 'at or after the initiation of adversary judicial criminal proceedings—whether by way of formal charge, preliminary hearing, indictment, information, or arraignment.' " And just as the right is offense specific, so also its *Michigan* v. *Jackson* effect of invalidating subsequent waivers in police-initiated interviews is offense specific.

> "The police have an interest ... in investigating new or additional crimes [after an individual is formally charged with one crime.] ... To exclude evidence pertaining to charges as to which the Sixth Amendment right to counsel had not attached at the time the evidence was obtained, simply because other charges were pending at that time, would unnecessarily frustrate the public's interest in the investigation of criminal activities.... "

> "Incriminating statements pertaining to other crimes, as to which the Sixth Amendment right has not yet attached, are, of course, admissible at a trial of those offenses."

Because petitioner provided the statements at issue here before his Sixth Amendment right to counsel with respect to the *Caledonia offenses* had been (or even could have been) invoked, that right poses no bar to the admission of the statements in this case.

Petitioner relies, however, upon a different "right to counsel," found not in the text of the Sixth Amendment, but in this Court's jurisprudence relating to the Fifth Amendment guarantee that "no person ... shall be compelled in any criminal case to be a witness against himself." In *Miranda v. Arizona,* 384 U.S. 436, 86 S.Ct. 1602, 16 L.Ed.2d 694 (1966), we established a number of prophylactic rights designed to counteract the "inherently compelling pressures" of custodial interrogation, including the right to have counsel present. *Miranda* did not hold, however, that those rights could not be waived. On the contrary, the opinion recognized that statements elicited during custodial interrogation would be admissible if the prosecution could establish that the suspect "knowingly and intelligently waived his privilege against self-incrimination and his right to retained or appointed counsel."

In *Edwards v. Arizona,* 451 U.S. 477, 101 S.Ct. 1880, 68 L.Ed.2d 378 (1981), we established a second layer of prophylaxis for the *Miranda* right to counsel: Once a suspect asserts the right, not only must the current interrogation cease, but he may not be approached for further interrogation "until counsel has been made available to him," which means* * * that counsel must be present. If the police do subsequently initiate an encounter in the absence of counsel (assuming there has been no break in custody), the suspect's statements are presumed involuntary and therefore inadmissible as substantive evidence at trial, even where the suspect executes a waiver and his statements would be considered voluntary under traditional standards. This is "designed to prevent police from badgering a defendant into waiving his previously asserted *Miranda* rights," The *Edwards* rule, moreover, is *not* offense specific: Once a suspect invokes the *Miranda* right to counsel for interrogation regarding one offense, he may not be reapproached regarding *any* offense unless counsel is present. *Arizona v. Roberson,* 486 U.S. 675, 108 S.Ct. 2093, 100 L.Ed.2d 704 (1988).

Having described the nature and effects of both the Sixth Amendment right to counsel and the *Miranda-Edwards* "Fifth Amendment" right to counsel, we come at last to the issue here: Petitioner seeks to prevail by combining the two of them. He contends that, although he expressly waived his *Miranda* right to counsel on every occasion he was interrogated, those waivers were the invalid product of impermissible approaches, because his prior invocation of the offense-specific Sixth Amendment right with regard to the West Allis burglary was also an invocation of the nonoffense-specific *Miranda-Edwards* right. We think that is false as a matter of fact and inadvisable (if even permissible) as a contrary-to-fact presumption of policy.

As to the former: The purpose of the Sixth Amendment counsel guarantee—and hence the purpose of invoking it—is to "protect the unaided layman at critical confrontations" with his "expert adversary," the government, *after* "the adverse positions of government and defendant have solidified" with respect to a particular alleged crime. The purpose of the *Miranda-Edwards* guarantee, on the other hand—and hence the purpose of invoking it—is to protect a quite different interest:

the suspect's "desire to deal with the police only through counsel." This is in one respect narrower than the interest protected by the Sixth Amendment guarantee (because it relates only to custodial interrogation) and in another respect broader (because it relates to interrogation regarding *any* suspected crime and attaches whether or not the "adversarial relationship" produced by a pending prosecution has yet arisen). To invoke the Sixth Amendment interest is, as a matter of *fact, not* to invoke the *Miranda-Edwards* interest. One might be quite willing to speak to the police without counsel present concerning many matters, but not the matter under prosecution. * * * The rule of [*Edwards v. Arizona*] applies only when the suspect "has *expressed*" his wish for the particular sort of lawyerly assistance that is the subject of *Miranda.* (emphasis added). It requires, at a minimum, some statement that can reasonably be construed to be an expression of a desire for the assistance of an attorney *in dealing with custodial interrogation by the police.* Requesting the assistance of an attorney at a bail hearing does not bear that construction. "To find that [the defendant] invoked his Fifth Amendment right to counsel on the present charges merely by requesting the appointment of counsel at his arraignment on the unrelated charge is to disregard the ordinary meaning of that request."

Our holding in *Michigan v. Jackson* does not, as petitioner asserts, contradict the foregoing distinction; to the contrary, it *rests* upon it. That case, it will be recalled, held that after the Sixth Amendment right to counsel attaches and is invoked, any statements obtained from the accused during subsequent police-initiated custodial questioning regarding the charge at issue (even if the accused purports to waive his rights) are inadmissible. The State in *Jackson* opposed that outcome on the ground that assertion of the Sixth Amendment right to counsel did not realistically constitute the *expression* (as *Edwards* required) of a wish to have counsel present during custodial interrogation. Our response to that contention was not that it *did* constitute such an expression, but that it *did not have to*, since the relevant question was not whether the *Miranda* "Fifth Amendment" right had been *asserted*, but whether the Sixth Amendment right to counsel had been *waived*. We said that since our "settled approach to questions of waiver requires us to give a broad, rather than a narrow, interpretation to a defendant's request for counsel, . . . we *presume* that the defendant requests the lawyer's services at every critical stage of the prosecution." (emphasis added). The holding of *Jackson* implicitly rejects any equivalence in fact between invocation of the Sixth Amendment right to counsel and the expression necessary to trigger *Edwards.* * * *

There remains to be considered the possibility that, even though the assertion of the Sixth Amendment right to counsel does not *in fact* imply an assertion of the *Miranda* "Fifth Amendment" right, we should declare it to be such as a matter of sound policy. Assuming we have such an expansive power under the Constitution, it would not wisely be exercised. Petitioner's proposed rule has only insignificant advantages. If a suspect does not wish to communicate with the police except through an attorney, he can simply tell them that when they give him the *Miranda* warnings. There is not the remotest chance that he will feel "badgered" by their asking to talk to him without counsel present, since the subject will not be the charge on which he has already requested counsel's assistance (for in that event *Jackson* would preclude initiation of the interview) and he will not have rejected uncounseled interrogation on *any* subject before (for in that event *Edwards* would preclude initiation of the interview). The proposed rule would, however, seriously impede effective law enforcement. The Sixth Amendment right to counsel attaches at the first formal proceeding against an accused, and in most States, at least with respect to serious offenses, free counsel is made available at that time and ordinarily requested. Thus, if we were to adopt petitioner's rule, most persons in pretrial custody for serious offenses would be *unapproachable* by police officers suspecting them of involvement in other crimes, *even though they have never expressed any unwillingness to be questioned.* Since the ready ability to obtain uncoerced confessions is not an evil but an unmitigated good, society would be the loser. Admissions of guilt resulting from valid *Miranda* waivers "are more than merely 'desirable'; they are essential to society's compelling interest in finding, convicting, and punishing those who violate the law."

Petitioner urges upon us the desirability of providing a "clear and unequivocal" guideline for the police: no police-initiated questioning of any person in custody who has requested counsel to assist him in defense or in interrogation. But the police do not need our assistance to establish such a guideline; they are free, if they wish, to adopt it on their own. Of course it *is* our task to establish guidelines for judicial review. We like *them* to be "clear and unequivocal," but only when they guide sensibly and in a direction we are authorized to go. Petitioner's proposal would in our view do much more harm than good, and is not contained within, or even in furtherance of, the Sixth Amendment's right to counsel or the Fifth Amendment's right against compelled self-incrimination.[3]

* * *

3. The dissent predicts that the result in this case will routinely be circumvented when, "in future preliminary hearings, competent counsel ... make sure that they, or their clients, make a statement on the record" invoking the *Miranda* right to counsel. We have in fact never held that a person can invoke his *Miranda* rights anticipatorily, in a context other than "custodial interrogation"—which a preliminary hearing will not always, or even usually, involve, cf. *Pennsylvania v. Muniz*, 496 U.S. 582, 601–602, 110 L.Ed.2d 528, 110 S.Ct. 2638 (1990) (plurality opinion); *Rhode Island v. Innis*, 446 U.S. 291, 298–303, 64 L.Ed.2d 297, 100 S.Ct. 1682 (1980). If the *Miranda* right to counsel can be invoked at a preliminary hearing, it could be argued, there is no logical reason why it could not be invoked by a letter prior to arrest, or indeed even prior to identification as a suspect. Most rights must be asserted when the government seeks to take the action they protect against. The fact that we have allowed the *Miranda* right to counsel, once asserted, to be effective with respect to future custodial interrogation does not necessarily mean that we will allow it to be asserted initially outside the context of custodial interrogation, with similar future effect. Assuming, however, that an assertion at arraignment would be effective, and would be routinely made, the mere fact that adherence to the principle of our decisions will not have substantial consequences is no reason to abandon that principle. It would

[JUSTICE KENNEDY'S concurring opinion is omitted.]

JUSTICE STEVENS, with whom JUSTICE MARSHALL and JUSTICE BLACKMUN join, dissenting.

The Court's opinion demeans the importance of the right to counsel. As a practical matter, the opinion probably will have only a slight impact on current custodial interrogation procedures. As a theoretical matter, the Court's innovative development of an "offense-specific" limitation on the scope of the attorney-client relationship can only generate confusion in the law and undermine the protections that undergird our adversarial system of justice. As a symbolic matter, today's decision is ominous because it reflects a preference for an inquisitorial system that regards the defense lawyer as an impediment rather than a servant to the cause of justice.

I

The predicate for the Court's entire analysis is the failure of the defendant at the preliminary hearing to make a "statement that can reasonably be construed to be expression of a desire for the assistance of an attorney *in dealing with custodial interrogation by the police.*" If petitioner in this case had made such a statement indicating that he was invoking his Fifth Amendment right to counsel as well as his Sixth Amendment right to counsel, the entire offense-specific house of cards that the Court has erected today would collapse, pursuant to our holding in *Arizona v. Roberson* that a defendant who invokes the right to counsel for interrogation on one offense may not be reapproached regarding any offense unless counsel is present.

In future preliminary hearings, competent counsel can be expected to make sure that they, or their clients, make a statement on the record that will obviate the consequences of today's holding. That is why I think this decision will have little, if any, practical effect on police practices.

II

The outcome of this case is determined by the Court's parsimonious "offense-specific" description of the right to counsel guaranteed by the Sixth Amendment. The Court's definition is inconsistent with the high value our prior cases have placed on this right, with the ordinary understanding of the scope of the right, and with the accepted practice of the legal profession.

In *Michigan v. Jackson* we held that the defendant's invocation of his right to the assistance of counsel at arraignment prohibited the police from initiating a postarraignment custodial interrogation without notice to his lawyer. After explaining that our prior cases required us "to give a broad, rather than a narrow, interpretation to a defendant's

remain intolerable that a person in custody who had expressed *no* objection to being questioned would be unapproachable.

request for counsel," we squarely rejected "the State's suggestion that respondents' requests for the appointment of counsel should be construed to apply only to representation in formal legal proceedings." Instead, we noted that "it is the State that has the burden of establishing a valid waiver [of the right to counsel]. Doubts must be resolved in favor of protecting the constitutional claim."

Today, however, the Court accepts a narrow, rather than a broad, interpretation of the same right. It accepts the State's suggestion that although, under our prior holding in *Michigan* v. *Jackson*, a request for the assistance of counsel at a formal proceeding such as an arraignment constitutes an invocation of the right to counsel at police-initiated custodial interrogation as well, such a request only covers interrogation about the specific charge that has already been filed and for which the formal proceeding was held. Today's approach of construing ambiguous requests for counsel narrowly and presuming a waiver of rights is the opposite of that taken in *Jackson*.

* * *

FELLERS v. UNITED STATES

Supreme Court of the United States, 2004.
540 U.S. 519, 124 S.Ct. 1019, 157 L.Ed.2d 1016.

JUSTICE O'CONNOR delivered the opinion of the Court.

* * *

I

On February 24, 2000, after a grand jury indicted petitioner for conspiracy to distribute methamphetamine, Lincoln Police Sergeant Michael Garnett and Lancaster County Deputy Sheriff Jeff Bliemeister went to petitioner's home in Lincoln, Nebraska, to arrest him. The officers knocked on petitioner's door and, when petitioner answered, identified themselves and asked if they could come in. Petitioner invited the officers into his living room.

The officers advised petitioner they had come to discuss his involvement in methamphetamine distribution. They informed petitioner that they had a federal warrant for his arrest and that a grand jury had indicted him for conspiracy to distribute methamphetamine. The officers told petitioner that the indictment referred to his involvement with certain individuals, four of whom they named. Petitioner then told the officers that he knew the four people and had used methamphetamine during his association with them.

After spending about 15 minutes in petitioner's home, the officers transported petitioner to the Lancaster County jail. There, the officers advised petitioner for the first time of his rights under *Miranda* v. *Arizona*, 384 U.S. 436, 16 L.Ed.2d 694, 86 S.Ct. 1602 (1966), and *Patterson* v. *Illinois*, 487 U.S. 285, 101 L.Ed.2d 261, 108 S.Ct. 2389

(1988). Petitioner and the two officers signed a *Miranda* waiver form, and petitioner then reiterated the inculpatory statements he had made earlier, admitted to having associated with other individuals implicated in the charged conspiracy, and admitted to having loaned money to one of them even though he suspected that she was involved in drug transactions.

Before trial, petitioner moved to suppress the inculpatory statements he made at his home and at the county jail. * * *

The District Court suppressed the "unwarned" statements petitioner made at his house but admitted petitioner's jailhouse statements pursuant to *Oregon* v. *Elstad,* 470 U.S. 298, 84 L.Ed.2d 222, 105 S.Ct. 1285 (1985), concluding petitioner had knowingly and voluntarily waived his *Miranda* rights before making the statements.

Following a jury trial at which petitioner's jailhouse statements were admitted into evidence, petitioner was convicted of conspiring to possess with intent to distribute methamphetamine. Petitioner appealed, arguing that his jailhouse statements should have been suppressed as fruits of the statements obtained at his home in violation of the Sixth Amendment. The Court of Appeals affirmed. * * *

* * *

II

The Sixth Amendment right to counsel is triggered "at or after the time that judicial proceedings have been initiated . . . 'whether by way of formal charge, preliminary hearing, indictment, information, or arraignment.' " *Brewer* v. *Williams,* 430 U.S. 387, 398, 51 L.Ed.2d 424, 97 S.Ct. 1232 (1977). We have held that an accused is denied "the basic protections" of the Sixth Amendment "when there [is] used against him at his trial evidence of his own incriminating words, which federal agents . . . deliberately elicited from him after he had been indicted and in the absence of his counsel." *Massiah* v. *United States,* 377 U.S. 201, 206, 12 L.Ed.2d 246, 84 S.Ct. 1199 (1964).

We have consistently applied the deliberate-elicitation standard in subsequent Sixth Amendment cases, and we have expressly distinguished this standard from the Fifth Amendment custodial-interrogation standard, see *Michigan* v. *Jackson,* 475 U.S. 625, 632, n. 5, 89 L.Ed.2d 631, 106 S.Ct. 1404 (1986) ("[T]he Sixth Amendment provides a right to counsel . . . even when there is no interrogation and no Fifth Amendment applicability"); *Rhode Island* v. *Innis,* 446 U.S. 291, 300, n. 4, 64 L.Ed.2d 297, 100 S.Ct. 1682 (1980) ("The definitions of 'interrogation' under the Fifth and Sixth Amendments, if indeed the term 'interrogation' is even apt in the Sixth Amendment context, are not necessarily interchangeable").

The Court of Appeals erred in holding that the absence of an "interrogation" foreclosed petitioner's claim that the jailhouse statements should have been suppressed as fruits of the statements taken from petitioner at his home. First, there is no question that the officers in this case "deliberately elicited" information from petitioner. Indeed, the officers, upon arriving at petitioner's house, informed him that their purpose in coming was to discuss his involvement in the distribution of methamphetamine and his association with certain charged co-conspirators. Because the ensuing discussion took place after petitioner had been indicted, outside the presence of counsel, and in the absence of any waiver of petitioner's Sixth Amendment rights, the Court of Appeals erred in holding that the officers' actions did not violate the Sixth Amendment standards established in *Massiah* and its progeny.

Second, because of its erroneous determination that petitioner was not questioned in violation of Sixth Amendment standards, the Court of Appeals improperly conducted its "fruits" analysis under the Fifth Amendment. Specifically, it applied *Elstad,* to hold that the admissibility of the jailhouse statements turns solely on whether the statements were " 'knowingly and voluntarily made.' " The Court of Appeals did not reach the question whether the Sixth Amendment requires suppression of petitioner's jailhouse statements on the ground that they were the fruits of previous questioning conducted in violation of the Sixth Amendment deliberate-elicitation standard. We have not had occasion to decide whether the rationale of *Elstad* applies when a suspect makes incriminating statements after a knowing and voluntary waiver of his right to counsel notwithstanding earlier police questioning in violation of Sixth Amendment standards. We therefore remand to the Court of Appeals to address this issue in the first instance.

Accordingly, the judgment of the Court of Appeals is reversed, and the case is remanded for further proceedings consistent with this opinion. It is so ordered.

Chapter 7

WHO CAN ASSERT A VIOLATION OF CONSTITUTIONAL RIGHTS? STANDING AND "FRUIT OF THE POISONOUS TREE"

A. STANDING TO SUPPRESS EVIDENCE

1. Personal Rights, Property and Fourth Amendment Standing

JONES v. UNITED STATES

Supreme Court of the United States, 1960.
362 U.S. 257, 80 S.Ct. 725, 4 L.Ed.2d 697.

MR. JUSTICE FRANKFURTER delivered the opinion of the Court.

This is a prosecution for violation of federal narcotics laws. * * * Possession was the basis of the Government's case against petitioner. The evidence against him may be briefly summarized. He was arrested in an apartment in the District of Columbia by federal narcotics officers, who were executing a warrant to search for narcotics. Those officers found narcotics, without appropriate stamps, and narcotics paraphernalia in a bird's nest in an awning just outside a window in the apartment. Another officer, stationed outside the building, had a short time before seen petitioner put his hand on the awning. Upon the discovery of the narcotics and the paraphernalia petitioner had admitted to the officers that some of these were his and that he was living in the apartment.

Prior to trial petitioner duly moved to suppress the evidence obtained through the execution of the search warrant on the ground that the warrant had been issued without a showing of probable cause. The Government challenged petitioner's standing to make this motion because petitioner alleged neither ownership of the seized articles nor an interest in the apartment greater than that of an "invitee or guest." The District Court agreed to take evidence on the issue of petitioner's standing. Only petitioner gave evidence. On direct examination he testi-

476

fied that the apartment belonged to a friend, Evans, who had given him the use of it, and a key, with which petitioner had admitted himself on the day of the arrest. On cross-examination petitioner testified that he had a suit and shirt at the apartment, that his home was elsewhere, that he paid nothing for the use of the apartment, that Evans had let him use it "as a friend," that he had slept there "maybe a night," and that at the time of the search Evans had been away in Philadelphia for about five days.

Solely on the basis of petitioner's lack of standing to make it, the district judge denied petitioner's motion to suppress [and] the seized items were offered in evidence at the trial. * * *

The issue of petitioner's standing is to be decided with reference to Rule 41(e) of the Federal Rules of Criminal Procedure. This is a statutory direction governing the suppression of evidence acquired in violation of the conditions validating a search. It is desirable to set forth the Rule.

"A person aggrieved by an unlawful search and seizure may move the district court for the district in which the property was seized for the return of the property and to suppress for use as evidence anything so obtained * * * If the motion is granted the property shall be restored unless otherwise subject to lawful detention and it shall not be admissible in evidence at any hearing or trial. * * *"

In order to qualify as a "person aggrieved by an unlawful search and seizure" one must have been a victim of a search or seizure, one against whom the search was directed, as distinguished from one who claims prejudice only through the use of evidence gathered as a consequence of a search or seizure directed at someone else. Rule 41(e) applies the general principle that a party will not be heard to claim a constitutional protection unless he "belongs to the class for whose sake the constitutional protection is given." The restrictions upon searches and seizures were obviously designed for protection against official invasion of privacy and the security of property. They are not exclusionary provisions against the admission of kinds of evidence deemed inherently unreliable or prejudicial. The exclusion in federal trials of evidence otherwise competent but gathered by federal officials in violation of the Fourth Amendment is a means for making effective the protection of privacy.

Ordinarily, then, it is entirely proper to require of one who seeks to challenge the legality of a search as the basis for suppressing relevant evidence that he allege, and if the allegation be disputed that he establish, that he himself was the victim of an invasion of privacy. But prosecutions like this one have presented a special problem. To establish "standing," Courts of Appeals have generally required that the movant claim either to have owned or possessed the seized property or to have had a substantial possessory interest in the premises searched. Since narcotics charges like those in the present indictment may be established through proof solely of possession of narcotics, a defendant seeking to comply with what has been the conventional standing requirement has been forced to allege facts the proof of which would tend, if indeed not be sufficient, to convict him. At the least, such a defendant has been placed in the criminally tendentious position of explaining his possession of the premises. He has been faced, not only with the chance that the allegations made on the motion to suppress may be used against him at the trial, although that they may is by no means an inevitable holding, but also with the encouragement that he perjure himself if he seeks to establish "standing" while maintaining a defense to the charge of possession.

[W]e are persuaded [that] to hold that petitioner's failure to acknowledge interest in the narcotics or the premises prevented his attack upon the search, would be to permit the Government to have the advantage of contradictory positions as a basis for conviction. Petitioner's conviction flows from his possession of the narcotics at the time of the search. Yet the fruits of that search, upon which the conviction depends, were admitted into evidence on the ground that petitioner did not have possession of the narcotics at that time. The prosecution here thus subjected the defendant to the penalties meted out to one in lawless possession while refusing him the remedies designed for one in that situation. It is not consonant with the amenities, to put it mildly, of the administration of criminal justice to sanction such squarely contradictory assertions of power by the Government. The possession on the basis of which petitioner is to be and was convicted suffices to give him standing under any fair and rational conception of the requirements of Rule 41(e). * * *

As a second ground sustaining "standing" here we hold that petitioner's testimony on the motion to suppress made out a sufficient interest in the premises to establish him as a "person aggrieved" by their search. That testimony established that at the time of the search petitioner was present in the apartment with the permission of Evans, whose apartment it was. The Government asserts that such an interest is insufficient to give standing. The Government does not contend that only ownership of the premises may confer standing. It would draw distinctions among various classes of possessors, deeming some, such as "guests" and "invitees" with only the "use" of the premises, to have too "tenuous" an interest although concededly having "some measure of control" through their "temporary presence," while conceding that others, who in a "realistic sense, have dominion of the apartment" or who are "domiciled" there, have standing. Petitioner, it is insisted, by his own testimony falls in the former class.

While this Court has never passed upon the interest in the searched premises necessary to maintain a motion to suppress, the Government's argument closely follows the prevailing view in the lower courts. * * *

We do not lightly depart from this course of decisions by the lower courts. We are persuaded, however, that it is unnecessary and ill-advised to import into the law surrounding the constitutional right to be free from unreasonable searches and seizures subtle distinctions, developed and refined by the common law in evolving the body of private property law which, more than almost any other branch of law, has been shaped by distinctions whose validity is largely historical. Even in the area from which they derive, due consideration has led to the discarding of these distinctions in the homeland of the common law. Distinctions such as those between "lessee," "licensee," "invitee" and "guest," often only of gossamer strength, ought not to be determinative in fashioning procedures ultimately referable to constitutional safeguards. * * *

[The Court held that the search warrant was valid, but vacated the judgment and remanded the case to the trial court for a hearing on petitioner's claim that the officers executed the warrant in an unlawful manner.]

Note

Prior to the Court's opinion in *Jones*, Fourth Amendment standing to challenge searches was linked closely to property rights. The decision to extend standing to "victims" of searches not entitled to assert claims under traditional property law concepts represented a profound change that continues to affect constitutional theory today. On the broadest theoretical level, *Jones* was a crucial step on the path to the free-floating idea of "reasonable expectations of privacy" that has dominated much of Fourth Amendment theory since 1967. As we saw in Chapter 2, during the 1960s the Warren Court abandoned property law in favor of ambiguous notions of privacy as the definitional source of the rights protected by the Fourth Amendment. *Jones* was one of the few authorities the Court could cite in Warden v. Hayden, 387 U.S. 294 (1967), to support the conclusion that "[t]he premise that property interests control the right of the Government to search and seize has been discredited." Warden v. Hayden was, in turn, a crucial authority for the opinion ultimately rejecting property law in favor of "reasonable expectations of privacy." Katz v. United States, 389 U.S. 347 (1967).

Jones also had a profound impact on the Court's subsequent treatment of the fundamental question at issue in that case: who has standing under the Fourth Amendment? By expanding the class of people with standing to challenge the constitutionality of some searches and seizures, the *Jones* opinion made it more likely that more evidence would be suppressed in favor of more defendants in more cases. The Supreme Court continued to extend standing even more widely during the 1960s. For example, the concept of automatic standing adopted in *Jones* did not accord standing to "victims" of searches and seizures who were not charged with possessory offenses. The Supreme Court filed this doctrinal gap in Simmons v. United States, 390 U.S. 377 (1968). In *Simmons*, the Court held that a defendant could not be forced to abandon his Fifth Amendment privilege against self-incrimination in order to assert his Fourth Amendment rights. Therefore, if a defendant testified at a suppression hearing that he had a possessory or ownership interest in property in order to gain standing, his testimony could not be used against him in the prosecution's case in chief. The *Simmons* Court did not, however, decide whether that testimony could be used to impeach a defendant who denied ownership or possession of the property during his trial testimony.

More than a decade after *Katz*, new Supreme Court majorities began to deploy the reasonable expectation of privacy concept to constrict the scope of Fourth Amendment standing. The most important opinions were published between 1978 and 1980, and frequently Associate Justice Rehnquist was the author.

The Supreme Court abolished the automatic standing rule in United States v. Salvucci, 448 U.S. 83 (1980). The majority opinion by Justice Rehnquist reasoned that the principal basis for the automatic standing rule announced in *Jones* was that the defendant should not have to give evidence that would incriminate him in order to establish standing to object to the search. Justice Rehnquist concluded that because *Simmons* decreed that testimony given by a defendant to establish standing may not be used against him at trial on the issue of guilt, the dilemma of choosing between Fourth and Fifth Amendment rights had been eliminated. Since the defendant's dilemma no longer existed, the automatic standing doctrine was no longer necessary. The dissenting opinion pointed out that the defendant's testimony on the search issue can still be used for impeachment if he later takes the stand and testifies to the contrary. To that extent, the dilemma continues to exist.

The opinion in *Jones* had also concluded that it was contradictory for the prosecution to charge the defendant with possession of seized property, but also to claim that he lacked a sufficient possessory interest to object to its seizure. The *Salvucci* opinion determined that there is no necessary contradiction, because a defendant may be in criminal possession of seized property without having a legitimate expectation of privacy in the area in which it was discovered.

The second theoretical innovation in *Jones*—"legitimately on the premises" standing—was overturned two years before *Salvucci* in another opinion authored by Justice Rehnquist. In *Rakas v. Illinois*, Justice Rehnquist's opinion left no doubt that expectations analysis would be a vehicle for minimizing the scope of Fourth Amendment standing.

2. Fourth Amendment Standing and "Expectations" Analysis

RAKAS v. ILLINOIS

Supreme Court of the United States, 1978.
439 U.S. 128, 99 S.Ct. 421, 58 L.Ed.2d 387.

Mr. Justice Rehnquist delivered the opinion of the Court.

Petitioners were convicted of armed robbery in the Circuit Court of Kankakee County, Ill., and their convictions were affirmed on appeal. At their trial, the prosecution offered into evidence a sawed-off rifle and rifle shells that had been seized by police during a search of an automobile in which petitioners had been passengers. Neither petitioner is the owner of the automobile and neither has ever asserted that he owned the rifle or shells seized. * * *

I

Because we are not here concerned with the issue of probable cause, a brief description of the events leading to the search of the automobile will suffice. A police officer on a routine patrol received a radio call notifying him of a robbery of a clothing store in Bourbonnais, Ill., and describing the getaway car. Shortly thereafter, the officer spotted an automobile which he thought might be the getaway car. After following the car for some time and after the arrival of assistance, he and several other officers stopped the vehicle. The occupants of the automobile, petitioners and two female companions, were ordered out of the car and, after the occupants had left the car, two officers searched the interior of the vehicle. They discovered a box of rifle shells in the glove compartment, which had been locked, and a sawed-off rifle under the front passenger seat. After discovering the rifle and the shells, the officers took petitioners to the station and placed them under arrest.

Before trial petitioners moved to suppress the rifle and shells seized from the car on the ground that the search violated the Fourth and Fourteenth Amendments. They conceded that they did not own the automobile and were simply passengers; the owner of the car had been the driver of the vehicle at the time of the search. Nor did they assert that they owned the rifle or the shells seized. The prosecutor challenged petitioners' standing to object to the lawfulness of the search of the car because neither the car, the shells nor the rifle belonged to them. [The Illinois courts agreed that petitioners lacked standing and denied the motion to suppress the evidence.]

II

Petitioners first urge us to relax or broaden the rule of standing enunciated in *Jones v. United States*, 362 U.S. 257, 80 S.Ct. 725, 4 L.Ed.2d 697 (1960), so that any criminal defendant at whom a search was "directed" would have standing to contest the legality of that search and object to the admission at trial of evidence obtained as a result of the search. Alternatively, petitioners argue that they have standing to object to the search under *Jones* because they were "legitimately on [the] premises" at the time of the search.

* * *

A

We decline to extend the rule of standing in Fourth Amendment cases in the manner suggested by petitioners. As we stated in *Alderman v. United States*, 394 U.S. 165, 174, 89 S.Ct. 961, 22 L.Ed.2d 176 (1969), "Fourth Amendment rights are personal rights which, like some other constitutional rights, may not be vicariously asserted." A person who is aggrieved by an illegal search and seizure only through the introduction of damaging evidence secured by a search of a third person's premises or property has not had any of his Fourth Amendment rights infringed. And since the exclusionary rule is an attempt to effectuate the guarantees of the Fourth Amendment, it is proper to permit only defendants whose Fourth Amendment rights have been violated to benefit from the rule's protections. * * *

* * *

In *Alderman v. United States*, Mr. Justice Fortas, in a concurring and dissenting opinion, argued that the Court should "include within the category of those who may object to the introduction of illegal evidence 'one against whom the search was directed.' " The Court did not directly comment on Mr. Justice Fortas' suggestion, but it left no doubt that it rejected this theory by holding that persons who were not parties to unlawfully overheard conversations or who did not own the premises on which such conversations took place did not have standing to contest the legality of the surveillance, regardless of whether or not they were the "targets" of the surveillance. Mr. Justice Harlan, concurring and dissenting, did squarely[reject] the target theory * * *.

* * *

Conferring standing to raise vicarious Fourth Amendment claims would necessarily mean a more widespread invocation of the exclusionary rule during criminal trials. The Court's opinion in *Alderman* counseled against such an extension of the exclusionary rule:

"The deterrent values of preventing the incrimination of those whose rights the police have violated have been considered sufficient to justify the suppression of probative evidence even though the case against the defendant is weakened or destroyed. We adhere to that judgment. But we are not convinced that the additional benefits of extending the exclusionary rule to other defendants would justify further encroachment upon the public interest in prosecuting those accused of crime and having them acquitted or convicted on the basis of all the evidence which exposes the truth."

Each time the exclusionary rule is applied it exacts a substantial social cost for the vindication of Fourth Amendment rights. Relevant and reliable evidence is kept from the trier of fact and the search for truth at trial is deflected. Since our cases generally have held that one whose Fourth Amendment rights are violated may successfully suppress evidence obtained in the course of an illegal search and seizure, misgivings as to the benefit of enlarging the class of persons who may invoke that rule are properly considered when deciding whether to expand standing to assert Fourth Amendment violations.

B

Had we accepted petitioners' request to allow persons other than those whose own Fourth Amendment rights were violated by a challenged search and seizure to suppress evidence obtained in the course of such police activity, it would be appropriate to retain *Jones'* use of standing in Fourth Amendment analysis. Under petitioners' target theory, a court could determine that a defendant had standing to invoke the exclusionary rule without having to inquire into the substantive question of whether the challenged search or seizure violated the Fourth Amendment rights of that particular defendant. However, having rejected petitioners' target theory and reaffirmed the principle that the "rights assured by the Fourth Amendment are personal rights, [which]... may be enforced by exclusion of evidence only at the instance of one whose own protection was infringed by the search and seizure," *Simmons v. United States*, 390 U.S. 377, 389, 88 S.Ct. 967, 19 L.Ed.2d 1247 (1968), the question necessarily arises whether it serves any useful analytical purpose to consider this principle a matter of standing, distinct from the merits of a defendant's Fourth Amendment claim. We can think of no decided cases of this Court that would have come out differently had we concluded, as we do now, that the type of standing requirement discussed in *Jones* and reaffirmed today is more properly subsumed under substantive Fourth Amendment doctrine. Rigorous application of the principle that the rights secured by this Amendment are personal, in place of a notion of "standing," will produce no additional situations in which evidence must be excluded. The inquiry under either approach is the same. But we think the better analysis forthrightly focuses on the extent of a particular defendant's rights under the Fourth Amendment, rather than on any theoretically separate, but invariably intertwined concept of standing. * * *

* * *

C

Here petitioners, who were passengers occupying a car which they neither owned nor leased, seek to analogize their position to that of the defendant in *Jones v. United States*, 362 U.S. 257, 80 S.Ct. 725, 4 L.Ed.2d 697 (1960). In *Jones*, petitioner was present at the time of the search of an apartment which was owned by a friend. The friend had given Jones permission to use the apartment and a key to it, with which Jones had admitted himself on the day of the search. He had a suit and shirt at the apartment and had slept there "maybe a night," but his home was elsewhere. At the time of the search, Jones was the only occupant of the apartment because the lessee was away for a period of several days. * * *

We do not question the conclusion in *Jones* that the defendant in that case suffered a violation of his personal Fourth Amendment rights if the search in question was unlawful. Nonetheless, we believe that the phrase "legitimately on premises" coined in *Jones* creates too broad a gauge for measurement of Fourth Amendment rights. For example, applied literally, this statement would permit a casual visitor who has never seen, or been permitted to visit, the basement of another's house to object to a search of the basement if the visitor happened to be in the kitchen of the house at the time of the search. Likewise, a casual visitor who walks into a house one minute before a search of the house commences and leaves one minute after the search ends would be able to contest the legality of the search. The first visitor would have absolutely no interest or legitimate expectation of privacy in the basement, the second would have none in the house, and it advances no purpose served by the Fourth Amendment to permit either of them to object to the lawfulness of the search.

We think that *Jones* on its facts merely stands for the unremarkable proposition that a person can have a legally sufficient interest in a place other than his own home so that the Fourth Amendment protects him from unreasonable governmental intrusion into that place. * * * Viewed in this manner, the holding in *Jones* can best be explained by the fact that Jones had a legitimate expectation of privacy in the premises he was using and therefore could claim the protection of the Fourth Amendment with respect to a governmental invasion of those premises, even though his "interest" in those premises might not have been a recognized property interest at common law.

* * *

D

Judged by the foregoing analysis, petitioners' claims must fail. They asserted neither a property nor a possessory interest in the automobile, nor an interest in the property seized. And as we have previously indicated, the fact that they were "legitimately on [the] premises" in the sense that they were in the car with the permission of its owner is not determinative of whether they had a legitimate expectation of privacy in the particular areas of the automobile searched. It is unnecessary for us to decide here whether the same expectations of privacy are warranted in a car as would be justified in a dwelling place in analogous circumstances. We have on numerous occasions pointed out that cars are not to be treated identically with houses or Apartments for Fourth Amendment purposes. But here petitioners' claim is one which would fail even in an analogous situation in a dwelling place, since they made no showing that they had any legitimate expectation of privacy in the glove compartment or area under the seat of the car in which they were merely passengers. Like the trunk of an automobile, these are areas in which a passenger *qua* passenger simply would not normally have a legitimate expectation of privacy. * * *

[The concurring opinion of JUSTICE POWELL, with whom THE CHIEF JUSTICE joined, is omitted.]

MR. JUSTICE WHITE, with whom MR. JUSTICE BRENNAN, MR. JUSTICE MARSHALL, and MR. JUSTICE STEVENS join, dissenting.

* * *

The Court's holding is contrary not only to our past decisions and the logic of the Fourth Amendment but also to the everyday expectations of privacy that we all share. Because of that, it is unworkable in all the various situations that arise in real life. If the owner of the car had not only invited petitioners to join her but had said to them, "I give you a temporary possessory interest in my vehicle so that you will share the right to privacy that the Supreme Court says that I own," then apparently the majority would reverse. But people seldom say such things, though they may mean their invitation to encompass them if only they had thought of the problem. If the nonowner were the spouse or child of the owner, would the Court recognize a sufficient interest? If so, would distant relatives somehow have more of an expectation of privacy than close friends? What if the nonowner were driving with the owner's permission? Would nonowning drivers have more of an expectation of privacy than mere passengers? What about a passenger in a taxicab? *Katz* expressly recognized protection for such passengers. Why should Fourth Amendment rights be present when one pays a cabdriver for a ride but be absent when one is given a ride by a friend?

The distinctions the Court would draw are based on relationships between private parties, but the Fourth Amendment is concerned with the relationship of one of those parties to the government. Divorced as it is from the purpose of the Fourth Amendment, the Court's essentially property-based rationale can satisfactorily answer none of the questions posed above. That is reason enough to reject it. The *Jones* rule is relatively easily applied by police and courts; the rule announced today will not provide law enforcement officials with a bright line between the protected and the unprotected. Only rarely will police know whether one private party has or has not been granted a sufficient possessory or other interest by another private party. Surely in this case the officers had no such knowledge. The Court's rule will ensnare defendants and police in needless litigation over factors that should not be determinative of Fourth Amendment rights.

More importantly, the ruling today undercuts the force of the exclusionary rule in the one area in which its use is most certainly justified—the deterrence of bad-faith violations of the Fourth Amendment. This decision invites police to engage in patently unreasonable searches every time an automobile contains more than one occupant. * * *

Of course, most police officers will decline the Court's invitation and will continue to do their jobs as best they can in accord with the Fourth Amendment. But the very purpose of the Bill of Rights was to answer the justified fear that governmental agents cannot be left totally to their own devices, and the Bill of Rights is enforceable in the courts because human experience teaches that not all such officials will otherwise adhere to the stated precepts. Some policemen simply do act in bad faith, even if for understandable ends, and some deterrent is needed. In the rush to limit the applicability of the exclusionary rule somewhere, anywhere, the Court ignores precedent, logic, and common sense to exclude the rule's operation from situations in which, paradoxically, it is justified and needed.

RAWLINGS v. KENTUCKY

Supreme Court of the United States, 1980.
448 U.S. 98, 100 S.Ct. 2556, 65 L.Ed.2d 633.

Mr. Justice Rehnquist delivered the opinion of the Court.

I

In the middle of the afternoon on October 18, 1976, six police officers armed with a warrant for the arrest of one Lawrence Marquess on charges of drug distribution arrived at Marquess' house in Bowling Green, Ky. In the house at the time the police arrived were one of Marquess' housemates, Dennis Saddler, and four visitors, Keith Northern, Linda Braden, Vanessa Cox, and petitioner David Rawlings. While searching unsuccessfully in the house for Marquess, several police officers smelled marihuana smoke and saw marihuana seeds on the mantel in one of the bedrooms. After conferring briefly, Officers Eddie Railey and John Bruce left to obtain a search warrant. While Railey and Bruce were gone, the other four officers detained the occupants of the house in the living room, allowing them to leave only if they consented to a body search. Northern and Braden did consent to such a search and were permitted to depart. Saddler, Cox, and petitioner remained seated in the living room.

Approximately 45 minutes later, Railey and Bruce returned with a warrant authorizing them to search the house. Railey read the warrant to Saddler, Cox, and petitioner, and also read *"Miranda"* warnings from a card he carried in his pocket. At that time, Cox was seated on a couch with petitioner seated to her left. In the space between them was Cox's handbag.

After Railey finished his recitation, he approached petitioner and told him to stand. Officer Don Bivens simultaneously approached Cox and ordered her to empty the contents of her purse onto a coffee table in front of the couch. Among those contents were a jar containing 1,800 tablets of LSD and a number of smaller vials containing benzphetamine, methamphetamine, methyprylan, and pentobarbital, all of which are controlled substances under Kentucky law.

Upon pouring these objects out onto the coffee table, Cox turned to petitioner and told him "to take what was his." Petitioner, who was standing in response to Officer Railey's command, immediately claimed ownership of the controlled substances. At that time, Railey searched petitioner's person and found $4,500 in cash in petitioner's shirt pocket and a knife in a sheath at petitioner's side. Railey then placed petitioner under formal arrest.

Petitioner was indicted for possession with intent to sell the various controlled substances recovered from Cox's purse. At the suppression hearing, he testified that he had flown into Bowling Green about a week before his arrest to look for a job and perhaps to attend the local university. He brought with him at that time the drugs later found in Cox's purse. Initially, petitioner stayed in the house where the arrest took place as the guest of Michael Swank, who shared the house with Marquess and Saddler. While at a party at that house, he met Cox and spent at least two nights of the next week on a couch at Cox's house.

On the morning of petitioner's arrest, Cox had dropped him off at Swank's house where he waited for her to return from class. At that time, he was carrying the drugs in a green bank bag. When Cox returned to the house to meet him, petitioner dumped the contents of the bank bag into Cox's purse. Although there is dispute over the discussion that took place, petitioner testified that he "asked her if she would carry this for me, and she said, 'yes'...." Petitioner then left the room to use the bathroom and, by the time he returned, discovered that the police had arrived to arrest Marquess.

The trial court denied petitioner's motion to suppress the drugs and the money and to exclude the statements made by petitioner when the police discovered the drugs. According to the trial court, the warrant obtained by the police authorized them to search Cox's purse. Moreover, even if the search of the purse was illegal, the trial court believed that petitioner lacked "standing" to contest that search. Finally, the trial court believed that the search that revealed the money and the knife was permissible "under the exigencies of the situation." After a bench trial, petitioner was found guilty of possession with intent to sell LSD and of possession of benzphetamine, methamphetamine, methyprylan, and pentobarbital.

[The Kentucky appellate courts affirmed the order denying suppression of the evidence.]

II

In this Court, [Rawlings] claims that he did have a reasonable expectation of privacy in Cox's purse so as to allow him to challenge the legality of the search of that purse [and] that his admission of ownership was the fruit of an illegal detention that began when the police refused to let the occupants of the house leave unless they consented to a search. * * *

A

In holding that petitioner could not challenge the legality of the search of Cox's purse, the Supreme Court of Kentucky looked primarily to our then recent decision in *Rakas* v. *Illinois,* 439 U.S. 128, 99 S.Ct. 421, 58 L.Ed.2d 387 (1978), where we abandoned a separate inquiry into a defendant's "standing" to contest an allegedly illegal search in favor of an inquiry that focused directly on the substance of the defendant's claim that he or she possessed a "legitimate expectation of privacy" in the area searched. See *Katz* v. *United States,* 389 U.S. 347, 88 S.Ct. 507, 19 L.Ed.2d 576 (1967). In the present case, the Supreme Court of Kentucky looked to the "totality of the circumstances," including petitioner's own admission at the suppression hearing that he did not believe that Cox's purse would be free from governmental intrusion, and held that petitioner "[had] not made a sufficient showing that his legitimate or reasonable expectations of privacy were violated" by the search of the purse.

We believe that the record in this case supports that conclusion. Petitioner, of course, bears the burden of proving not only that the search of Cox's purse was illegal, but also that he had a legitimate expectation of privacy in that purse. At the time petitioner dumped thousands of dollars worth of illegal drugs into Cox's purse, he had known her for only a few days. According to Cox's uncontested testimony, petitioner had never sought or received access to her purse prior to that sudden bailment. Nor did petitioner have any right to exclude other persons from access to Cox's purse. In fact, Cox testified that Bob Stallons, a longtime acquaintance and frequent companion of Cox's, had free access to her purse and on the very morning of the arrest had rummaged through its contents in search of a hairbrush. Moreover, even assuming that petitioner's version of the bailment is correct and that Cox did consent to the transfer of possession, the precipitous nature of the transaction hardly supports a reasonable inference that petitioner took normal precautions to maintain his privacy. In addition to all the foregoing facts, the record also contains a frank admission by petitioner that he had no subjective expectation that Cox's purse would remain free from governmental intrusion, an admission credited by both the trial court and the Supreme Court of Kentucky.

Petitioner contends nevertheless that, because he claimed ownership of the drugs in Cox's purse, he should be entitled to challenge the search regardless of his expectation of privacy. We disagree. While petitioner's ownership of the drugs is undoubtedly one fact to be considered in this case, *Rakas* emphatically rejected the notion that "arcane" concepts of property law ought to control the ability to claim the protections of the Fourth Amendment. Had petitioner placed his drugs in plain view, he would still have owned them, but he could not claim any legitimate expectation of privacy. Prior to *Rakas*, petitioner might have been given "standing" in such a case to challenge a "search" that netted those drugs but probably would have lost his claim on the merits. After *Rakas*, the two inquiries merge into one: whether governmental officials violated any legitimate expectation of privacy held by petitioner.

In sum, we find no reason to overturn the lower court's conclusion that petitioner had no legitimate expectation of privacy in Cox's purse at the time of the search.

* * *

[The concurring opinions of JUSTICE BLACKMUN, and of JUSTICE WHITE, with whom JUSTICE STEWART joined, concurring in part, are omitted.]

Mr. Justice Marshall, with whom Mr. Justice Brennan joins, dissenting.

* * *

I

The Court holds first that petitioner may not object to the introduction of the pills into evidence because the unconstitutional actions of the police officers did not violate his personal Fourth Amendment rights. To reach this result, the Court holds that the Constitution protects an individual against unreasonable searches and seizures only if he has "a 'legitimate expectation of privacy' in the area searched." This holding cavalierly rejects the fundamental principle, unquestioned until today, that an interest in either the place searched or the property seized is sufficient to invoke the Constitution's protections against unreasonable searches and seizures.

The Court's examination of previous Fourth Amendment cases begins and ends—as it must if it is to reach its desired conclusion—with *Rakas* v. *Illinois*. Contrary to the Court's assertion, however, *Rakas* did not establish that the Fourth Amendment protects individuals against unreasonable searches and seizures only if they have a privacy interest in the place searched. The question before the Court in *Rakas* was whether the defendants could establish their right to Fourth Amendment protection simply by showing that they were "legitimately on [the] premises" searched. Overruling that portion of *Jones*, the Court held that when a Fourth Amendment objection is based on an interest in the place searched, the defendant must show an actual invasion of his personal privacy interest. The petitioners in *Rakas* did not claim that they had standing either under the *Jones* automatic standing rule for persons charged with possessory offenses, which the Court overrules today, see *United States* v. *Salvucci* 448 U.S. 83, 100 S.Ct. 2547, 65 L.Ed.2d 619 (1980), or because their possessory interest in the items seized gave them "actual standing." No Fourth Amendment claim based on an interest in the property seized was before the Court, and, consequently, the Court did not and could not have decided whether such a claim could be maintained. In fact, the Court expressly disavowed any intention to foreclose such a claim * * * and suggested its continuing validity ("'[Petitioners]' claims must fail. They asserted neither a property nor a possessory interest in the automobile, *nor an interest in the property seized.*" (emphasis supplied)).

* * *

The Court's decision today is not wrong, however, simply because it is contrary to our previous cases. It is wrong because it is contrary to the Fourth Amendment, which guarantees that "[the] right of the people to be secure in their persons, houses, papers, and effects, against unreasonable searches and seizures, shall not be violated." The Court's reading of the Amendment is far too narrow. The Court misreads the guarantee of security "*in* their persons, houses, papers, and effects, *against* unreasonable searches and seizures" to afford protection only against unreasonable searches and seizures *of* persons and places.

The Fourth Amendment, it seems to me, provides in plain language that if one's security in one's "effects" is disturbed by an unreasonable search and seizure, one has been the victim of a constitutional violation; and so it has always been understood. Therefore the Court's insistence that in order to challenge the legality of the search one must also assert a protected interest in the premises is misplaced. The interest in the item seized is quite enough to establish that the defendant's personal Fourth Amendment rights have been invaded by the government's conduct.

* * *

When the government seizes a person's property, it interferes with his constitutionally protected right to be secure in his effects. That interference gives him the right to challenge the reasonableness of the government's conduct, including the seizure. If the defendant's property was seized as the result of an unreasonable search, the seizure cannot be other than unreasonable.

In holding that the Fourth Amendment protects only those with a privacy interest in the place searched, and not those with an ownership or possessory interest in the things seized, the Court has turned the development of the law of search and seizure on its head. The history of the Fourth Amendment shows that it was designed to protect property interests as well as privacy interests; in fact, until *Jones* the question whether a person's Fourth Amendment rights had been violated turned on whether he had a property interest in the place searched or the items seized. *Jones*, and *Katz v. United States, 389 U.S. 347 (1967)* expanded our view of the protections afforded by the Fourth Amendment by recognizing that privacy interests are protected even if they do not arise from property rights. But that recognition was never intended to exclude interests that had historically been sheltered by the Fourth Amendment from its protection. Neither *Jones* nor *Katz* purported to provide an exclusive definition of the interests protected by the Fourth Amendment. Indeed, as *Katz* recognized: "That Amendment protects individual privacy against certain kinds of governmental intrusion, but its protections go further, and often have nothing to do with privacy at all." Those decisions freed Fourth Amendment jurisprudence from the constraints of "subtle distinctions, developed and refined by the common law in evolving the body of private property law which, more than almost any other branch of law, has been shaped by distinctions whose validity is largely historical." Rejection of those finely drawn distinctions as irrelevant to the concerns of the Fourth Amendment did not render property rights wholly outside its protection, however. Not every concept involving property rights, we should remember, is "arcane."

In fact, the Court rather inconsistently denies that property rights may, by themselves, entitle one to the protection of the Fourth Amendment, but simultaneously suggests that a person may claim such protection only if his expectation of privacy in the premises searched is so strong that he may exclude all others from that place. Such a harsh threshold requirement was not imposed even in the heyday of a property rights oriented Fourth Amendment.

* * *

III

* * * Today a majority of the Court has substantially cut back the protection afforded by the Fourth Amendment and the ability of the people to claim that protection, apparently out of concern lest the government's ability to obtain criminal convictions be impeded. A slow and steady erosion of the ability of victims of unconstitutional searches and seizures to obtain a remedy for the invasion of their rights saps the constitutional guarantee of its life just as surely as would a substantive limitation. Because we are called on to decide whether evidence should be excluded only when a search has been "successful," it is easy to forget that the standards we announce determine what government conduct is reasonable in searches and seizures directed at persons who turn out to be innocent as well as those who are guilty. I continue to believe that ungrudging application of the Fourth Amendment is indispensable to preserving the liberties of a democratic society. Accordingly, I dissent.

MINNESOTA v. CARTER

Supreme Court of the United States, 1998.
525 U.S. 83, 119 S.Ct. 469, 142 L.Ed.2d 373.

CHIEF JUSTICE REHNQUIST delivered the opinion of the Court.

Respondents and the lessee of an apartment were sitting in one of its rooms, bagging cocaine. While so engaged they were observed by a police officer, who looked through a drawn window blind. The Supreme Court of Minnesota held that the officer's viewing was a search that violated respondents' Fourth Amendment rights. We hold that no such violation occurred.

James Thielen, a police officer in the Twin Cities' suburb of Eagan, Minnesota, went to an apartment building to investigate a tip from a confidential informant. The informant said that he had walked by the window of a ground-floor apartment and had seen people putting a white powder into bags. The officer looked in the same window through a gap in the closed blind and observed the bagging operation for several minutes. He then notified headquarters, which began preparing affidavits for a search warrant while he returned to the apartment building. When two men left the building in a previously identified Cadillac, the police stopped the car. Inside were respondents Carter and Johns. As the police opened the door of the car to let Johns out, they observed a black zippered pouch and a handgun, later determined to be loaded, on the vehicle's floor. Carter and Johns were arrested, and a later police search of the vehicle the next day discovered pagers, a scale, and 47 grams of cocaine in plastic sandwich bags.

After seizing the car, the police returned to Apartment 103 and arrested the occupant, Kimberly Thompson, who is not a party to this appeal. A search of the apartment pursuant to a warrant revealed cocaine residue on the kitchen table and plastic baggies similar to those found in the Cadillac. Thielen identified Carter, Johns, and Thompson as the three people he had observed placing the powder into baggies. The police later learned that while Thompson was the lessee of the apartment, Carter and Johns lived in Chicago and had come to the apartment for the sole purpose of packaging the cocaine. Carter and Johns had never been to the apartment before and were only in the apartment for approximately 2 1/2 hours. In return for the use of the apartment, Carter and Johns had given Thompson one-eighth of an ounce of the cocaine.

[After their motions to suppress evidence were denied Carter and Johns were convicted of controlled substances crimes. A divided Minnesota Supreme Court reversed, holding that respondents had "standing" to claim the protection of the Fourth Amendment because they had " 'a legitimate expectation of privacy in the invaded place.' "]

The Minnesota courts analyzed whether respondents had a legitimate expectation of privacy under the rubric of "standing" doctrine, an analysis which this Court expressly rejected 20 years ago in *Rakas*, 439 U.S. 128, 139–140, 99 S.Ct. 421, 58 L.Ed.2d 387 (1978). In that case, we held that automobile passengers could not assert the protection of the Fourth Amendment against the seizure of incriminating evidence from a vehicle where they owned neither the vehicle nor the evidence. Central to our analysis was the idea that in determining whether a defendant is able to show the violation of his (and not someone else's) Fourth Amendment rights, the "definition of those rights is more properly placed within the purview of substantive Fourth Amendment law than within that of standing." Thus, we held that in order to claim the protection of the Fourth Amendment, a defendant must demonstrate that he personally has an expectation of privacy in the place searched, and that his expectation is reasonable; *i.e.*, one that has "a source outside of the Fourth Amendment, either by reference to concepts of real or personal property law or to understandings that are recognized and permitted by society."

* * *

The text of the [Fourth] Amendment suggests that its protections extend only to people in "their" houses. But we have held that in some circumstances a person may have a legitimate expectation of privacy in the house of someone else. In *Minnesota* v. *Olson*, 495 U.S. 91, 110 S.Ct. 1684, 109 L.Ed.2d 85 (1990), for example, we decided that an overnight guest in a house had the sort of expectation of privacy that the Fourth Amendment protects. We said:

"To hold that an overnight guest has a legitimate expectation of privacy in his host's home merely recognizes the every day expectations of privacy that we all share. Staying overnight in another's home is a long standing social custom that serves functions recognized as valuable by society. We stay in others' homes when we travel to a strange city for business or pleasure, we visit our parents, children, or more distant relatives out of town, when we are in between jobs or homes, or when we house-sit for a friend. . . .

"From the overnight guest's perspective, he seeks shelter in another's home precisely because it provides him with privacy, a place where he and his possessions will not be disturbed by anyone but his host and those his host allows inside. We are at our most vulnerable when we are asleep because we cannot monitor our own safety or the security of our belongings. It is for this reason that, although we may spend all day in public places, when we cannot sleep in our own home we seek out another private place to sleep, whether it be a hotel room, or the home of a friend."

In *Jones* v. *United States*, 362 U.S. 257, 80 S.Ct. 725, 4 L.Ed.2d 697 (1960), the defendant seeking to exclude evidence resulting from a search of an apartment had been given the use of the apartment by a friend. He had clothing in the apartment, had slept there " 'maybe a night,' " and at the time was the sole occupant of the apartment. But while the holding of *Jones*—that a search of the apartment violated the defendant's Fourth Amendment rights—is still valid, its statement that "anyone legitimately on the premises where a search occurs may challenge its legality," was expressly repudiated in *Rakas* v. *Illinois*. Thus an overnight guest in a home may claim the protection of the Fourth Amendment, but one who is merely present with the consent of the householder may not.

Respondents here were obviously not overnight guests, but were essentially present for a business transaction and were only in the home a matter of hours. There is no suggestion that they had a previous relationship with Thompson, or that there was any other purpose to their visit. Nor was there anything similar to the overnight guest relationship in *Olson* to suggest a degree of acceptance into the household. While the apartment was a dwelling place for Thompson, it was for these respondents simply a place to do business.

Property used for commercial purposes is treated differently for Fourth Amendment purposes than residential property. "An expectation of privacy in commercial premises, however, is different from, and indeed less than, a similar expectation in an individual's home." And while it was a "home" in which respondents were present, it was not their home. Similarly, the Court has held that in some circumstances a worker can claim Fourth Amendment protection over his own workplace. But there is no indication that respondents in this case had nearly as significant a connection to Thompson's apartment as the worker in *O'Connor v.*

Ortega, 480 U.S. 709, 107 S.Ct. 1492, 94 L.Ed.2d 714 (1987), had to his own private office.

If we regard the overnight guest in *Minnesota* v. *Olson* as typifying those who may claim the protection of the Fourth Amendment in the home of another, and one merely "legitimately on the premises" as typifying those who may not do so, the present case is obviously somewhere in between. But the purely commercial nature of the transaction engaged in here, the relatively short period of time on the premises, and the lack of any previous connection between respondents and the householder, all lead us to conclude that respondents' situation is closer to that of one simply permitted on the premises. We therefore hold that any search which may have occurred did not violate their Fourth Amendment rights.

Because we conclude that respondents had no legitimate expectation of privacy in the apartment, we need not decide whether the police officer's observation constituted a "search." The judgment of the Supreme Court of Minnesota are accordingly reversed, and the cause is remanded for proceedings not inconsistent with this opinion. It is so ordered.

JUSTICE SCALIA, with whom joins JUSTICE THOMAS, concurring.

I join the opinion of the Court because I believe it accurately applies our recent case law, including *Minnesota* v. *Olson*. I write separately to express my view that that case law—like the submissions of the parties in this case—gives short shrift to the text of the Fourth Amendment, and to the well and long understood meaning of that text. Specifically, it leaps to apply the fuzzy standard of "legitimate expectation of privacy"—a consideration that is often relevant to whether a search or seizure covered by the Fourth Amendment is "unreasonable"—to the threshold question whether a search or seizure covered by the Fourth Amendment *has occurred.* * * *

* * *

* * * In my view, the only thing the past three decades have established about the *Katz,* 389 U.S. 347, 88 S.Ct. 507, 19 L.Ed.2d 576 (1967), test (which has come to mean the test enunciated by Justice Harlan's separate concurrence in *Katz*) is that, unsurprisingly, those "actual (subjective) expectations of privacy" "that society is prepared to recognize as 'reasonable'" bear an uncanny resemblance to those expectations of privacy that this Court considers reasonable. When that self-indulgent test is employed (as the dissent would employ it here) to determine whether a "search or seizure" within the meaning of the Constitution has *occurred* (as opposed to whether that "search or seizure" is an "unreasonable" one), it has no plausible foundation in the text of the Fourth Amendment. That provision did not guarantee some generalized "right of privacy" and leave it to this Court to determine which particular manifestations of the value of privacy "society is prepared to recognize as 'reasonable.'" Rather, it enumerated ("persons, houses, papers, and effects'') the objects of privacy protection to which the *Constitution* would extend, leaving further expansion to the good judgment, not of this Court, but of the people through their representatives in the legislature.

* * *

[The concurring opinions of JUSTICE KENNEDY and JUSTICE BREYER, and the dissenting opinion of JUSTICE GINSBERG, with whom JUSTICE STEVENS and JUSTICE SOUTER joined, are omitted.]

UNITED STATES v. PAYNER

Supreme Court of the United States, 1980.
447 U.S. 727, 100 S.Ct. 2439, 65 L.Ed.2d 468.

MR. JUSTICE POWELL delivered the opinion of the Court.

The question is whether the District Court properly suppressed the fruits of an unlawful search that did not invade the respondent's Fourth Amendment rights.

I

Respondent Jack Payner was indicted in September 1976 on a charge of falsifying his 1972 federal income tax return * * *. The indictment alleged that respondent denied maintaining a foreign bank account at a time when he knew that he had such an account at the Castle Bank and Trust Company of Nassau, Bahama Islands. The Government's case rested heavily on a loan guarantee agreement dated April 28, 1972, in which respondent pledged the funds in his Castle Bank account as security for a $100,000 loan.

* * *

The events leading up to the 1973 search are not in dispute. In 1965, the Internal Revenue Service launched an investigation into the financial activities of American citizens in the Bahamas. The project, known as "Operation Trade Winds," was headquartered in Jacksonville, Fla. Suspicion focused on the Castle Bank in 1972, when investigators learned that a suspected narcotics trafficker had an account there. Special Agent Richard Jaffe of the Jacksonville office asked Norman Casper, a private investigator and occasional informant, to learn what he could about the Castle Bank and its depositors. To that end, Casper cultivated his friendship with Castle Bank vice president Michael Wolstencroft. Casper introduced Wolstencroft to Sybol Kennedy, a private investigator and former employee. When Casper discovered that the banker intended to spend a few days in Miami in January 1973, he devised a scheme to gain access to the bank records he knew Wolstencroft would be carrying in his briefcase. Agent Jaffe approved the basic outline of the plan.

Wolstencroft arrived in Miami on January 15 and went directly to Kennedy's apartment. At about 7:30 p. m., the two left for dinner at a Key Biscayne restaurant. Shortly thereafter, Casper entered the apartment using a key supplied by Kennedy. He removed the briefcase and delivered it to Jaffe. While the agent supervised the copying of approximately 400 documents taken from the briefcase, a "lookout" observed Kennedy and Wolstencroft at dinner. The observer notified Casper when the pair left the restaurant, and the briefcase was replaced. The documents photographed that evening included papers evidencing a close working relationship between the Castle Bank and the Bank of Perrine, Fla. Subpoenas issued to the Bank of Perrine ultimately uncovered the loan guarantee agreement at issue in this case.

The District Court found that the United States, acting through Jaffe, "knowingly and willfully participated in the unlawful seizure of Michael Wolstencroft's briefcase.... " According to that court, "the Government affirmatively counsels its agents that the Fourth Amendment standing limitation permits them to purposefully conduct an unconstitutional search and seizure of one individual in order to obtain evidence against third parties.... " The District Court also found that the documents seized from Wolstencroft provided the leads that ultimately led to the discovery of the critical loan guarantee agreement. Although the search did not impinge upon the respondent's Fourth Amendment rights, the District Court believed that the Due Process Clause of the Fifth Amendment and the inherent supervisory power of the federal courts required it to exclude evidence tainted by the Government's "knowing and purposeful *bad faith hostility* to any person's fundamental constitutional rights."

* * *

II

This Court discussed the doctrine of "standing to invoke the [Fourth Amendment] exclusionary rule" in some detail last Term. *Rakas* v. *Illinois*, 439 U.S. 128, 138, 439 U.S. 128, 99 S.Ct. 421, 58 L.Ed.2d 387 (1978). We reaffirmed the established rule that a court may not exclude evidence under the Fourth Amendment unless it finds that an unlawful search or seizure violated the defendant's own constitutional rights. And the defendant's Fourth Amendment rights are violated only when the challenged conduct invaded *his* legitimate expectation of privacy rather than that of a third party.

The foregoing authorities establish, as the District Court recognized, that respondent lacks standing under the Fourth Amendment to suppress the documents illegally seized from Wolstencroft. The Court of Appeals did not disturb the District Court's conclusion that "Jack Payner possessed no privacy interest in the Castle Bank documents that were seized from Wolstencroft." * * *

* * *

The District Court and the Court of Appeals believed, however, that a federal court should use its supervisory power to suppress evidence tainted by gross illegalities that did not infringe the defendant's constitutional rights. * * *

III

We certainly can understand the District Court's commendable desire to deter deliberate intrusions into the privacy of persons who are unlikely to become defendants in a criminal prosecution. No court should condone the unconstitutional and possibly criminal behavior of those who planned and executed this "briefcase caper." Indeed, the decisions of this Court are replete with denunciations of willfully lawless activities undertaken in the name of law enforcement. But our cases also show that these unexceptional principles do not command the exclusion of evidence in every case of illegality. Instead, they must be weighed against the considerable harm that would flow from indiscriminate application of an exclusionary rule.

* * * Our cases have consistently recognized that unbending application of the exclusionary sanction to enforce ideals of governmental rectitude would impede unacceptably the truth-finding functions of judge and jury. After all, it is the defendant, and not the constable, who stands trial.

The same societal interests are at risk when a criminal defendant invokes the supervisory power to suppress evidence seized in violation of a third party's constitutional rights. The supervisory power is applied with some caution even when the defendant asserts a violation of his own rights. * * *

* * *

We conclude that the supervisory power does not authorize a federal court to suppress otherwise admissible evidence on the ground that it was seized unlawfully from a third party not before the court. Our Fourth Amendment decisions have established beyond any doubt that the interest in deterring illegal searches does not justify the exclusion of tainted evidence at the instance of a party who was not the victim of the challenged practices. *Rakas* v. *Illinois.* The values assigned to the competing interests do not change because a court has elected to analyze the question under the supervisory power instead of the Fourth Amendment. In either case, the need to deter the underlying conduct and the detrimental impact of excluding the evidence remain precisely the same.

* * *

The judgment of the Court of Appeals is *Reversed.*

[CHIEF JUSTICE BURGER's concurring opinion is omitted.]

MR. JUSTICE MARSHALL, with whom MR. JUSTICE BRENNAN and MR. JUSTICE BLACKMUN join, dissenting.

* * *

I

[The dissenting opinion reviewed the facts of the investigation, generally reiterating the facts set forth in the majority opinion, but also reciting additional facts. Some of the additional facts are presented in the following paragraphs.]

The illegalities of agents of the United States did not stop even at that point, however. During the following two weeks, Jaffe told Casper that the IRS needed additional information. Casper therefore sent Kennedy to visit Wolstencroft in the Bahamas. While there, acting pursuant to Casper's instructions, Kennedy stole a rolodex file from Wolstencroft's office. This file was turned over to Jaffe, who testified in the District Court that he had not cared how the rolodex file had been obtained.

The IRS paid Casper $8,000 in cash for the services he rendered in obtaining the information about Castle Bank. Casper in turn paid approximately $1,000 of this money to Kennedy for her role in the "briefcase caper" and the theft of the rolodex file.

The "briefcase caper" revealed papers which showed a close relationship between the Castle Bank and a Florida bank. Subpoenas issued to that Florida bank resulted in the uncovering of the loan guarantee agreement which was the principal piece of evidence against respondent at trial. It is that loan agreement and the evidence discovered as a result of it that the District Court reluctantly suppressed under the Due Process Clause of the Fifth Amendment and under its supervisory powers.

* * *

The most disturbing finding by the District Court, however, related to the intentional manipulation of the standing requirements of the Fourth Amendment by agents of the United States, who are, of course, supposed to uphold and enforce the Constitution and laws of this country. The District Court found:

"It is evident that the Government and its agents, including Richard Jaffe, were, and are, well aware that under the standing requirement of the Fourth Amendment, evidence obtained from a party pursuant to an unconstitutional search is admissible against third parties who's [sic] own privacy expectations are not subject to the search, even though the cause for the unconstitutional search was to obtain evidence incriminating those third parties. This Court finds that, in its desire to apprehend tax evaders, a desire the Court fully shares, the Government affirmatively counsels its agents that the Fourth Amendment standing limitation permits them to purposefully conduct an unconstitutional search and seizure of one individual in order to obtain evidence against third parties, who are the real targets of the governmental intrusion, and that the IRS agents in this case acted, and will act in the future, according to that counsel. Such governmental conduct compels the conclusion that Jaffe and Casper transacted the 'briefcase caper' with a purposeful, bad faith hostility toward the Fourth Amendment rights of Wolstencroft in order to obtain evidence against persons like Payner.''

* * * It is in the context of these findings—intentional illegal actions by Government agents taken in bad-faith hostility toward the constitutional rights of Wolstencroft for the purpose of obtaining evidence against persons such as the respondent through manipulation of the standing requirements of the Fourth Amendment—that the suppression issue must be considered.

II

This Court has on several occasions exercised its supervisory powers over the federal judicial system in order to suppress evidence that the Government obtained through misconduct. The Court has particularly stressed the need to use supervisory powers to prevent the federal courts from becoming accomplices to such misconduct.

* * *

Since the supervisory powers are exercised to protect the integrity of the *court*, rather than to vindicate the constitutional rights of the defendant, it is hard to see why the Court today bases its analysis entirely on Fourth Amendment standing rules. The point is that the federal judiciary should not be made accomplices to the crimes of Casper, Jaffe, and others. The only way the IRS can benefit from the evidence it chose to obtain illegally is if the evidence is admitted at trial against persons such as Payner; that was the very point of the criminal exercise in the first place. If the IRS is permitted to obtain a conviction in federal court based almost entirely on that illegally obtained evidence and its fruits, then the judiciary has given full effect to the deliberate wrongdoings of the Government. The federal court does indeed become the accomplice of the Government lawbreaker, an accessory after the fact, for without judicial use of the evidence the ''caper'' would have been for nought. Such a pollution of the federal courts should not be permitted.

It is particularly disturbing that the Court today chooses to allow the IRS deliberately to manipulate the standing rules of the Fourth Amendment to achieve its ends. * * * Whatever role those standing limitations may play, it is clear that they were never intended to be a sword to be used by the Government in its deliberate choice to sacrifice the constitutional rights of one person in order to prosecute another.

* * *

B. THE "FRUIT OF THE POISONOUS TREE" DOCTRINE

1. Fourth Amendment Violations

WONG SUN v. UNITED STATES

Supreme Court of the United States, 1963.
371 U.S. 471, 83 S.Ct. 407, 9 L.Ed.2d 441.

MR. JUSTICE BRENNAN delivered the opinion of the Court.

* * *

About 2 a. m. on the morning of June 4, 1959, federal narcotics agents in San Francisco, after having had one Hom Way under surveillance for six weeks, arrested him and found heroin in his possession. Hom Way, who had not before been an informant, stated after his arrest that he had bought an ounce of heroin the night before from one known to him only as "Blackie Toy," proprietor of a laundry on Leavenworth Street.

About 6 a. m. that morning six or seven federal agents went to a laundry at 1733 Leavenworth Street. The sign above the door of this establishment said "Oye's Laundry." It was operated by the petitioner James Wah Toy. There is, however, nothing in the record which identifies James Wah Toy and "Blackie Toy" as the same person. The other federal officers remained nearby out of sight while Agent Alton Wong, who was of Chinese ancestry, rang the bell. When petitioner Toy appeared and opened the door, Agent Wong told him that he was calling for laundry and dry cleaning. Toy replied that he didn't open until 8 o'clock and told the agent to come back at that time. Toy started to close the door. Agent Wong thereupon took his badge from his pocket and said, "I am a federal narcotics agent." Toy immediately "slammed the door and started running" down the hallway through the laundry to his living quarters at the back where his wife and child were sleeping in a bedroom. Agent Wong and the other federal officers broke open the door and followed Toy down the hallway to the living quarters and into the bedroom. Toy reached into a nightstand drawer. Agent Wong thereupon drew his pistol, pulled Toy's hand out of the drawer, placed him under arrest and handcuffed him. There was nothing in the drawer and a search of the premises uncovered no narcotics.

One of the agents said to Toy " . . . [Hom Way] says he got narcotics from you." Toy responded, "No, I haven't been selling any narcotics at all. However, I do know somebody who has." When asked who that was, Toy said, "I only know him as Johnny. I don't know his last name." However, Toy described a house on Eleventh Avenue where he said Johnny lived; he also described a bedroom in the house where he said "Johnny kept about a piece"[2] of heroin, and where he and Johnny had smoked some of the drug the night before. The agents left immediately for Eleventh Avenue and located the house. They entered and found one

2. A "piece" is approximately one ounce.

Johnny Yee in the bedroom. After a discussion with the agents, Yee took from a bureau drawer several tubes containing in all just less than one ounce of heroin, and surrendered them. Within the hour Yee and Toy were taken to the Office of the Bureau of Narcotics. Yee there stated that the heroin had been brought to him some four days earlier by petitioner Toy and another Chinese known to him only as "Sea Dog."

Toy was questioned as to the identity of "Sea Dog" and said that "Sea Dog" was Wong Sun. Some agents, including Agent Alton Wong, took Toy to Wong Sun's neighborhood where Toy pointed out a multi-family dwelling where he said Wong Sun lived. Agent Wong rang a downstairs door bell and a buzzer sounded, opening the door. The officer identified himself as a narcotics agent to a woman on the landing and asked "for Mr. Wong." The woman was the wife of petitioner Wong Sun. She said that Wong Sun was "in the back room sleeping." Alton Wong and some six other officers climbed the stairs and entered the apartment. One of the officers went into the back room and brought petitioner Wong Sun from the bedroom in handcuffs. A thorough search of the apartment followed, but no narcotics were discovered.

[James Toy, Johnny Yee, and Wong Sun were arraigned and charged with violating federal narcotics laws, and each was released on his own recognizance. Within a few days, all were interrogated at the office of the Narcotics Bureau. Following standard practice by federal agents even before *Miranda*, the interrogating agent advised each of the three of his rights to withhold incriminating information and to have the advice of counsel, although no attorney was present during the questioning of any of the three. After each interrogation, the agent prepared a statement from his notes. Both James Toy and Wong Sun refused to sign their statements. Only James Toy and Wong Sun were prosecuted. At the trial, Hom Way did not testify and the prosecution excused its principal witness, Johnny Yee, after he invoked the privilege against self-incrimination and repudiated his statement given during interrogation.]

The Government's evidence * * * consisted of four items which the trial court admitted over timely objections that they were inadmissible as "fruits" of unlawful arrests or of attendant searches: (1) the statements made orally by petitioner Toy in his bedroom at the time of his arrest; (2) the heroin surrendered to the agents by Johnny Yee; (3) petitioner Toy's pretrial unsigned statement; and (4) petitioner Wong Sun's similar statement. * * *

[Both defendants were convicted. The Court of Appeals held that the officers lacked probable cause, and therefore the arrests were illegal, but nonetheless affirmed the lower court because it concluded that the four items of evidence were not the fruits of the illegal arrests.]

* * *

I

The Court of Appeals found there was neither reasonable grounds nor probable cause for Toy's arrest. Giving due weight to that finding, we think it is amply justified by the facts clearly shown on this record. It is basic that an arrest with or without a warrant must stand upon firmer ground than mere suspicion, though the arresting officer need not have in hand evidence which would suffice to convict. The quantum of information which constitutes probable cause—evidence which would "warrant a man of reasonable caution in the belief" that a felony has been committed—must be measured by the facts of the particular case. The history of the use, and not infrequent abuse, of the power to arrest cautions that a relaxation of the fundamental requirements of probable cause would "leave law-abiding citizens at the mercy of the officers' whim or caprice."

Whether or not the requirements of reliability and particularity of the information on which an officer may act are more stringent where an arrest warrant is absent, they surely cannot be less stringent than where an arrest warrant is obtained. Otherwise, a principal incentive now existing for the procurement of arrest warrants would be destroyed. The threshold question in this case, therefore, is whether the officers could, on the information which impelled them to act, have procured a warrant for the arrest of Toy. We think that no warrant would have issued on evidence then available.

The narcotics agents had no basis in experience for confidence in the reliability of Hom Way's information; he had never before given information. And yet they acted upon his imprecise suggestion that a person described only as "Blackie Toy," the proprietor of a laundry somewhere on Leavenworth Street, had sold one ounce of heroin. We have held that identification of the suspect by a reliable informant may constitute probable cause for arrest where the information given is sufficiently accurate to lead the officers directly to the suspect. *Draper* v. *United States*, 358 U.S. 307, 79 S.Ct. 329, 3 L.Ed.2d 327 (1959). That rule does not, however, fit this case. For aught that the record discloses, Hom Way's accusation merely invited the officers to roam the length of Leavenworth Street (some 30 blocks) in search of one "Blackie Toy's" laundry—and whether by chance or other means (the record does not say) they came upon petitioner Toy's laundry, which bore not his name over the door, but the unrevealing label "Oye's." Not the slightest intimation appears on the record, or was made on oral argument, to suggest that the agents had information giving them reason to equate "Blackie" Toy and James Wah Toy—*e. g.*, that they had the criminal record of a Toy, or that they had consulted some other kind of official record or list, or had some information of some kind which had narrowed the scope of their search to this particular Toy.

It is conceded that the officers made no attempt to obtain a warrant for Toy's arrest. The simple fact is that on the sparse information at the officers' command, no arrest warrant could have issued * * *.

The Government contends, however, that any defects in the information which somehow took the officers to petitioner Toy's laundry were remedied by events which occurred after they arrived. Specifically, it is urged that Toy's flight down the hall when the supposed customer at the door revealed that he was a narcotics agent adequately corroborates the suspicion generated by Hom Way's accusation. * * * Agent Wong * * * affirmatively misrepresented his mission at the outset, by stating that he had come for laundry and dry cleaning. And before Toy fled, the officer never adequately dispelled the misimpression engendered by his own ruse.

* * *

A contrary holding here would mean that a vague suspicion could be transformed into probable cause for arrest by reason of ambiguous conduct which the arresting officers themselves have provoked. That result would have the same essential vice as a proposition we have consistently rejected—that a search unlawful at its inception may be validated by what it turns up. * * *

II

It is conceded that Toy's declarations in his bedroom are to be excluded if they are held to be "fruits" of the agents' unlawful action.

In order to make effective the fundamental constitutional guarantees of sanctity of the home and inviolability of the person, *Boyd* v. *United States*, 116 U.S. 616, this Court held nearly half a century ago that evidence seized during an unlawful search could not constitute proof against the victim of the search. *Weeks* v. *United States*, 232 U.S. 383. The exclusionary prohibition extends as well to the indirect as the direct products of such invasions. *Silverthorne Lumber Co.* v. *United States*, 251 U.S. 385. Mr. Justice Holmes, speaking for the Court in that case, in holding that the Government might not make use of information obtained during an unlawful search to subpoena from the victims the very documents illegally viewed, expressed succinctly the policy of the broad exclusionary rule:

> "The essence of a provision forbidding the acquisition of evidence in a certain way is that not merely evidence so acquired shall not be used before the Court but that it shall not be used at all. Of course this does not mean that the facts thus obtained become sacred and inaccessible. If knowledge of them is gained from an independent source they may be proved like any others, but the knowledge gained by the Government's own wrong cannot be used by it in the way proposed."

The exclusionary rule has traditionally barred from trial physical, tangible materials obtained either during or as a direct result of an unlawful invasion. It follows from our holding in *Silverman* v. *United States*, that the Fourth Amendment may protect against the overhearing of verbal statements as well as against the more traditional seizure of "papers and effects." Similarly, testimony as to matters observed during an unlawful invasion has been excluded in order to enforce the basic constitutional policies. Thus, verbal evidence which derives so immediately from an unlawful entry and an unauthorized arrest as the officers' action in the present case is no less the "fruit" of official illegality than the more common tangible fruits of the unwarranted intrusion. Nor do the policies underlying the exclusionary rule invite any logical distinction between physical and verbal evidence. Either in terms of deterring lawless conduct by federal officers, or of closing the doors of the federal courts to any use of evidence unconstitutionally obtained, the danger in relaxing the exclusionary rules in the case of verbal evidence would seem too great to warrant introducing such a distinction.

The Government argues that Toy's statements to the officers in his bedroom, although closely consequent upon the invasion which we hold unlawful, were nevertheless admissible because they resulted from "an intervening independent act of a free will." This contention, however, takes insufficient account of the circumstances. Six or seven officers had broken the door and followed on Toy's heels into the bedroom where his wife and child were sleeping. He had been almost immediately handcuffed and arrested. Under such circumstances it is unreasonable to infer that Toy's response was sufficiently an act of free will to purge the primary taint of the unlawful invasion.

* * *

III

We now consider whether the exclusion of Toy's declarations requires also the exclusion of the narcotics taken from Yee, to which those declarations led the police. The prosecutor candidly told the trial court that "we wouldn't have found those drugs except that Mr. Toy helped us to." Hence this is not the case envisioned by this Court where the exclusionary rule has no application because the Government learned of the evidence "from an independent source," nor is this a case in which the connection between the lawless conduct of the police and the discovery of the challenged evidence has "become so attenuated as to dissipate the taint." We need not hold that all evidence is "fruit of the poisonous tree" simply because it would not have come to light but for the illegal actions of the police. Rather, the more apt question in such a case is "whether, granting establishment of the primary illegality, the evidence to which instant objection is made has been come at by exploitation of that illegality or instead by means sufficiently distinguishable to be purged of the primary taint." We think it clear that the narcotics were "come at by the exploitation of that illegality" and hence that they may not be used against Toy.

* * *

V

We turn now to the case of the other petitioner, Wong Sun. We have no occasion to disagree with the finding of the Court of Appeals that his arrest, also, was without probable cause or reasonable grounds. At all events no evidentiary consequences turn upon that question. For Wong Sun's unsigned confession was not the fruit of that arrest, and was therefore properly admitted at trial. On the evidence that Wong Sun had been released on his own recognizance after a lawful arraignment, and had returned voluntarily several days later to make the statement, we hold that the connection between the arrest and the statement had "become so attenuated as to dissipate the taint." The fact that the statement was unsigned, whatever bearing this may have upon its weight and credibility, does not render it inadmissible; Wong Sun understood and adopted its substance, though he could not comprehend the English words. The petitioner has never suggested any impropriety in the interrogation itself which would require the exclusion of this statement.

We must then consider the admissibility of the narcotics surrendered by Yee. Our holding, that this ounce of heroin was inadmissible against Toy does not compel a like result with respect to Wong Sun. The exclusion of the narcotics as to Toy was required solely by their tainted relationship to information unlawfully obtained from Toy, and not by any official impropriety connected with their surrender by Yee. The seizure of this heroin invaded no right of privacy of person or premises which would entitle Wong Sun to object to its use at his trial.

However, for the reasons that Wong Sun's statement was incompetent to corroborate Toy's admissions contained in Toy's own statement, any references to Wong Sun in Toy's statement were incompetent to corroborate Wong Sun's admissions. Thus, the only competent source of corroboration for Wong Sun's statement was the heroin itself. * * *

[W]e cannot be sure that the scales were not tipped in favor of conviction by reliance upon the inadmissible Toy statement. This is particularly important because of the nature of the offense involved here.

Surely, under the narcotics statute, the discovery of heroin raises a presumption that someone—generally the possessor—violated the law. As to him, once possession alone is proved, the other elements of the offense—transportation and concealment with knowledge of the illegal importation of the drug—need not be separately demonstrated, much less corroborated. Thus particular care ought to be taken in this area, when the crucial element of the accused's possession is proved solely by his own admissions, that the requisite corroboration be found among the evidence which is properly before the trier of facts. We therefore hold that petitioner Wong Sun is also entitled to a new trial.

The judgment of the Court of Appeals is reversed and the case is remanded to the District Court for further proceedings consistent with this opinion. *It is so ordered.*

[The concurring opinion of JUSTICE DOUGLAS and the dissenting opinion of JUSTICE CLARK, with whom JUSTICE HARLAN, JUSTICE STEWART and JUSTICE WHITE joined, are omitted.]

BROWN v. ILLINOIS

Supreme Court of the United States, 1975.
422 U.S. 590, 95 S.Ct. 2254, 45 L.Ed.2d 416.

MR. JUSTICE BLACKMUN delivered the opinion of the Court.

This case lies at the crossroads of the Fourth and the Fifth Amendments. Petitioner was arrested without probable cause and without a warrant. He was given, in full, the warnings prescribed by *Miranda* v. *Arizona,* 384 U.S. 436, 86 S.Ct. 1602, 16 L.Ed.2d 694 (1966). Thereafter, while in custody, he made two inculpatory statements. The issue is whether evidence of those statements was properly admitted, or should have been excluded, in petitioner's subsequent trial for murder in state court. Expressed another way, the issue is whether the statements were to be excluded as the fruit of the illegal arrest, or were admissible because the giving of the *Miranda* warnings sufficiently attenuated the taint of the arrest. * * *

I

As petitioner Richard Brown was climbing the last of the stairs leading to the rear entrance of his Chicago apartment in the early evening of May 13, 1968, he happened to glance at the window near the door. He saw, pointed at him through the window, a revolver held by a stranger who was inside the apartment. The man said: "Don't move, you are under arrest." Another man, also with a gun, came up behind Brown and repeated the statement that he was under arrest. It was about 7:45 p.m. The two men turned out to be Detectives William Nolan and William Lenz of the Chicago police force. It is not clear from the record exactly when they advised Brown of their identity, but it is not disputed that they broke into his apartment, searched it, and then arrested Brown, all without probable cause and without any warrant, when he arrived. They later testified that they made the arrest for the purpose of questioning Brown as part of their investigation of the murder of a man named Roger Corpus.

Corpus was murdered one week earlier, on May 6, with a .38–caliber revolver in his Chicago West Side second-floor apartment. Shortly thereafter, Detective Lenz obtained petitioner's name, among others, from Corpus' brother. Petitioner and the others were identified as acquaintances of the victim, not as suspects.

* * *

As both officers held him at gunpoint, the three entered the apartment. Brown was ordered to stand against the wall and was searched. No weapon was found. He was asked his name. When he denied being Richard Brown, Detective Lenz showed him the photograph, informed him that he was under arrest for the murder of Roger Corpus, handcuffed him, and [took him to the police station for interrogation].

The officers warned Brown of his rights under *Miranda*. * * * At this point—it was about 8:45 p.m.—Lenz asked Brown whether he wanted to talk about the Corpus homicide. Petitioner answered that he did. For the next 20 to 25 minutes Brown answered questions put to him by Nolan, as Lenz typed.

This questioning produced a two-page statement [that] was signed by Brown.

* * *

Brown was again placed in the interrogation room. He was given coffee and was left alone, for the most part, until 2 a.m. when Assistant State's Attorney Crilly arrived.

Crilly, too, informed Brown of his *Miranda* rights. After a half hour's conversation, a court reporter appeared. Once again the *Miranda* warnings were given: "I read him the card." Crilly told him that he "was sure he would be charged with murder." Brown gave a second statement [which] was completed, at about 3 a.m. * * *. An hour later he made a phone call to his mother. At 9:30 that morning, about 14 hours after his arrest, he was taken before a magistrate.

[At trial, the State introduced evidence of both statements and Brown was found guilty of murder.]

Because of our concern about the implication of our holding in *Wong Sun* v. *United States*, 371 U.S. 471, 83 S.Ct. 407, 9 L.Ed.2d 441 (1963), to the facts of Brown's case, we granted certiorari.

II

* * *

The Court in *Wong Sun*, as is customary, emphasized that application of the exclusionary rule on Toy's behalf protected Fourth Amendment guarantees in two respects: "in terms of deterring lawless conduct by federal officers," and by "closing the doors of the federal courts to any use of evidence unconstitutionally obtained." These considerations of deterrence and of judicial integrity, by now, have become rather commonplace in the Court's cases. "The rule is calculated to prevent, not to repair. Its purpose is to deter—to compel respect for the constitutional guaranty in the only effectively available way—by removing the incentive to disregard it." But "[d]espite its broad deterrent purpose, the exclusionary rule has never been interpreted to proscribe the use of illegally seized evidence in all proceedings or against all persons."

III

* * *

This Court has described the *Miranda* warnings as a "prophylactic rule" and as a "procedural safeguard" employed to protect Fifth Amendment rights against "the compulsion inherent in custodial surroundings." The function of the warnings relates to the Fifth Amendment's guarantee against coerced self-incrimination, and the exclusion of a statement made in the absence of the warnings, it is said, serves to deter the taking of an incriminating statement without first informing the individual of his Fifth Amendment rights.

Although, almost 90 years ago, the Court observed that the Fifth Amendment is in "intimate relation" with the Fourth, *Boyd* v. *United States,* 116 U.S. 616, 633, 6 S.Ct. 524, 29 L.Ed. 746 (1886), the *Miranda* warnings thus far have not been regarded as a means either of remedying or deterring violations of Fourth Amendment rights. Frequently, as here, rights under the two Amendments may appear to coalesce since "the 'unreasonable searches and seizures' condemned in the Fourth Amendment are almost always made for the purpose of compelling a man to give evidence against himself, which in criminal cases is condemned in the Fifth Amendment." The exclusionary rule, however, when utilized to effectuate the Fourth Amendment, serves interests and policies that are distinct from those it serves under the Fifth. It is directed at all unlawful searches and seizures, and not merely those that happen to produce incriminating material or testimony as fruits. In short, exclusion of a confession made without *Miranda* warnings might be regarded as necessary to effectuate the Fifth Amendment, but it would not be sufficient fully to protect the Fourth. *Miranda* warnings, and the exclusion of a confession made without them, do not alone sufficiently deter a Fourth Amendment violation.

Thus, even if the statements in this case were found to be voluntary under the Fifth Amendment, the Fourth Amendment issue remains. In order for the causal chain, between the illegal arrest and the statements made subsequent thereto, to be broken, *Wong Sun* requires not merely that the statement meet the Fifth Amendment standard of voluntariness but that it be "sufficiently an act of free will to purge the primary taint." *Wong Sun* thus mandates consideration of a statement's admissibility in light of the distinct policies and interests of the Fourth Amendment.

If *Miranda* warnings, by themselves, were held to attenuate the taint of an unconstitutional arrest, regardless of how wanton and purposeful the Fourth Amendment violation, the effect of the exclusionary rule would be substantially diluted. Arrests made without warrant or without probable cause, for questioning or "investigation," would be encouraged by the knowledge that evidence derived therefrom could well be made admissible at trial by the simple expedient of giving *Miranda* warnings. Any incentive to avoid Fourth Amendment violations would be eviscerated by making the warnings, in effect, a "cure-all," and the constitutional guarantee against unlawful searches and seizures could be said to be reduced to "a form of words."

It is entirely possible, of course, as the State here argues, that persons arrested illegally frequently may decide to confess, as an act of free will unaffected by the initial illegality. But the *Miranda* warnings, *alone* and *per se,* cannot always make the act sufficiently a product of free will to break, for Fourth Amendment purposes, the causal connection between the illegality and the confession. They cannot assure in every case that the Fourth Amendment violation has not been unduly exploited.

    * * * The question whether a confession is the product of a free will under *Wong Sun* must be answered on the facts of each case. No single fact is dispositive. The workings of the human mind are too complex, and the possibilities of misconduct too diverse, to permit protection of the Fourth Amendment to turn on such a talismanic test. The *Miranda* warnings are an important factor, to be sure, in determining whether the confession is obtained by exploitation of an illegal arrest. But they are not the only factor to be considered. The temporal proximity of the arrest and the confession, the presence of intervening circumstances, and, particularly, the purpose and flagrancy of the official misconduct are all relevant. The voluntariness of the statement is a threshold requirement. And the burden of showing admissibility rests, of course, on the prosecution.

IV

    * * * We conclude that the State failed to sustain the burden of showing that the evidence in question was admissible under *Wong Sun*.

    Brown's first statement was separated from his illegal arrest by less than two hours, and there was no intervening event of significance whatsoever. In its essentials, his situation is remarkably like that of James Wah Toy in *Wong Sun*.[11] We could hold Brown's first statement admissible only if we overrule *Wong Sun*. We decline to do so. And the second statement was clearly the result and the fruit of the first.

    The illegality here, moreover, had a quality of purposefulness. The impropriety of the arrest was obvious; awareness of that fact was virtually conceded by the two detectives when they repeatedly acknowledged, in their testimony, that the purpose of their action was "for investigation" or for "questioning." The arrest, both in design and in execution, was investigatory. The detectives embarked upon this expedition for evidence in the hope that something might turn up. The manner in which Brown's arrest was effected gives the appearance of having been calculated to cause surprise, fright, and confusion.

* * *

    [The concurring opinions of JUSTICE WHITE, and of JUSTICE POWELL, with whom JUSTICE REHNQUIST joined, are omitted.]

---

    11. The situation here is thus in dramatic contrast to that of Wong Sun himself. Wong Sun's confession, which the Court held admissible, came several days after the illegality, and was preceded by a lawful arraignment and a release from custody on his own recognizance.

2. *Miranda* Violations and the "Fruits" Doctrine

OREGON v. ELSTAD

Supreme Court of the United States, 1985.
470 U.S. 298, 105 S.Ct. 1285, 84 L.Ed.2d 222.

JUSTICE O'CONNOR delivered the opinion of the Court. * * *

In December, 1981, the home of Mr. and Mrs. Gilbert Gross, in the town of Salem, Polk County, Ore., was burglarized. Missing were art objects and furnishings valued at $150,000. A witness to the burglary contacted the Polk County Sheriff's office, implicating respondent Michael Elstad, an 18-year-old neighbor and friend of the Grosses' teenage son. Thereupon, Officers Burke and McAllister went to the home of respondent Elstad, with a warrant for his arrest. Elstad's mother answered the door. She led the officers to her son's room where he lay on his bed, clad in shorts and listening to his stereo. The officers asked him to get dressed and to accompany them into the living room. Officer McAllister asked respondent's mother to step into the kitchen, where he explained that they had a warrant for her son's arrest for the burglary of a neighbor's residence. Officer Burke remained with Elstad in the living room. He later testified:

> "I sat down with Mr. Elstad and I asked him if he was aware of why Detective McAllister and myself were there to talk with him. He stated no, he had no idea why we were there. I then asked him if he knew a person by the name of Gross, and he said yes, he did, and also added that he heard that there was a robbery at the Gross house. And at that point I told Mr. Elstad that I felt he was involved in that, and he looked at me and stated, 'Yes, I was there.' "

The officers then escorted Elstad to the back of the patrol car. As they were about to leave for the Polk County Sheriff's office, Elstad's father arrived home and came to the rear of the patrol car. The officers advised him that his son was a suspect in the burglary. Officer Burke testified that Mr. Elstad became quite agitated, opened the rear door of the car and admonished his son: "I told you that you were going to get into trouble. You wouldn't listen to me. You never learn."

Elstad was transported to the Sheriff's headquarters and approximately one hour later, Officers Burke and McAllister joined him in McAllister's office. McAllister then advised respondent for the first time of his *Miranda* rights, reading from a standard card. Respondent indicated he understood his rights, and, having these rights in mind, wished to speak with the officers. Elstad gave a full statement, explaining that he had known that the Gross family was out of town and had been paid to lead several acquaintances to the Gross residence and show them how to gain entry through a defective sliding glass door. The statement was typed, reviewed by respondent, read back to him for correction, initialed and signed by Elstad and both officers. As an afterthought, Elstad added and initialed the sentence, "After leaving the house Robby & I went back to [the] van & Robby handed me a small bag of grass." Respondent concedes that the officers made no threats or promises either at his residence or at the Sheriff's office.

[Elstad contends] that the statement he made in response to questioning at his house "let the cat out of the bag," and tainted the subsequent confession as "fruit of the poisonous tree," citing *Wong Sun v. United States*, 371 U.S. 471, 83 S.Ct. 407, 9 L.Ed.2d 441 (1963). * * *

Prior to *Miranda*, 384 U.S. 436, 86 S.Ct. 1602, 16 L.Ed.2d 694 (1966), the admissibility of an accused's in custody statements was judged solely by whether they were "voluntary" within the meaning of the Due Process Clause. * * * The Court in *Miranda* required suppression of many statements that would have been admissible under traditional due process analysis by presuming that statements made while in custody and without adequate warnings were protected by the Fifth Amendment. * * * As the Court noted last Term in *New York v. Quarles*, 467 U.S. 649, 654, 104 S.Ct. 2626, 81 L.Ed.2d 550 (1984):

> "The *Miranda* Court, however, presumed that interrogation in certain custodial circumstances is inherently coercive and * * * that statements made under those circumstances are inadmissible unless the suspect is specifically informed of his *Miranda* rights and freely decides to forgo those rights. The prophylactic *Miranda* warnings therefore are 'not themselves rights protected by the Constitution but [are] instead measures to insure that the right against compulsory self-incrimination [is] protected.' *Michigan v. Tucker*, 417 U.S. 433, 444, 94 S.Ct. 2357, 41 L.Ed.2d 182 (1974) * * *."

Respondent's contention that his confession was tainted by the earlier failure of the police to provide *Miranda* warnings and must be excluded as "fruit of the poisonous tree" assumes the existence of a constitutional violation. This figure of speech is drawn from *Wong Sun*, in which the Court held that evidence and witnesses discovered as a result of a search in violation of the Fourth Amendment must be excluded, from evidence. The *Wong Sun* doctrine applies as well when the fruit of the Fourth Amendment violation is a confession. It is settled law that "a confession obtained through custodial interrogation after an illegal arrest should be excluded unless intervening events break the causal connection between the illegal arrest and the confession so that the confession is 'sufficiently an act of free will to purge the primary taint.' "

But as we explained in *Quarles* and *Tucker*, a procedural *Miranda* violation differs in significant respects from violations of the Fourth Amendment, which have traditionally mandated a broad application of the "fruits" doctrine. * * * The *Miranda* exclusionary rule, however, serves the Fifth Amendment and sweeps more broadly than the Fifth Amendment itself. It may be triggered even in the absence of a Fifth Amendment violation. The Fifth Amendment prohibits use by the prosecution in its case in chief only of *compelled* testimony. Failure to administer *Miranda* warnings creates a presumption of compulsion. Consequently, unwarned statements that are otherwise voluntary within the meaning of the Fifth Amendment must nevertheless be excluded from evidence under *Miranda*. Thus, in the individual case, *Miranda's* preventive medicine provides a remedy even to the defendant who has suffered no identifiable constitutional harm.

But the *Miranda* presumption, though irrebuttable for purposes of the prosecution's case in chief, does not require that the statements and their fruits be discarded as inherently tainted. Despite the fact that patently *voluntary* statements taken in violation of *Miranda* must be excluded from the prosecution's case, the presumption of coercion does not bar their use for impeachment purposes on cross-examination. *Harris v. New York*, 401 U.S. 222, 91 S.Ct. 643, 28 L.Ed.2d 1 (1971). * * *

In *Michigan v. Tucker*, the Court was asked to extend the *Wong Sun* fruits doctrine to suppress the testimony of a witness for the prosecution whose identity was discovered as the result of a statement taken from the accused without benefit of full *Miranda* warnings. As in respondent's case, the breach of the *Miranda* procedures in *Tucker* involved no actual compulsion. The Court concluded that the unwarned questioning "did not abridge respondent's constitutional privilege * * * but departed only from the prophylactic standards later laid down by this Court in *Miranda* to safeguard that privilege." Since there was no actual infringement of the suspect's constitutional rights, the case was not controlled by the doctrine expressed in *Wong Sun* that fruits of a constitutional violation must be suppressed. * * *

We believe that this reasoning applies with equal force when the alleged "fruit" of a noncoercive *Miranda* violation is neither a witness nor an article of evidence but the accused's own voluntary testimony. As in *Tucker*, the absence of any coercion or improper tactics undercuts the twin rationales—trustworthiness and deterrence—for a broader rule. Once warned, the suspect is free to exercise his own volition in deciding whether or not to make a statement to the authorities. * * * Because *Miranda* warnings may inhibit persons from giving information, this Court has determined that they need be administered only after the person is taken into "custody" or his freedom has otherwise been significantly restrained. Unfortunately, the task of defining "custody" is a slippery one, and policemen investigating serious crimes cannot realistically be expected to make no errors whatsoever. If errors are made by law enforcement officers in administering the prophylactic *Miranda* procedures, they should not breed the same irremediable consequences as police infringement of the Fifth Amendment itself. It is an unwarranted extension of *Miranda* to hold that a simple failure to administer the warnings, unaccompanied by any actual coercion or other circumstances calculated to undermine the suspect's ability to exercise his free will so taints the investigatory process that a subsequent voluntary and informed waiver is ineffective for some indeterminate period. Though *Miranda* requires that the unwarned admission must be suppressed, the admissibility of any subsequent statement should turn in these circumstances solely on whether it is knowingly and voluntarily made.

The Oregon court, however, believed that the unwarned remark compromised the voluntariness of respondent's later confession. It was the court's view that the prior *answer* and not the unwarned questioning impaired respondent's ability to give a valid waiver and that only lapse of time and change of place could dissipate what it termed the "coercive impact" of the inadmissible statement. When a prior statement is actually coerced, the time that passes between confessions, the change in place of interrogations, and the change in identity of the interrogators all bear on whether that coercion has carried over into the second confession. * * *

* * *

[A]bsent deliberately coercive or improper tactics in obtaining the initial statement, the mere fact that a suspect has made an unwarned admission does not warrant a presumption of compulsion. A subsequent administration of *Miranda* warnings to a suspect who has given a voluntary but unwarned statement ordinarily should suffice to remove the conditions that precluded admission of the earlier statement. In such circumstances, the finder of fact may reasonably conclude that the suspect made a rational and intelligent choice whether to waive or invoke his rights.

The state has conceded the issue of custody and thus we must assume that Burke breached *Miranda* procedures in failing to administer *Miranda* warnings before initiating the discussion in the living room. This breach may have been the result of confusion as to whether the brief exchange qualified as "custodial interrogation" or it may simply have reflected Burke's reluctance to initiate an alarming police procedure before McAllister had spoken with respondent's mother. Whatever the reason for Burke's oversight, the incident had none of the earmarks of coercion. Nor did the officers exploit the unwarned admission to pressure respondent into waiving his right to remain silent. * * * We find that the dictates of *Miranda* and the goals of the Fifth Amendment proscription against use of compelled testimony are fully satisfied in the circumstances of this case by barring use of the unwarned statement in the case in chief. No further purpose is served by imputing "taint" to subsequent statements obtained pursuant to a voluntary and knowing waiver. We hold today that a suspect who has once responded to unwarned yet uncoercive questioning is not thereby disabled from waiving his rights and confessing after he has been given the requisite *Miranda* warnings.

The judgment of the Court of Appeals of Oregon is reversed, and the case is remanded for further proceedings not inconsistent with this opinion.

JUSTICE BRENNAN, with whom JUSTICE MARSHALL joins, dissenting.

The Self–Incrimination Clause of the Fifth Amendment guarantees every individual that, if taken into official custody, he shall be informed of important constitutional rights and be given the opportunity knowingly and voluntarily to waive those rights before being interrogated about suspected wrongdoing. *Miranda v. Arizona.* This guarantee embodies our society's conviction that "no system of criminal justice can, or should, survive if it comes to depend for its continued effectiveness on the citizens' abdication through unawareness of their constitutional rights." *Escobedo v. Illinois,* 378 U.S. 478, 490, 84 S.Ct. 1758, 12 L.Ed.2d 977 (1964).

In the alternative, the Court asserts that neither the Fifth Amendment itself nor the judicial policy of deterring illegal police conduct requires the suppression of the "fruits" of a confession obtained in violation of *Miranda,* reasoning that to do otherwise would interfere with "legitimate law enforcement activity." As the Court surely understands, however, "[to] forbid the direct use of methods ... but to put no curb on their full indirect use would only invite the very methods deemed 'inconsistent with ethical standards and destructive of personal liberty.'" If violations of constitutional rights may not be remedied through the well-established rules respecting derivative evidence, as the Court has held today, there is a critical danger that the rights will be rendered nothing more than a mere "form of words."

* * *

I

The threshold question is this: What effect should an admission or confession of guilt obtained in violation of an accused's *Miranda* rights be presumed to have upon the voluntariness of subsequent confessions that are preceded by *Miranda* warnings? * * *

* * * Most federal courts have rejected the Court's approach and instead held that (1) there is a rebuttable presumption that a confession obtained in violation of *Miranda* taints subsequent confessions, and (2) the taint cannot be dissipated solely by giving *Miranda* warnings. * * * Although a handful have adopted the Court's approach, the overwhelming majority of state courts that have considered the issue have concluded that subsequent confessions are presumptively tainted by a first confession taken in violation of *Miranda* and that *Miranda* warnings alone cannot dissipate the taint.

* * *

(A)(2)

Our precedents did not develop in a vacuum. They reflect an understanding of the realities of police interrogation and the everyday experience of lower courts. Expert interrogators, far from dismissing a first admission or confession as creating merely a "speculative and attenuated" disadvantage for a suspect, understand that such revelations frequently lead directly to a full confession. Standard interrogation manuals advise that "[the] securing of the first admission is the biggest stumbling block...." If this first admission can be obtained, "there is every reason to expect that the first admission will lead to others, and eventually to the full confession."

* * *

There are numerous variations on this theme. Police may obtain a confession in violation of *Miranda* and then take a break for lunch or go home for the evening. When questioning is resumed, this time preceded by *Miranda* warnings, the suspect is asked to "clarify" the earlier illegal confession and to provide additional information. Or he is led by one of the interrogators into another room, introduced to another official, and asked to repeat his story. The new officer then gives the *Miranda* warnings and asks the suspect to proceed. Alternatively, the suspect might be questioned by arresting officers "in the field" and without *Miranda* warnings, as was young Elstad in the instant case. After making incriminating admissions or a confession, the suspect is then brought into the station house and either questioned by the same officers again or asked to repeat his earlier statements to another officer.

The variations of this practice are numerous, but the underlying problem is always the same: after hearing the witness testimony and considering the practical realities, courts have confirmed the time-honored wisdom of presuming that a first illegal confession "taints" subsequent confessions, and permitting such subsequent confessions to be admitted at trial *only* if the prosecution convincingly rebuts the presumption. They have discovered that frequently, "[having] once confessed [the accused] was ready to confess some more." For all practical purposes, the prewarning and postwarning questioning are often but stages of one overall interrogation. Whether or not the authorities explicitly confront the suspect with his earlier illegal admissions makes no significant difference, of course, because the suspect knows that the authorities know of his earlier statements and most frequently will believe that those statements already have sealed his fate. Thus a suspect in such circumstances is likely to conclude that "he might as well answer the questions put to him, since the [authorities are] already aware of the earlier answers," he will probably tell himself that "it's O.K., I have already told them." In such circumstances, courts have found, a suspect almost invariably asks himself, "What use is a lawyer? What good is a lawyer now? What benefit can a lawyer tell me? *[sic]* I have already told the police everything."

* * *

II

Not content merely to ignore the practical realities of police interrogation and the likely effects of its abolition of the derivative-evidence presumption, the Court goes on to assert that nothing in the Fifth Amendment or the general judicial policy of deterring illegal police conduct "ordinarily" requires the suppression of evidence derived proximately from a confession obtained in violation of *Miranda*. The Court does not limit its analysis to successive confessions, but recurrently refers generally to the "fruits" of the illegal confession. Thus the potential impact of the Court's reasoning might extend far beyond the "cat out of the bag" context to include the discovery of physical evidence and other derivative fruits of *Miranda* violations as well.

A

The Fifth Amendment requires that an accused in custody be informed of important constitutional rights before the authorities interrogate him. This requirement serves to combat the "inherently compelling pressures" of custodial questioning "which work to undermine the individual's will to resist and to compel him to speak where he would not otherwise do so freely," and is a prerequisite to securing the accused's informed and voluntary waiver of his rights. Far from serving merely as a prophylactic safeguard, "[the] requirement of warnings and waiver of rights is a fundamental with respect to the Fifth Amendment privilege. . . . " It is precisely because this requirement embraces rights that are deemed to serve a "central role in the preservation of basic liberties," that it is binding on the States through the Fourteenth Amendment.

* * *

JUSTICE STEVENS, dissenting.

* * *

For me, the most disturbing aspect of the Court's opinion is its somewhat opaque characterization of the police misconduct in this case. The Court appears ambivalent on the question whether there was any constitutional violation. This ambivalence is either disingenuous or completely lawless. This Court's power to require state courts to exclude probative self-incriminatory statements rests entirely on the premise that the use of such evidence violates the Federal Constitution. The same constitutional analysis applies whether the custodial interrogation is actually coercive or irrebuttably presumed to be coercive. If the Court does not accept that premise, it must regard the holding in the *Miranda* case itself, as well as all of the Federal jurisprudence that has evolved from that decision, as nothing more than an illegitimate exercise of raw judicial power. If the Court accepts the proposition that respondent's self-incriminatory statement was inadmissible, it must also acknowledge that the Federal Constitution protected him from custodial police interrogation without first being advised of his right to remain silent.

The source of respondent's constitutional protection is the Fifth Amendment's privilege against compelled self-incrimination that is secured against state invasion by the Due Process Clause of the Fourteenth Amendment. Like many other provisions of the Bill of Rights, that provision is merely a procedural safeguard. It is, however, the specific provision that protects all citizens from the kind of custodial interrogation that was once employed by the Star Chamber, by "the Germans of the 1930's and early 1940's," and by some of our own police departments only a few decades ago. Custodial interrogation that violates that provision of the Bill of Rights is a classic example of a violation of a constitutional right. I respectfully dissent.

MISSOURI v. SEIBERT

Supreme Court of the United States, 2004.
542 U.S. 600, 124 S.Ct. 2601, 159 L.Ed.2d 643.

JUSTICE SOUTER announced the judgment of the Court and delivered an opinion, in which JUSTICE STEVENS, JUSTICE GINSBURG, and JUSTICE BREYER join.

This case tests a police protocol for custodial interrogation that calls for giving no warnings of the rights to silence and counsel until interrogation has produced a confession. Although such a statement is generally inadmissible, since taken in violation of *Miranda* v. *Arizona*, 384 U. S 436 (1966), the interrogating officer follows it with *Miranda* warnings and then leads the suspect to cover the same ground a second time. The question here is the admissibility of the repeated statement. Because this midstream recitation of warnings after interrogation and unwarned confession could not effectively comply with *Miranda*'s constitutional requirement, we hold that a statement repeated after a warning in such circumstances is inadmissible.

I

Respondent Patrice Seibert's 12–year-old son Jonathan had cerebral palsy, and when he died in his sleep she feared charges of neglect because of bedsores on his body. In her presence, two of her teenage sons and two of their friends devised a plan to conceal the facts surrounding Jonathan's death by incinerating his body in the course of burning the family's mobile home, in which they planned to leave Donald Rector, a mentally ill teenager living with the family, to avoid any appearance that Jonathan had been unattended. Seibert's son Darian and a friend set the fire, and Donald died.

Five days later, the police awakened Seibert at 3 a.m. at a hospital where Darian was being treated for burns. In arresting her, Officer Kevin Clinton followed instructions from Rolla, Missouri, officer Richard Hanrahan that he refrain from giving *Miranda* warnings. After Seibert had been taken to the police station and left alone in an interview room for 15 to 20 minutes, Hanrahan questioned her without *Miranda* warnings for 30 to 40 minutes, squeezing her arm and repeating "Donald was also to die in his sleep." After Seibert finally admitted she knew Donald was meant to die in the fire, she was given a 20–minute coffee and cigarette break. Officer Hanrahan then turned on a tape recorder, gave Seibert the *Miranda* warnings, and obtained a signed waiver of rights from her. He resumed the questioning with "Ok, 'trice, we've been talking for a little while about what happened on Wednesday the twelfth, haven't we?," and confronted her with her prewarning statements [after which she confessed that her son was meant to die in his sleep].

After being charged with first-degree murder for her role in Donald's death, Seibert sought to exclude both her prewarning and postwarning statements. At the suppression hearing, Officer Hanrahan testified that he made a "conscious decision" to withhold *Miranda* warnings, thus resorting to an interrogation technique he had been taught: question first, then give the warnings, and then repeat the question "until I get the answer that she's already provided once." He acknowledged that Seibert's ultimate statement was "largely a repeat of information . . . obtained" prior to the warning.

The trial court suppressed the prewarning statement but admitted the responses given after the *Miranda* recitation. A jury convicted Seibert of second-degree murder. [The Supreme Court of Missouri reversed and the Supreme Court granted certiorari to resolve a split in the Courts of Appeals, and affirmed the state supreme court decision.]

II

* * *

* * * *Miranda* conditioned the admissibility at trial of any custodial confession on warning a suspect of his rights: failure to give the prescribed warnings and obtain a waiver of rights before custodial questioning generally requires exclusion of any statements obtained. Conversely, giving the warnings and getting a waiver has generally produced a virtual ticket of admissibility; maintaining that a statement is involuntary even though given after warnings and voluntary waiver of rights requires unusual stamina, and litigation over voluntariness tends to end with the finding of a valid waiver. To point out the obvious, this common consequence would not be common at all were it not that *Miranda* warnings are customarily given under circumstances allowing for a real choice between talking and remaining silent.

III

* * *

The technique of interrogating in successive, unwarned and warned phases raises a new challenge to *Miranda*. Although we have no statistics on the frequency of this practice, it is not confined to Rolla, Missouri. An officer of that police department testified that the strategy of withholding *Miranda* warnings until after interrogating and drawing out a confession was promoted not only by his own department, but by a national police training organization and other departments in which he had worked. Consistently with the officer's testimony, the Police Law Institute, for example, instructs that "officers may conduct a two-stage interrogation. . . . At any point during the pre-*Miranda* interrogation, usually after arrestees have confessed, officers may then read the *Miranda* warnings and ask for a waiver. If the arrestees waive their *Miranda* rights, officers will be able to repeat any *subsequent* incriminating statements later in court." Police Law Institute, Illinois Police Law Manual 83 (Jan. 2001–Dec. 2003), http://www.illinoispolicelaw.org/training/lessons/ ILPLMIR.pdf (hereinafter Police Law Manual).[2] The upshot of all this advice is a question-first practice of some popularity, as one can see from the reported cases describing its use, sometimes in obedience to departmental policy.

IV

When a confession so obtained is offered and challenged, attention must be paid to the conflicting objects of *Miranda* and question-first. *Miranda* addressed "interrogation practices ... likely ... to disable [an individual] from making a free and rational choice" about speaking, and held that a suspect must be "adequately and effectively" advised of the choice the Constitution guarantees. The object of question-first is to render *Miranda* warnings ineffective by waiting for a particularly opportune time to give them, after the suspect has already confessed.

Just as "no talismanic incantation [is] required to satisfy [*Miranda*'s] strictures," it would be absurd to think that mere recitation of the litany suffices to satisfy *Miranda* in every conceivable circumstance. "The inquiry is simply whether the warnings reasonably 'convey to [a suspect] his rights as required by *Miranda*.' " The threshold issue when interrogators question first and warn later is thus whether it would be reasonable to find that in these circumstances the warnings could function "effectively" as *Miranda* requires. Could the warnings effectively advise the suspect that he had a real choice about giving an admissible statement at that juncture? Could they reasonably convey that he could choose to stop talking even if he had talked earlier? For unless the warnings could place a suspect who has just been interrogated in a position to make such an informed choice, there is no practical justification for accepting the formal warnings as compliance with *Miranda*, or for treating the second stage of interrogation as distinct from the first, unwarned and inadmissible segment.

* * * By any objective measure, applied to circumstances exemplified here, it is likely that if the interrogators employ the technique of withholding warnings until after interrogation succeeds in eliciting a confession, the warnings will be ineffective in preparing the suspect for successive interrogation, close in time and similar in content. After all, the reason that question-first is catching on is as obvious as its manifest purpose, which is to get a confession the suspect would not make if he

---

2. Emphasizing the impeachment exception to the *Miranda* rule approved by this Court, *Harris* v. *New York*, 401 U.S. 222 (1971), some training programs advise officers to omit *Miranda* warnings altogether or to continue questioning after the suspect invokes his rights. See, *e.g.*, Police Law Manual 83 ("There is no need to give a *Miranda* warning before asking questions if ... the answers given ... will not be required by the prosecutor during the prosecution's case-in-chief"); California Commission on Peace Officer Standards and Training, Video Training Programs for California Law Enforcement, Miranda: Post–Invocation Questioning (broadcast July 11, 1996) ("We ... have been encouraging you to continue to question a suspect after they've invoked their *Miranda* rights"); * * *. This training is reflected in the reported cases involving deliberate questioning after invocation of *Miranda* rights. See, *e.g.*, *California Attorneys for Criminal Justice* v. *Butts*, 195 F.3d 1039, 1042–1044 (CA9 1999) * * *.

understood his rights at the outset; the sensible underlying assumption is that with one confession in hand before the warnings, the interrogator can count on getting its duplicate, with trifling additional trouble. Upon hearing warnings only in the aftermath of interrogation and just after making a confession, a suspect would hardly think he had a genuine right to remain silent, let alone persist in so believing once the police began to lead him over the same ground again. [T]elling a suspect that "anything you say can and will be used against you," without expressly excepting the statement just given, could lead to an entirely reasonable inference that what he has just said will be used, with subsequent silence being of no avail. Thus, when *Miranda* warnings are inserted in the midst of coordinated and continuing interrogation, they are likely to mislead and "deprive a defendant of knowledge essential to his ability to understand the nature of his rights and the consequences of abandoning them." By the same token, it would ordinarily be unrealistic to treat two spates of integrated and proximately conducted questioning as independent interrogations subject to independent evaluation simply because *Miranda* warnings formally punctuate them in the middle.

V

Missouri argues that a confession repeated at the end of an interrogation sequence envisioned in a question-first strategy is admissible on the authority of *Oregon* v. *Elstad*, 470 U.S. 298 (1985), but the argument disfigures that case. [The plurality discussed the facts of *Elstad*, concluded that the Supreme Court, treated the officer's initial failure to warn as an "oversight" that "may have been the result of confusion as to whether the brief exchange qualified as 'custodial interrogation' or . . . may simply have reflected . . . reluctance to initiate an alarming police procedure before [an officer] had spoken with respondent's mother," and distinguished this situation from an intentional and systematic attempt to circumvent *Miranda* during a station house interrogation. The plurality also concluded that "it is fair to read *Elstad* as treating the living room conversation as a good-faith *Miranda* mistake, not only open to correction by careful warnings before systematic questioning in that particular case, but posing no threat to warn-first practice generally."]

At the opposite extreme are the facts here, which by any objective measure reveal a police strategy adapted to undermine the *Miranda* warnings. The unwarned interrogation was conducted in the station house, and the questioning was systematic, exhaustive, and managed with psychological skill. When the police were finished there was little, if anything, of incriminating potential left unsaid. The warned phase of questioning proceeded after a pause of only 15 to 20 minutes, in the same place as the unwarned segment. When the same officer who had conducted the first phase recited the *Miranda* warnings, he said nothing to counter the probable misimpression that the advice that anything Seibert said could be used against her also applied to the details of the inculpatory statement previously elicited. In particular, the police did not advise that her prior statement could not be used. * * * Officer Hanrahan set the scene by saying "we've been talking for a little while about what happened on Wednesday the twelfth, haven't we?" The impression that the further questioning was a mere continuation of the earlier questions and responses was fostered by references back to the confession already given. * * *

VI

Strategists dedicated to draining the substance out of *Miranda* cannot accomplish by training instructions what *Dickerson* held Congress could not do by statute. Because the question-first tactic effectively threatens to thwart *Miranda*'s purpose of reducing the risk that a coerced confession would be admitted, and because the facts here do not reasonably support a conclusion that the warnings given could have served their purpose, Seibert's postwarning statements are inadmissible. The judgment of the Supreme Court of Missouri is affirmed. *It is so ordered.*

[The concurring opinions of JUSTICE BREYER and of JUSTICE KENNEDY are omitted.]

JUSTICE O'CONNOR, with whom THE CHIEF JUSTICE, JUSTICE SCALIA, and JUSTICE THOMAS join, dissenting.

* * *

I

On two preliminary questions I am in full agreement with the plurality. First, the plurality appropriately follows *Elstad* in concluding that Seibert's statement cannot be held inadmissible under a "fruit of the poisonous tree" theory. Second, the plurality correctly declines to focus its analysis on the subjective intent of the interrogating officer.

A

* * *

Although the analysis the plurality ultimately espouses examines the same facts and circumstances that a "fruits" analysis would consider (such as the lapse of time between the two interrogations and change of questioner or location), it does so for entirely different reasons. The fruits analysis would examine those factors because they are relevant to the balance of deterrence value versus the "drastic and socially costly course" of excluding reliable evidence. The plurality, by contrast, looks to those factors to inform the *psychological* judgment regarding whether the suspect has been informed effectively of her right to remain silent. The analytical underpinnings of the two approaches are thus entirely distinct, and they should not be conflated just because they function similarly in practice.

B

The plurality's rejection of an intent-based test is also, in my view, correct. Freedom from compulsion lies at the heart of the Fifth Amendment, and requires us to assess whether a suspect's decision to speak truly was voluntary. Because voluntariness is a matter of the suspect's state of mind, we focus our analysis on the way in which suspects experience interrogation.

* * *

Because the isolated fact of Officer Hanrahan's intent could not have had any bearing on Seibert's "capacity to comprehend and knowingly relinquish" her right to remain silent, it could not by itself affect the voluntariness of her confession. Moreover, recognizing an exception to *Elstad* for intentional violations would require focusing constitutional analysis on a police officer's subjective intent, an unattractive proposition that we all but uniformly avoid. In general, "we believe that 'sending state and federal courts on an expedition into the minds of police officers would produce a grave and fruitless misallocation of judicial resources.' " This case presents the uncommonly straightforward circumstance of an officer openly admitting that the violation was intentional. But the inquiry will be complicated in other situations probably more likely to occur. For example, different officers involved in an interrogation might claim different states of mind regarding the failure to give *Miranda* warnings. Even in the simple case of a single officer who claims that a failure to give *Miranda* warnings was inadvertent, the likelihood of error will be high.

* * *

UNITED STATES v. PATANE

Supreme Court of the United States, 2004.
542 U.S. 630, 124 S.Ct. 2620, 159 L.Ed.2d 667.

JUSTICE THOMAS announced the judgment of the Court and delivered an opinion, in which THE CHIEF JUSTICE and JUSTICE SCALIA join.

In this case we must decide whether a failure to give a suspect the warnings prescribed by *Miranda* v. *Arizona*, 384 U.S. 436 (1966), requires suppression of the physical fruits of the suspect's unwarned but voluntary statements. The Court has previously addressed this question but has not reached a definitive conclusion. Although we believe that the Court's decisions in *Oregon* v. *Elstad*, 470 U.S. 298 (1985), and *Michigan* v. *Tucker*, 417 U.S. 433 (1974), are instructive, the Courts of Appeals have split on the question after our decision in *Dickerson* v. *United States*, 530 U.S. 428 (2000). Because the *Miranda* rule protects against violations of the Self–Incrimination Clause, which, in turn, is not implicated by the introduction at trial of physical evidence resulting from voluntary statements, we answer the question presented in the negative.

I

[Patane, was arrested for harassing his ex-girlfriend, Linda O'Donnell. He was released on bond, subject to a temporary restraining order that prohibited him from contacting O'Donnell. At the time that the Colorado Springs Police Department began to investigate whether Patane had violated the restraining order, it was advised by the Bureau of Alcohol, Tobacco, and Firearms (ATF) that Patane, a convicted felon, might illegally possess a Glock pistol. Detective Benner and Officer Fox went to Patane's residence to investigate.]

After reaching the residence and inquiring into respondent's attempts to contact O'Donnell, Officer Fox arrested respondent for violating the restraining order. Detective Benner attempted to advise respondent of his *Miranda* rights but got no further than the right to remain silent. At that point, respondent interrupted, asserting that he knew his rights, and neither officer attempted to complete the warning.[1]

Detective Benner then asked respondent about the Glock. Respondent was initially reluctant to discuss the matter, stating: "I am not sure I should tell you anything about the Glock because I don't want you to take it away from me." Detective Benner persisted, and respondent told him that the pistol was in his bedroom. Respondent then gave Detective Benner permission to retrieve the pistol. Detective Benner found the pistol and seized it.

[The Court of Appeals affirmed the District Court's order suppressing the pistol.]

As we explain below, the *Miranda* rule is a prophylactic employed to protect against violations of the Self–Incrimination Clause. The Self–Incrimination Clause, however, is not implicated by the admission into evidence of the physical fruit of a voluntary statement. Accordingly, there is no justification for extending the *Miranda* rule to this context. And just as the Self–Incrimination Clause primarily focuses on the criminal trial, so too does the *Miranda* rule. The *Miranda* rule is not a code of police conduct, and police do not violate the Constitution (or even the *Miranda* rule, for that matter) by mere failures to warn. For this reason, the exclusionary rule articulated in cases such as *Wong Sun* does not apply. Accordingly, we reverse the judgment of the Court of Appeals and remand the case for further proceedings consistent with this opinion.

II

The Self–Incrimination Clause provides: "No person ... shall be compelled in any criminal case to be a witness against himself." We need not decide here the precise boundaries of the Clause's protection. For present purposes, it suffices to note that the core protection afforded by the Self–Incrimination Clause is a prohibition on compelling a criminal

---

1. The Government concedes that respondent's answers to subsequent on-the-scene questioning are inadmissible at trial under *Miranda* v. *Arizona,* despite the partial warning and respondent's assertions that he knew his rights.

defendant to testify against himself at trial. See, *e.g., Chavez* v. *Martinez,* 538 U.S. 760, 764–768 (2003) (plurality opinion). The Clause cannot be violated by the introduction of nontestimonial evidence obtained as a result of voluntary statements.

To be sure, the Court has recognized and applied several prophylactic rules designed to protect the core privilege against self-incrimination. For example, although the text of the Self–Incrimination Clause at least suggests that "its coverage [is limited to] compelled testimony that is used against the defendant in the trial itself," potential suspects may, at times, assert the privilege in proceedings in which answers might be used to incriminate them in a subsequent criminal case. We have explained that "the natural concern which underlies [these] decisions is that an inability to protect the right at one stage of a proceeding may make its invocation useless at a later stage."

Similarly, in *Miranda,* the Court concluded that the possibility of coercion inherent in custodial interrogations unacceptably raises the risk that a suspect's privilege against self-incrimination might be violated. To protect against this danger, the *Miranda* rule creates a presumption of coercion, in the absence of specific warnings, that is generally irrebuttable for purposes of the prosecution's case in chief.

But because these prophylactic rules (including the *Miranda* rule) necessarily sweep beyond the actual protections of the Self–Incrimination Clause, any further extension of these rules must be justified by its necessity for the protection of the actual right against compelled self-incrimination. Indeed, at times the Court has declined to extend *Miranda* even where it has perceived a need to protect the privilege against self-incrimination.

It is for these reasons that statements taken without *Miranda* warnings (though not actually compelled) can be used to impeach a defendant's testimony at trial, though the fruits of actually compelled testimony cannot. * * *

* * *

Finally, nothing in *Dickerson,* including its characterization of *Miranda* as announcing a constitutional rule, changes any of these observations. Indeed, in *Dickerson,* the Court specifically noted that the Court's "subsequent cases have reduced the impact of the *Miranda* rule on legitimate law enforcement while reaffirming [*Miranda*]'s core ruling that unwarned statements may not be used as evidence in the prosecution's case in chief." [N]othing in *Dickerson* calls into question our continued insistence that the closest possible fit be maintained between the Self–Incrimination Clause and any rule designed to protect it.

* * *

IV

In the present case, the Court of Appeals, relying on *Dickerson,* wholly adopted the position that the taking of unwarned statements violates a suspect's constitutional rights. And, of course, if this were so, a strong deterrence-based argument could be made for suppression of the fruits.

But *Dickerson*'s characterization of *Miranda* as a constitutional rule does not lessen the need to maintain the closest possible fit between the Self–Incrimination Clause and any judge-made rule designed to protect it. And there is no such fit here. Introduction of the nontestimonial fruit of a voluntary statement, such as respondent's Glock, does not implicate the Self–Incrimination Clause. The admission of such fruit presents no risk that a defendant's coerced statements (however defined) will be used against him at a criminal trial. In any case, "the exclusion of unwarned statements ... is a complete and sufficient remedy" for any perceived *Miranda* violation. There is simply no need to extend (and therefore no justification for extending) the prophylactic rule of *Miranda* to this context.

* * *

Accordingly, we reverse the judgment of the Court of Appeals and remand the case for further proceedings consistent with this opinion. It is so ordered.

[The opinion of JUSTICE KENNEDY concurring in the judgment, with whom JUSTICE O'CONNOR joined, is omitted.]

JUSTICE SOUTER, WITH WHOM JUSTICE STEVENS AND JUSTICE GINSBURG join, dissenting.

The majority repeatedly says that the Fifth Amendment does not address the admissibility of nontestimonial evidence, an overstatement that is beside the point. The issue actually presented today is whether courts should apply the fruit of the poisonous tree doctrine lest we create an incentive for the police to omit *Miranda* warnings. In closing their eyes to the consequences of giving an evidentiary advantage to those who ignore *Miranda*, the majority adds an important inducement for interrogators to ignore the rule in that case.

Miranda rested on insight into the inherently coercive character of custodial interrogation and the inherently difficult exercise of assessing the voluntariness of any confession resulting from it. Unless the police give the prescribed warnings meant to counter the coercive atmosphere, a custodial confession is inadmissible, there being no need for the previous time-consuming and difficult enquiry into voluntariness. That inducement to forestall involuntary statements and troublesome issues of fact can only atrophy if we turn around and recognize an evidentiary benefit when an unwarned statement leads investigators to tangible evidence. There is, of course, a price for excluding evidence, but the Fifth Amendment is worth a price, and in the absence of a very good reason, the logic of *Miranda* should be followed: a *Miranda* violation raises a presumption of coercion, and the Fifth Amendment privilege against compelled self-incrimination extends to the exclusion of derivative evidence. That should be the end of this case.

* * *

There is no way to read this case except as an unjustifiable invitation to law enforcement officers to flout *Miranda* when there may be physical evidence to be gained. The incentive is an odd one, coming from the Court on the same day it decides *Missouri* v. *Seibert, ante.* I respectfully dissent.

[JUSTICE BREYER's dissenting opinion is omitted.]

3. Deliberate Elicitation, the Sixth Amendment, and the "Fruits" Doctrine

FELLERS v. UNITED STATES

Supreme Court of the United States, 2004.
540 U.S. 519, 124 S.Ct. 1019, 157 L.Ed.2d 1016.

JUSTICE O'CONNOR delivered the opinion of the Court.

* * *

I

On February 24, 2000, after a grand jury indicted petitioner for conspiracy to distribute methamphetamine, Lincoln Police Sergeant Michael Garnett and Lancaster County Deputy Sheriff Jeff Bliemeister went to petitioner's home in Lincoln, Nebraska, to arrest him. The officers knocked on petitioner's door and, when petitioner answered, identified themselves and asked if they could come in. Petitioner invited the officers into his living room.

The officers advised petitioner they had come to discuss his involvement in methamphetamine distribution. They informed petitioner that they had a federal warrant for his arrest and that a grand jury had indicted him for conspiracy to distribute methamphetamine. The officers told petitioner that the indictment referred to his involvement with certain individuals, four of whom they named. Petitioner then told the officers that he knew the four people and had used methamphetamine during his association with them.

After spending about 15 minutes in petitioner's home, the officers transported petitioner to the Lancaster County jail. There, the officers advised petitioner for the first time of his rights under *Miranda* v. *Arizona,* 384 U.S. 436, 16 L.Ed.2d 694, 86 S.Ct. 1602 (1966), and *Patterson* v. *Illinois,* 487 U.S. 285, 101 L.Ed.2d 261, 108 S.Ct. 2389 (1988). Petitioner and the two officers signed a *Miranda* waiver form, and petitioner then reiterated the inculpatory statements he had made earlier, admitted to having associated with other individuals implicated in the charged conspiracy, and admitted to having loaned money to one of them even though he suspected that she was involved in drug transactions.

Before trial, petitioner moved to suppress the inculpatory statements he made at his home and at the county jail. * * *

The District Court suppressed the "unwarned" statements petitioner made at his house but admitted petitioner's jailhouse statements pursuant to *Oregon* v. *Elstad,* 470 U.S. 298, 84 L.Ed.2d 222, 105 S.Ct. 1285 (1985), concluding petitioner had knowingly and voluntarily waived his *Miranda* rights before making the statements.

Following a jury trial at which petitioner's jailhouse statements were admitted into evidence, petitioner was convicted of conspiring to possess with intent to distribute methamphetamine. Petitioner appealed, arguing that his jailhouse statements should have been suppressed as fruits of the statements obtained at his home in violation of the Sixth Amendment. The Court of Appeals affirmed. * * *

* * *

II

The Sixth Amendment right to counsel is triggered "at or after the time that judicial proceedings have been initiated ... 'whether by way of formal charge, preliminary hearing, indictment, information, or arraignment.'" *Brewer* v. *Williams,* 430 U.S. 387, 398, 51 L.Ed.2d 424, 97 S.Ct. 1232 (1977). We have held that an accused is denied "the basic protections" of the Sixth Amendment "when there [is] used against him at his trial evidence of his own incriminating words, which federal agents ... deliberately elicited from him after he had been indicted and in the absence of his counsel." *Massiah* v. *United States,* 377 U.S. 201, 206, 12 L.Ed.2d 246, 84 S.Ct. 1199 (1964).

We have consistently applied the deliberate-elicitation standard in subsequent Sixth Amendment cases, and we have expressly distinguished this standard from the Fifth Amendment custodial-interrogation standard, see *Michigan* v. *Jackson,* 475 U.S. 625, 632, n. 5, 89 L.Ed.2d 631, 106 S.Ct. 1404 (1986) ("[T]he Sixth Amendment provides a right to counsel ... even when there is no interrogation and no Fifth Amendment applicability"); *Rhode Island* v. *Innis,* 446 U.S. 291, 300, n. 4, 64 L.Ed.2d 297, 100 S.Ct. 1682 (1980) ("The definitions of 'interrogation' under the Fifth and Sixth Amendments, if indeed the term 'interrogation' is even apt in the Sixth Amendment context, are not necessarily interchangeable").

The Court of Appeals erred in holding that the absence of an "interrogation" foreclosed petitioner's claim that the jailhouse statements should have been suppressed as fruits of the statements taken from petitioner at his home. First, there is no question that the officers in this case "deliberately elicited" information from petitioner. Indeed, the officers, upon arriving at petitioner's house, informed him that their purpose in coming was to discuss his involvement in the distribution of methamphetamine and his association with certain charged co-conspirators. Because the ensuing discussion took place after petitioner had been indicted, outside the presence of counsel, and in the absence of any waiver of petitioner's Sixth Amendment rights, the Court of Appeals erred in holding that the officers' actions did not violate the Sixth Amendment standards established in *Massiah* and its progeny.

Second, because of its erroneous determination that petitioner was not questioned in violation of Sixth Amendment standards, the Court of Appeals improperly conducted its "fruits" analysis under the Fifth Amendment. Specifically, it applied *Elstad,* to hold that the admissibility of the jailhouse statements turns solely on whether the statements were " 'knowingly and voluntarily made.' " The Court of Appeals did not reach the question whether the Sixth Amendment requires suppression of petitioner's jailhouse statements on the ground that they were the fruits of previous questioning conducted in violation of the Sixth Amendment deliberate-elicitation standard. We have not had occasion to decide whether the rationale of *Elstad* applies when a suspect makes incriminating statements after a knowing and voluntary waiver of his right to counsel notwithstanding earlier police questioning in violation of Sixth Amendment standards. We therefore remand to the Court of Appeals to address this issue in the first instance. Accordingly, the judgment of the Court of Appeals is reversed, and the case is remanded for further proceedings consistent with this opinion. It is so ordered.

Part III

PRETRIAL PROCEEDINGS

Chapter 8

EYEWITNESS IDENTIFICATION, PHYSICAL CHARACTERISTICS, AND THE RIGHT TO COUNSEL

A. LINEUPS AND SHOWUPS

UNITED STATES v. WADE

Supreme Court of the United States, 1967.
388 U.S. 218, 87 S.Ct. 1926, 18 L.Ed.2d 1149.

MR. JUSTICE BRENNAN delivered the opinion of the Court.

The question here is whether courtroom identifications of an accused at trial are to be excluded from evidence because the accused was exhibited to the witnesses before trial at a post-indictment lineup conducted for identification purposes without notice to and in the absence of the accused's appointed counsel.

The federally insured bank in Eustace, Texas, was robbed on September 21, 1964. A man with a small strip of tape on each side of his face entered the bank, pointed a pistol at the female cashier and the vice president, the only persons in the bank at the time, and forced them to fill a pillowcase with the bank's money. The man then drove away with an accomplice who had been waiting in a stolen car outside the bank. [Wade was indicted for robbery and for conspiring to rob the bank. Wade was arrested, counsel was appointed to represent him, and] fifteen days later an FBI agent, without notice to Wade's lawyer, arranged to have the two bank employees observe a lineup made up of Wade and five or six other prisoners and conducted in a courtroom of the local county courthouse. Each person in the line wore strips of tape such as allegedly worn by the robber and upon direction each said something like "put the money in the bag," the words allegedly uttered by the robber. Both bank employees identified Wade in the lineup as the bank robber.

At trial, the two employees, when asked on direct examination if the robber was in the courtroom, pointed to Wade. The prior lineup identification was then elicited from both employees on cross-examination. At the close of testimony, Wade's counsel moved for a judgment of acquittal or, alternatively, to strike the bank officials' courtroom identifications on the ground that conduct of the lineup, without notice to and in the absence of his appointed counsel, violated his Fifth Amendment privilege against self-incrimination and his Sixth Amendment right to the assistance of counsel. The motion was denied, and Wade was convicted. [The Court of Appeals for the Fifth Circuit reversed the conviction and ordered a new trial at which the in-court identification evidence was to be excluded. The Supreme Court set the case for oral argument with *Gilbert* v. *California.* and *Stovall* v. *Denno,* which presented similar questions (and which are discussed in the Commentary following *Wade*), reversed the judgment of the Court of Appeals in *Wade*, and remanded to that court with direction to enter a new judgment vacating the conviction and remanding the case to the District Court for further proceedings.]

I.

Neither the lineup itself nor anything shown by this record that Wade was required to do in the lineup violated his privilege against self-incrimination. We have only recently reaffirmed that the privilege "protects an accused only from being compelled to testify against himself, or otherwise provide the State with evidence of a testimonial or communicative nature.... " *Schmerber* v. *California*, 384 U.S. 757, 761. We there held that compelling a suspect to submit to a withdrawal of a sample of his blood for analysis for alcohol content and the admission in evidence of the analysis report were not compulsion to those ends. That holding was supported by the opinion in *Holt* v. *United States*, 218 U.S. 245, in which case a question arose as to whether a blouse belonged to the defendant. A witness testified at trial that the defendant put on the blouse and it had fit him. The defendant argued that the admission of the testimony was error because compelling him to put on the blouse was a violation of his privilege. The Court rejected the claim as "an extravagant extension of the Fifth Amendment," Mr. Justice Holmes saying for the Court:

> "The prohibition of compelling a man in a criminal court to be witness against himself is a prohibition of the use of physical or moral compulsion to extort communications from him, not an exclusion of his body as evidence when it may be material.".

* * *

We have no doubt that compelling the accused merely to exhibit his person for observation by a prosecution witness prior to trial involves no compulsion of the accused to give evidence having testimonial significance. It is compulsion of the accused to exhibit his physical characteristics, not compulsion to disclose any knowledge he might have. It is no different from compelling Schmerber to provide a blood sample or Holt to wear the blouse, and, as in those instances, is not within the cover of the privilege. Similarly, compelling Wade to speak within hearing distance of the witnesses, even to utter words purportedly uttered by the robber, was not compulsion to utter statements of a "testimonial" nature; he was required to use his voice as an identifying physical characteristic, not to speak his guilt. We held in *Schmerber* that the distinction to be drawn under the Fifth Amendment privilege against self-incrimination is one between an accused's "communications" in whatever form, vocal or physical, and "compulsion which makes a suspect or accused the source of 'real or physical evidence.'" We recognized that "both federal and state courts have usually held that ... [the privilege] offers no protection against compulsion to submit to fingerprinting, photography, or measurements, to write or speak for identification, to appear in court, to stand, to assume a stance, to walk, or to make a particular gesture." *Id*. None of these activities becomes testimonial within the scope of the privilege because required of the accused in a pretrial lineup.

Moreover, it deserves emphasis that this case presents no question of the admissibility in evidence of anything Wade said or did at the lineup which implicates his privilege. The Government offered no such evidence as part of its case, and what came out about the lineup proceedings on Wade's cross-examination of the bank employees involved no violation of Wade's privilege.

II.

The fact that the lineup involved no violation of Wade's privilege against self-incrimination does not, however, dispose of his contention that the courtroom identifications should have been excluded because the lineup was conducted without notice to and in the absence of his counsel. * * *

* * *

As early as *Powell* v. *Alabama* [287 U.S. 45 (1931)], we recognized that the period from arraignment to trial was "perhaps the most critical period of the proceedings ... ," during which the accused "requires the guiding hand of counsel ... ," if the guarantee is not to prove an empty right. That principle has since been applied to require the assistance of counsel at the type of arraignment—for example, that provided by Alabama—where certain rights might be sacrificed or lost: "What happens there may affect the whole trial. Available defenses may be irretrievably lost, if not then and there asserted.... " The principle was also applied in *Massiah* v. *United States*, 377 U.S. 201, where we held that incriminating statements of the defendant should have been excluded from evidence when it appeared that they were overheard by federal agents who, without notice to the defendant's lawyer, arranged a meeting between the defendant and an accomplice turned informant. "[A]nything less ... might deny a defendant 'effective representation by counsel at the only stage when legal aid and advice would help him.'"

* * *

[I]n addition to counsel's presence at trial, the accused is guaranteed that he need not stand alone against the State at any stage of the prosecution, formal or informal, in court or out, where counsel's absence might derogate from the accused's right to a fair trial. The security of that right is as much the aim of the right to counsel as it is of the other guarantees of the Sixth Amendment—the right of the accused to a speedy and public trial by an impartial jury, his right to be informed of the nature and cause of the accusation, and his right to be confronted with the witnesses against him and to have compulsory process for obtaining witnesses in his favor. The presence of counsel at such critical confrontations, as at the trial itself, operates to assure that the accused's interests will be protected consistently with our adversary theory of criminal prosecution.

In sum, the principle of *Powell* v. *Alabama* and succeeding cases requires that we scrutinize *any* pretrial confrontation of the accused to determine whether the presence of his counsel is necessary to preserve the defendant's basic right to a fair trial as affected by his right meaningfully to cross-examine the witnesses against him and to have effective assistance of counsel at the trial itself. It calls upon us to analyze whether potential substantial prejudice to defendant's rights inheres in the particular confrontation and the ability of counsel to help avoid that prejudice.

III.

The Government characterizes the lineup as a mere preparatory step in the gathering of the prosecution's evidence, not different—for Sixth Amendment purposes—from various other preparatory steps, such as systematized or scientific analyzing of the accused's fingerprints, blood sample, clothing, hair, and the like. We think there are differences which preclude such stages being characterized as critical stages at which the accused has the right to the presence of his counsel. Knowledge of the techniques of science and technology is sufficiently available, and the variables in techniques few enough, that the accused has the opportunity for a meaningful confrontation of the Government's case at trial through the ordinary processes of cross-examination of the Government's expert witnesses and the presentation of the evidence of his own experts. The denial of a right to have his counsel present at such analyses does not therefore violate the Sixth Amendment; they are not critical stages since there is minimal risk that his counsel's absence at such stages might derogate from his right to a fair trial.

IV.

But the confrontation compelled by the State between the accused and the victim or witnesses to a crime to elicit identification evidence is peculiarly riddled with innumerable dangers and variable factors which might seriously, even crucially, derogate from a fair trial. The vagaries of eyewitness identification are well-known; the annals of criminal law are rife with instances of mistaken identification. Mr. Justice Frankfurter once said: "What is the worth of identification testimony even when uncontradicted? The identification of strangers is proverbially untrustworthy. The hazards of such testimony are established by a formidable number of instances in the records of English and American trials. These instances are recent—not due to the brutalities of ancient criminal procedure." The Case of Sacco and Vanzetti 30 (1927). A major factor contributing to the high incidence of miscarriage of justice from mistaken identification has been the degree of suggestion inherent in the manner in which the prosecution presents the suspect to witnesses for pretrial identification. A commentator has observed that "the influence of improper suggestion upon identifying witnesses probably accounts for more miscarriages of justice than any other single factor—perhaps it is responsible for more such errors than all other factors combined." Suggestion can be created intentionally or unintentionally in many subtle ways. And the dangers for the suspect are particularly grave when the witness' opportunity for observation was insubstantial, and thus his susceptibility to suggestion the greatest.

Moreover, "it is a matter of common experience that, once a witness has picked out the accused at the line-up, he is not likely to go back on his word later on, so that in practice the issue of identity may (in the absence of other relevant evidence) for all practical purposes be determined there and then, before the trial."

The pretrial confrontation for purpose of identification may take the form of a lineup, also known as an "identification parade" or "showup," as in the present case, or presentation of the suspect alone to the witness, as in *Stovall* v. *Denno*. It is obvious that risks of suggestion attend either form of confrontation and increase the dangers inhering in eyewitness identification. But as is the case with secret interrogations, there is serious difficulty in depicting what transpires at lineups and other forms of identification confrontations. "Privacy results in secrecy and this in turn results in a gap in our knowledge as to what in fact goes on.... " *Miranda* v. *Arizona*. For the same reasons, the defense can seldom reconstruct the manner and mode of lineup identification for judge or jury at trial. Those participating in a lineup with the accused may often be police officers; in any event, the participants' names are rarely recorded or divulged at trial. The impediments to an objective observation are increased when the victim is the witness. Lineups are prevalent in rape and robbery prosecutions and present a particular hazard that a victim's understandable outrage may excite vengeful or spiteful motives. In any event, neither witnesses nor lineup participants are apt to be alert for conditions prejudicial to the suspect. And if they were, it would likely be of scant benefit to the suspect since neither witnesses nor lineup participants are likely to be schooled in the detection of suggestive influences. Improper influences may go undetected by a suspect, guilty or not, who experiences the emotional tension which we might expect in one being confronted with potential accusers. Even when he does observe abuse, if he has a criminal record he may be reluctant to take the stand and open up the admission of prior convictions. Moreover, any protestations by the suspect of the fairness of the lineup made at trial are likely to be in vain; the jury's choice is between the accused's unsupported version and that of the police officers present. In short, the accused's inability effectively to reconstruct at trial any unfairness that occurred at the lineup may deprive him of his only opportunity meaningfully to attack the credibility of the witness' courtroom identification.

What facts have been disclosed in specific cases about the conduct of pretrial confrontations for identification illustrate both the potential for substantial prejudice to the accused at that stage and the need for its revelation at trial. A commentator provides some striking examples:

> "In a Canadian case ... the defendant had been picked out of a lineup of six men, of which he was the only Oriental. In other cases, a black-haired suspect was placed among a group of light-haired persons, tall suspects have been made to stand with short nonsuspects, and, in a case where the perpetrator of the crime was known to be a youth, a suspect under twenty was placed in a line-up with five other persons, all of whom were forty or over."

* * *

The potential for improper influence is illustrated by the circumstances, insofar as they appear, surrounding the prior identifications in the three cases we decide today. In the present case, the testimony of the identifying witnesses elicited on cross-examination revealed that those witnesses were taken to the courthouse and seated in the courtroom to await assembly of the lineup. The courtroom faced on a hallway observable to the witnesses through an open door. The cashier testified that she saw Wade "standing in the hall" within sight of an FBI agent. Five or six other prisoners later appeared in the hall. The vice president testified that he saw a person in the hall in the custody of the agent who "resembled the person that we identified as the one that had entered the bank."

The lineup in *Gilbert* was conducted in an auditorium in which some 100 witnesses to several alleged state and federal robberies charged to Gilbert made wholesale identifications of Gilbert as the robber in each other's presence, a procedure said to be fraught with dangers of suggestion. And the vice of suggestion created by the identification in *Stovall,* was the presentation to the witness of the suspect alone handcuffed to police officers. It is hard to imagine a situation more clearly conveying the suggestion to the witness that the one presented is believed guilty by the police.

* * *

Since it appears that there is grave potential for prejudice, intentional or not, in the pretrial lineup, which may not be capable of reconstruction at trial, and since presence of counsel itself can often avert prejudice and assure a meaningful confrontation at trial, there can be little doubt that for Wade the post-indictment lineup was a critical stage of the prosecution at which he was "as much entitled to such aid [of counsel]

... as at the trial itself." Thus both Wade and his counsel should have been notified of the impending lineup, and counsel's presence should have been a requisite to conduct of the lineup, absent an "intelligent waiver." No substantial countervailing policy considerations have been advanced against the requirement of the presence of counsel. Concern is expressed that the requirement will forestall prompt identifications and result in obstruction of the confrontations. As for the first, we note that in the two cases in which the right to counsel is today held to apply, counsel had already been appointed and no argument is made in either case that notice to counsel would have prejudicially delayed the confrontations. Moreover, we leave open the question whether the presence of substitute counsel might not suffice where notification and presence of the suspect's own counsel would result in prejudicial delay. And to refuse to recognize the right to counsel for fear that counsel will obstruct the course of justice is contrary to the basic assumptions upon which this Court has operated in Sixth Amendment cases. We rejected similar logic in *Miranda* v. *Arizona* concerning presence of counsel during custodial interrogation:

> "[A]n attorney is merely exercising the good professional judgment he has been taught. This is not cause for considering the attorney a menace to law enforcement. He is merely carrying out what he is sworn to do under his oath—to protect to the extent of his ability the rights of his client. In fulfilling this responsibility the attorney plays a vital role in the administration of criminal justice under our Constitution."

In our view counsel can hardly impede legitimate law enforcement; on the contrary, for the reasons expressed, law enforcement may be assisted by preventing the infiltration of taint in the prosecution's identification evidence. That result cannot help the guilty avoid conviction but can only help assure that the right man has been brought to justice.

* * *

V.

We come now to the question whether the denial of Wade's motion to strike the courtroom identification by the bank witnesses at trial because of the absence of his counsel at the lineup required, as the Court of Appeals held, the grant of a new trial at which such evidence is to be excluded. We do not think this disposition can be justified without first giving the Government the opportunity to establish by clear and convincing evidence that the in-court identifications were based upon observations of the suspect other than the lineup identification. Where, as here, the admissibility of evidence of the lineup identification itself is not involved, a *per se* rule of exclusion of courtroom identification would be unjustified. A rule limited solely to the exclusion of testimony concerning identification at the lineup itself, without regard to admissibility of the courtroom identification, would render the right to counsel an empty one. The lineup is most often used, as in the present case, to crystallize the witnesses' identification of the defendant for future reference. We have already noted that the lineup identification will have that effect. The State may then rest upon the witnesses' unequivocal courtroom identification, and not mention the pretrial identification as part of the State's case at trial. Counsel is then in the predicament in which Wade's counsel found himself—realizing that possible unfairness at the lineup may be the sole means of attack upon the unequivocal courtroom identification, and having to probe in the dark in an attempt to discover and reveal unfairness, while bolstering the government witness' courtroom identification by bringing out and dwelling upon his prior identification. Since counsel's presence at the lineup would equip him to attack not only the lineup identification but the courtroom identification as well, limiting the impact of violation of the right to counsel to exclusion of evidence only of identification at the lineup itself disregards a critical element of that right.

We think it follows that the proper test to be applied in these situations is that quoted in *Wong Sun* v. *United States*, 371 U.S. 471, 488, " 'Whether, granting establishment of the primary illegality, the evidence to which instant objection is made has been come at by exploitation of that illegality or instead by means sufficiently distinguishable to be purged of the primary taint.' " Application of this test in the present context requires consideration of various factors; for example, the prior opportunity to observe the alleged criminal act, the existence of any discrepancy between any pre-lineup description and the defendant's actual description, any identification prior to lineup of another person, the identification by picture of the defendant prior to the lineup, failure to identify the defendant on a prior occasion, and the lapse of time between the alleged act and the lineup identification. It is also relevant to consider those facts which, despite the absence of counsel, are disclosed concerning the conduct of the lineup.

* * *

On the record now before us we cannot make the determination whether the in-court identifications had an independent origin. This was not an issue at trial, although there is some evidence relevant to a determination. That inquiry is most properly made in the District Court. We therefore think the appropriate procedure to be followed is to vacate the conviction pending a hearing to determine whether the in-court identifications had an independent source, or whether, in any event, the introduction of the evidence was harmless error * * *.

[CHIEF JUSTICE WARREN and JUSTICE DOUGLAS joined the opinion of the Court except for Part I, from which they dissented. JUSTICE CLARK'S concurring opinion and the opinion of JUSTICE FORTAS, concurring in part and dissenting in part, with whom CHIEF JUSTICE WARREN and JUSTICE DOUGLAS joined, are omitted.]

Mr. Justice Black, dissenting in part and concurring in part.

* * *

I.

In rejecting Wade's claim that his privilege against self-incrimination was violated by compelling him to appear in the lineup wearing the tape and uttering the words given him by the police, the Court relies on the recent holding in *Schmerber* v. *California*. In that case the Court held that taking blood from a man's body against his will in order to convict him of a crime did not compel him to be a witness against himself. I dissented from that holding, and still dissent. The Court's reason for its holding was that the sample of Schmerber's blood taken in order to convict him of crime was neither "testimonial" nor "communicative" evidence. I think it was both. It seems quite plain to me that the Fifth Amendment's Self-incrimination Clause was designed to bar the Government from forcing any person to supply proof of his own crime, precisely what Schmerber was forced to do when he was forced to supply his blood. The Government simply took his blood against his will and over his counsel's protest for the purpose of convicting him of crime. So here, having Wade in its custody awaiting trial to see if he could or would be convicted of crime, the Government forced him to stand in a lineup, wear strips on his face, and speak certain words, in order to make it possible for government witnesses to identify him as a criminal. Had Wade been compelled to utter these or any other words in open court, it is plain that he would have been entitled to a new trial because of having been compelled to be a witness against himself. Being forced by the Government to help convict himself and to supply evidence against himself by talking outside the courtroom is equally violative of his constitutional right not to be compelled to be a witness against himself. Consequently, because of this violation of the Fifth Amendment, and not because of my own personal view that the Government's conduct was "unfair," "prejudicial," or "improper," I would prohibit the prosecution's use of lineup identification at trial.

* * *

Mr. Justice White, whom Mr. Justice Harlan and Mr. Justice Stewart join, dissenting in part and concurring in part.

* * *

* * * The Court apparently believes that improper police procedures are so widespread that a broad prophylactic rule must be laid down, requiring the presence of counsel at all pretrial identifications, in order to detect recurring instances of police misconduct. I do not share this pervasive distrust of all official investigations. * * *

* * *

[R]equiring counsel at pretrial identifications as an invariable rule trenches on other valid state interests. One of them is its concern with the prompt and efficient enforcement of its criminal laws. Identifications frequently take place after arrest but before an indictment is returned or an information is filed. The police may have arrested a suspect on probable cause but may still have the wrong man. Both the suspect and the State have every interest in a prompt identification at that stage, the suspect in order to secure his immediate release and the State because prompt and early identification enhances *accurate* identification and because it must know whether it is on the right investigative track. Unavoidably, however, the absolute rule requiring the presence of counsel will cause significant delay and it may very well result in no pretrial identification at all. Counsel must be appointed and a time arranged convenient for him and the witnesses. Meanwhile, it may be necessary to file charges against the suspect who may then be released on bail, in the federal system very often on his own recognizance, with neither the State nor the defendant having the benefit of a properly conducted identification procedure.

* * *

Commentary

1. Justice Brennan authored the Supreme Court's opinions in *Wade* and its two companion cases, Gilbert v. California, 388 U.S. 263 (1967) and Stovall v. Denno, 388 U.S. 293 (1967), but the results in the three companion cases were not identical. Gilbert was sentenced to death after being convicted of armed robbery and the murder of a police officer. In his arguments relying upon the Fifth and Sixth Amendments, Gilbert challenged the admissibility of testimony by witnesses that they had identified him at a lineup held without notice to Gilbert's attorney although the lineup occurred more than two weeks after his indictment and the appointment of defense counsel; the admissibility of in-court identification testimony by other witnesses; and the admissibility of handwriting exemplars taken from him after his arrest.

Citing *Schmerber* v. *California*, the Supreme Court held that the taking of the handwriting exemplars did not violate Gilbert's Fifth Amendment privilege against self-incrimination because "[t]he privilege reaches only compulsion of "an accused's communications, whatever form they might take, [and not] "compulsion which makes a suspect or accused the source of 'real or physical evidence'.... " The Court held that "[a] mere handwriting exemplar, in contrast to the content of what is written, like the voice or body itself, is an identifying physical characteristic outside its protection. In addition, the Court found that the Sixth Amendment was not violated because taking the exemplars was not a "critical stage" in the criminal proceedings at which Gilbert was entitled to have the assistance of counsel. The Court noted that these handwriting exemplars were taken before both his indictment and the appointment of defense counsel. Although those procedural facts would seem to be dispositive under other Sixth Amendment decisions, including *Massiah* and *Wade*, the Court offered another rationale, as well. It concluded that the absence of counsel at the taking of the exemplars did not threaten Gilbert's right to a fair trial. Because it was possible for the defendant to produce additional exemplars, defense counsel could demonstrate any defects in the exemplars produced by the government. Quoting from *Wade*, the Court concluded that "the accused has the opportunity for a meaningful confrontation of the [State's] case at trial through the ordinary processes of cross-examination of the [State's] expert [handwriting] witnesses and the presentation of the evidence of his own [handwriting] experts."

Conversely, the admission of testimony by nine witnesses that they had identified Gilbert at the post-indictment lineup violated Gilbert's rights and he was entitled to a new trial, at least at the penalty stage, where eight of these witnesses had testified. He was not entitled to a new trial on the issue of guilt, however, if the California Supreme Court found that it had been harmless error to allow a ninth witness to testify about his lineup identification and to identify Gilbert in the courtroom at the guilt phase of the trial. Citing *Wade* again, the Court also held that the State was entitled to have "the opportunity to establish that the in-court identifications" of Gilbert by three witnesses who also had observed him at the lineup "had an independent source, or that their introduction in evidence was in any event harmless error."

2.   The Supreme Court has applied the *Wade-Gilbert* doctrine to identification techniques other than lineups. In United States v. Ash, 413 U.S. 300 (1973), the majority held the right to counsel inapplicable when the Government conducts a post-indictment photographic display where the suspect is not present personally. The majority opinion likened the identification from photographs to other trial-preparation interviews between the prosecutor and witnesses, and refused to extend the right to counsel to such pretrial preparation.

3.   In *Stovall v. Denno*, 388 U.S. 293 (1967), police officers employed a "showup" rather than a lineup. Stovall was convicted and sentenced to death for murder in which the victims wife was seriously wounded by her husband's assailant. Stovall was arrested the day after the murder and without being given time to obtain counsel, was taken by police officers to the wife's hospital room, where she was recovering from life-saving surgery. Stovall was handcuffed to one of the officers. The Supreme Court description of the identification included the following passage: "Petitioner was the only Negro in the room. Mrs. Behrendt identified him from her hospital bed after being asked by an officer whether he "was the man" and after petitioner repeated at the direction of an officer a "few words for voice identification." At the trial, both Mrs. Behrendt and the officers testified about the hospital identification and she also made an in-court identification of Stovall.

Stovall argued that the hospital room confrontation was "so unnecessarily suggestive and conducive to irreparable mistaken identification" that it violated his Fourteenth Amendment due process rights. Justice Brennan's opinion acknowledged that "[t]he practice of showing suspects singly to persons for the purpose of identification, and not as part of a lineup, has been widely condemned," but also concluded that the totality of the circumstances made an immediate hospital confrontation "imperative." The Court agreed with the lower court that Mrs. Behrendt was the only person in the world who could possibly exonerate Stovall. * * * The hospital was not far distant from the courthouse and jail. No one knew how long Mrs. Behrendt might live. Faced with the responsibility of identifying the attacker, with the need for immediate action and with the knowledge that Mrs. Behrendt could not visit the jail, the police followed the only feasible procedure and took Stovall to the hospital room. Under these circumstances, the usual police station line-up * * * was out of the question.

In these circumstances, even such a suggestive showup was held not to violate Stovall's due process rights. *Stovall* is not the only case in which the Supreme Court has affirmed the validity of an extremely suggestive showup.

4. One of those cases was Kirby v. Illinois, 406 U.S. 682 (1972), in which the plurality opinion affirmed that a pre-indictment showup violated neither the privilege against self-incrimination nor the right to counsel. A showup in which the suspect displayed only physical characteristics did not implicate the Fifth Amendment, which protects only testimonial communications. The Sixth Amendment was not triggered because "a person's Sixth and Fourteenth Amendment right to counsel attaches only at or after the time that adversary judicial proceedings have been initiated against him." A pre-indictment showup is not, therefore, a critical stage of the proceedings at which the suspect in entitled to be represented by counsel. In the following case, decided later that same year, the Court also rejected a claim that an investigative showup violated the suspect's due process rights.

NEIL v. BIGGERS

Supreme Court of the United States, 1972.
409 U.S. 188, 93 S.Ct. 375, 34 L.Ed.2d 401.

MR. JUSTICE POWELL delivered the opinion of the Court.

In 1965, after a jury trial in a Tennessee court, respondent was convicted of rape and was sentenced to 20 years' imprisonment. The State's evidence consisted in part of testimony concerning a station-house identification of respondent by the victim. The Tennessee Supreme Court affirmed. * * * Respondent then brought a federal habeas corpus action raising several claims. The District Court held in an unreported opinion that the station-house identification procedure was so suggestive as to violate due process. The Court of Appeals affirmed. * * *

We proceed, then, to consider respondent's due process claim. As the claim turns upon the facts, we must first review the relevant testimony at the jury trial and at the habeas corpus hearing regarding the rape and the identification. The victim testified at trial that on the evening of January 22, 1965, a youth with a butcher knife grabbed her in the doorway to her kitchen:

"A. [H]e grabbed me from behind, and grappled—twisted me on the floor. Threw me down on the floor.

"Q. And there was no light in that kitchen?

"A. Not in the kitchen.

"Q. So you couldn't have seen him then?

"A. Yes, I could see him, when I looked up in his face.

"Q. In the dark?

"A. He was right in the doorway—it was enough light from the bedroom shining through. Yes, I could see who he was.

"Q. You could see? No light? And you could see him and know him then?

"A. Yes."

When the victim screamed, her 12–year-old daughter came out of her bedroom and also began to scream. The assailant directed the victim to "tell her [the daughter] to shut up, or I'll kill you both." She did so, and was then walked at knifepoint about two blocks along a railroad track, taken into a woods, and raped there. She testified that "the moon was shining brightly, full moon." After the rape, the assailant ran off, and she returned home, the whole incident having taken between 15 minutes and half an hour.

She then gave the police what the Federal District Court characterized as "only a very general description," describing him as "being fat and flabby with smooth skin, bushy hair and a youthful voice." Additionally, though not mentioned by the District Court, she testified at the habeas corpus hearing that she had described her assailant as being between 16 and 18 years old and between five feet ten inches and six feet tall, as weighing between 180 and 200 pounds, and as having a dark brown complexion. This testimony was substantially corroborated by that of a police officer who was testifying from his notes.

On several occasions over the course of the next seven months, she viewed suspects in her home or at the police station, some in lineups and others in showups, and was shown between 30 and 40 photographs. She told the police that a man pictured in one of the photographs had features similar to those of her assailant, but identified none of the suspects. On August 17, the police called her to the station to view respondent, who was being detained on another charge. In an effort to construct a suitable lineup, the police checked the city jail and the city juvenile home. Finding no one at either place fitting respondent's unusual physical description, they conducted a showup instead.

The showup itself consisted of two detectives walking respondent past the victim. At the victim's request, the police directed respondent to say "shut up or I'll kill you." The testimony at trial was not altogether clear as to whether the victim first identified him and then asked that he repeat the words or made her identification after he had spoken. In any event, the victim testified that she had "no doubt" about her identification. At the habeas corpus hearing, she elaborated in response to questioning.

"A. That I have no doubt, I mean that I am sure that when I—see, when I first laid eyes on him, I knew that it was the individual, because his face—well, there was just something that I don't think I could ever forget. I believe—

"Q. You say when you first laid eyes on him, which time are you referring to?

"A. When I identified him—when I seen him in the courthouse when I was took up to view the suspect."

We must decide whether, as the courts below held, this identification and the circumstances surrounding it failed to comport with due process requirements.

III

We have considered on four occasions the scope of due process protection against the admission of evidence deriving from suggestive identification procedures. In Stovall v. Denno, 388 U.S. 293 (1967), the Court held that the defendant could claim that "the confrontation conducted * * * was so unnecessarily suggestive and conducive to irreparable mistaken identification that he was denied due process of law." This we held, must be determined "on the totality of the circumstances." We went on to find that on the facts of the case then before us, due process was not violated, emphasizing that the critical condition of the injured witness justified a showup in her hospital room. At trial, the witness, whose view of the suspect at the time of the crime was brief, testified to the out-of-court identification, as did several police officers present in her hospital room, and also made an in-court identification.

Subsequently, in a case where the witnesses made in-court identifications arguably stemming from previous exposure to a suggestive photographic array, the Court restated the governing test:

"[W]e hold that each case must be considered on its own facts, and that convictions based on eye-witness identification at trial following a pretrial identification by photograph will be set aside on that ground only if the photographic identification procedure was so impermissibly suggestive as to give rise to a very substantial likelihood of irreparable misidentification." Simmons v. United States, 390 U.S. 377, 384 (1968).

Again we found the identification procedure to be supportable, relying both on the need for prompt utilization of other investigative leads and on the likelihood that the photographic identifications were reliable, the witnesses having viewed the bank robbers for periods of up to five minutes under good lighting conditions at the time of the robbery.

The only case to date in which this Court has found identification procedures to be violative of due process is Foster v. California, 394 U.S. 440 (1969). There, the witness failed to identify Foster the first time he confronted him, despite a suggestive lineup. The police then arranged a showup, at which the witness could make only a tentative identification. Ultimately, at yet another confrontation, this time a lineup, the witness was able to muster a definite identification. We held all of the identifications inadmissible, observing that the identifications were "all but inevitable" under the circumstances.

In the most recent case of Coleman v. Alabama, 399 U.S. 1 (1970), we held admissible an in-court identification by a witness who had a fleeting but "real good look" at his assailant in the headlights of a passing car. The witness testified at a pretrial suppression hearing that he identified one of the petitioners among the participants in the lineup before the police placed the participants in a formal line. Mr. Justice Brennan for four members of the Court stated that this evidence could support a finding that the in-court identification was "entirely based upon observations at the time of the assault and not at all induced by the conduct of the lineup."

Some general guidelines emerge from these cases as to the relationship between suggestiveness and misidentification. It is, first of all, apparent that the primary evil to be avoided is a very substantial likelihood of irreparable misidentification. * * * It is the likelihood of misidentification which violates a defendant's right to due process, and it is this which was the basis of the exclusion of evidence in *Foster*. Suggestive confrontations are disapproved because they increase the likelihood of misidentification, and unnecessarily suggestive ones are condemned for the further reason that the increased chance of misidentification is gratuitous. But as *Stovall* makes clear, the admission of evidence of a showup without more does not violate due process.

What is less clear from our cases is whether, as intimated by the District Court, unnecessary suggestiveness alone requires the exclusion of evidence. While we are inclined to agree with the courts below that the police did not exhaust all possibilities in seeking persons physically comparable to respondent, we do not think that the evidence must therefore be excluded. The purpose of a strict rule barring evidence of unnecessarily suggestive confrontations would be to deter the police from using a less reliable procedure where a more reliable one may be available, and would not be based on the assumption that in every instance the admission of evidence of such a confrontation offends due process. * * *

We turn, then, to the central question, whether under the "totality of the circumstances" the identification was reliable even though the confrontation procedure was suggestive. As indicated by our cases, the factors to be considered in evaluating the likelihood of misidentification include the opportunity of the witness to view the criminal at the time of the crime, the witness' degree of attention, the accuracy of the witness' prior description of the criminal, the level of certainty demonstrated by the witness at the confrontation, and the length of time between the crime and the confrontation. Applying these factors, we disagree with the District Court's conclusion.

* * *

We find that the District Court's conclusions on the critical facts are unsupported by the record and clearly erroneous. The victim spent a considerable period of time with her assailant, up to half an hour. She was with him under adequate artificial light in her house and under a full moon outdoors, and at least twice, once in the house and later in the woods, faced him directly and intimately. She was no casual observer, but rather the victim of one of the most personally humiliating of all crimes. Her description to the police, which included the assailant's approximate age, height, weight, complexion, skin texture, build, and voice, might not have satisfied Proust but was more than ordinarily thorough. She had "no doubt" that respondent was the person who raped her. In the nature of the crime, there are rarely witnesses to a rape other than the victim, who often has a limited opportunity of observation. The victim here, a practical nurse by profession, had an unusual opportunity to observe and identify her assailant. She testified at the habeas corpus hearing that there was something about his face "I don't think I could ever forget."

There was, to be sure, a lapse of seven months between the rape and the confrontation. This would be a seriously negative factor in most cases. Here, however, the testimony is undisputed that the victim made no previous identification at any of the showups, lineups, or photographic showings. Her record for reliability was thus a good one, as she had previously resisted whatever suggestiveness inheres in a showup. Weighing all the factors, we find no substantial likelihood of misidentification. The evidence was properly allowed to go to the jury.

Affirmed in part, reversed in part, and remanded.

[The opinion of JUSTICE BRENNAN, with whom JUSTICE DOUGLAS and JUSTICE STEWART joined, concurring in part, is omitted.]

Commentary

1. Eyewitness identifications to serve at least two important functions. First, identification of suspects by victims and eyewitnesses allows police officers to focus their investigations upon some suspects and to eliminate other people as suspects. Second, in-court identification of a defendant as the perpetrator of a crime by a victim or eyewitness can be persuasive evidence that the defendant is in fact the criminal. Given the importance of eyewitness identification in the decision-making by police, prosecutor, judge, and jury, it is surprising that actors in the criminal justice system long have recognized the unreliability of this evidence. Consider, for example, the characterization of eyewitness identification testimony by the California Supreme Court in People v. Wright, 43 Cal.3d 399, 233 Cal.Rptr. 89, 729 P.2d 280 (1987). Relying on an earlier decision, the court reaffirmed the rule "that in appropriate cases it is error to exclude expert testimony on psychological factors shown by the evidence that may affect the accuracy of an eyewitness identification of the defendant." The court then held that in addition, in appropriate cases defendants were entitled to request and obtain "instructions cautioning the jurors on the dangers of mistaken identification and focusing their attention on such factors."

In *Wright*, defense counsel had requested an instruction focusing the jury's attention on certain psychological factors that could affect the accuracy of the eyewitness identifications in this case. The proposal is based on a well-known model instruction originally promulgated in *United States v. Telfaire* (D.C.Cir.1972) 469 F.2d 552, 558–559, for use in the federal district court for the District of Columbia. The *Telfaire* instruction has been adopted in most federal circuits, and in the states of New York, Massachusetts, Kansas, and West Virginia; in other states it has met with resistance on various grounds.

The California Supreme reviewed the factors relied upon in its recent decision permitting expert testimony on the accuracy of eyewitness identification:

> * * * We began by recognizing, together with distinguished federal courts, that eyewitness identifications are often unreliable, particularly when a witness identifies a stranger on the basis of a single brief observation made in fear or under stress.

> Throughout our opinion we acknowledged, as numerous empirical studies have found, that certain psychological factors inherent in the observer or the event can adversely affect the accuracy of eyewitness identifications, and some of those factors "may be known only to some jurors, or may be imperfectly understood by many, or may be contrary to the intuitive beliefs of most." Such factors include "the effects or perception of an eyewitness' personal or cultural expectations or beliefs, the effects on memory of the witness' exposure to subsequent information or suggestions, and the effects on recall of bias or cues in identification procedures or methods of questioning." Others are "the pitfalls of cross-racial identification" and "the lack of correlation between the degree of confidence an eyewitness expresses in his identification and the accuracy of that identification."

2. In the following case, a defense attorney employed an unusual technique for challenging the reliability of the arresting officer's in-court identification of the defendant, his client. Was the attorney's conduct improper and deserving of sanctions? Or, was his behavior appropriate zealous advocacy designed to demonstrate the unreliability of eyewitness identification testimony? What should the court's fundamental concern be in reviewing this case? And what do the arresting officer's in-court identifications suggest about the effect of an earlier identification upon the witness's subsequent identification of the defendant at trial?

PEOPLE v. SIMAC (DAVID SOTOMAYOR, CONTEMNOR–APPELLANT)

Supreme Court of Illinois, 1994.
161 Ill.2d 297, 204 Ill.Dec. 192, 641 N.E.2d 416.

CHIEF JUSTICE BILANDIC delivered the opinion of the court:

The sole issue in this appeal is whether appellant, David Sotomayor, an attorney licensed to practice law in this State, was properly found in direct criminal contempt of court. * * *

The incident that gave rise to the contempt citation occurred during appellant's representation of defendant, Christopher Simac, for charges that arose from a car accident on March 20, 1990. Defendant was charged with driving with a revoked license and failure to yield while making a left-hand turn. After several delays, the case was called for trial on December 11, 1990. The State's only witness was Officer Ronald H. LaMorte. * * *

Before trial, appellant seated David P. Armanentos, a clerical worker employed at his law firm, next to him at counsel's table. Defendant was seated at another location in the courtroom. Armanentos and defendant shared similar physical characteristics, in that they were both tall, thin, dark blond-haired men who wore eyeglasses. On the date of trial, Armanentos wore a white shirt with blue stripes, while defendant was dressed in a white shirt with red stripes.

Appellant did not ask the court's permission, or notify the court that he had substituted Armanentos in the customary place for a defendant at counsel's table. The State's Attorney also was not notified of the substitution. The court ordered all witnesses who were going to testify to come forth and be sworn. The clerk asked appellant, "Is your defendant [going to be sworn]?" Appellant replied, "No."

In the State's case in chief Officer LaMorte testified regarding the automobile accident that he investigated on March 20, 1990, which resulted in injuries to a woman and her young child. He described the intersection where the accident occurred and the position of the cars. LaMorte testified that he asked defendant for identification; however, he believed that defendant was unable to produce his driver's license.

LaMorte identified Armanentos, who was seated next to appellant at counsel's table, as the person who was involved in the accident. The court noted LaMorte's identification of Armanentos as the defendant for the record. Appellant did not inform the court of the misidentification at this time or reveal that defendant was seated elsewhere in the courtroom.

After the State rested its case in chief appellant made a motion to exclude witnesses. The motion was granted, and LaMorte left the courtroom. Appellant then called Armanentos, the person whom LaMorte previously identified, as a witness. Armanentos was sworn at this time, as he did not come forward to be sworn when the court called for witnesses at the beginning of the trial. When Armanentos stated his name for the record, the court received the first indication that a misidentification had occurred.

On direct examination, Armanentos testified that he was not driving a motor vehicle at the intersection in question on March 20, 1990. The defense then rested. Under cross-examination, Armanentos testified that he had never met defendant. He stated that he temporarily worked as a clerical employee in the appellant's law firm. It was his understanding that he was brought to court by appellant and instructed to sit at counsel's table to see whether the testifying officer would identify him as the defendant. Armanentos testified that he was told that he resembled defendant. He further admitted that he looked similar to defendant, as they were both tall, thin, and Caucasian. In response to the court's inquiry, Armanentos admitted that he did not approach the clerk to be sworn in as a witness before the commencement of the trial.

Appellant stated for the record that Armanentos never approached the bench. He was not sworn in, and was seated in the corner of the courtroom until appellant directed him to sit in the chair next to him. Appellant argued that no fraud was perpetrated on the court, for defendant was in open court as required. He asked that a directed finding of not guilty be entered in the traffic case based on the misidentification.

After appellant said that he did not intend to call any further witnesses, the State called defendant to testify. After taking the stand and stating his name for the record, defendant invoked his fifth amendment privilege and was excused. The court refused the State's request to call appellant as a witness. The State then asked that defendant take his position next to his attorney. The court replied: "He can sit any place he wants to in the courtroom. He is here." Over appellant's objection, the court allowed the State to recall LaMorte. LaMorte again misidentified Armanentos as the defendant. The court granted appellant's request for a directed finding of not guilty based upon the misidentification. In addition, the court entered an order for contempt of court against the appellant for placing the witness in such a manner as to mislead the State's Attorney and the arresting officer. The court stated that the person seated next to appellant did not look like co-counsel or anyone employed in an attorney's office. The court stated that appellant had seated Armanentos next to him to purposely mislead the court. The order prepared by the court stated that "defense attorney is held in direct contempt of court for having a person bearing the likeness of [defendant] sit at the counsel table with him in the location usually occupied by defendant." The court imposed a $500 fine on appellant for direct criminal contempt.

* * *

On appeal, a divided appellate court affirmed the judgment of direct criminal contempt, but reduced the fine from $500 to $100. * * *

It is well established law that all courts have the inherent power to punish contempt; such power is essential to the maintenance of their authority and the administration of judicial powers. This court has defined criminal contempt of court " 'as conduct which is calculated to embarrass, hinder or obstruct a court in its administration of justice or derogate from its authority or dignity, thereby bringing the administration of law into disrepute.' "

Direct criminal contempt is contemptuous conduct occurring "in the very presence of the judge, making all of the elements of the offense matters within his own personal knowledge." On appeal, the standard of review for direct criminal contempt is whether there is sufficient evidence to support the finding of contempt and whether the judge considered facts outside of the judge's personal knowledge.

I. INTENT

In contending that the appellate court's holding violates principles of direct criminal contempt, appellant argues that the intent necessary to support a conviction of direct criminal contempt was not within the circuit court's personal knowledge and, therefore, his conviction must be overturned. In this regard, appellant argues that he has an ethical obligation to vigorously represent his client. Appellant asserts that, by placing a substitute at counsel's table, he merely intended in good faith to fulfill his ethical duties of zealous advocacy by testing the veracity of the State's identification testimony. Appellant argues that he was operating in unchartered waters, and that his intent was to facilitate rather than impede the administration of justice by preventing the conviction of a potentially innocent defendant based on a tainted in-court identification. He asserts that there was no evidence known to the court to establish an intent to obstruct the administration of justice or to derogate from the court's dignity or authority. Therefore, appellant asserts that, by its holding, the appellate court has improperly eliminated from the offense of direct criminal contempt the intent to embarrass, hinder, derogate, or obstruct the court. * * *

We find that appellant's conduct clearly reveals that his intent was not merely to test the State's identification testimony. Rather, we find that appellant intended to cause a misidentification, thereby misleading not only the State and its witness but also the court itself. Appellant commissioned a clerical employee from his office to sit with him at the defendant's customary place at counsel's table. Appellant's employee resembled the defendant in important identification characteristics. Moreover, both the substitute and the defendant wore glasses and were similarly dressed. Under these circumstances, we find that appellant calculated to cause a misidentification.

Additionally, appellant's conduct before the court indicates appellant's intent to create a misapprehension and thereby cause a misidentification. It is evident to us that appellant's conduct was intended to deceive. For instance, appellant responded in the negative to the clerk's direct inquiry as to whether his defendant would be sworn. Appellant responded negatively even though, at the same time, he obviously anticipated that the substitute would eventually testify as a witness concerning the misidentification. Clearly, appellant was aware that the only inference the court could draw from the totality of these circumstances was that the person sitting next to appellant at counsel's table was the defendant and that the defendant was not going to testify at trial.

Most revealing of appellant's intent to deceive, however, was appellant's failure to correct the court and the record upon the court's erroneous statement for the record that the witness had identified the defendant. At this point, as an officer of the court, appellant had a responsibility to the court and the integrity of the proceedings to correct the court and the record. When the court made the erroneous statement for the record, appellant clearly knew that the court was laboring wider a misconception as to the identity of the defendant, yet he took no action to correct the court's mistaken impression. If appellant had not calculated to cause such a misconception, he would have taken some action to clarify the defendant's identity.

As this court has stated, "An attorney's zeal to serve his client should never be carried to the extent of * * * seeking to secure from a court an order or judgment without a full and frank disclosure of all matters and facts which the court ought to know." The true identity of the defendant is clearly a fact "which the court ought to know" because it is the responsibility of the court to ensure the defendant's right to be present at all stages of the proceedings against him. Therefore, an attorney must not deceive the court as to the defendant's identity despite the attorney's obligation to vigorously represent his client. Such a deception prevents the court from fulfilling its obligation and derogates from the court's dignity and authority.

Furthermore, we reject appellant's claim that he merely intended in good faith to test the veracity of the State's identification testimony. Appellant could have easily achieved this purpose without resorting to deceptive and misleading practices. Many alternative methods are available to an attorney to test identification testimony. These available alternatives include conducting an in-court lineup, having defendant sit in the gallery without placing a substitute at counsel's table, or placing more than one person at counsel's table. It is readily apparent, therefore, that appellant could have achieved his goal as an advocate without misleading or deceiving the court, the State, and the witness and thereby remained within the bounds of his responsibilities as an officer of the court.

For the foregoing reasons, we conclude that there is sufficient evidence in the record to support appellant's conviction for direct criminal contempt. Appellant's actions derogated from the court's dignity and authority by causing the court to erroneously find for the record that the witness had identified the defendant, and his conduct delayed the proceedings. In view of appellant's actions and the surrounding circumstances, we find that appellant's conduct was calculated to and actually did embarrass, hinder, and obstruct the court and the proceedings.

II. PROFESSIONAL RESPONSIBILITY

* * *

Before closing, we note that our determination in this case is supported by cases decided in other jurisdictions. These decisions have refused to allow the practice of placing a substitute at counsel's table without notifying the court of the attorney's intent to do so. For instance, in United States v. Thoreen (9th Cir.1981), 653 F.2d 1332, an attorney representing a defendant accused of violating a preliminary injunction against salmon fishing decided to test the witness' identification by placing at counsel's table another person who resembled the defendant. The substitute was dressed in outdoor clothing, while the defendant was dressed in a business suit and sat behind the rail in a row normally reserved for the press. Defense counsel neither notified the prosecutor nor asked the court's permission to arrange this substitution. On defense counsel's motion at the start of the trial, the court ordered all witnesses excluded from the courtroom. However, the substitute remained seated next to defense counsel. Throughout the trial, defense counsel did not correct any mistaken representation of the court when it expressly referred to the substitute as the defendant for the record. Two government witnesses misidentified the substitute as the defendant. Following the prosecutor's case in chief, defense counsel called the substitute as a witness and disclosed the substitution. The prosecutor was allowed to reopen his case. Defendant was identified by an agent who had cited him for two of the violations, and was ultimately convicted.

Based upon defense counsel's substitution of another individual for defendant at counsel's table, the district court found him in criminal contempt. On review, the Ninth Circuit rejected defense counsel's argument that his conduct was a good-faith tactic to aid cross-examination. The court held that the substitution crossed over the line from zealous advocacy to actual obstruction because it delayed the proceedings in the time taken for the witnesses' misidentification of the defendant. In addition, it violated the custom practiced in Federal and State courts of general jurisdiction to allow only counsel, parties, and others having the court's permission to sit at counsel's table.

Most importantly, the defense counsel's subversive tactics impeded the court's ability to ascertain the truth. The *Thoreen* court noted that making misrepresentations to the court is inappropriate and unprofessional behavior. The guidelines promulgated in that State's code of professional responsibility to guide an attorney's conduct explicitly decree that an attorney's participation in the presentation or participation of false evidence is unprofessional and subjects him to discipline. * * *

* * *

For the reasons stated, the judgment of the appellate court, which affirmed the judgment of the circuit court in finding appellant guilty of direct criminal contempt but reduced the fine imposed to $100, is affirmed.

JUSTICE NICKELS, dissenting:

I do not agree that placing an individual in the defendant's customary place at counsel's table, without more, is a sufficient basis from which to infer an intent to hinder or obstruct the administration of justice or impugn the integrity of the court. After a thorough review of the record, I believe that defense counsel was acting in good faith to protect his client from a suggestive in-court identification. * * *

Under different circumstances, I agree that placing someone other than the defendant at counsel's table could evidence the contemptuous intent necessary to support a contempt charge. The *Thoreen* case relied upon by the appellate court and the majority provides an example. *Thoreen* involved the trial of a salmon fisherman for violating an injunction against salmon fishing. First, the character of the defense attorney's conduct in *Thoreen* showed an intent to mislead the court. The defense attorney in *Thoreen* actually disguised the person seated in defendant's place at counsel's table by dressing him in outdoor clothing, including heavy shoes, a plaid shirt and a jacket-vest. Unlike the contemnor below, the defense attorney in *Thoreen* actually gestured to the imposter as though he were the defendant and conferred with him during the trial.

Second, there were no circumstances in *Thoreen* showing a need to test the reliability of the State's identification, as identification was not in issue. In using a disguise where identification was not in issue and gesturing to the defendant as his client, the attorney in *Thoreen* was not acting in good-faith representation of his client but was engaging in conduct calculated to obstruct the administration of justice.

I recognize that several jurisdictions which have considered the issue require counsel to inform the court before testing an in-court identification by placing someone other than defendant at counsel's table. I agree with the majority that there are a variety of better ways to protect a defendant from such suggestive in-court identifications, including in-court lineups or other experiments done with the court's permission. The issue presented for review is not whether counsel made the best choice, but whether his specific conduct showed disregard for the court's authority and the administration of justice. A review of the record shows defense counsel was respectful at all times. Counsel did not misrepresent the identity of defendant in any way and attempted in good faith to test the veracity of the State's case. Under these facts, I believe counsel successfully charted a narrow pathway through a questionable course of conduct.

For the reasons stated, I would vacate the order finding defense counsel in direct criminal contempt of court. Therefore, I respectfully dissent.

JUSTICES HARRISON and MCMORROW join in this dissent.

Commentary

Treating the reliability of identification testimony as a constitutional issue is at odds with the tradition that it is for the jury to weigh credibility of witnesses and decide whether the defendant committed the crime. This central function of the jury has been relied upon by the Supreme Court in some of its identification decisions: "Juries are not so susceptible that they cannot measure intelligently the weight of identification testimony that has some questionable feature." Manson v. Brathwaite, 432 U.S. 98 (1977). Consequently, courts (especially appellate courts) are reluctant to find identification procedures unnecessarily suggestive, and still more reluctant to hold that testimony of a crime victim who made a positive identification was incurably tainted by some flaw in the way identification procedures were conducted.

For a case in which an appellate court did overturn a conviction on the basis of flaws in the identification procedure, see State v. Rosette, 653 So.2d 80 (La.App.1995). In *Rosette* an undercover narcotics officer (Lewis) made four "buys" within an hour from different persons whom she had never seen before. She then identified defendant as one of the sellers in a photo lineup. The state appellate court describe the problem with the photo lineup:

> Officer Lewis testified she perceived the defendant as being a black male, about 5'6" or 5'7", and weighing about 135 pounds. Four (4) photographs were shown to Officer Lewis. All of the photographs display black males. Two of the photographs display black males in front of a height chart, with both their heights being approximately 6'5". The defendant's photograph, the one selected by Officer Lewis, shows defendant in front of a height chart, with his height being about 5'6". The remaining photograph is of a black male with no height chart shown. However, the male in the remaining photograph appears to be in his mid-thirties while Officer Lewis' report describes defendant as a black male in his late teens. We find that the presence of the height chart in three of the four photographs, coupled with the significant difference in age between the suspect and the man in the fourth photograph, unduly focused attention on Rosette as the only person in the line-up whose height and age fit Officer Lewis' description. Because the photographs improperly singled out the defendant, this line-up was unduly suggestive.

The Louisiana court went on to explain that

> Assuming a suggestive identification procedure, courts must look to several factors to determine, from the totality of the circumstances, whether the suggestive identification presents a substantial likelihood of misidentification. These factors were initially set out in Neil v. Biggers, 409 U.S. 188, 199–200 (1972), and approved in *Brathwaite*, [432 U.S. 98 (1977)]. They include: (1) the opportunity of the witness to view the criminal at the time of the crime; (2) the witness's degree of attention; (3) the accuracy of his prior description of the criminal; (4) the level of certainty demonstrated at the confrontation; and (5) the time between the crime and the confrontation. "Against these factors is to be weighed the corrupting effect of the suggestive identification itself."

> In other words, even where an identification is considered suggestive it is usually still necessary to evaluate the likelihood of misidentification. It is only where the identification violates both of these tests that a defendant's right to due process has been violated.

The court then found that the second part of the constitutional identification test was met and the conviction should be reversed because

> Officer Lewis only had a brief opportunity to view the suspect. We further note that these transactions were occurring in rapid succession, lasting only minutes, and involving strangers. Even conceding that

Officer Lewis' attention was focused on each dealer during each transaction, the possibility for an erroneous identification is great under these circumstances.

Is a decision like *Rosette* likely to force the police to conduct these "drug buy" stings under circumstances which provide reliable identification of the identity of the drug seller?

B. *MIRANDA*, TESTIMONIAL COMMUNICATION, AND PHYSICAL CHARACTERISTICS

PENNSYLVANIA v. MUNIZ

Supreme Court of the United States, 1990.
496 U.S. 582, 110 S.Ct. 2638, 110 L.Ed.2d 528.

JUSTICE BRENNAN delivered the opinion of the Court, except as to Part III–C.

I

[Respondent Muniz was arrested for drunk driving after he failed field sobriety tests, and was taken to the local jail booking center.] Following its routine practice for receiving persons suspected of driving while intoxicated, the Booking Center videotaped the ensuing proceedings. Muniz was informed that his actions and voice were being recorded, but he was not at this time (nor had he been previously) advised of his [*Miranda*] rights. Officer Hosterman first asked Muniz his name, address, height, weight, eye color, date of birth, and current age. He responded to each of these questions, stumbling over his address and age. The officer then asked Muniz, "Do you know what the date was of your sixth birthday?" After Muniz offered an inaudible reply, the officer repeated, "When you turned six years old, do you remember what the date was?" Muniz responded, "No, I don't." Hosterman next requested Muniz to perform each of the three sobriety tests that Muniz had been asked to perform earlier during the initial roadside stop. The videotape reveals that his eyes jerked noticeably during the gaze test, that he did not walk a very straight line, and that he could not balance himself on one leg for more than several seconds. During the latter two tests, he did not complete the requested verbal counts from one to nine and from one to thirty. Moreover, while performing these tests, Muniz attempted to explain his difficulties in performing the various tasks, and often requested further clarification of the tasks he was to perform.

Finally, Officer Deyo asked Muniz to submit to a breathalyzer test. Officer Deyo read to Muniz the Commonwealth's Implied Consent Law, and explained that under the law his refusal to take the test would result in automatic suspension of his drivers' license for one year. Muniz asked a number of questions about the law, commenting in the process about his state of inebriation. Muniz ultimately refused to take the breath test. At this point, Muniz was for the first time advised of his *Miranda* rights. Muniz then signed a statement waiving his rights and admitted in response to further questioning that he had been driving while intoxicated. Both the video and audio portions of the videotape were admitted into evidence at Muniz's bench trial, along with the arresting officer's testimony that Muniz failed the roadside sobriety tests and made incriminating remarks at that time. Muniz was convicted of driving under the influence of alcohol. * * *

[The state appellate court reversed the conviction, holding that Muniz' statements on the videotape were testimonial and communicative, and that therefore the audio portion of the videotape should have been suppressed as obtained in violation of *Miranda*.]

II

* * * Because Muniz was not advised of his *Miranda* rights until after the videotaped proceedings at the Booking Center were completed, any verbal statements that were both testimonial in nature and elicited during custodial interrogation should have been suppressed. We focus first on Muniz's responses to the initial informational questions, then on his questions and utterances while performing the physical dexterity and balancing tests, and finally on his questions and utterances surrounding the breathalyzer test.

III

In the initial phase of the recorded proceedings, Officer Hosterman asked Muniz his name, address, height, weight, eye color, date of birth, current age, and the date of his sixth birthday. Both the delivery and content of Muniz's answers were incriminating. * * * The Commonwealth argues, however, that admission of Muniz's answers to these questions does not contravene Fifth Amendment principles because Muniz's statement regarding his sixth birthday was not "testimonial" and his answers to the prior questions were not elicited by custodial interrogation. We consider these arguments in turn.

A

We agree with the Commonwealth's contention that Muniz's answers are not rendered inadmissible by *Miranda* merely because the slurred nature of his speech was incriminating. * * * Under *Schmerber* and its progeny, any slurring of speech and other evidence of lack of muscular coordination revealed by Muniz's responses to Officer Hosterman's direct questions constitute nontestimonial components of those responses. Requiring a suspect to reveal the physical manner in which he articulates words, like requiring him to reveal the physical properties of the sound produced by his voice does not, without more, compel him to provide a testimonial response for purposes of the privilege.

B

This does not end our inquiry, for Muniz's answer to the sixth birthday question was incriminating, not just because of his delivery, but also because of his answer's content: the trier of fact could infer from

Muniz's answer (that he did not know the proper date) that his mental state was confused. The Commonwealth and United States as amicus curiae argue that this incriminating inference does not trigger the protections of the Fifth Amendment privilege because the inference concerns "the physiological functioning of Muniz's brain," which is asserted to be every bit as "real or physical" as the physiological makeup of his blood and the timbre of his voice.

But this characterization addresses the wrong question; that the "fact" to be inferred might be said to concern the physical status of Muniz's brain merely describes the way in which the inference is incriminating. The correct question for present purposes is whether the incriminating inference of mental confusion is drawn from a testimonial act or from physical evidence. * * *

We recently explained in Doe v. United States, 487 U.S. 201 (1988), that "in order to be testimonial, an accused's communication must itself, explicitly or implicitly, relate a factual assertion or disclose information." * * * At its core, the privilege reflects our fierce "unwillingness to subject those suspected of crime to the cruel trilemma of self-accusation, perjury or contempt," that defined the operation of the Star Chamber, wherein suspects were forced to choose between revealing incriminating private thoughts and forsaking their oath by committing perjury. * * * Whenever a suspect is asked for a response requiring him to communicate an express or implied assertion of fact or belief, the suspect confronts the "trilemma" of truth, falsity, or silence and hence the response (whether based on truth or falsity) contains a testimonial component.

* * * When Officer Hosterman asked Muniz if he knew the date of his sixth birthday and Muniz, for whatever reason, could not remember or calculate that date, he was confronted with the trilemma. By hypothesis the inherently coercive environment created by the custodial interrogation precluded the option of remaining silent. Muniz was left with the choice of incriminating himself by admitting that he did not then know the date of his sixth birthday, or answering untruthfully by reporting a date that he did not then believe to be accurate (an incorrect guess would be incriminating as well as untruthful). The content of his truthful answer supported an inference that his mental faculties were impaired, because his assertion (he did not know the date of his sixth birthday) was different from the assertion (he knew the date was [correct date]) that the trier of fact might reasonably have expected a lucid person to provide. Hence, the incriminating inference of impaired mental faculties stemmed, not just from the fact that Muniz slurred his response, but also from a testimonial aspect of that response. * * *

C

The Commonwealth argues that the seven questions asked by Officer Hosterman just prior to the sixth birthday question—regarding Muniz's name, address, height, weight, eye color, date of birth, and current age—did not constitute custodial interrogation. * * * In Rhode Island v. Innis, 446 U.S. 291 (1980), [we said that the functional equivalent of express questioning includes] "any words or actions on the part of the police (other than those normally attendant to arrest and custody) that the police should know are reasonably likely to elicit an incriminating response from the suspect. The latter portion of this definition focuses primarily upon the perceptions of the suspect, rather than the intent of the police." * * * We disagree with the Commonwealth's contention that Officer Hosterman's first seven questions regarding Muniz's name, address, height, weight, eye color, date of birth, and current age do not qualify as custodial interrogation as we defined the term in *Innis* merely because the questions were not intended to elicit information for investigatory purposes. * * * We agree with amicus United States, however, that Muniz's answers to these first seven questions are nonetheless admissible because the questions fall within a "routine booking question" exception which exempts from *Miranda's* coverage questions to secure the biographical data necessary to complete booking or pretrial services. * * * In this context, therefore, the first seven questions asked at the Booking Center fall outside the protections of *Miranda* and the answers thereto need not be suppressed.

IV

During the second phase of the videotaped proceedings, Officer Hosterman asked Muniz to perform the same three sobriety tests that he had earlier performed at roadside prior to his arrest. While Muniz was attempting to comprehend the instructions and then perform the requested sobriety tests, he made several audible and incriminating statements. [The majority opinion held that these statements, and the statements Muniz volunteered after being asked to submit to a breathalyzer examination, were not in response to interrogation and were admissible.]

V

We agree with the state court's conclusion that *Miranda* requires suppression of Muniz's response to the question regarding the date of his sixth birthday, but we do not agree that the entire audio portion of the videotape must be suppressed. Accordingly, the court's judgment reversing Muniz's conviction is vacated, and the case is remanded for further proceedings not inconsistent with this opinion.

CHIEF JUSTICE REHNQUIST, with whom JUSTICE WHITE, JUSTICE BLACKMUN and JUSTICE STEVENS join, concurring in part, concurring in the result in part, and dissenting in part.

I join Parts I, II, III–A, and IV of the Court's opinion. In addition, although I agree with the conclusion in Part III–C that the seven "booking" questions should not be suppressed, I do so for a reason different from that of Justice Brennan. I dissent from the Court's conclusion that Muniz' response to the "sixth birthday question" should have been suppressed. * * *

The sixth birthday question here was an effort on the part of the police to check how well Muniz was able to do a simple mathematical exercise. Indeed, had the question related only to the date of his birth, it presumably would have come under the "booking exception" to which the Court refers elsewhere in its opinion. The Court holds in this very case that Muniz may be required to perform a "horizontal gaze nystagmus" test, and "the walk and turn" test, and the "one leg stand" test, all of which are designed to test a suspect's physical coordination. If the police may require Muniz to use his body in order to demonstrate the level of his physical coordination, there is no reason why they should not be able to require him to speak or write in order to determine his mental coordination. * * *

For substantially the same reasons, Muniz' responses to the videotaped "booking" questions were not testimonial and do not warrant application to the privilege. Thus, it is unnecessary to determine whether the questions fall within the "routine booking question" exception to *Miranda* Justice Brennan recognizes.

I would reverse in its entirety the judgment of the Superior Court of Pennsylvania. But given the fact the five members of the Court agree that Muniz' response to the sixth birthday question should have been suppressed, I agree that the judgment of the Superior Court should be vacated so that on remand, the court may consider whether admission of the response at trial was harmless error.

JUSTICE MARSHALL, concurring in part and dissenting in part.

I concur in Part III–B of the Court's opinion that the "sixth birthday question" required a testimonial response from respondent Muniz. Because the police did not apprise Muniz of his Miranda rights before asking the question, his response should have been suppressed.

I disagree, however, with the plurality's recognition in Part III–C of a "routine booking question" exception to *Miranda*. Moreover, even were such an exception warranted, it should not extend to booking questions that the police should know are reasonably likely to elicit incriminating responses. Because the police in this case should have known that the seven booking questions were reasonably likely to elicit incriminating responses and because those questions were not preceded by *Miranda* warnings, Muniz's testimonial responses should have been suppressed.

I dissent from the Court's holding in Part IV that Muniz's testimonial statements in connection with the three sobriety tests and the breathalyzer test were not the products of custodial interrogation. The police should have known that the circumstances in which they confronted Muniz, combined with the detailed instructions and questions concerning the tests and the State's Implied Consent Law, were reasonably likely to elicit an incriminating response, and therefore constituted the "functional equivalent" of express questioning. Rhode Island v. Innis, 446 U.S. 291, 301 (1980). Muniz's statements to the police in connection with these tests thus should have been suppressed because he was not first given the Miranda warnings. Finally, the officer's directions to Muniz to count aloud during two of the sobriety tests sought testimonial responses, and Muniz's responses were incriminating. Because Muniz was not informed of his Miranda rights prior to the tests, those responses also should have been suppressed. * * *

Chapter 9

PRETRIAL DETENTION AND RELEASE

A. JUDICIAL REVIEW OF PRETRIAL DETENTION

GERSTEIN v. PUGH

Supreme Court of the United States, 1975.
420 U.S. 103, 95 S.Ct. 854, 43 L.Ed.2d 54.

MR. JUSTICE POWELL delivered the opinion of the Court.

The issue in this case is whether a person arrested under a prosecutor's information is constitutionally entitled to a judicial determination of probable cause for pretrial restraint of liberty.

I

In March 1971 respondents Pugh and Henderson were arrested in Dade County, Florida. Each was charged with several offenses under a prosecutor's information. Pugh was denied bail because one of the charges against him carried a potential life sentence, and Henderson remained in custody because he was unable to post a $4,500 bond.

In Florida, indictments are required only for prosecution of capital offenses. Prosecutors may charge all other crimes by information, without a prior preliminary hearing and without obtaining leave of court. At the time respondents were arrested, a Florida rule seemed to authorize adversary preliminary hearings to test probable cause for detention in all cases. But the Florida courts had held that the filing of an information foreclosed the suspect's right to a preliminary hearing. They had also held that habeas corpus could not be used, except perhaps in exceptional circumstances, to test the probable cause for detention under an information. The only possible methods for obtaining a judicial determination of probable cause were a special statute allowing a preliminary hearing after 30 days, and arraignment, which the District Court found was often delayed a month or more after arrest. As a result, a person charged by information could be detained for a substantial period solely on the decision of a prosecutor.

Respondents Pugh and Henderson filed a class action against Dade County officials in the Federal District Court, claiming a constitutional right to a judicial hearing on the issue of probable cause and requesting declaratory and injunctive relief. * * *

[The District Court granted the relief sought and the Court of Appeals affirmed. Gerstein, the prosecuting attorney of Dade County, petitioned for review in the Supreme Court.]

II

As framed by the proceedings below, this case presents two issues; whether a person arrested and held for trial on an information is entitled to a judicial determination of probable cause for detention, and if so, whether the adversary hearing ordered by the District Court and approved by the Court of Appeals is required by the Constitution.

A

Both the standards and procedures for arrest and detention have been derived from the Fourth Amendment and its common-law antecedents. The standard for arrest is probable cause, defined in terms of facts and circumstances "sufficient to warrant a prudent man in believing that the [suspect] had committed or was committing an offense." Beck v. Ohio, 379 U.S. 89, 91. This standard, like those for searches and seizures, represents a necessary accommodation between the individual's right to liberty and the State's duty to control crime. * * *

Maximum protection of individual rights could be assured by requiring a magistrate's review of the factual justification prior to any arrest but such a requirement would constitute an intolerable handicap for legitimate law enforcement. Thus, while the Court has expressed a preference for the use of arrest warrants when feasible, it has never invalidated an arrest supported by probable cause solely because the officers failed to secure a warrant.

Under this practical compromise, a policeman's on-the-scene assessment of probable cause provides legal justification for arresting a person suspected of crime, and for a brief period of detention to take the administrative steps incident to arrest. Once the suspect is in custody, however, the reasons that justify dispensing with the magistrate's neutral judgment evaporate. There no longer is any danger that the suspect will escape or commit further crimes while the police submit their evidence to a magistrate. And, while the State's reasons for taking summary action subside, the suspect's need for a neutral determination of probable cause increases significantly. The consequences of prolonged detention may be more serious than the interference occasioned by arrest. Pretrial confinement may imperil the suspect's job, interrupt his source of income, and impair his family relationships. Even pretrial release may be accompanied by burdensome conditions that effect a significant restraint on liberty. When the stakes are this high, the detached judgment of a neutral magistrate is essential if the Fourth

Amendment is to furnish meaningful protection from unfounded interference with liberty. Accordingly, we hold that the Fourth Amendment requires a judicial determination of probable cause as a prerequisite to extended restraint on liberty following arrest. * * *

B

Under the Florida procedures challenged here, a person arrested without a warrant and charged by information may be jailed or subjected to other restraints pending trial without any opportunity for a probable cause determination. Petitioner defends this practice on the ground that the prosecutor's decision to file an information is itself a determination of probable cause that furnishes sufficient reason to detain a defendant pending trial. Although a conscientious decision that the evidence warrants prosecution affords a measure of protection against unfounded detention, we do not think prosecutorial judgment standing alone meets the requirements of the Fourth Amendment. Indeed, we think the Court's previous decisions compel disapproval of the Florida procedure. In Albrecht v. United States, 273 U.S. 1, 5 (1927), the Court held that an arrest warrant issued solely upon a United States Attorney's information was invalid because the accompanying affidavits were defective. Although the Court's opinion did not explicitly state that the prosecutor's official oath could not furnish probable cause, that conclusion was implicit in the judgment that the arrest was illegal under the Fourth Amendment.[6] * * *

In holding that the prosecutor's assessment of probable cause is not sufficient alone to justify restraint on liberty pending trial, we do not imply that the accused is entitled to judicial oversight or review of the decision to prosecute. Instead, we adhere to the Court's prior holding that a judicial hearing is not prerequisite to prosecution by information. Nor do we retreat from the established rule that illegal arrest or detention does not void a subsequent conviction. Thus, as the Court of Appeals noted below, although a suspect who is presently detained may challenge the probable cause for that confinement, a conviction will not be vacated on the ground that the defendant was detained pending trial without a determination of probable cause.

III

Both the District Court and the Court of Appeals held that the determination of probable cause must be accompanied by the full panoply of adversary safeguards—counsel, confrontation, cross-examination, and compulsory process for witnesses. A full preliminary hearing of this sort is modeled after the procedure used in many States to determine whether the evidence justifies going to trial under an information or

6. By contrast, the Court has held that an indictment "fair upon its face," and returned by a "properly constituted grand jury" conclusively determines the existence of probable cause and requires issuance of an arrest warrant without further inquiry. The willingness to let a grand jury's judgment substitute for that of a neutral and detached magistrate is attributable to the grand jury's relationship to the courts and its historical role of protecting individuals from unjust prosecution.

presenting the case to a grand jury. The standard of proof required of the prosecution is usually referred to as "probable cause," but in some jurisdictions it may approach a prima facie case of guilt. When the hearing takes this form, adversary procedures are customarily employed. The importance of the issue to both the State and the accused justifies the presentation of witnesses and full exploration of their testimony on cross-examination. This kind of hearing also requires appointment of counsel for indigent defendants. And, as the hearing assumes increased importance and the procedures become more complex, the likelihood that it can be held promptly after arrest diminishes.

These adversary safeguards are not essential for the probable cause determination required by the Fourth Amendment. The sole issue is whether there is probable cause for detaining the arrested person pending further proceedings. This issue can be determined reliably without an adversary hearing. The standard is the same as that for arrest. That standard—probable cause to believe the suspect has committed a crime—traditionally has been decided by a magistrate in a nonadversary proceeding on hearsay and written testimony, and the Court has approved these informal modes of proof.

* * *

The use of an informal procedure is justified not only by the lesser consequences of a probable cause determination but also by the nature of the determination itself. It does not require the fine resolution of conflicting evidence that a reasonable-doubt or even a preponderance standard demands, and credibility determinations are seldom crucial in deciding whether the evidence supports a reasonable belief in guilt. This is not to say that confrontation and cross-examination might not enhance the reliability of probable cause determinations in some cases. In most cases, however, their value would be too slight to justify holding, as a matter of constitutional principle, that these formalities and safeguards designed for trial must also be employed in making the Fourth Amendment determination of probable cause.

Because of its limited function and its nonadversary character, the probable cause determination is not a "critical stage" in the prosecution that would require appointed counsel. The Court has identified as "critical stages" those pretrial procedures that would impair defense on the merits if the accused is required to proceed without counsel. Coleman v. Alabama, 399 U.S. 1 (1970). In Coleman v. Alabama, where the Court held that a preliminary hearing was a critical stage of an Alabama prosecution, the majority and concurring opinions identified two critical factors that distinguish the Alabama preliminary hearing from the probable cause determination required by the Fourth Amendment. First, under Alabama law the function of the preliminary hearing was to determine whether the evidence justified charging the suspect with an offense. A finding of no probable cause could mean that he would not be tried at all. The Fourth Amendment probable cause determination is addressed only to pretrial custody. To be sure, pretrial custody may affect to some extent the defendant's ability to assist in preparation of his defense, but this does not present the high probability of substantial harm identified as controlling in *Coleman*. Second, Alabama allowed the suspect to confront and cross-examine prosecution witnesses at the preliminary hearing. The Court noted that the suspect's defense on the merits could be compromised if he had no legal assistance for exploring or preserving the witnesses' testimony. This consideration does not apply when the prosecution is not required to produce witnesses for cross-examination. * * *

IV

We agree with the Court of Appeals that the Fourth Amendment requires a timely judicial determination of probable cause as a prerequisite to detention, and we accordingly affirm that much of the judgment. As we do not agree that the Fourth Amendment requires the adversary hearing outlined in the District Court's decree, we reverse in part and remand to the Court of Appeals for further proceedings consistent with this opinion.

[The concurring opinion of JUSTICE STEWART, with whom JUSTICE DOUGLAS, JUSTICE BRENNAN, and JUSTICE MARSHALL joined, is omitted.]

COUNTY OF RIVERSIDE v. McLAUGHLIN

Supreme Court of the United States, 1991.
500 U.S. 44 , 111 S.Ct. 1661, 114 L.Ed.2d 49.

JUSTICE O'CONNOR delivered the opinion of the Court.

In *Gerstein* v. *Pugh*, 420 U.S. 103, 43 L.Ed.2d 54, 95 S.Ct. 854 (1975), this Court held that the Fourth Amendment requires a prompt judicial determination of probable cause as a prerequisite to an extended pretrial detention following a warrantless arrest. This case requires us to define what is "prompt" under *Gerstein*.

I

This is a class action brought under 42 U. S. C. § 1983 challenging the manner in which the County of Riverside, California (County), provides probable cause determinations to persons arrested without a warrant. At issue is the County's policy of combining probable cause determinations with its arraignment procedures. Under County policy * * * arraignments must be conducted without unnecessary delay and, in any event, within two days of arrest. This 2–day requirement excludes from computation weekends and holidays. Thus, an individual arrested without a warrant late in the week may in some cases be held for as long as five days before receiving a probable cause determination. Over the Thanksgiving holiday, a 7–day delay is possible.

[The District Court issued a preliminary injunction requiring the County to provide all persons arrested without a warrant a judicial determination of probable cause within 36 hours of arrest. The United States Court of Appeals for the Ninth Circuit affirmed.]

* * *

III

A

In *Gerstein*, this Court held unconstitutional Florida procedures under which persons arrested without a warrant could remain in police custody for 30 days or more without a judicial determination of probable cause. In reaching this conclusion we attempted to reconcile important competing interests. On the one hand, States have a strong interest in protecting public safety by taking into custody those persons who are reasonably suspected of having engaged in criminal activity, even where there has been no opportunity for a prior judicial determination of probable cause. On the other hand, prolonged detention based on incorrect or unfounded suspicion may unjustly "imperil [a] suspect's job, interrupt his source of income, and impair his family relationships." We sought to balance these competing concerns by holding that States "must provide a fair and reliable determination of probable cause as a condition for any significant pretrial restraint of liberty, and this determination must be made by a judicial officer either before *or promptly after* arrest." (emphasis added).

The Court thus established a "practical compromise" between the rights of individuals and the realities of law enforcement. Under *Gerstein*, warrantless arrests are permitted but persons arrested without a warrant must promptly be brought before a neutral magistrate for a judicial determination of probable cause. Significantly, the Court stopped short of holding that jurisdictions were constitutionally compelled to provide a probable cause hearing immediately upon taking a suspect into custody and completing booking procedures. We acknowledged the burden that proliferation of pretrial proceedings places on the criminal justice system and recognized that the interests of everyone involved, including those persons who are arrested, might be disserved by introducing further procedural complexity into an already intricate system. Accordingly, we left it to the individual States to integrate prompt probable cause determinations into their differing systems of pretrial procedures.

In so doing, we gave proper deference to the demands of federalism. We recognized that "state systems of criminal procedure vary widely" in the nature and number of pretrial procedures they provide, and we noted that there is no single "preferred" approach. We explained further that "flexibility and experimentation by the States" with respect to integrating probable cause determinations was desirable and that each State should settle upon an approach "to accord with [the] State's pretrial procedure viewed as a whole." Our purpose in *Gerstein* was to make clear that the Fourth Amendment requires every State to provide prompt determinations of probable cause, but that the Constitution does not impose on the States a rigid procedural framework. Rather, individual States may choose to comply in different ways.

* * *

B

Given that *Gerstein* permits jurisdictions to incorporate probable cause determinations into other pretrial procedures, some delays are inevitable. For example, where, as in Riverside County, the probable cause determination is combined with arraignment, there will be delays caused by paperwork and logistical problems. Records will have to be reviewed, charging documents drafted, appearance of counsel arranged, and appropriate bail determined. On weekends, when the number of arrests is often higher and available resources tend to be limited, arraignments may get pushed back even further. In our view, the Fourth Amendment permits a reasonable postponement of a probable cause determination while the police cope with the everyday problems of processing suspects through an overly burdened criminal justice system.

But flexibility has its limits; *Gerstein* is not a blank check. A State has no legitimate interest in detaining for extended periods individuals who have been arrested without probable cause. The Court recognized in *Gerstein* that a person arrested without a warrant is entitled to a fair and reliable determination of probable cause and that this determination must be made promptly.

Unfortunately, as lower court decisions applying *Gerstein* have demonstrated, it is not enough to say that probable cause determinations must be "prompt." This vague standard simply has not provided sufficient guidance. Instead, it has led to a flurry of systemic challenges to city and county practices, putting federal judges in the role of making legislative judgments and overseeing local jailhouse operations.

Our task in this case is to articulate more clearly the boundaries of what is permissible under the Fourth Amendment. Although we hesitate to announce that the Constitution compels a specific time limit, it is important to provide some degree of certainty so that States and counties may establish procedures with confidence that they fall within constitutional bounds. Taking into account the competing interests articulated in *Gerstein*, we believe that a jurisdiction that provides judicial determinations of probable cause within 48 hours of arrest will, as a general matter, comply with the promptness requirement of *Gerstein*. For this reason, such jurisdictions will be immune from systemic challenges.

This is not to say that the probable cause determination in a particular case passes constitutional muster simply because it is provided within 48 hours. Such a hearing may nonetheless violate *Gerstein* if the arrested individual can prove that his or her probable cause determination was delayed unreasonably. Examples of unreasonable delay are delays for the purpose of gathering additional evidence to justify the arrest, a delay motivated by ill will against the arrested individual, or delay for delay's sake. In evaluating whether the delay in a particular case is unreasonable, however, courts must allow a substantial degree of flexibility. Courts cannot ignore the often unavoidable delays in transporting arrested persons from one facility to another, handling late-night bookings where no magistrate is readily available, obtaining the presence of an arresting officer who may be busy processing other suspects or securing the premises of an arrest, and other practical realities.

Where an arrested individual does not receive a probable cause determination within 48 hours, the calculus changes. In such a case, the arrested individual does not bear the burden of proving an unreasonable delay. Rather, the burden shifts to the government to demonstrate the existence of a bona fide emergency or other extraordinary circumstance. The fact that in a particular case it may take longer than 48 hours to consolidate pretrial proceedings does not qualify as an extraordinary circumstance. Nor, for that matter, do intervening weekends. A jurisdiction that chooses to offer combined proceedings must do so as soon as is reasonably feasible, but in no event later than 48 hours after arrest.

* * *

Everyone agrees that the police should make every attempt to minimize the time a presumptively innocent individual spends in jail. One way to do so is to provide a judicial determination of probable cause immediately upon completing the administrative steps incident to arrest—*i.e.*, as soon as the suspect has been booked, photographed, and fingerprinted. [S]everal States, laudably, have adopted this approach. The Constitution does not compel so rigid a schedule, however. Under *Gerstein*, jurisdictions may choose to combine probable cause determinations with other pretrial proceedings, so long as they do so promptly. This necessarily means that only certain proceedings are candidates for combination. Only those proceedings that arise very early in the pretrial process—such as bail hearings and arraignments—may be chosen. Even then, every effort must be made to expedite the combined proceedings.

IV

For the reasons we have articulated, we conclude that Riverside County is entitled to combine probable cause determinations with arraignments. The record indicates, however, that the County's current policy and practice do not comport fully with the principles we have outlined. The County's current policy is to offer combined proceedings within two days, exclusive of Saturdays, Sundays, or holidays. As a result, persons arrested on Thursdays may have to wait until the following Monday before they receive a probable cause determination. The delay is even longer if there is an intervening holiday. Thus, the County's regular practice exceeds the 48–hour period we deem constitutionally permissible, meaning that the County is not immune from systemic challenges, such as this class action.

As to arrests that occur early in the week, the County's practice is that "arraignment[s] usually take place on the last day" possible. There may well be legitimate reasons for this practice; alternatively, this may constitute delay for delay's sake. We leave it to the Court of Appeals and the District Court, on remand, to make this determination. The judgment of the Court of Appeals is vacated, and the case is remanded for further proceedings consistent with this opinion. *It is so ordered.*

[The dissenting opinion of Justice MARSHALL, with whom Justice BLACKMUN and Justice STEVENS joined, is omitted.]

Justice SCALIA, dissenting.

* * *

I

The Court views the task before it as one of "balancing [the] competing concerns" of "protecting public safety," on the one hand, and avoiding "prolonged detention based on incorrect or unfounded suspicion," on the other hand. It purports to reaffirm the " 'practical compromise' " between these concerns struck in *Gerstein* v. *Pugh*. There is assuredly room for such an approach in resolving novel questions of search and seizure under the "reasonableness" standard that the Fourth Amendment sets forth. But not, I think, in resolving those questions on which a clear answer already existed in 1791 and has been generally adhered to by the traditions of our society ever since. As to those matters, the "balance" has already been struck, the "practical compromise" reached—and it is the function of the Bill of Rights to *preserve* that judgment, not only against the changing views of Presidents and Members of Congress, but also against the changing views of Justices whom Presidents appoint and Members of Congress confirm to this Court.

The issue before us today is of precisely that sort. As we have recently had occasion to explain, the Fourth Amendment's prohibition of "unreasonable seizures," insofar as it applies to seizure of the person, preserves for our citizens the traditional protections against unlawful arrest afforded by the common law. One of those—one of the most important of those—was that a person arresting a suspect without a warrant must deliver the arrestee to a magistrate "as soon as he reasonably can." It was clear, moreover, that the only element bearing upon the reasonableness of delay was not such circumstances as the pressing need to conduct further investigation, but the arresting officer's ability, once the prisoner had been secured, to reach a magistrate who could issue the needed warrant for further detention. Any detention beyond the period within which a warrant could have been obtained rendered the officer liable for false imprisonment.

We discussed and relied upon this common-law understanding in *Gerstein*, holding that the period of warrantless detention must be limited to the time necessary to complete the arrest and obtain the magistrate's review.

"[A] policeman's on-the-scene assessment of probable cause provides legal justification for arresting a person suspected of crime, and for a *brief period of detention to take the administrative steps incident to arrest*. Once the suspect is in custody ... the reasons that justify dispensing with the magistrate's neutral judgment *evaporate*." (emphasis added).

We said that "the Fourth Amendment requires a judicial determination of probable cause as a prerequisite to extended restraint of liberty," "either before or promptly after arrest." Though *how* "promptly" we did not say, it was plain enough that the requirement left no room for intentional delay unrelated to the completion of "the administrative steps incident to arrest." Plain enough, at least, that all but one federal court considering the question understood *Gerstein* that way.

* * *

II

* * *

With one exception, no federal court considering the question has regarded 24 hours as an inadequate amount of time to complete arrest procedures, and with the same exception every court actually setting a limit for a probable-cause determination based on those procedures has selected 24 hours. (The exception would not count Sunday within the 24–hour limit.). Federal courts have reached a similar conclusion in applying Federal Rule of Criminal Procedure 5(a), which requires presentment before a federal magistrate "without unnecessary delay." And state courts have similarly applied a 24–hour limit under state statutes requiring presentment without "unreasonable delay." New York, for example, has concluded that no more than 24 hours is necessary from arrest to *arraignment*. Twenty-nine States have statutes similar to New York's, which require either presentment or arraignment "without unnecessary delay" or "forthwith"; eight States explicitly require presentment or arraignment within 24 hours; and only seven States have statutes explicitly permitting a period longer than 24 hours. Since the States requiring a probable-cause hearing within 24 hours include both New York and Alaska, it is unlikely that circumstances of population or geography demand a longer period. [T]he American Bar Association * * * has recently concluded that no more than six hours should be required, except at night. * * *

* * * I would treat the time limit as a presumption; when the 24 hours are exceeded the burden shifts to the police to adduce unforeseeable circumstances justifying the additional delay.

* * *

* * * One hears the complaint, nowadays, that the Fourth Amendment has become constitutional law for the guilty; that it benefits the career criminal (through the exclusionary rule) often and directly, but the ordinary citizen remotely if at all. By failing to protect the innocent arrestee, today's opinion reinforces that view. The common-law rule of *prompt* hearing had as its primary beneficiaries the innocent—not those whose fully justified convictions must be overturned to scold the police; nor those who avoid conviction because the evidence, while convincing, does not establish guilt beyond a reasonable doubt; but those so blameless that there was not even good reason to arrest them. While in recent years we have invented novel applications of the Fourth Amendment to release the unquestionably guilty, we today repudiate one of its core applications so that the presumptively innocent may be left in jail. Hereafter a law-abiding citizen wrongfully arrested may be compelled to await the grace of a Dickensian bureaucratic machine, as it churns its cycle for up to two days—never once given the opportunity to show a judge that there is absolutely no reason to hold him, that a mistake has been made. In my view, this is the image of a system of justice that has lost its ancient sense of priority, a system that few Americans would recognize as our own. I respectfully dissent.

B. PREVENTIVE DETENTION AND BAIL

Introduction

According to the Supreme Court's opinion in *Gerstein v. Pugh*, the constitutionally indispensable function of the preliminary hearing is not the review of the decision to prosecute, but the more limited determination that sufficient probable cause exists to require the defendant to post bond or otherwise guarantee appearance at trial. Given that probable cause can be established by evidence that falls considerably short of the proof needed to establish guilt at trial, the Constitution does little to protect a defendant from having to stand trial on weakly supported charges. The Constitution also does little to guarantee defendants a right to remain at liberty before conviction.

It is of crucial importance to a defendant to obtain release from custody during the period of weeks or months that intervenes between the arrest and the end of the trial. Pretrial confinement is itself a punishment, especially given the deplorable conditions that prevail in city and county jails. Although the time spent in custody is credited against the eventual sentence, defendants are sometimes tempted to plead guilty just to get to the relatively more comfortable environment of the prison system. Defendants in custody normally lose their jobs; if free, they might be able to support their families and earn enough money to retain private counsel.

Most important, pretrial liberty increases the prospects for an ultimately successful defense. It permits the defendant to assist counsel by finding witnesses or persuading them to cooperate. The defendant in custody is under pressure to plead guilty to "get it over with," but the free defendant enters plea bargaining negotiations from a stronger position and can consider employing delaying tactics. Delay often works to the benefit of the defense, because the prosecution's witnesses may become unavailable or forgetful, and because old crimes sometimes seem less serious than recent ones. After conviction, the defendant who is at liberty has a better chance of staying out of jail than the defendant in custody. If the defendant has held a job all along and stayed out of trouble, the attorney can make a powerful argument for probation or a fine as the appropriate penalty rather than a jail sentence.

On the other hand, law enforcement authorities around the world claim that, if all defendants were released prior to trial, a significant number would flee, tamper with the prosecution's witnesses, or commit "other" crimes while at liberty. As a result, magistrates in nearly every country have the discretionary authority to order pretrial confinement of persons accused of serious crimes upon substantial evidence, if they feel that such confinement is necessary to prevent flight or to protect the safety of individuals or the community. In many countries, most particularly including those where the investigating authorities rely heavily on interrogation of the accused person, lengthy pretrial detention is extremely common.

Until recently American law was the exception, because the American legal tradition has theoretically granted defendants an absolute right to pretrial release, except when the prosecution is for a crime punishable by death, if they can post sufficient security with the court to assure that they will not flee. The security is usually in the form of money bail that will be forfeited in the event of non-appearance. The system thus assumes that defendants will appear for trial if they have a sufficient financial incentive to do so. In the traditional view, the likelihood of non-appearance is the *only* proper consideration in setting the amount of bail to be required. Because so many criminal defendants are poor, and because even a defendant with substantial income may have difficulty in raising several thousand dollars in cash, many defendants cannot "make bail." The problem is compounded by the fact that bail is frequently set at an amount governed by the seriousness of the alleged offense, without much regard to the personal and financial circumstances of the offender.

Enter the bail bondsman. When the magistrate sets bail in the hundreds or thousands of dollars, few defendants have the resources or the inclination to post the entire amount in cash or equivalent security with the court. For a fee (usually a little more than 10% of the amount of the bail), the bondsman will post a surety bond with the court in the full amount of the bail and obtain the release of the client. The bondsman is in a sense betting that the accused will appear for trial, and of course the success of his business depends upon the accuracy of his judgment. As a practical matter, the accused will be at liberty before trial if he can afford to pay the bondsman's premium and if the bondsman trusts him not to flee.

But how does the money bail system operate to ensure the presence of the accused for trial if it is the bondsman who suffers the financial loss in the event of flight? The accused pays only the bondsman's fee, which is not refunded even if he does appear. Three factors explain how the bail system enforces the obligation to appear: (1) The bondsman would soon go out of business if many clients absconded, and so he refuses to post bond in doubtful cases. (2) The bondsman will often insist that the accused provide collateral to secure at least part of the risk, sometimes in the form of guarantees signed by solvent relatives or friends. Thus the accused himself or persons whose interests he presumably values will ultimately stand the financial loss in many cases. (3) The bondsman has a common law power to arrest a client and surrender him to the court at any time. Although the bond is forfeited when the defendant absconds, the forfeiture will normally be set aside if the bondsman brings him into court within a reasonable time. A bondsman who faces a substantial loss may exhibit great energy and employ resources not available to conventional law enforcement agencies to apprehend and return the fugitive.

The money bail system has been attacked on constitutional grounds, principally on the theory that setting a price for pretrial release invidiously discriminates between the rich and poor in violation of the Equal Protection Clause of the Fourteenth Amendment, or that bail in an amount higher than the accused can meet is "excessive" bail within the meaning of the Eighth Amendment. In Stack v. Boyle, 342 U.S. 1 (1951), the Supreme Court granted relief to certain Communist Party leaders whose bail had been set at an arbitrarily high figure, but the Court had no criticism for the money bail system itself. The reforms that have been made have come from legislative or administrative innovations, rather than from constitutional decisions by the courts. The reforms have been of three types:

(1) "O.R. release" programs. The laws of many jurisdictions now give magistrates discretionary authority to release an accused upon his "own recognizance," i.e. an unsecured written promise to appear. Willful violation of this promise is itself a criminal offense. Privately or publicly funded projects in many cities provide personnel who interview detainees at the jails to determine if they are good "O.R. risks." The "O.R. projects" have helped many arrested persons to obtain pretrial freedom without paying a bondsman, but they can do little to help those who do not have steady employment, stable family ties, lengthy residence in the community or other indicia of reliability.

(2) "Citation release" provisions in many jurisdictions give either the arresting officer or the booking officer at the jail discretion to release minor offenders upon their written promise to appear. Where the officer has and uses this authority, the accused obtains what is in effect an O.R. release without staying in custody for the hours or days that may intervene between the arrest and the first appearance in court. Statutes in some jurisdictions also require officers to issue a citation or summons rather than to arrest for minor offenses where the defendant can produce adequate identification.

(3) The Federal Bail Reform Act of 1966, applicable only in the federal courts but imitated in some of the states, required the judge to order O.R. release in the absence of some indication that "such a release will not reasonably assure the appearance of the person as required." If O.R. release was not appropriate, the judge was directed to consider in order the following possibilities short of outright custody for guaranteeing appearance at trial: (1) placing the person in the custody of another person or organization; (2) placing restrictions on the defendant's travel, association or place of residence; (3) setting bail but allowing the defendant to meet it by making a refundable deposit of 10 percent of the amount in cash (thus depositing with the court the amount that would otherwise be paid to a bondsman); (4) requiring a traditional bail bond;

or (5) requiring the person to be in custody during specified hours. Although the Bail Reform Act left judges with discretion to set bail in an amount higher than the defendant could pay, its procedures encouraged serious consideration of O.R. release and other conditions that would allow the defendant to remain out of custody.

The Federal Bail Reform Act was substantially revised in 1984. As amended, the Act gave magistrates a wide range of alternatives to ensure both appearance at trial and the safety of the public, but forbade the imposition of "a financial condition that results in the pretrial detention of the person." On the other hand, the revised Act gave magistrates substantial discretion in specified circumstances to impose pretrial detention where: (1) there is a serious risk that the person will flee; or (2) there is a serious risk that the person will attempt to influence a witness or juror; or (3) detention is necessary to protect the safety of other persons or the community.

As has previously been indicated, the tradition in the United States until recently was that assuring the appearance of the defendant at trial was the only legitimate purpose of bail, and judges had no authority to order pretrial confinement of defendants to protect the public from the crimes they might commit if released. The tradition was ambiguous, however, because it was an open secret that judges frequently imposed de facto detention by setting bail in an amount higher than the defendant could afford. Moreover, the recognition of a right to bail in non-capital cases grew up during a period in which most serious crimes were punishable by death. Routine denial of bail in capital cases may have been based on a theory that a potential death sentence creates an enormous inducement to flight, rather than an assumption that capital offenders are inherently dangerous, but undoubtedly the exception for capital cases helped the courts to avoid the question of whether dangerousness could be an independent ground for detention.

Opponents of preventive pretrial detention have argued that the practice violates not only the Eighth Amendment's prohibition of "excessive bail," but also the "presumption of innocence," a phrase which is not found in the Constitution but is concededly part of our due process tradition. Supporters of detention have argued that the presumption is merely an aphoristic way of stating the rule that the prosecution has the burden *at trial* of proving the defendant's guilt, rather than the defendant of proving innocence, and that it has no application to pretrial matters such as bail and detention. This view finds support in the decision of the Supreme Court in Bell v. Wolfish, 441 U.S. 520 (1979), where the Court held that the presumption of innocence does not place any limitations on the conditions of confinement that may be imposed on a person who is detained before trial for failure to post bail. The opinion stated specifically that the presumption "has no application to a determination of the rights of a pretrial detainee during confinement before his trial has even begun."

The traditional ban on explicit preventive detention was challenged by the Nixon Administration, which persuaded Congress to authorize preventive pretrial detention for criminal prosecutions in the District of Columbia. This statute provoked a vigorous academic debate about constitutional principles, but its provisions were at first rarely employed.

It seems that judges desiring to impose detention found it easier simply to set high bail.

The 1984 Bail Reform Act included a sweeping preventive detention statute applicable in the federal system as a whole, and the laws of many states now also provide for pretrial detention of categories of dangerous defendants. The federal statute is the subject of the following case.

UNITED STATES v. SALERNO

Supreme Court of the United States, 1987.
481 U.S. 739, 107 S.Ct. 2095, 95 L.Ed.2d 697.

CHIEF JUSTICE REHNQUIST delivered the opinion of the Court. * * *

Responding to "the alarming problem of crimes committed by persons on release," Congress formulated the Bail Reform Act of 1984, 18 U.S.C. § 3141 *et seq.,* as the solution to a bail crisis in the federal courts. The Act represents the National Legislature's considered response to numerous perceived deficiencies in the federal bail process. By providing for sweeping changes in both the way federal courts consider bail applications and the circumstances under which bail is granted, Congress hoped to "give the courts adequate authority to make release decisions that give appropriate recognition to the danger a person may pose to others if released."

To this end, § 3141(a) of the Act requires a judicial officer to determine whether an arrestee shall be detained. Section 3142(e) provides that "[i]f, after a hearing pursuant to the provisions of subsection (f), the judicial officer finds that no condition or combination of conditions will reasonably assure the appearance of the person as required and the safety of any other person and the community, he shall order the detention of the person prior to trial." Section 3142(f) provides the arrestee with a number of procedural safeguards. He may request the presence of counsel at the detention hearing, he may testify and present witnesses in his behalf, as well as proffer evidence, and he may cross-examine other witnesses appearing at the hearing. If the judicial officer finds that no conditions of pretrial release can reasonably assure the safety of other persons and the community, he must state his findings of fact in writing, § 3142(i), and support his conclusion with "clear and convincing evidence," § 3142(f).

The judicial officer is not given unbridled discretion in making the detention determination. Congress has specified the considerations relevant to that decision. These factors include the nature and seriousness of the charges, the substantiality of the government's evidence against the arrestee, the arrestee's background and characteristics, and the nature and seriousness of the danger posed by the suspect's release. § 3142(g). Should a judicial officer order detention, the detainee is entitled to expedited appellate review of the detention order. §§ 3145(b), (c).

Respondents Anthony Salerno and Vincent Cafaro were arrested on March 21, 1986, after being charged in a 29–count indictment alleging various Racketeer Influenced and Corrupt Organizations Act (RICO) violations, mail and wire fraud offenses, extortion, and various criminal gambling violations. The RICO counts alleged 35 acts of racketeering activity, including fraud, extortion, gambling, and conspiracy to commit murder. At respondents' arraignment, the Government moved to have Salerno and Cafaro detained pursuant to § 3142(e), on the ground that no condition of release would assure the safety of the community or any person. The District Court held a hearing at which the Government made a detailed proffer of evidence. The Government's case showed that Salerno was the "boss" of the Genovese Crime Family of La Cosa Nostra and that Cafaro was a "captain" in the Genovese Family. According to the Government's proffer, based in large part on conversations intercepted by a court-ordered wiretap, the two respondents had participated in wide-ranging conspiracies to aid their illegitimate enterprises through violent means. The Government also offered the testimony of two of its trial witnesses, who would assert that Salerno personally participated in two murder conspiracies. Salerno opposed the motion for detention, challenging the credibility of the Government's witnesses. He offered the testimony of several character witnesses as well as a letter from his doctor stating that he was suffering from a serious medical condition. Cafaro presented no evidence at the hearing, but instead characterized the wiretap conversations as merely "tough talk."

The District Court granted the Government's detention motion, concluding that the Government had established by clear and convincing evidence that no condition or combination of conditions of release would ensure the safety of the community or any person:

> "The activities of a criminal organization such as the Genovese Family do not cease with the arrest of its principals and their release on even the most stringent of bail conditions. The illegal businesses, in place for many years, require constant attention and protection, or they will fail. Under these circumstances, this court recognizes a strong incentive on the part of its leadership to continue business as usual. When business as usual involves threats, beatings, and murder, the present danger such people pose in the community is self-evident." 631 F.Supp. 1364, 1375 (S.D.N.Y.1986).

[The Court of Appeals held that the Due Process Clause does not permit detention of accused persons simply as a means of preventing future crimes.] * * *

Respondents first argue that the Act violates substantive due process because the pretrial detention it authorizes constitutes impermissible punishment before trial. * * *

[The majority opinion held that the detention authorized by the Act is not "punishment" because it furthers the "regulatory" purpose of protecting the community from crime.]

We have repeatedly held that the government's regulatory interest in community safety can, in appropriate circumstances, outweigh an individual's liberty interest. For example, in times of war or insurrection, when society's interest is at its peak, the government may detain individuals whom the government believes to be dangerous. Even outside the exigencies of war, we have found that sufficiently compelling governmental interests can justify detention of dangerous persons. Thus, we have found no absolute constitutional barrier to detention of potentially dangerous resident aliens pending deportation proceedings. We have also held that the government may detain mentally unstable individuals who present a danger to the public, and dangerous defendants who become incompetent to stand trial. We have approved of postarrest regulatory detention of juveniles when they present a continuing danger to the community. *Schall v. Martin*, 467 U.S. 253 (1984). Even competent adults may face substantial liberty restrictions as a result of the operation of our criminal justice system. If the police suspect an individual of a crime, they may arrest and hold him until a neutral magistrate determines whether probable cause exists. *Gerstein v. Pugh*. Finally, respondents concede and the Court of Appeals noted that an arrestee may be incarcerated until trial if he presents a risk of flight, or a danger to witnesses.

Respondents characterize all of these cases as exceptions to the "general rule" of substantive due process that the government may not detain a person prior to a judgment of guilt in a criminal trial. Such a "general rule" may freely be conceded, but we think that these cases show a sufficient number of exceptions to the rule that the congressional action challenged here can hardly be characterized as totally novel. Given the well-established authority of the government, in special circumstances, to restrain individuals' liberty prior to or even without criminal trial and conviction, we think that the present statute providing for pretrial detention on the basis of dangerousness must be evaluated in precisely the same manner that we evaluated the laws in the cases discussed above. * * *

Respondents also contend that the Bail Reform Act violates the Excessive Bail Clause of the Eighth Amendment. * * *

The Eighth Amendment addresses pretrial release by providing merely that "Excessive bail shall not be required." This Clause, of course, says nothing about whether bail shall be available at all. Respondents nevertheless contend that this Clause grants them a right to bail calculated solely upon considerations of flight. They rely on *Stack v. Boyle*, 342 U.S. 1, 5 (1951), in which the Court stated that "Bail set at a figure higher than an amount reasonably calculated [to ensure the defendant's presence at trial] is 'excessive' under the Eighth Amendment." In respondents' view, since the Bail Reform Act allows a court essentially to set bail at an infinite amount for reasons not related to the risk of flight, it violates the Excessive Bail Clause. Respondents concede that the right to bail they have discovered in the Eighth Amendment is not absolute. A court may, for example, refuse bail in capital cases. And, as the Court of Appeals noted and respondents admit, a court may refuse bail when the defendant presents a threat to the judicial process by intimidating witnesses. Respondents characterize these exceptions as consistent with what they claim to be the sole purpose of bail—to ensure integrity of the judicial process.

While we agree that a primary function of bail is to safeguard the courts' role in adjudicating the guilt or innocence of defendants, we reject the proposition that the Eighth Amendment categorically prohibits the government from pursuing other admittedly compelling interests through regulation of pretrial release. * * * Nothing in the text of the Bail Clause limits permissible government considerations solely to questions of flight. The only arguable substantive limitation of the Bail Clause is that the government's proposed conditions of release or detention not be "excessive" in light of the perceived evil. Of course, to determine whether the government's response is excessive, we must compare that response against the interest the government seeks to protect by means of that response. Thus, when the government has admitted that its only interest is in preventing flight, bail must be set by a court at a sum designed to ensure that goal, and no more. *Stack v. Boyle, supra.* We believe that when Congress has mandated detention on the basis of a compelling interest other than prevention of flight, as it has here, the Eighth Amendment does not require release on bail.

III

In our society liberty is the norm, and detention prior to trial or without trial is the carefully limited exception. We hold that the provisions for pretrial detention in the Bail Reform Act of 1984 fall within that carefully limited exception. The Act authorizes the detention prior to trial of arrestees charged with serious felonies who are found after an adversary hearing to pose a threat to the safety of individuals or to the community which no condition of release can dispel. The numerous procedural safeguards detailed above must attend this adversary hearing. We are unwilling to say that this congressional determination, based as it is upon that primary concern of every government—a concern for the safety and indeed the lives of its citizens—on its face violates either the Due Process Clause of the Fifth Amendment or the Excessive Bail Clause of the Eighth Amendment.

The judgment of the Court of Appeals is therefore *Reversed*.

JUSTICE MARSHALL, with whom JUSTICE BRENNAN joins, dissenting.
* * *

[The dissent began by pointing out that, while this case was pending, Salerno was convicted on other charges in a separate prosecution and sentenced to 100 years in prison. The court which imposed that sentence nonetheless delayed its imposition, apparently with the Government's consent so that the preventive detention issue in this case would not become moot. Respondent Cafaro was actually released on bail in this case when he secretly agreed to become an informer for the Government. Thus, the issue in both cases could well have been moot.]

III

The essence of this case may be found, ironically enough, in a provision of the Act to which the majority does not refer. Title 18 U.S.C. § 3142(j) provides that "[n]othing in this section shall be construed as modifying or limiting the presumption of innocence." But the very pith and purpose of this statute is an abhorrent limitation of the presumption of innocence. The majority's untenable conclusion that the present Act is constitutional arises from a specious denial of the role of the Bail Clause and the Due Process Clause in protecting the invaluable guarantee afforded by the presumption of innocence. * * *

The statute now before us declares that persons who have been indicted may be detained if a judicial officer finds clear and convincing evidence that they pose a danger to individuals or to the community. The statute does not authorize the government to imprison anyone it has evidence is dangerous; indictment is necessary. But let us suppose that a defendant is indicted and the government shows by clear and convincing evidence that he is dangerous and should be detained pending a trial, at which trial the defendant is acquitted. May the government continue to hold the defendant in detention based upon its showing that he is dangerous? The answer cannot be yes, for that would allow the government to imprison someone for uncommitted crimes based upon "proof" not beyond a reasonable doubt. The result must therefore be that once the indictment has failed, detention cannot continue. But our fundamental principles of justice declare that the defendant is as innocent on the day before his trial as he is on the morning after his acquittal. Under this statute an untried indictment somehow acts to permit a detention, based on other charges, which after an acquittal would be unconstitutional. The conclusion is inescapable that the indictment has been turned into evidence, if not that the defendant is guilty of the crime charged, then that left to his own devices he will soon be guilty of something else.

To be sure, an indictment is not without legal consequences. It establishes that there is probable cause to believe that an offense was committed, and that the defendant committed it. Upon probable cause a warrant for the defendant's arrest may issue; a period of administrative detention may occur before the evidence of probable cause is presented to a neutral magistrate. Once a defendant has been committed for trial he may be detained in custody if the magistrate finds that no conditions of release will prevent him from becoming a fugitive. * * * The finding of probable cause conveys power to try, and the power to try imports of necessity the power to assure that the processes of justice will not be evaded or obstructed. The detention purportedly authorized by this statute bears no relation to the government's power to try charges supported by a finding of probable cause, and thus the interests it serves are outside the scope of interests which may be considered in weighing the excessiveness of bail under the Eighth Amendment. * * *

IV

There is a connection between the peculiar facts of this case and the evident constitutional defects in the statute which the Court upholds today. Respondent Cafaro was originally incarcerated for an indeterminate period at the request of the Government, which believed (or professed to believe) that his release imminently threatened the safety of the community. That threat apparently vanished, from the Government's point of view, when Cafaro agreed to act as a covert agent of the Government. There could be no more eloquent demonstration of the coercive power of authority to imprison upon prediction, or of the dangers which the almost inevitable abuses pose to the cherished liberties of a free society. * * * I dissent.

[JUSTICE STEVENS' dissenting opinion is omitted.]

C. RIGHT TO COUNSEL AT PRELIMINARY HEARINGS

COLEMAN v. ALABAMA

Supreme Court of the United States, 1970.
399 U.S. 1, 90 S.Ct. 1999, 26 L.Ed.2d 387.

MR. JUSTICE BRENNAN announced the judgment of the Court and delivered the following opinion.*

[The defendants were convicted in an Alabama Circuit Court of assault with intent to murder in the shooting of one Reynolds after he and his wife parked their car on an Alabama highway to change a flat tire. The Alabama Court of Appeals affirmed, the Alabama Supreme Court denied review, and the United States Supreme Court vacated the judgment and remanded the case. One of the defendants' arguments was that the preliminary hearing prior to their indictment was a "critical stage" of the prosecution and that Alabama's failure to provide them with appointed counsel at the hearing therefore unconstitutionally denied them the assistance of counsel.

* * *

II

This Court has held that a person accused of crime "requires the guiding hand of counsel at every step in the proceedings against him," *Powell* v. *Alabama*, 287 U.S. 45, 69 (1932), and that that constitutional principle is not limited to the presence of counsel at trial. "It is central to that principle that in addition to counsel's presence at trial, the accused is guaranteed that he need not stand alone against the State at any stage of the prosecution, formal or informal, in court or out, where counsel's absence might derogate from the accused's right to a fair trial." *United States* v. *Wade.* Accordingly, "the principle of *Powell* v. *Alabama* and succeeding cases requires that we scrutinize *any* pretrial confrontation of the accused to determine whether the presence of his counsel is necessary to preserve the defendant's basic right to a fair trial as affected by his right meaningfully to cross-examine the witnesses against him and to have effective assistance of counsel at the trial itself. It calls upon us to analyze whether potential substantial prejudice to

---

* JUSTICES DOUGLAS, WHITE, and BRENNAN joined in Part I of JUSTICE BRENNAN's opinion. JUSTICES DOUGLAS, WHITE, and MARSHALL joined in Part II. JUSTICES BLACK, DOUGLAS, WHITE, and MARSHALL joined in Part III.

defendant's rights inheres in the particular confrontation and the ability of counsel to help avoid that prejudice." Applying this test, the Court has held that "critical stages" include the pretrial type of arraignment where certain rights may be sacrificed or lost, and the pretrial lineup * * *.

The preliminary hearing is not a required step in an Alabama prosecution. The prosecutor may seek an indictment directly from the grand jury without a preliminary hearing. The opinion of the Alabama Court of Appeals in this case instructs us that under Alabama law the sole purposes of a preliminary hearing are to determine whether there is sufficient evidence against the accused to warrant presenting his case to the grand jury, and, if so, to fix bail if the offense is bailable. The court continued:

> "At the preliminary hearing ... the accused is not required to advance any defenses, and failure to do so does not preclude him from availing himself of every defense he may have upon the trial of the case. Also Pointer v. State of Texas [380 U.S. 400 (1965)] bars the admission of testimony given at a pre-trial proceeding where the accused did not have the benefit of cross-examination by and through counsel. Thus, nothing occurring at the preliminary hearing in absence of counsel can substantially prejudice the rights of the accused on trial."

This Court is of course bound by this construction of the governing Alabama law. However, from the fact that in cases where the accused has no lawyer at the hearing the Alabama courts prohibit the State's use at trial of anything that occurred at the hearing, it does not follow that the Alabama preliminary hearing is not a "critical stage" of the State's criminal process. The determination whether the hearing is a "critical stage" requiring the provision of counsel depends, as noted, upon an analysis "whether potential substantial prejudice to defendant's rights inheres in the ... confrontation and the ability of counsel to help avoid that prejudice." *United States* v. *Wade*. Plainly the guiding hand of counsel at the preliminary hearing is essential to protect the indigent accused against an erroneous or improper prosecution. First, the lawyer's skilled examination and cross-examination of witnesses may expose fatal weaknesses in the State's case that may lead the magistrate to refuse to bind the accused over. Second, in any event, the skilled interrogation of witnesses by an experienced lawyer can fashion a vital impeachment tool for use in cross-examination of the State's witnesses at the trial, or preserve testimony favorable to the accused of a witness who does not appear at the trial. Third, trained counsel can more effectively discover the case the State has against his client and make possible the preparation of a proper defense to meet that case at the trial. Fourth, counsel can also be influential at the preliminary hearing in making effective arguments for the accused on such matters as the necessity for an early psychiatric examination or bail.

The inability of the indigent accused on his own to realize these advantages of a lawyer's assistance compels the conclusion that the

Alabama preliminary hearing is a "critical stage" of the State's criminal process at which the accused is "as much entitled to such aid [of counsel] . . . as at the trial itself." *Powell* v. *Alabama*.

III

There remains, then, the question of the relief to which petitioners are entitled. The trial transcript indicates that the prohibition against use by the State at trial of anything that occurred at the preliminary hearing was scrupulously observed. But on the record it cannot be said whether or not petitioners were otherwise prejudiced by the absence of counsel at the preliminary hearing. That inquiry in the first instance should more properly be made by the Alabama courts. The test to be applied is whether the denial of counsel at the preliminary hearing was harmless error under *Chapman* v. *California*, 386 U.S. 18 (1967).

We accordingly vacate the petitioners' convictions and remand the case to the Alabama courts for such proceedings not inconsistent with this opinion as they may deem appropriate to determine whether such denial of counsel was harmless error, and therefore whether the convictions should be reinstated or a new trial ordered. *It is so ordered.*

MR. JUSTICE BLACKMUN took no part in the consideration or decision of this case.

MR. JUSTICE BLACK, concurring.

I wholeheartedly agree with the conclusion in Part II of the prevailing opinion that an accused has a constitutional right to the assistance of counsel at the preliminary hearing which Alabama grants criminal defendants. The purpose of the preliminary hearing in Alabama is to determine whether an offense has been committed and, if so, whether there is probable cause for charging the defendant with that offense. If the magistrate finds that there is probable cause for charging the defendant with the offense, the defendant must, under Alabama law, be either incarcerated or admitted to bail. In the absence of such a finding of probable cause, the defendant must be released from custody. The preliminary hearing is therefore a definite part or stage of a criminal prosecution in Alabama, and the plain language of the Sixth Amendment requires that "in all criminal prosecutions, the accused shall enjoy the right . . . to have the Assistance of Counsel for his defence." Moreover, every attorney with experience in representing criminal defendants in a State which has a preliminary hearing similar to Alabama's knows— sometimes from sad experience—that adequate representation requires that counsel be present at the preliminary hearing to protect the interests of his client. The practical importance of the preliminary hearing is discussed in the prevailing opinion, and the considerations outlined there seem to me more than sufficient to compel the conclusion that the preliminary hearing is a "critical stage" of the proceedings during which the accused must be afforded the assistance of counsel if he is to have a meaningful defense at trial as guaranteed in the Bill of Rights.

I fear that the prevailing opinion seems at times to proceed on the premise that the constitutional principle ultimately at stake here is not the defendant's right to counsel as guaranteed by the Sixth and Fourteenth Amendments but rather a right to a "fair trial" as conceived by judges. While that phrase is an appealing one, neither the Bill of Rights nor any other part of the Constitution contains it. The pragmatic, government-fearing authors of our Constitution and Bill of Rights did not, and I think wisely did not, use any such vague, indefinite, and elastic language. Instead, they provided the defendant with clear, emphatic guarantees: counsel for his defense, a speedy trial, trial by jury, confrontation with the witnesses against him, and other such unequivocal and definite rights. The explicit commands of the Constitution provide a full description of the kind of "fair trial" the Constitution guarantees, and in my judgment that document leaves no room for judges either to add to or detract from these commands. * * *.

* * *

[The concurring opinions of JUSTICE DOUGLAS and JUSTICE WHITE, the opinion of JUSTICE HARLAN, concurring in part and dissenting in part, and the dissenting opinions of CHIEF JUSTICE BURGER and JUSTICE STEWART, are omitted.]

Commentary

The Fifth Amendment requires that prosecutions in federal cases for "infamous" crimes (i.e. felonies) be commenced by grand jury indictment. This is also the accepted practice in about one-third of the states. A majority of the states permit felony prosecutions to be brought by either information or indictment, and in these "information states" the use of the grand jury is exceptional. A few states permit the prosecutor to file an information directly in court without first going through a preliminary hearing, perhaps with supporting affidavits to establish probable cause, but the more common practice is to require that sufficient cause be established in a judicial proceeding prior to the filing of the information.

In California, for example, the prevailing practice is to begin the prosecution by filing a felony *complaint* in an inferior court, normally the court which handles misdemeanor trials and minor civil cases. If the magistrate in this court determines after a preliminary hearing that there is sufficient cause to believe that the defendant committed the crime, the defendant is held for trial in the superior court. The prosecutor may then file an *information* in the superior court: this document is the equivalent of a grand jury indictment. In misdemeanor cases the prosecutor may file a *complaint* directly in the inferior trial court and proceed to trial without any preliminary hearing or other review of the decision to prosecute. Once the complaint, information, or indictment has been filed, the defendant must be brought to court for arraignment on the charge. At arraignment the defendant appears with counsel or counsel is appointed, a plea is ordinarily entered, and the judge sets a date for the trial.

In some states, the preliminary hearing has developed into a full-fledged adversary proceeding, with the defense entitled to cross-examine prosecution witnesses and to put on witnesses for the defense. Occasionally, a defendant may be able to undermine the prosecution's case at this stage, and obtain dismissal of the charges without going through the greater ordeal of a jury trial. More often, the defense uses the preliminary hearing as an opportunity to discover the prosecution's evidence and cross-examine its witnesses for the purpose of "pinning them down" on matters of detail. In civil litigation, the parties may take the depositions of witnesses; in criminal litigation, the only comparable opportunity occurs at the preliminary hearing.

Defendants who exercise their right to subpoena witnesses rarely put on a complete defense at the preliminary hearing, since it is normally better tactics not to expose the defense case before trial. Instead, they subpoena and call to testify the prosecution witnesses whom the prosecutor had planned to save for the trial. The purpose usually is not so much to rebut probable cause as to find out what the witnesses will say and to build a record that may be useful in cross-examining them at trial. A thorough preliminary hearing also helps counsel to evaluate a case for purposes of plea bargaining.

A preliminary hearing may also be held in a felony case prosecuted in the federal courts or in one of the states which still requires a grand jury indictment, but it does not fulfil the same role. Where the grand jury has returned an indictment, no preliminary hearing is held because the grand jury has already determined that probable cause exists. The official purpose of the preliminary hearing in a jurisdiction that relies upon the grand jury for the ultimate decision on whether to prosecute is merely to decide whether the defendant should be held to answer (and thus required to remain in custody or give security for his appearance) until such time as the grand jury acts. Hence the prosecutor may avoid the preliminary hearing, and thus deprive the defendant of the discovery that the hearing would incidentally give him, by obtaining an indictment before the time of the hearing. The prosecutor may also be able to render moot any procedural errors occurring at the preliminary hearing by obtaining a supervening indictment. Compare Sciortino v. Zampano, 385 F.2d 132 (2d Cir.1967) and United States v. Coley, 441 F.2d 1299 (5th Cir.1971), with Coleman v. Burnett, 477 F.2d 1187 (D.C.Cir.1973). These cases contain useful discussions of the role of preliminary hearings in federal practice.

Lawyers in the information states have often argued that it is unfair to allow the prosecutor to avoid the preliminary hearing altogether by obtaining a grand jury indictment. Obviously, the grand jury procedure is far less favorable to the defense, and the prosecutor who wants to take a weak case to trial for some reason can probably do so by using the grand jury. Reacting against this denial of equal treatment, the Supreme Courts of California and Michigan have held that a defendant may have a preliminary hearing even if he has already been indicted by a grand jury. See, Hawkins v. Superior Court, 22 Cal.3d 584, 150 Cal.Rptr. 435, 586 P.2d 916 (1978); People v. Duncan, 388 Mich. 489, 201 N.W.2d 629 (1972); contra, State v. Clark, 291 Or. 231, 630 P.2d 810 (1981); State v. Sisneros, 137 Ariz. 323, 670 P.2d 721 (1983).

Although most preliminary hearings are routine affairs even in California, the California-style preliminary hearing can easily become a very extended proceeding when the issues are complex or when the defense chooses to do battle at this stage in the proceedings. The longest preliminary hearing in California history, in a complex sexual abuse case with numerous child witnesses, lasted 18 months. This case was exceptional, but preliminary hearings that take several days of court time are not uncommon. From the defense point of view, having so extensive a hearing is justified by the desirability of protecting an innocent defendant from undergoing the burden of a jury trial, and the desirability of providing an alternative to the civil deposition procedure for effective pretrial preparation.

On the other hand, granting an adversary-type preliminary examination substantially increases the burdens on the witnesses and on the judicial system. Testifying in a criminal case may be an ordeal for a witness, particularly one who is the victim of a sexual crime or who fears retaliation from the defendant. Delays and continuances in adversary hearings are common, and witnesses may be subjected to great inconvenience and frustration as a result. From the viewpoint of the witness, the adversary preliminary hearing may appear to be merely another opportunity for harassment.

D.　THE RIGHT TO A SPEEDY TRIAL

UNITED STATES v. LOUD HAWK

Supreme Court of the United States, 1986.
474 U.S. 302, 106 S.Ct. 648, 88 L.Ed.2d 640.

JUSTICE POWELL delivered the opinion of the Court.

In this case we must decide, first, whether the Speedy Trial Clause of the Sixth Amendment applies to time during which respondents were neither under indictment nor subjected to any official restraint, and, second, whether certain delays occasioned by interlocutory appeals were properly weighed in assessing respondents' right to a speedy trial. A divided panel of the Court of Appeals for the Ninth Circuit weighed most of the 90 months from the time of respondents' arrests and initial indictment in November 1975 until the District Court's dismissal of the indictment in May 1983 towards respondents' claims under the Speedy Trial Clause. We conclude that the time that no indictment was outstanding against respondents should not weigh towards respondents' speedy trial claims. We also find that in this case the delay attributable to interlocutory appeals by the Government and respondents do not establish a violation of the Speedy Trial Clause. Accordingly, we reverse the holding of the Court of Appeals that respondents were denied their right to a speedy trial.

I

In view of the nature of respondents' claim, we state the factual and procedural history of this case in some detail. On November 14, 1975, pursuant to a tip from the Federal Bureau of Investigation, Oregon State Troopers stopped two vehicles in search of several federal fugitives. After an exchange of gunfire and a motor chase, State Troopers captured all but one of the respondents, Dennis Banks. Both vehicles were locked and impounded while federal and state authorities obtained search warrants.

Searches of the vehicles over the next two days disclosed 350 pounds of dynamite, six partially assembled time bombs, 2,600 rounds of ammunition, 150 blasting caps, 9 empty hand grenades, and miscellaneous firearms. Oregon law enforcement officers, apparently unaware of the evidentiary consequences, adhered to their usual policy and destroyed the dynamite. A federal agent present at the destruction photographed the explosions. *United States v. Loud Hawk*, 628 F.2d 1139, 1142 (C.A.9 1979). State officials also preserved wrappers from the dynamite casings.

A federal grand jury indicted respondents on November 25, 1975, on charges of possessing firearms and explosives. Trial in the United States District Court for the District of Oregon was set for the week of February 9, 1976. On December 22, 1975, a grand jury returned a five-count superseding indictment. This indictment charged all respondents with three counts relating to possession and transportation in commerce of an unregistered destructive device (the dynamite counts) and two counts relating to unlawful possession of firearms (the firearms counts).

Two days later, respondents filed a motion to suppress all evidence concerning the dynamite, arguing that federal and state officials had intentionally and negligently destroyed the dynamite before the defense had the opportunity to examine it. After initially denying respondents' motion, and after two continuances at respondents' behest, the District Court granted respondents' motion to suppress on March 31, 1976. Three weeks later, the Government appealed the suppression order,[12] and moved that trial on all counts be continued pending the outcome of the appeal. The District Court denied the Government's request for a continuance, and when the case was called for trial, the Government answered not ready. Pursuant to Federal Rule of Criminal Procedure 48(b), the District Judge dismissed the indictment with prejudice. Six months had passed since the original indictment.

12. The Government is permitted to pursue some interlocutory appeals under 18 U.S.C. § 3731. That section as then in effect read:

"In a criminal case an appeal by the United States shall lie to a court of appeals from a decision, judgment, or order of a district court dismissing an indictment or information as to any one or more counts, except that no appeal shall lie where the double jeopardy clause of the United States Constitution prohibits further prosecution.

"An appeal by the United States shall lie to a court of appeals from a decision or order of a district courts [sic] suppressing or excluding evidence or requiring the return of seized property in a criminal proceeding, not made after the defendant has been put in jeopardy and before the verdict or finding on an indictment or information, if the United States attorney certifies to the district court that the appeal is not taken for purpose of delay and that the evidence is a substantial proof of a fact material in the proceeding.

"The appeal in all such cases shall be taken within thirty days after the decision, judgment or order has been rendered and shall be diligently prosecuted.

"Pending the prosecution and determination of the appeal in the foregoing instances, the defendant shall be released in accordance with chapter 207 of this title.

"The provisions of this section shall be liberally construed to effectuate its purposes."

The Government immediately appealed the dismissal, and the two appeals were consolidated. The Court of Appeals heard argument on October 15, 1976, and a divided panel affirmed in an unreported opinion on July 26, 1977. On the Government's motion, the court voted on October 17, 1977, to hear the case en banc. On March 6, 1978, the Court of Appeals en banc remanded for findings of fact on whether federal officials participated in the destruction of the dynamite and whether respondents were prejudiced by its destruction. The court retained jurisdiction over the appeal pending the District Court's findings. The District Court issued its findings on August 23, 1978, and the case returned to the Court of Appeals.

On August 7, 1979, the Court of Appeals reversed the suppression order and directed that the dynamite counts be reinstated. *United States v. Loud Hawk*. The court also held that although the Government could have gone to trial on the firearms counts pending the appeal, the District Court erred in dismissing those counts with prejudice. The Court of Appeals denied respondents' petition for rehearing on October 1, 1979. Respondents petitioned for certiorari; we denied the petition on March 3, 1980. The mandate of the Court of Appeals issued on March 12, 1980, 46 months after the Government filed its notice of appeal from the dismissal of the indictment. Respondents were unconditionally released during that time.

Following remand, the District Court ordered the Government to reindict on the firearms charges. Respondents filed a number of motions during June and July of 1980 in response to the superseding indictment, including a motion to dismiss for vindictive prosecution. On August 8, 1980, the District Court granted the vindictive prosecution motion as to KaMook Banks and denied it as to respondents Dennis Banks, Render, and Loud Hawk. Both sides appealed. Respondents remained free on their own recognizance during this appeal.

The appeals were consolidated, and the Court of Appeals ordered expedited consideration. The court heard argument on January 7, 1981, but did not issue its decision until July 29, 1982. The court sustained the Government's position on all issues. Respondents' petitions for rehearing were denied on October 5, 1982. Respondents again petitioned for certiorari, and we denied the petition on January 10, 1983. The Court of Appeals' mandate issued on January 31, 1983, almost 29 months after the appeals were filed.

The District Court scheduled trial to begin on April 11, 1983. The Government sought and received a continuance until May 3, 1983, because of alleged difficulties in locating witnesses more than seven years after the arrests. Subsequently, the court on its own motion continued the trial date until May 23, 1983, and then again rescheduled the trial for June 13. The record in this Court does not reveal the reasons for these latter two continuances. Defendants objected to each continuance.

On May 20, 1983, the District Court again dismissed the indictment, this time on the ground that respondents' Sixth Amendment right to a speedy trial had been violated. The Government appealed, and unsuccessfully urged the District Court to request that the Court of Appeals expedite the appeal. On its own motion the court treated the appeal as expedited, and heard argument on January 4, 1984. A divided panel affirmed on August 30, 1984. We granted certiorari, and now reverse.

II

The Government argues that under *United States v. MacDonald*, 456 U.S. 1 (1982), the time during which defendants are neither under indictment nor subject to any restraint on their liberty should be excluded—weighed not at all—when considering a speedy trial claim. Respondents contend that even during the time the charges against them were dismissed, the Government was actively pursuing its case and they continued to be subjected to the possibility that bail might be imposed. This possibility, according to respondents, is sufficient to warrant counting the time towards a speedy trial claim.

The Court has found that when no indictment is outstanding, only the "*actual* restraints imposed by arrest and holding to answer a criminal charge * * * engage the particular protections of the speedy trial provision of the Sixth Amendment." *United States v. Marion*, 404 U.S. 307, 320 (1971). As we stated in *MacDonald:* "The speedy trial guarantee is designed to minimize the possibility of lengthy incarceration prior to trial, to reduce the lesser, but nevertheless substantial, impairment of liberty imposed on an accused while released on bail, and to shorten the disruption of life caused by arrest and the presence of unresolved criminal charges."

During much of the litigation, respondents were neither under indictment nor subject to bail. Further judicial proceedings would have been necessary to subject the respondents to any actual restraints. * * *

Respondents argue that the speedy trial guarantee should apply to this period because the Government's desire to prosecute them was a matter of public record. Public suspicion, however, is not sufficient to justify the delay in favor of a defendant's speedy trial claim. We find that after the District Court dismissed the indictment against respondents and after respondents were freed without restraint, they were in the same position as any other subject of a criminal investigation. * * *

We therefore find that under the rule of *MacDonald*, when defendants are not incarcerated or subjected to other substantial restrictions on their liberty, a court should not weigh that time towards a claim under the Speedy Trial Clause.

III

The remaining issue is how to weigh the delay occasioned by an interlocutory appeal when the defendant is subject to indictment or restraint. As we have recognized, the Sixth Amendment's guarantee of a speedy trial is an important safeguard to prevent undue and oppressive incarceration prior to trial, to minimize anxiety and concern accompanying public accusation and to limit the possibilities that long delay will impair the ability of an accused to defend himself. These safeguards may be as important to the accused when the delay is occasioned by an unduly long appellate process as when the delay is caused by a lapse between the initial arrest and the drawing of a proper indictment, or by continuances in the date of trial, *Barker v. Wingo*, 407 U.S. 514, 517–518 (1972).

At the same time, there are important public interests in the process of appellate review. The assurance that motions to suppress evidence or to dismiss an indictment are correctly decided through orderly appellate review safeguards both the rights of defendants and the "rights of public justice." * * *

In *Barker*, we adopted a four-part balancing test to determine whether a series of continuances infringed upon the defendant's right to a speedy trial. That test assessed the "[l]ength of delay, the reason for the delay, the defendant's assertion of his right, and prejudice to the defendant." The *Barker* test furnishes the flexibility to take account of the competing concerns of orderly appellate review on the one hand, and a speedy trial on the other. * * *

A

Barker's first, third, and fourth factors present no great difficulty in application. The first factor, the length of delay, defines a threshold in the inquiry: there must be a delay long enough to be "presumptively prejudicial." Here, a 90–month delay in the trial of these serious charges is presumptively prejudicial and serves to trigger application of *Barker*'s other factors.

The third factor—the extent to which respondents have asserted their speedy trial rights—does not support their position. Although the Court of Appeals found that respondents have repeatedly moved for dismissal on speedy trial grounds, that finding alone does not establish that respondents have appropriately asserted their rights. * * *

Here, respondents' speedy trial claims are reminiscent of Penelope's tapestry. At the same time respondents were making a record of claims in the District Court for speedy trial, they consumed six months by filing indisputably frivolous petitions for rehearing and for certiorari * * * They also filled the District Courts docket with repetitive and unsuccessful motions.

The Court of Appeals gave "little weight" to the fourth factor, prejudice to respondents. At most, the court recognized the possibility of "impairment of a fair trial that may well result from the absence or loss of memory of witnesses in this case." That possibility of prejudice is not sufficient to support respondents' position that their speedy trial rights were violated. In this case, moreover, delay is a two-edged sword. It is the Government that bears the burden of proving its case beyond a reasonable doubt. The passage of time may make it difficult or impossible for the Government to carry this burden.

B

The flag all litigants seek to capture is the second factor, the reason for delay. * * *

Under *Barker*, delays in bringing the case to trial caused by the Government's interlocutory appeal may be weighed in determining whether a defendant has suffered a violation of his rights to a speedy trial. It is clear in this case, however, that respondents have failed to show a reason for according these delays any effective weight towards their speedy trial claims. There is no showing of bad faith or dilatory purpose on the Government's part. The Government's position in each of the appeals was strong, and the reversals by the Court of Appeals are prima facie evidence of the reasonableness of the Government's action. Moreover, despite the seriousness of the charged offenses, the District Court chose not to subject respondents to any actual restraints pending the outcome of the appeals. * * *

IV

We cannot hold, on the facts before us, that the delays asserted by respondents weigh sufficiently in support of their speedy trial claim to violate the Speedy Trial Clause. They do not justify the severe remedy of dismissing the indictment. Accordingly, the judgment of the Court of Appeals for the Ninth Circuit is reversed.

JUSTICE MARSHALL, with whom JUSTICE BRENNAN, JUSTICE BLACKMUN, and JUSTICE STEVENS join, dissenting.

* * *

I

The majority concludes that when an appeal arises out of the district court's dismissal of an indictment, the lack of an outstanding indictment absolves the Government of its responsibility to provide a speedy trial. However, we have never conditioned Sixth Amendment rights solely on the presence of an outstanding indictment. Those rights attach to anyone who is "accused," and we have until now recognized that one may stand publicly accused without being under indictment. * * *

Unlike one who has not been arrested, or one who has had the charges against him dropped, respondents did not enjoy the protection of the statute of limitations while the Government prosecuted its appeal. That protection was an important aspect of our holding in *Marion* that pre-arrest delay is not cognizable under the Speedy Trial Clause. See 404 U.S., at 322–323. More importantly, in contrast to *MacDonald*, the Government has not "dropped" anything in this case. There has been at all relevant times a case on a court docket captioned *United States v. Loud Hawk*—I can think of no more formal indication that respondents stand accused by the Government.

The most telling difference between this case and *MacDonald*, however, is the fact that respondents' liberty could have been taken from them at any time during the Government's appeal. One of the primary purposes of the speedy trial right, of course, is to prevent prolonged restraints on liberty, and the absence of any possibility of such restraints was a vital part of our *MacDonald* holding. In contrast, Congress has declared explicitly, in 18 U.S.C. § 3731, that a person in respondents' position shall be subject to the same restraints as an arrested defendant awaiting trial. Thus the District Court had the undoubted authority to condition respondents' release on the posting of bail, or indeed to keep them in jail throughout the appeal, see 18 U.S.C.A. § 3142(e) (1985). Respondents' release could have been accompanied by restrictions on travel, association, employment, abode, and firearms possession, or conditioned on their reporting regularly to law enforcement officers and/or keeping a curfew. Considering all the circumstances, therefore, I believe that respondents' position is most closely analogous to that of a defendant who has been arrested but not yet indicted. * * *

II

The majority also declines to hold the Government accountable for delay attributable to appeals during which respondents were under indictment. In doing so the majority emphasizes the second *Barker* factor—the reason for the delay. Because it concludes that "[t]here is no showing of bad faith or dilatory purpose on the Government's part," the majority declines to accord any "effective weight" to this factor in the speedy trial balance. In reaching this conclusion, it virtually ignores the most obvious "reason for the delay" in this case—the fact that the Court of Appeals was unable to decide these appeals in a reasonably prompt manner. * * *

The Court of Appeals frankly admitted that "most of the delay must be attributed to the processes of this court," a conclusion that is difficult to escape. This case involves appeals from pretrial rulings. The Court of Appeals had every reason to know that these appeals should have been ruled upon as expeditiously as possible. See that court's Rule 20. Yet it took over five years for the Court of Appeals to decide two appeals, one of them "expedited." No complicated analysis is needed to identify the reason for the delay in this case.

I would hold, simply, that a nonfrivolous appeal by any party permits a *reasonable* delay in the proceedings. The number and complexity of the issues on appeal, or the number of parties, might permit a greater or lesser delay in a given case. The Government, not the defendant, must suffer the ultimate consequences of delays attributable to "overcrowded courts," even at the appellate level. In the present case, the amount of time that the appeals consumed is patently unreasonable. I would therefore weigh the second *Barker* factor against the Government in this case. * * *

Note

In Doggett v. United States, 505 U.S. 647 (1992), the Supreme Court ordered dismissal of an indictment for violation of the Speedy Trial Clause even though the defendant could show no actual prejudice. Petitioner Doggett was indicted for conspiracy to smuggle and distribute cocaine. When DEA agents tried to arrest him at his parents' house, they found he had left the country. The agents later learned that he was in jail in Panama, and asked the Panamanian authorities to turn him over when their own proceedings were completed. Nonetheless, the Panamanians eventually released Doggett and allowed him to go to Colombia.

Doggett reentered the United States in 1982, settled in Virginia, married, earned a college degree, found a steady job as a computer operations manager, lived openly under his own name, and stayed within the law. The DEA made no serious effort to locate him, although doing so would not have been difficult. Doggett was apprehended in 1988, following a routine check by the U.S. Marshal's Service of the credit records of persons for whom there were outstanding arrest warrants. He was finally arrested more than 81/2 years after the indictment, and nearly 6 years after his return to the United States.

Although the Government claimed that it had pursued Doggett diligently, the lower courts and the Supreme Court had little difficulty finding that it had been negligent. The Government also contended unsuccessfully that Doggett must have known about the indictment all along, and thus could have invoked his Speedy Trial right. There was no evidence of knowledge, however, and Doggett's mother (who had spoken to the DEA agents in 1980), testified that she had not told her son or anyone else about the charge.

The case thus turned on the question of prejudice. Doggett's liberty was not affected by the pending charge, and he suffered no anxiety from it if he knew nothing about it. He also could not show that the delay had impaired his ability to defend. Because of the absence of demonstrated prejudice, the district court denied the motion to dismiss and Doggett entered a conditional plea of guilty (which preserved his ability to appeal on the Speedy Trial claim). The judge imposed a sentence of probation and a $1000 fine—the leniency presumably reflecting the judge's appreciation that the defendant had the equities on his side if not the law.

The Supreme Court granted certiorari, and had so much difficulty deciding the prejudice issue that it asked the parties to brief an additional issue: "whether the history of the Speedy Trial Clause of the Sixth Amendment supports the view that the Clause protects a right of citizens to repose, free from the fear of secret or unknown indictments for past crimes, independent of any interest in preventing lengthy pretrial incarceration or prejudice to the case of a criminal defendant." When the Supreme Court decided the case, however, the opinion for the 5–4 majority by Justice Souter ignored this additional issue. The majority instead applied the four-part balancing test of *Barker v. Wingo*. The delay was very long, the Government was negligently to blame, and the defendant asserted his Speedy Trial right as soon as he had notice. With respect to the fourth part of the test—prejudice to the defense—the majority held that under the circumstances there was "presumptive prejudice." The dissent by Justice Thomas concluded that "[b]y divorcing the Speedy Trial Clause from all considerations of prejudice to an accused, the Court positively invites the Nation's judges to indulge in ad hoc and result-driven second-guessing of the Government's investigatory efforts."

Chapter 10

THE RIGHT TO COUNSEL AND PLEA BARGAINING

A. THE RIGHT TO COUNSEL AND INDIGENT DEFENDANTS

GIDEON v. WAINWRIGHT

Supreme Court of the United States, 1963.
372 U.S. 335, 83 S.Ct. 792, 9 L.Ed.2d 799.

MR. JUSTICE BLACK delivered the opinion of the Court.

Petitioner was charged in a Florida state court with having broken and entered a poolroom with intent to commit a misdemeanor. This offense is a felony under Florida law. Appearing in court without funds and without a lawyer, petitioner asked the court to appoint counsel for him, whereupon the following colloquy took place:

The COURT: Mr. Gideon, I am sorry, but I cannot appoint Counsel to represent you in this case. Under the laws of the State of Florida, the only time the Court can appoint Counsel to represent a Defendant is when that person is charged with a capital offense. I am sorry, but I will have to deny your request to appoint Counsel to defend you in this case.

The DEFENDANT: The United States Supreme Court says I am entitled to be represented by Counsel.

Put to trial before a jury, Gideon conducted his defense about as well as could be expected from a layman. He made an opening statement to the jury, cross-examined the State's witnesses, presented witnesses in his own defense, declined to testify himself, and made a short argument "emphasizing his innocence to the charge contained in the Information filed in this case." The jury returned a verdict of guilty, and petitioner was sentenced to serve five years in the state prison. Later, petitioner filed in the Florida Supreme Court this habeas corpus petition attacking his conviction and sentence on the ground that the trial court's refusal to appoint counsel for him denied him rights "guaranteed by the Constitution and the Bill of Rights by the United States Government."

Treating the petition for habeas corpus as properly before it, the State Supreme Court, "upon consideration thereof" but without an opinion, denied all relief. Since 1942, when Betts v. Brady, 316 U.S. 455, was decided by a divided Court, the problem of a defendant's federal constitutional right to counsel in a state court has been a continuing source of controversy and litigation in both state and federal courts. To give this problem another review here, we granted certiorari. * * *

The Sixth Amendment provides, "In all criminal prosecutions, the accused shall enjoy the right * * * to have the Assistance of Counsel for his defence." We have construed this to mean that in federal courts counsel must be provided for defendants unable to employ counsel unless the right is competently and intelligently waived. Betts argued that this right is extended to indigent defendants in state courts by the Fourteenth Amendment. In response the Court stated that, while the Sixth Amendment laid down "no rule for the conduct of the states, the question recurs whether the constraint laid by the amendment upon the national courts expresses a rule so fundamental and essential to a fair trial, and so, to due process of law, that it is made obligatory upon the states by the Fourteenth Amendment." In order to decide whether the Sixth Amendment's guarantee of counsel is of this fundamental nature, the Court in Betts set out and considered "[r]elevant data on the subject * * * afforded by constitutional and statutory provisions subsisting in the colonies and the states prior to the inclusion of the Bill of Rights in the national Constitution, and in the constitutional, legislative, and judicial history of the states to the present date." On the basis of this historical data the Court concluded that "appointment of counsel is not a fundamental right essential to a fair trial." It was for this reason the Betts Court refused to accept the contention that the Sixth Amendment's guarantee of counsel for indigent federal defendants was extended to or, in the words of that Court, "made obligatory upon the states by the Fourteenth Amendment". Plainly, had the Court concluded that appointment of counsel for an indigent criminal defendant was "a fundamental right, essential to a fair trial," it would have held that the Fourteenth Amendment requires appointment of counsel in a state court, just as the Sixth Amendment requires in a federal court. * * *

We accept Betts v. Brady's assumption, based as it was on our prior cases, that a provision of the Bill of Rights which is "fundamental and essential to a fair trial" is made obligatory upon the States by the Fourteenth Amendment. We think the Court in Betts was wrong, however, in concluding that the Sixth Amendment's guarantee of counsel is not one of these fundamental rights. * * *

Governments, both state and federal, quite properly spend vast sums of money to establish machinery to try defendants accused of crime. Lawyers to prosecute are everywhere deemed essential to protect the public's interest in an orderly society. Similarly, there are few defendants charged with crime, few indeed, who fail to hire the best lawyers they can get to prepare and present their defenses. That government hires lawyers to prosecute and defendants who have the money hire lawyers to defend are the strongest indications of the widespread belief that lawyers in criminal courts are necessities, not luxuries. The right of one charged with crime to counsel may not be deemed fundamental and essential to fair trials in some countries, but it is in ours. From the very beginning, our state and national constitutions and laws have laid great emphasis on procedural and substantive safeguards designed to assure fair trials before impartial tribunals in which every defendant stands equal before the law. This noble ideal cannot be realized if the poor man charged with crime has to face his accusers without a lawyer to assist him. A defendant's need for a lawyer is nowhere better stated than in the moving words of Mr. Justice Sutherland in Powell v. Alabama:

> "The right to be heard would be, in many cases, of little avail if it did not comprehend the right to be heard by counsel. Even the intelligent and educated layman has small and sometimes no skill in the science of law. If charged with crime, he is incapable, generally, of determining for himself whether the indictment is good or bad. He is unfamiliar with the rules of evidence. Left without the aid of counsel he may be put on trial without a proper charge, and convicted upon incompetent evidence, or evidence irrelevant to the issue or otherwise inadmissible. He lacks both the skill and knowledge adequately to prepare his defense, even though he have a perfect one. He requires the guiding hand of counsel at every step in the proceedings against him. Without it, though he be not guilty, he faces the danger of conviction because he does not know how to establish his innocence." 287 U.S., at 68–69.

The Court in Betts v. Brady departed from the sound wisdom upon which the Court's holding in Powell v. Alabama rested. Florida, supported by two other States, has asked that Betts v. Brady by left intact. Twenty-two States, as friends of the Court, argue that Betts was "an anachronism when handed down" and that it should now be overruled. We agree.

The judgment is reversed and the cause is remanded to the Supreme Court of Florida for further action not inconsistent with this opinion. Reversed.

[A separate opinion by JUSTICE DOUGLAS and JUSTICE HARLAN'S concurring opinion, are omitted.]

ALABAMA v. SHELTON

Supreme Court of the United States, 2002.
535 U.S. 654, 122 S.Ct. 1764, 152 L.Ed.2d 888.

JUSTICE GINSBURG delivered the opinion of the Court.

This case concerns the Sixth Amendment right of an indigent defendant charged with a misdemeanor punishable by imprisonment, fine, or both, to the assistance of court-appointed counsel. Two prior decisions control the Court's judgment. First, in *Argersinger v. Hamlin*,

407 U.S. 25 (1972), this Court held that defense counsel must be appointed in any criminal prosecution, "whether classified as petty, misdemeanor, or felony," "that actually leads to imprisonment even for a brief period." Later, in *Scott v. Illinois*, 440 U.S. 367, 373–374 (1979), the Court drew the line at "actual imprisonment," holding that counsel need not be appointed when the defendant is fined for the charged crime, but is not sentenced to a term of imprisonment.

Defendant-respondent LeReed Shelton, convicted of third-degree assault, was sentenced to a jail term of 30 days, which the trial court immediately suspended, placing Shelton on probation for two years. The question presented is whether the Sixth Amendment right to appointed counsel, as delineated in *Argersinger* and *Scott*, applies to a defendant in Shelton's situation. We hold that a suspended sentence that may "end up in the actual deprivation of a person's liberty" may not be imposed unless the defendant was accorded "the guiding hand of counsel" in the prosecution for the crime charged.

* * *

II

Three positions are before us in this case. * * * Shelton argues that an indigent defendant may not receive a suspended sentence unless he is offered or waives the assistance of state-appointed counsel. Alabama now concedes that the Sixth Amendment bars *activation* of a suspended sentence for an uncounseled conviction, but maintains that the Constitution does not prohibit *imposition* of such a sentence as a method of effectuating probationary punishment. To assure full airing of the question presented, we invited an *amicus curiae* ("*amicus*") to argue in support of a third position, one Alabama has abandoned: Failure to appoint counsel to an indigent defendant "does not bar the imposition of a suspended or probationary sentence upon conviction of a misdemeanor, even though the defendant might be incarcerated in the event probation is revoked."

A

In *Gideon v. Wainwright*, 372 U.S. 335, 344 (1963), we held that the Sixth Amendment's guarantee of the right to state-appointed counsel, firmly established in federal-court proceedings in *Johnson v. Zerbst*, 304 U.S. 458 (1938), applies to state criminal prosecutions through the Fourteenth Amendment. We clarified the scope of that right in *Argersinger*, holding that an indigent defendant must be offered counsel in any misdemeanor case "that actually leads to imprisonment." Seven Terms later, *Scott* confirmed *Argersinger*'s "delimitation." Although the governing statute in *Scott* authorized a jail sentence of up to one year, we held that the defendant had no right to state-appointed counsel because the sole sentence actually imposed on him was a $50 fine. "Even were the matter *res nova*," we stated, "the central premise of *Argersinger*—that actual imprisonment is a penalty different in kind from fines or the mere threat of imprisonment—is eminently sound and warrants adoption of actual imprisonment as the line defining the constitutional right to appointment of counsel" in nonfelony cases.

Subsequent decisions have reiterated the *Argersinger-Scott* "actual imprisonment" standard. It is thus the controlling rule that "absent a knowing and intelligent waiver, no person may be imprisoned for any offense . . . unless he was represented by counsel at his trial."

B

Applying the "actual imprisonment" rule to the case before us, we take up first the question we asked *amicus* to address: Where the State provides no counsel to an indigent defendant, does the Sixth Amendment permit activation of a suspended sentence upon the defendant's violation of the terms of probation? We conclude that it does not. A suspended sentence is a prison term imposed for the offense of conviction. Once the prison term is triggered, the defendant is incarcerated not for the probation violation, but for the underlying offense. The uncounseled conviction at that point "results in imprisonment;" it "ends up in the actual deprivation of a person's liberty." This is precisely what the Sixth Amendment, as interpreted in *Argersinger* and *Scott*, does not allow.

* * *

Nor do we agree with *amicus* or the dissent that our holding will "substantially limit the states' ability" to impose probation, or encumber them with a "large, new burden." Most jurisdictions already provide a state-law right to appointed counsel more generous than that afforded by the Federal Constitution. All but 16 States, for example, would provide counsel to a defendant in Shelton's circumstances, either because he received a substantial fine or because state law authorized incarceration for the charged offense or provided for a maximum prison term of one year. There is thus scant reason to believe that a rule conditioning imposition of a suspended sentence on provision of appointed counsel would affect existing practice in the large majority of the States. * * *

* * * States unable or unwilling routinely to provide appointed counsel to misdemeanants in Shelton's situation are not without recourse to another option capable of yielding a similar result.

That option is pretrial probation, employed in some form by at least 23 States. Under such an arrangement, the prosecutor and defendant agree to the defendant's participation in a pretrial rehabilitation program, which includes conditions typical of post-trial probation. The adjudication of guilt and imposition of sentence for the underlying offense then occur only if and when the defendant breaches those conditions.

* * *

C

Alabama concedes that activation of a suspended sentence results in the imprisonment of an uncounseled defendant "for a term that relates to the original offense" and therefore "crosses the line of 'actual imprisonment'" established in *Argersinger* and *Scott*. Shelton cannot be imprisoned, Alabama thus acknowledges, "unless the State has afforded him the right to assistance of appointed counsel in his defense." Alabama maintains, however, that there is no constitutional barrier to *imposition* of a suspended sentence that can never be enforced; the State therefore urges reversal of the Alabama Supreme Court's judgment insofar as it vacated the term of probation Shelton was ordered to serve.

In effect, Alabama invites us to regard two years' probation for Shelton as a separate and independent sentence, which "the State would have the same power to enforce [as] a judgment of a mere fine." * * * Seen as a freestanding sentence, Alabama further asserts, probation could be enforced, as a criminal fine or restitution order could, in a contempt proceeding.

Alabama describes the contempt proceeding it envisions as one in which Shelton would receive "the full panoply of due process," including the assistance of counsel. Any sanction imposed would be for "postconviction wrongdoing," not for the offense of conviction. * * *

There is not so much as a hint, however, in the decision of the Supreme Court of Alabama, that Shelton's probation term is separable from the prison term to which it was tethered. Absent any prior presentation of the position the State now takes, we resist passing on it in the first instance. * * *

* * * It is for the Alabama Supreme Court to consider before this Court does whether the suspended sentence alone is invalid, leaving Shelton's probation term freestanding and independently effective. See *Hortonville Joint School Dist.* v. Hortonville Ed. Asso., 426 U.S. 482, 488, 49 L.Ed.2d 1, 96 S.Ct. 2308 (1976) ("We are, of course, bound to accept the interpretation of [the State's] law by the highest court of the State."). We confine our review to the ruling the Alabama Supreme Court made in the case as presented to it: "[A] defendant who receives a suspended or probated sentence *to imprisonment* has a constitutional right to counsel." We find no infirmity in that holding.

Satisfied that Shelton is entitled to appointed counsel at the critical stage when his guilt or innocence of the charged crime is decided and his vulnerability to imprisonment is determined, we affirm the judgment of the Supreme Court of Alabama.

It is so ordered.

* * *

JUSTICE SCALIA, with whom THE CHIEF JUSTICE, JUSTICE KENNEDY, and JUSTICE THOMAS join, dissenting.

* * *

* * * We are asked to decide whether "imposition of a suspended or conditional sentence in a misdemeanor case invokes a defendant's Sixth Amendment right to counsel." Since *imposition* of a suspended sentence does not deprive a defendant of his personal liberty, the answer to *that* question is plainly no. In the future, *if and when* the State of Alabama seeks to imprison respondent on the previously suspended sentence, we can ask whether the procedural safeguards attending the imposition of that sentence comply with the Constitution. But that question is *not* before us now.

* * *

Our prior opinions placed considerable weight on the practical consequences of expanding the right to appointed counsel beyond cases of actual imprisonment. * * * [T]he Court's decision imposes a large, new burden on a majority of the States, including some of the poorest (*e.g.*, Alabama, Arkansas, and Mississippi, see U.S. Census Bureau, Statistical Abstract of the United States 426 (2001)). That burden consists not only of the cost of providing state-paid counsel in cases of such insignificance that even financially prosperous defendants sometimes forgo the expense of hired counsel; but also the cost of enabling courts and prosecutors to respond to the "over-lawyering" of minor cases. * * *

DOUGLAS v. CALIFORNIA

Supreme Court of the United States, 1963.
372 U.S. 353, 83 S.Ct. 814, 9 L.Ed.2d 811.

MR. JUSTICE DOUGLAS delivered the opinion of the Court. * * *

Although several questions are presented in the petition for certiorari, we address ourselves to only one of them. The record shows that petitioners requested, and were denied, the assistance of counsel on appeal, even though it plainly appeared they were indigents. In denying petitioners' requests, the California District Court of Appeal stated that it had "gone through" the record and had come to the conclusion that "no good whatever could be served by appointment of counsel." The District Court of Appeal was acting in accordance with a California rule of criminal procedure which provides that state appellate courts, upon the request of an indigent for counsel, may make "an independent investigation of the record and determine whether it would be of advantage to the defendant or helpful to the appellate court to have counsel appointed. * * * After such investigation, appellate courts should appoint counsel if in their opinion it would be helpful to the defendant or the court, and should deny the appointment of counsel only if in their judgment such appointment would be of no value to either the defendant or the court." People v. Hyde, 51 Cal.2d 152, 154.

We agree, however, with Justice Traynor of the California Supreme Court, who said that the "[d]enial of counsel on appeal [to an indigent] would seem to be a discrimination at least as invidious as that condemned in Griffin v. People of State of Illinois * * *." In Griffin v. Illinois, 351 U.S. 12, we held that a State may not grant appellate review in such a way as to discriminate against some convicted defendants on account of their poverty. There, as in Draper v. Washington, 372 U.S. 487, the right to a free transcript on appeal was in issue. Here the issue is whether or not an indigent shall be denied the assistance of counsel on appeal. In either case the evil is the same: discrimination against the indigent. For there can be no equal justice where the kind of an appeal a man enjoys "depends on the amount of money he has."

In spite of California's forward treatment of indigents, under its present practice the type of an appeal a person is afforded in the District Court of Appeal hinges upon whether or not he can pay for the assistance of counsel. If he can the appellate court passes on the merits of this case only after having the full benefit of written briefs and oral argument by counsel. If he cannot the appellate court is forced to prejudge the merits before it can even determine whether counsel should be provided. At this stage in the proceedings only the barren record speaks for the indigent, and, unless the printed pages show that an injustice has been committed, he is forced to go without a champion on appeal. Any real chance he may have had of showing that his appeal has hidden merit is deprived him when the court decides on an *ex parte* examination of the record that the assistance of counsel is not required.

We are not here concerned with problems that might arise from the denial of counsel for the preparation of a petition for discretionary or mandatory review beyond the stage in the appellate process at which the claims have once been presented by a lawyer and passed upon by an appellate court. We are dealing only with the first appeal, granted as a matter of right to rich and poor alike, from a criminal conviction. We need not now decide whether California would have to provide counsel for an indigent seeking a discretionary hearing from the California Supreme Court after the District Court of Appeal had sustained his conviction or whether counsel must be appointed for an indigent seeking review of an appellate affirmance of his conviction in this Court by appeal as of right or by petition for a writ of certiorari which lies within the Court's discretion. But it is appropriate to observe that a State can, consistently with the Fourteenth Amendment, provide for differences so long as the result does not amount to a denial of due process or an invidious discrimination. Absolute equality is not required; lines can be and are drawn and we often sustain them. But where the merits of the one and only appeal an indigent has as of right are decided without benefit of counsel, we think an unconstitutional line has been drawn between rich and poor.

* * *

[Judgment vacated and case remanded.]

MR. JUSTICE HARLAN, whom MR. JUSTICE STEWART joins, dissenting.
* * *

To approach the present problem in terms of the Equal Protection Clause is, I submit, but to substitute resounding phrases for analysis. I dissented from this approach in Griffin v. Illinois, and I am constrained to dissent from the implicit extension of the equal protection approach here—to a case in which the State denies no one an appeal, but seeks only to keep within reasonable bounds the instances in which appellate counsel will be assigned to indigents.

The States, of course, are prohibited by the Equal Protection Clause from discriminating between "rich" and "poor" *as such* in the formulation and application of their laws. But it is a far different thing to suggest that this provision prevents the State from adopting a law of general applicability that may affect the poor more harshly than it does the rich, or, on the other hand, from making some effort to redress economic imbalances while not eliminating them entirely.

Every financial exaction which the State imposes on a uniform basis is more easily satisfied by the well-to-do than by the indigent. Yet I take it that no one would dispute the constitutional power of the State to levy a uniform sales tax, to charge tuition at a state university, to fix rates for the purchase of water from a municipal corporation, to impose a standard fine for criminal violations, or to establish minimum bail for various categories of offenses. Nor could it be contended that the State may not classify as crimes acts which the poor are more likely to commit than are the rich. And surely, there would be no basis for attacking a state law which provided benefits for the needy simply because those benefits fell short of the goods or services that others could purchase for themselves.

Laws such as these do not deny equal protection to the less fortunate for one essential reason: the Equal Protection Clause does not impose on the States "an affirmative duty to lift the handicaps flowing from differences in economic circumstances." To so construe it would be to read into the Constitution a philosophy of leveling that would be foreign to many of our basic concepts of the proper relations between government and society. The State may have a moral obligation to eliminate the evils of poverty, but it is not required by the Equal Protection Clause to give to some whatever others can afford. * * *

ANDERS v. CALIFORNIA

Supreme Court of the United States, 1967.
386 U.S. 738, 87 S.Ct. 1396, 18 L.Ed.2d 493.

Mr. Justice Clark delivered the opinion of the Court.

We are here concerned with the extent of the duty of a court-appointed appellate counsel to prosecute a first appeal from a criminal conviction, after that attorney has conscientiously determined that there is no merit to the indigent's appeal.

After he was convicted of the felony of possession of marijuana, petitioner sought to appeal and moved that the California District Court of Appeal appoint counsel for him. Such motion was granted; however, after a study of the record and consultation with petitioner, the appointed counsel concluded that there was no merit to the appeal. He so advised the court by letter and, at the same time, informed the court that petitioner wished to file a brief in his own behalf. At this juncture, petitioner requested the appointment of another attorney. This request was denied and petitioner proceeded to file his own brief *pro se*. The State responded and petitioner filed a reply brief. [T]he District Court of Appeal unanimously affirmed the conviction. * * *

The constitutional requirement of substantial equality and fair process can only be attained where counsel acts in the role of an active advocate in behalf of his client, as opposed to that of *amicus curiae*. The no-merit letter and the procedure it triggers do not reach that dignity. Counsel should, and can with honor and without conflict, be of more assistance to his client and to the court. His role as advocate requires that he support his client's appeal to the best of his ability. Of course, if counsel finds his case to be wholly frivolous, after a conscientious examination of it, he should so advise the court and request permission to withdraw. That request must, however, be accompanied by a brief referring to anything in the record that might arguably support the appeal. A copy of counsel's brief should be furnished the indigent and time allowed him to raise any points that he chooses; the court—not counsel—then proceeds, after a full examination of all the proceedings, to decide whether the case is wholly frivolous. If it so finds it may grant counsel's request to withdraw and dismiss the appeal insofar as federal requirements are concerned, or proceed to a decision on the merits, if state law so requires. On the other hand, if it finds any of the legal points arguable on their merits (and therefore not frivolous) it must, prior to decision, afford the indigent the assistance of counsel to argue the appeal.

This requirement would not force appointed counsel to brief his case against his client but would merely afford the latter that advocacy which a nonindigent defendant is able to obtain. It would also induce the court to pursue all the more vigorously its own review because of the ready references not only to the record, but also to the legal authorities as furnished it by counsel. The no-merit letter, on the other hand, affords neither the client nor the court any aid. The former must shift entirely for himself while the court has only the cold record which it must review without the help of an advocate. Moreover, such handling would tend to protect counsel from the constantly increasing charge that he was ineffective and had not handled the case with that diligence to which an indigent defendant is entitled. This procedure will assure penniless defendants the same rights and opportunities on appeal—as nearly as is practicable—as are enjoyed by those persons who are in a similar situation but who are able to afford the retention of private counsel.

* * *

[Judgment reversed and case remanded]

MR. JUSTICE STEWART, whom MR. JUSTICE BLACK and MR. JUSTICE HARLAN join, dissenting.

The system used by California for handling indigent appeals was described by the California Supreme Court in In re Nash, 61 Cal.2d 491, 495:

> "We believe that the requirement of the *Douglas* case is met * * * when, as in this case, counsel is appointed to represent the defendant on appeal, thoroughly studies the record, consults with the defendant and trial counsel, and conscientiously concludes that there are no meritorious grounds of appeal. If thereafter the appellate court is satisfied *from its own review* of the record in the light of any points raised by the defendant personally that counsel's assessment of the record is correct, it need not appoint another counsel to represent the defendant on appeal and may properly decide the appeal without oral argument." (Emphasis added.)

The Court today holds this procedure unconstitutional, and imposes upon appointed counsel who wishes to withdraw from a case he deems "wholly frivolous" the requirement of filing "a brief referring to anything in the record that might arguably support the appeal." But if the record did present any such "arguable" issues, the appeal would not be frivolous and counsel would not have filed a "no-merit" letter in the first place.

The quixotic requirement imposed by the Court can be explained, I think, only upon the cynical assumption that an appointed lawyer's professional representation to an appellate court in a "no-merit" letter is not to be trusted. That is an assumption to which I cannot subscribe. I cannot believe that lawyers appointed to represent indigents are so likely to be lacking in diligence, competence, or professional honesty. Certainly there was no suggestion in the present case that the petitioner's counsel was either incompetent or unethical.

But even if I could join in this degrading appraisal of the *in forma pauperis* bar, it escapes me how the procedure that the Court commands is constitutionally superior to the system now followed in California. The fundamental error in the Court's opinion, it seems to me, is its implicit assertion that there can be but a single inflexible answer to the difficult problem of how to accord equal protection to indigent appellants in each of the 50 States.

Believing that the procedure under which Anders' appeal was considered was free of constitutional error, I would affirm the judgment.

Note

A Wisconsin rule of Appellate Procedure requires appointed counsel who have conscientiously determined that an indigent's appeal is wholly frivolous to submit with the request to withdraw not only "a brief referring to anything in the record that might arguably support the appeal," but also "a discussion of why the issue lacks merit." This last requirement was challenged as inconsistent with *Anders* because it requires counsel to argue the case *against* the client. A closely divided Supreme Court upheld the Wisconsin rule in McCoy v. Court of Appeals of Wisconsin, District 1, 486 U.S. 429 (1988). The majority reasoned that requiring the explanation assists the court to determine that counsel has been diligent and that the appeal is indeed frivolous, and furnishing the explanation does not burden the right to effective representation on appeal any more than does stating the bald conclusion that the appeal is frivolous.

UNITED STATES v. ELY

United States Court of Appeals, Seventh Circuit, 1983.
719 F.2d 902.

POSNER, CIRCUIT JUDGE.

* * *

Ely was apprehended in 1982 and at the arraignment the district judge, after ascertaining that Ely was indigent and wanted counsel, appointed a lawyer named Brady to represent him. Ely requested the judge to appoint another lawyer instead, Bartley, who at Ely's request was in the courtroom. (Both Brady and Bartley are lawyers in private practice.) Ely stated, "Mr. Bartley had represented business of mine at one time and I have—I feel a more closer relationship with Mr. Bartley in understanding what is before me * * *." Although Bartley was willing to accept the appointment and had represented other indigent criminal defendants before the district judge, the judge refused to appoint him to represent Ely: "the Court appoints an attorney for you under the program that this Court has of attorneys on its list and in some relative degree of sequence and frequency. * * * I know that Mr. Brady is [a] thoroughly competent and experienced attorney in this Court. I don't have anything different to say about Mr. Bartley, but we cannot start the practice of allowing defendants to select attorneys to be appointed."
* * *

Ely argues that in denying him the counsel of his choice the judge violated the Sixth Amendment. Enacted against the background of the much criticized common law rule that forbade felony defendants to be represented by counsel, the Sixth Amendment removed that bar for federal trials and thus allowed federal criminal defendants to hire counsel—counsel of their choice, see, e.g., *United States v. Agosto*, 675 F.2d 965, 969 (8th Cir.1982). But as originally understood, the Sixth Amendment did not require the government to provide a lawyer to a criminal defendant too poor to be able to hire one. Although the Sixth Amendment has, of course, been reinterpreted in modern times to impose such a requirement, the government's constitutional obligation is exhausted "when 'the court appoints competent counsel who is uncommitted to any position or interest which would conflict with providing an effective defense.'" United States v. Davis, 604 F.2d 474, 479 (7th Cir.1979).

Ely does not argue that Brady was incompetent or had a conflict of interest. Brady was a natural choice to represent Ely, having been his counsel when he was first charged in 1979. Although he preferred Bartley, Ely expressed no dissatisfaction with Brady. It was not that Brady was not good but that Bartley was, in Ely's opinion, better. Our decision in *Davis* approved the district judge's refusal to allow the indigent defendant to choose his own court-appointed counsel. True, Davis had expressed dissatisfaction with four lawyers offered him in lieu of the one he wanted, but as Ely expressed no dissatisfaction with his substitute counsel we do not think *Davis* is a stronger case than this one for denying the indigent the counsel of his choice.

In relation to indigent criminal defendants, the Sixth Amendment seeks not to maximize free choice of counsel but to prevent anyone from being unjustly convicted or illegally sentenced. These are distinct goals. Not only is there no indication that Ely would have fared better with Bartley at his side than with Brady; even if Bartley is the better lawyer, some other indigent criminal defendant might have been denied his assistance had he been appointed in Brady's place.

There are practical reasons for not giving indigent criminal defendants their choice of counsel. Appointed counsel are not paid at munificent rates under the Criminal Justice Act, 18 U.S.C. § 3006A(d); in the Central District of Illinois, in the most recent year for which data are available (1980), the average fee per case under the Act was only $426.31. The best criminal lawyers who accept appointments therefore limit the amount of time they are willing to devote to this relatively unremunerative type of work; some criminal lawyers, indeed, only reluctantly agree to serve as appointed counsel, under pressure by district judges to whom they feel a sense of professional obligation. The services of the criminal defense bar cannot be auctioned to the highest bidder among the indigent accused—by definition, indigents are not bidders. But these services must be allocated somehow; indigent defendants cannot be allowed to paralyze the system by all flocking to one lawyer. The district judge in this case could not, realistically, be required to arbitrate a dispute between Ely and another indigent criminal defendant who wanted to be represented by Bartley.

Neither party presented any evidence regarding the list of attorneys available for appointment that this district judge uses, or, more generally, the supply of lawyers for indigents in the Central District relative to demand. The transcript of the hearing on appointment of counsel for Ely indicates that this judge uses a rotation system for handling the appointment of counsel for indigents. If Ely wanted to show that the judge's refusal to appoint Bartley to represent him nevertheless was unreasonable, he would have to produce evidence to this effect; he failed to produce any. Ely argues, no doubt correctly, that if he were rich he could have hired Bartley. But the government is not responsible for Ely's poverty, and could not, under any reasonable system for the appointment of counsel, rectify all the consequences of the inequality of wealth among criminal defendants. In general, the best criminal lawyers are retained by the most affluent defendants, who pay them on a much more generous scale than under the Criminal Justice Act. The government cannot eliminate the consequences of poverty; it can only limit them, as it did in this case by supplying Ely with the services of competent and experienced legal counsel. * * *

[Conviction affirmed.]*

Commentary

There are two distinct constitutional principles at work in these cases: (1) The "due process" principle that the state must provide an indigent defendant with a lawyer and whatever other resources are absolutely necessary to a fair trial; and (2) the "equal protection" principle, which requires the state to take affirmative steps to narrow the gap between the resources available to rich and poor criminal defendants. The second principle is plainly the more far-reaching, and indeed it appears to promise more than the courts and the rest of society are prepared to deliver. Fees for appointed defense counsel are typically quite low in comparison to the fees private litigants pay their lawyers. The problem is not only one of unwillingness to provide resources, however. As long as rich defendants are allowed to use all the resources at their command to retain the best lawyers and supporting services, it is difficult to see how any realistic program of public assistance could achieve anything like "equality." If we were truly dedicated to achieving this elusive goal, then we would probably have to consider "leveling down," by imposing a ceiling on what the rich can spend or by assigning defense counsel to rich and poor alike by random selection. The measures necessary to achieve equality might in themselves be unconstitutional.

The Supreme Court apparently felt it necessary to invoke the equal protection principle in the cases involving transcripts and counsel on appeal because the Constitution contains no explicit guarantee of a right to appeal. At common law there was no appeal in criminal cases, and the only remedy a convicted defendant had was executive clemency. The Supreme Court has said in *dicta* that the states are under no constitutional obligation to provide for appeal in criminal cases, although all states do. See McKane v. Durston, 153 U.S. 684 (1894). If there is no constitutional right to appeal, then it would seem that there can be no constitutional right to a transcript and a lawyer on appeal. Rather than declare that modern notions of "due process" require that there be a right to appeal in criminal cases, the Supreme Court chose to invoke the expansive equal protection principle. One wonders what the Court would do if a state actually chose to abolish all criminal appeals.

Given the proviso that "absolute equality is not required," what must a state do beyond providing free counsel to indigents at trial and on the first appeal to satisfy the Supreme Court's ban on invidious discrimination against the poor? The Supreme Court has held that a state is not required to provide counsel for an indigent defendant to seek discretionary review in the

---

* Compare, Harris v. Superior Court, 19 Cal.3d 786, 140 Cal.Rptr. 318, 567 P.2d 750 (1977), which held that the state trial court should have appointed the lawyers requested by the indigent defendants where defendants had previously established a close relationship with the requested lawyers.

state supreme court or in the United States Supreme Court, after his conviction has been initially affirmed in the state's intermediate court of appeals. Ross v. Moffitt, 417 U.S. 600 (1974). In its opinion, the Supreme Court observed that denial of appointed counsel at this stage would not deprive the indigent defendant of meaningful access to the state supreme court, because that court could determine whether or not to hear the case on the basis of the brief filed by appointed counsel in the intermediate court, together with the intermediate court's opinion and any supplemental materials that the defendant wished to submit *pro se*. The Court concluded that "The duty of the State under our cases is not to duplicate the legal arsenal that may be privately retained by a criminal defendant in a continuing effort to reverse his conviction, but only to assure the indigent defendant an adequate opportunity to present his claims fairly in the context of the State's appellate process." In dissent Mr. Justice Douglas noted that it would be a relatively easy matter for the attorney who had argued the first appeal to prepare a petition for further discretionary review, and repeated the admonition that "there can be no equal justice where the kind of appeal a man enjoys 'depends upon the amount of money he has.' "

Although the Constitution specifically provides for a right to counsel in all criminal trials but says nothing about a right to an appeal or a transcript, the Court has nonetheless given a broader scope to the equality-based right to a transcript than it has to the due process-based right to trial counsel. In Mayer v. Chicago, 404 U.S. 189 (1971), the Court unanimously held that an indigent defendant cannot be denied a record of sufficient completeness to permit proper consideration of his claims on appeal merely because he was convicted of ordinance violations punishable by a fine only. The opinion noted that a fine may bear as heavily on an indigent defendant as a jail sentence, and that the collateral consequences of a conviction may be substantial even in the absence of a jail term. These considerations are, of course, equally pertinent to the issue of a right to counsel at trial.

The absolute right to counsel extends to sentencing procedures, but not to probation or parole revocation hearings. See Gagnon v. Scarpelli, 411 U.S. 778 (1973); compare, Mempa v. Rhay, 389 U.S. 128 (1967). In such proceedings the probationer or parolee must be advised that he has a right to request counsel, but counsel is actually appointed only where the hearing officer makes a preliminary determination that the case involves issues which indicate a need for the assistance of counsel. In other words, the *Betts v. Brady* approach continues to be used for revocation hearings, with all its well-known disadvantages. A person who is unable to make a proper defense without counsel will often be unable to make a proper showing as to precisely why counsel is needed. In the opinion of most commentators, it is easier and more efficient simply to provide a lawyer upon request rather than to attempt to make a determination of whether counsel would be helpful.

Appointment of counsel to assist an inmate in collateral proceedings such as federal habeas corpus is also discretionary, although counsel is generally provided if the petition has sufficient merit to call for an evidentiary hearing. Prisoners generally have to prepare their own petitions in the first instance, relying on whatever legal materials are available to them and the assistance of fellow inmates. The Supreme Court has held that states may not arbitrarily prohibit such inmate "writ-writers" from providing assistance to other prisoners. Johnson v. Avery, 393 U.S. 483 (1969). States also have an obligation to provide minimally adequate law libraries or other legal assistance to allow prisoners to have meaningful access to the courts. See Bounds v. Smith, 430 U.S. 817 (1977); Hooks v. Wainwright, 716 F.2d 913 (11th Cir.1983). The need for post-appeal assistance of counsel is particularly acute for defendants sentenced to death, who may file petitions for stays of execution and other relief right up to the moment of execution.

Effective defense representation requires not only a lawyer and a transcript, but also in some cases resources like investigators or expert witnesses. The federal Criminal Justice Act, 18 U.S.C.A. Section 3006A, provides, in part: "(a) Each United States district court, with the approval of the judicial council of the circuit, shall place in operation throughout the district a plan for furnishing representation for any person financially unable to obtain adequate representation in accordance with this section. Representation under each plan shall include counsel and investigative, expert, and other services necessary for adequate representation." State laws also ordinarily provide some such discretionary authority, although of course they do not guarantee that defendants will receive fully adequate resources, especially in comparison to the resources available to the very rich. Free lawyers and other resources are ordinarily provided only to indigents; middle class defendants must pay for their own defense. The State does not pay these costs even if the defendant is found not guilty, and so a defendant may be ruined financially by a criminal prosecution regardless of the outcome. In this respect, indigents actually have an advantage over individuals with modest means, who may be deterred from pursuing all available remedies by cost considerations.

B. FORFEITURE OF ASSETS USED TO PAY FOR PRIVATE COUNSEL

CAPLIN & DRYSDALE, CHARTERED v. UNITED STATES

Supreme Court of the United States, 1989.
491 U.S. 617, 109 S.Ct. 2646, 105 L.Ed.2d 528.

JUSTICE WHITE delivered the opinion of the Court.

We are called on to determine whether the federal drug forfeiture statute includes an exemption for assets that a defendant wishes to use to pay an attorney who conducted his defense in the criminal case where forfeiture was sought. Because we determine that no such exemption exists, we must decide whether that statute, so interpreted, is consistent with the Fifth and Sixth Amendments. We hold that it is.

I

In January 1985, Christopher Reckmeyer was charged in a multi-count indictment with running a massive drug importation and distribution scheme. The scheme was alleged to be a continuing criminal enterprise (CCE), in violation of 21 U.S.C. section 848. Relying on a portion of the CCE statute that authorizes forfeiture to the government of "property constitution, or derived from * * * proceeds * * * obtained" from drug-law violations, 21 U.S.C. section 853(a), the indictment sought forfeiture of specified assets in Reckmeyer's possession. At this time, the District Court entered a restraining order forbidding Reckmeyer to transfer any of the listed assets that were potentially forfeitable. Sometime earlier, Reckmeyer had retained petitioner, a law firm, to represent him in the ongoing grand jury investigation which resulted in the January 1985 indictments. Notwithstanding the restraining order, Reckmeyer paid the firm $25,000 for preindictment legal services a few days after the indictment was handed down; this sum was placed by petitioner in an escrow account. Petitioner continued to represent Reckmeyer following the indictment. On March 7, 1985, Reckmeyer moved to modify the District Court's earlier restraining order to permit him to use some of the restrained assets to pay petitioner's fees; Reckmeyer also sought to exempt from any postconviction forfeiture order the assets that he intended to use to pay petitioner. However, one week later, before the District Court could conduct a hearing on this motion, Reckmeyer entered a plea agreement with the Government. Under the agreement, Reckmeyer pleaded guilty to the drug-related CCE charge, and agreed to forfeit all of the specified assets listed in the indictment. The day after the Reckmeyer's plea was entered, the District Court denied his earlier motion to modify the restraining order, concluding that the plea and forfeiture agreement rendered irrelevant any further consideration of the propriety of the court's pretrial restraints. Subsequently, an order forfeiting virtually all of the assets in Reckmeyer's possession was entered by the District Court in conjunction with his sentencing. After this order was entered petitioner filed a petition under 21 U.S.C. section 853(n), which permits third parties with an interest in forfeited property to ask the sentencing court for an adjudication of their rights to that property; specifically section 853(n)(6)(B) gives a third party who entered into a bona fide transaction with a defendant a right to make claims against forfeited property, if that third party was 'at the time of [the transaction] reasonably without cause to believe that the [defendant's assets were] subject to forfeiture.' Petitioner claimed an interest in $170,000 of Reckmeyer's assets, for services it had provided Reckmeyer in conducting his defense; petitioner also sought the $25,000 being held in the escrow account, as payment for preindictment legal services. Petitioner argued alternatively that assets used to pay an attorney were exempt from forfeiture under section 853, and if not, the failure of the statute to provide such an exemption rendered it unconstitutional. The District Court granted petitioner's claim for a share of the forfeited assets.

[The Court of Appeals reversed, en banc.] All the judges of the Fourth Circuit agreed that the language of the CCE statute acknowledged no exception to its forfeiture requirement that would recognize petitioner's claim to the forfeited assets. A majority found this statutory scheme constitutional; four dissenting judges, however, agreed with the panel's view that the statute so-construed violated the Sixth Amendment. * * *

II

Petitioner's first submission is that the statutory provision that authorizes pretrial restraining orders on potentially forfeitable assets in a defendant's possession, 21 U.S.C. section 853(e), grants district courts equitable discretion to determine when such orders should be imposed. This discretion should be exercised under "traditional equitable standards," petitioner urges, including a "weigh[ing] of the equities and competing hardships on the parties"; under this approach, a court "must invariably strike the balance so as to allow a defendant [to pay] * * * for bona fide attorneys fees," petitioner argues. Petitioner further submits that once a district court so exercises its discretion, and fails to freeze assets that a defendant then uses to pay an attorney, the statute's provision for recapture of forfeitable assets transferred to third parties, 21 U.S.C. section 853(c), may not operate on such sums.

Petitioner's argument, as it acknowledges, is based on the view of the statute expounded by Judge Winter of the Second Circuit in his concurring opinion in that Court of Appeals' en banc decision, United States v. Monsanto, 852 F.2d 1400, 1405–1411 (1988). We reject this interpretation of the statute today in our decision in *United States v. Monsanto*, which reverses the Second Circuit's holding in that case. As we explain in our *Monsanto* decision, whatever discretion section 853(e) provides district court judges to refuse to enter pretrial restraining orders, it does not extend as far as petitioner urges—nor does the exercise of that discretion "immunize" nonrestrained assets from subsequent forfeiture under section 853(c), if they are transferred to an attorney to pay legal fees. Thus, for the reasons provided in our opinion in Monsanto, we reject petitioner's statutory claim.

III

We therefore address petitioner's constitutional challenges to the forfeiture law. Petitioner contends that the statute infringes on criminal defendants' Sixth Amendment right to counsel of choice, and upsets the "balance of power" between the government and the accused in a manner contrary to the Due Process Clause of the Fifth Amendment. We consider these contentions in turn.

A

Petitioner's first claim is that the forfeiture law makes impossible, or at least impermissibly burdens, a defendant's right to select and be represented by one's preferred attorney. Petitioner does not, nor could it defensibly do so, assert that impecunious defendants have a Sixth Amendment right to choose their counsel. The amendment guarantees defendants in criminal cases the right to adequate representation, but those who do not have the means to hire their own lawyers have no cognizable complaint so long as they are adequately represented by attorneys appointed by the courts. * * *

The forfeiture statute does not prevent a defendant who has nonforfeitable assets from retaining any attorney of his choosing. Nor is it necessarily the case that a defendant who possesses nothing but assets the Government seeks to have forfeited will be prevented from retaining counsel of choice. Defendants like Reckmeyer may be able to find lawyers willing to represent them, hoping that their fees will be paid in the event of acquittal, or via some other means that a defendant might come by in the future. The burden placed on defendants by the forfeiture law is therefore a limited one. * * *

A defendant has no Sixth Amendment right to spend another person's money for services rendered by an attorney, even if those funds are the only way that that defendant will be able to retain the attorney of his choice. A robbery suspect for example, has no Sixth Amendment right to use funds he has stolen from a bank to retain an attorney to defend him if he is apprehended. The money, though in his possession, is not rightfully his; the government does not violate the Sixth Amendment if it seizes the robbery proceeds, and refuses to permit the defendant to use them to pay for his defense. * * * Petitioner seeks to distinguish such cases for Sixth Amendment purposes by arguing that the bank's claim to robbery proceeds rests on "pre-existing property rights," while the Government's claim to forfeitable assets rests on a "penal statute" which embodies the "fictive property-law concept of * * * relation-back" and is merely "a mechanism for preventing fraudulent conveyances of the defendant's assets, not * * * a device for determining true title to property." In light of this, petitioner contends, the burden placed on defendant's Sixth Amendment rights by the forfeiture statute outweighs the Government's interest in forfeiture. * * *

Petitioner's "balancing analysis" rests substantially on the view that the Government has only a modest interest in forfeitable assets that may be used to retain an attorney. Petitioner takes the position that, in large part, once assets have been paid over from client to attorney, the principal ends of forfeiture have been achieved: dispossessing a drug dealer or racketeer of the proceeds of his wrongdoing. We think that this view misses the mark for three reasons.

First, the Government has a pecuniary interest in forfeiture that goes beyond merely separating a criminal from his ill-gotten gains; that legitimate interest extends to recovering *all* forfeitable assets, for such assets are deposited in a Fund that supports law-enforcement efforts in a variety of important and useful ways. See 28 U.S.C. section 524(c), which establishes the Department of Justice Assets Forfeiture Fund. The sums of money that can be raised for law-enforcement activities this way are substantial, and the Government's interest in using the profits of crime to fund these activities should not be discounted.

Second, the statute permits "rightful owners" of forfeited assets to make claims for forfeited assets before they are retained by the government. The Government's interest in winning undiminished forfeiture thus includes the objective of returning property, in full, to those wrongfully deprived or defrauded of it. Where the Government pursues this restitutionary end, the government's interest in forfeiture is virtually indistinguishable from its interest in returning to a bank the proceeds of a bank robbery; and a forfeiture-defendant's claim of right to use such assets to hire an attorney, instead of having them returned to their rightful owners, is no more persuasive than a bank robber's similar claim.

Finally, as we have recognized previously, a major purpose motivating congressional adoption and continued refinement of the RICO and CCE forfeiture provisions has been the desire to lessen the economic power of organized crime and drug enterprises. This includes the use of such economic power to retain private counsel. As the Court of Appeals put it: "Congress has already underscored the compelling public interest in stripping criminals such as Reckmeyer of their undeserved economic power, and part of that undeserved power may be the ability to command high-priced legal talent." The notion that the government has a legitimate interest in depriving criminals of economic power, even insofar as that power is used to retain counsel of choice, may be somewhat unsettling. But when a defendant claims that he has suffered some substantial impairment of his Sixth Amendment rights by virtue of the seizure or forfeiture of assets in his possession, such a complaint is no more than the reflection of "the harsh reality that the quality of a criminal defendant's representation frequently may turn on his ability to retain the best counsel money can buy." Again, the Court of Appeals put it aptly: "The modern day Jean Valjean must be satisfied with appointed counsel. Yet the drug merchant claims that his possession of huge sums of money * * * entitles him to something more. We reject this contention, and any notion of a constitutional right to use the proceeds of crime to finance an expensive defense."

It is our view that there is a strong governmental interest in obtaining full recovery of all forfeitable assets, and interest that overrides any Sixth Amendment interest in permitting criminals to use assets adjudged forfeitable to pay for their defense. Otherwise, there would be an interference with a defendant's Sixth Amendment rights whenever the government freezes or takes some property in a defendant's possession before, during or after a criminal trial. So-called "jeopardy assessments"—IRS seizures of assets to secure potential tax liabilities—may impair a defendant's ability to retain counsel in a way similar to that complained of here. Yet these assessments have been upheld against constitutional attack, and we note that the respondent in *Monsanto* concedes their constitutionality. Moreover, petitioner's claim to a share of the forfeited assets postconviction would suggest that the government could never impose a burden on assets within a defendant's control that could be used to pay a lawyer. Criminal defendants, however, are not exempted from federal, state, and local taxation simply because these financial levies may deprive them of resources that could be used to hire an attorney. * * *

B

Petitioner's second constitutional claim is that the forfeiture statute is invalid under the Due Process Clause of the Fifth Amendment because it permits the Government to upset the balance of forces between the accused and his accuser. * * *

Forfeiture provisions are powerful weapons in the war on crime; like any such weapons, their impact can be devastating when used unjustly. But due process claims alleging such abuses are cognizable only in specific cases of prosecutorial misconduct (and petitioner has made no such allegation here) or when directed to a rule that is inherently unconstitutional. * * *

We rejected a claim similar to petitioner's last Term, in Wheat v. United States, 486 U.S. 153 (1988). In *Wheat*, the petitioner argued that permitting a court to disqualify a defendant's chosen counsel because of conflicts of interest—over that defendant's objection to the disqualification—would encourage the government to "manufacture" such conflicts to deprive a defendant of his chosen attorney. While acknowledging that this was possible, we declined to fashion the per se constitutional rule petitioner sought in Wheat, instead observing that "trial courts are undoubtedly aware of [the] possibility" of abuse, and would have to "take it into consideration," when dealing with disqualification motions. A similar approach should be taken here. The Constitution does not forbid the imposition of an otherwise permissible criminal sanction, such as forfeiture, merely because in some cases prosecutors may abuse the processes available to them, e.g., by attempting to impose them on persons who should not be subjected to that punishment. Cases involving particular abuses can be dealt with individually by the lower courts, when (and if) any such cases arise.

IV

For the reasons given above, we find that petitioner's statutory and constitutional challenges to the forfeiture imposed here are without merit. The judgment of the Court of Appeals is therefore Affirmed.

JUSTICE BLACKMUN, with whom JUSTICE BRENNAN, JUSTICE MARSHALL, and JUSTICE STEVENS join, dissenting.

Those jurists who have held forth against the result the majority reaches in these cases have been guided by one core insight: that it is unseemly and unjust for the Government to beggar those it prosecutes in order to disable their defense at trial. The majority trivializes the burden the forfeiture law imposes on a criminal defendant. Instead, it should heed the warnings of our district court judges, whose day-to-day exposure to the criminal-trial process enables them to understand, perhaps far better than we, the devastating consequences of attorney's fee forfeiture for the integrity of our adversarial system of justice.

[The dissent endorsed the argument of Judge Winter's opinion in the *Monsanto* case, reasoning that Congress did not explicitly consider the attorney's fee issue and the statute could be construed to allow otherwise forfeitable assets to be used to the reasonable fees of privately retained counsel.]

The majority has decided otherwise, however, and for that reason is compelled to reach the constitutional issue it could have avoided. But the majority pauses hardly long enough to acknowledge the Sixth Amendment's protection of one's right to retain counsel of his choosing, let alone to explore its "full extent." Instead, it moves rapidly from the observation that "a defendant may not insist on representation by an attorney he cannot afford," to the conclusion that the Government is free to deem the defendant indigent by declaring his assets "tainted" by criminal activity the Government has yet to prove. * * * The majority's decision in this case reveals that it has lost track of the distinct role of the right to counsel of choice in protecting the integrity of the judicial process, a role that makes "the right to be represented by privately retained counsel * * * the primary, preferred component of the basic right" protected by the Sixth Amendment. The right to retain private counsel serves to foster the trust between attorney and client that is necessary for the attorney to be a truly effective advocate. Not only are decisions crucial to the defendant's liberty placed in counsel's hands, but the defendant's perception of the fairness of the process, and his willingness to acquiesce in its results, depend upon his confidence in his counsel's dedication, loyalty, and ability. * * *

The right to privately chosen and compensated counsel also serves broader institutional interests. The "virtual socialization of criminal defense work in this country" that would be the result of a widespread abandonment of the right to retain chosen counsel, too readily would standardize the provision of criminal-defense services and diminish defense counsel's independence. There is a place in our system of criminal justice for the maverick and the risk-taker, for approaches that might not fit into the structured environment of a public defender's office, or that might displease a judge whose preference for nonconfrontational styles of advocacy might influence the judge's appointment decisions. * * *

Had it been Congress' express aim to undermine the adversary system as we know it, it could hardly have found a better engine of destruction that attorney's-fee forfeiture. The main effect of forfeitures under the Act, of course, will be to deny the defendant the right to retain counsel, and therefore the right to have his defense designed and presented by an attorney he has chosen and trusts. If the Government restrains the defendant's assets before trial, private counsel will be unwilling to continue or to take on the defense. Even if no restraining order is entered, the possibility of forfeiture after conviction will itself substantially diminish the likelihood that private counsel will agree to take the case. The message to private counsel is "Do not represent this defendant or you will lose your fee." That being the kind of message lawyers are likely to take seriously, the defendant will find it difficult or impossible to secure representation.

The resulting relationship between the defendant and his court-appointed counsel will likely begin in distrust, and be exacerbated to the extent that the defendant perceives his new-found "indigency" as a form of punishment imposed by the Government in order to weaken his defense. If the defendant had been represented by private counsel earlier in the proceedings, the defendant's sense that the Government has stripped him of his defenses will be sharpened by the concreteness of his loss. Appointed counsel may be inexperienced and undercompensated and, for that reason, may not have adequate opportunity or resources to deal with the special problems presented by what is likely to be a complex trial. The already scarce resources of a public defender's office will be stretched to the limit. Facing a lengthy trial against a better-armed adversary, the temptation to recommend a guilty plea will be great. The result, if the defendant is convicted, will be a sense, often well grounded, that justice was not done.

Even if the defendant finds a private attorney who is "so foolish, ignorant, beholden or idealistic as to take the business," the attorney-client relationship will be undermined by the forfeiture statute. Perhaps the attorney will be willing to violate ethical norms by working on a contingent fee basis in a criminal case. But if he is not—and we should question the integrity of any criminal-defense attorney who would violate the ethical norms of the profession by doing so—the attorney's own interests will dictate that he remain ignorant of the source of the assets from which he is paid. Under section 853(c), a third-party transferee may keep assets if "the transferee establishes * * * that he is a bona fide purchaser for value of such property who at the time of purchase was reasonably without cause to believe that the property was subject to forfeiture under this section." The less an attorney knows, the greater the likelihood that he can claim to have been an "innocent" third party. The attorney's interest in knowing nothing is directly adverse to his client's interest in full disclosure. The result of the conflict may be a less vigorous investigation of the defendant's circumstances, leading in turn to a failure to recognize or pursue avenues of inquiry necessary to the defense. Other conflicts of interest are also likely to develop. The attorney who fears for his fee will be tempted to make the Government's waiver of fee-forfeiture the sine qua non for any plea agreement, a position which conflicts with his client's best interests. Perhaps most troubling is the fact that forfeiture statutes place the Government in the position to exercise an intolerable degree of power over any private attorney who takes on the task of representing a defendant in a forfeiture case. The decision whether to seek a restraining order rests with the prosecution, as does the decision whether to waive forfeiture upon a plea of guilty or a conviction at trial. The Government will be ever tempted to use the forfeiture weapon against a defense attorney who is particularly talented or aggressive on the client's behalf—the attorney who is better than what, in the Government's view, the defendant deserves. The spectre of the Government's selectively excluding only the most talented defense counsel is a serious threat to the equality of forces necessary for the adversarial system to perform at its best. An attorney whose fees are potentially subject to forfeiture will be forced to operate in an environment in which the Government is not only the defendant's adversary, but also his own. The long-term effects of the fee-forfeiture practice will be to decimate the private criminal-defense bar. As the use of the forfeiture mechanism expands to new categories of federal crimes and spreads to the States, only one class of defendants will be free routinely to retain private counsel: the affluent defendant accused of a crime that generates no economic gain. As the number of private clients diminishes, only the most idealistic and the least skilled of young lawyers will be attracted to the field, while the remainder seek greener pastures elsewhere.

In short, attorney's fee-forfeiture substantially undermines every interest served by the Sixth Amendment right to chosen counsel, on the individual and institutional levels, over the short term and the long haul.
* * *

In my view, the Act as interpreted by the majority is inconsistent with the intent of Congress, and seriously undermines the basic fairness of our criminal-justice system. That a majority of this Court has upheld the constitutionality of the Act as so interpreted will not deter Congress, I hope, from amending the Act to make clear that Congress did not intend this result. This Court has the power to declare the Act constitutional, but it cannot thereby make it wise. I dissent.

C. APPOINTMENT OF EXPERT WITNESSES TO ASSIST INDIGENT DEFENDANTS

DE FREECE v. STATE

Court of Criminal Appeals of Texas, 1993.
848 S.W.2d 150.

CLINTON, JUDGE

Appellant was convicted by a jury of the offense of murder and his punishment assessed by the trial court at 60 years confinement in the penitentiary. On appeal he argued that the trial court erred in failing to appoint an expert to assist him in evaluation, preparation, and presentation of his insanity defense, in violation of his constitutional rights to due process, equal protection, effective assistance of counsel and compulsory process * * *.

I.

Appellant and the deceased, Juanita Rodriguez, had a five-month-old son. On the morning of February 17, 1989, appellant went to the home of Juanita's parents in Eagle Pass, where she and the baby were staying. Appellant was told by Juanita's sister that Juanita and her parents and brother had left that morning to drive to Pecos. Based upon statements he claimed Juanita's mother had made on prior occasions, appellant decided that the group intended to sell the baby in Pecos, and set out after them. He caught up with them on Highway 90 between Dryden and Sanderson, and ran them off the road. According to his testimony, at this time appellant heard voices he "couldn't overcome" which commanded him to "kill, kill." He forced Juanita into his car, where he stabbed her numerous times in the chest and abdomen, and then cut her throat. Texas Rangers apprehended him the next day a mile from the scene, and he readily confessed * * *.

On June 23, 1989, the State filed a motion requesting that appellant be examined both for competency to stand trial and sanity at the time of the offense. Pursuant to [statutes], the trial court ordered appellant sent to Vernon State Hospital "for observation, examination and treatment." There, Dr. D.F. Martinez, a psychiatrist, diagnosed him as suffering from "Schizophrenia, Chronic, Undifferentiated Type." Dr. F.E. Heynen, a clinical psychologist, opined that appellant was incompetent to stand trial, but that at the time of the offense he "had substantial capacity to appreciate the wrongfulness of his behavior and understood that his behavior was unlawful." On September 11, 1989, a jury found appellant presently incompetent, but capable of attaining competency in the foreseeable future; judgment to that effect was entered on September 13, 1989. Accordingly, appellant was returned to Vernon State Hospital, where he was re-evaluated every ninety days. On December 7, 1989, and again on March 12, 1990, the hospital reported that appellant had not yet attained competency, apparently on recommendations from Dr. Martinez. Finally, on June 1, 1990, the trial court was notified that appellant was competent to stand trial, although Dr. Martinez advised that "he should continue his present medications consisting of neuroleptics and antidepressants."

On August 20, 1990, counsel for appellant filed a motion requesting the appointment of a psychiatric expert to assist in preparing and presenting his insanity defense * * *. Counsel clarified that he sought no particular expert, but simply any competent psychiatrist who: "would be a member of the defense team, would be available for helping preparation of the case, preparation for cross examination, deciding which tests were needed, range and form, that sort of thing, as well as being present during trial to help the defendant."

The trial court stated, inter alia, that "I've already appointed a psychiatrist to conduct an evaluation, and I don't feel I have to appoint another one." Instead, the court assured appellant's counsel that he would be afforded an opportunity to interview Dr. Heynen, who was scheduled to testify for the State, prior to cross-examining her. Counsel for appellant complained that he "did not believe the ability to speak to this one doctor solves the problem, because number one, she's already on record in writing as supporting the State's position, and number two, she will give no assistance in how to cross-examine her * * *. We think that we still need the expert on the defense team." The trial court denied both appellant's motions.

Trial commenced that same day. Other than his testimony that he had heard voices commanding him to "kill, kill," appellant presented no direct evidence to show he was insane at the time of the offense. In rebuttal the State put Dr. Heynen on the witness stand to testify that any voices appellant may have heard would not be "sufficiently compelling to cause him to forget that this was a wrongful thing to do." After reading a number of reports from other clinics, conducting a battery of tests, and consulting with other staff members at Vernon State Hospital, she concluded that appellant had known the difference between right and wrong when he committed the offense. After this testimony the trial court adjourned for the day, and Dr. Heynen assured the court that she would be available to consult with appellant's counsel.

The next morning counsel took Dr. Heynen on cross-examination. She agreed that appellant's records from his stay at Vernon State Hospital "weigh several pounds." Out of the presence of the jury appellant then renewed his motion for expert assistance to help him interpret those voluminous records with a view to cross-examining Dr. Heynen * * *. The trial court again denied the motion.

As cross-examination continued, Dr. Heynen verified that Dr. Martinez had diagnosed appellant as suffering from undifferentiated schizophrenia, organic brain syndrome, and extreme psychosocial stressors. Dr. Heynen admitted that she herself had found that appellant had "diffuse organic brain damage." She believed his earlier history of commitment to mental hospitals, however, was "generally because of drug abuse." Disagreeing with Dr. Martinez' evaluation of appellant as schizophrenic, Dr. Heynen opined that her own diagnostic skills "far exceed those of Dr. Martinez." She acknowledged that another doctor had earlier found in appellant "the capacity * * * to decompensate and to be a danger to himself and others." She pointed out, however, that this doctor did not "give any reason why he thought he had decompensated." On redirect examination Dr. Heynen noted several typical characteristics of schizophrenia (e.g., incoherence, impaired personal hygiene, "flat affect") that appellant did not manifest.

During final argument appellant's counsel conceded that the evidence showed appellant caused the death of Rodriguez. Emphasizing appellant's history of mental health commitments and his apparently delusional belief that Rodriguez' family intended to sell his baby, counsel argued that the jury should find that when appellant killed Rodriguez, he did not appreciate the wrongfulness of his conduct. In rebuttal, the State stressed Dr. Heynen's testimony that appellant could distinguish right from wrong when he committed the offense. After deliberating for five hours, the jury returned a guilty verdict * * *.

We confront the question whether examination by "disinterested experts" at Vernon State Hospital, and testimony from at least one of those experts at trial about conclusions she drew from that examination, were sufficient to meet the due process minimum announced in Ake v. Oklahoma, 470 U.S. 68 (1985). Appellant does not claim he was deprived of the opportunity to be examined by a competent expert on the question of sanity, as was Ake. He does claim, however, that, having shown his sanity would be a significant factor at his trial, he should have been provided an expert of the court's choosing to help him evaluate and prepare his insanity defense, and meaningfully confront expert testimony adduced by the State. We agree, and hold that the trial court erred in denying him that assistance * * *.

Ake v. Oklahoma

Accused of capital murder, Glen Burton Ake displayed such odd behavior at his arraignment that the trial court ordered an examination to decide whether he should be observed to determine his competency to stand trial. The psychiatrist who examined Ake concluded he was a paranoid schizophrenic, and he was committed to a state hospital, where he was found incompetent. Six weeks later he was found to have regained competency, subject to continued treatment with an antipsychotic drug, Thorazine. Prior to trial his attorney indicated he would raise the defense of insanity, and requested psychiatric assistance, since Ake was indigent. Even though the state hospital had made no determination of Ake's sanity at the time of the offense, the trial court denied his request. "As a result there was no expert testimony for either side on Ake's sanity at the time of the offense." The Oklahoma Court of Criminal Appeals affirmed Ake's conviction, holding that the State had no obligation to provide psychiatric services to indigents in capital cases.

The United States Supreme Court reversed Ake's conviction. In its opinion the Court began by reaffirming the principle that due process requires that the indigent accused in a criminal trial must be equipped with the "basic tools" to ensure "a proper functioning of the adversary process." Deciding whether a psychiatric expert was necessary to that end, the Court considered three factors borrowed from cases involving questions of procedural due process, viz:

> "The first is the private interest that will be affected by the action of the State. The second is the governmental interest that will be affected if the safeguard is to be provided. The third is the probable value of the additional or substitute procedural safeguards that are sought, and the risk of an erroneous deprivation of the affected interest if those safeguards are not provided."

The accused's interest in maintaining the institutional presumption of innocence, the Court observed, "is obvious." The State, on the other hand, has more than the ordinary adversarial interest in prevailing; it has a concomitant interest in the fairness of the proceeding and the accuracy of the result. Moreover, because most states already provide some level of psychiatric assistance to the accused, that burden cannot be prohibitive. In these lights the Court concluded that the State's interest "is not substantial."

Assessing the third factor, the Court began "by considering the pivotal role that psychiatry has come to play in criminal proceedings." "In this role, psychiatrists gather facts, through professional examination, interviews, and elsewhere, that they will share with the judge and jury; they analyze the information gathered and from it draw plausible conclusions about the defendant's mental condition, and about the effects of any disorder on behavior; and they offer opinions about how the defendant's mental condition might have affected his behavior at the time in question. They know the probative questions to ask of the opposing party's psychiatrists and how to interpret their answers."

Thus, psychiatric experts may assist lay judges and jurors to make an informed decision about the sanity of the accused at the time of the offense. Because psychiatry is not "an exact science," however, juries remain the "primary factfinders," and, the Court suggested, it is important that the jury hear "the psychiatrists for each party" to equip it to make as informed a decision as possible. To avoid the risk of an inaccurate verdict, the Court concluded, an indigent accused must be provided an expert "to conduct a professional examination on issues relevant to the defense, to help determine whether the insanity defense is viable, to present testimony, and to assist in preparing the cross-examination of a State's psychiatric witnesses."

The Court concluded: "We therefore hold that when a defendant demonstrates to the trial judge that his sanity at the time of the offense is to be a significant factor at trial, the State must, at a minimum, assure the defendant access to a competent psychiatrist who will conduct an appropriate examination and assist in evaluation, preparation, and presentation of the defense. That is not to say, of course, that the indigent defendant has a constitutional right to choose a psychiatrist of his personal liking or to receive funds to hire his own. Our concern is that the indigent defendant have access to a competent psychiatrist for the purpose we have discussed, and as in the case of the provision of counsel we leave to the State the decision on how to implement this right."

Commentators have noted an "ambiguity" in *Ake,* a seeming internal contradiction between the express right to a single competent psychiatric expert not of the accused's choosing, on the one hand, and indications throughout the opinion, on the other, that the accused is entitled to an expert who will participate with him as a partisan in the case. Some courts have targeted the first aspect of *Ake* to hold that a single "neutral" expert is all the State need supply to ensure proper adversarial functioning. Thus, many courts have denied *Ake* claims where the accused has received an examination in a state mental institution pursuant to court order, holding that the state-sponsored examination met all due process requirements. In each of these cases, however, the state institution had found no reason to doubt the defendant's sanity, and therefore the court also found the defendant had not shown insanity would be a significant factor at trial in any event. Many other courts have held similarly that, where a state-sponsored examination reveals no likelihood of insanity at the time of the offense, a defendant has not met the threshold requirements for relief under *Ake.* [Almost every] court that has found the defendant did make an adequate showing that insanity would be a significant factor, however, has also held that *Ake* entitled him to more than an examination and testimony, if favorable, from a neutral psychiatric expert.

Thus, it is true that some jurisdictions have said, essentially in dicta, that the statutory provision of a single neutral psychiatrist to service both parties and the court is sufficient to meet the due process minimum of *Ake*. However, it appears that * * * the greater weight of authority holds otherwise. And, in our view, with good reason.

Ours is an adversarial system of criminal justice, not an inquisitorial one. Either mode of inquiry is aimed at assessing the truth. However, the adversarial model rests on the assumption that each party to a dispute, motivated by self-interest, will develop his position to the greatest extent possible within the boundaries of the rules of evidence and procedure, thus providing the factfinder an optimal vantage from which to gauge all relevant facts and make an informed decision on the merits. In *Ake* the Supreme Court reiterated that where the defendant is indigent, due process requires that the State guarantee he be at least minimally equipped to participate meaningfully in this adversarial process.

Where sanity of the indigent accused will be a significant factor at trial, psychiatry has come to play a "pivotal role." But since psychiatry "is not * * * an exact science," equally competent practitioners confronted with the same raw data often disagree in their diagnoses in an area that is "inevitably complex and foreign" to lawyers and juries alike. Although psychiatric testimony is undoubtedly useful in the resolution of many issues in the adversary trial context, including sanity at the time of the offense: "none of these issues * * * can be addressed by a psychiatrist with absolute certainty. Thus, to expect the 'objective' opinion of an amicus expert to yield 'the answer' in a particular case is unrealistic. Unless the choices made by the psychiatrist in the establishment and proof of his or her hypothesis are open to informed scrutiny, the psychiatrist's conclusions are of limited value. And, unless each party has access to psychiatric assistance in preparing and directing this scrutiny, it cannot be expected that the scrutiny will be adequately informed. Indeed, each party must have the opportunity to explore and explain the relevant psychiatric data in a case if the conclusions drawn from these data are properly to be understood by the judge or the jury and the 'truth' is to be most closely approximated. This is the teaching of *Ake v. Oklahoma*."

Because psychiatric evidence is at once esoteric and uncertain, the indigent accused needs a psychiatrist, inter alia, "to help determine whether the insanity defense is viable, to present testimony, and to assist in preparing the cross-examination of a State's psychiatric witness," if he is to present the factfinder with a perspective broad enough to ensure an informed resolution of the sanity question. Otherwise the risk of error is intolerably high, and due process will be offended * * *.

The State does not contest that in this cause appellant demonstrated to the trial court that insanity would be a significant factor at trial, as indeed it turned out to be * * *. Counsel for appellant did not ask for anything more than he was minimally entitled to under *Ake*. He did not request a particular psychiatrist, but only a single competent one. Nor did he seek a psychiatrist who would necessarily testify that his client was insane at the time of the offense. He simply sought expert guidance in evaluating the strength of appellant's defense, presenting it in the best possible light to the jury, and, in particular, in scrutinizing the testimony of Dr. Heynen, the only expert opinion then available that directly addressed the question of appellant's ability to distinguish right from wrong. Even a neutral "court's expert" cannot effectively prepare counsel to cross-examine herself. We hold that the trial court erred in denying appellant's request for the appointment of a psychiatrist to aid in the preparation and presentation of his insanity defense.

We therefore reverse the judgment and remand the cause for a new trial.

D. INEFFECTIVE ASSISTANCE OF COUNSEL

STRICKLAND v. WASHINGTON

Supreme Court of the United States, 1984.
466 U.S. 668, 104 S.Ct. 2052, 80 L.Ed.2d 674.

JUSTICE O'CONNOR delivered the opinion of the Court.

This case requires us to consider the proper standards for judging a criminal defendant's contention that the Constitution requires a conviction or death sentence to be set aside because counsel's assistance at the trial or sentencing was ineffective.

I

A

During a ten-day period in September 1976, respondent planned and committed three groups of crimes, which included three brutal stabbing murders, torture, kidnapping, severe assaults, attempted murders, attempted extortion, and theft. After his two accomplices were arrested, respondent surrendered to police and voluntarily gave a lengthy statement confessing to the third of the criminal episodes. The State of Florida indicted respondent for kidnapping and murder and appointed an experienced criminal lawyer to represent him.

Counsel actively pursued pretrial motions and discovery. He cut his efforts short, however, and he experienced a sense of hopelessness about the case, when he learned that, against his specific advice, respondent had also confessed to the first two murders. By the date set for trial, respondent was subject to indictment for three counts of first degree murder and multiple counts of robbery, kidnapping for ransom, breaking and entering and assault, attempted murder, and conspiracy to commit robbery. Respondent waived his right to a jury trial, again acting against counsel's advice, and pleaded guilty to all charges, including the three capital murder charges.

In the plea colloquy, respondent told the trial judge that, although he had committed a string of burglaries, he had no significant prior criminal record and that at the time of his criminal spree he was under extreme stress caused by his inability to support his family. He also stated, however, that he accepted responsibility for the crimes. The trial judge told respondent that he had "a great deal of respect for people who are willing to step forward and admit their responsibility" but that he was making no statement at all about his likely sentencing decision.

Counsel advised respondent to invoke his right under Florida law to an advisory jury at his capital sentencing hearing. Respondent rejected the advice and waived the right. He chose instead to be sentenced by the trial judge without a jury recommendation.

In preparing for the sentencing hearing, counsel spoke with respondent about his background. He also spoke on the telephone with respondent's wife and mother, though he did not follow up on the one unsuccessful effort to meet with them. He did not otherwise seek out character witnesses for respondent. Nor did he request a psychiatric examination, since his conversations with his client gave no indication that respondent had psychological problems.

Counsel decided not to present and hence not to look further for evidence concerning respondent's character and emotional state. That decision reflected trial counsel's sense of hopelessness about overcoming the evidentiary effect of respondent's confessions to the gruesome crimes. It also reflected the judgment that it was advisable to rely on the plea colloquy for evidence about respondent's background and about his claim of emotional stress: the plea colloquy communicated sufficient information about these subjects, and by foregoing the opportunity to present new evidence on these subjects, counsel prevented the State from cross-examining respondent on his claim and from putting on psychiatric evidence of its own.

Counsel also excluded from the sentencing hearing other evidence he thought was potentially damaging. He successfully moved to exclude respondent's "rap sheet." Because he judged that a presentence report might prove more detrimental than helpful, as it would have included respondent's criminal history and thereby undermined the claim of no significant history of criminal activity, he did not request that one be prepared.

At the sentencing hearing, counsel's strategy was based primarily on the trial judge's remarks at the plea colloquy as well as on his reputation as a sentencing judge who thought it important for a convicted defendant to own up to his crime. Counsel argued that respondent's remorse and acceptance of responsibility justified sparing him from the death penalty. Counsel also argued that respondent had no history of criminal activity and that respondent committed the crimes under extreme mental or emotional disturbance, thus coming within the statutory list of mitigating circumstances. He further argued that respondent should be spared death because he had surrendered, confessed, and offered to testify against a co-defendant and because respondent was fundamentally a good person who had briefly gone badly wrong in extremely stressful circumstances. The State put on evidence and witnesses largely for the purpose of describing the details of the crimes. Counsel did not cross-examine the medical experts who testified about the manner of death of respondent's victims.

The trial judge found several aggravating circumstances with respect to each of the three murders. He found that all three murders were especially heinous, atrocious, and cruel, all involving repeated stabbings. All three murders were committed in the course of at least one other dangerous and violent felony, and since all involved robbery, the murders were for pecuniary gain. All three murders were committed to avoid arrest for the accompanying crimes and to hinder law enforcement. In the course of one of the murders, respondent knowingly subjected numerous persons to a grave risk of death by deliberately stabbing and shooting the murder victim's sisters-in-law, who sustained severe—in one case, ultimately fatal—injuries.

With respect to mitigating circumstances, the trial judge made the same findings for all three capital murders. First, although there was no admitted evidence of prior convictions, respondent had stated that he had engaged in a course of stealing. In any case, even if respondent had no significant history of criminal activity, the aggravating circumstances "would still clearly far outweigh" that mitigating factor. Second, the judge found that, during all three crimes, respondent was not suffering from extreme mental or emotional disturbance and could appreciate the criminality of his acts. Third, none of the victims was a participant in, or consented to, respondent's conduct. Fourth, respondent's participation in the crimes was neither minor nor the result of duress or domination by an accomplice. Finally, respondent's age (26) could not be considered a factor in mitigation, especially when viewed in light of respondent's planning of the crimes and disposition of the proceeds of the various accompanying thefts.

In short, the trial judge found numerous aggravating circumstances and no (or a single comparatively insignificant) mitigating circumstance. * * * He therefore sentenced respondent to death on each of the three counts of murder and to prison terms for the other crimes. The Florida Supreme Court upheld the convictions and sentences on direct appeal.

B

Respondent subsequently sought collateral relief in state court on numerous grounds, among them that counsel had rendered ineffective assistance at the sentencing proceeding. Respondent challenged counsel's assistance in six respects. He asserted that counsel was ineffective because he failed to move for a continuance to prepare for sentencing, to request a psychiatric report, to investigate and present character witnesses, to seek a presentence investigation report, to present meaningful arguments to the sentencing judge, and to investigate the medical examiner's reports or cross-examine the medical experts. In support of the claim, respondent submitted fourteen affidavits from friends, neighbors, and relatives stating that they would have testified if asked to do so. He also submitted one psychiatric report and one psychological report stating that respondent, though not under the influence of extreme mental or emotional disturbance, was "chronically frustrated and depressed because of his economic dilemma" at the time of his crimes. * * *

[After the state courts denied relief, respondent brought this action for federal habeas corpus. The federal district court denied the petition, but the Court of Appeals ordered further hearings on the ineffective assistance of counsel claim. The Supreme Court granted the State's petition for certiorari "to consider the standards by which to judge a contention that the Constitution requires that a criminal judgment be overturned because of the actual ineffective assistance of counsel." * * *]

II

[T]he Court has recognized that "the right to counsel is the right to the effective assistance of counsel." *McMann v. Richardson*, 397 U.S. 759, 771 (1970). Government violates the right to effective assistance when it interferes in certain ways with the ability of counsel to make independent decisions about how to conduct the defense. See, *e.g., Geders v. United States*, 425 U.S. 80 (1976) (bar on attorney-client consultation during overnight recess); *Herring v. New York*, 422 U.S. 853 (bar on summation at bench trial); *Brooks v. Tennessee*, 406 U.S. 605 (requirement that defendant be first defense witness); *Ferguson v. Georgia*, 365 U.S. 570 (bar on direct examination of defendant). Counsel, however, can also deprive a defendant of the right to effective assistance, simply by failing to render "adequate legal assistance" (actual conflict of interest adversely affecting lawyer's performance renders assistance ineffective).

The Court has not elaborated on the meaning of the constitutional requirement of effective assistance in the latter class of cases—that is, those presenting claims of "actual ineffectiveness." In giving meaning to the requirement, however, we must take its purpose—to ensure a fair trial—as the guide. The benchmark for judging any claim of ineffectiveness must be whether counsel's conduct so undermined the proper functioning of the adversarial process that the trial cannot be relied on as having produced a just result.

The same principle applies to a capital sentencing proceeding such as that provided by Florida law. We need not consider the role of counsel in an ordinary sentencing, which may involve informal proceedings and standardless discretion in the sentencer, and hence may require a different approach to the definition of constitutionally effective assistance. A capital sentencing proceeding like the one involved in this case, however, is sufficiently like a trial in its adversarial format and in the existence of standards for decision, that counsel's role in the proceeding is comparable to counsel's role at trial—to ensure that the adversarial testing process works to produce a just result under the standards governing decision. For purposes of describing counsel's duties, therefore, Florida's capital sentencing proceeding need not be distinguished from an ordinary trial.

III

A convicted defendant's claim that counsel's assistance was so defective as to require reversal of a conviction or death sentence has two components. First, the defendant must show that counsel's performance was deficient. This requires showing that counsel made errors so serious that counsel was not functioning as the "counsel" guaranteed the defendant by the Sixth Amendment. Second, the defendant must show that the deficient performance prejudiced the defense. This requires showing that counsel's errors were so serious as to deprive the defendant of a fair trial, a trial whose result is reliable. Unless a defendant makes both showings, it cannot be said that the conviction or death sentence resulted from a breakdown in the adversary process that renders the result unreliable.

A

As all the Federal Courts of Appeals have now held, the proper standard for attorney performance is that of reasonably effective assistance. * * * Representation of a criminal defendant entails certain basic duties. Counsel's function is to assist the defendant, and hence counsel owes the client a duty of loyalty, a duty to avoid conflicts of interest. From counsel's function as assistant to the defendant derive the overarching duty to advocate the defendant's cause and the more particular duties to consult with the defendant on important decisions and to keep the defendant informed of important developments in the course of the prosecution. Counsel also has a duty to bring to bear such skill and knowledge as will render the trial a reliable adversarial testing process. * * *

Judicial scrutiny of counsel's performance must be highly deferential. It is all too tempting for a defendant to second-guess counsel's assistance after conviction or adverse sentence, and it is all too easy for a court, examining counsel's defense after it has proved unsuccessful, to conclude that a particular act or omission of counsel was unreasonable. * * *

These standards require no special amplification in order to define counsel's duty to investigate, the duty at issue in this case. As the Court of Appeals concluded, strategic choices made after thorough investigation of law and facts relevant to plausible options are virtually unchallengeable; and strategic choices made after less than complete investigation are reasonable precisely to the extent that reasonable professional judgments support the limitations on investigation. In other words, counsel has a duty to make reasonable investigations or to make a reasonable decision that makes particular investigations unnecessary. In any ineffectiveness case, a particular decision not to investigate must be directly assessed for reasonableness in all the circumstances, applying a heavy measure of deference to counsel's judgments. * * *

B

An error by counsel, even if professionally unreasonable, does not warrant setting aside the judgment of a criminal proceeding if the error had no effect on the judgment. The purpose of the Sixth Amendment guarantee of counsel is to ensure that a defendant has the assistance necessary to justify reliance on the outcome of the proceeding. Accordingly, any deficiencies in counsel's performance must be prejudicial to the defense in order to constitute ineffective assistance under the Constitution.

In certain Sixth Amendment contexts, prejudice is presumed. Actual or constructive denial of the assistance of counsel altogether is legally presumed to result in prejudice. So are various kinds of state interference with counsel's assistance. Prejudice in these circumstances is so likely that case by case inquiry into prejudice is not worth the cost. Moreover, such circumstances involve impairments of the Sixth Amendment right that are easy to identify and, for that reason and because the prosecution is directly responsible, easy for the government to prevent.

One type of actual ineffectiveness claim warrants a similar, though more limited, presumption of prejudice. [P]rejudice is presumed when counsel is burdened by an actual conflict of interest. In those circumstances, counsel breaches the duty of loyalty, perhaps the most basic of counsel's duties. Moreover, it is difficult to measure the precise effect on the defense of representation corrupted by conflicting interests. Given the obligation of counsel to avoid conflicts of interest and the ability of trial courts to make early inquiry in certain situations likely to give rise to conflicts, see, *e.g.*, Fed.Rule Crim.Proc. 44(c), it is reasonable for the criminal justice system to maintain a fairly rigid rule of presumed prejudice for conflicts of interest. Even so, the rule is not quite the *per se* rule of prejudice that exists for the Sixth Amendment claims mentioned above. Prejudice is presumed only if the defendant demonstrates that counsel "actively represented conflicting interests" and "that an actual conflict of interest adversely affected his lawyer's performance."

Conflict of interest claims aside, actual ineffectiveness claims alleging a deficiency in attorney performance are subject to a general requirement that the defendant affirmatively prove prejudice. * * *

[T]he appropriate test for prejudice finds its roots in the test for materiality of exculpatory information not disclosed to the defense by the prosecution, and in the test for materiality of testimony made unavailable to the defense by Government deportation of a witness. The defendant must show that there is a reasonable probability that, but for counsel's unprofessional errors, the result of the proceeding would have been different. A reasonable probability is a probability sufficient to undermine confidence in the outcome. * * *

V

Application of the governing principles is not difficult in this case. The facts as described above, make clear that the conduct of respondent's counsel at and before respondent's sentencing proceeding cannot be found unreasonable. They also make clear that, even assuming the challenged conduct of counsel was unreasonable, respondent suffered insufficient prejudice to warrant setting aside his death sentence.

With respect to the performance component, the record shows that respondent's counsel made a strategic choice to argue for the extreme emotional distress mitigating circumstance and to rely as fully as possible on respondent's acceptance of responsibility for his crimes. Although counsel understandably felt hopeless about respondent's prospects, nothing in the record indicates, that counsel's sense of hopelessness distorted his professional judgment. Counsel's strategy choice was well within the range of professionally reasonable judgments, and the decision not to seek more character or psychological evidence than was already in hand was likewise reasonable.

The trial judge's views on the importance of owning up to one's crimes were well known to counsel. The aggravating circumstances were utterly overwhelming. Trial counsel could reasonably surmise from his conversations with respondent that character and psychological evidence would be of little help. Respondent had already been able to mention at the plea colloquy the substance of what there was to know about his financial and emotional troubles. Restricting testimony on respondent's character to what had come in at the plea colloquy ensured that contrary character and psychological evidence and respondent's criminal history, which counsel had successfully moved to exclude, would not come in. On these facts, there can be little question, even without application of the presumption of adequate performance, that trial counsel's defense, though unsuccessful, was the result of reasonable professional judgment.

With respect to the prejudice component, the lack of merit of respondent's claim is even more stark. The evidence that respondent says his trial counsel should have offered at the sentencing hearing would barely have altered the sentencing profile presented to the sentencing judge. As the state courts and District Court found, at most this evidence shows that numerous people who knew respondent thought he was generally a good person and that a psychiatrist and a psychologist believed he was under considerable emotional stress that did not rise to the level of extreme disturbance. Given the overwhelming aggravating factors, there is no reasonable probability that the omitted evidence would have changed the conclusion that the aggravating circumstances outweighed the mitigating circumstances and, hence, the sentence imposed. Indeed, admission of the evidence respondent now offers might even have been harmful to his case: his "rap sheet" would probably have been admitted into evidence, and the psychological reports would have directly contradicted respondent's claim that the mitigating circumstance of extreme emotional disturbance applied to his case. * * *

We conclude, therefore, that the District Court properly declined to issue a writ of habeas corpus. The judgment of the Court of Appeals is accordingly reversed.

[The opinion of JUSTICE BRENNAN, concurring in part and dissenting in part, is omitted.]

JUSTICE MARSHALL, dissenting.

* * *

It is undisputed that respondent's trial counsel made virtually no investigation of the possibility of obtaining testimony from respondent's relatives, friends, or former employers pertaining to respondent's character or background. Had counsel done so, he would have found several persons willing and able to testify that, in their experience, respondent was a responsible, nonviolent man, devoted to his family, and active in the affairs of his church. Respondent contends that his lawyer could have and should have used that testimony to "humanize" respondent, to counteract the impression conveyed by the trial that he was little more than a cold-blooded killer. Had this evidence been admitted, respondent argues, his chances of obtaining a life sentence would have been significantly better. * * * The State makes a colorable—though in my view not compelling—argument that defense counsel in this case might have made a reasonable "strategic" decision not to present such evidence at the sentencing hearing on the assumption that an unadorned acknowledgement of respondent's responsibility for his crimes would be more likely to appeal to the trial judge, who was reputed to respect persons who accepted responsibility for their actions. But however justifiable such a choice might have been after counsel had fairly assessed the potential strength of the mitigating evidence available to him, counsel's failure to make any significant effort to find out what evidence might be garnered from respondent's relatives and acquaintances surely cannot be described as "reasonable." Counsel's failure to investigate is particularly suspicious in light of his candid admission that respondent's confessions and conduct in the course of the trial gave him a feeling of "hopelessness" regarding the possibility of saving respondent's life.

That the aggravating circumstances implicated by respondent's criminal conduct were substantial does not vitiate respondent's constitutional claim; judges and juries in cases involving behavior at least as egregious have shown mercy, particularly when afforded an opportunity to see other facets of the defendant's personality and life. Nor is respondent's contention defeated by the possibility that the material his counsel turned up might not have been sufficient to establish a statutory mitigating circumstance under Florida law; Florida sentencing judges and the Florida Supreme Court sometimes refuse to impose death sentences in cases in which, even though *statutory* mitigating circumstances do not outweigh statutory aggravating circumstances, the addition of nonstatutory mitigating circumstances tips the scales in favor of life imprisonment.

If counsel had investigated the availability of mitigating evidence, he might well have decided to present some such material at the hearing. If he had done so, there is a significant chance that respondent would have been given a life sentence. In my view, those possibilities, conjoined with the unreasonableness of counsel's failure to investigate, are more than sufficient to establish a violation of the Sixth Amendment and to entitle respondent to a new sentencing proceeding.

I respectfully dissent.

GLOVER v. UNITED STATES

Supreme Court of the United States, 2001.
531 U.S. 198, 121 S.Ct. 696, 148 L.Ed.2d 604.

JUSTICE KENNEDY delivered the opinion of the Court.

The issue presented rests upon the initial assumption, which we accept for analytic purposes, that the trial court erred in a Sentencing Guidelines determination after petitioner's conviction of a federal offense. The legal error, petitioner alleges, increased his prison sentence by at least 6 months and perhaps by 21 months. We must decide whether this would be "prejudice" under *Strickland* v. *Washington*, 466 U.S. 668 (1984). The Government is not ready to concede error in the sentencing determination but now acknowledges that if an increased prison term did flow from an error the petitioner has established *Strickland* prejudice. In agreement with the Government and petitioner on this point, we reverse and remand for further proceedings.

I

In the 1980's and early 1990's, petitioner Paul Glover was the Vice President and General Counsel of the Chicago Truck Drivers, Helpers, and Warehouse Workers Union (Independent). The evidence showed Glover used his control over the union's investments to enrich himself and his co-conspirators through kickbacks. When the malfeasance was discovered, he was tried [and convicted]. The presentence investigation report prepared by the probation office recommended that the convictions for labor racketeering, money laundering, and tax evasion be grouped together under United States Sentencing * * * Guidelines, which allow[] the grouping of "counts involving substantially the same harm." [The trial court agreed with the government's argument that the money laundering counts could not be grouped with the other counts. As a result, Glover's offense level was increased by two levels, and he was sentenced to 84 months in prison.] In the trial court, Glover's attorneys did not submit papers or offer extensive oral arguments contesting the no-grouping argument advanced by the Government. * * *

On appeal to the Seventh Circuit, Glover's counsel (the same attorneys who represented him in District Court) did not raise the grouping issue; instead, they concentrated on claims that certain testimony from his first trial should not have been admitted at his second trial and that he should not have been assessed a two-level increase for perjury at his first trial. [The Seventh Circuit rejected Glover's arguments and affirmed Glover's conviction and sentence.]

Glover filed a *pro se* motion to correct his sentence [arguing that the] failure of his counsel to press the grouping issue * * * was ineffective assistance * * *. He further argued that absent the ineffective assistance, his offense level would have been two levels lower, yielding a Guidelines sentencing range of 63 to 78 months. Under this theory, the 84–month sentence he received was an unlawful increase of anywhere between 6 and 21 months.

* * *

II

The Government no longer puts forth the proposition that a 6 to 21 month prison term increase is not prejudice under *Strickland*. It now acknowledges that such a rule, without more, would be "inconsistent with this Court's cases and unworkable."

It appears the Seventh Circuit drew the substance of its no-prejudice rule from our opinion in *Lockhart* v. *Fretwell,* 506 U.S. 364 (1993). *Lockhart* holds that in some circumstances a mere difference in outcome will not suffice to establish prejudice. * * * The Court explained last Term that our holding in *Lockhart* does not supplant the *Strickland* analysis. The Seventh Circuit was incorrect to rely on *Lockhart* to deny relief to persons attacking their sentence who might show deficient performance in counsel's failure to object to an error of law affecting the calculation of a sentence because the sentence increase does not meet some baseline standard of prejudice. Authority does not suggest that a minimal amount of additional time in prison cannot constitute prejudice. Quite to the contrary, our jurisprudence suggests that any amount of actual jail time has Sixth Amendment significance. * * *

The Seventh Circuit's rule is not well considered in any event, because there is no obvious dividing line by which to measure how much longer a sentence must be for the increase to constitute substantial prejudice. Indeed, it is not even clear if the relevant increase is to be measured in absolute terms or by some fraction of the total authorized sentence. Although the amount by which a defendant's sentence is increased by a particular decision may be a factor to consider in determining whether counsel's performance in failing to argue the point constitutes ineffective assistance, under a determinate system of constrained discretion such as the Sentencing Guidelines it cannot serve as a bar to a showing of prejudice. We hold that the Seventh Circuit erred in engrafting this additional requirement onto the prejudice branch of the *Strickland* test. This is not a case where trial strategies, in retrospect, might be criticized for leading to a harsher sentence. Here we consider the sentencing calculation itself, a calculation resulting from a ruling which, if it had been error, would have been correctable on appeal. We express no opinion on the ultimate merits of Glover's claim because the question of deficient performance is not before us, but it is clear that prejudice flowed from the asserted error in sentencing.

[The Supreme Court reversed the judgment of the Seventh Circuit and remanded the case for further proceedings.]

Commentary

[T]wo different approaches might be used to resolve claims of ineffective assistance of counsel. First, there is the approach employed by the Supreme Court in *Strickland*. This approach requires the defendant to demonstrate that counsel made very serious errors or inexcusable omissions, and that there is a reasonable probability that these errors or omissions affected the outcome. The fact that counsel was lazy, or inexperienced, or unprepared would not in itself indicate ineffective assistance unless specific errors of judgment or tactics resulted from these defects and caused prejudice to the defendant. Moreover, the reviewing court is careful to grant all reasonable deference to counsel's judgment, and to avoid second-guessing in the light of hindsight. Where this approach is taken, convicted defendants seldom obtain relief on the ground of ineffective assistance of counsel.

The alternative approach is more effective in protecting badly represented defendants, perhaps *too* effective. A court favoring this "categorical" approach looks to see if counsel did all the things which a well-prepared and diligent defense lawyer ought to have done. Did counsel interview and advise the defendant, make appropriate discovery motions, study the reports obtained, interview potential witnesses, and in general prepare all reasonable defense issues to the extent necessary to make informed tactical judgments? If the lawyer did not do all these things then the defendant did not have the effective assistance of counsel, however guilty he may have been and however richly he deserved the punishment imposed. Prejudice ought to be presumed, unless the *prosecution* can show beyond a reasonable doubt that counsel's inadequate performance could not have affected the outcome. Such a showing ought to be extremely difficult to make, because it is so inherently difficult to know for certain whether a better lawyer could have achieved a better result. The case for the categorical approach is argued in Judge Bazelon's dissenting opinion in United States v. Decoster, 624 F.2d 196 (D.C.Cir.1976) (en banc). The Supreme Court decisively rejected this approach in *Strickland* and in United States v. Cronic, 466 U.S. 648 (1984).

The categorical approach has some obvious advantages. An inquiry into whether a better lawyer could have won the case is not a satisfactory substitute for having the better lawyer in the first place. It may be difficult to provide every defendant with a dedicated and competent lawyer, but this is not a fully satisfactory response to the claim that due process of law requires no less. Even so, leading courts have found sufficient difficulties with the categorical approach to justify their consistent refusal to adopt it. The prospect that the defense attorney can cause a new trial by failing to perform some duty of preparation invites "extensive supervision by the trial judge through a pretrial 'checklist' to ensure that counsel has met his duties of preparation, and oversight of the conduct of the trial." United States v. Decoster, 624 F.2d 196, 216 (D.C.Cir.1976) (opinion of Judge Leventhal). According to Judge Leventhal, "the manifest consequence would be inevitable and increasing intrusion into the development and presentation of the defense case by the trial judge, and (out of self-protection) by the prosecution." The result might be a "reordering of the adversary system" in the direction of "the inquisitorial system of the Continent."

Whether a reordering of the adversary system would be altogether a bad thing is a matter of opinion. The adversary system at its best has great virtues, but there may be grounds to question whether it can be expected to operate effectively in the conditions of contemporary urban American society, with our enormous crime rates, overburdened courts, and poverty-impaired defendants. Lack of sufficient resources is not the only problem. The "sense of hopelessness" described by defense counsel in *Strickland* is not uncommon among attorneys who regularly defend persons who seem obviously guilty of serious crimes. On the other hand, if by some miracle we actually did succeed in providing every defendant with the kind of representation that an intelligent millionaire might purchase, the adversary system might have to be modified to protect the courts from the resulting profusion of motions and hearings.

The Supreme Court has said that ineffective assistance of counsel claims are judged by the same standard regardless of whether counsel is retained and chosen by the defendant or appointed by the court. According to an opinion for the Court by Justice Powell:

> A proper respect for the Sixth Amendment disarms petitioner's contention that defendants who retain their own lawyers are entitled to less protection than defendants for whom the State appoints counsel. We may assume with confidence that most counsel, whether retained or appointed, will protect the rights of an accused. But experience teaches that, in some cases, retained counsel will not provide adequate representation. The vital guarantee of the Sixth Amendment would stand for little if the often uninformed decision to retain a particular lawyer could reduce or forfeit the defendant's entitlement to constitutional protection. Since the State's conduct of a criminal trial itself implicates the State in the defendant's conviction, we see no basis for drawing a distinction between retained and appointed counsel that would deny equal justice to defendants who must choose their own lawyers. Cuyler v. Sullivan, 446 U.S. 335, 344–45 (1980).

The defendant in *Cuyler v. Sullivan* was charged with two other persons (Carchidi and DiPasquale) in a double murder. Originally represented by his own counsel, defendant Sullivan eventually accepted representation from two privately retained lawyers (DiBona and Peruto) who were paid by friends of the three defendants and represented all three throughout the proceedings. The three defendants were tried separately: Sullivan was convicted, and the other two were acquitted. The prosecution's circumstantial case was based entirely on the testimony of a janitor, who saw the three defendants in the building just before he heard sounds that must have been the fatal shots. Before the shooting the defendants had urged him to do his work another day, and after the shooting defendant Carchidi told the janitor to leave the building and say nothing. At the close of the prosecution's case in the Sullivan trial, the defense rested without presenting any evidence.

In subsequent federal habeas corpus proceedings, the constitutional question turned on whether the failure to present any defense evidence was a reasonable tactical decision in view of the circumstantial nature of the prosecution's case, or whether it was affected by counsel's concern to protect the interests of Carchidi and DiPasquale in their upcoming trials. Carchidi later claimed that he would have testified at Sullivan's trial to deny that he had directed the janitor to leave the building immediately after the shooting. The two lawyers gave conflicting testimony on whether the decision not to call Carchidi or present other evidence had been influenced by a desire to protect the other defendants (who of course could have refused to testify in any event). The federal Court of Appeals held that resting at the close of the prosecutor's case "would have been a legitimate tactical decision if made by independent counsel," but that in the circumstances the action provided sufficient indication of a conflict of interest to require a new trial.

The Supreme Court vacated and remanded. The opinion by Justice Powell first distinguished Holloway v. Arkansas, 435 U.S. 475 (1978). In *Holloway*, a single public defender represented three defendants at the same trial, and the state trial judge refused to consider the appointment of separate counsel despite the defense lawyer's timely and repeated assertions that the interests of the clients conflicted. The Supreme Court found that this failure to inquire into the need for separate representation unconstitutionally endangered the right to counsel, and required reversal of the resulting convictions without further determination of prejudice.

In *Cuyler v. Sullivan*, by way of contrast, no one had objected to the multiple representation and nothing in the circumstances indicated that there would be conflicting defenses. The trial court therefore had no constitutional duty to inquire into any possible conflict of interest. If, however, an *actual* conflict of interest adversely affected the defense lawyer's performance, the defendant should have a new trial without having to demonstrate further prejudice. In other words, if the failure to call defense witnesses was motivated by a desire to protect other clients, then Sullivan should have a new trial without the need to show that the defense might have been successful. On remand, the Court of Appeals found that counsel's performance had been adversely affected, and ordered a new trial despite the argument that Carchidi probably would have invoked the Fifth Amendment if he had been represented by independent counsel and called as a witness at Sullivan's trial.

Sometimes, two or more defendants desire to be represented by the same lawyer despite the existence of an apparent conflict of interest. The right to waive the conflict and proceed to trial with joint representation is not absolute, however. In Wheat v. United States, 486 U.S. 153 (1988), a closely divided Supreme Court held that trial courts have an independent responsibility to ensure compliance with the appropriate standards of professional responsibility for attorneys, and upheld a conviction where a federal district judge had exercised his discretion not to allow a defendant to substitute as trial counsel an attorney who was also representing co-defendants in the same prosecution. In *Wheat* it was the prosecution that objected to the substitution, and the defendant claimed that the prosecutor was imagining implausible possibilities for conflict of interest when its real motive was to deny this defendant the services of a particularly effective lawyer. Apart from the question of effectiveness, prosecutors may benefit when each defendant in a conspiracy is represented by separate counsel, because this arrangement increases the likelihood that each individual will be motivated to bargain for leniency and agree to testify against the others.

Counsel is an officer of the court as well as an advocate for a client, and this dual role may also give rise to conflicting loyalties. In the leading Supreme Court case, the defendant announced that he would embellish his testimony with a claim the lawyer knew to be a lie. The lawyer replied, according to his later testimony, that:

> "we could not allow him to [testify falsely] because that would be perjury, and as officers of the court we would be suborning perjury if we allowed him to do it; * * * I advised him that if he did so that it would be my duty to advise the Court of what he was going and that I felt he was committing perjury; also, that I probably would be allowed to attempt to impeach that particular testimony."

The defendant did testify without the proposed embellishment.

A federal Court of Appeals on habeas corpus held that this statement amounted to a threat to reveal confidential attorney-client communications, and created a conflict between the attorney's perceived ethical duty and his duty of loyalty to the client. This "actual conflict" affected his performance and thus eliminated the need to show further prejudice under *Cuyler*. Whiteside v. Scurr, 750 F.2d 713 (8th Cir.1984) (en banc). The Supreme Court unanimously reversed, holding that the attorney's ethical scruples created neither the kind of conflict of interest contemplated by the opinion in *Cuyler*, nor ineffective assistance as defined in *Strickland*. Nix v. Whiteside, 475 U.S. 157 (1986).

A defendant is not deprived of effective assistance because counsel refused to do something illegal or unethical, even though a defendant with sufficient resources could probably find a "mouthpiece" willing to take the risk. Further consideration of the ethical dimensions of the attorney's role is left to the course on professional responsibility.

E. THE RIGHT TO SELF–REPRESENTATION

FARETTA v. CALIFORNIA

Supreme Court of the United States, 1975.
422 U.S. 806, 95 S.Ct. 2525, 45 L.Ed.2d 562.

MR. JUSTICE STEWART delivered the opinion of the Court.

The Sixth and Fourteenth Amendments of our Constitution guarantee that a person brought to trial in any state or federal court must be afforded the right to the assistance of counsel before he can be validly convicted and punished by imprisonment. This clear constitutional rule has emerged from a series of cases decided here over the last 50 years. The question before us now is whether a defendant in a state criminal trial has a constitutional right to proceed *without* counsel when he voluntarily and intelligently elects to do so. Stated another way, the question is whether a State may constitutionally hale a person into its criminal courts and there force a lawyer upon him, even when he insists that he wants to conduct his own defense. It is not an easy question, but we have concluded that a State may not constitutionally do so.

I

Anthony Faretta was charged with grand theft in an information filed in the Superior Court of Los Angeles County, California. At the arraignment, the Superior Court Judge assigned to preside at the trial appointed the public defender to represent Faretta. Well before the date of trial, however, Faretta requested that he be permitted to represent himself. Questioning by the judge revealed that Faretta had once represented himself in a criminal prosecution, that he had a high school education, and that he did not want to be represented by the public defender because he believed that that office was "very loaded down with * * * a heavy case load." The judge responded that he believed Faretta was "making a mistake" and emphasized that in further proceedings Faretta would receive no special favors.[2] Nevertheless, after establishing that Faretta wanted to represent himself and did not want a lawyer, the judge, in a "preliminary ruling," accepted Faretta's waiver of the assistance of counsel. The judge indicated, however, that he might reverse this ruling if it later appeared that Faretta was unable adequately to represent himself.

Several weeks thereafter, but still prior to trial the judge *sua sponte* held a hearing to inquire into Faretta's ability to conduct his own defense, and questioned him specifically about both the hearsay rule and the state law governing the challenge of potential jurors. After consideration of Faretta's answers, and observation of his demeanor, the judge ruled that Faretta had not made an intelligent and knowing waiver of his right to the assistance of counsel, and also ruled that Faretta had no constitutional right to conduct his own defense. The judge accordingly reversed his earlier ruling permitting self-representation and again appointed the public defender to represent Faretta. Faretta's subsequent request for leave to act as co-counsel was rejected, as were his efforts to make certain motions on his own behalf. Throughout the subsequent trial, the judge required that Faretta's defense be conducted only through the appointed lawyer from the public defender's office. At the conclusion of the trial, the jury found Faretta guilty as charged, and the judge sentenced him to prison. [The conviction was affirmed on appeal, and the Supreme Court granted certiorari.]

---

2. The judge informed Faretta:

"You are going to follow the procedure. You are going to have to ask the questions right. If there is an objection to the form of the question and it is properly taken, it is going to be sustained. We are going to treat you like a gentleman. We are going to respect you. We are going to give you every chance, but you are going to play with the same ground rules that anybody plays. And you don't know those ground rules. You wouldn't know those ground rules any more than any other lawyer will know those ground rules until he gets out and tries a lot of cases. And you haven't done it."

There can be no blinking the fact that the right of an accused to conduct his own defense seems to cut against the grain of this Court's decisions holding that the Constitution requires that no accused can be convicted and imprisoned unless he has been accorded the right to the assistance of counsel. For it is surely true that the basic thesis of those decisions is that the help of a lawyer is essential to assure the defendant a fair trial. And a strong argument can surely be made that the whole thrust of those decisions most inevitably lead to the conclusion that a State may constitutionally impose a lawyer upon even an unwilling defendant.

But it is one thing to hold that every defendant, rich or poor, has the right to the assistance of counsel, and quite another to say that a State may compel a defendant to accept a lawyer he does not want. The value of state-appointed counsel was not unappreciated by the Founders, yet the notion of compulsory counsel was utterly foreign to them. And whatever else may be said of those who wrote the Bill of Rights, surely there can be no doubt that they understood the inestimable worth of free choice.

It is undeniable that in most criminal prosecutions defendants could better defend with counsel's guidance than by their own unskilled efforts. But where the defendant will not voluntarily accept representation by counsel, the potential advantage of a lawyer's training and experience can be realized, if at all, only imperfectly. To force a lawyer on a defendant can only lead him to believe that the law contrives against him. Moreover, it is not inconceivable that in some rare instances, the defendant might in fact present his case more effectively by conducting his own defense. Personal liberties are not rooted in the law of averages. The right to defend is personal. The defendant, and not his lawyer or the State, will bear the personal consequences of a conviction. It is the defendant, therefore, who must be free personally to decide whether in his particular case counsel is to his advantage. And although he may conduct his own defense ultimately to his own detriment, his choice must be honored out of that respect for the individual which is the lifeblood of the law.

When an accused manages his own defense, he relinquishes, as a purely factual matter, many of the traditional benefits associated with the right to counsel. For this reason, in order to represent himself, the accused must "knowingly and intelligently" forego those relinquished benefits. * * * Although a defendant need not himself have the skill and experience of a lawyer in order competently and intelligently to choose self-representation, he should be made aware of the dangers and disadvantages of self-representation, so that the record will establish that he knows what he is doing and his choice is made with eyes open.

Here, weeks before trial, Faretta clearly and unequivocally declared to the trial judge that he wanted to represent himself and did not want counsel. The record affirmatively shows that Faretta was literate, competent, and understanding and that he was voluntarily exercising his informed free will. The trial judge had warned Faretta that he thought it was a mistake not to accept the assistance of counsel, and that Faretta would be required to follow all the "ground rules" of trial procedure. We need make no assessment of how well or poorly Faretta had mastered the intricacies of the hearsay rule and the California code provisions that govern challenges of potential jurors on *voir dire*. For his technical legal knowledge, as such, was not relevant to an assessment of his knowing exercise of the right to defend himself.[3]

In forcing Faretta, under these circumstances, to accept against his will a state-appointed public defender, the California courts deprived him of his constitutional right to conduct his own defense. Accordingly, the judgment before us is vacated, and the case is remanded for further proceedings not inconsistent with this opinion. It is so ordered. Judgment vacated and case remanded.

[The dissenting opinion of CHIEF JUSTICE BURGER, with whom JUSTICE BLACKMUN and JUSTICE REHNQUIST joined, is omitted.]

MR. JUSTICE BLACKMUN, with whom THE CHIEF JUSTICE and MR. JUSTICE REHNQUIST join, dissenting.

* * *

I note briefly the procedural problems that, I suspect, today's decision will visit upon trial courts in the future. Although the Court indicates that a *pro se* defendant necessarily waives any claim he might otherwise make on ineffective assistance of counsel, the opinion leaves open a host of other procedural questions. Must every defendant be advised of his right to proceed *pro se*? If so, when must that notice be given? Since the right to assistance of counsel and the right to self-representation are mutually exclusive, how is the waiver of each right to be measured? If a defendant has elected to exercise his right to proceed *pro se*, does he still have a constitutional right to assistance of standby counsel? How soon in the criminal proceeding must a defendant decide between proceeding by counsel or *pro se*? Must he be allowed to switch in mid-trial? May a violation of the right to self-representation ever be harmless error? Must the trial court treat the *pro se* defendant differently than it would professional counsel? I assume that many of these questions will be answered with finality in due course. Many of them, however, such as the standards of waiver and the treatment of the *pro se* defendant, will haunt the trial of every defendant who elects to exercise his right to self-representation. The procedural problems spawned by an absolute right to self-representation will far outweigh whatever tactical

---

3. We are told that many criminal defendants representing themselves may use the courtroom for deliberate disruption of their trials. But the right of self-representation has been recognized from our beginnings by federal law and by most of the States, and no such result has thereby occurred. Moreover, the trial judge may terminate self-representation by a defendant who deliberately engages in serious and obstructionist misconduct. See Illinois v. Allen, 397 U.S. 337. Of course, a State may—even over objection by the accused—appoint a "standby counsel" to aid the accused if and when the accused requests help, and to be available to represent the accused in the event that termination of the defendant's self-representation is necessary. * * *

advantage the defendant may feel he has gained by electing to represent himself.

If there is any truth to the old proverb that "one who is his own lawyer has a fool for a client," the Court by its opinion today now bestows a *constitutional* right on one to make a fool of himself.

Commentary

Most appellate courts have had little difficulty deciding that there is no requirement that the defendant be advised of the right to self-representation, and they do not require trial courts to make special efforts to protect the *pro se* defendant from the consequences of a lack of professional skill. Defendants are ordinarily not allowed to "switch in mid-trial," or otherwise to manipulate the exercise of the right in a manner likely to disrupt the proceedings. Trial courts occasionally but rarely allow a defendant to "have it both ways" by acting as co-counsel along with a defense attorney who also participates in the proceedings. In many cases attorneys are unwilling to participate in such an arrangement, because it deprives the lawyer of the traditional prerogative of exercising independent professional judgment in managing the proceedings. Where the lawyer has no objection, courts are often unwilling to allow the defendant to give what amounts to unsworn testimony in the form of an opening or closing statement, and thus to avoid cross-examination by the prosecutor.

On the other hand, courts do frequently appoint "standby" counsel, to give the defendant advice and information on legal matters without directly participating in the trial. Although there is no right to the appointment of such counsel, at least one decision reversed a conviction for capital murder because the trial judge erroneously ruled that he did not have the discretionary authority to appoint standby counsel. People v. Bigelow, 37 Cal.3d 731 (1984). Standby counsel may also be appointed even over the defendant's objection, and this has sometimes led to claims that counsel's activities interfered with the defendant's right to self-representation. See *McKaskle v. Wiggins*, 465 U.S. 168 (1984).

Some of the most interesting problems raised by *Faretta* involve the allocation of authority between the defendant and counsel when the defendant does *not* elect to proceed *pro se*. If defendants should be allowed to control their own destiny, and to be assisted rather than dominated by counsel, then should the defendant rather than the lawyer have the final say about tactical decisions? The Supreme Court has held that appointed counsel on *appeal* may exercise professional judgment over which points to argue, and need not raise every non-frivolous issue urged by the client (who was permitted to file his own *pro se* brief in addition to the brief submitted by counsel). Jones v. Barnes, 463 U.S. 745 (1983). The majority opinion by Chief Justice Burger pointed out that effective advocacy requires concentrating on the strongest points, and that raising every colorable issue runs the risk of distracting the court from the most promising ones. Justice Brennan's dissent reasoned that "from the standpoint of effective administration of justice, the need to confer decisive authority on the attorney is paramount with regard to the hundreds of decisions that must be made quickly in the course of a trial. Decisions regarding which issues to press on appeal, in contrast, can and should be made more deliberately, in the course of deciding whether to appeal at all." Although counsel should try to persuade the client to defer to the lawyer's judgment on what issues to argue, the dissent reasoned that "the role of the defense lawyer should be above all to function as the instrument and defender of the client's autonomy and dignity in all phases of the criminal process."

The *Faretta* doctrine continues to generate disputes. In the following cases, the Supreme Court grappled with the application of *Faretta* at different stages in the criminal justice process.

MARTINEZ v. COURT OF APPEAL OF CALIFORNIA

Supreme Court of the United States, 2000.
528 U.S. 152, 120 S.Ct. 684, 145 L.Ed.2d 597.

JUSTICE STEVENS delivered the opinion of the Court.

The Sixth and Fourteenth Amendments of our Constitution guarantee that a person brought to trial in any state or federal court must be afforded the right to the assistance of counsel before he can be validly convicted and punished by imprisonment. In *Faretta* v. *California*, 422 U.S. 806 (1975), we decided that the defendant also "has a constitutional right to proceed *without* counsel when he voluntarily and intelligently elects to do so." Although that statement arguably embraces the entire judicial proceeding, we also phrased the question as whether a State may "constitutionally hale a person into its criminal courts and there force a lawyer upon him, even when he insists that he wants to conduct his own defense." Our conclusion in *Faretta* extended only to a defendant's "constitutional right to conduct his own defense." Accordingly, our specific holding was confined to the right to defend oneself at trial. We now address the different question whether the reasoning in support of that holding also applies when the defendant becomes an appellant * * * We have concluded that it does not.

I

Martinez describes himself as a self-taught paralegal with 25 years' experience at 12 different law firms. While employed as an office assistant at a firm in Santa Ana, California, Martinez was accused of converting $6,000 of a client's money to his own use * * * He chose to represent himself at trial before a jury, because he claimed " 'there wasn't an attorney on earth who'd believe me once he saw my past [criminal record].' " The jury acquitted him on * * * grand theft, but convicted him on * * * embezzlement. The jury also found that he had three prior convictions; accordingly, under California's "three strikes" law, the court imposed a mandatory sentence of 25–years-to-life in prison. * * *

* * *

II

* * *

The historical evidence relied upon by *Faretta* as identifying a right of self-representation is not always useful because it pertained to times when lawyers were scarce, often mistrusted, and not readily available to the average person accused of crime. For one who could not obtain a lawyer, self-representation was the only feasible alternative to asserting no defense at all. Thus, a government's recognition of an indigent defendant's right to represent himself was comparable to bestowing upon the homeless beggar a "right" to take shelter in the sewers of Paris. * * *

It has since been recognized, however, that an indigent defendant in a criminal trial has a constitutional right to the assistance of appointed counsel. Thus, an individual's decision to represent himself is no longer compelled by the necessity of choosing self-representation over incompetent or nonexistent representation; rather, it more likely reflects a genuine desire to " 'conduct his own cause in his own words.' " Therefore, * * * the original reasons for protecting that right do not have the same force when the availability of competent counsel for every indigent defendant has displaced the need—although not always the desire—for self-representation.

The scant historical evidence pertaining to the issue of self-representation on appeal is even less helpful. * * * Appellate courts have maintained the discretion to allow litigants to "manage their own causes"—and some such litigants have done so effectively. That opportunity, however, has been consistently subject to each court's own rules.

We are not aware of any historical consensus establishing a right of self-representation on appeal. * * * Historical silence, however, has no probative force in the appellate context because there simply was no long-respected right of self-representation on appeal. In fact, the right of appeal itself is of relatively recent origin.

Appeals as of right in federal courts were nonexistent for the first century of our Nation, and appellate review of any sort was "rarely allowed." The States, also, did not generally recognize an appeal as of right until Washington became the first to constitutionalize the right explicitly in 1889. There was similarly no right to appeal in criminal cases at common law, and appellate review of any sort was "limited" and "rarely used." Thus, unlike the inquiry in *Faretta,* the historical evidence does not provide any support for an affirmative constitutional right to appellate self-representation.

The *Faretta* majority's reliance on the structure of the Sixth Amendment is also not relevant. The Sixth Amendment identifies the basic rights that the accused shall enjoy in "all criminal prosecutions." They are presented strictly as rights that are available in preparation for trial and at the trial itself. The Sixth Amendment does not include any right to appeal. As we have recognized, "[t]he right of appeal, as we presently know it in criminal cases, is purely a creature of statute." * * *

* * *

Finally, the *Faretta* majority found that the right to self-representation at trial was grounded in part in a respect for individual autonomy. This consideration is, of course, also applicable to an appellant seeking to manage his own case. As we explained in *Faretta,* at the trial level "[t]o force a lawyer on a defendant can only lead him to believe that the law contrives against him." On appellate review, there is surely a similar risk that the appellant will be skeptical of whether a lawyer, who is employed by the same government that is prosecuting him, will serve his cause with undivided loyalty. Equally true on appeal is the related observation that it is the appellant personally who will bear the consequences of the appeal.

In light of our conclusion that the Sixth Amendment does not apply to appellate proceedings, any individual right to self-representation on appeal based on autonomy principles must be grounded in the Due Process Clause. Under the practices that prevail in the Nation today, however, we are entirely unpersuaded that the risk of either disloyalty or suspicion of disloyalty is a sufficient concern to conclude that a constitutional right of self-representation is a necessary component of a fair appellate proceeding. We have no doubt that instances of disloyal representation are rare. In both trials and appeals there are, without question, cases in which counsel's performance is ineffective. Even in those cases, however, it is reasonable to assume that counsel's performance is more effective than what the unskilled appellant could have provided for himself.

[E]xperience has taught us that "a pro se defense is usually a bad defense, particularly when compared to a defense provided by an experienced criminal defense attorney."

As the *Faretta* opinion recognized, the right to self-representation is not absolute. * * * Even at the trial level, therefore, the government's interest in ensuring the integrity and efficiency of the trial at times outweighs the defendant's interest in acting as his own lawyer.

In the appellate context, the balance between the two competing interests surely tips in favor of the State. The status of the accused defendant, who retains a presumption of innocence throughout the trial process, changes dramatically when a jury returns a guilty verdict. * * *

* * *

* * * Courts, of course, may still exercise their discretion to allow a lay person to proceed *pro se.* * * * Considering the change in position from defendant to appellant, the autonomy interests that survive a felony conviction are less compelling than those motivating the decision in *Faretta.* Yet the overriding state interest in the fair and efficient administration of justice remains as strong as at the trial level. Thus, the States are clearly within their discretion to conclude that the government's interests outweigh an invasion of the appellant's interest in self-representation.

* * *

[The concurring opinions of JUSTICE KENNEDY, JUSTICE BREYER and JUSTICE SCALIA are omitted.]

IOWA v. TOVAR

Supreme Court of the United States, 2004.
541 U.S. 77, 124 S.Ct. 1379, 158 L.Ed.2d 209.

JUSTICE GINSBURG delivered the opinion of the Court.

The Sixth Amendment safeguards to an accused who faces incarceration the right to counsel at all critical stages of the criminal process. *Maine* v. *Moulton,* 474 U.S. 159, 170, 88 L.Ed.2d 481, 106 S.Ct. 477 (1985). The entry of a guilty plea, whether to a misdemeanor or a felony charge, ranks as a "critical stage" at which the right to counsel adheres. Waiver of the right to counsel, as of constitutional rights in the criminal process generally, must be a "knowing, intelligent ac[t] done with sufficient awareness of the relevant circumstances." This case concerns the extent to which a trial judge, before accepting a guilty plea from an uncounseled defendant, must elaborate on the right to representation.

Beyond affording the defendant the opportunity to consult with counsel prior to entry of a plea and to be assisted by counsel at the plea hearing, must the court, specifically: (1) advise the defendant that "waiving the assistance of counsel in deciding whether to plead guilty [entails] the risk that a viable defense will be overlooked"; and (2) "admonis[h]" the defendant "that by waiving his right to an attorney he will lose the opportunity to obtain an independent opinion on whether, under the facts and applicable law, it is wise to plead guilty"? The Iowa Supreme Court held both warnings essential to the "knowing and intelligent" waiver of the Sixth Amendment right to the assistance of counsel..

We hold that neither warning is mandated by the Sixth Amendment. The constitutional requirement is satisfied when the trial court informs the accused of the nature of the charges against him, of his right to be counseled regarding his plea, and of the range of allowable punishments attendant upon the entry of a guilty plea.

I

[In November 1996, Tovar, then a 21–year-old college student, was arrested for operating a motor vehicle while under the influence of alcohol (OWI). An intoxilyzer test showed he had a blood alcohol level of 0.194. During subsequent proceedings, state court judges advised Tovar of his rights, including the right to counsel—and Tovar waived those rights—on more than one occasion. The first occurred at an appearance before a judge several hours after his arrest. At his subsequent arraignment, Tovar stated he wished to represent himself, and entered a guilty plea although the judge advised him of the rights he was giving up by pleading guilty. At his sentencing hearing, Tovar again represented himself. In 1998, Tovar was convicted of OWI a second time. He was represented by counsel, but again pleaded guilty. In December 2000,

Tovar was charged with OWI as a third offense, and additionally with driving while license barred. Iowa law classifies first-offense OWI as a serious misdemeanor and second-offense OWI as an aggravated misdemeanor. Third-offense OWI, and any OWI offenses thereafter, rank as class "D" felonies. Now represented by an attorney, Tovar pleaded not guilty to both December 2000 charges. Tovar filed a motion arguing that his 1996 OWI conviction could not be used to enhance the December 2000 OWI charge from a second-offense aggravated misdemeanor to a third-offense felony.]

* * * Significantly, Tovar did not allege that he was unaware at the November 1996 arraignment of his right to counsel prior to pleading guilty and at the plea hearing. Instead, he maintained that his 1996 waiver of counsel was invalid—not "full knowing, intelligent, and voluntary"—because he "was never made aware by the court ... of the dangers and disadvantages of self-representation."

[The court denied Tovar's motion, Tovar waived his right to a jury trial and was found guilty by the court of both the OWI third-offense charge and driving while license barred, and was sentenced to jail and fined on both charges. The Iowa Supreme Court reversed on Sixth Amendment grounds]

* * *

II

The Sixth Amendment secures to a defendant who faces incarceration the right to counsel at all "critical stages" of the criminal process. A plea hearing qualifies as a "critical stage." Because Tovar received a two-day prison term for his 1996 OWI conviction, he had a right to counsel both at the plea stage and at trial had he elected to contest the charge.

A person accused of crime, however, may choose to forgo representation. While the Constitution "does not force a lawyer upon a defendant," it does require that any waiver of the right to counsel be knowing, voluntary, and intelligent, see *Johnson* v. *Zerbst*, 304 U.S. 458, 464, 82 L.Ed. 1461, 58 S.Ct. 1019 (1938). Tovar contends that his waiver of counsel in November 1996, at his first OWI plea hearing, was insufficiently informed, and therefore constitutionally invalid. In particular, he asserts that the trial judge did not elaborate on the value, at that stage of the case, of an attorney's advice and the dangers of self-representation in entering a plea.

We have described a waiver of counsel as intelligent when the defendant "knows what he is doing and his choice is made with eyes open." We have not, however, prescribed any formula or script to be read to a defendant who states that he elects to proceed without counsel. The information a defendant must possess in order to make an intelligent election, our decisions indicate, will depend on a range of case-specific factors, including the defendant's education or sophistication, the complex or easily grasped nature of the charge, and the stage of the proceeding.

* * *

[I]n *Patterson* v. *Illinois,* 487 U.S. 285, 101 L.Ed.2d 261, 108 S.Ct. 2389 (1988), we elaborated on "the dangers and disadvantages of self-representation" * * *. "[A]t trial," we observed, "counsel is required to help even the most gifted layman adhere to the rules of procedure and evidence, comprehend the subtleties of *voir dire,* examine and cross-examine witnesses effectively . . . , object to improper prosecution questions, and much more." Warnings of the pitfalls of proceeding to trial without counsel, we therefore said, must be "rigorous[ly]" conveyed. We clarified, however, that at earlier stages of the criminal process, a less searching or formal colloquy may suffice.

Patterson concerned postindictment questioning by police and prosecutor. At that stage of the case, we held, the warnings required by *Miranda* v. *Arizona* adequately informed the defendant not only of his Fifth Amendment rights, but of his Sixth Amendment right to counsel as well. *Miranda* warnings, we said, effectively convey to a defendant his right to have counsel present during questioning. In addition, they inform him of the "ultimate adverse consequence" of making uncounseled admissions, *i.e.,* his statements may be used against him in any ensuing criminal proceeding. The *Miranda* warnings, we added, "also sufficed . . . to let [the defendant] know what a lawyer could 'do for him,'" namely, advise him to refrain from making statements that could prove damaging to his defense.

Patterson describes a "pragmatic approach to the waiver question," one that asks "what purposes a lawyer can serve at the particular stage of the proceedings in question, and what assistance he could provide to an accused at that stage," in order "to determine the scope of the Sixth Amendment right to counsel, and the type of warnings and procedures that should be required before a waiver of that right will be recognized." We require less rigorous warnings pretrial, *Patterson* explained, not because pretrial proceedings are "less important" than trial, but because, at that stage, "the full dangers and disadvantages of self-representation . . . are less substantial and more obvious to an accused than they are at trial."

* * *

[T]he State presents a narrow[] question: "Does the Sixth Amendment require a court to give a rigid and detailed admonishment to a *pro se* defendant pleading guilty of the usefulness of an attorney, that an attorney may provide an independent opinion whether it is wise to plead guilty and that without an attorney the defendant risks overlooking a defense?"

Training on that question, we turn to, and reiterate, the particular language the Iowa Supreme Court employed in announcing the warnings it thought the Sixth Amendment required: "[T]he trial judge [must] advise the defendant generally that there are defenses to criminal charges that may not be known by laypersons and that the danger in waiving the assistance of counsel in deciding whether to plead guilty is the risk that a viable defense will be overlooked," in addition, "[t]he defendant should be admonished that by waiving his right to an attorney he will lose the opportunity to obtain an independent opinion on whether, under the facts and applicable law, it is wise to plead guilty." Tovar did not receive such advice, and the sole question before us is whether the Sixth Amendment compels the two admonitions here in controversy. We hold it does not.

This Court recently explained, in reversing a lower court determination that a guilty plea was not voluntary: "[T]he law ordinarily considers a waiver knowing, intelligent, and sufficiently aware if the defendant fully understands the nature of the right and how it would likely apply *in general* in the circumstances—even though the defendant may not know the *specific detailed* consequences of invoking it." We similarly observed in *Patterson:* "If [the defendant] . . . lacked a full and complete appreciation of all of the consequences flowing from his waiver, it does not defeat the State's showing that the information it provided to him satisfied the constitutional minimum." The Iowa Supreme Court gave insufficient consideration to these guiding decisions. In prescribing scripted admonitions and holding them necessary in every guilty plea instance, we further note, the Iowa high court overlooked our observations that the information a defendant must have to waive counsel intelligently will "depend, in each case, upon the particular facts and circumstances surrounding that case."

* * *

* * * We hold only that the two admonitions the Iowa Supreme Court ordered are not required by the Federal Constitution.

* * *

F.   THE PLEA BARGAINING SYSTEM

BRADY v. UNITED STATES

Supreme Court of the United States, 1970.
397 U.S. 742, 90 S.Ct. 1463, 25 L.Ed.2d 747.

MR. JUSTICE WHITE delivered the opinion of the Court.

In 1959, petitioner was charged with kidnaping in violation of [the Lindbergh Act], 18 U.S.C.A. § 1201(a). Since the indictment charged that the victim of the kidnaping was not liberated unharmed, petitioner faced a maximum penalty of death if the verdict of the jury should so recommend. Petitioner, represented by competent counsel throughout, first elected to plead not guilty. Apparently because the trial judge was unwilling to try the case without a jury, petition made no serious attempt to reduce the possibility of a death penalty by waiving a jury trial. Upon learning that his codefendant, who had confessed to the authorities, would plead guilty and be available to testify against him, petitioner changed his plea to guilty. His plea was accepted after the trial judge twice questioned him as to the voluntariness of his plea. Petitioner was sentenced to 50 years' imprisonment, later reduced to 30.

In 1967, petitioner sought relief * * * claiming that his plea of guilty was not voluntarily given because § 1201(a) operated to coerce his plea, because his counsel exerted impermissible pressure upon him, and because his plea was induced by representations with respect to reduction of sentence and clemency. * * *

In United States v. Jackson, 390 U.S. 570 (1968) the defendants were indicted under § 1201(a). The District Court dismissed the § 1201(a) count of the indictment, holding the statute unconstitutional because it permitted imposition of the death sentence only upon a jury's recommendation and thereby made the risk of death the price of a jury trial. This Court held the statute valid, except for the death penalty provision; with respect to the latter, the Court agreed with the trial court "that the death penalty provision * * * imposes an impermissible burden upon the exercise of a constitutional right * * *." The problem was to determine "whether the Constitution permits the establishment of such a death penalty, applicable only to those defendants who assert the right to contest their guilt before a jury." The inevitable effect of the provision was said to be to discourage assertion of the Fifth Amendment right not to plead guilty and to deter exercise of the Sixth Amendment right to demand a jury trial. Because the legitimate goal of limiting the death penalty to cases in which a jury recommends it could be achieved without penalizing those defendants who plead not guilty and elect a jury trial, the death penalty provision "needlessly penalize[d] the assertion of a constitutional right," and was therefore unconstitutional.

Since the "inevitable effect" of the death penalty provision of § 1201(a) was said by the Court to be the needless encouragement of pleas of guilty and waivers of jury trial, Brady contends that *Jackson* requires the invalidation of every plea of guilty entered under that section, at least when the fear of death is shown to have been a factor in the plea. Petitioner, however, has read far too much into the *Jackson* opinion.

The Court made it clear in *Jackson* that it was not holding § 1201(a) inherently coercive of guilty pleas: "the fact that the Federal Kidnaping Act tends to discourage defendants from insisting upon their innocence and demanding trial by jury hardly implies that every defendant who enters a guilty plea to a charge under the Act does so involuntarily." * * *

It may be that Brady, faced with a strong case against him and recognizing that the chances for acquittal were slight, preferred to plead guilty and thus limit the penalty to life imprisonment rather than to elect a jury trial which could result in a death penalty. But even if we assume that Brady would not have pleaded guilty except for the death penalty provision of § 1201(a), this assumption merely identifies the penalty provision as a "but for" cause of his plea. That the statute caused the plea in this sense does not necessarily prove that the plea was coerced and invalid as an involuntary act.

The State to some degree encourages pleas of guilty at every important step in the criminal process. For some people, their breach of the State's law is alone sufficient reason for surrendering themselves and accepting punishment. For others, apprehension and charge, both threatening acts by the Government, jar them into admitting their guilt. In still other cases, the post-indictment accumulation of evidence may convince the defendant and his counsel that a trial is not worth the agony and expense to the defendant and his family. All these pleas of guilty are valid in spite of the State's responsibility for some of the factors motivating the pleas; the pleas are no more improperly compelled than is the decision by a defendant at the close of the State's evidence at trial that he must take the stand or face certain conviction.

Of course, the agents of the State may not produce a plea by actual or threatened physical harm or by mental coercion overbearing the will of the defendant. But nothing of the sort is claimed in this case; nor is there evidence that Brady was so gripped by fear of the death penalty or hope of leniency that he did not or could not, with the help of counsel, rationally weigh the advantages of going to trial against the advantages of pleading guilty. Brady's claim is of a different sort: that it violates the Fifth Amendment to influence or encourage a guilty plea by opportunity or promise of leniency and that a guilty plea is coerced and invalid if influenced by the fear of a possibly higher penalty for the crime charged if a conviction is obtained after the State is put to its proof.

Insofar as the voluntariness of his plea is concerned, there is little to differentiate Brady from (1) the defendant, in a jurisdiction where the judge and jury have the same range of sentencing power, who pleads guilty because his lawyer advises him that the judge will very probably be more lenient than the jury; (2) the defendant, in a jurisdiction where the judge alone has sentencing power, who is advised by counsel that the judge is normally more lenient with defendants who plead guilty than with those who go to trial; (3) the defendant who is permitted by prosecutor and judge to plead guilty to a lesser offense included in the offense charged; and (4) the defendant who pleads guilty to certain counts with the understanding that other charges will be dropped. In each of these situations, as in Brady's case, the defendant might never plead guilty absent the possibility or certainty that the plea will result in a lesser penalty than the sentence that could be imposed after a trial and a verdict of guilty. We decline to hold, however, that a guilty plea is compelled and invalid under the Fifth Amendment whenever motivated by the defendant's desire to accept the certainty or probability of a lesser penalty rather than face a wider range of possibilities extending from acquittal to conviction and a higher penalty authorized by law for the crime charged.

The issue we deal with is inherent in the criminal law and its administration because guilty pleas are not constitutionally forbidden, because the criminal law characteristically extends to judge or jury a range of choice in setting the sentence in individual cases, and because both the State and the defendant often find it advantageous to preclude the possibility of the maximum penalty authorized by law. For a defendant who sees slight possibility of acquittal, the advantages of pleading guilty and limiting the probable penalty are obvious—his exposure is reduced, the correctional processes can begin immediately, and the practical burdens of a trial are eliminated. For the State there are also advantages—the more promptly imposed punishment after an admission of guilt may more effectively attain the objectives of punishment; and with the avoidance of trial, scarce judicial and prosecutorial resources are conserved for those cases in which there is a substantial issue of the defendant's guilt or in which there is substantial doubt that the State can sustain its burden of proof. It is this mutuality of advantage that perhaps explains the fact that at present well over three-fourths of the criminal convictions in this country rest on pleas of guilty,[2] a great many of them no doubt motivated at least in part by the hope or assurance of a lesser penalty than might be imposed if there were a guilty verdict after a trial to judge or jury.

Of course, that the prevalence of guilty pleas is explainable does not necessarily validate those pleas or the system which produces them. But we cannot hold that it is unconstitutional for the State to extend a benefit to a defendant who in turn extends a substantial benefit to the State and who demonstrates by his plea that he is ready and willing to admit his crime and to enter the correctional system in a frame of mind that affords hope for success in rehabilitation over a shorter period of time than might otherwise be necessary.

A contrary holding would require the States and Federal Government to forbid guilty pleas altogether, to provide a single invariable penalty for each crime defined by the statutes, or to place the sentencing function in a separate authority having no knowledge of the manner in which the conviction in each case was obtained. In any event, it would be necessary to forbid prosecutors and judges to accept guilty pleas to selected counts, to lesser included offenses or to reduced charges. The Fifth Amendment does not reach so far.

Bram v. United States, 168 U.S. 532 (1897), held that the admissibility of a confession depended upon whether it was compelled within the meaning of the Fifth Amendment. To be admissible, a confession must be " 'free and voluntary: that is, must not be extracted by any sort of threats or violence, nor obtained by any direct or implied promises, however slight, nor by the exertion of any improper influence.' " More recently, *Malloy v. Hogan* carried forward the *Bram* definition of com-

---

2. It has been estimated that about 90%, and perhaps 95%, of all criminal convictions are by pleas of guilty; between 70% and 85% of all felony convictions are esti- mated to be by guilty plea. D. Newman, Conviction, The Determination of Guilt or Innocence Without Trial 3 and n. 1 (1966).

pulsion in the course of holding applicable to the States the Fifth Amendment privilege against compelled self-incrimination.

Bram is not inconsistent with our holding that Brady's plea was not compelled even though the law promised him a lesser maximum penalty if he did not go to trial. *Bram* dealt with a confession given by a defendant in custody, alone and unrepresented by counsel. In such circumstances, even a mild promise of leniency was deemed sufficient to bar the confession, not because the promise was an illegal act as such, but because defendants at such times are too sensitive to inducement and the possible impact on them too great to ignore and too difficult to assess. But *Bram* and its progeny did not hold that the possibly coercive impact of a promise of leniency could not be dissipated by the presence and advice of counsel, any more than *Miranda v. Arizona* held that the possibly coercive atmosphere of the police station could not be counteracted by the presence of counsel or other safeguards.

Brady's situation bears no resemblance to Bram's. Brady first pleaded not guilty; prior to changing his plea to guilty he was subjected to no threats or promises in face-to-face encounters with the authorities. He had competent counsel and full opportunity to assess the advantages and disadvantages of a trial as compared with those attending a plea of guilty; there was no hazard of an impulsive and improvident response to a seeming but unreal advantage. His plea of guilty was entered in open court and before a judge obviously sensitive to the requirements of the law with respect to guilty pleas. Brady's plea, unlike Bram's confession, was voluntary. * * *

It is true that Brady's counsel advised him that § 1201(a) empowered the jury to impose the death penalty and that nine years later in *United States v. Jackson*, the Court held that the jury had no such power as long as the judge could impose only a lesser penalty if trial was to the court or there was a plea of guilty. But these facts do not require us to set aside Brady's conviction.

Often the decision to plead guilty is heavily influenced by the defendant's appraisal of the prosecution's case against him and by the apparent likelihood of securing leniency should a guilty plea be offered and accepted. Considerations like these frequently present imponderable questions for which there are no certain answers; judgments may be made that in the light of later events seem improvident, although they were perfectly sensible at the time. The rule that a plea must be intelligently made to be valid does not require that a plea be vulnerable to later attack if the defendant did not correctly assess every relevant factor entering into his decision. A defendant is not entitled to withdraw his plea merely because he discovers long after the plea has been accepted that his calculus misapprehended the quality of the State's case or the likely penalties attached to alternative courses of action. More particularly, absent misrepresentation or other impermissible conduct by state agents, a voluntary plea of guilty intelligently made in the light of the then applicable law does not become vulnerable because later judicial decisions indicate that the plea rested on a faulty premise. A plea of guilty triggered by the expectations of a competently counseled defendant that the State will have a strong case against him is not subject to later attack because the defendant's lawyer correctly advised him with respect to the then existing law as to possible penalties but later pronouncements of the courts, as in this case, hold that the maximum penalty for the crime in question was less than was reasonably assumed at the time the plea was entered.

The fact that Brady did not anticipate *United States v. Jackson* does not impugn the truth or reliability of his plea. We find no requirement in the Constitution that a defendant must be permitted to disown his solemn admissions in open court that he committed the act with which he is charged simply because it later develops that the State would have had a weaker case than the defendant had thought or that the maximum penalty then assumed applicable has been held inapplicable in subsequent judicial decisions.

This is not to say that guilty plea convictions hold no hazards for the innocent or that the methods of taking guilty pleas presently employed in this country are necessarily valid in all respects. This mode of conviction is no more foolproof than full trials to the court or to the jury. Accordingly, we take great precautions against unsound results, and we should continue to do so, whether conviction is by plea or by trial. We would have serious doubts about this case if the encouragement of guilty pleas by offers of leniency substantially increased the likelihood that defendants, advised by competent counsel, would falsely condemn themselves. But our view is to the contrary and is based on our expectations that courts will satisfy themselves that pleas of guilty are voluntarily and intelligently made by competent defendants with adequate advice of counsel and that there is nothing to question the accuracy and reliability of the defendants' admissions that they committed the crimes with which they are charged. In the case before us, nothing in the record impeaches Brady's plea or suggests that his admissions in open court were anything but the truth.

Although Brady's plea of guilty may well have been motivated in part by a desire to avoid a possible death penalty, we are convinced that his plea was voluntarily and intelligently made and we have no reason to doubt that his solemn admission of guilt was truthful. Affirmed.

Mr. Justice Brennan, with whom Mr. Justice Douglas and Mr. Justice Marshall join, concurring in the result.

* * *

The Court attempts to submerge the issue of voluntariness of a plea under an unconstitutional capital punishment scheme in a general discussion of the pressures upon defendants to plead guilty which are said to arise from, *inter alia*, the venerable institution of plea bargaining. The argument appears to reduce to this: because the accused cannot be insulated from *all* inducements to plead guilty, it follows that he should be shielded from *none*.

The principal flaw in the Court's discourse on plea bargaining, however, is that it is, at best, only marginally relevant to the precise issues before us. There are critical distinctions between plea bargaining as commonly practiced and the situation presently under consideration— distinctions which, in constitutional terms, make a difference. Thus, whatever the merit, if any, of the constitutional objections to plea bargaining generally, those issues are not presently before us.

We are dealing here with the legislative imposition of a markedly more severe penalty if a defendant asserts his right to a jury trial and a concomitant legislative promise of leniency if he pleads guilty. This is very different from the give-and-take negotiation common in plea bargaining between the prosecution and defense, which arguably possess relatively equal bargaining power. No such flexibility is built into the capital penalty scheme where the government's harsh terms with respect to punishment are stated in unalterable form.

Furthermore, the legislatively ordained penalty scheme may affect any defendant, even one with respect to whom plea bargaining is wholly inappropriate because his guilt is uncertain. Thus the penalty scheme presents a clear danger that the innocent, or those not clearly guilty, or those who insist upon their innocence, will be induced nevertheless to plead guilty. This hazard necessitates particularly sensitive scrutiny of the voluntariness of guilty pleas entered under this type of death penalty scheme.

The penalty scheme involved here [is] also distinguishable from most plea bargaining because [it] involves the imposition of death—the most severe and awesome penalty known to our law. * * *

An independent examination of the record in the instant case convinces me that the conclusions of the lower courts are not clearly erroneous. Although Brady was aware that he faced a possible death sentence, there is no evidence that this factor alone played a significant role in his decision to enter a guilty plea. Rather, there is considerable evidence, which the District Court credited, that Brady's plea was triggered by the confession and plea decision of his codefendant and not by any substantial fear of the death penalty. Moreover, Brady's position is dependent in large measure upon his own assertions, years after the fact, that his plea was motivated by fear of the death penalty and thus rests largely upon his own credibility. For example, there is no indication, contemporaneous with the entry of the guilty plea, that Brady thought he was innocent and was pleading guilty merely to avoid possible execution. Furthermore, Brady's plea was accepted by a trial judge who manifested some sensitivity to the seriousness of a guilty plea and questioned Brady at length concerning his guilt and the voluntariness of the plea before it was finally accepted.

In view of the foregoing, I concur in the result reached by the Court * * *.

NORTH CAROLINA v. ALFORD

Supreme Court of the United States, 1970.
400 U.S. 25, 91 S.Ct. 160, 27 L.Ed.2d 162.

MR. JUSTICE WHITE delivered the opinion of the Court.

On December 2, 1963, Alford was indicted for first-degree murder, a capital offense under North Carolina law. The court appointed an attorney to represent him, and this attorney questioned all but one of the various witnesses who appellee said would substantiate his claim of innocence. The witnesses, however, did not support Alford's story but gave statements that strongly indicated his guilt. Faced with strong evidence of guilt and no substantial evidentiary support for the claim of innocence, Alford's attorney recommended that he plead guilty, but left the ultimate decision to Alford himself. The prosecutor agreed to accept a plea of guilty to a charge of second-degree murder, and on December 10, 1963, Alford pleaded guilty to the reduced charge.

Before the plea was finally accepted by the trial court, the court heard the sworn testimony of a police officer who summarized the State's case. Two other witnesses besides Alford were also heard. Although there was no eyewitness to the crime, the testimony indicated that shortly before the killing Alford took his gun from his house, stated his intention to kill the victim, and returned home with the declaration that he had carried out the killing. After the summary presentation of the State's case, Alford took the stand and testified that he had not committed the murder but that he was pleading guilty because he faced the threat of the death penalty if he did not do so.[3] In response to the questions of his counsel, he acknowledged that his counsel had informed him of the difference between second-and first-degree murder and of his rights in case he chose to go to trial. The trial court then asked appellee if, in light of his denial of guilt, he still desired to plead guilty to second-degree murder and appellee answered, "Yes, sir. I plead guilty on—from the circumstances that he [Alford's attorney] told me." After eliciting information about Alford's prior criminal record, which was a long one, the trial court sentenced him to 30 years' imprisonment, the maximum penalty for second-degree murder. * * *

[After extensive proceedings in the state and federal courts, a federal Court of Appeals held that Alford's guilty plea was involuntary. The State obtained review in the Supreme Court.]

State and lower federal courts are divided upon whether a guilty plea can be accepted when it is accompanied by protestations of innocence and hence contains only a waiver of trial but no admission of guilt. * * *

---

3. After giving his version of the events of the night of the murder, Alford stated:

"I pleaded guilty on second degree murder because they said there is too much evidence, but I ain't shot no man, but I take the fault for the other man. We never had an argument in our life and I just pleaded guilty because they said if I didn't they would gas me for it, and that is all." * * *

The issue in Hudson v. United States, 272 U.S. 451 (1926), was whether a federal court has power to impose a prison sentence after accepting a plea of *nolo contendere*, a plea by which a defendant does not expressly admit his guilt, but nonetheless waives his right to a trial and authorizes the court for purposes of the case to treat him as if he were guilty. The Court held that a trial court does have such power, and except for the cases which were rejected in *Hudson*, the federal courts have uniformly followed this rule, even in cases involving moral turpitude. Implicit in the *nolo contendere* cases is a recognition that the Constitution does not bar imposition of a prison sentence upon an accused who is unwilling expressly to admit his guilt but who, faced with grim alternatives, is willing to waive his trial and accept the sentence.

These cases would be directly in point if Alford had simply insisted on his plea but refused to admit the crime. The fact that his plea was denominated a plea of guilty rather than a plea of *nolo contendere* is of no constitutional significance with respect to the issue now before us, for the Constitution is concerned with the practical consequences, not the formal categorizations, of state law. Thus, while most pleas of guilty consist of both a waiver of trial and an express admission of guilt, the latter element is not a constitutional requisite to the imposition of criminal penalty. An individual accused of crime may voluntarily, knowingly, and understandingly consent to the imposition of a prison sentence even if he is unwilling or unable to admit his participation in the acts constituting the crime.

Nor can we perceive any material difference between a plea that refuses to admit commission of the criminal act and a plea containing a protestation of innocence when, as in the instant case, a defendant intelligently concludes that his interests require entry of a guilty plea and the record before the judge contains strong evidence of actual guilt. Here the State had a strong case of first-degree murder against Alford. Whether he realized or disbelieved his guilt, he insisted on his plea because in his view he had absolutely nothing to gain by a trial and much to gain by pleading. Because of the overwhelming evidence against him, a trial was precisely what neither Alford nor his attorney desired. Confronted with the choice between a trial for first-degree murder, on the one hand, and a plea of guilty to second-degree murder, on the other, Alford quite reasonably chose the latter and thereby limited the maximum penalty to a 30–year term. When his plea is viewed in light of the evidence against him, which substantially negated his claim of innocence and which further provided a means by which the judge could test whether the plea was being intelligently entered, its validity cannot be seriously questioned. In view of the strong factual basis for the plea demonstrated by the State and Alford's clearly expressed desire to enter it despite his professed belief in his innocence, we hold that the trial judge did not commit constitutional error in accepting it.[4]

* * *

4. Our holding does not mean that a trial judge must accept every constitutional-ly valid guilty plea merely because a defendant wishes so to plead. A criminal defen-

[The dissenting opinion of JUSTICE BRENNAN, with whom JUSTICE DOUGLAS and JUSTICE MARSHALL joined, is omitted.]

BORDENKIRCHER v. HAYES

Supreme Court of the United States, 1978.
434 U.S. 357, 98 S.Ct. 663, 54 L.Ed.2d 604.

MR. JUSTICE STEWART delivered the opinion of the Court.

* * *

The respondent, Paul Lewis Hayes, was indicted by a Fayette County, Ky., grand jury on a charge of uttering a forged instrument in the amount of $88.30, an offense then punishable by a term of two to 10 years in prison. After arraignment, Hayes, his retained counsel, and the Commonwealth's attorney met in the presence of the clerk of the court to discuss a possible plea agreement. During these conferences the prosecutor offered to recommend a sentence of five years in prison if Hayes would plead guilty to the indictment. He also said that if Hayes did not plead guilty and "save the court the inconvenience and necessity of a trial," he would return to the grand jury to seek an indictment under the Kentucky Habitual Criminal Act, (repealed 1975), which would subject Hayes to a mandatory sentence of life imprisonment by reason of his two prior felony convictions.[2] Hayes chose not to plead guilty, and the prosecutor did obtain an indictment charging him under the Habitual Criminal Act. It is not disputed that the recidivist charge was fully justified by the evidence, that the prosecutor was in possession of this evidence at the time of the original indictment, and that Hayes' refusal to plead guilty to the original charge was what led to his indictment under the habitual criminal statute.

A jury found Hayes guilty on the principal charge of uttering a forged instrument and, in a separate proceeding, further found that he had twice before been convicted of felonies. As required by the habitual offender statute, he was sentenced to a life term in the penitentiary. The Kentucky Court of Appeals rejected Hayes' constitutional objections to the enhanced sentence, holding in an unpublished opinion that imprisonment for life with the possibility of parole was constitutionally permissible in light of the previous felonies of which Hayes had been convicted,

dant does not have an absolute right under the Constitution to have his guilty plea accepted by the court * * *

2. At the time of Hayes' trial the statute provided that "[a]ny person convicted a * * * third time of felony * * * shall be confined in the penitentiary during his life." Ky.Rev.Stat. § 431.190 (repealed 1975). That statute has been replaced by Ky.Rev.Stat. § 532.080 (1977 Supp.) under which Hayes would have been sentenced to, at most, an indeterminate term of 10 to 20 years. In addition, under the new statute a previous conviction is a basis for enhanced sentencing only if a prison term of one year or more was imposed, the sentence or probation was completed within five years of the present offense, and the offender was over the age of 18 when the offense was committed. At least one of Hayes' prior convictions did not meet these conditions.

and that the prosecutor's decision to indict him as an habitual offender was a legitimate use of available leverage in the plea bargaining process.

On Hayes' petition for a federal writ of habeas corpus, the United States District Court for the Eastern District of Kentucky agreed that there had been no constitutional violation in the sentence or the indictment procedure, and denied the writ. The Court of Appeals for the Sixth Circuit reversed the District Court's judgment. * * *

This Court held in North Carolina v. Pearce, 395 U.S. 711, 725, that the Due Process Clause of the Fourteenth Amendment "requires that vindictiveness against a defendant for having successfully attacked his first conviction must play no part in the sentence he receives after a new trial." The same principle was later applied to prohibit a prosecutor from reindicting a convicted misdemeanant on a felony charge after the defendant had invoked an appellate remedy, since in this situation there was also a "realistic likelihood of 'vindictiveness.' "Blackledge v. Perry, 417 U.S., at 27.

In those cases the Court was dealing with the State's unilateral imposition of a penalty upon a defendant who had chosen to exercise a legal right to attack his original conviction—a situation "very different from the give-and-take negotiation common in plea bargaining between the prosecution and the defense, which arguably possess relatively equal bargaining power."

The Court has emphasized that the due process violation in cases such as *Pearce* and *Perry* lay not in the possibility that a defendant might be deterred from the exercise of a legal right, but rather in the danger that the State might be retaliating against the accused for lawfully attacking his conviction.

To punish a person because he has done what the law plainly allows him to do is a due process violation of the most basic sort, and for an agent of the State to pursue a course of action whose objective is to penalize a person's reliance on his legal rights is patently unconstitutional. But in the "give-and-take" of plea bargaining, there is no such element of punishment or retaliation so long as the accused is free to accept or reject the prosecution's offer.

Plea bargaining flows from "the mutuality of advantage" to defendants and prosecutors, each with his own reasons for wanting to avoid trial. Defendants advised by competent counsel and protected by other procedural safeguards are presumptively capable of intelligent choice in response to prosecutorial persuasion, and unlikely to be driven to false self-condemnation. Indeed, acceptance of the basic legitimacy of a plea bargaining necessarily implies rejection of any notion that a guilty plea is involuntary in a constitutional sense simply because it is the end result of the bargaining process. By hypothesis, the plea may have been induced by promises of a recommendation of a lenient sentence or a reduction of charges, and thus by fear of the possibility of a greater penalty upon conviction after a trial. * * * It follows that, by tolerating and encouraging the negotiation of pleas, this Court has necessarily accepted as constitutionally legitimate the simple reality that the prosecutor's interest at the bargaining table is to persuade the defendant to forego his right to plead not guilty.

It is not disputed here that Hayes was properly chargeable under the recidivist statute, since he had in fact been convicted of two previous felonies. In our system, so long as the prosecutor has probable cause to believe that the accused committed an offense defined by statute, the decision whether or not to prosecute, and what charge to file or bring before a grand jury, generally rests entirely in his discretion. Within the limits set by the legislature's constitutionally valid definition of chargeable offenses, "the conscious exercise of some selectivity in enforcement is not in itself a federal constitutional violation" so long as "the selection was [not] deliberately based upon an unjustifiable standard such as race, religion, or other arbitrary classification." Oyler v. Boles, 368 U.S. 448, 456. To hold that the prosecutor's desire to induce a guilty plea is an "unjustifiable standard," which, like race or religion, may play no part in his charging decision, would contradict the very premises that underlie the concept of plea bargaining itself. Moreover, a rigid constitutional rule that would prohibit a prosecutor from acting forthrightly in his dealings with the defense could only invite unhealthy subterfuge that would drive the practice of plea bargaining back into the shadows from which it has so recently emerged.

There is no doubt that the breadth of discretion that our country's legal system vests in prosecuting attorneys carries with it the potential for both individual and institutional abuse. And broad though that discretion may be, there are undoubtedly constitutional limits upon its exercise. We hold only that the course of conduct engaged in by the prosecutor in this case, which no more than openly presented the defendant with the unpleasant alternatives of foregoing trial or facing charges on which he was plainly subject to prosecution, did not violate the Due Process Clause of the Fourteenth Amendment.

Accordingly, the judgment of the Court of Appeals is

Reversed.

MR. JUSTICE BLACKMUN, with whom MR. JUSTICE BRENNAN and MR. JUSTICE MARSHALL join, dissenting. * * *

[In this case vindictiveness is present to the same extent as in North Carolina v. Pearce and Blackledge v. Perry.] The prosecutor here admitted that the sole reason for the new indictment was to discourage the respondent from exercising his right to a trial. Even had such an admission not been made, when plea negotiations, conducted in the face of the less serious charge under the first indictment, fail, charging by a second indictment a more serious crime for the same conduct creates a strong inference of vindictiveness. * * *

It might be argued that it really makes little difference how this case, now that it is here, is decided. The Court's holding gives plea bargaining full sway despite vindictiveness. A contrary result, however, merely would prompt the aggressive prosecutor to bring the greater charge initially in every case, and only thereafter to bargain. The consequences to the accused would still be adverse, for then he would bargain against a greater charge, face the likelihood of increased bail, and run the risk that the court would be less inclined to accept a bargained plea. Nonetheless, it is far preferable to hold the prosecution to the charge it was originally content to bring and to justify in the eyes of its public.[2]

* * *

[The dissenting opinion of Justice Powell is omitted.]

ALABAMA v. SMITH

Supreme Court of the United States, 1989.
490 U.S. 794, 109 S.Ct. 2201, 104 L.Ed.2d 865.

CHIEF JUSTICE REHNQUIST delivered the opinion of the Court.

* * * In 1985, an Alabama grand jury indicted Smith for burglary, rape, and sodomy. All the charges related to a single assault. Smith agreed to plead guilty to the burglary and rape charges in exchange for the State's agreement to dismiss the sodomy charge. The trial court granted the State's motion to dismiss the sodomy charge, accepted respondent's guilty pleas, and sentenced him to concurrent terms of 30–years' imprisonment on each conviction. Later, respondent moved to withdraw his guilty pleas, claiming that he had not entered them knowingly and voluntarily. The trial court denied this motion, but the Alabama Court of Criminal Appeals reversed, finding that respondent had not been properly informed of the penalties associated with the crimes to which he had pleaded guilty. The case was reassigned to the same trial judge. The State moved to reinstate the charge of first-degree sodomy; the trial court granted that motion, and respondent went to trial on all three original charges.

At trial, the victim testified that respondent had broken into her home in the middle of the night, clad only in his underwear and a ski mask and wielding a kitchen knife. Holding the knife to her chest, he had raped and sodomized her repeatedly and forced her to engage in oral sex with him. The attack, which lasted for more than an hour, occurred in the victim's own bedroom, just across the hall from the room in which her three young children lay sleeping. The State also offered respondent's postarrest statement, in which he admitted many of the details of the offenses. Respondent later took the stand and repudiated his postar-

---

2. That prosecutors, without saying so, may sometimes bring charges more serious than they think appropriate for the ultimate disposition of a case, in order to gain bargaining leverage with a defendant, does not add support to today's decision, for this Court, in its approval of the advantages to be gained from plea negotiations, has never openly sanctioned such deliberate over-charging or taken such a cynical view of the bargaining process. See *North Carolina v. Alford*, 400 U.S. 25 (1970); *Santobello v. New York*, 404 U.S. 257 (1971). Normally, of course, it is impossible to show that this is what the prosecutor is doing, and the courts necessarily have deferred to the prosecutor's exercise of discretion in initial charging decisions.

rest statement, testifying instead that he had been in bed with his girlfriend at the time the attack took place.

The jury returned a verdict of guilty on all three counts. This time, the trial judge imposed a term of life imprisonment for the burglary conviction, plus a concurrent term of life imprisonment on the sodomy conviction and a consecutive term of 150 years' imprisonment on the rape conviction. The trial court explained that it was imposing a harsher sentence than it had imposed following respondent's guilty pleas because the evidence presented at trial, of which it had been unaware at the time it imposed sentence on the guilty pleas, convinced it that the original sentence had been too lenient. As the court explained, at the time it imposed sentence on the guilty pleas, it had heard only "[respondent's] side of the story"; whereas now, it "has had a trial and heard all of the evidence," including testimony that respondent had raped the victim at least five times, forced her to engage in oral sex with him, and threatened her life with a knife. The court stated that this new information about the nature of respondent's crimes and their impact on the victim, together with its observations of his "mental outlook on [the offenses] and [his] position during the trial," convinced it that it was "proper to increase the sentence beyond that which was given to [him] on the plea bargain."

The Alabama Court of Criminal Appeals affirmed respondent's convictions, as well as the life sentences imposed for burglary and sodomy, but remanded the rape conviction for resentencing. The Supreme Court of Alabama then granted respondent's request for review of the burglary sentence, and reversed and remanded by a divided vote. The majority held that under our decision in North Carolina v. Pearce, 395 U.S. 711 (1969), there can be no increase in sentence upon reconviction at a second trial after the first conviction has been overturned on appeal and remanded for a new trial, unless the increase is justified by events subsequent to the first trial. Because the majority thought the trial court had increased respondent's sentence for the burglary conviction based on new information about events occurring prior to the imposition of the original sentence—e.g., new information about the nature of the crime and its effect on the victim—the majority held that *Pearce* required it to set aside that sentence.

* * * While the *Pearce* opinion appeared on its face to announce a rule of sweeping dimension, our subsequent cases have made clear that its presumption of vindictiveness does not apply in every case where a convicted defendant receives a higher sentence on retrial. As we explained in Texas v. McCullough, 475 U.S. 134 (1986), the evil *Pearce* sought to prevent was not the imposition of enlarged sentences after a new trial but vindictiveness of a sentencing judge. Because the *Pearce* presumption may operate in the absence of any proof of an improper motive and thus block a legitimate response to criminal conduct, we have limited its application, like that of other judicially created means of effectuating the rights secured by the Constitution, to circumstances where its objectives are thought most efficaciously served. * * *

In Colten v. Kentucky, 407 U.S. 104 (1972), for example, we refused to apply the presumption when the increased sentence was imposed by the second court in a two-tier system which gave a defendant convicted of a misdemeanor in an inferior court the right to trial de novo in a superior court. We observed that the trial de novo represented a completely fresh determination of guilt or innocence by a court that was not being "asked to do over what it thought it had already done correctly." * * * Consequently, we rejected the proposition that greater penalties on retrial were explained by vindictiveness with sufficient frequency to warrant the imposition of a prophylactic rule.[3] Similarly, in Chaffin v. Stynchcombe, 412 U.S. 17 (1973), we held that no presumption of vindictiveness arose when a second jury, on retrial following a successful appeal, imposed a higher sentence than a prior jury. We thought that a second jury was unlikely to have a "personal stake" in the prior conviction or to be "sensitive to the institutional interests that might occasion higher sentences."

We think the same reasoning leads to the conclusion that when a greater penalty is imposed after trial than was imposed after a prior guilty plea, the increase in sentence is not more likely than not attributable to the vindictiveness on the part of the sentencing judge. Even when the same judge imposes both sentences, the relevant sentencing information available to the judge after the plea will usually be considerably less than that available after a trial. * * * As this case demonstrates, in the course of the proof at trial the judge may gather a fuller appreciation of the nature and extent of the crimes charged. The defendant's conduct during trial may give the judge insights into his moral character and suitability for rehabilitation. See United States v. Grayson, 438 U.S. 41 (1978) (sentencing authority's perception of the truthfulness of a defendant testifying on his own behalf may be considered in sentencing). Finally, after trial, the factors that may have indicated leniency as consideration for the guilty plea are no longer present. * * *

Our conclusion here is not consistent with *Simpson v. Rice*, the companion case to *North Carolina v. Pearce*. In *Simpson v. Rice*, the complained of sentence followed trial after Rice had successfully attacked his previous guilty plea. We found that a presumption of vindictiveness arose when the State offered "no evidence attempting to justify the increase in Rice's original sentences * * *." With respect, it does not appear that the Court gave any consideration to a possible distinction between the *Pearce* case, in which differing sentences were imposed after

3. We adopted a prophylactic rule to guard against vindictiveness by the prosecutor at the post-conviction stage in Blackledge v. Perry, 417 U.S. 21 (1974). There the prosecutor charged the defendant with a felony when the latter availed himself of de novo review of his initial conviction of a misdemeanor for the same conduct. He received a sentence of five to seven years for the felony compared to the 6-month sentence he had received for the misdemeanor. On these facts, we concluded that a presumption of vindictiveness arose analogous to that in *Pearce* because the prosecutor clearly has a considerable stake in discouraging convicted misdemeanants from appealing. * * *

two trials, and the *Rice* case, in which the first sentence was entered on a guilty plea.

The failure in *Simpson v. Rice* to note the distinction just described stems in part from that case having been decided before some important developments in the constitutional law of guilty pleas. [The majority opinion discussed the endorsement of plea bargaining provided in decisions such as *Brady v. United States* and *Bordenkircher v. Hayes.*] Part of the reason for now reaching a conclusion different from that reached in *Simpson v. Rice*, therefore, is the later development of this constitutional law relating to guilty pleas. Part is the Court's failure in *Simpson* to note the greater amount of sentencing information that a trial generally affords as compared to a guilty plea. Believing as we do that there is no basis for a presumption of vindictiveness where a second sentence imposed after a trial is heavier than a first sentence imposed after a guilty plea, we overrule *Simpson v. Rice*, to that extent. Petitioner contends that there is evidence to support a finding of actual vindictiveness on the part of the sentencing judge in this case. This is not the question upon which we granted certiorari, and we decline to reach it here although it may be open to petitioner on our remand to the Supreme Court of Alabama.

The judgment of the Supreme Court of Alabama is reversed, and the cause remanded for further proceedings not inconsistent with this opinion.

JUSTICE MARSHALL, dissenting.

After successfully challenging the validity of his plea bargain on the grounds that the trial judge had misinformed him about the penalties he could face, respondent Smith went to trial. He was convicted and resentenced to a drastically longer sentence than the one he had initially received as a result of his plea bargain. The majority today finds no infirmity in this result. I, however, continue to believe that, "if for any reason a new trial is granted and there is a conviction a second time, the second penalty imposed cannot exceed the first penalty, if respect is had for the guarantee against double jeopardy." North Carolina v. Pearce, 395 U.S. 711, 727 (1969) (DOUGLAS, J., concurring, joined by MARSHALL, J.) I therefore dissent.

HILL v. LOCKHART

Supreme Court of the United States, 1985.
474 U.S. 52, 106 S.Ct. 366, 88 L.Ed.2d 203.

JUSTICE REHNQUIST delivered the opinion of the Court.

Petitioner William Lloyd Hill pleaded guilty in the Arkansas trial court to charges of first-degree murder and theft of property. More than two years later he sought federal habeas relief on the ground that his court-appointed attorney had failed to advise him that, as a second offender, he was required to serve one-half of his sentence before becoming eligible for parole.

* * *

Under Arkansas law, the murder charge to which petitioner pleaded guilty carried a potential sentence of 5 to 50 years or life in prison, along with a fine of up to $15,000. Petitioner's court-appointed attorney negotiated a plea agreement pursuant to which the State, in return for petitioner's plea of guilty to both the murder and theft charges, agreed to recommend that the trial judge impose concurrent prison sentences of 35 years for the murder and 10 years for the theft. Petitioner signed a written "plea statement" indicating that he understood the charges against him and the consequences of pleading guilty, that his plea had not been induced "by any force, threat, or promise" apart from the plea agreement itself, that he realized that the trial judge was not bound by the plea agreement and retained the sole "power of sentence," and that he had discussed the plea agreement with his attorney and was satisfied with his attorney's advice. The last two lines of the "plea statement," just above petitioner's signature, read: "I am aware of everything in this document. I fully understand what my rights are, and I voluntarily plead guilty because I am guilty as charged."

Petitioner appeared before the trial judge at the plea hearing, recounted the events that gave rise to the charges against him, affirmed that he had signed and understood the written "plea statement," reiterated that no "threats or promises" had been made to him other than the plea agreement itself, and entered a plea of guilty to both charges. The trial judge accepted the guilty plea and sentenced petitioner in accordance with the state's recommendations. The trial judge also granted petitioner credit for the time he had already served in prison, and told petitioner that "[y]ou will be required to serve at least one-third of your time before you are eligible for parole."

More than two years later petitioner filed a federal habeas corpus petition alleging, *inter alia*, that his guilty plea was involuntary by reason of ineffective assistance of counsel because his attorney had misinformed him as to his parole eligibility date. According to petitioner, his attorney had told him that if he pleaded guilty he would become eligible for parole after serving one-third of his prison sentence. In fact, because petitioner previously had been convicted of a felony in Florida, he was classified under Arkansas law as a "second offender" and was required to serve one-half of his sentence before becoming eligible for parole. Petitioner asked the United States District Court for the Eastern District of Arkansas to reduce his sentence to a term of years that would result in his becoming eligible for parole in conformance with his original expectations.

[The District Court denied relief, and the Court of Appeals affirmed by an evenly divided court.]

The long standing test for determining the validity of a guilty plea is "whether the plea represents a voluntary and intelligent choice among the alternative courses of action open to the defendant." Here petitioner does not contend that his plea was "involuntary" or "unintelligent" simply because the State through its officials failed to supply him with information about his parole eligibility date. We have never held that the United States Constitution requires the State to furnish a defendant with information about parole eligibility in order for the defendant's plea of guilty to be voluntary, and indeed such a constitutional requirement would be inconsistent with the current rules of procedure governing the entry of guilty pleas in the federal courts. See Fed.Rule Crim.Proc. 11(c); Advisory Committee's Notes on 1974 Amendment to Fed.Rule Crim. Proc. 11, 18 U.S.C.App., p. 22 (federal courts generally are not required to inform defendant about parole eligibility before accepting guilty plea). Instead, petitioner relies entirely on the claim that his plea was "involuntary" as a result of ineffective assistance of counsel because his attorney supplied him with information about parole eligibility that was erroneous. Where, as here, a defendant is represented by counsel during the plea process and enters his plea upon the advice of counsel, the voluntariness of the plea depends on whether counsel's advice "was within the range of competence demanded of attorneys in criminal cases." *McMann v. Richardson*, 397 U.S. 759, 771 (1970). As we explained in *Tollett v. Henderson*, 411 U.S. 258 (1973), a defendant who pleads guilty upon the advice of counsel "may only attack the voluntary and intelligent character of the guilty plea by showing that the advice he received from counsel was not within the standards set forth in *McMann*."

Our concern in *McMann v. Richardson* with the quality of counsel's performance in advising a defendant whether to plead guilty stemmed from the more general principle that all defendants facing felony charges are entitled to the effective assistance of competent counsel. Two Terms ago, in *Strickland v. Washington*, we adopted a two-part standard for evaluating claims of ineffective assistance of counsel. There, citing *McMann*, we reiterated that "[w]hen a convicted defendant complains of the ineffectiveness of counsel's assistance, the defendant must show that counsel's representation fell below an objective standard of reasonableness." We also held, however, that "[t]he defendant must show that there is a reasonable probability that, but for counsel's unprofessional errors, the result of the proceeding would have been different." This additional "prejudice" requirement was based on our conclusion that "[a]n error by counsel, even if professionally unreasonable, does not warrant setting aside the judgment of a criminal proceeding if the error had no effect on the judgment."

Although our decision in *Strickland v. Washington* dealt with a claim of ineffective assistance of counsel in a capital sentencing proceeding, and was premised in part on the similarity between such a proceeding and the usual criminal trial, the same two-part standard seems to us applicable to ineffective assistance claims arising out of the plea process. * * * In addition, we believe that requiring a showing of "prejudice" from defendants who seek to challenge the validity of their guilty pleas on the ground of ineffective assistance of counsel will serve the fundamental interest in the finality of guilty pleas we identified in *United States v. Timmreck*, 441 U.S. 780 (1979):

" 'Every inroad on the concept of finality undermines confidence in the integrity of our procedures; and, by increasing the volume of judicial work, inevitably delays and impairs the orderly administration of justice. The impact is greatest when new grounds for setting aside guilty pleas are approved because the vast majority of criminal convictions result from such pleas. Moreover, the concern that unfair procedures may have resulted in the conviction of an innocent defendant is only rarely raised by a petition to set aside a guilty plea.' "

We hold, therefore, that the two-part *Strickland v. Washington* test applies to challenges to guilty pleas based on ineffective assistance of counsel. In the context of guilty pleas, the first half of the *Strickland v. Washington* test is nothing more than a restatement of the standard of attorney competence already set forth in *Tollett v. Henderson* and *McMann v. Richardson*. The second, or "prejudice," requirement, on the other hand, focuses on whether counsel's constitutionally ineffective performance affected the outcome of the plea process. In other words, in order to satisfy the "prejudice" requirement, the defendant must show that there is a reasonable probability that, but for counsel's errors, he would not have pleaded guilty and would have insisted on going to trial.

In many guilty plea cases, the "prejudice" inquiry will closely resemble the inquiry engaged in by courts reviewing ineffective assistance challenges to convictions obtained through a trial. For example, where the alleged error of counsel is a failure to investigate or discover potentially exculpatory evidence, the determination whether the error "prejudiced" the defendant by causing him to plead guilty rather than go to trial will depend on the likelihood that discovery of the evidence would have led counsel to change his recommendation as to the plea. The assessment, in turn, will depend in large part on a prediction whether the evidence likely would have changed the outcome of a trial. Similarly, where the alleged error of counsel is a failure to advise the defendant of a potential affirmative defense to the crime charged, the resolution of the "prejudice" inquiry will depend largely on whether the affirmative defense likely would have succeeded at trial. * * *

In the present case the claimed error of counsel is erroneous advice as to eligibility for parole under the sentence agreed to in the plea bargain. We find it unnecessary to determine whether there may be circumstances under which erroneous advice by counsel as to parole eligibility may be deemed constitutionally ineffective assistance of counsel, because in the present case we conclude that petitioner's allegations are insufficient to satisfy the *Strickland v. Washington* requirement of "prejudice." Petitioner did not allege in his habeas petition that, had counsel correctly informed him about his parole eligibility date, he would have pleaded not guilty and insisted on going to trial. He alleged no special circumstances that might support the conclusion that he placed particular emphasis on his parole eligibility in deciding whether or not to plead guilty. Indeed, petitioner's mistaken belief that he would become eligible for parole after serving one-third of his sentence would seem to have affected not only his calculation of the time he likely would serve if sentenced pursuant to the proposed plea agreement, but also his calculation of the time he likely would serve if he went to trial and were convicted.

Because petitioner in this case failed to allege the kind of "prejudice" necessary to satisfy the second half of the *Strickland v. Washington* test, the District Court did not err in declining to hold a hearing on petitioner's ineffective assistance of counsel claim. The judgment of the Court of Appeals is therefore affirmed.

[The concurring opinion of JUSTICE WHITE, with whom JUSTICE STEVENS joined, is omitted.]

BOYKIN v. ALABAMA

Supreme Court of the United States, 1969.
395 U.S. 238, 89 S.Ct. 1709, 23 L.Ed.2d 274.

MR. JUSTICE DOUGLAS delivered the opinion of the Court.

In the spring of 1966, within the period of a fortnight, a series of armed robberies occurred in Mobile, Alabama. The victims, in each case, were local shopkeepers open at night who were forced by a gunman to hand over money. While robbing one grocery store, the assailant fired his gun once, sending a bullet through a door into the ceiling. A few days earlier in a drugstore, the robber had allowed his gun to discharge in such a way that the bullet, on ricochet from the floor, struck a customer in the leg. Shortly thereafter, a local grand jury returned five indictments against petitioner, a 27–year-old Negro, for common-law robbery—an offense punishable in Alabama by death.

Before the matter came to trial, the court determined that petitioner was indigent and appointed counsel to represent him. Three days later, at his arraignment, petitioner pleaded guilty to all five indictments. So far as the record shows, the judge asked no questions of petitioner concerning his plea, and petitioner did not address the court.

Trial strategy may of course make a plea of guilty seem the desirable course. But the record is wholly silent on that point and throws no light on it.

Alabama provides that when a defendant pleads guilty, "the court must cause the punishment to be determined by a jury" (except where it is required to be fixed by the court) and may "cause witnesses to be examined, to ascertain the character of the offense." Ala.Code, Tit. 15, § 277 (1958). In the present case a trial of that dimension was held, the prosecution presenting its case largely through eyewitness testimony. Although counsel for petitioner engaged in cursory cross-examination, petitioner neither testified himself nor presented testimony concerning his character and background. There was nothing to indicate that he had a prior criminal record.

In instructing the jury, the judge stressed that petitioner had pleaded guilty in five cases of robbery, defined as "the felonious taking of money * * * from another against his will * * * by violence or by putting him in fear * * * [carrying] from ten years minimum in the penitentiary to the supreme penalty of death by electrocution." The jury, upon deliberation, found petitioner guilty and sentenced him severally to die on each of the five indictments.

* * *

A plea of guilty is more than a confession which admits that the accused did various acts; it is itself a conviction; nothing remains but to give judgment and determine punishment. * * *

The requirement that the prosecution spread on the record the prerequisites of a valid waiver is no constitutional innovation. In Carnley v. Cochran, 369 U.S. 506, 516, we dealt with a problem of waiver of the right to counsel, a Sixth Amendment right. We held: "Presuming waiver from a silent record is impermissible. The record must show, or there must be an allegation and evidence which show, that an accused was offered counsel but intelligently and understandingly rejected the offer. Anything less is not waiver."

We think that the same standard must be applied to determining whether a guilty plea is voluntarily made. For, as we have said, a plea of guilty is more than an admission of conduct; it is a conviction. Ignorance, incomprehension, coercion, terror, inducements, subtle or blatant threats might be a perfect cover-up of unconstitutionality. The question of an effective waiver of a federal constitutional right in a proceeding is of course governed by federal standards.

Several federal constitutional rights are involved in a waiver that takes place when a plea of guilty is entered in a state criminal trial. First, is the privilege against compulsory self-incrimination guaranteed by the Fifth Amendment and applicable to the States by reason of the Fourteenth. Second, is the right to trial by jury. Third, is the right to confront one's accusers. We cannot presume a waiver of these three important federal rights from a silent record.

What is at stake for an accused facing death or imprisonment demands the utmost solicitude of which courts are capable in canvassing the matter with the accused to make sure he has a full understanding of what the plea connotes and of its consequence. When the judge discharges that function, he leaves a record adequate for any review that may be later sought, and forestalls the spin-off of collateral proceedings that seek to probe murky memories.

The three dissenting justices in the Alabama Supreme Court stated the law accurately when they concluded that there was reversible error "because the record does not disclose that the defendant voluntarily and understandingly entered his pleas of guilty."

Reversed.

[The dissenting opinion of JUSTICE HARLAN, in which JUSTICE BLACK joined, is omitted.]

Commentary

1. *Inadmissibility of Plea Discussions.* Federal Rule of Criminal Procedure 11(e)(6) provides generally that a defendant's statements during plea discussion may not be used against him. In United States v. Mezzanatto, 513 U.S. 196 (1995), the Supreme Court held that a defendant can waive this protection. Charged with drug selling, defendant asked to meet with the prosecutor to discuss terms of cooperation. The prosecutor insisted as a precondition that defendant would have to be absolutely truthful, and would have to agree that statements he made in the discussions could be used to impeach any contradictory testimony he might give at trial if the case should go that far. Defendant agreed to proceed under those terms. In the discussions defendant admitted knowing that the package he had delivered to an undercover agent contained methamphetamine, but made other false statements that led the prosecutor to terminate the discussions. At his subsequent trial defendant denied knowing that the package contained methamphetamine, and the prosecutor used his admission to impeach his testimony. The Supreme Court held (7–2) that the waiver was valid and the statement admissible for impeachment. Three Justices in the majority noted in the concurrence that the waiver might not be valid if employed to admit statements made during plea bargaining in the Government's case-in-chief.

2. *Withdrawing a Guilty Plea.* A defendant has an absolute right to withdraw a guilty plea before the court accepts it. When a defendant enters a plea of guilty pursuant to a bargain with the prosecution, the judge will typically accept the plea but defer acceptance of the bargain for a few weeks so that a presentence report can be prepared and considered. What if the defendant seeks to withdraw the plea in the meantime? Federal Rule of Criminal Procedure 32(e) says that the judge may allow a defendant to withdraw his plea for "any fair and just reason." The United States Court of Appeals for the Ninth Circuit held that, since the plea and the plea agreement "are inextricably bound together" the defendant retains his absolute right to withdraw the plea, "for any reason or for no reason," until the court accepts both the plea and the agreement.

This result would allow a defendant to plead guilty on the eve of trial, for example, and then withdraw the plea a few days or weeks later if it appeared that the prosecution's case had, for whatever reason, become weaker. If contract principles govern, prosecutors ready and willing to go to trial would presumably refuse to accept guilty pleas without some guarantee against subsequent withdrawal. In any case, the Supreme Court unanimously reversed the Ninth Circuit's decision in United States v. Hyde, 520 U.S. 670 (1997). The Supreme Court held that once the judge accepts the plea, and the defendant has stated in court that he is pleading guilty voluntarily and because he actually is guilty, the plea may be withdrawn only for good cause shown even though the judge has not yet decided whether to accept the plea agreement.

3. *Information Provided to the Defendant.* Two recent Supreme Court decisions emphasize that a defendant is not entitled to withdraw a guilty plea simply because he was not provided information that might have affected his decision:

In United States v. Benitez, 542 U.S. 74 (2004), the trial court failed to advise the defendant that he could not withdraw his guilty plea if the court did not accept the Government's recommendations. This warning is required by Federal Rule of Criminal Procedure 11. The pre-sentencing report revealed prior convictions that made the defendant ineligible for the sentence recommendation agreed upon during the plea negotiations, and the defendant received a longer sentence. The Supreme Court held that a defendant who seeks reversal of his conviction after a guilty plea, on the ground that the district court committed plain error under Rule 11, must show a reasonable probability that, but for the error, he would not have entered the plea. A defendant must demonstrate that the probability of a different result is " 'sufficient to undermine confidence in the outcome' " of the proceeding.

In United States v. Ruiz, 536 U.S. 622 (2002), the Supreme Court confirmed that a guilty plea can be voluntary, even if it is based upon incomplete information provided to the defendant, and held that the Constitution does not require federal prosecutors to disclose "impeachment information relating to any informants or other witnesses." before entering into a binding plea agreement with a criminal defendant. Ruiz rejected a plea agreement offered by federal prosecutors, who then obtained an indictment charging her without unlawful drug possession. Despite the absence of any plea agreement, Ruiz ultimately pleaded guilty.

The Supreme Court cited its prior decisions establishing that due process requires prosecutors to "avoid ... an unfair trial" by making available "upon request" evidence "favorable to an accused ... where the evidence is material either to guilt or to punishment" (Brady v. Maryland, 373 U.S. 83, 87 (1963); and subsequently, that a defense request is unnecessary (United States v. Agurs, 427 U.S. 97, 112–113 (1976); and that exculpatory evidence includes "evidence affecting" witness "credibility," where the witness'" reliability" is likely "determinative of guilt or innocence") (Giglio v. United States, 405 U.S. 150, 154 (1972)). The Supreme Court concluded, however that such disclosures were not constitutionally mandated during plea bargaining:

> "impeachment information is special in relation to the *fairness of a trial*, not in respect to whether a plea is *voluntary* ("knowing," "intelligent," and "sufficiently aware"). Of course, the more information the defendant has, the more aware he is of the likely consequences of a plea, waiver, or decision, and the wiser that decision will likely be. But the Constitution does not require the prosecutor to share all useful information with the defendant.

This was true, the Court held, because a waiver usually is considered knowing and intelligent if the defendant fully understood the nature of the right being waived, even though the defendant does not know "the *specific detailed* consequences of invoking it." The Court also emphasized that imposing on prosecutors a constitutional obligation to provide impeachment information during plea bargaining, prior to entry of a guilty plea, "could seriously interfere with the Government's interest in securing those guilty pleas that are factually justified, desired by defendants, and help to secure the efficient administration of justice," and could result in "premature disclosure of Government witness information, which * * * could "disrupt ongoing investigations" and expose prospective witnesses to serious harm."

Chapter 11

GRAND JURY PROCEEDINGS

A. PROSECUTORS AND GRAND JURY PROCEEDINGS

COSTELLO v. UNITED STATES

Supreme Court of the United States, 1956.
350 U.S. 359, 76 S.Ct. 406, 100 L.Ed. 397.

MR. JUSTICE BLACK delivered the opinion of the Court.

We granted certiorari in this case to consider a single question: " 'May a defendant be required to stand trial and a conviction be sustained where only hearsay evidence was presented to the grand jury which indicted him?' "

Petitioner, Frank Costello, was indicted for wilfully attempting to evade payment of income taxes due the United States for the years 1947, 1948, and 1949. The charge was that petitioner falsely and fraudulently reported less income than he and his wife actually received during the taxable years in question. Petitioner promptly filed a motion for inspection of the minutes of the grand jury and for a dismissal of the indictment. His motion was based on an affidavit stating that he was firmly convinced there could have been no legal or competent evidence before the grand jury which indicted him since he had reported all his income and paid all taxes due. The motion was denied. At the trial which followed the Government offered evidence designed to show increases in Costello's net worth in an attempt to prove that he had received more income during the years in question than he had reported. To establish its case the Government called and examined 144 witnesses and introduced 368 exhibits. All of the testimony and documents related to business transactions and expenditures by petitioner and his wife. The prosecution concluded its case by calling three government agents. Their investigations had produced the evidence used against petitioner at the trial. They were allowed to summarize the vast amount of evidence already heard and to introduce computations showing, if correct, that petitioner and his wife had received far greater income than they had reported. We have held such summarizations admissible in a "net worth" case like this.

Counsel for petitioner asked each government witness at the trial whether he had appeared before the grand jury which returned the indictment. This cross-examination developed the fact that the three investigating officers had been the only witnesses before the grand jury. After the Government concluded its case, petitioner again moved to dismiss the indictment on the ground that the only evidence before the grand jury was "hearsay," since the three officers had no firsthand knowledge of the transactions upon which their computations were based. Nevertheless the trial court again refused to dismiss the indictment, and petitioner was convicted. The Court of Appeals affirmed, holding that the indictment was valid even though the sole evidence before the grand jury was hearsay. Petitioner here urges: (1) that an indictment based solely on hearsay evidence violates that part of the Fifth Amendment providing that "No person shall be held to answer for a capital, or otherwise infamous crime, unless on a presentment or indictment of a Grand Jury * * * " and (2) that if the Fifth Amendment does not invalidate an indictment based solely on hearsay we should now lay down such a rule for the guidance of federal courts.

The Fifth Amendment provides that federal prosecutions for capital or otherwise infamous crimes must be instituted by presentments or indictments of grand juries. But neither the Fifth Amendment nor any other constitutional provision prescribes the kind of evidence upon which grand juries must act. The grand jury is an English institution, brought to this country by the early colonists and incorporated in the Constitution by the Founders. There is every reason to believe that our constitutional grand jury was intended to operate substantially like its English progenitor. The basic purpose of the English grand jury was to provide a fair method for instituting criminal proceedings against persons believed to have committed crimes. Grand jurors were selected from the body of the people and their work was not hampered by rigid procedural or evidential rules. In fact, grand jurors could act on their own knowledge and were free to make their presentments or indictments on such information as they deemed satisfactory. Despite its broad power to institute criminal proceedings the grand jury grew in popular favor with the years. It acquired an independence in England free from control by the Crown or judges. Its adoption in our Constitution as the sole method for preferring charges in serious criminal cases shows the high place it held as an instrument of justice. And in this country as in England of old the grand jury has convened as a body of laymen, free from technical rules, acting in secret, pledged to indict no one because of prejudice and to free no one because of special favor. As late as 1927 an English historian could say that English grand juries were still free to act on their own knowledge if they pleased to do so. And in 1852 Mr. Justice Nelson on circuit could say "no case has been cited, nor have we been able to find any, furnishing an authority for looking into and revising the judgment of the grand jury upon the evidence, for the purpose of determining whether or not the finding was founded upon sufficient proof * * *." United States v. Reed, 27 Fed.Cas. pages 727, 738, No. 16,134.

* * * If indictments were to be held open to challenge on the ground that there was inadequate or incompetent evidence before the grand jury, the resulting delay would be great indeed. The result of such a rule would be that before trial on the merits a defendant could always insist on a kind of preliminary trial to determine the competency and adequacy of the evidence before the grand jury. This is not required by the Fifth Amendment. An indictment returned by a legally constituted and unbiased grand jury, like an information drawn by the prosecutor, if valid on its face, is enough to call for trial of the charge on the merits. The Fifth Amendment requires nothing more.

Petitioner urges that this Court should exercise its power to supervise the administration of justice in federal courts and establish a rule permitting defendants to challenge indictments on the ground that they are not supported by adequate or competent evidence. No persuasive reasons are advanced for establishing such a rule. It would run counter to the whole history of the grand jury institution, in which laymen conduct their inquiries unfettered by technical rules. Neither justice nor the concept of a fair trial requires such a change. In a trial on the merits, defendants are entitled to a strict observance of all the rules designed to bring about a fair verdict. Defendants are not entitled, however, to a rule which would result in interminable delay but add nothing to the assurance of a fair trial.

Affirmed.

UNITED STATES v. HOGAN

United States Court of Appeals, Second Circuit, 1983.
712 F.2d 757.

CARDAMONE, CIRCUIT JUDGE:

On this appeal our principal concern is directed not at the jury trial where the accused were found guilty, but at earlier events—those that transpired before the grand jury which indicted the appellants. * * *

I

On July 24, 1981 appellants, Lawrence A. Hogan and Leonard J. Patricelli, were indicted by a grand jury sitting in the District of Connecticut for conspiracy to possess with intent to distribute heroin, in violation of 21 U.S.C. § 846. Hogan was also charged with five counts of using a telephone to facilitate an attempt to possess with intent to distribute heroin, in violation of 21 U.S.C. § 843(b). One of the § 843(b) counts was dismissed prior to trial.

After a nine-day trial held before then Chief Judge T. Emmet Clarie and a jury in the United States District Court for the District of Connecticut, the jury returned guilty verdicts as to both appellants on the conspiracy count and as to Hogan alone on three of the telephone facilitation counts, acquitting him on the remaining one. Although the appellants had moved before trial to dismiss the indictment on the basis of prosecutorial misconduct before the grand jury, that motion was denied. Both appellants were sentenced to five-year terms for the conspiracy conviction. Hogan also received three one-year terms on the telephone facilitation convictions, all of his sentences to run concurrently.

This case arose from a Federal Drug Enforcement Administration (DEA) undercover investigation of Hogan, a retired Stamford Connecticut Police Lieutenant with 22 years service, who had formerly served as head of the Southwestern Connecticut Regional Narcotics Crime Squad, and Patricelli, an associate of Hogan's with alleged ties to organized crime. Playing a central role in this investigation was Martin "Yogi" Ruggieri, a businessman who had allegedly borrowed $20,000 from Hogan. The record discloses that in late January 1981 Yogi persuaded Hogan and Patricelli to travel to the Hilton Hotel in Rye, New York for the purpose of obtaining repayment of the debt. While the government contends that the contemplated medium of repayment was narcotics, appellants assert that it was cash. In any event, upon arriving at the Hilton, Hogan and Patricelli were stopped by Rye Police Detective John Carlucci who was acting upon a request he had received from the DEA. Carlucci told Hogan and Patricelli that DEA agents were investigating a narcotics transaction and requested appellants to accompany him to Rye police headquarters for questioning. When it became clear at police headquarters that there was no basis to hold appellants, they were permitted to leave. We will return to this incident later.

On February 4, 1981 Yogi informed DEA Agent Paul Salute that Patricelli wanted to meet Yogi that evening to discuss the Rye, New York incident and Yogi's loan. Agent Salute, posing as Yogi's cousin from New Jersey, called Patricelli and had that meeting postponed. In the ensuing weeks a series of four meetings were held. At the first meeting, on February 11, Yogi, Hogan and DEA Agent Alleva, posing as a business partner of Yogi's cousin, met to discuss the money Yogi owed Hogan. During this meeting Alleva offered to sell to Hogan heroin at a discount price in exchange for forgiveness of Yogi's debt. The other meetings, between Hogan, Alleva, and on two occasions Patricelli, occurred on February 19, March 2 and March 11 at various area bars and restaurants. A number of telephone calls (perhaps nine or ten) between Hogan and Alleva also were made during February and March. The subject of these meetings and telephone calls concerned the proposed drug deal.

Through February and early March plans to implement the deal were in the discussion stage. No drugs were ever actually obtained or distributed. Then on March 13, when Alleva called him, Hogan terminated his involvement in the scheme, stating that he did not believe in it. In response to this statement by the principal subject of the undercover investigation, Alleva threatened Hogan with bodily harm if he did not change his mind and go through with the deal. DEA agents equipped Yogi with a recording device and sent him to see Hogan on May 12 to find out what had happened. Hogan told Yogi that he could not get involved in distributing heroin because it was against everything he ever believed in and that he wanted nothing to do with Alleva. Shortly thereafter the government sought and obtained the indictments at issue in this case.

II

* * *

Interposing a grand jury between the individual and the government serves the intended purpose of limiting indictments for higher crimes to those offenses charged by a group of one's fellow citizens acting independently of the prosecution and the court. In this independent position, a grand jury performs two distinct roles. It serves as an accuser sworn to investigate and present for trial persons suspected of wrongdoing. At the same time—and equally important—it functions as a shield, standing between the accuser and the accused, protecting the individual citizen against oppressive and unfounded government prosecution. It is true of course that prosecutors, by virtue of their position, have gained such influence over grand juries that these bodies' historic independence has been eroded. After all, it is the prosecutor who draws up the indictment, calls and examines the grand jury witnesses, advises the grand jury as to the law, and is in constant attendance during its proceedings. Nonetheless, there remain certain limitations on the presentation that a prosecutor may make to the grand jury. *See, e.g., United States v. Ciambrone,* 601 F.2d 616, 623 (2d Cir.1979) (prosecutor may not mislead grand jury or engage in fundamentally unfair tactics before it). In fact the gain in prosecutors' influence over grand juries is all the more reason to insist that these limitations be observed strictly. Due process considerations prohibit the government from obtaining an indictment based on known perjured testimony. *See United States v. Basurto,* 497 F.2d 781, 785 (9th Cir.1974). Courts have also held that a prosecutor may not make statements or argue in a manner calculated to inflame the grand jury unfairly against an accused. *See, e.g., United States v. Serubo,* 604 F.2d 807, 818 (3d Cir.1979). Under the applicable guidelines prosecutors have an ethical obligation strictly to observe the status of the grand jury as an independent legal body. In short, a prosecutor as an officer of the court is sworn to ensure that justice is done, not simply to obtain an indictment.

III

Bearing in mind these general obligations, we turn to the specific instances of prosecutorial misconduct which occurred before the grand jury in this case. At one point during the proceedings, a grand juror, apparently troubled by the proposed prosecution, posed the following question to the Assistant United States Attorney (AUSA):

What I don't understand is if this case fell through, in other words, if there was no deal made what is the purpose of us listening to this?

The AUSA's response, in pertinent part, was as follows:

If the deal would have gone forward we would have had a real hoodlum trying to sell heroin. * * * I think even though in a general case where somebody backs out and decides not to do the crime it probably shouldn't be prosecuted.

In a case like this I think is [sic] a matter of equity it should.

Having characterized Hogan as a real hoodlum, who should be indicted as "a matter of equity," the AUSA proceeded to present to the grand jury hearsay testimony to the effect that Connecticut police officials thought that Hogan had committed crimes wholly irrelevant to the alleged drug transaction then under federal investigation. Specifically, the prosecutor introduced testimony that Hogan was a "suspect" in the apparently unrelated murders of a drug dealer named David Avnayim and a Norwalk Connecticut policeman named Charles Dugan. The grand jury was never asked to consider returning indictments for any federal offenses relating to these two murders.

In addition to the testimony regarding the two murders, the AUSA suggested that Hogan was guilty of misconduct while he was a police officer. Making himself an unsworn witness, the prosecutor informed the grand jury that he had read various articles in a Stamford newspaper which accused "a high ranking officer" of receiving bribes from gamblers. Then the same AUSA went on to relate that Leo Tobin, a Stamford police officer, had told him that Stamford Police Chief Czankis had mentioned to Tobin that Hogan was "suspected of having been on the take from gambling establishments."

Further, the prosecutor, faced with explaining Hogan's refusal to go through with the drug deal, elicited the following testimony. In response to a question posed by the prosecutor, Agent Alleva testified that he had no direct knowledge of why Hogan had changed his mind, but that he had "heard why through other agents." The AUSA immediately followed up that question by asking Alleva whether "[t]he speculation is that Yogi told Hogan that this was an undercover deal?" To this Agent Alleva responded affirmatively. The identity of the persons so speculating and the basis for their conclusions were never explored. Moreover, evidence in the DEA's possession in the form of the recording of the May 12 conversation between Hogan and Yogi casts serious doubt on the accuracy of this speculation.

Concerned with the obvious possibility that the grand jury might not indict because no drugs were ever purchased, possessed or distributed, it was apparently the prosecution's view that it would be helpful to show appellants' predisposition to possess heroin; but much of the evidence it presented in this regard later proved to be false. This seems the only plausible explanation for the AUSA having elicited repeated testimony from Agents Salute and Alleva that in January 1981, prior to the proposed narcotics deal in question, Hogan and Patricelli had been caught in Rye, New York attempting to obtain heroin. Agent Salute categorically denied any DEA role in the Rye incident and Agent Alleva testified that he had thoroughly investigated the incident and that the stop of appellants by the Rye police was in no way caused by the DEA. But the facts in the record indicate just the opposite. Confronted with statements of the Rye police and writings made at the time of the stop, Agent Salute admitted in post trial proceedings that the DEA had in fact called the Rye police and *instigated* the detention of Hogan and Patricelli.

Additionally, Agent Salute told the grand jury that he had discussed heroin over the telephone with Patricelli prior to the first meeting with Hogan. This evidence, which tended to show that appellants were arranging a heroin deal even before the first meeting with DEA undercover agents, was later conceded by the government to be untrue. The subject of heroin was not mentioned until the first meeting in February. Similarly, Agent Alleva "mistakenly" testified before the grand jury that he had informed Hogan at the first meeting that Hogan would have to pay $50,000 prior to the heroin delivery. In fact, Hogan was initially offered nearly $2,000,000 worth of heroin for no cash down payment. This offer—one that Hogan admitted had tempted him—differed significantly from the offer Alleva described to the grand jury. At trial Agent Alleva conceded that on this particular point he had made an error. He testified that the $50,000 demand on Hogan was not made at the first meeting, but was in fact made several meetings later. His explanation was that he had "confused" the meetings during his grand jury testimony.

IV

The law of this Circuit is that dismissal of an indictment is justified to achieve either of two objectives: to eliminate prejudice to a defendant; or, pursuant to our supervisory power, to prevent prosecutorial impairment of the grand jury's independent role. Viewing the above-mentioned instances of conduct cumulatively, we believe that the latter function is implicated here.

Although there is no prohibition on the use of hearsay evidence before a grand jury, our decision in *United States v. Estepa*, 471 F.2d 1132 (2d Cir.1972), indicates that extensive reliance on hearsay testimony is disfavored. More particularly, the government prosecutor, in presenting hearsay evidence to the grand jury, must not deceive the jurors as to the quality of the testimony they hear. Heavy reliance on secondary evidence is disfavored precisely because it is not first-rate proof. It should not be used without cogent reason, and never be passed off to the grand jurors as quality proof when it is not. Here the prosecution presented extensive hearsay and double hearsay speculation regarding Hogan's involvement in two murders, corrupt activities as a policeman, and reason for terminating his participation in the proposed heroin deal.

Such secondary evidence added a false aura of factual support to the government's case and may well have deceived the grand jurors.

Additionally, the impartiality and independent nature of the grand jury process was seriously impaired by the AUSA's argument that Hogan was a real hoodlum who should be indicted as a matter of equity. Added to this inflammatory rhetoric were the numerous speculative references to other crimes of which Hogan was "suspected." None of these other crimes, the two murders and Hogan's alleged taking of bribes while a policeman, was under investigation by the grand jury. In fact, there is no indication that Hogan has ever been charged with these offenses by any state or federal body. These government accusations and others appear to have been made, not to support additional charges, but in order to depict appellants as bad persons and thereby obtain an indictment for independent crimes. This tactic is fundamentally unfair.

Finally, the DEA agents' false testimony to the grand jury on the issues of predisposition and inducement is most disturbing. Although the government was not required to anticipate a defense of entrapment and introduce evidence of predisposition, having elected to do so it was duty bound not to introduce false and misleading testimony. While the factual misstatements in the agents' testimony may have been inadvertent, as the government now argues, the fact remains that the appellants were prejudiced by the misstatements of important facts and the grand jury's independent role was impaired. * * *

In summary, the incidents related are flagrant and unconscionable. Taking advantage of his special position of trust, the AUSA impaired the grand jury's integrity as an independent body. Thus, based on the particular facts of this case, we believe that the indictment below must be dismissed.

Because of the determination reached, we need not decide the numerous other issues raised on appeal. The judgments of conviction are reversed and the case remanded to the district court with instructions to dismiss the underlying indictment against appellants.

Note

The Supreme Court held 5–4 in United States v. Williams, 504 U.S. 36 (1992), that the supervisory power of the federal courts does not permit a judge to dismiss an indictment on the ground that the prosecutor failed to submit "substantial exculpatory evidence" to the grand jury. The defendant Williams was charged with obtaining loans from banks by submitting financial statements that vastly overstated the value of his assets. The District Court granted his motion for disclosure of all exculpatory portions of the grand jury transcript under Brady v. Maryland, 373 U.S. 83 (1963).

After reviewing this material, Williams moved to dismiss the indictment on the ground that the government had chosen not to show other financial records to the grand jury. These records would have shown that he consistently accounted for the same assets in a similar manner for other purposes, and thus that the apparent inflation in their value was due to his peculiar accounting methods rather than to any intent to deceive the banks. The District Court granted the motion on the authority of United States v. Page, 808 F.2d 723 (10th Cir.1987), finding that the evidence was relevant and created a reasonable doubt as to Williams' guilt. The Court of Appeals affirmed, holding that it was not an abuse of discretion under the circumstances for the District Court to require the Government to begin anew before the grand jury.

The Supreme Court majority opinion by Justice Scalia observed that "it is axiomatic that the grand jury sits not to determine guilt or innocence, but to assess whether there is adequate basis for bringing a criminal charge * * *. As a consequence, neither in this country nor in England has the suspect under investigation by the grand jury ever been thought to have a right to testify, or to have exculpatory evidence presented." Moreover, the *Costello* rule does not allow a judge to dismiss an indictment on the ground that the grand jury indicted on incompetent or inadequate evidence. The majority concluded that to impose upon the prosecutor a legal obligation to present exculpatory evidence would be incompatible with this system.

UNITED STATES v. COX

United States Court of Appeals, Fifth Circuit, 1965.
342 F.2d 167 (en banc).

[A federal grand jury impaneled in the Southern District of Mississippi wished to indict two persons for perjury, but Hauberg, the United States Attorney, refused to prepare the necessary indictments. District Judge Cox ordered Hauberg to prepare and sign such indictments as the grand jury required but Hauberg, under instructions from Acting Attorney General Katzenbach, refused. Judge Cox found Hauberg guilty of contempt of court and ordered Katzenbach to show cause why he should not also be found guilty of contempt. Hauberg, Katzenbach, and the Department of Justice appealed.]

JONES, CIRCUIT JUDGE: * * *

The constitutional requirement of an indictment or presentment as a predicate to a prosecution for capital or infamous crimes has for its primary purpose the protection of the individual from jeopardy except on a finding of probable cause by a group of his fellow citizens, and is designed to afford a safeguard against oppressive actions of the prosecutor or a court. The constitutional provision is not to be read as conferring on or preserving to the grand jury, as such, any rights or prerogatives. The constitutional provision is, as has been said, for the benefit of the accused. The constitutional provision is not to be read as precluding, as essential to the validity of an indictment, the inclusion of requisites which did not exist at common law.

Traditionally, the Attorney for the United States had the power to enter a nolle prosequi of a criminal charge at any time after indictment and before trial, and this he could have done without the approval of the court or the consent of the accused. It may be doubted whether, before the adoption of the Federal Rules of Criminal Procedure, he had any authority to prevent the return of an indictment by a grand jury. There would be no constitutional barrier to a requirement that the signature of a United States Attorney upon an indictment is essential to its validity.

It is now provided by the Federal Rules of Criminal Procedure that the Attorney General or the United States Attorney may by leave of court file a dismissal of an indictment. Rule 48(a) Fed.Rules Crim.Proc. 18 U.S.C.A. In the absence of the Rule, leave of court would not have been required. The purpose of the Rule is to prevent harassment of a defendant by charging, dismissing and recharging without placing a defendant in jeopardy. Rule 7 eliminates the necessity for the inclusion in an indictment of many of the technical and prolix averments which were required at common law, by providing that the indictment shall be a plain, concise and definite written statement of the essential facts constituting the offense charged. The Rule also provides that "It shall be signed by the attorney for the government." Rule 7(c) Fed.Rules Crim. Proc. 18 U.S.C.A.

The judicial power of the United States is vested in the federal courts, and extends to prosecutions for violations of the criminal laws of the United States. The executive power is vested in the President of the United States, who is required to take care that the laws be faithfully executed. The Attorney General is the hand of the President in taking care that the laws of the United States in legal proceedings and in the prosecution of offenses, be faithfully executed. The role of the grand jury is restricted to a finding as to whether or not there is probable cause to believe that an offense has been committed. The discretionary power of the attorney for the United States in determining whether a prosecution shall be commenced or maintained may well depend upon matters of policy wholly apart from any question of probable cause. Although as a member of the bar, the attorney for the United States is an officer of the court, he is nevertheless an executive official of the Government, and it is as an officer of the executive department that he exercises a discretion as to whether or not there shall be a prosecution in a particular case. It follows, as an incident of the constitutional separation of powers, that the courts are not to interfere with the free exercise of the discretionary powers of the attorneys of the United States in their control over criminal prosecutions. The provision of Rule 7, requiring the signing of the indictment by the attorney for the Government, is a recognition of the power of Government counsel to permit or not to permit the bringing of an indictment. If the attorney refuses to sign, as he has the discretionary power of doing, we conclude that there is no valid indictment. It is not to be supposed that the signature of counsel is merely an attestation of the act of the grand jury. The signature of the foreman performs that function. It is not to be supposed that the signature of counsel is a certificate that the indictment is in proper form to charge an offense. The sufficiency of the indictment may be tested before the court. Rather, we think, the requirement of the signature is for the purpose of evidencing the joinder of the attorney for the United States with the grand jury in instituting a criminal proceeding in the Court. Without the signature there can be no criminal proceeding brought upon an indictment. * * *

If it were not for the discretionary power given to the United States Attorney to prevent an indictment by withholding his signature, there might be doubt as to the constitutionality of the requirement of Rule 48 for leave of court for a dismissal of a pending prosecution.

Because, as we conclude, the signature of the Government attorney is necessary to the validity of the indictment and the affixing or withholding of the signature is a matter of executive discretion which cannot be coerced or reviewed by the courts, the contempt order must be reversed. It seems that, since the United States Attorney cannot be required to give validity to an indictment by affixing his signature, he should not be required to indulge in an exercise of futility by the preparation of the form of an indictment which he is unwilling to vitalize with his signature. Therefore he should not be required to prepare indictments which he is unwilling and under no duty to sign.

Judges Tuttle, Jones, Brown and Wisdom join in the conclusion that the signature of the United States Attorney is essential to the validity of an indictment. Judge Brown, as appears in his separate opinion, is of the view that the United States Attorney is required, upon the request of the grand jury, to draft forms of indictments in accordance with its desires. The order before us for review is in the conjunctive; it requires the United States Attorney to prepare and sign. A majority of the court, having decided that the direction to sign is erroneous, the order on appeal will be reversed. * * *

Rives, Gewin and Griffin B. Bell, Circuit Judges (concurring in part and dissenting in part):

* * * [T]he basic issue before this Court is whether the controlling discretion as to the institution of a felony prosecution rests with the Attorney General or with the grand jury. The majority opinion would ignore the broad inquisitorial powers of the grand jury, and limit the constitutional requirement of Amendment V to the benefit of the accused. * * *

The grand jury may be permitted to function in its traditional sphere, while at the same time enforcing the separation of powers doctrine as between the executive and judicial branches of the government. This can best be done, indeed, it is mandatory, by requiring the United States Attorney to assist the grand jury in preparing indictments which they wish to consider or return, and by requiring the United States Attorney to sign any indictment that is to be returned. Then, once the indictment is returned, the Attorney General or the United States Attorney can refuse to go forward. That refusal will, of course, be in open court and not in the secret confines of the grand jury room. To permit the district court to compel the United States Attorney to proceed beyond this point would invest prosecutorial power in the judiciary, power which under the Constitution is reserved to the executive branch of the government. It may be that the court, in the interest of justice, may require a showing of good faith, and a statement of some rational basis for dismissal. In the unlikely event of bad faith or irrational action, not here present, it may be that the court could appoint counsel to prosecute the case. In brief, the court may have the same inherent power to administer justice to the government as it does to the defendant. That question is not now before us and may never arise. Except for a very limited discretion, however, the court's power to withhold leave to dismiss an indictment is solely for the protection of the defendant. * * *

For the Attorney General to prevent the grand jury from returning an indictment would, in effect, be to confine the grand jury to returning a mere presentment. That derogates from the grand jury its alternative power to return either "a presentment or indictment." U.S. Const. amend. V. The power of the grand jury cannot be limited in any case to a presentment; it may return an indictment.

Looking beyond the present controversy, one can foresee the grave danger inherent in such a restriction of the powers of a grand jury. If a grand jury is prevented from returning an indictment no more effective than a presentment, the statute of limitations may permanently bar prosecution for the crime. When the presentment is made public, the accused may flee or witnesses may get beyond the jurisdiction of the court. For all practical purposes, the case could be dead and there would be no point in any future Attorney General causing the presentment to be followed by an indictment. Worse still, this could be accomplished in the shadows of secrecy, with the Attorney General not being required to disclose his reasons. How much better is the constitutional system by which the grand jury can find and return an effective indictment upon which a prosecution for crime is instituted. At that point the power of the grand jury ceases. It is effectively checked and overbalanced by the power of the Attorney General, recognized in Rule 48(a), to move for a dismissal of the indictment. The court may then require such a motion to be heard in open court. Instead of a prevention in the shadows of secrecy, there would be a dismissal in a formal, public judicial proceeding.

* * *

By way of precaution, let us state that nothing here said is intended to reflect upon the present Acting Attorney General, in whose integrity we have the utmost confidence. Memory goes back, however, to days when we had an Attorney General suspected of being corrupt. There is no assurance that that will never again happen. We are establishing a precedent for other cases; we are construing a Constitution; we should retain intact that great constitutional bulwark, the institution of the grand jury.

On the cases before the Court, we agree with Judge Brown that the United States Attorney is required, upon the request of the grand jury, to draft forms of indictment in accordance with its desires. There is thus a majority of the Court in favor of that holding. We go further, and think that the United States Attorney is required to sign any indictment that may be found by the grand jury. * * * We would * * * affirm the judgment of civil contempt against the United States Attorney. * * *

[The concurring opinion of Judge John R. Brown is omitted.]

WISDOM, CIRCUIT JUDGE (concurring specially): * * *

The prosecution of offenses against the United States is an executive function within the exclusive prerogative of the Attorney General. * * *

This brings me to the facts. They demonstrate, better than abstract principles or legal dicta, the imperative necessity that the United States, through its Attorney General, have uncontrollable discretion to prosecute.

The crucial fact here is that Goff and Kendrick, two Negroes, testified in a suit by the United States against the Registrar of Clarke County, Mississippi, and the State of Mississippi, to enforce the voting rights of Negroes under the Fourteenth Amendment and the Civil Rights Act.

Goff and Kendrick testified that some seven years earlier at Stonewall, Mississippi, the registrar had refused to register them or give them application forms. They said that they had seen white persons registering, one of whom was a B. Floyd Jones. Ramsey, the registrar, testified that Jones had not registered at that time or place, but had registered the year before in Enterprise, Mississippi. He testified also that he had never discriminated against Negro applicants for registration. Jones testified that he was near the registration table in Stonewall in 1955, had talked with the registrar, and had shaken hands with him. The presiding judge, Judge W. Harold Cox, stated from the bench that Goff and Kendrick should be "bound over to await the action of the grand jury for perjury".

In January 1963 attorneys of the Department of Justice requested the Federal Bureau of Investigation to investigate the possible perjury. The FBI completed a full investigation in March 1963 and referred the matter to the Department's Criminal Division. In June 1963, the Criminal Division advised the local United States Attorney, Mr. Hauberg, that the matter presented "no basis for a perjury prosecution". Mr. Hauberg informed Judge Cox of the Department's decision. Judge Cox stated that in his view the matter was clearly one for the grand jury and that he would be inclined, if necessary, to appoint an outside attorney to present the matter to the grand jury. (I find no authority for a federal judge to displace the United States Attorney by appointing a special prosecutor.) On receiving this information, the Criminal Division again reviewed its files and concluded that the charge of perjury could not be sustained. General Katzenbach, then Deputy Attorney General, after reviewing the files, concurred in the Criminal Division's decision. In September 1963 General Katzenbach called on Judge Cox as a courtesy to explain why the Department had arrived at the conclusion that no perjury was involved. Judge Cox, unconvinced, requested the United States Attorney to present to the grand jury the Goff and Kendrick cases, which he regarded as cases of "palpable perjury".

[A Mississippi state grand jury indicted Goff and Kendrick for perjury for testifying falsely in the federal civil rights case, but the federal Department of Justice obtained an injunction against his prosecution. Judge Cox thereafter caused the federal grand jury to hear witnesses testify regarding the alleged perjury, and the grand jury decided to indict. Acting Attorney General Katzenbach directed the United States Attorney not to prepare or sign the indictments, and this contempt proceeding followed.]

Against the backdrop of Mississippi versus the Nation in the field of civil rights, we have a heated but bona fide difference of opinion between Judge Cox and the Attorney General as to whether two Negroes, Goff and Kendrick, should be prosecuted for perjury. Taking a narrow view of the case, we would be justified in holding that the Attorney General's implied powers, by analogy to the express powers of Rule 48(a), give him discretion to prosecute. Here there was a bona fide, reasonable exercise of discretion made after a full investigation and long consideration of the case—both sides of the case, not just the evidence tending to show guilt. If the grand jury is dissatisfied with that administrative decision, it may exercise its inquisitorial power and make a presentment in open court. It could be said, that is all there is to the case. But there is more to the case.

This Court, along with everyone else, knows that Goff and Kendrick, if prosecuted, run the risk of being tried in a climate of community hostility. They run the risk of a punishment that may not fit the crime. The Registrar, who provoked the original litigation, runs no risk, notwithstanding the fact that the district court, in effect, found that Ramsey did not tell the truth on the witness stand. In these circumstances, the very least demands of justice require that the discretion to prosecute be lodged with a person or agency insulated from local prejudices and parochial pressures. This is not the hard case that makes bad law. This is the type of case that comes up, in one way or another, whenever the customs, beliefs, or interests of a region collide with national policy as fixed by the Constitution or by Congress. It is not likely that the men who devised diversity jurisdiction expected to turn over to local juries the discretionary power to bring federal prosecutions. This case is unusual only for the clarity with which the facts, speaking for themselves, illuminate the imperative necessity in American Federalism that the discretion to prosecute be lodged in the Attorney General of United States.

My memory, too, goes back to the days, pointedly referred to by the dissenters, when we had "an Attorney General suspected of being corrupt." But I am not aware that we have had more lawless Attorneys General than lawless juries.

Commentary

In Inmates of Attica Correctional Facility v. Rockefeller, 477 F.2d 375 (2d Cir.1973) the plaintiffs sought to obtain a court order requiring federal and state officials to investigate and prosecute persons who allegedly had committed criminal acts in connection with the suppression of the uprising at the New York state prison. The Court of Appeals affirmed the dismissal of the action with the following comments:

In the absence of statutorily defined standards governing reviewability, or regulatory or statutory policies of prosecution, the problems inherent in the task of supervising prosecutorial decisions do not lend themselves to resolution by the judiciary. The reviewing courts would be placed in the undesirable and injudicious posture of becoming "superprosecutors." In the normal case of review of executive acts of discretion, the administrative record is open, public and reviewable on the basis of what it contains. The decision not to prosecute, on the other hand, may be based upon the insufficiency of the available evidence, in which event the secrecy of the grand jury and of the prosecutor's file may serve to protect the accused's reputation from public damage based upon insufficient, improper, or even malicious charges. *In camera* review would not be meaningful without access by the complaining party to the evidence before the grand jury or U.S. Attorney. Such interference with the normal operations of criminal investigations, in turn, based solely upon allegations of criminal conduct, raises serious questions of potential abuse by persons seeking to have other persons prosecuted. Any person, merely by filing a complaint containing allegations in general terms (permitted by the Federal Rules) of unlawful failure to prosecute, could gain access to the prosecutor's file and the grand jury's minutes, notwithstanding the secrecy normally attaching to the latter by law.

Nor is it clear what the judiciary's role of supervision should be were it to undertake such a review. At what point would the prosecutor be entitled to call a halt to further investigation as unlikely to be productive? What evidentiary standard would be used to decide whether prosecution should be compelled? How much judgment would the United States Attorney be allowed? Would he be permitted to limit himself to a strong "test" case rather than pursue weaker cases? What collateral factors would be permissible bases for a decision not to prosecute, e.g., the pendency of another criminal proceeding elsewhere against the same parties? What sort of review should be available in cases like the present one where the conduct complained of allegedly violates state as well as federal laws? With limited personnel and facilities at his disposal, what priority would the prosecutor be required to give to cases in which investigation or prosecution was directed by the court?

These difficult questions engender serious doubts as to the judiciary's capacity to review and as to the problem of arbitrariness inherent in any judicial decision to order prosecution. On balance, we believe that substitution of a court's decision to compel prosecution for the U.S. Attorney's decision not to prosecute, even upon an abuse of discretion standard of review and even if limited to directing that a prosecution be undertaken in good faith, would be unwise. Id. at 380–81.

The laws of some states permit a court to appoint a private prosecutor in exceptional cases but in general a prosecutor's decision not to bring charges is controlled only by his own superiors and, in highly visible cases, by public opinion. Even where state law expressly or impliedly permits a private individual to initiate a criminal prosecution without the approval of the public prosecutor, the practice has tended to fall into disuse. In People v. Municipal Court, 27 Cal.App.3d 193 (1972), the court refused to give a "literal" reading to a statute that appeared to allow private prosecution, explaining that it would violate the defendant's right to due process of law as well as the principle of separation of powers to permit a criminal prosecution to proceed without the approval of the District Attorney or Attorney General.

B. THE FIFTH AMENDMENT PRIVILEGE AND GRAND JURY SUBPOENAS FOR DOCUMENTS

MATTER OF GRAND JURY PROCEEDINGS OF GUARINO

Supreme Court of New Jersey, 1986.
104 N.J. 218, 516 A.2d 1063.

GARIBALDI, J.

* * *

Since 1959, respondent, Joseph Guarino, has been doing business as a sole proprietor under the name of Green Acres Estates, a real estate concern. In 1984, a state Grand Jury began an investigation of Green Acres Estates. During the course of that investigation, the Grand Jury served Guarino with a *subpoena duces tecum*. The subpoena directed him to produce [records of certain real estate transactions. He appeared before the Grand Jury but refused to produce the records, relying on the privilege against self-incrimination.]

We first examine whether, and to what extent, the Fifth Amendment privilege against self-incrimination applies to voluntarily-prepared business records of a sole proprietor. The constitutional privilege against self-incrimination is "essentially a personal one, applying only to natural individuals." *United States v. White*, 322 *U.S.* 694, 698 (1944). "[A]n individual cannot rely upon the privilege to avoid producing the records of a collective entity which are in his possession in a representative capacity, even if these records might incriminate him personally." *Bellis v. United States*, 417 *U.S.* 85, 88 (1974). Consequently, the privilege cannot be asserted by a collective group (such as a corporation or a union) or by a representative employee or agent of that collective group. [Citations]

Employing this principle, the Supreme Court in two recent cases, *Fisher v. United States*, 425 *U.S.* 391 (1976) and *United States v. Doe*, 465 *U.S.* 605 (1984), has substantially limited the application of the Fifth

Amendment privilege to business records, including those possessed by sole proprietors. Since *Boyd v. United States*, 116 *U.S.* 616 (1886) but prior to *Fisher*, the Supreme Court in a series of opinions consistently had repeated the axiom that an individual's private papers were protected by the Fifth Amendment from compelled disclosure. The prevailing rule was that "the Fifth Amendment privilege against compulsory self-incrimination protects an individual from compelled production of his personal papers and effects as well as compelled oral testimony." The protection of personal privacy, the fear that private thoughts recorded on paper might become the object of criminal sanctions, was the most prevalent rationale for this rule. And the privilege was viewed quite expansively, applying to the business records of the sole proprietor or sole practitioner as well as to the personal documents containing more intimate information about an individual's private life. *Bellis*, 417 *U.S.* at 87; Note, "Organizational Papers and the Privilege Against Self–Incrimination," 99 *Harv.L.Rev.* 640 (1986).

In *Fisher* and then again in *Doe*, the Court departed from these precedents. In *Fisher*, the Court held that a sole proprietor's tax records in the possession of his accountant were not protected. Justice White, writing in *Fisher* for himself and five other Justices, noted that "[s]everal of [the old] express or implicit declarations have not stood the test of time." He stated that "the prohibition against forcing the production of private papers has long been a rule searching for a rationale consistent with the proscriptions of the Fifth Amendment against compelling a person to give 'testimony' that incriminates him."

No longer constrained by the old rule, the *Fisher* Court fashioned a new one. The Court focused on the precise words of the Fifth Amendment—"[n]o person * * * shall be *compelled* in any criminal case to be a *witness against himself.*" Rather than existing to shield certain private writings from discovery by the Government, the Fifth Amendment "applies only when the accused is *compelled* to make a *testimonial* communication that is incriminating." In effect, the focus of the Court shifted from privacy to the process of compulsion.

Applying the new test to the facts of the *Fisher* case, the Court concluded that requiring a defendant-taxpayer to produce an accountant's workpapers in the taxpayer's possession would not violate the Fifth Amendment, regardless of how incriminating those papers might be to the taxpayer, because "the privilege protects a person only against being incriminated by his *own compelled testimonial communications.*" 425 *U.S.* at 409. * * *

The Court in *Fisher* recognized, however, that there were two situations where the act of producing evidence in response to a subpoena could have "communicative aspects of its own, wholly aside from the contents of the papers produced." First, the act of producing documents in some instances might amount to an admission of the existence of such documents and their possession or control by the taxpayer. Second, the act of production might resemble the act of testimonial self-incrimination if responding to a subpoena would in some sense "authenticate" the documents produced. Neither of these situations, however, was present in *Fisher*. Accordingly, the Court reiterated its conclusion that the Fifth Amendment did not prevent the Government from obtaining, through subpoena, an accountant's workpapers in the possession of a taxpayer or his attorney.

The Court subsequently employed the *Fisher* analysis in *U.S. v. Doe*, 465 *U.S.* 605 (1984), where the facts were virtually identical to those in this case. The respondent was a sole proprietor. He was served with five subpoenas during the course of a Grand Jury's investigation into corruption in the awarding of county and municipal contracts. The first two subpoenas demanded that he produce telephone records of several of his companies and all records pertaining to four of his banks. A third subpoena demanded the production of a list of virtually all the business records of one of his companies.

Respondent filed a motion in federal district court seeking to quash the subpoenas. The district court granted the motion, quashing all of the subpoenas except those that sought documents and records required by law to be kept or disclosed to a public agency. The Third Circuit affirmed.

In its opinion in *Doe*, the Supreme Court first stated that *Fisher's* rationale applied with equal force to a sole proprietor who prepared his own documents. As in *Fisher*, the Court found that a subpoena that demands the production of documents does not *compel* oral testimony. Doe did not contend, said the Court, that he prepared the documents involuntarily or that the subpoena would force him to restate, repeat, or affirm the truth of their contents. The fact that the records were in Doe's possession, as opposed to his accountant's, was irrelevant in determining whether the creation of the record was compelled. The Court, therefore reversed the Third Circuit in part and concluded that the *contents* of the records were not privileged.

The Court, however, continued to draw the distinction that it drew in *Fisher* between the *contents* of a document and the act of producing it. But in *Doe*, unlike in *Fisher*, the Court had the explicit findings of the District Court that the act of producing the documents would invoke testimonial self-incrimination. Declining to overturn that finding because it rested on a determination of factual issues that had some support in the record, it affirmed the lower courts insofar as they found the act of production to be privileged. The Court recognized that if the government wished to compel production of the documents, it could have sought a grant of use immunity with respect to the potentially incriminating evidence.

Following *Doe*, it is clear that the *contents* of business records, whether from a corporation, a partnership, or a sole proprietorship, are no longer privileged under the Fifth Amendment. The documents requested from the respondent in this case were far less extensive than those requested from Doe. The only request made of Guarino, doing business as Green Acres Estates, that was not made of Doe was for real estate contracts and documentation of real estate payments. Given the nature of Guarino's business, those contracts were clearly business, not personal, records, and they were related to the focus of the Grand Jury's investigation. Like Doe, Guarino does not contend that he prepared the requested records involuntarily or that the subpoena would force him to restate, repeat, or affirm the truth of the contents. Accordingly, under *Doe* the contents of respondent's business records are not protected by the Fifth Amendment privilege against self-incrimination. Furthermore, the prosecutors here, as the Supreme Court suggested in *Doe*, granted Guarino use immunity for *producing* the documents. Therefore, the production of the documents did not violate his Fifth Amendment privilege against self-incrimination.

III

We turn now to an examination of whether under independent principles of state law we might extend the privilege against self-incrimination to Guarino, doing business as Green Acres Estates. It is undisputed that State common law may provide greater protection to individual rights than afforded under the United States Constitution. * * *

We affirm our belief in the *Boyd* doctrine and hold that the New Jersey common law privilege against self-incrimination protects the individual's right "to a private enclave where he may lead a private life." *Murphy v. Waterfront Comm'n*, 378 U.S. 52, 55 (1964). To determine whether the evidence sought by the government lies within that sphere of personal privacy a court must look to the nature of the evidence. In the case of documents, therefore, a court must look to their contents, not to the testimonial compulsion involved in the act of producing them, as the Supreme Court has done in *Fisher* and *Doe*. Neither *Fisher* nor *Doe* recognize the fundamental privacy principles underlying the New Jersey common-law privilege against self-incrimination. Thus, in defining the scope of our common law privilege, we decline to follow the Court's rationale for its *Doe* decision.

IV

Nevertheless, as a matter of New Jersey common law, we agree with the result in *Fisher* and *Doe*. The subpoenaed documents in issue are the business records of Guarino, doing business as Green Acres Estates, a real estate concern. The business records of a sole proprietor do not lie within that special zone of privacy that forms the core of the documents protected by *Boyd* and its progeny, and that are protected by the New Jersey privilege against self-incrimination.[21]

* * *

---

21. If Guarino had contended that any part of these records invoked concerns of personal privacy, e.g. personal comments, telephone numbers, or the like that would warrant protection, the result might be different. No such issue has been raised.

The subpoenaed documents here illustrate that the business records of a sole proprietor are simply not private. They do not contain the requisite element of privacy or confidentiality essential to be privileged. The purpose of business records is frequently to record transactions with second and third parties. In today's highly computerized, commercialized and regulated world, there is little expectation of privacy for such records that touch so little on the intimate aspects of one's personal life. This is particularly true of the records requested here: contracts of sale, cash receipts, journals and general ledgers. They document payments made by purchasers of property from Guarino doing business as Green Acres Estates. Many of these documents of sale are presumably reviewed by the purchasers, their attorneys and their accountants, then used in preparing the purchaser's tax returns and possibly filed at county recording offices. Normally, such documents are disclosed to a significant number of individuals, to an extent totally inconsistent with any claim of privacy.

Moreover, we do not perceive any reason why the records of a sole proprietor kept in the ordinary course of business are entitled to any greater protection than the business records of a partnership or corporation. Sole proprietors may operate large, substantial business enterprises, in many instances more extensive than small one-person corporations or two-person partnership. * * *

[Order to produce documents upheld.]

Handler, J., dissenting.

* * *

Because of the unsoundness of [the Supreme Court's] new conceptualization of the Fifth Amendment, I am persuaded by Justice Brennan's reasoning that would keep the focus not solely upon the testimonial incidents that can be read into the act of producing personal records. Rather, the target should be the contents of documents, which are the heart of the Fifth Amendment's solicitude for privacy and the true object of the government's compulsory efforts. The Fifth Amendment's protection should attach to an individual's books and papers because their contents can be equated with an individual's mental notations.

The common-law and constitutional extension of the privilege to testimonial materials, such as books and papers, was inevitable. An individual's books and papers are generally little more than an extension of his person. They reveal no less than he could reveal upon being questioned directly. Many of the matters within an individual's knowledge may as easily be retained within his head as set down on a scrap of paper. I perceive no principle which does not permit compelling one to disclose the contents of one's mind but does permit compelling the disclosure of the contents of that scrap of paper by compelling its production. Under a contrary view, the constitutional protection would turn on fortuity, and persons would, at their peril, record their thoughts and the events of their lives.

The ability to think private thoughts, facilitated as it is by pen and paper, and the ability to preserve intimate memories would be curtailed through fear that those thoughts or the events of those memories would become the subject of criminal sanctions however invalidly imposed. Indeed, it was the very reality of those fears that helped provide the historical impetus for the privilege. [Citations] [*Fisher, supra*, 425 U.S. at 420 (Brennan., J., concurring).]

Assuming, moreover, that as a matter of logical analysis the contents of documents can be separated from their production, this analytical parsing should not serve to truncate or attenuate the substance of the privilege itself. There is nothing in the Fifth Amendment that insists that the contents of documents be created through compulsion in order to secure their protection—no more so than the thought which precedes the expression must itself be forced in order for the privilege to apply to a person's mental processes and verbalizations. As Justice Brennan observed, "it does not follow that the protection is necessarily unavailable if the papers were prepared voluntarily, for it is the compelled production of testimonial evidence, not just compelled creation of such evidence, against which the privilege protects." *Id.*, 425 U.S. at 423.

I am satisfied that the *Fisher-Doe* doctrine does not reflect a sound policy that can be commended as an interpretive source of the State's common-law privilege against self-incrimination. It is a doctrine that is problematic in its historical origins, contrary to constitutional tradition, a departure from long-standing constitutional philosophy, and productive of artificial and arbitrary applications. Our own common-law privilege against self-incrimination springs from a source that antedates *Fisher-Doe* and is nourished by constitutional principles alien to those that now dominate the Fifth Amendment. * * *

I am satisfied that the New Jersey common-law privilege against self-incrimination is fully protective of an individual's personal privacy interests, and would extend to the attempted prosecutorial use of any incriminating evidence that is of a testimonial nature. It would accord protection against the compelled production and resultant disclosure of the contents of an individual's personal business records. This common-law privilege is firmly grounded on sound principles of public policy that are solicitous of the personal privacy protected in the criminal law context. Further, these principles, which reflect a strong state tradition that respects individual privacy, have been consistently confirmed by decisional precedent. For these reasons I would hold that a subpoena may not be enforced to compel an individual to produce private and personal records relating to the conduct of his sole business.

* * *

JUSTICES CLIFFORD and POLLOCK join in this opinion.

Note

An additional Fifth Amendment issue arises when a grand jury subpoenas records in the custody of a foreign bank. Frequently the bank refuses to supply the records without the consent of its depositor, who is the subject of the grand jury investigation. May the prosecution obtain a court order directing the person who is the target of the investigation to sign a written consent to the production of the records? The Supreme Court held that such an order does not violate the suspect's Fifth Amendment rights, in Doe v. United States, 487 U.S. 201 (1988). The majority ruled that the consent directive was not testimonial in nature because executing it did not require the suspect to admit that any relevant records or accounts were in existence. Only Justice Stevens dissented, arguing that a suspect cannot "be compelled to use his mind to assist the Government in developing its case."

C. SELECTIVE PROSECUTION AND EQUAL PROTECTION

UNITED STATES v. ARMSTRONG

Supreme Court of the United States, 1996.
517 U.S. 456, 116 S.Ct. 1480, 134 L.Ed.2d 687.

CHIEF JUSTICE REHNQUIST delivered the opinion of the Court.

In this case, we consider the showing necessary for a defendant to be entitled to discovery on a claim that the prosecuting attorney singled him out for prosecution on the basis of his race. We conclude that respondents failed to satisfy the threshold showing: They failed to show that the Government declined to prosecute similarly situated suspects of other races.

In April 1992, respondents were indicted in the United States District Court for the Central District of California on charges of conspiring to possess with intent to distribute more than 50 grams of cocaine base (crack) and conspiring to distribute the same, in violation of 21 U.S.C. §§ 841 and 846, and federal firearms offenses. For three months prior to the indictment, agents of the Federal Bureau of Alcohol, Tobacco, and Firearms and the Narcotics Division of the Inglewood, California, Police Department had infiltrated a suspected crack distribution ring by using three confidential informants. On seven separate occasions during this period, the informants had bought a total of 124.3 grams of crack from respondents and witnessed respondents carrying firearms during the sales. The agents searched the hotel room in which the sales were transacted, arrested respondents Armstrong and Hampton in the room, and found more crack and a loaded gun. The agents later arrested the other respondents as part of the ring.

In response to the indictment, respondents filed a motion for discovery or for dismissal of the indictment, alleging that they were selected for federal prosecution because they are black. In support of their motion, they offered only an affidavit by a "Paralegal Specialist," employed by the Office of the Federal Public Defender representing one of the respondents. The only allegation in the affidavit was that, in every one of the 24 §§ 841 or 846 cases closed by the office during 1991, the defendant was black. Accompanying the affidavit was a "study" listing the 24 defendants, their race, whether they were prosecuted for dealing cocaine as well as crack, and the status of each case.

The Government opposed the discovery motion, arguing, among other things, that there was no evidence or allegation "that the Government has acted unfairly or has prosecuted non-black defendants or failed to prosecute them." The District Court granted the motion. It ordered the Government (1) to provide a list of all cases from the last three years in which the Government charged both cocaine and firearms offenses, (2) to identify the race of the defendants in those cases, (3) to identify what levels of law enforcement were involved in the investigations of those cases, and (4) to explain its criteria for deciding to prosecute those defendants for federal cocaine offenses.

The Government moved for reconsideration of the District Court's discovery order. With this motion it submitted affidavits and other evidence to explain why it had chosen to prosecute respondents and why respondents' study did not support the inference that the Government was singling out blacks for cocaine prosecution. The federal and local agents participating in the case alleged in affidavits that race played no role in their investigation. An Assistant United States Attorney explained in an affidavit that the decision to prosecute met the general criteria for prosecution, because

> "There was over 100 grams of cocaine base involved, over twice the threshold necessary for a ten year mandatory minimum sentence; there were multiple sales involving multiple defendants, thereby indicating a fairly substantial crack cocaine ring; * * * there were multiple federal firearms violations intertwined with the narcotics trafficking; the overall evidence in the case was extremely strong, including audio and videotapes of defendants; * * * and several of the defendants had criminal histories including narcotics and firearms violations."

The Government also submitted sections of a published 1989 Drug Enforcement Administration report which concluded that "large-scale, interstate trafficking networks controlled by Jamaicans, Haitians and Black street gangs dominate the manufacture and distribution of crack."

In response, one of respondents' attorneys submitted an affidavit alleging that an intake coordinator at a drug treatment center had told her that there are "an equal number of caucasian users and dealers to minority users and dealers." Respondents also submitted an affidavit from a criminal defense attorney alleging that in his experience many nonblacks are prosecuted in state court for crack offenses, and a newspaper article reporting that Federal "crack criminals * * * are being punished far more severely than if they had been caught with powder cocaine, and almost every single one of them is black," Newton, Harsher

Crack Sentences Criticized as Racial Inequity, Los Angeles Times, Nov. 23, 1992, p. 1; App. 208–210.

The District Court denied the motion for reconsideration. When the Government indicated it would not comply with the court's discovery order, the court dismissed the case.[23] The Court of Appeals [en banc] * * * affirmed the District Court's order of dismissal, holding that "a defendant is not required to demonstrate that the government has failed to prosecute others who are similarly situated."

[The Supreme Court held that Federal Rule of Criminal Procedure 16, which by its terms governs discovery in criminal cases, is not applicable to a claim of discriminatory prosecution.] * * *

A selective-prosecution claim is not a defense on the merits to the criminal charge itself, but an independent assertion that the prosecutor has brought the charge for reasons forbidden by the Constitution. Our cases delineating the necessary elements to prove a claim of selective prosecution have taken great pains to explain that the standard is a demanding one. These cases afford a "background presumption," that the showing necessary to obtain discovery should itself be a significant barrier to the litigation of insubstantial claims.

A selective-prosecution claim asks a court to exercise judicial power over a "special province" of the Executive. Heckler v. Chaney, 470 U.S. 821, 832 (1985). The Attorney General and United States Attorneys retain " 'broad discretion' " to enforce the Nation's criminal laws. Wayte v. United States, 470 U.S. 598, 607 (1985). They have this latitude because they are designated by statute as the President's delegates to help him discharge his constitutional responsibility to "take Care that the Laws be faithfully executed." As a result, "the presumption of regularity supports" their prosecutorial decisions and "in the absence of clear evidence to the contrary, courts presume that they have properly discharged their official duties." United States v. Chemical Foundation, Inc., 272 U.S. 1, 14–15 (1926). In the ordinary case, "so long as the prosecutor has probable cause to believe that the accused committed an offense defined by statute, the decision whether or not to prosecute, and what charge to file or bring before a grand jury, generally rests entirely in his discretion." Bordenkircher v. Hayes, 434 U.S. 357, 364 (1978).

Of course, a prosecutor's discretion is "subject to constitutional constraints." United States v. Batchelder, 442 U.S. 114, 125 (1979). One of these constraints, imposed by the equal protection component of the Due Process Clause of the Fifth Amendment, is that the decision whether to prosecute may not be based on "an unjustifiable standard such as race, religion, or other arbitrary classification," Oyler v. Boles, 368 U.S. 448, 456 (1962). A defendant may demonstrate that the

---

23. We have never determined whether dismissal of the indictment, or some other sanction, is the proper remedy if a court determines that a defendant has been the victim of prosecution on the basis of his race. Here, it was the government itself that suggested dismissal of the indictments to the district court so that an appeal might lie.

administration of a criminal law is "directed so exclusively against a particular class of persons * * * with a mind so unequal and oppressive" that the system of prosecution amounts to "a practical denial" of equal protection of the law. Yick Wo v. Hopkins, 118 U.S. 356, 373 (1886).

In order to dispel the presumption that a prosecutor has not violated equal protection, a criminal defendant must present "clear evidence to the contrary." [C]ourts are "properly hesitant to examine the decision whether to prosecute." Judicial deference to the decisions of these executive officers rests in part on an assessment of the relative competence of prosecutors and courts. "Such factors as the strength of the case, the prosecution's general deterrence value, the Government's enforcement priorities, and the case's relationship to the Government's overall enforcement plan are not readily susceptible to the kind of analysis the courts are competent to undertake." It also stems from a concern not to unnecessarily impair the performance of a core executive constitutional function. "Examining the basis of a prosecution delays the criminal proceeding, threatens to chill law enforcement by subjecting the prosecutor's motives and decisionmaking to outside inquiry, and may undermine prosecutorial effectiveness by revealing the Government's enforcement policy."

The requirements for a selective-prosecution claim draw on "ordinary equal protection standards." The claimant must demonstrate that the federal prosecutorial policy "had a discriminatory effect and that it was motivated by a discriminatory purpose." To establish a discriminatory effect in a race case, the claimant must show that similarly situated individuals of a different race were not prosecuted. This requirement has been established in our case law since Ah Sin v. Wittman, 198 U.S. 500 (1905). Ah Sin, a subject of China, petitioned a California state court for a writ of habeas corpus, seeking discharge from imprisonment under a San Francisco county ordinance prohibiting persons from setting up gambling tables in rooms barricaded to stop police from entering. He alleged in his habeas petition "that the ordinance is enforced 'solely and exclusively against persons of the Chinese race and not otherwise.' " We rejected his contention that this averment made out a claim under the Equal Protection Clause, because it did not allege "that the conditions and practices to which the ordinance was directed did not exist exclusively among the Chinese, or that there were other offenders against the ordinance than the Chinese as to whom it was not enforced."

The similarly situated requirement does not make a selective-prosecution claim impossible to prove. Twenty years before *Ah Sin*, we invalidated an ordinance, also adopted by San Francisco, that prohibited the operation of laundries in wooden buildings. Yick Wo, 118 U.S., at 374. The plaintiff in error successfully demonstrated that the ordinance was applied against Chinese nationals but not against other laundry-shop operators. The authorities had denied the applications of 200 Chinese subjects for permits to operate shops in wooden buildings, but granted the applications of 80 individuals who were not Chinese subjects

to operate laundries in wooden buildings "under similar conditions."
* * *

Having reviewed the requirements to prove a selective-prosecution claim, we turn to the showing necessary to obtain discovery in support of such a claim. If discovery is ordered, the Government must assemble from its own files documents which might corroborate or refute the defendant's claim. Discovery thus imposes many of the costs present when the Government must respond to a prima facie case of selective prosecution. It will divert prosecutors' resources and may disclose the Government's prosecutorial strategy. The justifications for a rigorous standard for the elements of a selective-prosecution claim thus require a correspondingly rigorous standard for discovery in aid of such a claim.

* * * The Courts of Appeals "require some evidence tending to show the existence of the essential elements of the defense," discriminatory effect and discriminatory intent.

In this case we consider what evidence constitutes "some evidence tending to show the existence" of the discriminatory effect element. The Court of Appeals held that a defendant may establish a colorable basis for discriminatory effect without evidence that the Government has failed to prosecute others who are similarly situated to the defendant. We think it was mistaken in this view. The vast majority of the Courts of Appeals require the defendant to produce some evidence that similarly situated defendants of other races could have been prosecuted, but were not, and this requirement is consistent with our equal protection case law. [Citations]

The Court of Appeals reached its decision in part because it started "with the presumption that people of all races commit all types of crimes—not with the premise that any type of crime is the exclusive province of any particular racial or ethnic group." It cited no authority for this proposition, which seems contradicted by the most recent statistics of the United States Sentencing Commission. Those statistics show that: More than 90% of the persons sentenced in 1994 for crack cocaine trafficking were black, United States Sentencing Comm'n, 1994 Annual Report 107 (Table 45); 93.4% of convicted LSD dealers were white; and 91% of those convicted for pornography or prostitution were white, id., at 41 (Table 13). Presumptions at war with presumably reliable statistics have no proper place in the analysis of this issue.

[T]he required threshold—a credible showing of different treatment of similarly situated persons—adequately balances the Government's interest in vigorous prosecution and the defendant's interest in avoiding selective prosecution.

In the case before us, respondents' "study" did not constitute "some evidence tending to show the existence of the essential elements of" a selective-prosecution claim. The study failed to identify individuals who were not black, could have been prosecuted for the offenses for which respondents were charged, but were not so prosecuted. This omission was not remedied by respondents' evidence in opposition to the Government's motion for reconsideration. The newspaper article, which discussed the discriminatory effect of federal drug sentencing laws, was not relevant to an allegation of discrimination in decisions to prosecute. Respondents' affidavits, which recounted one attorney's conversation with a drug treatment center employee and the experience of another attorney defending drug prosecutions in state court, recounted hearsay and reported personal conclusions based on anecdotal evidence. The judgment of the Court of Appeals is therefore reversed, and the case is remanded for proceedings consistent with this opinion.

[The concurring opinions of Justice Souter and Justice Ginsburg, joined by Justice Breyer, are omitted. They deal only with the scope of Federal Rule of Criminal Procedure 16.]

JUSTICE STEVENS, dissenting.

* * *

The District Judge's order should be evaluated in light of three circumstances that underscore the need for judicial vigilance over certain types of drug prosecutions. First, the Anti–Drug Abuse Act of 1986 and subsequent legislation established a regime of extremely high penalties for the possession and distribution of so-called "crack" cocaine. Those provisions treat one gram of crack as the equivalent of 100 grams of powder cocaine. The distribution of 50 grams of crack is thus punishable by the same mandatory minimum sentence of 10 years in prison that applies to the distribution of 5,000 grams of powder cocaine. The Sentencing Guidelines extend this ratio to penalty levels above the mandatory minimums: for any given quantity of crack, the guideline range is the same as if the offense had involved 100 times that amount in powder cocaine. These penalties result in sentences for crack offenders that average three to eight times longer than sentences for comparable powder offenders.

Second, the disparity between the treatment of crack cocaine and powder cocaine is matched by the disparity between the severity of the punishment imposed by federal law and that imposed by state law for the same conduct. For a variety of reasons, often including the absence of mandatory minimums, the existence of parole, and lower baseline penalties, terms of imprisonment for drug offenses tend to be substantially lower in state systems than in the federal system. The difference is especially marked in the case of crack offenses. The majority of States draw no distinction between types of cocaine in their penalty schemes; of those that do, none has established as stark a differential as the Federal Government. For example, if respondent Hampton is found guilty, his federal sentence might be as long as a mandatory life term. Had he been tried in state court, his sentence could have been as short as 12 years, less worktime credits of half that amount.

Finally, it is undisputed that the brunt of the elevated federal penalties falls heavily on blacks. While 65% of the persons who have used crack are white, in 1993 they represented only 4% of the federal offenders convicted of trafficking in crack. Eighty-eight percent of such defendants were black. During the first 18 months of full guideline implementation, the sentencing disparity between black and white defendants grew from preguideline levels: blacks on average received sentences over 40% longer than whites. See Bureau of Justice Statistics, Sentencing in the Federal Courts: Does Race Matter? 6–7 (Dec. 1993). Those figures represent a major threat to the integrity of federal sentencing reform, whose main purpose was the elimination of disparity (especially racial) in sentencing. The Sentencing Commission acknowledges that the heightened crack penalties are a "primary cause of the growing disparity between sentences for Black and White federal defendants."

The extraordinary severity of the imposed penalties and the troubling racial patterns of enforcement give rise to a special concern about the fairness of charging practices for crack offenses. Evidence tending to prove that black defendants charged with distribution of crack in the Central District of California are prosecuted in federal court, whereas members of other races charged with similar offenses are prosecuted in state court, warrants close scrutiny by the federal judges in that District. In my view, the District Judge, who has sat on both the federal and the state benches in Los Angeles, acted well within her discretion to call for the development of facts that would demonstrate what standards, if any, governed the choice of forum where similarly situated offenders are prosecuted. * * *

* * *

Commentary

The defense of selective or discriminatory prosecution is well established in principle, but rarely successful in practice. Courts generally shrink from the difficult task of assessing a prosecutor's motives, and defendants rarely succeed in establishing that a prosecutorial policy is so rationally indefensible as to be arbitrary. For example, selective prosecution of suspected organized crime figures has long been common and has been upheld. United States v. Sacco, 428 F.2d 264 (9th Cir.1970). The government has a policy of vigorously prosecuting notorious tax resisters on criminal tax charges, and the courts have approved because the policy is rationally related to legitimate enforcement goals. United States v. Catlett, 584 F.2d 864 (8th Cir. 1978). The tax protestors have been singled out for *tax* prosecutions, however, and a different issue might be presented if the government selectively pursued them for non-tax offenses. For example, an Illinois appellate court held unconstitutional the arrest of a suspected prostitute for failing to have a bell on her bicycle, where the arresting officer was acting pursuant to a departmental policy of strictly enforcing all laws against suspected prostitutes. The court observed that "The purpose of requiring a bell on a bicycle clearly does not envision the eradication of prostitution." People v. Kail, 150 Ill.App.3d 75 (1986).

Some cases hold that the defense of discriminatory prosecution is unavailable when the prosecution is under a statute which is generally enforced, even though the defendant asserts that the decision to prosecute in his case was based on some improper motive such as personal dislike. Determining motivation in such a situation is apt to be difficult, particularly where more than one person was involved in the charging decision. In rare cases, this difficulty may be overcome. In People v. Walker, 14 N.Y.2d 901 (1964), the defendant was granted a hearing and eventually prevailed on her claim that she was charged with violating several building code provisions (that were generally enforced against other persons) after she exposed corrupt practices in the enforcing department.

In addition to the "equal protection" claim of discriminatory enforcement, there is a limited due process doctrine against prosecutorial "vindictiveness." The doctrine stems from the Supreme Court's decision in Blackledge v. Perry, 417 U.S. 21 (1974), where the defendant was convicted of misdemeanor assault, exercised his right to trial *de novo* in a higher court, and then was charged with felony assault for the same conduct. The Supreme Court held that a person should be entitled to pursue his statutory right to a trial *de novo* without the fear that the State may retaliate by charging a higher offense to punish him for exercising that right. The doctrine is similar to the rule that prohibits a judge from imposing a higher sentence on retrial and reconviction to punish a defendant for successfully appealing his original conviction.

UNITED STATES v. BAGLEY

Supreme Court of the United States, 1985.
473 U.S. 667, 105 S.Ct. 3375, 87 L.Ed.2d 481.

JUSTICE BLACKMUN announced the judgment of the Court and delivered the opinion of the Court except as to Part III.

In *Brady v. Maryland*, 373 U.S. 83, 87 (1963), this Court held that "the suppression by the prosecution of evidence favorable to an accused upon request violates due process where the evidence is material either to guilt or punishment." The issue in the present case concerns the standard of materiality to be applied in determining whether a conviction should be reversed because the prosecutor failed to disclose requested evidence that could have been used to impeach Government witnesses.

I

In October 1977, respondent Hughes Anderson Bagley was indicted in the Western District of Washington on 15 charges of violating federal narcotics and firearms statutes. On November 18, 24 days before trial, respondent filed a discovery motion. The sixth paragraph of that motion requested:

> "The names and addresses of witnesses that the government intends to call at trial. Also the prior criminal records of witnesses, and any deals, promises or inducements made to witnesses in exchange for their testimony."

The Government's two principal witnesses at the trial were James F. O'Connor and Donald E. Mitchell. O'Connor and Mitchell were state law-enforcement officers employed by the Milwaukee Railroad as private security guards. Between April and June 1977, they assisted the federal Bureau of Alcohol, Tobacco and Firearms (ATF) in conducting an undercover investigation of respondent.

The Government's response to the discovery motion did not disclose that any "deals, promises or inducements" had been made to O'Connor or Mitchell. In apparent reply to a request in the motion's ninth paragraph for "[c]opies of all Jencks Act material,"[24] the Government produced a series of affidavits that O'Connor and Mitchell had signed between April 12 and May 4, 1977, while the undercover investigation was in progress. These affidavits recounted in detail the undercover dealings that O'Connor and Mitchell were having at the time with respondent. Each affidavit concluded with the statement, "I made this statement freely and voluntarily without any threats or rewards, or promises of reward having been made to me in return for it."

[O'Connor and Mitchell testified about both the firearms and the narcotics charges at Bagley's bench trial. Bagley was convicted on the narcotics charges, but acquitted on the firearms charges.]

[Two years later, Bagley] filed requests for information pursuant to the Freedom of Information Act and to the Privacy Act of 1974, 5 U.S.C. §§ 552 and 552a. He received in response copies of ATF form contracts that O'Connor and Mitchell had signed on May 3, 1977. Each form was entitled "Contract for Purchase of Information and Payment of Lump Sum Therefor." The printed portion of the form stated that the vendor "will provide" information to ATF and that "upon receipt of such information by the Regional Director, Bureau of Alcohol, Tobacco and Firearms, or his representative, and upon the accomplishment of the objective sought to be obtained by the use of such information to the satisfaction of said Regional Director, the United States will pay to said vendor a sum commensurate with services and information rendered." Each form contained the following typewritten description of services:

> "That he will provide information regarding T–I and other violations committed by Hughes A. Bagley, Jr.; that he will purchase evidence for ATF; that he will cut [sic] in an undercover capacity for ATF; that he will assist ATF in gathering of evidence and testify against the violator in federal court."

The figure "$300.00" was handwritten in each form on a line entitled "Sum to Be Paid to Vendor."

Because these contracts had not been disclosed to respondent in response to his pretrial discovery motion,[25] respondent moved under 28

---

24. The Jencks Act, 18 U.S.C. § 3500, requires the prosecutor to disclose, after direct examination of a Government witness and on the defendant's motion, any statement of the witness in the Govern-ment's possession that relates to the subject matter of the witness' testimony.

25. The Assistant United States Attorney who prosecuted respondent stated in stipulated testimony that he had not known

U.S.C. § 2255 to vacate his sentence. He alleged that the Government's failure to disclose the contracts, which he could have used to impeach O'Connor and Mitchell, violated his right to due process under *Brady v. Maryland*.

[After an evidentiary hearing before a magistrate, the District Court found that it was "probable" that O'Connor and Mitchell expected to receive compensation for their assistance, "though perhaps not for their testimony," that during pretrial discovery the United States withheld information as to any 'deals, promises or inducements' to these witnesses, and suppressed evidence favorable to the defendant, in violation of *Brady v. Maryland*. The trial court also found beyond a reasonable doubt that if the existence of the agreements had been disclosed during the trial, the disclosure would not have affected the its decision that the prosecution had proved that Bagley was guilty of the offenses for which he had been convicted beyond a reasonable doubt. It found, in particular, that the claimed impeachment evidence would not have been helpful to Bagley, and denied his motion to vacate his sentence. The Court of Appeals for the Ninth Circuit reversed, stating that the failure to provide the requested impeachment evidence "requires an automatic reversal." The Supreme Court granted certiorari.]

II

The holding in *Brady v. Maryland* requires disclosure only of evidence that is both favorable to the accused and "material either to guilt or punishment." See also *Moore v. Illinois*, 408 U.S. 786, 794–795 (1972). The Court explained in *United States v. Agurs*, 427 U.S. 97, 104 (1976): "A fair analysis of the holding in *Brady* indicates that implicit in the requirement of materiality is a concern that the suppressed evidence might have affected the outcome of the trial." The evidence suppressed in *Brady* would have been admissible only on the issue of punishment and not on the issue of guilt, and therefore could have affected only Brady's sentence and not his conviction. Accordingly, the Court affirmed the lower court's restriction of Brady's new trial to the issue of punishment.

The *Brady* rule is based on the requirement of due process. Its purpose is not to displace the adversary system as the primary means by which truth is uncovered, but to ensure that a miscarriage of justice does not occur. Thus, the prosecutor is not required to deliver his entire file to defense counsel, but only to disclose evidence favorable to the accused that, if suppressed, would deprive the defendant of a fair trial. * * *

The Court of Appeals treated impeachment evidence as constitutionally different from exculpatory evidence. According to that court, failure to disclose impeachment evidence is "even more egregious" than failure

that the contracts existed and that he
would have furnished them to respondent
had he known of them.

to disclose exculpatory evidence "because it threatens the defendant's right to confront adverse witnesses." * * *

This Court has rejected any such distinction between impeachment evidence and exculpatory evidence. * * *

* * *

The present case, in contrast, does not involve any direct restriction on the scope of cross-examination. The defense was free to cross-examine the witnesses on any relevant subject, including possible bias or interest resulting from inducements made by the Government. The constitutional error, if any, in this case was the Government's failure to assist the defense by disclosing information that might have been helpful in conducting the cross-examination. As discussed above, such suppression of evidence amounts to a constitutional violation only if it deprives the defendant of a fair trial. Consistent with our overriding concern with the justice of the finding of guilt, a constitutional error occurs, and the conviction must be reversed, only if the evidence is material in the sense that its suppression undermines confidence in the outcome of the trial.

III

A

It remains to determine the standard of materiality applicable to the nondisclosed evidence at issue in this case. Our starting point is the framework for evaluating the materiality of *Brady* evidence established in *United States v. Agurs*. The Court in *Agurs* distinguished three situations involving the discovery, after trial, of information favorable to the accused that had been known to the prosecution but unknown to the defense. The first situation was the prosecutor's knowing use of perjured testimony or, equivalently, the prosecutor's knowing failure to disclose that testimony used to convict the defendant was false. The Court noted the well-established rule that "a conviction obtained by the knowing use of perjured testimony is fundamentally unfair, and must be set aside if there is any reasonable likelihood that the false testimony could have affected the judgment of the jury." Although this rule is stated in terms that treat the knowing use of perjured testimony as error subject to harmless-error review, it may as easily be stated as a materiality standard under which the fact that testimony is perjured is considered material unless failure to disclose it would be harmless beyond a reasonable doubt. The Court in *Agurs* justified this standard of materiality on the ground that the knowing use of perjured testimony involves prosecutorial misconduct and, more importantly, involves "a corruption of the truth-seeking function of the trial process."

At the other extreme is the situation in *Agurs* itself, where the defendant does not make a *Brady* request and the prosecutor fails to disclose certain evidence favorable to the accused. The Court rejected a harmless-error rule in that situation, because under that rule every nondisclosure is treated as error, thus imposing on the prosecutor a constitutional duty to deliver his entire file to defense counsel. At the same time, the Court rejected a standard that would require the defendant to demonstrate that the evidence if disclosed probably would have resulted in acquittal. The Court reasoned: "If the standard applied to the usual motion for a new trial based on newly discovered evidence were the same when the evidence was in the State's possession as when it was found in a neutral source, there would be no special significance to the prosecutor's obligation to serve the cause of justice." The standard of materiality applicable in the absence of a specific *Brady* request is therefore stricter than the harmless-error standard but more lenient to the defense than the newly discovered evidence standard.

The third situation identified by the Court in *Agurs* is where the defense makes a specific request and the prosecutor fails to disclose responsive evidence. The Court did not define the standard of materiality applicable in this situation, but suggested that the standard might be more lenient to the defense than in the situation in which the defense makes no request or only a general request. The Court also noted: "When the prosecutor receives a specific and relevant request, the failure to make any response is seldom, if ever, excusable."

The Court has relied on and reformulated the *Agurs* standard for the materiality of undisclosed evidence in two subsequent cases arising outside the *Brady* context. In neither case did the Court's discussion of the *Agurs* standard distinguish among the three situations described in *Agurs*. In *United States v. Valenzuela–Bernal*, 458 U.S. 858, 874 (1982), the Court held that due process is violated when testimony is made unavailable to the defense by Government deportation of witnesses "only if there is a reasonable likelihood that the testimony could have affected the judgment of the trier of fact." And in *Strickland v. Washington* the Court held that a new trial must be granted when evidence is not introduced because of the incompetence of counsel only if "there is a reasonable probability that, but for counsel's unprofessional errors, the result of the proceeding would have been different." The *Strickland* Court defined a "reasonable probability" as "a probability sufficient to undermine confidence in the outcome."

We find the *Strickland* formulation of the *Agurs* test for materiality sufficiently flexible to cover the "no request," "general request," and "specific request" cases of prosecutorial failure to disclose evidence favorable to the accused: The evidence is material only if there is a reasonable probability that, had the evidence been disclosed to the defense, the result of the proceeding would have been different. A "reasonable probability" is a probability sufficient to undermine confidence in the outcome.

* * *

[U]nder the *Strickland* formulation the reviewing court may consider directly any adverse effect that the prosecutor's failure to respond might have had on the preparation or presentation of the defendant's case. The reviewing court should assess the possibility that such effect might have occurred in light of the totality of the circumstances and with an awareness of the difficulty of reconstructing in a post-trial proceeding the course that the defense and the trial would have taken had the defense not been misled by the prosecutor's incomplete response.

B

In the present case, we think that there is a significant likelihood that the prosecutor's response to respondent's discovery motion misleadingly induced defense counsel to believe that O'Connor and Mitchell could not be impeached on the basis of bias or interest arising from inducements offered by the Government. * * *

The District Court, nonetheless, found beyond a reasonable doubt that, had the information that the Government held out the possibility of reward to its witnesses been disclosed, the result of the criminal prosecution would not have been different. If this finding were sustained by the Court of Appeals, the information would be immaterial even under the standard of materiality applicable to the prosecutor's knowing use of perjured testimony. Although the express holding of the Court of Appeals was that the nondisclosure in this case required automatic reversal, the Court of Appeals also stated that it "disagreed" with the District Court's finding of harmless error. In particular, the Court of Appeals appears to have disagreed with the factual premise on which this finding expressly was based. The District Court reasoned that O'Connor's and Mitchell's testimony was exculpatory on the narcotics charges. The Court of Appeals, however, concluded, after reviewing the record, that O'Connor's and Mitchell's testimony was in fact inculpatory on those charges. [As a result, the Supreme Court reversed and remanded the case to the Court of Appeals for a determination of whether there was a reasonable probability that the outcome of the trial would have been different if the prosecution had disclosed the inducements it had offered to O'Connor and Mitchell to the defense.]

JUSTICE POWELL took no part in the decision of this case.

[The opinion of JUSTICE WHITE, with whom THE CHIEF JUSTICE and JUSTICE REHNQUIST joined, concurring in part and concurring in the judgment, is omitted.]

JUSTICE MARSHALL, with whom JUSTICE BRENNAN joins, dissenting.

When the Government withholds from a defendant evidence that might impeach the prosecution's *only witnesses*, that failure to disclose cannot be deemed harmless error. Because that is precisely the nature of the undisclosed evidence in this case, I would affirm the judgment of the Court of Appeals and would not remand for further proceedings.

I

The federal grand jury indicted the respondent, Hughes Anderson Bagley, on charges involving possession of firearms and controlled substances with intent to distribute. Following a bench trial, Bagley was found not guilty of the firearms charges, guilty of two counts of knowingly and intentionally distributing Valium, and guilty of several counts of a lesser included offense of possession of controlled substances. He was sentenced to six months' imprisonment and a special parole term of five years on the first count of distribution, and to three years of imprisonment, which were suspended, and five years' probation, on the second distribution count. He received a suspended sentence and five years' probation for the possession convictions.

The record plainly demonstrates that on the two counts for which Bagley received sentences of imprisonment, the Government's entire case hinged on the testimony of two private security guards who aided the Bureau of Alcohol, Tobacco and Firearms (BATF) in its investigation of Bagley. In 1977 the two guards, O'Connor and Mitchell, worked for the Milwaukee Railroad; for about three years, they had been social acquaintances of Bagley, with whom they often shared coffee breaks. At trial, they testified that on two separate occasions they had visited Bagley at his home, where Bagley had responded to O'Connor's complaint that he was extremely anxious by giving him Valium pills. In total, Bagley received $8 from O'Connor, representing the cost of the pills. At trial, Bagley testified that he had a prescription for the Valium because he suffered from a bad back. No testimony to the contrary was introduced. O'Connor and Mitchell each testified that they had worn concealed transmitters and body recorders at these meetings, but the tape recordings were insufficiently clear to be admitted at trial and corroborate their testimony. * * *

* * *

[The informants' testimony] was in fact the *only inculpatory testimony in the case* as to the two counts for which Bagley received a sentence of imprisonment. If, as the judge claimed, the testimony of the two information "vendors" was "very brief" and in part favorable to the defendant, that fact shows the weakness of the prosecutor's case, not the harmlessness of the error. If the testimony that might have been impeached is weak and also cumulative, corroborative or tangential, the failure to disclose the impeachment evidence could conceivably be held harmless. But when the testimony is the start and finish of the prosecution's case, and is weak nonetheless, quite a different conclusion must necessarily be drawn.

[T]he Government's failure to disclose the existence of any inducements to its witnesses, coupled with its disclosure of affidavits stating that no promises had been made, would lead all but the most careless lawyer to step wide and clear of questions about promises or inducements. The combination of nondisclosure and disclosure would simply lead any reasonable attorney to believe that the witness could not be impeached on that basis. Thus, a firm avowal that no payment is being received in return for assistance and testimony, if offered at trial by a witness who is not even a Government employee, could be devastating to the defense. A wise attorney would, of necessity, seek an alternative defense strategy.

* * *

* * * It simply cannot be denied that the existence of a contract signed by those witnesses, promising a reward whose size would depend on the Government's satisfaction with the end result, might sway the trier of fact, or cast doubt on the truth of all that the witnesses allege. In such a case, the trier of fact is absolutely entitled to know of the contract, and the defense counsel is absolutely entitled to develop his case with an awareness of it. Whatever the applicable standard of materiality, in this instance it undoubtedly is well met. * * *

JUSTICE STEVENS, dissenting.

* * *

[T]he *Brady* rule itself unquestionably applies to this case, because the Government failed to disclose favorable evidence that was clearly responsive to the defendant's specific request. Bagley's conviction therefore must be set aside if the suppressed evidence was "material"—and it obviously was—and if there is "any reasonable likelihood" that it could have affected the judgment of the trier of fact. Our choice, therefore, should be merely whether to affirm for the reasons stated in Part I of Justice Marshall's dissent, or to remand to the Court of Appeals for further review under the standard stated in *Brady*. I would follow the latter course, not because I disagree with Justice Marshall's analysis of the record, but because I do not believe this Court should perform the task of reviewing trial transcripts in the first instance. I am confident that the Court of Appeals would reach the appropriate result if it applied the proper standard.

The Court, however, today sets out a reformulation of the *Brady* rule in which I have no such confidence. * * * The Court's approach stretches the concept of "materiality" beyond any recognizable scope, transforming it from merely an evidentiary concept as used in *Brady* and *Agurs*, which required that material evidence be admissible and probative of guilt or innocence in the context of a specific request, into a result-focused standard that seems to include an independent weight in favor of affirming convictions despite evidentiary suppression. Evidence favorable to an accused and relevant to the dispositive issue of guilt apparently may still be found not "material," and hence suppressible by prosecutors prior to trial, unless there is a reasonable probability that its use would result in an acquittal. Justice Marshall rightly criticizes the incentives such a standard creates for prosecutors to gamble, to play the odds, and to take a chance that evidence will later turn out not to have been potentially dispositive.

Moreover, the Court's analysis reduces the significance of deliberate prosecutorial suppression of potentially exculpatory evidence to that merely of one of numerous factors that "may" be considered by a reviewing court. This is not faithful to our statement in *Agurs* that "[w]hen the prosecutor receives a specific and relevant request, the failure to make any response is seldom, if ever, excusable." Such suppression is far more serious than mere nondisclosure of evidence in which the defense has expressed no particular interest. A reviewing court should attach great significance to silence in the face of a specific request, when responsive evidence is later shown to have been in the Government's possession. Such silence actively misleads in the same way as would an affirmative representation that exculpatory evidence does not exist when, in fact, it does (*i.e.*, perjury)—indeed, the two situations are aptly described as "sides of a single coin."

Accordingly, although I agree that the judgment of the Court of Appeals should be vacated and that the case should be remanded for further proceedings, I disagree with the Court's statement of the correct standard to be applied. I therefore respectfully dissent from the judgment that the case be remanded for determination under the Court's new standard.

Commentary

The Brady Doctrine

The defendant in Brady v. Maryland, 373 U.S. 83 (1963), was found guilty of a felony murder committed with an accomplice named Boblit and sentenced to death. Prior to Brady's separate trial, defense counsel asked the prosecutor to produce all the statements that Boblit had given to the police. The prosecutor turned over some statements, but did not include one statement in which Boblit admitted that he had committed the actual killing. At trial Brady admitted his participation in the crime but claimed that he did not personally commit the killing, and defense counsel urged the jury to show leniency and not to impose the death penalty because of this fact. After the conviction and death sentence defense counsel learned of the undisclosed statement and sought a new trial. The Supreme Court affirmed a state court ruling granting a new trial on the issue of punishment alone. The identity of the actual killer had no effect on Brady's liability for felony murder, but withholding that information deprived Brady of a fair trial on the death penalty issue.

The *Brady* doctrine has been applied, interpreted or distinguished in a number of subsequent cases, including the following:

1. The defendant in Giglio v. United States, 405 U.S. 150 (1972), was convicted of passing forged money orders on the testimony of an unindicted co-conspirator named Taliento. Defense counsel tried to discredit Taliento's testimony by suggesting that he had been promised that he would not be prosecuted if he agreed to incriminate Giglio, but Taliento repeatedly denied on the stand that he had received any promises. After conviction the defense made a motion for a new trial on the basis of newly discovered evidence, specifically an affidavit from the Assistant United States Attorney who had presented the case to the grand jury relating that he had promised Taliento that he would not be prosecuted if Taliento testified for the Government at Giglio's trial. The AUSA who took over the case for trial filed an affidavit stating that the former prosecutor had told him that Taliento had *not* been

promised immunity but had not been prosecuted because he was very young at the time of the offense and "obviously had been overreached by the defendant Giglio."

The District Court did not try to resolve the conflict between the affidavits, but denied relief on the theory that disclosure of any promise that may have been made would not have affected the verdict. The Supreme Court reversed in a unanimous opinion by Chief Justice Burger, citing the "knowing use of false testimony" cases and holding that the prosecutor's office as an entity had an obligation to see that the jury was not misled as to the existence of a promise of non-prosecution. Because Taliento's testimony was the entire basis of the prosecution case, "evidence of any understanding or agreement as to a future prosecution would be relevant to his credibility and the jury was entitled to know of it." 405 U.S. at 155.

2. The defendant in Moore v. Illinois, 408 U.S. 786 (1972), was convicted and sentenced to death for murdering a bartender with a shotgun. Two eyewitnesses testified that they saw Moore commit the murder, and another witness (Sanders) testified that a man he knew as "Slick," whom he identified as Moore, admitted the killing in a conversation in another bar. The facts of the case are too complex to report completely here, but the allegedly suppressed exculpatory evidence essentially consisted of: (1) A statement and accompanying diagram by another person who was in the bar at the time of the murder. The diagram indicated that one of the eyewitnesses was seated at a card table facing away from the door, and the defense could have used this information to cast doubt upon this witness's testimony that he saw Moore enter and commit the killing. (2) Certain evidence indicating that the witness Sanders might have been confused about the identity of "Slick," and that therefore it could have been another person rather than Moore who admitted killing the bartender. The defense had made a general motion for discovery of all written witness statements, and the prosecutor had turned over his entire file. The missing items either were not in the file, or were turned over and not noted by the defense at the time. The Supreme Court affirmed the conviction (but reversed the death sentence on other grounds) by a 5–4 vote. The majority concluded that there had been no deliberate suppression, and that the evidence which subsequently came to light did not sufficiently undermine the state's case so as to call for relief on due process principles.

3. The opinion in United States v. Agurs, 427 U.S. 97 (1976), is discussed at some length in *Bagley*. The facts of the case were as follows: The defendant Agurs, apparently a prostitute, went to a motel room with the victim, Sewell. Sewell was wearing a bowie knife in a sheath and carried another knife in his pocket. He probably also had $360 in cash on his person. The evidence indicated that, after the parties completed an act of intercourse, Sewell had gone to the bathroom down the hall. Upon his return a violent struggle occurred. Motel employees responding to Agurs' screams for help entered the room and found Sewell on top of her struggling for possession of the bowie knife. While police were being summoned Agurs managed to depart, and Sewell died shortly afterward of wounds received in the struggle. The contents of his pockets were in disarray on the dresser and no money was found, indicating that the stabbing may have occurred after Sewell caught Agurs in the act of stealing his money.

The next day Agurs surrendered to the police. She was given a physical examination which showed no cuts or bruises, except for needle marks on her arm. An autopsy of Sewell disclosed that he had several deep stab wounds in his chest and abdomen, and a number of slashes on his arms and hands, characterized by the pathologist as "defensive wounds." Agurs did not testify, but her attorney argued that Sewell initially attacked her with a knife and that the killing was therefore in self-defense.

Following the murder conviction, defense counsel filed a motion for a new trial. It asserted that the prosecution had failed to disclose that Sewell had previously been convicted of assault and carrying a deadly weapon. The Government responded that the prior record could have been obtained by discovery, that there was no duty to tender such information to the defense in the absence of an appropriate request, and that the evidence was not material in any case. The Supreme Court majority affirmed the denial of the new trial motion because the victim's prior record was not requested, and because, in the context of the rest of the evidence, the record of prior convictions was not sufficient to create a reasonable doubt of the defendant's guilt. *Agurs* thus establishes that, in the absence of a defense request, prosecutorial suppression will not be found unless the withheld evidence is powerful enough to create a reasonable doubt.

4. The Supreme Court held that the *Brady* doctrine was not violated where the police failed to preserve important physical evidence, in Arizona v. Youngblood, 488 U.S. 51 (1988). In *Youngblood* the victim, a ten-year-old boy was abducted and sodomized by a middle-aged man. After the assault the boy was taken to a hospital where a physician used a swab from a "sexual assault kit" to collect semen samples from the victim's rectum. The police also collected the boy's clothing, which they failed to refrigerate. A police criminologist performed some tests on the rectal swab and the clothing, but he was unable to obtain information about the identity of the assailant. The boy later picked the defendant as the assailant from a photographic lineup; defendant was not arrested until several weeks after that. At trial the defense claimed mistaken identity, and experts testified that the defendant might have been completely exonerated by more thorough tests that could have been performed if the clothing had been refrigerated and the evidence preserved. The Supreme Court nonetheless held that the *Brady* doctrine was not violated where the failure to preserve evidence was at most negligent and there was no "bad faith on the part of the police." Three Justices dissented. Justice Stevens, concurring in the judgment, emphasized that defense counsel was allowed to argue the issue to the jury, and the judge instructed the jury that they could infer that any evidence lost or destroyed by the state would have been likely to be to the benefit of the defendant. Justice Stevens reasoned that "In declining defense counsel's and the court's invitations to draw the permissive inference, the jurors in effect indicated that, in their view, the other evidence at trial was so overwhelming that it was highly improbable that the lost evidence was exculpatory."

It is important to distinguish the *constitutional* issue (knowing use of perjured testimony or suppression of exculpatory evidence) from the *non-constitutional* question of when a defendant can obtain a new trial on the basis of newly discovered evidence. For example, Federal Rule of Criminal Procedure 33 provides that "A motion for a new trial based on the ground of newly discovered evidence may be made only before or within two years after final judgment, but if an appeal is pending the court may grant the motion only on remand of the case." The granting of such a motion is not dependent upon a finding that the prosecutor suppressed anything, and of course evidence may fail to come to light in time for trial without anyone being at fault. To obtain relief under Rule 33, however, the convicted defendant must "satisfy the severe burden of demonstrating that newly discovered evidence probably would have resulted in acquittal." *Agurs*, 427 U.S. at 111. Where the prosecutor (or the Government as an entity) was at fault, the burden of showing prejudice is not so severe.

When the time for making a new trial motion has passed, then a convicted person can obtain relief from a conviction or sentence only by showing a violation of the Constitution. In other words, it is not enough to establish that on the basis of current information there is a reasonable doubt as to guilt, if the trial was fairly conducted at the time. The defendant must show not only that new evidence casts doubt upon guilt, but also that the prosecution suppressed this evidence, or defense counsel was ineffective under the *Strickland* standard in failing to discover and present it. Unless either the prosecution or defense counsel was to blame there probably was no constitutional error, and the only avenue of relief is Executive Clemency.

Most cases have assumed that the *Brady* doctrine could be applied only where someone involved with the prosecutor's office was aware of the suppressed evidence or perjured testimony. In Sanders v. Sullivan, 863 F.2d 218 (2d Cir. 1988), the federal Court of Appeals held that a person convicted in a state court on the basis of perjured testimony could obtain relief on due process grounds in federal court even though the state prosecutor was unaware of the perjury. Defendant Sanders was convicted in a New York State court of shooting a drug dealer, on the testimony of Perez and Semiday, who were common-law husband and wife. After the conviction Semiday died, and Perez met Sanders in prison. Perez thereafter recanted his trial testimony, and gave Sanders several affidavits recounting that he had given false testimony in order to protect Semiday.

The state court and the federal district court denied relief on the grounds that, whether the recantation was credible or not, the prosecutor had had no knowledge of any perjury and thus there was no violation of the *Brady* doctrine. The Court of Appeals held that a defendant convicted on perjured testimony was entitled to habeas corpus relief whether or not the prosecutor knew of the perjury, and remanded for a determination by the district court of the credibility of the recantation. The district court was directed to vacate the conviction if it found that Perez did indeed commit perjury at the state trial, and if the court was convinced that the defendant would most likely not have been convicted but for the perjured testimony.

*

Part IV

THE CONSTITUTION IN A
TIME OF CRISIS: THE
WAR ON TERROR

Chapter 12

THE WAR ON TERROR

Introduction

The "war on terror" conducted by the United States government following the terrorist attacks on September 11, 2001, has generated disputes about the nature of government power to conduct searches and seizures, interrogate suspects, and detain suspected enemies. This Chapter includes materials on each of these subjects that are relevant to the discussions in earlier Chapters addressing analogous issues in the context of traditional domestic law enforcement. Some of the most significant materials include memoranda and other documents produced by the executive branch of the federal government and military authorities that define government power expansively. The Chapter commences with excerpts from such a document that was produced by the United States Department of Justice.

A. SEARCH AND SEIZURE

1. Racial Profiling and Particularized Suspicion

In the years leading up to the 2000 Presidential election, racial profiling by state and federal law enforcers became a topic of public debate and the practice was criticized by legal commentators, politicians, and law enforcement officials. In an Address to a Joint Session of Congress delivered a month after he took office, President Bush declared that racial profiling is "wrong and we will end it in America," and directed the Attorney General to review Federal law enforcement authorities' use of race as a factor in conducting stops, searches and other law enforcement investigative procedures. The Attorney General ordered the Civil Rights Division of the Department of Justice to develop guidance designed to end racial profiling by Federal law enforcement officials.

Before this "guidance" was issued, the terrorist attacks of September 11, 2001, changed the nature of the debate about racial profiling. Some legal commentators, politicians, and law enforcement officials now asserted that profiling was rational and necessary in the "war" against terrorism. The "guidance" finally was issued in June, 2003. The following excerpts from that document reveal a policy that condemns profiling in traditional law enforcement but attempts to preserve it as a tool for capturing terrorists.

Guidance Regarding the Use of Race by Federal Law Enforcement Agencies

United States Department of Justice, Civil Rights Division.
June 2003
Introduction and Executive Summary

* * *

"Racial profiling" at its core concerns the invidious use of race or ethnicity as a criterion in conducting stops, searches and other law enforcement investigative procedures. It is premised on the erroneous assumption that any particular individual of one race or ethnicity is more likely to engage in misconduct than any particular individual of another race or ethnicity.

Racial profiling in law enforcement is not merely wrong, but also ineffective. Race-based assumptions in law enforcement perpetuate negative racial stereotypes that are harmful to our rich and diverse democracy, and materially impair our efforts to maintain a fair and just society.

The use of race as the basis for law enforcement decision-making clearly has a terrible cost, both to the individuals who suffer invidious discrimination and to the Nation, whose goal of "liberty and justice for all" recedes with every act of such discrimination. For this reason, this guidance in many cases imposes more restrictions on the consideration of race and ethnicity in Federal law enforcement than the Constitution requires. This guidance prohibits racial profiling in law enforcement practices without hindering the important work of our Nation's public safety officials, particularly the intensified anti-terrorism efforts precipitated by the events of September 11, 2001.

* * *

The Constitutional Framework

"[T]he Constitution prohibits selective enforcement of the law based on considerations such as race." Whren v. United States, 517 U.S. 806, 813, 116 S.Ct. 1769, 135 L.Ed.2d 89 (1996). Thus, for example, the decision of federal prosecutors "whether to prosecute may not be based on 'an unjustifiable standard such as race, religion, or other arbitrary classification.' "[4] United States v. Armstrong, 517 U.S. 456, 464, 116 S.Ct. 1480, 134 L.Ed.2d 687 (1996). The same is true of Federal law enforcement officers. Federal courts repeatedly have held that any general policy of "utiliz[ing] impermissible racial classifications in deter-

4. These same principles do not necessarily apply to classifications based on alienage. For example, Congress, in the exercise of its broad powers over immigration, has enacted a number of provisions that apply only to aliens, and enforcement of such provisions properly entails consideration of a person's alien status.

mining whom to stop, detain, and search" would violate the Equal Protection Clause. Chavez v. Illinois State Police, 251 F.3d 612, 635 (7th Cir. 2001). As the Sixth Circuit has explained, "[i]f law enforcement adopts a policy, employs a practice, or in a given situation takes steps to initiate an investigation of a citizen based solely upon that citizen's race, without more, then a violation of the Equal Protection Clause has occurred." United States v. Avery, 137 F.3d 343, 355 (6th Cir. 1997). "A person cannot become the target of a police investigation solely on the basis of skin color. Such selective law enforcement is forbidden." [T]his constitutional prohibition against selective enforcement of the law based on race "draw[s] on 'ordinary equal protection standards.'" Thus, impermissible selective enforcement based on race occurs when the challenged policy has "'a discriminatory effect and ... was motivated by a discriminatory purpose.'"[5] Put simply, "to the extent that race is used as a proxy" for criminality, "a racial stereotype requiring strict scrutiny is in operation."

I. Guidance for Federal Officials Engaged in Law Enforcement Activities

A. Routine or Spontaneous Activities in Domestic Law Enforcement

In making routine or spontaneous law enforcement decisions, such as ordinary traffic stops, Federal law enforcement officers may not use race or ethnicity to any degree, except that officers may rely on race and ethnicity in a specific suspect description. This prohibition applies even where the use of race or ethnicity might otherwise be lawful.

* * *

Example: While parked by the side of the George Washington Parkway, a Park Police Officer notices that nearly all vehicles on the road are exceeding the posted speed limit. Although each such vehicle is committing an infraction that would legally justify a stop, the officer may not use race or ethnicity as a factor in deciding which motorists to pull over. Likewise, the officer may not use race or ethnicity in deciding which detained motorists to ask to consent to a search of their vehicles. Some have argued that overall discrepancies in certain crime rates among racial groups could justify using race as a factor in general traffic enforcement activities and would produce a greater number of arrests for non-traffic offenses (e.g., narcotics trafficking). We emphatically reject this view. * * * Even if there were overall statistical evidence of differential rates of commission of certain offenses among particular races, the affirmative use of such generalized notions by federal law enforcement

---

5. Invidious discrimination is not necessarily present whenever there is a "disproportion" between the racial composition of the pool of persons prosecuted and the general public at large; rather, the focus must be the pool of "similarly situated individuals of a different race [who] were not prosecuted." *Armstrong*, 517 U.S. at 465 (emphasis added). "[R]acial disproportions in the level of prosecutions for a particular crime may be unobjectionable if they merely reflect racial disproportions in the commission of that crime." *Bush v. Vera*, 517 U.S. 952, 968, 116 S.Ct. 1941, 135 L.Ed.2d 248 (1996) (plurality).

officers in routine, spontaneous law enforcement activities is tantamount to stereotyping. It casts a pall of suspicion over every member of certain racial and ethnic groups without regard to the specific circumstances of a particular investigation or crime, and it offends the dignity of the individual improperly targeted. * * * This is the core of "racial profiling" and it must not occur. The situation is different when an officer has specific information, based on trustworthy sources, to "be on the lookout" for specific individuals identified at least in part by race or ethnicity. In such circumstances, the officer is not acting based on a generalized assumption about persons of different races; rather, the officer is helping locate specific individuals previously identified as involved in crime.

Example: While parked by the side of the George Washington Parkway, a Park Police Officer receives an "All Points Bulletin" to be on the look-out for a fleeing bank robbery suspect, a man of a particular race and particular hair color in his 30s driving a blue automobile. The Officer may use this description, including the race of the particular suspect, in deciding which speeding motorists to pull over.

B. *Law Enforcement Activities Related to Specific Investigations*

In conducting activities in connection with a specific investigation, Federal law enforcement officers may consider race and ethnicity only to the extent that there is trustworthy information, relevant to the locality or time frame, that links persons of a particular race or ethnicity to an identified criminal incident, scheme, or organization. This standard applies even where the use of race or ethnicity might otherwise be lawful. As noted above, there are circumstances in which law enforcement activities relating to particular identified criminal incidents, schemes or enterprises may involve consideration of personal identifying characteristics of potential suspects, including age, sex, ethnicity or race. Common sense dictates that when a victim describes the assailant as being of a particular race, authorities may properly limit their search for suspects to persons of that race. Similarly, in conducting an ongoing investigation into a specific criminal organization whose membership has been identified as being overwhelmingly of one ethnicity, law enforcement should not be expected to disregard such facts in pursuing investigative leads into the organization's activities.

Example: In the course of investigating an auto theft in a federal park, law enforcement authorities could not properly choose to target individuals of a particular race as suspects, based on a generalized assumption that those individuals are more likely to commit crimes. This bar extends to the use of race-neutral pretexts as an excuse to target minorities. Federal law enforcement may not use such pretexts. This prohibition extends to the use of other, facially race-neutral factors as a proxy for overtly targeting persons of a certain race or ethnicity. This concern arises most frequently when aggressive law enforcement efforts are focused on "high crime areas." The issue is ultimately one of motivation and evidence; certain seemingly race-based efforts, if properly supported by reliable, empirical data, are in fact race-neutral.

* * *

3. The Information Must be Trustworthy

Where the information concerning potential criminal activity is unreliable or is too generalized and unspecific, use of racial descriptions is prohibited.

Example: ATF special agents receive an uncorroborated anonymous tip that a male of a particular race will purchase an illegal firearm at a Greyhound bus terminal in a racially diverse North Philadelphia neighborhood. Although agents surveilling the location are free to monitor the movements of whomever they choose, the agents are prohibited from using the tip information, without more, to target any males of that race in the bus terminal. Cf. Morgan v. Woessner, 997 F.2d 1244, 1254 (9th Cir. 1993) (finding no reasonable basis for suspicion where tip "made all black men suspect"). The information is neither sufficiently reliable nor sufficiently specific.

II. Guidance for Federal Officials Engaged in Law Enforcement Activities Involving Threats to National Security or the Integrity of the Nation's Borders

In investigating or preventing threats to national security or other catastrophic events (including the performance of duties related to air transportation security), or in enforcing laws protecting the integrity of the Nation's borders, *Federal law enforcement officers may not consider race or ethnicity except to the extent permitted by the Constitution and laws of the United States.* (emphasis supplied)

Since the terrorist attacks on September 11, 2001, the President has emphasized that federal law enforcement personnel must use every legitimate tool to prevent future attacks, protect our Nation's borders, and deter those who would cause devastating harm to our Nation and its people through the use of biological or chemical weapons, other weapons of mass destruction, suicide hijackings, or any other means. "It is 'obvious and unarguable' that no governmental interest is more compelling than the security of the Nation." Haig v. Agee, 453 U.S. 280, 307, 101 S.Ct. 2766, 69 L.Ed.2d 640 (1981).

The Constitution prohibits consideration of race or ethnicity in law enforcement decisions in all but the most exceptional instances. Given the incalculably high stakes involved in such investigations, however, Federal law enforcement officers who are protecting national security or preventing catastrophic events (as well as airport security screeners) may consider race, ethnicity, and other relevant factors to the extent permitted by our laws and the Constitution. Similarly, because enforcement of the laws protecting the Nation's borders may necessarily involve a consideration of a person's alienage in certain circumstances, the use of race or ethnicity in such circumstances is properly governed by existing statutory and constitutional standards. See, e.g., United States v. Brignoni–Ponce, 422 U.S. 873, 886–87, 95 S.Ct. 2574, 45 L.Ed.2d 607 (1975). This policy will honor the rule of law and promote vigorous protection of our national security.

As the Supreme Court has stated, all racial classifications by a governmental actor are subject to the "strictest judicial scrutiny." Adarand Constructors, Inc. v. Peña, 515 U.S. 200, 224–25, 115 S.Ct. 2097, 132 L.Ed.2d 158 (1995). The application of strict scrutiny is of necessity a fact-intensive process. Thus, the legality of particular, race-sensitive actions taken by Federal law enforcement officials in the context of national security and border integrity will depend to a large extent on the circumstances at hand. In absolutely no event, however, may Federal officials assert a national security or border integrity rationale as a mere pretext for invidious discrimination. Indeed, the very purpose of the strict scrutiny test is to "smoke out" illegitimate use of race, and law enforcement strategies not actually premised on bona fide national security or border integrity interests therefore will not stand. In sum, constitutional provisions limiting government action on the basis of race are wide-ranging and provide substantial protections at every step of the investigative and judicial process. Accordingly, and as illustrated below, when addressing matters of national security, border integrity, or the possible catastrophic loss of life, existing legal and constitutional standards are an appropriate guide for Federal law enforcement officers.

Example: The FBI receives reliable information that persons affiliated with a foreign ethnic insurgent group intend to use suicide bombers to assassinate that country's president and his entire entourage during an official visit to the United States. Federal law enforcement may appropriately focus investigative attention on identifying members of that ethnic insurgent group who may be present and active in the United States and who, based on other available information, might conceivably be involved in planning some such attack during the state visit.

Example: U.S. intelligence sources report that terrorists from a particular ethnic group are planning to use commercial jetliners as weapons by hijacking them at an airport in California during the next week. Before allowing men of that ethnic group to board commercial airplanes in California airports during the next week, Transportation Security Administration personnel, and other federal and state authorities, may subject them to heightened scrutiny.

Commentary

The DOJ Guidance concerning racial profiling apparently place greater restrictions on the activities of federal law enforcers than do the Supreme Court's contemporary decisions interpreting the Fourth Amendment. For example, the requirement of particularized suspicion described in the DOJ Guidance for traditional law enforcement activities would seem to preclude the suspicionless seizures and searches permitted in a number of the Court's opinions. Similarly, the DOJ's prohibition of pretextual seizures is more restrictive than the Supreme Court's treatment of this issue in its *Whren* decision—and the importance of this prohibition is emphasized by the repeated references to the strict scrutiny standard applied to government classifications based upon race. Does this mean that the executive branch actually will hold federal law enforcers to a different standard than is imposed by the courts on either federal or state agents? If not, what is the purpose of these guidelines?

2. Seizure of Suspects in Foreign Countries

The following case arises from crimes committed almost a decade before the September 11, 2001, terrorist attacks in the United States. Nonetheless, this decision (which was issued during the final week of the Supreme Court's October 2003, term along with decisions directly involving the detention of individuals seized during the "war on terror," discussed in Section C, *infra*) obviously is relevant to any discussion of the seizure and detention of suspects from foreign territory. The opinion also illustrates the difficulties facing United States courts attempting to apply both domestic and international law to law enforcement activities carried out by the government of the United States in foreign countries.

As you read the following opinion, consider whether it encourages United States officials to seize suspects in foreign countries, even if the seizures violate: (1) international human rights standards and conventions; (2) treaties ratified by the United States; and (3) the laws of the countries where the seizures occur.

SOSA v. ALVAREZ–MACHAIN

Supreme Court of the United States, 2004.
542 U.S. 692, 124 S.Ct. 2739, 159 L.Ed.2d 718.

JUSTICE SOUTER delivered the opinion of the Court.

The two issues are whether respondent Alvarez–Machain's allegation that the Drug Enforcement Administration instigated his abduction from Mexico for criminal trial in the United States supports a claim against the Government under the Federal Tort Claims Act (FTCA or Act), 28 U.S.C. § 1346(b)(1), § § 2671–2680, and whether he may recover under the Alien Tort Statute (ATS), 28 U.S.C. § 1350. We hold that he is not entitled to a remedy under either statute.

I

We have considered the underlying facts before, *United States* v. *Alvarez-Machain,* 504 U.S. 655, 119 L.Ed.2d 441, 112 S.Ct. 2188 (1992). In 1985, an agent of the Drug Enforcement Administration (DEA), Enrique Camarena–Salazar, was captured on assignment in Mexico and taken to a house in Guadalajara, where he was tortured over the course of a 2–day interrogation, then murdered. Based in part on eyewitness testimony, DEA officials in the United States came to believe that respondent Humberto Alvarez–Machain (Alvarez), a Mexican physician, was present at the house and acted to prolong the agent's life in order to extend the interrogation and torture.

In 1990, a federal grand jury indicted Alvarez for the torture and murder of Camarena–Salazar, and the United States District Court for the Central District of California issued a warrant for his arrest. The DEA asked the Mexican Government for help in getting Alvarez into the United States, but when the requests and negotiations proved fruitless, the DEA approved a plan to hire Mexican nationals to seize Alvarez and bring him to the United States for trial. As so planned, a group of Mexicans, including petitioner Jose Francisco Sosa, abducted Alvarez from his house, held him overnight in a motel, and brought him by private plane to El Paso, Texas, where he was arrested by federal officers.

Once in American custody, Alvarez moved to dismiss the indictment on the ground that his seizure was "outrageous governmental conduct," *Alvarez–Machain,* 504 U.S., at 658, 119 L.Ed.2d 441, 112 S.Ct. 2188, and violated the extradition treaty between the United States and Mexico. The District Court agreed, the Ninth Circuit affirmed, and we reversed, holding that the fact of Alvarez's forcible seizure did not affect the jurisdiction of a federal court. The case was tried in 1992, and ended at the close of the Government's case, when the District Court granted Alvarez's motion for a judgment of acquittal.

In 1993, after returning to Mexico, Alvarez began the civil action before us here. He sued Sosa, Mexican citizen and DEA operative Antonio Garate–Bustamante, five unnamed Mexican civilians, the United States, and four DEA agents. So far as it matters here, Alvarez sought damages from the United States under the FTCA, alleging false arrest, and from Sosa under the ATS, for a violation of the law of nations. The former statute authorizes suit "for ... personal injury ... caused by the negligent or wrongful act or omission of any employee of the Government while acting within the scope of his office or employment." 28 U.S.C. § 1346(b)(1). The latter provides in its entirety that "the district courts shall have original jurisdiction of any civil action by an alien for a tort only, committed in violation of the law of nations or a treaty of the United States." § 1350.

The District Court granted the Government's motion to dismiss the FTCA claim, but awarded summary judgment and $25,000 in damages to Alvarez on the ATS claim. A three-judge panel of the Ninth Circuit then affirmed the ATS judgment, but reversed the dismissal of the FTCA claim.

A divided en banc court came to the same conclusion. 331 F.3d at 641. As for the ATS claim, the court called on its own precedent, "that [the ATS] not only provides federal courts with subject matter jurisdiction, but also creates a cause of action for an alleged violation of the law of nations." The Circuit then relied upon what it called the "clear and universally recognized norm prohibiting arbitrary arrest and detention" to support the conclusion that Alvarez's arrest amounted to a tort in violation of international law. On the FTCA claim, the Ninth Circuit held that, because "the DEA had no authority to effect Alvarez's arrest and detention in Mexico," the United States was liable to him under California law for the tort of false arrest.

We granted certiorari in these companion cases to clarify the scope of both the FTCA and the ATS. We now reverse in each.

II

The Government seeks reversal of the judgment of liability under the FTCA on two principal grounds. It argues that the arrest could not have been tortious, because it was authorized by 21 U.S.C. § 878, setting out the arrest authority of the DEA, and it says that in any event the liability asserted here falls within the FTCA exception to waiver of sovereign immunity for claims "arising in a foreign country," 28 U.S.C. § 2680(k). We think the exception applies and decide on that ground.

A

The FTCA "was designed primarily to remove the sovereign immunity of the United States from suits in tort and, with certain specific exceptions, to render the Government liable in tort as a private individual would be under like circumstances." The Act accordingly gives federal district courts jurisdiction over claims against the United States for injury "caused by the negligent or wrongful act or omission of any employee of the Government while acting within the scope of his office or employment, under circumstances where the United States, if a private person, would be liable to the claimant in accordance with the law of the place where the act or omission occurred." But the Act also limits its waiver of sovereign immunity in a number of ways.

Here the significant limitation on the waiver of immunity is the Act's exception for "any claim arising in a foreign country," § 2680(k), a provision that on its face seems plainly applicable to the facts of this case. In the Ninth Circuit's view, once Alvarez was within the borders of the United States, his detention was not tortious; the appellate court suggested that the Government's liability to Alvarez rested solely upon a false arrest claim. Alvarez's arrest, however, was said to be "false," and thus tortious, only because, and only to the extent that, it took place and endured in Mexico. The actions in Mexico are thus most naturally understood as the kernel of a "claim arising in a foreign country," and barred from suit under the exception to the waiver of immunity.

Notwithstanding the straightforward language of the foreign country exception, the Ninth Circuit allowed the action to proceed under what has come to be known as the "headquarters doctrine." Some Courts of Appeals, reasoning that "the entire scheme of the FTCA focuses on the place where the negligent or wrongful act or omission of the government employee occurred," have concluded that the foreign country exception does not exempt the United States from suit "for acts or omissions occurring here which have their operative effect in another country." Headquarters claims "typically involve allegations of negligent guidance in an office within the United States of employees who cause damage while in a foreign country, or of activities which take place within a foreign country." In such instances, these courts have concluded that § 2680(k) does not bar suit.

The reasoning of the Ninth Circuit here was that, since Alvarez's abduction in Mexico was the direct result of wrongful acts of planning and direction by DEA agents located in California, "Alvarez's abduction fits the headquarters doctrine like a glove."

* * *

The potential effect of this sort of headquarters analysis flashes the yellow caution light. "It will virtually always be possible to assert that the negligent activity that injured the plaintiff [abroad] was the consequence of faulty training, selection or supervision—or even less than that, lack of careful training, selection or supervision—in the United States." * * * The headquarters doctrine threatens to swallow the foreign country exception whole, certainly at the pleadings stage.

* * *

C

[T]here is good reason to think that Congress understood a claim "arising in" a foreign country in such a way as to bar application of the headquarters doctrine. There is good reason, that is, to conclude that Congress understood a claim "arising in a foreign country" to be a claim for injury or harm occurring in a foreign country. * * *

* * *

The application of foreign substantive law [was] what Congress intended to avoid by the foreign country exception. * * *

* * *

* * * We therefore hold that the FTCA's foreign country exception bars all claims based on any injury suffered in a foreign country, regardless of where the tortious act or omission occurred.

III

Alvarez has also brought an action under the ATS against petitioner, Sosa, who argues (as does the United States supporting him) that there is no relief under the ATS because the statute does no more than vest federal courts with jurisdiction, neither creating nor authorizing the courts to recognize any particular right of action without further congressional action. Although we agree the statute is in terms only jurisdictional, we think that at the time of enactment the jurisdiction enabled federal courts to hear claims in a very limited category defined by the law of nations and recognized at common law. We do not believe, however, that the limited, implicit sanction to entertain the handful of international law *cum* common law claims understood in 1789 should be taken as authority to recognize the right of action asserted by Alvarez here.

A

Judge Friendly called the ATS a "legal Lohengrin," *IIT* v. *Vencap, Ltd.,* 519 F.2d 1001, 1015 (CA2 1975); "no one seems to know whence it came," and for over 170 years after its enactment it provided jurisdiction in only one case. The first Congress passed it as part of the Judiciary Act of 1789, in providing that the new federal district courts "shall also have cognizance, concurrent with the courts of the several States, or the circuit courts, as the case may be, of all causes where an alien sues for a tort only in violation of the law of nations or a treaty of the United States." Act of Sept. 24, 1789, ch. 20, § 9*(b),* 1 Stat. 79.

The parties and *amici* here advance radically different historical interpretations of this terse provision. Alvarez says that the ATS was intended not simply as a jurisdictional grant, but as authority for the creation of a new cause of action for torts in violation of international law. We think that reading is implausible. [W]e think the statute was intended as jurisdictional in the sense of addressing the power of the courts to entertain cases concerned with a certain subject.

But holding the ATS jurisdictional raises a new question, this one about the interaction between the ATS at the time of its enactment and the ambient law of the era. Sosa would have it that the ATS was stillborn because there could be no claim for relief without a further statute expressly authorizing adoption of causes of action. *Amici* professors of federal jurisdiction and legal history take a different tack, that federal courts could entertain claims once the jurisdictional grant was on the books, because torts in violation of the law of nations would have been recognized within the common law of the time. We think history and practice give the edge to this latter position.

1

"When the *United States* declared their independence, they were bound to receive the law of nations, in its modern state of purity and refinement." *Ware* v. *Hylton,* 3 Dall. 199, 281, 3 U.S. 199, 1 L.Ed. 568 (1796) (Wilson, J.). In the years of the early Republic, this law of nations comprised two principal elements, the first covering the general norms governing the behavior of national states with each other: *"the science which teaches the rights subsisting between nations or states, and the obligations correspondent to those rights,"* or "that code of public instruction which defines the rights and prescribes the duties of nations, in their intercourse with each other," This aspect of the law of nations thus occupied the executive and legislative domains, not the judicial.

The law of nations included a second, more pedestrian element, however, that did fall within the judicial sphere, as a body of judge-made law regulating the conduct of individuals situated outside domestic boundaries and consequently carrying an international savor. To Blackstone, the law of nations in this sense was implicated "in mercantile questions, such as bills of exchange and the like; in all marine causes, relating to freight, average, demurrage, insurances, bottomry ... ; [and] in all disputes relating to prizes, to shipwrecks, to hostages, and ransom bills." The law merchant emerged from the customary practices of international traders and admiralty required its own transnational regulation. And it was the law of nations in this sense that our precursors spoke about when the Court explained the status of coast fishing vessels in wartime grew from "ancient usage among civilized nations, beginning centuries ago, and gradually ripening into a rule of international law.... " *The Paquete Habana,* 175 U.S. 677, 686, 44 L.Ed. 320, 20 S.Ct. 290 (1900).

There was, finally, a sphere in which these rules binding individuals for the benefit of other individuals overlapped with the norms of state relationships. Blackstone referred to it when he mentioned three specific offenses against the law of nations addressed by the criminal law of England: violation of safe conducts, infringement of the rights of ambassadors, and piracy. An assault against an ambassador, for example, impinged upon the sovereignty of the foreign nation and if not adequately redressed could rise to an issue of war. It was this narrow set of violations of the law of nations, admitting of a judicial remedy and at the same time threatening serious consequences in international affairs, that was probably on minds of the men who drafted the ATS with its reference to tort.

* * *

IV

We think it is correct, then, to assume that the First Congress understood that the district courts would recognize private causes of action for certain torts in violation of the law of nations, though we have found no basis to suspect Congress had any examples in mind beyond those torts corresponding to Blackstone's three primary offenses: violation of safe conducts, infringement of the rights of ambassadors, and piracy. We assume, too, that no development in the two centuries from the enactment of § 1350 to the birth of the modern line of cases beginning with *Filartiga* v. *Pena–Irala,* 630 F.2d 876 (CA2 1980), has categorically precluded federal courts from recognizing a claim under the law of nations as an element of common law; Congress has not in any relevant way amended § 1350 or limited civil common law power by another statute. Still, there are good reasons for a restrained conception of the discretion a federal court should exercise in considering a new cause of action of this kind. Accordingly, we think courts should require any claim based on the present-day law of nations to rest on a norm of international character accepted by the civilized world and defined with a specificity comparable to the features of the 18th-century paradigms we have recognized. This requirement is fatal to Alvarez's claim.

* * *

C

* * *

Thus, Alvarez's detention claim must be gauged against the current state of international law, looking to those sources we have long, albeit cautiously, recognized.

> "[W]here there is no treaty, and no controlling executive or legislative act or judicial decision, resort must be had to the customs and usages of civilized nations; and, as evidence of these, to the works of jurists and commentators, who by years of labor, research and experience, have made themselves peculiarly well acquainted with the subjects of which they treat. Such works are resorted to by judicial tribunals, not for the speculations of their authors concerning what the law ought to be, but for trustworthy evidence of what the law really is." *The Paquete Habana,* 175 U.S., at 700, 44 L.Ed. 320, 20 S.Ct. 290.

To begin with, Alvarez cites two well-known international agreements that, despite their moral authority, have little utility under the standard set out in this opinion. He says that his abduction by Sosa was an "arbitrary arrest" within the meaning of the Universal Declaration of Human Rights (Declaration), G. A. Res. 217A (III), U. N. Doc. A/810 (1948). And he traces the rule against arbitrary arrest not only to the Declaration, but also to article nine of the International Covenant on Civil and Political Rights (Covenant), Dec. 19, 1996, 999 U. N. T. S. 171, to which the United States is a party, and to various other conventions to which it is not. But the Declaration does not of its own force impose obligations as a matter of international law. And, although the Covenant does bind the United States as a matter of international law, the United States ratified the Covenant on the express understanding that it was not self-executing and so did not itself create obligations enforceable in the federal courts. Accordingly, Alvarez cannot say that the Declaration and Covenant themselves establish the relevant and applicable rule of international law. He instead attempts to show that prohibition of arbitrary arrest has attained the status of binding customary international law.

Here, it is useful to examine Alvarez's complaint in greater detail. As he presently argues it, the claim does not rest on the cross-border feature of his abduction. [The] position that Alvarez takes now [is] that his arrest was arbitrary and as such forbidden by international law not because it infringed the prerogatives of Mexico, but because no applicable law authorized it.

Alvarez thus invokes a general prohibition of "arbitrary" detention defined as officially sanctioned action exceeding positive authorization to detain under the domestic law of some government, regardless of the circumstances. Whether or not this is an accurate reading of the Covenant, Alvarez cites little authority that a rule so broad has the status of a binding customary norm today. He certainly cites nothing to justify the federal courts in taking his broad rule as the predicate for a federal lawsuit, for its implications would be breathtaking. His rule would support a cause of action in federal court for any arrest, anywhere in the world, unauthorized by the law of the jurisdiction in which it took place, and would create a cause of action for any seizure of an alien in violation of the Fourth Amendment, supplanting the actions under Rev. Stat. § 1979, 42 U.S.C. § 1983 and *Bivens* v. *Six Unknown Fed. Narcotics Agents,* 403 U.S. 388, 29 L.Ed.2d 619, 91 S.Ct. 1999 (1971), that now provide damages remedies for such violations. It would create an action in federal court for arrests by state officers who simply exceed their authority; and for the violation of any limit that the law of any country might place on the authority of its own officers to arrest. And all of this assumes that Alvarez could establish that Sosa was acting on behalf of a government when he made the arrest, for otherwise he would need a rule broader still.

* * *

Whatever may be said for the broad principle Alvarez advances, in the present, imperfect world, it expresses an aspiration that exceeds any binding customary rule having the specificity we require. Creating a private cause of action to further that aspiration would go beyond any residual common law discretion we think it appropriate to exercise. It is enough to hold that a single illegal detention of less than a day, followed by the transfer of custody to lawful authorities and a prompt arraignment, violates no norm of customary international law so well defined as to support the creation of a federal remedy. The judgment of the Court of Appeals is *Reversed.*

[The opinions concurring in part and concurring in the judgment of JUSTICE SCALIA, with whom THE CHIEF JUSTICE and JUSTICE THOMAS joined, and of JUSTICE GINSBURG, with whom JUSTICE BREYER joined, and of JUSTICE BREYER, are omitted.]

B.　INTERROGATION AND TORTURE

Commentary

1.　*The Bybee Memorandum.* The threat of future terrorist attacks and reports that people captured during the military invasions of Afghanistan and Iraq were tortured by United States military personnel have triggered debates about the use of torture to interrogate captives suspected of being terrorists or enemy combatants. Under international law, torture is treated as a particularly abhorrent violation of human rights. Not surprisingly, torture is expressly prohibited by the fundamental human rights documents.[a]

The idea that governments can employ torture seems to defy the very essence of the concept of the rule of law. Yet in the wake of the September 11, 2001, terrorist murders in this country, some people have argued that torture is an acceptable technique to be used in the "war on terror."[b]

One frequently discussed scenario posits that a terrorist group is prepared to detonate a nuclear bomb in a crowded city, where the explosion will cause thousands, perhaps millions, of casualties. Authorities capture a man they suspect is a member of the terrorist group. Use of conventional interrogation techniques fails to produce a quick confession, which investigators believe is necessary because they fear the bombing is imminent. Some have argued that such a threatened emergency would justify torturing the suspect to obtain the information needed to stop the murders?[c] Does a threat of this magnitude justify torturing a suspect to gain information? If so, would torture also be permitted to save a single life from a non-terrorist crime.

The debate about the possible use of torture to fight terrorism has been fueled by two developments. The first is the fact that some members of the United States military have committed acts of torture upon prisoners captured during the post-September 11 military campaigns in the Middle East.[d] This has been confirmed by official inquiries[e] and by prosecutions which have produced guilty pleas and convictions.[f] Some of those charged with abusing prisoners have claimed that they were acting according to official policy,[g] although government officials have denied those allegations.

The Bybee Memorandum. The second development is epitomized by a memorandum, dated August 1, 2002, that was prepared for Alberto R. Gonzales, Counsel to the President (Gonzalez was subsequently appointed by President Bush to serve as Attorney General of the United States). The

a. The key documents include the Covenant on Civil and Political Rights, Dec. 16, 1966, art. 7, 999 U.N.T.S. 171, 175. The more recent Convention Against Torture and Other Cruel, Inhuman or Degrading Treatment or Punishment, Dec. 10, 1984, 1465 (1988), U.N.T.S. 85, which has been ratified by more than 120 nations, expressly prohibits torture.

b. For example, a prominent judge and legal scholar concluded that "if the stakes are high enough, torture is permissible." *See*, Richard A. Posner, *The Best Offense*, NEW REPUBLIC, Sept. 2, 2002, at 30.

c. *See* ALAN M. DERSHOWITZ, WHY TERRORISM WORKS: UNDERSTANDING THE THREAT, RESPONDING TO THE CHALLENGE 132–140, 159–161 (2002) (discussing a similar hypothetical scenario). Dershowitz proposes a chilling twist on the notion of the rule of law, by proffering the idea that torture could be authorized by a "torture warrant" issued by a judge.

d. *See, e.g.,* Douglas Jehl and David Johnston, *Within C.I.A., Growing Worry of Prosecution for Conduct*, N. Y. TIMES, February 27, 2005, A01.

e. *See, e.g., General: Some Abu Ghraib Abuse was Torture; Latest Report Finds Ties to Military Intelligence Personnel*, CNN.COM, Aug. 26, 2004, *available at* http://www.cnn.com/2004/US/08/25/abughraib.report/index.html; John H. Cushman, Jr., *Outside Panel Faults Leaders of Pentagon for Prisoner Abuse*, N. Y. TIMES, Aug. 24, 2004, *available at* http://www.ny-times.com/2004/08/24/politics/24CND–ABUS.html?hp

f. T.R. Reid, *Guard Convicted In the First Trial From Abu Ghraib: Graner Faces 15 Years for Abusing Iraqis*, THE WASHINGTON POST, January 15, 2005, A01.

g. *See, e.g., Iraq Abuse "Before MPs Arrived"*, CNN.COM, Aug. 24, 2004, *at* http://www.cnn.com/2004/WORLD/europe/08/24/abughraib.germany/index.html.

"Bybee Memorandum" was produced by the Office of Legal Counsel in the Department of Justice (and was commonly referred to by the name of its signatory, then Assistant Attorney General Jay S. Bybee, who was later appointed by President Bust to the Ninth Circuit Court of Appeals).

As you read the following excerpts from the Bybee Memorandum, consider whether its critics were correct in claiming that it authorizes the use of both physical and mental abuse. Would conduct that the Bybee Memorandum defines as *not* being torture nonetheless violate interrogation standards adopted under the Fifth and Fourteenth Amendments for traditional domestic law enforcement interrogations? Does the memorandum implicitly authorize the use of many forms of physical and mental abuse? Indeed, does it attempt to exempt even those who commit the most extreme forms of torture in support of the "war on terror" from criminal prosecution under the anti-torture statute?

Office of the Assistant Attorney General
August 1, 2002

Memorandum for Alberto R. Gonzales
Counsel to the President

Re: Standards of Conduct for Interrogation
under 18 U.S.C. §§ 2340–2340A

You have asked for our Office's views regarding the standards of conduct under the Convention Against Torture and Other Cruel, Inhuman and Degrading Treatment or Punishment as implemented by Sections 2340–2340A of title 18 of the United States Code. As we understand it, this question has arisen in the context of the conduct of interrogations outside of the United States. We conclude below that Section 2340A proscribes acts inflicting, and that are specifically intended to inflict, severe pain or suffering, whether mental or physical. Those acts must be of an extreme nature to rise to the level of torture within the meaning of Section 2340A and the Convention. We further conclude that certain acts may be cruel, inhuman, or degrading, but still not produce pain and suffering of the requisite intensity to fall within Section 2340A's proscription against torture. We conclude by examining possible defenses that would negate any claim that certain interrogation methods violate the statute.

* * * We conclude that for an act to constitute torture as defined in Section 2340A, it must inflict pain that is difficult to endure. Physical pain amounting to torture must be equivalent in intensity to the pain accompanying serious physical injury, such as organ failure, impairment of bodily function, or even death. For purely mental pain or suffering to amount to torture under Section 2340, it must result in significant psychological harm of significant duration, e.g., lasting for months or even years. We conclude that the mental harm also must result from one of the predicate acts listed in the statute, namely: threats of imminent death; threats of infliction of the kind of pain that would amount to physical torture; * * *. We conclude that the statute, taken as a whole, makes plain that it prohibits only extreme acts.

* * * We conclude that the treaty's text prohibits only the most extreme acts by reserving criminal penalties solely for torture and declining to require such penalties for "cruel, inhuman, or degrading treatment or punishment." This confirms our view that the criminal statute penalizes only the most egregious conduct. * * *

* * *

* * * We find that in the circumstances of the current war against al Qaeda and its allies, prosecution under Section 2340A may be barred because enforcement of the statute would represent an unconstitutional infringement of the President's authority to conduct war. * * * We [also] conclude that, under the current circumstances, necessity or self-defense may justify interrogation methods that might violate Section 2340A.

* * *

To violate Section 2340A, the statute requires that severe pain and suffering must be inflicted with specific intent. * * *

Here, because section 2340 requires that a defendant act with the specific intent to inflict severe pain, the infliction of such pain must be the defendant's precise objective. * * *

* * *

As a theoretical matter, therefore, knowledge alone that a particular result is certain to occur does not constitute specific intent. * * * Thus, even if the defendant knows that severe pain will result from his actions, if causing such harm is not his objective, he lacks the requisite specific intent even though the defendant did not act in good faith. Instead, a defendant is guilty of torture only if he acts with the express purpose of inflicting severe pain or suffering on a person within his custody or physical control. * * *

2. *Repudiation of the Bybee Memorandum.* By 2004, the press had reported both the torture of prisoners at the Abu Gharib prison in Iraq and elsewhere, as well as the contents of the Bybee Memorandum. The Bybee Memorandum was criticized widely in the press, by politicians, and by many members of the public. On December 30, 2004, the Office of Legal Counsel in the Department of Justice issued a new memorandum that repudiated much of the analysis it had previously adopted in the Bybee Memorandum. Compare the following passages, which address: (1) the definition of the harm that constitutes torture; (2) the mens rea of the torturer; and (3) potential liability of United States agents for acts alleged to be torture.

Office of the Assistant Attorney General
December 30, 2004

Memorandum for James B. Comey
Deputy Attorney General

Re: Standards of Conduct for Interrogation
under 18 U.S.C. §§ 2340–2340A

Torture is abhorrent both to American law and values and to international norms. This universal repudiation of torture is reflected in our criminal law, for example, 18 U.S.C. § § 2340–2340A; international agreements, exemplified by the United Nations Convention Against Torture (the "CAT"); customary international law; centuries of Anglo–American law; and the longstanding policy of the United States, repeatedly and recently reaffirmed by the President.

This Office interpreted the federal criminal prohibition against torture—codified at 18 U.S.C. § § 2340–234A—in [the August 1, 2002 Memorandum/Bybee Memorandum] and various defenses that might be asserted to avoid potential liability * * *.

Questions have since been raised, both by this Office and by others, about the * * * August 2002 Memorandum, * * * in particular the statement that "severe" pain under the statute was limited to pain "equivalent in intensity to the pain accompanying serious physical injury, such as organ failure, impairment of bodily function, or even death." We decided to withdraw the August 2002 Memorandum * * *.

This memorandum supersedes the August 2002 Memorandum in its entirety. * * *

We have also modified in some important respects our analysis of the legal standards applicable under 18 U.S.C. § 2340–2340A. For example, we disagree with statements in the August 2002 Memorandum limiting "severe" pain under the statute to "excruciating and agonizing" pain, or to pain "equivalent in intensity to the pain accompanying serious physical injury, such as organ, failure, impairment of bodily function, or even death. * * * "

* * *

Although Congress defined "torture" under sections 2340–2340A to require conduct specifically intended to cause "severe" pain or suffering, we do not believe Congress intended to reach only conduct involving "excruciating and agonizing" pain or suffering.

* * *

It is well recognized that the term "specific intent" is ambiguous and that the courts do not use it consistently. "Specific intent" is most commonly understood, however, "to designate a special mental element which is required above and beyond any mental state required with respect to the *actus reus* of the crime. * * *

* * *

We do not believe it is useful to try to define the precise meaning of "specific intent" in § 2340. In light of the President's directive that the United States not engage in torture, it would not be appropriate to rely on parsing the specific intent element of the statute to approve as lawful conduct that might otherwise amount to torture. [But it] is clear that the specific intent element of section 2340 would be met if a defendant performed an act and "consciously desire[d]" that act to inflict severe physical or mental pain or suffering. Conversely, if an individual acted in good faith, and only after reasonable investigation establishing that his conduct would not inflict severe physical or mental pain or suffering, it appears unlikely that he would have the specific intent necessary to violate sections §§ 2340–2340A. * * *

C. PRETRIAL DETENTION, DUE PROCESS, AND THE SCOPE OF JUDICIAL REVIEW

Commentary

On the day before the Supreme Court issued its decision in *Sosa v. Alvarez–Machain* (discussed in Section B, *supra*), the Court announced its decisions in the following two cases. The first case involved the detention of a United States citizen who was seized during the invasion of Afghanistan, and eventually held in custody in the United States. The second case involved the detention of foreign nationals also seized in Afghanistan, and held in custody at the Guantanamo Bay Naval Base in Cuba. In both cases, the detainees had been held in custody for long periods of time without receiving normal due process rights. As you read these cases, consider whether the Court was correct in its analysis of the nature of the respective rights of citizens and non-citizens held in custody. Also compare the Court's analysis of the government's power to detain Hamdi, a United States citizen, with the rules governing pretrial detention in criminal cases discussed in Chapter 9.

HAMDI v. RUMSFELD

Supreme Court of the United States, 2004.
542 U.S. 507, 124 S.Ct. 2633, 159 L.Ed.2d 578.

JUSTICE O'CONNOR announced the judgment of the Court and delivered an opinion, in which THE CHIEF JUSTICE, JUSTICE KENNEDY, and JUSTICE BREYER join.

At this difficult time in our Nation's history, we are called upon to consider the legality of the Government's detention of a United States citizen on United States soil as an "enemy combatant" and to address the process that is constitutionally owed to one who seeks to challenge his classification as such. The United States Court of Appeals for the Fourth Circuit held that petitioner's detention was legally authorized and that he was entitled to no further opportunity to challenge his enemy-combatant label. We now vacate and remand. We hold that although Congress authorized the detention of combatants in the narrow circumstances alleged here, due process demands that a citizen held in the United States as an enemy combatant be given a meaningful opportunity to contest the factual basis for that detention before a neutral decisionmaker.

I

On September 11, 2001, the al Qaeda terrorist network used hijacked commercial airliners to attack prominent targets in the United

States. Approximately 3,000 people were killed in those attacks. One week later, in response to these "acts of treacherous violence," Congress passed a resolution authorizing the President to "use all necessary and appropriate force against those nations, organizations, or persons he determines planned, authorized, committed, or aided the terrorist attacks" or "harbored such organizations or persons, in order to prevent any future acts of international terrorism against the United States by such nations, organizations or persons." Authorization for Use of Military Force ("the AUMF"), 115 Stat. 224. Soon thereafter, the President ordered United States Armed Forces to Afghanistan, with a mission to subdue al Qaeda and quell the Taliban regime that was known to support it.

This case arises out of the detention of a man whom the Government alleges took up arms with the Taliban during this conflict. His name is Yaser Esam Hamdi. Born an American citizen in Louisiana in 1980, Hamdi moved with his family to Saudi Arabia as a child. By 2001, the parties agree, he resided in Afghanistan. At some point that year, he was seized by members of the Northern Alliance, a coalition of military groups opposed to the Taliban government, and eventually was turned over to the United States military. The Government asserts that it initially detained and interrogated Hamdi in Afghanistan before transferring him to the United States Naval Base in Guantanamo Bay in January 2002. In April 2002, upon learning that Hamdi is an American citizen, authorities transferred him to a naval brig in Norfolk, Virginia, where he remained until a recent transfer to a brig in Charleston, South Carolina. The Government contends that Hamdi is an "enemy combatant," and that this status justifies holding him in the United States indefinitely—without formal charges or proceedings—unless and until it makes the determination that access to counsel or further process is warranted.

In June 2002, Hamdi's father, Esam Fouad Hamdi, filed the present petition for a writ of habeas corpus under 28 U.S.C. § 2241 in the Eastern District of Virginia, naming as petitioners his son and himself as next friend. The elder Hamdi alleges in the petition that he has had no contact with his son since the Government took custody of him in 2001, and that the Government has held his son "without access to legal counsel or notice of any charges pending against him." The petition contends that Hamdi's detention was not legally authorized. It argues that, "as an American citizen, ... Hamdi enjoys the full protections of the Constitution," and that Hamdi's detention in the United States without charges, access to an impartial tribunal, or assistance of counsel "violated and continues to violate the Fifth and Fourteenth Amendments to the United States Constitution." The habeas petition asks that the court, among other things, (1) appoint counsel for Hamdi; * * * (4) "to the extent Respondents contest any material factual allegations in this Petition, schedule an evidentiary hearing, at which Petitioners may adduce proof in support of their allegations"; and (5) order that Hamdi be released from his "unlawful custody." * * * Hamdi's father has asserted in documents found elsewhere in the record that his son went to Afghanistan to do "relief work," and that he had been in that country less than two months before September 11, 2001, and could not have received military training. The 20–year-old was traveling on his own for the first time, his father says, and "because of his lack of experience, he was trapped in Afghanistan once that military campaign began."

[The District Court ordered that counsel be given access to Hamdi. The United States Court of Appeals for the Fourth Circuit reversed, holding that the District Court had failed to extend appropriate deference to the Government's security and intelligence interests, and remanded for further proceedings.]

On remand, the Government filed a response and a motion to dismiss the petition. It attached to its response a declaration from one Michael Mobbs (hereinafter "Mobbs Declaration"), who identified himself as Special Advisor to the Under Secretary of Defense for Policy. Mobbs indicated that in this position, he has been "substantially involved with matters related to the detention of enemy combatants in the current war against the al Qaeda terrorists and those who support and harbor them (including the Taliban)." He expressed his "familiarity" with Department of Defense and United States military policies and procedures applicable to the detention, control, and transfer of al Qaeda and Taliban personnel, and declared that "based upon my review of relevant records and reports, I am also familiar with the facts and circumstances related to the capture of ... Hamdi and his detention by U.S. military forces."

Mobbs then set forth what remains the sole evidentiary support that the Government has provided to the courts for Hamdi's detention. The declaration states that Hamdi "traveled to Afghanistan" in July or August 2001, and that he thereafter "affiliated with a Taliban military unit and received weapons training." It asserts that Hamdi "remained with his Taliban unit following the attacks of September 11" and that, during the time when Northern Alliance forces were "engaged in battle with the Taliban," "Hamdi's Taliban unit surrendered" to those forces, after which he "surrendered his Kalishnikov assault rifle" to them. The Mobbs Declaration also states that, because al Qaeda and the Taliban "were and are hostile forces engaged in armed conflict with the armed forces of the United States," "individuals associated with" those groups "were and continue to be enemy combatants." Mobbs states that Hamdi was labeled an enemy combatant "based upon his interviews and in light of his association with the Taliban." According to the declaration, a series of "U.S. military screening teams" determined that Hamdi met "the criteria for enemy combatants," and "a subsequent interview of Hamdi has confirmed that he surrendered and gave his firearm to Northern Alliance forces, which supports his classification as an enemy combatant."

[The District Court found that the Mobbs Declaration fell "far short" of supporting Hamdi's detention, and criticized the affidavit as being generic and hearsay in nature and "little more than the government's 'say-so.'" The Fourth Circuit reversed the District Court.]

II

The threshold question before us is whether the Executive has the authority to detain citizens who qualify as "enemy combatants."

[F]or purposes of this case, the "enemy combatant" that [the government] is seeking to detain is an individual who, it alleges, was "'part of or supporting forces hostile to the United States or coalition partners'" in Afghanistan and who "'engaged in an armed conflict against the United States'" there. We therefore answer only the narrow question before us: whether the detention of citizens falling within that definition is authorized.

The Government maintains that no explicit congressional authorization is required, because the Executive possesses plenary authority to detain pursuant to Article II of the Constitution. We do not reach the question whether Article II provides such authority, however, because we agree with the Government's alternative position, that Congress has in fact authorized Hamdi's detention, through the AUMF.

* * *

The AUMF authorizes the President to use "all necessary and appropriate force" against "nations, organizations, or persons" associated with the September 11, 2001, terrorist attacks. There can be no doubt that individuals who fought against the United States in Afghanistan as part of the Taliban, an organization known to have supported the al Qaeda terrorist network responsible for those attacks, are individuals Congress sought to target in passing the AUMF. We conclude that detention of individuals falling into the limited category we are considering, for the duration of the particular conflict in which they were captured, is so fundamental and accepted an incident to war as to be an exercise of the "necessary and appropriate force" Congress has authorized the President to use.

* * *

In light of these principles, it is of no moment that the AUMF does not use specific language of detention. Because detention to prevent a combatant's return to the battlefield is a fundamental incident of waging war, in permitting the use of "necessary and appropriate force," Congress has clearly and unmistakably authorized detention in the narrow circumstances considered here.

Hamdi objects, nevertheless, that Congress has not authorized the *indefinite* detention to which he is now subject. The Government responds that "the detention of enemy combatants during World War II was just as 'indefinite' while that war was being fought." We take Hamdi's objection to be not to the lack of certainty regarding the date on which the conflict will end, but to the substantial prospect of perpetual detention. We recognize that the national security underpinnings of the "war on terror," although crucially important, are broad and malleable. As the Government concedes, "given its unconventional nature, the current conflict is unlikely to end with a formal cease-fire agreement." The prospect Hamdi raises is therefore not far-fetched. If the Government does not consider this unconventional war won for two generations, and if it maintains during that time that Hamdi might, if released, rejoin forces fighting against the United States, then the position it has taken throughout the litigation of this case suggests that Hamdi's detention could last for the rest of his life.

* * *

    * * * Active combat operations against Taliban fighters apparently are ongoing in Afghanistan. The United States may detain, for the duration of these hostilities, individuals legitimately determined to be Taliban combatants who "engaged in an armed conflict against the United States." If the record establishes that United States troops are still involved in active combat in Afghanistan, those detentions are part of the exercise of "necessary and appropriate force," and therefore are authorized by the AUMF.

* * *

III

    Even in cases in which the detention of enemy combatants is legally authorized, there remains the question of what process is constitutionally due to a citizen who disputes his enemy-combatant status. Hamdi argues that he is owed a meaningful and timely hearing and that "extrajudicial detention [that] begins and ends with the submission of an affidavit based on third-hand hearsay" does not comport with the Fifth and Fourteenth Amendments. The Government counters that any more process than was provided below would be both unworkable and "constitutionally intolerable." Our resolution of this dispute requires a careful examination both of the writ of habeas corpus, which Hamdi now seeks to employ as a mechanism of judicial review, and of the Due Process Clause, which informs the procedural contours of that mechanism in this instance.

A

    Though they reach radically different conclusions on the process that ought to attend the present proceeding, the parties begin on common ground. All agree that, absent suspension, the writ of habeas corpus remains available to every individual detained within the United States. U.S. Const., Art. I, § 9, cl. 2 ("The Privilege of the Writ of Habeas Corpus shall not be suspended, unless when in Cases of Rebellion or Invasion the public Safety may require it"). Only in the rarest of circumstances has Congress seen fit to suspend the writ. See, *e.g.*, Act of Mar. 3, 1863, ch. 81, § 1, 12 Stat. 755; Act of April 20, 1871, ch. 22, § 4, 17 Stat. 14. At all other times, it has remained a critical check on the Executive, ensuring that it does not detain individuals except in accordance with law. All agree suspension of the writ has not occurred here. Thus, it is undisputed that Hamdi was properly before an Article III court to challenge his detention under 28 U.S.C. § 2241. Further, all agree that § 2241 and its companion provisions provide at least a skeletal outline of the procedures to be afforded a petitioner in federal habeas review. Most notably, § 2243 provides that "the person detained may, under oath, deny any of the facts set forth in the return or allege any other material facts," and § 2246 allows the taking of evidence in habeas proceedings by deposition, affidavit, or interrogatories.

The simple outline of § 2241 makes clear both that Congress envisioned that habeas petitioners would have some opportunity to present and rebut facts and that courts in cases like this retain some ability to vary the ways in which they do so as mandated by due process. The Government recognizes the basic procedural protections required by the habeas statute, but asks us to hold that, given both the flexibility of the habeas mechanism and the circumstances presented in this case, the presentation of the Mobbs Declaration to the habeas court completed the required factual development. It suggests two separate reasons for its position that no further process is due.

B

First, the Government urges the adoption of the Fourth Circuit's holding below—that because it is "undisputed" that Hamdi's seizure took place in a combat zone, the habeas determination can be made purely as a matter of law, with no further hearing or factfinding necessary. This argument is easily rejected. As the dissenters from the denial of rehearing en banc noted, the circumstances surrounding Hamdi's seizure cannot in any way be characterized as "undisputed," as "those circumstances are neither conceded in fact, nor susceptible to concession in law, because Hamdi has not been permitted to speak for himself or even through counsel as to those circumstances." Further, the "facts" that constitute the alleged concession are insufficient to support Hamdi's detention. Under the definition of enemy combatant that we accept today as falling within the scope of Congress' authorization, Hamdi would need to be "part of or supporting forces hostile to the United States or coalition partners" and "engaged in an armed conflict against the United States" to justify his detention in the United States for the duration of the relevant conflict. The habeas petition states only that "when seized by the United States Government, Mr. Hamdi resided in Afghanistan." An assertion that one *resided* in a country in which combat operations are taking place is not a concession that one was "*captured* in a zone of active combat operations in a foreign theater of war," (emphasis added), and certainly is not a concession that one was "part of or supporting forces hostile to the United States or coalition partners" and "engaged in an armed conflict against the United States." Accordingly, we reject any argument that Hamdi has made concessions that eliminate any right to further process.

C

The Government's second argument requires closer consideration. This is the argument that further factual exploration is unwarranted and inappropriate in light of the extraordinary constitutional interests at stake. Under the Government's most extreme rendition of this argument, "respect for separation of powers and the limited institutional capabilities of courts in matters of military decision-making in connection with an ongoing conflict" ought to eliminate entirely any individual process, restricting the courts to investigating only whether legal authorization exists for the broader detention scheme. At most, the Government argues, courts should review its determination that a citizen is an enemy combatant under a very deferential "some evidence" standard. Under this review, a court would assume the accuracy of the Government's articulated basis for Hamdi's detention, as set forth in the Mobbs Declaration, and assess only whether that articulated basis was a legitimate one.

In response, Hamdi emphasizes that this Court consistently has recognized that an individual challenging his detention may not be held at the will of the Executive without recourse to some proceeding before a neutral tribunal to determine whether the Executive's asserted justifications for that detention have basis in fact and warrant in law. He argues that the Fourth Circuit inappropriately "ceded power to the Executive during wartime to define the conduct for which a citizen may be detained, judge whether that citizen has engaged in the proscribed conduct, and imprison that citizen indefinitely," and that due process demands that he receive a hearing in which he may challenge the Mobbs Declaration and adduce his own counter evidence. * * *

Both of these positions highlight legitimate concerns. And both emphasize the tension that often exists between the autonomy that the Government asserts is necessary in order to pursue effectively a particular goal and the process that a citizen contends he is due before he is deprived of a constitutional right. The ordinary mechanism that we use for balancing such serious competing interests, and for determining the procedures that are necessary to ensure that a citizen is not "deprived of life, liberty, or property, without due process of law," U.S. Const., Amdt. 5, is the test that we articulated in *Mathews* v. *Eldridge,* 424 U.S. 319 (1976). See, *e.g., United States* v. *Salerno,* 481 U.S. 739, 746 (1987); *Schall* v. *Martin,* 467 U.S. 253, 274–275 (1984). *Mathews* dictates that the process due in any given instance is determined by weighing "the private interest that will be affected by the official action" against the Government's asserted interest, "including the function involved" and the burdens the Government would face in providing greater process. The *Mathews* calculus then contemplates a judicious balancing of these concerns, through an analysis of "the risk of an erroneous deprivation" of the private interest if the process were reduced and the "probable value, if any, of additional or substitute safeguards." We take each of these steps in turn.

1

It is beyond question that substantial interests lie on both sides of the scale in this case. Hamdi's "private interest ... affected by the official action," is the most elemental of liberty interests—the interest in being free from physical detention by one's own government. "In our society liberty is the norm," and detention without trial "is the carefully limited exception." *Salerno, supra*, at 755. * * *

Nor is the weight on this side of the *Mathews* scale offset by the circumstances of war or the accusation of treasonous behavior, for "it is clear that commitment for *any* purpose constitutes a significant deprivation of liberty that requires due process protection," and at this stage in the *Mathews* calculus, we consider the interest of the *erroneously* detained individual. [A]s critical as the Government's interest may be in detaining those who actually pose an immediate threat to the national security of the United States during ongoing international conflict, history and common sense teach us that an unchecked system of detention carries the potential to become a means for oppression and abuse of others who do not present that sort of threat. Because we live in a society in which "mere public intolerance or animosity cannot constitutionally justify the deprivation of a person's physical liberty," our starting point for the *Mathews* v. *Eldridge* analysis is unaltered by the allegations surrounding the particular detainee or the organizations with which he is alleged to have associated. We reaffirm today the fundamental nature of a citizen's right to be free from involuntary confinement by his own government without due process of law, and we weigh the opposing governmental interests against the curtailment of liberty that such confinement entails.

2

On the other side of the scale are the weighty and sensitive governmental interests in ensuring that those who have in fact fought with the enemy during a war do not return to battle against the United States. As discussed above, the law of war and the realities of combat may render such detentions both necessary and appropriate, and our due process analysis need not blink at those realities. * * *

The Government also argues at some length that its interests in reducing the process available to alleged enemy combatants are heightened by the practical difficulties that would accompany a system of trial-like process. In its view, military officers who are engaged in the serious work of waging battle would be unnecessarily and dangerously distracted by litigation half a world away, and discovery into military operations would both intrude on the sensitive secrets of national defense and result in a futile search for evidence buried under the rubble of war. To the extent that these burdens are triggered by heightened procedures, they are properly taken into account in our due process analysis.

3

Striking the proper constitutional balance here is of great importance to the Nation during this period of ongoing combat. But it is equally vital that our calculus not give short shrift to the values that this country holds dear or to the privilege that is American citizenship. It is during our most challenging and uncertain moments that our Nation's commitment to due process is most severely tested; and it is in those times that we must preserve our commitment at home to the principles for which we fight abroad.

With due recognition of these competing concerns, we believe that neither the process proposed by the Government nor the process apparently envisioned by the District Court below strikes the proper constitutional balance when a United States citizen is detained in the United States as an enemy combatant. That is, "the risk of erroneous deprivation" of a detainee's liberty interest is unacceptably high under the Government's proposed rule, while some of the "additional or substitute procedural safeguards" suggested by the District Court are unwarranted in light of their limited "probable value" and the burdens they may impose on the military in such cases.

We therefore hold that a citizen-detainee seeking to challenge his classification as an enemy combatant must receive notice of the factual basis for his classification, and a fair opportunity to rebut the Government's factual assertions before a neutral decisionmaker. "For more than a century the central meaning of procedural due process has been clear: 'Parties whose rights are to be affected are entitled to be heard; and in order that they may enjoy that right they must first be notified.' It is equally fundamental that the right to notice and an opportunity to be heard 'must be granted at a meaningful time and in a meaningful manner.' " These essential constitutional promises may not be eroded.

At the same time, the exigencies of the circumstances may demand that, aside from these core elements, enemy combatant proceedings may be tailored to alleviate their uncommon potential to burden the Executive at a time of ongoing military conflict. Hearsay, for example, may need to be accepted as the most reliable available evidence from the Government in such a proceeding. Likewise, the Constitution would not be offended by a presumption in favor of the Government's evidence, so long as that presumption remained a rebuttable one and fair opportunity for rebuttal were provided. Thus, once the Government puts forth credible evidence that the habeas petitioner meets the enemy-combatant criteria, the onus could shift to the petitioner to rebut that evidence with more persuasive evidence that he falls outside the criteria. A burden-shifting scheme of this sort would meet the goal of ensuring that the errant tourist, embedded journalist, or local aid worker has a chance to prove military error while giving due regard to the Executive once it has put forth meaningful support for its conclusion that the detainee is in fact an enemy combatant. In the words of *Mathews*, process of this sort would sufficiently address the "risk of erroneous deprivation" of a detainee's liberty interest while eliminating certain procedures that have questionable additional value in light of the burden on the Government.

* * * [I]t does not infringe on the core role of the military for the courts to exercise their own time-honored and constitutionally mandated roles of reviewing and resolving claims like those presented here.

* * *

D

In so holding, we necessarily reject the Government's assertion that separation of powers principles mandate a heavily circumscribed role for the courts in such circumstances. Indeed, the position that the courts must forgo any examination of the individual case and focus exclusively on the legality of the broader detention scheme cannot be mandated by any reasonable view of separation of powers, as this approach serves only to *condense* power into a single branch of government. We have long since made clear that a state of war is not a blank check for the President when it comes to the rights of the Nation's citizens. Whatever power the United States Constitution envisions for the Executive in its exchanges with other nations or with enemy organizations in times of conflict, it most assuredly envisions a role for all three branches when individual liberties are at stake. Likewise, we have made clear that, unless Congress acts to suspend it, the Great Writ of habeas corpus allows the Judicial Branch to play a necessary role in maintaining this delicate balance of governance, serving as an important judicial check on the Executive's discretion in the realm of detentions. Thus, while we do not question that our due process assessment must pay keen attention to the particular burdens faced by the Executive in the context of military action, it would turn our system of checks and balances on its head to suggest that a citizen could not make his way to court with a challenge to the factual basis for his detention by his government, simply because the Executive opposes making available such a challenge. Absent suspension of the writ by Congress, a citizen detained as an enemy combatant is entitled to this process.

Because we conclude that due process demands some system for a citizen detainee to refute his classification, the proposed "some evidence" standard is inadequate. Any process in which the Executive's factual assertions go wholly unchallenged or are simply presumed correct without any opportunity for the alleged combatant to demonstrate otherwise falls constitutionally short. * * *

Today we are faced only with such a case. Aside from unspecified "screening" processes, and military interrogations in which the Government suggests Hamdi could have contested his classification, Hamdi has received no process. An interrogation by one's captor, however effective an intelligence-gathering tool, hardly constitutes a constitutionally adequate factfinding before a neutral decisionmaker. Plainly, the "process" Hamdi has received is not that to which he is entitled under the Due Process Clause.

There remains the possibility that the standards we have articulated could be met by an appropriately authorized and properly constituted military tribunal. Indeed, it is notable that military regulations already provide for such process in related instances, dictating that tribunals be made available to determine the status of enemy detainees who assert prisoner-of-war status under the Geneva Convention. In the absence of such process, however, a court that receives a petition for a writ of habeas corpus from an alleged enemy combatant must itself ensure that the minimum requirements of due process are achieved. * * * As we have discussed, a habeas court in a case such as this may accept affidavit evidence like that contained in the Mobbs Declaration, so long as it also permits the alleged combatant to present his own factual case to rebut the Government's return. * * *

IV

Hamdi * * * unquestionably has the right to access to counsel in connection with the proceedings on remand. No further consideration of this issue is necessary at this stage of the case.

* * *

The judgment of the United States Court of Appeals for the Fourth Circuit is vacated, and the case is remanded for further proceedings. It is so ordered.

JUSTICE SCALIA, with whom JUSTICE STEVENS joins, dissenting.

Petitioner, a presumed American citizen, has been imprisoned without charge or hearing in the Norfolk and Charleston Naval Brigs for more than two years, on the allegation that he is an enemy combatant who bore arms against his country for the Taliban. His father claims to the contrary, that he is an inexperienced aid worker caught in the wrong place at the wrong time. This case brings into conflict the competing demands of national security and our citizens' constitutional right to personal liberty. Although I share the Court's evident unease as it seeks to reconcile the two, I do not agree with its resolution.

Where the Government accuses a citizen of waging war against it, our constitutional tradition has been to prosecute him in federal court for treason or some other crime. Where the exigencies of war prevent that, the Constitution's Suspension Clause, Art. I, § 9, cl. 2, allows Congress to relax the usual protections temporarily. Absent suspension, however, the Executive's assertion of military exigency has not been thought sufficient to permit detention without charge. No one contends that the congressional Authorization for Use of Military Force, on which the Government relies to justify its actions here, is an implementation of the Suspension Clause. Accordingly, I would reverse the decision below.

I

The very core of liberty secured by our Anglo–Saxon system of separated powers has been freedom from indefinite imprisonment at the will of the Executive. * * *

* * *

The gist of the Due Process Clause, as understood at the founding and since, was to force the Government to follow those common-law procedures traditionally deemed necessary before depriving a person of life, liberty, or property. When a citizen was deprived of liberty because of alleged criminal conduct, those procedures typically required committal by a magistrate followed by indictment and trial. The Due Process Clause "in effect affirms the right of trial according to the process and proceedings of the common law."

* * *

These due process rights have historically been vindicated by the writ of habeas corpus. * * *

II

* * *

A

JUSTICE O'CONNOR, writing for a plurality of this Court, asserts that captured enemy combatants (other than those suspected of war crimes) have traditionally been detained until the cessation of hostilities and then released. That is probably an accurate description of wartime practice with respect to enemy *aliens*. The tradition with respect to American citizens, however, has been quite different. Citizens aiding the enemy have been treated as traitors subject to the criminal process.

* * *

[C]itizens have been charged and tried in Article III courts for acts of war against the United States, even when their noncitizen co-conspirators were not. * * * During World War II, the famous German saboteurs of *Ex parte Quirin,* 317 U.S. 1 (1942), received military process, but the citizens who associated with them (with the exception of one citizen-saboteur, discussed below) were punished under the criminal process. See *Haupt* v. *United States,* 330 U.S. 631 (1947); L. Fisher, Nazi Saboteurs on Trial 80–84 (2003); see also *Cramer* v. *United States,* 325 U.S. 1 (1945).

* * *

V

It follows from what I have said that Hamdi is entitled to a habeas decree requiring his release unless (1) criminal proceedings are promptly brought, or (2) Congress has suspended the writ of habeas corpus. A suspension of the writ could, of course, lay down conditions for continued detention, similar to those that today's opinion prescribes under the Due Process Clause. But there is a world of difference between the people's representatives' determining the need for that suspension (and prescribing the conditions for it), and this Court's doing so.

* * *

It should not be thought, however, that the plurality's evisceration of the Suspension Clause augments, principally, the power of Congress. As usual, the major effect of its constitutional improvisation is to increase the power of the Court. Having found a congressional authorization for detention of citizens where none clearly exists; and having discarded the categorical procedural protection of the Suspension Clause; the plurality then proceeds, under the guise of the Due Process Clause, to prescribe what procedural protections *it* thinks appropriate. It "weighs the private interest ... against the Government's asserted interest," and—just as though writing a new Constitution—comes up with an unheard-of system in which the citizen rather than the Government bears the burden of proof, testimony is by hearsay rather than live witnesses, and the presiding officer may well be a "neutral" military officer rather than judge and jury. It claims authority to engage in this sort of "judicious balancing" from *Mathews* v. *Eldridge,* a case involving ... *the withdrawal of disability benefits!* Whatever the merits of this technique when newly recognized property rights are at issue (and even there they are questionable), it has no place where the Constitution and the common law already supply an answer.

* * *

* * * The plurality seems to view it as its mission to Make Everything Come Out Right, rather than merely to decree the consequences, as far as individual rights are concerned, of the other two branches' actions and omissions. Has the Legislature failed to suspend the writ in the current dire emergency? Well, we will remedy that failure by prescribing the reasonable conditions that a suspension should have included. And has the Executive failed to live up to those reasonable conditions? Well, we will ourselves make that failure good, so that this dangerous fellow (if he is dangerous) need not be set free. The problem with this approach is not only that it steps out of the courts' modest and limited role in a democratic society; but that by repeatedly doing what it thinks the political branches ought to do it encourages their lassitude and saps the vitality of government by the people.

* * *

[The dissenting opinion of JUSTICE THOMAS, and the opinion of JUSTICE SOUTER, with whom JUSTICE GINSBURG joined, concurring in part, dissenting in part, and concurring in the judgment, are omitted.]

RASUL v. BUSH

Supreme Court of the United States, 2004.
542 U.S. 466, 124 S.Ct. 2686, 159 L.Ed.2d 548.

JUSTICE STEVENS delivered the opinion of the Court.

These two cases present the narrow but important question whether United States courts lack jurisdiction to consider challenges to the legality of the detention of foreign nationals captured abroad in connection with hostilities and incarcerated at the Guantanamo Bay Naval Base, Cuba.

I

On September 11, 2001, agents of the al Qaeda terrorist network hijacked four commercial airliners and used them as missiles to attack American targets. While one of the four attacks was foiled by the heroism of the plane's passengers, the other three killed approximately 3,000 innocent civilians, destroyed hundreds of millions of dollars of property, and severely damaged the U.S. economy. In response to the attacks, Congress passed a joint resolution authorizing the President to use "all necessary and appropriate force against those nations, organizations, or persons he determines planned, authorized, committed, or aided the terrorist attacks ... or harbored such organizations or persons." Authorization for Use of Military Force, Pub. L. 107–40, § § 1–2, 115 Stat. 224. Acting pursuant to that authorization, the President sent U.S. Armed Forces into Afghanistan to wage a military campaign against al Qaeda and the Taliban regime that had supported it.

Petitioners in these cases are 2 Australian citizens and 12 Kuwaiti citizens who were captured abroad during hostilities between the United States and the Taliban. Since early 2002, the U.S. military has held them—along with, according to the Government's estimate, approximately 640 other non-Americans captured abroad—at the Naval Base at Guantanamo Bay. The United States occupies the Base, which comprises 45 square miles of land and water along the southeast coast of Cuba, pursuant to a 1903 Lease Agreement executed with the newly independent Republic of Cuba in the aftermath of the Spanish–American War. Under the Agreement, "the United States recognizes the continuance of the ultimate sovereignty of the Republic of Cuba over the [leased areas]," while "the Republic of Cuba consents that during the period of the occupation by the United States ... the United States shall exercise complete jurisdiction and control over and within said areas." In 1934, the parties entered into a treaty providing that, absent an agreement to modify or abrogate the lease, the lease would remain in effect "so long as the United States of America shall not abandon the ... naval station of Guantanamo."

The two Australians, Mamdouh Habib and David Hicks, each filed a petition for writ of habeas corpus, seeking release from custody, access to counsel, freedom from interrogations, and other relief. Fawzi Khalid Abdullah Fahad Al Odah and the 11 other Kuwaiti detainees filed a complaint seeking to be informed of the charges against them, to be allowed to meet with their families and with counsel, and to have access to the courts or some other impartial tribunal. They claimed that denial of these rights violates the Constitution, international law, and treaties of the United States. Invoking the court's jurisdiction under 28 U.S.C. §§ 1331 and 1350, among other statutory bases, they asserted causes of action under the Administrative Procedure Act, 5 U.S.C. §§ 555, 702,

706; the Alien Tort Statute, 28 U.S.C. § 1350; and the general federal habeas corpus statute, §§ 2241–2243.

Construing all three actions as petitions for writs of habeas corpus, the District Court dismissed them for want of jurisdiction. The court held, in reliance on our opinion in *Johnson* v. *Eisentrager,* 339 U.S. 763 (1950), that "aliens detained outside the sovereign territory of the United States [may not] invoke a petition for a writ of habeas corpus.". The Court of Appeals affirmed. Reading *Eisentrager* to hold that " 'the privilege of litigation' does not extend to aliens in military custody who have no presence in 'any territory over which the United States is sovereign,' " it held that the District Court lacked jurisdiction over petitioners' habeas actions, as well as their remaining federal statutory claims that do not sound in habeas. We granted certiorari and now reverse.

II

Congress has granted federal district courts, "within their respective jurisdictions," the authority to hear applications for habeas corpus by any person who claims to be held "in custody in violation of the Constitution or laws or treaties of the United States." 28 U.S.C. § § 2241(a), (c)(3). The statute traces its ancestry to the first grant of federal court jurisdiction: Section 14 of the Judiciary Act of 1789 authorized federal courts to issue the writ of habeas corpus to prisoners "in custody, under or by colour of the authority of the United States, or committed for trial before some court of the same." Act of Sept. 24, 1789, ch. 20, § 14, 1 Stat. 82. In 1867, Congress extended the protections of the writ to "all cases where any person may be restrained of his or her liberty in violation of the constitution, or of any treaty or law of the United States." Act of Feb. 5, 1867, ch. 28, 14 Stat. 385. See *Felker* v. *Turpin,* 518 U.S. 651, 659–660 (1996).

Habeas corpus is, however, "a writ antecedent to statute, ... throwing its root deep into the genius of our common law." The writ appeared in English law several centuries ago, became "an integral part of our common-law heritage" by the time the Colonies achieved independence, and received explicit recognition in the Constitution, which forbids suspension of "the Privilege of the Writ of Habeas Corpus ... unless when in Cases of Rebellion or Invasion the public Safety may require it," Art. I, § 9, cl. 2.

As it has evolved over the past two centuries, the habeas statute clearly has expanded habeas corpus "beyond the limits that obtained during the 17th and 18th centuries." *Swain* v. *Pressley,* 430 U.S. 372, 380, n. 13 (1977). But "at its historical core, the writ of habeas corpus has served as a means of reviewing the legality of Executive detention, and it is in that context that its protections have been strongest." As Justice Jackson wrote in an opinion respecting the availability of habeas corpus to aliens held in U.S. custody:

"Executive imprisonment has been considered oppressive and lawless since John, at Runnymede, pledged that no free man should be imprisoned, dispossessed, outlawed, or exiled save by the judgment of his peers or by the law of the land. The judges of England developed the writ of habeas corpus largely to preserve these immunities from executive restraint."

Consistent with the historic purpose of the writ, this Court has recognized the federal courts' power to review applications for habeas relief in a wide variety of cases involving Executive detention, in wartime as well as in times of peace. The Court has, for example, entertained the habeas petitions of an American citizen who plotted an attack on military installations during the Civil War, *Ex parte Milligan,* 4 Wall. 2 (1866), and of admitted enemy aliens convicted of war crimes during a declared war and held in the United States, *Ex parte Quirin,* 317 U.S. 1 (1942), and its insular possessions, *In re Yamashita,* 327 U.S. 1 (1946).

The question now before us is whether the habeas statute confers a right to judicial review of the legality of Executive detention of aliens in a territory over which the United States exercises plenary and exclusive jurisdiction, but not "ultimate sovereignty."

III

Respondents' primary submission is that the answer to the jurisdictional question is controlled by our decision in *Eisentrager.* In that case, we held that a Federal District Court lacked authority to issue a writ of habeas corpus to 21 German citizens who had been captured by U.S. forces in China, tried and convicted of war crimes by an American military commission headquartered in Nanking, and incarcerated in the Landsberg Prison in occupied Germany. The Court of Appeals in *Eisentrager* had found jurisdiction, reasoning that "any person who is deprived of his liberty by officials of the United States, acting under purported authority of that Government, and who can show that his confinement is in violation of a prohibition of the Constitution, has a right to the writ." * * *

Petitioners in these cases differ from the *Eisentrager* detainees in important respects: They are not nationals of countries at war with the United States, and they deny that they have engaged in or plotted acts of aggression against the United States; they have never been afforded access to any tribunal, much less charged with and convicted of wrongdoing; and for more than two years they have been imprisoned in territory over which the United States exercises exclusive jurisdiction and control.

Not only are petitioners differently situated from the *Eisentrager* detainees, but the Court in *Eisentrager* made quite clear that all six of the facts critical to its disposition were relevant only to the question of the prisoners' *constitutional* entitlement to habeas corpus. The Court had far less to say on the question of the petitioners' *statutory* entitlement to habeas review. Its only statement on the subject was a passing reference to the absence of statutory authorization: "Nothing in the text of the Constitution extends such a right, nor does anything in our statutes."

* * *

Because subsequent decisions of this Court have filled the statutory gap that had occasioned *Eisentrager*'s resort to "fundamentals," persons detained outside the territorial jurisdiction of any federal district court no longer need rely on the Constitution as the source of their right to federal habeas review. In *Braden* v. *30th Judicial Circuit Court of Ky.*, 410 U.S. 484, 495 (1973), this Court held * * * that the prisoner's presence within the territorial jurisdiction of the district court is not "an invariable prerequisite" to the exercise of district court jurisdiction under the federal habeas statute. Rather, because "the writ of habeas corpus does not act upon the prisoner who seeks relief, but upon the person who holds him in what is alleged to be unlawful custody," a district court acts "within [its] respective jurisdiction" within the meaning of § 2241 as long as "the custodian can be reached by service of process." * * *

Because *Braden* overruled the statutory predicate to *Eisentrager*'s holding, *Eisentrager* plainly does not preclude the exercise of § 2241 jurisdiction over petitioners' claims.

IV

Putting *Eisentrager* and *Ahrens* to one side, respondents contend that we can discern a limit on § 2241 through application of the "longstanding principle of American law" that congressional legislation is presumed not to have extraterritorial application unless such intent is clearly manifested. Whatever traction the presumption against extraterritoriality might have in other contexts, it certainly has no application to the operation of the habeas statute with respect to persons detained within "the territorial jurisdiction" of the United States. By the express terms of its agreements with Cuba, the United States exercises "complete jurisdiction and control" over the Guantanamo Bay Naval Base, and may continue to exercise such control permanently if it so chooses. 1903 Lease Agreement, Art. III; 1934 Treaty, Art. III. Respondents themselves concede that the habeas statute would create federal-court jurisdiction over the claims of an American citizen held at the base. Considering that the statute draws no distinction between Americans and aliens held in federal custody, there is little reason to think that Congress intended the geographical coverage of the statute to vary depending on the detainee's citizenship. Aliens held at the base, no less than American citizens, are entitled to invoke the federal courts' authority under § 2241.

Application of the habeas statute to persons detained at the base is consistent with the historical reach of the writ of habeas corpus. At common law, courts exercised habeas jurisdiction over the claims of aliens detained within sovereign territory of the realm, as well as the claims of persons detained in the so-called "exempt jurisdictions," where ordinary writs did not run, and all other dominions under the sovereign's control. As Lord Mansfield wrote in 1759, even if a territory was "no part of the realm," there was "no doubt" as to the court's power to issue writs of habeas corpus if the territory was "under the subjection of the Crown." *King* v. *Cowle,* 2 Burr. 834, 854–855, 97 Eng. Rep. 587, 598–599 (K. B.). * * *

In the end, the answer to the question presented is clear. Petitioners contend that they are being held in federal custody in violation of the laws of the United States.[15] No party questions the District Court's jurisdiction over petitioners' custodians. Section 2241, by its terms, requires nothing more. We therefore hold that § 2241 confers on the District Court jurisdiction to hear petitioners' habeas corpus challenges to the legality of their detention at the Guantanamo Bay Naval Base.

V

* * *

[N]othing in *Eisentrager* or in any of our other cases categorically excludes aliens detained in military custody outside the United States from the " 'privilege of litigation' " in U.S. courts. The courts of the United States have traditionally been open to nonresident aliens. And indeed, 28 U.S.C. § 1350 explicitly confers the privilege of suing for an actionable "tort ... committed in violation of the law of nations or a treaty of the United States" on aliens alone. The fact that petitioners in these cases are being held in military custody is immaterial to the question of the District Court's jurisdiction over their nonhabeas statutory claims.

VI

Whether and what further proceedings may become necessary after respondents make their response to the merits of petitioners' claims are matters that we need not address now. What is presently at stake is only whether the federal courts have jurisdiction to determine the legality of the Executive's potentially indefinite detention of individuals who claim to be wholly innocent of wrongdoing. Answering that question in the affirmative, we reverse the judgment of the Court of Appeals and remand for the District Court to consider in the first instance the merits of petitioners' claims. It is so ordered.

[JUSTICE KENNEDY's opinion, concurring in the judgment, is omitted.]

JUSTICE SCALIA, with whom THE CHIEF JUSTICE and JUSTICE THOMAS join, dissenting.

---

15. Petitioners' allegations—that, although they have engaged neither in combat nor in acts of terrorism against the United States, they have been held in Executive detention for more than two years in territory subject to the long-term, exclusive jurisdiction and control of the United States, without access to counsel and without being charged with any wrongdoing—unquestionably describe "custody in violation of the Constitution or laws or treaties of the United States." 28 U.S.C. § 2241(c)(3). Cf. *United States* v. *Verdugo-Urquidez,* 494 U.S. 259, 277–278 (1990) (KENNEDY, J., concurring), and cases cited therein.

The Court today holds that the habeas statute, 28 U.S.C. § 2241, extends to aliens detained by the United States military overseas, outside the sovereign borders of the United States and beyond the territorial jurisdictions of all its courts. This is not only a novel holding; it contradicts a half-century-old precedent on which the military undoubtedly relied, *Johnson* v. *Eisentrager,* 339 U.S. 763 (1950). The Court's contention that *Eisentrager* was somehow negated by *Braden* v. *30th Judicial Circuit Court of Ky.,* 410 U.S. 484 (1973)—a decision that dealt with a different issue and did not so much as mention *Eisentrager*—is implausible in the extreme. This is an irresponsible overturning of settled law in a matter of extreme importance to our forces currently in the field. I would leave it to Congress to change § 2241, and dissent from the Court's unprecedented holding.

I

As we have repeatedly said: "Federal courts are courts of limited jurisdiction. They possess only that power authorized by Constitution and statute, which is not to be expanded by judicial decree. It is to be presumed that a cause lies outside this limited jurisdiction.... " The petitioners do not argue that the Constitution independently requires jurisdiction here. Accordingly, this case turns on the words of § 2241, a text the Court today largely ignores. Even a cursory reading of the habeas statute shows that it presupposes a federal district court with territorial jurisdiction over the detainee. * * *

[T]he statute could not be clearer that a necessary requirement for issuing the writ is that *some* federal district court have territorial jurisdiction over the detainee. Here, as the Court allows, the Guantanamo Bay detainees are not located within the territorial jurisdiction of any federal district court. One would think that is the end of this case.

* * *

II

In abandoning the venerable statutory line drawn in *Eisentrager,* the Court boldly extends the scope of the habeas statute to the four corners of the earth. Part III of its opinion asserts that *Braden* stands for the proposition that "a district court acts 'within [its] respective jurisdiction' within the meaning of § 2241 as long as 'the custodian can be reached by service of process.' " * * *

The consequence of this holding, as applied to aliens outside the country, is breathtaking. It permits an alien captured in a foreign theater of active combat to bring a § 2241 petition against the Secretary of Defense. Over the course of the last century, the United States has held millions of alien prisoners abroad. See, *e.g.,* Department of Army, G. Lewis & J. Mewha, History of Prisoner of War Utilization by the United States Army 1776–1945, Pamphlet No. 20–213, p. 244 (1955) (noting that, "by the end of hostilities [in World War II], U.S. forces had in custody approximately two million enemy soldiers"). A great many of these prisoners would no doubt have complained about the circumstances of their capture and the terms of their confinement. The military is currently detaining over 600 prisoners at Guantanamo Bay alone; each detainee undoubtedly has complaints—real or contrived—about those terms and circumstances. The Court's unheralded expansion of federal-court jurisdiction is not even mitigated by a comforting assurance that the legion of ensuing claims will be easily resolved on the merits. To the contrary, the Court says that the "petitioners' allegations ... unquestionably describe 'custody in violation of the Constitution or laws or treaties of the United States.'" From this point forward, federal courts will entertain petitions from these prisoners, and others like them around the world, challenging actions and events far away, and forcing the courts to oversee one aspect of the Executive's conduct of a foreign war.

* * *

Commentary

1.   Less than two weeks after the Supreme Court's opinion in *Rasul v. Bush*, the United States Department of Defense (DOD) established a tribunal for hearing the claims of detainees contesting their detention at Guantanamo Bay as enemy combatants. The DOD described the tribunal in the following press release. Do the tribunal procedures appear to be consistent with traditional notions of due process? Consider, for example, the nature of the hearing to be provided and the type of the representative to be appointed to assist the detainee.

"Combatant Status Review Tribunal Order Issued

"The Department of Defense announced today the formation of the Combatant Status Review Tribunal for detainees held at Guantanamo Bay, Cuba. This tribunal will serve as a forum for detainees to contest their status as enemy combatants.

"Detainees held at Guantanamo Bay will be notified within 10 days of their opportunity to contest their enemy combatant status under this process. The tribunal process will start as soon as possible. Detainees will also be notified of their right to seek a writ of habeas corpus in the courts of the United States. Habeas corpus is a writ ordering a person in custody to be brought before a court.

"An individual tribunal will be comprised of three neutral officers, none of whom were involved with the detainee. One of the tribunal members will be a judge advocate and the senior ranking officer will serve as the president of the tribunal.

"Each detainee will be assigned a military officer as a personal representative. That officer will assist the detainee in preparing for a tribunal hearing. Detainees will have the right to testify before the tribunal, call witnesses and introduce any other evidence. Following the hearing of testimony and other evidence, the tribunal will determine in a closed-door session whether the detainee is properly held as an enemy combatant. Any detainee who is determined not to be an enemy combatant will be transferred to their country of citizenship or other disposition consistent with domestic and international obligations and U.S. foreign policy.

"This tribunal does not replace the administrative review procedure announced earlier this year."

2. Unlike the preceding materials, the following case did not arise directly out of the government's activities during the "war on terror." Nonetheless, the Supreme Court's decision upholding the constitutionality of a statute mandating the detention of "criminal aliens" may have implications for future disputes about government detention of terror suspects. It is noteworthy that Kim was a lawful permanent resident accorded both procedural and substantive due process rights, yet the statute upheld by the Supreme Court mandated his detention without requiring either a hearing or evidence that the detention serves some government interest, like protecting the public from harm or preventing the detainee's flight.

DEMORE v. KIM

Supreme Court of the United States, 2003.
538 U.S. 510, 123 S.Ct. 1708, 155 L.Ed.2d 724.

CHIEF JUSTICE REHNQUIST delivered the opinion of the Court.

[T]he Immigration and Nationality Act, 8 U.S.C. § 1226(c), provides that "the Attorney General shall take into custody any alien who" is removable from this country because he has been convicted of one of a specified set of crimes. Respondent is a citizen of the Republic of South Korea. He entered the United States in 1984, at the age of six, and became a lawful permanent resident of the United States two years later. In July 1996, he was convicted of first-degree burglary in state court in California and, in April 1997, he was convicted of a second crime, "petty theft with priors." The Immigration and Naturalization Service (INS) charged respondent with being deportable from the United States in light of these convictions, and detained him pending his removal hearing. We hold that Congress, justifiably concerned that deportable criminal aliens who are not detained continue to engage in crime and fail to appear for their removal hearings in large numbers, may require that persons such as respondent be detained for the brief period necessary for their removal proceedings.

[Kim filed a habeas corpus action challenging the constitutionality of § 1226(c). The District Court held that the statute's requirement of mandatory detention for certain criminal aliens was unconstitutional. The Ninth Circuit Court of Appeals affirmed, holding that Kim's right to substantive due process was violated because he is a permanent resident alien, and concluding that the INS had not provided a justification "for no-bail civil detention sufficient to overcome a lawful permanent resident alien's liberty interest." Three other Circuits had reached the same conclusion, and another had rejected a similar constitutional claim. Resolving this split among the Circuits, the Supreme Court reversed the Ninth Circuit's decision. The Supreme Court rejected the argument that the statute deprived federal courts of jurisdiction to hear this type of case, and then turned to the constitutional issues.]

II

Having determined that the federal courts have jurisdiction to review a constitutional challenge to § 1226(c), we proceed to review respondent's claim. Section 1226(c) mandates detention during removal proceedings for a limited class of deportable aliens—including those convicted of an aggravated felony. Congress adopted this provision against a backdrop of wholesale failure by the INS to deal with increasing rates of criminal activity by aliens. Criminal aliens were the fastest growing segment of the federal prison population, already constituting roughly 25% of all federal prisoners, and they formed a rapidly rising share of state prison populations as well. Congress' investigations showed, however, that the INS could not even *identify* most deportable aliens, much less locate them and remove them from the country. One study showed that, at the then-current rate of deportation, it would take 23 years to remove every criminal alien already subject to deportation. Making matters worse, criminal aliens who were deported swiftly reentered the country illegally in great numbers.

[D]eportable criminal aliens who remained in the United States often committed more crimes before being removed. One 1986 study showed that, after criminal aliens were identified as deportable, 77% were arrested at least once more and 45%—nearly half—were arrested multiple times before their deportation proceedings even began.

Congress also had before it evidence that one of the major causes of the INS' failure to remove deportable criminal aliens was the agency's failure to detain those aliens during their deportation proceedings. * * *

Once released, more than 20% of deportable criminal aliens failed to appear for their removal hearings. * * *

* * *

"It is well established that the *Fifth Amendment* entitles aliens to due process of law in deportation proceedings." At the same time, however, this Court has recognized detention during deportation proceedings as a constitutionally valid aspect of the deportation process. As we said more than a century ago, deportation proceedings "would be vain if those accused could not be held in custody pending the inquiry into their true character." * * *

* * *

For the reasons set forth above, respondent's claim must fail. Detention during removal proceedings is a constitutionally permissible part of that process. The INS detention of respondent, a criminal alien who has conceded that he is deportable, for the limited period of his removal proceedings, is governed by these cases. The judgment of the Court of Appeals is Reversed.

JUSTICE SOUTER, with whom JUSTICE STEVENS and JUSTICE GINSBURG join, concurring in part and dissenting in part.

Respondent Kim is an alien lawfully admitted to permanent residence in the United States. He claims that the Constitution forbids the Immigration and Naturalization Service (INS) from detaining him under 8 U.S.C. § 1226(c) unless his detention serves a government interest, such as preventing flight or danger to the community. He contends that due process affords him a right to a hearing before an impartial official, giving him a chance to show that he poses no risk that would justify confining him between the moment the Government claims he is removable and the adjudication of the Government's claim.

I join Part I of the Court's opinion, which upholds federal jurisdiction in this case, but I dissent from the Court's disposition on the merits. The Court's holding that the Constitution permits the Government to lock up a lawful permanent resident of this country when there is concededly no reason to do so forgets over a century of precedent acknowledging the rights of permanent residents, including the basic liberty from physical confinement lying at the heart of due process. The INS has never argued that detaining Kim is necessary to guarantee his appearance for removal proceedings or to protect anyone from danger in the meantime. Instead, shortly after the District Court issued its order in this case, the INS, *sua sponte* and without even holding a custody hearing, concluded that Kim "would not be considered a threat" and that any risk of flight could be met by a bond of $5,000. He was released soon thereafter, and there is no indication that he is not complying with the terms of his release.

The Court's approval of lengthy mandatory detention can therefore claim no justification in national emergency or any risk posed by Kim particularly. The Court's judgment is unjustified by past cases or current facts, and I respectfully dissent.

* * *

II

A

It has been settled for over a century that all aliens within our territory are "persons" entitled to the protection of the Due Process Clause. Aliens "residing in the United States for a shorter or longer time, are entitled, so long as they are permitted by the government of the United States to remain in the country, to the safeguards of the Constitution, and to the protection of the laws, in regard to their rights of person and of property, and to their civil and criminal responsibility." * * *

The constitutional protection of an alien's person and property is particularly strong in the case of aliens lawfully admitted to permanent residence (LPRs). The immigration laws give LPRs the opportunity to establish a life permanently in this country by developing economic, familial, and social ties indistinguishable from those of a citizen. In fact, the law of the United States goes out of its way to encourage just such attachments by creating immigration preferences for those with a citizen as a close relation, and those with valuable professional skills or other assets promising benefits to the United States.

Once they are admitted to permanent residence, LPRs share in the economic freedom enjoyed by citizens: they may compete for most jobs in the private and public sectors without obtaining job-specific authorization, and apart from the franchise, jury duty, and certain forms of public assistance, their lives are generally indistinguishable from those of United States citizens. That goes for obligations as well as opportunities. * * * And if they choose, they may apply for full membership in the national polity through naturalization.

* * *

[O]nce an alien lawfully enters and resides in this country he becomes invested with the rights guaranteed by the Constitution to all people within our borders. Such rights include those protected by the First and the Fifth Amendments and by the due process clause of the Fourteenth Amendment. None of these provisions acknowledges any distinction between citizens and resident aliens. They extend their inalienable privileges to all "persons" and guard against any encroachment on those rights by federal or state authority. * * *

The law therefore considers an LPR to be at home in the United States, and even when the Government seeks removal, we have accorded LPRs greater protections than other aliens under the Due Process Clause. * * *

* * *

B

Kim's claim is a limited one: not that the Government may not detain LPRs to ensure their appearance at removal hearings, but that due process under the Fifth Amendment conditions a potentially lengthy detention on a hearing and an impartial decisionmaker's finding that detention is necessary to a governmental purpose. He thus invokes our repeated decisions that the claim of liberty protected by the Fifth Amendment is at its strongest when government seeks to detain an individual. THE CHIEF JUSTICE wrote in 1987 that "in our society liberty is the norm, and detention prior to trial or without trial is the carefully limited exception."

Accordingly, the *Fifth Amendment* permits detention only where "heightened, substantive due process scrutiny" finds a " 'sufficiently compelling' "governmental need. * * *

* * *

D

In sum, due process requires a "special justification" for physical detention that "outweighs the individual's constitutionally protected interest in avoiding physical restraint "as well as "adequate procedural protections." "There must be a 'sufficiently compelling' governmental interest to justify such an action, usually a punitive interest in imprisoning the convicted criminal or a regulatory interest in forestalling danger to the community." The class of persons subject to confinement must be commensurately narrow and the duration of confinement limited accordingly. [The Justices have] disapproved detention that is not "necessary" to counter a risk of flight or danger; it is "arbitrary or capricious" and violates the substantive component of the Due Process Clause. Finally, procedural due process requires, at a minimum, that a detainee have the benefit of an impartial decisionmaker able to consider particular circumstances on the issue of necessity.

By these standards, Kim's case is an easy one. "Heightened, substantive due process scrutiny," uncovers serious infirmities in § 1226(c). Detention is not limited to dangerous criminal aliens or those found likely to flee, but applies to all aliens claimed to be deportable for criminal convictions, even where the underlying offenses are minor. Detention under § 1226(c) is not limited by the kind of time limit imposed by the Speedy Trial Act, and while it lasts only as long as the removal proceedings, those proceedings have no deadline and may last over a year. Section 1226(c) neither requires nor permits an official to determine whether Kim's detention was necessary to prevent flight or danger.

Kim's detention without particular justification in these respects, or the opportunity to enquire into it, violates both components of due process, and I would accordingly affirm the judgment of the Court of Appeals requiring the INS to hold a bail hearing to see whether detention is needed to avoid a risk of flight or a danger to the community.
* * *

* * *

[JUSTICE O'CONNOR's opinion, concurring in part and concurring in the judgment, in which JUSTICE SCALIA AND JUSTICE THOMAS joined, JUSTICE BREYER's opinion, concurring in part and dissenting in part and JUSTICE KENNEDY's concurring opinion all are omitted.]

†